P9-DGB-724

The Earth and Its Peoples

A Global History

ADVANCED PLACEMENT* EDITION

The Earth and Its Peoples

A Global History

THIRD EDITION

Richard W. Bulliet
Columbia University

Pamela Kyle Crossley
Dartmouth College

Daniel R. Headrick
Roosevelt University

Steven W. Hirsch
Tufts University

Lyman L. Johnson
University of North Carolina–Charlotte

David Northrup
Boston College

Houghton Mifflin Company   Boston   New York

Document-Based Questions: Bard Keeler
Publisher: Charles Hartford
Editor-in-Chief: Jean L. Woy
Senior Sponsoring Editor: Nancy Blaine
Senior Development Editor: Jennifer Sutherland
Editorial Associate: Annette Fantasia
Senior Project Editor: Carol Newman
Editorial Assistant: Trinity Peacock-Broyles
Senior Design Coordinator: Jill Haber
Senior Designer: Henry Rachlin
Manufacturing Manager: Florence Cadran
Senior Marketing Manager: Sandra McGuire

Cover illustration: *New Year's Festival* (woodcut) by Utagawa Kunisada (1786–1864) Victoria and Albert Museum, London, UK / Bridgeman Art Library International, Ltd.

Part opener credits: Pt. 1, p. 1: Gian Berto Vanni/Corbis; Pt. 2, p. 89: © Corbis; Pt. 3, p. 193: Tokyo National Museum/DNP Archives; Pt. 4, p. 291: Bibliothèque nationale de France; Pt. 5, p. 401: Library of Congress; Pt. 6, p. 537: © Hulton-Deutsch/Corbis; Pt. 7, p. 677: Charles O'Rear/Corbis; Pt. 8, p. 817 © Corbis.

Chapter opener credits: Ch. 1, p. 4: Giraudon/Art Resource, NY; Ch. 2, p. 36: Courtesy of the Trustees of the British Museum; Ch. 3, p. 59: Woodfin Camp & Associates; Ch. 4, p. 92: Bibliothèque nationale de France; Ch. 5, p. 123: © Dennis Cox/ChinaStock; Ch. 6, p. 150: Dinodia Photo Library; Ch. 7, p. 173: Allan Eaton/Ancient Art & Architecture; Ch. 8, p. 196: Suleymaniye Library, Istanbul. Courtesy, Karen Pinto, History Department, Columbia University; Ch. 9, p. 218: Musée de Bayeaux/Michael Holford; Ch. 10, p. 248: Fujita Art Museum; Ch. 11, p. 267: Justin Kerr; Ch. 12, p. 294: Imperial Household Agency/International Society for Educational Information, Japan; Ch. 13, p. 324: Imperial Household Collection, Kyoto; Ch. 14, p. 349: Copyright Brussels, Royal Library of Belgium; Ch. 15, p. 375: G. Dagli Orti/The Art Archive; Ch. 16, p. 404: Kunsthistorisches Museum, Vienna/The Bridgeman Art Library, New York and London; Ch. 17, p. 430: Archivo General de la Nación, Buenos Aires; Ch. 18, p. 457: From William Clark, *Ten Views in the Islands of Antigua*, 1823. British Library; Ch. 19, p. 484: V&A Picture Library; Ch. 20, p. 510: Novosti; Ch. 21, p. 540: Jean-Loup Charmet/ The Bridgeman Art Library; Ch. 22, p. 568: Science & Society Picture Library; Ch. 23, p. 592: *Estación de Orizaba*, 1877. From Casimiro Castro, *Album del Ferro-Carril Mexicano: Coleccion de Vista Pintadas* (Victor Debray and Company, 1877); Ch. 24, p. 623: Eyre and Hobbs House Art Gallery; Ch. 25, p. 650: Mary Evans Picture Library; Ch. 26, p. 680: The Metropolitan Museum of Art, gift of Lincoln Kirstein, 1959 (JP 3346). Photograph by Otto E. Nelson. Photograph © 1986 The Metropolitan Museum of Art; Ch. 27, p. 707: Bildarchiv Preussischer Kulturbesitz; Ch. 28, p. 735: Imperial War Museum/The Art Archive; Ch. 29, p. 765: akg-images; Ch. 30, p. 793: Genevieve Naylor, photographer/Reznikoff Artistic Partnership, NY; Ch. 31, p. 820: Bettmann/Corbis; Ch. 32, p. 847: Paul Chesley/Getty Images; Ch. 33, p. 878: AFP Photo/ Doug Kanter/Getty Images.

*"Advanced Placement" and "AP" are registered trademarks of the College Board, which is not involved in the production of, and does not endorse, this product.

Copyright © 2005 by Houghton Mifflin Company. All rights reserved.

No part of this work may be reproduced or transmitted in any form or by any means, electronic or mechanical, including photocopying and recording, or by any information storage or retrieval system without the prior written permission of Houghton Mifflin Company unless such copying is expressly permitted by federal copyright law. Address inquiries to College Permissions, Houghton Mifflin Company, 222 Berkeley Street, Boston, MA 02116-3764.

Printed in U.S.A.

Library of Congress Catalog Card Number: 2003113993

ISBN: 0-618-42770-8

5 6 7 8 9—DW—09 08 07 06

Brief Contents

Contents

PART TWO
The Formation of New Cultural Communities, 1000 B.C.E.–600 C.E.
89

PART FIVE
The Globe Encompassed,
1500–1750
401

xiv   Contents

Maps

Environment and Technology

Diversity and Dominance

Document-Based Questions

Preface

Since the initial publication of *The Earth and Its Peoples* in 1997, our goal has remained unchanged: to produce a textbook that not only speaks for the past but speaks to today's student and today's teacher. Students and instructors alike should take away from this text a broad vision of human societies beginning as sparse and disconnected communities reacting creatively to local circumstances; experiencing ever more intensive stages of contact, interpenetration, and cultural expansion and amalgamation; and arriving at a twenty-first century world in which people increasingly visualize a single global community.

Process, not progress, is the keynote of this book: a steady process of change over time, at first differently experienced in various regions, but eventually connecting peoples and traditions from all parts of the globe. Students should come away from this book with a sense that the problems and promises of their world are rooted in a past in which people of every sort, in every part of the world, confronted problems of a similar character and coped with them as best they could. We believe that our efforts will help students see where their world has come from and learn thereby something useful for their own lives.

With the Third Edition of our text, we have created for the first time an Advanced Placement Edition intended for teachers and students preparing for the AP World History examination in 2004 and subsequent years. The first two parts of the book now correspond to the "Foundations" period of the AP World History course and end in 600 C.E. The book starts with the Neolithic period rather than with the emergence of hominids, making it possible to merge the first two chapters of the college edition, for a total of 33 chapters overall. In reorganizing Part Two to end at 600 C.E., some material in Part Three has been transferred to chapters in Part Two. In addition, the first eleven chapters have been abridged in order to concentrate on the key topics of the AP World History course.

Finally, a new "Document-Based Question" feature has been created specifically for the Advanced Placement Edition. Bard Keeler, AP World History teacher at Gulf Coast High School, Naples, Florida, has written a document-based question for every chapter. The questions help students learn how to analyze and assess the reliability of a variety of texts, photographs, charts, and maps in order to answer important historical questions.

For example, students are asked to analyze the factors that influenced the status and roles of women in Tang and Song China or later, to compare and contrast the role of nationalism in the struggles for independence in Vietnam and India from 1900 to 1949.

Central Themes

We subtitled *The Earth and Its Peoples* "A Global History" because the book explores the common challenges and experiences that unite the human past. Although the dispersal of early humans to every livable environment resulted in a myriad of different economic, social, political, and cultural systems, all societies displayed analogous patterns in meeting their needs and exploiting their environments. Our challenge was to select the particular data and episodes that would best illuminate these global patterns of human experience.

To meet this challenge, we adopted two themes to serve as the spinal cord of our history: "technology and the environment" and "diversity and dominance." The first theme represents the commonplace material bases of all human societies at all times. It grants no special favor to any cultural group even as it embraces subjects of the broadest topical, chronological, and geographical range. The second theme expresses the reality that every human society has constructed or inherited structures of domination. We examine practices and institutions of many sorts: military, economic, social, political, religious, and cultural, as well as those based on kinship, gender, and literacy. Simultaneously we recognize that alternative ways of life and visions of societal organization continually manifest themselves both within and in dialogue with every structure of domination.

With respect to the first theme, it is vital for students to understand that technology, in the broad sense of experience-based knowledge of the physical world, underlies all human activity. Writing is a technology, but so is oral transmission from generation to generation of lore about medicinal or poisonous plants. The magnetic compass is a navigational technology, but so is Polynesian mariners' hard-won knowledge of winds, currents, and tides that made possible the settlement of the Pacific islands.

All technological development has come about in interaction with environments, both physical and human, and has, in turn, affected those environments. The story of how humanity has changed the face of the globe is an integral part of our first theme. Yet technology and the environment do not explain or underlie all-important episodes of human experience. The theme of "diversity and dominance" informs all our discussions of politics, culture, and society. Thus when narrating the histories of empires, we describe a range of human experiences within and beyond the imperial frontiers without assuming that imperial institutions are a more fit topic for discussion than the economic and social organization of pastoral nomads or the lives of peasant women. When religion and culture occupy our narrative, we focus not only on the dominant tradition but also on the diversity of alternative beliefs and practices.

Changes in the Third Edition

The Advanced Placement Edition is based on the Third Edition of *The Earth and Its Peoples*, which introduced several important changes. In each chapter a two-page primary source feature, "Diversity and Dominance," has replaced the brief "Society and Culture" excerpts of the Second Edition. The new feature fills two needs. First, it gives students extended documentary selections on which to hone their analytical skills. Second, it provides a focus for students to consider the many forms of dominance that have developed over time and the many ways in which human diversity has continued to express itself regardless of these forms of dominance. The topics covered under "Diversity and Dominance" range from "Hierarchy and Conduct in the Analects of Confucius" (Chapter 2) and "Archbishop Adalbert of Hamburg and the Christianization of the Scandinavians and Slavs" (Chapter 9) to "The Afro-Brazilian Experience, 1828" (Chapter 23) and "Women, Family Values, and the Russian Revolution" (Chapter 29).

- Chapters 2 and 3 have been rethought and reorganized: Chapter 2 now deals with several civilizations that emerged independently in different parts of the world in the second and first millennia B.C.E., while Chapter 3 focuses on the same time period in Western Asia and the Mediterranean, giving greater stress to continuity and interaction in that region.
- Chapter 9, on early medieval Europe, has been reorganized so that it opens with Byzantium and proceeds from there to western Europe. Two new maps have been added—one on German kingdoms, ca. 530, and the other on Kievan Russia and the Byzantine Empire in the eleventh century.
- We greatly increased the coverage of Russian history, including expanded discussions in Chapters 9 and 20 and an entirely new section in Chapter 25.

- The history and impact of the Mongols are now covered in a single chapter, Chapter 12, "Mongol Eurasia and Its Aftermath, 1200-1500." Combining previously separated materials allowed us to make more evident the parallels and contrasts between the impact of the Mongols in the west and in the east.
- Coverage of the United States in the late nineteenth century, previously in two separate chapters, has been reorganized and consolidated in Chapter 23.
- Chapter 25 now includes an extended discussion of the beginnings of European impact on Egypt.
- Discussions of the modernization of Japan in the late nineteenth century have been combined in Chapter 26. The discussion of nationalism in that chapter now includes coverage of the unification of Italy as well as two new maps on the unifications of Italy and Germany.
- Chapter 32 brings the account of threats and strains to the global environment up to the present, including a new map showing stresses on the world's fresh water supplies.
- The final chapter, Chapter 33, "Globalization at the Turn of the Millennium," has been entirely rewritten to reflect current developments in global politics, the global economy, and global culture. New maps have been added showing regional trade associations and the unequal distribution of wealth around the world. The impact of the terrorist attacks of September 11 and the responses by the United States and other nations receive special attention.
- Suggested Reading lists were updated with important recent scholarship.

Organization

The *Earth and Its Peoples* uses eight broad chronological divisions to define its conceptual scheme of global historical development. In **Part One: The Emergence of Human Communities, to 500 B.C.E.,** we examine important patterns of human communal organization in both the Eastern and Western Hemispheres. Small, dispersed human communities living by foraging spread to most parts of the world over tens of thousands of years. They responded to enormously diverse environmental conditions, at different times in different ways, discovering how to cultivate plants and utilize the products of domestic animals. On the basis of these new modes of sustenance, population grew, permanent towns appeared, and political and religious authority, based on collection and control of agricultural surpluses, spread over extensive areas.

Part Two: The Formation of New Cultural Communities, 1000 B.C.E.–600 C.E., introduces the concept of a "cultural community," in the sense of a coherent pattern of activities and symbols pertaining to a specific human community. While all human communities develop distinctive cultures, including those discussed in Part One, historical development in this stage of global history prolonged and magnified the impact of some cultures more than others. In the geographically contiguous African-Eurasian land mass, the cultures that proved to have the most enduring influence traced their roots to the second and first millennia B.C.E.

Part Three: Competition Among Cultural Communities, 600–1200, deals with cultural consolidation on a broader scale than the episodes of imperial expansion previously considered. A melding of political rule with all-embracing ideological or religious concepts brought with it a variety of practices for indoctrinating peoples with the worldviews and beliefs of those controlling the structures of domination. Military and transportation technologies helped maintain large empires, and political consolidation brought technologies and currents of thought from different regions into fruitful contact. Of particular importance were technologies of language, from the invention of new scripts to the development of paper and printing.

In **Part Four: Interregional Patterns of Culture and Contact, 1200–1550,** we look at the world during the three and a half centuries that saw both intensified cultural and commercial contact and increasingly confident self-definition of cultural communities in Europe, Asia, and Africa. The Mongol conquest of a vast empire extending from the Pacific Ocean to eastern Europe greatly stimulated trade and interaction. In the West, strengthened European kingdoms began maritime expansion in the Atlantic, forging direct ties with sub-Saharan Africa and beginning the conquest of the civilizations of the Western Hemisphere.

Part Five: The Globe Encompassed, 1500–1750, treats a period dominated by the global effects of European expansion and continued economic growth. European ships took over, expanded, and extended the maritime trade of the Indian Ocean, coastal Africa, and the Asian rim of the Pacific Ocean. This maritime commercial enterprise had its counterpart in European colonial empires in the Americas and a new Atlantic trading system. The contrasting capacities and fortunes of traditional land empires and new maritime empires, along with the exchange of domestic plants and animals between the hemispheres, underline the technological and environmental dimensions of this first era of complete global interaction.

In **Part Six: Revolutions Reshape the World, 1750–1870,** the word revolution is used in several senses:

in the political sense of governmental overthrow, as in France and the Americas; in the metaphorical sense of radical transformative change, as in the Industrial Revolution; and in the broadest sense of a perception of a profound change in circumstances and worldview. Technology and environment lie at the core of these developments. With the rapid ascendancy of the Western belief that science and technology could overcome all challenges—environmental or otherwise—technology became an instrument not only of transformation but also of domination, to the point of threatening the integrity and autonomy of cultural traditions in nonindustrial lands.

Part Seven: Global Diversity and Dominance, 1850–1945, examines the development of a world arena in which people conceived of events on a global scale. Imperialism, world war, international economic connections, and world-encompassing ideological tendencies, such as nationalism and socialism, present the picture of a globe becoming increasingly interconnected. European dominance took on a worldwide dimension, seeming at times to threaten the diversity of human cultural experience with permanent subordination to European values and philosophies, while at other times triggering strong political or cultural resistance.

For Part Eight: Perils and Promises of a Global Community, 1945 to the Present, we divided the last half of the twentieth century into three time periods: 1945–1975, 1975–1991, and 1991 to the present. The challenges of the Cold War and post-colonial nation building dominated most of the period and unleashed global economic, technological, and political forces that became increasingly important in all aspects of human life. Technology plays a central role in Part Eight, because of its integral role in the growth of a global community and because its many benefits in improving the quality of life seem clouded by real and potential negative impacts on the environment.

Supplements

We have assembled an array of supplements to aid students in learning and instructors in teaching. These supplements, including the *History Companion*, a *Study Guide*, an *Instructor's Resource Manual*, *Test Items*, a *Teacher's Guide to the Advanced Placement World History Course*, and *Map Transparencies*, provide a tightly integrated program of teaching and learning. The *History Companion* has three components:

The *Instructor Companion* is an easily searchable CD-ROM that makes hundreds of historical images and maps instantly accessible in PowerPoint format. Each image is accompanied by notes that place it in its proper historical context and tips for ways it can be presented in the classroom. This CD is free to instructors with the adoption of the textbook. In addition to visual presentation materials, the CD includes our *HM Testing* program; a computerized version of the *Test Items* to enable instructors to alter, replace, or add questions; as well as resources from the *Instructor's Resource Manual.*

The *Student Research Companion* is a free Internet-based tool with 100 interactive maps and 500 primary sources. The primary sources include headnotes that provide pertinent background information and questions that students can answer and email to their instructors.

The *Student Study Companion* is a free online study guide that contains ACE self-tests, which feature 25 to 30 multiple-choice questions per chapter with feedback, an audio pronunciation guide, web-based flashcards, chapter chronologies, and web links. In addition, *History WIRED: Web Intensive Research Exercises and Documents,* updated by John Reisbord (Ph.D. Northwestern University), offers text-specific links to visual and written sources on the World Wide Web, along with exercises to enhance learning. These study tools will help make your students succeed in the classroom.

The *Study Guide,* written by Michele G. Scott James of Mira Costa College, contains learning objectives, chapter outlines (with space for students' notes on particular sections), key-term identifications, multiple-choice questions, short-answer and essay questions, and map exercises. Included too are distinctive "comparison charts" to help students organize the range of information about different cultures and events discussed in each chapter. The Study Guide is published in two volumes, to correspond to Volumes I and II of the college edition of the textbook: Volume I contains Chapters 1–16; Volume II, Chapters 16–34.

The *Instructor's Resource Manual,* thoroughly revised by John Reisbord (Ph.D. Northwestern University), provides useful teaching strategies for the global history course and tips for getting the most out of the text. Each chapter contains instructional objectives, a detailed chapter outline, discussion questions, in-depth learning projects, and audio-visual resources. Also available from your McDougal Littell representative is a correlation between the textbook and the Advanced Placement World History course description (the "acorn book").

Our *Test Items,* prepared by Jane Scimeca of Brookdale Community College, offers 20 to 25 key-term identifications, 5 to 10 essay questions with answer guidelines, 35 to 40 multiple-choice questions, and 2 to 3 history and geography exercises. The multiple-choice items each provide five possible answers, to parallel the format of the Advanced Placement examination.

In addition, Monty Armstrong of Cerritos High School, Cerritos, California, has prepared a *Teacher's Guide to the Advanced Placement World History Course,* to help teachers make optimal use of *The Earth and Its Peoples* in preparing for the AP exam.

Finally, a set of transparencies of all the maps in the textbook is available on adoption.

Acknowledgements

Our special thanks go to Bard Keeler, who wrote the "Document-Based Question" features. Mr. Keeler is an Advanced Placement World History teacher and Department Chair, History and Social Science, Gulf Coast High School, Naples, Florida.

In preparing the Third Edition, we benefited from the critical readings of many colleagues. Our sincere thanks go in particular to the following instructors: Joseph Adams, Walton High School, Cobb County, Georgia; William H. Alexander, Norfolk State University; Corinne Blake, Rowan University; Olwyn M. Blouet, Virginia State University; Eric Bobo, Hinds Community College; James Boyden, Tulane University; Craige B. Champion, Syracuse University; Eleanor A. Congdon, Youngstown State University; Philip Daileader, The College of William and Mary; Donald M. Fisher, Niagara County Community College; Nancy Fitch, California State University, Fullerton; Jay Harmon, Catholic High School, Baton Rouge, Louisiana; Carol A. Keller, San Antonio College; Susan Maneck, Jackson State University; Laurie S. Mannino, Magruder High School, North Potomac, Maryland; Margaret Malamud, New Mexico State University; Randall McGowen, University of Oregon; Diethelm Prowe, Carleton College; Michael D. Richards, Sweet Briar College; William Schell, Jr., Murray State University; Jeffrey M. Shumway, Brigham Young University; Jonathan Skaff, Shippensburg University of Pennsylvania; Tracy L. Steele, Sam Houston State University; and Peter von Sivers, University of Utah.

When textbook authors set out on a project, they are inclined to believe that 90 percent of the effort will be theirs and 10 percent that of various editors and production specialists employed by their publisher. How very naïve. This book would never have seen the light of day had it not been for the unstinting labors of the great team of professionals who turned the authors' words into beautifully presented print. Our debt to the staff of Houghton Mifflin remains undiminished in the third edition. Nancy Blaine, Senior Sponsoring Editor, has offered us firm but sympathetic guidance throughout the revision process. Jennifer Sutherland, Senior Development Editor, offered astute and sympathetic assistance as the authors worked to incorporate many new ideas and subjects into the text. Carol Newman, Senior Project Editor, moved the work through the production stages to meet what had initially seemed like an unachievable schedule. Carole Frolich did an outstanding job of photo research. Charlotte Miller excelled at developing and creating all the beautiful maps in the text. Jill Haber, Senior Production Design Coordinator, dealt with many of the technological issues that arise in producing a text of this size. We also recognize the invaluable contributions of Senior Designer Henry Rachlin, who created the book's elegant new design, Editorial Associate Annette Fantasia, who oversaw the review process and the preparation of supplemental material, and Florence Cadran, Manufacturing Manager, who saw to it that the text was printed on schedule.

We thank also the many students whose questions and concerns, expressed directly or through their instructors, shaped much of this revision. We continue to welcome all readers' suggestions, queries, and criticisms. Please contact us at our respective institutions or at this e-mail address: college_history@hmco.com.

About the Authors

Richard W. Bulliet   Professor of Middle Eastern History at Columbia University, Richard W. Bulliet received his Ph.D. from Harvard University. He has written scholarly works on a number of topics: the social history of medieval Iran *(The Patricians of Nishapur)*, the historical competition between pack camels and wheeled transport *(The Camel and the Wheel)*, the process of conversion to Islam *(Conversion to Islam in the Medieval Period)*, and the overall course of Islamic social history *(Islam: The View from the Edge)*. He is the editor of the *Columbia History of the Twentieth Century*. He has published four novels, co-edited *The Encyclopedia of the Modern Middle East*, and hosted an educational television series on the Middle East. He was awarded a fellowship by the John Simon Guggenheim Memorial Foundation.

Pamela Kyle Crossley   Pamela Kyle Crossley received her Ph.D. in Modern Chinese History from Yale University. She is Professor of History and Rosenwald Research Professor in the Arts and Sciences at Dartmouth College. Her books include *A Translucent Mirror: History and Identity in Qing Imperial Ideology; The Manchus; Orphan Warriors: Three Manchu Generations and the End of the Qing World;* and (with Lynn Hollen Lees and John W. Servos) *Global Society: The World Since 1900.* Her research, which concentrates on the cultural history of China, Inner Asia, and Central Asia, has been supported by the John Simon Guggenheim Memorial Foundation and the National Endowment for the Humanities.

Daniel R. Headrick   Daniel R. Headrick received his Ph.D. in History from Princeton University. Professor of History and Social Science at Roosevelt University in Chicago, he is the author of several books on the history of technology, imperialism, and international relations, including *The Tools of Empire: Technology and European Imperialism in the Nineteenth Century; The Tentacles of Progress: Technology Transfer in the Age of Imperialism; The Invisible Weapon: Telecommunications and International Politics;* and *When Information Came of Age: Technologies of Knowledge in the Age of Reason and Revolution, 1700–1850.* His articles have appeared in the *Journal of World History* and the *Journal of Modern History,* and he has been awarded fellowships by the National Endowment for the Humanities, the John Simon Guggenheim Memorial Foundation, and the Alfred P. Sloan Foundation.

Steven W. Hirsch   Steven W. Hirsch holds a Ph.D. in Classics from Stanford University and is currently Associate Professor Classics and History at Tufts University. He has received grants from the National Endowment for the Humanities and the Massachusetts Foundation for Humanities and Public Policy. His research and publications include *The Friendship of the Barbarians: Xenophon and the Persian Empire,* as well as articles and reviews in the *Classical Journal,* the *American Journal of Philology,* and the *Journal of Interdisciplinary History.* He is currently working on a comparative study of ancient Mediterranean and Chinese civilizations.

Lyman L. Johnson   Professor of History at the University of North Carolina at Charlotte, Lyman L. Johnson earned his Ph.D. in Latin American History from the University of Connecticut. A two-time Senior Fulbright-Hays Lecturer, he also has received fellowships from the Tinker Foundation, the Social Science Research Council, the National Endowment for the Humanities, and the American Philosophical Society. His recent books include *Death, Dismemberment, and Memory; The Faces of Honor* (with Sonya Lipsett-Rivera); *The Problem of Order in Changing Societies; Essays on the Price History of Eighteenth-Century Latin America* (with Enrique Tandeter); and *Colonial Latin America* (with Mark A. Burkholder). He also has published in journals, including the *Hispanic American Historical Review,* the *Journal of Latin American Studies,* the *International Review of Social History, Social History,* and *Desarrollo Económico.* He recently served as president of the Conference on Latin American History.

David Northrup   Professor of History at Boston College, David Northrup earned his Ph.D. in African and European History from the University of California at Los Angeles. He earlier taught in Nigeria with the Peace Corps and at Tuskegee Institute. Research supported by the Fulbright-Hays Commission, the National Endowment for the Humanities, and the Social Science Research Council led to publications concerning pre-colonial Nigeria, the Congo (1870–1940), the Atlantic slave trade, and Asian, African, and Pacific Islander indentured labor in the nineteenth century. A contributor to the *Oxford History of the British Empire* and *Blacks in the British Empire,* his latest book is *Africa's Discovery of Europe, 1450–1850.* For 2004 and 2005 he serves as president of the World History Association.

Note on Spelling and Usage

Where necessary for clarity, dates are followed by the letters C.E. or B.C.E. The abbreviation C.E. stands for "Common Era" and is equivalent to A.D. (*anno Domini,* Latin for "in the year of the Lord"). The abbreviation B.C.E stands for "before the Common Era" and means the same as B.C. ("before Christ"). In keeping with our goal of approaching world history without special concentration on one culture or another, we chose these neutral abbreviations as appropriate to our enterprise. Because many readers will be more familiar with English than with metric measurements, however, units of measure are generally given in the English system, with metric equivalents following in parentheses.

In general, Chinese has been romanized according to the *pinyin* method. Exceptions include proper names well established in English (e.g., Canton, Chiang Kai-shek) and a few English words borrowed from Chinese (e.g., kowtow). Spellings of Arabic, Ottoman Turkish, Persian, Mongolian, Manchu, Japanese, and Korean names and terms avoid special diacritical marks for letters that are pronounced only slightly differently in English. An apostrophe is used to indicate when two Chinese syllables are pronounced separately (e.g., Chang'an).

For words transliterated from languages that use the Arabic script—Arabic, Ottoman Turkish, Persian, Urdu—the apostrophe indicating separately pronounced syllables may represent either of two special consonants, the *hamza* or the *ain.* Because most English-speakers do not hear the distinction between these two, they have not been distinguished in transliteration and are not indicated when they occur at the beginning or end of a word. As with Chinese, some words and commonly used place-names from these languages are given familiar English spellings (e.g., Quran instead of Qur'an, Cairo instead of al-Qahira). Arabic romanization has normally been used for terms relating to Islam, even where the context justifies slightly different Turkish or Persian forms, again for ease of comprehension.

Before 1492 the inhabitants of the Western Hemisphere had no single name for themselves. They had neither a racial consciousness nor a racial identity. Identity was derived from kin groups, language, cultural practices, and political structures. There was no sense that physical similarities created a shared identity. America's original inhabitants had racial consciousness and racial identity imposed on them by conquest and the occupation of their lands by Europeans after 1492. All of the collective terms for these first American peoples are tainted by this history. *Indians, Native Americans, Amerindians, First Peoples, and Indigenous Peoples* are among the terms in common usage. In this book the names of individual cultures and states are used wherever possible. *Amerindian* and other terms that suggest transcultural identity and experience are used most commonly for the period after 1492.

There is an ongoing debate about how best to render Amerindian words in English. It has been common for authors writing in English to follow Mexican usage for Nahuatl and Yucatec Maya words and place-names. In this style, for example, the capital of the Aztec state is spelled Tenochtitlán, and the important late Maya city-state is spelled Chichén Itzá. Although these forms are still common even in the specialist literature, we have chosen to follow the scholarship that sees these accents as unnecessary. The exceptions are modern place-names, such as Mérida and Yucatán, which are accented. A similar problem exists for the spelling of Quechua and Aymara words from the Andean region of South America. Although there is significant disagreement among scholars, we follow the emerging consensus and use the spellings khipu (not quipu), Tiwanaku (not Tiahuanaco), and Wari (not Huari). However, we keep Inca (not Inka) and Cuzco (not Cusco), since these spellings are expected by most of our potential readers and we hope to avoid confusion.

The Earth and Its Peoples

A Global History

The Emergence of Human Communities, to 500 B.C.E.

Around 10,000 years ago, some human groups in various parts of the world began to cultivate plants, domesticate animals, and make pottery vessels for storage. One consequence of this shift from hunting and gathering to agriculture was the emergence of permanent settlements—at first small villages but eventually larger towns as well.

The earliest complex societies arose in the great river valleys of Asia and Africa, around 3100 B.C.E. in the valley between the Tigris and Euphrates Rivers in Mesopotamia and along the Nile River in Egypt, somewhat later in the valley of the Indus River in Pakistan, and on the floodplain of the Yellow River in China. In these arid regions, agriculture depended on irrigation with river water, and centers of political power arose to organize the massive human labor required to dig and maintain channels to carry water to the fields.

Kings and priests dominated these early societies. Kings controlled the military forces; priests managed the temples and the wealth of the gods. Within the urban centers—in the midst of palaces, temples, fortification walls, and other monumental buildings—lived administrators, soldiers, priests, merchants, craftsmen, and others with specialized skills. The production of surplus food grown on rural estates by a dependent peasantry sustained the activities of these groups. Professional scribes kept administrative and financial records and preserved their civilization's religious and scientific knowledge.

Over time, certain centers extended their influence and came to dominate broad expanses of territory. The rulers of these early empires were motivated primarily by the need to secure access to raw materials, especially tin and copper, from which to make bronze. A similar motive accounts for the development of long-distance trade and diplomatic relations between major powers. Fueling long-distance trade was the desire for bronze, which had both practical and symbolic importance. From bronze, artisans made weapons, tools and utensils, and ritual objects. Ownership of bronze items was a sign of wealth and power. Trade and diplomacy helped spread culture and technology from the core river-valley areas to neighboring regions, such as southern China, Nubia, Syria-Palestine, Anatolia, and the Aegean.

In the Western Hemisphere, different geographical circumstances called forth distinctive patterns of technological and cultural response in the early civilizations of the Olmec in southern Mexico and Chavín in the Andean region of South America. Nevertheless, the challenges of organizing agriculture and trade led to many of the same features of complex societies—social stratification, specialization of labor, urbanization, monumental building, technological development, and artistic achievement.

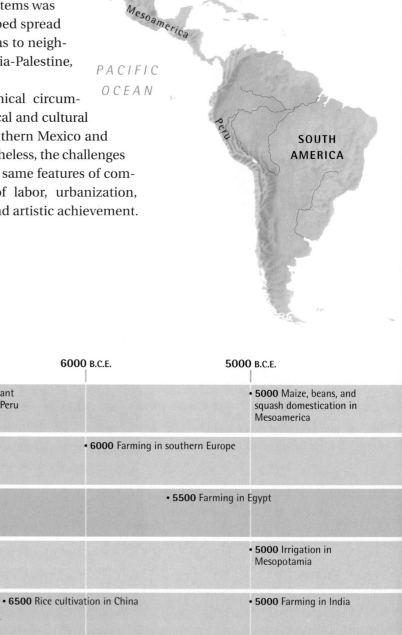

	8000 B.C.E.	7000 B.C.E.	6000 B.C.E.	5000 B.C.E.
Americas		• **7000** Incipient plant domestication in Peru		• **5000** Maize, beans, and squash domestication in Mesoamerica
Europe	Spread of Indo-European languages		• **6000** Farming in southern Europe	
Africa	• **8000** Farming in eastern Sahara		• **5500** Farming in Egypt	
Middle East	• **8000** Domestication of plants and animals in Fertile Crescent			• **5000** Irrigation in Mesopotamia
Asia and Oceania		• **6500** Rice cultivation in China		• **5000** Farming in India

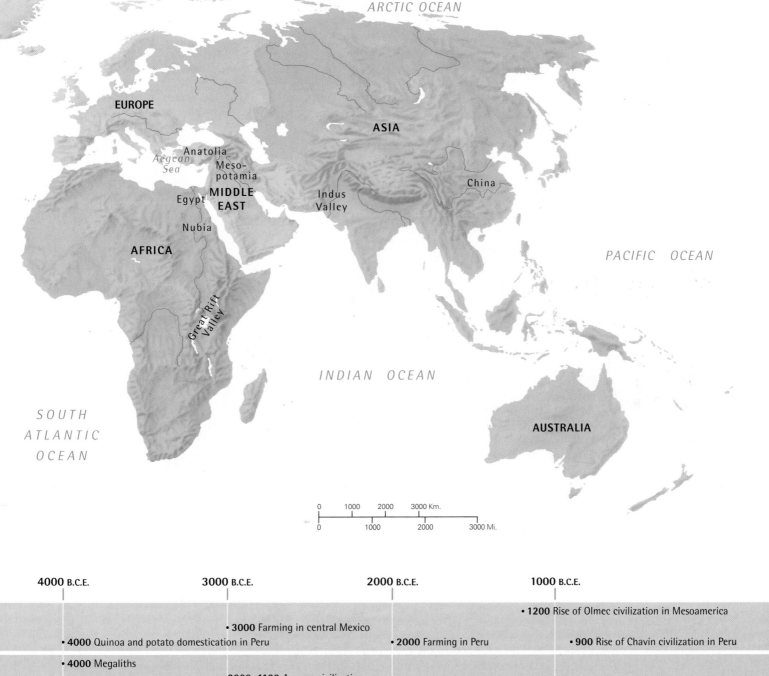

ARCTIC OCEAN

EUROPE

ASIA

Anatolia
Aegean
Sea
Meso-
potamia
Egypt
MIDDLE
EAST

China

Indus
Valley

Nubia

AFRICA

PACIFIC OCEAN

Great Rift
Valley

INDIAN OCEAN

SOUTH
ATLANTIC
OCEAN

AUSTRALIA

| 0 | 1000 | 2000 | 3000 Km. |
| 0 | 1000 | 2000 | 3000 Mi. |

4000 B.C.E.   **3000** B.C.E.   **2000** B.C.E.   **1000** B.C.E.

• 1200 Rise of Olmec civilization in Mesoamerica

• 3000 Farming in central Mexico

• 4000 Quinoa and potato domestication in Peru   • 2000 Farming in Peru   • 900 Rise of Chavín civilization in Peru

• 4000 Megaliths

3000–1100 Aegean civilization   • 1000 Iron metallurgy

• 3100 Unification of Egypt   2040–1640 Middle Kingdom Egypt

2575–2134 Old Kingdom Egypt   1532–1070 New Kingdom Egypt

• 2000 Rise of Kush in Nubia   • 800 Rise of Nubian kingdom at Napata

• 3100 Mesopotamian civilization   • 1750 Hammurabi's law code   • 911 Rise of Neo-Assyrian Empire

Advent of horses in western Asia 2000 •   1700–1200 Hittites dominant in Anatolia

• 2350 Akkadian kingdom

Bronze metallurgy in China 2000 •   1600–1027 Shang kingdom in China

2600–1900 Indus Valley civilization   1027–221 Zhou kingdom in China

1 From the Origins of Agriculture to the First River-Valley Civilizations 8000–1500 B.C.E.

Painted Wooden Models from the Tomb of an Egyptian Nobleman, ca. 2000 B.C.E.
Meketre, seated at right, oversees inspection of his cattle with the help of herdsmen and other servants.

Some five thousand years ago in Mesopotamia (present-day Iraq), people living in Sumer, the world's first urban civilization, cherished the story of Gilgamesh, superhero king of the city of Uruk. The goddess of creation, it recounted, fashioned the wild man Enkidu°:

> There was virtue in him of the god of war, of Ninurta himself. His body was rough, he had long hair like a woman's; it waved like the hair of Nisaba, the goddess of corn. His body was covered with matted hair like Samuqan's, the god of cattle. He was innocent of mankind; he knew nothing of the cultivated land. Enkidu ate grass in the hills with the gazelle and jostled with the wild beasts at the water-holes; he had joy of the water with the herds of wild game.

When Gilgamesh learns of Enkidu from a hunter, he sends a temple prostitute to tame him. After her seduction causes the wild beasts to shun him, she says:

> Come with me. I will take you to strong-walled Uruk,° to the blessed temple of Ishtar and of Anu, of love and of heaven . . . there all the people are dressed in their gorgeous robes, every day is holiday, the young men and the girls are wonderful to see. How sweet they smell! . . . O Enkidu, you who live life, I will show you Gilgamesh.[1]

She clothes Enkidu and teaches him to eat cooked food, drink beer, and bathe and oil his body. Her words and actions signal the principal traits of civilized life in Sumer, just as the divine comparisons of the wild Enkidu show Sumer's dependence on grain and livestock.

The Sumerians, like other peoples, equated civilization with their own way of life. But lifestyles varied. Given the ambiguity of the term *civilization*, therefore, the common understanding that the first civilizations arose in Mesopotamia and Egypt sometime before 3000 B.C.E. needs examination.

Scholars agree that settled agricultural life and certain political, social, economic, and technological traits are indicators of **civilization,** if not of every civilization. These traits include (1) cities as administrative centers, (2) a political system based on defined territory rather than kinship, (3) many people engaged in specialized, non-food-producing activities, (4) status distinctions based largely on accumulation of wealth, (5) monumental building, (6) a system for keeping permanent records, (7) long-distance trade, and (8) sophisticated interest in science and art.

The earliest societies exhibiting these traits appeared in the floodplains of great rivers: the Tigris° and Euphrates° in Iraq, the Indus in Pakistan, the Yellow (Huang He°) in China, and the Nile in Egypt (see Map 1.2). Periodic flooding fertilized the land with silt and provided water for agriculture but also threatened lives and property. To control the floods, the peoples living near the rivers created new technologies and forms of political and social organization.

In this chapter, we describe the origins of domestication among the scattered groups of foragers living at the end of the last Ice Age and the slow development of farming and herding societies. We then trace the rise of complex societies in Mesopotamia, Egypt, and the Indus River Valley from approximately 3500 to 1500 B.C.E. (China, developing slightly later, is discussed in Chapter 2). This story roughly coincides with the origins of writing, allowing us to document aspects of human life not revealed by archaeological evidence alone.

As you read this chapter, ask yourself the following questions:

- How did plant and animal domestication set the scene for the emergence of civilization?

- Why did the earliest civilizations arise in river valleys?

Enkidu (EN-kee-doo)   Uruk (OO-rook)

Tigris (TIE-gris)   Euphrates (you-FRAY-teez)
Huang He (hwang huh)

- How did the organization of labor shape political and social structures?

- How did metallurgy, writing, and monumental construction contribute to the power and wealth of elite groups?

- How do religious beliefs reflect interaction with the environment?

BEFORE CIVILIZATION

Evidence of human artistic creativity first came to light in 1940 near Lascaux in southwestern France with the discovery of a vast underground cavern. The cavern walls were covered with paintings of animals, including many that had been extinct for thousands of years. Similar cave paintings have been found in Spain and elsewhere in southern France.

To even the most skeptical person, these artistic troves reveal rich imaginations and sophisticated skills, qualities also apparent in the stone tools and evidence of complex social relations uncovered from prehistoric sites. The production of such artworks and tools over wide areas and long periods of time demonstrates that skills and ideas were not simply individual but were deliberately passed along within societies. These learned patterns of action and expression constitute **culture.** Culture includes material objects, such as dwellings, clothing, tools, and crafts, along with nonmaterial values, beliefs, and languages. Although it is true that some animals also learn new ways, their activities are determined primarily by inherited instincts. Only human communities trace profound cultural developments over time. The development, transmission, and transformation of cultural practices and events are the subject of **history.**

Food Gathering and Stone Technology

Stone toolmaking, the first recognizable cultural activity, first appeared around 2 million years ago. The **Stone Age,** which lasted from then until around 4,000 years ago, can be a misleading label. Stone tools abound at archaeological sites, but not all tools were of stone. They were made as well of bone, skin, and wood, materials that survive poorly. In addition, this period encompasses many cultures and subperiods. Among the major subdivisions, the **Paleolithic°** (Old Stone Age)

lasted until 10,000 years ago, about 3,000 years after the end of the last Ice Age, long periods when glaciers covered much of North America, Europe, and Asia. The **Neolithic°** (New Stone Age), which is associated with the origins of agriculture, followed.

Fossilized animal bones bearing the marks of butchering tools testify to the scavenging and hunting activities of Stone Age peoples, but anthropologists do not believe that early humans lived primarily on meat. Modern **foragers** (hunting and food-gathering peoples) in the Kalahari Desert of southern Africa and Ituri Forest of central Africa derive the bulk of their day-to-day nourishment from wild vegetable foods. They eat meat at feasts. Stone Age peoples probably did the same, even though the tools and equipment for gathering and processing vegetable foods have left few archaeological traces.

Like modern foragers, ancient humans would have used skins and mats woven from leaves for collecting fruits, berries, and wild seeds, and they would have dug up edible roots with wooden sticks. Archaeologists suspect that the doughnut-shaped stones often found at Stone Age sites served as weights to make wooden digging sticks more effective.

Cooking makes both meat and vegetables tastier and easier to digest, something early humans may have discovered inadvertently after wildfires. Humans may have begun setting fires deliberately 1 million to 1.5 million years ago, but proof of cooking does not appear until some 12,500 years ago, when clay cooking pots came into use in East Asia.

Studies of present-day foragers also indicate that Ice Age women probably did most of the gathering and cooking, which they could do while caring for small children. Women past child-bearing age would have been the most knowledgeable and productive food gatherers. Men, with stronger arms and shoulders, would have been better suited for hunting, particularly for large animals. Some early cave art suggests male hunting activities.

The same studies, along with archaeological evidence from Ice Age campsites, indicate that early foragers lived in groups that were big enough to defend themselves from predators and divide responsibility for food collection and preparation, but small enough not to exhaust the food resources within walking distance. Even bands of around fifty men, women, and children would have moved regularly to follow migrating animals or collect seasonally ripening plants in different places.

In regions with severe climates or lacking in natural shelters like caves, people built huts of branches, stones,

---

Paleolithic (pay-lee-oh-LITH-ik)

Neolithic (nee-oh-LITH-ik)

C H R O N O L O G Y			
	Mesopotamia	**Egypt**	**Indus Valley**
3500 B.C.E.		3100–2575 B.C.E. Early Dynastic	
3000 B.C.E.	3000–2350 B.C.E. Early Dynastic (Sumerian)	2575–2134 B.C.E. Old Kingdom	2600 B.C.E. Beginning of Indus Valley civilization
2500 B.C.E.	2350–2230 B.C.E. Akkadian (Semitic)	2134–2040 B.C.E. First Intermediate Period	
2000 B.C.E.	2112–2004 B.C.E. Third Dynasty of Ur (Sumerian) 1900–1600 B.C.E. Old Babylonian (Semitic)	2040–1640 B.C.E. Middle Kingdom	1900 B.C.E. End of Indus Valley civilization
		1640–1532 B.C.E. Second Intermediate Period 1532–1070 B.C.E. New Kingdom	
1500 B.C.E.	1500–1150 B.C.E. Kassite		

bones, skins, and leaves as seasonal camps. Animal skins served as clothing, with the earliest evidence of woven cloth appearing about 26,000 years ago. Groups living in the African grasslands and other game-rich areas probably spent only three to five hours a day securing food, clothing, and shelter. This would have left a great deal of time for artistic endeavors, tool-making, and social life.

The foundations of what later ages called science, art, and religion also date to the Stone Age. Gatherers learned which local plants were edible and when they ripened, as well as which natural substances were effective for medicine, consciousness altering, dyeing, and other purposes. Hunters learned the habits of game animals. People experimented with techniques of using plant and animal materials for clothing, twine, and construction. Knowledge of the environment included identifying which minerals made good paints and which stones made good tools. All of these aspects of culture were passed orally from generation to generation.

Early music and dance have left no traces, but visual artwork has survived abundantly. Cave paintings appear as early as 32,000 years ago in Europe and North Africa and somewhat later in other parts of the world. Because many feature food animals like wild oxen, reindeer, and horses, some scholars believe the art records hunting scenes or played a magical and religious role in hunting.

A newly discovered cave at Vallon Pont-d'Arc° in southern France, however, features rhinoceros, panthers, bears, owls, and a hyena, which probably were not hunted for food. Other drawings include people dressed in animal skins and smeared with paint and stencils of human hands. Some scholars suspect that other marks in cave paintings and on bones may represent efforts at counting or writing.

Some cave art suggests that Stone Age people had well-developed religions, but without written texts, it is hard to know what they believed. Some graves from about 100,000 years ago contain stone implements, food, clothing, and red-ochre powder, indicating that early people revered their leaders enough to honor them in death and may have believed in an afterlife.

The Agricultural Revolutions

Around 10,000 years ago, some human groups began to meet their food needs by raising domesticated plants and animals. Gradually over the next millennium, most people became food producers, although hunting and gathering continued in some places.

Vallon Pont-d'Arc (vah-LON pon-DAHRK)

The term *Neolithic Revolution,* commonly given to the changeover from food gathering to food producing, can be misleading. *Neolithic* means "new stone," but the new tool designs that accompanied the beginnings of agriculture did not define it. Nor was the "revolution" a single event. The changeover occurred at different times in different parts of the world. The term **Agricultural Revolutions** is more precise because it emphasizes the central role of food production and signals that the changeover occurred several times. The adoption of agriculture often included the domestication of animals for food (see Map 1.1).

Food gathering gave way to food production over hundreds of generations. The process may have begun when forager bands, returning year after year to the same seasonal camps, scattered seeds and cleared away weeds to encourage the growth of foods they liked. Such semicultivation could have supplemented food gathering without the permanent settlement of the group. Families choosing to concentrate their energies on food production, however, would have had to settle permanently near their fields.

Specialized stone tools first alerted archaeologists to new food-producing practices: polished or ground stone heads to work the soil, sharp stone chips embedded in bone or wooden handles to cut grasses, and stone mortars to pulverize grain. Early farmers used fire to clear fields of shrubs and trees and discovered that ashes were a natural fertilizer. After the burn-off, farmers used blades and axes to keep the land clear.

Selection of the highest-yielding strains of wild plants led to the development of domesticated varieties over time. As the principal gatherers of wild plant foods, women probably played a major role in this transition to plant cultivation, but the task of clearing fields probably fell to the men.

In the Middle East, the region with the earliest evidence of agriculture, human selection had transformed certain wild grasses into higher-yielding domesticated grains, now known as emmer wheat and barley, by 8000 B.C.E. Farmers there also discovered that alternating the cultivation of grains and pulses (plants yielding edible seeds such as lentils and peas) helped maintain fertility.

Plants domesticated in the Middle East spread to adjacent lands, but in many parts of the world, agriculture arose independently. Exchanges of crops and techniques occurred between regions, but societies that had already turned to farming borrowed new plants, animals, and farming techniques more readily than foraging groups did.

The eastern Sahara, which went through a wet period after 8000 B.C.E., preserves the oldest traces of food

Domestication of Wheat Through selection of the largest seeds of this wild grass, early farmers in the Middle East were able to develop varieties with larger edible kernels. Bread wheat was grown in the Nile Valley by 5000 B.C.E. (From Iris Barn, *Discovering Archaeology,* © 1981)

production in northern Africa. As in the Middle East, emmer wheat and barley became the principal crops and sheep, goats, and cattle the main domestic animals. When drier conditions returned around 5000 B.C.E., many Saharan farmers moved to the Nile Valley, where the river's annual flood provided water for crops.

In Greece, wheat and barley cultivation, beginning as early as 6000 B.C.E., combined local experiments with Middle Eastern borrowings. Shortly after 4000 B.C.E., farming developed in the light-soiled plains of Central Europe and along the Danube River. As forests receded because of climate changes and human clearing efforts, agriculture spread to other parts of Europe over the next millennium.

Early farmers in Europe and elsewhere practiced shifting cultivation, also known as swidden agriculture. After a few growing seasons, farmers left the fields fallow (abandoned to natural vegetation) and cleared new fields nearby. Between 4000 and 3000 B.C.E., for example, communities of from forty to sixty people in the Danube Valley supported themselves on about 500 acres (200 hectares) of farmland, cultivating a third or less each year while leaving the rest fallow to regain its fertility. From around 2600 B.C.E., people in Central Europe began using ox-drawn wooden plows to till heavier and richer soils.

Although the lands around the Mediterranean seem to have shared a complex of crops and farming techniques, geographical barriers blocked the spread elsewhere. Rainfall patterns south of the Sahara favored locally domesticated grains—sorghums, millets, and (in

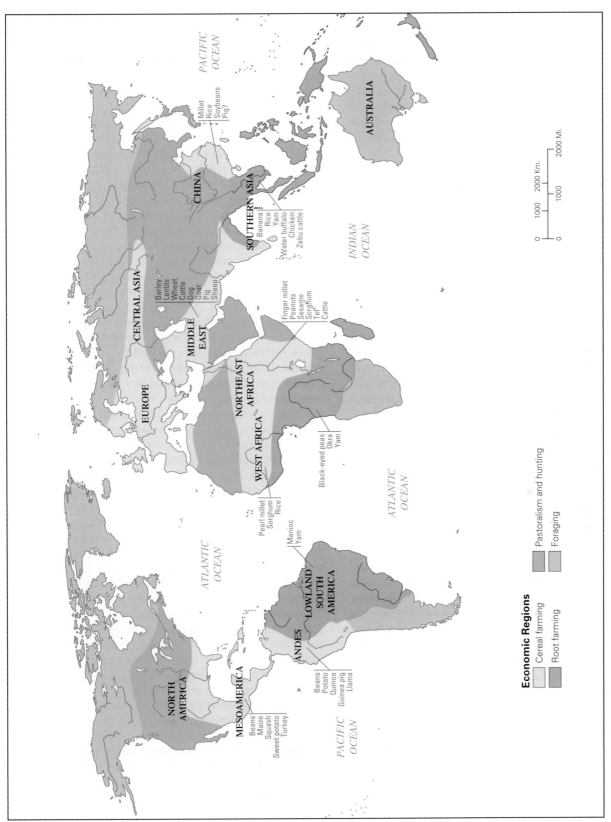

Map 1.1 Early Centers of Plant and Animal Domestication Many different parts of the world made original contributions to domestication during the Agricultural Revolutions that began about 10,000 years ago. Later interactions helped spread these domesticated animals and plants to new locations. In lands less suitable for crop cultivation, pastoralism and hunting remained more important for supplying food.

Ethiopia) teff—over wheat and barley. Middle Eastern grains did not grow at all in the humidity of equatorial West Africa; there, yams became an early domestic crop.

Domestic rice originated in southern China, the northern half of Southeast Asia, or northern India, possibly as early as 10,000 B.C.E. but more likely closer to 5000 B.C.E. The warm, wet climate of southern China particularly favored rice. Indian farmers cultivated hyacinth beans, green grams, and black grams along with rice by about 2000 B.C.E.

In the Americas a decline of game animals in the Tehuacán° Valley of Mexico after 8000 B.C.E. increased people's dependence on wild plants. Agriculture based on maize° (corn) developed there about 3000 B.C.E. and gradually spread. At about the same time, the inhabitants of Peru developed a food production pattern based on potatoes and quinoa°, a protein-rich seed grain. People in the more tropical parts of Mesoamerica cultivated tomatoes, peppers, squash, and potatoes. In South America's tropical forests, the root crop manioc became the staple food after 1500 B.C.E. Manioc and maize then spread to the Caribbean islands.

The domestication of animals expanded rapidly during these same millennia. The first domesticated animal, the dog, may have helped hunters track game well before the Neolithic period. Later, animals initially provided meat but eventually supplied milk, wool, and energy as well.

Refuse dumped outside Middle East villages shows a gradual decline in the number of wild gazelle bones after 7000 B.C.E. This probably reflects the depletion of wild game through overhunting by local farmers. Meat eating, however, did not decline. Sheep and goat bones gradually replaced gazelle bones. Possibly wild sheep and goats learned to graze around agricultural villages to take advantage of the suppression of predators by humans. The tamer animals may gradually have accepted human control and thus become themselves a ready supply of food. The bones of tame animals initially differ so little from those of their wild ancestors that the early stages of domestication are hard to date. However, selective breeding for characteristics like a wooly coat and high milk production eventually yielded distinct breeds of domestic sheep and goats.

Elsewhere, other wild species were evolving domestic forms during the centuries before 3000 B.C.E.: cattle in northern Africa or the Middle East, donkeys in northern Africa, water buffalo in China, humped-back Zebu° cattle in India, horses and two-humped camels in Central Asia, one-humped camels in Arabia, chickens in Southeast Asia, and pigs in several places. Like domestic plant species, varieties of domesticated animals spread from one region to another. The Zebu cattle originally domesticated in India, for example, became important in sub-Saharan Africa about 2,000 years ago.

Once cattle and water buffalo had become sufficiently tame to be yoked to plows, long after their initial domestication, they became essential to the agricultural cycle of grain farmers. In addition, animal droppings provided valuable fertilizer. Wool and milk production also followed initial domestication by a substantial period.

In the Americas, domestic llamas provided meat, transport, and wool, while guinea pigs and turkeys provided meat. Dogs assisted hunters and also provided meat. Some scholars believe that no other American species could have been domesticated, but this cannot be proven. Domestic species could not be borrowed from elsewhere, however, because of the geographical isolation of the Americas.

Pastoralism, a way of life dependent on large herds of grazing livestock, came to predominate in arid regions. As the Sahara approached its maximum dryness around 2500 B.C.E., pastoralists replaced farmers who migrated southward (see Chapter 7). Moving herds to new pastures and watering places throughout the year made pastoralists almost as mobile as foragers and discouraged accumulation of bulky possessions and substantial dwellings. Like modern pastoralists, early cattle keepers probably relied more heavily on milk than on meat, since killing animals diminished the size of their herds. During wet seasons, they may also have engaged in semicultivation or bartered meat and skins for plant foods with nearby farming communities.

Why did the Agricultural Revolutions occur? Some theories assume that growing crops had obvious advantages. Grain, for example, provided both a dietary staple and the makings of beer. Beer drinking appears frequently in ancient Middle Eastern art and can be dated to as early as 3500 B.C.E. Most researchers today, however, believe that climate change drove people to abandon hunting and gathering in favor of pastoralism and agriculture. So great was the global warming that ended the last Ice Age that geologists gave the era since about 9000 B.C.E. a new name: the **Holocene°**. Scientists have also found evidence that temperate lands were exceptionally warm between 6000 and 2000 B.C.E., when people in many parts of the world adopted agriculture. The precise nature of the climatic crisis probably varied. In the Middle East, shortages of wild food caused by dry-

---

Tehuacán (teh-wah-KAHN) **maize** (mayz)
quinoa (kee-NOH-uh) **Zebu** (ZEE-boo)

Holocene (HAWL-oh-seen)

ness or population growth may have stimulated food production. Elsewhere, a warmer, wetter climate could have turned grasslands into forest and thereby reduced supplies of game and wild grains.

In many drier parts of the world, where wild food remained abundant, agriculture did not arise. The inhabitants of Australia relied exclusively on foraging until recent centuries, as did some peoples on the other continents. Amerindians in the arid grasslands from Alaska to the Gulf of Mexico hunted bison, and salmon fishing sustained groups in the Pacific Northwest. Ample supplies of fish, shellfish, and aquatic animals permitted food gatherers east of the Mississippi River to become increasingly sedentary. In the equatorial rain forest and in the southern part of Africa, conditions also favored retention of older ways.

Whatever the causes, the gradual adoption of food production transformed most parts of the world. A hundred thousand years ago, world population, mostly living in the temperate and tropical regions of Africa and Eurasia, did not exceed 2 million. The population may have fallen still lower during the last glacial epoch, between 32,000 and 13,000 years ago. Agriculture supported a gradual population increase, perhaps to 10 million by 5000 B.C.E., and then a mushrooming to between 50 million and 100 million by 1000 B.C.E.[2]

Life in Neolithic Communities

Evidence that an ecological crisis may have triggered the transition to food production has prompted reexamination of the assumption that farmers enjoyed a better life than foragers did. Early farmers probably had to work much harder and for much longer periods than food gatherers. Long days spent clearing and cultivating the land yielded meager harvests. Guarding herds from predators, guiding them to fresh pastures, and tending to their needs imposed similar burdens.

Although early farmers commanded a more reliable food supply, their diet contained less variety and nutrition than that of foragers. Skeletons show that Neolithic farmers were shorter on average than earlier foragers. Death from contagious diseases ravaged farming settlements, which were contaminated by human waste, infested by disease-bearing vermin and insects, and inhabited by domesticated animals—especially pigs and cattle—whose diseases could infect people.

A dependable supply of food that could be stored between harvests to see people through nonproductive seasons, droughts, and other calamities proved decisive in the long run, however. Over several millennia, farmers

came to outnumber nonfarmers, permanent settlements generated cultural changes, and specialized crafts appeared in fledgling towns.

Some researchers envision violent struggles between farmers and foragers. Others see a more peaceful transition. Violence may well have accompanied land clearance that constrained the foragers' food supplies. And farmers probably fought for control of the best land. In most cases, however, farmers seem to have displaced foragers by gradual infiltration rather than by conquest.

The archaeologist Colin Renfrew maintains that over a few centuries, farming populations in Europe could have increased by a factor of fifty to one hundred just on the basis of the dependability of their food supply. In his view, as population densities rose, individuals with fields farthest away from their native village formed new settlements, leading to a steady, nonviolent expansion of agriculture consistent with the archaeological record. An expansion by only 12 to 19 miles (20 to 30 kilometers) in a generation could have brought farming to every corner of Europe between 6500 and 3500 B.C.E.[3] Yet it would have happened so gradually as to minimize sharp conflicts with foragers, who would simply have stayed clear of the agricultural frontier or gradually adopted agriculture themselves. Studies that map similar genetic changes in the population also suggest a gradual spread of agricultural people across Europe from southeast to northwest.[4]

Like forager bands, kinship and marriage bound farming communities together. Nuclear family size (parents and their children) may not have risen, but kinship relations traced back over more generations brought distant cousins into a common kin network. This encouraged the holding of land by large kinship units known as lineages° or clans.

Because each person has two parents, four grandparents, eight great-grandparents, and so on, each individual has a bewildering number of ancestors. Some societies trace descent equally through both parents, but most give greater importance to descent through either the mother (matrilineal° societies) or the father (patrilineal° societies).

Some scholars believe descent through women and perhaps rule by women prevailed in early times. The traditions of Kikuyu° farmers on Mount Kenya in East Africa, for example, relate that women ruled until the Kikuyu men conspired to get all the women pregnant at once and then overthrew them while they were unable to fight back. No specific evidence can prove or disprove

---

lineage (LIN-ee-ij)　**matrilineal** (mat-ruh-LIN-ee-uhl)
patrilineal (pat-ruh-LIN-ee-uhl)　**Kikuyu** (Ki-KOO-yoo)

legends such as this, but it is important not to confuse tracing descent through women (matrilineality) with rule by women (matriarchy°).

Religiously, kinship led to reverence for departed ancestors. Old persons often received elaborate burials. A plastered skull from Jericho° in the Jordan Valley of modern Israel may be evidence of early ancestor reverence or worship at the dawn of agriculture.

The religions of foragers tended to center on sacred groves, springs, and wild animals. In contrast, the rituals of farmers often centered on the Earth Mother, a deity believed to be the source of new life, an all-powerful (and usually male) Sky God, and divinities representing fire, wind, and rain.

Assemblages of **megaliths** (meaning "big stones") seem to relate to religious beliefs. One complex built in the Egyptian desert before 5000 B.C.E. includes stone burial chambers, a calendar circle, and pairs of upright stones that frame the rising sun on the summer solstice. Stonehenge, a famous megalithic site in England constructed about 2000 B.C.E., marked the position of the sun and other celestial bodies at key points in the year. In the Middle East, the Americas, and other parts of the world, giant earth burial mounds may have served similar ritual and symbolic functions.

In some parts of the world, a few Neolithic villages grew into towns, which served as centers of trade and specialized crafts. Two towns in the Middle East, Jericho on the west bank of the Jordan River and Çatal Hüyük° in central Anatolia (modern Turkey), have been extensively excavated (Map 1.2 shows their location). Jericho revealed an elaborate early agricultural settlement. The round mud-brick dwellings characteristic of Jericho around 8000 B.C.E. may have imitated the shape of the tents of foragers who once had camped near Jericho's natural spring. A millennium later, rectangular rooms with finely plastered walls and floors and wide doorways opened onto central courtyards. Surrounding the 10-acre (4-hectare) settlement, a massive stone wall protected against attacks.

The ruins of Çatal Hüyük, an even larger Neolithic town, date to between 7000 and 5000 B.C.E. and cover 32 acres (13 hectares). Its residents lived in plastered mud-brick rooms with elaborate decorations, but Çatal Hüyük had no wall. Instead, the outer walls of its houses formed a continuous barrier without doors or large windows. Residents entered their houses by climbing down ladders through a hole in the roof.

Long-distance trade at Çatal Hüyük featured obsidian, a hard volcanic rock that artisans chipped, ground,

Neolithic Goddess   Many versions of a well-nourished and pregnant female figure were found at Çatal Hüyük. Here she is supported by twin leopards whose tails curve over her shoulders. To those who inhabited the city some 8,000 years ago the figure likely represented fertility and power over nature.   (C. M. Dixon)

and polished into tools, weapons, mirrors, and ornaments. Other residents made fine pottery, wove baskets and woolen cloth, made stone and shell beads, and worked leather and wood. House sizes varied, but nothing indicates that Çatal Hüyük had a dominant class or a centralized political structure.

Representational art at Çatal Hüyük makes it clear that hunting retained a powerful hold on people's minds. Wall paintings of hunting scenes closely resemble earlier cave paintings. Many depict men and women adorned with leopard skins. Men were buried with weapons rather than with farm tools, and bones from rubbish heaps prove that wild game featured prominently in their diet.

Yet Çatal Hüyük's economy rested on agriculture. The surrounding fields produced barley and emmer wheat, as well as legumes° and other vegetables. Pigs

---

matriarchy (MAY-tree-ahr-key)   **Jericho** (JER-ih-koe)
Çatal Hüyük (cha-TAHL hoo-YOOK)

legume (LEG-yoom)

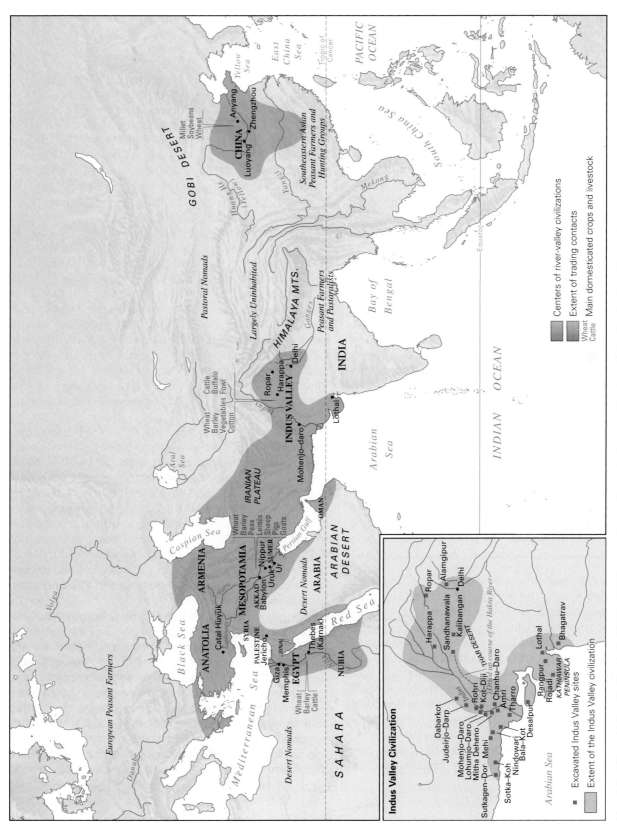

Map 1.2 River-Valley Civilizations, 3500–1500 B.C.E. The earliest complex societies arose in the floodplains of large rivers: in the fourth millennium B.C.E. in the valley of the Tigris and Euphrates Rivers in Mesopotamia and the Nile River in Egypt, in the third millennium B.C.E. in the valley of the Indus River in Pakistan, and in the second millennium B.C.E. in the valley of the Yellow River in China.

were kept along with goats and sheep. Nevertheless, foragers' foods, such as acorns and wild grains, had not yet disappeared.

Çatal Hüyük had one religious shrine for every two houses. At least forty rooms contained shrines with depictions of horned wild bulls, female breasts, goddesses, leopards, and handprints. Rituals involved burning dishes of grain, legumes, and meat but not sacrifice of live animals. Statues of plump female deities far outnumber statues of male deities, suggesting that the inhabitants venerated a goddess as their principal deity. The large number of females who were buried elaborately in shrine rooms may have been priestesses of this cult. The site's principal excavator maintains that although male priests existed, "it seems extremely likely that the cult of the goddess was administered mainly by women."[5]

Metalworking became a specialized occupation in the late Neolithic period. At Çatal Hüyük, objects of copper and lead, which occur naturally in fairly pure form, date to about 6400 B.C.E. Silver and gold also appear at early dates in various parts of the world. Because of their rarity and their softness, these metals did not replace stone tools and weapons. The discovery of decorative and ceremonial objects of metal in graves indicates that they became symbols of status and power.

Towns, specialized crafts, and religious shrines forced the farmers to produce extra food for nonfarmers like priests and artisans. The building of permanent houses, walls, and towers, not to mention megalithic monuments, also called for added labor. Stonehenge, for example, took some 30,000 person-hours to build. Whether these tasks were performed freely or coerced is unknown.

MESOPOTAMIA

Because of the unpredictable nature of the Tigris and Euphrates Rivers, the peoples of ancient Mesopotamia saw themselves at the mercy of gods, who embodied the forces of nature. The Babylonian Creation Myth (**Babylon** was the most important city in southern Mesopotamia in the second and first millennia B.C.E.) climaxes in a cosmic battle between Marduk, the chief god of Babylon, and Tiamat°, a female figure who personifies the salt sea. Marduk cuts up Tiamat and from her body fashions the earth and sky. He then creates the divisions of time, the celestial bodies, rivers, and weather phenomena. From the blood of a defeated rebel god, he creates human beings. Myths of this sort explained to the ancient inhabitants of Mesopotamia the environment in which they were living.

Settled Agriculture in an Unstable Landscape

Mesopotamia means "land between the rivers" in Greek. It reflects the centrality of the Euphrates and Tigris Rivers to the way of life in this region (see Map 1.3). The plain alongside and between the rivers, which originate in the mountains of eastern Anatolia (modern Turkey) and empty into the Persian Gulf, gains fertility from the silt deposited by river floods over many millennia.

Today mostly in Iraq, the Mesopotamian plain gives way to mountains in the north and east: an arc extending from northern Syria through southeastern Anatolia to the Zagros° Mountains that separate the plain from the Iranian Plateau. To the west and southwest lie the Syrian and Arabian deserts, to the southeast the Persian Gulf. Floods caused by snow melting in the northern mountains can be sudden and violent. They come inconveniently in the spring when crops, planted in winter to avoid the torrid summer temperatures, are ripening. Floods sometimes cause the rivers to change course, abruptly cutting off fields and towns from water and river communication.

Although the first domestication of plants and animals around 8000 B.C.E. occurred nearby, in the "Fertile Crescent" region of northern Syria and southeastern Anatolia, agriculture did not reach Mesopotamia until approximately 5000 B.C.E. "Dry" (unirrigated) farming requires at least 8 inches (20 centimeters) of rain a year. The hot, arid climate of southern Mesopotamia calls for irrigation, the artificial provision of water to crops. Initially, people probably channeled floodwater into nearby fields, but shortly after 3000 B.C.E., they learned to construct canals to supply water as needed and carry it to more distant fields.

Ox-drawn plows, developed by around 4000 B.C.E., cut a furrow in the earth into which carefully measured amounts of seed dropped from an attached funnel. Farmers favored barley as a cereal crop because it could tolerate the Mesopotamian climate and withstand the toxic effects of salt drawn to the surface of the soil by evaporation. Fields stood fallow (unplanted) every other year to replenish the nutrients in the soil. Date palms provided food, fiber, and wood. Garden plots produced vegetables. Reeds growing along the rivers and in the marshy southern delta yielded raw material for mats,

---

Tiamat (TIE-ah-mat)

Zagros (ZAG-ruhs)

Reed Huts in the Marshes of Southern Iraq   Reeds growing along the riverbanks or in the swampy lands at the head of the Persian Gulf were used in antiquity—and continue to be used today—for a variety of purposes, including baskets and small watercraft as well as dwellings.   (Courtesy, Dominique Collon)

baskets, huts, and boats. Fish was a dietary staple. Herds of sheep and goats, which grazed on fallow land or the nearby desert, provided wool, milk, and meat. Donkeys, originally domesticated in northeast Africa, joined cattle as beasts of burden in the third millennium B.C.E., as did camels from Arabia and horses from the mountains in the second millennium B.C.E.

The written record begins with the **Sumerians** and marks the division, by some definitions, between prehistory and history. Archaeological evidence places the Sumerians in southern Mesopotamia at least by 5000 B.C.E. and perhaps even earlier. They created the framework of civilization in Mesopotamia during a long period of dominance in the third millennium B.C.E. Other peoples lived in Mesopotamia as well. As early as 2900 B.C.E., personal names recorded in inscriptions from the more northerly cities reveal a non-Sumerian **Semitic°** language. (*Semitic* refers to a family of languages spoken in parts of western Asia and northern Africa. They include the Hebrew, Aramaic°, and Phoenician° of the ancient world and the Arabic of today.) Possibly the descendants of nomads from the desert west of Mesopotamia, these Semites seem to have lived in peace with the Sumerians, adopting their culture and sometimes achieving positions of wealth and power.

By 2000 B.C.E., the Semitic peoples had become politically dominant. From this time on, Akkadian°, a Semitic language, took precedence over Sumerian, although the Sumerian cultural legacy survived in translation. The

Sumerian-Akkadian dictionaries compiled at the time to facilitate translations from Sumerian allow us today to read the language, which has no known relatives. The characteristics and adventures of the Semitic gods also indicate cultural borrowing. This cultural synthesis parallels a biological merging of Sumerians and Semites

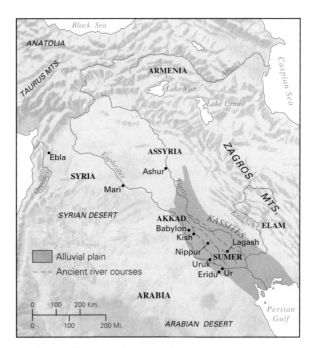

Map 1.3   Mesopotamia   The Sumerians of southern Mesopotamia developed new technologies, complex political and social institutions, and distinctive cultural practices, responding to the need to organize labor resources to create and maintain an irrigation network in the Tigris-Euphrates Valley, a land of little rain.

Semitic (suh-MIT-ik)   **Aramaic** (ar-uh-MAY-ik)
Phoenician (fi-NEE-shuhn)   **Akkadian** (uh-KAY-dee-uhn)

through intermarriage. Though other ethnic groups, including Kassites° from the eastern mountains and Elamites° and Persians from farther south in Iran, played roles in Mesopotamian history, the Sumerian/Semitic cultural heritage remained fundamentally unaltered until the arrival of Greeks in the late fourth century B.C.E.

Cities, Kings, and Trade

Mesopotamian farmers usually lived in villages. A group of families, totaling a few hundred persons perhaps, could protect one another, work together at key times in the agricultural cycle, and share tools, barns, and threshing floors. Village society also provided companionship and a pool of potential marriage partners.

Occasionally, as a particularly successful village grew, small satellite villages developed nearby and eventually merged with the main village to form an urban center. Cities depended on agriculture and therefore on the villages. Many early Mesopotamian city dwellers went out each day to labor in nearby fields. Other city dwellers, however, depended for food on the surplus food production of the villagers. Some specialized in crafts—for example, pottery, artwork, and forging weapons, tools, and other objects out of metal. Others served the gods or carried out administrative duties. Mesopotamian cities controlled the agricultural land and collected crop surpluses from villages in their vicinity. In return, the city provided rural districts with military protection against bandits and raiders and a market where villagers could acquire manufactured goods produced by urban specialists.

The term **city-state** refers to a self-governing urban center and the agricultural territories it controlled. Stretches of uncultivated land, either desert or swamp, served as buffers between the many small city-states of early Mesopotamia. Nevertheless, disputes over land, water rights, and movable property often sparked hostilities between neighboring cities and the building of protective° walls of sun-dried bricks. At other times, cities cooperated, sharing water and allowing traders safe passage through their territories.

Mesopotamians opened new land to agriculture by building and maintaining irrigation networks. Canals brought water from river to field; drainage ditches carried the water back to the river before evaporation could draw harmful salt and minerals to the surface. Weirs (partial dams) raised the water level of the river so that water could flow by gravity into the canals. Dikes along the riverbanks protected against floods. The silt carried by floods clogged the canals, which required frequent

dredging. In some places, levers with counterweights lifted buckets of irrigation water out of a river or canal.

Successful operation of such sophisticated irrigation systems depended on leaders compelling or persuading large numbers of people to work together. Other projects called for similar cooperation: harvesting, sheep shearing, building of fortifications and large public buildings, and warfare. Two centers of power, the temple and the palace of the king, have left written records, but details of governmental life remain scanty, as are the hints at some sort of citizens' assembly that may have evolved from traditional village councils.

One or more temples, centrally located, housed each city-state's deity or deities and their associated cults—sets of religious rituals. Temples owned agricultural lands and stored the gifts that worshipers donated. The central location of the temple buildings confirms the importance of cults. Head priests, who controlled each shrine and managed its wealth, played prominent political and economic roles.

In the third millennium B.C.E., Sumerian documents show the emergence of a *lugal*° or "big man"—what we would call a king. An increase in warfare as ever-larger communities quarreled over land, water, and raw materials may have prompted this development, but details are lacking. According to one theory, communities chose certain men to lead their armies in time of war, and these individuals found ways to prolong their authority in peacetime and assume judicial and ritual functions. Although the lugal's position was not hereditary, it often passed from a father to a capable son.

The location of the temple in the city's heart and the less prominent siting of the king's palace symbolize the later emergence of royalty. The king's power grew at the expense of the priesthood, however, because the army backed him. The priests and temples retained influence because of their wealth and religious mystique, but they gradually became dependent on the palace. Some Mesopotamian kings claimed divinity, but this concept did not take root. Normally the king portrayed himself as the deity's earthly representative.

By the late third millennium B.C.E., kings assumed responsibility for the upkeep and building of temples and the proper performance of ritual. Other royal responsibilities included maintaining city walls and defenses, extending and repairing irrigation channels, guarding property rights, warding off foreign attacks, and establishing justice.

The *Epic of Gilgamesh* referred to at the beginning of this chapter shows both the ambition and the value to the community of the kings. Gilgamesh, who is probably

---

Kassite (KAS-ite)   **Elamite** (EE-luh-mite)

lugal (LOO-guhl)

based on a historical king of Uruk, stirs resentment by demanding sexual favors from new brides, but the community relies on his immense strength, wisdom, and courage. In quest of everlasting glory, Gilgamesh walls the city magnificently, stamping his name on every brick. His journey to the faraway Cedar Mountains reflects the king's role in accessing valuable resources.

A few city-states became powerful enough to dominate their neighbors. Sargon°, ruler of Akkad° around 2350 B.C.E., pioneered in uniting many cities under one king and capital. His title, King of Sumer and Akkad, symbolized this claim to universal dominion. Sargon and the four family members who succeeded him over 120 years secured their power in several ways. They razed the walls of conquered cities and installed governors backed by garrisons of Akkadian troops. They gave soldiers land to ensure their loyalty. Being of Semitic stock, they adapted the cuneiform° system of writing used for Sumerian (discussed later in the chapter) to express their own language. Their administration featured a uniform system of weights and measures and standardized formats for official documents. These measures facilitated assessment and collection of taxes, recruitment of soldiers, and organization of labor projects.

For reasons that remain obscure, the Akkadian state fell around 2230 B.C.E. The Sumerian language and culture revived in the cities of the southern plain under the Third Dynasty of Ur (2112–2004 B.C.E.), a five-king dynasty that maintained itself for a century through campaigns of conquest and prudent marriage alliances. The Akkadian state had controlled more territory, but tighter government control based on a rapidly expanding bureaucracy and obsessive recordkeeping now secured Ur's dominance. Messengers and well-maintained road stations speeded up communications; and an official calendar, standardized weights and measures, and uniform writing practices improved central administration. To protect against nomadic Semitic Amorites° from the northwest, the kings erected a wall 125 miles (201 kilometers) long. Eventually, however, nomad incursions combined with an Elamite attack from the southeast toppled the Third Dynasty of Ur.

The Amorites founded a new city at Babylon, not far from Akkad. Toward the end of a long reign, **Hammurabi**° (r. 1792–1750 B.C.E.) initiated a series of aggressive military campaigns, and Babylon became the capital of what historians have named the "Old Babylonian" state, which eventually stretched beyond Sumer and Akkad into the north and northwest, from 1900 to 1600 B.C.E. Hammurabi's famous Law Code, inscribed on a polished black stone pillar, provided judges with a lengthy set of examples illustrating the principles to be used in deciding cases. Some examples call for severe physical punishments to compensate for crimes. These Amorite notions of justice differed from the monetary penalties prescribed in earlier codes from Ur.

Conquest gave some Mesopotamian city-states access to vital resources. Trade offered an alternative, and long-distance commerce flourished in most periods. Evidence of seagoing vessels appears as early as the fifth millennium B.C.E. Wood, metals, and stone came from foreign lands in exchange for wool, cloth, barley, and vegetable oil. Cedar forests in Lebanon and Syria yielded wood, Anatolia produced silver, Egypt gold, and the eastern Mediterranean and Oman (on the Arabian peninsula) copper. Tin, which in alloy with copper made bronze, came from Afghanistan (in south-central Asia), and chlorite, a greenish, easily carved stone, from the Iranian plateau. Jewelers and stone-carvers used black diorite from the Persian Gulf, blue lapis lazuli° from Afghanistan, and reddish carnelian° from Pakistan.

Most merchants worked for the palace or the temple in the third millennium B.C.E. These institutions alone commanded the financial resources and organizational skills needed for acquiring, transporting, and protecting valuable commodities. Merchants exchanged surpluses from the royal or temple farmlands for raw materials and luxury goods. In the second millennium B.C.E., independent merchants and merchant guilds gained increasing influence.

Sources do not reveal whether the most important commercial transactions took place in the area just inside the city gates or in the vicinity of the docks. Wherever they occurred, coined money played no role. Coins—stamped metal pieces of state-guaranteed value—first appeared in the sixth century B.C.E. and did not reach Mesopotamia until several centuries later. For most of Mesopotamian history, items that could not be bartered—traded for one another—had their value calculated in relation to fixed weights of precious metal, primarily silver, or measures of grain.

Mesopotamian Society

Urbanized civilizations foster social division, that is, obvious variation in the status and privileges of different groups according to wealth, social function, and legal and political rights. Urbanization, specialization of function,

---

Sargon (SAHR-gone)   Akkad (AH-kahd)
cuneiform (kyoo-NEE-uh-form)   Amorite (AM-uh-rite)
Hammurabi (HAM-uh-rah-bee)

---

lapis lazuli (LAP-is LAZ-uh-lee)   carnelian (kahr-NEEL-yuhn)

centralization of power, and use of written records enabled certain groups to amass unprecedented wealth. Temple leaders and the kings controlled large agricultural estates, and the palace administration collected taxes from subjects. How elite individuals acquired large private landholdings is unknown, since land was rarely put up for sale. In some cases, however, debtors lost their land to creditors, or soldiers and priests received land in return for their services.

The Law Code of Hammurabi in the eighteenth century B.C.E. reflects social divisions that may have been valid for other places and times despite inevitable fluctuations. It identifies three classes: (1) the free landowning class—royalty, high-ranking officials, warriors, priests, merchants, and some artisans and shopkeepers; (2) the class of dependent farmers and artisans, whose legal attachment to royal, temple, or private estates made them the primary rural work force; and (3) the class of slaves, primarily employed in domestic service. Penalties prescribed in the Law Code depend on the class of the offender. The lower orders received the most severe punishments. Slaves, many of them prisoners of war from the mountains and others, insolvent debtors, played a lesser economic role than they would in the later societies of Greece and Rome (see Chapters 4 and 5). Identified by a distinctive hair style rather than chains or brands, they would have a barber shave off the telltale mark if they were lucky enough to regain their freedom. Because commodities such as food and oil were distributed to all people in proportion to their age, gender, and task, documents do not always distinguish between slaves or dependent workers and free laborers. In the Old Babylonian period, the class of people who were not dependent on the temple or palace grew, the amount of land and other property in private hands increased, and free laborers became more common.

The daily lives of ordinary Mesopotamians, especially those in villages or on large estates, left few archaeological or literary traces. Peasants built with mud brick and reeds, which quickly disintegrate, and they had few metal possessions. Being illiterate, they left no written record of their lives. Male domination of the position of **scribe**—an administrator or scholar charged by the temple or palace with reading and writing tasks—further complicates efforts to reconstruct the lives of women. For the most part, their writings reflect elite male activities. Archaeology only partially fills this gap.

Anthropologists theorize that women lost social standing and freedom with the spread of agriculture. In hunting and gathering societies, they believe, women's foraging provided most of the community's food. But in Mesopotamia, food production depended on the heavy physical labor of plowing, harvesting, and digging irrigation channels, jobs usually performed by men. Since food surpluses made larger families possible, bearing and raising children became the primary occupation of many women, leaving them little time to acquire the specialized skills of a scribe or artisan.

Women could own property, maintain control of their dowry, and even engage in trade, but men monopolized political life. Some women worked outside the household in textile factories and breweries or as prostitutes, tavern keepers, bakers, or fortune-tellers. Home tasks for nonelite women probably included helping with farming, growing vegetables, cooking, cleaning, fetching water, tending the household fire, and weaving baskets and textiles.

The standing of women seems to have declined further in the second millennium B.C.E., perhaps because of the rise of an urbanized middle class and an increase in private wealth. Husbands gained authority in the household and benefited from marriage and divorce laws. A man normally took just one wife, but he could obtain a second if the first gave him no children. In later Mesopotamian history, kings and rich men had several wives. Marriage alliances arranged between families made women instruments for preserving and enhancing family wealth. Alternatively, a family might decide to avoid a daughter's marriage, with the resulting loss of a dowry, by dedicating her to temple service as "god's bride." Constraints on women's lives that eventually became part of Islamic tradition, such as remaining at home and wearing veils in public, may date back to the second millennium B.C.E. (see Chapter 8).

Gods, Priests, and Temples

The Sumerian gods embodied the forces of nature: Anu the sky, Enlil the air, Enki the water, Utu the sun, Nanna the moon. The goddess Inanna governed sexual attraction and violence. When the Semitic peoples became dominant, they equated their deities with those of the Sumerians. The Sumerian gods Nanna and Utu, for example, became the Semitic Sin and Shamash, while the goddess Inanna became Ishtar. The Semitic gods took over the myths and many of the rituals of their Sumerian predecessors.

People imagined their gods as anthropomorphic°, that is, like humans in form and conduct. The gods had bodies and senses, sought nourishment from sacrifice, enjoyed the worship and obedience of humanity, and ex-

anthropomorphic (an-thruh-phu-MORE-fik)

perienced the human emotions of lust, love, hate, anger, and envy. Religious beliefs instilled fear of the gods, who could alter the landscape, and a desire to appease them.

Public, state-organized religion stands out in the archaeological record. Cities built temples and showed devotion to the divinity or divinities who protected the community. All the peoples of Sumer regarded Nippur (see Map 1.3) as a religious center because of its temple to the air god Enlil. As with other temples, they considered it the god's residence and believed the cult statue in its interior shrine embodied his life-force. Priests attended this divine image, trying to anticipate and meet its every need in a daily cycle of waking, bathing, dressing, feeding, moving around, entertaining, soothing, and revering. These rituals reflected the message of the Babylonian Creation Myth that humankind existed only to serve the gods. Several thousand priests may have staffed a large temple like that of the god Marduk at Babylon.

Priests passed their office and sacred lore to their sons, and their families lived on rations of food from the deity's estates. The amount an individual received depended on his rank within a complicated hierarchy of status and specialized function. The high priest performed the central acts in the great rituals. Certain priests pleasured the gods with music. Others exorcised evil spirits. Still others interpreted dreams and divined the future by examining the organs of sacrificed animals, reading patterns in rising incense smoke, or casting dice.

A high wall surrounded the temple precinct, which contained the shrine of the chief deity; open plazas; chapels for lesser gods; housing, dining facilities, and offices for priests and other temple staff; and buildings for crafts, storage, and other services. The compound focused on the **ziggurat**°, a multistory, mud-brick, pyramid-shaped tower approached by ramps and stairs. Scholars are still debating the ziggurat's function and symbolic meaning.

Scholars similarly debate whether common people had much access to temple buildings and how religious practices and beliefs affected their everyday lives. Individuals placed votive statues in the sanctuaries in the belief that these miniature replicas of themselves could continually seek the deity's favor. The survival of many **amulets** (small charms meant to protect the bearer from evil) and representations of a host of demons suggests widespread belief in magic—the use of special words and rituals to manipulate the forces of nature. They believed, for example, that a demon caused headaches and could be driven out of the ailing body. Lamashtu, the demon who caused miscarriages, could be frightened off if

ziggurat (ZIG-uh-rat)

a pregnant woman wore an amulet with the likeness of the hideous but beneficent demon Pazuzu. A god or goddess might also be persuaded to reveal the future in return for a gift or sacrifice.

Elite and common folk came together in great festivals such as the twelve-day New Year's festival held each spring in Babylon as the new grain was beginning to sprout in the fields. In the early days of the festival, in conjunction with rituals of purification and invocations of Marduk, a priest read to the god's image the text of the Babylonian Creation Epic. Many subsequent activities in the temple courtyard and streets reenacted the events of the myth. Following their belief that time moved in a circular path through a cycle of birth, growth, maturity, and death, they hoped through this ritual to persuade the gods to grant a renewal of time and life at winter's end (see Diversity and Dominance: Violence and Order in the Babylonian New Year's Festival).

Technology and Science

The term *technology* comes from the Greek word *techne*, meaning "skill" or "specialized knowledge." It normally refers to the tools and processes by which humans manipulate the physical world. However, many scholars also use it more broadly for any specialized knowledge used to transform the natural environment and human society. Ancient Mesopotamian irrigation techniques that expanded agricultural production fit the first definition, priestly belief in their ability to enhance prosperity through prayers and rituals the second.

Writing, which first appeared in Mesopotamia before 3300 B.C.E., partakes more of the second definition than of the first. The earliest inscribed tablets, found in the chief temple at Uruk, date from a time when the temple was the community's most important economic institution. The most plausible current theory maintains that writing originated from a system of tokens used to keep track of property—sheep, cattle, wagon wheels—as wealth accumulated and the volume and complexity of commerce strained people's memories. The shape and number of tokens inserted in clay "envelopes" (balls of clay) indicated the contents of a shipment or storeroom, and pictures of the tokens incised on the outside of the envelope reminded the reader of what was inside.

Eventually people realized that the incised pictures, the first written symbols, provided an adequate record of the transaction and made the tokens inside the envelope redundant. Each early symbol represented a thing, but it could also stand for the sound of the word for that thing when that sound was a syllable of a longer word. For

우세인 은신처 방

파운드폭탄 4발 투하… 두 아들과 함께 사망 가

심진지 구축… 이틀째 시가戰

령이 대중 앞에 나타나거나 애국심
을 고취하는 노래만을 내보내던 방
송마저 중단됐다.

라크 전후 대책
의에서는 전후
영국 주도로

DIVERSITY AND DOMINANCE

VIOLENCE AND ORDER IN THE BABYLONIAN NEW YEAR'S FESTIVAL

The twelve-day Babylonian New Year's Festival was one of the grandest and most important religious celebrations in ancient Mesopotamia. Complex rituals, both private and public, were performed in accordance with detailed formulas. Fragmentary Babylonian documents of the third century B.C.E. (fifteen hundred years after Hammurabi) provide most of our information about the festival, but because of the continuity of culture over several millennia, the later Babylonian New Year's Festival is likely to preserve many of the beliefs and practices of earlier epochs.

In the first days of the festival, most of the activity took place in inner chambers of the temple of Marduk, patron deity of Babylon, attended only by ranking members of the priesthood. A particularly interesting ceremony was a ritualized humiliation of the king, followed by a renewal of the institution of divinely sanctioned kingship:

On the fifth day of the month Nisannu . . . they shall bring water for washing the king's hands and then shall accompany him to the temple Esagil. The *urigallu*-priest shall leave the sanctuary and take away the scepter, the circle, and the sword from the king. He shall bring them before the god Bel [Marduk] and place them on a chair. He shall leave the sanctuary and strike the king's cheek. He shall accompany the king into the presence of the god Bel. He shall drag him by the ears and make him bow to the ground. The king shall speak the following only once: "I did not sin, lord of the countries. I was not neglectful of the requirements of your godship. I did not destroy Babylon. The temple Esagil, I did not forget its rites. I did not rain blows on the cheek of a subordinate." . . . [The *urigallu*-priest responds:] "The god Bel will listen to your prayer. He will exalt your kingship. The god Bel will bless you forever. He will destroy your enemy, fell your adversary." After the *urigallu*-priest says this, the king shall regain his composure. The scepter, circle, and sword shall be restored to the king.

Also in the early days of the festival, in conjunction with rituals of purification and invocations to Marduk, a priest recited the entire text of the Babylonian Creation Epic to the image of the god. After relating the origins of the gods from the mating of two primordial creatures, Tiamat, the female embodiment of the salt sea, and Apsu, the male embodiment of fresh water, the myth tells how Tiamat gathered an army of old gods and monsters to destroy the younger generation of gods.

When her labor of creation was ended, against her children Tiamat began preparations of war . . . all the Anunnaki [the younger gods], the host of gods gathered into that place tongue-tied; they sat with mouths shut for they thought, "What other god can make war on Tiamat? No one else can face her and come back" . . . Lord Marduk exulted, . . . with racing spirits he said to the father of gods, "Creator of the gods who decides their destiny, if I must be your avenger, defeating Tiamat, saving your lives, call the Assembly, give me precedence over all the rest; . . . now and for ever let my word be law; I, not you, will decide the world's nature, the things to come. My decrees shall never be altered, never be annulled, but my creation endures to the ends of the world" . . . He took his route towards the rising sound of Tiamat's rage, and all the gods besides, the fathers of the gods pressed in around him, and the lord approached Tiamat. . . . When Tiamat heard him her wits scattered, she was possessed and shrieked aloud, her legs shook from the crotch down, she gabbled spells, muttered maledictions, while the gods of war sharpened their weapons. . . . The lord shot his net to entangle Tiamat, and the pursuing tumid wind, Imhullu, came from behind and beat in her face. When the mouth gaped open to suck him down he drove Imhullu in, so that the mouth would not shut but wind raged through her belly; her carcass blown up, tumescent. She gaped. And now he shot the arrow that split the belly, that pierced the gut and cut the womb.

Now that the Lord had conquered Tiamat he ended her life, he flung her down and straddled the carcass; the leader was killed, Tiamat was dead her rout was shattered, her band dispersed. . . . The lord rested; he gazed at the huge body, pondering how to use it, what to create from the dead carcass. He split it apart like a cockle-shell; with the upper half he constructed the arc of sky, he pulled down the bar and set a watch on the waters, so they should never escape. . . . He projected positions for the Great Gods conspicuous in the sky, he gave them a starry aspect as constellations; he measured the year, gave it a beginning and an end, and to each month of the twelve three rising stars. . . . Through her ribs he opened gates in the east and west, and gave them strong bolts on the right and left; and high in the belly of Tiamat he set the zenith. He gave the moon the luster of a jewel, he gave him all the night, to mark off days, to watch by night each month the circle of a waxing waning light. . . . When Marduk had sent out the moon, he took the sun and set him to complete the cycle from this one to the next New Year. . . .

Then Marduk considered Tiamat. He skimmed spume from the bitter sea, heaped up the clouds, spindrift of wet and wind and cooling rain, the spittle of Tiamat. With his own hands from the steaming mist he spread the clouds. He pressed hard down the head of water, heaping mountains over it, opening springs to flow: Euphrates and Tigris rose from her eyes, but he closed the nostrils and held back their springhead. He piled huge mountains on her paps and through them drove water-holes to channel the deep sources; and high overhead he arched her tail, locked-in to the wheel of heaven; the pit was under his feet, between was the crotch, the sky's fulcrum. Now the earth had foundations and the sky its mantle. . . . When it was done, when they had made Marduk their king, they pronounced peace and happiness for him, "Over our houses you keep unceasing watch, and all you wish from us, that will be done."

Marduk considered and began to speak to the gods assembled in his presence. This is what he said, "In the former time you inhabited the void above the abyss, but I have made Earth as the mirror of Heaven, I have consolidated the soil for the foundations, and there I will build my city, my beloved home. A holy precinct shall be established with sacred halls for the presence of the king. When you come up from the deep to join the Synod you will find lodging and sleep by night. When others from heaven descend to the Assembly, you too will find lodging and sleep by night. It shall be BABYLON the home of the gods. The masters of all crafts shall build it according to my plan". . . . Now that Marduk has heard what it is the gods are saying, he is moved with desire to create a work of consummate art. He told Ea the deep thought in his heart.

> "Blood to blood
> I join,
> blood to bone
> I form
> an original thing,
> its name is MAN,
> aboriginal man
> is mine in making.

> "All his occupations
> are faithful service . . ."

Ea answered with carefully chosen words, completing the plan for the gods' comfort. He said to Marduk, "Let one of the kindred be taken; only one need die for the new creation. Bring the gods together in the Great Assembly; there let the guilty die, so the rest may live."

Marduk called the Great Gods to the Synod; he presided courteously, he gave instructions and all of them listened with grave attention. The king speaks to the rebel gods, "Declare on your oath if ever before you spoke the truth, who instigated rebellion? Who stirred up Tiamat? Who led the battle? Let the instigator of war be handed over; guilt and retribution are on him, and peace will be yours for ever."

The great Gods answered the Lord of the Universe, the king and counselor of gods, "It was Kingu who instigated rebellion, he stirred up that sea of bitterness and led the battle for her." They declared him guilty, they bound and held him down in front of Ea, they cut his arteries and from his blood they created man; and Ea imposed his servitude. . . .

*M*uch of the subsequent activity of the festival, which took place in the temple courtyard and streets, was a reenactment of the events of the Creation Myth. The festival occurred at the beginning of spring, when the grain shoots were beginning to emerge, and the essential symbolism of the event concerns the return of natural life to the world. The Babylonians believed that time moved in a circular path and that the natural world had a life cycle consisting of birth, growth, maturity, and death. In winter the cycle drew to a close, and there was no guarantee that it would repeat and that life would return to the world. Babylonians hoped that the New Year's Festival would encourage the gods to grant a renewal of time and life, in essence to recreate the world.

QUESTIONS FOR ANALYSIS

1. According to the Creation Epic, how did the present order of the universe come into being? What does the violent nature of this creation tell us about the Mesopotamian view of the physical world and the gods?

2. How did the symbolism of the events of the New Year's Festival, with its ritual reading and recreation of the story of the Creation Myth, validate such concepts as kingship, the primacy of Babylon, and mankind's relationship to the gods?

3. What is the significance of the distinction between the "private" ceremonies celebrated in the temple precincts and the "public" ceremonies that took place in the streets of the city? What does the festival tell us about the relationship of different social groups to the gods?

Source: Adapted from James B. Pritchard, ed., *Ancient Near Eastern Texts Relating to the Old Testament*, 3d ed. (Princeton, NJ: Princeton University Press, 1969), 332–334. Copyright © 1969 by Princeton University Press. Reprinted by permission of Princeton University Press.

Mesopotamian Cylinder Seal   Seals indicated the identity of an individual and were impressed into wet clay or wax to "sign" legal documents or to mark ownership of an object. This seal, produced in the period of the Akkadian Empire, depicts Ea (second from right), the god of underground waters, symbolized by the stream with fish emanating from his shoulders; Ishtar, whose attributes of fertility and war are indicated by the date cluster in her hand and the pointed weapons showing above her wings; and the sun-god Shamash, cutting his way out of the mountains with a jagged knife, an evocation of sunrise.   (Courtesy of the Trustees of the British Museum)

example, the symbols *shu* for "hand" and *mu* for "water" could be combined to form *shumu*, the word for "name."

The usual method of writing involved pressing the point of a sharpened reed into a moist clay tablet. Because the reed made wedge-shaped impressions, the early pictures, which were more or less realistic, evolved into stylized combinations of strokes and wedges, a system known as **cuneiform** (Latin for "wedge-shaped") writing. Mastering cuneiform, which in any particular period involved several hundred signs, as compared to the twenty-five or so in an alphabetic system, required years of practice. In the "tablet-house" attached to a temple or palace, students learned writing and mathematics under a stern headmaster and endured bullying by older student tutors called "big brothers." The prestige and regular employment that went with their position may have made scribes reluctant to simplify the cuneiform system. In the Old Babylonian period, the growth of private commerce brought an increase in the number of people who could read and write, but literacy remained a rare accomplishment.

Developed originally for the Sumerian language, cuneiform—a system of writing rather than a language— later served to express the Akkadian language of the Mesopotamian Semites as well as other languages of western Asia such as Hittite, Elamite, and Persian. The remains of the ancient city of Ebla° in northern Syria illustrate the Mesopotamian influence on other parts of western Asia. Ebla's buildings and artifacts follow Mesopotamian models, and thousands of tablets inscribed with cuneiform symbols bear messages in both Sumerian and the local Semitic dialect. The high point of Ebla's wealth and power occurred from 2400 to 2250 B.C.E., roughly contemporary with the Akkadian Empire. Ebla then controlled extensive territory and derived wealth from agriculture, manufacture of woolen cloth, and trade with Mesopotamia and the Mediterranean coast.

Economic concerns predominate in the earliest Sumerian documents, but cuneiform came to have wide-ranging uses beyond the recordkeeping that apparently inspired its invention. Legal acts that had formerly been validated by the recitation of oral formulas and performance of symbolic acts came to be accompanied by written documents marked with the seals of the participants. Cuneiform similarly served political, literary, religious, and scientific purposes.

In the physical realm, irrigation, the basis of Mesopotamian agriculture, required the construction and

Ebla (EH-bluh)

maintenance of canals, weirs, and dikes. Cattle drew carts and sledges in some locations. In the south, where numerous water channels cut up the landscape, boats and barges predominated. In northern Mesopotamia, donkeys served as pack animals for overland caravans in the centuries before the advent of the camel around 1200 B.C.E.

To improve on stone tools, the Mesopotamians imported ores containing copper, tin, and arsenic. From these they made bronze, a form of copper alloyed with either of the other two elements. Craftsmen poured molten bronze into molds shaped like weapons or tools. The cooled metal took a sharper edge than stone, was less likely to break, and was more easily repaired. Yet stone implements remained in use among poor people who could not afford bronze.

Clay, Mesopotamia's most abundant resource, went into the making of mud bricks. Whether dried in the sun or baked in an oven for greater durability, these constituted the main building material. Construction of city walls, temples, and palaces required practical knowledge of architecture and engineering. For example, the reed mats that Mesopotamian builders laid between the mud-brick layers of ziggurats served the same stabilizing purpose as girders in modern high-rise construction. Abundance of good clay also made pottery the most common material for dishes and storage vessels. By 4000 B.C.E., potters had begun to use a revolving platform called a potter's wheel. Spun by hands or feet, the potter's wheel made possible rapid manufacture in precise and complex shapes.

Military technology changed as armies evolved from militias called up for short periods in the earliest periods to well-trained and well-paid full-time soldiers by the late third and second millennia B.C.E. In the early second millennium B.C.E., horses appeared in western Asia, and the horse-drawn chariot, a technically complicated device, came into vogue. Infantry found themselves at the mercy of swift chariots carrying a driver and an archer who could easily overtake them. Using increasingly effective siege machinery, Mesopotamian soldiers learned to climb over, undermine, or knock down the walls protecting the cities of their enemies.

In another area where the Mesopotamians sought to gain control of their physical environment, they used a base-60 number system (the origin of the seconds and minutes we use today), in which numbers were expressed as fractions or multiples of 60 (in contrast to our base-10 system). Such advances in mathematics along with careful observation of the skies made the Mesopotamians sophisticated practitioners of astronomy. Mesopotamian priests compiled lists of omens or unusual

sightings on earth and in the heavens, together with a record of the events that coincided with them. They consulted these texts at critical times, for they believed that the recurrence of such phenomena could provide clues to future developments. The underlying premise was that the elements of the material universe, from the microcosmic to the macrocosmic, were interconnected in mysterious but undeniable ways.

EGYPT

No other place exhibits the impact of the natural environment on the history and culture of a society better than ancient Egypt. Though located at the intersection of Asia and Africa, Egypt was less a crossroads than an isolated land protected by surrounding barriers of desert and a harborless, marshy seacoast. Where Mesopotamia was open to migration or invasion and was dependent on imported resources, Egypt's natural isolation and material self-sufficiency fostered a unique culture that for long periods had relatively little to do with other civilizations.

The Land of Egypt: "Gift of the Nile"

The world's longest river, the Nile flows northward from Lake Victoria and draws water from several large tributaries in the highlands of tropical Africa. Carving a narrow valley between a chain of hills on either side, it terminates at the Mediterranean Sea (see Map 1.4). Though bordered mostly by desert, the banks of the river support lush vegetation. About 100 miles (160 kilometers) from the Mediterranean, the river divides into channels to form a triangular delta. Most of Egypt's population lives on the twisting, green ribbon of land along the river or in the Nile Delta. Bleak deserts of mountains, rocks, and dunes occupy the remaining 90 percent of the country. The ancient Egyptians distinguished between the low-lying, life-sustaining "Black Land" with its dark soil and the elevated, deadly "Red Land" of the desert. The fifth-century B.C.E. Greek traveler Herodotus° demonstrated insight when he called Egypt the "gift of the Nile."

Travel and communication centered on the river, with the most important cities located upstream away from the Mediterranean. Because the river flows from south to north, the Egyptians called the southern part of

---

Herodotus (he-ROD-uh-tuhs)

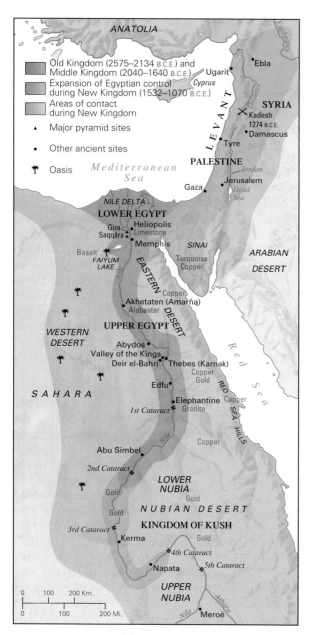

Map 1.4   Ancient Egypt   The Nile River, flowing south to north, carved out of the surrounding desert a narrow green valley that became heavily settled in antiquity.

most periods, but Egyptian control sometimes extended farther south into what they called "Kush" (later Nubia, today part of southern Egypt and northern Sudan). The Egyptians also settled certain large oases, green and habitable "islands" in the midst of the desert, which lay west of the river.

The hot, sunny climate favored agriculture. Though rain rarely falls south of the delta, the river provided water to irrigation channels that carried water out into the valley and increased the area suitable for planting. In one large depression west of the Nile, drainage techniques reduced the size of Lake Faiyum° and allowed land to be reclaimed for agriculture.

Each September, the river overflowed its banks, spreading water into the bordering valley. Unlike the Mesopotamians, the Egyptians needed no dams or weirs to raise the level of the river and divert water into channels. Moreover, the Nile, unlike the Tigris and Euphrates, flooded at the best time for grain agriculture. When the flood receded and its waters drained back into the river, the land had a fertile new layer of mineral-rich silt, and farmers could easily plant their crops in the moist soil. The Egyptians' many creation myths commonly featured the emergence of a life-supporting mound of earth from a primeval swamp.

The level of the flood's crest determined the abundance of the following harvest. "Nilometers," stone staircases with incised units of height along the river's edge, recorded each flood. Too much water washed out the dikes protecting inhabited areas and caused much damage. Too little water left fertile land unirrigated and hence uncultivable, plunging the country into famine. The ebb and flow of successful and failed regimes seems linked to the cycle of floods. Nevertheless, remarkable stability characterized most eras, and Egyptians viewed the universe as an orderly and beneficent place.

Egypt's other natural resources offered further advantages. Papyrus reeds growing in marshy areas yielded fibers that made good sails, ropes, and a kind of paper. The wild animals and birds of the marshes and desert fringe and the abundant river fish attracted hunters and fishermen. Building stone could be quarried and floated downstream from a number of locations in southern Egypt. Clay for mud bricks and pottery could be found almost everywhere. Copper and turquoise deposits in the Sinai desert to the east and gold from Nubia to the south were within reach, and the state organized armed expeditions and forced labor to exploit these resources. Thus, Egypt was substantially more self-sufficient than Mesopotamia.

the country "Upper Egypt" and the northern delta "Lower Egypt." The First Cataract of the Nile, the northernmost of a series of impassable rocks and rapids below Aswan° (about 500 miles [800 kilometers] south of the Mediterranean), formed Egypt's southern boundary in

---

Aswan (AS-wahn)

Faiyum (fie-YOOM)

The farming villages that appeared in Egypt as early as 5500 B.C.E. relied on domesticated plant and animal species that had emerged several millennia earlier in western Asia. Egypt's emergence as a focal point of civilization, however, stemmed at least partially from a gradual change in climate from the fifth to the third millennium B.C.E. Before that time, the Sahara, today the world's largest desert, had a relatively mild and wet climate. Its lakes and grasslands supported a variety of plant and animal species as well as populations of hunter-gatherers (see Chapter 7). As the climate changed and the Sahara began to dry up, displaced groups migrated into the then marshy Nile Valley, where they developed a sedentary way of life.

Divine Kingship

The increasing population called for greater complexity in political organization, including a form of local kingship. Later generations of Egyptians saw the unification of such smaller units into a single state by Menes°, a ruler from the south, as a pivotal event. Scholars question whether this event, dated to around 3100 B.C.E., took place at the hands of a historical or a mythical figure, but many authorities equate Menes with Narmer, a historical ruler who is shown on a decorated slate palette exulting over defeated enemies. Later kings of Egypt bore the title "Ruler of the Two Lands"—Upper and Lower Egypt—and wore two crowns symbolizing the unification of the country. Unlike Mesopotamia, Egypt discovered unity early in its history.

Following the practice of Manetho, an Egyptian priest from the fourth century B.C.E., historians divide Egyptian history into thirty dynasties (sequences of kings from the same family). The rise and fall of dynasties often reflects the dominance of one or another part of the country. Scholars also divide Egyptian history into "Old," "Middle," and "New Kingdoms," each a period of centralized political power and brilliant cultural achievement. "Intermediate Periods" signal political fragmentation and cultural decline. Although experts debate the specific dates, the chronology (on page 7) reflects current opinion.

The Egyptian state centered on the king, often known by the New Kingdom term **pharaoh,** from an Egyptian phrase meaning "palace." From the Old Kingdom on, if not earlier, Egyptians considered the king a god on earth, the incarnation of Horus and the son of the sun-god Re°. In this role he maintained **ma'at°,** the divinely authorized order of the universe. As a link between the people and the gods, his benevolent rule ensured the welfare and prosperity of the country. The Egyptians' conception of a divine king, the source of law and justice, may explain the apparent absence in Egypt of an impersonal code of law comparable to Hammurabi's Code in Mesopotamia.

So much depended on the kings that their deaths evoked elaborate efforts to ensure the well-being of their spirits on their journey to rejoin the gods. Carrying out funerary rites, constructing royal tombs, and sustaining the kings' spirits in the afterlife by perpetual offerings in adjoining funerary chapels demanded massive resources. Flat-topped, rectangular tombs made of mud brick sufficed for the earliest rulers, but around 2630 B.C.E., Djoser°, a Third Dynasty king, ordered the construction of a stepped **pyramid**—a series of stone platforms laid one on top of the other—at Saqqara°, near Memphis. Rulers of the Fourth Dynasty filled in the steps of Djoser's tomb to create the smooth-sided, limestone pyramids that most often symbolize ancient Egypt. Between 2550 and 2490 B.C.E., the pharaohs Khufu° and Khefren° erected huge pyramids at Giza, several miles north of Saqqara, the largest stone structures ever built. Khufu's pyramid originally reached a height of 480 feet (146 meters).

Egyptians accomplished this construction with stone tools (bronze was still expensive and rare) and no machinery other than simple levers, pulleys, and rollers. Calculations of the human muscle power needed to build a pyramid within a ruler's lifetime indicate that large numbers of people must have been pressed into service for part of each year, probably during the flood season, when no agricultural work could be done. The Egyptian masses probably considered this demand for labor a kind of religious service that would help ensure prosperity. Most of Egypt's surplus resources went into constructing these artificial mountains of stone. The age of the great pyramids lasted about a century, though construction of pyramids on a smaller scale continued for two millennia.

Administration and Communication

Ruling dynasties usually placed their capitals in the area of their original power base. **Memphis,** near today's Cairo at the apex of the Nile delta, held this central position during the Old Kingdom; but **Thebes,** far to the south, often supplanted it during the Middle and New Kingdom periods (see Map 1.4). A complex

---

Menes (MEH-neez)   **Re** (ray)   **ma'at** (muh-AHT)

Djoser (JO-sur)   **Saqqara** (suh-KAHR-uh)   **Khufu** (KOO-foo)
Khefren (KEF-ren)

bureaucracy kept detailed records of the country's resources. Beginning at the village level and progressing to the district level and finally to the central government based in the capital, bureaucrats kept track of land, labor, products, and people, extracting as taxes a substantial portion—as much as 50 percent—of the annual revenues of the country. This income supported the palace, bureaucracy, and army; paid for building and maintaining temples; and made possible great monuments celebrating the king's grandeur. The government maintained a monopoly over key sectors of the economy and controlled long-distance trade. The urban middle-class traders who increasingly managed the commerce of Mesopotamia had no parallel in Egypt.

Literacy according to a writing system developed before the Early Dynastic period marked the administrative class. **Hieroglyphics°**, the earliest form of this system, featured picture symbols standing for words, syllables, or individual sounds. We can read ancient Egyptian writing today only because of the discovery in the early nineteenth century C.E. of the Rosetta Stone, an inscription from the second century B.C.E. that gave hieroglyphic and Greek versions of the same text.

Hieroglyphic writing long continued in use on monuments and ornamental inscriptions. By 2500 B.C.E., however, administrators and copyists had developed a cursive script, in which the original pictorial nature of the symbol was less apparent, for their everyday needs. They wrote with ink on a writing material called **papyrus°**, made from the stems of the papyrus reed that grew in the Nile marshes. Papyrus makers laid out the stems in a vertical and horizontal grid pattern, moistened them, and then pounded them with a soft mallet until they adhered into a sheet of writing material. A uniquely Egyptian product, papyrus served scribes throughout the ancient world and was exported in large quantities. The word *paper* comes from Greek and Roman words for papyrus.

Apart from administrative recordkeeping, Egyptian literary compositions included tales of adventure and magic, love poetry, religious hymns, and instruction manuals on technical subjects. Scribes in workshops attached to the temples made copies of traditional texts.

Strong monarchs appointed and promoted officials on the basis of merit and accomplishment, giving them grants of land cultivated by dependent peasants. Low-level officials worked in villages and district capitals; high-ranking officials served in the royal capital. During the Old Kingdom, the tombs of officials lay near the monumental tomb of the king so they could serve him in death as they had in life.

Egyptian history exhibits a recurring tension between the centralizing power of the monarchy and the decentralizing tendencies of the bureaucracy. The shift of officials' tombs from the vicinity of the royal tomb to home districts where they spent much of their time and exercised power more or less independently signaled the breakdown of centralized power in the late Old Kingdom and First Intermediate Period. Inheritance of administrative posts similarly indicated a decline in centralized power. The early monarchs of the Middle Kingdom restored centralized power by reducing the power and prerogatives of the old elite and creating a new middle class of administrators.

The common observation that Egypt was a land of villages without real cities stems from its capitals being primarily extensions of the palace and central administration. Compared to Mesopotamia, a far larger percentage of the Egyptian population lived in farming villages, and Egypt's wealth derived to a higher degree from cultivating the land. The towns and cities that did exist unfortunately lie buried beneath modern urban sites, since Egypt has too little land in its cultivable region to afford abandonment of a large area.

Egypt largely stuck to itself during the Old and Middle Kingdoms, all foreigners being technically regarded as enemies. When necessary, local militia units backed up a small standing army of professional soldiers. Nomadic groups in the eastern and western deserts and Libyans to the northwest posed a nuisance more than a real danger. The king maintained limited contact with other advanced civilizations in the region. Egypt's interests abroad focused on maintaining access to resources rather than on acquiring territory. Trade with the Levant° coast (modern Israel, Lebanon, and Syria) brought in cedar wood in return for grain, papyrus, and gold.

Egypt's strongest interests involved goods from the south. Nubia contained gold mines (in Chapter 2 we examine the rise in Nubia of a civilization influenced by Egypt but also vital, original, and long lasting), and the southern course of the Nile offered access to sub-Saharan Africa. In the Old Kingdom, Egyptian noblemen living at Aswan on the southern border led donkey caravans south in search of gold, incense, and products from tropical Africa such as ivory, ebony, and exotic animals. Forts along the border protected Egypt from attack. In the early second millennium B.C.E., Egyptian forces invaded Nubia and extended the Egyptian border as far as

---

hieroglyphics (high-ruh-GLIF-iks)   **papyrus** (puh-PIE-ruhs)

Levant (luh-VANT)

the Third Cataract of the Nile, taking possession of the gold fields.

The People of Egypt

The estimated million to a million and half inhabitants of Egypt included various physical types, ranging from dark-skinned people related to the populations of sub-Saharan Africa to lighter-skinned people akin to the populations of North Africa and western Asia who spoke Berber and Semitic languages, respectively. Though Egypt experienced no migrations or invasions on a scale common in Mesopotamian history, settlers periodically trickled into the Nile Valley and mixed with the local people.

Egypt had less pronounced social divisions than Mesopotamia, where a formal class structure emerged. The king and high-ranking officials enjoyed status, wealth, and power. Below them came lower-level officials, local leaders, priests and other professionals, artisans, and well-to-do farmers. Peasants, at the bottom, constituted the vast majority of the population.

Peasants lived in rural villages and devoted themselves to the seasonally changing tasks of agriculture: plowing, sowing, tending emerging shoots, reaping, threshing, and storing. They maintained irrigation channels, basins, and dikes. Fish and meat from domesticated animals—cattle, sheep, goats, and poultry—supplemented a diet based on wheat or barley, beer, and vegetables. Villages probably shared implements, work animals, and storage facilities and helped one another at peak times in the agricultural cycle and in building projects. Festivals to the local gods and other public celebrations occasionally brought feasting and ceremonies into their lives; labor conscripted for pyramid construction and other state projects brought hardship. If the burden of taxation or compulsory service proved too great, flight into the desert usually offered the only escape.

This account of village life depends on guesswork and bits and pieces of archaeological and literary evidence. Tomb paintings of the elite sometimes depict the lives of common folk. The artists employed conventions to indicate status: obesity for the rich and comfortable, baldness and deformity for the working classes. Egyptian poets frequently employed metaphors of farming and hunting, and papyrus documents preserved in the hot, dry sands tell of property transactions and legal disputes among ordinary people.

Slavery existed on a limited scale and was of little economic significance. Prisoners of war, condemned criminals, and debtors could be found on country estates or in the households of the king and wealthy families. But humane treatment softened the burden of slavery, as did the possibility of being freed.

Scarceness of sources also clouds the experiences of women. What is known about the lives of elite women derives from the possibly distorted impressions of male artists and scribes. Tomb paintings, rendered with dignity and affection, show women of the royal family and elite classes accompanying their husbands and engaging in domestic activities. Subordination to men is evident. The convention of depicting men with a dark red and women with a yellow flesh tone implies that elite women stayed indoors, away from the searing sun. In the beautiful love poetry of the New Kingdom, lovers address each other in terms of apparent equality and express emotions akin to our own ideal of romantic love. Whether this poetry represents the attitudes prevalent in other periods or among nonelite groups remains unknown.

Legal documents show that Egyptian women could own property, inherit from their parents, and will their property to whomever they wished. Marriage, usually monogamous, arose from a couple's decision to establish a household together rather than through legal or religious ceremony. Either party could dissolve the relationship, and the woman retained rights over her dowry in case of divorce. At certain times, queens and queen-mothers played significant behind-the-scenes roles in the politics of the royal court, and priestesses sometimes supervised the cults of female deities. In general, the limited evidence suggests that women in ancient Egypt enjoyed greater respect and more legal rights and social freedom than women in Mesopotamia and other ancient societies.

Belief and Knowledge

Egyptian religion evoked the landscape of the Nile Valley and the vision of cosmic order that this environment fostered. The sun rose every day into a clear and cloudless sky, and the river flooded on schedule every year, ensuring a bounteous harvest. Recurrent cycles and periodic renewal seemed a part of the natural world. Egyptians imagined the sky to be a great ocean surrounding the inhabited world. The sun-god Re traversed its waters in a boat by day, then returned through the Underworld at night, fighting off the attacks of demonic serpents so that he could be born anew each morning. In one especially popular story, Osiris°, a god who once ruled the land of Egypt, dies at the hand of his jealous brother Seth, who

Osiris (oh-SIGH-ris)

scatters his dismembered remains. Isis, Osiris's sister and wife, finds and reassembles the pieces, while Horus, his son, takes revenge on Seth. Restored to life and installed as king of the Underworld, Osiris represented hope for a new life in a world beyond this one.

The king, represented as Horus and as the son of Re, fit into the pattern of the dead returning to life and the sun-god renewing life. As Egypt's chief priest, he intervened with the gods on behalf of his land and people. When a particular town became the capital of a ruling dynasty, the chief god of that town gained prominence throughout the land. Thus did Ptah° of Memphis, Re of Heliopolis°, and Amon° of Thebes become gods of all Egypt, serving to unify the country and strengthen the monarchy.

Egyptian rulers zealously built new temples, refurbished old ones, and made lavish gifts to the gods, at the same time overseeing construction of their own tombs. Thus, much of the country's wealth went for religious purposes in the ceaseless effort to win the gods' favor, maintain the continuity of divine kingship, and ensure the renewal of life-giving forces.

Some deities normally appear with animal heads; others always take human form. Few myths about the origins and adventures of the gods have survived, but there must have been a rich oral tradition. Many towns had temples in which locally prominent deities were thought to reside. Such local deities could be viewed as manifestations of the great gods, and gods could merge to form hybrids, such as Amon-Re. Ordinary believers were excluded from cult activities in the inner reaches of the temples, where priests served the daily needs of the deity by attending to his or her statue. Food offered to the image was later distributed to temple staff. As in Mesopotamia, some temples possessed extensive landholdings worked by dependent peasants, and the priests who administered the deity's wealth played an influential role locally and sometimes throughout the land.

During great festivals, the priests paraded a boat-shaped litter carrying the shrouded statue and cult items of the deity around the town. This brought large numbers of people into contact with the deity in an outpouring of devotion and celebration. Little is known about the day-to-day beliefs and practices of the common people, however. At home, family members revered and made small offerings to Bes, the grotesque god of marriage and domestic happiness, to local deities, and to the family's ancestors. They relied on amulets and depictions of demonic figures to ward off evil forces. In later

times, Greeks and Romans commented on the Egyptian devotion to magic.

Egyptians believed in the afterlife. They prepared extensively for a safe passage and a comfortable existence once they arrived. Hazards abounded on the soul's journey after death. The Egyptian Book of the Dead, present in many excavated tombs, contained rituals and spells to protect the journeying spirit. The weighing of the deceased's heart (believed to be the source of personality, intellect, and emotion) in the presence of the judges of the Underworld presented the ultimate challenge—the one that determined whether the deceased had led a good life and deserved to reach the blessed destination.

The Egyptian obsession with the afterlife produced concerns about the physical condition of the dead body and a perfection of mummification techniques for preserving it. The idea probably derived from the slow decomposition of bodies buried in hot, dry sand on the edge of the desert, an early practice. The elite classes spent the most on mummification. Specialists removed vital organs for preservation and storage in stone jars laid out around the corpse and filled the body cavities with various packing materials. After immersing the cadaver for long periods in dehydrating and preserving chemicals, they wrapped it in linen. They then placed the **mummy** in one or more decorated wooden caskets with a tomb.

Building tombs at the edge of the desert left the lowlands free for farming. Pictures and samples of food and objects from everyday life accompanied the mummy to provide whatever he or she might need in the next life. Much of what is now known about ancient Egyptian life comes from examining utilitarian and luxury household objects found in tombs. Small figurines called shawabtis° represented the servants whom the deceased might need or the laborers he might send as substitutes if asked to provide compulsory labor. The elite classes ordered chapels attached to their tombs and left endowments to subsidize the daily attendance of a priest and offerings of foodstuffs to sustain their spirits for eternity.

The form of the tomb also reflected wealth and status. Simple pit graves or small mud-brick chambers sufficed for the common people. Members of the privileged classes built larger tombs and covered the walls with pictures and inscriptions. Kings erected pyramids and other grand edifices, employing trickery to hide the sealed chamber containing the body and treasures, as well as curses and other magical precautions to foil tomb robbers. Rarely did they succeed, however. Archaeologists have seldom discovered an undisturbed royal tomb.

Ptah (puh-TAH)   **Heliopolis** (he-lee-OP-uh-lis)
Amon (AH-muhn)

---

shawabtis (shuh-WAB-tees)

Scene from the Egyptian Book of the Dead, ca. 1300 B.C.E.   The mummy of a royal scribe named Hunefar is approached by members of his household before being placed in the tomb. Behind Hunefar is jackel-headed Anubis, the god who will conduct the spirit of the deceased to the afterlife. The Book of the Dead provided Egyptians with the instructions they needed to complete this arduous journey and gain a blessed existence in the afterlife.   (Courtesy of the Trustees of the British Museum)

The ancient Egyptians explored many areas of knowledge and developed advantageous technologies. They learned about chemistry through developing the mummification process, which also provided opportunities to learn about human anatomy. Egyptian doctors served in royal courts throughout western Asia because of their relatively advanced medical knowledge and techniques.

The endless cycle of flooding and irrigation spurred the development of mathematics for determining the dimensions of fields and calculating the quantity of agricultural produce owed to the state. Through careful observation of the stars, they constructed the most accurate calendar in the world, and they knew that when the star Sirius appeared on the horizon shortly before sunrise, the Nile flood surge was imminent.

For pyramids, temple complexes, and other monumental building projects, vast quantities of earth had to be moved and the construction site made level. Large stones had to be quarried, dragged on rollers, floated downstream on barges, lifted into place along ramps of packed earth, carved to the exact size needed, and then made smooth. Long underground passageways connected mortuary temples by the river with tombs near the desert's edge. More practically, several Egyptian kings dredged a canal more than 50 miles (80 kilometers) long to connect the Nile Valley to the Red Sea and expedite the transport of goods.

Besides river barges for transporting building stones, the Nile carried lightweight ships equipped with sails and oars. These sometimes ventured into the Mediterranean and Red Seas. Canals and flooded basins limited the use of carts and sledges, but archaeologists have discovered an 8-mile (13-kilometer) road made of slabs of sandstone and limestone connecting a rock quarry with Faiyum Lake. The oldest known paved road in the world, it dates to the second half of the third millennium B.C.E.

THE INDUS VALLEY CIVILIZATION

Civilization developed almost as early in South Asia as in Mesopotamia and Egypt. Just as each Middle Eastern civilization centered on a great river valley, so civilization in the Indian subcontinent originated on a fertile floodplain. In the valley of the Indus River, settled farming created the agricultural surplus essential to urbanized society.

Natural Environment

A plain of more than 1 million acres (400,000 hectares) stretches between the mountains of western Pakistan and the Thar° Desert to the east in the central portion of the Indus Valley, the province of Sind° in modern Pakistan (see Map 1.2). Silt carried downstream and deposited on the land by the Indus River over many centuries has elevated the riverbed and its banks above the level of the plain. Twice a year, the river overflows and inundates surrounding land as far as 10 miles (16 kilometers) distant. Snowmelt from the Pamir° and Himalaya° mountains feeds the flood in March and April. In August, seasonal winds called monsoons (see Chapter 13) bring rains from the southwest that feed a second flood. Though extremely dry for the rest of the year, Sind's floods make two crops a year possible. In ancient times, the Hakra° River (sometimes referred to as the Saraswati), which has since dried up, ran parallel to the Indus about 25 miles (40 kilometers) to the east and supplied water to a second cultivable area.

Adjacent regions shared distinctive cultural traits with this core area. In Punjab (literally "five waters"), to the northeast, five rivers converge to feed the main stream of the Indus. Closer to the northern mountains, the Punjab receives more rainfall but less floodwater than Sind. Culturally similar settlements extend from the Punjab as far east as Delhi° in northwest India. Settlement also extended through the Indus delta in southern Sind down into India's hook-shaped Kathiawar° Peninsula, an area of alluvial plains and coastal marshes. The Indus Valley civilization, as scholars labeled this area of cultural homogeneity when they first discovered it eighty years ago, covered an area roughly equivalent to modern France.

Material Culture

Although archaeologists have located several hundred communities that flourished from approximately 2600 to 1900 B.C.E., the remains of two urban sites, known by the modern names **Harappa** and **Mohenjo-Daro°**, best typify the Indus Valley civilization. Unfortunately, the high water table at these sites makes excavation of the earliest levels of settlement nearly impossible.

Scholars once believed that the people who created this civilization spoke Dravidian° languages related to those spoken today in southern India. Invaders from the northwest speaking Indo-European languages, they thought, conquered these people around 1500 B.C.E., causing some of them to migrate to the southeast. Skeletal evidence, however, indicates that the population of the Indus Valley has remained stable from ancient times to the present. Settled agriculture in this region seems to date back to at least 5000 B.C.E. Archaeological investigations have not yet revealed the relations between the Indus Valley civilization and earlier cultural complexes in the Indus Valley and the hilly lands to the west or the forces that gave rise to the urbanization, population increase, and technological advances that occurred in the mid-third millennium B.C.E. Nevertheless, the case for continuity with earlier cultures seems stronger than the case for a sudden transformation due to the arrival of new peoples.

The writing system of the Indus Valley people contained more than four hundred signs to represent syllables and words. Archaeologists have recovered thousands of inscribed seal stones and copper tablets. The inscriptions are so brief, however, that no one has yet deciphered them, though some scholars believe they represent an early Dravidian language.

Harappa, 3½ miles (5.6 kilometers) in circumference, may have housed a population of 35,000 and Mohenjo-Daro several times that. These cities show marked similarities in planning and construction: high, thick, encircling walls of brick; streets laid out in a rectangular grid; and covered drainpipes to carry away waste. The consistent width of streets and length of city blocks, and the uniformity of the mud bricks used in construction, suggest a strong central authority, located possibly in the citadel—an elevated, enclosed compound containing large buildings. Scholars think the well-ventilated structures near the citadel stored grain for local use and for export. The presence of barracks may point to some regimentation of skilled artisans.

Though it is presumed that these urban centers controlled the surrounding farmlands, different centers may have served different functions, which might account for their locations. Mohenjo-Daro seems to dominate the great floodplain of the Indus. Harappa, which is nearly 500 miles (805 kilometers) to the north, sits in the zone where farmlands give way to pasturelands. No settlements have been found west of Harappa, which may have served as a gateway for copper, tin, precious stones,

---

Thar (tahr) **Sind** (sinned) **Pamir** (pah-MEER)
Himalaya (him-uh-LAY-uh) **Hakra** (HAK-ruh)
Delhi (DEL-ee) **Kathiawar** (kah-tee-uh-WAHR)
Mohenjo-Daro (moe-hen-joe-DAHR-oh)

Dravidian (druh-VID-ee-uhn)

and other resources coming from the northwest. Coastal towns to the south engaged in seaborne trade with Sumer and lands around the Persian Gulf, as well as fishing and gathering highly prized seashells.

While published accounts of the Indus Valley civilization tend to treat Mohenjo-Daro and Harappa, the most extensively excavated sites, as the norm, most people surely lived in smaller settlements, which exhibit the same artifacts and the same standardization of styles and shapes as the large cities. Some scholars attribute this standardization to extensive exchange of goods within the zone of Indus Valley civilization rather than to a strong and authoritarian central government.

Metal appears more frequently in Indus Valley sites than in Mesopotamia or Egypt. Tools and other useful objects outweigh in importance the decorative objects—jewelry and the like—so often found in those other regions. Largely the possessions of elite groups in the Middle East, metal goods belonged to a broad cross-section of the population in the Indus Valley.

Technologically, the Indus Valley people showed skill in irrigation, used the potter's wheel, and fired bricks to rocky hardness in kilns for use in the foundations of large public buildings (sun-dried bricks exposed to floodwaters would have dissolved quickly). Smiths worked with various metals—gold, silver, copper, and tin. The varying ratios of tin to copper in their bronze objects suggest awareness of the hardness of different mixtures. They used less tin, a relatively scarce metal, in objects that did not require maximum hardness, like knives, and more tin in things like axes that had to be harder.

Archaeological finds point to widespread trading contacts. Mountain passes through the northwest granted access to the valuable resources of eastern Iran and Afghanistan, as well as to ore deposits in western India. These resources included metals (such as copper and tin), precious stones (lapis lazuli, jade, and turquoise), building stone, and timber. Rivers provided thoroughfares for transporting goods within the zone of Indus Valley culture. The undeciphered writing on the many seal stones, some scholars feel, may represent the names of merchants who stamped their wares.

Inhabitants of the Indus Valley and of Mesopotamia obtained raw materials from some of the same sources. The discovery of Indus Valley seal stones in the Tigris-Euphrates Valley indicates that merchants from the former region may have acted as middlemen in long-distance trade, obtaining raw materials from the northwest and shipping them to the Persian Gulf.

We know little about the political, social, economic, and religious structures of Indus Valley society. Efforts to link artifacts and images to cultural features characteris-

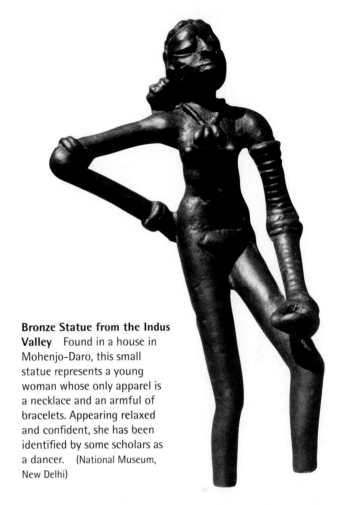

Bronze Statue from the Indus Valley Found in a house in Mohenjo-Daro, this small statue represents a young woman whose only apparel is a necklace and an armful of bracelets. Appearing relaxed and confident, she has been identified by some scholars as a dancer. (National Museum, New Delhi)

tic of later periods of Indian history (see Chapter 7), including sociopolitical institutions (a system of hereditary occupational groups, the predominant role of priests), architectural forms (bathing tanks like those later found in Hindu temples, private interior courtyards in houses), and religious beliefs and practices (depictions of gods and sacred animals on the seal stones, a cult of the mother-goddess), remain speculative. Further knowledge on these matters awaits additional archaeological finds and deciphering of the Indus Valley script.

Transformation of the Indus Valley Civilization

The Indus Valley cities were abandoned sometime after 1900 B.C.E. Archaeologists once thought that invaders destroyed them, but they now believe this civilization suffered "systems failure"—a breakdown of the fragile interrelationship of political, social, and

ENVIRONMENT + TECHNOLOGY

Environmental Stress in the Indus Valley

The three river-valley civilizations discussed in this chapter were located in arid or semiarid regions. Such regions are particularly vulnerable to changes in the environment. Scholars' debates about the existence and impact of changes in the climate and landscape of the Indus Valley illuminate some of the possible factors at work, as well as the difficulties of verifying and interpreting such long-ago changes.

One of the points at issue is climatic change. An earlier generation of scholars believed that the climate of the Indus Valley was considerably wetter during the height of that civilization than it is now. As evidence, they cited the enormous quantities of timber, cut from extensive forests, that would have been needed to bake the millions of mud bricks used to construct the cities (see photo), the distribution of human settlements on land that is now unfavorable for agriculture, and the representation of jungle and marsh animals on decorated seals. This approach assumes that the growth of population, prosperity, and complexity in the Indus Valley in the third millennium B.C.E. required wet conditions, and it concludes that the change to a drier climate in the early second millennium B.C.E. pushed this civilization into decline.

Other experts, skeptical about radical climate change, countered with alternative calculations of the amount of timber needed and evidence of plant remains—particularly barley, a grain that is tolerant of dry conditions. However, recent studies of the stabilization of sand dunes, which occurs in periods of heavy rainfall, and analysis of the sediment deposited by rivers and winds have been used to strengthen the claim that the Indus Valley used to be wetter and that in the early- to mid-second millennium B.C.E. it entered a period of relatively dry conditions that have persisted to the present.

A much clearer case can be made for changes in the landscape caused by shifts in the courses of rivers. These shifts are due, in many cases, to tectonic forces such as earthquakes. Dry channels, whether detected in satellite photographs or by on-the-ground inspection, reveal the location of old riverbeds, and it appears that a second major river system, the Hakra, once ran parallel to the Indus some distance to the east. The Hakra, with teeming towns and fertile fields along its banks, appears to have been a second axis of this civilization. Either the Sutlej, which now feeds into the Indus, or the Yamuna, which now pours into the Ganges, may have been the main source of water for this long-gone system before undergoing a change of course. The consequences of the drying-up of this major waterway must have been immense—the loss of huge amounts of arable land and the food that it

Mud–Brick Fortification Wall of the Citadel at Harappa
Built upon a high platform, this massive and towering construction required large numbers of bricks and enormous man-hours of labor. *The Cambridge History of India: The Indus Civilization,* 3d ed. (1968), by Sir Mortimer Wheeler. With permission of the Syndics of the Cambridge University Press.

produced, the abandonment of cities and villages and consequent migration of their populations, shifts in the trade routes, and desperate competition for shrinking resources.

As for the Indus itself, the present-day course of the lower reaches of the river has shifted 100 miles (161 kilometers) to the west since the arrival of the Greek conqueror Alexander the Great in the late fourth century B.C.E., and the deposit of massive volumes of silt has pushed the mouth of the river 50 miles (80 kilometers) farther south. Such a shift of the river bed and buildup of alluvial deposits also may have occurred in the third and second millennia B.C.E.

A recent study concludes: "It is obvious that ecological stresses, caused both climatically and technically, played an important role in the life and decay" of the Indus civilization.

Source: Quotation from D. P. Agarwal and R. K. Sood in Gregory L. Possehl, ed., *Harappan Civilization: A Contemporary Perspective* (Warminster, England: Aris and Phillips, 1982), 229.

economic systems that sustained order and prosperity. The precipitating cause may have been one or more natural disasters, such as an earthquake or massive flooding. Gradual ecological changes may also have played a role as the Hakra river system dried up and salinization (an increase in the amount of plant-inhibiting salt in the soil) and erosion increased (see Environment and Technology: Environmental Stress in the Indus Valley).

Towns left dry by a change of riverbed, seaports removed from the coast by silt deposited in deltas, and regions suffering loss of fertile soil would have necessitated the relocation of populations and a change in the livelihood of those who remained. The causes, patterns, and pace of change probably varied, with urbanization persisting longer in some regions than in others. The urban centers eventually succumbed, however, and village-based farming and herding took their place. As the interaction between regions lessened, regional variation replaced the standardization of technology and style of the previous era.

Historians can do little more than speculate about the causes behind the changes and the experiences of the people who lived in the Indus Valley around 1900 B.C.E. Two tendencies bear remembering, however. In most cases like this, the majority of the population adjusts to the new circumstances. But members of the political and social elite, who depend on urban centers and complex political and economic structures, lose the source of their authority and merge with the population as a whole.

CONCLUSION

Tens of thousands of years elapsed between the first appearance of the earliest ancestors of humankind and the agricultural revolutions that made possible the transition to civilization. Domesticated plants and animals contributed to the settling down of wandering groups of foragers and, in time, produced sufficient surplus food to relieve a small minority of people from the labor of tilling fields and watching flocks. Some of these people availed themselves of this opportunity to advance already existing skills—painting, stone-working, weaving, building—to higher levels requiring more specialized techniques. Others specialized in warfare, administration, religious ceremonies, and accumulation of knowledge. Thus did humanity pass from the prehistoric era to the era of civilized history.

The first civilizations developed high levels of political centralization, urbanization, and technology because their situations in river valleys too arid to support agriculture through rainfall forced communities to work together on constructing and maintaining canals, dams, weirs, and dikes. Crops harvested from irrigated fields not only fed the farming populations of Mesopotamia, Egypt, and the Indus Valley, but produced enough surplus to support artisans with specialized expertise in engineering, mathematics, and metallurgy.

Unpredictable and violent floods constantly threatened communities in the Tigris-Euphrates Basin, but the opportune and gradual Nile floods usually brought joy and satisfaction to those in Egypt. Relationships with nature stamped the worldview of both peoples. Mesopotamians tried to appease their harsh deities in order to survive in an unpredictable world. Egyptians trusted in and nurtured the supernatural powers they believed guaranteed orderliness and prosperity.

In both Egypt and Mesopotamia, kingship emerged as the dominant political form. The Egyptian king's divine origins and symbolic association with the forces of renewal made him central to the welfare of the entire country and gave him a religious monopoly, superseding the authority of the temples and priests. Egyptian monarchs lavished much of the country's wealth on their tombs, believing that a proper burial would ensure the continuity of kingship and the attendant blessings that it brought to the land and people. Mesopotamian rulers, who were not normally regarded as divine, built new cities, towering walls, splendid palaces, and religious edifices as lasting testaments to their power.

Both cultures revered a hierarchy of gods, ranging from protective demons and local deities to gods of the state, whose importance rose or fell with the power of the political centers with which they were associated. Cheered by the stability of their environment, Egyptians conceived a positive notion of the gods' designs for humankind. They believed that despite hazards, the righteous spirit could journey to the next world and look forward to a blessed existence. In contrast, terrifying visions of the afterlife torment Gilgamesh, the Mesopotamian hero: disembodied spirits of the dead stumbling around in the darkness of the Underworld for all eternity, eating dust and clay, and slaving for the heartless gods of that realm.

Cultural continuity marked both Egypt and Mesopotamia despite substantial ethnic diversity. Immigrants assimilated to the dominant language, belief system, and lifestyles of the civilization. Culture, not physical appearance, served as the criterion of personal identification. Reduced freedom and legal privilege for Mesopotamian women in the second millennium B.C.E. may relate to a high degree of urbanization and class stratification. In contrast, Egyptian pictorial documents, love poems, and legal records indicate an attitude of respect and a higher degree of equality for women in the valley of the Nile.

In the second millennium B.C.E., as the societies of Mesopotamia and Egypt consolidated their cultural achievements and entered new phases of political expansion, and as the Indus Valley centers went into irreversible decline, a new and distinctive civilization, based on exploiting the agricultural potential of a floodplain, emerged in the valley of the Yellow River in eastern China. We turn to that area in Chapter 2.

■ Key Terms

civilization	scribe
culture	ziggurat
history	amulet
Stone Age	cuneiform
Paleolithic	pharaoh
Neolithic	ma'at
foragers	pyramid
Agricultural Revolutions	Memphis
Holocene	Thebes
megalith	hieroglyphics
Babylon	papyrus
Sumerians	mummy
Semitic	Harappa
city-state	Mohenjo-Daro
Hammurabi	

■ Suggested Reading

Reliable textbooks are Brian Fagan's *People of the Earth: An Introduction to World Prehistory*, 9th ed. (1997), and Robert J. Wenke, *Patterns in Prehistory: Humankind's First Three Million Years,* 4th ed. (1999).

Ann Sieveking, *The Cave Artists* (1979), Mario Ruspoli, *The Cave Art of Lascaux* (1986), and N. K. Sanders, *Prehistoric Art in Europe* (1968) provide overviews of major European sites.

For ideas on the transition to food production, see Jared Diamond, *Guns, Germs, and Steel: The Fates of Human Societies* (1997), and Allen W. Johnson and Timothy Earle, *The Evolution of Human Societies: From Foraging Group to Agrarian State* (1987). Jean-Pierre Mohen, *The World of Megaliths* (1990), analyzes early monumental architecture. James Mellaart, the principal excavator of Çatal Hüyük, discusses his work for the general reader in *Çatal Hüyük: A Neolithic Town in Anatolia* (1967).

Jack M. Sasson, ed., *Civilizations of the Ancient Near East*, 4 vols. (1993), contains up-to-date articles and a bibliography on a wide range of topics. An excellent starting point for geogra-

phy, chronology, and basic institutions and cultural concepts in ancient western Asia is Michael Roaf, *Cultural Atlas of Mesopotamia and the Ancient Near East* (1990). Amelie Kuhrt, *The Ancient Near East, c. 3000–330 B.C.*, 2 vols. (1995), is the best and most up-to-date introduction to the historical development of western Asia and Egypt, offering a clear and concise historical outline and a balanced presentation of continuing controversies. Other general historical introductions can be found in A. Bernard Knapp, *The History and Culture of Ancient Western Asia and Egypt* (1988); Hans J. Nissen, *The Early History of the Ancient Near East, 9000–2000 B.C.* (1988); H. W. F. Saggs, *Civilization Before Greece and Rome* (1989); and Georges Roux, *Ancient Iraq*, 3d ed. (1992). Joan Oates, *Babylon* (1979), focuses on the most important of all the Mesopotamian cities. J. N. Postgate, *Early Mesopotamia: Society and Economy at the Dawn of History* (1992), offers deep insights into political, social, and economic dynamics. Daniel C. Snell, *Life in the Ancient Near East 3100–322 B.C.E.* (1997), emphasizes social and economic matters for advanced students. Stephanie Dalley, ed., *The Legacy of Mesopotamia* (1998), explores Mesopotamian interactions with other parts of the ancient world.

David Ferry's *Gilgamesh: A New Rendering in English Verse* (1992) is an attractive translation. The evolving mentality of Mesopotamian religion comes through in Thorkild Jacobsen, *The Treasures of Darkness: A History of Mesopotamian Religion* (1976). Stephanie Dalley, *Myths from Mesopotamia* (1989), Henrietta McCall, *Mesopotamian Myths* (1990), and Jeremy Black and Anthony Green, *Gods, Demons and Symbols of Ancient Mesopotamia* (1992), cover myth, religion, and religious symbolism. Pierre Amiet, *Art of the Ancient Near East* (1980), introduces various arts with good illustrations. Dominique Collon, *First Impressions: Cylinder Seals in the Ancient Near East* (1988), reveals much about art and daily life.

C. B. F. Walker, *Cuneiform* (1987), is a concise guide to the Mesopotamian writing system. James B. Pritchard, *Ancient Near Eastern Texts Relating to the Old Testament,* 3d ed. (1969), contains translated documents and texts from western Asia and Egypt. For women's matters, see Barbara Lesko, "Women of Egypt and the Ancient Near East," in *Becoming Visible: Women in European History*, 2d ed., ed. Renata Bridenthal, Claudia Koonz, and Susan Stuard (1994), and Guity Nashat, "Women in the Ancient Middle East," in *Restoring Women to History* (1988). Harvey Weiss, ed., *Ebla to Damascus: Art and Archaeology of Ancient Syria* (1985), and Giovanni Pettinato, *Ebla: A New Look at History* (1991), discuss Syria's relationship with Mesopotamia.

A lavishly illustrated introduction to ancient Egyptian civilization is David P. Silverman, ed., *Ancient Egypt* (1997). John Baines and Jaromir Malek, *Atlas of Ancient Egypt* (1980), and T. G. H. James, *Ancient Egypt: The Land and Its Legacy* (1988), are organized around the sites of ancient Egypt and provide general introductions. Historical treatments include B. G. Trigger, B. J. Kemp, D. O'Connor, and A. B. Lloyd, *Ancient Egypt: A Social History* (1983); Barry J. Kemp, *Ancient Egypt: Anatomy of a Civilization* (1989); and Nicholas-Cristophe Grimal, *A History of Ancient Egypt* (1992). John Romer, *People of the Nile: Everyday Life in*

Ancient Egypt (1982); Miriam Stead, *Egyptian Life* (1986); and Eugen Strouhal, *Life of the Ancient Egyptians* (1992), emphasize social history. For women, see the chapter by Lesko cited above; Barbara Watterson, *Women in Ancient Egypt* (1991); Gay Robins, *Women in Ancient Egypt* (1993); and the articles and museum exhibition catalogue in Anne K. Capel and Glenn E. Markoe, eds., *Mistress of the House, Mistress of Heaven: Women in Ancient Egypt* (1996).

Stephen Quirke, *Ancient Egyptian Religion* (1990), is a highly regarded treatment of a complex subject. George Hart, *Egyptian Myths* (1990), presents evidence for what must have been a thriving oral tradition. Pritchard's collection, cited above, and Miriam Lichtheim, *Ancient Egyptian Literature: A Book of Readings,* Vol. 1, *The Old and Middle Kingdoms* (1973), provide translated texts and documents. William Stevenson Smith, *The Art and Architecture of Ancient Egypt* (1998), and Gay Robins, *The Art of Ancient Egypt* (1997), cover the visual record.

For the Indus Valley civilization, see the brief treatment by Stanley Wolpert, *A New History of India,* 3d ed. (1989). Jonathan Mark Kenoyer, *Ancient Cities of the Indus Valley Civilization* (1998), supersedes the occasionally still useful works of Mortimer Wheeler, *Civilizations of the Indus Valley and Beyond* (1966) and *The Indus Civilization,* 3d ed. (1968). Gregory L. Poschl has edited two collections of articles: *Ancient Cities of the Indus* (1979) and *Harappan Civilization: A Contemporary Perspective* (1982).

■ Notes

1. N. K. Sandars, *The Epic of Gilgamesh* (Baltimore: Penguin Books, 1960), 61–63.
2. Colin McEvedy and Richard Jones, *Atlas of World Population History* (New York: Penguin Books, 1978), 13–15.
3. Colin Renfrew, *Archaeology and Language: The Puzzle of Indo-European Origins* (Cambridge: Cambridge University Press, 1988), 125, 150.
4. Luigi Cavalli-Sforza, L. Luca, Paolo Menozzi, and Alberto Piazza, *The History and Geography of Human Genes* (Princeton, NJ: Princeton University Press, 1994).
5. James Mellaart, *Çatal Hüyük: A Neolithic Town in Anatolia* (New York: McGraw-Hill, 1967), 202.

Document-Based Question
Early Civilizations and the Physical Environment

Using the following documents, analyze the role of the physical environment in the development of early civilizations in Mesopotamia, Egypt, and the Indus Valley.

DOCUMENT 1
Excerpt from the story of Gilgamesh (p. 5)

DOCUMENT 2
Map 1.2 River-Valley Civilizations, 3500–1500 B.C.E (p. 13)

DOCUMENT 3
Reed Huts in the Marshes of Southern Iraq (photo, p. 15)

DOCUMENT 4
Violence and Order in the Babylonian New Year's Festival (Diversity and Dominance, p. 20)

DOCUMENT 5
Mesopotamian Cylinder Seal (photo, p. 22)

DOCUMENT 6
Map 1.4 Ancient Egypt (p. 24)

DOCUMENT 7
Mud-Brick Fortification Wall of the Citadel at Harappa (photo, p. 32)

Evaluate the ways in which the documents demonstrate the human ability to modify the physical environment. What additional types of documents would help you understand the importance of the physical environment in early civilizations?

2 New Civilizations in the Eastern and Western Hemispheres, 2200–250 B.C.E.

Wall Painting of Nubians Arriving in Egypt with Rings and Bags of Gold, Fourteenth Century B.C.E.
This image decorated the tomb of an Egyptian administrator in Nubia.

CHAPTER OUTLINE

Early China, 2000–221 B.C.E.

Nubia, 3100 B.C.E.–350 C.E.

First Civilizations of the Americas: The Olmec and Chavín, 1200–250 B.C.E.

ENVIRONMENT AND TECHNOLOGY: Divination in Ancient Societies

DIVERSITY AND DOMINANCE: Hierarchy and Conduct in the Analects of Confucius

Around 2200 B.C.E. an Egyptian official named Harkhuf°, who lived at Aswan° on the southern boundary of Egypt, set out for a place called Yam, far to the south in the land that later came to be called Nubia. He had made this trek three times before, so he was familiar with the route and skillful in dealing with various Nubian chieftains along the way. He brought gifts from the Egyptian pharaoh for the ruler of Yam, and he returned home with three hundred donkeys loaded with incense, dark ebony wood, ivory, panthers, and other exotic products from tropical Africa. While this exchange was couched in the diplomatic fiction of gifts, we should probably regard it as a form of trade and Harkhuf as a brave and enterprising caravan leader. On this particular trip he returned with something so special that the eight-year-old boy pharaoh, Pepi II, could not contain his excitement. He wrote:

> Come north to the residence at once! Hurry and bring with you this pygmy whom you brought from the land of the horizon-dwellers live, hale, and healthy, for the dances of the god, to gladden the heart, to delight the heart of king Neferkare [Pepi] who lives forever! When he goes down with you into the ship, get worthy men to be around him on deck, lest he fall into the water! When he lies down at night, get worthy men to lie around him in his tent. Inspect ten times at night! My majesty desires to see this pygmy more than the gifts of the mine-land and of Punt![1]

Although the precise location of Yam is uncertain, scholars are beginning to identify it with Kerma, later the capital of the kingdom of Nubia, on the upper Nile in modern Sudan. From the Egyptian point of view, Nubia was a wild and dangerous place. Yet we can see that it was developing features of more complex political organization, and that the burgeoning trade between Nubia and Egypt was important to both societies.

In contrast to the river-valley civilizations of Mesopotamia, Egypt, and the Indus Valley surveyed in the previous chapter, the complex societies examined in this chapter subsequently emerged in ecological conditions quite a bit more diverse, sometimes independently, sometimes under the influence of the older centers. Whereas the river-valley civilizations were originally largely self-sufficient, each of the new civilizations discussed in this chapter and the next was shaped by the development of networks of long-distance trade.

In the second millennium B.C.E. a civilization based on irrigation agriculture arose along the valley of the Yellow River and its tributaries in northern China. In the same epoch, in Nubia (southern Egypt and northern Sudan), the first complex society in tropical Africa continued to develop from the roots observed earlier by Harkhuf. The first millennium B.C.E. witnessed the flourishing of the earliest complex societies of the Western Hemisphere, the Olmec of Mesoamerica and the Chavín culture on the flanks of the Andes Mountains in South America. These societies had no contact with one another, and they represent a variety of responses to different environmental and historical circumstances. Thus, their stories will necessarily be separate. However, as we shall see, they have certain features in common and collectively point to a distinct stage in the development of human societies.

As you read this chapter, ask yourself the following questions:

- How did the peoples of early China, Nubia, and the Olmec and Chavín civilizations each develop distinctive political and social institutions, cultural patterns, and technologies in response to the challenges of the environment?

- What was the basis of the status, power, and wealth of elite groups in each society, and how did they dominate the rest of the population?

- How did the technological and cultural influences of older centers affect the formation of the new civilizations?

- Why did societies in the Eastern and Western Hemispheres acquire complex organizations and potent technologies at different times and in different sequences?

Harkhuf (HAHR-koof)   **Aswan** (AS-wahn)

EARLY CHINA, 2000–221 B.C.E.

On the eastern edge of the great Eurasian landmass, Neolithic cultures developed as early as 8000 B.C.E. A more complex civilization evolved in the second millennium B.C.E. Under the Shang and Zhou monarchs many of the institutions and values of classical Chinese civilization emerged and spread south and west. As in Mesopotamia, Egypt, and the Indus Valley, the rise of cities, specialization of labor, bureaucratic government, writing, and other advanced technologies depended on the exploitation of a great river system—the Yellow River (Huang He°) and its tributaries—to support intensive agriculture. Although there is archaeological evidence of some movement of goods and ideas between western and eastern Asia, developments in China were largely independent of the complex societies in the Middle East and the Indus Valley.

Geography and Resources

China is isolated from the rest of the Eastern Hemisphere by formidable natural barriers: the Himalaya° mountain range on the southwest; the Pamir° and Tian° mountains and the Takla Makan° Desert on the west; the Gobi° Desert and the treeless and grassy hills and plains of the Mongolian steppe on the northwest (see Map 2.1). To the east lies the Pacific Ocean. Although China's separation was not total—trade goods, people, and ideas moved back and forth between China, India, and Central Asia—in many respects its development was distinctive.

Most of East Asia is covered with mountains, making overland travel, transport, and communications difficult and slow. The great river systems of eastern China, however—the Yellow and the Yangzi° Rivers and their tributaries—facilitate east-west movement. In the eastern river valleys dense populations could practice intensive agriculture; on the steppe lands of Mongolia, the deserts and oases of Xinjiang°, and the high plateau of Tibet sparser populations engaged in different forms of livelihood. The climate zones of East Asia range from the dry, subarctic reaches of Manchuria in the north to the lush, subtropical forests of the south, and support a rich variety of plant and animal life adapted to these zones.

Within the eastern agricultural zone, the north and the south have strikingly different environments. Each

zone produced distinctive patterns for the use of the land, the kinds of crops that could flourish, and the organization of agricultural labor. The monsoons that affect India and Southeast Asia (see Chapter 1) drench southern China with heavy rainfall in the summer, the most beneficial time for agriculture. Northern China, in contrast, where rainfall is much more erratic, receives less moisture. As in Mesopotamia and the Indus Valley, where technological and social developments unfolded in relatively adverse conditions, China's early history unfolded on the northern plains, a demanding environment that stimulated important technologies and political traditions as well as the philosophical and religious views that became hallmarks of Chinese civilization. By the third century C.E., however, the gradual flow of population toward the warmer southern lands caused the political and intellectual center to move south.

The eastern river valleys and North China Plain contained timber, stone, scattered deposits of metals, and, above all, potentially productive land. Since prehistoric times, winds blowing from Central Asia have deposited a yellowish-brown dust called **loess**° (these particles suspended in the water give the Yellow River its distinctive hue and name). Over the ages a thick mantle of soil has accumulated that is extremely fertile and soft enough to be worked with wooden digging sticks. The lack of compactness of this soil accounts for the severity of earthquake damage in this region.

In this landscape, agriculture demanded the coordinated efforts of large groups of people. In parts of northern China forests had to be cleared. Recurrent floods on the Yellow River necessitated the construction of earthen dikes and channels to carry off the overflow. To cope with the periodic droughts, catch basins (reservoirs) were dug to store river water and rainfall. As the population grew, people built retaining walls to partition the hillsides into tiers of flat arable terraces.

The staple crops in the northern region were millet, a grain indigenous to China, and wheat, which had spread to East Asia from the Middle East. Rice requires a warmer climate and prospered in the south. The cultivation of rice in the Yangzi River Valley and the south required a great outlay of labor. Rice paddies—the fields where rice is grown—must be absolutely flat and surrounded by water channels to bring and lead away water according to a precise schedule. Seedlings sprout in a nursery, and are transplanted one by one to the paddy, which is then flooded. Flooding eliminates weeds and rival plants and supports microscopic organisms that keep the soil fertile. When the crop is ripe, the paddy is drained; the rice stalks are harvested with a sickle; and

---

Huang He (hwahng-HUH)   **Himalaya** (him-uh-LAY-uh)
Pamir (pah-MEER)   **Tian** (tee-en)
Takla Makan (TAH-kluh muh-KAHN)   **Gobi** (GO-bee)
Yangzi (yang-zuh)   **Xinjiang** (shin-jyahng)

---

loess (less)

C H R O N O L O G Y

	China	Nubia	Americas
2500 B.C.E.	**8000–2000 B.C.E.** Neolithic cultures	**4500 B.C.E.** Early agriculture in Nubia **2200 B.C.E.** Harkhuf's expeditions to Yam	**3500 B.C.E.** Early agriculture in Mesoamerica and Andes **2600 B.C.E.** Rise of Caral
2000 B.C.E.	**2000 B.C.E.** Bronze metallurgy **1750–1027 B.C.E.** Shang dynasty	**1750 B.C.E.** Rise of kingdom of Kush based on Kerma	
1500 B.C.E.		**1500 B.C.E.** Egyptian conquest of Nubia	
1000 B.C.E.	**1027–221 B.C.E.** Zhou dynasty **600 B.C.E.** Iron Metallurgy	**1000 B.C.E.** Decline of Egyptian control in Nubia **750 B.C.E.** Rise of kingdom based on Napata **712–660 B.C.E.** Nubian kings rule Egypt	**1200–900 B.C.E.** Rise of Olmec civilization, centered on San Lorenzo **900–600 B.C.E.** La Venta, the dominant Olmec center **900–250 B.C.E.** Chavín civilization in the Andes **600–400 B.C.E.** Ascendancy of Tres Zapotes and Olmec decline
500 B.C.E		**300 B.C.E.–350 C.E.** Kingdom of Meroë	**500 B.C.E.** Early metallurgy in Andes

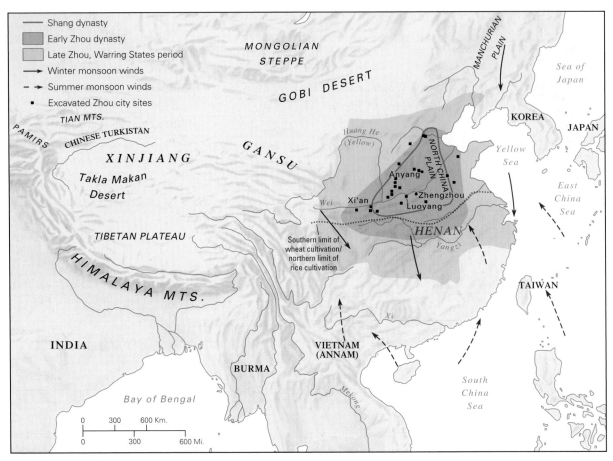

Map 2.1   China in the Shang and Zhou Periods, 1750–221 B.C.E.   The Shang dynasty arose in the second millennium B.C.E. in the floodplain of the Yellow River. While southern China benefits from the monsoon rains, northern China depends on irrigation. As population increased, the Han Chinese migrated from their eastern homeland to other parts of China, carrying their technologies and cultural practices. Other ethnic groups predominated in more outlying regions, and the nomadic peoples of the northwest constantly challenged Chinese authority.

the edible kernels are separated out. The reward for this effort is a spectacular yield. Rice can feed more people per cultivated acre than any other grain, which explains why the south eventually became more populous and important than the north.

The Shang Period, 1750–1027 B.C.E.

Archaeologists have identified several Neolithic cultural complexes in China, primarily on the basis of styles of pottery and forms of burial. These early populations grew millet, raised pigs and chickens, and used stone tools. They made pottery on a wheel and fired it in high-temperature kilns. They pioneered the production of silk cloth, first raising silkworms on mul-

berry trees, then carefully unraveling their cocoons to produce silk thread. The early Chinese built walls of pounded earth by hammering the soil inside temporary wooden frames until it became hard as cement. By 2000 B.C.E. they had begun to make bronze (roughly a thousand years after the beginnings of bronze-working in the Middle East).

Later generations of Chinese told stories about the ancient dynasty of the Xia, said to have ruled the core region of the Yellow River Valley. The validity of those stories is difficult to gauge, though some archaeologists identify the Xia with the Neolithic Longshan cultural complex in the centuries before and after 2000 B.C.E. Chinese history proper begins with the rise to power of the Shang clans, which coincides with the earliest written records anywhere in China.

Bronze Vessel from the Shang Period, 13th–11th Century B.C.E.
Vessels such as this large wine jar were used in rituals that allowed members of the Shang ruling class to make contact with their ancestors. Signifying both the source and the proof of the elite's authority, these vessels were often buried in Shang tombs. The complex shapes and elaborate decorations testify to the artisans' skill. (Tokyo National Museum Image: TNM Image)

The **Shang°** originated in the part of the Yellow River Valley that lies in the present-day province of Henan°. After 1750 B.C.E. they extended their control north into Mongolia, west as far as Gansu°, and south to the Yangzi River Valley. Shang society was dominated by a warrior aristocracy whose greatest pleasures were warfare, hunting (for recreation and to fine-tune skills required for war), exchanging gifts, feasting, and wine-filled revelry.

The king and his court ruled the core area of the Shang state directly. Aristocrats served as generals, ambassadors, and supervisors of public projects. Other members of the royal family and high-ranking nobility governed outlying provinces. The most distant regions were governed by native rulers who swore allegiance to the Shang king. The king was often on the road, traveling to the courts of his subordinates to reinforce their loyalty.

Frequent military campaigns provided the warrior aristocracy with a theater for brave achievements and yielded considerable plunder. The nomadic peoples who occupied the steppe and desert regions to the north and west were periodically rolled back and given a demon-

stration of Shang power. (Chinese sources refer to these peoples as "barbarians." Modern readers should be wary of the Chinese claim that these nomads were culturally backward and morally inferior to the Chinese.) Large numbers of prisoners of war were taken in these campaigns and used as slaves in the Shang capital.

Various cities served as the capital of the Shang kingdom. The last and most important was near modern Anyang° (see Map 2.1). Shang cities were centers of political control and religion. Surrounded by massive walls of pounded earth, they contained palaces, administrative buildings and storehouses, royal tombs, shrines of gods and ancestors, and houses of the nobility. The common people lived in agricultural villages outside these centers. Because stone was in short supply, buildings were set on foundation platforms of pounded earth and constructed with wooden posts and dried mud. These cities, which were laid out on a grid plan aligned with the north polar star and had gates opening to the cardinal directions, are an early manifestation of the Chinese concern with the orientation of buildings known as *feng shui*,° and they symbolized the order imposed by gods and monarchs.

A key to effective administration was the form of writing developed in this era. Pictograms (pictures representing objects and concepts) and phonetic symbols representing the sounds of syllables were combined to form a complex system of hundreds of signs. Only a small, educated elite had the time to master this system. Despite substantial changes through the ages, the fundamental principles of the Chinese system still endure today. As a result, people speaking essentially different languages, such as Mandarin and Cantonese, can read and understand the same text. In contrast, the cuneiform of Mesopotamia and the hieroglyphics of Egypt were eventually replaced by simpler alphabetic scripts.

The Shang ideology of kingship glorified the king as the indispensable intermediary between the people and the gods. The Shang royal family and aristocracy worshiped the spirits of their male ancestors. They believed that these ancestors were intensely interested in the fortunes of their descendants and had special influence with the gods. Before taking any action, the Shang rulers used **divination** to determine the will of the gods (see Environment and Technology: Divination in Ancient Societies). They made ritual sacrifices to their gods and ancestors in order to win divine favor. Burials of kings also entailed sacrifices, not only of animals but also of humans, including noble officials of the court, women, servants, soldiers, and prisoners of war.

Possession of bronze objects was a sign of authority

Shang (shahng)   **Henan** (heh-nahn)   **Gansu** (gahn-soo)

Anyang (ahn-yahng)   **feng shui** (fung shway)

Divination in Ancient Societies

The ancient inhabitants of China, the Middle East, Europe, and the Americas, as well as many other peoples throughout history, believed that the gods controlled the forces of nature and shaped destinies. Starting from this premise, they practiced various techniques of divination—the effort to interpret phenomena in the natural world as signs of the gods' will and intentions. Through divination the ancients sought to communicate with the gods and thereby anticipate—even influence—the future.

The Shang ruling class in China frequently sought information from shamans, individuals who claimed the ability to make direct contact with ancestors and other higher powers. The Shang monarch himself often functioned as a shaman. Chief among the tools of divination used by a shaman were oracle bones. The shaman touched a tortoiseshell or the shoulder bone of an animal (sometimes holes had been drilled in it ahead of time) with the heated point of a stick. The shell or bone would crack, and the cracks were "read" as a message from the spirit world.

Tens of thousands of oracle bones survive. They are a major source of information about Shang life; usually the question, the resulting answer, and often confirmation of the accuracy of the prediction were inscribed on the back of the shell or bone. The rulers asked about the proper performance of ritual, the likely outcome of wars or hunting expeditions, the prospects for rainfall and the harvest, and the meaning of strange occurrences.

In Mesopotamia in the third and second millennia B.C.E. the most important divination involved the close inspection of the form, size, and markings of the organs of sacrificed animals. Archaeologists have found models of sheep's livers accompanied by written explanations of the meaning of various features. Two other techniques of divination were following the trail of smoke from burning incense and examining the patterns that resulted when oil was thrown on water.

From about 2000 B.C.E. Mesopotamian diviners foretold the future from their observation of the movements of the sun, moon, planets, stars, and constellations. In the centuries after 1000 B.C.E. celestial omens were the most important source of predictions about the future, and specialists maintained precise records of astronomical events. Mesopotamian mathematics, essential for calculations of the movements of celestial bodies, was the most sophisticated in the ancient Middle East. Astrology, with its division of the sky into the

and nobility. Bronze weapons allowed the state to assert its authority, and bronze vessels were used in rituals seeking the support of ancestors and gods. The quantity of bronze objects found in Shang tombs is impressive. The relatively modest tomb of one queen contained 450 bronze articles (ritual vessels, bells, weapons, and mirrors)—remarkable because copper and tin, the principal ingredients of bronze, were not plentiful in northern China. (Also found in the same tomb were numerous objects in jade, bone, ivory, and stone; seven thousand cowrie shells; sixteen sacrificed men, women, and children; and six dogs!) The Shang elite expended huge effort to find and mine deposits of copper and tin, refine them into pure metal, transport the ingots to the capital, and commission the creation of weapons and beautifully decorated objects.

Artisans worked in foundries outside the main cities. They poured the molten bronze into clay molds, and joined together the hardened pieces as necessary.

Shang artisans made weapons, chariot fittings, musical instruments, and the ritual vessels used in religious ceremonies. Many of these elegant vessels were vividly decorated with stylized depictions of real and imaginary animals.

Far-reaching networks of trade sprang up across China, bringing the Shang valued commodities such as jade, ivory, and mother of pearl (a hard, shiny substance from the interior of mollusk shells) used for jewelry, carved figurines, and decorative inlays. Some evidence suggests that Shang China may have exchanged goods and ideas with distant Mesopotamia. The horse-drawn chariot, which the Shang may have adopted from Western Asia, was a formidable instrument of war.

The Zhou Period, 1027–221 B.C.E.

Shang domination of central and northern China lasted more than six centuries. In the

twelve segments of the zodiac and its use of the position of the stars and planets to predict an individual's destiny, developed out of long-standing Mesopotamian attention to the movements of celestial objects. Horoscopes—charts with calculations and predictions based on an individual's date of birth—have been found from shortly before 400 B.C.E. In the Hellenistic period (323–30 B.C.E.), Greek settlers flooding into western Asia built on this Mesopotamian foundation and greatly advanced the study of astrology.

Little is known for certain about the divinatory practices of early American peoples. The Olmec produced polished stone mirrors whose concave surfaces gave off reflected images that were thought to emanate from a supernatural realm. Painted basins found in Olmec households have been compared to those attested for later Meso-

american groups. In the latter, women threw maize kernels onto the surface of water-filled basins and noted the patterns by which they floated or sank, in order to ascertain information useful to the family, such as the cause and cure of illness, the right time for agricultural tasks or marriage, and propitious names for newborn children.

It may seem surprising that divination is being treated here as a form of technology. Most modern people would regard such interpretations of patterns in everyday phenomena as mere superstition. However, within the context of the laws of nature as understood by ancient societies (the gods control and direct events in the natural world), divination involved the application of principles of causation to the socially beneficial task of acquiring information about what would happen in the future. These techniques were usually known only to a class of experts whose special training and knowledge gave them high status in their society.

Chinese Divination Shell After inscribing questions on a bone or shell, the diviner applied a red-hot point and interpreted the resulting cracks as a divine response. (Institute of History and Philology, Academia Sinica)

eleventh century B.C.E. the last Shang king was defeated by Wu, the ruler of **Zhou**°, a dependent state in the Wei° River Valley. The Zhou line of kings (ca. 1027–221 B.C.E.) was the longest lasting and most revered of all dynasties in Chinese history. Just as the Semitic peoples in Mesopotamia had adopted and adapted the Sumerian legacy (see Chapter 1), the Zhou preserved the essentials of Shang culture and added new elements of ideology and technology.

The positive image of Zhou rule was skillfully constructed by propagandists for the new regime. The early Zhou monarchs had to justify their seizure of power to the restive remnants of the Shang clans. The chief deity was now referred to as "Heaven"; the monarch was called the "Son of Heaven"; and his rule was called the "**Mandate of Heaven.**" According to the new theory, the ruler

had been chosen by the supreme deity and would retain his backing as long as he served as a wise, principled, and energetic guardian of his people. The proof of divine favor was the prosperity and the stability of the kingdom. If the ruler misbehaved, as the last Shang ruler had done, his right to rule could be withdrawn. Corruption, violence, arrogance, and insurrection, such as had occurred under the last Shang king, were signs of divine displeasure and validated the ruler's replacement by a new dynasty that was committed to just rule.

The Zhou kings continued some of the Shang rituals, but there was a marked decline in the practice of divination and in extravagant and bloody sacrifices and burials. The priestly power of the ruling class, the only ones who had been able to make contact with the spirits of ancestors during the Shang period, faded away. The resulting separation of religion and government promoted the development of important philosophical and mystical systems in the Zhou period. The bronze vessels

Zhou (joe)   **Wei** (way)

Women Beating Chimes   This scene, from a bronze vessel of the Zhou era, illustrates the important role of music in festivals, religious rituals, and court ceremonials. During the politically fragmented later (Eastern) Zhou era, many small states marked their independence by having their own musical scales and distinctive arrangements of orchestral instruments.   (Courtesy, Sichuan Museum)

that had been sacred implements in the Shang period now became family treasures.

The early period of Zhou rule, the eleventh through ninth centuries B.C.E., is sometimes called the Western Zhou era because of the location of the capitals in the western part of the kingdom. These centuries saw the development of a sophisticated administrative apparatus. The Zhou built a series of capital cities with pounded-earth foundations and walls. The major buildings all faced south, in keeping with an already ancient concern to orient structures so that they would be in a harmonious relationship with the terrain, the forces of wind, water, and sunlight, and the invisible energy perceived to be flowing through the natural world. All government officials, including the king, were supposed to be models of morality, fairness, and concern for the welfare of the people.

Like the Shang, the Zhou regime was highly decentralized. Members and allies of the royal family ruled more than a hundred largely autonomous territories. The court was the scene of elaborate ceremonials, embellished by music and dance, that impressed on observers the glory of Zhou rule and reinforced the bonds of obligation between rulers and ruled.

Around 800 B.C.E. Zhou power began to wane. Ambitious local rulers operated ever more independently and waged war on one another, while nomadic peoples attacked the northwest frontiers (see Map 2.1). The following five hundred years are sometimes referred to as the Eastern Zhou era. In 771 B.C.E. members of the Zhou lineage relocated to a new, more secure, eastern capital near

Luoyang°, where they continued to hold the royal title and received at least nominal homage from the real power brokers of the age. This was a time of political fragmentation, rapidly shifting centers of power, and fierce competition and warfare among numerous small and independent states. Historians conventionally divide Eastern Zhou into the "Spring and Autumn Period," from 771 to 481 B.C.E., after a collection of chronicles that give annual entries for those two seasons, and the "Warring States Period," from 480 to the unification of China in 221 B.C.E.

The many states of the Eastern Zhou era contended with one another for leadership. Cities, some of them quite large, spread across the Chinese landscape. Long walls of pounded earth, the ancestors of the Great Wall of China, protected the kingdoms from each other and from northern nomads. The Chinese also learned from the steppe nomads to put fighters on horseback. By 600 B.C.E. iron began to replace bronze as the primary metal for tools and weapons. There is mounting evidence that ironworking came to China from the nomadic peoples of the northwest. Subsequently, metalworkers in southern China, which had limited access to copper and tin for making bronze, were the first in the world to forge steel by removing carbon during the iron-smelting process.

In many of the states, bureaucrats expanded in number and function. Codes of law were written down. Governments collected taxes from the peasants directly, imposed standardized money, and managed large-scale

Luoyang (LWOE-yahng)

public works projects. The wealth and power of the state and its demands for obedience were justified by an authoritarian political philosophy that came to be called **Legalism.** Legalist thinkers maintained that human nature is essentially wicked and that people behave in an orderly fashion only if compelled by strict laws and harsh punishments. Legalists believed that every aspect of human society ought to be controlled and personal freedom sacrificed for the good of the state.

Confucianism, Daoism, and Chinese Society

The governments of the major Zhou states took over many of the traditional functions of the aristocracy. To maintain their influence, aristocrats sought a new role as advisers to the rulers. One who lived through the political flux and social change of this anxious time was Kongzi (551–479 B.C.E.)—known in the West by the Latin form of his name, **Confucius.** Coming from one of the smaller states, he had not been particularly successful in obtaining administrative posts. His doctrine of duty and public service, initially aimed at fellow aristocrats, was to become a central influence in Chinese thought (see Diversity and Dominance: Hierarchy and Conduct in the Analects of Confucius).

Many elements in Confucius's teaching had roots in earlier Chinese belief, including folk religion and the rites of the Zhou royal family, such as the veneration of ancestors and elders and worship of the deity Heaven. Confucius drew a parallel between the family and the state. Just as the family is a hierarchy, with the father at its top, sons next, then wives and daughters in order of age, so too the state is a hierarchy, with the ruler at the top, the public officials as the sons, and the common people as the women.

Confucius took a traditional term for the feelings between family members (*ren*) and expanded it into a universal ideal of benevolence toward all humanity, which he believed was the foundation of moral government. Government exists, he said, to serve the people, and the administrator or ruler gains respect and authority by displaying fairness and integrity. Confucian teachings emphasized benevolence, avoidance of violence, justice, rationalism, loyalty, and dignity. Confucius, who held a far more optimistic view of the basic goodness of human nature than the adherents of Legalism, sought to affirm and maintain the political and social order by improving it.

It is ironic that Confucius, whose ideas were to become so important in Chinese thought, actually had little influence in his own time. His later follower Mencius (Mengzi, 371–289 B.C.E.), who opposed despotism and argued against the authoritarian political ideology of the Legalists, made Confucius's teachings much better known. In the era of the early emperors, Confucianism became the dominant political philosophy and the core of the educational system for government officials (see Chapter 5).

The Warring States Period also saw the rise of the school of thought known as **Daoism°.** According to tradition, Laozi°, the originator of Daoism (believed to have lived in the sixth century B.C.E., though some scholars doubt his existence), sought to stop the warfare of the age by urging humanity to follow the *Dao,* or "path." Daoists accept the world as they find it, avoiding useless struggles and adhering to the "path" of nature. They avoid violence if at all possible and take the minimal action necessary for a task. Rather than fight the current of a stream, a wise man allows the onrushing waters to pass around him. This passivity arises from the Daoist's sense that the world is always changing and lacks any absolute morality or meaning. In the end, Daoists believe, all that matters is the individual's fundamental understanding of the "path."

The original Daoist philosophy was greatly expanded in subsequent centuries to incorporate popular beliefs, magic, and mysticism. Daoism represented an important stream of thought throughout Chinese history. By idealizing individuals who find their own "path" to right conduct, it offered an alternative to the Confucian emphasis on hierarchy and duty and to the Legalist approval of force.

Social organization also changed in this period. The kinship structures of the Shang and early Zhou periods, based on the clan (a relatively large group of related families), gave way to the three-generation family of grandparents, parents, and children as the fundamental social unit. A related development was the emergence of the concept of private property. Land was considered to belong to the men of the family and was divided equally among the sons when the father died.

Little is known about the conditions of life for women in early China. Some scholars believe that women may have acted as shamans, entering into trances to communicate with supernatural forces, making requests on behalf of their communities, and receiving predictions of the future. By the time written records begin to illuminate our knowledge of women's experiences, they show women in a subordinate position in the strongly patriarchal family.

Confucian thought codified this male-female hierar-

Daoism (DOW-izm) **Laozi** (low-zuh)

우세인 은신처

파운드폭탄 4발 투하… 두 아들과 함께 사망 가

실진지 구축… 이틀째 시가戰

령이 대중 앞에 나타나거나 애국심
을 고취하는 노래만을 내보내던 방
송마저 중단됐다.

라크 전후 대체
의에서는 전후
영국 주도로 이

DIVERSITY AND DOMINANCE

HIERARCHY AND CONDUCT IN THE ANALECTS OF CONFUCIUS

The Analects are a collection of sayings of Confucius, probably compiled and written down several generations after he lived, though some elements may have been added even later. They cover a wide range of matters, including ethics, government, education, music, and rituals. Taken as a whole, they are a guide to living a proper, honorable, virtuous, useful, and satisfying life. While subject to reinterpretation according to the circumstances of the times, Confucian principles have had a great influence on Chinese values and behavior ever since.

Chinese society in Confucius's time was very attuned to distinctions of status. Confucius assumed that hierarchy is innate in the order of the universe and that human society should echo and harmonize with the natural world. Each person has a role to play, with prescribed rules of conduct and proper ceremonial behavior, in order to maintain the social order. The following selections illuminate the particular attention paid by Confucius to the important status categories in his society, the proper way for individuals to treat others, and the necessity of hierarchy and inequality.

1:6 Confucius said: "A young man should serve his parents at home and be respectful to elders outside his home. He should be earnest and truthful, loving all, but become intimate with *ren* [an inner capacity, possessed by all human beings, to do good]. After doing this, if he has energy to spare, he can study literature and the arts."

4:18 Confucius said: "When you serve your mother and father it is okay to try to correct them once in a while. But if you see that they are not going to listen to you, keep your respect for them and don't distance yourself from them. Work without complaining."

2:5 Meng Yi Zi asked about the meaning of filial piety. Confucius said, "It means 'not diverging (from your parents).'" Later, when Fan Chi was driving him, Confucius told Fan Chi, "Meng asked me about the meaning of filial piety, and I told him 'not diverging.'" Fan Chi said, "What did you mean by that?" Confucius said, "When your parents are alive, serve them with propriety; when they die, bury them with propriety, and then worship them with propriety."

1:2 Master You said: "There are few who have developed themselves filially and fraternally who enjoy offending their superiors. Those who do not enjoy offending superiors are never troublemakers. The Superior Man concerns himself with the fundamentals. Once the fundamentals are established, the proper way (*dao*) appears. Are not filial piety and obedience to elders fundamental to the enactment of *ren*?"

1:8 Confucius said: "If the Superior Man is not 'heavy,' then he will not inspire awe in others. If he is not learned, then he will not be on firm ground. He takes loyalty and good faith to be of primary importance, and has no friends who are not of equal (moral) caliber. When he makes a mistake, he doesn't hesitate to correct it."

4:5 Confucius said, "Riches and honors are what all men desire. But if they cannot be attained in accordance with the *dao* they should not be kept. Poverty and low status are what all men hate. But if they cannot be avoided while staying in accordance with the *dao*, you should not avoid them. If a Superior Man departs from *ren*, how can he be worthy of that name? A Superior Man never leaves *ren* for even the time of a single meal. In moments of haste he acts according to it. In times of difficulty or confusion he acts according to it."

15:20 Confucius said: "The Superior Man seeks within himself. The inferior man seeks within others."

16:8 Confucius said: "The Superior Man stands in awe of three things:

(1) He is in awe of the decree of Heaven.
(2) He is in awe of great men.
(3) He is in awe of the words of the sages.

The inferior man does not know the decree of Heaven; takes great men lightly and laughs at the words of the sages."

4:14 Confucius said: "I don't worry about not having a good position; I worry about the means I use to gain position. I don't worry about being unknown; I seek to be known in the right way."

7:15 Confucius said: "I can live with coarse rice to eat, water for drink and my arm as a pillow and still be happy. Wealth and honors that one possesses in the midst of injustice are like floating clouds."

4:17 Confucius said: "When you see a good person, think of becoming like her/him. When you see someone not so good, reflect on your own weak points."

13:6 Confucius said: "When you have gotten your own life straightened out, things will go well without your giving orders. But if your own life isn't straightened out, even if you give orders, no one will follow them."

12:2 Zhonggong asked about the meaning of *ren*. The Master said: "Go out of your home as if you were receiving an important guest. Employ the people as if you were assisting at a great ceremony. What you don't want done to yourself, don't do to others. Live in your town without stirring up resentments, and live in your household without stirring up resentments."

1:5 Confucius said: "If you would govern a state of a thousand chariots (a small-to-middle-size state), you must pay strict attention to business, be true to your word, be economical in expenditure and love the people. You should use them according to the seasons."

2:3 Confucius said: "If you govern the people legalistically and control them by punishment, they will avoid crime, but have no personal sense of shame. If you govern them by means of virtue and control them with propriety, they will gain their own sense of shame, and thus correct themselves."

12:7 Zigong asked about government.
The Master said, "Enough food, enough weapons and the confidence of the people."
Zigong said, "Suppose you had no alternative but to give up one of these three, which one would be let go of first?"
The Master said, "Weapons."
Zigong said "What if you had to give up one of the remaining two which one would it be?"
The Master said, "Food. From ancient times, death has come to all men, but a people without confidence in its rulers will not stand."

12:19 Ji Kang Zi asked Confucius about government saying: "Suppose I were to kill the unjust, in order to advance the just. Would that be all right?"
Confucius replied: "In doing government, what is the need of killing? If you desire good, the people will be good. The nature of the Superior Man is like the wind, the nature of the inferior man is like the grass. When the wind blows over the grass, it always bends."

2:19 The Duke of Ai asked: "How can I make the people follow me?" Confucius replied: "Advance the upright and set aside the crooked, and the people will follow you. Advance the crooked and set aside the upright, and the people will not follow you."

2:20 Ji Kang Zi asked: "How can I make the people reverent and loyal, so they will work positively for me?" Confucius said, "Approach them with dignity, and they will be reverent. Be filial and compassionate and they will be loyal. Promote the able and teach the incompetent, and they will work positively for you."

QUESTIONS FOR ANALYSIS

1. What are the important social categories and status distinctions in early China? What kinds of behaviors are expected of individuals in particular social categories toward individuals in other categories?

2. How does Confucius explain and justify the inequalities among people? Why is it important for people to behave in appropriate ways toward others?

3. How does the experience of family life prepare an individual to conduct himself or herself properly in the wider spheres of community and state?

4. Which personal qualities and kinds of actions will allow a ruler to govern successfully? Why might Confucius's passionate concern for ethical behavior on the part of officials and rulers arise at a time when the size and power of governments was growing?

Source: From "Hierarchy and Conduct in the Analects of Confucius," translated by Charles Muller, as seen at http://www.human.toyogakuen-u.ac.jp/~acmuller/contao/analects.htm.

chy. Only men could conduct rituals and make offerings to the ancestors, though women could help maintain the household's ancestral shrines. Fathers held authority over the women and children, arranged marriages for their offspring, and could sell the labor of family members. A man was limited to one wife but was permitted additional sexual partners, who had the lower status of concubines. The elite classes used marriage to create political alliances, and it was common for the groom's family to offer a substantial "bride-gift," a proof of the wealth and standing of his family, to the family of the prospective bride. A man whose wife died had a duty to remarry in order to produce male heirs to keep alive the cult of the ancestors.

These differences in male and female activities were explained by the concept of **yin** and **yang,** the complementary nature of female and male roles in the natural order. The male principle (yang) was equated with the sun, active, bright, and shining; the female principle (yin) corresponded to the moon, passive, shaded, and reflective. Male toughness was balanced by female gentleness, male action and initiative by female endurance and need for completion, and male leadership by female supportiveness. In its earliest form, the theory considered yang and yin as equal and alternately dominant, like day and night, creating balance in the world. However, as a result of the changing role of women in the Zhou period and the pervasive influence of Confucian ideology, the male principle came to be seen as superior to the female.

The classical Chinese patterns of family, property, and bureaucracy took shape during the long centuries of Zhou rule and the competition among small states. At the end of this period the state of Qin°, whose aggressive and disciplined policies made it the premier power among the warring states, defeated all rivals and unified China (see Chapter 6).

NUBIA, 3100 B.C.E.–350 C.E.

Since the first century B.C.E. the name *Nubia* has been applied to a thousand-mile (1,600-kilometer) stretch of the Nile Valley lying between Aswan and Khartoum° and straddling the southern part of the modern nation of Egypt and the northern part of Sudan (see Map 2.2). The ancient Egyptians called it Ta-sety, meaning "Land of the Bow," after the favorite weapon of its warriors. Nubia is the only continuously inhabited stretch of territory connecting sub-Saharan Africa (the lands south of the vast

Qin (chin)   **Khartoum** (kahr-TOOM)

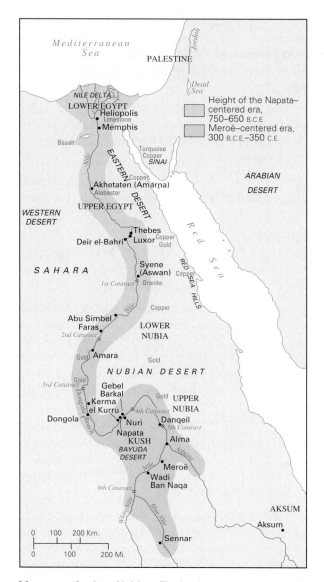

Map 2.2   Ancient Nubia   The land route alongside the Nile River as it flows through Nubia has long served as a corridor connecting sub-Saharan Africa with North Africa. The centuries of Egyptian occupation, as well as time spent in Egypt by Nubian hostages, mercenaries, and merchants, led to a marked Egyptian cultural influence in Nubia.   (Based on Map 15 from *The Historical Atlas of Africa,* ed. by J. F. Ajyi and Michael Crowder. Reprinted by permission of Addison Wesley Longman Ltd.)

Sahara Desert) with North Africa. For thousands of years it has served as a corridor for trade between tropical Africa and the Mediterranean. Nubia was richly endowed with natural resources such as gold, copper, and semi-precious stones.

Nubia's location and natural wealth, along with

Temple of the Lion-Headed God Apedemak at Naqa in Nubia, First Century C.E. Queen Amanitore (right) and her husband, Natakamani, are shown slaying their enemies. The architectural forms are Egyptian, but the deity is Nubian. The costumes of the monarchs and the important role of the queen also reflect the trend in the Meroitic era to draw upon sub-Saharan cultural practices. (P. L. Shinnie)

Egypt's quest for Nubian gold, explain the early rise of a civilization with a complex political organization, social stratification, metallurgy, monumental building, and writing. Nubia traditionally was considered a periphery, or outlying region, of Egypt, and its culture was regarded as derivative. Now, however, most scholars emphasize the interactions between Egypt and Nubia and the mutually beneficial borrowings and syntheses that took place, and there is growing evidence that Nubian culture drew on influences from sub-Saharan Africa.

Early Cultures and Egyptian Domination, 2300–1100 B.C.E.

The central geographical feature of Nubia, as of Egypt, is the Nile River. This part of the Nile flows through a landscape of rocky desert, grassland, and fertile plain. River irrigation was essential for agriculture in a climate that was severely hot and, in the north, nearly without rainfall. Six cataracts, barriers formed by large boulders and rapids, obstructed boat traffic. Commerce and travel were achieved by boats operating between the cataracts and by caravan tracks alongside the river or across the desert.

In the fourth millennium B.C.E. bands of people in northern Nubia made the transition from seminomadic hunting and gathering to a settled life based on grain

agriculture and cattle herding. From this time on, the majority of the population lived in agricultural villages alongside the river. Even before 3000 B.C.E. Nubia served as a corridor for long-distance commerce. Egyptian craftsmen of the period were working in ivory and in ebony wood—products of tropical Africa that had to have come through Nubia.

Nubia enters the historical record around 2300 B.C.E. in Old Kingdom Egyptian accounts of trade missions to southern lands. At that time Aswan, just north of the First Cataract, was the southern limit of Egyptian control. As we saw with the journey of Harkhuf at the beginning of this chapter, Egyptian noblemen stationed there led donkey caravans south in search of gold, incense, ebony, ivory, slaves, and exotic animals from tropical Africa. This was dangerous work, requiring delicate negotiations with local Nubian chiefs in order to secure protection, but it brought substantial rewards to those who succeeded.

During the Middle Kingdom (ca. 2040–1640 B.C.E.), Egypt adopted a more aggressive stance toward Nubia. Egyptian rulers sought to control the gold mines in the desert east of the Nile and to cut out the Nubian middlemen who drove up the cost of luxury goods from the tropics. The Egyptians erected a string of mud-brick forts on islands and riverbanks south of the Second Cataract. The forts protected the southern frontier of Egypt against

Nubians and nomadic raiders from the desert, and regulated the flow of commerce. There seem to have been peaceable relations but little interaction between the Egyptian garrisons and the indigenous population of northern Nubia, which continued to practice its age-old farming and herding ways.

Farther south, where the Nile makes a great U-shaped turn in the fertile plain of the Dongola Reach (see Map 2.2), a more complex political entity was evolving from the chiefdoms of the third millennium B.C.E. The Egyptians gave the name **Kush** to the kingdom whose capital was located at Kerma, one of the earliest urbanized centers in tropical Africa. Beginning around 1750 B.C.E. the kings of Kush marshaled a labor force to build monumental walls and structures of mud brick. The dozens or even hundreds of servants and wives sacrificed for burial with the kings, as well as the rich objects found in their tombs, testify to the wealth and power of the rulers of Kush and suggest a belief in some sort of afterlife in which attendants and possessions would be useful. Kushite craftsmen were skilled in metalworking, whether for weapons or jewelry, and their pottery surpassed anything produced in Egypt.

During the expansionist New Kingdom (ca. 1532–1070 B.C.E.) the Egyptians penetrated more deeply into Nubia (see Chapter 3). They destroyed Kush and its capital and extended their frontier to the Fourth Cataract. A high-ranking Egyptian official called "Overseer of Southern Lands" or "King's Son of Kush" ruled Nubia from a new administrative center at Napata°, near Gebel Barkal°, the "Holy Mountain," believed to be the home of a local god. In an era of intense commerce among the states of the Middle East, when everyone was looking to Egypt as the prime source of gold, Egypt exploited the mines of Nubia at considerable human cost. Fatalities were high among native workers in the brutal desert climate, and the army had to ward off attacks from desert nomads.

Five hundred years of Egyptian domination in Nubia left many marks. The Egyptian government imposed Egyptian culture on the native population. Children from elite families were brought to the Egyptian royal court to guarantee the good behavior of their relatives in Nubia; they absorbed Egyptian language, culture, and religion, which they later carried home with them. Other Nubians served as archers in the Egyptian armed forces. The manufactured goods that they brought back to Nubia have been found in their graves. The Nubians built towns on the Egyptian model and erected stone temples

to Egyptian gods, particularly Amon. The frequent depiction of Amon with the head of a ram may reflect a blending of the chief Egyptian god with a Nubian ram deity.

The Kingdom of Meroë, 800 B.C.E.–350 C.E.

Egypt's weakness after 1200 B.C.E. led to the collapse of its authority in Nubia. In the eighth century B.C.E. a powerful new native kingdom emerged in southern Nubia. The story of this civilization, which lasted for over a thousand years, can be divided into two parts. During the early period, between the eighth and fourth centuries B.C.E., Napata, the former Egyptian headquarters, was the primary center. During the later period, from the fourth century B.C.E. to the fourth century C.E., the center was farther south, at **Meroë**°, near the Sixth Cataract.

For half a century, from around 712 to 660 B.C.E., the kings of Nubia ruled all of Egypt as the Twenty-fifth Dynasty. They conducted themselves in the age-old manner of Egyptian rulers. They were addressed by royal titles, depicted in traditional costume, and buried according to Egyptian custom. However, they kept their Nubian names and were depicted with physical features suggesting peoples of sub-Saharan Africa. They inaugurated an artistic and cultural renaissance, building on a monumental scale for the first time in centuries and reinvigorating Egyptian art, architecture, and religion. The Nubian kings resided at Memphis, the Old Kingdom capital, while Thebes, the New Kingdom capital, was the residence of a celibate female member of the king's family who was titled "God's Wife of Amon."

The Nubian dynasty made a disastrous mistake in 701 B.C.E. when it offered help to local rulers in Palestine who were struggling against the Assyrian Empire. The Assyrians retaliated by invading Egypt and driving the Nubian monarchs back to their southern domain by 660 B.C.E. Napata again became the chief royal residence and religious center of the kingdom. Egyptian cultural influences remained strong. Court documents continued to be written in Egyptian hieroglyphs, and the mummified remains of the rulers were buried in modestly sized sandstone pyramids along with hundreds of shawabti° figurines.

By the fourth century B.C.E. the center of gravity had shifted south to Meroë, perhaps because Meroë was better situated for agriculture and trade, the economic main-

---

Napata (nah-PAH-tuh) **Gebel Barkal** (JEB-uhl BAHR-kahl)

Meroë (MER-oh-ee) **shawabti** (shuh-WAB-tee)

stays of the Nubian kingdom. As a result, sub-Saharan cultural patterns gradually replaced Egyptian ones. Egyptian hieroglyphs gave way to a new set of symbols, still essentially undeciphered, for writing the Meroitic language. People continued to worship Amon as well as Isis, an Egyptian goddess connected to fertility and sexuality. But those deities had to share the stage with Nubian deities like the lion-god Apedemak, and elephants had some religious significance. Meroitic art combined Egyptian, Greco-Roman, and indigenous traditions.

Women of the royal family played an important role in Meroitic politics, another reflection of the influence of sub-Saharan Africa. The Nubians employed a matrilineal system in which the king was succeeded by the son of his sister. Nubian queens sometimes ruled by themselves and sometimes in partnership with their husbands. Greek, Roman, and biblical sources refer to a queen of Nubia named Candace. Since these sources relate to different times, *Candace* was probably a title rather than a proper name. At least seven queens ruled between 284 B.C.E. and 115 C.E. They played a part in warfare, diplomacy, and the building of temples and pyramid tombs. They are depicted in scenes reserved for male rulers in Egyptian imagery, smiting enemies in battle and being suckled by the mother-goddess Isis. Roman sources marvel at the fierce resistance put up by a one-eyed warrior-queen.

Meroë was a huge city for its time, more than a square mile in area, overlooking fertile grasslands and dominating converging trade routes. Much of the city is still buried under the sand. In 2002 archaeologists using a magnetometer to detect buried structures discovered a large palace and will soon begin excavation. Great reservoirs were dug to catch precious rainfall. The city was a major center for iron smelting (after 1000 B.C.E. iron had replaced bronze as the primary metal for tools and weapons). The Temple of Amon was approached by an avenue of stone rams, and the enclosed "Royal City" was filled with palaces, temples, and administrative buildings. The ruler, who may have been regarded as divine, was assisted by a professional class of officials, priests, and army officers.

Meroë collapsed in the early fourth century C.E. It may have been overrun by nomads from the western desert who had become more mobile because of the arrival of the camel in North Africa. Meroë had already been weakened when profitable commerce with the Roman Empire was diverted to the Red Sea and to the rising kingdom of Aksum° (in present-day Ethiopia). In any case, the end of the Meroitic kingdom, and of this phase of civilization in

Nubia, was as closely linked to Nubia's role in long-distance commerce as had been its beginning.

FIRST CIVILIZATIONS OF THE AMERICAS: THE OLMEC AND CHAVÍN, 1200–250 B.C.E.

Humans reached the Western Hemisphere through a series of migrations from Asia. Some scholars believe that the first migrations occurred as early as 35,000 to 25,000 B.C.E., but most accept a later date of 20,000 to 13,000 B.C.E. Although some limited contacts with other cultures—for example, with Polynesians—may have occurred later, the peoples in the Western Hemisphere were virtually isolated from the rest of the world for at least fifteen thousand years. The duration and comprehensiveness of their isolation distinguishes the Americas from the world's other major cultural regions. While technological innovations passed back and forth among the civilizations of Asia, Africa, and Europe, the peoples of the Americas faced the challenges of the natural environment on their own.

Over thousands of years the population of the Americas grew and spread throughout the hemisphere, responding to environments that included frozen regions of the polar extremes, tropical rain forests, and high mountain ranges as well as deserts, woodlands, and prairies. Two of the hemisphere's most impressive cultural traditions developed in Mesoamerica (Mexico and northern Central America) and in the mountainous Andean region of South America. Well before 1000 B.C.E. the domestication of new plant varieties, the introduction of new technologies, and a limited development of trade led to greater social stratification and the beginnings of urbanization in both regions. Cultural elites associated with these changes used their increased political and religious authority to organize great numbers of laborers to construct large-scale irrigation and drainage works, to clear forests, and to unleash the productive potential of floodplains and steeply pitched hillsides. These transformed environments provided the economic platform for the construction of urban centers dominated by monumental structures devoted to religious purposes and to housing for members of the elite. By 1000 B.C.E. the major urban centers of Mesoamerica and the Andes had begun to project their political and cultural power over broad territories: they had become civilizations. The cultural legacies of the two most important of these early civilizations, the Olmec of Mesoamerica and Chavín

---

Aksum (AHK-soom)

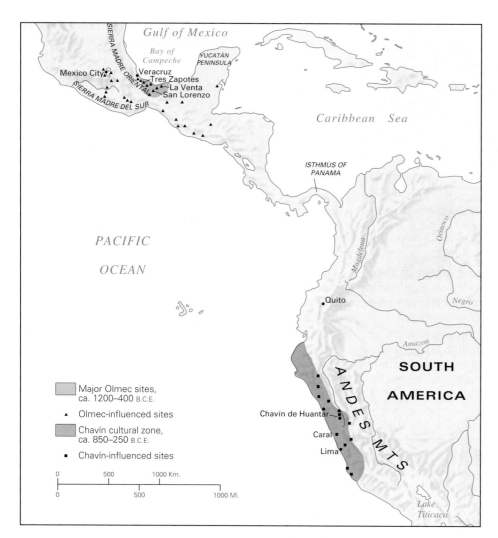

Map 2.3 Olmec and Chavín Civilizations The regions of Mesoamerica (most of modern Mexico and Central America) and the Andean highlands of South America have hosted impressive civilizations since early times. The civilizations of the Olmec and Chavín were the originating civilizations of these two regions, providing the foundations of architecture, city planning, and religion.

of the Andes, would persist for more than a thousand years.

The Mesoamerican Olmec, 1200–400 B.C.E.

Mesoamerica is a region of great geographic and climatic diversity. It is extremely active geologically, experiencing both earthquakes and volcanic eruptions. Mountain ranges break the region into micro environments, including the temperate climates of the Valley of Mexico and the Guatemalan highlands, the tropical forests of the Peten and Gulf of Mexico coast, the rain forest of the southern Yucatán and Belize, and the drier scrub forest of the northern Yucatán (see Map 2.3).

Within these ecological niches, Amerindian peoples developed specialized technologies that exploited indigenous plants and animals, as well as minerals like obsidian, quartz, and jade. Eventually, contacts across these environmental boundaries led to trade and cultural exchange. Enhanced trade, increasing agricultural productivity, and rising population led, in turn, to urbanization and the gradual appearance of powerful political and religious elites. Although a number of militarily powerful civilizations developed in Mesoamerica, the region was never unified politically. All Mesoamerican civilizations, however, shared fundamental elements of material culture, technology, religious belief and ritual, political organization, art, architecture, and sports.

The most influential early Mesoamerican civilization was the **Olmec,** flourishing between 1200 and 400

Olmec Head   Giant heads sculpted from basalt are a widely recognized legacy of Olmec culture. Sixteen heads have been found, the largest approximately 11 feet (3.4 meters) tall. Experts in Olmec archaeology believe the heads are portraits of individual rulers, warriors, or ballplayers.   (Georg Gerster/Photo Researchers, Inc.)

B.C.E. (see Map 2.3). The center of Olmec civilization was located near the tropical Atlantic coast of what are now the Mexican states of Veracruz and Tabasco. Olmec cultural influence reached as far as the Pacific coast of Central America and the Central Plateau of Mexico.

Olmec urban development was made possible by earlier advances in agriculture. Original settlements depended on the region's rich plant diversity and on fishing. Later, by 3500 B.C.E or earlier, the staples of the Mesoamerican diet—corn, beans, and squash—were domesticated. Recent research indicates that manioc, a calorie-rich root crop, was also grown in the floodplains of the region, multiplying food resources. The ability of farmers to produce dependable surpluses of these products permitted the first stages of craft specialization and social stratification. As religious and political elites emerged, they used their prestige and authority to organize the population to dig irrigation and drainage canals, develop raised fields in wetlands that could be farmed more intensively, and construct the large-scale religious and civic buildings that became the cultural signature of Olmec civilization.

The cultural core of the early Olmec civilization was located at San Lorenzo but included smaller centers

nearby (1200–900 B.C.E.). La Venta°, which developed at about the same time, became the most important Olmec center after 900 B.C.E. when San Lorenzo was abandoned or destroyed. Tres Zapotes° was the last dominant center, rising to prominence after La Venta collapsed or was destroyed around 600 B.C.E. The relationship among these centers is unclear. Scholars have found little evidence to suggest that they were either rival city-states or dependent centers of a centralized political authority. It appears that each center developed independently to exploit and exchange specialized products like salt, cacao (chocolate beans), clay for ceramics, and limestone. Each major Olmec center was eventually abandoned, its monuments defaced and buried and its buildings destroyed. Archaeologists interpret these events differently; some see them as evidence of internal upheavals or military defeat by neighboring peoples, and others suggest that they were rituals associated with the death of a ruler.

Large artificial platforms and mounds of packed earth dominated Olmec urban centers and served to frame the collective ritual and political activities that brought the rural population to the cities at special times in the year. Some of the platforms also served as foundations for elite residences, in effect lifting the elite above the masses. The Olmec laid out their cities in alignment with the paths of certain stars, reflecting their strong belief in the significance of astronomical events. Since these centers had small permanent populations, the scale of construction suggests that the Olmec elite was able to require and direct the labor of thousands of men and women from surrounding settlements and dispersed family plots in the region. This labor pool was used primarily for low-skill tasks like moving dirt and stone construction materials. Skilled artisans who lived in or near the urban core decorated the buildings with carvings and sculptures. They also produced the high-quality crafts, such as exquisite carved jade figurines, necklaces, and ceremonial knives and axes, that distinguished Olmec culture. Archaeological evidence suggests the existence of a class of merchants who traded with distant peoples for obsidian, jade, and pottery.

Little is known about Olmec political structure, but it seems likely that the rise of major urban centers coincided with the appearance of a form of kingship that combined religious and secular roles. Finely crafted objects decorated the households of the elite and distinguished their dress from that of the commoners who lived in dispersed small structures constructed of sticks

La Venta (LA BEN-tah)   **Tres Zapotes** (TRACE zah-POE-tace)

and mud. The authority of the rulers and their kin groups is suggested by a series of colossal carved stone heads, some as large as 11 feet (3.4 meters) high. Since each head is unique and suggestive of individual personality, most archaeologists believe they were carved to memorialize individual rulers. This theory is reinforced by the location of the heads close to the major urban centers, especially San Lorenzo. These remarkable stone sculptures are the best-known monuments of Olmec culture.

The organization of collective labor by the Olmec elites benefited the commoners by increasing food production and making it more reliable. People also enjoyed a more diverse diet. Ceramic products such as utilitarian pots and small figurines as well as small stone carvings associated with religious belief have been found in commoner households. This suggests that at least some advantages gained from urbanization and growing elite power were shared broadly in the society.

The Olmec elite used elaborate religious rituals to control this complex society. Thousands of commoners were drawn from the countryside to attend awe-inspiring ceremonies at the centers. The elevated platforms and mounds with carved stone veneers served as potent backdrops for these rituals. Rulers and their close kin came to be associated with the gods through bloodletting and human sacrifice, evidence of which is found in all the urban centers. The Olmec were polytheistic, and most of their deities had dual (male and female) natures. Human and animal characteristics were also blended. Surviving representations of jaguars, crocodiles, snakes, and sharks suggest that these powerful animals provided the most enduring images used in Olmec religious representation. The ability of humans to transform themselves into these animals is a common decorative motif. Rulers were especially associated with the jaguar.

An important class of shamans and healers attached to the elite organized religious life and provided practical advice about the periodic rains essential to agricultural life. They directed the planning of urban centers to reflect astronomical observations and were responsible for developing a form of writing that may have influenced later innovations among the Maya (see Chapter 11). From their close observation of the stars, they produced a calendar that was used to organize ritual life and agriculture. The Olmec were also the likely originators of a ritual ball game that became an enduring part of Mesoamerican ceremonial life.

There is little evidence for the existence of an Olmec empire. Given the limited technological and agricultural base of the society, it is unlikely that the power of the Olmecs could have been projected over significant distances militarily. However, the discovery of Olmec products and images, such as jade carvings decorated with the jaguar-god, as far away as central Mexico provides evidence that the Olmec did exercise cultural influence over a wide area. This influence would endure for centuries.

Early South American Civilization: Chavín, 900–250 B.C.E.

Geography played an important role in the development of human society in the Andes. The region's diverse environment—a mountainous core, arid coastal plain, and dense interior jungles—challenged human populations, encouraging the development of specialized regional production as well as complex social institutions and cultural values that facilitated interregional exchanges and shared labor responsibilities. These adaptations to environmental challenge became enduring features of Andean civilization.

The earliest urban centers in the Andean region were villages of a few hundred people built along the coastal plain or in the foothills near the coast. The abundance of fish and mollusks along the coast of Peru provided a dependable supply of food that helped make the development of early cities possible. The coastal populations traded these products as well as decorative shells for corn, other foods, and eventually textiles produced in the foothills. The two regions also exchanged ceremonial practices, religious motifs, and aesthetic ideas. Recent discoveries demonstrate that as early as 2600 B.C.E. the vast site called Caral in the Supe Valley had developed many of the characteristics now viewed as the hallmarks of later Andean civilization, including ceremonial plazas, pyramids, elevated platforms and mounds, and extensive irrigation works. The scale of the public works in Caral suggests a population of thousands and a political structure capable of organizing the production and distribution of maritime and agricultural products over a broad area.

Chavín, one of the most impressive of South America's early urban civilizations (see Map 2.3), inherited many of the cultural and economic characteristics of Caral. Its capital, Chavín de Huantar°, was located at 10,300 feet (3,139 meters) in the eastern range of the Andes north of the modern city of Lima. Between 900 and 250 B.C.E., a period roughly coinciding with Olmec civilization in Mesoamerica, Chavín dominated a densely populated region that included large areas of the Peruvian coastal plain and Andean foothills. Chavín de

Chavín de Huantar (cha-BEAN day WAHN-tar)

Huantar's location at the intersection of trade routes connecting the coast with populous mountain valleys and the tropical lowlands on the eastern flank of the Andes allowed the city's rulers to control trade among these distinct ecological zones and gain an important economic advantage over regional rivals.

Chavín's dominance as a ceremonial and commercial center depended on earlier developments in agriculture and trade, including the introduction of maize cultivation from Mesoamerica. Maize increased the food supplies of the coast and interior foothills, allowing greater levels of urbanization. As Chavín grew, its trade linked the coastal economy with the producers of quinoa (a local grain), potatoes, and llamas in the high mountain valleys and, to a lesser extent, with Amazonian producers of coca (the leaves were chewed, producing a mild narcotic effect) and fruits.

These developments were accompanied by the evolution of reciprocal labor obligations that permitted the construction and maintenance of roads, bridges, temples, palaces, and large irrigation and drainage projects as well as textile production. The exact nature of these reciprocal labor obligations at Chavín is unknown. In later times groups of related families who held land communally and claimed descent from a common ancestor organized these labor obligations. Group members thought of each other as brothers and sisters and were obligated to aid each other, providing a model for the organization of labor and the distribution of goods at every level of Andean society.

The increased use of **llamas** to move goods from one ecological zone to another promoted specialization of production and increased trade. Llamas were the only domesticated beasts of burden in the Americas, and they played an important role in the integration of the Andean region. They were first domesticated in the mountainous interior of Peru and were crucial to Chavín's development, not unlike the camel in the evolution of trans-Saharan trade (see Chapter 7). Llamas provided meat and wool and decreased the labor needed to transport goods. A single driver could control ten to thirty animals, each carrying up to 70 pounds (32 kilograms); a human porter could carry only about 50 pounds (22.5 kilograms).

The enormous scale of the capital and the dispersal of Chavín's pottery styles, religious motifs, and architectural forms over a wide area suggest that Chavín imposed some form of political integration and trade dependency on its neighbors that may have relied in part on military force. Most modern scholars believe that, as in the case of the Olmec civilization, Chavín's influence depended more on the development of an attractive and convincing religious belief system and related rituals. Chavín's most

potent religious symbol, a jaguar deity, was dispersed over a broad area, and archaeological evidence suggests that Chavín de Huantar served as a pilgrimage site.

The architectural signature of Chavín was a large complex of multilevel platforms made of packed earth or rubble and faced with cut stone or adobe (sun-dried brick made of clay and straw). Small buildings used for ritual purposes or as elite residences were built on these platforms. Nearly all the buildings were decorated with relief carvings of serpents, condors, jaguars, or human forms. The largest building at Chavín de Huantar measured 250 feet (76 meters) on each side and rose to a height of 50 feet (15 meters). About one-third of its interior is hollow, containing narrow galleries and small rooms that may have housed the remains of royal ancestors.

American metallurgy was first developed in the Andean region. The later introduction of metallurgy in Mesoamerica, like the appearance of maize agriculture in the Andes, suggests sustained trade and cultural contacts between the two regions. Archaeological investigations of Chavín de Huantar and smaller centers have revealed remarkable three-dimensional silver, gold, and gold alloy ornaments that represent a clear advance over earlier technologies. Improvements in both the manufacture and the decoration of textiles are also associated with the rise of Chavín. The quality of these products, probably used only by the elite or in religious rituals, added to the reputation and prestige of the culture and aided in the projection of its power and influence. The most common decorative motif in sculpture, pottery, and textiles was a jaguar-man similar in conception to the Olmec symbol. In both civilizations and in many other cultures in the Americas, this powerful predator provided an enduring image of religious authority and a vehicle through which the gods could act in the world of men and women.

Class distinctions appear to have increased during this period of expansion. A class of priests directed religious life. Modern scholars also see evidence that both local chiefs and a more powerful chief or king dominated Chavín's politics. Excavations of graves reveal that superior-quality textiles as well as gold crowns, breastplates, and jewelry distinguished rulers from commoners. These rich objects, the quality and abundance of pottery, and the monumental architecture of the major centers all suggest the presence of highly skilled artisans as well.

There is no convincing evidence, like defaced buildings or broken images, that the eclipse of Chavín (unlike the Olmec centers) was associated with conquest or rebellion. However, recent investigations have suggested that increased warfare throughout the region around 200

B.C.E. disrupted Chavín's trade and undermined the authority of the governing elite. Regardless of what caused the collapse of this powerful culture, the technologies, material culture, statecraft, architecture, and urban planning associated with Chavín influenced the Andean region for centuries.

CONCLUSION

The civilizations of early China, Nubia, the Olmec, and Chavín emerged in very different ecological contexts in widely separated parts of the globe, and the patterns of organization, technology, behavior, and belief that they developed were, in large part, responses to the challenges and opportunities of those environments.

In the north China plain, as in the river-valley civilizations of Mesopotamia and Egypt, the presence of great, flood-prone rivers and the lack of dependable rainfall led to the formation of powerful institutions capable of organizing large numbers of people to dig and maintain irrigation channels and build dikes. An authoritarian central government has been a recurring feature of Chinese history, beginning with the Shang monarchy and warrior elite.

In Nubia, the initial impetus for the formation of a strong state was the need for protection from desert nomads and from the Egyptian rulers who coveted Nubian gold and other resources. Control of these resources and of the trade route between sub-Saharan Africa and the north, as well as the agricultural surplus to feed administrators and specialists in the urban centers, made the rulers of Kush, Napata, and Meroë wealthy and formidable.

While the ecological zones in Mesoamerica and South America in which the Olmec and Chavín cultures emerged were quite different, both societies created networks that brought together the resources and products of disparate regions. Little is known about the political and social organization of these societies, but archaeological evidence makes clear the existence of ruling elites that gathered wealth and organized labor for the construction of monumental centers.

In most complex societies small groups achieve a level of wealth and prestige that allows them to dominate the majority. It is important to understand how these elite groups maintain and justify their position.

Among the early Chinese a warrior aristocracy, with wealth based on land and flocks, controlled significant numbers of human laborers. When the Zhou overthrew the Shang, they curtailed the power of the warrior elite, and over time a new elite of educated government officials evolved. Much less is known about the emergence of

elite groups in Nubia and the states of the Olmec and Chavín. However, it is likely that they played key roles in the organization of trade and the construction of the irrigation networks that greatly increased the food supply available to their communities.

In the Eastern Hemisphere, the production of metal tools, weapons, and luxury and ceremonial implements was vital to the success of elite groups. Bronze metallurgy began at different times—in western Asia around 2500 B.C.E., in East Asia around 2000 B.C.E., in northeastern Africa around 1500 B.C.E. Possession of bronze weapons with hard, sharp edges enabled the warriors of Shang and Zhou China, like the royal armies of Egypt and Mesopotamia, to dominate the peasant masses. In Shang China bronze was also used to craft the vessels that played a vital role in the rituals of contact with the spirits of ancestors.

Throughout history, elites have used religion to bolster their position. The Shang rulers of China were indispensable intermediaries between their kingdom and powerful and protective gods and ancestors. Their Zhou successors developed the concept of the ruler as divine Son of Heaven who ruled in accord with the Mandate of Heaven. The rulers of Nubia, drawing on Egyptian concepts, claimed to be gods on earth. In the Olmec and Chavín zones there is some evidence of religious rituals performed to affirm the position of the ruling class. Human sacrifice was practiced in Shang China, Nubia, and Olmec Mesoamerica. This, too, was a mechanism by which ruling elites inspired fear and obedience in their subjects.

The construction and use of "urban" centers and monumental spaces and structures for dramatic religious rituals and colorful political events also propagated the ideologies of power. Ceremonies involving impressive pageantry communicated a message of the "superiority" of the elite and the desirability of being associated with them. In early China and the Olmec and Chavín civilizations, the centers appear to have been the sites of palaces, shrines, and the dwellings of the elite.

Scholars have debated why powerful civilizations appeared many centuries later in the Western Hemisphere than in the Eastern Hemisphere. Recent theories have focused on environmental differences. The Eastern Hemisphere was home to a far larger number of wild plant and animal species that were particularly well suited to domestication. In addition, the natural east-west axis of the huge landmass of Europe and Asia allowed for the relatively rapid spread of domesticated plants and animals to climatically similar zones along the same latitudes. Settled agriculture led to population growth, more complex political and social organization, and increased technological sophistication. In the Americas, by contrast, there were fewer wild plant and animal species that could be domesticated, and the north-south axis of the continents made it more difficult for domesticated species to spread because of variations in climate at different latitudes. As a result, the processes that foster the development of complex societies evolved somewhat more slowly.

The comparison of the two hemispheres leads to another important realization. The complex societies of the Western Hemisphere did not necessarily develop technologies in the same sequence as their Eastern Hemisphere counterparts. The Olmec and Chavín peoples did not possess large draft animals, wheeled vehicles, or metal weapons and tools. Nevertheless, they created sophisticated political, social, and economic institutions that rivaled those developed in the Eastern Hemisphere in the third and second millennia B.C.E.

■ Key Terms

loess	Legalism	Meroë
Shang	Confucius	Olmec
divination	Daoism	Chavín
Zhou	yin/yang	llama
Mandate of Heaven	Kush	

■ Suggested Reading

Caroline Blunden and Mark Elvin, *Cultural Atlas of China* (1983), contains general geographic, ethnographic, and historical information about China through the ages, as well as many maps and illustrations. Conrad Schirokauer, *A Brief History of Chinese Civilization* (1991), and John King Fairbank, *China: A New History* (1992), offer useful chapters on early China. Edward L. Shaughnessy and Michael Loewe, eds., *The Cambridge History of Ancient China* (1998), approaches the subject in far greater depth. Nicola Di Cosmo, *Ancient China and Its Enemies: The Rise of Nomadic Power in East Asian History* (2002), sets the development of Chinese civilization in the broader context of interactions with nomadic neighbors. Jessica Rawson, *Ancient China: Art and Archaeology* (1980), Kwang-chih Chang, *The Archaeology of Ancient China*, 4th ed. (1986), and Ronald G. Knapp, *China's Walled Cities* (2000), emphasize archaeological evidence. W. Thomas Chase, *Ancient Chinese Bronze Art: Casting the Precious Sacral Vessel* (1991), contains a brief but useful discussion of the importance of bronzes in ancient China, as well as a detailed discussion of bronze-casting techniques. Robert Temple, *The Genius of China: 3,000 Years of Science, Discovery, and Invention* (1986), explores many aspects of Chinese technology, using a division into general topics such as agriculture, engineering, and medicine. Anne Behnke Kinney, "Women in Ancient China," in *Women's Roles in Ancient Civilizations: A Reference Guide*, ed. Bella Vivante (1999), and Patricia Ebrey, "Women, Marriage, and the Family in Chinese History," in *Heritage of China: Contemporary Perspectives on Chinese Civiliza-*

tion, ed. Paul S. Ropp (1990), address the very limited evidence for women in early China. Michael Loewe and Carmen Blacker, *Oracles and Divination* (1981), addresses practices in China and other ancient civilizations. Simon Leys, *The Analects of Confucius* (1997), provides a translation of and a commentary on this fundamental text. Benjamin I. Schwartz, *The World of Thought in Ancient China* (1985), is a broad introduction to early Chinese ethical and spiritual concepts.

After a long period of scholarly neglect, with an occasional exception such as Bruce G. Trigger, *Nubia Under the Pharaohs* (1976), the study of ancient Nubia is now receiving considerable attention. David O'Connor, *Ancient Nubia: Egypt's Rival in Africa* (1993); Joyce L. Haynes, *Nubia: Ancient Kingdoms of Africa* (1992); Karl-Heinz Priese, *The Gold of Meroë* (1993); P. L. Shinnie, *Ancient Nubia* (1996); Derek A. Welsby, *The Kingdom of Kush: The Napatan and Meroitic Empires* (1996); and Timothy Kendall, *Kerma and the Kingdom of Kush, 2500-1500 B.C.: The Archaeological Discovery of an Ancient Nubian Empire* (1997), all reflect the new interest of major museums in the art and artifacts of this society. Robert Morkot, "Egypt and Nubia," in *Empires: Perspectives from Archaeology and History*, ed. Susan E. Alcock (2001), examines the political dimension of Egyptian domination, while John H. Taylor, *Egypt and Nubia* (1991), also emphasizes the fruitful interaction of the Egyptian and Nubian cultures.

A number of useful books provide an introduction to the early Americas. In *Prehistory of the Americas* (1987) Stuart Fiedel provides an excellent summary of the early history of the Western Hemisphere. *Early Man in the New World*, ed. Richard Shutler, Jr. (1983), is also a useful general work. *Atlas of Ancient America* (1986), by Michael Coe, Elizabeth P. Benson, and Dean R. Snow, offers a compendium of maps and information. George Kubler, *The Art and Architecture of Ancient America: The Mexican, Maya, and Andean Peoples* (1984), is an essential tool, though dated.

For the Olmecs see Jacques Soustelle, *The Olmecs: The Oldest Civilization in Mexico* (1984). More reliable is Michael Coe, *The Olmec World* (1996). Richard W. Keatinge, ed., *Peruvian Prehistory* (1988), provides a helpful introduction to the scholarship on Andean societies. The most useful summary of recent research on Chavín is Richard L. Burger, *Chavín and the Origins of Andean Civilization* (1992).

Jared Diamond, *Guns, Germs, and Steel: The Fates of Human Societies* (1997), tackles the difficult question of why technological development occurred at different times and took different paths of development in the Eastern and Western Hemispheres.

■ Notes

1. Quoted in Miriam Lichtheim, ed., *Ancient Egyptian Literature: A Book of Readings* (Berkeley: University of California Press 1978).

Document-Based Question
Social Status in Early Complex Societies

Using the following documents, analyze the various ways that early China and Nubia defined and marked social status.

DOCUMENT 1
Wall Painting of Nubians Arriving in Egypt with Rings and Bags of Gold, Fourteenth Century B.C.E (photo, p. 36)

DOCUMENT 2
Quote from Pharaoh Pepi II (p. 37)

DOCUMENT 3
Bronze Vessel from the Shang Period, 13th–11th Century B.C.E. (photo, p. 41)

DOCUMENT 4
Chinese Divination Shell (Environment and Technology, p. 43)

DOCUMENT 5
Hierarchy and Conduct in the Analects of Confucius (Diversity and Dominance, pp. 46–47)

DOCUMENT 6
Temple of the Lion-Headed God Apedemak at Naqa in Nubia, First Century C.E. (photo, p. 49)

What factors shape point of view in Documents 2 and 5? What additional types of documents would help you analyze social status in early China and Nubia?

The Mediterranean and Middle East, 2000–500 B.C.E.

3

The Mortuary Temple of Queen Hatshepsut at Deir el-Bahri, Egypt, ca. 1460 B.C.E.
This beautiful complex of terraces, ramps, and colonnades featured relief sculptures
and texts commemorating the famous expedition to Punt.

CHAPTER OUTLINE

The Cosmopolitan Middle East, 1700–1100 B.C.E.

The Aegean World, 2000–1100 B.C.E.

The Assyrian Empire, 911–612 B.C.E.

Israel, 2000–500 B.C.E.

Phoenicia and the Mediterranean, 1200–500 B.C.E.

Failure and Transformation, 750–550 B.C.E.

DIVERSITY AND DOMINANCE: An Israelite Prophet Chastizes the Ruling Class

ENVIRONMENT AND TECHNOLOGY: Ancient Textiles and Dyes

Ancient peoples' stories—even those that are not historically accurate—provide valuable insights into how people thought about their origins and identity. One famous story concerned the city of Carthage° in present-day Tunisia, which for centuries dominated the commerce of the western Mediterranean. Tradition held that Dido, a member of the royal family of the Phoenician city-state of Tyre° in southern Lebanon, fled with her supporters to the western Mediterranean after her husband was murdered by her brother, the king of Tyre. Landing on the North African coast, the refugees made friendly contact with local people, who agreed to give them as much land as a cow's hide could cover. By cleverly cutting the hide into narrow strips, they were able to mark out a substantial piece of territory for Kart Khadasht, the "New City" (called *Carthago* by their Roman enemies). Later, faithful to the memory of her dead husband, Dido committed suicide rather than marry a local chieftain.

This story highlights the spread of cultural patterns from older centers to new regions, and the migration and resettlement of Late Bronze Age and Early Iron Age peoples in the Mediterranean lands and western Asia. Just as Egyptian cultural influences helped transform Nubian society, influences from the older centers in Mesopotamia and Egypt penetrated throughout western Asia and the Mediterranean. Far-flung trade, diplomatic contacts, military conquests, and the relocation of large numbers of people spread knowledge, beliefs, practices, and technologies.

By the end of the second millennium B.C.E. many of the societies of the Eastern Hemisphere had entered the **Iron Age:** they had begun to use iron instead of bronze for tools and weapons. Iron offered several advantages. It was a single metal rather than an alloy and thus was simpler to obtain; and there were many potential sources of iron ore. Once the technology of iron making had been mastered—iron has to be heated to a higher temperature than bronze, and its hardness depends on the amount of carbon added during the forging process—iron tools were found to have harder, sharper edges than bronze tools.

The first part of this chapter resumes the story of Mesopotamia and Egypt in the Late Bronze Age, the second millennium B.C.E.: their complex relations with neighboring peoples, the development of a prosperous, "cosmopolitan" network of states in the Middle East, and the period of destruction and decline that set in around 1200 B.C.E. We also look at how the Minoan and Mycenaean civilizations of the Aegean Sea were inspired by the technologies and cultural patterns of the older Middle Eastern centers and prospered from participation in long-distance networks of trade. The remainder of the chapter examines the resurgence of this region in the early Iron Age, from 1000 to 500 B.C.E. The focus is on three societies: the Assyrians of northern Mesopotamia; the Israelites of Israel; and the Phoenicians of Lebanon and Syria and their colonies in the western Mediterranean, mainly Carthage. After the decline or demise of the ancient centers dominant throughout the third and second millennia B.C.E., these societies evolved into new political, cultural, and commercial centers.

As you read this chapter, ask yourself the following questions:

- What environmental, technological, political, and cultural factors led these societies to develop their distinctive institutions and values?

- In what ways were the societies of this era more interconnected and interdependent than before, and what were the consequences—positive and negative—of these connections?

- What were the causes and consequences of large-scale movements of peoples to new homes during this era?

- Why were certain cultures destroyed or assimilated while others survived?

Carthage (KAHR-thuhj)   **Tyre** (tire)

	Western Asia	Egypt	Syria–Palestine	Mediterranean
2000 B.C.E.	**2000 B.C.E.** Horses in use	**2040–1640 B.C.E.** Middle Kingdom		**2000 B.C.E.** Rise of Minoan civilization on Crete; early Greeks arrive in Greece
	1700–1200 B.C.E. Hittites dominant in Anatolia	**1640–1532 B.C.E.** Hyksos dominate northern Egypt		**1600 B.C.E.** Rise of Mycenaean civilization in Greece
		1532 B.C.E. Beginning of New Kingdom		
1500 B.C.E.	**1500 B.C.E.** Hittites develop iron metallurgy		**1500 B.C.E.** Early "alphabetic" script developed at Ugarit	
	1460 B.C.E. Kassites assume control of southern Mesopotamia	**1470 B.C.E.** Queen Hatshepsut dispatches expedition to Punt		**1450 B.C.E.** Destruction of Minoan palaces in Crete
		1353 B.C.E. Akhenaten launches reforms	**1250–1200 B.C.E.** Israelite occupation of Canaan	
	1200 B.C.E. Destruction of Hittite kingdom	**1200–1150 B.C.E.** Sea Peoples attack Egypt	**1150 B.C.E.** Philistines settle southern coast of Israel	**1200–1150 B.C.E.** Destruction of Mycenaean centers in Greece
		1070 B.C.E. End of New Kingdom		
1000 B.C.E.	**1000 B.C.E.** Iron metallurgy begins		**1000 B.C.E.** David establishes Jerusalem as Israelite capital	**1000 B.C.E.** Iron metallurgy
	911 B.C.E. Rise of Neo-Assyrian Empire		**969 B.C.E.** Hiram of Tyre comes to power	**814 B.C.E.** Foundation of Carthage
	744–727 B.C.E. Reforms of Tiglath-pileser	**750 B.C.E.** Kings of Kush control Egypt	**960 B.C.E.** Solomon builds First Temple	
	668–627 B.C.E. Reign of Ashurbanipal	**671 B.C.E.** Assyrian conquest of Egypt	**920 B.C.E.** Division into two kingdoms of Israel and Judah	
	626–539 B.C.E. Neo-Babylonian kingdom		**721 B.C.E.** Assyrian conquest of northern kingdom	
	612 B.C.E. Fall of Assyria		**701 B.C.E.** Assyrian humiliation of Tyre	
600 B.C.E.			**587 B.C.E.** Neo-Babylonian capture of Jerusalem	**550–300 B.C.E.** Rivalry of Carthaginians and Greeks in western Mediterranean
			515 B.C.E. Deportees from Babylon return to Jerusalem	
			450 B.C.E. Completion of Hebrew Bible; Hanno the Phoenician explores West Africa	

THE COSMOPOLITAN MIDDLE EAST, 1700–1100 B.C.E.

Both Mesopotamia and Egypt succumbed to outside invaders in the seventeenth century B.C.E. (see Chapter 1). Eventually the outsiders were either ejected or assimilated, and conditions of stability and prosperity were restored. Between 1500 and 1200 B.C.E. a number of large territorial states dominated the Middle East (see Map 3.1). These centers of power controlled the smaller city-states, kingdoms, and kinship groups as they competed with, and sometimes fought against, one another for control of valuable commodities and trade routes.

Historians have called the Late Bronze Age in the Middle East a "cosmopolitan" era, meaning a time of widely shared cultures and lifestyles. Extensive diplomatic relations and commercial contacts between states fostered the flow of goods and ideas, and elite groups shared similar values and enjoyed a relatively high standard of living. The peasants in the countryside who comprised the majority of the population may have seen some improvement in their standard of living, but they reaped far fewer benefits from the increasing contacts and trade.

Western Asia

By 1500 B.C.E. Mesopotamia was divided into two distinct political zones: Babylonia in the south and Assyria in the north (see Map 3.1). The city of Babylon had gained political and cultural ascendancy over the southern plain under the dynasty of Hammurabi in the eighteenth and seventeenth centuries B.C.E. Subsequently there was a persistent inflow of Kassites°, peoples from the Zagros° Mountains to the east who spoke a non-Semitic language, and by 1460 B.C.E a Kassite dynasty had come to power in Babylon. The Kassites retained names in their native language but otherwise embraced Babylonian language and culture and intermarried with the native population. During their 250 years in power, the Kassite lords of Babylonia defended their core area and traded for raw materials, but they did not pursue territorial conquest.

The Assyrians of the north had more ambitious designs. As early as the twentieth century B.C.E. the city of Ashur,° the leading urban center on the northern Tigris, anchored a busy trade route across the northern Mesopotamian plain and onto the Anatolian Plateau. Repre-

sentatives of Assyrian merchant families maintained settlements outside the walls of important Anatolian cities. The Assyrians exported textiles and tin, used since about 2500 B.C.E. to make bronze, which they exchanged for silver from Anatolia. In the eighteenth century B.C.E. an Assyrian dynasty briefly gained control of the upper Euphrates River near the present-day border of Syria and Iraq. This "Old Assyrian" kingdom, as it is now called, illustrates the importance of the trade routes connecting Mesopotamia to Anatolia and the Syria-Palestine coast. After 1400 B.C.E. a resurgent "Middle Assyrian" kingdom again engaged in campaigns of conquest and expansion of its economic interests.

Other ambitious states emerged on the periphery of the Mesopotamian heartland, including Elam in southwest Iran and Mitanni° in the broad plain between the upper Euphrates and Tigris Rivers. Most formidable of all were the **Hittites°**, speakers of an Indo-European language, who became the foremost power in Anatolia from around 1700 to 1200 B.C.E. From their capital at Hattusha°, near present-day Ankara° in central Turkey, they deployed the fearsome new technology of horse-drawn war chariots. The Hittites exploited Anatolia's rich deposits of copper, silver, and iron to play an indispensable role in international commerce. Many historians believe that the Hittites were the first to develop a technique for making tools and weapons of iron. They heated the ore until it was soft enough to shape, pounded it to remove impurities, and then plunged it into cold water to harden. The Hittites were anxious to keep knowledge of this process secret, since it provided both military and economic advantages.

During the second millennium B.C.E. Mesopotamian political and cultural concepts spread across much of western Asia. Akkadian° became the language of diplomacy and correspondence between governments. The Elamites° and Hittites, among others, adapted the cuneiform system to write their own languages. In the Syrian coastal city of Ugarit° thirty cuneiform symbols were used to write consonant sounds, an early use of the alphabetic principle and a considerable advance over the hundreds of signs required in conventional cuneiform and hieroglyphic writing. Mesopotamian myths and legends and styles of art and architecture were widely imitated. Newcomers who had learned and improved on the lessons of Mesopotamian civilization often put pressure on the old core area. The small, fractious city-states

---

Kassite (KAS-ite)   **Zagros** (ZAH-groes)   **Ashur** (AH-shoor)

Mitanni (mih-TAH-nee)   **Hittite** (HIT-ite)
Hattusha (haht-tush-SHAH)   **Ankara** (ANG-kuh-ruh)
Akkadian (uh-KAY-dee-uhn)   **Elamite** (EE-luh-mite)
Ugarit (OO-guh-reet)

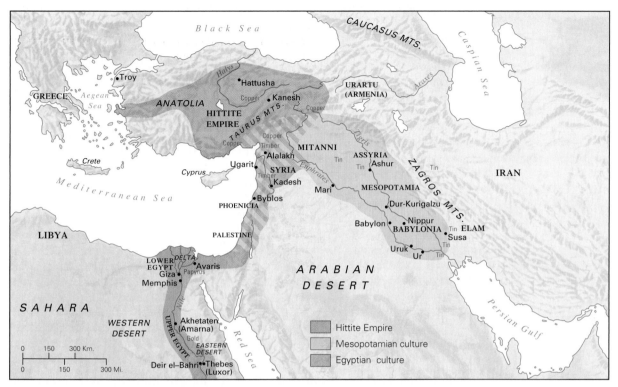

Map 3.1   The Middle East in the Second Millennium B.C.E.   Although warfare was not uncommon, treaties, diplomatic missions, and correspondence in Akkadian cuneiform fostered cooperative relationships between states. All were tied together by extensive networks of exchange centering on the trade in metals, and peripheral regions, such as Nubia and the Aegean Sea, were drawn into the web of commerce.

of the third millennium B.C.E. had been concerned only with their immediate neighbors in southern Mesopotamia. In contrast, the larger states of the second millennium B.C.E. interacted politically, militarily, and economically in a geopolitical sphere encompassing all of western Asia.

New Kingdom Egypt

After flourishing for nearly four hundred years (see Chapter 1), the Egyptian Middle Kingdom declined in the seventeenth century B.C.E. As high-level officials in the countryside became increasingly independent and new groups migrated into the Nile Delta, central authority broke down, and Egypt entered a period of political fragmentation and economic decline. Around 1640 B.C.E. Egypt came under foreign rule for the first time, at the hands of the Hyksos°, or "Princes of Foreign Lands."

Historians are uncertain about who the Hyksos were and how they came to power. Semitic peoples had been migrating from the Syria-Palestine region (sometimes called the Levant, present-day Syria, Lebanon, Israel, and the Palestinian territories) into the eastern Nile Delta for centuries. In the chaotic conditions of this time, other peoples may have joined them and established control, first in the delta and then in the middle of the country. The Hyksos possessed military technologies that gave them an advantage over the Egyptians, such as the horse-drawn war chariot and a composite bow, made of wood and horn, that had greater range and velocity than the simple wooden bow. The process by which the Hyksos came to dominate much of Egypt may not have been far different from that by which the Kassites first settled and gained control in Babylonia. The Hyksos intermarried with Egyptians and assimilated to native ways. They used the Egyptian language and maintained Egyptian institutions and culture. Nevertheless, in contrast to the relative ease with which outsiders were assimilated in Mesopotamia, the Egyptians, with their

Hyksos (HICK-soes)

strong ethnic identity, continued to regard the Hyksos as "foreigners."

As with the formation of the Middle Kingdom five hundred years earlier, the reunification of Egypt under a native dynasty was accomplished by princes from Thebes. After three decades of warfare, Kamose° and Ahmose° expelled the Hyksos from Egypt and inaugurated the New Kingdom, which lasted from about 1532 to 1070 B.C.E.

A century of foreign domination had shaken Egyptian pride and shattered the isolationist mindset of earlier eras. New Kingdom Egypt was an aggressive and expansionist state, extending its territorial control north into Syria-Palestine and south into Nubia and winning access to timber, gold, and copper (bronze metallurgy took hold in Egypt around 1500 B.C.E.) as well as taxes and tribute (payments from the territories it had conquered). The occupied territories provided a buffer zone, protecting Egypt from attack. In Nubia, Egypt imposed direct control and pressed the native population to adopt Egyptian language and culture. In the Syria-Palestine region, in contrast, the Egyptians stationed garrisons at strategically placed forts and supported local rulers willing to collaborate.

The New Kingdom was a period of innovation. Egypt fully participated in the diplomatic and commercial networks that linked the states of western Asia. Egyptian soldiers, administrators, diplomats, and merchants traveled widely, exposing Egypt to exotic fruits and vegetables, new musical instruments, and new technologies, such as an improved potter's wheel and weaver's loom.

At least one woman held the throne of New Kingdom Egypt. When Pharaoh Tuthmosis° II died, his queen, **Hatshepsut°,** served as regent for her young stepson and soon claimed the royal title for herself (r. 1473–1458 B.C.E.). In inscriptions she often used the male pronoun to refer to herself, and drawings and sculptures show her wearing the long, conical beard of the ruler of Egypt.

Around 1460 B.C.E. Hatshepsut sent a naval expedition down the Red Sea to the fabled land that the Egyptians called "Punt°." Historians believe that Punt may have been near the coast of eastern Sudan or Eritrea. Hatshepsut was seeking the source of myrrh°, a reddish-brown resin from the hardened sap of a local tree, which the Egyptians burned on the altars of their gods and used as an ingredient in medicines and cosmetics. She hoped to bypass the middlemen who drove up the price exorbitantly, and establish direct trade between Punt and Egypt. When the expedition returned with myrrh and various sub-Saharan luxury goods—ebony and other rare woods, ivory, cosmetics, live monkeys, panther skins—Hatshepsut celebrated the achievement in a great public display and in words and pictures on the walls of the mortuary temple she built for herself at Deir el-Bahri°. She may have used the success of this expedition to bolster her claim to the throne. After her death, in a reaction that reflected some official opposition to a woman ruler, her image was defaced and her name blotted out wherever it appeared.

Another ruler who departed from traditional ways ascended the throne as Amenhotep° IV. He soon began to refer to himself as **Akhenaten°** (r. 1353–1335 B.C.E.), meaning "beneficial to the Aten°" (the disk of the sun). Changing his name was one of the ways in which he sought to spread his belief in Aten as the supreme deity. He closed the temples of other gods, challenging the age-old supremacy of the chief god Amon° and the power and influence of the priests of Amon.

Some scholars have credited Akhenaten with the invention of monotheism—the belief in one exclusive god. It is likely, however, that Akhenaten was attempting to reassert the superiority of the king over the priests and to renew belief in the king's divinity. Worship of Aten was confined to the royal family: the people of Egypt were pressed to revere the divine ruler.

Akhenaten built a new capital at modern-day Amarna°, halfway between Memphis and Thebes (see Map 3.1). He transplanted thousands of Egyptians to construct the site and serve the ruling elite. Akhenaten and his artists created a new style that broke with the conventions of earlier art: the king, his wife Nefertiti°, and their daughters were depicted in fluid, natural poses with strangely elongated heads and limbs and swelling abdomens.

Akhenaten's reforms were strongly resented by government officials, priests, and others whose privileges and wealth were linked to the traditional system. After his death the temples were reopened; Amon was reinstated as chief god; the capital returned to Thebes; and the institution of kingship was weakened to the advantage of the priests. The boy-king Tutankhamun° (r. 1333–1323 B.C.E.), one of the immediate successors of Akhenaten and famous solely because his was the only royal tomb found by archaeologists that had not been pillaged

---

Kamose (KAH-mose)   Ahmose (AH-mose)
Tuthmosis (tuth_MOE-sis)   Hatshepsut (hat-SHEP-soot)
Punt (poont)   myrrh (murr)

Deir el-Bahri (DARE uhl–BAH-ree)
Amenhotep (ah-muhn-HOE-tep)   Akhenaten (ah-ken-AHT-n)
Aten (AHT-n)   Amon (AH-muhn)   Amarna (uh-MAHR-nuh)
Nefertiti (nef-uhr-TEE-tee)
Tutankhamun (tuht-uhnk-AH-muhn)

Colossal Statues of Ramesses II at Abu Simbel   Strategically placed at a bend in the Nile River so as to face the southern frontier, this monument was an advertisement of Egyptian power. A temple was carved into the cliff behind the gigantic statues of the pharaoh. Within the temple, a corridor decorated with reliefs of military victories leads to an inner shrine containing images of the divine ruler seated alongside three of the major gods. In a modern marvel of engineering, the monument was moved to higher ground in the 1960s C.E. to protect it from rising waters when a dam was constructed upriver.   (Susan Lapides/Woodfin Camp & Associates)

by tomb robbers, reveals both in his name (meaning "beautiful in life is Amon") and in his insignificant reign the ultimate failure of Akhenaten's revolution.

In 1323 B.C.E. the general Haremhab seized the throne and established a new dynasty, the Ramessides°. The rulers of this line renewed the policy of conquest and expansion that Akhenaten had neglected. The greatest of these monarchs, **Ramesses° II**—sometimes called Ramesses the Great—ruled for sixty-six years (r. 1290–1224 B.C.E.) and dominated his age. Ramesses looms large in the archaeological record because he undertook monumental building projects all over Egypt. Living into his nineties, he had many wives and concubines and may have fathered more than a hundred children. Since 1990 archaeologists have been excavating a network of more than a hundred corridors and chambers carved deep into a hillside in the Valley of the Kings where many sons of Ramesses were buried.

Commerce and Communication

Early in his reign Ramesses II fought a major battle against the Hittites at Kadesh in northern Syria (1285 B.C.E.). Although Egyptian scribes presented this encounter as a great victory, the lack of territorial gains suggests that it was essentially a draw. In subsequent years Egyptian and Hittite diplomats negotiated a treaty, which was strengthened by Ramesses' marriage to a Hittite princess. At issue was control of Syria-Palestine, strategically located at a crossroads between the great powers of the Middle East and at the end of the east-west trade route across Asia. The inland cities of Syria-Palestine—such as Mari° on the upper Euphrates and Alalakh° in western Syria—were active centers of international trade. The coastal towns—particularly Ugarit and the Phoenician towns of the Lebanese seaboard—served as transshipment points for trade to and from the lands ringing the Mediterranean Sea.

Ramesside (RAM-ih-side)   **Ramesses** (RAM-ih-seez)

Mari (MAH-ree)   **Alalakh** (UH-luh-luhk)

In the eastern Mediterranean, northeastern Africa, and western Asia in the Late Bronze Age, any state that wanted to project its power needed metal to make tools and weapons. Commerce in metals energized the long-distance trade of the time.

New modes of transportation expedited communications and commerce across great distances and inhospitable landscapes. Horses arrived in western Asia around 2000 B.C.E. Domesticated by nomadic peoples in Central Asia, they were brought into Mesopotamia through the Zagros mountains and reached Egypt by 1600 B.C.E. The speed of travel and communication made possible by horses contributed to the creation of large states and empires. Soldiers and government agents could cover great distances quickly, and swift, maneuverable horse-drawn chariots became the premier instrument of war. The team of driver and archer could ride forward and unleash a volley of arrows or trample terrified foot soldiers.

THE AEGEAN WORLD, 2000–1100 B.C.E.

In this era of far-flung trade and communication, the influence of Mesopotamia and Egypt was felt as far away as the Aegean Sea, a gulf of the eastern Mediterranean. The emergence of the Minoan° civilization on the island of Crete and the Mycenaean° civilization of Greece is another manifestation of the fertilizing influence of older centers on outlying lands and peoples, who then struck out on their own unique paths of cultural evolution.

The landscape of southern Greece and the Aegean islands is mostly rocky and arid, with small plains lying between ranges of hills. The limited arable land is suitable for grains, grapevines, and olive trees. Flocks of sheep and goats graze the slopes. Sharply indented coastlines, natural harbors, and small islands within sight of one another made the sea the fastest and least costly mode of travel and transport. With few deposits of metals and little timber, Aegean peoples had to import these commodities, as well as food, from abroad. As a result, the rise, success, and eventual fall of the Minoan and Mycenaean societies were closely tied to their commercial and political relations with other peoples in the region.

Minoan Crete

By 2000 B.C.E. the island of Crete (see Map 3.2) housed the first European civilization to have complex political and social structures and advanced technologies like those found in western Asia and northeastern Africa. The **Minoan** civilization had centralized government, monumental building, bronze metallurgy, writing, and recordkeeping. Archaeologists named this civilization after Greek legends about King Minos, who was said to have ruled a vast naval empire, including the southern Greek mainland, and to have kept the monstrous Minotaur° (half-man, half-bull) beneath his palace in a mazelike labyrinth built by the ingenious inventor Daedalus°. Thus later Greeks recollected a time when Crete was home to many ships and skilled craftsmen.

The ethnicity of the Minoans is uncertain, and their writing has not been deciphered. But their sprawling palace complexes at Cnossus°, Phaistos°, and Mallia° and the distribution of Cretan pottery and other artifacts around the Mediterranean and Middle East testify to widespread trading connections. Egyptian, Syrian, and Mesopotamian influences can be seen in the design of the Minoan palaces, centralized government, and system of writing. The absence of identifiable representations of Cretan rulers, however, contrasts sharply with the grandiose depictions of kings in the Middle East and suggests a different conception of authority. Also noteworthy is the absence of fortifications at the palace sites and the presence of high-quality indoor plumbing.

Statuettes of women with elaborate headdresses and serpents coiling around their limbs may represent fertility goddesses. Colorful frescoes (paintings done on a moist plaster surface) on the walls of Cretan palaces portray groups of women in frilly, layered skirts engaged in conversation or watching rituals or entertainment. We do not know whether pictures of young acrobats vaulting over the horns and back of an onrushing bull show a religious activity or mere sport. Scenes of servants carrying jars and fishermen throwing nets and hooks from their boats suggest a joyful attitude toward work, but this portrayal may say more about the tastes of the elite than about the reality of daily toil. The stylized depictions of plants and animals on Minoan vases—plants with swaying leaves and playful octopuses whose tentacles wind around the surface of the vase—seem to reflect a delight in the beauty and order of the natural world.

Minoan (mih-NO-uhn)   **Mycenaean** (my-suh-NEE-uhn)

Minotaur (MIN-uh-tor)   **Daedalus** (DED-ih-luhs)
Cnossus (NOSS-suhs)   **Phaistos** (FIE-stuhs)   **Mallia** (mahl-YAH)

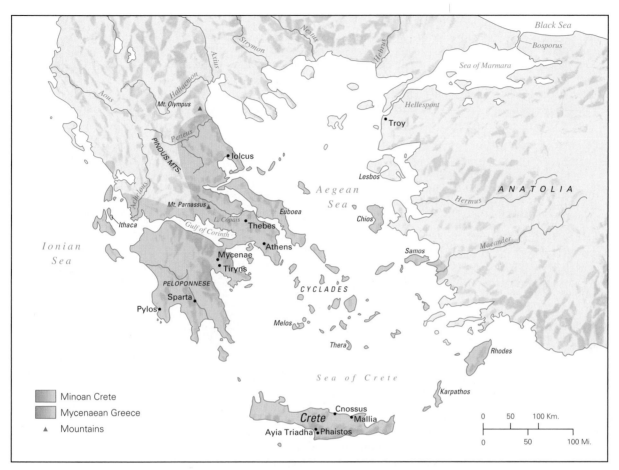

Map 3.2   Minoan and Mycenaean Civilizations of the Aegean   The earliest complex civilizations in Europe arose in the Aegean Sea. The Minoan civilization on the island of Crete evolved in the later third millennium B.C.E. and had a major cultural influence on the Mycenaean Greeks. Palaces decorated with fresco paintings, a centrally controlled economy, and the use of a system of writing for recordkeeping are some of the most conspicuous features of these societies.

All the Cretan palaces except Cnossus, along with the houses of the elite and peasants in the countryside, were deliberately destroyed around 1450 B.C.E. Because Mycenaean Greeks took over at Cnossus, most historians regard them as the likely culprits.

Mycenaean Greece

Most historians believe that speakers of an Indo-European language ancestral to Greek migrated into the Greek peninsula around 2000 B.C.E., although some argue for earlier and later dates. Through intermarriage, blending of languages, and melding of cultural practices, the indigenous population and the newcomers created the first Greek culture. For centuries this society remained simple and static. Farmers and shepherds lived in Stone Age conditions, wringing a bare living from the land. Then, sometime around 1600 B.C.E., life changed relatively suddenly.

More than a century ago a German businessman, Heinrich Schliemann°, set out to prove that the *Iliad* and the *Odyssey* were true. These epics attributed to the poet Homer, who probably lived shortly before 700 B.C.E., spoke of Agamemnon°, the king of **Mycenae**° in southern Greece. In 1876 Schliemann stunned the scholarly world by discovering at Mycenae a circle of graves at the base of deep, rectangular shafts. These **shaft graves** contained the bodies of men, women, and children and

---

Schliemann (SHLEE-muhn)   **Agamemnon** (ag-uh-MEM-non)
Mycenae (my-SEE-nee)

Fresco from the Aegean Island of Thera, ca. 1650 b.c.e. This picture, originally painted on wet plaster, depicts the arrival of a fleet in a harbor as people watch from the walls of the town. The Minoan civilization of Crete was famous in later legend for its naval power. The fresco reveals the appearance and design of ships in the Bronze Age Aegean. In the seventeenth century b.c.e., the island of Thera was devastated by a massive volcanic explosion, thought by many to be the origin of the myth of Atlantis sinking beneath the sea. (Archaeological Receipts Fund, Athens)

were filled with gold jewelry and ornaments, weapons, and utensils. Clearly, some people in this society had acquired wealth, authority, and the capacity to mobilize human labor. Subsequent excavation uncovered a large palace complex, massive walls, more shaft graves, and other evidence of a rich and technologically advanced civilization that lasted from around 1600 to 1150 b.c.e.

Despite legends about the power of King Minos of Crete, there is no archaeological evidence of Cretan political control of the Greek mainland. But Crete exerted a powerful cultural influence. The Mycenaeans borrowed the Minoan idea of the palace, centralized economy, and administrative bureaucracy, as well as the Minoan writing system. They adopted Minoan styles and techniques of architecture, pottery making, and fresco and vase painting. This explains where the Mycenaean Greeks got their technology. But how did they suddenly accumulate power and wealth? Most historians look to the profits

from trade and piracy and perhaps also to the pay and booty brought back by mercenaries (soldiers who served for pay in foreign lands).

The first advanced civilization in Greece is called "Mycenaean" largely because Mycenae was the first site excavated. Excavations at other centers have revealed that Mycenae exemplifies the common pattern of these citadels: built at a commanding location on a hilltop and surrounded by high, thick fortification walls made of stones so large that later Greeks believed that the giant, one-eyed Cyclopes° of legend had lifted them into place. The fortified enclosure provided a place of refuge for the entire community in time of danger and contained the palace and administrative complex. The large central hall with an open hearth and columned porch was sur-

---

Cyclopes (SIGH-kloe-pees)

rounded by courtyards, living quarters for the royal family and their retainers, and offices, storerooms, and workshops. The palace walls were covered with brightly painted frescoes depicting scenes of war, the hunt, and daily life, as well as decorative motifs from nature.

Nearby lay the tombs of the rulers and leading families: shaft graves at first; later, grand beehive-shaped structures made of stone and covered with a mound of earth. Large houses, probably belonging to the aristocracy, lay just outside the walls. The peasants lived on the lower slopes and in the plain below, close to the land they worked.

Additional information about Mycenaean life is provided by over four thousand baked clay tablets written in a script now called **Linear B.** Like its predecessor, the undeciphered Minoan script called Linear A, Linear B uses pictorial signs to represent syllables, but it is recognizably an early form of Greek. The extensive palace bureaucracy kept track of people, animals, and objects in exhaustive detail and exercised a high degree of control over the economy of the kingdom. The tablets list everything from the number of chariot wheels in palace storerooms, the rations paid to textile workers, and the gifts dedicated to various gods, to the ships stationed along the coasts.

The government organized and coordinated grain production and controlled the wool industry from raw material to finished product. Scribes kept track of the flocks in the field, the sheared wool, the allocation of raw wool to spinners and weavers, and the production, storage, and distribution of cloth articles.

The tablets say almost nothing about individual people—not even the name of a single Mycenaean king—and very little about the political and legal systems, social structures, gender relations, and religious beliefs. They tell nothing about particular historical events and relations with other Mycenaean centers or peoples overseas.

The evidence for a broad political organization of Greece in this period is contradictory. In Homer's *Iliad*, Agamemnon, the king of Mycenae, leads a great expedition of Greeks from different regions against the city of Troy in northwest Anatolia. To this can be added the cultural uniformity of all the Mycenaean centers: a remarkable similarity in the shapes, decorative styles, and production techniques of buildings, tombs, utensils, tools, clothing, and works of art. Some scholars argue that such cultural uniformity could have occurred only in a context of political unity. The plot of the *Iliad*, however, revolves around the difficulties Agamemnon has in asserting control over other Greek leaders. Moreover, the archaeological remains and the Linear B tablets give

Lion Gate at Mycenae   View over the massive fortification wall encircling the citadel. Above the entrance a large stone depicts a Minoan-style column with lions on either side, thought to signify royal power. Just inside the gate on the right is one of the shaft grave circles containing the treasure-filled tombs of the elite. (Dimitrios Harissiadis/Benaki Museum)

strong indications of independent centers of power at Mycenae, Pylos°, and elsewhere.

Long-distance contact and trade were made possible by the seafaring skill of Minoans and Mycenaeans. Commercial vessels depended primarily on wind and sail. In general, ancient sailors preferred to sail in daylight hours and keep the land in sight. Their light, wooden vessels had little storage area and decking, so the crew had to go ashore to eat and sleep every night. With their low keels the ships could run up onto the beach.

Cretan and Greek pottery and crafted goods are found not only in the Aegean but also in other parts of the Mediterranean and Middle East. At certain sites the quantity and range of artifacts suggest settlements of Aegean peoples. The oldest artifacts are Minoan; then Minoan and Mycenaean objects are found side by side;

Pylos (PIE-lohs)

and eventually Greek wares replace Cretan goods altogether. Such evidence indicates that Cretan merchants pioneered trade routes and established trading posts and then admitted Mycenaean traders, who eventually supplanted them in the fifteenth century B.C.E.

The numerous Aegean pots found throughout the Mediterranean and Middle East must once have contained such products as wine and olive oil. Other possible exports include weapons and other crafted goods, as well as slaves and mercenary soldiers. Minoan and Mycenaean sailors also may have made tidy profits by transporting the trade goods of other peoples.

As for imports, amber (a hard, translucent, yellowish-brown fossil resin used for jewelry) from northern Europe and ivory carved in Syria have been discovered at Aegean sites, and the large population of southwest Greece and other regions probably relied on imports of grain. Above all, the Aegean lands needed metals, both the gold prized by rulers and the copper and tin needed to make bronze. A number of sunken ships carrying copper ingots have been found on the floor of the Mediterranean. Scholars believe that these ships were transporting metals from Cyprus to the Aegean (see Map 3.2). As in early China, the elite classes were practically the only people who owned metal goods, which may have been symbols of their superior status.

In this era, trade and piracy were closely linked. Mycenaeans were tough, warlike, and acquisitive. They traded with those who were strong and took from those who were weak. This may have led to conflict with the Hittite kings of Anatolia in the fourteenth and thirteenth centuries B.C.E. Documents found in the archives at Hattusha, the Hittite capital, refer to the king and land of Ahhijawa°, most likely a Hittite rendering of *Achaeans*°, the term used most frequently by Homer for the Greeks. The documents indicate that relations were sometimes friendly, sometimes strained, and that the people of Ahhijawa were aggressive and tried to take advantage of Hittite preoccupation or weakness.

The Fall of Late Bronze Age Civilizations

Hittite difficulties with Ahhijawa and the Greek attack on Troy foreshadowed the troubles that culminated in the destruction of many of the old centers of the Middle East and Mediterranean around 1200 B.C.E. In this period, for reasons that historians do not completely understand, large numbers of people were on the move. As migrants swarmed into one region, they displaced other peoples, who then joined the tide of refugees.

Around 1200 B.C.E. unidentified invaders destroyed Hattusha, and the Hittite kingdom in Anatolia came crashing down. The tide of destruction moved south into Syria, and the great coastal city of Ugarit was swept away. Around 1190 Ramesses III of Egypt checked a major invasion of Palestine by the "Sea Peoples." Although he claimed to have won a great victory, the Philistines° were able to occupy the coast of Palestine. Egypt soon surrendered all its territory in Syria-Palestine and lost contact with the rest of western Asia. The Egyptians also lost their foothold in Nubia, opening the way for the emergence of the native kingdom centered on Napata (see Chapter 2).

Among the invaders listed in the Egyptian inscriptions are the Ekwesh°, who could be Achaeans—that is, Greeks. Whether or not the Mycenaeans participated in the destructions elsewhere, their own centers collapsed in the first half of the twelfth century B.C.E. The rulers had seen trouble coming; at some sites they began to build more extensive fortifications and took steps to guarantee the water supply of the citadels. But their efforts were in vain, and nearly all the palaces were destroyed.

The end of Mycenaean civilization illustrates the consequences of political and economic collapse. The deconstruction of the palaces ended the domination of the ruling class. The massive administrative apparatus revealed in the Linear B tablets disappeared, and the technique of writing was forgotten, since it had been known only to a few palace officials and was no longer useful. Archaeological studies indicate the depopulation of some regions of Greece and an inflow of people to other regions that had escaped destruction. The Greek language persisted, and a thousand years later people were still worshiping gods mentioned in the Linear B tablets. People also continued to make the vessels and implements that they were familiar with, although there was a marked decline in artistic and technical skill in the new, much poorer society. The cultural uniformity of the Mycenaean Age gave way to regional variations in shapes, styles, and techniques, reflecting increased isolation of different parts of Greece.

Thus perished the cosmopolitan world of the Late Bronze Age in the Mediterranean and Middle East. Societies that had long prospered through complex links of trade, diplomacy, and shared technologies now collapsed in the face of external violence and internal weakness,

---

Ahhijawa (uh-key-YAW-wuh)   **Achaeans** (uh-KEY-uhns)

Philistine (FIH-luh-steen)   **Ekwesh** (ECK-wesh)

and the peoples of the region entered a centuries-long "Dark Age" of poverty, isolation, and loss of knowledge.

THE ASSYRIAN EMPIRE, 911–612 B.C.E.

A number of new centers emerged in western Asia and the eastern Mediterranean in the centuries after 1000 B.C.E. The chief force for change was the powerful and aggressive **Neo-Assyrian Empire** (911–612 B.C.E.). Although historians sometimes apply the term *empire* to earlier regional powers, the Assyrians of this era were the first to rule over far-flung lands and diverse peoples (see Map 3.3).

The Assyrian homeland in northern Mesopotamia differs in essential respects from the flat expanse of Sumer and Akkad to the south. It is hillier, has a more temperate climate and greater rainfall, and is more exposed to raiders from the mountains to the east and north and from the arid plain to the west. Peasant farmers, accustomed to defending themselves against marauders, provided the foot-soldiers for the revival of Assyrian power in the ninth century B.C.E. The rulers of the Neo-Assyrian Empire struck out in a ceaseless series of campaigns: westward across the steppe and desert as far as the Mediterranean, north into mountainous Urartu° (modern Armenia), east across the Zagros range onto the Iranian Plateau, and south along the Tigris River to Babylonia.

These campaigns largely followed the most important long-distance trade routes in western Asia and provided immediate booty and the prospect of tribute and taxes. They also secured access to vital resources such as iron and silver and brought the Assyrians control of international commerce. As noted earlier in this chapter, Assyria already had a long tradition of commercial and political interests in Syria and Anatolia. What started out as an aggressive program of self-defense and reestablishment of old claims soon became far more ambitious. Driven by pride, greed, and religious conviction, the Assyrians defeated all the great kingdoms of the day—Elam (southwest Iran), Urartu, Babylon, and Egypt. At its peak their empire stretched from Anatolia, Syria-Palestine, and Egypt in the west, across Armenia and Mesopotamia, as far as western Iran. The Assyrians created a new kind of empire, larger in extent than anything seen

---

Urartu (ur-RAHR-too)

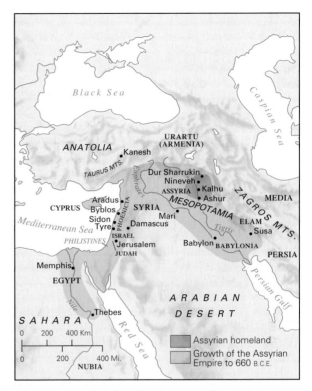

Map 3.3 The Assyrian Empire From the tenth to the seventh century B.C.E. the Assyrians of northern Mesopotamia created the largest empire the world had yet seen, extending from the Iranian Plateau to the eastern shore of the Mediterranean and containing a diverse array of peoples.

before and dedicated to the enrichment of the imperial center at the expense of the subjugated periphery.

God and King

The king was literally and symbolically the center of the Assyrian universe. All the land belonged to him, and all the people, even the highest-ranking officials, were his servants. Assyrians believed that the gods chose the king to rule as their earthly representative. Normally the king chose one of his sons to be his successor, and his choice was confirmed by divine oracles and the Assyrian elite. In the revered ancient city of Ashur the high priest anointed the new king by sprinkling his head with oil and gave him the insignia of kingship: a crown and scepter. The kings were buried in Ashur.

Every day messengers and spies brought the king information from every corner of the empire. He made decisions, appointed officials, and heard complaints. He dictated his correspondence to an army of scribes and received and entertained foreign envoys and high-ranking government figures. He was the military leader, responsible for planning campaigns, and he often was away from the capital commanding operations in the field.

Among the king's chief responsibilities was supervision of the state religion. He devoted much of his time to elaborate public and private rituals and to overseeing the upkeep of the temples. He made no decisions of state without consulting the gods through elaborate rituals. All state actions were carried out in the name of Ashur, the chief god. Military victories were cited as proof of Ashur's superiority over the gods of the conquered peoples.

Relentless government propaganda secured popular support for military campaigns that mostly benefited the king and the nobility. Royal inscriptions posted throughout the empire catalogued recent military victories, extolled the charisma and relentless will of the king, and promised ruthless punishments to anyone who resisted him. Art, too, served the Assyrian state. Relief sculptures depicting hunts, battles, sieges, executions, and deportations covered the walls of the royal palaces at Kalhu° and Nineveh°. Looming over most scenes was the king, larger than anyone else, muscular and fierce, with the appearance of a god. Few visitors to the Assyrian court could fail to be awed—and intimidated.

Conquest and Control

The Assyrians' unprecedented conquests were made possible by their superior military organization and technology. Early Assyrian armies consisted of men who served in return for grants of land, and peasants and slaves whose service was contributed by large landowners. Later, King Tiglathpileser° (r. 744–727 B.C.E.) created a core army of professional soldiers made up of Assyrians and the most formidable subject peoples. At its peak the Assyrian state could mobilize a half-million troops, including light-armed bowmen and slingers who launched stone projectiles, armored spearmen, cavalry equipped with bows or spears, and four-man chariots.

Iron weapons gave Assyrian soldiers an advantage over many opponents, and cavalry provided unprecedented speed and mobility. Assyrian engineers developed machinery and tactics for besieging fortified towns. They dug tunnels under the walls, built mobile towers for their archers, and applied battering rams to weak points. The Assyrians destroyed some of the best-fortified cities of the Middle East—Babylon, Thebes in Egypt, Tyre in Phoenicia, and Susa in Elam (see Map 3.3). Couriers and signal fires provided long-distance communication, while a network of spies gathered intelligence.

The Assyrians used terror tactics to discourage resistance and rebellion, inflicting swift and harsh retribution and publicizing their brutality: civilians were thrown into fires, prisoners were skinned alive, and the severed heads of defeated rulers hung on city walls. **Mass deportation**—forcibly uprooting entire communities and resettling them elsewhere—broke the spirit of rebellious peoples. This tactic had a long history in the ancient Middle East—in Sumer, Babylon, Urartu, Egypt, and the Hittite Empire—but the Neo-Assyrian monarchs used it on an unprecedented scale. Surviving documents record the relocation of over 1 million people, and historians estimate that the true figure exceeds 4 million. Deportation also shifted human resources from the periphery to the center, where the deportees worked on royal and noble estates, opened new lands for agriculture, and built new palaces and cities.

The Assyrians never found a single, enduring method of governing an empire that included nomadic and sedentary kinship groups, temple-states, city-states, and kingdoms. Control tended to be tight and effective at the center and in lands closest to the core area, and less so farther away. The Assyrian kings waged many campaigns to reimpose control on territories subdued in previous wars.

Assyrian provincial officials oversaw the payment of tribute and taxes, maintained law and order, raised troops, undertook public works, and provisioned armies and administrators that were passing through their territory. Provincial governors were subject to frequent inspections by royal overseers.

The elite class was bound to the monarch by oaths of obedience, fear of punishment, and the expectation of rewards, such as land grants or shares of booty and taxes. Skilled professionals—priests, diviners, scribes, doctors, and artisans—were similarly bound.

The Assyrians ruthlessly exploited the wealth and resources of their subjects. Military campaigns and administration had to be funded by plunder and tribute. Wealth from the periphery was funneled to the center, where the king and nobility grew rich. Proud kings used their riches to expand the ancestral capital and religious center at Ashur and to build magnificent new royal cities. Dur Sharrukin°, the "Fortress of Sargon," was completed in a

---

Kalhu (KAL-oo)   **Nineveh** (NIN-uh-vuh)
Tiglathpileser (TIG-lath-pih-LEE-zuhr)

Dur Sharrukin (DOOR SHAH-roo-keen)

Wall Relief from the Palace of Sennacherib at Nineveh   Against a backdrop of wooded hills representing the landscape of Assyria, workers are hauling a huge stone sculpture from the riverbank to the palace under the watchful eyes of officials and soldiers. They accomplish this task with simple equipment—a lever, a sledge, and thick ropes—and a lot of human muscle power.   (Courtesy of the Trustees of the British Museum)

mere ten years, thanks to a massive labor force composed of prisoners of war and Assyrian citizens who owed periodic service to the state.

Nevertheless, the Assyrian Empire was not simply parasitic. There is some evidence of royal investment in provincial infrastructure. The cities and merchant classes thrived on expanded long-distance commerce, and some subject populations were surprisingly loyal to their Assyrian rulers.

Assyrian Society and Culture

A few things are known about the lives and activities of the millions of Assyrian subjects. In the core area people belonged to the same three classes that had existed in Hammurabi's Babylon a millennium before (see Chapter 1): (1) free, landowning citizens, (2) farmers and artisans attached to the estates of the king or other rich landholders, and (3) slaves. Slaves—debtors and prisoners of war—had legal rights and, if sufficiently talented, could rise to positions of influence.

The government normally did not distinguish between native Assyrians and the increasingly large number of immigrants and deportees residing in the Assyrian homeland. All were referred to as "human beings," entitled to the same legal protections and liable for the same labor and military service. Over time the inflow of outsiders changed the ethnic makeup of the core area.

The vast majority of subjects worked on the land. The agricultural surpluses they produced allowed substantial numbers of people—the standing army, government officials, religious experts, merchants, artisans, and all manner of professionals in the towns and cities—to engage in specialized activities.

Individual artisans and small workshops in the towns manufactured pottery, tools, and clothing, and most trade took place at the local level. The state fostered long-distance trade, since imported luxury goods—metals, fine textiles, dyes, gems, and ivory—brought in substantial customs revenues and found their way to the royal family and elite classes. Silver was the basic medium of exchange, weighed out for each transaction in a time before the invention of coins.

Building on the achievements of their Mesopotamian ancestors, Assyrian scholars created and preserved lists of plant and animal names, geographic terms, and astronomical occurrences, and made original contributions in mathematics and astronomy. Their assumption that gods or demons caused disease obstructed the investigation of natural causes, but in addition to exorcists trained to expel demons, another type of physician experimented with medicines and surgical treatments to relieve symptoms.

Some Assyrian temples may have had libraries. When archaeologists excavated the palace of Ashurbanipal° (r. 668–627 B.C.E.), one of the last Assyrian kings, at Nineveh, they discovered more than twenty-five thousand tablets or fragments of tablets. The **Library of Ashurbanipal** contained official documents as well as literary and scientific texts. Some were originals that had been brought to the capital; others were copies made at the king's request. Ashurbanipal was an avid collector of the literary and scientific heritage of Mesopotamia, and the "House of Knowledge" referred to in some of the documents may have been an academy that attracted learned men to the imperial center.

ISRAEL, 2000–500 B.C.E.

On the western edge of the Assyrian Empire lived a people who probably seemed of no great significance to the masters of western Asia but were destined to play an important role in world history. The history of ancient Israel is marked by two grand and interconnected dramas that played out from around 2000 to 500 B.C.E. First, a loose collection of nomadic kinship groups engaged in herding and caravan traffic became a sedentary, agricultural people, developed complex political and social institutions, and became integrated into the commercial and diplomatic networks of the Middle East. Second, these people transformed the austere cult of a desert god into the concept of a single, all-powerful, and all-knowing deity, in the process creating the ethical and intellectual traditions that underlie the beliefs and values of Judaism and Christianity.

The land and the people at the heart of this story have gone by various names: Canaan, Israel, Palestine; Hebrews, Israelites, Jews. For the sake of consistency, the people are referred to here as *Israelites*, the land they occupied in antiquity as **Israel.**

Israel is a crossroads, linking Anatolia, Egypt, Arabia, and Mesopotamia (see Map 3.4). Its location has given

Map 3.4   Phoenicia and Israel   The lands along the eastern shore of the Mediterranean Sea—sometimes called the Levant or Syria-Palestine—have always been a crossroads, traversed by migrants, nomads, merchants, and armies moving between Egypt, Arabia, Mesopotamia, and Anatolia.

Israel an importance in history out of all proportion to its size. Its natural resources are few. The Negev Desert and the vast wasteland of the Sinai° lie to the south. The Mediterranean coastal plain was usually in the hands of others, particularly the Philistines, throughout much of this period. At the center are the rock-strewn hills of the Shephelah°. Galilee to the north, with its sea of the same name, was a relatively fertile land of grassy hills and small plains. The narrow ribbon of the Jordan River runs down the eastern side of the region into the Dead Sea, so named because its high salt content is toxic to life.

Origins, Exodus, and Settlement   Information about ancient Israel comes partly from archaeological excavations and references in contemporary documents such as the royal annals of Egypt and Assyria. However, the fundamental source is the collection of

---

Ashurbanipal (ah-shur-BAH-nee-pahl)

Sinai (SIE-nie)   **Shephelah** (sheh-FEH-luh)

writings preserved in the **Hebrew Bible** (called the Old Testament by Christians). The Hebrew Bible is a compilation of several collections of materials that originated with different groups, employed distinctive vocabularies, and advocated particular interpretations of past events. Traditions about the Israelites' early days were long transmitted orally. Not until the tenth century B.C.E. were they written down in a script borrowed from the Phoenicians. The text that we have today dates from the fifth century B.C.E., with a few later additions, and reflects the point of view of the priests who controlled the Temple in Jerusalem. Historians disagree about how accurately this document represents Israelite history. In the absence of other written sources, however, it provides a foundation to be used critically and modified in light of archaeological discoveries.

The Hebrew language of the Bible reflects the speech of the Israelites until about 500 B.C.E. It is a Semitic language, most closely related to Phoenician and Aramaic (which later supplanted Hebrew in Israel), more distantly related to Arabic and the Akkadian language of the Assyrians. This linguistic affinity probably parallels the Israelites' ethnic relationship to the neighboring peoples.

The Hebrew Bible tells the story of the family of Abraham. Born in the city of Ur in southern Mesopotamia, Abraham rejected the traditional idol worship of his homeland and migrated with his family and livestock across the Syrian desert. Eventually he arrived in the land of Israel, which, according to the biblical account, had been promised to him and his descendants as part of a "covenant," or pact, with the Israelite god, Yahweh.

These "recollections" of the journey of Abraham (who, if he was a real person, probably lived in the twentieth century B.C.E.) may compress the experiences of generations of pastoralists who migrated from the grazing lands between the upper reaches of the Tigris and Euphrates Rivers to the Mediterranean coastal plain. Abraham, his family, and his companions were following the usual pattern in this part of the world. They camped by a permanent water source in the dry season, then drove herds of domesticated animals (sheep, cattle, donkeys) to a well-established sequence of grazing areas during the rest of the year.

Abraham's son Isaac and then his grandson Jacob became the leaders of this wandering group of herders. In the next generation the squabbling sons of Jacob's several wives sold their brother Joseph as a slave to passing merchants heading for Egypt. According to the biblical account, through luck and ability Joseph became a high official at Pharaoh's court. Thus he was in a position to help his people when drought struck Israel and forced the Israelites to migrate to Egypt. The sophisticated Egyptians feared and looked down on these rough herders and eventually reduced the Israelites to slaves, putting them to work on the grand building projects of the pharaoh.

That is the version of events given in the Hebrew Bible. Several points need to be made about it. First, the biblical account glosses over the period from 1700 to 1500 B.C.E., when Egypt was dominated by the Hyksos. Since the Hyksos are thought to have been Semitic groups that infiltrated the Nile Delta from the northeast, the Israelite migration to Egypt and later enslavement could have been connected to the Hyksos' rise and fall. Second, although the surviving Egyptian sources do not refer to Israelite slaves, they do complain about Apiru°, a derogatory term applied to caravan drivers, outcasts, bandits, and other marginal groups. The word seems to designate a class of people rather than a particular ethnic group, but some scholars believe there may be a connection between the similar-sounding terms *Apiru* and *Hebrew*. Third, the period of alleged Israelite slavery coincided with the era of ambitious building programs launched by several New Kingdom pharaohs.

According to the Hebrew Bible, the Israelites were led out of captivity by Moses, an Israelite with connections to the Egyptian royal family. It is possible that oral tradition may have preserved memories of a real emigration from Egypt followed by years of wandering in the wilderness of Sinai.

During their reported forty years in the desert, the Israelites became devoted to a stern and warlike god. According to the Hebrew Bible, Yahweh made a covenant with the Israelites: they would be his "Chosen People" if they promised to worship him exclusively. This pact was confirmed by tablets that Moses brought down from the top of Mount Sinai. Written on the tablets were the Ten Commandments, which set out the basic tenets of Jewish belief and practice. The Commandments prohibited murder, adultery, theft, lying, and envy, and demanded respect for parents and rest from work on the Sabbath, the seventh day of the week.

The biblical account tells how Joshua, Moses's successor, led the Israelites from the east side of the Jordan River into the land of Canaan° (modern Israel and the Palestinian territories). They attacked and destroyed Jericho° and other Canaanite° cities. Archaeological evidence confirms the destruction of some Canaanite towns between 1250 and 1200 B.C.E., though not precisely the towns mentioned in the biblical account. Shortly thereafter, lowland sites were resettled and new

---

Apiru (uh-PEE-roo)　**Canaan** (KAY-nuhn)　**Jericho** (JEH-rih-koe)
Canaanite (KAY-nuh-nite)

sites were established in the hills, thanks to the development of cisterns carved into nonporous rock to hold rainwater and the construction of leveled terraces on the slopes to expand the cultivable area. The material culture of the new settlers was cruder but continued Canaanite patterns.

Most scholars doubt that Canaan was conquered by a unified Israelite army. In a time of widespread disruption, movements of peoples, and decline and destruction of cities throughout this region, it is more likely that Israelite migrants took advantage of the disorder and were joined by other loosely organized groups and even refugees from the Canaanite cities.

In a pattern common throughout history, the new coalition of peoples invented a common ancestry. The "Children of Israel," as they called themselves, were divided into twelve tribes supposedly descended from the sons of Jacob and Joseph. Each tribe installed itself in a different part of the country and was led by one or more chiefs. Such leaders usually had limited power and were primarily responsible for mediating disputes and seeing to the welfare and protection of the group. Certain charismatic figures, famed for their daring in war or genius in arbitration, were called "Judges" and enjoyed a special standing that transcended tribal boundaries. The tribes also shared access to a shrine in the hill country at Shiloh°, which housed the Ark of the Covenant, a sacred chest containing the tablets that Yahweh had given Moses.

Rise of the Monarchy

The time of troubles that struck the eastern Mediterranean around 1200 B.C.E. also brought the Philistines to Israel. Possibly related to the pre-Greek population of the Aegean Sea region and likely participants in the Sea People's attack on Egypt, the Philistines occupied the coastal plain of Israel and came into frequent conflict with the Israelites. Their wars were memorialized in Bible stories about the long-haired strongman Samson, who toppled a Philistine temple, and the shepherd boy David, whose slingshot felled the towering warrior Goliath.

A religious leader named Samuel recognized the need for a stronger central authority to lead the Israelites against the Philistine city-states and anointed Saul as the first king of Israel around 1020 B.C.E. When Saul perished in battle, the throne passed to David (r. ca. 1000–960 B.C.E.).

A gifted musician, warrior, and politician, David oversaw Israel's transition from a tribal confederacy to a unified monarchy. He strengthened royal authority by making the captured hill city of Jerusalem, which lay outside tribal boundaries, his capital. Soon after, David brought the Ark to Jerusalem, making the city the religious as well as the political center of the kingdom. A census was taken to facilitate the collection of taxes, and a standing army, with soldiers paid by and loyal to the king, was instituted. These innovations enabled David to win a string of military victories and expand Israel's borders.

The reign of David's son Solomon (r. ca. 960–920 B.C.E.) marked the high point of the Israelite monarchy. Alliances and trade linked Israel with near and distant lands. Solomon and Hiram, the king of Phoenician Tyre, together commissioned a fleet that sailed into the Red Sea and brought back gold, ivory, jewels, sandalwood, and exotic animals. The story of the visit to Solomon by the queen of Sheba, who brought gold, precious stones, and spices, may be mythical, but it reflects the reality of trade with Saba° in south Arabia (present-day Yemen) or the Horn of Africa (present-day Somalia). Such wealth supported a lavish court life, a sizeable bureaucracy, and an intimidating chariot army that made Israel a regional power. Solomon undertook an ambitious building program employing slaves and the compulsory labor of citizens. To strengthen the link between religious and secular authority, he built the **First Temple** in Jerusalem. The Israelites now had a central shrine and an impressive set of rituals that could compete with other religions in the area.

The Temple priests became a powerful and wealthy class, receiving a share of the annual harvest in return for making animal sacrifices to Yahweh on behalf of the community. The expansion of Jerusalem, new commercial opportunities, and the increasing prestige of the Temple hierarchy changed the social composition of Israelite society. A gap between urban and rural, rich and poor, polarized a people that previously had been relatively homogeneous. Fiery prophets, claiming revelation from Yahweh, accused the monarchs and aristocracy of corruption, impiety, and neglect of the poor (see Diversity and Dominance: An Israelite Prophet Chastizes the Ruling Class).

The Israelites lived in extended families, several generations residing together under the authority of the eldest male. Marriage, usually arranged between families, was an important economic as well as social institution. When the groom, in order to prove his financial worthiness, gave a substantial gift to the father of the bride, her entire family participated in the ceremonial weighing out of silver or gold. The wife's dowry often included a slave girl who attended her for life.

Shiloh (SHIE-loe)

Saba (SUH-buh)

Artist's Rendering of Solomon's Jerusalem Strategically located in the middle of lands occupied by the Israelite tribes and on a high plateau overlooking the central hills and the Judaean desert, Jerusalem was captured around 1000 B.C.E. by King David, who made it his capital (the City of David is at left, the citadel and palace complex at center). The next king, Solomon, built the First Temple to serve as the center of worship of the Israelite god, Yahweh. Solomon's Temple (at upper right) was destroyed during the Neo-Babylonian sack of the city in 587 B.C.E. The modest structure soon built to take its place was replaced by the magnificent Second Temple, erected by King Herod in the last decades of the first century B.C.E. and destroyed by the Romans in 70 C.E. (Ritmeyer Archaeological Design, London)

Male heirs were of paramount importance, and first-born sons received a double share of the inheritance. If a couple had no son, they could adopt one, or the husband could have a child by the wife's slave attendant. If a man died childless, his brother was expected to marry his widow and sire an heir.

In early Israel women provided a vital portion of the goods and services that sustained the family. As a result, women were respected and enjoyed relative equality with their husbands. Unlike men, however, they could not inherit property or initiate divorce, and a woman caught in extramarital relations could be put to death. Working-class women labored with other family members in agriculture or herding in addition to caring for the house and children. As the society became urbanized, some women worked outside the home as cooks, bakers, perfumers, wet nurses (usually a recent mother, still producing milk, hired to provide nourishment to another person's child), prostitutes, and singers of laments at funerals. A few women reached positions of influence, such as Deborah the Judge, who led troops in battle against the Canaanites. Women known collectively as "wise women" appear to have composed sacred texts in poetry and prose. This reality has been obscured, in part by the male bias of the Hebrew Bible, in part because the status of women declined as Israelite society became more urbanized.

Fragmentation and Dispersal

After Solomon's death around 920 B.C.E., resentment over royal demands and the neglect of tribal prerogatives split the monarchy into two kingdoms: Israel in the north, with its capital at Samaria°; and Judah° in the southern territory

Samaria (suh-MAH-ree-yuh) **Judah** (JOO-duh)

DIVERSITY AND DOMINANCE

AN ISRAELITE PROPHET CHASTIZES THE RULING CLASS

Israelite society underwent profound changes in the period of the monarchy. A loosely organized society of village-based farmers and herders was transformed relatively rapidly into a centrally controlled state with urban centers, a standing army, an administrative bureaucracy supported by taxation, and involvement in long-distance trade networks. A central religious shrine emerged, with a hierarchy of priests and other religious specialists maintained at public expense. The new opportunities for some to acquire considerable wealth led to greater disparities between rich and poor.

Throughout this period a series of prophets publicly challenged the behavior of the Israelite ruling elite. They denounced the changes in Israelite society as corrupting people and separating them from the religious devotion and moral rectitude of an earlier, better time. The prophets often spoke out on behalf of the uneducated, inarticulate, illiterate, and powerless lower classes, and thus provide valuable information about the experiences of different social groups. Theirs was not objective reporting, but rather the angry, anguished visions of unconventional individuals.

The following excerpts from the Hebrew Bible are taken from the book of Amos. A herdsman from the southern kingdom of Judah (in the era of the divided monarchy), Amos was active in the northern kingdom of Israel in the mid-eighth century B.C.E., when Assyria threatened the Syria-Palestine region.

1:1 The following is a record of what Amos prophesied. He was one of the herdsmen from Tekoa. These prophecies about Israel were revealed to him during the time of King Uzziah of Judah and King Jeroboam son of Joash of Israel, two years before the earthquake. . . .

3:1 Listen, you Israelites, to this message which the Lord is proclaiming against you. This message is for the entire clan I brought up from the land of Egypt:
3:2 "I have chosen you alone from all the clans of the earth. Therefore I will punish you for all your sins" . . .
3:9 Make this announcement in the fortresses of Ashdod and in the fortresses in the land of Egypt. Say this: "Gather on the hills around Samaria! [capital of the northern kingdom]

Observe the many acts of violence taking place within the city, the oppressive deeds occurring in it."
3:10 "They do not know how to do what is right. They store up the spoils of destructive violence in their fortresses."
3:11 "Therefore," says the sovereign Lord, "an enemy will encircle the land. Your power, Samaria, will be taken away; your fortresses will be looted."
3:12 This is what the Lord says: "Just as a shepherd salvages from the lion's mouth a couple of leg bones or a piece of an ear, so the Israelites who live in Samaria will be salvaged. They will be left with just a corner of a bed, and a part of a couch" . . .
3:14 "Certainly when I punish Israel for their treaty violations, I will destroy Bethel's altars. The horns of the altars will be cut off and fall to the ground.
3:15 I will destroy both the winter and summer houses. The houses filled with ivory will be ruined, the great houses will be swept away." The Lord is speaking!
4:1 Listen to this message, you "cows of Bashan" who live on Mount Samaria! You oppress the poor; you crush the needy. You say to your husbands, "Bring us more to drink so we can party!"
4:2 The sovereign Lord confirms this oath by his own holy character: "Certainly the time is approaching! You will be carried away in baskets, every last one of you in fishermen's pots.
4:3 Each of you will go straight through the gaps in the walls; you will be thrown out toward Harmon" . . .

5:10 The Israelites hate anyone who arbitrates at the city gate; they despise anyone who speaks honestly.
5:11 Therefore, because you make the poor pay taxes on their crops and exact a grain tax from them, you will not live in the houses you built with chiseled stone, nor will you drink the wine from the fine vineyards you planted.
5:12 Certainly I am aware of your many rebellious acts and your numerous sins. You torment the innocent, you take bribes, and you deny justice to the needy at the city gate.
5:13 For this reason whoever is smart keeps quiet in such a time, for it is an evil time.

5:15 Hate what is wrong, love what is right! Promote justice at the city gate! Maybe the Lord, the God who leads armies, will have mercy on those who are left from Joseph [the Israelites] . . .

5:21 "I absolutely despise your festivals. I get no pleasure from your religious assemblies.

5:22 Even if you offer me burnt and grain offerings, I will not be satisfied; I will not look with favor on the fattened calves you offer in peace.

5:23 Take away from me your noisy songs; I don't want to hear the music of your stringed instruments.

5:24 Justice must flow like water, right actions like a stream that never dries up . . ."

6:3 You refuse to believe a day of disaster will come, but you establish a reign of violence.

6:4 They lie around on beds decorated with ivory, and sprawl out on their couches. They eat lambs from the flock, and calves from the middle of the pen.

6:5 They sing to the tune of stringed instruments; like David they invent musical instruments.

6:6 They drink wine from sacrificial bowls, and pour the very best oils on themselves.

6:7 Therefore they will now be the first to go into exile, and the religious banquets where they sprawl out on couches will end.

7:10 Amaziah the priest of Bethel sent this message to King Jeroboam of Israel: "Amos is conspiring against you in the very heart of the kingdom of Israel! The land cannot endure all his prophecies.

7:11 As a matter of fact, Amos is saying this: 'Jeroboam will die by the sword and Israel will certainly be carried into exile away from its land.'"

7:12 Amaziah then said to Amos, "Leave, you visionary! Run away to the land of Judah! Earn money and prophesy there!

7:13 Don't prophesy at Bethel any longer, for a royal temple and palace are here!"

7:14 Amos replied to Amaziah, "I was not a prophet by profession. No, I was a herdsman who also took care of sycamore fig trees.

7:15 Then the Lord took me from tending flocks and gave me this commission, 'Go! Prophesy to my people Israel!'

7:16 So now listen to the Lord's message! You say, 'Don't prophesy against Israel! Don't preach against the family of Isaac!'

7:17 "Therefore this is what the Lord says: 'Your wife will become a prostitute in the streets and your sons and daughters will die violently. Your land will be given to others and you will die in a foreign land. Israel will certainly be carried into exile away from its land.'"

8:4 Listen to this, you who trample the needy, and get rid of the destitute in the land.

8:5 You say, "When will the new moon festival be over, so we can sell grain? When will the Sabbath end, so we can open up the grain bins? We're eager to sell less for a higher price, and to cheat the buyer with rigged scales.

8:6 We're eager to trade silver for the poor, a pair of sandals for the needy. We want to mix in some chaff with the grain."

8:7 The Lord confirms this oath by the arrogance of Jacob: "I swear I will never forget all you have done!

8:8 Because of this the earth will quake, and all who live in it will mourn. The whole earth will rise like the River Nile, it will surge upward and then grow calm, like the Nile in Egypt.

8:9 In that day," says the sovereign Lord, "I will make the sun set at noon, and make the earth dark in the middle of the day.

8:10 I will turn your festivals into funerals, and all your songs into funeral dirges. I will make everyone wear funeral clothes and cause every head to be shaved bald. I will make you mourn as if you had lost your only son; when it ends it will indeed have been a bitter day.

8:11 Be certain of this, the time is coming," says the sovereign Lord, "when I will send a famine through the land. I'm not talking about a shortage of food or water, but an end to divine revelation.

8:12 People will stagger from sea to sea, and from the north around to the east. They will wander around looking for a revelation from the Lord, but they will not find any . . ."

9:8 "Look, the sovereign Lord is watching the sinful nation, and I will destroy it from the face of the earth. But I will not completely destroy the family of Jacob," says the Lord.

9:9 "For look, I am giving a command and I will shake the family of Israel together with all the nations. It will resemble a sieve being shaken, when not even a pebble falls to the ground.

9:10 All the sinners among my people will die by the sword, the ones who say, 'Disaster will not come near, it will not confront us.'

9:11 In that day I will rebuild the collapsing hut of David. I will seal its gaps, repair its ruins, and restore it to what it was like in days gone by."

QUESTIONS FOR ANALYSIS

1. For whom is Amos's message primarily intended? How does the ruling class react to Amos's prophetic activity, and how does he respond to their tactics?

2. What does Amos see as wrong in Israelite society, and who is at fault? Why are even the religious practices of the elite criticized?

3. What will be the means by which God punishes Israel, and why does God punish them this way? What grounds for hope remain?

Source: http://www.netbible.com. Reprinted courtesy of Biblical Studies Press, L.L.C.

around Jerusalem (see Map 3.4). The two were sometimes at war, sometimes allied. This period saw the final formulation of **monotheism,** the absolute belief in Yahweh as the one and only god.

The small states of Syria and the two Israelite kingdoms laid aside their rivalries to mount a joint resistance to the Neo-Assyrian Empire, but to no avail. In 721 B.C.E. the Assyrians destroyed the northern kingdom of Israel and deported much of its population to the east. New settlers were brought in from Syria, Babylon, and Iran, changing the area's ethnic, cultural, and religious character and removing it from the mainstream of Jewish history. The kingdom of Judah survived for more than a century longer, sometimes rebelling, sometimes paying tribute to the Assyrians or the Neo-Babylonian kingdom (626–539 B.C.E.) that succeeded them. When the Neo-Babylonian monarch Nebuchadnezzar° captured Jerusalem in 587 B.C.E., he destroyed the Temple and deported to Babylon the royal family, the aristocracy, and many skilled workers such as blacksmiths and scribes.

The deportees prospered so well in their new home "by the waters of Babylon" that half a century later most of their descendants refused the offer of the Persian monarch Cyrus (see Chapter 4) to return to their homeland. This was the origin of the **Diaspora°**—a Greek word meaning "dispersion" or "scattering." This dispersion outside the homeland of many Jews—as we may now call these people, since an independent Israel no longer existed—continues to this day. To maintain their religion and culture outside the homeland, the Diaspora communities developed institutions like the synagogue (Greek for "bringing together"), a communal meeting place that served religious, educational, and social functions.

Several groups of Babylonian Jews did make the long trek back to Judah, where they met with a cold reception from the local population. Persevering, they rebuilt the Temple in modest form and drafted the Deuteronomic° Code (*deuteronomic* is Greek for "second set of laws") of law and conduct. The fifth century B.C.E. also saw the compilation of much of the Hebrew Bible in roughly its present form.

The loss of political autonomy and the experience of exile had sharpened Jewish identity, with an unyielding monotheism as the core belief. Jews lived by a rigid set of rules. Dietary restrictions forbade the eating of pork and

shellfish and mandated that meat and dairy products not be consumed together. Ritual baths were used to achieve spiritual purity, and women were required to take ritual baths after menstruation. The Jews venerated the Sabbath (Saturday, the seventh day of the week) by refraining from work and from fighting, following the example of Yahweh, who, according to the Bible, rested on the seventh day after creating the world (this is the origin of the concept of the weekend). These strictures and others, including a ban on marrying non-Jews, tended to isolate the Jews from other peoples, but they also fostered a powerful sense of community and the belief that they were protected by a watchful and beneficent deity.

PHOENICIA AND THE MEDITERRANEAN, 1200–500 B.C.E.

While the Israelite tribes were being forged into a united kingdom, the people who occupied the coast of the Mediterranean to the north were developing their own distinctive civilization. Historians refer to a major element of the ancient population of Syria-Palestine as **Phoenicians°,** though they referred to themselves as "Can'ani"—Canaanites. Despite the sparse written record and the disturbance of the archaeological record by frequent migrations and invasions, enough of their history survives to reveal major transformations.

The Phoenician City-States

When the eastern Mediterranean entered a period of violent upheaval and mass migrations around 1200 B.C.E. (discussed earlier), many Canaanite settlements were destroyed. Aramaeans°—nomadic pastoralists similar to the early Israelites—migrated into the interior portions of Syria.

By 1100 B.C.E. Canaanite territory had shrunk to a narrow strip of present-day Lebanon between the mountains and the sea (see Map 3.4). The inhabitants of this densely populated area adopted new political forms and turned to seaborne commerce and new kinds of manufacture for their survival. Sometime after 1000 B.C.E. the Canaanites encountered the Greeks, who referred to them as *Phoinikes,* or Phoenicians. The term may mean "red men" and refer to the color of their skin, or it may re-

---

Nebuchadnezzar (NAB-oo-kuhd-nez-uhr)
Diaspora (die-ASS-peh-rah)
Deuteronomic (doo-tuhr-uh-NAHM-ik)

Phoenician (fi-NEE-shun)   **Aramaean** (ah-ruh-MAY-uhn)

fer to the highly valued purple dye they extracted from the murex snail (see Environment and Technology: Ancient Textiles and Dyes).

Rivers and rocky spurs of Mount Lebanon sliced the coastal plain into a series of small city-states, chief among them Byblos°, Berytus°, Sidon°, and Tyre. A thriving trade in raw materials (cedar and pine, metals, incense, papyrus), foodstuffs (wine, spices, salted fish), and crafted luxury goods (textiles, carved ivory, glass) brought considerable wealth to the Phoenician city-states and gave them an important role in international politics.

The Phoenicians developed earlier Canaanite models into an "alphabetic" system of writing with about two dozen symbols, in which each symbol represented a sound. (The Phoenicians represented only consonants, leaving the vowel sounds to be inferred by the reader. The Greeks added symbols for vowel sounds, thereby creating the first truly alphabetic system of writing—see Chapter 4.) Little Phoenician writing survives, however, probably because scribes used perishable papyrus. Some information in Greek and Roman documents may be based on Phoenician sources.

Before 1000 B.C.E. Byblos had been the most important Phoenician city-state. It was a distribution center for cedar timber from the slopes of Mount Lebanon and for papyrus from Egypt. The English word *bible* comes from the Greek *biblion*, meaning "book written on papyrus from Byblos." After 1000 B.C.E. Tyre, in southern Lebanon, surpassed Byblos. King Hiram, who came to power in 969 B.C.E., was responsible for Tyre's rise to prominence. According to the Bible, he formed a close alliance with the Israelite king Solomon and provided skilled Phoenician craftsmen and cedar wood for building the Temple in Jerusalem. In return, Tyre gained access to silver, food, and trade routes to the east and south. In the 800s B.C.E. Tyre took control of nearby Sidon and monopolized the Mediterranean coastal trade.

Located on an offshore island, Tyre was practically impregnable. It had two harbors, one facing north, the other south, connected by a canal. The city boasted a large marketplace, a magnificent palace complex with treasury and archives, and temples to the gods. Some of its thirty thousand or more inhabitants lived in suburbs on the mainland. Its one weakness was its dependence on the mainland for food and fresh water.

Little is known about the internal affairs of Tyre and other Phoenician cities. The names of a series of kings are preserved, and the scant evidence suggests that the political arena was dominated by leading merchant families.

Between the ninth and seventh centuries B.C.E. the Phoenician city-states contended with Assyrian aggression, followed in the sixth century B.C.E. by the expansion of the Neo-Babylonian kingdom and later the Persian Empire (see Chapter 4).

Expansion into the Mediterranean

After 900 B.C.E. Tyre began to turn its attention westward, establishing colonies on Cyprus, a copper-rich island 100 miles (161 kilometers) from the Syrian coast (see Map 3.4) that was strategically located on a major trade route. Phoenician merchants sailing into the Aegean Sea are mentioned in Homer's *Iliad* and *Odyssey* around 700 B.C.E. By that time a string of settlements in the western Mediterranean formed a "Phoenician triangle" composed of the North African coast from western Libya to Morocco; the south and southeast coast of Spain, including Gades° (modern Cadiz°) on the Strait of Gibraltar, controlling passage between the Mediterranean and the Atlantic Ocean; and the islands of Sardinia, Sicily, and Malta off the coast of Italy (see Map 3.5). Many of these new settlements were situated on promontories or offshore islands in imitation of Tyre. The Phoenician trading network spanned the entire Mediterranean.

Overseas settlement provided an outlet for excess population, new sources of trade goods, and new trading partners. Tyre maintained its autonomy until 701 B.C.E. by paying tribute to the Assyrian kings. In that year it finally fell to an Assyrian army that stripped it of much of its territory and population, allowing Sidon to become the leading city in Phoenicia.

The Phoenicians' activities in the western Mediterranean often brought them into conflict with the Greeks, who were also expanding trade and establishing colonies. The focal point of this rivalry was Sicily. Phoenicians occupied the western end of the island, Greeks its eastern and central parts. For centuries Greeks and Phoenicians fought for control of Sicily in some of the most savage wars in the history of the ancient Mediterranean. The Phoenicians controlled all of Sicily by the mid-third century B.C.E.

Carthage's Commercial Empire

Historians know far more about **Carthage** and the other Phoenician colonies than they do about the Phoenician homeland. Much of this knowledge

---

Byblos (BIB-loss)   **Berytus** (buh-RIE-tuhs)   **Sidon** (SIE-duhn)

Gades (GAH-days)   **Cadiz** (kuh-DEEZ)

Ancient Textiles and Dyes

Throughout human history the production of textiles—cloth for clothing, blankets, carpets, and coverings of various sorts—may have required an expenditure of human labor second only to the amount of work necessary to provide food. Nevertheless, textile production in antiquity has left few traces in the archaeological record. The plant fibers and animal hair used for cloth are organic and quickly decompose except in rare and special circumstances. Some textile remains have been found in the hot, dry conditions of Egypt, the cool, arid Andes of South America, and the peat bogs of northern Europe. But most of our knowledge of ancient textiles depends on the discovery of equipment used in textile production—such as spindles, loom weights, and dyeing vats—and on pictorial representations and descriptions in texts.

The production of cloth usually has been the work of women for a simple but important reason. Responsibility for child rearing limits women's ability to participate in other activities but does not consume all their time and energy. In many societies textile production has been complementary to child-rearing activities, for it can be done in the home, is relatively safe, does not require great concentration, and can be interrupted without consequence. For many thousands of years cloth production has been one of the great common experiences of women around the globe. The growing and harvesting of plants such as cotton or flax (from which linen is made) and the shearing of wool from sheep and, in the Andes, llamas are outdoor activities, but the subsequent stages of production can be carried out inside the home. The basic methods of textile production did not change much from early antiquity until the late eighteenth century C.E., when the fabrication of textiles was transferred to mills and mass production began.

When textile production has been considered "women's work," most of the output has been for household consumption. One exception was in the early civilizations of Peru,

Ancient Peruvian Textiles The weaving of Chavín was famous for its color and symbolic imagery. Artisans both wove designs into the fabric and used paint or dyes to decorate plain fabric. This early Chavín painted fabric was used in a burial. Notice how the face suggests a jaguar and the headdress includes the image of a serpent. (Private collection)

where women weavers developed new raw materials, new techniques, and new decorative motifs around three thousand years ago. They began to use the wool of llamas and alpacas in addition to cotton. Three women worked side by side and passed the weft from hand to hand in order to overcome limitations to the width of woven fabric imposed by the back-strap loom. Women weavers also introduced embroidery, and they decorated garments with new religious motifs, such as the jaguar-god of Chavín. Their high-quality textiles were given as tribute to the elite and were used in trade to acquire luxury goods as well as dyes and metals.

More typically, men dominated commercial production. In ancient Phoenicia, fine textiles with bright, permanent colors became a major export product. These striking colors were produced by dyes derived from several species of snail. Most prized was the red-purple known as Tyrian purple because Tyre was the major source. Persian and Hellenistic kings wore robes dyed this color, and a white toga with a purple border was the sign of a Roman senator.

The production of Tyrian purple was an exceedingly laborious process. The spiny dye-murex snail lives on the sandy Mediterranean bottom at depths ranging from 30 to 500 feet (10 to 150 meters). Nine thousand snails were needed to produce 1 gram (0.035 ounce) of dye. The dye was made from a colorless liquid in the snail's hypobranchial gland. The gland sacs were removed, crushed, soaked with salt, and exposed to sunlight and air for some days; then they were subject to controlled boiling and heating.

Huge mounds of broken shells on the Phoenician coast are testimony to the ancient industry. It is likely that the snail was rendered nearly extinct at many locations, and some scholars have speculated that Phoenician colonization in the Mediterranean may have been motivated in part by the search for new sources of snails.

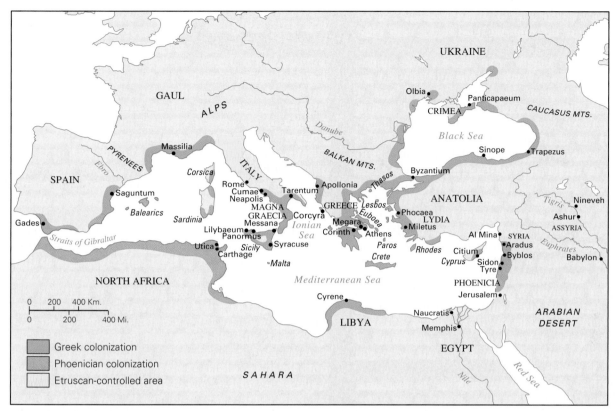

Map 3.5   Colonization of the Mediterranean   In the ninth century B.C.E., the Phoenicians of Lebanon began to explore and colonize parts of the western Mediterranean, including the coast of North Africa, southern and eastern Spain, and the islands of Sicily and Sardinia. The Phoenicians were primarily interested in access to valuable raw materials and trading opportunities.

comes from Greek and Roman reports of their wars with the western Phoenician communities. For example, the account of the origins of Carthage that begins this chapter comes from Roman sources (most famously Virgil's epic poem *The Aeneid*) but probably is based on a Carthaginian original. Archaeological excavation has roughly confirmed the city's traditional foundation date of 814 B.C.E. Just outside the present-day city of Tunis in Tunisia, Carthage controlled the middle portion of the Mediterranean where Europe comes closest to Africa. The new settlement grew rapidly and soon dominated other Phoenician colonies in the west.

Located on a narrow promontory jutting into the Mediterranean, Carthage stretched between Byrsa°, the original hilltop citadel of the community, and a double harbor. The inner harbor could accommodate up to 220 warships. A watchtower allowed surveillance of the sur-

rounding area, and high walls made it impossible to see in from the outside. The outer commercial harbor was filled with docks for merchant ships and shipyards. In case of attack, the harbor could be closed off by a huge iron chain.

Government offices ringed a large central square where magistrates heard legal cases outdoors. The inner city was a maze of narrow, winding streets, multistory apartment buildings, and sacred enclosures. Farther out was a sprawling suburban district where the wealthy built spacious villas amid fields and vegetable gardens. This entire urban complex was enclosed by a wall 22 miles (35 kilometers) in length.

With a population of roughly 400,000, Carthage was one of the largest cities in the world by 500 B.C.E. The population was ethnically diverse, including people of Phoenician stock, indigenous peoples likely to have been the ancestors of modern-day Berbers, and immigrants from other Mediterranean lands and sub-Saharan

---

Byrsa (BURR-suh)

Africa. Contrary to the story of Dido's reluctance to remarry, Phoenicians intermarried quite readily with other peoples.

Each year two "judges" were elected from upper-class families to serve as heads of state and carry out administrative and judicial functions. The real seat of power was the Senate, where members of the leading merchant families, who sat for life, formulated policy and directed the affairs of the state. An inner circle of thirty or so senators made the crucial decisions. From time to time the leadership convened an Assembly of the citizens to elect public officials or vote on important issues, particularly when the leaders were divided or wanted to stir up popular enthusiasm for some venture.

Carthaginian power rested on its navy, which dominated the western Mediterranean for centuries. Phoenician towns provided a chain of friendly ports. The Carthaginian fleet consisted of fast, maneuverable galleys—oared warships. A galley had a sturdy, pointed ram in front that could pierce the hull of an enemy vessel below the water line, while marines (soldiers aboard a ship) fired weapons. Innovations in the placement of benches and oars made room for 30, 50, and eventually as many as 170 rowers.

Carthaginian foreign policy reflected its economic interests. Protection of the sea lanes, access to raw materials, and fostering trade mattered most to the dominant merchant class. Indeed, Carthage claimed the waters of the western Mediterranean as its own. Foreign merchants were free to sail to Carthage to market their goods, but if they tried to operate on their own, they risked having their ships sunk by the Carthaginian navy. Treaties between Carthage and other states included formal recognition of this maritime commercial monopoly.

The archaeological record provides few clues about the commodities traded by the Carthaginians. Commerce may have included perishable goods—foodstuffs, textiles, animal skins, slaves—and raw metals such as silver, lead, iron, and tin, whose Carthaginian origin would not be evident. We know that Carthaginian ships carried goods manufactured elsewhere and that products brought to Carthage by foreign traders were reexported.

There is also evidence for trade with sub-Saharan Africa. Hanno°, a Carthaginian captain of the fifth century B.C.E., claimed to have sailed through the Strait of Gibraltar into the Atlantic Ocean and to have explored the West African coast (see Map 3.5). Other Carthaginians explored the Atlantic coast of Spain and France and secured control of an important source of tin in the "Tin Islands," probably Cornwall in southwestern England.

War and Religion

Unlike Assyria, Carthage did not directly rule a large amount of territory. A belt of fertile land in northeastern Tunisia, worked by native peasants and imported slaves, provided a secure food supply. Beyond this core area the Carthaginians ruled most of their "empire" indirectly, and allowed other Phoenician communities in the western Mediterranean to remain independent. These Phoenician communities looked to Carthage for military protection and followed its lead in foreign policy. Only Sardinia and southern Spain were put under the direct control of a Carthaginian governor and garrison, presumably to safeguard their agricultural, metal, and manpower resources.

Carthage's focus on trade may explain the unusual fact that citizens were not required to serve in the army: they were of more value in other capacities, such as trading activities and the navy. Since the indigenous North African population was not politically or militarily well organized, Carthage had little to fear from potential enemies close to home. When Carthage was drawn into a series of wars with the Greeks and Romans from the fifth through third centuries B.C.E., it relied on mercenaries from the most warlike peoples in its dominions or from neighboring areas—Numidians from North Africa, Iberians from Spain, Gauls from France, and various Italian peoples. These well-paid mercenaries were under the command of Carthaginian officers.

Carthaginian religion fascinated Greek and Roman writers. Like the deities of Mesopotamia (see Chapter 1), the gods of the Carthaginians—chief among them Baal Hammon°, a male storm-god, and Tanit°, a female fertility figure—were powerful and capricious entities who had to be appeased by anxious worshipers. Roman sources report that members of the Carthaginian elite would sacrifice their own male children in times of crisis. Excavations at Carthage and other western Phoenician towns have turned up *tophets*°—walled enclosures where thousands of small, sealed urns containing the burned bones of children lay buried. Although some scholars argue that these were infants born prematurely or taken by childhood illnesses, most maintain that the western Phoenicians practiced child sacrifice on a more or less regular basis. Originally practiced by the upper classes, child sacrifice seems to have become more common and to have involved broader elements of the population after 400 B.C.E.

Hanno (HA-noe)

Baal Hammon (BAHL ha-MOHN)   Tanit (TAH-nit)
tophet (TOE-fet)

The Tophet of Carthage   Here, from the seventh to second centuries B.C.E., the cremated bodies of sacrificed children were buried. Archaeological excavation has confirmed the claim in ancient sources that the Carthaginians sacrificed children to their gods at times of crisis. Stone markers, decorated with magical signs and symbols of divinities as well as family names, were placed over ceramic urns containing the ashes and charred bones of one or more infants or, occasionally, older children.   (Martha Cooper/Peter Arnold, Inc.)

FAILURE AND TRANSFORMATION, 750–550 B.C.E.

The extension of Assyrian power over the entire Middle East had enormous consequences for all the peoples of this region and caused the stories of Mesopotamia, Israel, and Phoenicia to converge.

By 650 B.C.E. Assyria stood unchallenged in western Asia. But the arms race with Urartu, the frequent expensive campaigns, and the protection of lengthy borders had sapped Assyrian resources. Assyrian brutality and exploitation aroused the hatred of conquered peoples. At the same time, changes in the ethnic composition of the army and the population of the homeland had reduced popular support for the Assyrian state.

Two new political entities spearheaded resistance to Assyria. First, Babylonia had been revived by the Neo-Babylonian, or Chaldaean°, dynasty (the Chaldaeans had infiltrated southern Mesopotamia around 1000 B.C.E.). Second, the Medes°, an Iranian people, were extending their kingdom eastward across the Iranian Plateau in the seventh century B.C.E. The two powers launched a series of attacks on the Assyrian homeland that destroyed the chief cities by 612 B.C.E.

The rapidity of the Assyrian fall is stunning. The destruction systematically carried out by the victorious attackers led to the depopulation of northern Mesopotamia. Two centuries later, when a corps of Greek mercenaries passed by mounds that concealed the ruins of the Assyrian capitals, the Athenian chronicler Xenophon° had no inkling that their empire had ever existed.

The Medes took over the Assyrian homeland and the northern steppe as far as eastern Anatolia, but most of the territory of the old empire fell to the **Neo-Babylonian kingdom** (626–539 B.C.E.), thanks to the energetic campaigns of kings Nabopolassar° (r. 625–605 B.C.E.) and

Chaldaean (chal-DEE-uhn)

Mede (MEED)   **Xenophon** (ZEN-uh-fahn)
Nabopolassar (NAB-oh-poe-lass-uhr)

Nebuchadnezzar (r. 604–562 B.C.E.). Babylonia underwent a cultural renaissance. The city of Babylon was enlarged and adorned, becoming the greatest metropolis of the world in the sixth century B.C.E. Old cults were revived, temples rebuilt, festivals resurrected. The related pursuits of mathematics, astronomy, and astrology reached new heights.

CONCLUSION

This chapter traces developments in the Middle East and the Mediterranean from 2000 to 500 B.C.E. The patterns of culture that originated in the river-valley civilizations of Egypt and Mesopotamia persisted into this era. Peoples such as the Amorites, Kassites, and Chaldaeans, who migrated into the Tigris-Euphrates plain, were largely assimilated into the Sumerian-Semitic cultural tradition, adopting the language, religious beliefs, political and social institutions, and forms of artistic expression. Similarly, the Hyksos, who migrated into the Nile Delta and controlled much of Egypt for a time, adopted the ancient ways of Egypt. When the founders of the New Kingdom finally ended Hyksos domination, they reinstituted the united monarchy and the religious and cultural traditions of earlier eras.

Yet the Middle East was in many important respects a different place after 2000 B.C.E. New centers of political and economic power had emerged—the Elamites in southwest Iran, the Assyrians in northern Mesopotamia, Urartu in present-day Armenia, the Hittites of Anatolia, and the Minoan and Mycenaean peoples of the Aegean Sea. These new centers often borrowed heavily from the technologies and cultural practices of Mesopotamia and Egypt, creating dynamic syntheses of imported and indigenous elements. The entire Middle East was drawn together by networks of trade and diplomacy, a situation that provided general stability and raised the standard of living for many. Ultimately, though, the very interdependence of these societies made them vulnerable to the destructions and disorder of the decades around 1200 B.C.E. The entire region slipped into a "Dark Age" of isolation, stagnation, and decline that lasted several centuries.

The early centuries after 1000 B.C.E. saw a resurgence of political organization and international commerce, and the spread of technologies and ideas. The Neo-Assyrian Empire, the great power of the time, represented a continuation of the Mesopotamian tradition, though the center of empire moved to the north. Israel and Phoenicia, on the other hand, reflected the influence of Mesopotamia and Egypt but also evolved distinctive cultural traditions.

Throughout this era people were on the move, sometimes voluntarily and sometimes under compulsion. The Assyrians deported large numbers of prisoners of war from outlying subject territories to the core area in northern Mesopotamia. The Phoenicians left their overpopulated homeland to establish new settlements in North Africa, Spain, and islands off the coast of Italy. In their new homes the Phoenician colonists tried to duplicate familiar ways of life from the old country. In contrast, the Israelites who settled in Canaan and, at a later time, emigrated to the Diaspora underwent significant political, social, and cultural transformations as they adapted to new zones of settlement.

■ Key Terms

Iron Age	mass deportation
Hittites	Library of Ashurbanipal
Hatshepsut	Israel
Akhenaten	Hebrew Bible
Ramesses II	First Temple
Minoan	monotheism
Mycenae	Diaspora
shaft graves	Phoenicians
Linear B	Carthage
Neo-Assyrian Empire	Neo-Babylonian kingdom

■ Suggested Reading

Fundamental for all periods in the ancient Middle East is Jack M. Sasson, ed., *Civilizations of the Ancient Near East*, 4 vols. (1995), containing nearly two hundred articles by contemporary experts and bibliography on a wide range of topics. John Boardman, I. E. S. Edwards, N. G. L. Hammond, and E. Sollberger, *The Cambridge Ancient History*, 2d ed., vols. 3.1–3.3 (1982–1991), provides extremely detailed historical coverage of the entire Mediterranean and western Asia. Barbara Lesko, ed., *Women's Earliest Records: From Ancient Egypt and Western Asia* (1989), is a collection of papers on the experiences of women in the ancient Middle East.

Many of the books recommended in the Suggested Reading list for Chapter 1 are useful for Mesopotamia, Syria, and Egypt in the Late Bronze Age. In addition, see Miriam Lichtheim, *Ancient Egyptian Literature: A Book of Readings*, vol. 2, *The New Kingdom* (1978); Donald B. Redford, *Egypt, Canaan, and Israel in Ancient Times* (1992), which explores the relations of Egypt with the Syria-Palestine region in this period; Erik Hornung, *Akhenaten and the Religion of Light* (1999), which, while focusing on the religious innovations, deals with many facets of the reign of Akhenaten; Karol Mysliwiec, *The Twilight of Ancient Egypt: First Millennium B.C.E.* (2000), which traces the story of Egyptian civilization after the New Kingdom; and H. W. F. Saggs, *Babylonians* (1995), which devotes several chapters to this more thinly documented epoch in the history of southern

Mesopotamia. The most up-to-date treatment of the Hittites can be found in Trevor Boyce, *The Kingdom of the Hittites* (1998) and *Life and Society in the Hittite World* (2002). Also useful are O. R. Gurney, *The Hittites*, 2d ed., rev. (1990), and J. G. Macqueen, *The Hittites and Their Contemporaries in Asia Minor* (1975).

R. A. Higgins, *The Archaeology of Minoan Crete* (1973) and *Minoan and Mycenaean Art*, new rev. ed. (1997); Rodney Castleden, *Minoans: Life in Bronze Age Crete* (1990); J. Walter Graham, *The Palaces of Crete* (1987); O. Krzyszkowska and L. Nixon, *Minoan Society* (1983); and N. Marinatos, *Minoan Religion* (1993), examine the archaeological evidence for the Minoan civilization. The brief discussion of M. I. Finley, *Early Greece: The Bronze and Archaic Ages* (1970), and the much fuller accounts of Emily Vermeule, *Greece in the Bronze Age* (1972), and J. T. Hooker, *Mycenaean Greece* (1976), are still useful treatments of Mycenaean Greece, based primarily on archaeological evidence. Robert Drews, *The Coming of the Greeks: Indo-European Conquests in the Aegean and the Near East* (1988), examines the evidence for the earliest Greeks. For the Linear B tablets see John Chadwick, *Linear B and Related Scripts* (1987) and *The Mycenaean World* (1976). J. V. Luce, *Homer and the Heroic Age* (1975), and Carol G. Thomas, *Myth Becomes History: Pre-Classical Greece* (1993), examine the usefulness of the Homeric poems for reconstructing the Greek past. For the disruptions and destructions of the Late Bronze Age in the eastern Mediterranean, see N. K. Sandars, *The Sea Peoples: Warriors of the Ancient Mediterranean* (1978), and Trude Dothan and Moshe Dothan, *People of the Sea: The Search for the Philistines* (1992).

For general history and cultural information about the Neo-Assyrian Empire, Mesopotamia, and western Asia in the first half of the first millennium B.C.E. see Michael Roaf, *Cultural Atlas of Mesopotamia and the Ancient Near East* (1990); Amelie Kuhrt, *The Ancient Near East, c. 3000–300 B.C.* (1995); H. W. F. Saggs, *Civilization Before Greece and Rome* (1989); and A. Bernard Knapp, *The History and Culture of Ancient Western Asia and Egypt* (1988). H. W. F. Saggs, *Babylonians* (1995), has coverage of the fate of the old centers in southern Mesopotamia during this era in which the north attained dominance. Primary texts in translation for Assyria and other parts of western Asia can be found in James B. Pritchard, ed., *Ancient Near Eastern Texts Relating to the Old Testament*, 3d ed. (1969). Jeremy Black and Anthony Green, *Gods, Demons and Symbols of Ancient Mesopotamia: An Illustrated Dictionary* (1992), is valuable for religious concepts, institutions, and mythology. Julian Reade, *Assyrian Sculpture* (1983), provides a succinct introduction to the informative relief sculptures from the Assyrian palaces. J. E. Curtis and J. E. Reade, eds., *Art and Empire: Treasures from Assyria in the British Museum* (1995), relates the art to many facets of Assyrian life. Andre Parrot, *The Arts of Assyria* (1961), provides full coverage of all artistic media.

For general historical introductions to ancient Israel see Michael Grant, *The History of Israel* (1984); J. Maxwell Miller and John H. Hayes, *A History of Ancient Israel and Judah* (1986); and J. Alberto Soggin, *A History of Israel: From the Beginnings to the Bar Kochba Revolt, A.D. 135* (1984). Amnon Ben-Tor, *The Archaeology of Ancient Israel* (1991), and Amihai Mazar, *Archaeology of the Land of the Bible, 10,000–586 B.C.E.* (1990), provide overviews of the discoveries of archaeological excavation in Israel. William G. Dever, *What Did the Biblical Writers Know, and When Did They Know It? What Archaeology Can Tell Us About the Reality of Ancient Israel* (2001), and B. J. S. Isserlin, *The Israelites* (2001), both review the archaeological evidence and take moderate positions in the heated debate about the value of the biblical text for reconstructing the history of Israel. Hershel Shanks, *Jerusalem, an Archaeological Biography* (1995), explores the long and colorful history of the city. For social and economic issues see Shunya Bendor, *The Social Structure of Ancient Israel: The Institution of the Family (beit 'ab) from the Settlement to the End of the Monarchy* (1996), and Moses Aberbach, *Labor, Crafts and Commerce in Ancient Israel* (1994). Carol Meyers, *Discovering Eve: Ancient Israelite Women in Context* (1998), carefully sifts through literary and archaeological evidence to reach a balanced assessment of the position of women in the period before the monarchy. Victor H. Matthews, *The Social World of the Hebrew Prophets* (2001), provides social and historical contexts for all the prophets. For the Philistines see Trude Dothan, *The Philistines and Their Material Culture* (1982).

Glenn Markoe, *Phoenicians* (2000), Sabatino Moscati, *The Phoenicians* (1988), and Gerhard Herm, *The Phoenicians: The Purple Empire of the Ancient World* (1975), are general introductions to the Phoenicians in their homeland. Maria Eugenia Aubet, *The Phoenicians and the West: Politics, Colonies and Trade* (2001), is an insightful investigation of the dynamics of Phoenician expansion into the western Mediterranean. Lionel Casson, *The Ancient Mariners: Seafarers and Sea Fighters of the Mediterranean in Ancient Times*, 2d ed. (1991), 75–79, discusses the design of warships and merchant vessels. For Carthage see Serge Lancel, *Carthage: A History* (1995), and David Soren, Aicha Ben Abed Ben Khader, and Hedi Slim, *Carthage: Uncovering the Mysteries and Splendors of Ancient Tunisia* (1990). Aicha Ben Abed Ben Khader and David Soren, *Carthage: A Mosaic of Ancient Tunisia* (1987), includes articles by American and Tunisian scholars as well as the catalog of a museum exhibition. R. C. C. Law, "North Africa in the Period of Phoenician and Greek Colonization, c. 800 to 323 B.C.," Chapter 2 in *The Cambridge History of Africa*, vol. 2 (1978), places the history of Carthage in an African perspective.

Elizabeth Wayland Barber, *Women's Work: The First 20,000 Years: Women, Cloth, and Society in Early Times* (1994), is an intriguing account of textile manufacture in antiquity, with emphasis on the social implications and primary role of women. I. Irving Ziderman, "Seashells and Ancient Purple Dyeing," *Biblical Archaeologist* 53 (June 1990): 98–101, is a convenient summary of Phoenician purple-dyeing technology.

Document-Based Question

The Power of the Ruling Class in Ancient Egypt, Greece, and Israel

Using the following documents, analyze the various ways ruling classes demonstrated power in ancient Egypt, Greece, and Israel.

DOCUMENT 1
The Mortuary Temple of Queen Hatshepsut at Deir el-Bahri, Egypt, ca. 1460 B.C.E (photo, p. 59)

DOCUMENT 2
Colossal Statues of Ramesses II at Abu Simbel (photo, p. 65)

DOCUMENT 3
Fresco from the Aegean Island of Thera, ca. 1600 B.C.E. (photo, p. 68)

DOCUMENT 4
Lion Gate at Mycenae (photo, p. 69)

DOCUMENT 5
Artist's Rendering of Solomon's Jerusalem (photo, p. 77)

DOCUMENT 6
An Israelite Prophet Chastizes the Ruling Class (Diversity and Dominance, pp. 78–79)

What is the tone of Document 6? How does the document's tone help you to determine its point of view? What additional types of documents would help you understand the power of the ruling class in ancient Egypt, Greece, and Israel?

PART TWO

The Formation of New Cultural Communities, 1000 B.C.E.–600 C.E.

The sixteen centuries from 1000 B.C.E. to 600 C.E. mark a new chapter in the story of humanity. Important changes in the ways of life established in the river-valley civilizations in the two previous millennia occurred, and the scale of human institutions and activities increased.

The political and social structure of the earliest river-valley centers reflected the importance of irrigation for agriculture. Powerful kings, hereditary priesthoods, dependent laborers, limited availability of metals, and very restricted literacy are hallmarks of the complex societies described in Part One. In the first millennium B.C.E., new centers arose, in lands watered by rainfall and worked by a free peasantry, on the shores of the Mediterranean, in Iran, India, Southeast Asia, and in Central and South America. Shaped by the natural environments in which they arose, they developed new patterns of political and social organization and economic activity, and moved in new intellectual, artistic, and spiritual directions, though under the influence of the older centers.

The rulers of the empires of this era took steps intended to control and tax their subjects: they constructed extensive networks of roads and promoted urbanization. These measures brought incidental benefits: more rapid communication, the transport of trade goods over greater distances, and the broad diffusion of religious ideas, artistic styles, and technologies. Large cultural zones unified by common traditions emerged. A number of these cultural traditions—Iranian, Hellenistic, Roman—were to exercise substantial influence on subsequent ages. The influence of some—Hindu, Chinese, African, Buddhist—persists into our own time.

The expansion of agriculture and trade and improvements in technology led to population increases, the spread of cities, and the growth of a comfortable middle class. In many parts of the world iron replaced bronze as the preferred metal for weapons, tools, and utensils. People using iron tools cleared extensive forests around the Mediterranean, in India, and in eastern China. Iron weapons gave an advantage to the armies of Greece, Rome, and imperial China. Metal, still an important item of long-distance trade, was available to more people than it had been in the preceding age. Metal coinage, which originated in Anatolia, was adopted by many peoples. Metal coins facilitated commercial transactions and the acquisition of wealth along new trade routes crossing the Indian Ocean and Central and Inner Asia.

New systems of writing also developed. Because these systems were more easily and rapidly learned, writing moved out of the control of specialists. The vast majority of people remained illiterate, but writing became an increasingly important medium for preserving and transmitting cultural knowledge. The spread of literacy gave birth to new ways of thinking, new genres of literature, and new types of scientific endeavor.

ARCTIC OCEAN

NORTH AMERICA

NORTH ATLANTIC OCEAN

Mesoamerica

PACIFIC OCEAN

Peru

SOUTH AMERICA

	1000 B.C.E.	700 B.C.E.	400 B.C.E.
Americas	1200–400 Olmec civilization in Mesoamerica		• 500 Gold metallurgy in Chavín
	900–250 Chavín civilization in Peru		
Europe	• 1000 Iron metallurgy	• 700 Hoplite warfare	477–404 Athenian empire and democracy
		Roman Republic 507 •	
	800–500 Archaic period in Greece		• 399 Trial and death of Socrates
Africa	Rise of Nubian kingdom at Napata 800 •	712–660 Nubian domination of Egypt	400 B.C.E.–300 C.E. Kingdom of Meroë in Nubia
		Hanno of Carthage explores West African coast 465 •	323–30 Ptolemies rule Hellenistic kingdom in Egypt
	Carthage founded 814 •		500 B.C.E.–1000 C.E. Bantu migrations
Middle East	• 1000 David establishes Jerusalem as capital of Israel	• 701 Assyrian attack on Phoenician Tyre	334–323 Alexander of Macedonia conquers western Asia
			522–486 Darius I rules Persian Empire
	911–612 Neo-Assyrian Empire	• 587 Babylonian conquest of Jerusalem	301–64 Seleucid kingdom in western Asia
Asia and Oceania	1027–221 Zhou kingdom in China		
		Iron metallurgy in China 600 • 551–479 Life of Confucius	
	• 1000 Aryans settle Ganges Plain	563–483 Life of the Buddha	324–184 Mauryan Empire in India

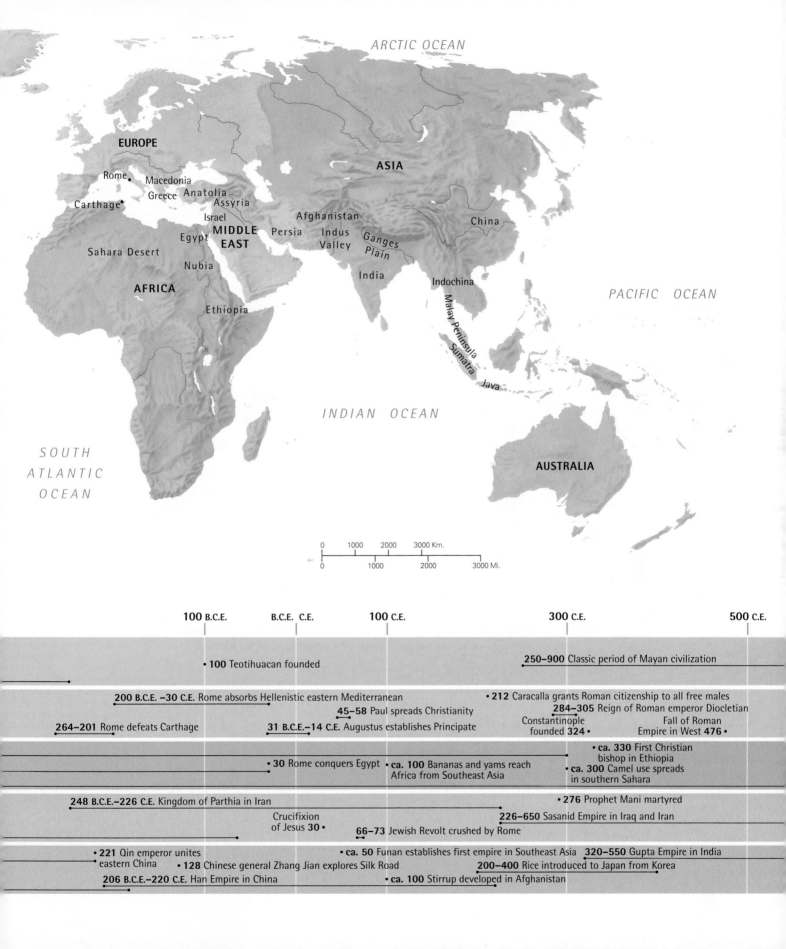

ARCTIC OCEAN

EUROPE

Rome •
Macedonia
Greece
Carthage •
Anatolia
Assyria
Israel
Egypt
MIDDLE
EAST
Persia
Afghanistan
Indus
Valley
Ganges
Plain
India
Indochina
Malay Peninsula
Sumatra
Java

ASIA

China

Sahara Desert
Nubia
AFRICA
Ethiopia

PACIFIC
OCEAN

INDIAN OCEAN

SOUTH
ATLANTIC
OCEAN

AUSTRALIA

| 0 | 1000 | 2000 | 3000 Km. |
| 0 | 1000 | 2000 | 3000 Mi. |

100 B.C.E.   B.C.E. C.E.   100 C.E.   300 C.E.   500 C.E.

• 100 Teotihuacan founded

250–900 Classic period of Mayan civilization

200 B.C.E. –30 C.E. Rome absorbs Hellenistic eastern Mediterranean

• 212 Caracalla grants Roman citizenship to all free males

45–58 Paul spreads Christianity

284–305 Reign of Roman emperor Diocletian

264–201 Rome defeats Carthage

31 B.C.E.–14 C.E. Augustus establishes Principate

Constantinople
founded 324 •

Fall of Roman
Empire in West 476 •

• 30 Rome conquers Egypt

• ca. 100 Bananas and yams reach
Africa from Southeast Asia

• ca. 330 First Christian
bishop in Ethiopia

• ca. 300 Camel use spreads
in southern Sahara

248 B.C.E.–226 C.E. Kingdom of Parthia in Iran

• 276 Prophet Mani martyred

Crucifixion
of Jesus 30 •

226–650 Sasanid Empire in Iraq and Iran

66–73 Jewish Revolt crushed by Rome

• 221 Qin emperor unites
eastern China

• ca. 50 Funan establishes first empire in Southeast Asia

320–550 Gupta Empire in India

• 128 Chinese general Zhang Jian explores Silk Road

200–400 Rice introduced to Japan from Korea

206 B.C.E.–220 C.E. Han Empire in China

• ca. 100 Stirrup developed in Afghanistan

4

Greece and Iran, 1000–30 B.C.E.

Painted Cup of Arcesilas of Cyrene   The ruler of this Greek community in North Africa supervises the weighing and export of silphium, a valuable medicinal plant.

The Greek historian Herodotus° (ca. 485–425 B.C.E.), chronicler of the struggles of the city-states of Greece with the Persian Empire in the sixth and fifth centuries B.C.E., teaches a lesson about cultural differences. The Persian king Darius° I, whose vast empire stretched from eastern Europe to Pakistan, summoned the Greek and Indian wise men who served him at court. He first asked the Greeks whether under any circumstances they would be willing to eat the bodies of their deceased fathers. The Greeks, who cremated their dead, recoiled at the impiety of such an act. Darius then asked the Indians whether they would be prepared to burn the bodies of their dead parents. The Indians were repulsed; their practice was to ritually partake of the bodies of the dead. The point, as Herodotus noted, was that different peoples have very different practices, but each regards its own way as "natural" and superior.

Distinguishing between what was natural and what was cultural convention created much discomfort among Greeks in Herodotus's lifetime, for it called into question the validity of their fundamental beliefs. Herodotus's story also reminds us that the Persian Empire (and the Hellenistic Greek kingdoms that succeeded it) brought together peoples and cultural systems that previously had known little direct contact, and that this new cross-cultural interaction could be alarming even while it stimulated new and exciting cultural syntheses.

In this chapter we look at the eastern Mediterranean and western Asia in the first millennium B.C.E., emphasizing the experiences of the Persians and Greeks. The rivalry and wars of Greeks and Persians from the sixth to fourth centuries B.C.E. are traditionally seen as the clash of the civilizations of East and West, of two peoples and two ways of life that were fundamentally different and thus almost certain to come into conflict.

Ironically, Greeks and Persians had far more in common than they realized. Both spoke in tongues belonging to the same Indo-European family of languages found throughout Europe and western and southern Asia. Many scholars believe that all the ancient peoples who spoke languages belonging to this family inherited fundamental cultural traits, forms of social organization, and religious outlooks from their shared past.

As you read this chapter, ask yourself the following questions:

- How did geography, environment, and contacts with other peoples shape the institutions and values of Persians and Greeks?

- What brought the Greek city-states and the Persian Empire into conflict, and which factors dictated the outcome of their rivalry?

- In what ways were the lands and peoples of the eastern Mediterranean and western Asia influenced—culturally, economically, and politically—by the domination of the Persian Empire and the Greek kingdoms that succeeded it?

ANCIENT IRAN, 1000–500 B.C.E.

Iran, the "land of the Aryans," links western Asia and southern and Central Asia, and its history has been marked by this mediating position (see Map 4.1). In the sixth century B.C.E. the vigorous Persians of southwest Iran created the largest empire the world had yet seen.

Relatively little written material from within the Persian Empire has survived, so we are forced to view it mostly through the eyes of the ancient Greeks—outsiders who were ignorant at best, usually hostile, and interested primarily in events that affected themselves. (Iranian groups and individuals are known in the western world by Greek approximations of their names; thus these familiar forms are used here, with the original Iranian names given in parentheses.) This Greek perspective leaves us unaware of developments in the central and eastern portions of the Persian Empire. Nevertheless, recent archaeological discoveries and close analysis of the limited written material from within the empire can supplement and correct the perspective of the Greek sources.

Herodotus (heh-ROD-uh-tuhs)   **Darius** (duh-RIE-uhs)

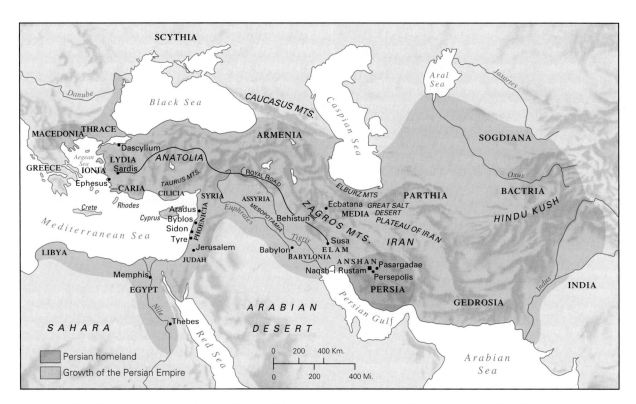

Map 4.1   The Persian Empire   Between 550 and 522 B.C.E., the Persians of southwest Iran, under their first two kings, Cyrus and Cambyses, conquered each of the major states of western Asia—Media, Babylonia, Lydia, and Egypt. The third king, Darius I, extended the boundaries as far as the Indus Valley to the east and the European shore of the Black Sea to the west. The first major setback came when the fourth king, Xerxes, failed in his invasion of Greece in 480 B.C.E. The Persian Empire was considerably larger than its recent predecessor, the Assyrian Empire. For their empire, the Persian rulers developed a system of provinces, governors, regular tribute, and communication by means of royal roads and couriers that allowed for efficient operations for almost two centuries.

Geography and Resources

Iran is bounded by the Zagros° Mountains to the west, the Caucasus° Mountains and Caspian Sea to the northwest and north, the mountains of Afghanistan and the desert of Baluchistan° to the east and southeast, and the Persian Gulf to the southwest. The northeast is less protected by natural boundaries, and from that direction Iran was open to attacks by the nomads of Central Asia.

The fundamental topographical features of Iran are high mountains at the edges, salt deserts in the interior depressions, and mountain streams crossing a sloping plateau and draining into seas or interior salt lakes and marshes. Humans trying to survive in these harsh lands had to find ways to exploit limited water resources. Un-

like the valleys of the Nile, Tigris-Euphrates, Ganges, and Yellow Rivers, ancient Iran never had a dense population. The best-watered and most populous parts of the country lie to the north and west; aridity increases and population decreases as one moves south and east. The Great Salt Desert, which covers most of eastern Iran, and Baluchistan in the southeast corner were extremely inhospitable. Scattered settlements in the narrow plains beside the Persian Gulf were cut off from the interior plateau by mountain barriers.

In the first millennium B.C.E. irrigation enabled people to move down from the mountain valleys and open the plains to agriculture. To prevent evaporation in the hot, dry climate, they devised underground irrigation channels. Constructing and maintaining these subterranean channels and the vertical shafts that provided access to them was labor-intensive. Normally, local leaders oversaw the expansion of the network in each district. Activ-

---

Zagros (ZUHG-roes)   **Caucasus** (KAW-kuh-suhs)
Baluchistan (buh-loo-chi-STAN)

CHRONOLOGY

	Greece and the Hellenistic World	Persian Empire
1000 B.C.E.	**1150–800 B.C.E.** Greece's "Dark Age"	**ca. 1000 B.C.E.** Persians settle in southwest Iran
800 B.C.E.	**ca. 800 B.C.E.** Resumption of Greek contact with eastern Mediterranean **800–480 B.C.E.** Greece's Archaic Period **ca. 750–550 B.C.E.** Era of colonization **ca. 700 B.C.E.** Beginning of hoplite warfare **ca. 650–500 B.C.E.** Era of tyrants	
600 B.C.E.	**594 B.C.E.** Solon reforms laws at Athens **546–510 B.C.E.** Pisistratus and sons hold tyranny at Athens	**550 B.C.E.** Cyrus overthrows Medes **550–530 B.C.E.** Reign of Cyrus **546 B.C.E.** Cyrus conquers Lydia **539 B.C.E.** Cyrus takes control of Babylonia **530–522 B.C.E.** Reign of Cambyses; Conquest of Egypt **522–486 B.C.E.** Reign of Darius
500 B.C.E.	**499–494 B.C.E.** Ionian Greeks rebel against Persia **490 B.C.E.** Athenians check Persian punitive expedition at Marathon **480–323 B.C.E.** Greece's classical period **477 B.C.E.** Athens becomes leader of Delian League **461–429 B.C.E.** Pericles dominant at Athens; Athens completes evolution to democracy	**480–479 B.C.E.** Xerxes' invasion of Greece
400 B.C.E.	**431–404 B.C.E.** Peloponnesian War **399 B.C.E.** Trial and execution of Socrates **359 B.C.E.** Philip II becomes king of Macedonia **338 B.C.E.** Philip takes control of Greece	**387 B.C.E.** King's Peace makes Persia arbiter of Greek affairs **334–323 B.C.E.** Alexander the Great defeats Persia and creates huge empire **323–30 B.C.E.** Hellenistic period
300 B.C.E.	**317 B.C.E.** End of democracy in Athens **ca. 300 B.C.E.** Foundation of the Museum in Alexandria	
100 B.C.E.	**200 B.C.E.** First Roman intervention in the Hellenistic East **30 B.C.E.** Roman annexation of Egypt, the last Hellenistic kingdom	

ity accelerated when a strong central authority was able to organize large numbers of laborers. The connection between royal authority and prosperity is evident in the ideology of the first Persian Empire (discussed below). Even so, human survival depended on a delicate ecological balance, and a buildup of salt in the soil or a falling water table sometimes forced the abandonment of settlements.

Iran's mineral resources—copper, tin, iron, gold, and silver—were exploited on a limited scale in antiquity. Mountain slopes, more heavily wooded than they are now, provided fuel and materials for building and crafts. Because this austere land could not generate much of an agricultural surplus, objects of trade tended to be minerals and crafted goods.

The Rise of the Persian Empire

In antiquity many groups of people, whom historians refer to collectively as "Iranians" because they spoke related languages and shared certain cultural features, spread out across western and Central Asia. Several of these groups arrived in western Iran near the end of the second millennium B.C.E. The first to achieve a complex level of political organization was the Medes (Mada in Iranian). They settled in the northwest and came under the influence of the ancient centers in Mesopotamia and Urartu (modern Armenia and northeast Turkey). The Medes played a major role in the destruction of the Assyrian Empire in the late seventh century B.C.E. and extended their control westward across Assyria into Anatolia (modern Turkey). They also projected their power southeast toward the Persian Gulf, a region occupied by another Iranian people, the Persians (Parsa).

The Persian rulers—now called Achaemenids° because they traced their lineage back to an ancestor named Achaemenes—cemented their relationship with the Median court through marriage. **Cyrus** (Kurush), the son of a Persian chieftain and a Median princess, united the various Persian tribes and overthrew the Median monarch sometime around 550 B.C.E. Cyrus placed both Medes and Persians in positions of responsibility and retained the framework of Median rule. The differences between these two Iranian peoples—principally differences in the dialects they spoke and the way they dressed—were not great. The Greeks could not readily tell the two apart.

Like most Indo-European peoples, the early inhabitants of western Iran had a patriarchal family organization: the male head of the household had nearly absolute authority over family members. Society was divided into three social and occupational classes: warriors, priests, and peasants. Warriors were the dominant element. A landowning aristocracy, they took pleasure in hunting, fighting, and gardening. The king was the most illustri-

ous member of this group. The priests, or Magi (*magush*), were ritual specialists who supervised the proper performance of sacrifices. The common people—peasants—were primarily village-based farmers and shepherds.

Over the course of two decades the energetic Cyrus (r. 550–530 B.C.E.) redrew the map of western Asia. In 546 B.C.E. he prevailed in a cavalry battle outside the gates of Sardis, the capital of the kingdom of Lydia in western Anatolia, reportedly because the smell of his camels caused a panic among his opponents' horses. All Anatolia, including the Greek city-states on the western coast, came under Persian control. In 539 B.C.E. he swept into Mesopotamia, where the Neo-Babylonian dynasty had ruled since the collapse of Assyrian power (see Chapter 3). Cyrus made a deal with disaffected elements within Babylon, and when he and his army approached, the gates of the city were thrown open to him without a struggle. A skillful propagandist, Cyrus showed respect to the Babylonian priesthood and had his son crowned king in accordance with native traditions.

After Cyrus lost his life in 530 B.C.E. while campaigning against a coalition of nomadic Iranians in the northeast, his son Cambyses° (Kambujiya, r. 530–522 B.C.E.) set his sights on Egypt, the last of the great ancient kingdoms of the Middle East. The Persians prevailed over the Egyptians in a series of bloody battles; then they sent exploratory expeditions south to Nubia and west to Libya. Greek sources depict Cambyses as a cruel and impious madman, but contemporary documents from Egypt show him operating in the same practical vein as his father, cultivating local priests and notables and respecting native traditions.

When Cambyses died in 522 B.C.E., **Darius I** (Darayavaush) seized the throne. His success in crushing many early challenges to his rule was a testimony to his skill, energy, and ruthlessness. From this reign forward, Medes played a lesser role, and the most important posts went to members of leading Persian families. Darius (r. 522–486 B.C.E.) extended Persian control eastward as far as the Indus Valley and westward into Europe, where he bridged the Danube River and chased the nomadic Scythian° peoples north of the Black Sea. The Persians erected a string of forts in Thrace (modern-day northeast Greece and Bulgaria) and by 500 B.C.E. were on the doorstep of Greece. Darius also promoted the development of maritime routes. He dispatched a fleet to explore the waters from the Indus Delta to the Red Sea, and he completed a canal linking the Red Sea with the Nile.

Achaemenid (a-KEY-muh-nid)

Cambyses (kam-BIE-sees)   **Scythian** (SITH-ee-uhn)

Imperial Organization and Ideology

The empire of Darius I was the largest the world had yet seen (see Map 4.1). Stretching from eastern Europe to Pakistan, from southern Russia to Sudan, it encompassed a multitude of ethnic groups and many forms of social and political organization, from nomadic kinship group to subordinate kingdom to city-state. Darius can rightly be considered a second founder of the Persian Empire, after Cyrus, because he created a new organizational structure that was maintained throughout the remaining two centuries of the empire's existence.

Darius divided the empire into twenty provinces. Each was under the supervision of a Persian **satrap°**, or governor, who was likely to be related or connected by marriage to the royal family. The satrap's court was a miniature version of the royal court. The tendency for the position of satrap to become hereditary meant that satraps' families lived in the province governed by their head, acquired a fund of knowledge about local conditions, and formed connections with the local native elite. The farther a province was from the center of the empire, the more autonomy the satrap had, because slow communications made it impractical to refer most matters to the central administration. This system of administration brought significant numbers of Persians and other peoples from the center of the empire to the provinces, resulting in intermarriage and cultural and technological exchanges.

One of the satrap's most important duties was to collect and send tribute to the king. Darius prescribed how much precious metal each province was to contribute annually. This amount was forwarded to the central treasury. Some of it was disbursed for necessary expenditures, but most was hoarded. As more and more precious metal was taken out of circulation, the price of gold and silver rose, and provinces found it increasingly difficult to meet their quotas. Evidence from Babylonia indicates a gradual economic decline setting in by the fourth century B.C.E.

Well-maintained and patrolled royal roads connected the outlying provinces to the heart of the empire. Way stations were built at intervals to receive important travelers and couriers carrying official correspondence. At strategic points, such as mountain passes, river crossings, and important urban centers, garrisons controlled people's movements. The administrative center of the empire was Susa, the ancient capital of Elam, in southwest Iran near the present-day border with Iraq.

The king lived and traveled with his numerous wives and children. The little information that we have about the lives of Persian royal women comes from foreign sources and is thus suspect. The Book of Esther in the Hebrew Bible tells a romantic story of how King Ahasuerus° (Xerxes° to the Greeks) picked the beautiful Jewish woman Esther to be one of his wives and how the courageous and clever queen later saved the Jewish people from a plot to massacre them. Greek sources show women of the royal family being used as pawns in the struggle for power. Darius strengthened his claim to the throne by marrying a daughter of Cyrus, and later the Greek conqueror Alexander the Great married a daughter of the last Persian king. Greek sources portray Persian queens as vicious intriguers. However, a recent study suggests that the Greek stereotype misrepresents the important role played by Persian women in protecting family members and mediating conflicts. Both Greek sources and documents within the empire reveal that Persian elite women were politically influential, possessed substantial property, traveled, and were prominent on public occasions.

Besides the royal family, the king's large entourage included several other groups: (1) the sons of Persian aristocrats, who were educated at court and also served as hostages for their parents' good behavior; (2) many noblemen, who were expected to attend the king when they were not otherwise engaged; (3) the central administration, including officials and employees of the treasury, secretariat, and archives; (4) the royal bodyguard; and (5) countless courtiers and slaves. Long gone were the simple days when the king hunted and caroused with his warrior companions. Inspired by Mesopotamian conceptions of monarchy, the king of Persia had become an aloof figure of majesty and splendor: "The Great King, King of Kings, King in Persia, King of countries." He referred to everyone, even the Persian nobility, as "my slaves," and anyone who approached him had to bow down before him.

The king owned vast tracts of land throughout the empire. Some of it he gave to his supporters. Donations called "bow land," "horse land," and "chariot land" in Babylonian documents obliged the recipient to provide military service. Scattered around the empire were gardens, orchards, and hunting preserves belonging to the king and the high nobility. The *paradayadam* (meaning "walled enclosure"—the term has come into English as *paradise*), a green oasis in an arid landscape, advertised the prosperity that the king could bring to those who loyally served him.

---

satrap (SAY-trap)

Ahasuerus (uh-HAZZ-yoo-ear-uhs)   **Xerxes** (ZERK-sees)

View of the East Front of the Apadana (Audience Hall) at Persepolis, ca. 500 B.C.E.   To the right lies the Gateway of Xerxes. Persepolis, in the Persian homeland, was built by Darius I and his son Xerxes, and it was used for ceremonies of special importance to the Persian king and people—coronations, royal weddings, funerals, and the New Year's festival. The stone foundations, walls, and stairways of Persepolis are filled with sculpted images of members of the court and embassies bringing gifts, offering a vision of the grandeur and harmony of the Persian Empire.   (Courtesy of the Oriental Institute, University of Chicago)

Surviving administrative records from the Persian homeland give us a glimpse of how the complex tasks of administration were managed. The **Persepolis°** Treasury and Fortification Texts, inscribed in Elamite cuneiform on baked clay tablets, show that government officials distributed food and other essential commodities to large numbers of workers of many different nationalities. Some of these workers may have been prisoners of war brought to the center of the empire to work on construction projects, maintain and expand the irrigation network, and farm the royal estates. Workers were divided into groups of men, women, and children. Women received less than men of equivalent status, but pregnant women and women with babies received more. Men and women performing skilled jobs received more than their unskilled counterparts.

Tradition remembered Darius as a lawgiver who created a body of "laws of the King" and a system of royal judges operating throughout the empire, as well as encouraging the codification and publication of the laws of the various subject peoples. In a manner that typifies the decentralized character of the Persian Empire, he allowed each people to live in accordance with its own traditions and ordinances.

The central administration was based in Elam and Mesopotamia. This location allowed the kings to employ the trained administrators and scribes of those ancient civilizations. However, on certain occasions the kings returned to one special place back in the homeland. Darius began construction of a ceremonial capital at Persepolis (Parsa). An artificial platform was erected, and on it were built a series of palaces, audience halls, treasury buildings, and barracks. Here, too, Darius and his son Xerxes, who completed the project, were inspired by Mesopotamian traditions, for the great Assyrian kings had created new fortress-cities as advertisements of wealth and power.

Darius's approach to governing can be seen in the luxuriant relief sculpture that covers the foundations, walls, and stairwells of the buildings at Persepolis. Representatives of all the peoples of the empire—recognizable by their distinctive hair, beards, dress, hats, and

---

Persepolis (Per-SEH-poe-lis)

footwear—are depicted in the act of bringing gifts to the king. Historians used to think that the sculpture represented a real event that transpired each year at Persepolis, but now they see it as an exercise in what today we would call public relations or propaganda. It is Darius's carefully crafted vision of an empire of vast extent and abundant resources in which all the subject peoples willingly cooperate.

What actually took place at Persepolis? This opulent retreat in the homeland probably was the scene of events of special significance for the king and his people: the New Year's Festival, coronation, marriage, death, and burial. The kings from Darius on were buried in elaborate tombs cut into the cliffs at nearby Naqsh-i Rustam°.

Another perspective on what the Persian monarchy claimed to stand for is provided by the several dozen inscriptions that have survived (see Diversity and Dominance: The Persian Idea of Kingship).

These inscriptions make it clear that behind Darius and the empire stands the will of god. Ahuramazda° made Darius king and gave him a mandate to bring order to a world in turmoil, and, despite his reasonable and just disposition, the king will brook no opposition. Ahuramazda is the great god of a religion called **Zoroastrianism°**, and it is nearly certain that Darius and his successors were Zoroastrians.

The origins of this religion are shrouded in uncertainty. The Gathas, hymns in an archaic Iranian dialect, are said to be the work of Zoroaster° (Zarathushtra). The dialect and physical setting of the hymns indicate that Zoroaster lived in eastern Iran. Scholarly guesses about when he lived range from 1700 to 500 B.C.E. He revealed that the world had been created by Ahuramazda, "the wise lord," and was threatened by Angra Mainyu°, "the hostile spirit," backed by a host of demons. In this dualistic universe, the struggle between good and evil plays out over twelve thousand years, after which good is destined to prevail, and the world will return to the pure state of creation. In the meantime, humanity is a participant in the cosmic struggle, and individuals are rewarded or punished in the afterlife for their actions.

In addition to Zoroastrianism, the Persians drew on moral and metaphysical conceptions with deep roots in the Iranian past. They were sensitive to the beauties of nature and venerated beneficent elements, such as water, which was not to be sullied, and fire, which was worshiped at fire altars. They were greatly concerned about the purity of the body. Corpses were exposed to wild beasts and the elements to prevent them from putrefying in the earth or tainting the sanctity of fire. The Persians still revered major deities from the polytheist past, such as Mithra, associated with the sun and defender of oaths and compacts. They were expected to keep promises and tell the truth. In his inscriptions at Persepolis, Darius castigated evildoers as followers of "the Lie."

Zoroastrianism was one of the great religions of the ancient world. It preached belief in one supreme deity, held humans to a high ethical standard, and promised salvation. It traveled across western Asia with the advance of the Persian Empire, and it may have exerted a major influence on Judaism and thus, indirectly, on Christianity. God and the Devil, Heaven and Hell, reward and punishment, the Messiah and the End of Time all appear to be legacies of this profound belief system.

THE RISE OF THE GREEKS, 1000–500 B.C.E.

Because Greece was a relatively resource-poor region, the cultural features that emerged there in the first millennium B.C.E. came into being only because the Greeks had access to foreign sources of raw materials and to markets abroad. Greeks were in contact with other peoples, and Greek merchants and mercenaries brought home not only raw materials and crafted goods but also ideas. Under the pressure of population, poverty, war, or political crisis, Greeks moved to other parts of the Mediterranean and western Asia, bringing their language and culture and exerting a powerful influence on other societies. Encounters with the different practices and beliefs of other peoples stimulated the formation of a Greek identity and sparked interest in geography, ethnography, and history. A two-century-long rivalry with the Persian Empire also played a large part in shaping the destinies of the Greek city-states.

Geography and Resources

Greece is part of a large ecological zone that encompasses the Mediterranean Sea and the lands surrounding it (see Map 3.5). This zone is bounded by the Atlantic Ocean to the west, the several ranges of the Alps to the north, the Syrian desert to the east, and the Sahara to the south. The lands lying within this zone have a roughly uniform climate, experience a similar sequence of seasons, and

Naqsh-i Rustam (NUHK-shee ROOS-tuhm)
Ahuramazda (ah-HOOR-uh-MAZZ-duh)
Zoroastrianism (zo-roe-ASS-tree-uh-niz-uhm)
Zoroaster (zo-roe-ASS-ter)   **Angra Mainyu** (ANG-ruh MINE-yoo)

우세연 은신처 방
파운드폭탄 4발 투하… 두 아들과 함께 사망 기
중심진지 구축… 이틀째 시가戰
령이 대중 앞에 나타나거나 애국심
을 고취하는 노래만을 내보내던 방
송마저 중단됐다.
라크 전후 대
의에서는 전제
영국 주도로

DIVERSITY AND DOMINANCE

THE PERSIAN IDEA OF KINGSHIP

Our most important internal source of information about the Persian Empire is a group of inscriptions commissioned by several kings. The most extensive and informative of these is the inscription that Darius had carved into a cliff face at Behistun (Beh-HISS-toon), high above the road leading from Mesopotamia to northwest Iran through a pass in the Zagros mountain range. It is written in three versions— Old Persian, the language of the ruling people (quite possibly being put into written form for the first time); Elamite, the language native to the ancient kingdom lying between southern Mesopotamia and the Persian homeland and used in Persia for local administrative documents; and Akkadian, the language of Babylonia, widely used for administrative purposes throughout western Asia. The multilingual inscription accompanied a monumental relief representing Darius looming over a line of bound prisoners, the leaders of the many forces he had to defeat in order to secure the throne after the death of Cambyses in 522 B.C.E.

I am Darius, the great king, king of kings, the king of Persia, the king of countries, the son of Hystaspes, the grandson of Arsames, the Achaemenid . . . from antiquity we have been noble; from antiquity has our dynasty been royal . . .

King Darius says: By the grace of Ahuramazda am I king; Ahuramazda has granted me the kingdom.

King Darius says: These are the countries which are subject unto me, and by the grace of Ahuramazda I became king of them: Persia, Elam, Babylonia, Assyria, Arabia, Egypt, the countries by the Sea, Lydia, the Greeks, Media, Armenia, Cappadocia, Parthia, Drangiana, Aria, Chorasmia, Bactria, Sogdiana, Gandara, Scythia, Sattagydia, Arachosia and Maka; twenty-three lands in all.

King Darius says: These are the countries which are subject to me; by the grace of Ahuramazda they became subject to me; they brought tribute unto me. Whatsoever commands have been laid on them by me, by night or by day, have been performed by them.

King Darius says: Within these lands, whosoever was a friend, him have I surely protected; whosoever was hostile, him have I utterly destroyed. By the grace of Ahuramazda these lands have conformed to my decrees; as it was commanded unto them by me, so was it done.

King Darius says: Ahuramazda has granted unto me this empire. Ahuramazda brought me help, until I gained this empire; by the grace of Ahuramazda do I hold this empire.

King Darius says: The following is what was done by me after I became king.

A lengthy description of the many battles Darius and his supporters fought against a series of other claimants to power follows.

King Darius says: This is what I have done. By the grace of Ahuramazda have I always acted. After I became king, I fought nineteen battles in a single year and by the grace of Ahuramazda I overthrew nine kings and I made them captive . . .

King Darius says: As to these provinces which revolted, lies made them revolt, so that they deceived the people. Then Ahuramazda delivered them into my hand; and I did unto them according to my will.

King Darius says: You who shall be king hereafter, protect yourself vigorously from lies; punish the liars well, if thus you shall think, 'May my country be secure!' . . .

King Darius says: On this account Ahuramazda brought me help, and all the other gods, all that there are, because I was not wicked, nor was I a liar, nor was I a tyrant, neither I nor any of my family. I have ruled according to righteousness. Neither to the weak nor to the powerful did I do wrong. Whosoever helped my house, him I favored; he who was hostile, him I destroyed . . .

King Darius says: By the grace of Ahuramazda this is the inscription which I have made. Besides, it was in Aryan script, and it was composed on clay tablets and on parchment. Besides, a sculptured figure of myself I made. Besides, I made my lineage. And it was inscribed and was read off before me. Afterwards this inscription I sent off everywhere among the provinces. The people unitedly worked upon it.

This is an extremely important historical document. For all practical purposes, it is the only version we have of the circumstances by which Darius, who was not a member of the family of Cyrus, took over the Persian throne and established a new dynasty. The account of these events given by the Greek historian Herodotus, for all its additional (and often suspect) detail, is clearly based, however indirectly, on Darius' own account. While scholars have doubted the truthfulness of Darius's claims, the inscription is a resounding example of how the victors often get to impose their version of events on the historical record.

The Behistun inscription is certainly propaganda, but that does not mean that it lacks value. To be effective, propaganda must be predicated on the moral values, political principles, and religious beliefs that are familiar and acceptable in a society, and thus it can provide us with a window on those views. The Behistun inscription also allows us to glimpse something of the personality of Darius and how he wished to be perceived.

Another document, found at Persepolis, the magnificent ceremonial center built by Darius and his son Xerxes, expands on the qualities of an exemplary ruler. While it purports to be the words of Xerxes, it is almost an exact copy of an inscription of Darius from nearby Naqsh-i Rustam, where Darius and subsequent kings were buried in monumental tombs carved into the sheer cliff. This shows the continuity of concepts through several reigns.

A great god is Ahuramazda, who created this excellent thing which is seen, who created happiness for man, who set wisdom and capability down upon King Xerxes.

Proclaims Xerxes the King: By the will of Ahuramazda I am of such a sort, I am a friend of the right, of wrong I am not a friend. It is not my wish that the weak should have harm done him by the strong, nor is it my wish that the strong should have harm done him by the weak.

The right, that is my desire. To the man who is a follower of the lie I am no friend. I am not hot-tempered. Whatever befalls me in battle, I hold firmly. I am ruling firmly my own will.

The man who is cooperative, according to his cooperation thus I reward him. Who does harm, him according to the harm I punish. It is not my wish that a man should do harm; nor indeed is it my wish that if he does harm he should not be punished.

What a man says against a man, that does not persuade me, until I hear the sworn statements of both.

What a man does or performs, according to his ability, by that I become satisfied with him, and it is much to my desire, and I am well pleased, and I give much to loyal men.

Of such a sort are my understanding and my judgment: if what has been done by me you see or hear of, both in the palace and in the expeditionary camp, this is my capability over will and understanding.

This indeed my capability: that my body is strong. As a fighter of battles I am a good fighter of battles. When ever with my judgment in a place I determine whether I behold or do not behold an enemy, both with understanding and with judgment, then I think prior to panic, when I see an enemy as when I do not see one.

I am skilled both in hands and in feet. A horseman, I am a good horseman. A bowman, I am a good bowman, both on foot and on horseback. A spearman, I am a good spearman, both on foot and on horseback.

These skills that Ahuramazada set down upon me, and which I am strong enough to bear, by the will of Ahuramazda, what was done by me, with these skills I did, which Ahuramazda set down upon me.

May Ahuramazda protect me and what was done by me.

QUESTIONS FOR ANALYSIS

1. How does Darius justify his assumption of power in the Behistun inscription? What is his relationship to Ahuramazda, the Zoroastrian god, and what role does divinity play in human affairs?

2. How does Darius conceptualize his empire (look at a map and follow the order in which he lists the provinces), and what are the expectations and obligations that he places on his subjects? What does his characterization of his opponents as "Lie-followers" tell us about his view of human nature?

3. Looking at the document of Xerxes from Persepolis, what qualities (physical, mental, and moral) are desirable in a ruler? What is the Persian concept of justice?

4. To what audiences are Darius and Xerxes directing their messages, and in what media are they being disseminated? Given that Darius himself is, in all likelihood, illiterate, and that so are most of his subjects, what is the effect of the often repeated phrase: "Darius the King says"?

Sources: Behistun inscription translated by L. W. King and R. C. Thompson, *The Sculptures and Inscription of Darius the Great on the Rock of Behistun in Persia,* London, 1907 (http://www.livius.org/be-bm/behistun03.html); document from Naqsh-i Rustam (http://www.livius.org/x/xerxes/xerxes_texts.htm#daeva)

are home to similar plants and animals. In the summer a weather front stalls near the entrance of the Mediterranean, impeding the passage of storms from the Atlantic and allowing hot, dry air from the Sahara to creep up over the region. In winter the front dissolves and the ocean storms roll in, bringing waves, wind, and cold. It was relatively easy for people to migrate to new homes within this ecological zone without having to alter familiar cultural practices and means of livelihood.

Greek civilization arose in the lands bordering the Aegean Sea: the Greek mainland, the islands of the Aegean, and the western coast of Anatolia (see Map 4.2). The small islands dotting the Aegean were inhabited from early times. People could cross the water from Greece to Anatolia almost without losing sight of land. From about 1000 B.C.E. Greeks began to settle on the western edge of Anatolia. Rivers that formed broad and fertile plains near the coast made Ionia, as the ancient Greeks called this region, a comfortable place. The interior of Anatolia is rugged plateau, and the Greeks of the coast were in much closer contact with their fellows across the Aegean than with the native peoples of the interior. The sea was always a connector, not a barrier.

Without large rivers, Greek farmers on the mainland depended entirely on rainfall to water their crops (see Environment and Technology: The Farmer's Year). The limited arable land, thin topsoil, and sparse rainfall in the south could not sustain large populations. In the historical period farmers usually planted grain (mostly barley, which was hardier than wheat) in the flat plain, olive trees at the edge of the plain, and grapevines on the terraced lower slopes of the foothills. Sheep and goats grazed in the hills during the growing season. In northern Greece, where the rainfall is greater and the land opens out into broad plains, cattle and horses were more abundant. These Greek lands had few metal deposits and little timber, although both building stone, including some fine marble, and clay for the potter were abundant.

The difficulty of overland transport, the availability of good anchorages, and the need to import metals, timber, and grain drew the Greeks to the sea. They obtained timber from the northern Aegean, gold and iron from Anatolia, copper from Cyprus, tin from the western Mediterranean, and grain from the Black Sea, Egypt, and Sicily. Sea transport was much cheaper and faster than overland transport.

The Emergence of the Polis

The first flowering of Greek culture in the Mycenaean civilization was largely an adaptation of the imported institutions of Middle Eastern palace-dominated states to the Greek terrain. For several centuries after the destruction of the Mycenaean palace-states, Greece lapsed into a "Dark Age" (ca. 1150–800 B.C.E.), during which Greece and the whole Aegean region were largely isolated from the rest of the world.

Within Greece, regions that had little contact with one another developed distinctive local styles in pottery and other crafts. With fewer people to feed, the land was largely given over to grazing flocks of sheep, goats, and cattle. While there was continuity of language, religion, and other aspects of culture, there was a sharp break with the authoritarian Mycenaean political structure and centralized control of the economy.

The isolation of Greece ended around 800 B.C.E. when Phoenician ships began to visit the Aegean (see Chapter 3). By reestablishing contact between the Aegean and the Middle East, the Phoenicians gave Greek civilization an important push and inaugurated what scholars now term the "Archaic" period of Greek history (ca. 800–480 B.C.E.). Soon Greek ships were also plying the waters of the Mediterranean in search of raw materials, trade opportunities, and fertile farmland.

Various evidence reveals the influx of new ideas from the east, such as the appearance of naturalistic human and animal figures and imaginative mythical beasts on painted Greek pottery. The most auspicious gift of the Phoenicians was a writing system. The Phoenicians used a set of twenty-two symbols to represent the consonants in their language, leaving the vowel sounds to be inferred by the reader. To represent Greek vowel sounds, the Greeks utilized some of the Phoenician symbols for which there were no equivalent sounds in the Greek language. This was the first true alphabet, a system of writing that fully represents the sounds of spoken language. An alphabet offers tremendous advantages over systems of writing such as cuneiform and hieroglyphics, whose signs represent entire words or syllables. Because cuneiform and hieroglyphics required years of training and the memorization of several hundred signs, they remained the preserve of a scribal class whose elevated social position stemmed from their mastery of the technology. An alphabet opens the door for more widespread literacy because people can learn an alphabet in a relatively short period of time.

Some scholars maintain that the Greeks first used the alphabet for economic purposes. Others propose that it originated as a vehicle for preserving the oral poetic epics so important to the Greeks. Whatever its first use, the Greeks soon came to employ the new technology to produce new forms of literature, law codes, religious dedications, and epitaphs on gravestones. This

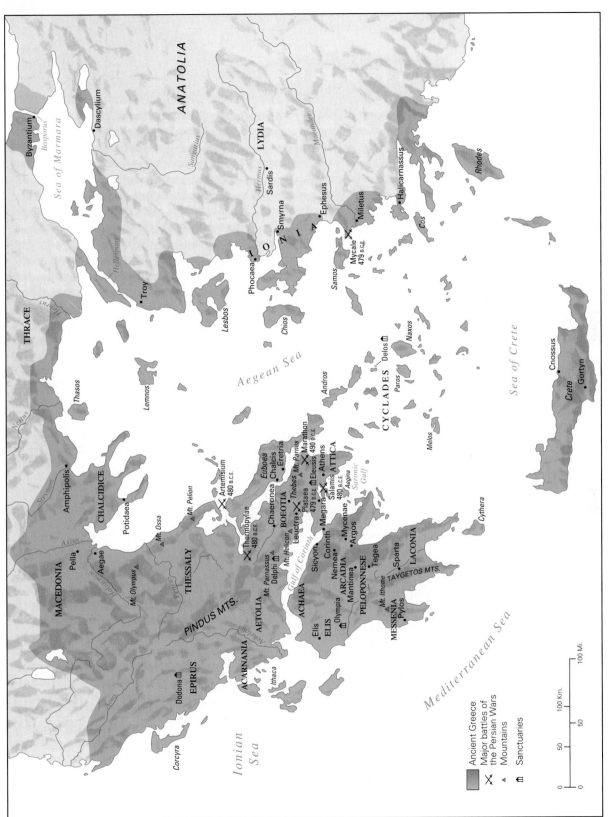

Map 4.2 Ancient Greece By the early first millennium B.C.E. Greek-speaking peoples were dispersed throughout the Aegean region, occupying the Greek mainland, most of the islands, and the western coast of Anatolia. The rough landscape of central and southern Greece, with small plains separated by ranges of mountains, and the many islands in the Aegean favored the rise of hundreds of small, independent communities. The presence of adequate rainfall meant that agriculture was organized on the basis of self-sufficient family farms. As a result of the limited natural resources of this region, the Greeks had to resort to sea travel and trade with other lands in the Mediterranean to acquire metals and other vital raw materials.

The Farmer's Year

Perhaps the first Greek we can get to know as an individual is Hesiod (HEE-see-uhd). Hesiod lived near a village in Boeotia, in central Greece, around 700 B.C.E. In his poem *Works and Days*, we learn about his work as a farmer and about his relationships with family members and neighbors. The poem is presented as advice to his good-for-nothing brother, stressing the necessity of hard and perpetual work in order to survive. Much of the poem is a kind of farmer's almanac, describing the annual cycle of tasks on a Greek farm.

As Hesiod makes clear, it was very important for farmers to perform work at the right time. How did Greeks of the Archaic period, with no clocks, calendars, or newspapers, know where they were in the cycle of the year? They oriented themselves by acute observation of natural phenomena such as the flowering of plants and trees and the behavior of animals, the migration of birds and changes in the weather, and the movements of planets, stars, and constellations in the night sky.

Hesiod gives the following advice for determining the proper times for planting and harvesting grain:

> Pleiades rising in the dawning sky,
>   Harvest is nigh.
> Pleiades setting in the waning night,
>   Plowing is right.

The Pleiades (PLEE-uh-dees) is a cluster of seven stars visible to the naked eye. In Greek mythology, the Pleiades were seven sisters whom the gods placed in the sky to help them escape from the hunter Orion. The ancient Greeks observed that individual stars and constellations (groups of stars perceived by the human eye to form images in the sky) moved from east to west during the night and appeared in different parts of the sky at different times of the year. (In fact, the apparent movement of the stars is due to the earth's rotation on its axis and orbit around the sun against a background of unmoving stars. To earthly observers, however, the stars appear to move.) Hesiod is telling his audience that, when the Pleiades appear above the eastern horizon just before the light of the rising sun makes all the other stars invisible (in May on the modern calendar), a sensible farmer will cut down his grain crop. Some months later (in our September), when the Pleiades dip below the western horizon just before sunrise, it is time to plow the fields and plant seeds for the next year's harvest.

Other events in nature provide similar indicators:

> Mind now, when you hear the call of the crane
> Coming from the clouds, as it does year by year:
> That's the sign for plowing . . .

---

does not mean, however, that Greek society immediately became literate in the modern sense. For many centuries, Greece remained a primarily oral culture: people used storytelling, rituals, and performances to preserve and transmit information. Many of the distinctive intellectual and artistic creations of Greek civilization, such as theatrical drama, philosophical dialogues, and political and courtroom oratory, are products of the dynamic interaction of speaking and writing.

One indicator of the powerful new forces at work in the Archaic period was a veritable explosion of population. Studies of cemeteries in the vicinity of Athens show that there was a dramatic population increase (perhaps as much as fivefold or sevenfold) during the eighth century B.C.E. Its causes are not fully understood but probably include the more intensive use of land as farming replaced herding and independent farmers and their families began to work previously unused land on the margins of the plains. A second factor was increasing prosperity based on the importation of food and raw materials. Rising population density led villages to merge and become urban centers.

Greece at this time consisted of hundreds of independent political entities. The Greek **polis**° (usually translated "city-state") consisted of an urban center and the

---

polis (POE-lis)

And even the stern Hesiod allows himself a break at the height of summer:

> But when the thistle's in bloom, and the cicada
> Chirps from its perch in a branch, pouring down
> Shrill song from its wings in the withering heat,
> Then goats are plumpest, wine at its best, women
> Most lustful, but men at their feeblest, since Sirius
> Scorches head and knees, and skin shrivels up....
>   Time to drink sparkling wine
> Sitting in the shade, heart satisfied with food,
> Face turned toward the cooling West Wind...

Sirius (SIH-ree-uhs), the brightest star in the sky, rose with the sun in late July. The ancients believed that the addition of its heat to the heat already provided by the sun accounted for sizzling temperatures at this time of year. (The ancient Egyptians connected the rising of Sirius with the beginning of the Nile flood.)

It is clear to any reader of Hesiod's poem that he and his fellow Greek farmers were intimately attuned to their environment. Their extensive knowledge of the natural world provided them with information vital for survival.

Source: From *Hesiod: Works and Days and Theogony*, translated by Stanley Lombardo (Indianapolis/Cambridge: Hackett Publishing, 1993) Reprinted by permission of Hackett Publishing Company, Inc. All rights reserved.

Black-Figure Vase from Athens, Late Sixth Century B.C.E. In this rare depiction of the activities of the working class, one man is up in an olive tree shaking the branches, two others knock olives down with sticks, while a fourth picks them off the ground. Olives were an important agricultural product, not only for eating, but also for the oil that was used for lamps, cooking, and cleaning and moisturizing the skin. Olive oil was a major export product at Athens. (Courtesy of the Trustees of the British Museum)

rural territory that it controlled. City-states came in various sizes, with populations as small as several thousand or as large as several hundred thousand in the case of Athens.

Most urban centers had certain characteristic features. A hilltop *acropolis*° ("top of the city") offered a place of refuge in an emergency. The town spread out around the base of this fortified high point. An *agora*° ("gathering place") was an open area where citizens came together to ratify the decisions of their leaders or to line up with their weapons before military ventures. Government buildings were located there, but the agora soon developed into a marketplace as well (vendors everywhere are eager to set out their wares wherever crowds gather). Fortified walls surrounded the urban center; but as the population expanded, new buildings went up beyond the perimeter.

Each polis was fiercely jealous of its independence and suspicious of its neighbors, and this state of mind led to frequent conflict. By the early seventh century B.C.E. the Greeks had developed a new kind of warfare, waged by **hoplites**°—heavily armored infantrymen who

---

acropolis (uh-KRAW-poe-lis)   agora (ah-go-RAH)

hoplite (HAWP-lite)

The Acropolis at Athens   This steep, defensible plateau jutting up from the Attic Plain served as a Mycenaean fortress in the second millennium B.C.E., and the site of Athens has been continuously occupied since that time. In the mid-sixth century B.C.E. the tyrant Pisistratus built a temple to Athena, the patron goddess of the community. It was destroyed by the Persians when they invaded Greece in 480 B.C.E. The Acropolis was left in ruins for three decades as a reminder of what the Athenians sacrificed in defense of Greek freedom, but in the 440s B.C.E. Pericles initiated a building program, using funds from the naval empire that Athens headed. These construction projects, including a new temple to Athena—the Parthenon—brought glory to the city and popularity to Pericles and to the new democracy that he championed.   (Robert Harding Picture Library)

fought in close formation. Protected by a helmet, a breastplate, and leg guards, each hoplite held a round shield over his own left side and the right side of the man next to him and brandished a thrusting spear, keeping a sword in reserve. In this style of combat, the key to victory was maintaining the cohesion of one's own formation while breaking open the enemy's line. Most of the casualties were suffered by the defeated army in flight.

Recent studies have emphasized the close relationship of hoplite warfare to the agricultural basis of Greek society. Greek states were defended by armies of private citizens—mostly farmers—called up for brief periods of crisis, rather than by a professional class of soldiers. Although this kind of fighting called for strength to bear the weapons and armor, and courage to stand one's ground in battle, no special training was needed by the citizen-soldiers. Campaigns took place when farmers were available, in the windows of time between major tasks in the agricultural cycle. When a hoplite army

marched into the fields of another community, the enraged farmers of that community, who had expended a lot of hard labor on their land and buildings, could not fail to meet the challenge. Though brutal and terrifying, the clash of two hoplite lines did offer a quick decision. Battles rarely lasted more than a few hours, and the survivors could promptly return home to tend their farms.

The expanding population soon surpassed the capacity of the small plains, and many communities sent excess population abroad to establish independent "colonies" in distant lands. Not every colonist left willingly. Sources tell of people being chosen by lot and forbidden to return on pain of death. Others, seeing an opportunity to escape from poverty, avoid the constraints of family, or find adventure, voluntarily set out to seek their fortunes on the frontier. After obtaining the approval of the god Apollo from his sanctuary at Delphi, the colonists departed, carrying fire from the communal hearth of the "mother-city," a symbol of the kinship and religious ties that would connect the two communities. They settled by the sea in the vicinity of a hill or other natural refuge. The "founder," a prominent member of the mother-city, allotted parcels of land and drafted laws for the new community. In some cases the indigenous population was driven away or reduced to a semiservile status; in other cases there was intermarriage and mixing between colonists and natives.

A wave of colonization from the mid-eighth through mid-sixth centuries B.C.E. spread Greek culture far beyond the land of its origins. New settlements sprang up in the northern Aegean area, around the Black Sea, and on the Libyan coast of North Africa. In southern Italy and on the island of Sicily (see Map 3.5) another Greek core area was established. Although the creation of new homes, farms, and communities undoubtedly posed many challenges for the Greek settlers, they were able to transplant their entire way of life, mostly because of the general similarity in climate and ecology in the Mediterranean lands.

Greeks began to use the term *Hellenes°* (*Graeci* is what the Romans later called them) to distinguish themselves from *barbaroi* (the root of the English word *barbarian*). Interaction with new peoples and exposure to their different practices made the Greeks aware of the factors that bound them together: their language, religion, and lifestyle. It also introduced them to new ideas and technologies.

Another significant development was the invention of coins in the early sixth century B.C.E., probably in Lydia (western Anatolia). They soon spread throughout the Greek world and beyond. In the ancient world a coin was a piece of metal whose weight and purity, and thus value, were guaranteed by the state. Silver, gold, bronze, and other metals were attractive choices for a medium of exchange: sufficiently rare to be valuable, relatively lightweight and portable (at least in the quantities available to most individuals), seemingly indestructible and therefore permanent, yet easily divided. Prior to the invention of coinage, people in the lands of the eastern Mediterranean and western Asia weighed out quantities of gold, silver, or bronze in exchange for the items they wanted to buy. Coinage allowed for more rapid exchanges of goods as well as for more efficient recordkeeping and storage of wealth. It stimulated trade and increased the total wealth of the society. Even so, international commerce could still be confusing because different states used different weight standards that had to be reconciled, just as people have to exchange currencies when traveling today.

By reducing surplus population, colonization helped relieve pressures within the Archaic Greek world. Nevertheless, this was an era of political instability. Kings ruled the Dark Age societies depicted in Homer's *Iliad* and *Odyssey*, but at some point councils composed of the heads of noble families superseded the kings. This aristocracy derived its wealth and power from ownership of large tracts of land. Peasant families worked this land; they were allowed to occupy a plot and keep a portion of what they grew. Debt-slaves, too, worked the land. They were people who had borrowed money or seed from the lord and lost their freedom when they were unable to repay the loan. Also living in a typical community were free peasants, who owned small farms, and urban-based craftsmen and merchants, who began to constitute a "middle class."

In the mid-seventh and sixth centuries B.C.E. in one city-state after another, an individual **tyrant**—a person who seized and held power in violation of the normal political institutions and traditions of the community—gained control. Greek tyrants were often disgruntled or ambitious members of the aristocracy, backed by the emerging middle class. New opportunities for economic advancement and the declining cost of metals meant that more and more men could acquire arms. These individuals, who already played an important role as hoplite soldiers in the local militias, must have demanded some political rights as the price of their support for their local tyrant.

Ultimately, the tyrants of this age were unwitting catalysts in an evolving political process. Some were able to pass their positions on to their sons, but eventually the tyrant-family was ejected. Authority in the community developed along one of two lines: toward oligarchy°, the exercise of political privilege by the wealthier members of society, or toward **democracy,** the exercise of political power by all free adult males. In any case, the absence of a professional military class in the early Greek states was essential to broadening the base of political participation.

Greek religion encompassed a wide range of cults and beliefs. The ancestors of the Greeks brought a collection of sky-gods with them when they entered the Greek peninsula at the end of the third millennium B.C.E. Some of the gods represented forces in nature: for example, Zeus sent storms and lightning, and Poseidon was master of the sea and earthquakes. The two great epic poems, the *Iliad* and *Odyssey*, which Greek schoolboys memorized and professional performers recited, put a distinctive stamp on the personalities and characters of

Hellenes (HELL-leans)

oligarchy (OLL-ih-gahr-key)

Vase Painting Depicting a Sacrifice to the God Apollo, ca. 440 B.C.E. For the Greeks, who believed in a multitude of gods who looked and behaved like humans, the central act of worship was the sacrifice, the ritualized offering of a gift. Sacrifice created a relationship between the human worshiper and the deity and raised expectations that the god would bestow favors in return. Here we see a number of male devotees, wearing their finest clothing and garlands in their hair, near a sacred outdoor altar and statue of Apollo. The god is shown at the far right, standing on a pedestal and holding his characteristic bow and laurel branch. The first worshiper offers the god bones wrapped in fat. All of the worshipers will feast on the meat carried by the boy. (Museum für Vor-und. Frühgeschichte, Frankfurt)

these deities. The gods that Homer portrayed were anthropomorphic°—that is, conceived as humanlike in appearance (though they were taller, more beautiful, and more powerful than mere mortals and had a supernatural radiance) and humanlike in their displays of emotion.

The worship of the gods at state-sponsored festivals was as much an expression of civic identity as of personal piety. **Sacrifice,** the central ritual of Greek religion, was performed at altars in front of the temples that the Greeks built to be the gods' places of residence. Greeks gave their gods gifts, often as humble as a small cake or a cup of wine poured on the ground, in the hope that the gods would favor and protect them. In more spectacular forms of sacrifice, a group of people would kill one or more animals, spray the altar with the victim's blood, burn parts of its body so that the aroma would ascend to the gods on high, and enjoy a rare feast of meat. In this way the Greeks created a sense of community out of shared participation in the taking of life.

Greek individuals and communities sought information, advice, or predictions about the future from oracles—sacred sites where they believed the gods communicated with humans. Especially prestigious was the oracle of Apollo at Delphi in central Greece. Petitioners left gifts in the treasuries, and the god responded to their questions through his priestess, the Pythia°, who gave forth obscure, ecstatic utterances. Because most Greeks were farmers, fertility cults, whose members worshiped and sought to enhance the productive forces in nature (usually conceived as female), were popular, though

often hidden from modern view because of our dependence on literary texts expressing the values of an educated, urban elite.

New Intellectual Currents

One distinctive feature of the Archaic period was a growing emphasis on the individual. In early Greek communities the family enveloped the individual, and land belonged collectively to the family, including ancestors and descendants. Ripped out of this communal network and forced to establish new lives on a distant frontier, the colonist became a model of rugged individualism, as did the tyrant who seized power for himself alone. These new patterns led toward the concept of humanism—a valuing of the uniqueness, talents, and rights of the individual—which remains a central tenet of Western civilization.

We see clear signs of individualism in the new lyric poetry—short verses in which the subject matter is intensely personal, drawn from the experience of the poet and expressing his or her feelings and views. Archilochus°, a soldier and poet living in the first half of the seventh century B.C.E., made a surprising admission:

> Some barbarian is waving my shield, since I was
>   obliged to
> leave that perfectly good piece of equipment behind
> under a bush. But I got away, so what does it matter?
> Let the shield go; I can buy another one equally good.[1]

anthropomorphic (an-thruh-puh-MORE-fik)
Pythia (PITH-ee-uh)

Archilochus (ahr-KIL-uh-kuhs)

Here Archilochus is poking fun at the heroic ideal that scorned a soldier who ran away from the enemy. In challenging traditional values and exploiting the medium to express personal feeling and opinion, lyric poets paved the way for the modern Western conception of poetry.

There were also challenges to traditional religion from thinkers now known as pre-Socratic philosophers (the term *pre-Socratic* refers to philosophers before Socrates, who in the later fifth century B.C.E. shifted the focus of philosophy to ethical questions). In the sixth century B.C.E. Xenophanes° called into question the kind of gods that Homer had popularized.

> But if cattle and horses or lions had hands, or were able to draw with their hands and do the works that men can do, horses would draw the forms of the gods like horses, and cattle like cattle, and they would make their bodies such as they each had themselves.[2]

The pre-Socratic philosophers rejected traditional religious explanations of the origins and nature of the world and sought rational explanations. They were primarily concerned with learning how the world was created, what it is made of, and why changes occur. Some pre-Socratic thinkers postulated various combinations of earth, air, fire, and water as the primal elements that combine or dissolve to form the numerous substances found in nature. One advanced the theory that the world is composed of microscopic *atoms* (from a Greek word meaning "indivisible") that move through the void of space, colliding randomly and combining in various ways to form the many substances of the natural world. In some respects startlingly similar to modern atomic theory, this model was essentially a lucky intuition, but it is a testament to the sophistication of these thinkers. It is probably no coincidence that most of them came from Ionia and southern Italy, two zones in which Greeks were in close contact with non-Greek peoples. The shock of encountering people with very different ideas may have stimulated new lines of inquiry.

Another important intellectual development also took place in Ionia in the sixth century B.C.E. A group of men later referred to as logographers° ("writers of prose accounts"), taking full advantage of the nearly infinite capacity of writing to store information, began gathering data on a wide range of topics, including ethnography (description of a people's physical characteristics and cultural practices), the geography of Mediterranean lands, the foundation stories of important cities, and the origins of famous Greek families. They were the first to write in prose—the language of everyday speech—rather than poetry, which had long facilitated the memorization essential to an oral society. *Historia*, "investigation/research," was the name they gave to the method they used to collect, sort, and select information. In the mid-fifth century B.C.E. **Herodotus** (ca. 485–425 B.C.E.), from Halicarnassus in southwest Anatolia, published his *Histories*. Early parts of the work are filled with the geographic and ethnographic reports, legends, folktales, and marvels dear to the logographers, but in later sections Herodotus focuses on the great event of the previous generation: the wars between the Greeks and the Persian Empire.

Herodotus declared his new conception of his mission in the first lines of the book:

> I, Herodotus of Halicarnassus, am here setting forth my history, that time may not draw the color from what man has brought into being, nor those great and wonderful deeds, manifested by both Greeks and barbarians, fail of their report, and, together with all this, the reason why they fought one another.[3]

In stating that he wants to find out *why* Greeks and Persians came to blows, he reveals that he has become a historian seeking the causes behind historical events. Herodotus directed the all-purpose techniques of *historia* to the service of *history* in the modern sense of the term, thereby narrowing the meaning of the word. For this achievement he is known as the "father of history."

Athens and Sparta

The two preeminent Greek city-states of the late Archaic and Classical periods were Athens and Sparta. The different character of these two communities underscores the potential for diversity in the evolution of human societies, even those arising in similar environmental and cultural contexts.

The ancestors of the Spartans migrated into the Peloponnese°, the southernmost part of the Greek mainland, around 1000 B.C.E. For a time Sparta followed a typical path of development, participating in trade and fostering the arts. Then in the seventh century B.C.E. something happened to alter the destiny of the Spartan state. Instead of sending out colonists when confronted by population pressure, the Spartans crossed their mountainous western frontier and invaded the fertile plain of Messenia (see Map 4.2). Hoplite tactics may

---

Xenophanes (zeh-NOFF-uh-nees)
logographer (loe-GOG-ruff-er)

Peloponnese (PELL-uh-puh-neze)

have given the Spartans the edge they needed to prevail over fierce Messenian resistance. The result was the takeover of Messenia and the domination of the native population, who descended to the status of helots°, the most abused and exploited population on the Greek mainland.

Fear of a helot uprising led to the evolution of the unique Spartan way of life. The Spartan state became a military camp in a permanent state of preparedness. Territory in Messenia and Laconia (the Spartan homeland) was divided into several thousand lots, which were assigned to Spartan citizens. Helots worked the land and turned over a portion of what they grew to their Spartan masters, who were thereby freed from food production and able to spend their lives in military training and service.

The professional Spartan soldier was the best in Greece, and the Spartan army was superior to all others, since the other Greek states relied on citizen militias called out only in time of crisis. The Spartans, however, paid a huge personal price for their military readiness. At age seven, boys were taken from their families and put into barracks, where they were toughened by a severe regimen of discipline, beatings, and deprivation. A Spartan male's whole life was subordinated to the demands of the state. Sparta essentially stopped the clock, declining to participate in the economic, political, and cultural renaissance taking place in the Archaic Greek world. There were no longer any poets or artists at Sparta. In an attempt to maintain equality among citizens, precious metals and coinage were banned, and Spartans were forbidden to engage in commerce. The fifth-century B.C.E. historian Thucydides°, a native of Athens, remarked that in his day Sparta appeared to be little more than a large village and that no future observer of the ruins of the site would be able to guess its power.

The Spartans rarely put their reputation to the test, practicing a foreign policy that was cautious and isolationist. Reluctant to march far from home for fear of a helot uprising, the Spartans sought to maintain peace in the Peloponnese through the Peloponnesian League, a system of alliances between Sparta and its neighbors.

Athens followed a different path. In comparison with other Greek city-states, it possessed an unusually large and populous territory: the entire region of Attica. Attica contained a number of moderately fertile plains and was ideally suited for cultivation of olive trees. In addition to the urban center of Athens, located some 5 miles (8 kilometers) from the sea where the sheer-sided

Acropolis towered above the Attic Plain, the peninsula was dotted with villages and a few larger towns.

Attica's large land area provided a buffer against the initial stresses of the Archaic period, but by the early sixth century B.C.E. things had reached a critical point. In 594 B.C.E. Solon was appointed lawgiver and was granted extraordinary powers to avert a civil war. He divided Athenian citizens into four classes based on the annual yield of their farms. Those in the top three classes could hold state offices. Members of the lowest class, who had little or no property, could not hold office but were allowed to participate in meetings of the Assembly. This arrangement, which made rights and privileges a function of wealth, was far from democratic. But it broke the absolute monopoly on power of a small circle of aristocratic families, and it allowed for social and political mobility. By abolishing the practice of enslaving individuals for failure to repay their debts, Solon guaranteed the freedom of Athenian citizens.

Despite Solon's efforts to defuse the crisis, political turmoil continued until 546 B.C.E., when an aristocrat named Pisistratus° seized power. To strengthen his position and weaken the aristocracy, the tyrant Pisistratus tried to shift the allegiance of the still largely rural population to the urban center of Athens, where he was the dominant figure. He undertook a number of monumental building projects, including a Temple of Athena on the Acropolis. He also instituted or expanded several major festivals that drew people to Athens for religious processions, performances of plays, and athletic and poetic competitions.

Pisistratus passed the tyranny on to his sons, but with Spartan assistance the Athenians turned the tyrant-family out in the last decade of the sixth century B.C.E. In the 460s and 450s B.C.E. **Pericles**° and his political allies took the last steps in the evolution of Athenian democracy, transferring all power to popular organs of government: the Assembly, Council of 500, and People's Courts. From that time on, men of moderate or little means could hold office and participate in the political process. Men were selected by lot to fill even the highest offices, and they were paid for public service so they could afford to take time off from their work. The focal point of Athenian political life became the Assembly of all citizens. Several times a month proposals were debated there; decisions were openly made, and any citizen could speak to the issues of the day.

---

helot (HELL-ut)   **Thucydides** (thoo-SID-ih-dees)

Pisistratus (pie-SIS-truh-tuhs)
Pericles (PER-eh-kleez)

THE STRUGGLE OF PERSIA AND GREECE, 546–323 B.C.E.

For the Greeks of the fifth and fourth centuries B.C.E., Persia was the great enemy and the wars with Persia were the decisive historical event. The Persians probably were more concerned about developments farther east and did not regard the wars with the Greeks as so consequential. Nevertheless, the encounter with the Greeks over a period of two centuries was of profound importance for the history of the eastern Mediterranean and western Asia.

Early Encounters Cyrus's conquest of Lydia in 546 B.C.E. led to the subjugation of the Greek cities on the Anatolian seacoast. In the years that followed, these cities were ruled by local groups or individuals who collaborated with the Persian government so as to maintain themselves in power and allow their cities to operate with minimal Persian interference. All this changed when the Ionian Revolt, a great uprising of Greeks and other subject peoples on the western frontier, broke out in 499 B.C.E. The Persians needed five years and a massive infusion of troops and resources to stamp out the insurrection.

The failed revolt led to the **Persian Wars**—two Persian attacks on Greece in the early fifth century B.C.E. In 490 B.C.E. Darius dispatched a naval fleet to punish Eretria° and Athens, two states on the Greek mainland that had given assistance to the Ionian rebels, and to warn others about the foolhardiness of crossing the Persian king. Eretria was betrayed to the Persians by several of its own citizens, and the survivors were marched off to permanent exile in southwest Iran. Next on the Persians' list were the Athenians, who probably would have suffered a similar fate if their hoplites had not defeated the lighter-armed Persian troops in a short, sharp engagement at Marathon, 26 miles (42 kilometers) from Athens.

Xerxes (Khshayarsha, r. 486–465 B.C.E.) succeeded his father on the Persian throne and soon turned his attention to the troublesome Greeks. In 480 B.C.E. he set out with a huge invasionary force consisting of the Persian army, contingents summoned from all the peoples of the Persian Empire, and a large fleet of ships drawn from maritime subjects. Crossing the Hellespont (the narrow strait at the edge of the Aegean separating Europe and Asia), Persian forces descended into central and southern Greece (see Map 4.2). Xerxes sent messengers ahead to most of the Greek states, bidding them to offer up "earth and water"—tokens of submission.

Many Greek communities acknowledged Persian overlordship. But in southern Greece an alliance of states bent on resistance was formed under the leadership of the Spartans. This Hellenic League, as modern historians call it, initially failed to halt the Persian advance. At the pass of Thermopylae° in central Greece, three hundred Spartans and their king gave their lives to buy time for their fellows to escape. However, after seizing and sacking the city of Athens in 480 B.C.E., the Persians allowed their navy to be lured into the narrow straits of nearby Salamis°, where they lost their advantage in numbers and maneuverability and suffered a devastating defeat. The following spring (479 B.C.E.), the Persian land army was routed at Plataea°, and the immediate threat to Greece receded.

The collapse of the threat to the Greek mainland did not mean an end to war. The Greeks went on the offensive. Athens's stubborn refusal to submit to the Persian king, even after the city was sacked twice in two successive years, and the vital role played by the Athenian navy, which made up fully half of the allied Greek fleet, earned the city a large measure of respect. The next phase of the war, designed to drive the Persians away from the Aegean and liberate Greek states still under Persian control, was naval. Thus Athens replaced land-based, isolationist Sparta as leader of the campaign against Persia.

In 477 B.C.E. the Delian° League was formed. It was initially a voluntary alliance of Greek states eager to prosecute the war against Persia. In less than twenty years, League forces led by Athenian generals swept the Persians from the waters of the eastern Mediterranean and freed all Greek communities except those in distant Cyprus (see Map 3.5).

The Height of Athenian Power By scholarly convention, the Classical period of Greek history (480–323 B.C.E.) begins with the successful defense of the Greek homeland against the forces of the Persian Empire. Ironically, the Athenians, who had played such a crucial role, exploited these events to become an imperial power. A string of successful campaigns and the passage of time led many of their Greek allies to grow complacent and contribute money instead of military forces. The Athenians used the money to build up and

Eretria (er-EH-tree-uh)

Thermopylae (thuhr-MOP-uh-lee)   Salamis (SAH-lah-miss)
Plataea (pluh-TEE-uh)   Delian (DEE-lih-yuhn)

Replica of Ancient Greek Trireme   Greek warships had a metal-tipped ram in front to pierce the hulls of enemy vessels and a pair of steering rudders in the rear. Though equipped with masts and sails, in battle these warships were propelled by 170 rowers. This modern, full-size replica represents one solution to the puzzle of how three tiers of oars could operate simultaneously without becoming entangled. Volunteer crews are helping scholars to determine attainable speeds and maneuvering techniques.   (Courtesy, the Trireme Trust)

staff their navy. Eventually they saw the other members of the Delian League as their subjects and demanded annual contributions and other signs of submission from them. States that tried to leave the League were brought back by force, stripped of their defenses, and rendered subordinate to Athens.

Athens's mastery of naval technology transformed Greek warfare and politics and brought power and wealth to Athens itself. Unlike commercial ships, whose stable, round-bodied hulls were propelled by a single square sail, military vessels could not risk depending on the wind. By the late sixth century B.C.E. the **trireme°,** a sleek, fast vessel powered by 170 rowers, had become the premier warship. The design of the trireme has long been a puzzle, but the unearthing of the slips where these vessels were moored at Athens and recent experiments with a full-scale replica manned by international

volunteers have revealed much about the trireme's design and the battle tactics it made possible. Rowers using oars of different lengths and carefully positioned on three levels so as not to run afoul of one another were able to achieve short bursts of speed of up to 7 knots. Athenian crews, by constant practice, became the best in the eastern Mediterranean.

The emergence at Athens of a democratic system in which each male citizen had, at least in principle, an equal voice is connected to the new primacy of the fleet. Hoplites were members of the middle and upper classes (they had to provide their own protective gear and weapons). Rowers, in contrast, came from the lower classes, but because they were providing the chief protection for the community and were the source of its power, they could insist on full rights.

Possession of a navy allowed Athens to project its power farther than it could have done with a citizen militia (which could be kept in arms for only short periods of time). In previous Greek wars, the victorious state

---

trireme (TRY-reem)

had little capability to occupy a defeated neighbor permanently (with the exception, as we have seen, of Sparta's takeover of Messenia). Usually the victor was satisfied with booty and, perhaps, minor adjustments to boundary lines. Athens was able to continually dominate and exploit other, weaker communities in an unprecedented way.

Athens did not hesitate to use military and political power to promote its commercial interests. Athens's port, Piraeus°, grew into the most important commercial center in the eastern Mediterranean. The money collected each year from the subject states helped subsidize the increasingly expensive Athenian democracy as well as underwrite the construction costs of the beautiful buildings on the Acropolis, including the majestic new temple of Athena, the Parthenon. Many Athenians worked on the construction and decoration of these monuments. Indeed, the building program was a means by which the Athenian leader Pericles redistributed the profits of empire to the Athenian people and gained extraordinary popularity.

In other ways as well, Athens's cultural achievements were dependent on the profits of empire. The economic advantages that empire brought to Athens indirectly subsidized the festivals at which the great dramatic tragedies of Aeschylus, Sophocles, and Euripides and the comedies of Aristophanes° were performed. Money is a prerequisite for support of the arts and sciences, and the brightest and most creative artists and thinkers in the Greek world were drawn to Athens. Traveling teachers called Sophists ("wise men") provided instruction in logic and public speaking to pupils who could afford their fees. The new discipline of rhetoric—the construction of attractive and persuasive arguments—gave those with training and quick wits a great advantage in politics and the courts. The Greek masses became connoisseurs of oratory, eagerly listening for each innovation, yet so aware of the power of words that *sophist* came to mean one who uses cleverness to distort and manipulate reality.

These new intellectual currents came together in 399 B.C.E. when the philosopher **Socrates** (ca. 470–399 B.C.E.) was brought to trial. A sculptor by trade, Socrates spent most of his time in the company of young men who enjoyed conversing with him and observing him deflate the pretensions of those who thought themselves wise. He wryly commented that he knew one more thing than everyone else: that he knew nothing. At his trial, Socrates was easily able to dispose of the charges of corrupting the youth of Athens and not believing in the gods

of the city. He argued that the real basis of the hostility he faced was twofold: (1) He was being held responsible for the actions of several of his aristocratic students who had tried to overthrow the Athenian democracy. (2) He was being blamed unfairly for the controversial teachings of the Sophists, which were widely believed to be contrary to traditional religious beliefs and to undermine morality. In Athenian trials, juries of hundreds of citizens decided guilt and punishment, often motivated more by emotion than by legal principles. The vote that found Socrates guilty was fairly close. But his lack of contrition in the penalty phase—he proposed that he be rewarded for his services to the state—led the jury to condemn him to death by drinking hemlock. Socrates' disciples regarded his execution as a martyrdom, and smart young men such as Plato withdrew from public life and dedicated themselves to the philosophical pursuit of knowledge and truth.

This period encompasses the last stage in Greece of the transition from orality to literacy. Socrates himself wrote nothing, preferring to converse with people he met in the street. His disciple Plato (ca. 428–347 B.C.E.) may represent the first generation to be truly literate. He gained much of his knowledge from books and habitually wrote down his thoughts. On the outskirts of Athens, Plato founded the Academy, a school where young men could pursue a course of higher education. Yet even Plato retained traces of the orality of the world in which he had grown up. He wrote dialogues—an oral form—in which his protagonist, Socrates, uses the "Socratic method" of question and answer to reach a deeper understanding of the meaning of values such as justice, excellence, and wisdom. Plato refused to write down the most advanced stages of the philosophical and spiritual training that took place at his Academy. He believed that full apprehension of a higher reality, of which our own sensible world is but a pale reflection, could be entrusted only to "initiates" who had completed the earlier stages.

The third of the great classical philosophers, Aristotle (384–322 B.C.E.), came from Stagira, a community on the Thracian coast. After several decades of study at Plato's Academy in Athens, he was chosen by the king of Macedonia, Philip II, who had a high regard for Greek culture, to be the tutor of his son Alexander. Later, Aristotle returned to Athens to found his own school, the Lyceum. Of a very different temperament than Plato, who had been drawn to mysticism and metaphysical speculation, Aristotle sought to collect and categorize a vast array of knowledge. He lectured and wrote about politics, philosophy, ethics, logic, poetry, rhetoric, physics, astronomy, meteorology, zoology, and psychology, laying the foundations for many modern disciplines.

Piraeus (pih-RAY-uhs)   **Aristophanes** (ah-ruh-STOFF-eh-neze)

Inequality in Classical Greece

Athenian democracy, the inspiration for the concept of democracy in the Western tradition, was a democracy only for the relatively small percentage of the inhabitants of Attica who were truly citizens—free adult males of pure Athenian ancestry. Excluding women, children, slaves, and foreigners, this group amounted to 30,000 or 40,000 people out of a total population of approximately 300,000—only 10 or 15 percent.

Slaves, mostly of foreign origin, constituted perhaps one-third of the population of Attica in the fifth and fourth centuries B.C.E., and the average Athenian family owned one or more. Slaves were needed to run the shop or work on the farm while the master was attending meetings of the Assembly or serving on one of the boards that oversaw the day-to-day activities of the state. The slave was a "living piece of property," required to do any work, submit to any sexual acts, and receive any punishments that the owner ordained. In the absence of huge estates, there were no rural slave gangs, and most Greek slaves were domestic servants, often working on the same tasks as the master or mistress. Close daily contact between owners and slaves meant, in many cases, that a relationship developed, making it hard for Greek slave owners to deny the essential humanity of their slaves. Still, Greek thinkers rationalized the institution of slavery by arguing that barbaroi (non-Greeks) lacked the capacity to reason and thus were better off under the direction of rational Greek owners.

The position of women varied across Greek communities. The women of Sparta, who were expected to bear and raise strong children, were encouraged to exercise, and they enjoyed a level of public visibility and outspokenness that shocked other Greeks. Athens may have been at the opposite extreme as regards the confinement and suppression of women. Ironically, the exploitation of women in Athens, as of slaves, is linked to the high degree of freedom enjoyed by Athenian men in the democratic state.

Athenian marriages were unequal affairs. A new husband might be thirty, reasonably well educated, a veteran of war, and experienced in business and politics. Under law he had nearly absolute authority over the members of his household. He arranged his marriage with the parents of his prospective wife, who was likely to be a teenager brought up with no formal education and only minimal training in weaving, cooking, and household management. Coming into the home of a husband she hardly knew, she had no political rights and limited legal protection. Given the differences in age, social experience, and authority, the relationship between husband and wife was in many ways similar to that of father and daughter.

Vase Painting Depicting Women at an Athenian Fountain House, ca. 520 B.C.E. Paintings on Greek vases provide the most vivid pictorial record of ancient Greek life. The subject matter usually reflects the interests of the aristocratic males who purchased the vases—warfare, athletics, mythology, drinking parties—but sometimes we are given glimpses into the lives of women and the working classes. These women are presumably domestic servants sent to fetch water for the household from the public fountain. The large water jars they are filling are like the one on which this scene is depicted. (William Francis Warden Fund, Courtesy, Museum of Fine Arts Boston)

The primary function of marriage was to produce children, preferably male. It is impossible to prove the extent of infanticide—the killing through exposure of unwanted children—because the ancients were sufficiently ashamed to say little about it. But it is likely that more girls than boys were abandoned.

Husbands and wives had limited daily contact. The man spent the day outdoors attending to work or political responsibilities; he dined with male friends at night; and usually he slept alone in the men's quarters. The woman stayed home to cook, clean, raise the children, and supervise the servants. The closest relationship in the family was likely to be between the wife and her slave attendant. These women, often roughly the same age, spent enormous amounts of time together. The servant could be sent into town on errands. The wife stayed in the house, except to attend funerals and certain festivals and to make discreet visits to the houses of female relatives. Greek men justified the confinement of women by claiming that they were naturally promiscuous and likely to introduce other men's children into the household—an action that would threaten the family property and violate the strict regulation of citizenship rights.

Without any documents written by women in this period, we cannot tell the extent to which Athenian women resented their situation or accepted it because they knew little else. Women's festivals provided rare opportunities for women to get out. During the three-day Thesmophoria° festival, the women of Athens lived together and managed their own affairs in a great encampment, carrying out mysterious rituals meant to enhance the fertility of the land. The appearance of bold and self-assertive women on the Athenian stage is also suggestive: the defiant Antigone° of Sophocles' play who buried her brother despite the prohibition of the king; and the wives in Aristophanes' comedy *Lysistrata*° who refused to have sex with their husbands until the men ended a war. Although these plays were written by men and probably reflect a male fear of strong women, the playwrights must have had models in their mothers, sisters, and wives.

The inequality of men and women posed obstacles to creating a "meaningful" relationship between the sexes. To find his intellectual and emotional equal, a man often looked to other men. Bisexuality was common in ancient Greece, as much a product of the social structure as of biological inclinations. A common pattern was that of an older man serving as admirer, pursuer, and mentor of a youth. Bisexuality became part of a system by which young men were educated and initiated into the community of adult males. At least this was true of the elite intellectual groups that loom large in the written sources. It is hard to say how prevalent bisexuality and the confinement of women were among the Athenian masses.

Failure of the City-State and Triumph of the Macedonians

The emergence of Athens as an imperial power in the half-century after the Persian invasion aroused the suspicions of other Greek states and led to open hostilities between for-

Thesmophoria (thes-moe-FOE-ree-uh)
Antigone (an-TIG-uh-nee)   Lysistrata (lis-uh-STRAH-tuh)

mer allies. In 431 B.C.E. the **Peloponnesian War** broke out. This nightmarish struggle for survival between the Athenian and Spartan alliance systems encompassed most of the Greek world. It was a war unlike any previous Greek war because the Athenians used their naval power to insulate themselves from the dangers of an attack by land. In midcentury they had built three long walls connecting the city with the port of Piraeus and the adjacent shoreline. At the start of the war, Pericles formulated an unprecedented strategy, refusing to engage the Spartan-led armies that invaded Attica each year. Pericles knew that, as long as Athens controlled the sea lanes and was able to provision itself, the enemy hoplites must soon return to their farms and the city could not be starved into submission by a land-based siege. Thus, instead of culminating in a short, decisive battle like most Greek hoplite warfare, the Peloponnesian War dragged on for nearly three decades with great loss of life and squandering of resources. It sapped the morale of all of Greece and ended only with the defeat of Athens in a naval battle in 404 B.C.E. The Persian Empire had bankrolled the construction of ships by the Spartan alliance, so Sparta finally was able to take the conflict into Athens's own element, the sea.

The victorious Spartans, who had entered the war championing "the freedom of the Greeks," took over Athens's overseas empire until their own increasingly highhanded behavior aroused the opposition of other city-states. Indeed, the fourth century B.C.E. was a time of nearly continuous skirmishing among Greek states. One can make the case that the independent polis, from one point of view the glory of Greek culture, was also the fundamental structural flaw because it fostered rivalry, fear, and mistrust among neighboring communities.

Internal conflict in the Greek world allowed the Persians to recoup old losses. By the terms of the King's Peace of 387 B.C.E., to which most of the states of war-weary Greece subscribed, all of western Asia, including the Greek communities of the Anatolian seacoast, were conceded to Persia. The Persian king became the guarantor of a status quo that kept the Greeks divided and weak. Luckily for the Greeks, rebellions in Egypt, Cyprus, and Phoenicia as well as trouble with some of the satraps in the western provinces diverted Persian attention from thoughts of another Greek invasion.

Meanwhile, in northern Greece developments were taking place that would irrevocably alter the balance of power in the eastern Mediterranean and western Asia. Philip II (r. 359–336 B.C.E.) was transforming his previously backward kingdom of Macedonia into the premier military power in the Greek world. (Although southern Greeks had long doubted the "Greekness" of the rough and rowdy Macedonians, modern scholarship is inclined to regard their language and culture as Greek at base, though much influenced by contact with non-Greek neighbors.) Philip had made a number of improvements to the traditional hoplite formation. He increased the striking power and mobility of his force by equipping soldiers with longer thrusting spears and less armor. Because horses thrived in the broad, grassy plains of the north, he experimented with the coordinated use of infantry and cavalry. His engineers had also developed new kinds of siege equipment, including the first catapults—machines using the power of twisted cords that, when released, hurled arrows or stones great distances. For the first time it became possible to storm a fortified city rather than wait for starvation to take effect.

In 338 B.C.E. Philip defeated a coalition of southern states and established the Confederacy of Corinth as an instrument for controlling the Greek city-states. Philip had himself appointed military commander for a planned all-Greek campaign against Persia, and his generals established a bridgehead on the Asiatic side of the Hellespont. It appears that Philip was following the advice of Greek thinkers who had pondered the lessons of the Persian Wars of the fifth century B.C.E. and had urged a crusade against the national enemy as a means of unifying their quarrelsome countrymen.

We will never know how far Philip's ambitions extended, for an assassin killed him in 336 B.C.E. When **Alexander** (356–323 B.C.E.), his son and heir, crossed over into Asia in 334 B.C.E., his avowed purpose was to exact revenge for Xerxes' invasion a century and half before. He defeated the Persian forces of King Darius III (r. 336–330 B.C.E.) in three pitched battles in Anatolia and Mesopotamia, and ultimately campaigned as far as the Punjab region of modern Pakistan.

Alexander the Great, as he came to be called, maintained the framework of Persian administration in the lands he conquered. He realized that it was well adapted to local circumstances and familiar to the subject peoples. At first, however, he replaced Persian officials with his own Macedonian and Greek comrades. To control strategic points in his expanding empire, he established a series of Greek-style cities, beginning with Alexandria in Egypt, and he settled wounded and aged former soldiers in them. After his decisive victory at Gaugamela in northern Mesopotamia (331 B.C.E.), he began to experiment with leaving cooperative Persian officials in place. He also admitted some Persians and other Iranians into his army and into the circle of his courtiers, and he adopted elements of Persian dress and court ceremonial. Finally, he married several Iranian women who had useful royal or aristocratic connections, and he pressed his leading subordinates to do the same.

THE HELLENISTIC SYNTHESIS, 323–30 B.C.E.

At the time of his sudden death in 323 B.C.E. at the age of thirty-two, Alexander apparently had made no plans for the succession. Thus his death ushered in a half-century of chaos as the most ambitious and ruthless of his officers struggled for control of the vast empire. When the dust cleared, the empire had been broken up into three major kingdoms, each ruled by a Macedonian dynasty—the Seleucid°, Ptolemaic°, and Antigonid° kingdoms (see Map 4.3). Each major kingdom faced a unique set of problems, and although the three frequently were at odds with one another, a rough balance of power prevented any one from gaining the upper hand and enabled smaller states to survive by playing off the great powers.

Historians call the epoch ushered in by the conquests of Alexander the **"Hellenistic Age"** (323–30 B.C.E.) because the lands in northeastern Africa and western Asia that came under Greek rule tended to be "Hellenized"—that is, powerfully influenced by Greek culture. This was a period of large kingdoms with heterogeneous populations, great cities, powerful rulers, pervasive bureaucracies, and vast disparities in wealth—a far cry from the small, homogeneous, independent city-states of Archaic and Classical Greece. It was a cosmopolitan age of long-distance trade and communications, which saw the rise of new institutions like libraries and universities, new kinds of scholarship and science, and the cultivation of sophisticated tastes in art and literature. In many respects, in comparison with the preceding Classical era, it was a world much more like our own.

Of all the successor states, the kingdom of the Seleucids, who took over the bulk of Alexander's conquests, faced the greatest challenges. The Indus Valley and Afghanistan soon split off, and over the course of the third and second centuries B.C.E. Iran was lost to the Parthians. What remained for the Seleucids was a core in Mesopotamia, Syria, and parts of Anatolia, which the Seleucid monarchs ruled from their capital at Syrian Antioch°. Their sprawling territories were open to attack from many directions, and, like the Persians before them, they had to administer lands inhabited by many different ethnic groups organized under various political and social forms. In the countryside, where most of the

---

Seleucid (sih-LOO-sid)   **Ptolemaic** (tawl-uh-MAY-ik)
Antigonid (an-TIG-uh-nid)   **Antioch** (AN-tee-awk)

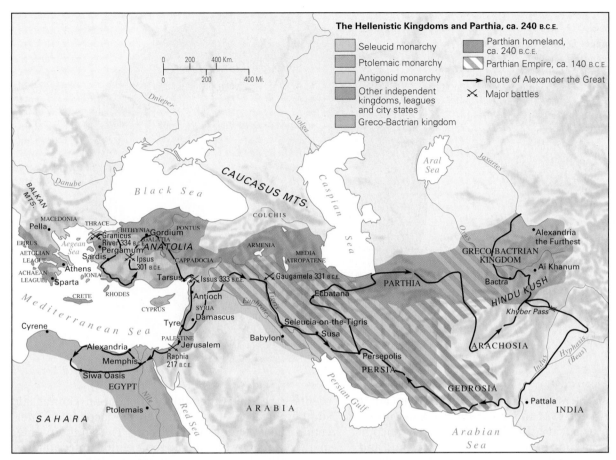

Map 4.3   Hellenistic Civilization   After the death of Alexander the Great in 323 B.C.E., his vast empire soon split apart into a number of large and small political entities. A Macedonian dynasty was established on each continent: the Antigonids ruled the Macedonian homeland and tried with varying success to extend their control over southern Greece: the Ptolemies ruled Egypt; and the Seleucids inherited the majority of Alexander's conquests in Asia, though they lost control of the eastern portions because of the rise of the Parthians of Iran in the second century B.C.E. This period saw Greeks migrating in large numbers from their overcrowded homeland to serve as a privileged class of soldiers and administrators on the new frontiers, where they replicated the lifestyle of the city-state.

native peoples resided, the Seleucids maintained an administrative structure modeled on the Persian system. They also continued Alexander's policy of founding Greek-style cities throughout their domains. These cities served as administrative centers and were also the lure that the Seleucids used to attract colonists from Greece. The Seleucids desperately needed Greek soldiers, engineers, administrators, and other professionals.

The dynasty of the **Ptolemies**° ruled Egypt and sometimes laid claim to adjacent Syria-Palestine. The people of Egypt belonged to only one ethnic group and

were fairly easily controlled because the vast majority of them were farmers living in villages alongside the Nile. The Ptolemies were able to take over much of the administrative structure of the pharaohs and to extract the surplus wealth of this populous and productive land. The Egyptian economy was centrally planned and highly controlled. Vast revenues poured into the royal treasury from rents (the king owned most of the land), taxes of all sorts, and royal monopolies on olive oil, salt, papyrus, and other key commodities.

The Ptolemies ruled from **Alexandria,** the first of the new cities laid out by Alexander himself. Alexandria was situated near to where the westernmost branch of the

Ptolemies (TAWL-uh-meze)

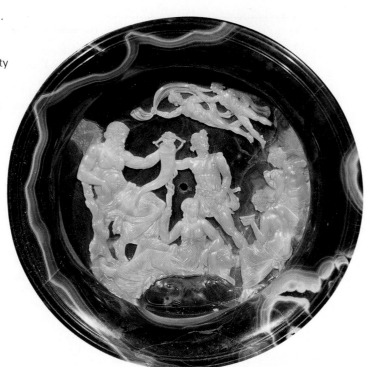

Hellenistic Cameo, Second Century B.C.E.
This sardonyx cameo is an allegory of the prosperity of Ptolemaic Egypt. At left, the bearded river-god Nile holds a horn of plenty while his wife, seated on a sphinx and dressed like the Egyptian goddess Isis, raises a stalk of grain. Their son, at center, carries a seed bag and the shaft of a plow. The Seasons are seated at right. Two wind-gods float overhead. The style is entirely Greek, but the motifs are a blending of Greek and Egyptian elements.
(G. Dagli-Orti, Paris)

Nile runs into the Mediterranean Sea and was meant to be a link between Egypt and the Mediterranean world.

Like the Seleucids, the Ptolemies actively encouraged the immigration of Greeks from the homeland and, in return for their skills and collaboration in the military or civil administration, gave them land and a privileged position in the new society. But the Ptolemies did not seek to plant Greek-style cities throughout the Egyptian countryside, and they made no effort to encourage the native population to adopt the Greek language or ways. In fact, so separate was the Greek ruling class from the subject population that only the last Ptolemy, Queen Cleopatra (r. 51–30 B.C.E.), even bothered to learn the language of the Egyptians. For the Egyptian peasant population laboring on the land, life was little changed by the advent of new masters. Yet from the early second century B.C.E., periodic native insurrections in the countryside, which government forces in cooperation with Greek and Hellenized settlers quickly stamped out, were signs of Egyptians' growing resentment of the Greeks' exploitation and arrogance.

In Europe, the Antigonid dynasty ruled the Macedonian homeland and adjacent parts of northern Greece. This was a compact and ethnically homogeneous kingdom, so there was little of the hostility and occasional resistance that the Seleucid and Ptolemaic ruling classes faced. Macedonian garrisons at strong-

points gave the Antigonids a toehold in central and southern Greece, and the shadow of Macedonian intervention always hung over the south. The southern states met the threat by banding together into confederations, such as the Achaean° League in the Peloponnese, in which the member-states maintained local autonomy but pooled resources and military power.

Athens and Sparta, the two leading cities of the Classical period, stood out from these confederations. The Spartans never quite abandoned the myth of their own invincibility and made a number of heroic but futile stands against Macedonian armies. Athens, which held a special place in the hearts of all Greeks because of the artistic and literary accomplishments of the fifth century B.C.E., pursued a policy of neutrality. The city became a large museum, filled with the relics and memories of a glorious past, as well as a university town that attracted the children of the well-to-do from all over the Mediterranean and western Asia.

In an age of cities, the greatest city of all was Alexandria, with a population of nearly half a million. At the heart of this city was the royal compound, containing the palace and administrative buildings for the ruling dynasty and its massive bureaucracy. The centerpiece

---

Achaean (uh-KEY-uhn)

was the magnificent Mausoleum of Alexander. The first Ptolemy had stolen the body of Alexander while it was being brought back to Macedonia for burial. The theft was aimed at gaining legitimacy for Ptolemaic rule by claiming the blessing of the great conqueror, who was declared to be a god. Two harbors served the needs of the many trading ventures that linked the commerce of the Mediterranean with the Red Sea and Indian Ocean. A great lighthouse—the first of its kind, a multistory tower with a fiery beacon visible at a distance of 30 miles (48 kilometers)—was one of the wonders of the ancient world.

Alexandria gained further luster from its famous Library, which had several hundred thousand volumes, and from its Museum, or "House of the Muses" (divinities who presided over the arts and sciences), a research institution that supported the work of the greatest poets, philosophers, doctors, and scientists of the day. The existence of such well-funded institutions made possible significant advances in science, both in the systematization and extension of earlier work. Some of the greatest achievements were in mathematics and astronomy. The mathematical writings of Euclid° (ca. 276–194 B.C.E.) and the astronomical text of Claudius Ptolemy (second century C.E.), each a grand synthesis of Greek accomplishments in these areas, were highly influential in Europe and the Islamic world into early modern times. Aristarchus° (ca. 310–230 B.C.E.) calculated the distances and relative sizes of the moon and sun. He also argued against the prevailing notion that the earth was the center of the universe, asserting that the earth and other planets revolved around the sun, a view that would not be accepted for another 1,800 years. Eratosthenes° (ca. 276–194 B.C.E.) made a surprisingly accurate calculation of the circumference of the earth. While the claim is often made that the Greeks had a strong predilection for abstract theorizing rather than experimental verification and practical application, experience was put to use in some fields. Archimedes° (ca. 287–211 B.C.E.) invented many mechanical devices, including the screw pump for extracting underground water, and developed a technique for determining the volume of an object. Galen° (ca. 129–210 C.E.), a Greek physician of the Roman era, conveyed the legacy of Greek medical knowledge to subsequent ages.

Greek residents of Alexandria enjoyed citizenship in a Greek-style polis with an Assembly, a Council, and officials who dealt with purely local affairs, and they took advantage of public works and institutions that signified the Greek way of life. Public baths and shaded arcades were places to relax and socialize with friends. Ancient plays were revived in the theaters, and musical performances and demonstrations of oratory took place in the concert halls. Gymnasiums offered facilities for exercise and fitness and were places where young men of the privileged classes were schooled in athletics, music, and literature. Jews had their own civic corporation, officials, and courts and predominated in two of the five main residential districts. Other quarters were filled with the sights, sounds, and smells of ethnic groups from Syria, Anatolia, and the Egyptian countryside.

In all the Hellenistic states, ambitious members of the indigenous populations learned the Greek language and adopted elements of the Greek way of life, because doing so put them in a position to become part of the privileged and wealthy ruling class. For the ancient Greeks, to be Greek was primarily a matter of language and lifestyle rather than physical traits. In the Hellenistic Age there was a spontaneous synthesis of Greek and indigenous ways. Egyptians migrated to Alexandria, and Greeks and Egyptians intermarried in the villages of the countryside. Greeks living amid the monuments and descendants of the ancient civilizations of Egypt and western Asia were exposed to the mathematical and astronomical wisdom of Mesopotamia, the elaborate mortuary rituals of Egypt, and the many attractions of foreign religious cults. With little official planning or blessing, stemming for the most part from the day-to-day experiences and actions of ordinary people, a great multicultural experiment unfolded as Greek and Middle Eastern cultural traits clashed and merged.

CONCLUSION

Profound changes took place in the lands of the eastern Mediterranean and western Asia in the first millennium B.C.E. Persians and Greeks played pivotal roles. Let us compare the impacts of these two peoples and assess the broad significance of these centuries.

The empire of the Achaemenid Persians was the largest empire yet to appear in the world. It was also a new kind of empire because it encompassed such a wide variety of landscapes, peoples, and social, political, and economic systems. How did the Persians manage to hold together this diverse collection of lands for more than two centuries?

The answer did not lie entirely in brute force. The

Euclid (YOO-klid)   **Aristarchus** (ah-ris-TAWR-kiss)
Eratosthenes (eh-ruh-TOSS-thih-nees)
Archimedes (ahr-kih-MEE-dees)   **Galen** (GAY-luhn)

Persians lacked the manpower to install garrisons everywhere, and communication between the central administration and provincial officials was sporadic and slow. They managed to co-opt leaders among the subject peoples who were willing to collaborate in return for being allowed to retain their power and influence. The Persian government demonstrated flexibility and tolerance in its handling of the laws, customs, and beliefs of subject peoples. Persian administration, superimposed on top of local structures, left a considerable role for local institutions.

The Persians also displayed a flair for public relations. The Zoroastrian religion underlined the authority of the king as the appointee of god and upholder of world order. In their art and inscriptions, the Persian kings broadcast an image of a benevolent empire in which the dependent peoples contributed to the welfare of the realm. Certain peoples with long and proud traditions, such as the Egyptians and Babylonians, revolted from time to time. But most subjects found the Persians to be decent enough masters and a great improvement over earlier Middle Eastern empires such as that of the Assyrians.

Western Asia underwent significant changes in the period of Persian supremacy. First, the early Persian kings put an end to the ancient centers of power in Mesopotamia, Anatolia, and Egypt. Then, by imposing a uniform system of law and administration and by providing security and stability, the Persian government fostered commerce and prosperity, at least for some. Some historians have argued that this period was a turning point in the economic history of western Asia.

Most difficult to assess is the cultural impact of Persian rule. The long-dominant culture of Mesopotamia fused with some Iranian elements. The resulting new synthesis is most visible in the art, architecture, and inscriptions of the Persian monarchs. The lands east of the Zagros Mountains as far as northwest India were brought within this cultural sphere. It has been suggested that the Zoroastrian religion spread across the empire and influenced other religious traditions, such as Judaism, but Zoroastrianism does not appear to have had broad, popular appeal. The Persian administration relied heavily on the scribes and written languages of its Mesopotamian, Syrian, and Egyptian subjects, and literacy remained the preserve of a small, professional class. Thus the Persian language does not seem to have been widely adopted by inhabitants of the empire.

Nearly two centuries of trouble with the Greeks on their western frontier vexed the Persians but was probably not their first priority. It appears that Persian kings were always more concerned about the security of their eastern and northeastern frontiers, where they were vulnerable to attack by the nomads of Central Asia. The technological differences between Greece and Persia were not great. The only difference that seems to have been of significance was a set of arms and a military formation used by the Greeks that often allowed them to prevail over the Persians. The Persian king's response in the later fifth and fourth centuries B.C.E. was to hire Greek mercenaries to use hoplite tactics for his benefit.

The shadow of Persia loomed large over the affairs of the Greek city-states for more than two centuries, and even after the repulse of Xerxes' great expeditionary force there was perpetual fear of another Persian invasion. The victories in 480 and 479 B.C.E. did allow the Greek city-states to continue to evolve politically and culturally at a critical time. Athens, in particular, vaulted into power, wealth, and intense cultural creativity as a result of its role in the Greek victory. It evolved into a new kind of Greek state, upsetting the rough equilibrium of the Archaic period by threatening the autonomy of other city-states and changing the rules of war. The result was the Peloponnesian War, which squandered lives and resources for a generation, raised serious doubts about the viability of the city-state, and diminished many people's allegiance to it.

Alexander's conquests brought changes to the Greek world almost as radical as those suffered by the Persians. Greeks spilled out into the sprawling new frontiers in northeastern Africa and western Asia, and the independent city-state became inconsequential in a world of large kingdoms. The centuries of Greek domination had a far more pervasive cultural impact on the Middle East than did the Persian period. Alexander had been inclined to preserve the Persian administrative apparatus, leaving native institutions and personnel in place. His successors relied almost exclusively on a privileged class of Greek soldiers, officers, and administrators.

Equally significant were the foundation of Greek-style cities, which exerted a powerful cultural influence on important elements of the native populations, and a system of easily learned alphabetic Greek writing, which led to more widespread literacy and far more effective dissemination of information. The result was that the Greeks had a profound impact on the peoples and lands of the Middle East, and Hellenism persisted as a cultural force for a thousand years.

■ Key Terms

Cyrus

Darius I

satrap

Persepolis

Zoroastrianism

polis

hoplite

tyrant

democracy

sacrifice

Herodotus

Pericles

Persian Wars

trireme

Socrates

Peloponnesian War

Alexander

Hellenistic Age

Ptolemies

Alexandria

■ Suggested Reading

The most up-to-date treatment of ancient Persia is Pierre Briant, *From Cyrus to Alexander: A History of the Persian Empire* (2002). Also useful is J. M. Cook, *The Persian Empire* (1983). Josef Wiesehofer, *Ancient Persia: From 550 B.C. to 650 A.D.* (1996); Richard N. Frye, *The History of Ancient Iran* (1984); and volume 2 of *The Cambridge History of Iran*, ed. Ilya Gershevitch (1985), are written by Iranian specialists and have abundant bibliographies. John Curtis, *Ancient Persia* (1989), emphasizes the archaeological record. Roland G. Kent, *Old Persian: Grammar, Texts, Lexicon*, 2d ed. (1953), contains translations of the royal inscriptions.

Maria Brosius, *Women in Ancient Persia, 559–331 B.C.* (1996), gathers and evaluates the scattered evidence. William W. Malandra, *An Introduction to Ancient Iranian Religion: Readings from the Avesta and Achaemenid Inscriptions* (1983), contains documents in translation pertaining to religious subjects. Vesta Sarkhosh Curtis, *Persian Myths* (1993), is a concise, illustrated introduction to Iranian myths and legends. John Boardman, *Persia and the West: An Archaeological Investigation of the Genesis of Achaemenid Persian Art* (2000), explores the complex question of Greek influence on Persian art and architecture.

The fullest treatment of Greek history and civilization in this period is in *The Cambridge Ancient History*, 3d ed., vols. 3–7 (1970–). Sarah B. Pomeroy, Stanley M. Burstein, Walter Donlan, and Jennifer Tolbert Roberts, *Ancient Greece: A Political, Social, and Cultural History* (1999), is a fine one-volume treatment of Greek civilization. Bella Vivante, ed., *Events That Changed Ancient Greece* (2002), contains an overview, interpretative essay, and up-to-date bibliography for each period of Greek history. Other general treatments include J. B. Bury and Russell Meiggs, *A History of Greece* (1975), and Nancy Demand, *A History of Ancient Greece* (1996). For the Archaic period see Oswyn Murray, *Early Greece*, 2d ed. (1993), and Robin Osborne, *Greece in the Making, 1200–479 B.C.* (1996).

Social history is emphasized by Frank J. Frost, *Greek Society*, 3d ed. (1987). Robert Morkot, *The Penguin Historical Atlas of Ancient Greece* (1996), and Peter Levi, *Atlas of the Greek World* (1980), are filled with maps, pictures, and general information about Greek civilization, as is Lesley Adkins and Roy A. Adkins, *Handbook to Life in Ancient Greece* (1997). Michael Grant and Rachel Kitzinger, eds., *Civilization of the Ancient Mediterranean* (1987), is a three-volume collection of essays by contemporary experts on nearly every aspect of ancient Greco-Roman civilization and includes select bibliographies.

We are fortunate to have an abundant written literature from ancient Greece, and the testimony of the ancients themselves should be the starting point for any inquiry. Herodotus, Thucydides, and Xenophon chronicled the history of the Greeks and their Middle Eastern neighbors from the sixth through fourth centuries B.C.E. Arrian, who lived in the second century C.E., provides the most useful account of the career of Alexander the Great. Among the many collections of documents in translation, see Michael Crawford and David Whitehead, eds., *Archaic and Classical Greece: A Selection of Ancient Sources in Translation* (1983). David G. Rice and John E. Stambaugh, eds., *Sources for the Study of Greek Religion* (1979); Mary R. Lefkowitz and Maureen B. Fant, eds., *Women's Life in Greece and Rome: A Source Book in Translation* (1982); Thomas Wiedemann, ed., *Greek and Roman Slavery* (1981); Michael M. Sage, *Warfare in Ancient Greece: A Sourcebook* (1996), and Michael Gagarin and Paul Woodruff, *Early Greek Political Thought from Homer to the Sophists* (1995), are specialized collections. The Perseus Project (*www.perseus.tufts.edu*) is a remarkable internet site containing hundreds of ancient texts, thousands of photographs of artifacts and sites, maps, encyclopedias, dictionaries, and other resources for the study of Greek (and Roman) civilization.

Victor Davis Hanson, *The Other Greeks: The Family Farm and the Agrarian Roots of Western Civilization* (1995), emphasizes the centrality of farming to the development of Greek institutions and values. Eric A. Havelock, *The Muse Learns to Write: Reflections on Orality and Literacy from Antiquity to the Present* (1986), and Rosalind Thomas, *Literacy and Orality in Ancient Greece* (1992), explore the profound effects of alphabetic literacy on the Greek mind.

Valuable treatments of other key topics include Elaine Fantham, Helene Peet Foley, Natalie Boymel Kampen, Sarah B. Pomeroy, and H. Alan Shapiro, *Women in the Classical World* (1994); Cynthia Patterson, *The Family in Greek History* (1998); Yvon Garlan, *Slavery in Ancient Greece* (1988); Walter Burkert, *Greek Religion* (1985); Victor Davis Hanson, *The Western Way of War: Infantry Battle in Classical Greece* (1989); Lionel Casson, *The Ancient Mariners: Seafarers and Sea Fighters of the Mediterranean in Ancient Times*, 2d ed. (1991); Michail Yu Treister, *The Role of Metals in Ancient Greek History* (1996); Joint Association of Classical Teachers, *The World of Athens: An Introduction to Classical Athenian Culture* (1984); N. G. L. Hammond, *The Macedonian State: The Origins, Institutions and History* (1989); Joseph Roisman, ed., *Alexander the Great: Ancient and Modern Perspectives* (1995); and William R. Biers, *The Archaeology of*

Greece: An Introduction (1990). Mary R. Lefkowitz and Guy MacLean Rogers, *Black Athena Revisited* (1996), explores the controversies surrounding the Greek cultural obligation to Egypt and western Asia. For the Hellenistic world see F. W. Walbank, *The Hellenistic World*, rev. ed. (1993), and Michael Grant, *From Alexander to Cleopatra: The Hellenistic World* (1982). M. M. Austin, ed., *The Hellenistic World from Alexander to the Roman Conquest: A Selection of Ancient Sources in Translation* (1981), provides sources in translation. Jean-Yves Empereur, *Alexandria Rediscovered* (1998), summarizes exciting new finds from the palace precinct in the waters off Alexandria.

■ Notes

1. Richmond Lattimore, *Greek Lyrics*, 2d ed. (Chicago: University of Chicago Press, 1960), 2.
2. G. S. Kirk and J. E. Raven, *The Presocratic Philosophers: A Critical History with a Selection of Texts* (Cambridge, England: Cambridge University Press, 1957), 169.
3. Herodotus, *The History*, trans. David Grene (Chicago: University of Chicago Press, 1988), 33. (Herodotus 1.1)

Document-Based Question
Power and Authority in Iran and Greece

Drawing on the following documents, analyze the methods used by Persian and Greek rulers to exert and legitimize their authority.

DOCUMENT 1
Painted Cup of Arcesilas of Cyrene (photo, p. 92)

DOCUMENT 2
Map 4.1 The Persian Empire (p. 94)

DOCUMENT 3
View of the East Front of the Apadana (Audience Hall) at Persepolis, ca. 500 B.C.E. (photo, p. 98)

DOCUMENT 4
The Persian Idea of Kingship (Diversity and Dominance, pp. 100–101)

DOCUMENT 5
The Acropolis at Athens (photo, p. 106)

DOCUMENT 6
Excerpt from Herodotus (p. 109)

DOCUMENT 7
Hellenistic Cameo, Second Century B.C.E. (photo, p. 118)

How do Documents 3 through 7 demonstrate the importance of cultural continuity in establishing power and authority? What additional types of documents would help you understand how Greek and Persian rulers legitimized their authority?

An Age of Empires: Rome and Han China, 753 B.C.E.–600 C.E.

5

Terracotta Soldiers from the Tomb of Shi Huangdi, "First Emperor" of China   Thousands of these life-size, baked-clay figures—each with distinctive features—have been unearthed.

CHAPTER OUTLINE

Rome's Mediterranean Empire, 753 B.C.E.–600 C.E.

The Origins of Imperial China, 221 B.C.E.–220 C.E.

Imperial Parallels

DIVERSITY AND DOMINANCE: The Treatment of Slaves in Rome and China

ENVIRONMENT AND TECHNOLOGY: Water Engineering in Rome and China

123

According to Chinese sources, in the year 166 C.E. a group of travelers identifying themselves as delegates from Andun, the king of distant Da Qin, arrived at the court of the Chinese emperor Huan, one of the Han rulers. Andun was Marcus Aurelius Antoninus, the emperor of Rome.

As far as we know, these travelers were the first "Romans" to reach China, although they probably were residents of one of the eastern provinces of the Roman Empire, perhaps Egypt or Syria, and they may have stretched the truth in claiming to be official representatives of the Roman emperor. More likely they were merchants hoping to set up a profitable trading arrangement at the source of the silk so highly prized in the West. Chinese officials, however, were in no position to disprove their claim, since there was no direct contact between the Roman and Chinese Empires.

We do not know what became of these travelers, and their mission apparently did not lead to more direct or regular contact between the empires. Even so, the episode raises some interesting points. First, in the early centuries C.E. Rome and China were linked by far-flung international trading networks encompassing the entire Eastern Hemisphere, and were dimly aware of each other's existence. Second, the last centuries B.C.E. and the first centuries C.E. saw the emergence of two manifestations of a new kind of empire.

The Roman Empire encompassed all the lands surrounding the Mediterranean Sea as well as substantial portions of continental Europe and the Middle East. The Han Empire stretched from the Pacific Ocean to the oases of Central Asia. The largest empires the world had yet seen, they managed to centralize control to a greater degree than earlier empires; their cultural impact on the lands and peoples they dominated was more pervasive; and they were remarkably stable and lasted for many centuries.

Thousands of miles separated Rome and Han China; neither influenced the other. Why did two such unprecedented political entities flourish at the same time? Historians have put forth theories stressing supposedly common factors—such as climate change and the pressure of nomadic peoples from Central Asia on the Roman and Chinese frontiers—but no theory has won the support of most scholars.

As you read this chapter, ask yourself the following questions:

- How did the Roman and Han Empires come into being?
- What were the sources of their stability or instability?
- What benefits and liabilities did these empires bring to the rulers and their subjects?
- What were the most important similarities and differences between these two empires, and what do the similarities and differences tell us about the circumstances and the character of each?

ROME'S MEDITERRANEAN EMPIRE, 753 B.C.E.–600 C.E.

Rome's central location contributed to its success in unifying Italy and then all the lands ringing the Mediterranean Sea (see Map 5.1). Italy was a crossroads in the Mediterranean, and Rome was a crossroads within Italy. Rome lay at the midpoint of the peninsula, about 15 miles (24 kilometers) from the western coast, where a north-south road intersected an east-west river route. The Tiber River on one side and a double ring of seven hills on the other afforded natural protection to the site.

Italy is a land of hills and mountains. The Apennine range runs along its length like a spine, separating the eastern and western coastal plains, while the arc of the Alps shields it on the north. Many of Italy's rivers are navigable, and passes through the Apennines and the Alps allowed merchants and armies to travel overland. The mild Mediterranean climate affords a long growing season and conditions suitable for a wide variety of crops. The hillsides were well forested in ancient times, providing timber for construction and fuel. The region of Etruria in the northwest was rich in iron and other metals.

Even though 75 percent of the total area of the Italian peninsula is hilly, there is still ample arable land in the coastal plains and river valleys. Much of this land has fertile volcanic soil and sustained a much larger population than was possible in Greece. While expanding within Italy, the Roman state created effective mechanisms for tapping the human resources of the countryside.

C H R O N O L O G Y

	Rome	China
1000 B.C.E.	**1000 B.C.E.** First settlement on site of Rome	
500 B.C.E.	**507 B.C.E.** Establishment of the Republic	**480–221 B.C.E.** Warring States Period
300 B.C.E.	**290 B.C.E.** Defeat of tribes of Samnium gives Romans control of Italy	
	264–202 B.C.E. Wars against Carthage guarantee Roman control of western Mediterranean	**221 B.C.E.** Qin emperor unites eastern China
		206 B.C.E. Han dynasty succeeds Qin
200 B.C.E.	**200–146 B.C.E.** Wars against Hellenistic kingdoms lead to control of eastern Mediterranean	
		140–87 B.C.E. Emperor Wu expands the Han Empire
100 B.C.E.	**88–31 B.C.E.** Civil wars and failure of the Republic	
	31 B.C.E.–14 C.E. Augustus establishes the Principate	
		23 C.E. Han capital transferred from Chang'an to Luoyang
	45–58 C.E. Paul spreads Christianity in the eastern Mediterranean	
100 C.E.		
200 C.E.	**235–284 C.E.** Third-century crisis	**220 C.E.** Fall of Han Empire
300 C.E.		
500 C.E.	**324 C.E.** Constantine moves capital to Constantinople	
	476 Deposing of the last Roman emperor in the West	
	527–565 Justinian and Theodora rule Byzantine Empire; imperial edicts collected in single law code	

A Republic of Farmers, 753–31 B.C.E

According to popular legend, Romulus, who was cast adrift on the Tiber River as a baby and was nursed by a she-wolf, founded the city of Rome in 753 B.C.E. Archaeological research, however, shows that the Palatine Hill—one of the seven hills on the site of Rome—was occupied as early as 1000 B.C.E. The merging of several hilltop communities to form an urban nucleus, made possible by the draining of a swamp on the site of the future Roman Forum (civic center), took place shortly before 600 B.C.E.

The Latin speech and cultural patterns of the original inhabitants of the site were typical of the indigenous

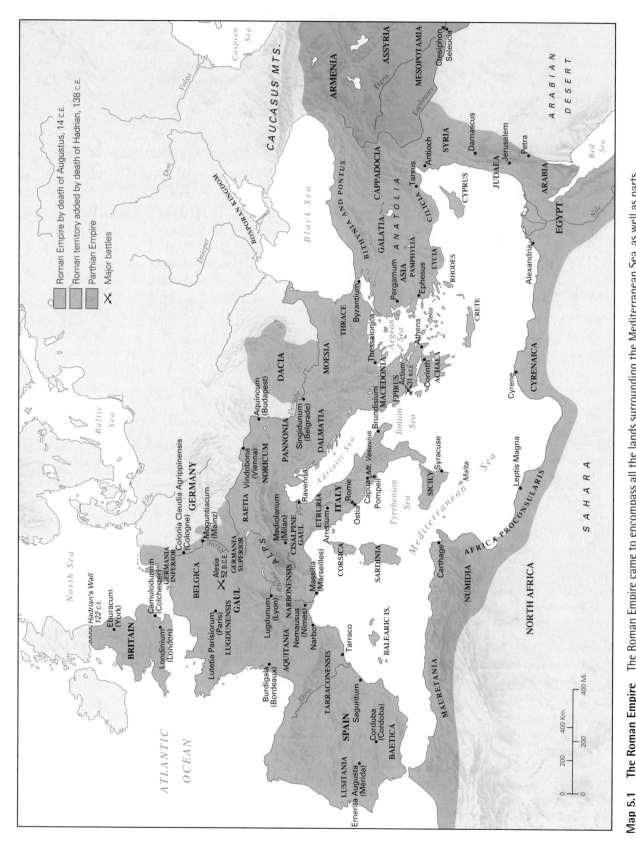

Map 5.1   The Roman Empire   The Roman Empire came to encompass all the lands surrounding the Mediterranean Sea, as well as parts of continental Europe. When Augustus died in 14 C.E., he left instructions to his successors not to expand beyond the limits he had set, but Claudius invaded southern Britain in the mid-first century and the soldier-emperor Trajan added Romania early in the second century. Deserts and seas provided solid natural boundaries, but the long and vulnerable river border in central and eastern Europe would eventually prove expensive to defend and vulnerable to invasion by Germanic and Central Asian peoples.

population of most of the peninsula. However, tradition remembered Etruscan immigrants arriving in the seventh century B.C.E., and Rome came to pride itself on offering hospitality to exiles and outcasts.

Agriculture was the essential economic activity in the early Roman state, and land was the basis of wealth. As a consequence, social status, political privilege, and fundamental values were related to landownership. The vast majority of early Romans were self-sufficient independent farmers who owned small plots of land. A relatively small number of families managed to acquire large tracts of land. The heads of these wealthy families were members of the Senate—a "Council of Elders" that played a dominant role in the politics of the Roman state. These families constituted the senatorial class.

According to tradition, there were seven kings of Rome between 753 and 507 B.C.E. The first was Romulus; the last was the tyrannical Tarquinius Superbus. In 507 B.C.E. members of the senatorial class, led by Brutus "the Liberator," deposed Tarquinius Superbus and instituted a *res publica*, a "public possession," or republic.

The **Roman Republic,** which lasted from 507 to 31 B.C.E., was not a democracy. Sovereign power resided in several assemblies, and while all male citizens were eligible to attend, the votes of the wealthy classes counted for more than the votes of poor citizens. A slate of civic officials was elected each year, and a hierarchy of state offices evolved. The culmination of a political career was to be selected as one of the two consuls who presided over meetings of the Senate and assemblies and commanded the army on military campaigns.

The real center of power was the **Roman Senate.** Technically an advisory council, first to the kings and later to the annually changing Republican officials, the Senate increasingly made policy and governed. Senators nominated their sons for public offices and filled Senate vacancies from the ranks of former officials. This self-perpetuating body, whose members served for life, brought together the state's wealth, influence, and political and military experience.

The inequalities in Roman society led to periodic unrest and conflict between the elite (called "patricians°") and the majority of the population (called "plebeians°"), a struggle known as the Conflict of the Orders. On a number of occasions the plebeians refused to work or fight, and even physically withdrew from the city, in order to pressure the elite to make political concessions. One result was publication of the laws on twelve stone tablets ca. 450 B.C.E., a check on arbitrary decisions by judicial officials. Another important reform was the creation of

Statue of a Roman Carrying Busts of His Ancestors, First Century B.C.E. Roman society was extremely conscious of status, and the status of an elite Roman family was determined in large part by the public achievements of ancestors and living members. A visitor to a Roman home found portraits of distinguished ancestors in the entry hall, along with labels listing the offices they held. Portrait heads were carried in funeral processions. (Alinari/Art Resource, NY)

new officials, the tribunes°, who were drawn from and elected by the lower classes, and who had the power to veto, or block, any action of the Assembly or patrician officials that they deemed to be against the interests of the lower orders. The elite, though forced to give in on key points, found ways to blunt the reforms, in large part by bringing the plebeian leadership into an expanded elite.

---

patrician (puh-TRISH-uhn)   **plebeian** (pluh-BEE-uhn)

tribune (TRIH-byoon)

The basic unit of Roman society was the family, made up of several generations of family members plus domestic slaves. The oldest living male, the *paterfamilias,* exercised absolute authority over other family members.

Complex ties of obligation, such as the **patron/client relationship,** bound together individuals and families. Clients sought the help and protection of patrons, men of wealth and influence. A senator might have dozens or even hundreds of clients, to whom he provided legal advice and representation, physical protection, and loans of money in tough times. In turn, the client was expected to follow his patron into battle, support him in the political arena, work on his land, and even contribute toward the dowry of his daughter. Throngs of clients awaited their patrons in the morning and accompanied them to the Forum for the day's business. Especially large retinues brought great prestige. Middle-class clients of aristocrats might be patrons of poorer men. In Rome inequality was accepted, institutionalized, and turned into a system of mutual benefits and obligations.

Nearly all our information about Roman women pertains to those in the upper classes. In early Rome, a woman never ceased to be a child in the eyes of the law. She started out under the absolute authority of her paterfamilias. When she married, she came under the jurisdiction of the paterfamilias of her husband's family. Unable to own property or represent herself in legal proceedings, she had to depend on a male guardian to advocate her interests.

Despite the limitations put on them, Roman women seem to have been less constrained than their counterparts in the Greek world (see Chapter 4). Over time they gained greater personal protection and economic freedom: for instance, some took advantage of a form of marriage that left a woman under the jurisdiction of her father and independent after his death. There are many stories of strong women who had great influence on their husbands or sons and thereby helped shape Roman history. Roman poets confess their love for women who appear to have been educated and outspoken, and the accounts of the careers of the early emperors are filled with tales of self-assured and assertive queen-mothers and consorts.

Like other Italian peoples, early Romans believed in invisible, shapeless forces known as *numina.* Vesta, the living, pulsating energy of fire, dwelled in the hearth. Janus guarded the door. The Penates watched over food stored in the cupboard. Other deities resided in nearby hills, caves, grottoes, and springs. Romans made small offerings of cakes and liquids to win the favor of these spirits. Certain gods had larger spheres of operation—for example, Jupiter was the god of the sky, and Mars initially was a god of agriculture as well as of war.

The Romans tried to maintain the *pax deorum* ("peace of the gods"), a covenant between the gods and the Roman state. Boards of priests drawn from the aristocracy performed sacrifices and other rituals to win the gods' favor. In return, the gods were expected to bring success to the undertakings of the Roman state. When the Romans came into contact with the Greeks of southern Italy (see Chapter 4), they equated their major deities with gods from the Greek pantheon, such as Zeus (Jupiter) and Ares (Mars), and they took over the myths attached to those gods.

Expansion in Italy and the Mediterranean

The expansion of the Roman Republic began slowly, then picked up momentum, reaching a peak in the third and second centuries B.C.E. Some scholars attribute this expansion to the greed and aggressiveness of a people fond of war. Others observe that the structure of the Roman state encouraged war, because the two consuls had only one year in office in which to gain military glory. The Romans invariably claimed that they were only defending themselves. It is possible that, as fear drove the Romans to expand the territory under their control in order to provide a buffer against attack, each new conquest became vulnerable and a sense of insecurity led to further expansion.

All male citizens who owned a specified amount of land were subject to military service. The Roman soldiers' equipment—body armor, shield, spear, and sword—was not far different from that of Greek hoplites, but the Roman battle line was more flexible than the phalanx, being subdivided into units that could maneuver independently. Roman armies were famous for their training and discipline. One observer noted that, whereas a Greek army would minimize its exertions by finding a hill or some other naturally defended location to camp for the night, a Roman army would go to the trouble of fortifying an identical camp in the plain on every occasion.

Rome's conquest of Italy was sparked by ongoing friction between the pastoral hill tribes of the Apennines, whose livelihood depended on driving their herds to seasonal grazing grounds, and the farmers of the coastal plains. In the fifth century B.C.E. Rome rose to a position of leadership within a league of central Italian cities organized for defense against the hill tribes.

Unlike the Greeks, who were reluctant to share the privileges of citizenship with outsiders (see Chapter 4), the Romans granted the political, legal, and economic privileges of Roman citizenship to conquered populations. Rome also demanded soldiers from its Italian subjects, and a seemingly inexhaustible reservoir of manpower was a key element of its military success. In a number of crucial wars, Rome was able to endure higher casualties than the enemy and to prevail by sheer numbers.

Between 264 and 202 B.C.E. Rome fought two protracted and bloody wars against the Carthaginians, those energetic descendants of Phoenicians from Lebanon who had settled in present-day Tunisia and dominated the commerce of the western Mediterranean (see Chapter 3). The Roman state emerged as the unchallenged master of the western Mediterranean and acquired its first overseas provinces in Sicily, Sardinia, and Spain (see Map 5.1). Between 200 and 146 B.C.E. a series of wars pitted the Roman state against the major Hellenistic kingdoms in the eastern Mediterranean. The Romans were at first reluctant to occupy such distant territories and withdrew their troops at the conclusion of several wars. But when the settlements that they imposed failed to take root, the frustrated Roman government took over direct administration of the turbulent lands. The conquest of the Celtic peoples of Gaul (modern France) by Rome's most brilliant general, Gaius Julius Caesar, between 59 and 51 B.C.E. led to its first territorial acquisitions in Europe's heartland.

At first the Romans resisted extending their system of governance and citizenship rights to the distant provinces. Indigenous elite groups willing to collaborate with the Roman authorities were given considerable autonomy, including responsibility for local administration and tax collection. Every year a senator, usually someone who recently had held a high public post, was dispatched to each province to serve as governor. The governor was primarily responsible for defending the province against outside attack and internal disruption, overseeing the collection of taxes and other revenues due Rome, and deciding legal cases.

Over time, this system of provincial administration proved inadequate. Officials were chosen because of their political connections and often lacked competence or experience. Yearly changes of governor meant that incumbents had little time to gain experience or make local contacts. Also, although many governors were honest, some were unscrupulous and extorted huge sums of money from the provincial populace.

Scene from Trajan's Column, Rome, ca. 113 C.E.   The Roman emperor Trajan erected a marble column 125 feet (38 meters) in height to commemorate his triumphant campaign in Dacia (modern Romania). The relief carving, which snakes around the column for 656 feet (200 meters), illustrates numerous episodes of the conquest and provides a detailed pictorial record of the equipment and practices of the Roman army in the field. This panel depicts soldiers building a fort.   (Peter Rockwell, Rome)

The Failure of the Republic

Rome's success in creating a vast empire unleashed forces that eventually destroyed the Republican system of government. In the third and second centuries B.C.E., Italian peasant farmers were away from home on military service for long periods of time. While they were away, it was easy for investors to take possession of their farms by purchase, deception, or intimidation. Most of the wealth generated by the conquest and control of new provinces ended up in the hands of the upper classes, who used it to purchase Italian land. As a result, the small, self-sufficient farms of the Italian countryside, whose peasant owners had been the backbone of the Roman legions (units of 6,000 soldiers), were replaced by *latifundia*, literally "broad estates."

The owners of these large estates found it more lucrative to graze herds or to make wine, undertakings that brought in big profits, than to grow wheat, the staple food of ancient Italy. Much of Italy, especially the burgeoning cities, became dependent on imported grain. Meanwhile, the cheap slave labor provided by prisoners of war (see Diversity and Dominance: The Treatment of Slaves in Rome and China) made it hard for peasants who had lost their farms to find work in the countryside.

DIVERSITY AND DOMINANCE

THE TREATMENT OF SLAVES IN ROME AND CHINA

Although slaves were found in most ancient societies, Rome was one of the few in which slave labor became the indispensable foundation of the economy. In the course of the frequent wars of the second century B.C.E., large numbers of prisoners were carried into slavery. The prices of such slaves were low, and landowners and manufacturers found they could compel slaves to work longer and harder than hired laborers. Periodically, the harsh working and living conditions resulted in slave revolts.

The following excerpt, from one of several surviving manuals on agriculture, gives advice about controlling and efficiently exploiting slaves:

When the head of a household arrives at his estate, after he has prayed to the family god, he must go round his farm on a tour of inspection on the very same day, if that is possible, if not, then on the next day. When he has found out how his farm has been cultivated and which jobs have been done and which have not been done, then on the next day after that he must call in his manager and ask him which are the jobs that have been done and which remain, and whether they were done on time, and whether what still has to be done can be done, and how much wine and grain and anything else has been produced. When he has found this out, he must make a calculation of the labor and the time taken. If the work doesn't seem to him to be sufficient, and the manager starts to say how hard he tried, but the slaves weren't any good, and the weather was awful, and the slaves ran away, and he was required to carry out some public works, then when he has finished mentioning these and all sorts of other excuses, you must draw his attention to your calculation of the labor employed and time taken. If he claims that it rained all the time, there are all sorts of jobs that can be done in rainy weather—washing wine-jars, coating them with pitch, cleaning the house, storing grain, shifting muck, digging a manure pit, cleaning seed, mending ropes or making new ones; the slaves ought to have been mending their patchwork cloaks and their hoods. On festival days they would have been able to clean out old ditches, work on the public highway, prune back brambles,

dig up the garden, clear a meadow, tie up bundles of sticks, remove thorns, grind barley and get on with cleaning. If he claims that the slaves have been ill, they needn't have been given such large rations. When you have found out about all these things to your satisfaction, make sure that all the work that remains to be done will be carried out. . . The head of the household [on his tour of inspection] should examine his herds and arrange a sale; he should sell the oil if the price makes it worthwhile, and any wine and rain that is surplus to needs; he should sell any old oxen, cattle or sheep that are not up to standard, wool and hides, an old cart or old tools, an old slave, a sick slave—anything else that is surplus to requirements. The head of a household ought to sell, and not to buy. (Cato the Elder, *Concerning Agriculture*, bk. 2, second century B.C.E.)

Cato, the Roman author of that excerpt, was notorious for his stern manner and hard-edged traditionalism, and he expresses a point of view that Roman society found acceptable. In reality, the treatment of slaves by Roman masters varied widely.

Slavery was far less prominent in ancient China. During the Warring States Period, dependent peasants as well as slaves worked the large holdings of the landowning aristocracy. The Qin government sought to abolish slavery, but the institution persisted into the Han period, although it involved only a small fraction of the population and was not a central component of the economy. The relatives of criminals could be seized and enslaved, and poor families sometimes sold unwanted children into slavery. In China slaves, whether they belonged to the state or to individuals, generally performed domestic tasks, as can be seen in the following text:

Wang Ziyuan of Shu Commandery went to the Jian River on business, and went up to the home of the widow Yang Hui, who had a male slave named Bianliao. Wang Ziyuan requested him to go and buy some wine. Picking up a big stick, Bianliao climbed to the top of the grave mound and said: "When my master bought me, Bianliao, he only contracted for me to care for the grave and did not contract for me to buy wine for some other gentleman."

Wang Ziyuan was furious and said to the widow: "Wouldn't you prefer to sell this slave?"

Yang Hui said: "The slave's father offered him to people, but no one wanted him."

Wang Ziyuan immediately settled on the sale contract.

The slave again said: "Enter in the contract everything you wish to order me to do. I, Bianliao, will not do anything not in the contract."

Wang Ziyuan said: "Agreed."

The text of the contract said:

Third year of Shenjiao , the first month, the fifteenth day, the gentleman Wang Ziyuan, of Zizhong, purchases from the lady Yang Hui of Anzhi village in Zhengdu, the bearded male slave, Bianliao, of her husband's household. The fixed sale [price] is 15,000 [cash]. The slave shall obey orders about all kinds of work and may not argue.

He shall rise at dawn and do an early sweeping. After eating he shall wash up. Ordinarily he should pound the grain mortar, tie up broom straws, carve bowls and bore wells, scoop out ditches, tie up fallen fences, hoe the garden, trim up paths and dike up plots of land, cut big flails, bend bamboos to make rakes, and scrape and fix the well pulley. In going and coming he may not ride horseback or in the cart, [nor may he] sit crosslegged or make a hubbub. When he gets out of bed he shall shake his head [to wake up], fish, cut forage, plait reeds and card hemp, draw water for gruel, and help in making zumo [drink]. He shall weave shoes and make [other] coarse things . . .

In the second month at the vernal equinox he shall bank the dikes and repair the boundary walls [of the fields]; prune the mulberry trees, skin the palm trees, plant melons to make gourd [utensils], select eggplant [seeds for planting], and transplant onion sets; burn plant remains to generate the fields, pile up refuse and break up lumps [in the soil]. At midday he shall dry out things in the sun. At cockcrow he shall rise and pound grain in the mortar, exercise and curry the horses, the donkeys, and likewise the mules . . . [The list of tasks continues for two-and-a-half pages.]

He shall be industrious and quick-working, and he may not idle and loaf. When the slave is old and his strength spent, he shall plant marsh grass and weave mats. When his work is over and he wishes to rest he should pound a picul [of grain]. Late at night when there is no work he shall wash clothes really white. If he has private savings they shall be the master's gift, or from guests. The slave may not have evil secrets; affairs should be open and reported. If the slave does not heed instructions, he shall be whipped a hundred strokes.

The reading of the text of the contract came to an end.

The slave was speechless and his lips were tied. Wildly he beat his head on the ground, and beat himself with his hands; from his eyes the tears streamed down, and the drivel from his nose hung a foot long.

He said: "If it is to be exactly as master Wang says, I would rather return soon along the yellow-soil road, with the grave worms boring through my head. Had I known before I would have bought the wine for master Wang. I would not have dared to do that wrong." (Wang Bao, first century B.C.E.)

*T*his story shows that Chinese slaves could be forced to work hard and engaged in many of the same menial tasks as their Roman counterparts. However, it is hard to imagine a Roman slave daring to refuse a request and arguing publicly with a nobleman, for fear of severe punishment. It also appears that slaves in China had legal protections provided by contracts specifying and limiting what could be demanded of them.

QUESTIONS FOR ANALYSIS

1. Why might slavery have been less important in Han China than in the Roman Empire? Why would the treatment of slaves have been less harsh in China than in Rome?

2. In what ways were slaves treated like other forms of property, such as animals and tools? In what ways was a slave's "humanity" taken into account?

3. What are some of the passive-resistance tactics that slaves resorted to, and what did they achieve by these actions?

Source: First selection from Thomas Wiedemann, *Greek and Roman Slavery,* (Baltimore: Johns Hopkins University Press (1981), 183–184. Reprinted with the permission of Thomas Publishing Services. Second selection reprinted with permission of Scribner, an imprint of Simon and Schuster Adult Publishing Group, from *Slavery in China During the Former Han Dynasty, 206 B.C.–A.D. 25* by Clarence Martin Wilbur (New York: Russell & Russell, 1967).

When they moved to Rome and other cities, they found no work there either, and they lived in dire poverty. The growing urban masses, idle and prone to riot, would play a major role in the political struggles of the late Republic.

One consequence of the decline of peasant farmers in Italy was a shortage of men who owned the minimum amount of property required for military service. During a war in North Africa at the end of the second century B.C.E., Gaius Marius—a "new man," as the Romans called politically active individuals who did not belong to the traditional ruling class—achieved political prominence by accepting into the Roman legions poor, propertyless men to whom he promised farms upon retirement from military service. These troops became devoted to Marius and helped him get elected to an unprecedented (and illegal) six consulships.

Between 88 and 31 B.C.E., a series of ambitious individuals—Sulla, Pompey, Julius Caesar, Mark Antony, and Octavian—commanded armies that were more loyal to them than to the state. Their use of Roman troops to increase their personal power and influence led to bloody civil wars between military factions. The city of Rome itself was taken by force on several occasions, and victorious commanders executed political opponents and exercised dictatorial control of the state.

The Roman Principate, 31 B.C.E.–330 C.E.

Julius Caesar's grandnephew and heir, Octavian (63 B.C.E.–14 C.E.), eliminated all rivals by 31 B.C.E. and painstakingly set about refashioning the Roman system of government. He was careful to maintain the forms of the Republic—the offices, honors, and social prerogatives of the senatorial class—but he fundamentally altered the realities of power. A military dictator in fact, he never called himself king or emperor, claiming merely to be *princeps*, "first among equals," in a restored Republic. For this reason, the period following the Roman Republic is called the **Roman Principate.**

Augustus, one of the many honorific titles that the Roman Senate gave Octavian, connotes prosperity and piety, and it became the name by which he is best known to posterity. Augustus's ruthlessness, patience, and intuitive grasp of psychology enabled him to manipulate all the groups that made up Roman society. When he died in 14 C.E., after forty-five years of rule, almost no one could remember the Republic. During his reign Egypt and parts of the Middle East and Central Europe were added to the empire, leaving only the southern half of Britain and modern Romania to be added later.

Augustus had allied himself with the **equites°**, the class of well-to-do Italian merchants and landowners second in wealth and social status only to the senatorial class. This body of competent and self-assured individuals became the core of a new civil service that helped run the Roman Empire. At last Rome had an administrative bureaucracy up to the task of managing a large empire with considerable honesty, consistency, and efficiency.

So popular was Augustus when he died that four members of his family succeeded to the position of "emperor" (as we call it) despite their serious personal and political shortcomings. However, due to Augustus's calculated ambiguity about his role, the position of emperor was never automatically regarded as hereditary, and after the mid-first century C.E. other families obtained the post. In theory the early emperors were affirmed by the Senate; in reality they were chosen by the armies. By the second century C.E. a series of very capable emperors instituted a new mechanism of succession: each adopted a mature man of proven ability as his son, designated him as his successor, and shared offices and privileges with him.

While Augustus had felt it important to appeal to Republican traditions and conceal the source and extent of his power, this became less necessary over time, and later emperors exercised their authority more overtly. In imitation of Alexander the Great and the Hellenistic kings, many Roman emperors were officially deified (regarded as gods) after death. A cult of worship of the living emperor developed as a useful way to increase the loyalty of subjects.

The terse Law of the Twelve Tables, ca. 450 B.C.E., was supplemented by decrees of the Senate, bills passed in the Assembly, and the annual proclamations of the praetors°, elected public officials responsible for hearing cases and administering the law. In the later Republic a small group of legal experts began to emerge who analyzed laws and legal procedures to determine the underlying principles, then applied these principles to the creation of new laws required by a changing society. These experts were less lawyers in the modern sense than teachers, though they were sometimes consulted by magistrates or the parties to legal actions.

During the Principate the emperor became a major source of new laws. In this period the law was studied and codified with a new intensity by the class of legal experts, and their opinions and interpretations often were given the force of law.

---

equites (EH-kwee-tays)   **praetor** (PRAY-tuhr)

Roman Shop Selling Food and Drink
The bustling town of Pompeii on the Bay of Naples was buried in ash by the eruption of Mt. Vesuvius in 79 C.E. Archaeologists have unearthed the streets, stores, and houses of this typical Roman town. Shops such as this sold hot food and drink served from clay vessels set into the counter. Shelves and niches behind the counter contained other items. In the background can be seen a well-paved street and a public fountain where the inhabitants could fetch water. (Courtesy, Leo C. Curran)

An Urban Empire

The Roman Empire of the first three centuries C.E. was an "urban" empire. This does not mean that most people were living in cities and towns. Perhaps 80 percent of the 50 to 60 million people living within the borders of the empire engaged in agriculture and lived in villages or on isolated farms in the countryside. The empire, however, was administered through a network of towns and cities, and the urban populace benefited most.

Numerous towns had several thousand inhabitants. A handful of major cities—Alexandria in Egypt, Antioch in Syria, and Carthage—had populations of several hundred thousand. Rome itself had approximately a million residents. The largest cities strained the limited technological capabilities of the ancients; providing adequate food and water and removing sewage were always problems.

In Rome the upper classes lived in elegant townhouses on one or another of the seven hills. Such a house was centered around an *atrium,* a rectangular courtyard with a skylight that let in light and rainwater for drinking and washing. Surrounding the atrium were a dining room for dinner and drinking parties, an interior garden, a kitchen, and possibly a private bath. Bedrooms were on the upper level. The floors were decorated with peb-

ble mosaics, and the walls and ceilings were covered with frescoes (paintings done directly on wet plaster) of mythological scenes or outdoor vistas, giving a sense of openness in the absence of windows.

The poor lived in crowded slums in the low-lying parts of the city. Damp, dark, and smelly, with few furnishings, their wooden tenements were susceptible to frequent fires.

The cities, towns, and even the ramshackle settlements that sprang up on the edge of frontier forts were miniature replicas of the capital city in political organization, physical layout, and appearance. A town council and two annually elected officials drawn from prosperous members of the community maintained law and order and collected both urban and rural taxes. In their desire to imitate the manners and values of Roman senators, this "municipal aristocracy" endowed cities and towns, which had very little revenue of their own, with attractive elements of Roman urban life—a forum (an open plaza that served as a civic center), government buildings, temples, gardens, baths, theaters, amphitheaters, and games and public entertainments of all sorts.

The concentration of ownership of the land in ever fewer hands was temporarily reversed during the civil wars that brought an end to the Roman Republic, but it resumed in the era of the emperors. However, after the era of conquest ended in the early second century C.E., slaves were no longer plentiful or inexpensive, and landowners needed a new source of labor. Over time, the independent farmers were replaced by "tenant farmers" who were allowed to live on and cultivate plots of land in return for a portion of their crops. The landowners still lived in the cities and hired foremen to manage their estates. Thus wealth was concentrated in the cities but was based on the productivity of rural agricultural laborers.

Some urban dwellers got rich from manufacture and trade. Commerce was greatly enhanced by the **pax romana** ("Roman peace"), the safety and stability guaranteed by Roman might. Grain, meat, vegetables, and other bulk foodstuffs usually could be exchanged only locally because transportation was expensive and many products spoiled quickly. However, the city of Rome depended on the import of massive quantities of grain from Sicily and Egypt.

Glass, metalwork, delicate pottery, and other fine manufactured products were exported throughout the empire. Roman armies stationed on the frontiers were a large market, and their presence promoted the prosperity of border provinces. Other merchants traded in luxury items from far beyond the boundaries of the empire, especially silk from China and spices from India and Arabia.

Romanization—the spread of the Latin language and Roman way of life—was one of the most enduring consequences of empire, primarily in the western provinces. Greek language and culture, a legacy of the Hellenistic kingdoms, continued to dominate the eastern Mediterranean (see Chapter 4). As towns sprang up and acquired the features of Roman urban life, they served as magnets for ambitious members of the indigenous populations. The empire gradually and reluctantly granted Roman citizenship, with its attendant privileges, legal protections, and exemptions from some types of taxation, to people living outside Italy. Men who completed a twenty-six-year term of service in the native military units that backed up the Roman legions were granted citizenship and could pass this status on to their descendants. Emperors made grants of citizenship to individuals or entire communities as rewards for good service. In 212 C.E. the emperor Caracalla granted citizenship to all free, adult, male inhabitants of the empire.

The gradual extension of citizenship mirrored the empire's transformation from an Italian dominion over Mediterranean lands into a commonwealth of peoples. As early as the first century C.E. some of the leading literary and intellectual figures came from the provinces. By the second century even the emperors hailed from Spain, Gaul, and North Africa.

The Rise of Christianity

The Jewish homeland of Judaea (see Chapter 3), roughly equivalent to present-day Israel, was put under direct Roman rule in 6 C.E. Over the next half-century Roman governors insensitive to the Jewish belief in one god managed to increase tensions, and opposition to Roman rule sprang up. Many waited for the arrival of the Messiah, the "Anointed One," presumed to be a military leader who would liberate the Jewish people and drive the Romans out of the land.

It is in this context that we must see the career of **Jesus,** a young carpenter from the Galilee region in northern Israel. While scholars largely agree that the portrait of Jesus found in the New Testament reflects the viewpoint of followers a half-century after his death, it is difficult to determine the motives and teachings of the historical Jesus. Some experts believe that he was essentially a rabbi, or teacher, and that, offended by what he perceived as Jewish religious and political leaders' excessive concern with money and power and by the perfunctory nature of mainstream Jewish religious practice in his time, he prescribed a return to the personal faith and spirituality of an earlier age. Others stress his connections to the apocalyptic fervor found in certain circles of Judaism, such as John the Baptist and the community that authored the Dead Sea Scrolls. They view Jesus as a fiery prophet who urged people to prepare themselves for the imminent end of the world and God's ushering in of a blessed new age. Still others see him as a political revolutionary, upset by the downtrodden condition of the peasants in the countryside and the poor in the cities, who was determined to drive out the Roman occupiers and their collaborators among the Jewish elite. Whatever his real motivations, the charismatic Jesus eventually attracted the attention of the Jewish authorities in Jerusalem, who regarded popular reformers as potential troublemakers. They turned him over to the Roman governor, Pontius Pilate. Jesus was imprisoned, condemned, and executed by crucifixion, a punishment usually reserved for common criminals. His followers, the Apostles, carried on after his death and sought to spread his teachings and their belief that he was the Messiah and had been resurrected (returned from death to life) among their fellow Jews.

Paul, a Jew from the city of Tarsus in southeast Anatolia, converted to the new creed. Between 45 and 58 C.E. he threw his enormous energy into spreading the word. Traveling throughout Syria-Palestine, Anatolia, and Greece, he became increasingly frustrated with the refusal of most Jews to accept his claim that Jesus was the Messiah and had ushered in a new age. Many Jews, on the other hand, were appalled by the failure of the followers of Jesus to maintain traditional Jewish practices. Discovering a spiritual hunger among many non-Jews (sometimes called "gentiles"), Paul redirected his efforts toward them and set up a string of Christian (from the Greek name *christos,* meaning "anointed one," given to Jesus by his followers) communities in the eastern Mediterranean. Speaking both Greek and Aramaic, he moved comfortably between the Greco-Roman and Jewish worlds.

In 66 C.E. long-building tensions in Roman Judaea erupted into a full-scale revolt that lasted until 73. One of the casualties of the Roman reconquest of Judaea was the Jerusalem-based Christian community, which focused on converting the Jews. This left the field clear for Paul's non-Jewish converts, and Christianity began to diverge more and more from its Jewish roots.

For more than two centuries, the sect grew slowly but steadily. Many of the first converts were from disenfranchised groups—women, slaves, the urban poor. However, as the religious movement grew and prospered, it developed a hierarchy of priests and bishops and became subject to bitter disputes over theological doctrine (see Chapter 9).

As monotheists forbidden to worship other gods, early Christians were persecuted by Roman officials who regarded their refusal to worship the emperor as a sign of disloyalty. Despite occasional government-sponsored attempts at suppression and spontaneous mob attacks, or perhaps because of them, the young Christian movement continued to gain strength and attract converts. By the late third century C.E. its adherents were a sizable minority within the Roman Empire and included many educated and prosperous people with posts in the local and imperial governments.

The expansion of Christianity should be seen as part of a broader religious tendency. By the Greek Classical period a number of "mystery" cults had gained popularity by claiming to provide secret information about the nature of life and death and promising a blessed afterlife to their adherents. In the Hellenistic and Roman periods, a number of cults making similar promises arose in the eastern Mediterranean and spread throughout the Greco-Roman lands, presumably in response to a growing spiritual and intellectual hunger not satisfied by traditional pagan practices. As we shall see, the ultimate victory of Christianity over these rivals had as much to do with historical circumstances as with its spiritual appeal.

Technology and Transformation

The relative ease and safety of travel brought about by Roman arms and engineering enabled merchants to sell their wares and helped the early Christians spread their faith. Surviving remnants of roads, fortification walls, aqueducts, and buildings testify to the engineering expertise of the ancient Romans. Some of the best engineers served with the army, building bridges, siege works, and ballistic weapons that hurled stones and shafts. In peacetime soldiers were often put to work on construction projects. **Aqueducts**—long elevated or underground conduits—carried water from a source to an urban center, using only the force of gravity (see Environment and Technology: Water Engineering in Rome and China). The Romans were pioneers in the use of arches, which allow the even distribution of great weights without thick supporting walls. The invention of concrete—a mixture of lime powder, sand, and water that could be poured into molds—allowed the Romans to create vast vaulted and domed interior spaces.

Defending borders that stretched for thousands of miles was a great challenge. In a document released after his death, Augustus advised against expanding the empire because the costs of administering and defending subsequent acquisitions would be greater than the revenues. The Roman army was reorganized and redeployed to reflect the shift from an offensive to a defensive strategy. At most points the empire was protected by mountains, deserts, and seas. But the lengthy Rhine and Danube river frontiers in Germany and Central Europe were vulnerable. They were guarded by a string of forts with relatively small garrisons, adequate for dealing with raiders. On particularly desolate frontiers, such as in Britain and North Africa, the Romans built long walls to keep out the peoples who lived beyond.

The Roman state prospered for two-and-a-half centuries after Augustus stabilized the internal political situation and addressed the needs of the empire with an ambitious program of reforms. In the third century C.E. cracks in the edifice became visible. Historians use the expression **"third-century crisis"** to refer to the period from 235 to 284 C.E., when political, military, and economic problems beset and nearly destroyed the Roman Empire. The most visible symptom of the crisis was the frequent change of rulers. Twenty or more men claimed the office of emperor during this period. Most reigned for only a few months or years before being overthrown by rivals or killed by their own troops. Germanic tribesmen on the Rhine/Danube frontier took advantage of the frequent civil wars and periods of anarchy to raid deep into the empire. For the first time in centuries, Roman cities began to erect walls for protection.

The political and military emergencies had a devastating impact on the empire's economy. Buying the loyalty of the army and paying to defend the increasingly permeable frontiers drained the treasury. The unending demands of the central government for more tax revenues from the provinces, as well as the interruption of commerce by fighting, eroded the towns' prosperity. Shortsighted emperors, desperate for cash, reduced the amount of precious metal in Roman coins. As the devalued coinage became less and less acceptable in the marketplace, parts of the empire reverted to a barter economy, a far less efficient system that further curtailed large-scale and long-distance commerce.

The municipal aristocracy, once the most vital and public-spirited class in the empire, was slowly crushed out of existence. As town councilors, its members were personally liable for shortfalls in taxes owed to the state. The decline in trade eroded their wealth, which often was based on manufacture and commerce, and many began to evade their civic duties and even went into hid-

ing. Population shifted out of the cities and into the countryside. Many people sought employment and protection from both raiders and government officials on the estates of wealthy and powerful country landowners.

Just when things looked bleakest, one man pulled the empire back from the brink of self-destruction. Of humble origins, Diocletian had risen through the ranks of the army and gained power in 284. His success is indicated by the fact that he ruled for more than twenty years and died in bed.

Diocletian implemented radical reforms that saved the Roman state by transforming it. To halt inflation (the process by which prices rise as money becomes worth less), Diocletian issued an edict that specified the maximum prices that could be charged for various commodities and services. To ensure an adequate supply of workers in vital services, he froze many people into their

Roman Aqueduct Near Tarragona, Spain   How to provide an adequate supply of water was a problem posed by the growth of Roman towns and cities. Aqueducts channeled water from a source, sometimes many miles away, to an urban complex, using only the force of gravity. To bring an aqueduct from high ground into the city, Roman engineers designed long, continuous rows of arches that maintained a steady downhill slope. Roman troops were often used in such large-scale construction projects. Scholars sometimes can roughly estimate the population of an ancient city by calculating the amount of water that was available to it.   (Robert Frerck/Woodfin Camp & Associates)

Water Engineering in Rome and China

People needed water to drink; it was vital for agriculture; and it provided a rapid and economical means for transporting people and goods. Some of the most impressive technological achievements of ancient Rome and China involved hydraulic (water) engineering.

Roman cities, with their large populations, required abundant and reliable sources of water. One way to obtain it was to build aqueducts—stone channels to bring water from distant lakes and streams to the cities. The water flowing in these conduits was moved only by the force of gravity. Surveyors measured the land's elevation and plotted a course that very gradually moved downhill.

Some conduits were elevated atop walls or bridges, which made it difficult for unauthorized parties to tap the water line for their own use. Portions of some aqueducts were built underground. Still-standing aboveground segments indicate that the Roman aqueducts were well-built structures made of large cut stones closely fitted and held together by a cement-like mortar. Construction of the aqueducts was labor-intensive, and often both design and construction were carried out by military personnel. This was one of the ways in which the Roman government could keep large numbers of soldiers busy in peacetime.

Sections of aqueduct that crossed rivers presented the same construction challenges as bridges. Roman engineers lowered prefabricated wooden cofferdams—large, hollow cylinders—into the riverbed and pumped out the water so workers could descend and construct cement piers to support the arched segments of the bridge and the water channel itself. This technique is still used for construction in water.

When an aqueduct reached the outskirts of a city, the water flowed into a reservoir, where it was stored. Pipes connected the reservoir to different parts of the city. Even within the city, gravity provided the motive force until the water reached the public fountains used by the poor and the private storage tanks of individuals wealthy enough to have plumbing in their houses.

In ancient China, rivers running generally in an east-west direction were the main thoroughfares. The earliest development of complex societies centered on the Yellow River Valley, but by the beginning of the Qin Empire the Yangzi River Valley and regions farther south were becoming increasingly important to China's political and economic vitality. In this era the Chinese began to build canals connecting the northern and southern zones, at first for military purposes but eventually for transporting commercial goods as well. In later periods, with the acquisition of more advanced engineering skills, an extensive network of canals was built, including the 1,100-mile-long (1,771-kilometer-long) Grand Canal.

One of the earliest efforts was the construction of the Magic Canal. A Chinese historian tells us that the Qin emperor Shi Huangdi ordered his engineers to join two rivers by a 20-mile-long (32.2-kilometer-long) canal so that he could more easily supply his armies of conquest in the south. Construction of the canal posed a difficult engineering challenge, because the rivers Hsiang and Li, though coming within 3 miles (4.8 kilometers) of one another, flowed in opposite directions and with a strong current.

The engineers took advantage of a low point in the chain of hills between the rivers to maintain a relatively level grade. The final element of the solution was to build a snout-shaped mound to divide the waters of the Hsiang, funneling part of that river into an artificial channel. Several spillways further reduced the volume of water flowing into the canal, which was 15 feet wide and 3 feet deep (about 4.5 meters wide and 1 meter deep). The joining of the two rivers completed a network of waterways that permitted continuous inland water transport of goods between the latitudes of Beijing and Guangzhou (Canton), a distance of 1,250 miles (2,012 kilometers). Modifications were made in later centuries, but the Magic Canal is still in use.

The Magic Canal Engineers of Shi Huangdi, "First Emperor" of China, exploited the contours of the landscape to connect the river systems of northern and southern China. (From Robert Temple, *The Genius of China* [1986]. Photographer: Robert Temple)

professions and required them to train their sons to succeed them. This unprecedented government regulation of prices and vocations had unforeseen consequences. A "black market" arose among buyers and sellers who chose to ignore the government's price controls and establish their own prices for goods and services. Many inhabitants of the empire began to see the government as an oppressive entity that no longer deserved their loyalty.

When Diocletian resigned in 305, the old divisiveness reemerged as various claimants battled for the throne. The eventual winner was **Constantine** (r. 306–337), who reunited the entire empire under his sole rule by 324.

In 312 Constantine won a key battle at the Milvian Bridge over the Tiber River near Rome. He later claimed that he had seen a cross (the sign of the Christian God) superimposed on the sun before this battle. Believing that the Christian God had helped him achieve the victory, in the following year Constantine issued the so-called Edict of Milan, ending the persecution of Christianity and guaranteeing freedom of worship to Christians and all others. Throughout his reign he supported the Christian church, although he tolerated other beliefs as well. Historians disagree about whether Constantine was spiritually motivated or was pragmatically seeking to unify the peoples of the empire under a single religion. In either case his embrace of Christianity was of tremendous historical significance. Large numbers of people began to convert when they saw that Christians seeking political office or favors from the government had clear advantages over non-Christians.

In 324 Constantine transferred the imperial capital from Rome to Byzantium, an ancient Greek city on the Bosporus° strait leading from the Mediterranean into the Black Sea. The city was renamed Constantinople°, "City of Constantine." This move both reflected and accelerated changes already taking place. Constantinople was closer than Rome to the most-threatened borders in eastern Europe (see Map 5.1). The urban centers and prosperous middle class in the eastern half of the empire had better withstood the third-century crisis than had those in the western half. In addition, more educated people and more Christians were living in the eastern provinces.

Byzantines and Germans

Though conversion to the Christian faith affected all parts of the empire, a deep gulf opened between the eastern, Greek-speaking lands and the lands in the west that came under the influence of Germanic rulers. The term **Byzantine Empire,** derived from Constantinople's original name, came into use for the eastern realm. Constantine (and his pious mother Helena) studded the city with churches, controlled the appointment of the newly created Christian patriarch of Constantinople, and involved himself in doctrinal disputes over which beliefs constituted heresy.

In 325 he called hundreds of bishops to a council at the city of Nicaea° (modern Iznik in northwestern Turkey) to resolve disputes over religious doctrine. The bishops rejected the views of a priest from Alexandria named Arius, who maintained that Jesus was of lesser importance than God the Father. However, the Arian doctrine enjoyed great, though temporary, popularity among the Germanic peoples then migrating along the Danube frontier and into the western Roman lands.

The next several centuries were crowded with disputes over theology and quarrels among the patriarchs, or paramount church officials, of Constantinople, Alexandria, Antioch, Jerusalem, and Rome. The patriarchs appointed bishops, and each bishop consecrated priests within his area of jurisdiction, called a diocese. Church rules set by the patriarch or by councils of bishops guided priests in serving ordinary believers.

Christianity progressed most rapidly in urban centers. Though the country folk (Latin *pagani*, whence the word *pagan* used as a negative label for polytheists) long retained customs deriving from worship of the old gods, the emperor Julian (r. 361–363) tried in vain to restore the old polytheism as the state cult. In 392 the emperor Theodosius banned all pagan ceremonies.

The heavy involvement with religion of the emperors in Constantinople did not prevent them from playing the traditional roles of conqueror and lawmaker. The emperor Justinian (r. 527–565) sent armies to regain control of Roman North Africa, which had been conquered by Germans invading from Spain, and of parts of Italy. His historians celebrated these deeds, but his collection of Roman laws proved more enduring. At his command a team of seventeen legal scholars made a systematic compilation, in Latin, of a thousand years of Roman legal tradition. The *Corpus Juris Civilis (Body of Civil Law),* as it came to be called, began to be studied in western Europe under the influence of a legal scholar named Irnerius (ca. 1055–ca. 1130), whose establishment of legal studies at the University of Bologna° in Italy laid the foundation for most modern European legal systems.

Bosporus (BAHS-puhr-uhs)
Constantinople (cahn-stan-tih-NO-pul)

Nicaea (nye-SEE-uh)   Bologna (boe-LOAN-yuh)

Continuing imperial vitality in the eastern empire contrasted with deepening decline in the western empire, which formally became a separate entity after 395. Byzantine armies and diplomats warded off most assaults on the comparatively short Danube River frontier, thereby persuading migrating German warrior bands to keep moving westward. Crossing the Rhine, they overwhelmed the Roman legions in the west. Gaul, Britain, Spain, and North Africa fell to various Germanic peoples in the early fifth century. Visigoths sacked Rome itself in 410, and the last Roman emperor was deposed in 476.

By 530, with the old Roman economy and urban centers in shambles, the Western Roman Empire had fragmented into a handful of kingdoms under Germanic rulers. The city of Rome had lost its political importance but retained prominence as the seat of the most influential Western churchman, the patriarch of Rome. Local noble families competed for control of this position, which over several centuries acquired the title *Pope* along with supreme power in the Latin-speaking church.

The educated few, increasingly only Christian priests and monks, still spoke and wrote a somewhat simplified form of Latin. But the Latin of the uneducated masses who had lived under Roman rule rapidly evolved into the Romance dialects that eventually became modern Portuguese, Spanish, French, Italian, and Romanian. In the north and east of the Rhine River, where Roman culture had scarcely penetrated, people spoke Germanic and related Scandinavian languages. East of the Elbe River, speakers of Slavic languages formed a third major group.

From a Roman point of view, the rise of the Germanic kingdoms represented the triumph of the barbarians. Yet the society that developed on the ruins of Rome in the west was to prove more dynamic and creative than the Byzantine realm that preserved intact much more of the Roman tradition.

THE ORIGINS OF IMPERIAL CHINA, 221 B.C.E.–220 C.E.

The early history of China (see Chapter 2) was characterized by the fragmentation that geography seemed to dictate. The Shang (ca. 1750–1027 B.C.E.) and Zhou (1027–221 B.C.E.) dynasties ruled over a relatively compact zone in northeastern China. The last few centuries of nominal Zhou rule—the Warring States Period—saw rivalry and belligerence among a group of small states with somewhat different languages and cultures. As in the contemporary Greek city-states (see Chapter 4), com-

petition and conflict gave rise to many distinctive elements of a national culture.

In the second half of the third century B.C.E. one of the warring states—the **Qin**° state of the Wei° Valley—rapidly conquered its rivals and created China's first empire (221–206 B.C.E.). Built at a great cost in human lives and labor, the Qin Empire barely survived the death of its founder, **Shi Huangdi**°. Power soon passed to a new dynasty, the **Han,** which ruled China from 206 B.C.E. to 220 C.E. (see Map 5.2). Thus began the long history of imperial China—a tradition of political and cultural unity and continuity that lasted into the early twentieth century.

Resources and Population

Agriculture produced the wealth and taxes that supported the institutions of imperial China. The main tax, a percentage of the annual harvest, funded government activities ranging from the luxurious lifestyle of the royal court to the daily tasks of officials and military units throughout the country and on the frontiers. Large populations in China's capital cities, first Chang'an° and later Luoyang°, had to be fed. As intensive agriculture spread in the Yangzi River Valley, the need to transport southern crops to the north spurred the construction of canals to connect the Yangzi with the Yellow River (see Environment and Technology: Water Engineering in Rome and China). During prosperous times, the government also collected and stored surplus grain that could be sold at reasonable prices in times of shortage.

The government periodically conducted a census of inhabitants, and the results for 2 C.E. and 140 C.E. are available today. The earlier survey counted approximately 12 million households and 60 million people; the later, not quite 10 million households and 49 million people. The average household contained 5 persons. Then, as now, the vast majority of the people lived in the eastern portion of the country, the river-valley regions where intensive agriculture could support a dense population. At first the largest concentration was in the Yellow River Valley and North China Plain, but by early Han times the demographic center had begun to shift to the Yangzi River Valley.

In the intervals between seasonal agricultural tasks, every able-bodied man donated one month of labor a year to public works projects—building palaces, temples,

---

Qin (chin)   **Wei** (way)   **Shi Huangdi** (shee wahng-dee)
Chang'an (chahng-ahn)   **Luoyang** (LWOE-yahng)

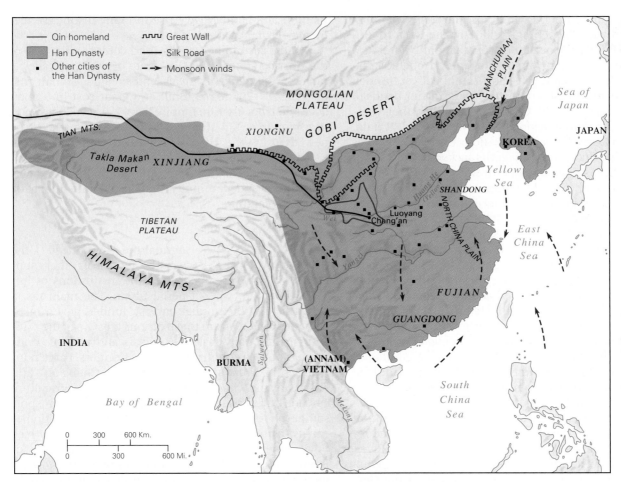

Map 5.2   Han China   The Qin and Han rulers of northeast China extended their control over all of eastern China and extensive territories to the west. A series of walls in the north and northwest, built to check the incursions of nomadic peoples from the steppes, were joined together to form the ancestor of the present-day Great Wall of China. An extensive network of roads connecting towns, cities, and frontier forts promoted rapid communication and facilitated trade. The Silk Road carried China's most treasured product to Central, South, and West Asia and the Mediterranean lands.

fortifications, and roads; transporting goods; excavating and maintaining canal channels; laboring on imperial estates; or working in the mines. The state also required two years of military service. On the frontiers, young conscripts built walls and forts, kept an eye on barbarian neighbors, fought when necessary, and grew crops to support themselves. Annually updated registers of land and households enabled imperial officials to keep track of money and services due. Like the Romans, the Chinese government depended on a large population of free peasants to contribute taxes and services to the state.

The Han Chinese gradually but persistently expanded at the expense of other ethnic groups. Population growth

in the core regions and a shortage of good, arable land spurred pioneers to push into new areas. Sometimes the government organized new settlements, at militarily strategic sites and on the frontiers, for example. Neighboring kingdoms also invited Chinese settlers so as to exploit their skills and learn their technologies.

Han people preferred regions suitable for the kind of agriculture they had practiced in the eastern river valleys. They took over land on the northern frontier, pushing back nomadic populations. They also expanded into the tropical forests of southern China and settled in the western oases. In places not suitable for their preferred kind of agriculture, particularly the steppe and the desert, Han Chinese did not displace other groups.

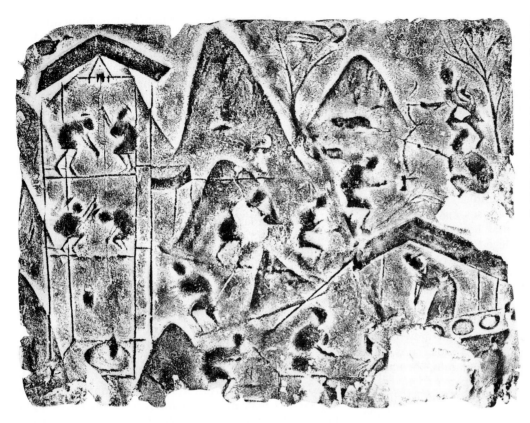

Rubbing of Salt Mining
Found in a Chinese tomb of the first century C.E., this rubbing illustrates a procedure for mining salt. The tower on the left originally served as a derrick for drilling a deep hole through dirt and rock. In this scene workers are hauling up buckets full of brine (saltwater) from underground deposits. In the background are hunters in the mountains.   (Courtesy of the Trustees of the British Museum)

Hierarchy, Obedience, and Belief

As the Han Chinese expanded into new regions, they took along their social organization, values, language, and other cultural practices. The basic unit of Chinese society was the family, which included not only the living generations but also all the previous generations—the ancestors. The Chinese believed that their ancestors maintained an ongoing interest in the fortunes of living family members, so they consulted, appeased, and venerated them in order to maintain their favor. The family was viewed as a living, self-renewing organism, and each generation was required to have sons to perpetuate the family and maintain the ancestor cult that provided a kind of immortality to the deceased.

The doctrine of Confucius (Kongzi), which had its origins in the sixth century B.C.E. (see Chapter 2), became very influential in the imperial period. Confucianism regarded hierarchy as a natural aspect of human society and laid down rules of appropriate conduct. People saw themselves as part of an interdependent unit rather than as individual agents. Each person had a place and responsibilities within the family hierarchy, based on his or her gender, age, and relationship to other family members. Absolute authority rested with the father, who was an intermediary between the living members and the ancestors, presiding over the rituals of ancestor worship.

The same concepts operated in society as a whole. Peasants, soldiers, administrators, and rulers all made distinctive and necessary contributions to the welfare of society. Confucianism optimistically maintained that people could be guided to the right path through education, imitation of proper role models, and self-improvement. The family inculcated the basic values of Chinese society: loyalty, obedience to authority, respect for elders and ancestors, and concern for honor and appropriate conduct. Because the hierarchy in the state mirrored the hierarchy in the family, these same attitudes carried over into the relationship between individuals and the state.

The experiences of women in ancient Chinese society are hard to pinpoint because, as elsewhere, contemporary written sources tell us little. Confucian ethics stressed the impropriety of women participating in public life. Traditional wisdom about conduct appropriate for women is preserved in an account of the life of the mother of the Confucian philosopher Mencius (Mengzi):

A woman's duties are to cook the five grains, heat the wine, look after her parents-in-law, make clothes, and that is all! . . . [She] has no ambition to manage affairs outside the house. . . . She must follow the "three submissions." When she is young, she must submit to her parents. After her marriage, she must submit to her husband. When she is widowed, she must submit to her son.[1]

That is an ideal perpetuated by males of the upper classes, the social stratum that is the source of most of the written texts. Upper-class females probably were under considerable pressure to conform to those expectations. Women of the lower classes, less affected by Confucian ways of thinking, may have been less constrained than their more "privileged" counterparts.

After her parents arranged her marriage, a young bride went to live with her husband's family, where she was a stranger who had to prove herself. Ability and force of personality—as well as the capacity to produce sons—could make a difference. Dissension between the wife and her mother-in-law and sisters-in-law grew out of competition for influence with husbands, sons, and brothers and for a larger share of the family's economic resources.

Like the early Romans, the ancient Chinese believed that divinity resided within nature rather than outside and above it, and they worshiped and tried to appease the forces of nature. The state erected and maintained shrines to the lords of rain and winds as well as to certain great rivers and high mountains. Gathering at mounds or altars where the local spirit of the soil was thought to reside, people sacrificed sheep and pigs and beat drums loudly to promote the fertility of the earth. Strange or disastrous natural phenomena, such as eclipses or heavy rains, called for symbolic restraint of the deity by tying a red cord around the sacred spot. Because it was believed that supernatural forces flowed through the landscape, bringing good and evil fortune, experts in *feng shui*, meaning "earth divination," were consulted to determine the most favorable location and orientation for buildings and graves. The faithful learned to adapt their lives to the complex rhythms they perceived in nature.

The First Chinese Empire, 221–207 B.C.E.

For centuries eastern China was divided among rival states whose frequent hostilities gave rise to the label "Warring States Period" (480–221 B.C.E.). In the second half of the third century B.C.E. the state of the Qin suddenly burst forth and took over the other states one by one. By 221 B.C.E., the first emperor had united the northern plain and the Yangzi River Valley under one rule, marking the creation of China and the inauguration of the imperial age. Many scholars maintain that the name "China," by which this land has been known in the Western world, is derived from "Qin."

Several factors account for the meteoric rise of the Qin. The Qin ruler, who took the title *Shi Huangdi* ("First Emperor"), and his adviser and prime minister Li Si° were able and ruthless men who exploited the exhaustion resulting from the long centuries of interstate rivalry. The Qin homeland in the valley of the Wei, a tributary of the Yellow River, was less urbanized and commercialized than the kingdoms farther east, with a large pool of sturdy peasants to serve in the army. Moreover, long experience in mobilizing manpower for the construction of irrigation and flood-control works had strengthened the authority of the Qin king at the expense of the nobles and endowed his government with superior organizational skills.

Shi Huangdi and Li Si created a totalitarian structure that subordinated the individual to the needs of the state. By publicly burning large numbers of books, they symbolically expressed a radical break with the past. They cracked down on Confucianism, regarding its demands for benevolent and nonviolent conduct from rulers to be a check on the absolute power they sought. They instead drew from a stream of political thought known as Legalism (see Chapter 2). Developing earlier Legalist thinking, Li Si insisted that the will of the ruler was supreme, and that it was necessary to impose discipline and obedience on the subjects through the rigid application of rewards and punishments.

The new regime was determined to eliminate rival centers of authority. Its first target was the landowning aristocracy of the conquered rival states and the system on which aristocratic wealth and power had been based. Because primogeniture—the right of the eldest son to inherit all the landed property—allowed a small number of individuals to accumulate vast tracts of land, the Qin government abolished it, instead requiring estates to be broken up and passed on to several heirs.

The large estates of the aristocracy had been worked by slaves (see Diversity and Dominance: The Treatment of Slaves in Rome and China) and peasant serfs, who gave their landlords a substantial portion of their harvest. The Qin abolished slavery and took steps to create a free peasantry who paid taxes and provided labor, as well as military service, to the state.

The Qin government's commitment to standardization helped create a unified Chinese civilization. During the Warring States Period, small states had found many ways to emphasize their independence. For example, states had had their own forms of music, with different

Li Si (luh suh)

scales, systems of notation, and instruments. The Qin imposed standard weights, measures, and coinage; a uniform law code; a common system of writing; and even regulations governing the axle length of carts so as to leave just one set of ruts on the roads.

The Qin built thousands of miles of roads—comparable in scale to the roads of the Roman Empire—to connect the parts of the empire and to move Qin armies quickly. They also built canals connecting the river systems of northern and southern China (see Environment and Technology: Water Engineering in Rome and China). The frontier walls of the old states began to be linked into a continuous barricade, the precursor of the Great Wall), to protect cultivated lands from raids by northern nomads. Large numbers of people were forced to donate their labor and often their lives to build the walls and roads. So oppressive were the financial exploitation and demands for forced labor that a series of rebellions broke out when Shi Huangdi died in 210 B.C.E., bringing down the Qin dynasty.

The Long Reign of the Han, 206 B.C.E.–220 C.E.

When the dust cleared, Liu Bang°, who may have been born a peasant, had outlasted his rivals and established a new dynasty, the Han (206 B.C.E.–220 C.E.). The new emperor promised to reject the excesses and mistakes of the Qin and to restore the institutions of a venerable past. To sustain and protect a large empire, however, the Han administration maintained much of the Qin's structure and Legalist ideology, though with less fanatical zeal. The Han tempered Legalist government with a Confucianism revised to serve a large, centralized political entity. This Confucianism emphasized the government's benevolence and the appropriateness of particular rituals and behaviors in a manifestly hierarchical society. The Han system of administration became the standard for later ages, and the Chinese people today refer to themselves ethnically as "Han."

After eighty years of imperial consolidation, Emperor Wu (r. 140–87 B.C.E.) launched a period of military expansion, south into Fujian, Guangdong, and present-day north Vietnam, and north into Manchuria and present-day North Korea. Han armies also went west to inner Mongolia and Xinjiang° to secure the lucrative Silk Road (see Chapter 7). Controlling the newly acquired territories was expensive, however, so Wu's successors curtailed further expansion.

The Han Empire endured, with a brief interruption between 9 and 23 C.E., for more than four hundred years.

From 202 B.C.E. to 8 C.E.—the period of the Early, or Western, Han—the capital was at Chang'an, in the Wei Valley, an ancient seat of power from which the Zhou and Qin dynasties had emerged. From 23 to 220 C.E. the Later, or Eastern, Han established its base farther east, in the more centrally located Luoyang.

Protected by a ring of hills but with ready access to the fertile plain, **Chang'an** was surrounded by a wall of pounded earth and brick 15 miles (24 kilometers) in circumference. Contemporaries described it as a bustling place, filled with courtiers, officials, soldiers, merchants, craftsmen, and foreign visitors. In 2 C.E. its population was 246,000. Part of the city was carefully planned. Broad thoroughfares running north and south intersected with others running east and west. High walls protected the palaces, administrative offices, barracks, and storehouses of the imperial compound, and access was restricted. Temples and marketplaces were scattered about the civic center. Chang'an became a model of urban planning, and its main features were imitated in the cities and towns that sprang up throughout the Han Empire.

Moralizing writers who criticized the elite provide glimpses of their private lives. Living in multistory houses, wearing fine silks, and traveling about Chang'an in ornate horse-drawn carriages, well-to-do officials and merchants devoted their leisure time to art and literature, occult religious practices, elegant banquets, and various entertainments—music and dance, juggling and acrobatics, dog and horse races, cock and tiger fights. In stark contrast, the common people inhabited a sprawling warren of alleys, living in dwellings packed "as closely as the teeth of a comb," as one poet put it.

As in the Zhou monarchy (see Chapter 2), the emperor was the "Son of Heaven," chosen to rule in accordance with the Mandate of Heaven. He stood at the center of government and society. As the father held authority in the family and was a link between the living generations and the ancestors, so was the emperor supreme in the state. He brought the support of powerful imperial ancestors and guaranteed the harmonious interaction of heaven and earth. To a much greater degree than his Roman counterpart, he was regarded as a divinity and his word was law.

Living in seclusion within the walled palace compound, surrounded by his many wives, children, servants, courtiers, and officials, the emperor presided over unceasing pomp and ritual emphasizing the worship of Heaven and imperial ancestors as well as the practical business of government. The royal compound was also a hive of intrigue, no more so than when the emperor died and his chief widow chose his heir from among the male members of the ruling clan.

The central government was run by a prime minister,

Lui Bang (le-oo bahng)   **Xinjiang** (SHIN-jyahng)

a civil service director, and nine ministers with military, economic, legal, and religious responsibilities. Like the imperial Romans, the Han depended on local officials for day-to-day administration of their far-flung territories. Local people collected taxes and dispatched revenues to the central government, regulated conscription for the army and for labor projects, provided protection, and settled disputes. The remote central government rarely impinged on the lives of most citizens.

As part of their strategy to weaken the rural aristocrats and exclude them from political posts, the Qin and Han emperors allied themselves with the **gentry**—the class next in wealth below the aristocrats. To serve as local officials the central government chose members of this class of moderately prosperous landowners, usually men with education and valued expertise who resembled the Roman equites favored by Augustus and his successors. These officials were a privileged and respected group within Chinese society, and they made the government more efficient and responsive than it had been in the past.

The guiding philosophy of the new gentry class was a modified Confucianism that provided a system for training officials to be intellectually capable and morally worthy of their role and set forth a code of conduct for measuring their performance. According to Chinese tra-

dition, an imperial university with as many as thirty thousand students was located outside Chang'an, and provincial centers of learning were established. (Some scholars doubt that such a complex institution existed this early.) Students from these centers were chosen to enter various levels of government service.

In theory, young men from any class could rise in the state hierarchy. In practice, sons of the gentry had an advantage because they were most likely to receive the necessary training in the Confucian classics. As civil servants advanced in the bureaucracy, they received distinctive emblems and privileges of rank, including preferential treatment in the legal system and exemption from military service. Over time, the gentry became a new aristocracy of sorts, banding together in cliques and family alliances that had considerable clout and worked to advance the careers of group members.

Daoism, which also had its origins in the Warring States Period (see Chapter 2), took deeper root, becoming popular with the common people. Daoism emphasized the search for the *Dao,* or "path," of nature and the value of harmonizing with the cycles and patterns of the natural world. Enlightenment was achieved not so much by education as by solitary contemplation and physical and mental discipline. Daoism was skeptical, questioning age-old beliefs and values and rejecting the hierar-

Han-Era (First Century B.C.E.) Stone Rubbing of a Horse-Drawn Carriage The "trace harness," a strap running across the horse's chest, was a Chinese invention that allowed horses to pull far heavier loads than were possible with the constricting throat harness used in Europe. In the Han period, officials, professionals, and soldiers who served the regime enjoyed a lifestyle made pleasant by fine clothing, comfortable transportation, servants, and delightful pastimes, but at the same time they were guided by a Confucian emphasis on duty, honesty, and appropriate behavior. (From Wu family shrine, Jiaxiang, Shantung. From *Chin-shih-so* [Jinshisuo])

chy, rules, and rituals of the Confucianism of the elite classes. It urged passive acceptance of the disorder of the world, denial of ambition, contentment with simple pleasures, and trusting one's own instincts.

Technology and Trade

Chinese tradition recognized the importance of technology for the success and spread of Chinese civilization, crediting legendary rulers of the distant past with the introduction of major technologies.

The advent of bronze tools around 1500 B.C.E. helped clear the forests and open land for agriculture on the North China Plain. Almost a thousand years later iron arrived. Chinese metallurgists employed more advanced techniques than did their counterparts elsewhere in the hemisphere. Whereas Roman blacksmiths produced wrought-iron tools and weapons by hammering heated iron, the Chinese hammered ores with a higher carbon content to produce steel, and they mastered the technique of liquefying iron and pouring it into molds. The resulting steel and cast-iron tools and weapons were considerably stronger.

In the succeeding centuries, the crossbow and the use of cavalry helped the Chinese military repel nomads from the steppe regions. The watermill, which harnessed the power of running water to turn a grindstone, was used in China long before it appeared in Europe. The development of a horse collar that did not constrict the animal's breathing allowed Chinese horses to pull much heavier loads than European horses could. The Chinese also were the first to make paper, perhaps as early as the second century B.C.E. They pounded soaked plant fibers and bark with a mallet, then poured the mixture through a porous mat. Once the residue left on the mat surface dried out, it provided a relatively smooth, lightweight medium for writing.

The Qin began and the Han rulers continued an extensive program of road building. Roads enabled rapid movement of military forces and supplies. The network of couriers that carried messages to and from the central administration used horses, boats, and even footpaths, and they found food and shelter at relay stations. The network of navigable rivers was improved and connected by canals (see Environment and Technology: Water Engineering in Rome and China).

Population growth and increasing trade gave rise to local market centers. These thriving towns grew to become county seats from which imperial officials operated. Between 10 and 30 percent of the population lived in Han towns and cities.

China's most important export commodity was silk. For a long time the fact that silk cocoons are secreted onto the leaves of mulberry trees by silkworms was a closely guarded secret that gave the Chinese a monopoly on the manufacture of silk. As silk was carried on a perilous journey westward through the Central Asian oases to the Middle East, India, and the Mediterranean, it passed through the hands of middlemen who raised the price to make a profit. The value of a beautiful textile may have increased a hundredfold by the time it reached its destination. The Chinese government sought to control the Silk Road by launching periodic campaigns into Central Asia. Garrisons were installed, and colonies of Chinese settlers were sent out to occupy the oases.

Decline of the Han Empire

For the Han government, as for the Romans, maintaining the security of the frontiers—particularly the north and northwest frontiers—was a primary concern. In general, the Han Empire successfully controlled lands occupied by farming peoples, but met resistance from nomadic groups whose livelihood depended on their horses and herds. The different ways of life of farmers and herders gave rise to insulting stereotypes on both sides. The settled Chinese thought of nomads as "barbarians"—rough, uncivilized peoples—much as the inhabitants of the Roman Empire looked down on the Germanic tribes living beyond their frontier.

Along the boundary, the closeness of the herders and farmers often led to significant commercial activity. The nomadic herders sought the food and crafted goods produced by the farmers and townsfolk, and the settled farmers depended on the nomads for horses and other herd animals and products. Sometimes, however, nomads raided the settled lands and took what they needed or wanted. Tough and warlike because of the demands of their way of life, mounted nomads could strike swiftly and just as swiftly disappear.

Although nomadic groups tended to be relatively small and often fought with one another, from time to time circumstances and a charismatic leader could create a large coalition. In response, the Chinese developed cavalry forces that could match the mobility of the nomads, and made access to good stocks of horses and pasture lands a state priority. Other strategies included maintaining colonies of soldier-farmers and garrisons on the frontier; settling compliant nomadic groups inside the borders to serve as a buffer against warlike groups; paying bribes to promote dissension among the nomad leadership; and paying protection money. One frequently successful approach was a "tributary system" in which nomad rulers nominally accepted Chinese supremacy and paid tribute, for which they were rewarded with marriages to Chinese princesses, dazzling receptions at court, and gifts from the Han emperor that exceeded the value of the tribute.

In the end, continuous military vigilance along the frontier burdened Han finances and worsened the economic troubles of later Han times. Despite the earnest efforts of Qin and Early Han emperors to reduce the power and wealth of the aristocracy and to turn land over to a free peasantry, by the end of the first century B.C.E. nobles and successful merchants again controlled huge tracts of land, and many peasants sought their protection against the demands of the imperial government. Over the next two centuries strongmen who were largely independent of imperial control emerged, and the central government was deprived of tax revenues and manpower. The system of military conscription broke down, forcing the government to hire more and more foreign soldiers and officers. These men were willing to serve for pay, but they were not very loyal to the Han state.

Several factors contributed to the fall of the Han dynasty in 220 C.E.: factional intrigues within the ruling clan, official corruption and inefficiency, uprisings of desperate and hungry peasants, the spread of banditry, attacks by nomadic groups on the northwest frontier, and the ambitions of rural warlords. China entered a period of political fragmentation and economic and cultural regression that lasted until the rise of the Sui° and Tang° dynasties in the late sixth and early seventh centuries C.E.

IMPERIAL PARALLELS

The similarities between the Roman and Han Empires begin at the level of the family. In both cultures the family was headed by an all-powerful patriarch. Strong loyalties and obligations bound family members. Values first learned in the family—obedience, respect for superiors, piety, and a strong sense of duty and honor—created a pervasive social cohesion.

Agriculture was the fundamental economic activity and source of wealth in both civilizations. Government revenues were primarily derived from a percentage of the annual harvest. Both empires depended on a free peasantry—sturdy farmers who could be pressed into military service or other forms of compulsory labor. Conflicts over who owned the land and how it was to be used were at the heart of the political and social turmoil

in both places. The autocratic rulers of the Roman and Chinese states secured their positions by breaking the power of the old aristocratic families, seizing their excess land, and giving land to small farmers (as well as keeping extensive tracts for themselves). They veiled the revolutionary nature of these changes by claiming to restore the institutions of a venerable past. The later reversal of this process, when wealthy noblemen once again gained control of vast tracts of land and reduced the peasants to dependent tenant farmers, signaled the erosion of the authority of the state.

Both empires spread out from an ethnically homogeneous core to encompass widespread territories containing diverse ecosystems, populations, and ways of life. Both brought those regions a cultural unity that has persisted, at least in part, to the present day. This development involved far more than military conquest and political domination. The skill of Roman and Chinese farmers and the high yields that they produced led to a dynamic expansion of population. As the population of the core areas outstripped the available resources, Italian and Han settlers moved into new regions, bringing their languages, beliefs, customs, and technologies with them. Many people in the conquered lands were attracted to the culture of the ruler nation and chose to adopt these practices and attach themselves to a "winning cause."

Both empires found similar solutions to the problems of administering far-flung territories and large populations in an age when men on horseback or on foot carried messages. The central government had to delegate considerable autonomy to local officials. These local elites identified their own interests with the central government they loyally served. In both empires a kind of civil service developed, staffed by educated and capable members of a prosperous middle class.

Technologies that facilitated imperial control also fostered cultural unification and improvements in the general standard of living. Roads built to expedite the movement of troops became the highways of commerce and the thoroughfares by which imperial culture spread. A network of cities and towns served as the nerve center of each empire, providing local administrative bases, further promoting commerce, and radiating imperial culture out into the surrounding countryside.

Cities and towns modeled themselves on the capital cities of Rome and Chang'an. Travelers could find the same types and styles of buildings and public spaces, as well as other attractive features of urban life, in outlying regions that they had seen in the capital. The majority of the population still resided in the countryside, but most of the advantages of empire were enjoyed by people living in urban centers.

Sui (sway)   **Tang** (tahng)

The empires of Rome and Han China faced similar problems of defense: long borders located far from the administrative center and aggressive neighbors who coveted the prosperity of the empire. Both empires had to build walls and maintain a chain of forts and garrisons to protect against incursions. The cost of frontier defense was staggering and eventually eroded the economic prosperity of the two empires. As the imperial governments became ever more beholden to the military and demanded more taxes and services from the hard-pressed civilian population, they lost the loyalty of their own people, many of whom sought protection on the estates of powerful rural landowners. Eventually, both empires were so weakened that their borders were overrun and their central governments collapsed.

In referring to the eventual failure of these two empires, we are brought up against different long-term consequences. In China the imperial model was revived in subsequent eras, but the lands of the Roman Empire never again achieved the same level of unification. Several interrelated factors help account for the different outcomes.

First, these cultures had different attitudes about the relationship of individuals to the state. In China the individual was deeply embedded in the larger social group. The Chinese family, with its emphasis on a precisely defined hierarchy, unquestioning obedience, and solemn rituals of deference to elders and ancestors, served as the model for society and the state. Respect for authority was (and remains) deeply seated. Confucianism, which sanctified hierarchy and provided a code of conduct for professionals and public officials, had arisen long before the imperial system and could be revived and tailored to fit subsequent political circumstances. Although the Roman family had its own hierarchy and traditions of obedience, the cult of ancestors was not as strong as among the Chinese, and the family was not the organizational model for Roman society and the Roman state. Also, there was no Roman equivalent of Confucianism—no ideology of political organization and social conduct that could survive the dissolution of the Roman state.

It is probably also fair to say that economic and social mobility, which allows some people to rise dramatically in wealth and status, enhances a society's sense of the significance of the individual. Opportunities for individuals to improve their economic status were more limited in ancient China than in the Roman Empire, and the merchant class in China was frequently disparaged and constrained by the government. The greater importance of commerce in the Roman Empire and the absence of government interference resulted in greater economic mobility. Roman law gave great weight to the sanctity of property and the rights of the individual. To a much greater extent than the Chinese emperor, the Roman emperor had to resort to persuasion, threats, and promises in order to forge a consensus for his initiatives.

Although Roman emperors tried to create an ideology to bolster their position, they were hampered by the persistence of Republican traditions and the ambiguities about the position of emperor deliberately cultivated by Augustus. As a result, Roman rulers were likely to be chosen by the army or by the Senate; the dynastic principle never took deep root; and the cult of the emperor had little spiritual content. This stands in sharp contrast to the clear-cut Chinese belief that the emperor was the divine Son of Heaven with privileged access to the beneficent power of the royal ancestors.

Finally, Christianity, with its insistence on monotheism and one doctrine of truth, negated the Roman emperors' pretensions to divinity and was essentially unwilling to come to terms with pagan beliefs. The spread of Christianity through the provinces during the Late Roman Empire, and the decline of the western half of the empire in the fifth century C.E., constituted an irreversible break with the past. On the other hand, Buddhism, which came to China in the early centuries C.E. and flourished in the post-Han era (see Chapter 10), was more easily reconciled with traditional Chinese values and beliefs.

CONCLUSION

Both the Roman Empire and the first Chinese empire arose from relatively small states that, because of their discipline and military toughness, were initially able to subdue small and quarreling neighbors. Ultimately they unified widespread territories under strong central governments.

In China the Qin Empire emerged rapidly, in the reign of a single ruler, because many of the elements for unification were already in place. The "First Emperor" looked back to the precedents of the Shang and Zhou states, which had controlled large core areas in the North China Plain. He drew upon the preexisting concept of the Mandate of Heaven, a claim to divine backing for the ruler, who was himself the Son of Heaven; and the Legalist political philosophy justified authoritarian measures. The harshness of the new order generated discontent and resistance that soon brought down the Qin dynasty, but Han successors were able to moderate and build on Qin structures to create a durable imperial regime.

The early Roman state had no such precedents to draw upon. The creation of the Roman Empire was a much slower process in which solutions were discovered by trial and error. The Republican form of government, developed to meet the needs of an Italian city-state, proved inadequate to the demands of empire, and Rome's military success led to social and economic disruption and an acute political struggle. Out of this crisis emerged the Principate, which persevered for several centuries. Even so, the Roman emperors were never able to develop an effective ideology of rule.

In the end, both empires succumbed to a combination of external pressures and internal divisions. In China the imperial tradition and the class structure and value system that maintained it were eventually revived (see Chapters 10 and 13), and they survived with remarkable continuity into the twentieth century C.E. In Europe, North Africa, and the Middle East, in contrast, there was no restoration of the Roman Empire, and the later history of those lands was marked by great political changes and cultural diversity.

■ Key Terms

Roman Republic	aqueduct
Roman Senate	third-century crisis
patron/client relationship	Constantine
Roman Principate	Byzantine Empire
Augustus	Qin
equites	Shi Huangdi
pax romana	Han
Romanization	Chang'an
Jesus	gentry
Paul	

■ Suggested Reading

Tim Cornell and John Matthews, *Atlas of the Roman World* (1982), offers a general introduction, pictures, and maps to illustrate many aspects of Roman civilization. Michael Grant and Rachel Kitzinger, eds., *Civilization of the Ancient Mediterranean*, 3 vols. (1988), is an invaluable collection of essays with bibliographies by specialists on every major facet of life in the Greek and Roman worlds. Among the many good surveys of Roman history are Michael Grant, *History of Rome* (1978), and M. Cary and H. H. Scullard, *A History of Rome Down to the Reign of Constantine* (1975). Naphtali Lewis and Meyer Reinhold, eds., *Roman Civilization*, 2 vols. (1951), contains extensive ancient sources in translation.

For Roman political and legal institutions, attitudes, and values see J. A. Crook, *Law and Life of Rome: 90 B.C.–A.D. 212* (1967). Michael Crawford, *The Roman Republic*, 2d ed. (1993), and Chester G. Starr, *The Roman Empire, 27 B.C.–A.D. 476: A Study in Survival* (1982), assess the evolution of the Roman state during the Republic and Principate. Fergus Millar, *The Emperor in the Roman World (31 B.C.–A.D. 337)* (1977), is a comprehensive study of the position of the princeps. Barbara Levick, *The Government of the Roman Empire: A Sourcebook* (2000), presents original texts in translation.

For Roman military expansion and defense of the frontiers see W. V. Harris, *War and Imperialism in Republican Rome* (1979), and Stephen L. Dyson, *The Creation of the Roman Frontier* (1985). For military technology see M. C. Bishop, *Roman Military Equipment: From the Punic Wars to the Fall of Rome* (1993). David Macaulay, *City: A Story of Roman Planning and Construction* (1974), uses copious illustrations to reveal the wonders of Roman engineering; more depth and detail are found in K. D. White, *Greek and Roman Technology* (1984). The characteristics of Roman urban centers are highlighted in John E. Stambaugh, *The Ancient Roman City* (1988).

Kevin Greene, *The Archaeology of the Roman Economy* (1986), showcases new approaches to social and economic history. Suzanne Dickson, *The Roman Family* (1992) explores this most basic social group. Lionel Casson, *Everyday Life in Ancient Rome* (1998), and U. E. Paoli, *Rome: Its People, Life and Customs* (1983), look at the features that typified daily life. Jo-Ann Shelton, ed., *As the Romans Did: A Sourcebook in Roman Social History* (1998), offers a selection of translated ancient sources. Elaine Fantham, Helene Peet Foley, Natalie Boymel Kampen, Sarah B. Pomeroy, and H. Alan Shapiro, *Women in the Classical World: Image and Text* (1994), provide an up-to-date discussion of women in the Roman world. Many of the ancient sources on Roman women can be found in Mary R. Lefkowitz and Maureen B. Fant, eds., *Women's Life in Greece and Rome: A Source Book in Translation* (1982). Thomas Wiedemann, ed., *Greek and Roman Slavery* (1981), contains the ancient sources in translation. Donald G. Kyle, *Spectacles of Death in Ancient Rome* (1998), explores the nature and significance of blood sports in the arena.

A number of the chapters in John Boardman, Jasper Griffin, and Oswyn Murray, eds., *The Roman World* (1988), survey the intellectual and literary achievements of the Romans. Ronald Mellor, ed., *The Historians of Ancient Rome* (1998), provides context for reading the historical sources. Michael von Albrecht, *History of Roman Literature: From Livius Andronicus to Boethius: With Special Regard to Its Influence on World Literature* (1997), Michael Grant, *Art in the Roman Empire* (1995), and Nancy H. Ramage and Andrew Ramage, *The Cambridge Illustrated History of Roman Art* (1991) are surveys of Roman creative arts. Robert Turcan, *The Gods of Ancient Rome: Religion in Everyday Life from Archaic to Imperial Times* (2000), and R. M. Ogilvie, *The Romans and Their Gods in the Age of Augustus* (1969), are accessible introductions to Roman religion in its public and private manifestations. Michael Grant, *The Jews in the Roman World* (1973), and Erich S. Gruen, *Diaspora: Jews Amidst Greeks and Romans* (2002), explore the complicated situation of Jews in the Roman Empire. Joseph F. Kelly, *The World of the Early Christians* (1997), W. H. C. Frend, *The Rise of Christianity* (1984), and R. A. Markus, *Christianity in the Roman World* (1974), investigate the rise of Christianity. Everett Ferguson, ed., *Encyclopedia of Early Christianity* (2d ed., 1998), contains articles and bibliographies on a wide range of topics.

For the geography and demography of China see the well-illustrated *Cultural Atlas of China* (1983) by Caroline Blunden and Mark Elvin. Valerie Hansen, *The Open Empire: A History of China to 1600* (2000), emphasizes social history and China's interactions with other societies. Other basic surveys of Chinese history include Jacques Gernet, *A History of Chinese Civilization* (1982), and John K. Fairbank, *China: A New History* (1992). In greater depth for the ancient period are Edward L. Shaughnessy and Michael Loewe, eds., *The Cambridge History of Ancient China* (1998); Denis Twitchett and Michael Loewe, eds., *The Cambridge History of China*, vol. 1, *The Ch'in and Han Empires, 221 B.C.–A.D. 220* (1986); and Michele Pirazzoli-t'Serstevens, *The Han Dynasty* (1982). Nicola Di Cosmo, *Ancient China and Its Enemies: The Rise of Nomadic Power in East Asian History* (2002), explores the interactions of Chinese and nomads on the northern frontier. Kwang-chih Chang, *The Archaeology of Ancient China*, 4th ed. (1986), emphasizes the archaeological record. Patricia Buckley Ebrey, *Chinese Civilization: A Sourcebook* (2d ed., 1993), and W. de Bary, W. Chan, and B. Watson, eds., *Sources of Chinese Tradition* (1960), are collections of sources in translation. Sima Qian, *Historical Records* (1994), translated by Raymond Dawson, provides a very readable selection of varied material pertaining to the Qin dynasty compiled by the premier historian of the Han period.

For social history see Michael Loewe, *Everyday Life in Early Imperial China During the Han Period, 202 B.C.–A.D. 220* (1988), and Anne Behnke Kinney, "Women in Ancient China," in Bella Vivante, ed., *Women's Roles in Ancient Civilizations: A Reference Guide* (1999). For economic history and foreign relations see Xinru Liu, *Ancient India and Ancient China: Trade and Religious Exchanges, A.D. 1–600* (1994), and Ying-shih Yu, *Trade and Expansion in Han China* (1967). For scientific and technological achievements see Robert Temple, *The Genius of China: 3,000 Years of Science, Discovery, and Invention* (1986).

Benjamin I. Schwartz addresses intellectual history in *The World of Thought in Ancient China* (1985). Spiritual matters are taken up by Laurence G. Thompson, *Chinese Religion: An Introduction*, 3d ed. (1979). For art see Michael Sullivan, *A Short History of Chinese Art*, rev. ed. (1970), and Jessica Rawson, *Ancient China: Art and Archaeology* (1980).

For a stimulating comparison of the Roman and Han Empires that emphasizes the differences, see the first chapter of S. A. M. Adshead, *China in World History*, 2d ed. (1995).

■ Notes

1. Patricia Buckley Ebrey, ed., *Chinese Civilization and Society: A Sourcebook* (New York: Free Press, 1981), 33–34.

Document-Based Question
Economic Development in the Roman and Han Empires

Using the following documents, compare and contrast the geographic factors that affected economic development in the Roman and Han empires.

DOCUMENT 1
Map 5.1 The Roman Empire (p. 126)

DOCUMENT 2
The Treatment of Slaves in Rome and China (Diversity and Dominance, pp. 130–131)

DOCUMENT 3
Roman Aqueduct Near Tarragona, Spain (photo, p. 136)

DOCUMENT 4
The Magic Canal (Environment and Technology, p. 137)

DOCUMENT 5
Map 5.2 Han China (p. 140)

DOCUMENT 6
Rubbing of Salt Mining (photo, p. 141)

How did geography affect the economic value of slaves in the Roman and Han empires? What additional types of documents would help you understand the geographic factors affecting economic development in the two empires?

6 India and Southeast Asia, 1500 B.C.E.–600 C.E.

The Thousand Pillared Hall in the Temple of Minakshi at Madurai
At the annual Chittarai Festival, the citizens of this city in south India
celebrate the wedding of their patron goddess, Minakshi, to Shiva.

CHAPTER OUTLINE

Foundations of Indian Civilization, 1500 B.C.E.–600 C.E.

Imperial Expansion and Collapse, 324 B.C.E.–650 C.E.

Southeast Asia, 50–600 C.E.

ENVIRONMENT AND TECHNOLOGY: Indian Mathematics

DIVERSITY AND DOMINANCE: The Situation of Women in the *Kama Sutra*

In the *Bhagavad-Gita*°, the most renowned of all Indian sacred texts, Arjuna°, the greatest warrior of Indian legend, rides out in his chariot to the open space between two armies preparing for battle. Torn between his social duty to fight for his family's claim to the throne and his conscience, which balks at the prospect of killing the relatives, friends, and former teachers who are in the enemy camp, Arjuna slumps down in his chariot and refuses to fight. But his chariot driver, the god Krishna° in disguise, persuades him, in a carefully structured dialogue, both of the necessity to fulfill his duty as a warrior and of the proper frame of mind for performing these acts. In the climactic moment of the dialogue Krishna endows Arjuna with a "divine eye" and permits him to see the true appearance of god:

It was a multiform, wondrous vision,
with countless mouths and eyes
and celestial ornaments,
Everywhere was boundless divinity
containing all astonishing things,
wearing divine garlands and garments,
anointed with divine perfume.
If the light of a thousand suns
were to rise in the sky at once,
it would be like the light
of that great spirit.
Arjuna saw all the universe
in its many ways and parts,
standing as one in the body
of the god of gods.[1]

In all of world literature, this is one of the most compelling attempts to depict the nature of deity. Graphic images emphasize the vastness, diversity, and multiplicity of the god, but in the end we learn that Krishna is the organizing principle behind all creation, that behind diversity and multiplicity lies a higher unity.

This is an apt metaphor for Indian civilization. If one word can characterize India in both ancient and modern times, it is *diversity*. The enormous variety of the Indian landscape is mirrored in the patchwork of ethnic and linguistic groups that occupy it, the political fragmentation that has marked most of Indian history, the elaborate hierarchy of social groups into which the Indian population is divided, and the thousands of deities who are worshiped at the innumerable holy places that dot the subcontinent. Yet, in the end, one can speak of an Indian civilization that is united by a set of shared views and values.

In this chapter we survey the history of South and Southeast Asia from approximately 1500 B.C.E. to 600 C.E., focusing on the evolution of defining features of Indian civilization. Considerable attention is given to Indian religious conceptions. This coverage is due, in part, to religion's profound role in shaping Indian society. It is also a consequence of the sources of information available to historians. Lengthy epic poems, such as the *Mahabharata*° and *Ramayana*°, preserve useful information about early Indian society, but most of the earliest texts are religious documents—such as the *Vedas*°, *Upanishads*°, and Buddhist dialogues and stories—that were preserved and transmitted orally long before they were written down. In addition, Indian civilization held a conception of vast expanses of time during which creatures were repeatedly reincarnated and lived many lives. This belief may be why ancient Indians did not develop a historical consciousness like that of their Israelite and Greek contemporaries and took little interest in recording specific historical events: such events seemed relatively insignificant when set against the long cycles of time and lives.

As you read this chapter, ask yourself the following questions:

- What historical forces led to the development of complex social groupings in ancient India?

Bhagavad-Gita (BUH-guh-vahd GEE-tuh)
Arjuna (AHR-joo-nuh)   **Krishna** (KRISH-nuh)

Mahabharata (muh-huh-BAH-ruh-tuh)
Ramayana (ruh-muh-YAH-nuh)   **Vedas** (VAY-duhs)
Upanishads (oo-PAHN-ih-shahds)

- Why did Indian civilization develop religious traditions with such distinctive conceptions of space, time, gods, and the life cycle, and how did these beliefs shape nearly every aspect of South Asian culture?

- How, in the face of powerful forces that tended to keep India fragmented, did two great empires—the Mauryan° Empire of the fourth to second centuries B.C.E. and the Gupta° Empire of the fourth to sixth centuries C.E.—succeed in unifying much of India?

FOUNDATIONS OF INDIAN CIVILIZATION, 1500 B.C.E.–300 C.E.

India is called a *subcontinent* because it is a large—roughly 2,000 miles (3,200 kilometers) in both length and breadth—and physically isolated landmass within the continent of Asia. It is set off from the rest of Asia by the Himalayas°, the highest mountains on the planet, to the north, and by the Indian Ocean on its eastern, southern, and western sides (see Map 6.1). The most permeable frontier, and the one used by a long series of invaders and migrating peoples, lies to the northwest. But people using this corridor must cross over the mountain barrier of the Hindu Kush° (via the Khyber° Pass) and the Thar° Desert east of the Indus River.

The Indian Subcontinent

The subcontinent—which encompasses the modern nations of Pakistan, Nepal, Bhutan, Bangladesh, India, and the adjacent island of Sri Lanka—can be divided into three topographical zones. The mountainous northern zone takes in the heavily forested foothills and high meadows on the edge of the Hindu Kush and Himalaya ranges. Next come the great basins of the Indus and Ganges° Rivers. Originating in the ice of the Tibetan mountains to the north, these rivers have repeatedly overflowed their banks and deposited layer upon layer of silt, creating large alluvial plains. Northern India is divided from the third zone, the peninsula proper, by the Vindhya range and the Deccan°, an arid, rocky plateau that brings to mind parts of the American southwest. The tropical coastal strip of

Kerala (Malabar) in the west, the Coromandel Coast in the east with its web of rivers descending from the central plateau, the flatlands of Tamil Nadu on the southern tip of the peninsula, and the island of Sri Lanka often have followed paths of political and cultural development separate from those of northern India.

The rim of mountains looming above India's northern frontier shelters the subcontinent from cold Arctic winds and gives it a subtropical climate. The most dramatic source of moisture is the **monsoon** (seasonal wind). The Indian Ocean is slow to warm or cool, and the vast landmass of Asia swings rapidly between seasonal extremes of heat and cold. The temperature difference between the water and the land acts like a bellows, producing a great wind in this and adjoining parts of the globe. The southwest monsoon begins in June. It picks up huge amounts of moisture from the Indian Ocean and drops it over a swath of India that encompasses the rain-forest belt on the western coast and the Ganges Basin. Three harvests a year are possible in some places. Rice is grown in the moist, flat Ganges Delta (the modern region of Bengal). Elsewhere the staples are wheat, barley, and millet. The Indus Valley, in contrast, gets little precipitation (see Chapter 1). In this arid region agriculture depends on extensive irrigation. Moreover, the volume of water in the Indus is irregular, and the river has changed course from time to time.

Although invasions and migrations usually came by land through the northwest corridor, the ocean surrounding the peninsula has not been a barrier to travel and trade. Indian Ocean mariners learned to ride the monsoon winds across open waters from northeast to southwest in January and to make the return voyage in July. Ships made their way west across the Arabian Sea to the Persian Gulf, the southern coast of Arabia, and East Africa, and east across the Bay of Bengal to Indochina and Indonesia (see Chapter 7).

It is tempting to trace many of the characteristic features of later Indian civilization back to the Indus Valley civilization of the third and early second millennia B.C.E., but proof is hard to come by because the writing from that period has not yet been deciphered. That society, which responded to the challenge of an arid terrain by developing high levels of social organization and technology, seems to have succumbed around 1900 B.C.E. to some kind of environmental crisis (see Chapter 1).

The Vedic Age

Historians call the period from 1500 to 500 B.C.E. the "Vedic Age," after the *Vedas*, religious texts that are our main source of information about the period. The foundations for Indian civilization were laid

Mauryan (MORE-yuhn) Gupta (GOOP-tuh)
Himalayas (him-uh-LAY-uhs) Hindu Kush (HIHN-doo KOOSH)
Khyber (KIE-ber) Thar (tahr) Ganges (GAHN-jeez)
Deccan (de-KAN)

C H R O N O L O G Y

	India	Southeast Asia
2000 B.C.E.		**ca. 2000 B.C.E.** Swidden agriculture
		ca. 1600 B.C.E. Beginning of migrations from mainland Southeast Asia to islands in Pacific and Indian Oceans
1500 B.C.E.	**ca. 1500 B.C.E.** Migration of Indo-European peoples into northwest India	
1000 B.C.E.	**ca. 1000 B.C.E.** Indo-European groups move into the Ganges Plain	
500 B.C.E.	**ca. 500 B.C.E.** Siddhartha Gautama founds Buddhism; Mahavira founds Jainism	
	324 B.C.E. Chandragupta Maurya becomes king of Magadha and lays foundation for Mauryan Empire	
1 C.E.	**184 B.C.E.** Fall of Mauryan Empire	
	320 C.E. Chandra Gupta establishes Gupta Empire	**ca. 50–560 C.E.** Funan dominates southern Indochina and the Isthmus of Kra
500 C.E.	**550 C.E.** Collapse of Gupta Empire	**ca. 500 C.E.** Trade route develops through Strait of Malacca
	606–647 C.E. Reign of Harsha Vardhana	

in the Vedic Age. Most historians believe that new groups of people—nomadic warriors speaking Indo-European languages—migrated into northwest India around 1500 B.C.E. Some argue for a much earlier Indo-European presence in this region in conjunction with the spread of agriculture. In any case, in the mid-second millennium B.C.E. northern India entered a new historical period associated with the dominance of Indo-European groups.

After the collapse of the Indus Valley civilization there was no central authority to direct irrigation efforts. The region became home to kinship groups that depended mostly on their herds of cattle for sustenance and perhaps supplemented their diet by doing some gardening. These societies, like those of other Indo-European peoples—Greeks, Iranians, Romans—were patriarchal. The father dominated the family as the king ruled the tribe. Members of the warrior class boasted of their martial skill and courage, relished combat, celebrated with lavish feasts and heavy drinking, and filled their leisure time with chariot racing and gambling.

After 1000 B.C.E. some of these groups pushed east into the Ganges Plain. New technologies made this advance possible. Iron tools—harder than bronze and able to hold a sharper edge—allowed settlers to fell trees and work the newly cleared land with plows pulled by oxen. The soil of the Ganges Plain was fertile, well watered by the annual monsoon, and able to sustain two or three crops a year. As in Greece at roughly the same time (see Chapter 4), the use of iron tools to open new land for agriculture must have led to a significant increase in population.

Stories about this era, written down much later but preserved by memorization and oral recitation, speak of bitter rivalry and warfare between two groups of people:

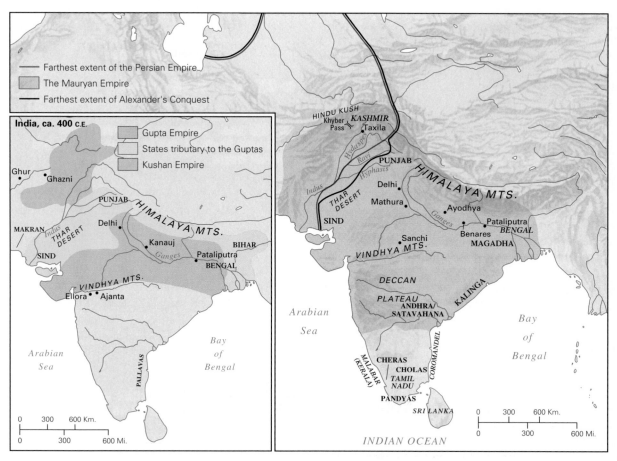

Map 6.1   Ancient India   Mountains and ocean largely separate the Indian subcontinent from the rest of Asia. Migrations and invasions usually came through the Khyber Pass in the northwest. Seaborne commerce with western Asia, Southeast Asia, and East Asia often flourished. Peoples speaking Indo-European languages migrated into the broad valleys of the Indus and Ganges Rivers in the north. Dravidian-speaking peoples remained the dominant population in the south. The diversity of the Indian landscape, the multiplicity of ethnic groups, and the primary identification of people with their class and caste lie behind the division into many small states that has characterized much of Indian political history.

the Aryas, relatively light-skinned speakers of Indo-European languages, and the Dasas, dark-skinned speakers of Dravidian languages. Some scholars contend that some Dasas were absorbed into Arya populations and elites from both groups merged. For the most part, however, the Aryas pushed the Dasas south into central and southern India, where their descendants still live. Indo-European languages are primarily spoken in northern India today. Dravidian speech prevails in the south.

Skin color has been a persistent concern of Indian society and is one of the bases for its historically sharp internal divisions. Over time there evolved a system of **varna**—literally "color," though the word came to indicate something akin to "class." Individuals were born into one of four classes: *Brahmin*, the group comprising priests and scholars; *Kshatriya°*, warriors and officials; *Vaishya°*, merchants, artisans, and landowners; or *Shudra°*, peasants and laborers. The designation *Shudra* originally may have been reserved for Dasas, who were given the menial jobs in society. Indeed, the very term *dasa* came to mean "slave." Eventually a fifth group was marked off: the Untouchables. They were excluded from the class system, and members of the other groups literally avoided them because of the demeaning or pollut-

Kshatriya (kshuh-TREE-yuh)   **Vaishya** (VIESH-yuh)
Shudra (SHOOD-ra)

ing work to which they were relegated—such as leather tanning, which involved touching dead animals, and sweeping away ashes after cremations.

People at the top of the social pyramid in ancient India could explain why this hierarchy existed. According to one creation myth, a primordial creature named Purusha allowed itself to be sacrificed. From its mouth sprang the class of Brahmin priests, the embodiment of intellect and knowledge. From its arms came the Kshatriya warrior class, from its thighs the Vaishya landowners and merchants, and from its feet the Shudra workers.

The varna system was just one of the mechanisms that Indian society developed to regulate relations between different groups. Within the broad class divisions, the population was further subdivided into numerous **jati,** or birth groups (sometimes called *castes,* from a Portuguese term meaning "breed"). Each jati had its proper occupation, duties, and rituals. Individuals who belonged to a given jati lived with members of their group, married within the group, and ate only with members of the group. Elaborate rules governed their interactions with members of other groups. Members of higher-status groups feared pollution from contact with lower-caste individuals and had to undergo elaborate rituals of purification to remove any taint.

The class and caste systems came to be connected to a widespread belief in reincarnation. The Brahmin priests taught that every living creature had an immortal essence: the *atman,* or "breath." Separated from the body at death, the atman was later reborn in another body. Whether the new body was that of an insect, an animal, or a human depended on the **karma,** or deeds, of the atman in its previous incarnations. People who lived exemplary lives would be reborn into the higher classes. Those who misbehaved would be punished in the next life by being relegated to a lower class or even a lower life form. The underlying message was: You are where you deserve to be, and the only way to improve your lot in the next cycle of existence is to accept your current station and its attendant duties.

The dominant deities in Vedic religion were male and were associated with the heavens. To release the dawn, Indra, god of war and master of the thunderbolt, daily slew the demon encasing the universe. Varuna, lord of the sky, maintained universal order and dispensed justice. Agni, the force of fire, consumed the sacrifice and bridged the spheres of gods and humans.

Sacrifice—the dedication to a god of a valued possession, often a living creature—was the essential ritual. The purpose of these offerings was to invigorate the gods and thereby sustain their creative powers and promote stability in the world.

Brahmin priests controlled the technology of sacrifice, for only they knew the rituals and prayers. The *Rig Veda,* a collection of more than a thousand poetic hymns to various deities, and the *Brahmanas,* detailed prose descriptions of procedures for ritual and sacrifice, were collections of priestly lore couched in the Sanskrit language of the Arya upper classes. This information was handed down orally from one generation of priests to the next. Some scholars have hypothesized that the Brahmins opposed the introduction of writing. Such opposition would explain why this technology did not come into widespread use in India until the Gupta period (320–550 C.E.), long after it had begun to play a conspicuous role in other societies of equivalent complexity. The priests' "knowledge" (the term *veda* means just that) was the basis of their economic well-being. They were amply rewarded for officiating at sacrifices, and their knowledge gave them social and political power because they were the indispensable intermediaries between gods and humans.

As in nearly all ancient societies, it is difficult to uncover the experiences of women in ancient India. Limited evidence indicates that women in the Vedic period studied sacred lore, composed religious hymns, and participated in the sacrificial ritual. They had the opportunity to own property and usually were not married until they reached their middle or late teens. A number of strong and resourceful women appear in the epic poem *Mahabharata.* One of them, the beautiful and educated Draupadi, married—by her own choice—the five royal Pandava brothers. This probably should not be taken as evidence of the regular practice of polyandry (having more than one husband). In India, as in Greece, legendary figures had their own rules.

The sharp internal divisions of Indian society, the complex hierarchy of groups, and the claims of some to superior virtue and purity served important social functions. They provided each individual with a clear identity and role and offered the benefits of group solidarity and support. There is evidence that groups sometimes were able to upgrade their status. Thus the elaborate system of divisions was not static and provided a mechanism for working out social tensions.

Challenges to the Old Order: Jainism and Buddhism

After 700 B.C.E. various forms of reaction against Brahmin power and privilege emerged. People who objected to the rigid hierarchy of classes and castes or the community's demands on the individual could retreat to the forest. Despite the clearing of

Carved Stone Gateway Leading to the Great Stupa at Sanchi   Pilgrims traveled long distances to visit stupas, mounds containing relics of the Buddha. The complex at Sanchi, in central India, was begun by Ashoka in the third century B.C.E., though the gates probably date to the first century C.E. This relief shows a royal procession bringing the remains of the Buddha to the city of Kushinagara.   (Dinodia Photo Library)

extensive tracts of land for agriculture, much of ancient India was covered with forest. Never very far from civilized areas, these wild places served as a refuge and symbolized freedom from societal constraints.

Certain charismatic individuals who abandoned their town or village and moved to the forest attracted bands of followers. Calling into question the priests' exclusive claims to wisdom and the necessity of Vedic chants and sacrifices, they offered an alternative path to salvation: the individual pursuit of insight into the nature of the self and the universe through physical and mental discipline (*yoga*), special dietary practices, and meditation. They taught that by distancing oneself from desire for the things of this world, one could achieve **moksha,** or "liberation." This release from the cycle of reincarnations and union with the divine force that animates the universe sometimes was likened to "a deep, dreamless sleep." The *Upanishads*—a collection of more than one hundred mystical dialogues between teachers and disciples—reflect this questioning of the foundations of Vedic religion.

The most serious threat to Vedic religion and to the prerogatives of the Brahmin priestly class came from two new religions that emerged around this time: Jainism° and Buddhism. Mahavira (540–468 B.C.E.) was known to his followers as Jina, "the Conqueror," from which is derived *Jainism*, the name of the belief system that he established. Emphasizing the holiness of the life force that animates all living creatures, Mahavira and his followers practiced strict nonviolence. They wore masks to pre-

Jainism (JINE-iz-uhm)

vent themselves from accidentally inhaling small insects, and they carefully brushed off a seat before sitting down. Those who gave themselves over completely to Jainism practiced extreme asceticism and nudity, ate only what they were given by others, and eventually starved themselves to death. Less zealous Jainists, restricted from agricultural work by the injunction against killing, tended to be city dwellers engaged in commerce and banking.

Of far greater significance for Indian and world history was the rise of Buddhism. So many stories have been told about Siddhartha Gautama (563–483 B.C.E.), known as the **Buddha,** "the Enlightened One," that it is difficult to separate fact from legend. He came from a Kshatriya family of the Sakyas, a people in the foothills of the Himalayas. As a young man he enjoyed the princely lifestyle to which he had been born, but at some point he experienced a change of heart and gave up family and privilege to become a wandering ascetic. After six years of self-deprivation, he came to regard asceticism as no more likely than the luxury of his previous life to produce spiritual insight, and he decided to adhere to a "Middle Path" of moderation. Sitting under a tree in a deer park near Benares on the Ganges River, he gained a sudden and profound insight into the true nature of reality, which he set forth as "Four Noble Truths": (1) life is suffering; (2) suffering arises from desire; (3) the solution to suffering lies in curbing desire; and (4) desire can be curbed if a person follows the "Eightfold Path" of right views, aspirations, speech, conduct, livelihood, effort, mindfulness, and meditation. Rising up, the Buddha preached his First Sermon, a central text of Buddhism, and set into motion the "Wheel of the Law." He soon at-

Sculpture of the Buddha, Second or Third Century C.E. This depiction of the Buddha, showing the effects of a protracted fast before he abandoned asceticism for the path of moderation, is from Gandhara in the northwest. It displays the influence of Greek artistic styles emanating from Greek settlements established in that region by Alexander the Great in the late fourth century B.C.E. (Robert Fisher)

Buddhism regarded the individual as a composite without any soul-like component that survived upon entering nirvana.

When the Buddha died, he left no final instructions, instead urging his disciples to "be their own lamp." As the Buddha's message—contained in philosophical discourses memorized by his followers—spread throughout India and into Central, Southeast, and East Asia, its very success began to subvert the individualistic and essentially atheistic tenets of the founder. Buddhist monasteries were established, and a hierarchy of Buddhist monks and nuns came into being. Worshipers erected *stupas*° (large earthen mounds that symbolized the universe) over relics of the cremated founder and walked around them in a clockwise direction. Believers began to worship the Buddha himself as a god. Many Buddhists also revered *bodhisattvas*°, men and women who had achieved enlightenment and were on the threshold of nirvana but chose to be reborn into mortal bodies to help others along the path to salvation.

The makers of early pictorial images had refused to show the Buddha as a living person and represented him only indirectly, through symbols such as his footprints, his begging bowl, or the tree under which he achieved enlightenment, as if to emphasize his achievement of a state of nonexistence. From the second century C.E., however, statues of the Buddha and bodhisattvas began to proliferate, done in native sculptural styles and in a style that showed the influence of the Greek settlements established in Bactria (modern Afghanistan) by Alexander the Great (see Chapter 4). A schism emerged within Buddhism. Devotees of **Mahayana**° ("Great Vehicle") **Buddhism** embraced the popular new features, while practitioners of **Theravada**° ("Teachings of the Elders") **Buddhism** followed most of the original teachings of the founder.

tracted followers, some of whom took vows of celibacy, nonviolence, and poverty.

In its original form, Buddhism centered on the individual. Although it did not quite reject the existence of gods, it denied their usefulness to a person seeking enlightenment. What mattered was living one's life with moderation, in order to minimize desire and suffering, and searching for spiritual truth through self-discipline and meditation. The ultimate reward was *nirvana*, literally "snuffing out the flame." With nirvana came release from the cycle of reincarnations and achievement of a state of perpetual tranquility. The Vedic tradition emphasized the eternal survival of the atman, the "breath" or nonmaterial essence of the individual. In contrast,

The Rise of Hinduism

Challenged by new, spiritually satisfying, and egalitarian movements, Vedic religion made important adjustments, evolving into **Hinduism,** the religion of hundreds of millions of people in South Asia today. (The term *Hinduism,* however, was imposed from outside. Islamic invaders who reached India in the eleventh century C.E. labeled the diverse range of practices they saw there as Hinduism: "what the Indians do.") The foundation of

stupa (STOO-puh)   bodhisattva (boe-dih-SUT-vuh)
Mahayana (mah-huh-YAH-nuh)   Theravada (there-uh-VAH-duh)

Hindu Temple at Khajuraho   This sandstone temple of the Hindu deity Shiva, representing the celestial mountain of the gods, was erected at Khajuraho, in central India, around 1000 C.E., but it reflects the architectural symbolism of Hindu temples developed in the Gupta period. Worshipers made their way through several rooms to the image of the deity, located in the innermost "womb-chamber" directly beneath the tallest tower.   (Jean-Louis Nou)

Hinduism is the Vedic religion of the Arya peoples of northern India. But Hinduism also incorporated elements drawn from the Dravidian cultures of the south, such as an emphasis on intense devotion to the deity and the prominence of fertility rituals and symbolism. Also present are elements of Buddhism.

The process by which Vedic religion was transformed into Hinduism by the fourth century C.E. is largely hidden from us. The Brahmin priests maintained their high social status and influence. But sacrifice, though still part of traditional worship, was less central, and there was much more opportunity for direct contact between gods and individual worshipers.

The gods were altered, both in identity and in their relationships with humanity. Two formerly minor deities, Vishnu° and Shiva°, assumed preeminent positions in the Hindu pantheon. Hinduism emphasized the worshiper's personal devotion to a particular deity, usually Vishnu, Shiva, or Devi° ("the Goddess"). Both Shiva and Devi appear to be derived from the Dravidian tradition,

in which a fertility cult and female deities played a prominent role. Their Dravidian origin is a telling example of how Arya and non-Arya cultures fused to form classic Hindu civilization. It is interesting to note that Vishnu, who has a clear Arya pedigree, remains more popular in northern India, while Shiva is dominant in the Dravidian south. These gods can appear in many guises. They are identified by various cult names and are represented by a complex symbolism of stories, companion animals, birds, and objects.

Vishnu, the preserver, is a benevolent deity who helps his devotees in time of need. Hindus believe that whenever demonic forces threaten the cosmic order, Vishnu appears on earth in one of a series of *avataras*, or incarnations. Among his incarnations are the legendary hero Rama, the popular cowherd-god Krishna, and the Buddha (a clear attempt to co-opt the rival religion's founder). Shiva, who lives in ascetic isolation on Mount Kailasa in the Himalayas, is a more ambivalent figure. He represents both creation and destruction, for both are part of a single, cyclical process. He often is represented performing dance steps that symbolize the acts of cre-

Vishnu (VIHSH-noo)   Shiva (SHEE-vuh)   Devi (DEH-vee)

ation and destruction. Devi manifests herself in various ways—as a full-bodied mother-goddess who promotes fertility and procreation, as the docile and loving wife Parvati, and as the frightening deity who, under the name Kali or Durga, lets loose a torrent of violence and destruction.

The multiplicity of gods (330 million according to one tradition), sects, and local practices within Hinduism is dazzling, reflecting the ethnic, linguistic, and cultural diversity of India. Yet within this variety there is unity. A worshiper's devotion to one god or goddess does not entail denial of the other main deities or the host of lesser divinities and spirits. Ultimately, all are seen as manifestations of a single divine force that pervades the universe. This sense of underlying unity is expressed in texts, such as the passage from the Bhagavad-Gita quoted at the beginning of this chapter; in the different potentials of women represented in the various manifestations of Devi; and in composite statues that are split down the middle—half Shiva, half Vishnu—as if to say that they are complementary aspects of one cosmic principle.

Hinduism offers the worshiper a variety of ways to approach god and obtain divine favor—through special knowledge of sacred truths, mental and physical discipline, or extraordinary devotion to the deity. Worship centers on the temples, which range from humble village shrines to magnificent, richly decorated stone edifices built under royal patronage. Beautifully proportioned statues beckon the deity to take up temporary residence within the image, to be reached and beseeched by eager worshipers. A common form of worship is *puja*, service to the deity, which can take the form of bathing, clothing, or feeding the statue. Potent blessings are conferred on the man or woman who glimpses the divine image.

Pilgrimage to famous shrines and attendance at festivals offer worshipers additional opportunities to show devotion. The entire Indian subcontinent is dotted with sacred places where a worshiper can directly sense and benefit from the inherent power of divinity. Mountains, caves, and certain trees, plants, and rocks are enveloped in an aura of mystery and sanctity. The literal meaning of *tirthayatra*, the term for a pilgrimage site, is "journey to a river-crossing," pointing out the frequent association of Hindu sacred places with flowing water. Hindus consider the Ganges River to be especially sacred, and each year millions of devoted worshipers travel to its banks to bathe and receive the restorative and purifying power of its waters. The habit of pilgrimage to the major shrines has promoted contact and the exchange of ideas among people from different parts of India and has helped create a broad Hindu identity and the concept of India as a single civilization, despite enduring political fragmentation.

Religious duties may vary, depending not only on the

Stone Relief Depicting Vishnu Asleep and Dreaming on the Ocean Floor, Fifth Century C.E. In this relief from a temple at Deogarh, in central India, Vishnu reclines on the coiled body of a giant multiheaded serpent that he subdued. The beneficent god of preservation, Vishnu appears in a new incarnation whenever demonic forces threaten the world. The Indian view of the vastness of time is embodied in this mythic image, which conceives of Vishnu as creating and destroying universes as he exhales and inhales. (John C. Huntington)

worshiper's social standing and gender but also on his or her stage of life. A young man from one of the three highest classes (Brahmin, Kshatriya, or Vaishya) undergoes a ritual rebirth through the ceremony of the sacred thread, marking the attainment of manhood and readiness to receive religious knowledge. From this point, the ideal life cycle passes through four stages: (1) the young man becomes a student and studies the sacred texts; (2) he then becomes a householder, marries, has children, and acquires material wealth; (3) when his grandchildren are born, he gives up home and family and becomes a forest dweller, meditating on the nature and meaning of existence; (4) he abandons his personal identity altogether and becomes a wandering ascetic awaiting death. In the course of a virtuous life he has fulfilled first his duties to society and then his duties to himself, so that by the end of his life he is so disconnected from the world that he can achieve moksha (liberation).

The successful transformation of a religion based on Vedic antecedents and the ultimate victory of Hinduism over Buddhism—Buddhism was driven from the land of its birth, though it maintains deep roots in Central, East, and Southeast Asia (see Chapters 7 and 10)—are remarkable phenomena. Hinduism responded to the needs of people for personal deities with whom they could establish direct connections. The austerity of Buddhism in its most authentic form, its denial of the importance of gods, and its expectation that individuals find their own path to enlightenment may have demanded too much of ordinary people. The very features that made Mahayana Buddhism more accessible to the populace—gods, saints, and myths—also made it more easily absorbed into the vast social and cultural fabric of Hinduism.

IMPERIAL EXPANSION AND COLLAPSE, 324 B.C.E.–650 C.E.

Political unity in India, on those rare occasions when it has been achieved, has not lasted long. A number of factors have contributed to India's habitual political fragmentation. Different terrains—mountains, foothills, plains, forests, steppes, deserts—called forth different forms of organization and economic activity, and peoples occupying topographically diverse zones differed from one another in language and cultural practices. Perhaps the most significant barrier to political unity lay in the complex social hierarchy. Individuals identified themselves primarily in terms of their class and caste (birth group); allegiance to a higher political authority was of secondary concern.

Despite these divisive factors, two empires arose in the Ganges Plain: the Mauryan Empire of the fourth to second centuries B.C.E. and the Gupta Empire of the fourth to sixth centuries C.E. Each extended political control over a substantial portion of the subcontinent and fostered the formation of a common Indian civilization.

The Mauryan Empire, 324–184 B.C.E.

Around 600 B.C.E. separate kinship groups and independent states dotted the landscape of north India. The kingdom of Magadha, in eastern India south of the Ganges (see Map 6.1), began to play an increasingly influential role, however, thanks to wealth based on agriculture, iron mines, and its strategic location astride the trade routes of the eastern Ganges Basin. In the late fourth century B.C.E. Chandragupta Maurya°,

a young man who may have belonged to the Vaishya or Shudra class, gained control of the kingdom of Magadha and expanded it into the **Mauryan Empire**—India's first centralized empire. He may have been inspired by the example of Alexander the Great, who had followed up his conquest of the Persian Empire with a foray into the Punjab (northern Pakistan) in 326 B.C.E. (see Chapter 4). Indeed, Greek tradition claimed that Alexander met a young Indian native by the name of "Sandracottus," an apparent corruption of "Chandragupta."

The collapse of Greek rule in the Punjab after the death of Alexander created a power vacuum in the northwest. Chandragupta (r. 324–301 B.C.E.) and his successors Bindusara (r. 301–269 B.C.E.) and Ashoka (r. 269–232 B.C.E.) extended Mauryan control over the entire subcontinent except for the southern tip of the peninsula. Not until the height of the Mughal Empire of the seventeenth century C.E. was so much of India again under the control of a single government.

Tradition holds that Kautilya, a crafty elderly Brahmin, guided Chandragupta in his conquests and consolidation of power. Kautilya is said to have written a surviving treatise on government, the *Arthashastra*°. Although recent studies have shown that the *Arthashastra* in its present form is a product of the third century C.E., its core text may well go back to Kautilya. This coldly pragmatic guide to political success and survival advocates the so-called *mandala*° (circle) theory of foreign policy: "My enemy's enemy is my friend." It also relates a long list of schemes for enforcing and increasing the collection of tax revenues, and it prescribes the use of spies to keep watch on everyone in the kingdom.

A tax equivalent to one-fourth the value of the harvest supported the Mauryan kings and government. Close relatives and associates of the king governed administrative districts based on traditional ethnic boundaries. A large imperial army—with infantry, cavalry, chariot, and elephant divisions—and royal control of mines, shipbuilding, and the manufacture of armaments further secured power. Standard coinage issued throughout the empire fostered support for the government and military and promoted trade.

The Mauryan capital was at Pataliputra (modern Patna), where five tributaries join the Ganges. Several extant descriptions of the city composed by foreign visitors provide valuable information and testify to the international connections of the Indian monarchs. Surrounded by a timber wall and moat, the city extended along the river for 8 miles (13 kilometers). It was governed by six committees with responsibility for features of urban life

---

Maurya (MORE-yuh)

Arthashastra (ahr-thuh-SHAHS-truh) **mandala** (man-DAH-luh)

such as manufacturing, trade, sales, taxes, the welfare of foreigners, and the registration of births and deaths.

Ashoka, Chandragupta's grandson, is an outstanding figure in early Indian history. At the beginning of his reign he engaged in military campaigns that extended the boundaries of the empire. During his conquest of Kalinga (modern Orissa, a coastal region southeast of Magadha), hundreds of thousands of people were killed, wounded, or deported. Overwhelmed by the brutality of this victory, the young monarch became a convert to Buddhism and preached nonviolence, morality, moderation, and religious tolerance in both government and private life.

Ashoka publicized this program by inscribing edicts on great rocks and polished pillars of sandstone scattered throughout his enormous empire. Among the inscriptions that have survived—they constitute the earliest decipherable Indian writing—is the following:

> For a long time in the past, for many hundreds of years have increased the sacrificial slaughter of animals, violence toward creatures, unfilial conduct toward kinsmen, improper conduct toward Brahmins and ascetics. Now with the practice of morality by King [Ashoka], the sound of war drums has become the call to morality. . . . You [government officials] are appointed to rule over thousands of human beings in the expectation that you will win the affection of all men. All men are my children. Just as I desire that my children will fare well and be happy in this world and the next, I desire the same for all men. . . . King [Ashoka] . . . desires that there should be the growth of the essential spirit of morality or holiness among all sects. . . . There should not be glorification of one's own sect and denunciation of the sect of others for little or no reason. For all the sects are worthy of reverence for one reason or another.[2]

Ashoka, however, was not naive. Despite his commitment to employing peaceful means whenever possible, he hastened to remind potential transgressors that "the king, remorseful as he is, has the strength to punish the wrongdoers who do not repent."

Commerce and Culture in an Era of Political Fragmentation

The Mauryan Empire prospered for a time after Ashoka's death in 232 B.C.E. Then, weakened by dynastic disputes, it collapsed from the pressure of attacks in the northwest in 184 B.C.E. Five hundred years passed before another indigenous state was able to extend its control over northern India.

In the meantime, a series of foreign powers dominated the northwest, present-day Afghanistan and Pakistan, and extended their influence east and south. The first was the Greco-Bactrian kingdom (180–50 B.C.E.), descended from troops and settlers left in Afghanistan by Alexander the Great. Greek influence is especially evident in the art of this period and in the designs of coins. Occupation by two nomadic peoples from Central Asia followed. The Shakas, an Iranian people known as Scythians in the Mediterranean world, were dominant from 50 B.C.E. to 50 C.E. They were followed by the Kushans°, originally from Xinjiang in northwest China, who were preeminent from 50 to 240 C.E. At its height the Kushan kingdom controlled much of present-day Uzbekistan, Afghanistan, Pakistan, and northwest India, fostering trade and prosperity by connecting to both the overland Silk Road and Arabian seaports (see Chapter 7). Several foreign kings—most notably the Greco-Bactrian Milinda (Menander in Greek) and the Kushan Kanishka—were converts to Buddhism, a logical choice because of the lack of an easy mechanism for working foreigners into the Hindu system of class and caste. The eastern Ganges region reverted to a patchwork of small principalities, as it had been before the Mauryan era.

Despite the political fragmentation of India in the five centuries after the collapse of the Mauryan Empire, there were many signs of economic, cultural, and intellectual development. The network of roads and towns that had sprung up under the Mauryans fostered lively commerce within the subcontinent, and India was at the heart of international land and sea trade routes that linked China, Southeast Asia, Central Asia, the Middle East, East Africa, and the lands of the Mediterranean. In the absence of a strong central authority, guilds of merchants and artisans became politically powerful in the Indian towns. Their wealth enabled them to serve as patrons of culture and to endow the religious sects to which they adhered—particularly Buddhism and Jainism—with richly decorated temples and monuments.

During the last centuries B.C.E. and first centuries C.E. the two greatest Indian epics, the *Ramayana* and the *Mahabharata*, based on oral predecessors dating back many centuries, achieved their final form. The events that both epics describe are said to have occurred several million years in the past, but the political forms, social organization, and other elements of cultural context—proud kings, beautiful queens, wars among kinship groups, heroic conduct, and chivalric values—seem to reflect the conditions of the early Vedic period, when Arya warrior societies were moving onto the Ganges Plain.

Kushan (KOO-shahn)

The *Ramayana* relates the exploits of Rama, a heroic prince, who is an incarnation of the god Vishnu. When his beautiful wife is kidnapped, aided by his loyal brother and the king of the monkeys, he defeats and destroys the chief of the demons and his evil horde. The vast pageant of the **Mahabharata** (it is eight times the length of the Greek *Iliad* and *Odyssey* combined) tells the story of two sets of cousins, the Pandavas and Kauravas, whose quarrel over succession to the throne leads them to a cataclysmic battle at the field of Kurukshetra. The battle is so destructive on all sides that the eventual winner, Yudhishthira, is reluctant to accept the fruits of so tragic a victory.

The **Bhagavad-Gita,** quoted at the beginning of this chapter, is a self-contained (and perhaps originally separate) episode set in the midst of those events. The great hero Arjuna, at first reluctant to fight his own kinsmen, is tutored by the god Krishna and learns the necessity of fulfilling his duty as a warrior. Death means nothing in a universe in which souls will be reborn again and again. The climactic moment comes when Krishna reveals his true appearance—awesome and overwhelmingly powerful—and his identity as time itself, the force behind all creation and destruction. The Bhagavad-Gita offers an attractive resolution to the tension in Indian civilization between duty to society and duty to one's own soul. Disciplined action—that is, action taken without regard for any personal benefits that might derive from it—is a form of service to the gods and will be rewarded by release from the cycle of rebirths.

This era also saw significant advances in science and technology. Indian doctors had a wide knowledge of herbal remedies and were in demand in the courts of western and southern Asia. Indian scholars made impressive strides in linguistics. Panini (late fourth century B.C.E.) undertook a detailed analysis of Sanskrit word forms and grammar. The work of Panini and later linguists led to the standardization of Sanskrit, which arrested its natural development and turned it into a formal, literary language. Prakrits—popular dialects—emerged to become the ancestors of the modern Indo-European languages of northern and central India.

This period of political fragmentation in the north also saw the rise of important states in central India, particularly the Andhra dynasty in the Deccan Plateau (from the second century B.C.E. to the second century C.E.), and the three **Tamil kingdoms** of Cholas, Pandyas, and Cheras in southern India (see Map 6.1). The three Tamil kingdoms were in frequent conflict with one another and experienced periods of ascendancy and decline, but they persisted in one form or another for over two thousand years. Historians regard the period from the third century B.C.E. to the third century C.E. as a "classical" period of great literary and artistic productivity in Tamil society. Under the patronage of the Pandya kings and the intellectual leadership of an academy of five hundred authors, works of literature on a wide range of topics—grammatical treatises, collections of ethical proverbs, epics, and short poems about love, war, wealth, and the beauty of nature—were produced, and music, dance, and drama were performed.

The Gupta Empire, 320–550 C.E.

In the early fourth century C.E. a new imperial entity took shape in northern India. Like its Mauryan predecessor, the **Gupta Empire** grew out of the kingdom of Magadha on the Ganges Plain and had its capital at Pataliputra. Clear proof that the founder of this empire consciously modeled himself on the Mauryans is the fact that he called himself Chandra Gupta (r. 320–335), borrowing the very name of the Mauryan founder. A claim to wide dominion was embodied in the title that the monarchs of this dynasty assumed—"Great King of Kings"—although they never controlled territories as extensive as those of the Mauryans. Nevertheless, over the fifteen-year reign of Chandra Gupta and the forty-year reigns of his three successors—Samudra Gupta, Chandra Gupta II, and Kumara Gupta—Gupta power and influence reached across northern and central India, west to Punjab and east to Bengal, north to Kashmir, and south into the Deccan Plateau (see Map 6.1).

This new empire, like its Mauryan predecessor, sat astride important trade routes, exploited the agricultural productivity of the Ganges Plain, and controlled nearby iron deposits. It adopted similar methods for raising revenue and administering broad territories. The chief source of revenue was a 25 percent tax on agriculture. Those who used the irrigation network also had to pay for the service, and there were special taxes on particular commodities. The state maintained monopolies in key areas such as the mining of metals and salt. The state also owned extensive tracts of farmland and demanded a specified number of days of labor annually from the subjects for the construction and upkeep of roads, wells, and the irrigation network.

Gupta control, however, was never as effectively centralized as Mauryan authority. The Gupta administrative bureaucracy and intelligence network were smaller and less pervasive. A powerful army maintained tight control in the core of the empire, but governors had a free hand in organizing the outlying areas. The position of governor offered tempting opportunities to exploit the populace.

It often was hereditary, passed from father to son in families of high-ranking members of the civil and military administrations. Distant subordinate kingdoms and areas inhabited by kinship groups were expected to make annual donations of tribute, and garrisons were stationed at certain key frontier points to keep open the lines of trade and expedite the collection of customs duties.

Limited in its ability to enforce its will on outlying areas, the empire found ways to "persuade" others to follow its lead. One medium of persuasion was the splendor, beauty, and orderliness of life at the capital and royal court. The constant round of solemn rituals, dramatic ceremonies, and exciting cultural events was such a potent advertisement for the benefits of association with the empire that modern historians point to the Gupta Empire as a good example of a **"theater-state."** The relationship of ruler and subjects in a theater-state also has an economic base. The center collects luxury goods and profits from trade and redistributes them to its dependents through the exchange of gifts and other means. Subordinate princes gained prestige by emulating the Gupta center on whatever scale they could manage, and maintained close ties through visits, gifts, and marriages to the Gupta royal family.

Astronomers, mathematicians, and other scientists received royal Gupta support. Indian mathematicians invented the concept of zero and developed the "Arabic" numerals and system of place-value notation that are in use in most parts of the world today (see Environment and Technology: Indian Mathematics).

Because the moist climate of the Ganges Plain does not favor the preservation of buildings and artifacts, there is relatively little archaeological data for the Gupta era. An eyewitness account, however, provides valuable information about the Gupta kingdom and Pataliputra, its capital city. A Chinese Buddhist monk named Faxian° made a pilgrimage to the homeland of his faith around 400 C.E. and left a record of his journey:

The royal palace and halls in the midst of the city, which exist now as of old, were all made by spirits which [King Ashoka] employed, and which piled up the stones, reared the walls and gates, and executed the elegant carving and inlaid sculpture-work—in a way which no human hands of this world could accomplish. . . . By the side of the stupa of Ashoka, there has been made a Mahayana [Buddhist] monastery, very grand and beautiful; there is also a Hinayana [Theravada] one; the two together containing six hundred or seven hundred monks. The rules of demeanor

and the scholastic arrangements in them are worthy of observation. . . . The cities and towns of this country are the greatest of all in the Middle Kingdom. The inhabitants are rich and prosperous, and vie with one another in the practice of benevolence and righteousness. . . . The heads of the Vaishya families in them establish in the cities houses for dispensing charity and medicines. All the poor and destitute in the country, orphans, widowers, and childless men, maimed people and cripples, and all who are diseased, go to those houses, and are provided with every kind of help.[3]

Various kinds of evidence point to a decline in the status of women in this period (see Diversity and Dominance: The Situation of Women in the *Kama Sutra*). As in Mesopotamia, Greece, and China (see Chapters 3, 4, and 5), urbanization, the formation of increasingly complex political and social structures, and the emergence of a nonagricultural middle class that placed high value on the acquisition and inheritance of property led to a loss of women's rights and an increase in male control over women's behavior.

Over time, women in India lost the right to own or inherit property. They were barred from studying sacred texts and participating in the sacrificial ritual. In many respects, they were treated as equivalent to the lowest class, the Shudra. As in Confucian China, a woman was expected to obey first her father, then her husband, and finally her sons (see Chapter 5). Indian girls were married at an increasingly early age, sometimes as young as six or seven. This practice meant that the prospective husband could be sure of his wife's virginity and, by bringing her up in his own household, could train and shape her to suit his purposes. The most extreme form of control of women's conduct took place in parts of India where a widow was expected to cremate herself on her husband's funeral pyre. This ritual, called *sati*°, was seen as a way of keeping a woman "pure." Women who declined to make this ultimate gesture of devotion were forbidden to remarry, shunned socially, and given little opportunity to earn a living.

Some women escaped these instruments of male control. One way to do so was by entering a Jainist or Buddhist religious community. Status also gave women more freedom. Women who belonged to powerful families and courtesans who were trained in poetry and music as well as in ways of providing sexual pleasure had high social standing and sometimes gave money for the erection of Buddhist stupas and other shrines.

Faxian (fah-shee-en)

sati (suh-TEE)

Indian Mathematics

The so-called Arabic numerals used in most parts of the world today were developed in India. The Indian system of place-value notation was far more efficient than the unwieldy numerical systems of Egyptians, Greeks, and Romans, and the invention of zero was a profound intellectual achievement. Indeed, it has to be ranked as one of the most important and influential discoveries in human history. This system is used even more widely than the alphabet derived from the Phoenicians (see Chapter 4) and is, in one sense, the only truly global language.

In its fully developed form the Indian method of arithmetic notation employed a base-10 system. It had separate columns for ones, tens, hundreds, and so forth, as well as a zero sign to indicate the absence of units in a given column. This system makes possible the economical expression of even very large numbers. And it allows for the performance of calculations not possible in a system like the numerals of the Romans, where any real calculation had to be done mentally or on a counting board.

A series of early Indian inscriptions using the numerals from 1 to 9 are deeds of property given to religious institutions by kings or other wealthy individuals. They were incised in the Sanskrit language on copper plates (see below). The earliest known example has a date equivalent to 595 C.E. A sign for zero is attested by the eighth century. Other textual evidence leads to the inference that a place-value system and the zero concept were already known in the fifth century.

This Indian system spread to the Middle East, Southeast Asia, and East Asia by the seventh century. Other peoples quickly recognized its capabilities and adopted it, sometimes using indigenous symbols. Europe received the new technology somewhat later. Gerbert of Aurillac, a French Christian monk, spent time in Spain between 967 and 970, where he was exposed to the mathematics of the Arabs. A great scholar and teacher who eventually became Pope Sylvester II (r. 999–1003), he spread word of the "Arabic" system in the Christian West.

Knowledge of the Indian system of mathematical notation eventually spread throughout Europe, in part through the use of a mechanical calculating device—an improved version of the Roman counting board, with counters inscribed with variants of the Indian numeral forms. Because the counters could be turned sideways or upside down, at first there was considerable variation in the forms. But by the twelfth century they had become standardized into forms close to those in use today. As the capabilities of the place-value system for written calculations became clear, the counting board fell into disuse. The abandonment of this device led to the adoption of the zero sign—not necessary on the counting board, where a column could be left empty—by the twelfth century. Leonardo Fibonacci, a thirteenth century C.E. Italian who learned algebra in Muslim North Africa and employed the Arabic numeral system in his mathematical treatise, gave additional impetus to the movement to discard the traditional system of Roman numerals.

Why was this marvelous system of mathematical notation invented in ancient India? The answer may lie in the way in which its range and versatility correspond to elements of Indian cosmology. The Indians conceived of immense spans of time—trillions of years (far exceeding current scientific estimates of the age of the universe as approximately 14 billion years old)—during which innumerable universes like our own were created, existed for a finite time, then were destroyed. In one popular creation myth, Vishnu is slumbering on the coils of a giant serpent at the bottom of the ocean, and worlds are being created and destroyed as he exhales and inhales. In Indian thought our world, like others, has existed for a series of epochs lasting more than 4 million years, yet the period of its existence is but a brief and insignificant moment in the vast sweep of time. The Indians developed a number system that allowed them to express concepts of this magnitude.

Copper Plate with Indian Numerals
This property deed from western India shows an early form of the symbol system for numbers that spread to the Middle East and Europe, and today is used all over the world. (Facsimile by Georges Ifrah. Reproduced by permission of Georges Ifrah.)

Wall Painting from the Caves at Ajanta, Fifth or Sixth Century C.E During and after the Gupta period, natural caves in the Deccan were turned into complexes of shrines decorated with sculpture and painting. This painting depicts one of the earlier lives of the Buddha, a king named Mahajanaka who lost and regained his kingdom, here listening to his queen, Sivali. While representing scenes from the earlier lives of the Buddha, the artists also give us a glimpse of life at the royal court in their own times. (Benoy K. Behl)

The Mauryans had been Buddhists, but the Gupta monarchs were Hindus. They revived ancient Vedic practices to bring an aura of sanctity to their position. This period also saw a reassertion of the importance of class and caste and the influence of Brahmin priests. Nevertheless, it was an era of religious tolerance. The Gupta kings were patrons for Hindu, Buddhist, and Jain endeavors. Buddhist monasteries with hundreds or even thousands of monks and nuns in residence flourished in the cities. Northern India was the destination of Buddhist pilgrims from Southeast and East Asia, traveling to visit the birthplace of their faith.

The classic form of the Hindu temple evolved during the Gupta era. Sitting atop a raised platform surmounted by high towers, the temple was patterned on the sacred mountain or palace in which the gods of mythology resided, and it represented the inherent order of the universe. From an exterior courtyard worshipers approached the central shrine, where the statue of the deity stood. Paintings or sculptured depictions of gods and mythical events covered the walls of the best-endowed sanctuaries. Cave-temples carved out of rock were also richly adorned with frescoes or with sculpture.

The vibrant commerce that had grown up after the fall of the Mauryan Empire continued into the Gupta period. Coined money served as the medium of exchange, and artisan guilds played an influential role in the economic, political, and religious life of the towns. The Gup-

tas sought control of the ports on the Arabian Sea but saw a decline in trade with the weakened Roman Empire. In compensation, trade with Southeast and East Asia was on the rise. Adventurous merchants from the ports of eastern and southern India made the sea voyage to the Malay° Peninsula and islands of Indonesia in order to exchange Indian cotton cloth, ivory, metalwork, and exotic animals for Chinese silk or Indonesian spices.

By the later fifth century C.E. the Gupta Empire was coming under pressure from the Huns. These nomadic invaders from the steppes of Central Asia poured into the northwest corridor. Defense of this distant frontier region eventually exhausted the imperial treasury, and the empire collapsed by 550. Save for a brief revival of imperial unity under Harsha Vardhana (r. 606–647), northern India reverted to its customary state of political fragmentation.

SOUTHEAST ASIA, 50–600 C.E.

Southeast Asia consists of three geographical zones: the Indochina mainland, the Malay Peninsula, and thousands of islands extending on an east-west axis far out into the Pacific Ocean. Encompassing a vast area of

Malay (muh-LAY)

우세인 은신처 방...

파운드폭탄 4발 투하··· 두 아들과 함께 사망 기

심진지 구축··· 이틀째 시가戰

령이 대중 앞에 나타나거나 애국심   라크 전후 대
을 고취하는 노래만을 내보내던 방   의에서는 전
송마저 중단됐다.   영국 주도로

DIVERSITY AND DOMINANCE

THE SITUATION OF WOMEN IN THE *KAMA SUTRA*

The ancient Indians articulated three broad areas of human concern: Dharma—the realm of religious and moral behavior; Artha—the acquisition of wealth and property; and Kama—the pursuit of pleasure. The Kama Sutra, which means "Treatise on Pleasure," while best known in the West for its detailed descriptions of erotic activities, is actually far more than a sex manual. It addresses, in a very broad sense, the relations between women and men in ancient Indian society, providing valuable information about the character and activities of men and women, the psychology of relationships, the forms of courtship and marriage, the household responsibilities of married women, appropriate behavior, and much more. The author of this text, Vatsyayana, lived in the third century C.E. He claims to be abridging and sharpening a series of earlier texts on the subject.

When a girl of the same caste, and a virgin, is married in accordance with the precepts of Holy Writ, the results of such a union are the acquisition of Dharma and Artha, offspring, affinity, increase of friends, and untarnished love. For this reason a man should fix his affections upon a girl who is of good family, whose parents are alive, and who is three years or more younger than himself. She should be born of a highly respectable family, possessed of wealth, well connected, and with many relations and friends. She should also be beautiful, of a good disposition, with lucky marks on her body, and with good hair, nails, teeth, ears, eyes and breasts, neither more nor less than they ought to be, and no one of them entirely wanting, and not troubled with a sickly body. The man should, of course, also possess these qualities himself. But at all events, says Ghotakamukha [an earlier writer], a girl who has been already joined with others (i.e. no longer a maiden) should never be loved, for it would be reproachable to do such a thing.

Now in order to bring about a marriage with such a girl as described above, the parents and relations of the man should exert themselves, as also such friends on both sides as may be desired to assist in the matter. These friends should bring to the notice of the girl's parents the faults, both present and future, of all the other men that may wish to marry her, and should at the same time extol even to exaggeration all the excellencies, ancestral, and paternal, of their friend, so as to endear him to them, and particularly to those that may be liked by the girl's mother. One of the friends should also disguise himself as an astrologer, and declare the future good fortune and wealth of his friend by showing the existence of all the lucky omens and signs, the good influence of planets, the auspicious entrance of the sun into a sign of the Zodiac, propitious stars and fortunate marks on his body. Others again should rouse the jealousy of the girl's mother by telling her that their friend has a chance of getting from some other quarter even a better girl than hers.

A girl should be taken as a wife, as also given in marriage, when fortune, signs, omens, and the words of others are favourable, for, says Ghotakamukha, a man should not marry at any time he likes. A girl who is asleep, crying, or gone out of the house when sought in marriage, or who is betrothed to another, should not be married. The following also should be avoided:

- One who is kept concealed
- One who has an ill-sounding name
- One who has her nose depressed
- One who has her nostril turned up
- One who is formed like a male
- One who is bent down
- One who has crooked thighs
- One who has a projecting forehead
- One who has a bald head
- One who does not like purity
- One who has been polluted by another
- One who is affected with the Gulma [glandular enlargement]
- One who is disfigured in any way
- One who has fully arrived at puberty
- One who is a friend
- One who is a younger sister
- One who is a Varshakari [prone to extreme perspiration]

In the same way a girl who is called by the name of one of the twenty-seven stars, or by the name of a tree, or of a river, is considered worthless, as also a girl whose name ends in "r" or "l." But some authors say that prosperity is gained only by marrying that girl to whom one becomes attached, and that therefore no other girl but the one who is loved should be married by anyone.

When a girl becomes marriageable her parents should dress her smartly, and should place her where she can be easily seen by all. Every afternoon, having dressed her and decorated her in a becoming manner, they should send her with her female companions to sports, sacrifices, and marriage ceremonies, and thus show her to advantage in society, because she is a kind of merchandise. They should also receive with kind words and signs of friendliness those of an auspicious appearance who may come accompanied by their friends and relations for the purpose of marrying their daughter, and under some pretext or other having first dressed her becomingly, should then present her to them. . . .

When a girl, possessed of good qualities and well-bred, though born in a humble family, or destitute of wealth, and not therefore desired by her equals, or an orphan girl, or one deprived of her parents, but observing the rules of her family and caste, should wish to bring about her own marriage when she comes of age, such a girl should endeavour to gain over a strong and good looking young man, or a person whom she thinks would marry her on account of the weakness of his mind, and even without the consent of his parents. She should do this by such means as would endear her to the said person, as well as by frequently seeing and meeting him. Her mother also should constantly cause them to meet by means of her female friends, and the daughter of her nurse. The girl herself should try to get alone with her beloved in some quiet place, and at odd times should give him flowers, betel nut, betel leaves and perfumes. She should also show her skill in the practice of the arts, in shampooing, in scratching and in pressing with the nails. She should also talk to him on the subjects he likes best, and discuss with him the ways and means of gaining over and winning the affections of a girl . . .

To the girl also she [the daughter of the girl's nurse, essentially a friend of the same age serving as a go-between] should speak about the excellent qualities of the man, especially of those qualities which she knows are pleasing to the girl. She should, moreover, speak with disparagement of the other lovers of the girl, and talk about the avarice and indiscretion of their parents, and the fickleness of their relations. She should also quote samples of many girls of ancient times, such as Sakoontala and others, who, having united themselves with lovers of their own caste and their own choice, were ever happy afterwards in their society. And she should also tell of other girls who married into great families, and being troubled by rival wives, became wretched and miserable, and were finally abandoned. She should further speak of the good fortune, the continual happiness, the chastity, obedience, and affection of the man, and if the girl gets amorous about him, she should endeavour to allay her shame and her fear as well as her suspicions about any disaster that might result from her marriage. In a word, she should act the whole part of a female messenger by telling the girl all about the man's affection for her, the places he frequented, and the endeavours he made to meet her, and by frequently repeating, "It will be all right if the man will take you away forcibly and unexpectedly." . . .

A virtuous woman, who has affection for her husband, should act in conformity with his wishes as if he were a divine being, and with his consent should take upon herself the whole care of his family. She should keep the whole house well cleaned, and arrange flowers of various kinds in different parts of it, and make the floor smooth and polished so as to give the whole a neat and becoming appearance. She should surround the house with a garden, and place ready in it all the materials required for the morning, noon and evening sacrifices. Moreover she should herself revere the sanctuary of the Household Gods, for, says Gonardiya [another earlier writer], "nothing so much attracts the heart of a householder to his wife as a careful observance of the things mentioned above." . . .

The wife should always avoid the company of female beggars, female Buddhist mendicants, unchaste and roguish women, female fortune tellers and witches. As regards meals, she should always consider what her husband likes and dislikes and what things are good for him, and what are injurious to him. When she hears the sounds of his footsteps coming home she should at once get up and be ready to do whatever he may command her, and either order her female servant to wash his feet, or wash them herself. When going anywhere with her husband, she should put on her ornaments, and without his consent she should not either give or accept invitations, or attend marriages and sacrifices, or sit in the company of female friends, or visit the temples of the Gods. And if she wants to engage in any kind of games or sports, she should not do it against his will. In the same way she should always sit down after him, and get up before him, and should never awaken him when he is asleep.

QUESTIONS FOR ANALYSIS

1. In what ways are women given essentially equal treatment to men in these excerpts? In what ways are they treated unequally?

2. On what bases do men and women choose spouses and lovers?

3. What were the most important household responsibilities of ancient Indian women? What social, intellectual, and cultural activities did they engage in?

4. In light of the treatise's prescriptions for how a married woman should treat her husband, what do you think was the nature of the emotional relationship of husband and wife? How might this differ from marriages in our society?

Source: Sir Richard Burton and F. F. Arbuthnot, *The Kama Sutra of Vatsyayana* (1883), sections III.1, III.4, III.5, IV.1, found at http://www.sacred-texts.com/sex/kama/index.htm.

land and water, this region is now occupied by the countries of Myanmar° (Burma), Thailand, Laos, Cambodia, Vietnam, Malaysia, Singapore, Indonesia, Brunei°, and the Philippines. Poised between the ancient centers of China and India, Southeast Asia has been influenced by the cultures of both civilizations. The region first rose to prominence and prosperity because of its intermediate role in the trade exchanges between southern and eastern Asia.

The strategic importance of Southeast Asia is enhanced by the region's natural resources. This is a geologically active zone; the islands are the tops of a chain of volcanoes. Lying along the equator, Southeast Asia has a tropical climate. The temperature hovers around 80 degrees Fahrenheit (30 degrees Celsius), and the monsoon winds provide dependable rainfall throughout the year. Thanks to several growing cycles each year, the region is capable of supporting a large human population. The most fertile agricultural lands lie along the floodplains of the largest silt-bearing rivers or contain rich volcanic soil deposited by ancient eruptions.

Rain forest covers much of Southeast Asia. Rainforest ecosystems are particularly fragile because of the great local variation of plant forms within them and because of the vulnerability of their soil to loss of fertility if the protective forest canopy is removed. As early as 2000 B.C.E. people in this region were clearing land for farming by cutting and burning the vegetation growing on it. The cleared land, known as swidden, was farmed for several growing seasons. When the soil was exhausted, the farmers abandoned the patch, allowing the forest to reclaim it before they cleared it again for agriculture. In the meantime, they cleared and cultivated other nearby fields in similar fashion.

A number of plant and animal species spread from Southeast Asia to other regions. Among them were wet rice (rice cultivated in deliberately flooded fields), soybeans, sugar cane, yams, bananas, coconuts, cocoyams, chickens, and pigs. Rice was the staple food product, for even though rice cultivation is labor-intensive (see Chapter 2), it can support a large population.

Historians believe that the **Malay peoples** who became the dominant population in this region were the product of several waves of migration from southern China beginning around 3000 B.C.E. In some cases the indigenous peoples merged with the Malay newcomers; in other cases they retreated to remote mountain and forest zones. Subsequently, rising population and disputes within communities prompted streams of people

---

Myanmar (myahn-MAH) **Brunei** (broo-NIE)

to leave the Southeast Asian mainland in the longest-lasting colonization movement in human history. By the first millennium B.C.E. the inhabitants of Southeast Asia had developed impressive navigational skills. They knew how to ride the monsoon winds and interpret the patterns of swells, winds, clouds, and bird and sea life. Over a period of several thousand years groups of Malay peoples in large, double outrigger canoes spread out across the Pacific and Indian Oceans—half the circumference of the earth—to settle thousands of islands.

The inhabitants of Southeast Asia tended to cluster along riverbanks or in fertile volcanic plains. Their fields and villages were never far from the rain forest, with its wild animals and numerous plant species. Forest trees provided fruit, wood, and spices. The shallow waters surrounding the islands teemed with fish. This region was also an early center of metallurgy, particularly bronze. Metalsmiths heated copper and tin ore to the right temperature for producing and shaping bronze implements by using hollow bamboo tubes to funnel a stream of oxygen to the furnace.

The first political units were small. The size of the fundamental unit reflected the number of people who drew water from the same source. Water resource "boards," whose members were representatives of the leading families of the different villages involved, met periodically to allocate and schedule the use of this critical resource.

Northern Indochina, by its geographic proximity, was particularly vulnerable to Chinese pressure and cultural influences, and was under Chinese political control for a thousand years (111 B.C.E.–939 C.E.). Farther south, larger states emerged in the early centuries C.E. in response to two powerful forces: commerce and Hindu-Buddhist culture. Southeast Asia was strategically situated along a new trade route that merchants used to carry Chinese silk westward to India and the Mediterranean. The movements of nomadic peoples had disrupted the old land route across Central Asia. But in India demand for silk was increasing—both for domestic use and for transshipment to the Arabian Gulf and Red Sea to satisfy the fast-growing luxury market in the Roman Empire. At first, a route developed across the South China Sea, by land over the Isthmus of Kra on the Malay peninsula, and across the Bay of Bengal to India. Over time, merchants extended this exchange network to include not only silk but also goods from Southeast Asia, such as aromatic woods, resins, and cinnamon, pepper, cloves, nutmeg, and other spices. By serving this trade network and controlling key points, Southeast Asian centers rose to prominence.

The other force leading to the rise of larger political entities was the influence of Hindu-Buddhist culture imported from India. Commerce brought Indian merchants and sailors into the ports of Southeast Asia. As Buddhism spread, Southeast Asia became a way station for Indian missionaries and East Asian pilgrims going to and coming from the birthplace of their faith. Indian cosmology, rituals, art, and statecraft constituted a rich treasury of knowledge and a source of prestige and legitimacy for local rulers who adopted them. The use of Sanskrit terms such as *maharaja*° (great king), the adaptation of Indian ceremonial practices and forms of artistic representation, and the employment of scribes skilled in writing all proved invaluable to the most ambitious and capable Southeast Asian rulers.

The first major Southeast Asian center, called **"Funan°"** by Chinese visitors, flourished between the first and sixth centuries C.E. Its capital was at the modern site of Oc-Eo in southern Vietnam. Funan occupied the delta of the Mekong° River, a "rice bowl" capable of supporting a large population. The rulers mobilized large numbers of laborers to dig irrigation channels and prevent destructive floods. By extending its control over most of southern Indochina and the Malay Peninsula, Funan was able to dominate the Isthmus of Kra—a key point on the trade route from India to China. Seaborne merchants from the ports of northeast India found that offloading their goods from ships and carrying them across the narrow strip of land was safer than making the 1,000-mile (1,600-kilometer) voyage around the Malay Peninsula—a dangerous trip marked by treacherous currents, rocky shoals, and pirates. Once the portage across the isthmus was finished, the merchants needed food and lodging while they waited for the monsoon winds to shift so that they could make the last leg of the voyage to China by sea. Funan stockpiled food and provided security for those engaged in this trade—in return, most probably, for customs duties and other fees.

According to one legend (a sure indicator of the influence of Indian culture in this region), the kingdom of Funan arose out of the marriage of an Indian Brahmin and a local princess. Chinese observers have left reports of the prosperity and sophistication of Funan, emphasizing the presence of walled cities, palaces, archives, systems of taxation, and state-organized agriculture. Nevertheless, for reasons not yet clear to modern historians, Funan declined in the sixth century. The most likely explanation is that international trade routes changed and Funan no longer held a strategic position.

---

maharaja (mah-huh-RAH-juh)   **Funan** (FOO-nahn)
Mekong (MAY-kawng)

CONCLUSION

This chapter traces the emergence of complex societies in India and Southeast Asia between the second millennium B.C.E. and the first millennium C.E. Because of migrations, trade, and the spread of belief systems, an Indian style of civilization spread throughout the subcontinent and adjoining regions and eventually made its way to the mainland and island chains of Southeast Asia. In this period were laid cultural foundations that in large measure still endure.

The development and spread of belief systems—Vedism, Buddhism, Jainism, and Hinduism—have a central place in this chapter because nearly all the sources for this area are religious. A visitor to a museum who examines artifacts from ancient Mesopotamia, Egypt, the Greco-Roman Mediterranean, China, and India will find that a prominent part of the collection consists of objects from religious shrines or with cultic function. Only the Indian artifacts, however, will be almost exclusively from the religious sphere.

The prolific use of writing came later to India than to other parts of the Eastern Hemisphere, for reasons particular to the Indian situation. Like Indian artifacts, most of the ancient Indian texts are of a religious nature. Ancient Indians did not generate historiographic texts of the kind written elsewhere in the ancient world, primarily because they held a strikingly different view of time. Mesopotamian scribes compiled lists of political and military events and the strange celestial and earthly phenomena that coincided with them. They were inspired by a cyclical conception of time and believed that the recurrence of an omen at some future date potentially signaled a repetition of the historical event associated with it. Greek and Roman historians described and analyzed the progress of wars and the character of rulers. They believed that these accounts would prove useful because of the essential constancy of human nature and the value of understanding the past as a sequence of causally linked events. Chinese annalists set down the deeds and conduct of rulers as inspirational models of right conduct and cautionary tales of the consequences of impropriety. In contrast, the distinctive Indian view of time—as vast epochs in which universes are created and destroyed again and again and the essential spirit of living creatures is reincarnated repeatedly—made the particulars of any brief moment seem relatively unilluminating.

The tension between divisive and unifying forces can be seen in many aspects of Indian life. Political and social division has been the norm throughout much of the history of India. It is a consequence of the topographical and environmental diversity of the subcontinent and the complex mix of ethnic and linguistic groups inhabiting it. The elaborate structure of classes and castes was a response to this diversity—an attempt to organize the population and position individuals within an accepted hierarchy, as well as to regulate group interactions. Strong central governments, such as those of the Mauryan and Gupta kings, gained ascendancy for a time and promoted prosperity and development. They rose to dominance by gaining control of metal resources and important trade routes, developing effective military and administrative institutions, and creating cultural forms that inspired admiration and emulation. However, as in Archaic Greece and Warring States China, the periods of fragmentation and multiple small centers of power seemed as economically and intellectually fertile and dynamic as the periods of unity.

India possessed many of the advanced technologies available elsewhere in the ancient world—agriculture, irrigation, metallurgy, textile manufacture, monumental construction, military technology, writing, and systems of administration. But of all the ancient societies, India made the most profound contribution to mathematics, devising the so-called Arabic numerals and place-value notation.

Many distinctive social and intellectual features of Indian civilization—the class and caste system, models of kingship and statecraft, and Vedic, Jainist, and Buddhist belief systems—originated in the great river valleys of the north, where descendants of Indo-European immigrants came to dominate. Hinduism embraced elements drawn from the Dravidian cultures of the south as well as from Buddhism. Hindu beliefs and practices are less fixed and circumscribed than the beliefs and practices of Judaism, Christianity, and Islam, which rely on clearly defined textual and organizational sources of authority. The capacity of the Hindu tradition to assimilate a wide range of popular beliefs facilitated the spread of elements of a common Indian civilization across the subcontinent, although there was, and is, considerable variation from one region to another.

This same malleable quality also came into play as the pace of international commerce quickened in the first millennium C.E. and Indian merchants embarking by sea for East Asia passed through Funan and other commercial centers in Southeast Asia. Indigenous elites in Southeast Asia came into contact with Indian merchants, sailors, and pilgrims. Involvement in the lucrative long-distance commerce and adoption of Indian political and religious ideas and methods brought wealth, power, and prestige to able and ambitious leaders. Finding elements of Indian civilization attractive and useful, they fused it with their own traditions to create a culture unique to

Southeast Asia. Chapter 7 describes how the networks of long-distance trade and communication established in the Eastern Hemisphere in antiquity continued to expand and foster technological and cultural development in the subsequent era.

■ Key Terms

monsoon
Vedas
varna
jati
karma
moksha
Buddha
Mahayana Buddhism
Theravada Buddhism
Hinduism
Mauryan Empire
Ashoka
Mahabharata
Bhagavad-Gita
Tamil kingdoms
Gupta Empire
theater-state
Malay peoples
Funan

■ Suggested Reading

A useful starting point for the Indian subcontinent is Karl J. Schmidt, *An Atlas and Survey of South Asian History* (1995), with maps and facing text illustrating geographic, environmental, cultural, and historical features of South Asian civilization. Concise discussions of the history of ancient India can be found in Stanley Wolpert, *A New History of India*, 3d ed. (1989), and Romila Thapar, *A History of India*, vol. 1 (1966). D. D. Kosambi, *Ancient India: A History of Its Culture and Civilization* (1965), and Paul Masson-Oursel, *Ancient India and Indian Civilization* (1998), are fuller presentations.

Ainslie T. Embree, *Sources of Indian Tradition*, vol. 1, 2d ed. (1988), contains translations of primary texts, with the emphasis almost entirely on religion and few materials from southern India. Barbara Stoler Miller, *The Bhagavad-Gita: Krishna's Counsel in Time of War* (1986), is a readable translation of this ancient classic with a useful introduction and notes. An abbreviated version of the greatest Indian epic can be found in R. K. Narayan, *The Mahabharata: A Shortened Modern Prose Version of the Indian Epic* (1978). The filmed version of Peter Brook's stage production of *The Mahabharata* (3 videos, 1989) generated much controversy because of its British director and multicultural cast, but it is a painless introduction to the plot and main characters. Robert Goldman, *The Ramayana of Valmiki: An Epic of Ancient India* (1984), makes available the other Indian epic. To sample the fascinating document on state building supposedly composed by the adviser to the founder of the Mauryan Empire, see T. N. Ramaswamy, *Essentials of Indian Statecraft: Kautilya's Arthasastra for Contemporary Readers* (1962). James Legge, *The Travels of Fa-hien [Faxian]: Fa-hien's Record of Buddhistic Kingdoms* (1971), and John W. McCrindle, *Ancient India as Described by Megasthenes and Arrian* (1877), provide translations of reports of foreign visitors to ancient India.

A number of works explore political institutions and ideas in ancient India: Charles Drekmeier, *Kingship and Community in Early India* (1962); John W. Spellman, *Political Theory of Ancient India: A Study of Kingship from the Earliest Times to Circa A.D. 300* (1964); and R. S. Sharma, *Aspects of Political Ideas and Institutions in Ancient India,* 2d ed. (1968). Romila Thapar, *Asoka and the Decline of the Mauryas* (1963), is a detailed study of the most interesting and important Maurya king.

For fundamental Indian social and religious conceptions see David R. Kinsley, *Hinduism: A Cultural Perspective* (1982). See also David G. Mandelbaum, *Society in India,* 2 vols. (1970), who provides essential insights into the complex relationship of class and caste. Kevin Trainor, ed., *Buddhism: The Illustrated Guide* (2001), devotes several chapters to Buddhism in ancient India. Jacob Pandian, *The Making of India and Indian Tradition* (1995), contains much revealing historical material, with particular attention to often neglected regions such as southern India, in its effort to explain the diversity of contemporary India. The chapter on ancient India by Karen Lang in Bella Vivante, ed., *Women's Roles in Ancient Civilizations: A Reference Guide* (1999), provides an up-to-date overview and bibliography. Stephanie W. Jamison, *Sacrificed Wife/Sacrificer's Wife: Women, Ritual, and Hospitality in Ancient India* (1996), deals with the roles early Indian women filled in ritual practices and the creation and maintenance of social relations, including several forms of marriage. Stella Kramrisch, *The Hindu Temple,* 2 vols. (1946), and Surinder M. Bhardwaj, *Hindu Places of Pilgrimage in India: A Study in Cultural Geography* (1973), examine important elements of worship in the Hindu tradition.

Roy C. Craven, *Indian Art* (1976), is a clear, historically organized treatment of its subject. Mario Bussagli and Calembus

Sivaramamurti, *5000 Years of the Art of India* (1971), is lavishly illustrated.

For the uniqueness and decisive historical impact of Indian mathematics see Georges Ifrah, *From One to Zero: A Universal History of Numbers* (1985).

Kameshwar Prasad, *Cities, Crafts, and Commerce under the Kusanas* (1984), discusses the dynamic, multicultural domain of the Kushans. Jean W. Sedlar, *India and the Greek World: A Study in the Transmission of Culture* (1980), relates the interaction of Greek and Indian civilizations. Lionel Casson, *The Periplus Maris Erythraei: Text with Introduction, Translation and Commentary* (1989), explicates a fascinating mariner's guide to the ports, trade goods, and human and navigational hazards of Indian Ocean commerce in the Roman era. Xinru Liu, *Ancient India and Ancient China: Trade and Religious Exchanges, A.D. 1–600* (1994), covers interactions with East Asia.

Richard Ulack and Gyula Pauer, *Atlas of Southeast Asia* (1989), provides a very brief introduction and maps for the environment and early history of Southeast Asia. Nicholas Tarling, ed., *The Cambridge History of Southeast Asia,* vol. 1 (1999); D. R. SarDeSai, *Southeast Asia: Past and Present,* 3d ed. (1994); and Milton E. Osborne, *Southeast Asia: An Introductory History* (1995), provide general accounts of Southeast Asian history. Lynda Shaffer, *Maritime Southeast Asia to 1500* (1996), focuses on early Southeast Asian history in a world historical context. Also useful is Kenneth R. Hall, *Maritime Trade and State Development in Early Southeast Asia* (1985).

The art of Southeast Asia is taken up by Maud Girard-Geslan et al., *Art of Southeast Asia* (1998), and Daigoro Chihara, *Hindu-Buddhist Architecture in Southeast Asia* (1996).

◼ Notes

1. Barbara Stoler Miller, *The Bhagavad-Gita: Krishna's Counsel in Time of War* (New York: Bantam, 1986), 98–99.
2. B. G. Gokhale, *Asoka Maurya* (New York: Twayne, 1966), 152–153, 156–157, 160.
3. James Legge, *The Travels of Fa-hien: Fa-hien's Record of Buddhistic Kingdoms* (Delhi: Oriental Publishers, 1971), 77–79.

Document-Based Question
Religion and Society in Ancient India

Using the following documents, assess the role of religion in the development of Indian society before 600 C.E.

DOCUMENT 1
The Thousand Pillared Hall in the Temple of Minakshi at Madurai (p. 150)

DOCUMENT 2
Excerpt from the *Bhagavad-Gita* (p. 151)

DOCUMENT 3
Hindu Temple at Khajuraho (p. 158)

DOCUMENT 4
Stone Relief Depicting Vishnu Asleep and Dreaming on the Ocean Floor, Fifth Century C.E. (p. 159)

DOCUMENT 5
Excerpt from an edict of King Ashoka (p. 161)

DOCUMENT 6
Excerpt from the Buddhist monk Faxian (p. 163)

DOCUMENT 7
The Situation of Women in the *Kama Sutra* (Diversity and Dominance, pp. 166–167)

DOCUMENT 8
Wall Painting from the Caves at Ajanta, Fifth or Sixth Century, C.E. (photo, p. 165)

How did religion shape the authors' points of view in Documents 5 through 7? What additional types of documents would help you assess the role of religion in Indian society before 600 C.E.?

Networks of Communication and Exchange, 300 B.C.E.–600 C.E.

7

Indian Ocean Sailing Vessel   Ships like this one, in a rock carving on the Buddhist temple of Borobodur in Java, probably carried colonists from Indonesia to Madagascar.

Inspired by the tradition of the Silk Road, a Chinese poet named Po Zhuyi° nostalgically wrote:

> Iranian whirling girl, Iranian whirling girl—
> Her heart answers to the strings,
> Her hands answer to the drums.
> At the sound of the strings and drums, she raises
>   her arms,
> Like whirling snowflakes tossed about, she turns
>   in her twirling dance.
> Iranian whirling girl,
> You came from Sogdiana°.
> In vain did you labor to come east more than ten
>   thousand tricents.
> For in the central plains there were already some
>   who could do the Iranian whirl,
> And in a contest of wonderful abilities, you
>   would not be their equal.[1]

The western part of Central Asia, the region around Samarkand° and Bukhara° known in the eighth century C.E. as Sogdiana, was 2,500 miles (4,000 kilometers) from the Chinese capital of Chang'an°. Caravans took more than four months to trek across the mostly unsettled deserts, mountains, and grasslands.

The Silk Road connecting China and the Middle East across Central Asia fostered the exchange of agricultural goods, manufactured products, and ideas. Musicians and dancing girls traveled, too—as did camel pullers, merchants, monks, and pilgrims. The Silk Road was not just a means of bringing peoples and parts of the world into contact; it was a social system.

With every expansion of territory, the growing wealth of temples, kings, and emperors enticed traders to venture ever farther afield for precious goods. For the most part, the customers were wealthy elites. But the new products, agricultural and industrial processes, and foreign ideas and customs these long-distance traders brought with them sometimes affected an entire society.

Po Zhuyi (boh joo-yee)   **Sogdiana** (sog-dee-A-nuh)
Samarkand (SAM-mar-kand)   **Bukhara** (boo-CAR-ruh)
Chang'an (chahng-ahn)

Travelers and traders seldom owned much land or wielded political power. Socially isolated (sometimes by law) and secretive because any talk about markets, products, routes, and travel conditions could help their competitors, they nevertheless contributed more to drawing the world together than did all but a few kings and emperors.

This chapter examines the social systems and historical impact of exchange networks that developed between 300 B.C.E. and 600 C.E. in Europe, Asia, and Africa. The Silk Road and the Indian Ocean maritime system illustrate the nature of long-distance trade in this era.

Trading networks were not the only medium for the spread of new ideas, products, and customs. This chapter compares developments along trade routes with folk migration by looking at the beginnings of contact across the Sahara and the simultaneous spread of Bantu-speaking peoples within sub-Saharan Africa. Chapter 5 discussed a third pattern of cultural contact and exchange, that taking place with the beginning of Christian missionary activity in the Roman Empire. This chapter further explores the process by examining the spread of Buddhism in Asia and Christianity in Africa and Asia.

As you read this chapter, ask yourself the following questions:

- What role does technology play in long-distance trade?
- How does geography affect trade patterns?
- How do human groups affect communication between regions?
- Why do some goods and ideas travel more easily than others?
- How do the three modes of cultural contact and exchange affect patterns of dominance and diversity?

THE SILK ROAD

Archaeology and linguistic studies show that the peoples of Central Asia engaged in long-distance movement and exchange from at least 1500 B.C.E. In Roman times Europeans became captivated by the idea of a

C H R O N O L O G Y		
Silk Road	**Indian Ocean Trade**	**Saharan Trade**

	Silk Road	Indian Ocean Trade	Saharan Trade
300 B.C.E.	**247 B.C.E.** Parthian rule begins in Iran **128 B.C.E.** General Zhang Jian reaches Ferghana		**500 B.C.E.–ca. 1000 C.E.** Bantu migrations **ca. 200 B.C.E.** Camel nomads in southern Sahara
1 C.E.	**100 B.C.E.–300 C.E.** Kushans rule northern Afghanistan and Sogdiana	**1st cent. C.E.** *Periplus of the Erythraean Sea;* Indonesian migration to Madagascar	**46 B.C.E.** First mention of camels in northern Sahara
300 C.E.	**ca. 400** Buddhist pilgrim Faxian travels Silk Road		**ca. 300** Beginning of camel nomadism in northern Sahara

trade route linking the lands of the Mediterranean with China by way of Mesopotamia, Iran, and Central Asia. The **Silk Road,** as it came to be called in modern times, experienced several periods of heavy use (see Map 7.1). The first began around 100 B.C.E.

Origins and Operations

The Seleucid kings who succeeded to the eastern parts of Alexander the Great's empire in the third century B.C.E. focused their energies on Mesopotamia and Syria. This allowed an Iranian nomadic leader to establish an independent kingdom in northeastern Iran. The **Parthians,** a people originally from east of the Caspian Sea, had become a major force by 247 B.C.E. They left few written sources, and recurring wars with Greeks and Romans to the west prevented travelers from the Mediterranean region from gaining firm knowledge of their kingdom. It seems likely, however, that their being located on the threshold of Central Asia and sharing customs with steppe nomads farther to the east helped foster the Silk Road.

In 128 B.C.E. a Chinese general named Zhang Jian° made his first exploratory journey across the deserts and mountains of Inner Asia on behalf of Emperor Wu of the Han dynasty. After crossing the broad and desolate Tarim Basin north of Tibet, he reached the fertile valley of Ferghana° and for the first time encountered westward-flowing rivers. There he found horse breeders whose animals far outclassed any horses he had seen. Later Chinese historians looked on General Zhang, who ultimately led eighteen expeditions, as the originator of overland trade with the western lands, and they credited him with personally introducing a whole garden of new plants and trees to China.

Long-distance travel suited the people of the steppes more than the Chinese. The populations of Ferghana and neighboring regions included many nomads who followed their herds. Their migrations had little to do with trade, but they provided pack animals and controlled transit across their lands. The trading demands that brought the Silk Road into being were Chinese eagerness for western products, especially horses, and on the western end, the organized Parthian state, which had captured the flourishing markets of Mesopotamia from the Seleucids.

By 100 B.C.E., Greeks could buy Chinese silk from Parthian traders in Mesopotamian border entrepôts. Yet caravans also bought and sold goods along the way in prosperous Central Asian cities like Samarkand and Bukhara. These cities grew and flourished, often under the rule of local princes.

General Zhang definitely seems to have brought two plants to China: alfalfa and wine grapes. The former

Zhang Jian (jahng jee-en)

Ferghana (fer-GAH-nuh)

Iranian Musicians from Silk Road This three-color glazed pottery figurine, 23 inches (58.4 centimeters) high, comes from a northern Chinese tomb of the Tang era (sixth to ninth centuries C.E.). The musicians playing Iranian instruments confirm the migration of Iranian culture across the Silk Road. At the same time, dishes decorated by the Chinese three-color glaze technique were in vogue in northern Iran. (The National Museum of Chinese History)

provided the best fodder for horses. In addition, Chinese farmers adopted pistachios, walnuts, pomegranates, sesame, coriander, spinach, and other new crops. Chinese artisans and physicians made good use of other trade products, such as jasmine oil, oak galls (used in tanning animal hides, dyeing, and making ink), sal ammoniac (for medicines), copper oxides, zinc, and precious stones.

Traders going west from China carried new fruits such as peaches and apricots, which the Romans mistakenly attributed to other eastern lands, calling them Persian plums and Armenia plums, respectively. They also carried cinnamon, ginger, and other spices that could not be grown in the West.

THE SASANID EMPIRE, 224–600

The rise of the **Sasanid Empire** in Iran brought a continuation of the rivalry between Rome and the Parthians along the Euphrates frontier and an intensification of trade along the Silk Road; but otherwise it differed greatly from its Parthian predecessor. Ardashir, a descendant of an ancestor named Sasan, defeated the Parthians around 224. Unlike the Parthians, who originated as nomads in northeastern Iran, the Sasanids came from the southwest, the same region that earlier gave rise to the Achaemenids (see Chapter 4).

In contrast to the sparse material remains of the Parthian period, Sasanid silver work and silk fabrics testify to the sumptuous and sedentary lifestyle of the warrior elite. Cities in Iran were small walled communities that served more as military strongpoints protecting long-distance trade than as centers of population and production.

The Silk Road now brought many new crops to Mesopotamia. Sasanid farmers pioneered in planting cotton, sugar cane, rice, citrus trees, eggplants, and other crops adopted from India and China. Although the acreage devoted to new crops increased slowly, these products became important consumption and trade items in later centuries.

The Sasanids established their Zoroastrian faith (see Chapter 4), which the Parthians had not particularly stressed, as a state religion similar to Christianity in the Byzantine Empire (see Chapter 5). The proclamation of Christianity and Zoroastrianism as official faiths marked the fresh emergence of religion as an instrument of politics both within and between the empires. This politicization of religion greatly affected the culture of the Silk Road.

Both Zoroastrianism and Christianity practiced intolerance. A late-third-century inscription in Iran boasts of the persecutions of Christians, Jews, and Buddhists carried out by the Zoroastrian high priest. Yet sizable Christian and Jewish communities remained, especially in Mesopotamia. Similarly, from the fourth century onward, councils of Christian bishops declared many theological beliefs heretical—so unacceptable that they were un-Christian.

Christians became pawns in the political rivalry with the Byzantines and were sometimes persecuted, sometimes patronized by the Sasanid kings. In 431 a council of bishops called by the Byzantine emperor declared the Nestorian Christians heretics for overemphasizing the humanness of Christ. The Nestorians believed that a human nature and a divine nature coexisted in Jesus and that Mary was not the mother of God, as many other

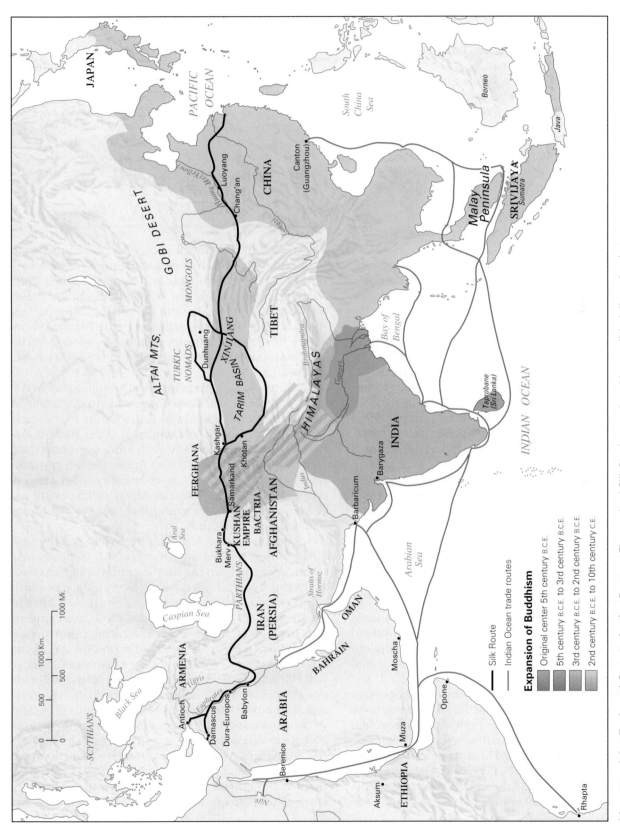

Map 7.1 Asian Trade and Communication Routes The overland Silk Road was vulnerable to political disruption, but was much shorter than the maritime route from the South China Sea to the Red Sea, and ships were more expensive than pack animals. Moreover, China's political centers were in the north.

Christians maintained, but the mother of the human Jesus. After the bishops' ruling, the Nestorians sought refuge under the Sasanid shah and engaged in missionary activities along the Silk Road.

A parallel episode within Zoroastrianism transpired in the third century. A preacher named Mani founded a new religion in Mesopotamia: Manichaeism. He preached a dualist faith—a struggle between Good and Evil—theologically derived from Zoroastrianism. Although at first Mani enjoyed the favor of the shah, he and many of his followers were martyred in 276. His religion survived and spread widely, particularly along the Silk Road. Nestorian missionaries thus competed with Manichaean missionaries for converts in Central Asia.

The Impact of the Silk Road

As trade became a more important part of Central Asian life, the Iranian-speaking peoples increasingly settled in trading cities and surrounding farm villages. By the sixth century C.E., nomads originally from the Altai Mountains farther east had spread across the steppes and become the dominant pastoral group. These peoples spoke Turkic languages unrelated to the Iranian tongues. The nomads continued to live in the round, portable felt huts called yurts that can still occasionally be seen in Central Asia, but prosperous individuals, both Turks and Iranians, built stately homes decorated with brightly colored wall paintings. The paintings show people wearing Chinese silks and Iranian brocades and riding on richly outfitted horses and camels. They also indicate an avid interest in Buddhism (see below), which competed with Nestorian Christianity, Manichaeism, and Zoroastrianism in a lively and inquiring intellectual milieu.

Missionary influences exemplify the impact of foreign customs and beliefs on the peoples along the Silk Road. Military technology affords an example of the opposite phenomenon, steppe customs radiating into foreign lands. Chariot warfare and the use of mounted bowmen originated in Central Asia and spread eastward and westward through military campaigns and folk migrations that began in the second millennium B.C.E. and recurred throughout the period of the Silk Road.

Evidence of the **stirrup,** one of the most important inventions, comes first from the Kushan people who ruled northern Afghanistan in approximately the first century C.E. At first a solid bar, then a loop of leather to support the rider's big toe, and finally a device of leather and metal or wood supporting the instep, the stirrup gave riders far greater stability in the saddle—which itself was in all likelihood an earlier Central Asian invention.

Using stirrups, a mounted warrior could supplement his bow and arrow with a long lance and charge his enemy at a gallop without fear that the impact of his attack would push him off his mount. Far to the west, the stirrup made possible the armored knights who dominated the battlefields of Europe (see Chapter 9), and it contributed to the superiority of the Tang cavalry in China (see Chapter 10).

THE INDIAN OCEAN MARITIME SYSTEM

A multilingual, multiethnic society of seafarers established the **Indian Ocean Maritime System,** a trade network across the Indian Ocean and the South China Sea. These people left few records and seldom played a visible part in the rise and fall of kingdoms and empires, but they forged increasingly strong economic and social ties between the coastal lands of East Africa, southern Arabia, the Persian Gulf, India, Southeast Asia, and southern China.

This trade took place in three distinct regions: (1) In the South China Sea, Chinese and Malays (including Indonesians) dominated trade. (2) From the east coast of India to the islands of Southeast Asia, Indians and Malays were the main traders. (3) From the west coast of India to the Persian Gulf and the east coast of Africa, merchants and sailors were predominantly Persians and Arabs. However, Chinese and Malay sailors could and did voyage to East Africa, and Arab and Persian traders reached southern China.

From the time of Herodotus in the fifth century B.C.E., Greek writers regaled their readers with stories of marvelous voyages down the Red Sea into the Indian Ocean and around Africa from the west. Most often, they attributed such trips to the Phoenicians, the most fearless of Mediterranean seafarers. Occasionally a Greek appears. One such was Hippalus, a Greek ship's pilot who was said to have discovered the seasonal monsoon winds that facilitate sailing across the Indian Ocean (see Diversity and Dominance: The Indian Ocean Trading World).

Of course, the regular, seasonal alternation of steady winds could not have remained unnoticed for thousands of years, waiting for an alert Greek to happen along. The great voyages and discoveries made before written records became common should surely be attributed to the peoples who lived around the Indian Ocean rather than to interlopers from the Mediterranean Sea. The story of Hippalus resembles the Chinese story of Gen-

Asklepios, the Greek God of Medicine This representation, found in the sea off the coast of Bahrain in the Persian Gulf, reflects the extension of Greek culture along sea routes into distant lands. Greek medical knowledge and principles became known as far away as India. The crude craftsmanship of this effigy indicates that it was locally made and not imported from Greece. (Courtesy, Bahrain National Museum)

eral Zhang Jian, whose role in opening trade with Central Asia overshadows the anonymous contributions made by the indigenous peoples. The Chinese may indeed have learned from General Zhang and the Greeks from Hippalus, but other people played important roles anonymously.

Mediterranean sailors of the time of Alexander used square sails and long banks of oars to maneuver among the sea's many islands and small harbors. Indian Ocean vessels relied on roughly triangular lateen sails and normally did without oars in running before the wind on long ocean stretches. Mediterranean shipbuilders nailed their vessels together. The planks of Indian Ocean ships were pierced, tied together with palm fiber, and caulked with bitumen. Mediterranean sailors rarely ventured out of sight of land. Indian Ocean sailors, thanks to the monsoon winds, could cover long reaches entirely at sea.

These technological differences prove that the world of the Indian Ocean developed differently from the world of the Mediterranean Sea, where the Phoenicians and Greeks established colonies that maintained con-

tact with their home cities (see Chapters 3 and 4). The traders of the Indian Ocean, where distances were greater and contacts less frequent, seldom retained political ties with their homelands. The colonies they established were sometimes socially distinctive but rarely independent of the local political powers.

Origins of Contact and Trade

By 2000 B.C.E. Sumerian records indicate regular trade between Mesopotamia, the islands of the Persian Gulf, Oman, and the Indus Valley. However, this early trading contact broke off, and later Mesopotamian trade references mention East Africa more often than India.

A similarly early chapter in Indian Ocean history concerns migrations from Southeast Asia to Madagascar, the world's fourth largest island, situated off the southeastern coast of Africa. About two thousand years ago, people from one of the many Indonesian islands of Southeast Asia established themselves in that forested, mountainous land 6,000 miles (9,500 kilometers) from home. They could not possibly have carried enough supplies for a direct voyage across the Indian Ocean, so their route must have touched the coasts of India and southern Arabia. No physical remains of their journeys have been discovered, however.

Apparently, the sailing canoes of these people plied the seas along the increasingly familiar route for several hundred years. Settlers farmed the new land and entered into relations with Africans who found their way across the 250-mile-wide (400-kilometer-wide) Mozambique° Channel around the fifth century C.E. Descendants of the seafarers preserved the language of their homeland and some of its culture, such as the cultivation of bananas, yams, and other native Southeast Asian plants. These food crops spread to mainland Africa. But the memory of their distant origins gradually faded, not to be recovered until modern times, when scholars established the linguistic link between the two lands.

The Impact of Indian Ocean Trade

The demand for products from the coastal lands inspired mariners to persist in their long ocean voyages. Africa produced exotic animals, wood, and ivory. Since ivory also came from India, Mesopotamia, and North Africa, the extent of African ivory exports cannot be determined. The highlands of northern Somalia and

Mozambique (moe-zam-BEEK)

우세인 은신처 방
파운드폭탄 4발 투하… 두 아들과 함께 사망
진지 구축… 이틀째 시가戰
령이 대중 앞에 나타나거나 애국심   라크 전후 대
을 고취하는 노래만을 내보내던 방   의에서는 전
송마저 중단됐다.   영국 주도로

DIVERSITY AND DOMINANCE

THE INDIAN OCEAN TRADING WORLD

The most revealing description of ancient trade in the Indian Ocean and of the diversity and economic forces shaping the Indian Ocean trading system, "The Periplus of the Erythraean Sea," a sailing itinerary (periplus in Greek), was composed in the first century C.E. by an unknown Greco-Egyptian merchant. It highlights the diversity of peoples and products from the Red Sea to the Bay of Bengal and illustrates the comparative absence of a dominating political force in the Indian Ocean trading system. Historians believe that the descriptions of market towns were based on first-hand experience. Information on more remote regions was probably hearsay (see Map 7.1).

Of the designated ports on the Erythraean Sea [Indian Ocean], and the market-towns around it, the first is the Egyptian port of Mussel Harbor. To those sailing down from that place, on the right hand . . . there is Berenice. The harbors of both are at the boundary of Egypt. . . .

On the right-hand coast next below Berenice is the country of the Berbers. Along the shore are the Fish-Eaters, living in scattered caves in the narrow valleys. Further inland are the Berbers, and beyond them the Wild-flesh-Eaters and Calf-Eaters, each tribe governed by its chief; and behind them, further inland, in the country towards the west, there lies a city called Meroe.

Below the Calf-Eaters there is a little market-town on the shore . . . called Ptolemais of the Hunts, from which the hunters started for the interior under the dynasty of the Ptolemies . . . But the place has no harbor and is reached only by small boats . . . .

Beyond this place, the coast trending toward the south, there is the Market and Cape of Spices, an abrupt promontory, at the very end of the Berber coast toward the east. . . . A sign of an approaching storm . . . is that the deep water becomes more turbid and changes its color. When this happens they all run to a large promontory called Tabae, which offers safe shelter. . . .

Beyond Tabae [lies] . . . another market-town called Opone . . . [I]n it the greatest quantity of cinnamon is produced . . . and slaves of the better sort, which are brought to Egypt in increasing numbers. . . .

[Ships also come] from the places across this sea, from . . . Barygaza, bringing to these . . . market-towns the products of their own places; wheat, rice, clarified butter, sesame oil, cotton cloth . . . and honey from the reed called sacchari [sugar cane]. Some make the voyage especially to these market-towns, and others exchange their cargoes while sailing along the coast. This country is not subject to a King, but each market-town is ruled by its separate chief.

Beyond Opone, the shore trending more toward the south . . . this coast [the Somali region of Azania, or East Africa] is destitute of harbors . . . until the Pyralax islands [Zanzibar] . . . . [A] little to the south of south-west . . . is the island Menuthias [Madagascar], about three hundred stadia from the mainland, low and wooded, in which there are rivers and many kinds of birds and the mountain-tortoise. There are no wild beasts except the crocodiles; but there they do not attack men. In this place there are sewed boats, and canoes hollowed from single logs. . . .

Two days' sail beyond, there lies the very last market-town of the continent of Azania, which is called Rhapta [Dar es-Salaam]; which has its name from the sewed boats (*rhapton ploiarion*) . . . ; in which there is ivory in great quantity, and tortoise-shell. Along this coast live men of piratical habits, very great in stature, and under separate chiefs for each place. [One] chief governs it under some ancient right that subjects it to the sovereignty of the state that is become first in Arabia. And the people of Muza [Mocha in Yemen] now hold it under his authority, and send thither many large ships; using Arab captains and agents, who are familiar with the natives and intermarry with them, and who know the whole coast and understand the language.

There are imported into these markets the lances made at Muza especially for this trade, and hatchets and daggers and awls, and various kinds of glass; and at some places a little wine, and wheat, not for trade, but to serve for getting the good-will of the savages. There are exported from these places a great quantity of ivory . . . and rhinoceros-horn. . . .

And these markets of Azania are the very last of the continent that stretches down on the right hand from Berenice; for beyond these places the unexplored ocean curves around toward the west, and running along by the regions to the south of Aethiopia and Libya and Africa, it mingles with the western sea. . . .

Beyond the harbor of Moscha [Musqat in Oman] . . . a mountain range runs along the shore; at the end of which, in a row, lie seven islands. . . . Beyond these there is a barbarous region which is no longer of the same Kingdom, but now belongs to Persia. Sailing along this coast well out at sea . . . there meets you an island called Sarapis. . . . It is about two hundred stadia wide and six hundred long, inhabited by three settlements of Fish-Eaters, a villainous lot, who use the Arabian language and wear girdles of palm-leaves. . . .

[T]here follows not far beyond, the mouth of the Persian Gulf, where there is much diving for the pearl-mussel. . . . At the upper end of this Gulf there is a market-town designated by law called Apologus, situated near . . . the River Euphrates.

Sailing [southeast] through the mouth of the Gulf, after a six-days' course there is another market-town of Persia called Ommana . . . . [L]arge vessels are regularly sent from Barygaza, loaded with copper and sandalwood and timbers of teakwood and logs of blackwood and ebony. . . .

Beyond this region . . . there follows the coast district of Scythia, which lies above toward the north; the whole marshy; from which flows down the river Sinthus [Indus], the greatest of all the rivers that flow into the Erythraean Sea, bringing down an enormous volume of water. . . . This river has seven mouths, very shallow and marshy, so that they are not navigable, except the one in the middle; at which by the shore, is the market-town, Barbaricum. . . . [I]nland behind it is the metropolis of Scythia . . . it is subject to Parthian princes who are constantly driving each other out.

Now the whole country of India has very many rivers, and very great ebb and flow of the tides. . . . But about Barygaza [Broach] it is much greater, so that the bottom is suddenly seen, and now parts of the dry land are sea, and now it is dry where ships were sailing just before; and the rivers, under the inrush of the flood tide, when the whole force of the sea is directed against them, are driven upwards more strongly against their natural current. . . .

The country inland from Barygaza is inhabited by numerous tribes. . . . Above these is the very warlike nation of the Bactrians, who are under their own king. And Alexander, setting out from these parts, penetrated to the Ganges. . . . [T]o the present day ancient drachmae are current in Barygaza, coming from this country, bearing inscriptions in Greek letters, and the devices of those who reigned after Alexander. . . .

Inland from this place and to the east, is the city called Ozene [Ujjain]. . . . [F]rom this place are brought down all things needed for the welfare of the country about Barygaza, and many things for our trade: agate and carnelian, Indian muslins . . . .

There are imported into this market-town, wine, Italian preferred, also Laodicean and Arabian; copper, tin, and lead; coral and topaz; thin clothing and inferior sorts of all kinds . . . gold and silver coin, on which there is a profit when exchanged for the money of the country. . . . And for the King there are brought into those places very costly vessels of silver, singing boys, beautiful maidens for the harem, fine wines, thin clothing of the finest weaves, and the choicest ointments. There are exported from these places [spices], ivory, agate and carnelian . . . cotton cloth of all kinds, silk cloth. . . .

Beyond Barygaza the adjoining coast extends in a straight line from north to south. . . . The inland country back from the coast toward the east comprises many desert regions and great mountains; and all kinds of wild beasts—leopards, tigers, elephants, enormous serpents, hyenas, and baboons of many sorts; and many populous nations, as far as the Ganges. . . .

This whole voyage as above described . . . they used to make in small vessels, sailing close around the shores of the gulfs; and Hippalus was the pilot who by observing the location of the ports and the conditions of the sea, first discovered how to lay his course straight across the ocean. . . .

About the following region, the course trending toward the east, lying out at sea toward the west is the island Palaesimundu, called by the ancients Taprobane [Sri Lanka]. . . . It produces pearls, transparent stones, muslins, and tortoiseshell. . . .

Beyond this, the course trending toward the north, there are many barbarous tribes, among whom are the Cirrhadae, a race of men with flattened noses, very savage; another tribe, the Bargysi; and the Horse-faces and the Long-faces, who are said to be cannibals.

After these, the course turns toward the east again, and sailing with the ocean to the right and the shore remaining beyond to the left, Ganges comes into view. . . . And just opposite this river there is an island in the ocean, the last part of the inhabited world toward the east, under the rising sun itself; it is called Chryse; and it has the best tortoise-shell of all the places on the Erythraean Sea.

After this region under the very north, the sea outside ending in a land called This, there is a very great inland city called Thinae, from which raw silk and silk yarn and silk cloth are brought on foot. . . . But the land of This is not easy of access; few men come from there, and seldom.

QUESTIONS FOR ANALYSIS

1. Of what importance were political organization and ethnicity to a traveling merchant?

2. How might a manual like this have been used?

3. To what extent can the observations of a Greco-Egyptian merchant be taken as evidence for understanding how merchants from other lands saw the trade in the Indian Ocean?

Source: Excerpts from W. H. Schoff (tr. & ed.), *The Periplus of the Erythraean Sea: Travel and Trade in the Indian Ocean by a Merchant of the First Century* (London, Bombay & Calcutta, 1912).

southern Arabia grew the scrubby trees whose aromatic resins were valued as frankincense and myrrh. Pearls abounded in the Persian Gulf, and evidence of ancient copper mines has been found in Oman in southeastern Arabia. India shipped spices and manufactured goods, and more spices came from Southeast Asia, along with manufactured items, particularly pottery, obtained in trade with China. In sum, the Indian Ocean trading region had a great variety of highly valued products. Given the long distances and the comparative lack of islands, however, the volume of trade there was undoubtedly much lower than in the Mediterranean Sea.

Furthermore, the culture of the Indian Ocean ports was often isolated from the hinterlands, particularly in the west. The coasts of the Arabian peninsula, the African side of the Red Sea, southern Iran, and northern India (today's Pakistan) were mostly barren desert. Ports in all these areas tended to be small, and many suffered from meager supplies of fresh water. Farther south in India, the monsoon provided ample water, but steep mountains cut off the coastal plain from the interior of the country. Thus few ports between Zanzibar and Sri Lanka had substantial inland populations within easy reach. The head of the Persian Gulf was one exception: ship-borne trade was possible from the port of Apologus (later called Ubulla, the precursor of modern Basra) as far north as Babylon and, from the eighth century C.E., nearby Baghdad.

By contrast, eastern India, the Malay Peninsula, and Indonesia afforded more hospitable and densely populated shores with easier access to inland populations. Though the fishers, sailors, and traders of the western Indian Ocean system supplied a long series of kingdoms and empires, none of these consumer societies became primarily maritime in orientation, as the Greeks and Phoenicians did in the Mediterranean. In the east, in contrast, sea-borne trade and influence seem to have been important even to the earliest states of Southeast Asia (see Chapter 6).

In coastal areas throughout the Indian Ocean system, small groups of seafarers sometimes had a significant social impact despite their usual lack of political power. Women seldom accompanied the men on long sea voyages, so sailors and merchants often married local women in port cities. The families thus established were bilingual and bicultural. As in many other situations in world history, women played a crucial though not well-documented role as mediators between cultures. Not only did they raise their children to be more cosmopolitan than children from inland regions, but they also introduced the men to customs and attitudes that they carried with them when they returned to sea. As a consequence, the designation of specific seafarers

as Persian, Arab, Indian, or Malay often conceals mixed heritages and a rich cultural diversity.

ROUTES ACROSS THE SAHARA

The windswept Sahara, a desert stretching from the Red Sea to the Atlantic Ocean and broken only by the Nile River, isolates sub-Saharan Africa from the Mediterranean world (see Map 7.2). The current dryness of the Sahara dates only to about 2500 B.C.E. The period of drying out that preceded that date lasted twenty-five centuries and encompassed several cultural changes. During that time, travel between a slowly shrinking number of grassy areas was comparatively easy. However, by 300 B.C.E., scarcity of water was restricting travel to a few difficult routes initially known only to desert nomads. Trade over **trans-Saharan caravan routes,** at first only a trickle, eventually expanded into a significant stream.

Early Saharan Cultures

Sprawling sand dunes, sandy plains, and vast expanses of exposed rock make up most of the great desert. Stark and rugged mountain and highland areas separate its northern and southern portions. The cliffs and caves of these highlands, the last spots where water and grassland could be found as the climate changed, preserve rock paintings and engravings that constitute the primary evidence for early Saharan history.

Though dating is difficult, what appear to be the earliest images, left by hunters in much wetter times, include elephants, giraffes, rhinoceros, crocodiles, and other animals that have long been extinct in the region. Overlaps in the artwork indicate that the hunting societies were gradually joined by new cultures based on cattle breeding and well adapted to the sparse grazing that remained. Domestic cattle may have originated in western Asia or in North Africa. They certainly reached the Sahara before it became completely dry. The beautiful paintings of cattle and scenes of daily life seen in the Saharan rock art depict pastoral societies that bear little similarity to any in western Asia. The people seem physically akin to to-

Map 7.2 Africa and the Trans-Saharan Trade Routes The Sahara and the surrounding oceans isolated most of Africa from foreign contact before 1000 C.E. The Nile Valley, a few trading points on the east coast, and limited transdesert trade provided exceptions to this rule; but the dominant forms of sub-Saharan African culture originated far to the west, north of the Gulf of Guinea.

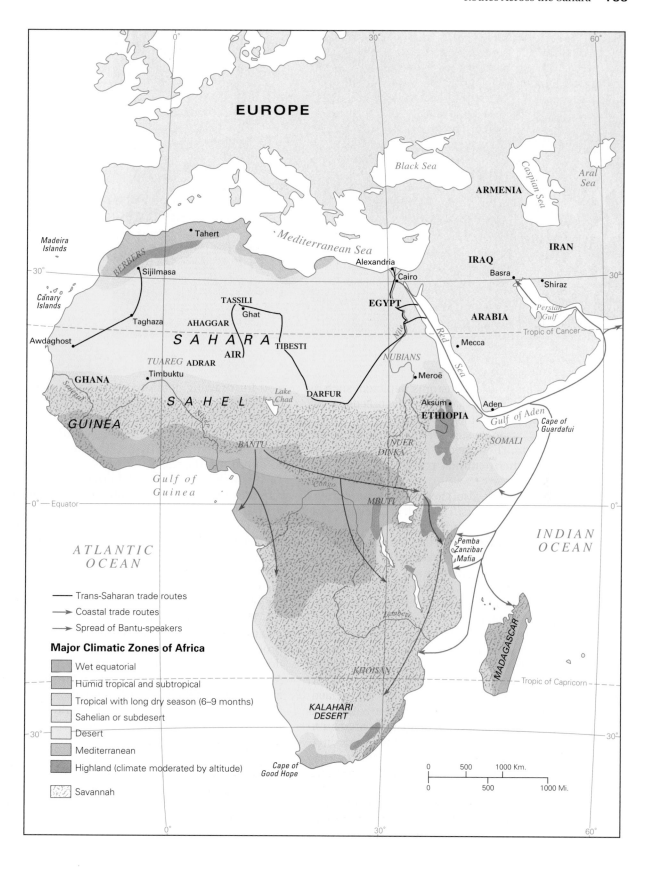

Cattle Herders in Saharan Rock Art These paintings represent the most artistically accomplished type of Saharan art. Herding societies of modern times living in the Sahel region south of the Sahara strongly resemble the society depicted here. (Henri Lhote)

day's West Africans, and the customs depicted, such as dancing and wearing masks, as well as the breeds of cattle, particularly those with piebald coloring (splotches of black and white), strongly suggest later societies to the south of the Sahara. These factors support the hypothesis that some southern cultural patterns originated in the Sahara.

Overlaps in artwork also show that horse herders succeeded the cattle herders. The rock art changes dramatically in style, from the superb realism of the cattle pictures to sketchier images that are often strongly geometric. Moreover, the horses are frequently shown drawing light chariots. According to the most common theory, intrepid charioteers from the Mediterranean shore drove their flimsy vehicles across the desert and established societies in the few remaining grassy areas of the central Saharan highlands. Some scholars suggest possible chariot routes that refugees from the collapse of the Mycenaean and Minoan civilizations of Greece and Crete (see Chapter 3) might have followed deep into the desert around the twelfth century B.C.E. However, no archaeological evidence of actual chariot use in the Sahara has been discovered, and it is difficult to imagine large numbers of refugees from the politically chaotic Mediterranean region driving chariots into a waterless, trackless desert in search of a new homeland somewhere to the south.

As with the cattle herders, therefore, the identity of the Saharan horse breeders and the source of their pas-

sion for drawing chariots remain a mystery. Only with the coming of the camel is it possible to make firm connections with the Saharan nomads of today through the depiction of objects and geometric patterns still used by the veiled, blue-robed Tuareg° people of the highlands in southern Algeria, Niger, and Mali.

Some historians maintain that the Romans inaugurated an important trans-Saharan trade, but they lack firm archaeological evidence. More plausibly, Saharan trade relates to the spread of camel domestication. Supporting evidence comes from rock art, where overlaps of images imply that camel riders in desert costume constitute the latest Saharan population. The camel-oriented images are decidedly the crudest to be found in the region.

The first mention of camels in North Africa comes in a Latin text of 46 B.C.E. Since the native camels of Africa probably died out before the era of domestication, the domestic animals probably reached the Sahara from Arabia, probably by way of Egypt in the first millennium B.C.E. They could have been adopted by peoples farther and farther to the west, from one central Saharan highland to the next, only much later spreading northward and coming to the attention of the Romans (see Environment and Technology: Camel Saddles). Camel herding made it easier for people to move away from the Saharan highlands and roam the deep desert.

Tuareg (TWAH-reg)

Trade Across the Sahara

Linkage between two different trading systems, one in the south, the other in the north, developed slowly. Southern traders concentrated on supplying salt from large deposits in the southern desert to the peoples of sub-Saharan Africa. Traders from the equatorial forest zone brought forest products, such as kola nuts (a condiment and source of caffeine) and edible palm oil, to trading centers near the desert's southern fringe. Each received the products they needed in their homelands from the other, or from the farming peoples of the Sahel°—literally "the coast" in Arabic, the southern borderlands of the Sahara (see Map 7.2). Middlemen who were native to the Sahel played an important role in this trade, but precise historical details are lacking.

In the north, Roman colonists supplied Italy with agricultural products, primarily wheat and olives. Surviving mosaic pavements depicting scenes from daily life show that people living on the farms and in the towns of the interior consumed Roman manufactured goods and shared Roman styles. This northern pattern began to change only in the third century C.E. with the decline of the Roman Empire, the abandonment of many Roman farms, the growth of nomadism, and a lessening of trade across the Mediterranean.

Sub-Saharan Africa

The Indian Ocean network and later trade across the Sahara provided sub-Saharan Africa, the portion of Africa south of the Sahara, with a few external contacts. The most important African network of cultural exchange from 300 B.C.E. to 1100 C.E., however, arose within the region and took the form of folk migration. These migrations and exchanges put in place enduring characteristics of African culture.

A Challenging Geography

Many geographic obstacles impede access to and movement within sub-Saharan Africa (see Map 7.2). The Sahara, the Atlantic and Indian Oceans, and the Red Sea form the boundaries of the region. With the exception of the Nile, a ribbon of green traversing the Sahara from south to north, the major river systems empty into the Atlantic, in the case of the Senegal, Niger, and Zaire° Rivers, or into

Sahel (SAH-hel) Zaire (zah-EER)

the Mozambique Channel of the Indian Ocean, in the case of the Zambezi. Rapids limit the use of these rivers for navigation.

Stretching over 50 degrees of latitude, sub-Saharan Africa encompasses dramatically different environments. A 4,000-mile (6,500-kilometer) trek from the southern edge of the Sahara to the Cape of Good Hope would take a traveler from the flat, semiarid **steppes** of the Sahel region to tropical **savanna** covered by long grasses and scattered forest, and then to **tropical rain forest** on the lower Niger and in the Zaire Basin. The rain forest gives way to another broad expanse of savanna, followed by more steppe and desert, and finally by a region of temperate highlands at the southern extremity, located as far south of the equator as Greece and Sicily are to its north. East-west travel is comparatively easy in the steppe and savanna regions—a caravan from Senegal to the Red Sea would have traversed a distance comparable to that of the Silk Road—but difficult in the equatorial rain-forest belt and across the mountains and deep rift valleys that abut the rain forest to the east and separate East from West Africa.

The Development of Cultural Unity

Cultural heritages shared by the educated elites within each region—heritages that some anthropologists call **"great traditions"**—typically include a written language, common legal and belief systems, ethical codes, and other intellectual attitudes. They loom large in written records as traditions that rise above the diversity of local customs and beliefs commonly distinguished as **"small traditions."**

By the year 1 C.E. sub-Saharan Africa had become a distinct cultural region, though one not shaped by imperial conquest or characterized by a shared elite culture, a "great tradition." The cultural unity of sub-Saharan Africa rested on similar characteristics shared to varying degrees by many popular cultures, or "small traditions." These had developed during the region's long period of isolation from the rest of the world and had been refined, renewed, and interwoven by repeated episodes of migration and social interaction. Historians know little about this complex prehistory. Thus, to a greater degree than in other regions, they call on anthropological descriptions, oral history, and comparatively late records of various "small traditions" to reconstruct the broad outlines of cultural formation.

Sub-Saharan Africa's cultural unity is less immediately apparent than its diversity. By one estimate, Africa is home to two thousand distinct languages, many

Camel Saddles

As seemingly simple a technology as saddle design can indicate a society's economic structure. The South Arabian saddle, a Tunisian example of which is shown to the right, was good for riding, and baggage could easily be tied to the wooden arches at its front. It was militarily inefficient, however, because the rider knelt on the cushion behind the camel's hump, which made it difficult to use weapons.

The North Arabian saddle was a significant improvement that came into use in the first centuries B.C.E. The two arches anchoring the front end of the South Arabian saddle were separated and greatly enlarged, one arch going in front of the hump and the other behind. This formed a solid wooden framework to which loads could easily be attached, but the placement of the prominent front and back arches seated the rider on top of the camel's hump instead of behind it and thereby gave warriors a solid seat and the advantage of height over enemy horsemen. Arabs in northern Arabia used these saddles to take control of the caravan trade through their lands.

The lightest and most efficient riding saddles, shown below, come from the southern Sahara, where personal travel and warfare took priority over trade. These excellent war saddles could not be used for baggage because they did not offer a convenient place to tie bundles.

Camel Saddles The militarily inefficient south Arabian saddle (above) seats the rider behind the animal's hump atop its hindquarters. The rider controls his mount by tapping its neck with a long camelstick. The Tuareg saddle (below) seats the rider over the animal's withers, leaving his hands free to wield a sword and letting him control his mount with his toes. (above: Private collection; below: Fred Bavendam/Peter Arnold, Inc.)

corresponding to social and belief systems endowed with distinctive rituals and cosmologies. There are likewise numerous food production systems, ranging from hunting and gathering—very differently carried out by the Mbuti° Pygmies of the equatorial rain forest and the Khoisan° peoples of the southwestern deserts—to the cultivation of bananas, yams, and other root crops in forest clearings and of sorghum and other grains in the savanna lands. Pastoral societies, particularly those depending on cattle, display somewhat less diversity across the Sahel and savanna belt from Senegal to Kenya.

Sub-Saharan Africa covered a larger and more diverse area than any other cultural region of the first millennium C.E. and had a lower overall population density. Thus societies and polities had ample room to form and reform, and a substantial amount of space separated different groups. The contacts that did occur did not last long enough to produce rigid cultural uniformity.

In addition, for centuries external conquerors could not penetrate the region's natural barriers and impose a uniform culture. The Egyptians occupied Nubia, and

---

Mbuti (m-BOO-tee)   **Khoisan** (KOI-sahn)

some traces of Egyptian influence appear in Saharan rock art farther west, but the Nile cataracts and the vast swampland in the Nile's upper reaches blocked movement farther south. The Romans sent expeditions against pastoral peoples living in the Libyan Sahara but could not incorporate them into the Roman world. Not until the nineteenth century did outsiders gain control of the continent and begin the process of establishing an elite culture—that of European imperialism.

African Cultural Characteristics

European travelers who got to know the sub-Saharan region well in the nineteenth and twentieth centuries observed broad commonalities underlying African life and culture. In agriculture, the common technique was cultivation by hoe and digging stick. Musically, different groups of Africans played many instruments, especially types of drums, but common features, particularly in rhythm, gave African music as a whole a distinctive character. Music played an important role in social rituals, as did dancing and wearing masks, which often showed great artistry in their design.

African kingdoms varied, but kingship displayed common features, most notably the ritual isolation of the king himself (see Diversity and Dominance: Personal Styles of Rule in India and Mali in Chapter 13). Fixed social categories—age groupings, kinship divisions, distinct gender roles and relations, and occupational groupings—also show resemblances from one region to another, even in societies too small to organize themselves into kingdoms. Though not hierarchical, these categories played a role similar to the divisions between noble, commoner, and slave prevalent where kings ruled. Such indications of underlying cultural unity have led modern observers to identify a common African quality throughout most of the region, even though most sub-Saharan Africans themselves did not perceive it. An eminent Belgian anthropologist, Jacques Maquet, has called this quality "Africanity."

Some historians hypothesize that this cultural unity emanated from the peoples who once occupied the southern Sahara. In Paleolithic times, periods of dryness alternated with periods of wetness as the Ice Age that locked up much of the world's fresh water in glaciers and icecaps came and went. When European glaciers receded with the waning of the Ice Age, a storm belt brought increased wetness to the Saharan region. Rushing rivers scoured deep canyons. Now filled with fine sand, those canyons are easily visible on flights over the southern parts of the desert. As the glaciers receded farther, the storm belt moved northward to Europe, and dryness set in after 5000 B.C.E. As a consequence, runs the hypothesis, the region's population migrated southward, becoming increasingly concentrated in the Sahel, which may have been the initial incubation center for Pan-African cultural patterns.

Increasing dryness and the resulting difficulty in supporting the population would have driven some people out of this core into more sparsely settled lands to the east, west, and south. In a parallel development farther to the east, migration away from the growing aridity of the desert seems to have contributed to the settling of the Nile Valley and the emergence of the Old Kingdom of Egypt (see Chapter 1).

The Advent of Iron and the Bantu Migrations

Archaeology confirms that agriculture had become common between the equator and the Sahara by the early second millennium B.C.E. It then spread southward, displacing hunting and gathering as a way of life. Moreover, botanical evidence indicates that banana trees, probably introduced to southeastern Africa from Southeast Asia, made their way north and west, retracing in the opposite direction the presumed migration routes of the first agriculturists.

Archaeology has also uncovered traces of copper mining in the Sahara from the early first millennium B.C.E. Copper appears in the Niger Valley somewhat later, and in the Central African copper belt after 400 C.E. Most important of all, iron smelting began in northern sub-Saharan Africa in the early first millennium C.E. and spread southward from there.

Many historians believe that the secret of smelting iron, which requires very high temperatures, was discovered only once, by the Hittites of Anatolia (modern Turkey) around 1500 B.C.E. (see Chapter 3). If that is the case, it is hard to explain how iron smelting reached sub-Saharan Africa. The earliest evidence of ironworking from the kingdom of Meroë, situated on the upper Nile and in cultural contact with Egypt, is no earlier than the evidence from West Africa (northern Nigeria). Even less plausible than the Nile Valley as a route of technological diffusion is the idea of a spread southward from Phoenician settlements in North Africa, since archaeological evidence has failed to substantiate the vague Greek and Latin accounts of Phoenician excursions to the south.

A more plausible scenario focuses on Africans' discovering for themselves how to smelt iron. Some historians suggest that they might have done so while firing pottery in kilns. No firm evidence exists to prove or disprove this theory.

Linguistic analysis provides the strongest evidence of extensive contacts among sub-Saharan Africans in the first millennium C.E.—and offers suggestions about the spread of iron. More than three hundred languages spoken south of the equator belong to the branch of the Niger-Congo family known as **Bantu,** after the word meaning "people" in most of the languages.

The distribution of the Bantu languages both north and south of the equator is consistent with a divergence beginning in the first millennium B.C.E. By comparing core words common to most of the languages, linguists have drawn some conclusions about the original Bantu-speakers, whom they call "proto-Bantu." These people engaged in fishing, using canoes, nets, lines, and hooks. They lived in permanent villages on the edge of the rain forest, where they grew yams and grains and harvested wild palm nuts from which they pressed oil. They possessed domesticated goats, dogs, and perhaps other animals. They made pottery and cloth. Linguists surmise that the proto-Bantu homeland was near the modern boundary of Nigeria and Cameroon.

Because the presumed home of the proto-Bantu lies near the known sites of early iron smelting, migration by Bantu-speakers seems a likely mechanism for the southward spread of iron. The migrants probably used iron axes and hoes to hack out forest clearings and plant crops. According to this scenario, their actions would have established an economic basis for new societies capable of sustaining much denser populations than could earlier societies dependent on hunting and gathering alone. Thus the period from 500 B.C.E. to 600 C.E. saw a massive transfer of Bantu traditions and practices southward, eastward, and westward and their transformation, through intermingling with preexisting societies, into Pan-African traditions and practices.

THE SPREAD OF IDEAS

Ideas, like social customs, religious attitudes, and artistic styles, can spread along trade routes and through folk migrations. In both cases, documenting the dissemination of ideas, particularly in preliterate societies, poses a difficult historical problem.

Ideas and Material Evidence

Historians know about some ideas only through the survival of written sources. Other ideas do not depend on writing but are inherent in material objects studied by archaeologists and anthropologists. Customs surrounding the eating of pork are a case in point. Scholars disagree about whether pigs became domestic in only one place, from which the practice of pig keeping spread elsewhere, or whether several peoples hit on the same idea at different times and in different places.

Southeast Asia was an important early center of pig domestication. Anthropological studies tell us that the eating of pork became highly ritualized in this area and that it was sometimes allowed only on ceremonial occasions. On the other side of the Indian Ocean, wild swine were common in the Nile swamps of ancient Egypt. There, too, pigs took on a sacred role, being associated with the evil god Set, and eating them was prohibited. The biblical prohibition on the Israelites' eating pork, echoed later by the Muslims, probably came from Egypt in the second millennium B.C.E.

In a third locale in eastern Iran, an archaeological site dating from the third millennium B.C.E. provides evidence of another religious taboo relating to pork. Although the area around the site was swampy and home to many wild pigs, not a single pig bone has been found. Yet small pig figurines seem to have been used as symbolic religious offerings, and the later Iranian religion associates the boar with an important god.

What accounts for the apparent connection between domestic pigs and religion in these far-flung areas? There is no way of knowing. It has been hypothesized that pigs were first domesticated in Southeast Asia by people who had no herd animals—sheep, goats, cattle, or horses—and who relied on fish for most of their animal protein. The pig therefore became a special animal to them. The practice of pig herding, along with religious beliefs and rituals associated with the consumption of pork, could conceivably have spread from Southeast Asia along the maritime routes of the Indian Ocean, eventually reaching Iran and Egypt. But no evidence survives to support this hypothesis. In this case, therefore, material evidence can only hint at the spread of religious ideas, leaving the door open for other explanations.

A more certain example of objects' indicating the spread of an idea is the practice of hammering a carved die onto a piece of precious metal and using the resulting coin as a medium of exchange. From its origin in the Lydian kingdom in Anatolia in the first millennium B.C.E. (see Chapter 4), the idea of trading by means of struck coinage spread rapidly to Europe, North Africa, and India. Was the low-value copper coinage of China, made by pouring molten metal into a mold, also inspired by this practice from far away? It may have been, but it might also derive from indigenous Chinese metalworking. There is no way to be sure.

The Spread of Buddhism

While material objects associated with religious beliefs and rituals are important indicators of the spread of spiritual ideas, written sources deal with the spread of today's major religions. Buddhism grew to become, with Christianity and Islam (see Chapter 8), one of the most popular and widespread religions in the world. In all three cases, the religious ideas spread without dependency on a single ethnic or kinship group.

King Ashoka, the Maurya ruler of India, and Kanishka, the greatest king of the Kushans of northern Afghanistan, promoted Buddhism between the third century B.C.E. and the second century C.E. However, monks, missionaries, and pilgrims who crisscrossed India, followed the Silk Road, or took ships on the Indian Ocean brought the Buddha's teachings to Southeast Asia, China, Korea, and ultimately Japan (see Map 7.1).

The Chinese pilgrim Faxian° (died between 418 and 423 C.E.) left a written account of his travels. Faxian began his trip in the company of a Chinese envoy to an unspecified ruler or people in Central Asia. After traveling from one Buddhist site to another across Afghanistan and India, he reached Sri Lanka, a Buddhist land, where he lived for two years. He then embarked for China on a merchant ship with two hundred men aboard. A storm drove the ship to Java, which he chose not to describe since it was Hindu rather than Buddhist. After five months ashore, Faxian finally reached China on another ship.

Less reliable accounts make reference to missionaries traveling to Syria, Egypt, and Macedonia, as well as to Southeast Asia. One of Ashoka's sons allegedly led a band of missionaries to Sri Lanka. Later, his sister brought a company of nuns there, along with a branch of the sacred Bo tree under which the Buddha had received enlightenment. At the same time, there are reports of other monks traveling to Burma, Thailand, and Sumatra. Ashoka's missionaries may also have reached Tibet by way of trade routes across the Himalayas.

The different lands that received the story and teachings of the Buddha preserved or adapted them in different ways. Theravada Buddhism, "Teachings of the Elder," was centered in Sri Lanka. Holding closely to the Buddha's earliest teachings, it maintained that the goal of religion, available only to monks, is *nirvana,* the total absence of suffering and the end of the cycle of rebirth (see Chapter 6). This teaching contrasted with Mahayana, or "Great Vehicle" Buddhism, which stressed the goal of becoming a *bodhisattva,* a person who attains nirvana but chooses to remain in human company to help and guide others.

Faxian (fah-shee-en)

Statue of a Bodhisattva at Bamian This is one of two monumental Buddhist sculptures near the top of a high mountain pass connecting Kabul, Afghanistan, with the northern parts of the country. Carved into the side of a cliff in the sixth or seventh century, C.E., the sculptures were surrounded by cave dwellings of monks and rock sanctuaries, some dating to the first century B.C.E. This statue and the one alongside it were blown to pieces by the intolerant Taliban regime in Afghanistan in 2001. (Ian Griffiths/ Robert Harding Picture Library)

The Spread of Christianity

The post-Roman development of Christianity in Europe is discussed in Chapter 9. The Christian faith enjoyed an earlier spread in Asia and Africa before its confrontation with Islam (described in Chapter 8). Jerusalem in Palestine, Antioch in Syria, and Alexandria in Egypt became centers of Christian authority soon after the crucifixion, but the spread of Christianity to Armenia and Ethiopia illustrates the connections between religion, trade, and imperial politics.

Stele of Aksum   This 70-foot (21-meter) stone is the tallest remnant of a field of stelae, or standing stones, marking the tombs of Aksumite kings. The carvings of doors, windows, and beam ends imitate common features of Aksumite architecture, suggesting that each stele symbolized a multistory royal palace. The largest stelae date from the fourth century C.E.   (J. Allan Cash)

Situated in eastern Anatolia (modern Turkey), **Armenia** served recurrently as a battleground between Iranian states to the south and east and Mediterranean states to the west. Each imperial power wanted to control this region so close to the frontier where Silk Road traders met their Mediterranean counterparts. In Parthian times, Armenia's kings favored Zoroastrianism. The invention of an Armenian alphabet in the early fifth century opened the way to a wider spread of Christianity. The

Iranians did not give up domination easily, but within a century the Armenian Apostolic Church had become the center of Armenian cultural life.

Far to the south Christians similarly sought to outflank Iran. The Christian emperors in Constantinople (see Chapter 5) sent missionaries along the Red Sea trade route to seek converts in Yemen and **Ethiopia.** In the fourth century C.E. a Syrian philosopher traveling with two young relatives sailed to India. On the way back the ship docked at a Red Sea port occupied by Ethiopians from the prosperous kingdom of Aksum. Being then at odds with the Romans, the Ethiopians killed everyone on board except the two boys, Aedisius—who later narrated this story—and Frumentius. Impressed by their learning, the king made the former his cupbearer and the latter his treasurer and secretary.

When the king died, his wife urged Frumentius to govern Aksum on her behalf and that of her infant son, Ezana. As regent Frumentius sought out Roman Christians among the merchants who visited the country and helped them establish Christian communities. When he became king, Ezana, who may have become a Christian, permitted Aedisius and Frumentius to return to Syria. The patriarch of Alexandria, on learning about the progress of Christianity in Aksum, elevated Frumentius to the rank of bishop, though he had not previously been a clergyman, and sent him back to Ethiopia as the first leader of its church.

The spread of Christianity into Nubia, the land south of Egypt along the Nile River, proceeded from Ethiopia rather than Egypt. Politically and economically, Ethiopia became a power at the western end of the Indian Ocean trading system, occasionally even extending its influence across the Red Sea and asserting itself in Yemen (see Map 7.2).

CONCLUSION

Exchange facilitated by the early long-distance trading systems differed in many ways from the ebb and flow of culture, language, and custom that folk migrations brought about. Transportable goods and livestock and ideas about new technologies and agricultural products sometimes worked great changes on the landscape and in people's lives. But nothing resembling the Africanity observed south of the Sahara can be attributed to the societies involved in the Silk Road, Indian Ocean, or trans-Saharan exchanges. Not only were few people directly involved in these complex social systems of travel and trade compared with the populations with whom they were brought into contact, but their lifestyles as pastoral nomads or seafarers isolated them still more. Communities of traders contributed to this isolation by their reluctance to share knowledge with people who might become commercial competitors.

The Bantu, however, if current theories are correct, spread far and wide in sub-Saharan Africa with the deliberate intent of settling and implanting a lifestyle based on iron implements and agriculture. The metallurgical skills and agricultural techniques they brought with them permitted much denser habitation and helped ensure that the languages of the immigrants would supplant those of their hunting and gathering predecessors. Where the trading systems encouraged diversity by introducing new products and ideas, the Bantu migrations brought a degree of cultural dominance that strongly affected later African history.

An apparent exception to the generalization that trading systems have less impact than folk migrations on patterns of dominance lies in the intangible area of ideas. Christianity and Buddhism both spread along trade routes, at least to some degree. Each instance of spread, however, gave rise to new forms of cultural diversity even as overall doctrinal unity made these religions dominant. As "great traditions," the new faiths based on conversion linked priests, monks, nuns, and religious scholars across vast distances. However, these same religions merged with myriad "small traditions" to provide for the social and spiritual needs of peoples living in many lands under widely varying circumstances.

Key Terms

Silk Road

Parthians

Sasanid Empire

stirrup

Indian Ocean Maritime System

trans-Saharan caravan routes

Sahel

sub-Saharan Africa

steppes

savanna

tropical rain forest

"great traditions"

"small traditions"

Bantu

Armenia

Ethiopia

Suggested Reading

For broad and suggestive overviews on cross-cultural exchange see Philip D. Curtin, *Cross-Cultural Trade in World History* (1985), and C. G. F. Simkin, *The Traditional Trade of Asia* (1968).

Readable overviews of the Silk Road include Luce Boulnois, *The Silk Road* (1966), and Irene M. Franck and David M. Brownstone, *The Silk Road: A History* (1986). For products traded across Central Asia based on an eighth-century Japanese collection, see Ryoichi Hayashi, *The Silk Road and the Shoso-in* (1975). Xinru Liu, *Silk and Religion* (1996), covers one specific product. Owen Lattimore gives a first-person account of traveling by camel caravan in *The Desert Road to Turkestan* (1928). More generally on Central Asia, see Denis Sinor, *Inner Asia, History-Civilization-Languages: A Syllabus* (1987), and Karl Jettmar, *Art of the Steppes*, rev. ed. (1967). Richard Foltz, *Religions of the Silk Road* (1999), is an excellent brief introduction.

For a readable but sketchy historical overview see August Toussaint, *History of the Indian Ocean* (1966). Alan Villiers recounts what it was like to sail dhows between East Africa and the Persian Gulf in *Sons of Sinbad* (1940).

On a more scholarly plane, see K. N. Chaudhuri's *Trade and Civilization in the Indian Ocean: An Economic History from the Rise of Islam to 1750* (1985). Archaeologist Pierre Vérin treats the special problem of Madagascar in *The History of Civilisation in North Madagascar* (1986). For Rome and India see E. H. Warmington's *The Commerce Between the Roman Empire and India* (1974); J. Innes Miller's *The Spice Trade of the Roman Empire, 29 B.C. to A.D. 641* (1969); and Vimala Begley and Richard Daniel De Puma's edited collection of articles, *Rome and India: The Ancient Sea Trade* (1991), along with the primary source *The Periplus Maris Erythraei: Text with Introduction, Translation, and Commentary* (1989), edited and translated by Lionel Casson. George F. Hourani's brief *Arab Seafaring in the Indian Ocean in Ancient and Early Medieval Times* (1975) covers materials in Arabic sources.

Nicholas Tarling, ed., *The Cambridge History of Southeast Asia*, vol. 1 (1992); D. R. Sardesai, *Southeast Asia: Past and Present*, 3d ed. (1994); and Milton E. Osborne, *Southeast Asia: An Introductory History* (1995), provide general accounts of Southeast Asian history. Lynda Shaffer, *Maritime Southeast Asia to 1500* (1996), focuses on the world historical context. Also useful is Kenneth R. Hall, *Maritime Trade and State Development in Early Southeast Asia* (1985).

On art see Maud Girard-Geslan et al., *Art of Southeast Asia* (1998), and Daigoro Chihara, *Hindu-Buddhist Architecture in Southeast Asia* (1996).

Richard W. Bulliet's *The Camel and the Wheel* (1975) deals with camel use in the Middle East, along the Silk Road, and in North Africa and the Sahara. For a well-illustrated account of Saharan rock art see Henri Lhote, *The Search for the Tassili Frescoes: The Story of the Prehistoric Rock-Paintings of the Sahara* (1959).

J. F. A. Ajayi and Michael Crowder, *A History of West Africa*, vol. 1 (1976), and G. Mokhtar, ed., *General History of Africa II: Ancient*

Civilizations of Africa (1981), include many articles by numerous authors; the latter work specifically treats ironworking and the Bantu migrations. On African cultural unity see Jacques Maquet, *Africanity: The Cultural Unity of Black Africa* (1972).

Of special importance on Christianity in Asia and Africa is Garth Fowden, *Empire to Commonwealth: Consequences of Monotheism in Late Antiquity* (1993). For specific topics treated in this chapter see Stuart Munro-Hay, *Aksum: An African Civilisation of Late Antiquity* (1991); Xinru Liu, *Ancient India and Ancient China: Trade and Religious Exchanges, A.D. 1–600* (1998); Rolf A. Stein, *Tibetan Civilization* (1972); and Tilak Hettiarachchy, *History of Kingship in Ceylon up to the Fourth Century A.D.* (1972). *The Travels of Fahsien (399–414 A.D.), or, Record of the Buddhistic Kingdoms*, trans. H. A. Giles (1923; reprint, 1981) recounts the experiences of a Chinese pilgrim.

◼ Notes

1. Victor H. Mair, ed., *The Columbia Anthology of Traditional Chinese Literature* (New York: Columbia University Press, 1994), 485; translated by Victor H. Mair.

Document-Based Question
Indian Ocean and Silk Road Trade Before 1100 C.E.

Using the following documents, analyze the character of communication and exchange on the Indian Ocean and Silk Road trade routes. Consider the geography of the trade routes, the modes of transportation, the people involved, and the nature of goods and ideas exchanged.

DOCUMENT 1
Indian Ocean Sailing Vessel (photo, p. 173)

DOCUMENT 2
Excerpt from Po Zhuyi (p. 174)

DOCUMENT 3
Iranian Musicians from Silk Road (photo, p. 176)

DOCUMENT 4
Map 7.1 Asian Trade and Communication Routes (p. 177)

DOCUMENT 5
The Indian Ocean Trading World (Diversity and Dominance, pp. 180–181)

DOCUMENT 6
Camel Saddles (photo, p. 186)

DOCUMENT 7
Statue of a Bodhisattva at Bamian (p. 189)

The author of Document 5 is a Greco-Egyptian merchant. What experiences would have shaped this merchant's view of Indian Ocean trade? What additional types of documents would help you assess the reliability of Document 5?

PART THREE

Competition Among Cultural Communities, 600–1200

The six centuries from 600 to 1200 witnessed a consolidation of cultural communities, as previously separated religious, ethnic, and linguistic traditions became incorporated into larger cultural units. The nature of the consolidated communities varied. In Europe and the Middle East the defining feature was religion—Catholic or Orthodox Christianity, or Islam. In East Asia, the political and social teachings of Confucianism guided the creation of new states and societies. In the Americas, ethnic ties shaped the cultures of new communities.

In the 600s and early 700s, the Arabs of the Arabian peninsula, under the inspiration of Islam, conquered an empire that stretched from Spain to India. The unified empire they established proved short-lived, but it provided a framework for implanting the Muslim faith and accompanying cultural values, including a vibrant urban-based style of life. At about the same time, the expansion of the Tang Empire spread Chinese culture and technologies throughout Inner and East Asia, while simultaneously introducing Buddhism and Inner Asian cultural practices into China. The southward migration of people from northern China played an important role in this process.

In Europe, missionaries labored to convert the Celtic, Germanic, and Slavic peoples to Christianity. Christian beliefs became enmeshed in new

193

political and social structures. In western Europe, this produced a struggle between royal and church authority. In the eastern Mediterranean, religious and imperial authority came together in the Byzantine Empire, although many eastern Christians lost their imperial connection when Egypt, Syria, and North Africa fell to Arab armies. In Kievan Russia, the Byzantine imperial tradition produced a look-alike offshoot that split the Slavic peoples between Catholics (e.g., Poland) and Orthodox (e.g., Russia). Competition between Islam and Christianity climaxed in the Crusades, which also opened contacts between western Europe and lands to the east after centuries of isolation.

The development of a significant level of trade across the Sahara desert brought sub-Saharan Africa into contact with some of these developments. The Muslim principalities in North Africa that pioneered the trade also began the long process of converting sub-Saharan African peoples to Islam. Other North Africans maintained close contact with Muslim Spain and other parts of southern Europe.

By the end of the period, the major cultural regions in Europe, North Africa, and Asia had come into a substantial degree of contact. The knowledge that increasingly circulated about distant lands contributed to the first era of world-encompassing political and economic development after 1200.

Unexplored seas still separated the Eastern and Western Hemispheres. The European voyagers who would find their way across the Atlantic Ocean in the ensuing period would encounter developed urban and agricultural civilizations in the Andes, the Yucatán lowlands, and the central plateau of Mexico as well as less intensely developed areas of settled agricultural life in parts of North America.

	600 C.E.	700 C.E.	800 C.E.
Americas	250–800 Classic period of Maya civilization		• ca. 750 Teotihuacan destroyed
	600–1000 Tiwanaku and Wari control Peruvian highlands		800–900 Maya centers abandoned
	• 600 Teotihuacan at height of its power	700–1200 Anasazi culture in North America	
Europe	ca. 400–800 Decline of cities and monetary economy in west	• 732 Battle of Tours	
		• 711 Muslim conquest of Spain	• 800 Charlemagne crowned emperor
		Treaty of Verdun divides Carolingian empire 843 •	
Africa	500 B.C.E.–1000 C.E. Bantu migrations		
		• ca. 750 Trans-Saharan trade routes become active	
Middle East	570–632 Life of Muhammad		750–850 Abbasid Caliphate at its height
	634–711 Islamic conquests of western Asia, North Africa		
	661–750 Umayyad Caliphate		• 836 City of Samarra founded
Asia and Oceania	589–618 Sui Empire reunites China	An Lushan rebellion in China 755–757	Buddhism suppressed in China 840 •
	645–655 Taika reforms in Japan	Battle of	794–1185 Heian era in Japan
	618–907 Tang Empire in China and Inner Asia	Talas River 751 •	Buddhist political power secured in Tibet ca. 850 •

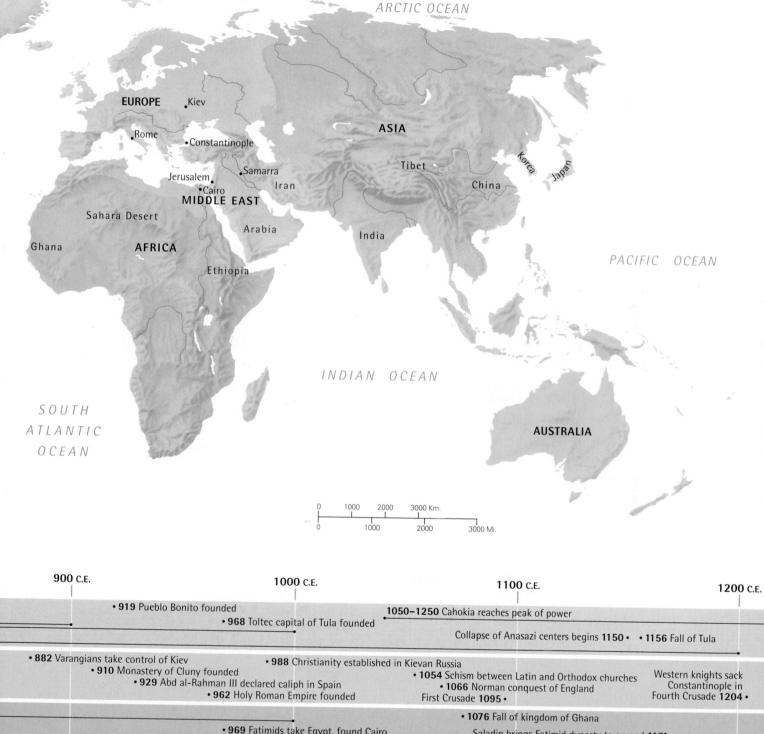

ARCTIC OCEAN

EUROPE
•Kiev

•Rome
•Constantinople

ASIA

Samarra
Jerusalem
•Cairo
MIDDLE EAST
Iran

Korea
Japan

Tibet
China

Sahara Desert
Ghana
AFRICA
Arabia

India

Ethiopia

PACIFIC OCEAN

INDIAN OCEAN

SOUTH
ATLANTIC
OCEAN

AUSTRALIA

```
0    1000   2000   3000 Km.

0    1000   2000   3000 Mi.
```

900 C.E.   1000 C.E.   1100 C.E.   1200 C.E.

• 919 Pueblo Bonito founded   1050–1250 Cahokia reaches peak of power
            • 968 Toltec capital of Tula founded
                                        Collapse of Anasazi centers begins 1150 •   • 1156 Fall of Tula

• 882 Varangians take control of Kiev   • 988 Christianity established in Kievan Russia
      • 910 Monastery of Cluny founded   • 1054 Schism between Latin and Orthodox churches   Western knights sack
            • 929 Abd al-Rahman III declared caliph in Spain   • 1066 Norman conquest of England   Constantinople in
                  • 962 Holy Roman Empire founded   First Crusade 1095 •   Fourth Crusade 1204 •

                                                            • 1076 Fall of kingdom of Ghana
            • 969 Fatimids take Egypt, found Cairo   Saladin brings Fatimid dynasty to an end 1171 •
• 909 Fatimid dynasty founded in Tunisia

      945–1055 Caliphate controlled by Shi'ite dynasty from Iran   • 1099 Crusaders take Jerusalem
                        • 1036 Seljuks found Turkish state in northeast Iran   Saladin recaptures
                                                                  Jerusalem 1187
                        • 1071 Turks defeat Byzantines at Manzikert   Mongols invade Iran 1218 •

      • 918 Koryo kingdom founded in Korea   • ca. 1000 The Tale of Genji
                                              Kamakura Shogunate founded in Japan 1185 •

            960–1127 Song Empire reunites China   1127–1279 Southern Song Empire

8

The Rise of
Islam, 600–1200

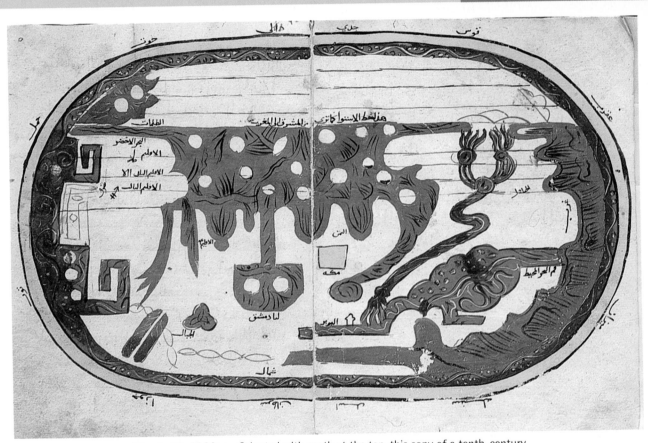

Islamic World Map Oriented with south at the top, this copy of a tenth-century original was probably made in the fourteenth century.

CHAPTER OUTLINE

The Origins of Islam

The Rise and Fall of the Caliphate, 632–1258

Islamic Civilization

DIVERSITY AND DOMINANCE: Beggars, Con Men, and Singing-girls

ENVIRONMENT AND TECHNOLOGY: Automata

The story is told that in the early days of Islam, at the time of the Prophet Muhammad's last pilgrimage to Mecca in 630, a dispute over distribution of booty arose between his daughter's husband, Ali, who was also Muhammad's first cousin, and some troops Ali commanded. Muhammad quelled the grumbling and later on the same journey, at a place named Ghadir al-Khumm°, drew his followers together, took Ali's hand, and declared: "Am I not nearer to the believers than their own selves? Whomever I am nearest to, so likewise is Ali. O God, be the friend of him who is his friend, and the foe of him who is his foe."

Written narratives of Muhammad's praise of Ali, like all stories of Muhammad's life, date to well over a century after the event. By that time, Ali had served as leader of Muhammad's community for a brief time and had then been defeated in a civil war and assassinated. Subsequently, his son Husayn, along with his family, died in a hopelessly lopsided battle while trying to claim leadership as the Prophet's grandson.

Out of these events grew a division in the Islamic community: some believers, called **Shi'ites**°, from the Arabic term *Shi'at Ali* ("Party of Ali"), thought that religious leadership rightfully belonged to Ali and his descendants; others, eventually called **Sunnis**°, followers of the sunna, or "tradition" of the community, felt that the community should choose its leaders more broadly. Sunnis and Shi'ites agreed that Muhammad commended Ali at Ghadir al-Khumm. But the Sunnis considered his remarks to relate only to the distribution of the booty, and the Shi'ites understood them to be Muhammad's formal and public declaration of Ali's special and elevated position, and hence of his right to rule.

Shi'ite rulers rarely achieved power, but those who ruled from Cairo between 969 and 1171 made the commemoration of Ghadir al-Khumm a major festival. At the beginning of every year, Shi'ites everywhere also engaged in public mourning over the deaths of Husayn and his family. Sunni rulers, in contrast, sometimes ordered that Ali be cursed in public prayers.

Muhammad's Arab followers conquered an enormous territory in the seventh century. In the name of Islam, they created an empire that encompassed many peoples speaking many languages and worshiping in many ways. Its immediate forerunners, the realms of the Byzantine emperors (see Chapter 5) and Iran's Sasanid° shahs (see Chapter 7), closely linked religion with imperial politics.

Although urbanism, science, manufacturing, trade, and architecture flourished in the lands of Islam while medieval Europe was enduring hardship and economic contraction, religion shaped both societies. Just as the medieval Christian calendar revolved around Easter and Christmas, Islamic fasts, pilgrimages, and political religious observances like Ghadir al-Khumm marked the yearly cycle in the lands of Muhammad's followers.

As you read this chapter, ask yourself the following questions:

- How did the Arab conquests grow out of the career of Muhammad?

- Why did the caliphate break up?

- How did Muslim societies differ from region to region?

- What was the relationship between urbanization and the development of Islamic culture?

THE ORIGINS OF ISLAM

The Arabs of 600 C.E. lived exclusively in the Arabian peninsula and on the desert fringes of Syria, Jordan, and Iraq. Along their Euphrates frontier, the Sasanids subsidized nomadic Arab chieftains to protect their empire from invasion. The Byzantines did the same with Arabs on their Jordanian frontier. Arab pastoralists farther to the south remained isolated and independent, seldom engaging the attention of the shahs and emperors. It was precisely in these interior Arabian lands that the religion of Islam took form.

Ghadir al-Khumm (ga-DEER al-KUM)
Shi'ite (SHE-ite)
Sunni (SUN-nee)

Sasanid (suh-SAH-nid)

Sasanid Silver Vase The Sasanid aristocracy, based in the countryside, invested part of its wealth in silver plates and vessels. The image is of the fertility goddess Anahita, a deity acceptable to the Zoroastrian faith. One inscription in Pahlavi (a Middle Persian language) gives the weight, 116.9 grams in modern terms, while another in Sogdian, a language common along the Silk Road, gives the owner's name, Mithrak. (The State Heritage Museum, St Petersburg)

The Arabian Peninsula Before Muhammad

Throughout history more people living on the Arabian peninsula have subsisted as farmers or sailors than as pastoral nomads. Farming villages support the comparatively dense population of Yemen, where the highlands receive abundant rainfall during the spring monsoon. Small inlets along the southern coast favored fishing and trading communities. However, the enormous sea of sand known as the "Empty Quarter" isolated many southern regions from the Arabian interior. In the seventh century, most people in southern Arabia knew more about Africa, India, and the Persian Gulf (see Chapter 7, Diversity and Dominance: "The Indian Ocean Trading World") than about the for-

bidding interior and the scattered camel- and sheep-herding nomads who lived there.

Exceptions to this pattern mostly involved caravan trading. Nomads derived income from providing camels, guides, and safe passage to merchants wanting to transport northward the primary product of the south: the aromatic resins frankincense and myrrh that were burned in religious rituals. Return caravans brought manufactured products from Mesopotamia and the Mediterranean.

Nomad dominance of the caravan trade received a boost from the invention of militarily efficient camel saddles (see Chapter 7, Environment and Technology: Camel Saddles). This contributed to the rise of Arab-dominated caravan cities and to Arab pastoralists becoming the primary suppliers of animal power throughout the region. By 600 C.E., wheeled vehicles—mostly ox carts and horse-drawn chariots—had all but disappeared from the Middle East, replaced by pack camels and donkeys.

Arabs who accompanied the caravans became familiar with the cultures and lifestyles of the Sasanid and Byzantine Empires, and many of those who pastured their herds on the imperial frontiers adopted one form or another of Christianity. Even in the interior deserts, Semitic polytheism, with its worship of natural forces and celestial bodies, began to encounter more sophisticated religions.

Mecca, a late-blooming caravan city, lies in a barren mountain valley halfway between Yemen and Syria and a short way inland from the Red Sea coast of Arabia (see Map 8.1). A nomadic kin group known as the Quraysh° settled in Mecca in the fifth century and assumed control of trade. Mecca rapidly achieved a measure of prosperity, partly because it was too far from Byzantine Syria, Sasanid Iraq, and Ethiopian-controlled Yemen for them to attack it.

A cubical shrine called the Ka'ba°, containing idols, a holy well called Zamzam, and a sacred precinct surrounding the two wherein killing was prohibited contributed to the emergence of Mecca as a pilgrimage site. Some Meccans associated the shrine with stories known to Jews and Christians. They regarded Abraham (Ibrahim in Arabic) as the builder of the Ka'ba, and they identified a site outside Mecca as the location where God asked Abraham to sacrifice his son. The son was not Isaac (Ishaq in Arabic), the son of Sarah, but Ishmael (Isma'il in Arabic), the son of Hagar, cited in the Bible as the forefather of the Arabs.

Quraysh (koo-RYYSH)   **Ka'ba** (KAH-buh)

C H R O N O L O G Y

	The Arab Lands	Iran and Central Asia
600	**570–632** Life of the Prophet Muhammad	
	634 Conquests of Iraq and Syria commence	
	639–42 Conquest of Egypt by Arabs	
	656–61 Ali caliph; first civil war	
	661–750 Umayyad Caliphate rules from Damascus	
700		
	711 Berbers and Arabs invade Spain from North Africa	**711** Arabs capture Sind in India
	750 Beginning of Abbasid Caliphate	**747** Abbasid revolt begins in Khurasan
	755 Umayyad state established in Spain	
	776–809 Caliphate of Harun al-Rashid	
800		
	835–92 Abbasid capital moved from Baghdad to Samarra	
900		**875** Independent Samanid state founded in Bukhara
	909 Fatimids seize North Africa, found Shi'ite Caliphate	
	929 Abd al-Rahman III declares himself caliph in Cordoba	
	945 Shi'ite Buyids take control in Baghdad	**945** Buyids from northern Iran take control of Abbasid Caliphate
	969 Fatimids conquer Egypt	
1000		
	1055 Seljuk Turks take control in Baghdad	**1036** Beginning of Turkish Seljuk rule in Khurasan
	1099 First Crusade captures Jerusalem	
	1171 Fall of Fatimid Egypt	
	1187 Saladin recaptures Jerusalem	
	1250 Mamluks control Egypt	
	1258 Mongols sack Baghdad and end Abbasid Caliphate	
	1260 Mamluks defeat Mongols at Ain Jalut	

Muhammad in Mecca

Born in Mecca in 570, **Muhammad** grew up an orphan in the house of his uncle. He engaged in trade and married a Quraysh widow named Khadija°, whose caravan interests he superintended. Their son died in childhood, but several daughters survived. Around 610 Muhammad began meditating at night in the mountainous terrain around Mecca. During one night vigil, known to later tradition as the "Night of Power and Excellence," a being whom Muhammad later understood to be the angel Gabriel (Jibra'il in Arabic) spoke to him:

Proclaim! In the name of your Lord who created.
Created man from a clot of congealed blood.
Proclaim! And your Lord is the Most Bountiful.

Khadija (kah-DEE-juh)

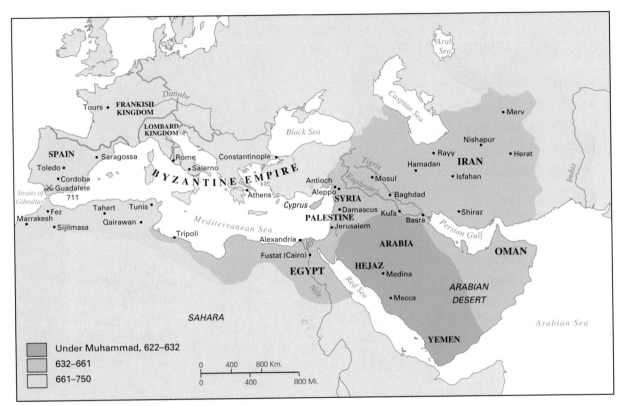

Map 8.1   Early Expansion of Muslim Rule   Arab conquests of the first Islamic century brought vast territory under Muslim rule, but conversion to Islam proceeded slowly. In most areas outside the Arabian peninsula, the only region where Arabic was then spoken, conversion did not accelerate until the third century after the conquest.

He who has taught by the pen.
Taught man that which he knew not.[1]

For three years he shared this and subsequent revelations only with close friends and family members. This period culminated in Muhammad's conviction that he was hearing the words of God (Allah° in Arabic). Khadija, his uncle's son Ali, his friend Abu Bakr°, and others close to him shared this conviction. The revelations continued until Muhammad's death in 632.

Like most people of the time, including Christians and Jews, the Arabs believed in unseen spirits: gods, desert spirits called *jinns*, demonic *shaitans*, and others. They further believed that certain individuals had contact with the spirit world, notably seers and poets, who were thought to be possessed by jinns. Therefore, when Muhammad began to recite his rhymed revelations in public, many people believed he was inspired by an unseen spirit, even if it was not, as Muhammad asserted, the one true god.

Muhammad's earliest revelations called on people to witness that one god had created the universe and everything in it, including themselves. At the end of time, their souls would be judged, their sins balanced against their good deeds. The blameless would go to paradise; the sinful would taste hellfire:

> By the night as it conceals the light;
> By the day as it appears in glory;
> By the mystery of the creation of male and female;
> Verily, the ends ye strive for are diverse.
> So he who gives in charity and fears God,
> And in all sincerity testifies to the best,
> We will indeed make smooth for him the path to Bliss.
> But he who is a greedy miser and thinks himself
>   self-sufficient,
> And gives the lie to the best,
> We will indeed make smooth for him the path to
>   misery.[2]

The revelation called all people to submit to God and accept Muhammad as the last of his messengers. Doing so

---

Allah (AH-luh)   **Abu Bakr** (ah-boo BAK-uhr)

made one a **muslim,** meaning one who makes "submission," **Islam,** to the will of God.

Because earlier messengers mentioned in the revelations included Noah, Moses, and Jesus, Muhammad's hearers felt that his message resembled the Judaism and Christianity they were already somewhat familiar with. Yet his revelations charged the Jews and Christians with being negligent in preserving God's revealed word. Thus, even though they identified Abraham/Ibrahim, whom Muslims consider the first Muslim, as the builder of the Ka'ba, which superseded Jerusalem as the focus of Muslim prayer in 624, Muhammad's followers considered his revelation more perfect than the Bible because it had not gone through an editing process.

Some scholars maintain that Muhammad's revelations appealed especially to people distressed over wealth replacing kinship as the most important aspect of social relations. They see a message of social reform in verses criticizing taking pride in money and neglecting obligations to orphans and other powerless people. Other scholars, along with most Muslims, put less emphasis on a social message and stress the power and beauty of Muhammad's revelations. Forceful rhetoric and poetic vision, coming in the Muslim view directly from God, go far to explain Muhammad's early success.

The Formation of the Umma

Mecca's leaders feared that accepting Muhammad as the sole agent of the one true God would threaten their power and prosperity. They pressured his kin to disavow him and persecuted the weakest of his followers. Stymied by this hostility, Muhammad and his followers fled Mecca in 622 to take up residence in the agricultural community of **Medina** 215 miles (346 kilometers) to the north. This hijra° marks the beginning of the Muslim calendar.

Prior to the hijra, Medinan representatives had met with Muhammad and agreed to accept and protect him and his followers because they saw him as an inspired leader who could calm their perpetual feuding. Together, the Meccan migrants and major groups in Medina bound themselves into a single **umma**°, a community defined solely by acceptance of Islam and of Muhammad as the "Messenger of God," his most common title. Three Jewish kin groups chose to retain their own faith, thus contributing to the Muslims' changing the direction of their prayer toward the Ka'ba, now thought of as the "House of God."

During the last decade of his life, Muhammad took active responsibility for his umma. Having left their Meccan kin groups, the immigrants in Medina felt vulnerable. Fresh revelations provided a framework for regulating social and legal affairs and stirred the Muslims to fight against the still-unbelieving city of Mecca. Sporadic war, largely conducted by raiding and negotiation with desert nomads, sapped Mecca's strength and convinced many Meccans that God favored Muhammad. In 630 Mecca surrendered. Muhammad and his followers made the pilgrimage to the Ka'ba unhindered.

Muhammad did not return to Mecca again. Medina had grown into a bustling city-state. He had charged the Jewish kin groups with disloyalty at various points during the war and had expelled or eliminated them. Delegations from all over Arabia came to meet Muhammad, and he sent emissaries back with them to teach about Islam and collect their alms. Muhammad's mission to bring God's message to humanity had brought him unchallenged control of a state that was coming to dominate the Arabian peninsula. But the supremacy of the Medinan state, unlike preceding short-lived nomadic kingdoms, depended not on kinship but on a common faith in a single god.

In 632, after a brief illness, Muhammad died. Within twenty-four hours a group of Medinan leaders, along with three of Muhammad's close friends, determined that Abu Bakr, one of the earliest believers and the father of Muhammad's favorite wife A'isha°, should succeed him. They called him the *khalifa*°, or "successor," the English version of which is *caliph*. But calling Abu Bakr a successor did not clarify his powers. Everyone knew that neither Abu Bakr nor anyone else could receive revelations, and they likewise knew that Muhammad's revelations made no provision for succession or for any government purpose beyond maintaining the umma.

Abu Bakr continued and confirmed Muhammad's religious practices, notably the so-called Five Pillars of Islam: (1) avowal that there is only one god and Muhammad is his messenger, (2) prayer five times a day, (3) fasting during the lunar month of Ramadan, (4) paying alms, and (5) making the pilgrimage to Mecca at least once during one's lifetime. He also reestablished and expanded Muslim authority over Arabia's nomadic and settled communities. After Muhammad's death, some had abandoned their allegiance to Medina or followed various would-be prophets. Muslim armies fought hard to confirm the authority of the newborn **caliphate.** In the process, some fighting spilled over into non-Arab areas in Iraq.

Abu Bakr ordered those who had acted as secretaries for Muhammad to organize the Prophet's revelations into a book. Hitherto written haphazardly on pieces of

hijra (HIJ-ruh)   umma (UM-muh)

A'isha (AH-ee-shah)   khalifa (kah-LEE-fuh)

leather or bone, the verses of revelation became a single document gathered into chapters. This resulting book, which Muslims believe acquired its final form around the year 650, was called the **Quran°**, or the Recitation. Muslims regard it not as the words of Muhammad but as the unalterable word of God. As such, it compares not so much to the Bible, a book written by many hands over many centuries, as to the person of Jesus Christ, whom Christians consider a human manifestation of God.

Though united in its acceptance of God's will, the umma soon disagreed over the succession to the caliphate. The first civil war in Islam followed the assassination of the third caliph, Uthman°, in 656. To succeed him, his assassins, rebels from the army, nominated Ali, Muhammad's first cousin and the husband of his daughter Fatima. Ali had been passed over three times previously, even though many people considered him to be the Prophet's natural heir. As mentioned previously, Ali and his supporters felt that Muhammad had indicated as much at Ghadir al-Khumm.

When Ali accepted the nomination to be caliph, two of Muhammad's close companions and his favorite wife A'isha challenged him. Ali defeated them in the Battle of the Camel (656), so called because the fighting raged around the camel on which A'isha was seated in an enclosed woman's saddle.

After the battle, the governor of Syria, Mu'awiya°, a kinsman of the slain Uthman from the Umayya clan of the Quraysh, renewed the challenge. Inconclusive battle gave way to arbitration. The arbitrators decided that Uthman, whom his assassins considered corrupt, had not deserved death and that Ali had erred in accepting the nomination. Ali rejected the arbitrators' findings, but before he could resume fighting, one of his own supporters killed him for agreeing to the arbitration. Mu'awiya then offered Ali's son Hasan a dignified retirement and thus emerged as caliph in 661.

Mu'awiya chose his own son, Yazid, to succeed him, thereby instituting the **Umayyad° Caliphate.** When Hasan's brother Husayn revolted in 680 to reestablish the right of Ali's family to rule, Yazid ordered Husayn and his family killed. Sympathy for Husayn's martyrdom helped transform Shi'ism from a political movement into a religious sect.

Several variations in Shi'ite belief developed, but Shi'ites have always agreed that Ali was the rightful successor to Muhammad and that God's choice as Imam, leader of the Muslim community, has always been one or another of Ali's descendants. They see the office of caliph as more secular than religious. Because the Shi'ites seldom held power, their religious feelings came to focus on outpourings of sympathy for Husayn and other martyrs and on messianic dreams that one of their Imams would someday triumph.

Those Muslims who supported the first three caliphs gradually came to be called "People of Tradition and Community"—in Arabic, *Ahl al-Sunna wa'l-Jama'a,* Sunnis for short. Sunnis consider the caliphs to be Imams. As for Ali's followers who had abhorred his acceptance of arbitration, they evolved into small and rebellious Kharijite sects (from *kharaja,* meaning "to secede or rebel") claiming righteousness for themselves alone. These three divisions of Islam, the last now quite minor, still survive.

THE RISE AND FALL OF THE CALIPHATE, 632–1258

The Islamic caliphate built on the conquests the Arabs carried out after Muhammad's death gave birth to a dynamic and creative religious society. By the late 800s, however, one piece after another of this huge realm broke away. Yet the idea of a caliphate, however unrealistic it became, remained a touchstone of Sunni belief in the unity of the umma.

Sunni Islam never gave a single person the power to define true belief, expel heretics, and discipline clergy. Thus, unlike Christian popes and patriarchs, the caliphs had little basis for reestablishing their universal authority once they lost political and military power.

The Islamic Conquests, 634–711

Arab conquests outside Arabia began under the second caliph, Umar (r. 634–644), possibly prompted by earlier forays into Iraq. Arab armies wrenched Syria (636) and Egypt (639–642) away from the Byzantine Empire and defeated the last Sasanid shah, Yazdigird III (r. 632–651) (see Map. 8.1). After a decade-long lull, expansion began again. Tunisia fell and became the governing center from which was organized, in 711, the conquest of Spain by an Arab-led army mostly composed of Berbers from North Africa. In the same year, Sind—the southern Indus Valley and westernmost region of India—succumbed to invaders from Iraq. The Muslim dominion remained roughly stable for the next

---

Quran (kuh-RAHN) **Uthman** (ooth-MAHN)
Mu'awiya (moo-AH-we-yuh) **Umayyad** (oo-MY-ad)

three centuries. In the eleventh century, conquest began anew in India, Anatolia, and sub-Saharan Africa. Islam also expanded peacefully by trade in these and other areas both before and after the year 1000.

The close Meccan companions of the Prophet, men of political and economic sophistication inspired by his charisma, guided the conquests. The social structure and hardy nature of Arab society lent itself to flexible military operations; and the authority of Medina, reconfirmed during the caliphate of Abu Bakr, ensured obedience.

The decision made during Umar's caliphate to prohibit Arabs from assuming ownership of conquered territory proved important. Umar tied army service, with its regular pay and windfalls of booty, to residence in large military camps—two in Iraq (Kufa and Basra), one in Egypt (Fustat), and one in Tunisia (Qairawan). East of Iraq, Arabs settled around small garrison towns at strategic locations and in one large garrison at Marv in present-day Turkmenistan. Down to the early eighth century, this policy kept the armies together and ready for action and preserved life in the countryside, where some three-fourths of the population lived, virtually unchanged. Only a tiny proportion of the Syrian, Egyptian, and Iraqi populations understood the Arabic language.

The million or so Arabs who participated in the conquests over several generations constituted a small, self-isolated ruling minority living on the taxes paid by a vastly larger non-Arab, non-Muslim subject population. The Arabs had little material incentive to encourage conversion, and there is no evidence of coherent missionary efforts to spread Islam during the conquest period.

The Umayyad and Early Abbasid Caliphates, 661–850

The Umayyad caliphs presided over an ethnically defined Arab realm rather than a religious empire. Ruling from Damascus, their armies consisted almost entirely of Muslim Arabs. They adopted and adapted the administrative practices of their Sasanid and Byzantine predecessors, as had the caliphs who preceded them. Only gradually did they replace non-Muslim secretaries and tax officials with Muslims and introduce Arabic as the language of government. The introduction of distinctively Muslim silver and gold coins early in the eighth century symbolized the new order. From that time on, silver dirhams and gold dinars bearing Arabic religious phrases circulated in monetary exchanges from Morocco to the frontiers of China.

The Umayyad dynasty fell in 750 after a decade of growing unrest. Converts to Islam, by that date no more than 10 percent of the indigenous population, were numerically significant because of the comparatively small number of Arab warriors. They resented not achieving equal status with the Arabs. The Arabs of Iraq and elsewhere envied the Syrian Arab influence in caliphal affairs. Pious Muslims looked askance at the secular and even irreligious behavior of the caliphs. Shi'ites and Kharijites attacked the Umayyad family's legitimacy as rulers, launching a number of rebellions.

In 750 one such rebellion, in the region of Khurasan° in what is today northeastern Iran, overthrew the last Umayyad caliph, though one family member escaped to Spain and founded an Umayyad principality there in 755. Many Shi'ites supported the rebellion, thinking they were fighting for the family of Ali. As it turned out, the family of Abbas, one of Muhammad's uncles, controlled the secret organization that coordinated the revolt. Upon victory they established the **Abbasid° Caliphate.** Some of the Abbasid caliphs who ruled after 750 befriended their relatives in Ali's family, and one even flirted with transferring the caliphate to them. The Abbasid family, however, held on to the caliphate until 1258, when Mongol invaders killed the last of them in Baghdad (see Chapter 12).

At its outset the Abbasid dynasty made a fine show of leadership and concern for Islam. Theology and religious law became preoccupations at court and among a growing community of scholars, along with interpretation of the Quran, collecting the sayings of the Prophet, and Arabic grammar. (In recent years, some western scholars have maintained that the Quran, the sayings of the Prophet, and the biography of the Prophet were all composed around this time to provide a legendary base for the regime. This reinterpretation of Islamic origins has not been generally accepted either in the scholarly community or among Muslims.) Some caliphs sponsored ambitious projects to translate great works of Greek, Persian, and Indian thought into Arabic.

With its roots among the semi-Persianized Arabs of Khurasan, the new dynasty gradually adopted the ceremonies and customs of the Sasanid shahs. Government grew increasingly complex in Baghdad, the newly built capital city on the Tigris River. As more non-Arabs converted to Islam, the ruling elite became more cosmopolitan. Greek, Iranian, Central Asian, and African cultural currents met in the capital and gave rise to an abundance of literary works, a process facilitated by the introduction of papermaking from China. Arab poets neglected the traditional odes extolling life in the desert and wrote

Khurasan (kor-uh-SAHN) **Abbasid** (ah-BASS-id)

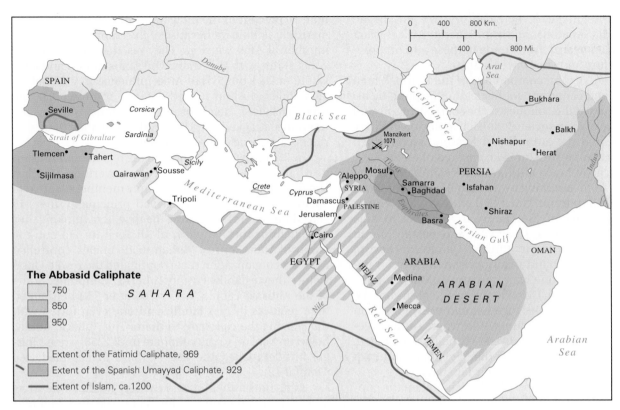

Map 8.2   Rise and Fall of the Abbasid Caliphate   Though Abbasid rulers occupied the caliphal seat in Iraq from 750 to 1258, when Mongol armies destroyed Baghdad, real political power waned sharply and steadily after 850. The rival caliphates of the Fatimids (909–1171) and Spanish Umayyads (929–976) were comparatively short-lived.

instead wine songs (despite Islam's prohibition of alcohol) or poems in praise of their patrons.

The translation of Aristotle into Arabic, the founding of the main currents of theology and law, and the splendor of the Abbasid court—reflected in stories of *The Arabian Nights* set in the time of the caliph Harun al-Rashid° (r. 776–809)—in some respects warrant calling the early Abbasid period a "golden age." Yet the refinement of Baghdad culture only slowly made its way into the provinces. Egypt remained predominantly Christian and Coptic-speaking in the early Abbasid period. Iran never adopted Arabic as a spoken tongue. Most of Berber-speaking North Africa rebelled and freed itself of direct caliphal rule after 740.

Gradual conversion to Islam among the conquered population accelerated in the second quarter of the ninth century. Social discrimination against non-Arab converts gradually faded, and the Arabs themselves—at least those living in cosmopolitan urban settings—lost

their previously strong attachment to kinship and ethnic identity.

Political Fragmentation, 850–1050

Abbasid decline became evident in the second half of the ninth century as the conversion to Islam accelerated (see Map 8.2). No government ruling so vast an empire could hold power easily. Caravans traveled only 20 miles (32 kilometers) a day, and the couriers of the caliphal post system usually did not exceed 100 miles (160 kilometers) a day. News of frontier revolts took weeks to reach Baghdad. Military responses might take months. Administrators struggled to centralize tax payments, often made in grain or other produce rather than cash, and ensure that provincial governors forwarded the proper amounts to Baghdad.

During the first two Islamic centuries, revolts against Muslim rule had been a concern. The Muslim umma had therefore clung together, despite the long distances. But

Harun al-Rashid (hah-ROON al–rah-SHEED)

Mosque of Ibn Tulun in Fustat   Completed in 877, this mosque symbolized Egypt becoming for the first time a quasi-independent province under its governor. The kiosk in the center of the courtyard contains fountains for washing before prayer. Before its restoration in the thirteenth century, the mosque had a spiral minaret and a door to an adjoining governor's palace. (Ellen Rooney/Robert Harding Picture Library)

with the growing conversion of the population to Islam, fears that Islamic dominion might be overthrown faded. Once they became the overwhelming majority, Muslims realized that a highly centralized empire did not necessarily serve the interests of all the people.

By the middle of the ninth century, revolts targeting Arab or Muslim domination gave way to movements within the Islamic community concentrating on seizure of territory and formation of principalities. None of the states carved out of the Abbasid Caliphate after 850 repudiated or even threatened Islam. They did, however, cut the flow of tax revenues to Baghdad, thereby increasing local prosperity.

Increasingly starved for funds by breakaway provinces and by an unexplained fall in revenues from Iraq itself, the caliphate experienced a crisis in the late ninth century. Distrusting generals and troops from outlying areas, the caliphs purchased Turkic slaves, **mamluks°**, from Central Asia and established them as a standing army. Well trained and hardy, the Turks proved an effec-

tive but expensive military force. When the government could not pay them, the mamluks took it on themselves to seat and unseat caliphs, a process made easier by the construction of a new capital at Samarra, north of Baghdad on the Tigris River.

The Turks dominated Samarra without interference from an unruly Baghdad populace that regarded them as rude and highhanded. However, the money and effort that went into the huge city, which was occupied only from 835 to 892, further sapped the caliphs' financial strength and deflected labor from more productive pursuits.

In 945, after several attempts to find a strongman to reform government administration and restore military power, the Abbasid Caliphate fell under the control of rude mountain warriors from the province of Daylam in northern Iran. Led by the Shi'ite Buyid° family, they conquered western Iran as well as Iraq. Each Buyid commander ruled his own principality. After almost two centuries of glory, the sun began to set on Baghdad. The

mamluk (MAM-luke)

Buyid (BOO-yid)

Abbasid caliph remained, but the Buyid princes controlled him. Being Shi'ites, the Buyids had no special reverence for the Sunni caliph. According to their particular Shi'ite sect, the twelfth and last divinely appointed Imam had disappeared around 873 and would return as a messiah only at the end of the world. Thus they had no Shi'ite Imam to defer to and retained the caliph only to help control their predominantly Sunni subjects.

Dynamic growth in outlying provinces paralleled the caliphate's gradual loss of temporal power. In the east in 875, the dynasty of the Samanids°, one of several Iranian families to achieve independence, established a glittering court in Bukhara, a major city on the Silk Road (see Map 8.2). Samanid princes patronized literature and learning, but the language they favored was Persian written in Arabic letters. For the first time, a non-Arabic literature rose to challenge the eminence of Arabic within the Islamic world.

In the west, the Berber revolts against Arab rule led to the appearance after 740 of the city-states of Sijilmasa° and Tahert° on the northern fringe of the Sahara. The Kharijite beliefs of these states' rulers interfered with their east-west overland trade and led them to develop the first regular trade across the Sahara desert. Once traders looked to the desert, they discovered that Berber speakers in the southern Sahara were already carrying salt from the desert into the Sahel region. The northern traders discovered that they could trade salt for gold by providing the southern nomads, who controlled the salt sources but had little use for gold, with more useful products, such as copper and manufactured goods. Sijilmasa and Tahert became wealthy cities, the former minting gold coins that circulated as far away as Egypt and Syria.

The earliest known sub-Saharan beneficiary of the new exchange system was the kingdom of **Ghana**°. It first appears in an Arabic text of the late eighth century as the "land of gold." Few details survive about the early years of this realm, which was established by the Soninke° people and covered parts of Mali, Mauritania, and Senegal, but it prospered until 1076, when it was conquered by nomads from the desert. It was one of the first lands outside the orbit of the caliphate to experience a gradual and peaceful conversion to Islam.

The North African city-states lost their independence after the Fatimid° dynasty, whose members claimed (perhaps falsely) to be Shi'ite Imams descended from Ali, established itself in Tunisia in 909. After consolidat-

ing their hold on northwest Africa, the Fatimids culminated their rise to power by conquering Egypt in 969. Claiming the title of caliph in a direct challenge to the Abbasids, the Fatimid rulers governed from a palace complex outside the old conquest-era garrison city of Fustat°. They named the complex Cairo. For the first time Egypt became a major cultural, intellectual, and political center of Islam. The abundance of Fatimid gold coinage, now channeled to Egypt from West Africa, made the Fatimids an economic power in the Mediterranean.

Cut off from the rest of the Islamic world by the Strait of Gibraltar and, from 740 onward, by independent city-states in Morocco and Algeria, Umayyad Spain developed a distinctive Islamic culture blending Roman, Germanic, and Jewish traditions with those of the Arabs and Berbers (see Map 8.1). Historians disagree on how rapidly and completely the Spanish population converted to Islam. If we assume a process similar to that in the eastern regions, it seems likely that the most rapid surge in Islamization occurred in the middle of the tenth century.

As in the east, governing cities symbolized the Islamic presence in al-Andalus, as the Muslims called their Iberian territories. Cordoba, Seville, Toledo, and other cities grew substantially, becoming much larger and richer than contemporary cities in neighboring France. Converts to Islam and their descendants, unconverted Arabic-speaking Christians, and Jews joined with the comparatively few descendants of Arab settlers to create new architectural and literary styles. In the countryside, where the Berbers preferred to settle, a fusion of preexisting agricultural technologies with new crops, notably citrus fruits, and irrigation techniques from the east gave Spain the most diverse and sophisticated agricultural economy in Europe.

The rulers of al-Andalus took the title *caliph* only in 929, when Abd al-Rahman° III (r. 912–961) did so in response to a similar declaration by the newly established (909) Fatimid ruler in Tunisia. By the century's end, however, this caliphate encountered challenges from breakaway movements that eventually splintered al-Andalus into a number of small states. Political decay did not impede cultural growth. Some of the greatest writers and thinkers in Jewish history worked in Muslim Spain in the eleventh and twelfth centuries, sometimes writing in Arabic, sometimes in Hebrew. Judah Halevi (1075–1141) composed exquisite poetry and explored questions of religious philosophy. Maimonides (1135–1204) made a major compilation of Judaic law and expounded on Aristotelian philosophy. At the same time, Islamic thought in Spain attained its loftiest peaks in Ibn Hazm's (994–1064)

Samanid (sah-MAN-id)   **Sijilmasa** (sih-jil-MAS-suh)
Tahert (TAH-hert)   **Ghana** (GAH-nuh)   **Soninke** (soh-NIN-kay)
Fatimid (FAT-uh-mid)

Fustat (fuss-TAHT)   **Abd al-Rahman** (AHB-d al–ruh-MAHN)

treatises on love and other subjects, the Aristotelian philosophical writings of Ibn Rushd° (1126–1198, known in Latin as Averroës°) and Ibn Tufayl° (d. 1185), and the mystic speculations of Ibn al-Arabi° (1165–1240). Christians, too, shared in the intellectual and cultural dynamism of al-Andalus. Translations from Arabic to Latin made during this period had a profound effect on the later intellectual development of western Europe (see Chapter 9).

The Samanids, Fatimids, and Spanish Umayyads, three of many regional principalities, represent the political diversity and awakening of local awareness that coincided with Abbasid decline. Yet drawing and redrawing political boundaries did not result in the rigid division of the Islamic world into kingdoms. Religious and cultural developments, particularly the rise in cities of a social group of religious scholars known as the **ulama**°—Arabic for "people with (religious) knowledge"—worked against any permanent division of the Islamic umma.

Spanish Muslim Textile of the Twelfth Century   This fragment of woven silk, featuring peacocks and Arabic writing, is one of the finest examples of Islamic weaving. The cotton industry flourished in the early Islamic centuries, but silk remained a highly valued product. Some fabrics were treasured in Christian Europe. (Victoria & Albert Museum)

Assault from Within and Without, 1050–1258

The role played by Turkish mamluks in the decline of Abbasid power established an enduring stereotype of the Turk as a ferocious, unsophisticated warrior. This image gained strength in the 1030s when the Seljuk° family established a Turkish Muslim state based on nomadic power. Taking the Arabic title *Sultan,* meaning "power," and the revived Persian title *Shahan-shah,* or King of Kings, the Seljuk ruler Tughril° Beg created a kingdom that stretched from northern Afghanistan to Baghdad, which he occupied in 1055. After a century under the thumb of the Shi'ite Buyids, the Abbasid caliph breathed easier under the slightly lighter thumb of the Sunni Turks. The Seljuks pressed on into Syria and Anatolia, administering a lethal blow to Byzantine power at the Battle of Manzikert° in 1071. The Byzantine army fell back on Constantinople, leaving Anatolia open to Turkish occupation.

Under Turkish rule, cities shrank as pastoralists overran their agricultural hinterlands. Irrigation works suffered from lack of maintenance in the unsettled countryside. Tax revenues fell. Twelfth-century Seljuk princes contesting for power fought over cities, but few Turks participated in urban cultural and religious life.

Ibn Rushd (IB-uhn RUSHED)   Averroës (uh-VERR-oh-eez)
Ibn Tufayl (IB-uhn too-FILE)
Ibn al-Arabi (IB-uhn ahl-AH-rah-bee)   ulama (oo-leh-MAH)
Seljuk (sel-JOOK)   Tughril (TUUG-ruhl)
Manzikert (MANZ-ih-kuhrt)

The gulf between a religiously based urban society and the culture and personnel of the government deepened. When factional riots broke out between Sunnis and Shi'ites, or between rival schools of Sunni law, rulers generally remained aloof, even as destruction and loss of life mounted. Similarly, when princes fought for the title *sultan,* religious leaders advised citizens to remain neutral.

By the early twelfth century, unrepaired damage from floods, fires, and civil disorder had reduced old Baghdad on the west side of the Tigris to ruins. The withering of Baghdad reflected a broader environmental problem: the collapse of the canal system on which agriculture in the Tigris and Euphrates Valley depended. For millennia a center of world civilization, Mesopotamia underwent substantial population loss and never again regained its geographical importance.

The Turks alone cannot be blamed for the demographic and economic misfortunes of Iran and Iraq. Too-robust urbanization had strained food resources, and political fragmentation had dissipated revenues. The growing practice of using land grants to pay soldiers and courtiers also played a role. When absentee grant holders used agents to collect taxes, the agents tended to gouge villagers and take little interest in improving production, all of which weakened the agricultural base of the economy.

The Seljuk Empire was beset by internal quarrels when the first crusading armies of Christians reached the Holy Land. The First Crusade captured Jerusalem in 1099 (see Chapter 9). Though charged with the stuff of romance, the Crusades had little lasting impact on the Islamic lands. The four crusader principalities of Edessa, Antioch, Tripoli, and Jerusalem simply became pawns in the shifting pattern of politics already in place. Newly arrived knights eagerly attacked the Muslim enemy, whom they called "Saracens°"; but veteran crusaders recognized that diplomacy and seeking partners of convenience among rival Muslim princes offered a sounder strategy.

The Muslims finally unified to face the European enemy in the mid-twelfth century. Nur al-Din ibn Zangi° established a strong state based in Damascus and sent an army to terminate the Fatimid Caliphate in Egypt. A nephew of the Kurdish commander of that expedition, Salah-al-Din, known in the West as Saladin, took advantage of Nur al-Din's timely death to seize power and unify Egypt and Syria. The Fatimid dynasty fell in 1171. In 1187 Saladin recaptured Jerusalem from the Europeans.

Saladin's descendants fought off subsequent Crusades. After one such battle, however, in 1250, Turkish mamluk troops seized control of the government in Cairo, ending Saladin's dynasty. In 1260 these mamluks rode east to confront a new invading force. At the Battle of Ain Jalut° (Spring of Goliath) in Syria, they met and defeated an army of Mongols from Central Asia (see Chapter 12), thus stemming an invasion that had begun several decades before and legitimizing their claim to dominion over Egypt and Syria.

A succession of Mamluk sultans ruled Egypt and Syria until 1517. Fear of new Mongol attacks receded after 1300, but by then the new ruling system had become fixed. Young Turkish or Circassian slaves, the latter from the eastern end of the Black Sea, were imported from non-Muslim lands, raised in military training barracks, and converted to Islam. Owing loyalty to the Mamluk officers who purchased them, they formed a military ruling class that was socially disconnected from the Arabic-speaking native population.

The Mongol invasions, especially their destruction of the Abbasid Caliphate in Baghdad in 1258, shocked the world of Islam. The Mamluk sultan placed a relative of the last Baghdad caliph on a caliphal throne in Cairo, but the Egyptian Abbasids were never more than puppets serving Mamluk interests. In the Muslim lands from Iraq eastward, non-Muslim rule lasted for much of the thirteenth century. Although the Mongols left few ethnic or linguistic traces in these lands, their initial destruction of cities and slaughter of civilian populations, their diversion of Silk Road trade from the traditional route terminating in Baghdad to more northerly routes ending at ports on the Black Sea, and their casual disregard, even after their conversion to Islam, of Muslim religious life and urban culture hastened currents of change already under way.

ISLAMIC CIVILIZATION

Though increasingly unsettled in its political dimension and subject to economic disruptions caused by war, the ever-expanding Islamic world underwent a fruitful evolution in law, social structure, and religious expression. Religious conversion and urbanization reinforced each other to create a distinct Islamic civilization. The immense geographical and human diversity of the Muslim lands allowed many "small traditions" to coexist with the developing "great tradition" of Islam.

Law and Dogma

The Shari'a, the law of Islam, provides the foundation of Islamic civilization. Yet aside from certain Quranic verses conveying specific divine ordinances—most pertaining to personal and family matters—Islam had no legal system in the time of Muhammad. Arab custom and the Prophet's own authority offered the only guidance. After Muhammad died, the umma tried to follow his example. This became harder and harder to do, however, as those who knew Muhammad best passed away, and many Arabs found themselves living in far-off lands. Non-Arab converts to Islam, who at first tried to follow Arab customs they had little familiarity with, had an even harder time.

Saracen (SAR-uh-suhn)
Nur al-Din ibn Zangi (NOOR-al-DEEN ib-uhn ZAN-gee)
Ain Jalut (ine jah-LOOT)

Scholarly Life in Medieval Islam Books being scarce and expensive, teachers dictated to their students, as shown on the right. Notice that the student is writing on a single sheet of paper while the scholar in the center holds an entire book. On the left, an author presents his work to a wealthy patron. (Bibliothèque nationale de France)

Islam slowly developed laws to govern social and religious life. The full sense of Islamic civilization, however, goes well beyond the basic Five Pillars mentioned earlier. Some Muslim thinkers felt that the reasoned consideration of a mature man offered the best resolution of issues not covered by Quranic revelation. Others argued for the sunna, or tradition, of the Prophet as the best guide. To understand that sunna they collected and studied thousands of reports, called **hadith**°, purporting to convey the precise words or deeds of Muhammad. It became customary to precede each hadith with a chain of oral authorities leading back to the person who had direct acquaintance with the Prophet.

Many hadith dealt with ritual matters, such as how to wash before prayer. Others provided answers to legal questions not covered by Quranic revelation or suggested principles for deciding such matters. By the eleventh century most legal thinkers had accepted the idea that Muhammad's personal behavior provided the best role model, and that the hadith constituted the most authoritative basis for law after the Quran itself.

Yet the hadith posed a problem because the tens of thousands of anecdotes included both genuine and invented reports, the latter sometimes politically motivated, as well as stories derived from non-Muslim religious tra-

ditions. Only a specialist could hope to separate a sound from a weak tradition. As the hadith grew in importance, so did the branch of learning devoted to their analysis. Scholars discarded thousands for having faulty chains of authority. The most reliable they collected into books that gradually achieved authoritative status. Sunnis placed six books in this category; Shi'ites, four.

As it gradually evolved, the Shari'a embodied a vision of an umma in which all subscribed to the same moral values and political and ethnic distinctions lost importance. Every Muslim ruler was expected to abide by and enforce the religious law. In practice, this expectation often lost out in the hurly-burly of political life. But the Shari'a proved an important basis for an urban lifestyle that varied surprisingly little from Morocco to India.

Converts and Cities

Conversion to Islam, more the outcome of people's learning about the new rulers' religion than an escape from the tax on non-Muslims, as some scholars have suggested, helped spur urbanization. Conversion did not require extensive knowledge of the faith. To become a Muslim, a person simply stated, in the presence of a Muslim: "There is no God but God, and Muhammad is the Messenger of God."

Few converts spoke Arabic, and fewer could read the

hadith (hah-DEETH)

Quran. Many converts knew no more of the Quran than the verses they memorized for daily prayers. Muhammad had established no priesthood to define and spread the faith. Thus new converts, whether Arab or non-Arab, faced the problem of finding out for themselves what Islam was about and how they should act as Muslims. This meant spending time with Muslims, learning their language, and imitating their practices.

In many areas, conversion involved migrating to an Arab governing center. The alternative, converting to Islam but remaining in one's home community, was difficult because religion had become the main component of social identity in Byzantine and Sasanid times. Converts to Islam thus encountered discrimination if they stayed in their Christian, Jewish, or Zoroastrian communities. Migration both averted discrimination and took advantage of the economic opportunities opened up by tax revenues flowing into the Arab governing centers.

The Arab military settlements of Kufa and Basra in Iraq blossomed into cities and became important centers for Muslim cultural activities. As conversion rapidly spread in the mid-ninth century, urbanization accelerated in other regions, most visibly in Iran, where most cities previously had been quite small. Nishapur in the northeast grew from fewer than 10,000 pre-Islamic inhabitants to between 100,000 and 200,000 by the year 1000. Other Iranian cities experienced similar growth. In Iraq, Baghdad and Mosul joined Kufa and Basra as major cities. In Syria, Aleppo and Damascus flourished under Muslim rule. Fustat in Egypt developed into Cairo, one of the largest and greatest Islamic cities. The primarily Christian patriarchal cities of Jerusalem, Antioch, and Alexandria, not being Muslim governing centers, shrank and stagnated.

Conversion-related migration meant that cities became heavily Muslim before the countryside. This reinforced the urban orientation deriving from the fact that Muhammad and his first followers came from the commercial city of Mecca. Mosques in large cities served both as ritual centers and as places for learning and social activities.

Islam colored all aspects of urban social life (see Diversity and Dominance: Beggars, Con Men, and Singing-girls). Initially the new Muslims imitated Arab dress and customs and emulated people they regarded as particularly pious. In the absence of a central religious authority, local variations developed in the way people practiced Islam and in the hadith they attributed to the Prophet. This gave the rapidly growing religion the flexibility to accommodate many different social situations.

By the tenth century, urban growth was affecting the countryside by expanding the consumer market. Citrus fruits, rice, and sugar cane, introduced by the Sasanids, increased in acreage and spread to new areas. Cotton became a major crop in Iran and elsewhere and stimulated textile production. Irrigation works expanded. Abundant coinage facilitated a flourishing intercity and long-distance trade that provided regular links between isolated districts and integrated the pastoral nomads, who provided pack animals, into the region's economy. Trade encouraged the manufacture of cloth, metal goods, and pottery.

Science and technology also flourished (see Environment and Technology: Automata). Building on Hellenistic traditions and their own observations and experience, Muslim doctors and astronomers developed skills and theories far in advance of their European counterparts. Working in Egypt in the eleventh century, the mathematician and physicist Ibn al-Haytham° wrote more than a hundred works. Among other things, he determined that the Milky Way lies far beyond earth's atmosphere, proved that light travels from a seen object to the eye and not the reverse, and explained why the sun and moon appear larger on the horizon than overhead.

Islam, Women, and Slaves

Women seldom traveled. Those living in rural areas worked in the fields and tended animals. Urban women, particularly members of the elite, lived in seclusion and did not leave their homes without covering themselves. Seclusion of women and veiling in public already existed in Byzantine and Sasanid times. Through interpretation of specific verses from the Quran, these practices now became fixtures of Muslim social life. Although women sometimes became literate and studied with relatives, they did so away from the gaze of unrelated men. Although women played influential roles within the family, public roles were generally barred. Only slave women could perform before unrelated men as musicians and dancers. A man could have sexual relations with as many slave concubines as he pleased, in addition to marrying as many as four wives.

Islamic law granted women greater status than did Christian or Jewish law. Muslim women inherited property and retained it in marriage. They had a right to remarry, and they received a cash payment upon divorce. Although a man could divorce his wife without stating a cause, a woman could initiate divorce under specified conditions. Women could practice birth control. They could testify in court, although their testimony counted

Ibn al-Haytham (IB-uhn al–HY-tham)

Women Playing Chess in Muslim Spain As shown in this thirteenth-century miniature, women in their own quarters, without men present, wore whatever clothes and jewels they liked. Notice the henna decorating the hands of the woman in the middle. The woman on the left, probably a slave, plays an oud. (Institute Amatller d'Art Hispanic. © Patrimonio Nacional, Madrid)

as half that of a man. They could go on pilgrimage. Nevertheless, a misogynistic tone sometimes appears in Islamic writings. One saying attributed to the Prophet observed: "I was raised up to heaven and saw that most of its denizens were poor people; I was raised into the hellfire and saw that most of its denizens were women."[3]

In the absence of writings by women from this period, the status of women must be deduced from the writings of men. Two episodes involving the Prophet's wife A'isha, the daughter of Abu Bakr, demonstrate how Muslim men appraised women in society. As a fourteen-year-old she had become separated from a caravan and rejoined it only after traveling through the night with a man who found her alone in the desert. Gossips accused her of being untrue to the Prophet, but a revelation from God proved her innocence. The second event was her participation in the Battle of the Camel, fought to derail Ali's caliphate. These two episodes came to epitomize what Muslim men feared most about women: sexual infidelity and meddling in politics.

The earliest literature dealing with A'isha stresses her position as Muhammad's favorite and her role as a prolific transmitter of hadith. In time, however, his first wife, Khadija, and his daughter, Ali's wife Fatima, surpassed A'isha as ideal women. Both appear as model wives and mothers with no suspicion of sexual irregularity or political manipulation.

As the seclusion of women became commonplace in urban Muslim society, some writers extolled homosexual relationships, partly because a male lover could appear in public or go on a journey. Although Islam deplored homosexuality, one ruler wrote a book advising his son to follow moderation in all things and thus share his affections equally between men and women. Another ruler and his slave-boy became models of perfect love in the verses of mystic poets.

Islam allowed slavery but forbade Muslims from enslaving other Muslims or so-called People of the Book—Jews, Christians, and Zoroastrians, who revered holy books respected by the Muslims. Being enslaved as a prisoner of war constituted an exception. Later centuries saw a constant flow of slaves into Islamic territory from Africa and Central Asia. A hereditary slave society, however, did not develop. Usually slaves converted to Islam, and many masters then freed them as an act of piety. The offspring of slave women and Muslim men were born free.

The Recentering of Islam

Early Islam centered on the caliphate, the political expression of the unity of the umma. No formal organization or hierarchy, however, directed the process of conversion. Thus there emerged a multitude of local Islamic

DIVERSITY AND DOMINANCE

BEGGARS, CON MEN, AND SINGING-GIRLS

Though rulers, warriors, and religious scholars dominate the traditional narratives, the society that developed over the early centuries of Islam was remarkably diverse. Beggars, tricksters, and street performers belonged to a single loose fraternity: the Banu Sasan, or Tribe of Sasan. Tales of their tricks and exploits amused staid, pious Muslims, who often encountered them in cities and on their scholarly travels. The tenth-century poet Abu Dulaf al-Khazraji, who lived in Iran, studied the jargon of the Banu Sasan and their way of life and composed a long poem in which he cast himself as one of the group. However, he added a commentary to each verse to explain the jargon words that his sophisticated court audience would have found unfamiliar.

> We are the beggars' brotherhood, and no one can deny
>   us our lofty pride . . .
> And of our number if the feigned madman and mad
>   woman, with metal charms strung from their [sic] necks.
> And the ones with ornaments drooping from their ears,
>   and with collars of leather or brass round their necks . . .
> And the one who simulates a festering internal wound,
>   and the people with false bandages round their heads
>   and sickly, jaundiced faces.
> And the one who slashes himself, alleging that he has
>   been mutilated by assailants, or the one who darkens
>   his skin artificially pretending that he has been
>   beaten up and wounded . . .
> And the one who practices as a manipulator and quack
>   dentist, or who escapes from chains wound round his
>   body, or the one who uses almost invisible silk thread
>   mysteriously to draw off rings . . .
> And of our number are those who claim to be refugees
>   from the Byzantine frontier regions, those who go
>   round begging on pretext of having left behind cap-
>   tive families . . .
> And the one who feigns an internal discharge, or who
>   showers the passers-by with his urine, or who farts in
>   the mosque and makes a nuisance of himself, thus
>   wheedling money out of people . . .
> And of our number are the ones who purvey objects of
>   veneration made from clay, and those who have their
>   beards smeared with red dye.

> And the one who brings up secret writing by immersing it
>   in what looks like water, and the one who similarly
>   brings up the writing by exposing it to burning embers.

One of the greatest masters of Arabic prose, Jahiz (776–869), was a famously ugly man—his name means "Popeyed"—of Abyssinian family origin. Spending part of his life in his native Basra, in southern Iraq, and part in Baghdad, the Abbasid capital, he wrote voluminously on subjects ranging from theology to zoology to miserliness. These excerpts come from his book devoted to the business of training slave girls as musicians, a lucrative practice of suspect morality but great popularity among men of wealth. He pretends that he is not the author, but merely writing down the views of the owners of singing-girls.

Now I will describe for you the definition of the passion of love, so that you may understand what exactly it is. It is a malady which smites the spirit, and affects the body as well by contagion: just as physical weakness impairs the spirit and low spirits in a man make him emaciated . . . The stronger the constituent causes of the malady are, the more inveterate it is, and the slower to clear up . . .

Passion for singing-girls is dangerous, in view of their manifold excellences and the satisfaction one's soul finds in them. . . . The singing-girl is hardly ever sincere in her passion, or wholehearted in her affection. For both by training and by innate instinct her nature is to set up snares and traps for the victims, in order that they may fall into her toils. As soon as the observer notices her, she exchanges provocative glances with him, gives him playful smiles, dallies with him in verses set to music, falls in with his suggestions, is eager to drink when he drinks, expresses her fervent desire for him to stay a long while, her yearning for his prompt return, and her sorrow at his departure. Then when she perceives that her sorcery has worked on him and that he has become entangled in the net, she redoubles the wiles she had used at first, and leads him to suppose that she is more in love than he is . . .

But it sometimes happens that this pretence leads her on to turning it into reality, and she in fact shares her lover's torments . . . Sometimes she may renounce her craft, in order for her to be cheaper for him [to buy], and makes a show of illness and is sullen towards her guardians and asks the owners to sell her . . . specially if she finds [her lover] to be sweet-tempered, clever in expressing himself, pleasant-tongued, with a fine apprehension and delicate sensibility, and light-hearted; while if he can compose and quote poetry or warble a tune, that gives him all the more favour in her eyes . . .

How indeed could a singing-girl be saved from falling prey to temptation, and how is it possible for her to be chaste? It is in the very place where she is brought up that she acquires unbridled desires, and learns her modes of speech and behaviour. From cradle to grave she is nourished by such idle talk, and all sorts of frivolous and impure conversation, as must hinder her from recollection of God; among abandoned and dissolute persons, who never utter a serious word, from whom she could never look for any trustworthiness, religion, or safe-guarding of decent standards.

An accomplished singing-girl has a repertoire of upwards of four thousands songs, each of them two to four verses long, so that the total amount . . . comes to ten thousand verses, in which there is not one mention of God (except by inadvertence). . . . They are all founded on references to fornication, pimping, passion, yearning, desire, and lust. Later on she continues to study her profession assiduously, learning from music teachers whose lessons are all flirting and whose directives are a seduction . . .

Among the advantages enjoyed by each man among us [i.e., speaking as a keeper of singing-girls] is that other men seek him out eagerly in his abode, just as one eagerly seeks out caliphs and great folk; is visited without having the trouble of visiting; receives gifts and is not compelled to give; has presents made to him and none required from him. Eyes remain wakeful, tears flow, minds are agitated, emotions lacerated, and hopes fixed—all on the property which he has under his control: which is something that does not occur with anything [else] that is sold or bought. . . . [F]or who could reach anything like the price fetched by an Abyssinian girl, the slave of Awn, namely 120,000 dinars [i.e., gold coins]?

The owner of singing-girls . . . takes the substance and gives the appearance, gets the real thing and gives the shadow, and sells the gusty wind for solid ore and pieces of silver and gold. Between the suitors and what they desire lies the thorniest of obstacles. For the owner, were he not to abstain from granting the dupe his desire for motives of purity and decency, would at any rate do so out of sharp-wittedness and wiliness, and to safeguard his trade and defend the sanctity of his estate. For when the lover once possesses himself of the beloved, nine-tenths of his ardour disappear, and his liberality and contributions [to the owner] diminish on the same scale. What is there, consequently, to induce the owner of the singing-girls to give you his girl, spiting his own face and causing himself to be no longer sought after?

If he were not a past-master in this splendid and noble profession, why is it that he abandons jealous surveillance of the girls (though choosing his spies well), accepts the room rent, pretends to doze off before supper, takes no notice of winkings, is indulgent to a kiss, ignores signs [passing between the pair of lovers], turns a blind eye to the exchange of billets-doux, affects to forget all about the girl on the day of the visit, does not scold her for retiring to a private place, does not pry into her secrets or cross-examine her about how she passed the night, and does not bother to lock the doors and draw close the curtains? He reckons up each victim's income separately, and knows how much money he is good for; just as the trader sorts out his various kinds of merchandise and prices them according to their value . . . When he has an influential customer, he takes advantage of his influence and makes requests from him; if the customer is rich but not influential, he borrows money from him without interest. If he is a person connected with the authorities, such a one can be used as a shield against the unfriendly attentions of the police; and when such a one comes on a visit, drums and hautbois [i.e., double-reed pipes] are sounded.

*B*oth of these passages fall into the category of Arabic literature known as* adab, *or belles-lettres. The purpose of adab was to entertain and instruct through a succession of short anecdotes, verses, and expository discussions. It attracted the finest writers of the Abbasid era and affords one of the richest sources for looking at everyday life, always keeping in mind that the intended readers were a restricted class of educated men, including merchants, court and government officials, and even men of religion.*

QUESTIONS FOR ANALYSIS

1. What do the authors' portrayals of beggars, con men, singing-girls, and keepers of singing-girls indicate about the diversity of life in the city?
2. Taken together, what do these passages indicate about the conventional portrayal of religious laws and moral teachings dominating everyday life?
3. In the discussion of singing-girls, what do you see as the importance of the practices of veiling and seclusion among urban, free-born, Muslim women?
4. In evaluating these as historical sources, is it necessary to take the tastes of the intended audience into account?

Sources: First selection excerpts from Clifford Edmund Bosworth, *The Mediaeval Islamic Underworld: The Banu Sasan in Arabic Society and Literature* (Leiden: E. I. Brill, 1976), 191–199. Copyright © 1976. With kind permission of Koninklijke Brill N.V. Leiden, the Netherlands. Second selection excerpts from Jahiz, *The Epistle on Singing-Girls,* tr. and ed. A. F. L. Beeston (Warminster: Aris and Phillips, 1980), 28–37. Reprinted with permission of Oxbow Books, Ltd.

ENVIRONMENT + TECHNOLOGY

Automata

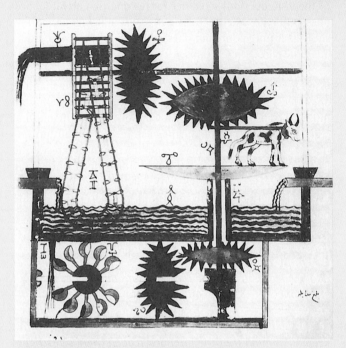

Model of a Water-Lifting Device   The artist's effort to render a three-dimensional construction in two dimensions shows a talent for schematic drawing.   (Widener Library Photographic Services)

Muslim scientists made discoveries and advances in almost every field, from mathematics and astronomy to chemistry and optics. Many worked under the patronage of rulers who paid for translations from Greek and other languages into Arabic and built libraries and observatories to facilitate their work. Fascination with science and technology also manifested itself in designs for elaborate mechanical devices—automata—intended for the entertainment of rulers and amazement of court visitors. In this example, a conventional-looking device for drawing water from a well, known as a saqiya (suh-KEY-yuh) and still in use from Morocco to Afghanistan, appears to be powered by a wooden cow that actually is moved by the force of the beam it is attached to rather than providing the motion itself.

A saqiya is a chain of buckets descending to a water source from a spoked drum attached to interlocking gears. In real life, an animal walks in a circle turning the first gear above it and thereby setting the drum in motion by way of a connecting gear that turns horizontal rotation into vertical rotation. In this automaton, real power comes from a water wheel with cups on its arms and hidden beneath the pool of water and connected by gears to the platform the wooden cow is standing on. The water flowing into the pond at left and right provides the hydraulic pressure needed to keep the apparatus in motion, causing the gears above to operate the chain of buckets lifting water to the outlet trough on the upper left.

communities so disconnected from each other that numerous competing interpretations of the developing religion arose. Inevitably, the centrality of the caliphate diminished (see Map 8.2). The appearance of rival caliphates in Tunisia and Cordoba accentuated the problem of decentralization.

The rise of the ulama as community leaders did not prevent growing fragmentation because the ulama themselves divided into contentious factions. During the twelfth century factionalism began to abate, and new socioreligious institutions emerged to provide the umma with a different sort of religious center. These new developments stemmed in part from an exodus of religious scholars from Iran in response to economic and political disintegration during the late eleventh and twelfth centuries. The flow of Iranians to the Arab lands and to newly conquered territories in India and Anatolia increased after the Mongol invasion.

Fully versed in Arabic as well as their native Persian, immigrant scholars were warmly received. They brought with them a view of religion developed in Iran's urban centers. A type of religious college, the *madrasa*°, gained sudden popularity outside Iran, where madrasas had been known since the tenth century. Scores of madrasas, many founded by local rulers, appeared throughout the Islamic world.

Iranians also contributed to the growth of mystic groups known as *Sufi* brotherhoods in the twelfth and thirteenth centuries. The doctrines and rituals of certain Sufis spread from city to city, giving rise to the first geo-

madrasa (MAH-dras-uh)

Quran Page Printed from a Woodblock Printing from wood-blocks or tin plates existed in Islamic lands between approximately 800 and 1400. Most prints were narrow amulets designed to be rolled and worn around the neck in cylindrical cases. Less valued than handwritten amulets, many prints came from Banu Sasan con men. Why blockprinting had so little effect on society in general and eventually disappeared is unknown. (Cambridge University Library)

graphically extensive Islamic religious organizations. Sufi doctrines varied, but a quest for a sense of union with God through rituals and training was a common denominator. Sufism had begun in early Islamic times and had doubtless benefited from the ideas and beliefs of people from religions with mystic traditions who converted to Islam.

The early Sufis had been saintly individuals given to ecstatic and poetic utterances and wonderworking. They attracted disciples but did not try to organize them. The growth of brotherhoods, a less ecstatic form of Sufism, set a tone for society in general. It soon became common for most Muslim men, particularly in the cities, to belong to at least one brotherhood.

A sense of the social climate the Sufi brotherhoods fostered can be gained from a twelfth-century manual:

> Every limb has its own special ethics. . . . The ethics of the tongue. The tongue should always be busy in reciting God's names (*dhikr*) and in saying good things of the brethren, praying for them, and giving them counsel. . . . The ethics of hearing. One should not listen to indecencies and slander. . . . The ethics of sight. One should lower one's eyes in order not to see forbidden things.[4]

Special dispensations allowed people who merely wanted to emulate the Sufis and enjoy their company to follow less demanding rules:

> It is allowed by way of dispensation to possess an estate or to rely on a regular income. The Sufis' rule in this matter is that one should not use all of it for himself, but should dedicate this to public charities and should take from it only enough for one year for himself and his family. . . .
>
> There is a dispensation allowing one to be occupied in business; this dispensation is granted to him who has to support a family. But this should not keep him away from the regular performance of prayers. . . .
>
> There is a dispensation allowing one to watch all kinds of amusement. This is, however, limited by the rule: What you are forbidden from doing, you are also forbidden from watching.[5]

Some Sufi brotherhoods spread in the countryside. Local shrines and pilgrimages to the tombs of Muhammad's descendants and saintly Sufis became popular. The end of the Abbasid Caliphate enhanced the religious centrality of Mecca, which eventually became an important center of madrasa education, and gave renewed importance to the annual pilgrimage.

CONCLUSION

The inspiration of Muhammad's teachings and the leadership his close followers provided after his death helped unite the Arabs and guide their conquests. But the formation of Islamic society was a more gradual affair. The caliphate was the culmination of a transformation, begun in Byzantine and Sasanid times, from ethnically and religiously diverse societies held together by the power and grandeur of kings to a unified realm based on religious identity. The concept of the umma, as set forth in the Quran, united Muslims in a universal community embracing enormous diversity of language and social custom. Though Muslim communities adapted to local "small traditions," by the twelfth century a religious scholar could travel throughout the Islamic world and blend easily into the local Muslim community.

By the ninth century, the forces of conversion and urbanization fostered social and religious experimentation in urban settings. But from the eleventh century onward, political disruption and the spread of pastoral nomadism slowed this early economic and technological dynamism. The Muslim community then turned to new religious institutions, such as the madrasas and Sufi brotherhoods, to create the flexible and durable community structures that carried Islam into new regions and protected ordinary believers from capricious political rule.

■ Key Terms

Shi'ites	caliphate
Sunnis	Quran
Mecca	Umayyad Caliphate
Muhammad	Abbasid Caliphate
muslim	mamluks
Islam	Ghana
Medina	ulama
umma	hadith

■ Suggested Reading

Ira M. Lapidus, *A History of Islamic Societies* (1988), focuses on social developments and includes the histories of Islam in India, Southeast Asia, sub-Saharan Africa, and other parts of the world. Marshall G. S. Hodgson, *The Venture of Islam*, 3 vols. (1974), critiques traditional ways of studying the Islamic Middle East while offering an alternative interpretation. Bernard Lewis's *The Middle East: A Brief History of the Last 2,000 Years* (1995) provides a lively narration from the time of Christ.

For a shorter survey see J. J. Saunders, *History of Medieval Islam* (1965; reprint, 1990). Richard W. Bulliet, *Islam: The View from the Edge* (1993), offers, in brief form, an approach that concentrates on the lives of converts to Islam and local religious notables.

Muslims regard the Quran as untranslatable because they consider the Arabic in which it is couched to be inseparable from God's message. Most "interpretations" in English adhere reasonably closely to the Arabic text.

Martin Lings, *Muhammad: His Life Based on the Earliest Sources*, rev. ed. (1991), offers a readable biography reflecting Muslim viewpoints. Standard Western treatments include W. Montgomery Watt's *Muhammad at Mecca* (1953) and *Muhammad at Medina* (1956; reprint, 1981); and the one-volume summary: *Muhammad, Prophet and Statesman* (1974). Michael A. Cook, *Muhammad* (1983), intelligently discusses historiographical problems and source difficulties. Karen Armstrong's *Muham-*

mad: A Biography of the Prophet (1993) achieves a sympathetic balance.

For information on the new school of thought that rejects the traditional accounts of Muhammad's life and of the origins of the Quran, see Patricia Crone and Michael Cook, *Hagarism* (1977), Patricia Crone, *Meccan Trade and the Rise of Islam* (1987), and Fred Donner, *Narratives of Islamic Origins* (1998).

Wilfred Madelung's *The Succession to Muhammad: A Study of the Early Caliphate* (1997) gives an interpretation unusually sympathetic to Shi'ite viewpoints. G. R. Hawting, *The First Dynasty of Islam: The Umayyad Caliphate, A.D. 661–750* (1987), offers a more conventional and easily readable history of a crucial century.

Western historians have debated the beginnings of the Abbasid Caliphate. Moshe Sharon, *Black Banners from the East: The Establishment of the 'Abbasid State—Incubation of a Revolt* (1983), and Jacob Lassner, *Islamic Revolution and Historical Memory: An Inquiry into the Art of Abbasid Apologetics* (1987), give differing accounts based on newly utilized sources. For a broader history that puts the first three centuries of Abbasid rule into the context of the earlier periods, see Hugh N. Kennedy, *The Prophet and the Age of the Caliphates: The Islamic Near East from the Sixth to the Eleventh Century* (1986). Harold Bowen, *The Life and Times of Ali ibn Isa "The Good Vizier"* (1928; reprint, 1975), supplements Kennedy's narrative superbly with a detailed study of corrupt caliphal politics in the tumultuous early tenth century.

Articles in Michael Gervers and Ramzi Jibran Bikhazi, eds., *Conversion and Continuity: Indigenous Christian Communities in Islamic Lands, Eighth to Eighteenth Centuries* (1990), detail Christian responses to Islam. For a Zoroastrian perspective see Jamsheed K. Choksy, *Conflict and Cooperation: Zoroastrian Subalterns and Muslim Elites in Medieval Iranian Society* (1997). Jacob Lassner summarizes S. D. Goitein's definitive multivolume study of the Jews of medieval Egypt in *A Mediterranean Society: An Abridgement in One Volume* (1999). On the process of conversion see the work in quantitative history of Richard W. Bulliet, *Conversion to Islam in the Medieval Period* (1979).

With the fragmentation of the Abbasid Caliphate beginning in the ninth century, studies of separate areas become more useful than general histories. Richard N. Frye, *The Golden Age of Persia: The Arabs in the East* (1975), skillfully evokes the complicated world of early Islamic Iran and the survival and revival of Persian national identity. Thomas F. Glick, *Islamic and Christian Spain in the Early Middle Ages* (1979) and *From Muslim Fortress to Christian Castle: Social and Cultural Change in Medieval Spain* (1995), questions standard ideas about Christians and Muslims in Spain from a geographical and technological standpoint. For North Africa, Charles-André Julien, *History of North Africa: Tunisia, Algeria, Morocco, from the Arab Conquest to 1830* (1970), summarizes a literature primarily written in French. This same French historiographical tradition is challenged and revised by Abdallah Laroui, *The History of the Maghrib: An Interpretive Essay* (1977). For a detailed primary source, see the English translation of the most important chronicle of early Islamic history, *The History of al-Tabari*, published in thirty-eight volumes under the general editorship of Ehsan Yarshater.

Roy P. Mottahedeh, *Loyalty and Leadership in an Early Islamic Society* (1980); Richard W. Bulliet, *The Patricians of Nishapur* (1972); and Ira Marvin Lapidus, *Muslim Cities in the Later Middle Ages* (1984), discuss social history in tenth-century Iran, eleventh-century Iran, and fourteenth-century Syria, respectively. Jonathan Berkey, *The Transmission of Knowledge in Medieval Cairo: A Social History of Islamic Education* (1992), and Michael Chamberlain, *Knowledge and Social Practice in Medieval Damascus, 1190–1350* (1994), put forward competing assessments of education and the ulama. For urban geography see Paul Wheatley, *The Places Where Men Pray Together* (2001).

Ahmad Y. al-Hassan and Donald R. Hill, *Islamic Technology: An Illustrated History* (1986), introduce a little-studied field. For a more crafts-oriented look see Hans E. Wulff, *The Traditional Crafts of Persia: Their Development, Technology, and Influence on Eastern and Western Civilizations* (1966). Jonathan Bloom's *Paper Before Print* (2001) details the great impact of papermaking in many cultural areas.

Denise Spellberg, *Politics, Gender, and the Islamic Past: The Legacy of A'isha bint Abi Bakr* (1994), provides pathbreaking guidance on women's history. Basim Musallam, *Sex and Society in Islamic Civilization* (1983), treats the social, medical, and legal history of birth control. On race and slavery see Bernard Lewis, *Race and Slavery in the Middle East: A Historical Enquiry* (1992).

Among the numerous introductory books on Islam as a religion, a reliable starting point is David Waines, *An Introduction to Islam* (1995). For more advanced work, Fazlur Rahman, *Islam*, 2d ed. (1979), skillfully discusses some of the subject's difficulties. Islamic law is well covered in Noel J. Coulson, *A History of Islamic Law* (1979). For Sufism see Annemarie Schimmel, *Mystical Dimensions of Islam* (1975).

Two religious texts available in translation are Abu Hamid al-Ghazali, *The Faith and Practice of al-Ghazali*, trans. W. Montgomery Watt (1967; reprint, 1982), and Abu al-Najib al-Suhrawardi, *A Sufi Rule for Novices*, trans. Menahem Milson (1975).

For detailed and abundant maps see William C. Brice, ed., *An Historical Atlas of Islam* (1981). The most complete reference work for people working in Islamic studies is *The Encyclopedia of Islam*, new ed. (Leiden: E. J. Brill, 1960–), now available in CD-ROM format. For encyclopedia-type articles on pre-Islamic topics see G.W. Bowersock, Peter Brown, and Oleg Grabar, *Late Antiquity: A Guide to the Postclassical World* (1999). On Iran see the excellent but still unfinished *Encyclopedia Iranica*, edited by Ehsan Yarshater.

◼ Notes

1. Quran. Sura 96, verses 1–5.
2. Quran. Sura 92, verses 1–10.
3. Richard W. Bulliet, *Islam: The View from the Edge* (New York: Columbia University Press, 1994), 87.
4. Abu Najib al-Suhrawardi, *A Sufi Rule for Novices*, trans. Menahem Milson (Cambridge, MA: Harvard University Press, 1975), 45–58.
5. Ibid., 73–82.

Document-Based Question
Moral and Social Behavior in the Islamic World before 1250

Using the following documents, evaluate the standards of moral and social behavior in the Islamic World before 1250. Compare and contrast the application of these standards to men and women.

DOCUMENT 1
Excerpt from the Quran (pp. 199–200)

DOCUMENT 2
Mosque of Ibn Tulun in Fustat (photo, p. 205)

DOCUMENT 3
Scholarly Life in Medieval Islam (photo, p. 209)

DOCUMENT 4
Women Playing Chess (photo, p. 211)

DOCUMENT 5
Beggars, Con Men, and Singing-girls (Diversity and Dominance, pp. 212–213)

DOCUMENT 6
Excerpts from a Sufi manual (p. 215)

To what degree is each document an accurate portrayal of Islamic society? (Note that there are two different forms of writing—poetry and prose—in Document 5.) What additional types of documents would help you evaluate the standards of moral and social behavior in the Islamic world before 1250?

9 Christian Europe Emerges, 600–1200

Boatbuilding Scene from the Bayeaux Tapestry   Eleventh-century shipwrights prepare vessels for William of Normandy's invasion of England.

CHAPTER OUTLINE

Christmas Day in 800 found Charles, king of the Franks, in Rome instead of at his palace at Aachen in northwestern Germany. At six-foot-three, Charles towered over the average man of his time, and his royal career had been equally gargantuan. Crowned king in his mid-twenties in 768, he had crisscrossed Europe for three decades, waging war on Muslim invaders from Spain, Avar° invaders from Hungary, and a number of German princes.

Charles had subdued many enemies and had become protector of the papacy. So not all historians believe the eyewitness report of his secretary and biographer that Charles was surprised when, as the king rose from his prayers, Pope Leo III placed a new crown on his head. "Life and victory to Charles the August, crowned by God the great and pacific Emperor of the Romans," proclaimed the pope.[1] Then, amid the cheers of the crowd, he humbly knelt before the new emperor.

Charlemagne° (from Latin *Carolus magnus,* "Charles the Great") was the first in western Europe to bear the title *emperor* in over three hundred years. Rome's decline and Charlemagne's rise marked a shift of focus for Europe—away from the Mediterranean and toward the north and west. German custom and Christian piety transformed the Roman heritage to create a new civilization. Irish monks preaching in Latin became important intellectual influences in some parts of Europe, while the memory of Greek and Roman philosophy faded. Urban life continued the decline that had begun in the later days of the Roman Empire. Historians originally called this era **"medieval,"** literally "middle age," because it comes between the era of Greco-Roman civilization and the intellectual, artistic, and economic changes of the Renaissance in the fourteenth century; but research has uncovered many aspects of medieval culture that are as rich and creative as those that came earlier and later.

Charlemagne was not the only ruler in Europe to claim the title emperor. Another emperor held sway in the Greek-speaking east, where Rome's political and legal heritage continued. The Eastern Roman Empire was often called the **Byzantine Empire** after the seventh century, and was known to the Muslims as Rum. Western Europeans lived amid the ruins of empire, while the Byzantines maintained and reinterpreted Roman traditions. The authority of the Byzantine emperors blended with the influence of the Christian church to form a cultural synthesis that helped shape the emerging kingdom of **Kievan Russia.** Byzantium's centuries-long conflict with Islam helped spur the crusading passion that overtook western Europe in the eleventh century.

The comparison between western and eastern Europe appears paradoxical. Byzantium inherited a robust and self-confident late Roman society and economy, while western Europe could not achieve political unity and suffered severe economic decline. Yet by 1200 western Europe was showing renewed vitality and flexing its military muscles, while Byzantium was showing signs of decline and military weakness. As we explore the causes and consequences of these different historical paths, we must remember that the emergence of Christian Europe included both developments.

As you read this chapter, ask yourself the following questions:

- What role did Christianity play in reshaping European society in east and west?
- How did the Roman heritage differently affect the east and the west?
- How can one compare Kievan Russia's resemblances to western Europe and to the Byzantine Empire?
- How did Mediterranean trade and the Crusades help revive western Europe?

THE BYZANTINE EMPIRE, 600–1200

The Byzantine emperors established Christianity as their official religion (see Chapter 5). They also represented a continuation of Roman imperial rule and tradition that was largely absent in the kingdoms that succeeded Rome in the west. Byzantium inherited imperial law intact; only provincial forms of Roman law

---

Avar (ah-vahr)   Charlemagne (SHAHR-leh-mane)

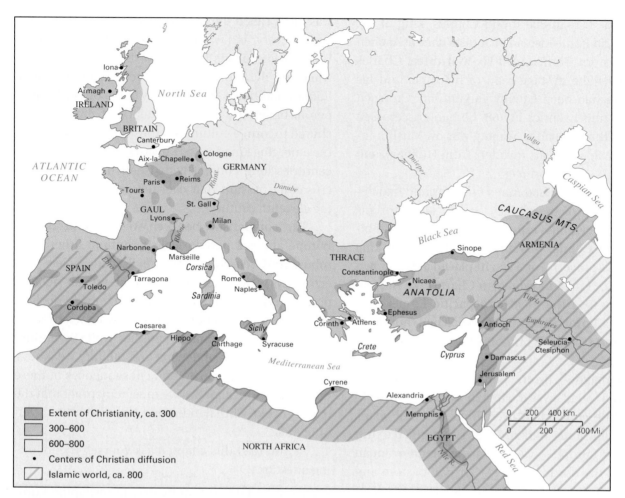

Map 9.1   The Spread of Christianity   By the early eighth century, Christian areas around the southern Mediterranean from northern Syria to northern Spain, accounting for most of the Christian population, had fallen under Muslim rule; the slow process of conversion to Islam had begun. This accentuated the importance of the patriarchs of Constantinople, the popes in Rome, and the later converting regions of northern and eastern Europe.

survived in the west. Combining the imperial role with political oversight over the Christian church, the emperors made a comfortable transition into the role of all-powerful Christian monarchs. The Byzantine drama, however, played on a steadily shrinking stage. Territorial losses and almost constant military pressure from north and south deprived the empire of long periods of peace.

An Empire Beleaguered

Having a single ruler endowed with supreme legal and religious authority prevented the breakup of the Eastern Empire into petty principalities, but a series of territorial losses sapped the empire's strength. Between 634 and 650, Arab armies destroyed the Sasanid Empire and captured Byzantine Egypt, Syria, and Tunisia (see Chapter 8). Islam posed a religious as well as a political challenge. By the end of the twelfth century, some two-thirds of the Christians in these former Byzantine territories had adopted the Muslim faith (see Map 9.1).

The loss of such populous and prosperous provinces shook the empire and reduced its power. Although it had largely recovered and reorganized militarily by the tenth century, it never regained the lost lands. Though Crusaders from western Europe established short-lived Christian principalities at the eastern end of the Mediterranean Sea in the eleventh century, the Byzantines found them almost as hostile as the Muslims (see

CHRONOLOGY

	Western Europe	Eastern Europe
600		**634–650** Muslims conquer Byzantine provinces of Syria, Egypt, and Tunisia
	711 Muslim conquest of Spain **732** Battle of Tours	
800	**800** Coronation of Charlemagne **843** Treaty of Verdun divides Carolingian Empire among Charlemagne's grandsons	
	910 Monastery of Cluny founded **962** Beginning of Holy Roman Empire	**882** Varangians take control of Kiev **980** Vladimir becomes grand prince of Kievan Russia
1000	**1054** Formal schism between Latin and Orthodox Churches **1066** Normans under William the Conqueror invade England **1077** Climax of investiture controversy **1095** Pope Urban II preaches First Crusade	
1200		**1081–1118** Alexius Comnenus rules Byzantine Empire, calls for western military aid against Muslims **1204** Western knights sack Constantinople in Fourth Crusade

the section below on the Crusades). Eventually the empire succumbed to Muslim conquest in 1453.

The later Byzantine emperors faced new enemies in the north and south. Following the wave of Germanic migrations (see Chapter 5), Slavic and Turkic peoples appeared on the northern frontiers as part of centuries-long and poorly understood population migrations in Eurasian steppe lands. Other Turks led by the Seljuk family became the primary foe in the south (see Chapter 8).

At the same time, relations with the popes and princes of western Europe steadily worsened. In the mid-ninth century the patriarchs of Constantinople had challenged the territorial jurisdiction of the popes of Rome and some of the practices of the Latin Church. These arguments worsened over time and in 1054 culminated in a formal **schism°** between the Latin Church and the Orthodox Church—a break that has been only partially mended.

Schism (SKIZ-uhm)

Society and Urban Life

Imperial authority and urban prosperity in the eastern provinces of the late Roman Empire initially sheltered Byzantium from many of the economic reverses and population losses suffered by western Europe. However, the two regions shared a common demographic crisis during a sixth-century epidemic of bubonic plague known as "the plague of Justinian," named after the emperor who ruled from 527 to 565. A similar though gradual and less pronounced social transformation set in around the seventh century, possibly sparked by further epidemics and the loss of Egypt and Syria to the Muslims. Narrative histories tell us little, but popular narratives of saints' lives show a transition from stories about educated saints hailing from cities to stories about saints who originated as peasants. In many areas, barter replaced money transactions; some cities declined in population and wealth; and the traditional class of local urban notables nearly disappeared.

Byzantine Church from a Twelfth-Century Manuscript
The upper portion shows the church façade and domes. The lower portion shows the interior with a mosaic of Christ enthroned at the altar end.   (Bibliothèque nationale de France)

As the urban elite class shrank, the importance of high-ranking aristocrats at the imperial court and of rural landowners increased. Power organized by family began to rival power from class-based officeholding. By the end of the eleventh century, a family-based military aristocracy had emerged. Of Byzantine emperor Alexius Comnenus° (r. 1081–1118) it was said: "He considered himself not a ruler, but a lord, conceiving and calling the empire his own house."[2] The situation of women changed, too. Although earlier Roman family life was centered on a legally all-powerful father, women had enjoyed comparative freedom in public. After the seventh century women increasingly found themselves confined to the home. Some sources indicate that when they went out, they concealed their faces behind veils. The only men they socialized with were family members. Para-

Alexius Comnenus (uh-LEX-see-uhs kom-NAY-nuhs)

doxically, however, from 1028 to 1056 women ruled the Byzantine Empire alongside their husbands. These social changes and the apparent increase in the seclusion of women resemble simultaneous developments in neighboring Islamic countries, but historians have not uncovered any firm linkage between them.

Economically, the Byzantine emperors continued the Late Roman inclination to set prices, organize grain shipments to the capital, and monopolize trade in luxury goods like Tyrian purple cloth. Such government intervention may have slowed technological development and economic innovation. So long as merchants and pilgrims hastened to Constantinople from all points of the compass, aristocrats could buy rare and costly goods. Just as the provisioning and physical improvement of Rome overshadowed the development of other cities at the height of the Roman Empire, so other Byzantine cities suffered from the intense focus on Constantinople. In the countryside, Byzantine farmers continued to use slow oxcarts and light scratch plows, which were efficient for many, but not all, soil types, long after farmers in western Europe had begun to adopt more efficient techniques (see below).

Because Byzantium's Roman inheritance remained so much more intact than western Europe's, few people recognized the slow deterioration. Gradually, however, pilgrims and visitors from the west saw the reality beyond the awe-inspiring, incense-filled domes of cathedrals and beneath the glitter and silken garments of the royal court. An eleventh-century French visitor wrote:

> The city itself [Constantinople] is squalid and fetid and in many places harmed by permanent darkness, for the wealthy overshadow the streets with buildings and leave these dirty, dark places to the poor and to travelers; there murders and robberies and other crimes which love the darkness are committed. Moreover, since people live lawlessly in this city, which has as many lords as rich men and almost as many thieves as poor men, a criminal knows neither fear nor shame, because crime is not punished by law and never entirely comes to light. In every respect she exceeds moderation; for, just as she surpasses other cities in wealth, so too, does she surpass them in vice.[3]

A Byzantine contemporary, Anna Comnena, the brilliant daughter of Emperor Alexius Comnenus, expressed the view from the other side. She scornfully described a prominent churchman and philosopher who happened to be from Italy: "Italos . . . was unable with his barbaric, stupid temperament to grasp the profound truths of philosophy; even in the act of learning he utterly rejected the teacher's guiding hand, and full of temerity and barbaric folly, [believed] even before study that he excelled all others."[4]

Cultural Achievements

Though the greatest Byzantine architectural monument, Constantinople's Hagia Sophia° ("Sacred Wisdom") cathedral, dates to the reign of Justinian, artistic creativity continually manifested itself in the design and ornamentation of other churches and monasteries. Byzantine religious art, featuring stiff but arresting images of holy figures against gold backgrounds, strongly influenced painting in western Europe down to the thirteenth century, and Byzantine musical traditions strongly affected the chanting employed in medieval Latin churches.

Another important Byzantine achievement dates to the empire's long period of political decline. In the ninth century brothers named Cyril and Methodius embarked on a highly successful mission to the Slavs of Moravia (part of the modern Czech Republic). They preached in the local language, and their followers perfected a writing system, called Cyrillic°, that came to be used by Slavic Christians adhering to the Orthodox—that is, Byzantine—rite. Their careers also mark the beginning of a competition between the Greek and Latin forms of Christianity for the allegiance of the Slavs. The use today of the Cyrillic alphabet among the Russians and other Slavic peoples of Orthodox Christian faith, and of the Roman alphabet among the Poles, Czechs, and Croatians, testifies to this competition (see the section below on Kievan Russia).

EARLY MEDIEVAL EUROPE, 600–1000

The disappearance of the imperial legal framework that had persisted to the final days of the Western Roman Empire (see Chapter 5) and the rise of various kings, nobles, and chieftains changed the legal and political landscape of western Europe. In region after region, the family-based traditions of the Germanic peoples, which often fit local conditions better than previous practices, supplanted the edicts of the Roman emperors.

Fear and physical insecurity led communities to seek the protection of local strongmen. In places where looters and pillagers might appear at any moment, a local lord with a castle at which peasants could take refuge counted for more than a distant king. Dependency of weak people on strong people became a hallmark of the post-Roman period in western Europe.

A Time of Insecurity

In 711 a frontier raiding party of Arabs and Berbers, acting under the authority of the Umayyad caliph in Syria, crossed the Strait of Gibraltar and overturned the kingdom of the Visigoths in Spain (see Chapter 8). The disunited Europeans could not stop them from consolidating their hold on the Iberian Peninsula. After pushing the remaining Christian chieftains into the northern mountains, the Muslims moved on to France. They occupied much of the southern coast and penetrated as far north as Tours, less than 150 miles (240 kilometers) from the English Channel, before Charlemagne's grandfather, Charles Martel, stopped their most advanced raiding party in 732.

Military effectiveness was the key element in the rise of the Carolingian° family (from Latin *Carolus*, "Charles"), first as protectors of the Frankish kings, then as kings themselves under Charlemagne's father Pepin (r. 751–768), and finally, under Charlemagne, as emperors. At the peak of Charlemagne's power, the Carolingian Empire encompassed all of Gaul and parts of Germany and Italy, with the pope ruling part of the latter. When Charlemagne's son, Louis the Pious, died, the Germanic tradition of splitting property among sons led to the Treaty of Verdun (843), which split the empire into three parts. French-speaking in the west (France) and middle (Burgundy), and German-speaking in the east (Germany), the three regions never reunited. Nevertheless, the Carolingian economic system based on landed wealth and a brief intellectual revival sponsored personally by Charlemagne—though he himself was illiterate—provided a common heritage.

A new threat to western Europe appeared in 793, when the Vikings, sea raiders from Scandinavia, attacked and plundered a monastery on the English coast, the first of hundreds of such raids. Local sources from France, the British Isles, and Muslim Spain attest to widespread dread of Viking warriors descending from multi-oared, dragon-prowed boats to pillage monasteries, villages, and towns. Viking shipbuilders made versatile vessels that could brave the stormy North Atlantic and also maneuver up rivers to attack inland towns. In the ninth century raiders from Denmark and Norway

---

Hagia Sophia (AH-yah SOH-fee-uh)   **Cyrillic** (sih-RIL-ik)   **Carolingian** (kah-roe-LIN-gee-uhn)

harried the British and French coasts (see Diversity and Dominance: Archbishop Adalbert of Hamburg and the Christianization of the Scandinavians and Slavs) while Varangians° (Swedes) pursued raiding and trading interests, and eventually the building of kingdoms, along the rivers of eastern Europe and Russia, as we shall see. Although many Viking raiders sought booty and slaves, in the 800s and 900s Viking captains organized the settlement of Iceland, Greenland, and, around the year 1000, Vinland on the northern tip of Newfoundland.

Vikings long settled on lands they had seized in Normandy (in northwestern France) organized the most important and ambitious expeditions in terms of numbers of men and horses and long-lasting impact. William the Conqueror, the duke of Normandy, invaded England in 1066 and brought Anglo-Saxon domination of the island to an end. Other Normans (from "north men") attacked Muslim Sicily in the 1060s and, after thirty years of fighting, permanently severed it from the Muslim world.

A Self-Sufficient Economy

Archaeology and records kept by Christian monasteries and convents reveal a profound economic transformation that accompanied the new Germanic political order. The new rulers cared little for the urban-based civilization of the Romans, which accordingly shrank in importance. Though the pace of change differed from region to region, most cities lost population, in some cases becoming villages. Roman roads fell into disuse and disrepair. Small thatched houses sprang up beside abandoned villas, and public buildings made of marble became dilapidated in the absence of the laborers, money, and civic leadership needed to maintain them. Paying for purchases in coin largely gave way to bartering goods and services.

Trade across the Mediterranean did not entirely stop after the Muslim conquests; occasional shipments from Egypt and Syria continued to reach western ports. But most of western Europe came to rely on meager local resources. These resources, moreover, underwent redistribution.

Roman centralization had channeled the wealth and production of the empire to the capital, which in turn radiated Roman cultural styles and tastes to the provinces. As Roman governors were replaced by Germanic territorial lords who found the riches of their own culture more appealing than those of Rome, local self-sufficiency became more important. The decline of literacy and other aspects of Roman life made room for the growth of Germanic cultural traditions.

The diet in the northern countries featured beer, lard or butter, and bread made of barley, rye, or wheat, all supplemented by pork from herds of swine fed on forest acorns and beechnuts, and by game from the same forests. Nobles ate better than peasants, but even the peasant diet was reasonably balanced. The Roman diet based on wheat, wine, and olive oil persisted in the south. The average western European of the ninth century was probably better nourished than his or her descendants three hundred years later, when population was increasing and the nobility monopolized the resources of the forests.

In both north and south, self-sufficient farming estates known as **manors** became the primary centers of agricultural production. Fear of attack led many common farmers in the most vulnerable regions to give their lands to large landowners in return for political and physical protection. The warfare and instability of the post-Roman centuries made unprotected country houses especially vulnerable to pillaging. Isolated by poor communications and lack of organized government, landowners depended on their own resources for survival. Many became warriors or maintained a force of armed men. Others swore allegiance to landowners who had armed forces to protect them.

A well-appointed manor possessed fields, gardens, grazing lands, fish ponds, a mill, a church, workshops for making farm and household implements, and a village where the farmers dependent on the lord of the manor lived. Depending on local conditions, protection ranged from a ditch and wooden stockade to a stone wall surrounding a fortified keep (a stone building). Fortification tended to increase until the twelfth century, when stronger monarchies made it less necessary.

Manor life reflected personal status. Nobles and their families exercised almost unlimited power over the **serfs**—agricultural workers who belonged to the manor, tilled its fields, and owed other dues and obligations. Serfs could not leave the manor where they were born and attach themselves to another lord. Most peasants in England, France, and western Germany were unfree serfs in the tenth and eleventh centuries. In Bordeaux°, Saxony, and a few other regions free peasantry survived based on the egalitarian social structure of the Germanic peoples during their period of migration. Outright slavery, the mainstay of the Roman economy (see Chapter

---

Varangians (va-RAN-gee-anz)

Bordeaux (bore-DOE)

5), diminished as more and more peasants became serfs in return for a lord's protection. The enslavement of prisoners to serve as laborers became less important as an object of warfare.

Early Medieval Society in the West

Europe's reversion to a self-sufficient economy limited the freedom and potential for personal achievement of most people, but an emerging class of nobles reaped great benefits. During the Germanic migrations and later among the Vikings of Scandinavia, men regularly answered the call to arms issued by war chiefs, to whom they swore allegiance. All warriors shared in the booty gained from raiding. As settlement enhanced the importance of agricultural tasks, laying down the plow and picking up the sword at the chieftain's call became harder.

Those who, out of loyalty or desire for adventure, continued to join the war parties included a growing number of horsemen. Mounted warriors became the central force of the Carolingian army. At first, fighting from horseback did not make a person either a nobleman or a landowner. By the tenth century, however, nearly constant warfare to protect land rights or support the claims of a lord brought about a gradual transformation in the status of the mounted warrior, which led, at different rates in different areas, to landholding becoming almost inseparable from military service.

In trying to understand long-standing traditions of landholding and obligation, lawyers in the sixteenth century and later simplified thousands of individual agreements into a neat system they called "feudalism," from Latin *feodum,* meaning a land awarded for military service. It became common to refer to medieval Europe as a "feudal society" in which kings and lords gave land to "vassals" in return for sworn military support. By analyzing original records, more recent historians have discovered this to be an oversimplification. Relations between landholders and serfs and between lords and vassals differed too much from one place to another, and from one time to another, to fit together in anything resembling a system.

The German foes of the Roman legions had equipped themselves with helmets, shields, and swords, spears, or throwing axes. Some rode horses, but most fought on foot. Before the invention of the stirrup by Central Asian pastoralists in approximately the first century C.E., horsemen had gripped their mounts with their legs and fought with bows and arrows, throwing javelins, stabbing spears, and swords. Stirrups allowed a rider to stand in the saddle and absorb the impact when his lance struck an enemy at full gallop. This type of warfare required grain-fed horses that were larger and heavier than the small, grass-fed animals of the Central Asian nomads, though smaller and lighter than the draft horses bred in later times for hauling heavy loads. Thus agricultural Europe rather than the grassy steppes produced the charges of armored knights that came to dominate the battlefield.

By the eleventh century, the knight, called by different terms in different places, had emerged as the central figure in medieval warfare. He wore an open-faced helmet and a long linen shirt, or hauberk°, studded with small metal disks. A century later, knightly equipment commonly included a visored helmet that covered the head and neck and a hauberk of chain mail.

Each increase in armor for knight and horse entailed a greater financial outlay. Since land was the basis of wealth, a knight needed financial support from land revenues. Accordingly, kings began to reward armed service with grants of land from their own property. Lesser nobles with extensive properties built their own military retinues the same way.

A grant of land in return for a pledge to provide military service was often called a **fief.** At first, kings granted fiefs to their noble followers, known as **vassals,** on a temporary basis. By the tenth century, most fiefs could be inherited as long as the specified military service continued to be provided. Though patterns varied greatly, the association of landholding with military service made the medieval society of western Europe quite different from the contemporary city-based societies of the Islamic world.

Kings and lords might be able to command the service of their vassals for only part of the year. Vassals could hold land from several different lords and owe loyalty to each one. Moreover, the allegiance that a vassal owed to one lord could entail military service to that lord's master in time of need.

A "typical" medieval realm—actual practices varied between and within realms—consisted of lands directly owned by a king or a count and administered by his royal officers. The king's or count's major vassals held and administered other lands, often the greater portion, in return for military service. These vassals, in turn, granted land to their own vassals.

The lord of a manor provided governance and justice, direct royal government being quite limited. The king had few financial resources and seldom exercised legal jurisdiction at a local level. Members of the clergy, as well as the extensive agricultural lands owned by

---

hauberk (HAW-berk)

DIVERSITY AND DOMINANCE

ARCHBISHOP ADALBERT OF HAMBURG AND THE CHRISTIANIZATION OF THE SCANDINAVIANS AND SLAVS

*A*dam of Bremen's History of the Archbishops of Hamburg-Bremen, *consists of four sections. The third is devoted to the Archbishop Adalbert, whose death in 1072 stirred Adam to write. References to classical poets, the lives of saints, and royal documents show that Adam, a churchman, had a solid education and access to many sources. He also drew on living informants, in particular the Danish king Svein Estrithson, a nephew of Canute, king of England from 1015 to 1035, and father-in-law of Gottschalk, a lord over the Slavs mentioned below. The excerpts below illustrate the close connection between political and religious institutions in establishing a structure of domination in lands on the European frontier.*

Archbishop Adalbert held the see for twenty-nine years. He received the pastoral staff from the [Holy Roman] Emperor Henry, the son of Conrad, who was, counting from Caesar Augustus, the ninetieth Roman emperor to sit upon the throne . . . The archiepiscopal pallium [i.e., bishop's cloak] was brought to him . . . by legates from the Pope Benedict . . . [who] was the one hundred and forty-seventh after the Apostles in the succession of Roman pontiffs. His consecration took place in Aachen in the presence of Caesar and of the princes of the realm. Twelve bishops assisted and laid their hands on him . . .

This remarkable man may for all that be extolled with praise of every kind in that he was noble, handsome, wise, eloquent, chaste, temperate. All these qualities he comprised in himself and others besides, such as one is wont to attach to the outer man: that he was rich, that he was successful, that he was glorious, that he was influential. All these things were his in abundance. Moreover, in respect of the mission to the heathen, which is the first duty of the Church at Hamburg, no one so vigorous could ever be found . . . Although he was such in the beginning, he seemed to fail toward the end. Not being well on his guard against any defect in his virtue, the man met with ruin as much through his own negligence as through the driving malice of others . . .

Keen and well trained of mind, he was skillful in many arts. In things divine and human he was possessed of great prudence and was well known for retaining in memory and setting forth with matchless eloquence what he had acquired by hearing or by study. Then, besides, although handsome in physical form, he was a lover of chastity. His generosity was of a kind that made him regard asking favors as unworthy, that made him slow and humble in accepting them but prompt and cheerful in giving, often generously, to those who had not asked. His humility appears doubtful in that he exhibited it only in respect of the servants of God, the poor, and pilgrims, and it went to such lengths that before retiring he often would on bended knees personally wash the feet of thirty or more beggars. To the princes of the world, however, and to his peers he would in no way stoop. Toward them he even broke out at times with a vehemence that at last spared no one he thought outstanding. Some he upbraided for luxury, others for greed, still others for infidelity . . .

On seeing that the basilica [i.e., cathedral] which had lately been started was an immense structure requiring very great resources, he with too precipitate judgment immediately had the city wall, begun by his predecessors, pulled down, as if it were not at all necessary, and ordered its stones built into the temple. Even the beautiful tower, . . . fitted out with seven chambers, was then razed to its foundations . . . Alebrand before him had begun [the cathedral] in the style of the church at Cologne [in western Germany], but he planned to carry it out in the manner of the cathedral at Benevento [in southern Italy] . . .

And because the great prelate saw that his Church and bishopric . . . was troubled again by the iniquitous might of the dukes, he made a supreme effort to restore to that Church its former freedom, that thus neither the duke nor the count nor any person of judicial position would have any right or power in his diocese. But this objective could not be attained without incurring hatred, since the wrath of the princes, rebuked for their wickedness, would be further inflamed. And they say that Duke Bernhard, who held the archbishop under suspicion because of his nobility and wisdom, often said that Adalbert had been stationed in this country like a spy, to betray the weaknesses of the land to the aliens and to Caesar. Consequently the duke declared that as long as he or any of his sons lived, the bishop should not have a happy day in the bishopric . . .

As soon as the metropolitan [i.e., Archbishop Adalbert] had entered upon his episcopate, he sent legates to the kings of the north in the interest of friendship. There were also dispersed throughout all Denmark and Norway and Sweden and to the ends of the earth admonitory letters in which he exhorted the bishops and priests living in those parts . . . fearlessly to forward the conversion of the pagans . . . [Svein, the Danish king who died after invading England in 1013 and left his throne to his son Canute] forgot the heavenly King as things prospered with him and married a blood relative from Sweden. This mightily displeased the lord archbishop, who sent legates to the rash king, rebuking him severely for his sin, and who stated finally that if he did not come to his senses, he would have to be cut off with the sword of excommunication. Beside himself with rage, the king then threatened to ravage and destroy the whole diocese of Hamburg. Unperturbed by these threats, our archbishop, reproving and entreating, remained firm, until at length the Danish tyrant was prevailed upon by letters from the pope to give his cousin a bill of divorce. Still the king would not give ear to the admonitions of the priests. Soon after he had put aside his cousin he took to himself other wives and concubines, and again still others . . .

While these events were taking place there, the most Christian king of the Swedes, James, departed this world, and his brother, Edmund the Bad, succeeded him. He was born of a concubine by Olaf [the Lapp King] and, although he had been baptized, took little heed of our religion. He had with him a certain bishop named Osmund, of irregular status, whom the bishop of the Norwegians, Sigefrid, had once commended to the school at Bremen for instruction. But later he forgot these kindnesses and went to Rome for consecration. When he was rejected there, he wandered about through many parts and so finally secured consecration from a Polish archbishop. Going to Sweden then, he boasted that he had been consecrated archbishop for those parts. But when our archbishop sent his legates to King [Edmund], they found this same vagabond Osmund there, having the cross borne before him after the manner of an archbishop. They also heard that he had by his unsound teaching of our faith corrupted the barbarians, who were still neophytes [i.e., beginners] . . .

In Norway . . . King Harold surpassed all the madness of tyrants in his savage wildness. Many churches were destroyed by that man; many Christians were tortured to death by him. But he was a mighty man and renowned for the victories he had previously won in many wars with barbarians in Greece and in the Scythian regions [i.e., while assisting the Byzantine empress Zoë fight the Seljuk Turks]. After he came into his fatherland, however, he never ceased from warfare;

he was the thunderbolt of the north . . . And so, as he ruled over many nations, he was odious to all on account of his greed and cruelty. He also gave himself up to the magic arts and, wretched man that he was, did not heed the fact that his most saintly brother [i.e., Saint Olaf, one of Harold's predecessors] had eradicated such illusions from the realm and striven even unto death for the adoption of the precepts of Christianity . . .

Across the Elbe [i.e., east of the river Hamburg is on] and in Slavia our affairs were still meeting with great success. For Gottschalk . . . married a daughter of the Danish king and so thoroughly subdued the Slavs that they feared him like a king, offered to pay tribute, and asked for peace with subjection. Under these circumstances our Church at Hamburg enjoyed peace, and Slavia abounded in priests and churches . . . Gottschalk is said to have been inflamed with such ardent zeal for the faith that, forgetting his station, he frequently made discourse in church in exhortation of the people—in church because he wished to make clearer in the Slavic speech what was abstrusely preached by the bishops or priests. Countless was the number of those who were converted every day; so much so that he sent into every province for priests. In the several cities were then also founded monasteries for holy men who lived according to canonical rule . . .

I have also heard the most veracious king of the Danes say . . . that the Slavic peoples without doubt could easily have been converted to Christianity long ago but for the avarice of the Saxons. "They are," he said, "more intent on the payment of tribute than on the conversion of the heathen." Nor do these wretched people realize with what great danger they will have to atone for their cupidity, they who through their avarice in the first place threw Christianity in Slavia into disorder, in the second place have by their cruelty forced their subjects to rebel, and who now by their desire only for money hold in contempt the salvation of a people who wish to believe" . . .

QUESTIONS FOR ANALYSIS

1. Using this work as a historical source, what would you consider the main concerns of the church in northern Germany?

2. How does Adam distinguish Christians from pagans in his descriptive passages?

3. What appears to be the relationship between ecclesiastical lords like the archbishop and the secular kings and dukes?

Source: Excerpts from *History of the Archbishops of Hamburg-Bremen*, tr. Francis J. Tschan (New York: Columbia University Press, 1959 [new ed. 2002]), 114–133. Reprinted with the permission of the publisher.

Noblewoman Directing Construction of a Church   This picture of Berthe, wife of Girat de Rouissillion, acting as mistress of the works comes from a tenth-century manuscript that shows a scene from the ninth century. Wheelbarrows rarely appear in medieval building scenes.   (Copyright Brussels, Royal Library of Belgium)

monasteries and nunneries, fell under the jurisdiction of the church, which further limited the reach and authority of the monarch.

Noblewomen became enmeshed in this tangle of obligations as heiresses and as candidates for marriage. A man who married the widow or daughter of a lord with no sons could gain control of that lord's property. Marriage alliances affected entire kingdoms. Noble daughters and sons had little say in marriage matters; issues of land, power, and military service took precedence. Noblemen guarded the women in their families as closely as their other valuables.

Nevertheless, women could own land. A noblewoman sometimes administered her husband's estates when he was away at war. Nonnoble women usually worked alongside their menfolk, performing agricultural tasks such as raking and stacking hay, shearing sheep, and picking vegetables. As artisans, women spun, wove, and sewed clothing. The Bayeux° Tapestry, a piece of embroidery 230 feet (70 meters) long and 20 inches (51 centimeters) wide depicting William the Conqueror's

Bayeux (bay-YUH)

invasion of England in 1066, was designed and executed entirely by women, though historians do not agree on who those women were.

THE WESTERN CHURCH

Just as the Christian populations in eastern Europe followed the religious guidance of the patriarch of Constantinople appointed by the Byzantine emperor, so the pope commanded similar authority over church affairs in western Europe. And just as missionaries in the east spread Christianity among the Slavs, so missionaries in the west added territory to Christendom with forays into the British Isles and the lands of the Germans. Throughout the period covered by this chapter Christian society was emerging and changing in both areas.

In the west Roman nobles lost control of the **papacy**—the office of the pope—and it became a more powerful international office after the tenth century. Councils of bishops—which normally set rules, called canons, to regulate the priests and laypeople (men and women who were not members of the clergy) under their jurisdiction—became increasingly responsive to papal direction.

Nevertheless, regional disagreements over church regulations, shortages of educated and trained clergy, difficult communications, political disorder, and the general insecurity of the period posed formidable obstacles to unifying church standards and practices. Clerics in some parts of western Europe were still issuing prohibitions against the worship of rivers, trees, and mountains as late as the eleventh century. Church problems included lingering polytheism, lax enforcement of prohibitions against marriage of clergy, nepotism (giving preferment to one's close kin), and simony (selling ecclesiastical appointments, often to people who were not members of the clergy). The persistence of the papacy in asserting its legal jurisdiction over clergy, combating polytheism and heretical beliefs, and calling on secular rulers to recognize the pope's authority, including unpopular rulings like a ban on first-cousin marriage, constituted a rare force for unity and order in a time of disunity and chaos.

Politics and the Church

In politically fragmented western Europe, the pope needed allies. Like his son, Charlemagne's father Pepin was a strong supporter of the papacy. The relationship between kings and popes was tense, however, since both thought of themselves as ultimate authorities. In 962 the pope crowned the first "Holy Roman Emperor" (Charlemagne never held this full title). This designation of a secular political authority as the guardian of general Christian interests proved more apparent then real. Essentially a loose confederation of German princes who named one of their own to the highest office, the **Holy Roman Empire** had little influence west of the Rhine River.

Although the pope crowned the early Holy Roman emperors, this did not signify political superiority. The law of the church (known as canon law because each law was called a canon) gave the pope exclusive legal jurisdiction over all clergy and church property wherever located. But bishops who held land as vassals owed military support or other services and dues to kings and princes. The secular rulers argued that they should have the power to appoint those bishops because that was the only way to guarantee fulfillment of their duties as vassals. The popes disagreed.

In the eleventh century, this conflict over the control of ecclesiastical appointments came to a head.

Hildebrand°, an Italian monk, capped a career of reorganizing church finances when the cardinals (a group of senior bishops) meeting in Rome selected him to be Pope Gregory VII in 1073. His personal notion of the papacy (preserved among his letters) represented an extreme position, stating among other claims, that

§ The pope can be judged by no one;
§ The Roman church has never erred and never will err till the end of time;
§ The pope alone can depose and restore bishops;
§ He alone can call general councils and authorize canon law;
§ He can depose emperors;
§ He can absolve subjects from their allegiance;
§ All princes should kiss his feet.[5]

Such claims antagonized lords and monarchs, who had become accustomed to *investing*—that is, conferring a ring and a staff as symbols of authority on bishops and abbots in their domains. Historians apply the term **investiture controversy** to the medieval struggle between the church and the lay lords to control ecclesiastical appointments; the term also refers to the broader conflict of popes versus emperors and kings. When Holy Roman Emperor Henry IV defied Gregory's reforms, Gregory excommunicated him in 1076, thereby cutting him off from church rituals. Stung by the resulting decline in his influence, Henry stood barefoot in the snow for three days outside a castle in northern Italy waiting for Gregory, a guest there, to receive him. Henry's formal act of penance induced Gregory to forgive him and restore him to the church; but the reconciliation, an apparent victory for the pope, did not last. In 1078 Gregory declared Henry deposed. The emperor then forced Gregory to flee from Rome to Salerno, where he died two years later.

The struggle between the popes and the emperors continued until 1122, when a compromise was reached at Worms, a town in Germany. In the Concordat of Worms, Emperor Henry V renounced his right to choose bishops and abbots or bestow spiritual symbols upon them. In return, Pope Calixtus II permitted the emperor to invest papally appointed bishops and abbots with any lay rights or obligations before their spiritual consecration. Such compromises did not fully solve the problem, but they reduced tensions between the two sides.

Assertions of royal authority triggered other conflicts as well. Though barely twenty when he became king of England in 1154, Henry II, a great-grandson of William the Conqueror, instituted reforms designed to strengthen the power of the Crown and weaken the

---

Hildebrand (HILL-de-brand)

nobility. He appointed traveling justices to enforce his laws. He made juries, a holdover from traditional Germanic law, into powerful legal instruments. He established the principle that criminal acts violated the "king's peace" and should be tried and punished in accordance with charges brought by the Crown instead of in response to charges brought by victims.

Henry had a harder time controlling the church. His closest friend and chancellor, or chief administrator, Thomas à Becket (ca. 1118–1170), lived the grand and luxurious life of a courtier. In 1162 Henry persuaded Becket to become a priest and assume the position of archbishop of Canterbury, the highest church office in England. Becket agreed but cautioned that from then on he would act solely in the interest of the church if it came into conflict with the Crown. When Henry sought to try clerics accused of crimes in royal instead of ecclesiastical courts, Archbishop Thomas, now leading an austere and pious life, resisted.

In 1170 four of Henry's knights, knowing that the king desired Becket's death, murdered the archbishop in Canterbury Cathedral. Their crime backfired, and an outpouring of sympathy caused Canterbury to become a major pilgrimage center. In 1173 the pope declared the martyred Becket a saint. Henry allowed himself to be publicly whipped twice in penance for the crime, but his authority had been badly damaged.

Henry II's conflict with Thomas à Becket, like the Concordat of Worms, yielded no clear victor. The problem of competing legal traditions made political life in western Europe more complicated than in Byzantium or the lands of Islam (see Chapter 8). Feudal law, rooted in Germanic custom, gave supreme power to the king. Canon law, based on Roman precedent, visualized a single hierarchical legal institution with jurisdiction over all of Western Christendom. In the eleventh century Roman civil law, contained in the *Corpus Juris Civilis* (see Chapter 5), added a third tradition.

Monasticism

Monasticism featured prominently in the religious life of almost all medieval Christian lands. The origins of group monasticism lay in the eastern lands of the Roman Empire. Pre-Christian practices such as celibacy, continual devotion to prayer, and living apart from society (alone or in small groups) came together in Christian form in Egypt.

The most important form of monasticism in western Europe, however, involved groups of monks or nuns living together in organized communities. The person most responsible for introducing this originally Egyp-

Illuminated Manuscript from Monastic Library This page from the Book of Kells, written around 800 in Ireland, contains the Greek letters chi and rho, or CR, a monogram for Jesus Christ. The intricate interwoven forms that fill the background derive from pagan design traditions that featured intertangled dragons, snakes, and other beasts. (The Board of Trinity College, Dublin)

tian practice in the Latin west was Benedict of Nursia (ca. 480–547) in Italy. Benedict began his pious career as a hermit in a cave but eventually organized several monasteries, each headed by an abbot. In the seventh century monasteries based on his model spread far beyond Italy. The Rule Benedict wrote to govern the monks' behavior envisions a balanced life of devotion and work, along with obligations of celibacy, poverty, and obedience to the abbot. Those who lived by this or other monastic rules became *regular clergy,* in contrast to *secular clergy,* priests who lived in society instead of in seclusion and did not follow a formal code of regulations. The Rule of Benedict was the starting point for most forms of western European monastic life and remains in force today in Benedictine monasteries.

Though monks and nuns, women who lived by monastic rules in convents, made up a small percentage of the total population, their secluded way of life reinforced the separation of religious affairs from ordinary politics and economics. Monasteries followed Jesus' axiom to "render unto Caesar what is Caesar's and unto God what is God's" better than the many town-based bishops who behaved like lords.

Monasteries preserved literacy and learning in the early medieval period, although some rulers, like Charlemagne, encouraged scholarship at court. Many illiterate lay nobles interested themselves only in warfare and hunting. Monks (but seldom nuns) saw copying manuscripts and even writing books as a religious calling. Monastic scribes preserved many ancient Latin works that would otherwise have disappeared. The survival of Greek works depended more on Byzantine and Muslim scribes in the east.

Monasteries and convents served other functions as well (see Environment and Technology: Cathedral Organs). A few planted Christianity in new lands, as Irish monks did in parts of Germany. Most serviced the needs of travelers, organized agricultural production on their lands, and took in infants abandoned by their parents. Convents provided refuge for widows and other women who lacked male protection in the harsh medieval world or who desired a spiritual life. These religious houses presented problems of oversight to the church, however. A bishop might have authority over an abbot or abbess (head of a convent), but he could not exercise constant vigilance over what went on behind monastery walls.

The failure of some abbots to maintain monastic discipline led to the growth of a reform movement centered on the Benedictine abbey of Cluny° in eastern France. Founded in 910 by William the Pious, the first duke of Aquitaine, who completely freed it of lay authority, Cluny gained similar freedom from the local bishop a century later. Its abbots pursued a vigorous campaign, eventually in alliance with reforming popes like Gregory VII, to improve monastic discipline and administration. A magnificent new abbey church symbolized Cluny's claims to eminence. With later additions, it became the largest church in the world.

At the peak of Cluny's influence, nearly a thousand Benedictine abbeys and priories (lower-level monastic houses) in various countries accepted the authority of its abbot. The Benedictine Rule had presumed that each monastery would be independent; the Cluniac reformers stipulated that every abbot and every prior (head of a priory) be appointed by the abbot of Cluny and have

personal experience of the religious life of Cluny. Monastic reform gained new impetus in the second half of the twelfth century with the rapid rise of the Cistercian order, which emphasized a life of asceticism and poverty. These movements set the pattern for the monasteries, cathedral clergy, and preaching friars that would dominate ecclesiastical life in the thirteenth century.

KIEVAN RUSSIA, 900–1200

Though Latin and Orthodox Christendom followed different paths in later centuries, which had a more promising future was not apparent in 900. The Poles and other Slavic peoples living in the north eventually accepted the Christianity of Rome as taught by German priests and missionaries (see Diversity and Dominance: Archbishop Adalbert of Hamburg and the Christianization of Scandinavians and Slavs). The Serbs and other southern Slavs took their faith from Constantinople.

The conversion of Kievan Russia, farther to the east, shows how economics, politics, and religious life were closely intertwined. The choice of orthodoxy over Catholicism had important consequences for later European history.

The Rise of the Kievan State

The territory between the Black and Caspian Seas in the south and the Baltic and White Seas in the north divides into a series of east-west zones. Frozen tundra in the far north gives way to a cold forest zone, then to a more temperate forest, then to a mix of forest and steppe grasslands, and finally to grassland only. Several navigable rivers, including the Volga, the Dnieper°, and the Don, run from north to south across these zones.

Early historical sources reflect repeated linguistic and territorial changes, seemingly under pressure from poorly understood population migrations. Most of the Germanic peoples, along with some Iranian and west Slavic peoples, migrated into eastern Europe from Ukraine and Russia in Roman times. The peoples who remained behind spoke eastern Slavic languages, except in the far north and south: Finns and related peoples lived in the former region, Turkic-speakers in the latter.

Forest dwellers, farmers, and steppe nomads complemented each other economically. Nomads traded animals for the farmers' grain; and honey, wax, and furs from

---

Cluny (KLOO-nee)

Dnieper (d-NYEP-er)

Cathedral of Saint Dmitry in Vladimir Built between 1193 and 1197, this Russian Orthodox cathedral shows Byzantine influence. The three-arch façade, small dome, and symmetrical Greek-cross floor plan strongly resemble features of the Byzantine church shown on page 222.   (Sovfoto)

the forest became important exchange items. Traders could travel east and west by steppe caravan (see Chapters 7 and 12), or they could use boats on the rivers to move north and south.

Hoards containing thousands of Byzantine and Islamic coins buried in Poland and on islands in the Baltic Sea where fairs were held attest to the trading activity of Varangians (Swedish Vikings) who sailed across the Baltic and down Russia's rivers. They exchanged forest products and slaves for manufactured goods and coins, which they may have used as jewelry rather than as money, at markets controlled by the Khazar Turks. The powerful Khazar kingdom centered around the mouth of the Volga River.

Historians debate the early meaning of the word *Rus* (from which *Russia* is derived), but at some point it came to refer to Slavic-speaking peoples ruled by Varangians. Unlike western European lords, the Varangian princes and their *druzhina* (military retainers) lived in cities, while the Slavs farmed. The princes occupied themselves with trade and fending off enemies. The Rus of the city of Kiev° controlled trade on the Dnieper River and dealt more with Byzantium than with the Muslim world because the Dnieper flows into the Black Sea. The Rus of Novgorod° played the same role on the Volga. The semi-

Kiev (KEE-yev)   **Novgorod** (NOHV-goh-rod)

ENVIRONMENT + TECHNOLOGY

Cathedral Organs

The Christian church directly encouraged musical development. Pope Gregory I (d. 604) is traditionally credited with making a standard collection of chants then in use. Later, a special school in Rome trained choir directors who were sent out to teach the chants in cathedrals and monasteries. Organ accompaniment, initially in the form of long, sustained bass notes, came into common use by the end of the seventh century. The organ worked by directing a current of air to a set of pipes of different lengths that could be opened or closed at one end. Each pipe sounded a tone as long as the air was flowing past its open end.

A monk named Wulstan (d. 963) described the organ installed in Winchester Cathedral in England:

> Twice six bellows above are ranged in a row, and fourteen lie below. These, by alternate blasts, supply an immense quantity of wind, and are worked by 70 strong men, laboring with their arms, covered with perspiration, each inciting his companions to drive the wind up with all his strength, that the full-bosomed box may speak with its 400 pipes, which the hand of the organist governs. Some when closed he opens, others when open he closes, as the individual nature of the varied sound requires. Two brethren of concordant spirit sit at the instrument . . . Like thunder their tones batter the ear, so that it may receive no sound but that alone. To such an amount does it reverberate, echoing in every direction, that everyone stops with his hand his gaping ears, being in no wise able to draw near and bear the sound, which so many combinations produce.

A century later huge levers or keys came into use for opening and closing the pipes. Each was several inches in width, one or two inches thick, and up to three feet in length. So much muscle was required to operate the keys that organists were called "organ pounders." Over time, organs became smaller and capable of playing magnificent music.

Cathedral Organ Note the unhappy faces on the men assigned the dreary and noisy job of pumping the bellows for an organ. Note also the ping-pong paddle shaped keys that are more appropriate to pounding with a fist than pressing with a finger. (St. John's College Library, Cambridge Manuscript, B.18)

Source: Alexander Russell, "Organ," *The International Cyclopedia of Music and Musicians*, ed. Oscar Thompson (New York: Dodd, Mead, 1943), 1315.

legendary account of the Kievan Rus conversion to Christianity must be seen against this background.

In 980 Vladimir° I, a ruler of Novgorod who had fallen from power, returned from exile to Kiev with a band of Varangians and made himself the grand prince of Kievan Russia (see Map 9.2). Though his grandmother Olga had been a Christian, Vladimir built a temple on Kiev's heights and placed there the statues of the six gods his Slavic subjects worshipped. The earliest Russian chronicle reports that Vladimir and his advisers decided against Islam as the official religion because of its ban on alcohol, rejected Judaism (the religion to which the Khazars had converted) because they thought that a truly powerful god would not have let the ancient Jewish kingdom be destroyed, and

Vladimir (VLAD-ih-mir)

even spoke with German emissaries advocating Latin Christianity. Why Vladimir chose Orthodox Christianity over the Latin version is not precisely known. The magnificence of Constantinople seems to have been a consideration. After visiting Byzantine churches, his agents reported: "We knew not whether we were in heaven or on earth, for on earth there is no such splendor of [sic] such beauty, and we are at a loss how to describe it. We know only that God dwells there among men, and their service is finer than the ceremonies of other nations."[6]

After choosing a reluctant bride from the Byzantine imperial family, Vladimir converted to Orthodox Christianity, probably in 988, and opened his lands to Orthodox clerics and missionaries. The patriarch of Constantinople appointed a metropolitan (chief bishop) at Kiev to govern ecclesiastical affairs. Churches arose in Kiev, one of them on the ruins of Vladimir's earlier hilltop temple. Writing was introduced, using the Cyrillic alphabet devised earlier for the western Slavs. This extension of Orthodox Christendom northward provided a barrier against the eastward expansion of Latin Christianity. Kiev became firmly oriented toward trade with Byzantium and turned its back on the Muslim world, though the Volga trade continued through Novgorod.

Struggles within the ruling family and with other enemies, most notably the steppe peoples of the south, marked the later political history of Kievan Russia. But down to the time of the Mongols in the thirteenth century (see Chapter 12), the state remained and served as an instrument for the Christianization of the eastern Slavs.

Society and Culture

In Kievan Russia political power derived from trade rather than from landholding, so the manorial agricultural system of western Europe never developed. Farmers practiced shifting cultivation of their own lands. They would burn a section of forest, then lightly scratch the ash-strewn surface with a plow. When fertility waned, they would move to another section of forest. Poor land and a short growing season in the most northerly latitudes made food scarce. Living on their own estates, the druzhina evolved from infantry into cavalry and focused their efforts more on horse breeding than on agriculture.

Large cities like Kiev and Novgorod may have reached thirty thousand or fifty thousand people—roughly the size of contemporary London or Paris, but far smaller than Constantinople or major Muslim metropolises like Baghdad and Nishapur. Many cities amounted to little more than fortified trading posts. Yet they served as centers for the development of crafts, some, such as

Map 9.2   Kievan Russia and the Byzantine Empire in the Eleventh Century   By the mid-eleventh century, the princes of Kievan Russia had brought all the eastern Slavs under their rule. The loss of Egypt, Syria, and Tunisia to Arab invaders in the seventh to eighth century had turned Byzantium from a far-flung empire into a fairly compact state. From then on the Byzantine rulers looked to the Balkans and Kievan Russia as the primary arena for extending their political and religious influence.

glassmaking, based on skills imported from Byzantium. Artisans enjoyed higher status in society than peasant farmers. Construction relied on wood from the forests, although Christianity brought the building of stone cathedrals and churches on the Byzantine model.

Christianity penetrated the general population slowly. Several polytheist uprisings occurred in the eleventh century, particularly in times of famine. Passive resistance led some groups to reject Christian burial and persist in cremating the dead and keeping the bones of the deceased in urns. Women continued to use polytheist designs on their clothing and bracelets, and as late as the twelfth century they were still turning to polytheist priests for charms to cure sick children. Traditional Slavic marriage practices involving casual and polygamous relations particularly scandalized the clergy.

Christianity eventually triumphed, and its success led to increasing church engagement in political and economic affairs. In the twelfth century, Christian clergy became involved in government administration, some of them collecting fees and taxes related to trade. Direct and indirect revenue from trade provided the rulers with the money they needed to pay their soldiers. The rule of law also spread as Kievan Russia experienced its peak of culture and prosperity in the century before the Mongol invasion of 1237.

WESTERN EUROPE REVIVES, 1000–1200

Between 1000 and 1200 western Europe slowly emerged from nearly seven centuries of subsistence economy—in which most people who worked on the land could meet only their basic needs for food, clothing, and shelter. Population and agricultural production climbed, and a growing food surplus found its way to town markets, speeding the return of a money-based economy and providing support for larger numbers of craftspeople, construction workers, and traders.

Historians have attributed western Europe's revival to population growth spurred by new technologies and to the appearance in Italy and Flanders, on the coast of the North Sea, of self-governing cities devoted primarily to seaborne trade. For monarchs, the changes facilitated improvements in central administration, greater control over vassals, and consolidation of realms on the way to becoming stronger kingdoms.

The Role of Technology

A lack of concrete evidence confirming the spread of technological innovations frustrates efforts to relate the exact course of Europe's revival to technological change. Nevertheless, most historians agree that technology played a significant role in the near doubling of the population of western Europe between 1000 and 1200. The population of England seems to have risen from 1.1 million in 1086 to 1.9 million in 1200, and the population of the territory of modern France seems to have risen from 5.2 million to 9.2 million over the same period.

Examples that illustrate the difficulty of drawing historical conclusions from scattered evidence of technological change were a new type of plow and the use of efficient draft harnesses for pulling wagons. The Roman plow, which farmers in southern Europe and Byzantium continued to use, scratched shallow grooves, as was appropriate for loose, dry Mediterranean soils. The new plow cut deep into the soil with a knife-like blade, while a curved board mounted behind the blade lifted the cut layer and turned it over. This made it possible to farm the heavy, wet clays of the northern river valleys. Pulling the new plow took more energy, which could mean harnessing several teams of oxen or horses.

Horses plowed faster than oxen but were more delicate. Iron horseshoes, which were widely adopted in this period, helped protect their feet, but like the plow itself, they added to the farmer's expenses. Roman horse harnesses, inefficiently modeled on the yoke used for oxen, put such pressure on the animal's neck that a horse pulling a heavy load risked strangulation. A mystery surrounds the adoption of more efficient designs. The **horse collar,** which moves the point of traction from the animal's throat to its shoulders, first appeared around 800 in a miniature painting, and it is shown clearly as a harness for plow horses in the Bayeux Tapestry, embroidered after 1066. The breast-strap harness, which is not as well adapted for the heaviest work but was preferred in southern Europe, seems to have appeared around 500. In both cases, linguists have tried to trace key technical terms to Chinese or Turko-Mongol words and have argued for technological diffusion across Eurasia. Yet third-century Roman farmers in Tunisia and Libya used both types of harness to hitch horses and camels to plows and carts. This technology, which is still employed in Tunisia, appears clearly on Roman bas-reliefs and lamps; but there is no more evidence of its movement northward into Europe than there is of similar harnessing moving across Asia. Thus the question of where efficient harnessing came from and whether it began in 500 or in 800, or was known even earlier but not extensively used, cannot be easily resolved.

Hinging on this problem is the question of when and why landowners in northern Europe began to use teams of horses to pull plows through moist, fertile river-valley soils that were too heavy for teams of oxen. Stronger and faster than oxen, horses increased productivity by reducing the time needed for plowing, but they cost more to feed and equip. Thus, while agricultural surpluses did grow and better plowing did play a role in this growth, areas that continued to use oxen and even old-style plows seem to have shared in the general population growth of the period.

Cities and the Rebirth of Trade

Independent cities governed and defended by communes appeared first in Italy and Flanders and then elsewhere. Communes were groups of leading citizens who banded together to defend their cities and demand the privilege of self-government from their lay or ecclesiastical lord. Lords who granted such privileges benefited from the commune's economic dynamism. Lacking extensive farmlands, these cities turned to manufacturing and trade, which they encouraged through the laws they enacted. Laws making serfs free once they came into the city, for example, attracted many workers from the countryside. Cities in Italy that had shrunk within walls built by the Romans now pressed against those walls, forcing the construction of new ones. Pisa built a new wall in 1000 and expanded it in 1156. Other twelfth-century cities that built new walls include Florence, Brescia°, Pavia, and Siena°.

Settlers on a group of islands at the northern end of the Adriatic Sea that had been largely uninhabited in Roman times organized themselves into the city of Venice. In the eleventh century it became the dominant sea power in the Adriatic. Venice competed with Pisa and Genoa, its rivals on the western side of Italy, for leadership in the trade with Muslim ports in North Africa and the eastern Mediterranean. A somewhat later merchant's

---

Brescia (BREH-shee-uh)   **Siena** (see-EN-uh)

Vertical Two-Beam Loom These women weavers set up their loom out-of-doors. The vertical strands are the warp threads around which the weft is interwoven. The pole across the bottom of the loom holds the warp threads taut. The kneeling weaver holds a beater to compact the weft at the loom's bottom. In Europe, horizontal looms were more common and paved the way for the mechanization of weaving. (Courtesy, Master and Fellows of Trinity College, Cambridge, Ms. R17.I.f.260 [detail])

list mentions trade in some three thousand "spices" (including dyestuffs, textile fibers, and raw materials), some of them products of Muslim lands and some coming via the Silk Road or the Indian Ocean trading system (see Chapter 7). Among them were eleven types of alum (for dyeing), eleven types of wax, eight types of cotton, four types of indigo, five types of ginger, four types of paper, and fifteen types of sugar, along with cloves, caraway, tamarind, and fresh oranges. By the time of the Crusades (see below), maritime commerce throughout the Mediterranean had come to depend heavily on ships from Genoa, Venice, and Pisa.

Ghent, Bruges°, and Ypres° in Flanders rivaled the Italian cities in prosperity, trade, and industry. Enjoying comparable independence based on privileges granted by the counts of Flanders, these cities centralized the fishing and wool trades of the North Sea region. Around 1200 raw wool from England began to be woven into woolen cloth for a very large market.

More abundant coinage also signaled the upturn in economic activity. In the ninth and tenth centuries most gold coins had come from Muslim lands and the Byzantine Empire. Being worth too much for most trading purposes, they seldom reached Germany, France, and England. The widely imitated Carolingian silver penny sufficed. With the economic revival of the twelfth century, minting of silver coins began in Scandinavia,

Poland, and other outlying regions. In the following century the reinvigoration of Mediterranean trade made possible a new and abundant gold coinage.

THE CRUSADES, 1095–1204

Western European revival coincided with and contributed to the **Crusades,** a series of religiously inspired Christian military campaigns against Muslims in the eastern Mediterranean that dominated the politics of Europe from 1095 to 1204 (see Chapter 8 and Map 9.3). Four great expeditions, the last redirected against the Byzantines and resulting in the Latin capture of Constantinople, constituted the region's largest military undertakings since the fall of Rome. The cultural impact of the Crusades upon western Europe resulted in noble courts and burgeoning cities consuming more goods from the east. This set the stage for the later adoption of ideas, artistic styles, and industrial processes from Byzantium and the lands of Islam.

The Roots of the Crusades

Several social and economic currents of the eleventh century contributed to the Crusades. First, reforming leaders of the Latin Church, seeking to soften the warlike tone of society, popularized the Truce of God. This movement

Bruges (broozh) **Ypres** (EEP-r)

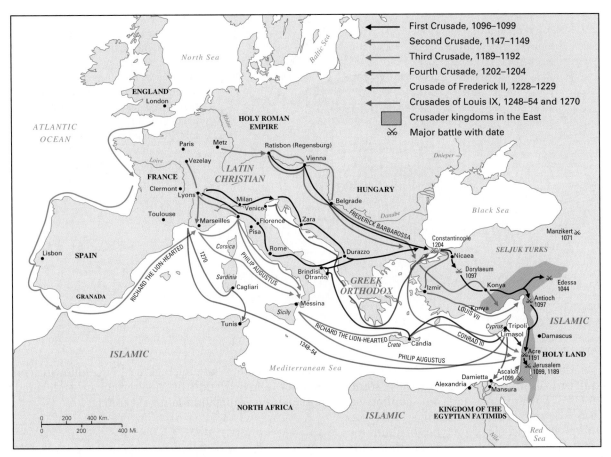

Map 9.3 The Crusades The first two Crusades proceeded overland through Byzantine territory. The Third Crusade included contingents under the French and English kings, Philip Augustus and Richard the Lion-Hearted, that traveled by sea, and a contingent under the Holy Roman Emperor Frederick Barbarossa that took the overland route. Frederick died in southern Anatolia. Later Crusades were mostly seaborne, with Sicily, Crete, and Cyprus playing important roles.

limited fighting between Christian lords by specifying times of truce, such as during Lent (the forty days before Easter) and on Sundays. Many knights welcomed a religiously approved alternative to fighting other Christians. Second, ambitious rulers, like the Norman chieftains who invaded England and Sicily, were looking for new lands to conquer. Nobles, particularly younger sons in areas where the oldest son inherited everything, were hungry for land and titles to maintain their status. Third, Italian merchants wanted to increase trade in the eastern Mediterranean and acquire trading posts in Muslim territory. However, without the rivalry between popes and kings already discussed, and without the desire of the church to demonstrate political authority over western Christendom, the Crusades might never have occurred.

Several factors focused attention on the Holy Land, which had been under Muslim rule for four centuries. **Pilgrimages** played an important role in European religious life. In western Europe, pilgrims traveled under royal protection, a few actually being tramps, thieves, beggars, peddlers, and merchants for whom pilgrimage was a safe way of traveling. Genuinely pious pilgrims often journeyed to visit the old churches and sacred relics preserved in Rome or Constantinople. The most intrepid went to Jerusalem, Antioch, and other cities under Muslim control to fulfill a vow or to atone for a sin.

Knights who followed a popular pilgrimage route across northern Spain to pray at the shrine of Santiago de Compostela learned of the expanding efforts of Christian kings to dislodge the Muslims. The Umayyad

Caliphate in al-Andalus had broken up in the eleventh century, leaving its smaller successor states prey to Christian attacks from the north (see Chapter 8). This was the beginning of a movement of reconquest that culminated in 1492 with the surrender of the last Muslim kingdom. The word *crusade*, taken from Latin *crux* for "cross," was first used in Spain. Stories also circulated of the war conducted by seafaring Normans against the Muslims in Sicily, whom they finally defeated in the 1090s after thirty years of fighting.

The tales of pilgrims returning from Palestine further induced both churchmen and nobles to consider the Muslims a proper target for Christian militancy. Muslim rulers, who had controlled Jerusalem, Antioch, and Alexandria since the seventh century, generally tolerated and protected Christian pilgrims. But after 1071, when a Seljuk army defeated the Byzantine emperor at the Battle of Manzikert (see Chapter 8), Turkish nomads spread throughout the region, and security along the pilgrimage route through Anatolia, already none too good, deteriorated further. The decline of Byzantine power threatened ancient centers of Christianity, such as Ephesus in Anatolia, previously under imperial control.

Despite the theological differences between the Orthodox and Roman churches, the Byzantine emperor Alexius Comnenus asked the pope and western European rulers to help him confront the Muslim threat and reconquer what the Christians termed the Holy Land, the early centers of Christianity in Palestine and Syria. Pope Urban II responded at the Council of Clermont in 1095. He addressed a huge crowd of people gathered in a field and called on them, as Christians, to stop fighting one another and go to the Holy Land to fight Muslims.

"God wills it!" exclaimed voices in the crowd. People cut cloth into crosses and sewed them on their shirts to symbolize their willingness to march on Jerusalem. Thus began the holy war now known as the "First Crusade." People at the time more often used the word *peregrinatio,* "pilgrimage." Urban promised to free crusaders who had committed sins from their normal penance, or acts of atonement, the usual reward for peaceful pilgrims to Jerusalem.

The First Crusade captured Jerusalem in 1099 and established four crusader principalities, the most important being the Latin Kingdom of Jerusalem. The next two expeditions strove with diminishing success to protect these gains. Muslim forces retook Jerusalem in 1187. By the time of the Fourth Crusade in 1204, the original religious ardor had so diminished that the commanders agreed, at the urging of the Venetians, to sack Constantinople first to help pay the cost of transporting the army by ship.

Armored Knights in Battle   This painting from around 1135 shows the armament of knights at the time of the Crusades. Chain mail, a helmet, and a shield carried on the left side protect the rider. The lance carried underarm and the sword are the primary weapons. Notice that riders about to make contact with lances have their legs straight and braced in the stirrups, while riders with swords and in flight have bent legs.   (Pierpont Morgan Library/ Art Resource, NY)

The Impact of the Crusades

Exposure to Muslim culture in Spain, Sicily, and the crusader principalities established in the Holy Land made many Europeans aware of things lacking in their own lives. Borrowings from Muslim society occurred gradually and are not always easy to date, but Europeans eventually learned how to manufacture pasta, paper, refined sugar, colored glass, and many other items that had formerly been imported. Arabic translations of and commentaries on Greek philosophical and scientific works, and equally important original works by Arabs and Iranians, provided a vital stimulus to European thought.

Some works were brought directly into the Latin world through the conquests of Sicily, parts of Spain and the Holy Land, and Constantinople (for Greek texts). Others were rendered into Latin by translators who worked in parts of Spain that continued under Muslim rule. Generations passed before all these works were studied and understood, but they eventually transformed the intellectual world of the western Europeans, who previously had had little familiarity with Greek writings. The works of Aristotle and the Muslim commentaries on them were of particular importance to theologians, but Muslim writers like Avicenna (980–1037) were of parallel importance in medicine.

Changes affecting the lifestyle of the nobles took place more quickly. Eleanor of Aquitaine (1122?–1204), one of the most influential women of the crusading era, accompanied her husband, King Louis VII of France, on the Second Crusade (1147–1149). The court life of her uncle Raymond, ruler of the crusader principality of Antioch, particularly appealed to her. After her return to France, a lack of male offspring led to an annulment of her marriage with Louis, and she married Henry of Anjou in 1151. He inherited the throne of England as Henry II three years later. Eleanor's sons Richard Lion-Heart, famed in romance as the chivalrous foe of Saladin during the Third Crusade (1189–1192), and John rebelled against their father but eventually succeeded him as kings of England.

In Aquitaine, a powerful duchy in southern France, Eleanor maintained her own court for a time. The poet-singers called troubadours who enjoyed her favor made her court a center for new music based on the idea of "courtly love," an idealization of feminine beauty and grace that influenced later European ideas of romance. Thousands of troubadour melodies survive in manuscripts, and some show the influence of the poetry styles then current in Muslim Spain. The favorite troubadour instrument, moreover, was the lute, a guitar-like instrument with a bulging shape whose design and name (Arabic *al-ud*) come from Muslim Spain. In centuries to come the lute would become the mainstay of Renaissance music in Italy.

CONCLUSION

The legacy of Roman rule affected eastern and western Europe in different ways. Byzantium inherited the grandeur, pomp, and legal supremacy of the imperial office and merged it with leadership of the Christian church. Byzantium guarded its shrinking frontiers against foreign invasion but gradually contracted around Constantinople, its imperial capital, as more and more territory was lost. By contrast, no Roman core survived in the west. The Germanic peoples overwhelmed the legions guarding the frontiers and established kingdoms based on their own traditions. The law of the king and the law of the church did not echo each other. Yet memories of Roman grandeur and territorial unity resurfaced with the idea of a Holy Roman Empire, however unworkable that empire proved to be.

The competition between the Orthodox and Catholic forms of Christianity complicated the role of religion in the emergence of medieval European society and culture. The Byzantine Empire, constructed on a Roman political and legal heritage that had largely passed away in the west, was generally more prosperous than the Germanic kingdoms of western Europe, and its arts and culture were initially more sophisticated. Furthermore, Byzantine society became deeply Christian well before a comparable degree of Christianization had been reached in western Europe. Yet despite their success in transmitting their version of Christianity and imperial rule to Kievan Russia, and in the process erecting a barrier between the Orthodox Russians and the Catholic Slavs to their west, the Byzantines failed to demonstrate the dynamism and ferment that characterized both the Europeans to their west and the Muslims to their south. Byzantine armies played only a supporting role in the Crusades, and the emperors lost their capital and their power, at least temporarily, to western crusaders in 1204.

Technology and commerce deepened the political and religious gulf between the two Christian zones. Changes in military techniques in western Europe increased battlefield effectiveness, while new agricultural technologies led to population increases that revitalized urban life and contributed to the crusading movement by making the nobility hunger for new lands. At the same time, the need to import food for growing urban populations contributed to the growth of maritime commerce in the Mediterranean and North Seas. Culture and manufacturing benefited greatly from the increased pace of communication and exchange. Lacking parallel developments of a similar scale, the Byzantine Empire steadily lost the dynamism of its early centuries and by the end of the period had clearly fallen behind western Europe in prosperity and cultural innovation.

■ Key Terms

Charlemagne

medieval

Byzantine Empire

Kievan Russia

schism

manor

serf

fief

vassal

papacy

Holy Roman Empire

investiture controversy

monasticism

horse collar

Crusades

pilgrimage

■ Suggested Reading

Standard Byzantine histories include Dimitri Obolensky, *The Byzantine Commonwealth* (1971), and Warren Treadgold, *A History of Byzantine State and Society* (1997). Cyril Mango's *Byzantium: The Empire of New Rome* (1980) emphasizes cultural matters. For later Byzantine history see A. P. Kazhdan and Ann Wharton Epstein in *Change in Byzantine Culture in the Eleventh and Twelfth Centuries* (1985), which stresses social and economic issues, and D. M. Nicol, *Byzantium and Venice* (1988).

Roger Collins's *Early Medieval Europe, 300–1000* (1991) surveys institutional and political developments, while Robert Merrill Bartlett, *The Making of Europe* (1994), emphasizes frontiers. For the later part of the period see Susan Reynolds, *Kingdoms and Communities in Western Europe, 900–1300*, 2d ed. (1997). Jacques Le Goff, *Medieval Civilization, 400–1500* (1989), stresses questions of social structure. Among many books on religious matters see Richard W. Southern, *Western Society and the Church in the Middle Ages* (1970), and Richard Fletcher, *The Barbarian Conversion* (1997). Susan Reynolds makes the case for avoiding the term *feudalism* in *Fiefs and Vassals* (1994).

More specialized economic and technological studies begin with the classic Lynn White, Jr., *Medieval Technology and Social Change* (1962). See also Michael McCormick, *Origins of the European Economy: Communications and Commerce, AD 300–900* (2002); C. M. Cipolla, *Money, Prices and Civilization in the Mediterranean World, Fifth to Seventeenth Century* (1956); and Georges Duby, *Rural Economy and Country Life in the Medieval West* (1990), which includes translated documents. J. C. Russell, *The Control of Late Ancient and Medieval Population* (1985), analyzes demographic history and the problems of data.

On France see the numerous works of Rosamond McKitterick, including *The Frankish Kingdoms Under the Carolingians, 751–987* (1983). On England see Peter Hunter Blair, *An Introduction to Anglo-Saxon England* (1977), and Christopher Brooke, *The Saxon and Norman Kings*, 3d ed. (2001). On Italy see Chris Wickham, *Early Medieval Italy: Central Power and Local Society, 400–1000* (1981), and Edward Burman, *Emperor to Emperor:*

Italy Before the Renaissance (1991). On Germany and the Holy Roman Empire see Timothy Reuter, *Germany in the Early Middle Ages, c. 800–1056* (1991). On Spain see J. F. O'Callaghan, *A History of Medieval Spain* (1975), and R. Collins, *Early Medieval Spain: Unity and Diversity 400–1000* (1983). On Viking Scandinavia see John Haywood's illustrated *Encyclopaedia of the Viking Age* (2000).

Amy Keller's popularly written *Eleanor of Aquitaine and the Four Kings* (1950) tells the story of an extraordinary woman. Dhuoda, *Handbook for William: A Carolingian Woman's Counsel for Her Son*, trans. Carol Neel (1991), offers a firsthand look at a Carolingian noblewoman. More general works include Margaret Wade's *A Small Sound of the Trumpet: Women in Medieval Life* (1986) and Bonnie S. Anderson and Judith P. Zinsser's *A History of Their Own: Women in Europe from Prehistory to the Present* (1989). In the area of religion, Caroline Bynum's *Jesus as Mother: Studies in the Spirituality of the High Middle Ages* (1982) illustrates new views about women.

On Kievan Russia see Janet Martin, *Medieval Russia, 980–1584* (1995); Simon Franklin and Jonathan Shepard, *The Emergence of Rus: 750–1200* (1996); and Thomas S. Noonan, *The Islamic World, Russia and the Vikings, 750–900: The Numismatic Evidence* (1998).

Jonathan Riley-Smith, *The Crusades: A Short History* (1987), is a standard work. He has also a more colorful version in *The Oxford Illustrated History of the Crusades* (1995). For other views see Jonathan Phillips, *The Crusades, 1095–1197* (2002), and Norman Housley, *Crusading and Warfare in Medieval and Renaissance Europe* (2001). For a masterful account with a Byzantine viewpoint, see Steven Runciman, *A History of the Crusades*, 3 vols. (1987). For accounts from the Muslim side see Carole Hillenbrand, *The Crusades: Islamic Perspectives* (1999).

Henri Pirenne, *Medieval Cities: Their Origins and the Revival of Trade* (1952), and Robert S. Lopez, *The Commercial Revolution of the Middle Ages, 950–1350* (1971), masterfully discuss the revival of trade. Lopez and Irving W. Raymond compile and translate primary documents in *Medieval Trade in the Mediterranean World: Illustrative Documents with Introductions and Notes* (1990).

■ Notes

1. Lewis G. M. Thorpe, *Two Lives of Charlemagne* (Harmondsworth, England: Penguin, 1969).
2. A. P. Kazhdan and Ann Wharton Epstein, *Change in Byzantine Culture in the Eleventh and Twelfth Centuries* (Berkeley: University of California Press, 1985), 71.
3. Ibid., 248.
4. Ibid., 255.
5. R. W. Southern, *Western Society and the Church in the Middle Ages* (Harmondsworth, England: Penguin, 1970), 102.
6. S. A. Zenkovsky, ed., *Medieval Russia's Epics, Chronicles, and Tales* (New York: New American Library, 1974), 67.

Document-Based Question
Religion and Politics in Early Christian Europe

Using the following documents, analyze the relationship between rulers and religious leaders in early Christian Europe.

DOCUMENT 1
Quote from Pope Leo III at the coronation of Charlemagne (p. 219)

DOCUMENT 2
Excerpt about Emperor Alexius Comnenus (p. 222)

DOCUMENT 3
Quote from Anna Comnena (p. 222)

DOCUMENT 4
Archbishop Adalbert of Hamburg and the Christianization of the Scandinavians and Slavs (Diversity and Dominance, p. 226)

DOCUMENT 5
Excerpt from Pope Gregory VII (p. 229)

DOCUMENT 6
Map 9.3 The Crusades (p. 238)

How did Adam of Bremen's education and religious beliefs affect his view of the Scandinavians and the Slavs (Document 4)? What additional types of documents would balance your understanding of the relationship between rulers and religious leaders in early Christian Europe?

10

Inner and East Asia, 600–1200

Buddhism at a Distance   The Buddhist monk Xuanzang returns to the Tang capital Chang'an from Tibet in 645, his ponies laden with Sanskrit texts.

CHAPTER OUTLINE

The Early Tang Empire, 618–755

Rivals for Power in Inner Asia and China, 600–907

The Emergence of East Asia, to 1200

New Kingdoms in East Asia

DIVERSITY AND DOMINANCE: Law and Society in Tang China

ENVIRONMENT AND TECHNOLOGY: Writing in East Asia, 600–1200

The powerful and expansive Tang° Empire (618–907) ended four centuries of rule by short-lived and competing states that had repeatedly brought turmoil to China after the fall of the Han Empire in 220 C.E. (see Chapter 5) but had also encouraged the spread of Buddhism. The Tang left an indelible mark on the Chinese imagination long after it too fell.

According to surviving memoirs, people could watch shadow plays and puppet shows, listen to music and scholarly lectures, or take in less edifying spectacles like wrestling and bear baiting in the entertainment quarters of the cities that flourished in southern China under the succeeding Song° Empire. Song-stories provided a novel and popular entertainment from the 1170s onward. Singer-storytellers spun long romantic narratives that alternated prose passages with sung verse.

Master Tung's *Western Chamber Romance* stood out for its literary quality. Little is known of Master Tung° beyond a report that he lived at the end of the twelfth century. In 184 prose passages and 5,263 lines of verse the narrator tells the story of a love affair between Chang, a young Confucian scholar, and Ying-ying, a ravishing damsel. Secondary characters include Ying-ying's shrewd and worldly mother, a general who practices just and efficient administration, and a fighting monk named Fa-ts'ung°. It is based on *The Story of Ying-ying* by the Tang period author Yüan Chen° (779–831).

As the tale begins, the abbot of a Buddhist monastery responds to Chang's request to rent him a study room, singing:

> Sir, you're wrong to offer me rent.
> We Buddhists and Confucians are of one family.
> As things stand, I can't give you
> A place in our dormitory,
> But you're welcome to stay
> In one of the guest apartments.

As soon as Chang spies Ying-ying, who lives there with her mother, thoughts of studying flee his mind.

The course of romance takes a detour, however, when bandits attack the monastery. A prose passage explains:

> During the T'ang dynasty, troops were stationed in the P'u prefecture. The year of our story, the commander of the garrison, Marshal Hun, died. Because the second-in-command, Ting Wen-ya, did not have firm control of the troops, Flying Tiger Sun, a subordinate general, rebelled with five thousand soldiers. They pillaged and plundered the P'u area. How do I know this to be true? It is corroborated by *The Ballad of the True Story of Ying-ying*.

As the monks dither, one of them lifts his robe to reveal his "three-foot consecrated sword."

> Who was this monk? He was none other than Fa-ts'ung. Fa-ts'ung was a descendant of a tribesman from western Shensi. When he was young he took great pleasure in archery, fencing, hunting, and often sneaked into foreign states to steal. He was fierce and courageous. When his parents died, it suddenly became clear to him that the way of the world was frivolous and trivial, so he became a monk in the Temple of Universal Salvation.
> . . .

> [Song]   He didn't know how to read sutras;
>   He didn't know how to follow rituals;
>   He was neither pure nor chaste
>   But indomitably courageous . . .[1]

Amidst the love story, the ribaldry, and the derring-do, the author implants historical vignettes that mingle fact and fiction. Sophisticates of the Song era, living a life of ease, enjoyed these romanticized portrayals of Tang society.

As you read this chapter, ask yourself the following questions:

- What is the importance of Inner and Central Asia as a region of interchange during the Tang period?

- On what were new relationships among East Asian societies based after the fall of the Tang?

Tang (tahng)   Song (soong)   Tung (toong)
Fa-ts'ung (fa-soong)   Yüan Chen (you-ahn shen)

C H R O N O L O G Y

	Inner Asia	China	Northeast Asia	Japan
600	**620–640** Tibetan Empire emerges under Songsam Gyampo	**581–618** Sui unification **618** Tang Empire founded **627–649** Li Shimin reign **690–705** Wu Zhao reign	**668** Silla victory in Korea	**645–655** Taika era **710–784** Nara as capital **752** "Eye-Opening" ceremony **794–1185** Heian era
800	**744** Uighur empire founded **751** Battle of Talas River **ca. 850** Buddhist political power secured in Tibet	**755–757** An Lushan rebellion **840** Suppression of Buddhism **879–881** Huang Chao rebellion **907** End of Tang Empire		
1000		**938** Liao capital at Beijing **960** Song Empire Founded **1127–1279** Southern Song period	**916** Liao Empire founded **918** Koryo founded **1115** Jin Empire founded	**ca. 950–1180** Fujiwara influence **ca. 1000** *The Tale of Genji* **1185** Kamakura shogunate founded

- Why do Buddhism and Confucianism play different political roles in Tang and Song China, and in Tibet, Korea, and Japan?

- What accounts for the scientific and economic advancement that contributed to the thriving urban life of Song China?

THE EARLY TANG EMPIRE, 618–755

The reunification of China after centuries of division into small principalities took place under the Sui° dynasty. But after only 34 years in power the Sui collapsed in 615, paving the way for the powerful and long-lasting Tang dynasty. Just as the Qin, who built the first powerful Chinese state but ruled for only 14 years, influenced their Han successors (see Chapter 2), so Sui practices strongly influenced the Tang.

Tang Origins

In 618 the powerful Li family took advantage of Sui disorder to carve out an empire of similar scale and ambition. They adopted the dynastic name Tang (Map 10.1). The brilliant emperor **Li Shimin°** (r. 627–649) extended his power primarily westward into Inner Asia. Though he and succeeding rulers of the **Tang Empire** retained many Sui governing practices, they avoided overcentralization by allowing local nobles,

Sui (sway)

Li Shimin (lee shir-meen)

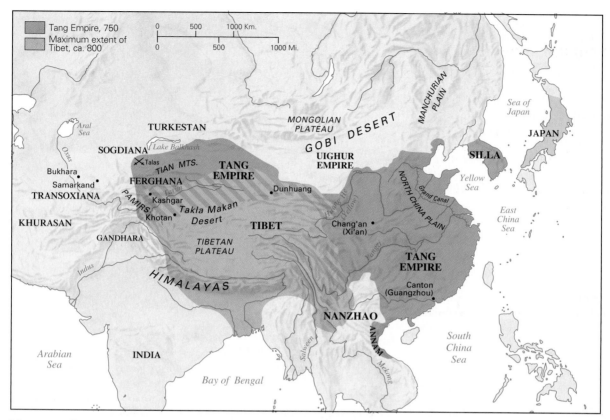

Map 10.1 The Tang Empire in Inner and Eastern Asia, 750 For over a century the Tang Empire controlled China and a very large part of Inner Asia. The defeat of Tang armies in 751 by a force of Arabs, Turks, and Tibetans at the Talas River in present-day Kirgizstan ended Tang westward expansion. To the east the Tang dominated Annam, and Japan and the Silla kingdom in Korea were leading tributary states of the Tang.

gentry, officials, and religious establishments to exercise significant power. (See Diversity and Dominance: Law and Society in Tang China).

The Tang emperors and nobility descended from the Turkic elites that built small states in northern China after the Han, and from Chinese officials and settlers who had settled there. They continued the Confucian system of examining candidates for bureaucratic office on the classic Confucian texts, a practice that had been reinstituted by the Sui. But they also appreciated the Turkic culture of Inner Asia (the part of the Eurasian steppe east of the Pamir Mountains). Some of the most impressive works of Tang sculpture, for example, are large pottery figurines of the horses and two-humped camels used along the Silk Road. In warfare, the Tang combined Chinese weapons—the crossbow and armored infantrymen—with Inner Asian expertise in horsemanship and the use of iron stirrups. At their peak, from about 650 to 751, when they were defeated in Central Asia (present-day Kirgizstan) by an Arab Muslim army at the Battle of the Talas River, the Tang armies were a formidable force.

Buddhism and the Tang Empire

The Tang rulers followed Inner Asian precedents in their political use of Buddhism. State cults based on Buddhism had flourished in Inner Asia and north China since the fall of the Han. Some interpretations of Buddhist doctrine accorded kings and emperors the spiritual function of welding humankind into a harmonious Buddhist society. Protecting spirits were to help the ruler govern and prevent harm from coming to his people.

Mahayana°, or "Great Vehicle," Buddhism predominated. Mahayana fostered faith in enlightened beings—bodhisattvas—who postpone nirvana (see Chapter 6) to

Mahayana (mah-HAH-YAH-nah)

Iron Stirrups   This bas-relief from the tomb of Li Shimin depicts the type of horse on which the Tang armies conquered China and Inner Asia. Saddles with high supports in front and back, breastplates, and cruppers (straps beneath the tail that help keep the saddle in place) point to the importance of high speeds and quick maneuvering. Central and Inner Asian horsemen had iron stirrups available from the time of the Huns (fifth century). Earlier stirrups were of leather or wood. Stirrups could support the weight of shielded and well-armed soldiers rising in the saddle to shoot arrows or use lances.   (University of Pennsylvania Museum, neg. #S8-62844)

help others achieve enlightenment. This permitted the absorption of local gods and goddesses into Mahayana sainthood and thereby made conversion more attractive to the common people. Mahayana also encouraged translating Buddhist scripture into local languages, and it accepted religious practices not based on written texts. The tremendous reach of Mahayana views, which proved adaptable to different societies and classes of people, invigorated travel, language learning, and cultural exchange.

Early Tang princes competing for political influence enlisted monastic leaders to pray for them, preach on their behalf, counsel aristocrats to support them, and—perhaps most important—contribute monastic wealth to their war chests. In return, the monasteries received tax exemptions, land privileges, and gifts.

As the Tang Empire expanded westward, contacts with Central Asia and India increased, and so did the complexity of Buddhist influence throughout China. Chang'an°, the Tang capital, became the center of a continentwide system of communication. Central Asians, Tibetans, Vietnamese, Japanese, and Koreans regularly visited the capital and took away with them the most recent ideas and styles. Thus the Mahayana network connecting Inner Asia and China intersected a vigorous commercial world in which material goods and cultural influences mixed. Though Buddhism and Confucianism proved attractive to many different peoples, regional cultures and identities remained strong, just as regional commitments to Tibetan, Uighur, and other languages and writing systems coexisted with the widespread use of written Chinese. Textiles reflected Persian, Korean, and Vietnamese styles, while influences from every part of Asia appeared in sports, music, and painting. Many historians characterize the Tang Empire as "cosmopolitan" because of its breadth and diversity.

To Chang'an by Land and Sea

The Sui called their new capital Chang'an in honor of the old Han capital nearby in the Wei° River Valley (modern Shaanxi province). The Tang retained it as their capital, and it became the hub of Tang communications.

Well-maintained roads and water transport connected Chang'an to the coastal towns of south China, most importantly Canton (Guangzhou°). Though the 1,100-mile (1771 kilometers) **Grand Canal,** built by the Sui to link the Yellow River with the Yangzi°, did not reach Chang'an, it was a key component of this transportation network. Chang'an became the center of what is often called the **tributary system,** a type of political relationship dating from Han times by which independent countries acknowledged the Chinese emperor's supremacy. Each tributary state sent regular embassies to the capital to pay tribute (see Chapter 5). As symbols of

Chang'an (chahng-ahn)

Wei (way)   **Guangzhou** (gwahng-jo)   **Yangzi** (yahng-zeh)

파운드폭탄 4발 투하… 두 아들과 함께 사망 가

실전지 구축… 이틀째 시가戰

령이 대중 앞에 나타나거나 애국심
을 고취하는 노래만을 내보내던 방
송마저 중단했다.

라크 전후 대체
의에서는 전후
영국 주도로

DIVERSITY AND DOMINANCE

LAW AND SOCIETY IN TANG CHINA

The Tang law code, compiled in the early seventh century, served as the basis for the Tang legal system and as a model for later dynastic law codes. It combined the centralized authority of the imperial government, as visualized in the legalist tradition dating back to Han times, with Confucian concern for status distinctions and personal relationships. Like contemporary approaches to law in Christian Europe and the Islamic world, it did not fully distinguish between government as a structure of domination and law as an echo of religious and moral values.

Following a Preface, 502 articles, each with several parts, are divided into twelve books: (1) General Principles, (2) Imperial Guard and Prohibitions, (3) Administrative Regulations, (4) Household and Marriage, (5) Public Stables and Granaries, (6) Unauthorized Levies, (7) Violence and Robberies, (8) Assaults and Accusations, (9) Fraud and Counterfeiting, (10) Miscellaneous Articles, (11) Arrest and Flight, and (12) Judgment and Imprisonment. Each article contained a basic ordinance with commentary, subcommentary, and sometimes additional questions. Excerpts from a single Article from Book 1 follow.

THE TEN ABOMINATIONS

Text: The first is called plotting rebellion.

Subcommentary: The *Gongyang* [GON-gwang] *Commentary* states: "The ruler or parent has no harborers [of plots]. If he does have such harborers, he must put them to death." This means that if there are those who harbor rebellious hearts that would harm the ruler or father, he must then put them to death.

The king occupies the most honorable position and receives Heaven's precious decrees. Like Heaven and Earth, he acts to shelter and support, thus serving as the father and mother of the masses. As his children, as his subjects, they must be loyal and filial. Should they dare to cherish wickedness and have rebellious hearts, however, they will run counter to Heaven's constancy and violate human principle. Therefore this is called plotting rebellion.

Text: The second is called plotting great sedition.

Subcommentary: This type of person breaks laws and destroys order, is against traditional norms, and goes contrary to virtue . . .

Commentary: Plotting great sedition means to plot to destroy the ancestral temples, tombs, or palaces of the reigning house.

Text: The third is called plotting treason.

Subcommentary: The kindness of father and mother is like "great heaven, illimitable" . . . Let one's heart be like the *xiao* bird or the *jing* beast, and then love and respect both cease. Those whose relationship is within the five degrees of mourning are the closest of kin. For them to kill each other is the extreme abomination and the utmost in rebellion, destroying and casting aside human principles. Therefore this is called contumacy.

Commentary: Contumacy means to beat or plot to kill [without actually killing] one's paternal grandparents or parents; or to kill one's paternal uncles or their wives, or one's elder brothers or sisters, or one's maternal grandparents, or one's husband, or one's husband's paternal grandparents, or his parents . . . .

Text: The fifth is called depravity.

Subcommentary: This article describes those who are cruel and malicious and who turn their backs on morality. Therefore it is called depravity.

Commentary: Depravity means to kill three members of a single household who have not committed a capital crime, or to dismember someone . . .

Commentary: The offense also includes the making or keeping of poison or sorcery.

Subcommentary: This means to prepare the poison oneself, or to keep it, or to give it to others in order to harm people. But if the preparation of the poison is not yet completed, this offense does not come under the ten abominations. As to sorcery, there are a great many methods, not all of which can be described.

Text: The sixth is called great irreverence . . .

Commentary: Great irreverence means to steal the objects of the great sacrifices to the spirits or the carriage or possessions of the emperor.

Text: The seventh is called lack of filiality.

Subcommentary: Serving one's parents well is called filiality. Disobeying them is called lack of filiality.

Text: The ninth is called what is not right . . .
Commentary: [This] means to kill one's department head, prefect, or magistrate, or the teacher from whom one has received one's education . . .

Text: The tenth is called incest.
Subcommentary: The *Zuo Commentary* states: "The woman has her husband's house; the man has his wife's chamber; and there must be no defilement on either side." If this is changed, then there is incest. If one behaves like birds and beasts and introduces licentious associates into one's family, the rules of morality are confused. Therefore this is called incest.

Commentary: This section includes having illicit sexual intercourse with relatives who are of the fourth degree of mourning or closer . . . .

The following are the titles of 26 of the 46 articles in Book 4 of the Code entitled "The Household and Marriage."

- Omitting to File a Household Register
- Unauthorized Ordainment as a Buddhist or Daoist Priest
- Sons and Grandsons in the Male Line Are Not Permitted to Have a Separate Household Register
- Having a Child During the Period of Mourning for Parents
- Adopted Sons Who Reject Their Adoptive Parents
- Falsely Combining Households
- Possession of More than the Permitted Amount of Land
- Illegal Cultivation of Public or Private Land
- Wrongfully Laying Claim to or Selling Public or Private Land
- Officials Who Encroach Upon Private Land
- Illegal Cultivation of Other Persons' Grave Plots
- Not Allowing Rightful Exemption from Taxes and Labor Services
- Betrothal of a Daughter and Announcement of the Marriage Contract
- Wrongful Substitution by the Bride's Family in a Marriage
- Taking a Second Wife
- Making the Wife a Concubine
- Marriage During the Period of Mourning for Parents or Husband
- Marriage While Parents Are in Prison
- Marriage by Those of the Same Surname
- Marrying a Runaway Wife
- Marriage of Officials with Women Within Their Area of Jurisdiction
- Marrying Another Man's Wife by Consent
- Divorcing a Wife Who Has Not Given Any of the Seven Causes for Repudiation
- Divorce
- Slaves Who Take Commoners as Wives
- General Bondsmen Are Not Permitted to Marry Commoners
- Marriages That Violate the Code

The day-to-day realities of country life appear in the following account by a scholar living during the late 700s.

Wealthy landowning families bought townhouses and engaged in conspicuous consumption while farmers, whose high rents and low pay contributed to the gentry's growing wealth, enjoyed few direct benefits.

When a farmer falls on bad times, he has to sell his field and his hut. If it is a good year, he might be able to pay his debts by selling out. But no sooner will the harvest be in than his storage bins will be empty again, and he will have to try to contract a new debt promising his labor for the next year. Each time he indentures himself he incurs higher interest rates, and soon will be destitute again.

If it is a bad year, and there is a famine, then the situation is hopeless. Families break up, parents separate, and all try to sell themselves into slavery. But in a bad year nobody will buy them.

In these circumstances land prices fall low enough that the rich buy up tens of thousands of acres, or simply seize the land of defaulted farmers. The poor then have no land, and try for places as servants, bodyguards, or enforcers for the rich families. If they manage to attach themselves to the organization of a gentry family, they can borrow seed and grain, and rent land as tenants. Then they will work themselves to death, all year round, without a day off. If they should manage to clear their debts, they live in constant anxiety about when the next bad patch will leave them destitute again.

The gentry, however, live off their rents, with no troubles and no cares. Wealth and poverty are very clearly divided.

This is how we have reached the situation where the rents from private land are much higher, and collected more ruthlessly, than the government's taxes. In areas around the capital, rents are twenty times higher than taxes. Even rents in more remote areas are ten times what the government collects in tax.

QUESTIONS FOR ANALYSIS

1. Comparing these historical documents, what would seem to have been the relationship between law and equity under the Tang?
2. Did the Confucian concern for family relations and social status manifested in the law code prevent injustice?
3. Does the law code appear more an expression of ideals and compilation of past philosophical ideas than a practical guide to a just society?

Sources: The first two selections are from Theodore de Bary and Irene Bloom, eds., *Sources of Chinese Tradition*, vol. 1, 2d ed. Copyright © 1999 by Columbia University Press. Reprinted with permission of the publisher. The third selection is adapted from Etienne Balazs, *Chinese Civilization and Bureaucracy: Variations on a Theme*, trans. by H. M. Wright, ed. by Arthur F. Wright. Copyright © 1964. Reprinted by permission of Yale University Press.

China's political supremacy, these embassies sometimes meant more to the Chinese than to the tribute-payers, who might see them more as a means of accessing the Chinese trading system.

During the Tang period, Chang'an had something over a million people, only a minority of whom lived in the central city. Most people lived in suburbs that extended beyond the main gates. Others dwelt in separate outlying towns that had special responsibilities like maintaining nearby imperial tombs or operating the imperial resort, where aristocrats relaxed in sunken tile tubs while the steamy waters of natural springs swirled around them.

Foreigners, whether merchants, students, or ambassadors, resided in special compounds in Chang'an and other entrepôts. These included living accommodations and general stores. By the end of the Tang period, West Asians in Chang'an probably numbered over 100,000.

In the main parts of the city, restaurants, inns, temples, mosques, and street stalls along the main thoroughfares kept busy every evening. At curfew, generally between eight and ten o'clock, commoners returned to their neighborhoods, which were enclosed by brick walls and wooden gates that guards locked until dawn to control crime.

Of the many routes converging on Chang'an, the Grand Canal commanded special importance, with its own army patrols, boat design, canal towns, and maintenance budget. It conveyed vital supplies and contributed to the economic and cultural development of eastern China, where later capitals were built within easier reach.

The Tang consolidated Chinese control of the southern coastal region, increasing access to the Indian Ocean and facilitating the spread of Islamic and Jewish influences. A legend credits an uncle of Muhammad with erecting the Red Mosque at Canton in the mid-seventh century.

Chinese mariners and shipwrights excelled in compass design and the construction of very large oceangoing vessels. The government took direct responsibility for outfitting grain transport vessels for the Chinese coastal cities and the Grand Canal. Commercial ships, built to sail from south China to the Philippines and Southeast Asia, carried twice as much as contemporary vessels in the Mediterranean Sea (see Chapter 7).

The sea route linking the Red Sea and Persian Gulf with Canton also brought East Asia the "plague of Justinian" (see Chapter 9). Historical sources mention the **bubonic plague** in Canton and south China in the early 600s. As in certain other parts of the world, the plague bacillus became endemic among rodent populations in parts of southwestern China and thus lingered long after its disappearance in West Asia and Europe. The disease

Tang Women at Polo   The Tang Empire, like the Sui, was strongly influenced by Inner Asian as well as Chinese traditions. As in many Inner Asian cultures, women in Tang China were likely to exercise greater influence in the management of property, in the arts, and in politics than women in Chinese society at later times. They were not excluded from public view, and noblewomen could even compete at polo. The game, widely known in various forms in Central and Inner Asia from a very early date, combined the Tang love of riding, military arts, and festive spectacles.   (The Nelson-Atkins Museum of Art, Kansas City, Missouri)

followed trade and embassy routes to Korea, Japan, and Tibet, where initial outbreaks followed the establishment of diplomatic ties in the seventh century.

Trade and Cultural Exchange

Influences from Central Asia and the Islamic world introduced lively new motifs to ceramics, painting, and silk designs. Clothing styles changed in north China; working people switched from robes to the pants favored by horse-riding Turks from Central Asia. Cotton imported from Central Asia, where production boomed in the early Islamic centuries, gradually replaced hemp in clothes worn by commoners. The Tang court promoted polo, a pastime from the steppes, and followed the Inner Asian tradition of allowing noblewomen to compete. Various stringed instruments reached China across the Silk Road, along with Turkic folk melodies. Grape wine from West Asia and tea, sugar, and spices from India and Southeast Asia transformed the Chinese diet.

By about the year 1000 the magnitude of exports from Tang territories, facilitated by China's excellent transportation systems, dwarfed Chinese imports from Europe, West Asia, and South Asia. Stories of ships carrying Chinese exports outnumbering those laden with South Asian, West Asian, European, or African goods by a hundred to one cannot be relied on. Tang exports did, however, tilt the trade balance with both the Central Asia caravan cities and the lands of the Indian Ocean, causing precious metal to flow into China in return for export goods.

China remained the source of superior silks. Tang factories created more and more complex styles, partly to counter foreign competition. China became the sole supplier of porcelain—a fine, durable ceramic made from a special clay—to West Asia. As travel along the Silk Road and to the various ports of the Indian Ocean trading system increased, the economies of seaports and entrepôts involved in the trade—even distant ones—became increasingly commercialized, leading to networks of private traders devising new instruments of credit and finance. As we shall see, these networks would later contribute to the prosperity of the Song era.

RIVALS FOR POWER IN INNER ASIA AND CHINA, 600–907

Li Bo, the most renowned Tang poet and one of the greatest ever to write in the Chinese language, wrote in 751 of the seemingly endless succession of wars:

> The beacons are always alight, fighting and marching
>   never stop.
> Men die in the field, slashing sword to sword;
> The horses of the conquered neigh piteously to
>   Heaven.
> Crows and hawks peck for human guts,
> Carry them in their beaks and hang them on the
>   branches of withered trees.
> Captains and soldiers are smeared on the bushes and
>   grass;
> The General schemed in vain.
> Know therefore that the sword is a cursed thing
> which the wise man uses only if he must.[2]

Between 600 and 751, when the Tang Empire was at its height, the Turkic-speaking Uighurs° and the Tibetans built large rival states in Inner Asia. The power of the former centered on the basin of the Tarim River, a largely desert area north of Tibet that formed a vital link on the

Silk Road. The Tibetan empire at its peak stretched well beyond modern Tibet into northeastern India, southwestern China, and the Tarim Basin. The contest between these states and the Tang for control of the land routes west of China reached a standoff by the end of the period. Mutually beneficial trade required diplomatic accommodation more than political unity. By the mid-800s all three empires were experiencing political decay and military decline. The problems of one aggravated those of the others, since governmental collapse allowed soldiers, criminals, and freebooters to roam without hindrance into neighboring territories.

Centralization and integration being most extensively developed in Tang territory, the impact fell most heavily there. Nothing remained of Tang power but pretense by the early 800s, the period reflected in the original romance of Ying-ying described at the start of this chapter. In the provinces military governors suppressed the rebellion of General An Lushan°, a commander of Sogdian (Central Asian) and Turkic origin, which raged from 755 to 763, and then seized power for themselves.

The nomads of the steppe survived the social disorder and agricultural losses best. The caravan cities that had prospered from overland trade, and that lay at the heart of the Uighur state in the Tarim Basin, had as much to lose as China itself. Eventually, the urban and agricultural economies of Inner Asia and China recovered. In the short term, however, the debilitating contest for power with the Inner Asian states prompted a strong cultural backlash, particularly in China, where disillusionment with northern neighbors combined with social and economic anxieties to fuel an antiforeign movement.

The Uighur and Tibetan Empires

The original homeland of the Turks lay in the northern part of modern Mongolia. After the fall of the Han Empire, Turkic peoples began moving south and west, through Mongolia, then west to Central Asia, on the long migration that eventually brought them to what is today modern Turkey (see Chapter 8). In the seventh century the Tang Emperor Li Shimin took advantage of Turkic disunity to establish control over the Tarim Basin. Yet within a century, a new Turkic group, the **Uighurs,** had taken much of Inner Asia.

Under the Uighurs, caravan cities like Kashgar and Khotan (see Map 10.1) displayed a literate culture with strong ties to both the Islamic world and China. The Uighurs excelled as merchants and as scribes able to transact business in many languages. They adapted the

Uighur (WEE-ger)

An Lushan (ahn loo-shahn)

Women of Turfan Grinding Flour   Women throughout Inner and East Asia were critical to all facets of economic life. In the Turkic areas of Central and Inner Asia, women commonly headed households, owned property, and managed businesses. These small figurines, made to be placed in tombs, portray women of Turfan—an Inner Asian area crossed by the Silk Road—performing tasks in the preparation of wheat flour.   (Xinjiang Uighur Autonomous District Museum)

syllabic script of the Sogdians, who lived to the west of them in Central Asia, to writing Turkic. Their flourishing urban culture exhibited a cosmopolitan enthusiasm for Buddhist teachings, religious art derived from northern India, and a mixture of East Asian and Islamic tastes in dress.

Unified Uighur power collapsed after half a century, leaving only Tibet as a rival to the Tang in Inner Asia. A large, stable empire critically positioned where China, Southeast Asia, South Asia, and Central Asia meet, **Tibet** experienced a variety of cultural influences. In the seventh century Chinese Buddhists on pilgrimage to India advanced contacts between India and Tibet. The Tibetans derived their alphabet from India, as well as a variety of artistic and architectural styles. India and China both contributed to Tibetan knowledge of mathematics, astronomy, divination, farming, and milling of grain. Islam and the monarchical traditions of Iran became familiar through Central Asian trading connections. The Tibetan royal family favored Greek medicine transmitted through Iran.

Under Li Shimin, cautious friendliness had prevailed between China and Tibet. A Tang princess, called Kongjo by the Tibetans, came to Tibet in 634 to marry the Tibetan king and cement an alliance. She brought Mahayana Buddhism, which combined with the native religion to create a distinctive form of Buddhism. Tibet sent ambassadors and students to the Tang imperial capital. Regular contact and Buddhist influences consolidated the Tang-Tibet relationship for a time. The Tibetan kings encouraged Buddhist religious establishments and prided themselves on being cultural intermediaries between India and China.

Tibet also excelled at war. Horses and armor, techniques borrowed from the Turks, raised Tibetan forces to a level that startled even the Tang. By the late 600s the Tang emperor and the Tibetan king were rivals for religious leadership and political dominance in Inner Asia, and Tibetan power reached into what are now Qinghai°, Sichuan°, and Xinjiang° provinces in China. War weariness affected both empires after 751, however.

In the 800s a new king in Tibet decided to follow the Tang lead and eliminate the political and social influence of the monasteries (see below). He was assassinated by Buddhist monks, and control of the Tibetan royal family passed into the hands of religious leaders. In the centuries that followed down to modern times, monastic domination isolated Tibet from surrounding regions.

Upheavals and Repression, 750–879

The Tang elites came to see Buddhism as undermining the Confucian idea of the family as the model for the state. The Confucian scholar Han Yu (768–824) spoke powerfully for a return to traditional Confucian practices. In "Memorial on the Bone of Buddha," written to the emperor in 819 on the occasion of ceremonies to receive a bone of the Buddha in the imperial palace, he scornfully disparages the Buddha and his followers:

> Now Buddha was a man of the barbarians who did not speak the language of China and wore clothes of a different fashion. His sayings did not concern the ways of our ancient kings, nor did his manner of dress conform to their laws. He understood neither the duties that bind sovereign and subject nor the affections of father and son. If he were still alive today and came to our court by order of his ruler, Your Majesty might condescend to receive him, but . . . he would then be escorted to the borders of the state, dismissed, and not allowed to delude the masses. How then, when he has long been dead, could his rotten bones, the foul and

Qinghai (CHING-hie)   **Sichuan** (SUH-chwahn)
Xinjiang (shin-jee-yahng)

unlucky remains of his body, be rightly admitted to the palace? Confucius said, "Respect spiritual beings, while keeping at a distance from them."[3]

Buddhism was also attacked for encouraging women in politics. Wu Zhao°, a woman who had married into the imperial family, seized control of the government in 690 and declared herself emperor. She based her legitimacy on claiming to be a bodhisattva, an enlightened soul who had chosen to remain on earth to lead others to salvation. She also favored Buddhists and Daoists over Confucianists in her court and government.

Later Confucian writers expressed contempt for Wu Zhao and other powerful women, such as the concubine Yang Guifei°. Bo Zhuyi°, in his poem "Everlasting Remorse," lamented the influence of women at the Tang court, which had caused "the hearts of fathers and mothers everywhere not to value the birth of boys, but the birth of girls."[4] Confucian elites heaped every possible charge on prominent women who offended them, accusing Emperor Wu of grotesque tortures and murders, including tossing the dismembered but still living bodies of enemies into wine vats and cauldrons. They blamed Yang Guifei for the outbreak of the An Lushan rebellion in 755.

Serious historians dismiss the stories about Wu Zhao as stereotypical characterizations of "evil" rulers. Eunuchs (castrated palace servants), charged by historians with controlling Chang'an and the Tang court and publicly executing rival bureaucrats, represent a similar stereotype. In fact Wu seems to have ruled effectively and was not deposed until 705, when extreme old age (eighty-plus) incapacitated her. Nevertheless, traditional Chinese historians commonly describe unorthodox rulers and all-powerful women as evil, and the truth about Wu will never be known.

Even Chinese gentry living in safe and prosperous localities associated Buddhism with social ills. People who worried about "barbarians" ruining their society pointed to Buddhism as evidence of the foreign evil, since it had such strong roots in Inner Asia and Tibet. They claimed that eradicating Buddhist influence would restore the ancient values of hierarchy and social harmony. Because Buddhism shunned earthly ties, monks and nuns severed relations with the secular world in search of enlightenment. They paid no taxes, served in no army. They deprived their families of advantageous marriage alliances and denied descendants to their ancestors. The Confucian elites saw all this as threatening

to the family, and to the family estates that underlay the Tang economic and political structure.

In 840 (a year of disintegration on many fronts) the government moved to crush the monasteries. An imperial edict of 845 reports the demolition of 4,600 temples and the forcible conversion of 26,500 monks and nuns into ordinary workers. The tax exemption of monasteries had allowed them to purchase land and precious objects and to employ large numbers of serfs. Wealthy believers had given the monasteries large tracts of land, and poor people had flocked to the Buddhist institutions to work as artisans, fieldworkers, cooks, housekeepers, and guards. By the ninth century, hundreds of thousands of people had entered tax exempt Buddhist institutions. Now an enormous amount of land and 150,000 workers were returned to the tax rolls.

Though some Buddhist cultural centers, such as the cave monasteries at Dunhuang, were protected by local warlords dependent on the favor of Buddhist rulers in Inner Asia, the dissolution of the monasteries was an incalculable loss to China's cultural heritage. Some sculptures and grottoes survived only in defaced form. Wooden temples and façades sheltering great stone carvings burned to the ground. Monasteries became legal again in later times, but Buddhism never recovered the social, political, and cultural influence of early Tang times.

The End of the Tang Empire, 879–907

The Tang order succumbed to the very forces that were essential to its creation and maintenance. The campaigns of expansion in the seventh century had left the empire dependent on local military commanders and a complex tax collection system. Such reverses as the Battle of the Talas River in 751, which halted the drive westward into Central Asia, led to military demoralization and underfunding. In 755 An Lushan, a Tang general appointed as regional commander on the northeast frontier, led about 200,000 soldiers in a rebellion that forced the emperor to flee Chang'an and execute his favorite concubine, Yang Guifei, whom some accused of being An Lushan's lover. Though he was killed by his own son in 757, An Lushan's rebellion lasted for eight years and resulted in new powers and greater independence for the provincial military governors who helped suppress it. The Uighurs also helped bring the disorder to an end.

Despite continuing prosperity, political disintegration and the elite's sense of cultural decay created an unsettled environment that encouraged aspiring dictators.

Wu Zhao (woo jow)　**Yang Guifei** (yahng gway-fay)
Bo Zhuyi (baw joo-ee)

A disgruntled member of the gentry, Huang Chao°, led the most devastating uprising between 879 and 881. Despite ruthless and violent domination of the villages he controlled, his rebellion attracted hundreds of thousands of poor farmers and tenants who could not protect themselves from local bosses, or who sought escape from oppressive landlords or taxes, or who simply did not know what else to do in the deepening chaos. The new hatred of "barbarians" spurred the rebels to murder thousands of foreign residents in Canton and Beijing°.

Local warlords finally wiped out the rebels, using the same violent tactics. But Tang society did not find peace. Refugees, migrant workers, and homeless people became common sights in both city and country. Residents of northern China fled to the southern frontiers as groups from Inner Asia took advantage of the flight of population to move into localities in the north. Though Tang emperors continued to rule in Chang'an until their line was terminated by one of the warlords in 907, they never regained effective power after Huang Chao's rebellion.

THE EMERGENCE OF EAST ASIA, TO 1200

In the aftermath of the Tang, three new states emerged and competed to inherit its legacy (see Map 10.2). The Liao° Empire of the Khitan° people, pastoral nomads related to the Mongols living on the northeastern frontier, established their rule in the north. They centered their government on several cities, but the emperors preferred to spend their time in their nomad encampments. In western China, the Minyak people (closely related to the Tibetans) established a second successor state. They called themselves "Tangguts°" to show their connection with the former empire. The third state, the Chinese-speaking **Song Empire,** came into being in 960 in central China.

Competition among these states was unavoidable. They embodied the political ambitions of peoples who spoke very different languages and subscribed to different religious and philosophical systems—Mahayana Buddhism among the Liao, Tibetan Buddhism among the Tangguts, and Confucianism among the Song. The Liao and especially the Tangguts maintained some continuing relationship with Inner and Central Asia, but the Song were cut off. Instead they developed their sea connections with other states in East Asia, West Asia, and

Silk Painting Depicting Khitan Hunters Resting Their Horses
The artist shows the Khitans' soft riding boots, leggings, and robes (much like those used by the Mongols) and the Khitans' patterned hairstyle, with part of the skull shaved and some of the hair worn long. Men in Inner and North Asia (including Japan) used patterned hairstyles to indicate their political allegiance. The custom was documented in the 400s (but is certainly much older) and continued up to the twentieth century.   (National Palace Museum, Taipai, Taiwan, Republic of China)

Southeast Asia. This effort led to advanced seafaring and sailing technologies. The Song elite shared the late Tang dislike of "barbaric" or "foreign" influences as they tried to cope with multiple enemies that heavily taxed their military capacities.

The Liao and Jin Challenge

The Liao Empire of the Khitan people extended from Siberia to Central Asia, connecting China with societies to the north and west. Variations on the Khitan name became the name for China in these distant regions: "Kitai" for the Mongols, "Khitai" for the Russians, and "Cathay" for those, like contemporaries of the Italian merchant Marco Polo, who reached China from Europe (see Chapter 12).

The Liao rulers prided themselves on their pastoral traditions, the continuing source of their military might, and made no attempt to create a single elite culture. They encouraged Chinese elites to use their own language, study their own classics, and see the emperor through Confucian eyes; and they encouraged other peoples to

---

Huang Chao (wang show)   **Liao** (lee-OW)   **Khitan** (kee-THAN)   **Beijing** (bay-jeeng)   **Tanggut** (TAHNG-gut)

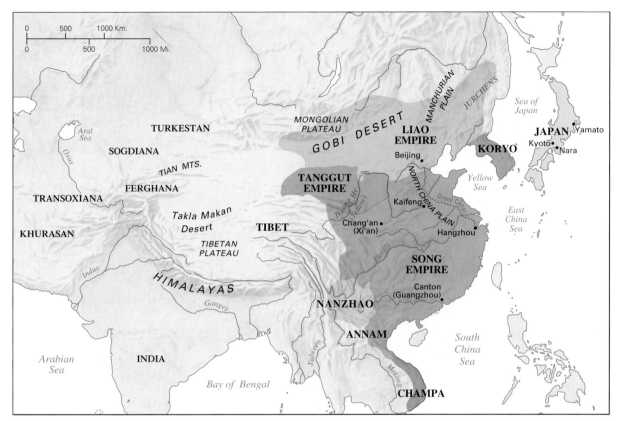

Map 10.2   Liao and Song Empires, ca. 1100   The states of Liao in the north and Song in the south generally ceased open hostilities after a treaty in 1005 stabilized the border and imposed an annual payment on Song China.

use their own languages and see the emperor as a champion of Buddhism or as a nomadic leader. On balance, Buddhism far outweighed Confucianism in this and other northern states, where rulers depended on their roles as bodhisattvas or as Buddhist kings to legitimate power. Liao rule lasted from 916 to 1121.

Superb horsemen and archers, the Khitans added siege machines from China and Central Asia to their armory for challenging the Song. In 1005 the Song emperor agreed to a truce that included enormous annual payments in cash and silk to the Liao. This lasted for more than a century, but eventually the Song tired of paying the annual tribute and entered into a secret alliance with the Jurchens of northeastern Asia, who were also chafing under Liao rule. In 1125 the Jurchens destroyed the Liao capital in Mongolia and proclaimed their own empire—the Jin. Then they turned against their former Song ally.

The Jurchens grew rice, millet, and wheat, but they also spent a good deal of time hunting, fishing, and tending livestock. Though their language was unrelated to that of the Khitan, the Jurchens nevertheless learned

much from the Khitan about the military arts and political organization. This helped them become formidable enemies of the Song Empire, against whom they mounted an all-out campaign in 1127. They laid siege to the Song capital, Kaifeng°, and captured the Song emperor. Within a few years the Song withdrew south of the Yellow River and established a new capital at Hangzhou°, leaving central as well as northern China in Jurchen control (Map 10.3). The Song made annual payments to the Jin Empire to avoid open warfare. Historians generally refer to this period as the "Southern Song" (1127–1279).

Song Industries

Historians look upon the Southern Song as the premodern state and society that came closest to initiating an industrial revolution. Divided into three separate states from 907 to 1279, China did not exhibit the military expansionism and exploitation of

Kaifeng (kie-fuhng)   **Hangzhou** (hahng-jo)

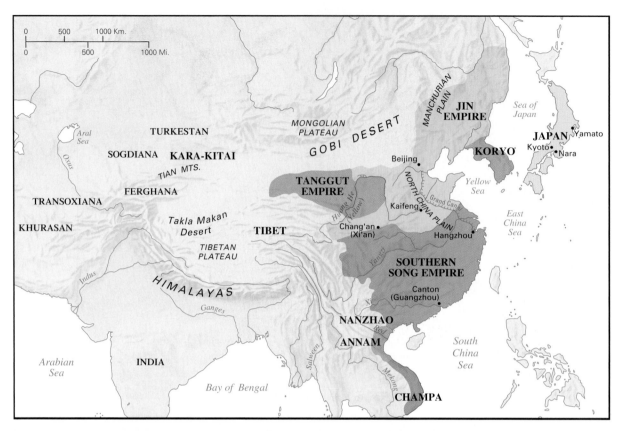

Map 10.3   Jin and Southern Song Empires, ca. 1200   After 1127 Song abandoned its northern territories to Jin. The Southern Song continued the policy of annual payments—to Jin rather than Liao—and maintained high military preparedness to prevent further invasions.

far-flung networks of communication that had characterized the Tang at their height. Yet many of the advances in technology, medicine, astronomy, and mathematics for which the Song is famous derived from information that had come to China in Tang times, sometimes from very distant places.

Chinese scholars made great strides in the arts of measurement and observation, drawing on the work of Indian and West Asian mathematicians and astronomers who had migrated to the Tang Empire. Song mathematicians introduced the use of fractions, first employing them to describe the phases of the moon. From lunar observations, Song astronomers constructed a very precise calendar and, alone among the world's astronomers, noted the explosion of the Crab Nebula in 1054. Chinese scholars used their work in astronomy and mathematics to make significant contributions to timekeeping and the development of the compass.

In 1088 the engineer Su Song constructed a gigantic mechanical celestial clock in Kaifeng. Escapement mechanisms for controlling the revolving wheels in water-powered clocks had appeared under the Tang, as had the application of water wheels to weaving and threshing. But this knowledge had not been widely applied. Su Song adapted the escapement and water wheel to his clock, which featured the first known chain-drive mechanism. The clock told the time of day and the day of the month, and it indicated the movement of the moon and certain stars and planets across the night sky. An observation deck and a mechanically rotated armillary sphere crowned the 80-foot (24-meter) structure.

Song inventors drew on their knowledge of celestial coordinates, particularly the Pole Star, to refine the design of the compass. Long known in China, the magnetic compass shrank in size in Song times and gained a fixed pivot point for the needle, and sometimes even a small protective case with a glass covering. These changes made the compass suitable for seafaring, a use first attested in 1090. The Chinese compass and the Greek astrolabe, in-

Su Song's Astronomical Clock This gigantic clock built at Kaifeng between 1088 and 1092 combined mathematics, astronomy, and calendar-making with skillful engineering. The team overseen by Su Song placed an armillary sphere on the observation platform and linked it with chains to the water-driven central mechanism shown in the cutaway view. The water wheel also rotated the buddha statues in the multistory pagoda the spectators are looking at. Other devices displayed the time of the day, the month, and the year. (Courtesy, Joseph Needham, *Science and Civilization in China*)

troduced later, improved navigation throughout Southeast Asia and the Indian Ocean.

Development of the seaworthy compass coincided with new techniques in building China's main oceangoing ship, the **junk.** A stern-mounted rudder improved the steering of the large ship in uneasy seas, and watertight bulkheads helped keep it afloat in emergencies. The shipwrights of the Persian Gulf soon copied these features in their ship designs.

Song innovation carried over into military affairs as well, though military pressure from the Liao and Jin Empires remained a serious challenge. The Song fielded an army four times as large as that of the Tang—about 1.25 million men (roughly the size of the present-day army of the United States)—though it occupied less than half the territory of the Tang. Song commanders were specially educated for the task, examined on military subjects, and paid regular salaries.

Because of the need for iron and steel to make weapons, the Song rulers fought their northern rivals for control of iron and coal mines in north China. The volume of Song mining and iron production, which again became a government monopoly in the eleventh century, soared. By the end of that century cast iron production reached about 125,000 tons (113,700 metric tons) annually, putting it on a par with the output of eighteenth-century Britain. Engineers became skilled at high-temperature metallurgy. They produced steel weapons of unprecedented strength by using enormous bellows, often driven by water wheels, to superheat the molten ore. Military engineers used iron to buttress defensive works because it was impervious to fire or concussion. Armorers used it in mass-produced body armor (in small, medium, and large sizes). Iron construction also appeared in bridges and small buildings. Mass-production techniques for bronze and ceramics in use in China for nearly two thousand years were adapted to iron casting and assembly.

To counter cavalry assaults, the Song experimented with **gunpowder,** which they initially used to propel clusters of flaming arrows. During the wars against the Jurchens in the 1100s the Song introduced a new and terrifying weapon. Shells launched from Song fortifications exploded in the midst of the enemy, blowing out shards of iron and dismembering men and horses. The short

Going up the River Song cities hummed with commercial and industrial activity, much of it concentrated on the rivers and canals linking the capital Kaifeng to the provinces. This detail from *Going Upriver at the Qingming [Spring] Festival* shows a tiny portion of the scroll painting's panorama. Painted by Zhang Zeduan sometime before 1125, its depiction of daily life makes it an important source of information on working people. Before open shop fronts and tea houses a camel caravan departs, donkey carts are unloaded, a scholar rides loftily (if gingerly) on horseback, and women of wealth go by in closed sedan-chairs. (The Palace Museum, Beijing)

range of the shells limited them to defensive uses, and they had no major impact on the overall conduct of war.

Economy and Society in Song China

Despite the continuous military threats and the vigor of Song responses, Song elite culture idealized civil pursuits. Socially, the civil man outranked the military man. Private academies, designed to train young men for the official examinations and develop intellectual interests, became influential in culture and politics. New interpretations of Confucian teachings became so important and influential that the term **neo-Confucianism** is used for Song and later versions of Confucian thought.

Zhu Xi° (1130–1200), the most important early neo-Confucian thinker, wrote in reaction to the many centuries during which Buddhism and Daoism had often overshadowed the precepts of Confucius. He and others worked out a systematic approach to cosmology that focused on the central conception that human nature is moral, rational, and essentially good. To combat the Buddhist dismissal of worldly affairs as a transitory dis-

Zhu Xi (jew she)

traction, they reemphasized individual moral and social responsibility. Their human ideal was the sage, a person who could preserve mental stability and serenity while dealing conscientiously with troubling social problems. Where earlier Confucian thinkers had written about sage kings and political leaders, the neo-Confucians espoused the spiritual idea of universal sagehood, a state that could be achieved through proper study of the new Confucian principles and cosmology.

Despite the vigor and pervasiveness of neo-Confucianism, popular Buddhist sects persisted during the Song. The excerpt from a Song song-story quoted at the beginning of this chapter contained the line "We Buddhists and Confucians are of one family." While historically suitable for the time when the original version of the story of Ying-ying was written, before the Tang abolition of the Buddhist monasteries in 845, it is unlikely that the line would have pleased a Song audience if anti-Buddhist feelings had remained so ferocious. Some Buddhists elaborated upon Tang-era folk practices derived from India and Tibet. The best known, Chan Buddhism (known as **Zen** in Japan and as Son in Korea), asserted that mental discipline alone could win salvation.

Meditation, a key Chan practice, could be employed by Confucians as well as Buddhists. It could afford prospective officials relief from their preparation for civil service examinations, which continued into the Song from the Tang period. Dramatically different from the Han policy of hiring and promoting on the basis of recommendations, Song-style examinations persisted for nearly a thousand years. A large bureaucracy oversaw their design and administration. Test questions, which changed each time the examinations were given, even though they were always based on Confucian classics, often related to economic management or foreign policy.

The examinations had social implications, for hereditary class distinctions meant less than they had in Tang times, when noble lineages played a greater role in the structure of power. The new system recruited the most talented men for government service, whatever their origin. Men from wealthy families, however, succeeded most often. The tests required memorization of classics believed to date from the time of Confucius; preparation consumed so much time that peasant boys could rarely compete.

Success in the examinations brought good marriage prospects, the chance for a high salary, and enormous prestige. Failure could bankrupt a family and ruin a man both socially and psychologically. This put great pressure on candidates, who spent days at a time in tiny, dim, airless examination cells, attempting to produce their answers—in beautiful calligraphy.

Changes in printing, from woodblock to an early form of **movable type,** allowed cheaper printing of many kinds of informative books and of test materials. The Song government realized that the examination system schooled millions of ambitious young men in Confucian ideals of state service—many times the number who eventually passed the tests. To promote its ideological goals, the government authorized the mass production of preparation books in the years before 1000. Though a man had to be literate to read the preparation books and basic education was still not common, some people of limited means were now able to take the examinations; and a moderate number of candidates entered the Song bureaucracy without noble, gentry, or elite backgrounds.

The availability of printed books changed country life as well, since landlords now had access to expert advice on planting and irrigation techniques, harvesting, tree cultivation, threshing, and weaving. Landlords frequently gathered their tenants and workers to show them illustrated texts and explain their meaning. This dissemination of knowledge, along with new technologies, furthered the development of new agricultural land south of the Yangzi River. Iron implements such as plows and rakes, first used in the Tang era, were adapted to wet-rice cultivation as the population moved south. Landowners and village leaders learned from books how

to fight the mosquitoes that carried malaria. Control of the disease became one of the factors encouraging northerners to move south, which led to a sharp increase in population.

The increasing profitability of agriculture caught the attention of some ambitious members of the gentry. Still a frontier for Chinese settlers under the Tang, the south saw increasing concentration of land in the hands of a few wealthy families. In the process, the indigenous inhabitants of the region, related to the modern-day populations of Malaysia, Thailand, and Laos, retreated into the mountains or southward toward Vietnam.

During the 1100s the total population of the Chinese territories, spurred by prosperity, rose above 100 million. An increasing proportion lived in large towns and cities, though the leading Song cities had fewer than a million inhabitants. This still put them among the largest cities in the world.

Health and crowding posed problems in the Song capitals. Multistory wooden apartment houses fronted on narrow streets—sometimes only 4 or 5 feet (1.2 to 1.5 meters) wide—clogged by peddlers or families spending time outdoors. The crush of people called for new techniques in waste management, water supply, and firefighting. Controlling urban rodent and insect infestations improved health and usually kept the bubonic plague isolated in a few rural areas.

In Hangzhou engineers diverted the nearby river to flow through the city, flushing away waste and disease. Arab and European travelers who had firsthand experience with the Song capital, and who were sensitive to the urban crowding in their own societies, expressed amazement at the way Hangzhou city officials sheltered the densely packed population from danger so that they could enjoy the abundant pleasures of the city: restaurants, parks, bookstores, wine shops, tea houses, theaters, and the various entertainments mentioned at the start of this chapter.

The idea of credit, originating in the robust long-distance trade of the Tang period, spread widely under the Song. Intercity or interregional credit—what the Song called "flying money"—depended on the acceptance of guarantees that the paper could be redeemed for coinage at another location. The public accepted the practice because credit networks tended to be managed by families, so that brothers and cousins were usually honoring each other's certificates.

"Flying money" certificates differed from government-issued paper money, which the Song pioneered. In some years, military expenditures consumed 80 percent of the government budget. The state responded to this financial pressure by distributing paper money. But this

The Players   Women—often enslaved—entertained at Chinese courts from early times. Tang art often depicts women with slender figures, but Tang taste also admired more robust physiques. Song women, usually pale with willowy figures, appear as here with bound feet. The practice appeared in Tang times but was not widespread until the Song, when the image of weak, housebound women unable to work became a status symbol and pushed aside the earlier enthusiasm for healthy women who participated in family business.   (The Palace Museum, Beijing)

made inflation so severe that by the beginning of the 1100s paper money was trading for only 1 percent of its face value. Hard-pressed for revenue to maintain the army, canals, roads, and waterworks, the government eventually withdrew paper money and resorted to tax farming, selling the rights to tax collection to private individuals. Tax farmers made their profit by collecting the maximum amount and sending an agreed-upon smaller sum to the government. This meant exorbitant rates for taxable services, such as tolls.

Rapid economic growth undermined the remaining government monopolies and the traditional strict regulation of business. Now merchants and artisans as well as gentry and officials could make fortunes. With land no longer the only source of wealth, the traditional social hierarchy common to an agricultural economy weakened, while cities, commerce, consumption, and the use of money and credit boomed. Urban life reflected the elite's growing taste for fine fabrics, porcelain, exotic foods, large houses, and exquisite paintings and books. Because the government and traditional elites did not

control much of the new commercial and industrial development, historians sometimes describe Song China as "modern," using the term to refer to the era of private capitalism and the growth of an urban middle class in eighteenth-century Europe.

In conjunction with the backlash against Buddhism and revival of Confucianism that began under the Tang and intensified under the Song, women entered a long period of cultural subordination, legal disenfranchisement, and social restriction. Merchants spent long periods away from home, and many maintained several wives in different locations. Frequently they depended on wives to manage their homes and even their businesses in their absence. But though women took on responsibility for the management of their husbands' property, their own property rights suffered legal erosion. Under Song law, a woman's property automatically passed to her husband, and women could not remarry if their husbands divorced them or died.

The subordination of women proved compatible with Confucianism, and it became fashionable to educate girls just enough to read simplified versions of Confucian philosophy that emphasized the lowly role of women. Modest education made these young women more desirable as companions for the sons of gentry or noble families, and as literate mothers in lower ranking families aspiring to improve their status. Only rarely did a woman of extremely high station with unusual personal determination, as well as uncommon encouragement from father and husband, manage to acquire extensive education and freedom to pursue the literary arts. The poet Li Qingzhao° (1083–1141) acknowledged and made fun of her unusual status as a highly celebrated female writer:

> Although I've studied poetry for thirty years
> I try to keep my mouth shut and avoid reputation.
> Now who is this nosy gentleman talking about my
>   poetry
> Like Yang Ching-chih°
> Who spoke of Hsiang Ssu° everywhere he went.[5]

Her reference is to a hermit poet of the ninth century who was continually and extravagantly praised by a court official, Yang Ching-chih.

Female footbinding first appeared among slave dancers at the Tang court, but it did not become widespread until the Song period. The bindings forced the toes under and toward the heel, so that the bones even-

---

Li Qingzhao (lee CHING-jow)
Yang Ching-chih (yahng SHING-she)   **Hsiang Ssu** (sang sue)

tually broke and the woman could not walk on her own. In noble and gentry families, footbinding began between ages five and seven. In less wealthy families, girls worked until they were older, so footbinding began only in a girl's teens.

Many literate men condemned the maiming of innocent girls and the general uselessness of footbinding. Nevertheless, bound feet became a status symbol. By 1200 a woman with unbound feet had become undesirable in elite circles, and mothers of elite status, or aspiring to such status, almost without exception bound their daughters' feet. They knew that girls with unbound feet faced rejection by society, by prospective husbands, and ultimately by their own families. Working women and the indigenous peoples of the south, where northern practices took a longer time to penetrate, did not practice footbinding. As a consequence, they enjoyed considerably more mobility and economic independence than did elite Chinese women.

NEW KINGDOMS IN EAST ASIA

With the rival states to the northeast and northwest strongly oriented toward Buddhism, the best possibilities for expanding the Confucian worldview of the Song lay with newly emerging kingdoms to the east and south. Korea, Japan, and Vietnam, like Song China, depended on agriculture. The cultivation of rice, an increasingly widespread crop, fit well with Confucian social ideas. Tending the young rice plants, irrigating the rice paddies, and managing the harvest required coordination among many village and kin groups and rewarded hierarchy, obedience, and self-discipline.

Since Han times Confucianism had spread through East Asia with the spread of the Chinese writing system. Political ideologies in Korea, Japan, and Vietnam varied somewhat from those of Song China, however. These three East Asian neighbors had first centralized power under ruling houses in the early Tang period, and their state ideologies continued to resemble that of the early Tang, when Buddhism and Confucianism were still seen as compatible.

Government offices in Korea, Japan, and Vietnam went to noble families and did not depend on passing an elaborate set of examinations on Confucian texts. Nevertheless, members of the ruling and landholding elite sought to instill Confucian ideals of hierarchy and harmony among the general population. The elite in every country learned to read Chinese and the Confucian classics, and Chinese characters contributed to locally invented writing systems (see Environment and Technology: Writing in East Asia, 600–1200).

Korea

A land of mountains, particularly in the east and north, Korea was largely covered by forest until modern times. Less than 20 percent of the land, mostly in the warmer south, is suitable for agriculture. In the early 500s the dominant landholding families made inherited status—the "bone ranks"—permanent in Silla°, a kingdom in the southeast of the peninsula. In 668 the larger Koguryo kingdom in the north came to an end after prolonged conflict with the Sui and Tang, and with Tang encouragement, Silla took control of much of the Korean peninsula. Silla could not stand by itself without Tang support, however, so after the fall of the Tang in the early 900s, the ruling house of **Koryo°,** from which the modern name "Korea" derives, united the peninsula. At constant threat from the Liao and then the Jin, Koryo pursued amicable relations with Song China. The Koryo kings supported Buddhism and made superb printed editions of Buddhist texts.

Woodblock printing exemplifies the technological exchanges that Korea enjoyed with China. The oldest surviving woodblock print in Chinese characters comes from Korea in the middle 700s. Commonly used during the Tang period, woodblock printing required great technical skill. A calligrapher would write the text on thin paper, which would then be pasted upside down on a block of wood. When the paper was wetted, the characters showed through from the back, and an artisan would carve away the wooden surface surrounding each character. A fresh block had to be carved for each printed page. Korean artisans developed their own advances in printing. By Song times, Korean experiments with movable type reached China, where further improvements led to metal or porcelain type from which texts could be cheaply printed.

Japan

Japan consists of four main islands and many smaller ones stretching in an arc from as far south as Georgia to as far north as Maine. The nearest point of contact with the Asian mainland lies 100 miles away in southern Korea. In early times Japan was even more mountainous and heavily forested than Korea, and only 11 percent of its land area was suitable for cultivation.

Silla (SILL-ah or SHILL-ah)   **Koryo** (KAW-ree-oh)

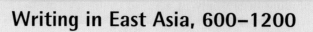

Writing in East Asia, 600–1200

An ideographic writing system that originated in China became a communications tool throughout East Asia. Variations on this system, based more on depictions of meanings than representations of sound, spread widely by the time of the Sui and Tang Empires. Many East Asian peoples adapted ideographic techniques to writing languages unrelated to Chinese in grammar or sound.

The Vietnamese, Koreans, and Japanese often simplified Chinese characters and associated them with the sounds of their own non-Chinese languages. For instance, the Chinese character *an*, meaning "peace" (Fig. 1), was pronounced "an" in Japanese and was familiar as a Chinese character to Confucian scholars in Japan's Heian (hay-ahn) period. However, nonscholars simplified the character and used it to write the Japanese sound "a" (Fig. 2). A set of more than thirty of these syllabic symbols adapted from Chinese characters could represent the inflected forms (forms with grammatical endings) of any Japanese word. Murasaki Shikibu used such a syllabic system when she wrote *The Tale of Genji*.

In Vietnam and later in northern Asia, phonetic and ideographic elements combined in new ways. The apparent circles in some *chu nom* writing from Vietnam (Fig. 3) derive from the Chinese character for "mouth" and indicate a primary sound association for the word. The Khitans, who spoke a language related to Mongolian, developed an ideographic system of

their own, inspired by Chinese characters. The Chinese character *wang* (Fig. 4), meaning "king, prince, ruler," was changed to represent the Khitan word for "emperor" by adding an upward stroke representing a "superior" ruler (Fig. 5). Because the system was ideographic, we do not know the pronunciation of this Khitan word. The Khitan character for "God" or "Heaven" adds a top stroke representing the "supreme" ruler or power to the character meaning "ruler" (Fig. 6). Though inspired by Chinese characters, Khitan writings could not be read by anyone who was not specifically educated in them.

The Khitans developed another system to represent the sounds and grammar of their language. They used small, simplified elements arranged within an imaginary frame to indicate the sounds in any word. This idea might have come from the phonetic script used by the Uighurs. Here (Fig. 7) we see the word for horse in a Khitan inscription. Fitting sound elements within a frame also occurred later in *hangul*, the Korean phonetic system introduced in the 1400s. Here (Fig. 8) we see the two words making up the country name "Korea."

The Chinese writing system served the Chinese elite well. But peoples speaking unrelated languages continually experimented with the Chinese invention to produce new ways of expressing themselves. Some of the resulting sound-based writing systems remain in common use; others are still being deciphered.

   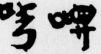   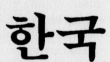

Figure 1　**Figure 2**　**Figure 3**　**Figure 4**　**Figure 5**　**Figure 6**　**Figure 7**　**Figure 8**

Japan's earliest history, like Korea's, comes from Chinese records. In the mid-600s the rulers based at Yamato, on the central plain of Honshu island, implemented the Taika° and other reforms, giving the Yamato regime the key features of Tang government, which they knew of through embassies to Chang'an: a legal code, an official variety of Confucianism, and an official reverence for Buddhism. Within a century a centralized government

with a complex system of law had emerged, as attested by a massive history in the Confucian style. The Japanese mastered Chinese building techniques so well that Nara° and Kyoto, Japan's early capitals, provide invaluable evidence of the wooden architecture long since vanished from China. During the eighth century Japan in some ways surpassed China in Buddhist studies. In 752 dignitaries from all over Mahayana Buddhist Asia gathered at

---

Taika (TIE-kah)

Nara (NAH-rah)

the enormous Todaiji temple, near Nara, to celebrate the "eye-opening" of the "Great Buddha" statue.

Japanese admiration of Chinese culture did not extend to everything, however. Though the Japanese adopted Chinese building styles and some street plans, Japanese cities were built without walls. Unlike China, central Japan was not plagued by constant warfare. Also, the Confucian Mandate of Heaven, which justified dynastic changes, played no role in legitimating Japanese government. The *tenno*—often called "emperor" in English—belonged to a family believed to have ruled Japan since the beginning of known history. The dynasty never changed. The royal family endured because the emperors seldom wielded political power. A prime minister and the leaders of the native religion, in later times called Shinto, the "way of the gods," exercised real control.

In 794 the central government moved to Kyoto, usually called by its ancient name, Heian. Legally centralized government lasted there until 1185, though power became decentralized toward the end. Members of the **Fujiwara°** family—an ancient family of priests, bureaucrats, and warriors—controlled power and protected the emperor. Fujiwara dominance favored men of Confucian learning over the generally illiterate warriors. Noblemen of the Fujiwara period read the Chinese classics, appreciated painting and poetry, and refined their sense of wardrobe and interior decoration.

Pursuit of an aesthetic way of life prompted the Fujiwara nobles to entrust responsibility for local government, policing, and tax collection to their warriors. Though often of humble origins, a small number of warriors had achieved wealth and power by the late 1000s. By the middle 1100s the nobility had lost control, and civil war between rival warrior clans engulfed the capital.

Like other East Asian states influenced by Confucianism, the elite families of Fujiwara Japan did not encourage education for women. However, this did not prevent the exceptional woman from having a strong cultural impact. The hero of the celebrated Japanese novel *The Tale of Genji,* written around the year 1000 by the noblewoman Murasaki Shikibu, remarks: "Women should have a general knowledge of several subjects, but it gives a bad impression if they show themselves to be attached to a particular branch of learning."[6]

Fujiwara noblewomen lived in near-total isolation, generally spending their time on cultural pursuits and the study of Buddhism. To communicate with their families or among themselves, they depended on writing.

The simplified syllabic script that they used represented the Japanese language in its fully inflected form (the Chinese classical script used by Fujiwara men could not do so). Loneliness, free time, and a ready instrument for expression produced an outpouring of poetry, diaries, and storytelling by women of the Fujiwara era. Their best-known achievement, however, remains Murasaki's portrait of Fujiwara court culture.

Military values acquired increasing importance during the period 1156–1185, when warfare between rival clans culminated in the establishment of the **Kamakura° shogunate,** the first of three decentralized military governments, in eastern Honshu, far from the old religious and political center at Kyoto. The standing of the Fujiwara family fell as nobles and the emperor hurried to accommodate the new warlords. *The Tale of the Heike,* an anonymously composed thirteenth-century epic account of the clan war, reflects an appreciation of the Buddhist doctrine of the impermanence of worldly things, a view that became common at that time among a new warrior class. This new class, in later times called *samurai,* eventually absorbed some of the Fujiwara aristocratic values, but the ascendancy of the nonmilitary civil elite had come to an end.

Vietnam

Occupying the coastal regions east of the mountainous spine of mainland Southeast Asia, Vietnam's economic and political life centered on two fertile river valleys, the Red River in the north and the Mekong° in the south. Agriculture was also possible in many smaller coastal areas where streams from the mountains—torrents during the monsoon season—flowed down to the sea. The rice-based agriculture of Vietnam made the region well suited for integration with southern China. As in southern China, the wet climate and hilly terrain of Vietnam demanded expertise in irrigation.

In Tang and Song times the elites of "Annam°"—as the Chinese called early Vietnam—adopted Confucian bureaucratic training, Mahayana Buddhism, and other aspects of Chinese culture. Annamese elites continued to rule in the Tang style after that dynasty's fall. Annam assumed the name Dai Viet° in 936 and maintained good relations with Song China as an independent country.

Champa, located largely in what is now southern Vietnam, rivaled the Dai Viet state. The cultures of India and Malaya strongly influenced Champa through

---

Fujiwara (foo-jee-WAH-rah)

Kamakura (kah-mah-KOO-rah)   **Mekong** (may-KONG)
Annam (ahn-nahm)   **Dai Viet** (die vee-yet)

the networks of trade and communication that encompassed the Indian Ocean. During the Tang period Champa had hostile relations with Dai Viet, but both kingdoms cooperated with the less threatening Song, the former as a voluntary tributary state. Among the tribute gifts brought to the Song court by Champa emissaries was **Champa rice** (originally from India). Chinese farmers soon made use of this fast-maturing variety to improve their yields of the essential crop.

Vietnam shared the Confucian interest in hierarchy that was also evident in Korea and Japan, but attitudes toward women, like those in the other two countries, differed from the Chinese model. None of the societies adopted the Chinese practice of footbinding. In Korea strong family alliances that functioned like political and economic organizations allowed women a role in negotiating and disposing of property. Before the adoption of Confucianism, Annamese women had enjoyed higher status than women in China, perhaps because both women and men participated in wet-rice cultivation.

CONCLUSION

The reunification of China under the Sui and Tang triggered major changes both within China and in neighboring lands. Connections across Inner Asia and Tibet facilitated the flow of cultural and economic influences into China. Diversity within the empire produced great wealth and new ideas, and the dominant position of the Tang in the entire region led neighboring peoples in Korea, Japan, and Vietnam to imitate their practices. In time, however, internal tensions and foreign military pressure from the Uighurs and Tibetans weakened the Tang political structure and touched off rebellions that eventually doomed the empire.

The post-Tang fragmentation reduced the degree of Chinese domination in East Asia. Combining indigenous traditions and ideas borrowed from the Tang, neighboring peoples experimented with and often improved upon Tang military, architectural, and scientific technologies. The Jin, Tangguts, and Jurchens pursued these refinements on the basis of Buddhism as the state ideology. But they were not averse to adopting bureaucratic practices based on Chinese traditions and military techniques combining nomadic horsemanship and strategies with Chinese armaments and weapons. Korea, Japan, and Vietnam became much more closely wedded to Confucian models of state and society.

In Song China the spread of Tang technological knowledge resulted in the privatization of commerce,

major advances in technology and industry, increased productivity in agriculture, and deeper exploration of ideas relating to time, cosmology, and mathematics. The brilliant achievements of the Song period came from mutually reinforcing developments in economy and technology. Avoiding the Tang's discouragement of innovation and competition, the Song economy, though much smaller than its predecessor, showed great productivity, circulating goods and money throughout East Asia and stimulating the economies of neighboring states. In terms of industrial specialization, Song China excelled in military technology, engineering of all kinds, and production of iron and coal.

All the East Asian societies made advances in agricultural technology and productivity. All raised their literacy rates after the improvement of printing. Building on knowledge derived from Tang and Song sources, Japan went beyond China in developing advanced techniques in steel making, and Korea excelled in textiles and agriculture and produced major innovations in printing.

In the long run Song China could not maintain the equilibrium necessary to sustain its own prosperity and that of the region. Constant military challenges from the north eventually overwhelmed Song finances, and the need to buy high-quality steel from Japan caused a drain of copper coinage. When historians compare Song China with eighteenth-century Great Britain, another society that achieved unprecedented industrial production and technological innovation, they speculate about the reasons China progressed to such high levels of achievement and then tapered off while developments in Britain interacted with those in other European countries to produce an industrial revolution. No one can answer such questions conclusively, but the complex character of interrelationships among the East Asian and Inner Asian states as a whole, and the differing views of the world presented by Buddhism and neo-Confucianism surely played important roles.

■ Key Terms

Li Shimin

Tang Empire

Grand Canal

tributary system

bubonic plague

Uighurs

Tibet

Song Empire

junk

gunpowder

neo-Confucianism

Zen

movable type

Koryo

Fujiwara

Kamakura shogunate

Champa rice

■ Suggested Reading

On Inner Asia see the bibliography for Chapter 7 relating to the Silk Road. In addition, Denis Sinor, ed., *The Cambridge History of Early Inner Asia* (1990), and M. S. Asimov and C. E. Bosworth, eds., *History of Civilizations of Central Asia: Volume IV—The Age of Achievement, A.D. 750 to the End of the Fifteenth Century—Part Two, the Achievements* (2000), contain articles on many topics. Thomas Barfield, *The Perilous Frontier: Nomadic Empires and China* (1992), is an anthropologist's view of the broad relationship between pastoralists and agriculturists in the region. Susan Whitfield's *Life Along the Silk Road* (2001) uses fictional travelers as a narrative device but is solidly based on documentary research.

Arthur F. Wright, *The Sui Dynasty* (1978), is a very readable narrative of the reunification of China in the sixth century. The Tang Empire is the topic of a huge literature, but for a variety of enduring essays see Arthur F. Wright and David Twitchett, eds., *Perspectives on the T'ang* (1973). On Tang contacts with the cultures of Central, South, and Southeast Asia see Edward Schaeffer, *The Golden Peaches of Samarkand* (1963), *The Vermilion Bird* (1967), and *Pacing the Void* (1977). For an introduction to medieval Tibet see Rolf Stein, *Tibetan Civilization* (1972). On the Uighurs see Colin MacKarras, *The Uighur Empire* (1968).

There is comparatively little secondary work in English on the Central and northern Asian empires that succeeded the Tang. But for a classic text see Karl Wittfogel and Chia-sheng Feng, *History of Chinese Society: Liao* (1949). On the Jurchen Jin, see Jin-sheng Tao, *The Jurchens in Twelfth Century China,* and on the Tangguts see Ruth Dunnell, *The State of High and White: Buddhism and the State in Eleventh-Century Xia* (1996). Morris Rossabi, ed., *China Among Equals: The Middle Kingdom and Its Neighbors, 10th–14th Centuries* (1983), deals with post-Tang relationships more broadly.

On the Song there is a large volume of material, particularly relating to technological achievements. For an introduction to the monumental work of Joseph Needham see *Science in Traditional China* (1981). A classic thesis on Song advancement (and Ming backwardness) is Mark Elvin, *The Pattern of the Chinese Past* (1973), particularly Part II. Joel Mokyr, *The Lever of Riches* (1990), is a more recent comparative treatment. Agriculture is the special concern of Francesca Bray, *The Rice Economies: Technology and Development in Asian Societies* (1994).

For neo-Confucianism and Buddhism see W. T. de Bary, W-T Chan, and B. Watson, compilers, *Sources of Chinese Tradition,* vol. 1, 2d ed. (1999), as well as Arthur F. Wright, *Buddhism in Chinese History* (1983). On religion more broadly see Robert P. Hymes, *Way and Byway: Taoism, Local Religion, and Models of Divinity in Sung China* (2002). On social and economic history see Miyazaki Ichisada, *China's Examination Hell* (1971); Richard von Glahn, *The Land of Streams and Grottoes* (1987); and Patricia Ebery, *The Inner Quarters: Marriage and the Lives of Chinese Women in the Sung Period* (1993). On the poet Li Qingzhao see Hu Pin-ch'ing, *Li Ch'ing-chao* (1966).

On the history of Korea see Andrew C. Nahm, *Introduction to Korean History and Culture* (1993), and Ki-Baik Kim, *A New History of Korea* (1984). Yongho Ch'oe et al., eds., include excerpts from many historical works in *Sources of Korean Tradition* (2000). An excellent introduction to Japanese history is Paul H. Varley, *Japanese Culture* (1984). Selections of relevant documents may be found in David John Lu, *Sources of Japanese History,* vol. 1 (1974), and R. Tsunoda, W. T. de Bary, and D. Keene, compilers, *Sources of Japanese Tradition,* vol. 1 (1964). Ivan Morris, *The World of the Shining Prince: Court Life in Ancient Japan* (1979), is a classic introduction to the literature and culture of Fujiwara Japan at the time of the composition of Murasaki Shikibu's *The Tale of Genji.* For Vietnam see Keith Weller Taylor, *The Birth of Vietnam* (1983).

■ Notes

1. *Master Tung's Western Chamber Romance,* tr. Li-li Ch'en (New York: Columbia University Press, 1994), 22, 42–43, 45–46.
2. Arthur Waley, *Poetry and Career of Li Po* (London: Unwin Hyman, 1954), 35.
3. Theodore de Bary, ed., *Sources of Chinese Tradition,* vol. 1, 2d ed. (New York: Columbia University Press, 1999), 584.
4. Quoted in David Lattimore, "Allusion in T'ang Poetry," in *Perspectives on the T'ang,* ed. Arthur F. Wright and David Twitchett (New Haven, CT: Yale University Press, 1973), 436.
5. Quoted at "Women's Early Music, Art, Poetry," http://music.acu.edu/www/iawm/pages/reference/tzusongs.html.
6. Quoted in Ivan Morris, *The World of the Shining Prince: Court Life in Ancient Japan* (New York: Penguin Books, 1979), 221–222.

Document-Based Question

Women in Tang and Song China

Using the following documents, analyze the factors that influenced the status and roles of women in Tang and Song China.

DOCUMENT 1
Law and Society in Tang China (Diversity and Dominance, pp. 248–249)

DOCUMENT 2
Tang Women at Polo (photo, p. 250)

DOCUMENT 3
Women of Turfan Grinding Flour (photo, p. 252)

DOCUMENT 4
Going up the River (photo, p. 258)

DOCUMENT 5
The Players (photo, p. 260)

DOCUMENT 6
Excerpt from a poem by Li Qingzhao (p. 260)

Which documents seem to provide an idealized or sanitized representation of women in Tang and Song China? What additional types of documents would provide a more realistic view of their status and roles?

11

Peoples and Civilizations of the Americas, 600–1500

Maya Scribe   Mayan scribes used a complex writing system to record religious concepts and memorialize the actions of their kings. This picture of a scribe was painted on a ceramic plate.

In late August 682 C.E. the Maya° princess Lady Wac-Chanil-Ahau° walked down the steep steps from her family's residence and mounted a sedan chair decorated with rich textiles and animal skins. As the procession exited from the urban center of Dos Pilas°, her military escort spread out through the fields and woods along its path to prevent ambush by enemies. Lady Wac-Chanil-Ahau's destination was the Maya city of Naranjo°, where she was to marry a powerful nobleman. Her marriage had been arranged to re-establish the royal dynasty that had been eliminated when Caracol, the region's major military power, had defeated Naranjo. Lady Wac-Chanil-Ahau's passage to Naranjo symbolized her father's desire to forge a military alliance that could resist Caracol. For us, the story of Lady Wac-Chanil-Ahau illustrates the importance of marriage and lineage in the politics of the classic-period Maya.

Smoking Squirrel, the son of Lady Wac-Chanil-Ahau, ascended the throne of Naranjo as a five-year-old in 693 C.E. During his long reign he proved to be a careful diplomat and formidable warrior. He was also a prodigious builder, leaving behind an expanded and beautified capital as part of his legacy. Mindful of the importance of his mother and her lineage from Dos Pilas, he erected numerous stelae (carved stone monuments) that celebrated her life.[1]

When population increased and competition for resources grew more violent, warfare and dynastic crisis convulsed the world of Wac-Chanil-Ahau. The defeat of the city-states of Tikal and Naranjo by Caracol undermined long-standing commercial and political relations in much of southern Mesoamerica and led to more than a century of conflict. Caracol, in turn, was challenged by the dynasty created at Dos Pilas by the heirs of Lady Wac-Chanil-Ahau. Despite a shared culture and religion, the great Maya cities remained divided by the dynastic ambitions of their rulers and by the competition for resources.

As the story of Lady Wac-Chanil-Ahau's marriage and her role in the development of a Maya dynasty suggests, the peoples of the Americas were in constant competition for resources. Members of hereditary elites organized their societies to meet these challenges, even as their ambition for greater power predictably ignited new conflicts. No single set of political institutions or technologies worked in every environment, and enormous cultural diversity existed in the ancient Americas. In Mesoamerica (Mexico and northern Central America) and in the Andean region of South America, Amerindian peoples developed an extraordinarily productive and diversified agriculture.[2] They also built great cities that rivaled the capitals of the Chinese and Roman Empires in size and beauty. The Olmecs of Mesoamerica and Chavín° of the Andes were among the earliest civilizations of the Americas (see Chapter 2). In the rest of the hemisphere, indigenous peoples adapted combinations of hunting and agriculture to maintain a wide variety of settlement patterns, political forms, and cultural traditions. All the cultures and civilizations of the Americas experienced cycles of expansion and contraction as they struggled with the challenges of environmental changes, population growth, social conflict, and war.

As you read this chapter, ask yourself the following questions:

- How did differing environments influence the development of Mesoamerican, Andean, and northern peoples?

- What technologies were developed to meet the challenges of these environments?

- How were the civilizations of Mesoamerica and the Andean region similar? How did they differ?

- How did religious belief and practice influence political life in the ancient Americas?

Maya (MY-ah)   **Wac-Chanil-Ahau** (wac-cha-NEEL-ah-HOW)
Dos Pilas (dohs PEE-las)   **Naranjo** (na-ROHN-hoe)

Chavín (cha-VEEN)

C H R O N O L O G Y

	Mesoamerica	Northern peoples	Andes
600	**600** Teotihuacan at height of power		**600–1000** Tiwanaku and Wari control Peruvian highlands
700	**ca. 750** Teotihuacan destroyed **800–900** Maya centers abandoned, end of classic period **968** Toltec capital of Tula founded	**700–1200** Anasazi culture **919** Pueblo Bonito founded	**700** End of Moche control of Peruvian coast
1000	**1156** Tula destroyed	**1050–1250** Cahokia reaches peak power **1150** Collapse of Anasazi centers begins	
1300	**1325** Aztec capital Tenochtitlan founded		**1438** Inca expansion begins
1500	**1502** Moctezuma II crowned Aztec ruler	**1500** Mississippian culture declines	**1500–1525** Inca conquer Ecuador

CLASSIC-ERA CULTURE AND SOCIETY IN MESOAMERICA, 600–900

The Mesoamerican civilization of the period 600 to 900 C.E. was the culmination of several centuries of growth involving several peoples speaking different languages. Though no regionwide political integration developed, Mesoamericans were unified by similarities in material culture, religious beliefs and practices, and social structures. Building on the earlier achievements of the Olmecs and others (see Chapter 2), the peoples of today's Central America and south and central Mexico developed new forms of political organization, made advances in astronomy and mathematics, and improved agricultural productivity. Population grew, traders exchanged a variety of products over longer distances, and social hierarchies became more complex, giving rise to great cities that served as centers of political and spiritual life.

Classic-period cities, as archaeologists call those of the period ending in about 900 C.E., continued to be feature platforms and pyramids devoted to religious functions. They had large full-time populations divided into classes and dominated by hereditary political and religious elites who controlled nearby towns and villages and imposed their will on the rural peasantry.

Political and cultural innovations did not depend on new technologies. The agricultural foundation of Mesoamerican civilization was centuries old. Irrigation, the draining of wetlands, and the terracing of hillsides had all been in place for more than a thousand years. Instead, the achievements of the classic era depended on the ability of increasingly powerful elites to organize and command growing numbers of laborers and soldiers. What changed was the reach and power of religious and political leaders.

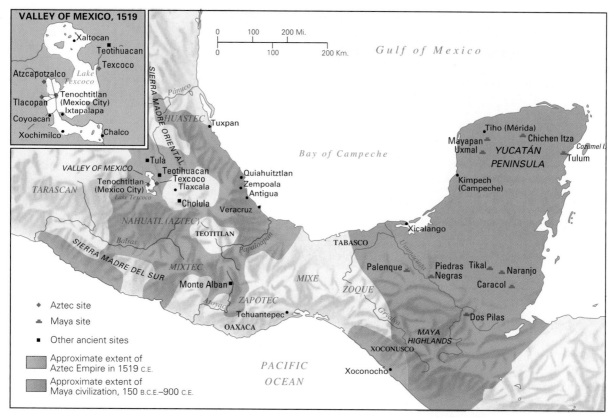

Map 11.1   Major Mesoamerican Civilizations, 1000 B.C.E.–1519 C.E.   From their island capital of Tenochtitlan, the Aztecs militarily and commercially dominated a large region. Aztec achievements were built on the legacy of earlier civilizations such as the Olmecs and Maya.

Teotihuacan

Located about 30 miles (48 kilometers) northeast of modern Mexico City, **Teotihuacan°** (see Map 11.1) was at the height of its power in 600 C.E. and verging on decline. With between 125,000 and 200,000 inhabitants, it was the largest city in the Americas and larger than all but a few contemporary European and Asian cities.

Religious architecture rose above a city center aligned with nearby sacred mountains and reflecting the movement of the stars. Enormous pyramids dedicated to the Sun and Moon and more than twenty smaller temples devoted to other gods were arranged along a central avenue. The people recognized and worshiped many gods and lesser spirits. Among the gods were the Sun, the Moon, a storm-god, and Quetzalcoatl°, the feathered serpent. Quetzalcoatl was a culture-god believed to be the originator of agriculture and the arts. Like the earlier

Olmecs, people living at Teotihuacan practiced human sacrifice. More than a hundred sacrificial victims were found during the excavation of the temple of Quetzalcoatl at Teotihuacan. Sacrifice was viewed as a sacred duty toward the gods and as essential to the well-being of human society.

The rapid growth in urban population initially resulted from a series of volcanic eruptions that disrupted agriculture. Later, as the city elite increased its power, farm families from the smaller villages in the region were forced to relocate to the urban core. As a result, more than two-thirds of the city's residents retained their dependence on agriculture, walking out from urban residences to their fields. The elite of Teotihuacan used the city's growing labor resources to bring marginal lands into production. Swamps were drained, irrigation works were constructed, terraces were built into hillsides, and the use of chinampas was expanded. **Chinampas°**, sometimes called "floating gardens," were narrow artificial is-

Teotihuacan (teh-o-tee-WAH-kahn)
Quetzalcoatl (kate-zahl-CO-ah-tal)

chinampas (chee-NAM-pahs)

lands constructed along lakeshores or in marshes. They were created by heaping lake muck and waste material on beds of reeds that were then anchored to the shore by trees. Chinampas permitted year-round agriculture—because of subsurface irrigation and resistance to frost—and thus played a crucial role in sustaining the region's growing population. The productivity of the city's agriculture made possible its accomplishments in art, architecture, and trade.

As population grew, the housing of commoners underwent dramatic change. Apartment-like stone buildings were constructed for the first time. These apartment compounds were unique to Teotihuacan. They commonly housed members of a single kinship group, but some were used to house craftsmen working in the same trade. The two largest craft groups produced pottery and obsidian tools, the most important articles of long-distance trade. It appears that more than 2 percent of the urban population was engaged in making obsidian tools and weapons. The city's pottery and obsidian have been found throughout central Mexico and even in the Maya region of Guatemala.

The city's role as a religious center and commercial power provided both divine approval of and a material basis for the elite's increased wealth and status. Members of the elite controlled the state bureaucracy, tax collection, and commerce. Their prestige and wealth were reflected in their style of dress and diet and in the separate residence compounds built for aristocratic families. The central position and great prestige of the priestly class were evident in temple and palace murals. Teotihuacan's economy and religious influence drew pilgrims from as far away as Oaxaca and Veracruz. Some of them became permanent residents.

Unlike the other classic-period civilizations, the people of Teotihuacan did not concentrate power in the hands of a single ruler. Although the ruins of their impressive housing compounds demonstrate the wealth and influence of the city's aristocracy, there is no clear evidence that individual rulers or a ruling dynasty gained overarching political power. In Teotihuacan the deeds of individual rulers were not featured in public art, nor were their images represented by statues or other monuments as in other Mesoamerican civilizations. In fact, some scholars suggest that Teotihuacan was ruled by alliances forged among elite families or by weak kings who were the puppets of these powerful families. Regardless of what form political decision making took, we know that this powerful classic-period civilization achieved regional preeminence without subordinating its political life to the personality of a powerful individual ruler or lineage.

Historians debate the role of the military in the de-velopment of Teotihuacan. The city walls of 600 C.E. had not been there a century and a half earlier, suggesting that Teotihuacan enjoyed relative peace during its early development. Archaeological evidence, however, reveals that the city created a powerful military to protect long-distance trade and to compel peasant agriculturalists to transfer their surplus production to the city. The discovery of representations of soldiers in typical Teotihuacan dress in the Maya region of Guatemala suggests to some that Teotihuacan used its military to expand trade relations. Unlike later postclassic civilizations, however, Teotihuacan was not an imperial state controlled by a military elite.

It is unclear what forces brought about the collapse of Teotihuacan about 650 C.E. Pictorial evidence from murals suggests that the city's final decades were violent. Early scholars suggested that the city was overwhelmed militarily by a nearby rival city or by nomadic warriors from the northern frontier. More recent investigators have uncovered evidence of conflict within the ruling elite and the mismanagement of resources. This, they argue, led to class conflict and the breakdown of public order. As a result, most important temples in the city center were pulled down and religious images defaced. Elite palaces were also systematically burned and many of the residents killed.

The Maya

During Teotihuacan's ascendancy in the north, the **Maya** developed an impressive civilization in the region that today includes Guatemala, Honduras, Belize, and southern Mexico (see Map 11.1). Given the difficulties imposed by a tropical climate and fragile soils, the cultural and architectural achievements of the Maya were remarkable. Although they shared a single culture, they were never unified politically. Instead, rival kingdoms led by hereditary rulers struggled with each other for regional dominance.

Today Maya farmers prepare their fields by cutting down small trees and brush and then burning the dead vegetation to fertilize the land. Swidden agriculture (also called shifting agriculture or slash and burn agriculture) can produce high yields for a few years. However, it uses up the soil's nutrients, eventually forcing people to move to more fertile land. The high population levels of the Maya classic period, which ended about 900 C.E., required more intensive forms of agriculture. Maya living near the major urban centers achieved high agricultural yields by draining swamps and building elevated fields. They used irrigation in areas with long dry seasons, and they terraced hillsides in the cooler highlands. Nearly every household planted a garden to provide condiments

The Great Plaza at Tikal   Still visible in the ruins of Tikal, in modern Guatemala, are the impressive architectural and artistic achievements of the classic-era Maya. Maya centers provided a dramatic setting for the rituals that dominated public life. Construction of Tikal began before 150 B.C.E.; the city was abandoned about 900 C.E. A ball court and residences for the elite were part of the Great Plaza.   (Martha Cooper/Peter Arnold, Inc.)

and fruits to supplement dietary staples. Maya agriculturists also managed nearby forests, favoring the growth of the trees and shrubs that were most useful to them.

The most powerful cities of the classic period controlled groups of smaller dependent cities and a broad agricultural zone by building impressive religious temples and by creating rituals that linked the power of kings to the gods. High pyramids, commonly aligned with the movements of the sun and Venus, and elaborately decorated palaces surrounding open plazas awed the masses drawn to the centers for religious and political rituals.

Bas-reliefs painted in bright colors covered most public buildings. Religious allegories, the genealogies of rulers, and important historical events were the most common motifs. Beautifully carved altars and stone monoliths were erected near major temples. Everything

was constructed without the aid of wheels—no pulleys, wheelbarrows, or carts—or metal tools. Masses of men and women aided only by levers and stone tools cut and carried construction materials and lifted them into place.

The Maya cosmos was divided into three layers connected along a vertical axis that traced the course of the sun. The earthly arena of human existence held an intermediate position between the heavens, conceptualized by the Maya as a sky-monster, and a dark underworld. A sacred tree rose through the three layers; its roots were in the underworld, and its branches reached into the heavens. The temple precincts of Maya cities physically represented essential elements of this religious cosmology. The pyramids were sacred mountains reaching to the heavens. The doorways of the pyramids were portals to the underworld.

The Mesoamerican Ball Game   From Guatemala to Arizona, archaeologists have found evidence of an ancient ball game played with a solid rubber ball on slope-sided courts shaped like a capital T. Among the Maya the game was associated with a creation myth and thus had deep religious meaning. There is evidence that some players were sacrificed. In this scene from a ceramic jar, players wearing elaborate ritual clothing—which includes heavy, protective pads around the chest and waist—play with a ball much larger than the ball actually used in such games. Some representations show balls drawn to suggest a human head. (Chrysler Museum of Art/Justin Kerr)

Rulers and other members of the elite served both priestly and political functions. They decorated their bodies with paint and tattoos and wore elaborate costumes of textiles, animal skins, and feathers to project both secular power and divine sanction. Kings communicated directly with the supernatural residents of the other worlds and with deified royal ancestors through bloodletting rituals and hallucinogenic trances. Scenes of rulers drawing blood from lips, ears, and penises are common in surviving frescoes and on painted pottery.

Warfare in particular was infused with religious meaning and attached to elaborate rituals. Battle scenes and the depiction of the torture and sacrifice of captives were frequent decorative themes. Typically, Maya military forces fought to secure captives rather than territory. Days of fasting, sacred ritual, and rites of purification preceded battle. The king, his kinsmen, and other ranking nobles actively participated in war. Elite captives were nearly always sacrificed; captured commoners were more likely to be forced to labor for their captors.

Only two women are known to have ruled Maya kingdoms. Maya women of the ruling lineages did play important political and religious roles, however. The consorts of male rulers participated in bloodletting rituals and in other important public ceremonies, and their noble blood helped legitimate the rule of their husbands. Although Maya society was patrilineal (tracing descent in the male line), there is evidence that some male rulers traced their lineages bilaterally (in both the male and the female lines). Like Lady Wac-Chanil-Ahau's son Smoking Squirrel, some rulers emphasized the female line if it held higher status. Much less is known about the lives of the women of the lower classes, but scholars believe that women played a central role in the religious rituals of the home. They were also healers and shamans. Women were essential to the household economy, maintaining essential garden plots and weaving, and in the management of family life.

Building on what the Olmecs had done, the Maya made important contributions to the development of the Mesoamerican calendar and to mathematics and writing. Their interest in time and in the cosmos was reflected in the complexity of their calendric system. Each day was identified by three separate dating systems. Like other peoples throughout Mesoamerica, the Maya had a calendar that tracked the ritual cycle (260 days divided into thirteen months of 20 days) as well as a solar calendar (365 days divided into eighteen months of 20 days, plus 5 unfavorable days at the end of the year). The concurrence of these two calendars every fifty-two years was believed to be especially ominous. Alone among Mesoamerican peoples, the Maya also maintained a continuous "long count" calendar, which began at a fixed date in the past that scholars have identified as 3114 B.C.E., a date that the Maya probably associated with creation.

Both the calendars and the astronomical observations on which they were based depended on Maya mathematics and writing. Their system of mathematics incorporated the concept of the zero and place value but had limited notational signs. Maya writing was a form of hieroglyphic inscription that signified whole words or concepts as well as phonetic cues or syllables. Aspects of public life, religious belief, and the biographies of rulers and their ancestors were recorded in deerskin and bark-paper books, on pottery, and on the stone columns and monumental buildings of the urban centers.

Between 800 and 900 C.E. many of the major urban centers of the Maya were abandoned or destroyed, although a small number of classic-period centers survived for centuries. In some areas, decades of urban population decline and increased warfare preceded abandonment. Some scholars have proposed, on little evidence, that epidemic disease played a role in this catastrophe. Others contend that the earlier destruction of Teotihuacan around 650 C.E. disrupted trade, thus undermining the legitimacy of Maya rulers who had used the goods in rituals. There is growing consensus that the population expansion led to environmental degradation and declining agricultural productivity, which, in turn, provoked social conflict and warfare.

THE POSTCLASSIC PERIOD IN MESOAMERICA, 900–1500

The division between the classic and postclassic periods is somewhat arbitrary. Not only is there no single explanation for the collapse of Teotihuacan and many of the major Maya centers, but these events occurred over more than a century and a half. In fact, some important classic-period civilizations survived unscathed. Moreover, the essential cultural characteristics of the classic period were carried over to the postclassic. The two periods are linked by similarities in religious belief and practice, architecture, urban planning, and social organization.

There were, however, some important differences between the periods. There is evidence that the population of Mesoamerica expanded during the postclassic period. Resulting pressures led to an intensification of agricultural practices and to increased warfare. The governing elites of the major postclassic states—the Toltecs and the Aztecs—responded to these harsh realities by increasing the size of their armies and by developing political institutions that facilitated their control of large and culturally diverse territories acquired through conquest.

The Toltecs

Little is known about the **Toltecs°** prior to their arrival in central Mexico. Some scholars speculate that they were originally a satellite population that Teotihuacan had placed on the northern frontier to protect against the incursions of nomads. After their migration south, the Toltecs borrowed from the cultural legacy of Teotihuacan and created an important postclassic civilization. Memories of their military achievements and the violent imagery of their political and religious rituals dominated the Mesoamerican imagination in the late postclassic period. In the fourteenth century, the Aztecs and their contemporaries erroneously believed that the Toltecs were the source of nearly all the great cultural achievements of the Mesoamerican world. As one Aztec source later recalled:

> In truth [the Toltecs] invented all the precious and marvelous things. . . . All that now exists was their discovery. . . . And these Toltecs were very wise; they were thinkers, for they originated the year count, the day count. All their discoveries formed the book for interpreting dreams. . . . And so wise were they [that] they understood the stars which were in the heavens.[3]

In fact, all these contributions to Mesoamerican culture were in place long before the Toltecs gained control of central Mexico. The most important Toltec innovations were instead political and military.

The Toltecs created the first conquest state based largely on military power, and they extended their political influence from the area north of modern Mexico City to Central America. Established about 968 C.E., the Toltec capital of Tula° was constructed in a grand style (see Map 11.1). Its public architecture featured colonnaded patios and numerous temples. Although the population of Tula never reached the levels of classic-period Teotihuacan, the Toltec capital dominated central Mexico.

Toltec (TOLL-tek)   **Tula** (TOO-la)

Toltec decoration had a more warlike and violent character than did the decoration of earlier Mesoamerican cultures. Nearly all Toltec public buildings and temples were decorated with representations of warriors or with scenes suggesting human sacrifice.

Two chieftains or kings apparently ruled the Toltec state together. Evidence suggests that this division of responsibility eventually weakened Toltec power and led to the destruction of Tula. Sometime after 1000 C.E. a struggle between elite groups identified with rival religious cults undermined the Toltec state. According to legends that survived among the Aztecs, Topiltzin°—one of the two rulers and a priest of the cult of Quetzalcoatl—and his followers bitterly accepted exile in the east, "the land of the rising sun." These legendary events coincided with growing Toltec influence among the Maya of the Yucatán Peninsula. One of the ancient texts relates these events in the following manner:

> Thereupon he [Topiltzin] looked toward Tula, and then wept. . . . And when he had done these things . . . he went to reach the seacoast. Then he fashioned a raft of serpents. When he had arranged the raft, he placed himself as if it were his boat. Then he set off across the sea.[4]

After the exile of Topiltzin, the Toltec state began to decline, and around 1156 C.E. northern invaders overcame Tula itself. After its destruction, a centuries-long process of cultural and political assimilation produced a new Mesoamerican political order based on the urbanized culture and statecraft of the Toltecs. Like Semitic peoples of the third millennium B.C.E. interacting with Sumerian culture (see Chapter 1), the new Mesoamerican elites were drawn in part from the invading cultures. The Aztecs of the Valley of Mexico became the most important of these late postclassic peoples.

The Aztecs

The Mexica°, more commonly known as the **Aztecs,** were among the northern peoples who pushed into central Mexico in the wake of the collapse of Tula. At the time of their arrival they had a clan-based social organization. In their new environment they began to adopt the political and social practices that they found among the urbanized agriculturalists of the valley. At first, the Aztecs served their more powerful neighbors as serfs and mercenaries. As their strength grew, they relocated to small islands near the shore of Lake Texcoco, and around 1325 C.E. they began the construction of their twin capitals, **Tenochtitlan°** and Tlatelolco (together the foundation for modern Mexico City).

Military successes allowed the Aztecs to seize control of additional agricultural land along the lakeshore. With the increased economic independence and greater political security that resulted from this expansion, the Aztecs transformed their political organization by introducing a monarchical system similar to that found in more powerful neighboring states. The kinship-based organizations that had organized political life earlier survived to the era of Spanish conquest, but lost influence relative to monarchs and hereditary aristocrats. Aztec rulers did not have absolute power, and royal succession was not based on primogeniture. A council of powerful aristocrats selected new rulers from among male members of the ruling lineage. Once selected, the ruler was forced to renegotiate the submission of tribute dependencies and then demonstrate his divine mandate by undertaking a new round of military conquests. War was infused with religious meaning, providing the ruler with legitimacy and increasing the prestige of successful warriors.

With the growing power of the ruler and aristocracy, social divisions were accentuated. These alterations in social organization and political life were made possible by Aztec military expansion. Territorial conquest allowed the warrior elite of Aztec society to seize land and peasant labor as spoils of war (see Map 11.1). In time, the royal family and highest-ranking members of the aristocracy possessed extensive estates that were cultivated by slaves and landless commoners. The Aztec lower classes received some material rewards from imperial expansion but lost most of their ability to influence or control decisions. Some commoners were able to achieve some social mobility through success on the battlefield or by entering the priesthood, but the highest social ranks were always reserved for hereditary nobles.

The urban plan of Tenochtitlan and Tlatelolco continued to be organized around the clans, whose members maintained a common ritual life and accepted civic responsibilities such as caring for the sick and elderly. Clan members also fought together as military units. Nevertheless, the clans' historical control over common agricultural land and other scarce resources, such as fishing and hunting rights, declined. By 1500 C.E. great inequalities in wealth and privilege characterized Aztec society.

Aztec kings and aristocrats legitimated their ascendancy by creating elaborate rituals and ceremonies to

Costumes of Aztec Warriors
In Mesoamerican warfare individual warriors sought to gain prestige and improve their status by taking captives. This illustration from the sixteenth-century Codex Mendoza was drawn by an Amerindian artist. It shows the Aztecs' use of distinctive costumes to acknowledge the prowess of warriors. These costumes indicate the taking of two (top left) to six captives (bottom center). The individual on the bottom right shown without a weapon was a military leader. As was common in Mesoamerican illustrations of military conflict, the captives, held by their hair, are shown kneeling before the victors. (The Bodleian Library, University of Oxford, Selder. A.I. fol. 64r)

distinguish themselves from commoners. One of the Spaniards who participated in the conquest of the Aztec Empire remembered his first meeting with the Aztec ruler Moctezuma° II (r. 1502–1520): "many great lords walked before the great Montezuma [Moctezuma II], sweeping the ground on which he was to tread and laying down cloaks so that his feet should not touch the earth. Not one of these chieftains dared look him in the face."[5] Commoners lived in small dwellings and ate a limited diet of staples, but members of the nobility lived in large, well-constructed two-story houses and consumed a diet rich in animal protein and flavored by condiments and expensive imports like chocolate from the Maya region to the south. Rich dress and jewelry also set apart the elite. Even in marriage customs the two groups were different. Commoners were monogamous, great nobles polygamous.

The Aztec state met the challenge of feeding an urban population of approximately 150,000 by efficiently organizing the labor of the clans and additional laborers sent by defeated peoples to expand agricultural land. The construction of a dike more than 5½ miles (9 kilometers)

long by 23 feet (7 meters) wide to separate the freshwater and saltwater parts of Lake Texcoco was the Aztecs' most impressive land reclamation project. The dike allowed a significant extension of irrigated fields and the construction of additional chinampas. One expert has estimated that the project consumed 4 million person-days to complete. Aztec chinampas contributed maize, fruits, and vegetables to the markets of Tenochtitlan. The imposition of a **tribute system** on conquered peoples also helped relieve some of the pressure of Tenochtitlan's growing population. Unlike the tribute system of Tang China, where tribute had a more symbolic character (see Chapter 10), one-quarter of the Aztec capital's food requirements was satisfied by tribute payments of maize, beans, and other foods sent by nearby political dependencies. The Aztecs also demanded cotton cloth, military equipment, luxury goods like jade and feathers, and sacrificial victims as tribute. Trade supplemented these supplies.

A specialized class of merchants controlled long-distance trade. Given the absence of draft animals and wheeled vehicles, this commerce was dominated by lightweight and valuable products like gold, jewels, feathered garments, cacao, and animal skins. Merchants

Moctezuma (mock-teh-ZU-ma)

also provided essential political and military intelligence for the Aztec elite. Operating outside the protection of Aztec military power, merchant expeditions were armed and often had to defend themselves. Although merchants became wealthy and powerful as the Aztecs expanded their empire, they were denied the privileges of the high nobility, which was jealous of its power. As a result, the merchants feared to publicly display their affluence.

Like commerce throughout the Mesoamerican world, Aztec commerce was carried on without money and credit. Barter was facilitated by the use of cacao, quills filled with gold, and cotton cloth as standard units of value to compensate for differences in the value of bartered goods. Aztec expansion facilitated the integration of producers and consumers in the central Mexican economy. As a result, the markets of Tenochtitlan and Tlatelolco offered a rich array of goods from as far away as Central America and what is now the southwestern border of the United States. Hernán Cortés (1485–1547), the Spanish adventurer who eventually conquered the Aztecs, expressed his admiration for the abundance of the Aztec marketplace:

> One square in particular is twice as big as that of Salamanca and completely surrounded by arcades where there are daily more than sixty thousand folk buying and selling. Every kind of merchandise such as may be met with in every land is for sale. . . . There is nothing to be found in all the land which is not sold in these markets, for over and above what I have mentioned there are so many and such various things that on account of their very number . . . I cannot detail them.[6]

The Aztecs succeeded in developing a remarkable urban landscape. The combined population of Tenochtitlan and Tlatelolco and the cities and hamlets of the surrounding lakeshore was approximately 500,000 by 1500 C.E. The island capital was designed so that canals and streets intersected at right angles. Three causeways connected the city to the lakeshore.

Religious rituals dominated public life in Tenochtitlan. Like the other cultures of the Mesoamerican world, the Aztecs worshiped a large number of gods. Most of these gods had a dual nature—both male and female. The major contribution of the Aztecs to the religious life of Mesoamerica was the cult of Huitzilopochtli°, the southern hummingbird. As the Aztec state grew in power and wealth, the importance of this cult grew as well. Huitzilopochtli was originally associated with war, but eventually the Aztecs identified this god with the Sun, worshiped as a divinity throughout Mesoamerica. Huit-

Huitzilopochtli (wheat-zeel-oh-POSHT-lee)

zilopochtli, they believed, required a diet of human hearts to sustain him in his daily struggle to bring the Sun's warmth to the world. Tenochtitlan was architecturally dominated by a great twin temple devoted to Huitzilopochtli and Tlaloc, the rain god, symbolizing the two bases of the Aztec economy: war and agriculture.

War captives were the preferred sacrificial victims, but large numbers of criminals, slaves, and people provided as tribute by dependent regions were also sacrificed. Although human sacrifice had been practiced since early times in Mesoamerica, the Aztecs and other societies of the late postclassic period transformed this religious ritual by dramatically increasing its scale. There are no reliable estimates for the total number of sacrifices, but the numbers clearly reached into the thousands each year. This form of violent public ritual had political consequences and was not simply the celebration of religious belief. Some scholars have emphasized the political nature of the rising tide of sacrifice, noting that sacrifices were carried out in front of large crowds that included leaders from enemy and subject states as well as the masses of Aztec society. The political subtext must have been clear: rebellion, deviancy, and opposition were extremely dangerous.

NORTHERN PEOPLES

By the end of the classic period in Mesoamerica, around 900 C.E., important cultural centers had appeared in the southwestern desert region and along the Ohio and Mississippi river valleys of what is now the United States. The introduction of maize, beans, and squash from Mesoamerica played an important role in the development of complex societies. Once established, these useful food crops were adopted throughout North America.

As growing populations came to depend on maize as a dietary staple, large-scale irrigation projects were undertaken in both the southwestern desert and the eastern river valleys. This development is a sign of increasingly centralized political power and growing social stratification. The two regions, however, evolved different political traditions.

Southwestern Desert Cultures

Of all the southwestern cultures, the Hohokam of the Salt and Gila river valleys of southern Arizona show the strongest Mexican influence. Hohokam sites have platform mounds and ball courts similar to those of Mesoamerica.

Mesa Verde Cliff Dwelling Located in southern Colorado, the Anasazi cliff dwellings of the Mesa Verde region hosted a population of about 7,000 in 1250 C.E. The construction of housing complexes and religious buildings in the area's large caves was probably prompted by increased warfare in the region. (David Muench Photography)

Hohokam pottery, clay figurines, cast copper bells, and turquoise mosaics also reflect Mexican influence. By 1000 C.E. the Hohokam had constructed an elaborate irrigation system that included one canal more than 18 miles (30 kilometers) in length. Hohokam agricultural and ceramic technology spread over the centuries to neighboring peoples, but it was the Anasazi to the north who left the most vivid legacy of these desert cultures.

Archaeologists use **Anasazi°,** a Navajo word meaning "ancient ones," to identify a number of dispersed, though similar, desert cultures located in what is now the Four Corners region of Arizona, New Mexico, Colorado, and Utah (see Map 11.2). By 600 C.E. the Anasazi

had a well-established economy based on maize, beans, and squash. Their successful adaptation of these crops permitted the formation of larger villages and led to an enriched cultural life centered in underground buildings called kivas. Evidence suggests that the Anasazi may have used kivas for weaving and pottery making, as well as for religious rituals. They produced pottery decorated with geometric patterns, learned to weave cotton

Map 11.2 Culture Areas of North America In each of the large ecological regions of North America, native peoples evolved distinctive cultures and technologies. Here the Anasazi of the arid southwest and the mound-building cultures of the Ohio and Mississippi river valleys are highlighted.

Anasazi (ah-nah-SAH-zee)

A
R
C
T
I
C

S
U
B
A
R
C
T
I
C

NORTHWEST

PLATEAU

CALIFORNIA

GREAT
BASIN

PLAINS

NORTHEAST

Cahokia

Mesa
Verde
Kiet Siel
Canyon
de Chelly
Chaco
Canyon

SOUTHEAST

SOUTHWEST

0   300   600 Km.

0   300   600 Mi.

Approximate extent of Anasazi culture

Approximate extent of mound-building cultures

cloth, and, after 900 C.E., began to construct large multistory residential and ritual centers.

One of the largest Anasazi communities was located in Chaco Canyon in northwestern New Mexico. Eight large towns were built in the canyon and four more on surrounding mesas, suggesting a regional population of approximately 15,000. Many smaller villages were located nearby. Each town contained hundreds of rooms arranged in tiers around a central plaza. At Pueblo Bonito, the largest town, more than 650 rooms were arranged in a four-story block of residences and storage rooms. Pueblo Bonito had thirty-eight kivas, including a great kiva more than 65 feet (19 meters) in diameter. Social life and craft activities were concentrated in small open plazas or common rooms. Hunting, trade, and the need to maintain irrigation works often drew men away from the village. Women shared in agricultural tasks and were specialists in many crafts. They also were responsible for food preparation and childcare. If the practice of the modern Pueblos, cultural descendants of the Anasazi, is a guide, houses and furnishings may have belonged to the women, who formed extended families with their mothers and sisters.

At Chaco Canyon high-quality construction, the size and number of kivas, and the system of roads linking the canyon to outlying towns all suggest that Pueblo Bonito and its nearest neighbors exerted some kind of political or religious dominance over a large region. Some archaeologists have suggested that the Chaco Canyon culture originated as a colonial appendage of Mesoamerica, but the archaeological record provides little evidence for this theory. Merchants from Chaco provided Toltec-period peoples of northern Mexico with turquoise in exchange for shell jewelry, copper bells, macaws, and trumpets. But these exchanges occurred late in Chaco's development, and more important signs of Mesoamerican influence such as pyramid-shaped mounds and ball courts are not found at Chaco. Nor is there evidence from the excavation of burials and residences of clear class distinctions, a common feature of Mesoamerican culture. Instead, it appears that the Chaco Canyon culture developed from earlier societies in the region.

The abandonment of the major sites in Chaco Canyon in the twelfth century most likely resulted from a long drought that undermined the culture's fragile agricultural economy. Nevertheless, the Anasazi continued in the Four Corners region for more than a century after the abandonment of Chaco Canyon. There were major centers at Mesa Verde in present-day Colorado and at Canyon de Chelly and Kiet Siel in Arizona. Anasazi settlements on the Colorado Plateau and in Arizona were constructed in large natural caves high above valley floors. This hard-to-reach location suggests increased levels of warfare, probably provoked by population pressure on limited arable land.

Mound Builders: The Mississippian Culture

Building large mounds for elite burials, the residences of chiefs, and as platforms for temples had been a feature of village life in an area stretching from New York to Illinois and from Ontario to Florida for a period of a thousand years before the development of Mississippian culture (700–1500 C.E.). Economically, the early mound builders depended on hunting and gathering supplemented by limited cultivation of locally domesticated seed crops.

As in the case of the Anasazi, some experts have suggested that contacts with Mesoamerica influenced Mississippian culture, but there is no convincing evidence to support this theory. It is true that maize, beans, and squash, all first domesticated in Mesoamerica, were closely associated with the development of the urbanized Mississippian culture. But these plants and related technologies were probably passed along through numerous intervening cultures.

Mississippian political organization continued the earlier North American **chiefdom** tradition, wherein a territory that had a population as large as 10,000 was ruled by a chief, a hereditary leader with both religious and secular responsibilities. Chiefs organized periodic rituals of feasting and gift giving that established bonds among diverse kinship groups and guaranteed access to specialized crops and craft goods. They also managed long-distance trade, which provided luxury goods and additional food supplies.

Urbanized Mississippian sites developed from the accumulated effects of small increases in agricultural productivity, the adoption of the bow and arrow, and the expansion of trade networks. An improved economy led to population growth and social stratification. The largest towns shared a common urban plan based on a central plaza surrounded by large platform mounds. Major towns were trade centers where people bartered essential commodities, such as the flint used for weapons and tools.

The Mississippian culture reached its highest stage of evolution at the great urban center of Cahokia, located near the modern city of East St. Louis, Illinois (see Map 11.2). At the center of this site was the largest mound constructed in North America, a terraced structure 100 feet (30 meters) high and 1,037 by 790 feet (316 by 241 meters) at the base. Areas where commoners lived ringed the center area of elite housing and temples. At its height in about 1200 C.E., Cahokia had a population of about 20,000—about the same as some of the largest postclassic Maya cities.

Cahokia controlled surrounding agricultural lands and a number of secondary towns ruled by subchiefs. The urban center's political and economic influence depended on its location on the Missouri, Mississippi, and Illinois Rivers. This location permitted canoe-based commercial exchanges as far away as the coasts of the Atlantic and the Gulf of Mexico. Sea shells, copper, mica, and flint were drawn to the city by trade and tribute from distant sources and converted into ritual goods and tools. Burial evidence suggests that the rulers of Cahokia enjoyed most of the benefits of this exalted position. In one burial more than fifty young women and retainers were apparently sacrificed to accompany a ruler on his travels after death.

No evidence links the decline and eventual abandonment of Cahokia, which occurred after 1250 C.E., with military defeat or civil war. Climate changes and population pressures undermined the center's vitality. Environmental degradation caused by deforestation, as more land was cleared to feed the growing population, and more intensive farming practices played roles as well. After the decline of Cahokia, smaller Mississippian centers continued to flourish in the southeast of the present-day United States until the arrival of Europeans.

ANDEAN CIVILIZATIONS, 600–1500

The Andean region of South America was an unlikely environment for the development of rich and powerful civilizations (see Map 11.3). Much of the region's mountainous zone is at altitudes that seem too high for agriculture and human habitation. Along the Pacific coast an arid climate posed a difficult challenge to the development of agriculture. To the east of the Andes Mountains, the hot and humid tropical environment of the Amazon headwaters also offered formidable obstacles to the organization of complex societies. Yet the Amerindian peoples of the Andean area produced some of the most socially complex and politically advanced societies of the Western Hemisphere. The very harshness of the environment compelled the development of productive and reliable agricultural technologies and attached them to a complex fabric of administrative structures and social relationships that became the central features of Andean civilization.

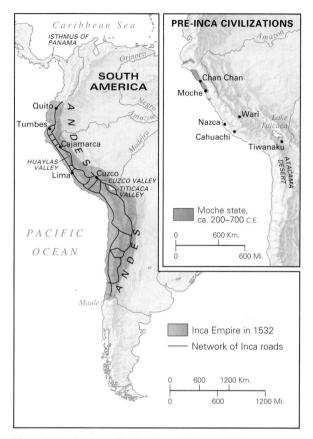

Map 11.3   Andean Civilizations, 600 C.E.–1532 C.E.   In response to environmental challenges posed by an arid coastal plain and high interior mountain ranges, Andean peoples made complex social and technological adaptations. Irrigation systems, the domestication of the llama, metallurgy, and shared labor obligations helped provide a firm economic foundation for powerful, centralized states. In 1532 the Inca Empire's vast territory stretched from modern Chile in the south to Colombia in the north.

Cultural Response to Environmental Challenge

From the time of Chavín (see Chapter 2) all of the great Andean civilizations succeeded in connecting the distinctive resources of the coastal region, with its abundant fisheries and irrigated maize fields, to the mountainous interior, with its herds of llamas and rich mix of grains and tubers. Both regions faced significant environmental challenges. The coastal region's fields were periodically overwhelmed by droughts or shifting sands that clogged irrigation works. The mountainous interior presented some of the greatest environmental challenges, averaging between 250 and 300 frosts per year.

The development of compensating technologies required an accurate calendar to time planting and harvests and the domestication of frost-resistant varieties of potatoes and grains. Native peoples learned to practice dispersed farming at different altitudes to reduce risks from frosts, and they terraced hillsides to create micro environments within a single area. They also discovered how to use the cold, dry climate to produce freeze-dried vegetable and meat products that prevented famine when crops failed. The domestication of the llama and alpaca also proved crucial, providing meat, wool, and long-distance transportation that linked coastal and mountain economies. Even though the Andean environment was harsher than that of Mesoamerica, the region's agriculture proved more dependable, and Andean peoples faced fewer famines.

The effective organization of human labor allowed the peoples of both the high mountain valleys and dry coastal plain to overcome the challenges posed by their environments. The remarkable collective achievements of Andean peoples were accomplished with a record-keeping system more limited than the one found in Mesoamerica. A system of knotted colored cords, **khipus°**, was used to aid administration and record population counts and tribute obligations. Large-scale drainage and irrigation works and the terracing of hillsides to control erosion and provide additional farmland led to an increase in agricultural production. Andean people also collectively undertook road building, urban construction, and even textile production.

The sharing of responsibilities began at the household level. But it was the clan, or **ayllu°**, that provided the foundation for Andean achievement. Members of an ayllu held land communally. Although they claimed descent from a common ancestor, they were not necessarily related. Ayllu members thought of each other as brothers and sisters and were obligated to aid each other in tasks that required more labor than a single household could provide. These reciprocal obligations provided the model for the organization of labor and the distribution of goods at every level of Andean society. Just as individuals and families were expected to provide labor to kinsmen, members of an ayllu were expected to provide labor and goods to their hereditary chief.

With the development of territorial states ruled by hereditary aristocracies and kings, these obligations were organized on a larger scale. The **mit'a°** was a rotational labor draft that organized members of ayllus to work the fields and care for the llama and alpaca herds owned by religious establishments, the royal court, and the aristocracy. Each ayllu contributed a set number of workers for specific tasks each year. Mit'a laborers built and maintained roads, bridges, temples, palaces, and large irrigation and drainage projects. They produced textiles and goods essential to ritual life, such as beer made from maize and coca (dried leaves chewed as a stimulant and now also the source of cocaine). The mit'a system was an essential part of the Andean world for more than a thousand years.

Work was divided along gender lines, but the work of men and women was interdependent. Hunting, military service, and government were largely reserved for men. Women had numerous responsibilities in textile production, agriculture, and the home. One early Spanish commentator described the responsibilities of Andean women in terms that sound very modern:

> [T]hey did not just perform domestic tasks, but also [labored] in the fields, in the cultivation of their lands, in building houses, and carrying burdens. . . . [A]nd more than once I heard that while women were carrying these burdens, they would feel labor pains, and giving birth, they would go to a place where there was water and wash the baby and themselves. Putting the baby on top of the load they were carrying, they would then continue walking as before they gave birth. In sum, there was nothing their husbands did where their wives did not help.[7]

The ayllu was intimately tied to a uniquely Andean system of production and exchange. Because the region's mountain ranges created a multitude of small ecological areas with specialized resources, each community sought to control a variety of environments so as to guarantee access to essential goods. Coastal regions produced maize, fish, and cotton. Mountain valleys contributed quinoa (the local grain) as well as potatoes and other tubers. Higher elevations contributed the wool and meat of llamas and alpacas, and the Amazonian region provided coca and fruits. Ayllus sent out colonists to exploit the resources of these ecological niches. Colonists remained linked to their original region and kin group by marriage and ritual. Historians commonly refer to this system of controlled exchange across ecological boundaries as vertical integration, or verticality.

The historical periodization of Andean history is similar to that of Mesoamerica. Both regions developed highly integrated political and economic systems long before 1500. The pace of agricultural development, urbanization, and state formation in the Andes also approximated that in Mesoamerica. Due to the unique environmental challenges in the Andean region, however,

---

khipus (KEY-pooz) **ayllu** (aye-YOU) **mit'a** (MEET-ah)

distinctive highland and coastal cultures appeared. In the Andes, more than in Mesoamerica, geography influenced regional cultural integration and state formation.

Moche

By 600 C.E. the **Moche°** had developed cultural and political tools that allowed them to dominate the north coastal region of Peru. Moche identity was cultural in character. They did not establish a formal empire or create unified political structures. The Moche and the Chimu° who followed them cultivated maize, quinoa, beans, manioc, and sweet potatoes with the aid of massive irrigation works. At higher elevations they also produced coca, which they used ritually. Complex networks of canals and aqueducts connected fields with water sources as far away as 75 miles (121 kilometers). These hydraulic works were maintained by mit'a labor imposed on Moche commoners or on subject peoples. The Moche maintained large herds of alpacas and llamas to transport goods across the region's difficult terrain. Their wool, along with cotton provided by farmers, provided the raw material for the thriving Moche textile production. Their meat provided an important part of the diet.

Evidence from surviving murals and decorated ceramics suggests that Moche society was highly stratified and theocratic. The need to organize large numbers of laborers to construct and maintain the irrigation system helped promote class divisions. Wealth and power among the Moche was concentrated, along with political control, in the hands of priests and military leaders. The residences of the elite were constructed atop large platforms at Moche ceremonial centers. Rich clothing and jewelry confirmed their divine status and set them farther apart from commoners. Moche rulers and other members of the elite wore tall headdresses. Gold and gold alloy jewelry marked their social position: gold plates suspended from their noses concealed the lower portion of their faces, and large gold plugs decorated their ears (see Diversity and Dominance: Burials as Historical Texts).

Most commoners devoted their time to subsistence farming and to the payment of labor dues owed to their ayllu and to the elite. Both men and women were involved in agriculture, care of llama herds, and the household economy. They lived with their families in one-room buildings clustered in the outlying areas of cities and in surrounding agricultural zones.

Moche (MO-che) **Chimu** (chee-MOO)

Moche Portrait Vase   The Moche of ancient Peru were among the most accomplished ceramic artists of the Americas. Moche potters produced representations of gods and spirits, scenes of daily life, and portrait vases of important people. This man wears a headdress adorned by two birds and seashells. The stains next to the eyes of the birds represent tears.   (Museo de Arqueologica y Antropologia, Lima/Lee Bolton Picture Library)

Among craft workers, women had a special role in the production of textiles; even elite women devoted time to weaving. Moche potters produced highly individualized portrait vases and decorated other vessels with line drawings representing myths and rituals. The most original Moche ceramic vessels depict explicit sexual acts. In addition to gold jewelry, metalworkers produced a range of tools made of heavy copper and copper alloy for agricultural and military purposes.

Without written sources, a detailed history of the Moche cannot be written. The archaeological record reveals, however, that the rapid decline of the major centers coincided with a succession of natural disasters in the sixth century. When an earthquake altered the course of the Moche River, major flooding seriously damaged urban centers. In addition, a thirty-year drought expanded the area of coastal sand dunes, and powerful winds pushed sand onto fragile agricultural lands, overwhelming the irrigation system. As the land dried, periodic heavy rains caused erosion that damaged fields and

[Korean newspaper headers within the photograph]

우세인 은신서

파운드폭탄 4발 투하… 두 아들과 함께 사망

실전지 구축… 이틀째 시가戰

령이 대중 앞에 나타나거나 애국심
을 고취하는 노래만을 내보내던 방
송마저 중단됐다.

라크 전후
의에서는
영국 주도

DIVERSITY AND DOMINANCE

BURIALS AS HISTORICAL TEXTS

Efforts to reveal the history of the Americas before the arrival of Europeans depend on the work of archaeologists. The burials of rulers and other members of elites can be viewed as historical texts that describe how textiles, precious metals, beautifully decorated ceramics, and other commodities were used to reinforce the political and cultural power of ruling lineages. In public, members of the elite were always surrounded by the most desirable and rarest products as well as by elaborate rituals and ceremonies. The effect was to create an aura of godlike power. The material elements of political and cultural power were integrated into the experience of death and burial as members of the elite were sent into the afterlife.

The first photograph is of an excavated Moche tomb in Sipán, Peru. The Moche (100 C.E.–ca. 700 C.E.) were one of the most important of the pre-Inca civilizations of the Andean region. They were masters of metallurgy, ceramics, and textiles. The excavations at Sipán revealed a "warrior/priest" buried with an amazing array of gold ornaments, jewels, textiles, and ceramics. He was also buried with two women, perhaps wives or concubines, two male servants, and a warrior. The warrior, one woman, and one man are missing feet, as if this deformation would guarantee their continued faithfulness to the deceased ruler.

The second photograph shows the excavation of a Classic-Era (250 C.E.–ca. 800 C.E.) Maya burial at Río Azul in Guatemala. Here a member of the elite was laid out on a carved wooden platform and cotton mattress; his body painted with decorations. He was covered in beautifully woven textiles and surrounded by valuable goods. Among the discoveries were a necklace of individual stones carved in the shape of heads, perhaps a symbol of his prowess in battle, high-quality ceramics, some filled with foods consumed by the elite like cacao. The careful preparation of the burial chamber had required the work of numerous artisans and laborers, as was the case in the burial of the Moche warrior/priest. In death, as in life, these early American civilizations acknowledged the high status, political power, and religious authority of their elites.

QUESTIONS FOR ANALYSIS

1. If these burials are texts, what are stories?
2. Are there any visible differences in the two burials?
3. What questions might historians ask of these burials that cannot be answered?
4. Are modern burials texts in similar ways to these ancient practices?

---

weakened the economy. This succession of disasters undermined the authority of the religious and political leaders, whose privileges were based on their ability to control natural forces through rituals. Despite massive efforts to keep the irrigation canals open and construct new urban centers in less vulnerable areas, Moche civilization never recovered.

Tiwanaku and Wari

In the Andean highlands the Tiwanaku and Wari cultures paralleled that of Moche of the coastal regions. At nearly 13,000 feet (3,962 meters) on the high treeless plain near Lake Titicaca in modern Bolivia stand the ruins of Tiwanaku° (see Map 11.3). Modern excavations provide the outline of vast drainage projects that reclaimed nearly 200,000 acres (8,000 hectares) of rich lakeside marshes for agriculture. This system of raised fields and ditches permitted intensive cultivation similar to that achieved by the use of chinampas in Mesoamerica. Fish from the nearby lake and llamas added protein to a diet largely dependent on potatoes and grains. Llamas were also crucial for the maintenance of long-distance trade relationships that brought in corn, coca, tropical fruits, and medicinal plants.

The urban center of Tiwanaku was distinguished by the scale of its construction and by the high quality of its

---

Tiwanaku (tee-wah-NA-coo)

Burials Reveal Ancient Civilizations (Left) Buried around 300 C.E., this Moche warrior-priest was buried amid rich tribute at Sipán in Peru. Also, buried were the bodies of retainers or kinsmen probably sacrificed to accompany this powerful man. The body lies with the head on the right and the feet on the left. (Right) Similarly, the burial of a member of the Maya elite at Río Azul in northern Guatemala indicates the care taken to surround the powerful with fine ceramics, jewelry and other valuable goods. (*left:* Heinze Plenge/NGS Image Collection; *right:* George Mobley/NGS Image Collection)

stone masonry. Large stones and quarried blocks were moved many miles to construct a large terraced pyramid, walled enclosures, and a reservoir—projects that probably required the mobilization of thousands of laborers over a period of years. Despite a limited metallurgy that produced only tools of copper alloy, Tiwanaku's artisans built large structures of finely cut stone that required little mortar to fit the blocks. They also produced gigantic human statuary. The largest example, a stern figure with a military bearing, is cut from a single block of stone 24 feet (7 meters) high.

Many scholars portray Tiwanaku as the capital of a vast empire, a precursor to the later Inca state. It is clear that the elite controlled a large, disciplined labor force in the surrounding region. Military conquests and the es-

tablishment of colonial populations provided the highland capital with dependable supplies of products from ecologically distinct zones. Tiwanaku cultural influence extended eastward to the jungles and southward to the coastal regions and oases of the Atacama Desert in Chile. But archaeological evidence suggests that Tiwanaku, in comparison with contemporary Teotihuacan in central Mexico, had a relatively small full-time population of around 30,000. It was not a metropolis like the largest Mesoamerican cities; it was a ceremonial and political center for a large regional population.

The contemporary site of **Wari**° was located about 450 miles (751 kilometers) to the northwest of Tiwanaku,

Wari (WAH-ree)

near the modern Peruvian city of Ayacucho. Wari shared elements of the culture and technology of Tiwanaku, but the exact nature of this relationship remains unclear. Some scholars argue that Wari began as a dependency of Tiwanaku, while others suggest that they were joint capitals of a single empire. Wari was larger than Tiwanaku, measuring nearly 4 square miles (10 square kilometers). The city center was surrounded by a massive wall and included a large temple. The center had numerous multi-family housing blocks. Less-concentrated housing for commoners was located in a sprawling suburban zone.

Perhaps as a consequence of military conflict, both Tiwanaku and Wari declined to insignificance by about 1000 C.E. The Inca inherited their political legacy.

The Inca

In little more than a hundred years, the **Inca** developed a vast imperial state, which they called "Land of Four Corners." By 1525 the empire had a population of more than 6 million and stretched from the Maule River in Chile to northern Ecuador and from the Pacific coast across the Andes to the upper Amazon and, in the south, into Argentina (see Map 11.3). In the early fifteenth century the Inca were one of many competing military powers in the southern highlands, an area of limited political significance after the collapse of Wari. Centered in the valley of Cuzco, the Inca were initially organized as a chiefdom based on reciprocal gift giving and the redistribution of food and textiles. Strong and resourceful leaders consolidated political authority in the 1430s and undertook an ambitious campaign of military expansion.

The Inca state, like earlier highland powers, was built on traditional Andean social customs and economic practices. Tiwanaku had relied in part on the use of colonists to provide supplies of resources from distant, ecologically distinct zones. The Inca built on this legacy by conquering additional distant territories and increasing the scale of forced exchanges. Crucial to this process was the development of a large, professional military. Unlike the peoples of Mesoamerica, who distributed specialized goods by developing markets and tribute relationships, Andean peoples used state power to broaden and expand the vertical exchange system that had permitted ayllus to exploit a range of ecological niches.

Like earlier highland civilizations, the Inca were pastoralists. Inca prosperity and military strength depended on vast herds of llamas and alpacas, which provided food and clothing as well as transport for goods. Both men and women were involved in the care of these herds. Women were primarily responsible for weaving; men

were drivers in long-distance trade. This pastoral tradition provided the Inca with powerful metaphors that helped shape their political and religious beliefs. They believed that the gods and their ruler shared the obligations of the shepherd to his flock—an idea akin to references to "The Lord is my Shepherd."

Collective efforts by mit'a laborers made the Inca Empire possible. Cuzco, the imperial capital, and the provincial cities, the royal court, the imperial armies, and the state's religious cults all rested on this foundation. The mit'a system also created the material surplus that provided the bare necessities for the old, weak, and ill of Inca society. Each ayllu contributed approximately one-seventh of its adult male population to meet these collective obligations. These draft laborers served as soldiers, construction workers, craftsmen, and runners to carry messages along post roads. They also drained swamps, terraced mountainsides, filled in valley floors, built and maintained irrigation works, and built storage facilities and roads. Inca laborers constructed 13,000 miles (20,930 kilometers) of road, facilitating military troop movements, administration, and trade (see Environment and Technology: Inca Roads).

Imperial administration was similarly superimposed on existing political structures and established elite groups. The hereditary chiefs of ayllus carried out administrative and judicial functions. As the Inca expanded, they generally left local rulers in place. By leaving the rulers of defeated societies in place, the Inca risked rebellion, but they controlled these risks by means of a thinly veiled system of hostage taking and the use of military garrisons. The rulers of defeated regions were required to send their heirs to live at the Inca royal court in Cuzco. Inca leaders even required that representations of important local gods be brought to Cuzco and made part of the imperial pantheon. These measures promoted imperial integration while at the same time providing hostages to ensure the good behavior of subject peoples.

Conquests magnified the authority of the Inca ruler and led to the creation of an imperial bureaucracy drawn from among his kinsmen. The royal family claimed descent from the Sun, the primary Inca god. Members of the royal family lived in palaces maintained by armies of servants. The lives of the ruler and members of the royal family were dominated by political and religious rituals that helped legitimize their authority. Among the many obligations associated with kingship was the requirement to extend imperial boundaries by warfare. Thus each new ruler began his reign with conquest.

Tenochtitlan, the Aztec capital, had a population of about 150,000 in 1520. At the height of Inca power in 1530, Cuzco had a population of less than 30,000. Never-

Inca Roads

From the time of Chavín (900–250 B.C.E.), Andean peoples built roads to facilitate trade across ecological boundaries and to project political power over conquered peoples. In the fifteenth and sixteenth centuries, the Inca extended and improved the networks of roads constructed in earlier eras. Roads were crucially important to Inca efforts to collect and redistribute tribute paid in food, textiles, and chicha (corn liquor).

Two roads connected Cuzco, the Inca capital in southern Peru, to Quito, Ecuador, in the north and to Chile farther south. One ran along the flat and arid coastal plain, the other through the mountainous interior. Shorter east-west roads connected important coastal and interior cities. Evidence suggests that administrative centers were sited along these routes to expedite rapid communication with the capital. Rest stops at convenient distances provided shelter and food to traveling officials and runners who carried messages between Cuzco and the empire's cities and towns. Warehouses were constructed along the roads to provide food and military supplies for passing Inca armies or to supply local laborers working on construction projects or cultivating the ruler's fields.

Because communication with regional administrative centers and the movement of troops were the central objectives of the Inca leadership, routes were selected to avoid natural obstacles and to reduce travel time. Mit'a laborers recruited from nearby towns and villages built and maintained the roads. Roads were commonly paved with stone or packed earth and often were bordered by stone or adobe walls to keep soldiers or pack trains of llamas from straying into farmers' fields. Whenever possible, roadbeds were made level. In mountainous terrain some roads were little more than improved paths, but in flat country three or four people could walk abreast. Care was always taken to repair damage caused by rain runoff or other drainage problems.

The achievement of Inca road builders is clearest in the mountainous terrain of the interior. They built suspension bridges across high gorges and cut roadbeds into the face of cliffs. A Spanish priest living in Peru in the seventeenth century commented that the Inca roads "were magnificent constructions, which could be compared favorably with the most superb roads of the Romans."

Source: Quotation from Father Bernabe Cobo, *History of the Inca Empire. An account of the Indians' customs and origin together with a treatise on Inca legends, history, and social institutions* (Austin: University of Texas Press, 1983), 223.

Inca Road The Inca built roads to connect distant parts of the empire to Cuzco, the Inca capital. These roads are still used in Peru. (Loren McIntyre/Woodfin Camp & Associates)

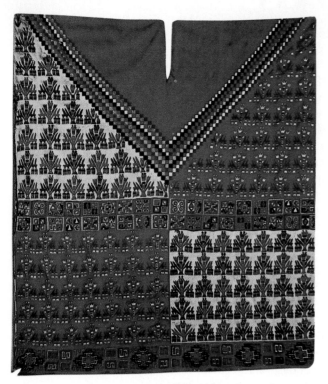

Inca Tunic   Andean weavers produced beautiful textiles from cotton and from the wool of llamas and alpacas. The Inca inherited this rich craft tradition and produced some of the world's most remarkable textiles. The quality and design of each garment indicated the weaver's rank and power in this society. This tunic was an outer garment for a powerful male.   (From *Textile Art of Peru*. Collection created and directed by Jose Antonio de Lavalle and Jose Alejandro Gonzalez Garcia [L. L. Editores, 1989])

theless, Cuzco was a remarkable place. The Inca were highly skilled stone craftsmen: their most impressive buildings were constructed of carefully cut stones fitted together without mortar. The city was laid out in the shape of a giant puma (a mountain lion). At the center were the palaces that each ruler built when he ascended to the throne, as well as the major temples. The richest was the Temple of the Sun. Its interior was lined with sheets of gold, and its patio was decorated with golden representations of llamas and corn. The ruler made every effort to awe and intimidate visitors and residents alike with a nearly continuous series of rituals, feasts, and sacrifices. Sacrifices of textiles, animals, and other goods sent as tribute dominated the city's calendar. The destruction of these valuable commodities, and a small number of human sacrifices, helped give the impression of splendor and sumptuous abundance that appeared to demonstrate the ruler's claimed descent from the Sun.

Inca cultural achievement rested on the strong foundation of earlier Andean civilizations. We know that astronomical observation was a central concern of the priestly class, as in Mesoamerica; the Inca calendar, however, is lost to us. All communication other than oral was transmitted by the khipus borrowed from earlier Andean civilizations. In weaving and metallurgy, Inca technology, building on earlier regional developments, was more advanced than in Mesoamerica. Inca craftsmen produced utilitarian tools and weapons of copper and bronze as well as decorative objects of gold and silver. Inca women produced textiles of extraordinary beauty from cotton and the wool of llamas and alpacas.

Although the Inca did not introduce new technologies, they increased economic output and added to the region's prosperity. The conquest of large populations in environmentally distinct regions allowed the Inca to multiply the yields produced by the traditional exchanges between distinct ecological niches. But the expansion of imperial economic and political power was purchased at the cost of reduced equality and diminished local autonomy. The imperial elite, living in richly decorated palaces in Cuzco and other urban centers, was increasingly cut off from the masses of Inca society. The royal court held members of the provincial nobility at arm's length, and commoners were subject to execution if they dared to look directly at the ruler's face.

After only a century of regional dominance, the Inca Empire faced a crisis in 1525. The death of the Inca ruler Huayna Capac at the conclusion of the conquest of Ecuador initiated a bloody struggle for the throne. Powerful factions coalesced around two sons, whose rivalry compelled both the professional military and the hereditary Inca elite to choose sides. Civil war was the result. The Inca state controlled a vast territory spread over more than 3,000 miles (4,830 kilometers) of mountainous terrain. Regionalism and ethnic diversity had always posed a threat to the empire. Civil war weakened imperial institutions and ignited the resentments of conquered peoples. On the eve of the arrival of Europeans, the destructive consequences of this violent conflict undermined the institutions and economy of Andean civilizations.

CONCLUSION

The indigenous societies of the Western Hemisphere developed unique technologies and cultural forms in mountainous regions, tropical rain forests, deserts, woodlands, and arctic regions. In Mesoamerica, North

America, and the Andean region, the natural environment powerfully influenced cultural development. The Maya of southern Mexico, for example, developed agricultural technologies that compensated for the tropical cycle of heavy rains followed by long dry periods. On the coast of Peru the Moche used systems of trade and mutual labor obligation to meet the challenge of an arid climate and mountainous terrain, while the mound builders of North America expanded agricultural production by utilizing the rich floodplains of the Ohio and Mississippi Rivers. Across the Americas, hunting and gathering peoples and urbanized agricultural societies produced rich religious and aesthetic traditions as well as useful technologies and effective social institutions in response to local conditions. Once established, these cultural traditions proved very durable.

The Aztec and Inca Empires represented the culmination of a long developmental process that had begun before 1000 B.C.E. Each imperial state controlled extensive and diverse territories with populations that numbered in the millions. The capital cities of Tenochtitlan and Cuzco were great cultural and political centers that displayed some of the finest achievements of Amerindian technology, art, and architecture. Both states were based on conquests and were ruled by powerful hereditary elites who depended on the tribute of subject peoples. In both traditions religion met spiritual needs while also organizing collective life and legitimizing political authority.

The Aztec and Inca Empires were created militarily, their survival depending as much on the power of their armies as on the productivity of their economies or the wisdom of their rulers. Both empires were ethnically and environmentally diverse, but there were important differences. Elementary markets had been developed in Mesoamerica to distribute specialized regional production, although the forced payment of goods as tribute remained important. In the Andes reciprocal labor obligations and managed exchange relationships were used to allocate goods. The Aztecs used their military to force defeated peoples to provide food, textiles, and even sacrificial captives as tribute, but they left local hereditary elites in place. The Incas, in contrast, created a more centralized administrative structure managed by a trained bureaucracy.

As the Western Hemisphere's long isolation drew to a close in the late fifteenth century, both empires were challenged by powerful neighbors or internal revolts. In earlier periods similar challenges had contributed to the decline of great civilizations in both Mesoamerica and the Andean region. In those cases, a long period of adjustment and the creation of new indigenous institutions followed the collapse of dominant powers such as the Toltecs in Mesoamerica and Tiwanaku in the Andes. With the arrival of Europeans, this cycle of crisis and adjustment would be transformed, and the future of Amerindian peoples would become linked to the cultures of the Old World.

Key Terms

Teotihuacan
chinampas
Maya
Toltecs
Aztecs
Tenochtitlan
tribute system
Anasazi
chiefdom
khipu
ayllu
mit'a
Moche
Tiwanaku
Wari
Inca

Suggested Reading

In *Prehistory of the Americas* (1987) Stuart Fiedel provides an excellent summary of the early history of the Western Hemisphere. Alvin M. Josephy, Jr., in *The Indian Heritage of America* (1968), also provides a thorough introduction to the topic. *Canada's First Nations* (1992) by Olive Patricia Dickason is a well-written survey that traces the history of Canada's Amerindian peoples to the modern era. *Early Man in the New World*, ed. Richard Shutler, Jr. (1983), provides a helpful addition to these works. *Atlas of Ancient America* (1986) by Michael Coe, Elizabeth P. Benson, and Dean R. Snow is a useful compendium of maps and information. George Kubler, *The Art and Architecture of Ancient America* (1962), is a valuable resource, though now dated.

Eric Wolf provides an enduring synthesis of Mesoamerican history in *Sons of the Shaking Earth* (1959). A good summary of recent research on Teotihuacan is found in Esther Pasztori, *Teotihuacan* (1997). Linda Schele and David Freidel summarize the most recent research on the classic-period Maya in their excellent *A Forest of Kings* (1990). See also David Drew, *The Lost Chronicles of the Maya Kings* (1999). The best summary of Aztec history is Nigel Davies, *The Aztec Empire: The Toltec Resurgence* (1987). Jacques Soustelle, *Daily Life of the Aztecs,* trans. Patrick O'Brian (1961), is a good introduction. Though controversial in some of its analysis, Inga Clendinnen's *Aztecs* (1991) is also an important contribution.

Chaco and Hohokam (1991), ed. Patricia L. Crown and W. James Judge, is a good summary of research issues. Robert Silverberg, *Mound Builders of Ancient America* (1968), supplies a good introduction to this topic. See also *Understanding Complexity in the Prehistoric Southwest,* ed. George J. Gumerman and Murray Gell-Mann (1994).

A helpful introduction to the scholarship on early Andean societies is provided by Karen Olsen Bruhns, *Ancient South America* (1994). For the Moche see Garth Bawden, *The Moche* (1996). *The History of the Incas* (1970) by Alfred Metraux is dated but offers a useful summary. The best recent modern synthesis is María Rostworowski de Diez Canseco, *History of the Inca Realm,* trans. by Harry B. Iceland (1999). John Murra, *The Economic Organization of the Inca State* (1980), and Irene Silverblatt, *Moon, Sun, and Witches: Gender Ideologies and Class in Inca and Colonial Peru* (1987), are challenging, important works on Peru before the arrival of Columbus in the Western Hemisphere. Frederich Katz, *The Ancient Civilizations of the Americas* (1972), offers a useful comparative perspective on ancient American developments.

■ Notes

1. This summary closely follows the historical narrative and translation of names offered by Linda Schele and David Freidel in *A Forest of Kings: The Untold Story of the Ancient Maya* (New York: Morrow, 1990), 182–186.
2. From the Florentine Codex, quoted in Inga Clendinnen, *Aztecs* (New York: Cambridge University Press, 1991), 213.
3. Quoted in Nigel Davies, *The Toltec Heritage: From the Fall of Tula to the Rise of Tenochtitlán* (Norman: University of Oklahoma Press, 1980), 3.
4. Bernal Díaz del Castillo, *The Conquest of New Spain,* trans. J. M. Cohen (London: Penguin Books, 1963), 217.
5. Hernando Cortés, *Five Letters, 1519–1526,* trans. J. Bayard Morris (New York: Norton, 1991), 87.
6. Quoted in Irene Silverblatt, *Moon, Sun, and Witches: Gender Ideologies and Class in Inca and Colonial Peru* (Princeton, NJ: Princeton University Press, 1987), 10.
7. Quoted in Irene Silverblatt, *Moon, Sun, and Witches: Gender Ideologies and Class in Inca and Colonial Peru* (Princeton, N.J.: Princeton University Press, 1987), 10.

Document-Based Question
Rituals in Mesoamerican and Andean Societies

Using the following illustrations of art and archaeological sites, evaluate the importance of rituals in the public life of Mesoamerican and Andean societies.

DOCUMENT 1
Maya Scribe (photo, p. 267)

DOCUMENT 2
The Great Plaza at Tikal (photo, p. 272)

DOCUMENT 3
The Mesoamerican Ball Game (photo, p. 273)

DOCUMENT 4
Costumes of Aztec Warriors (photo, p. 276)

DOCUMENT 5
Moche Portrait Vase (photo, p. 283)

DOCUMENT 6
Burials Reveal Ancient Civilizations (Diversity and Dominance, p. 285)

What special problems do historians face when they have to rely on such archaeological evidence to reconstruct the past? What additional types of archaeological evidence would help you understand the importance of rituals in the public life of Mesoamerican and Andean societies?

PART FOUR

Interregional Patterns of Culture and Contact, 1200–1550

In Eurasia, overland trade along the Silk Road, which had begun before the Roman and Han empires, reached its peak during the era of the Mongol empires. Beginning in 1206 with the rise of Genghis Khan, the Mongols tied Europe, the Middle East, Russia, and East Asia together with threads of conquest and trade centered on Central and Inner Asia. For over a century and a half, some communities thrived on the continental connections that the Mongols fostered, while others groaned under the tax burdens and physical devastation of Mongol rule. But whether for good or ill, Mongol power was based on the skills, strategies, and technologies of the overland trade and life on the steppes.

The impact of the Mongols was also felt by societies that escaped conquest. In Eastern Europe, the Mediterranean coastal areas of the Middle East, Southeast Asia, and Japan, fear of Mongol attack stimulated societies to organize more intensively in their own defense, accelerating processes of urbanization, technological development, and political centralization that in many cases were already underway.

By 1500, Mongol dominance was past, and new powers had emerged. A new Chinese empire, the Ming, was expanding its influence in Southeast

Asia. The Ottomans had captured Constantinople and overthrown the Byzantine Empire. And the Christian monarchs who had defeated the Muslims in Spain and Portugal were laying the foundations of new overseas empires. With the fall of the Mongol Empire, Central and Inner Asia were no longer at the center of Eurasian trade.

As the overland trade of Eurasia faded, merchants, soldiers, and explorers took to the seas. The most spectacular of the early state-sponsored long-distance ocean voyages were undertaken by the Chinese admiral Zheng He. The 1300s and 1400s also saw African exploration of the Atlantic and Polynesian colonization of the central and eastern Pacific. By 1500 the navigator Christopher Columbus, sailing for Spain, had reached the Americas; within twenty-five years a Portuguese ship would sail all the way around the world. New sailing technologies and a sounder knowledge of the size of the globe and the contours of its shorelines made sub-Saharan Africa, the Indian Ocean, Asia, Europe, and finally the Americas more accessible to each other than ever before.

The great overland routes of Eurasia had generated massive wealth in East Asia and a growing hunger for commerce in Europe. These factors animated the development of the sea trade, too. Exposure to the achievements, wealth, and resources of societies in the Americas, sub-Saharan Africa, and Asia enticed the emerging European monarchies to pursue further exploration and control of the seas.

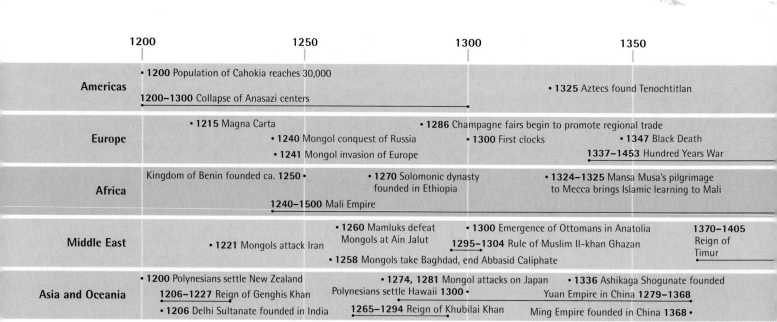

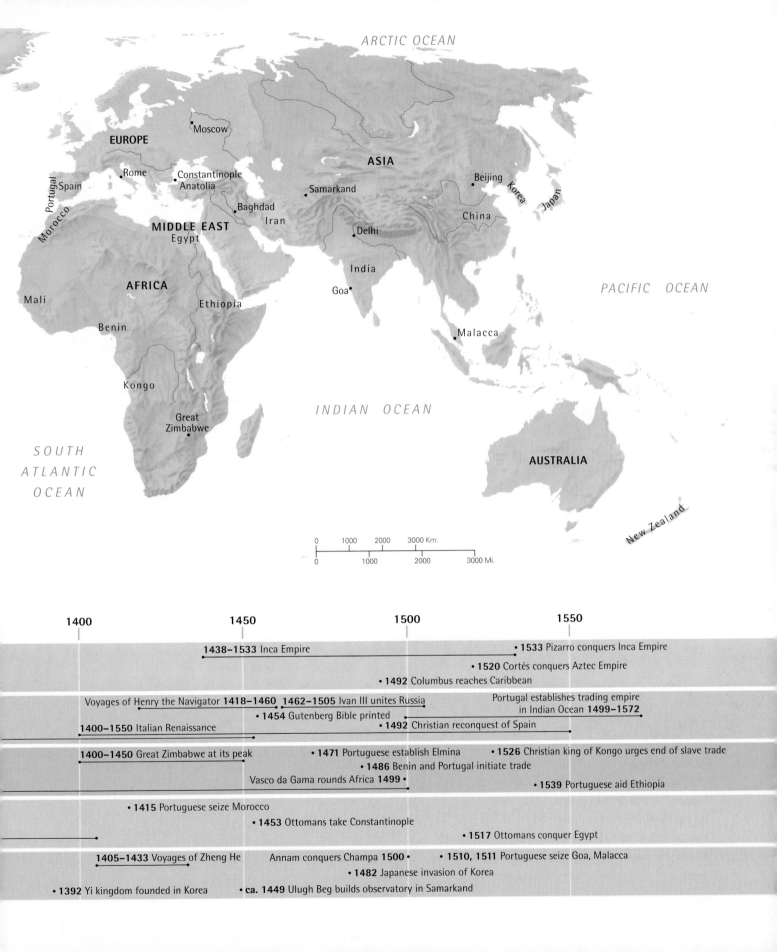

ARCTIC OCEAN

EUROPE
Moscow
Rome
Spain
Portugal
Morocco
Constantinople
Anatolia
Baghdad
Iran
MIDDLE EAST
Egypt

ASIA
Samarkand
Beijing
Korea
Japan
China
Delhi
India
Goa

PACIFIC OCEAN

AFRICA
Mali
Ethiopia
Benin
Kongo
Great
Zimbabwe

Malacca

INDIAN OCEAN

SOUTH
ATLANTIC
OCEAN

AUSTRALIA

New Zealand

| 0 | 1000 | 2000 | 3000 Km. |
| 0 | 1000 | 2000 | 3000 Mi. |

| 1400 | 1450 | 1500 | 1550 |

1438–1533 Inca Empire   • 1533 Pizarro conquers Inca Empire

• 1520 Cortés conquers Aztec Empire

• 1492 Columbus reaches Caribbean

Voyages of Henry the Navigator 1418–1460   1462–1505 Ivan III unites Russia   Portugal establishes trading empire in Indian Ocean 1499–1572

• 1454 Gutenberg Bible printed

1400–1550 Italian Renaissance   • 1492 Christian reconquest of Spain

1400–1450 Great Zimbabwe at its peak   • 1471 Portuguese establish Elmina   • 1526 Christian king of Kongo urges end of slave trade

• 1486 Benin and Portugal initiate trade

Vasco da Gama rounds Africa 1499 •

• 1539 Portuguese aid Ethiopia

• 1415 Portuguese seize Morocco

• 1453 Ottomans take Constantinople

• 1517 Ottomans conquer Egypt

1405–1433 Voyages of Zheng He   Annam conquers Champa 1500 •   • 1510, 1511 Portuguese seize Goa, Malacca

• 1482 Japanese invasion of Korea

• 1392 Yi kingdom founded in Korea   • ca. 1449 Ulugh Beg builds observatory in Samarkand

12

Mongol Eurasia and Its Aftermath, 1200–1500

Defending Japan Japanese warriors board Mongol warships with swords to prevent the landing of the invasion force in 1281.

CHAPTER OUTLINE

When the Mongol leader Temüjin° was a boy, a rival group murdered his father. Temüjin's mother tried to shelter him (and protect him from dogs, which he feared), but she could not find a safe haven. At fifteen Temüjin sought refuge with the leader of the Keraits°, one of Mongolia's many warring confederations. The Keraits spoke Turkic and respected both Christianity and Buddhism. Gifted with strength, courage, and intelligence, Temüjin learned the importance of religious tolerance, the necessity of dealing harshly with enemies, and the variety of Central Asia's cultural and economic traditions.

In 1206 the **Mongols** and their allies acknowledged Temüjin as **Genghis Khan°,** or supreme leader. His advisers included speakers of many languages and adherents of all the major religions of the Middle East and East Asia. His deathbed speech, which cannot be literally true even though a contemporary recorded it, captures the strategy behind Mongol success: "If you want to retain your possessions and conquer your enemies, you must make your subjects submit willingly and unite your diverse energies to a single end."[1] By implementing this strategy, Genghis Khan became the most famous conqueror in history, initiating an expansion of Mongol dominion that by 1250 stretched from Poland to northern China.

Scholars today stress the immense impact Temüjin and his successors had on the later medieval world, and the positive developments that transpired under Mongol rule. European and Asian sources of the time, however, vilify the Mongols as agents of death, suffering, and conflagration, a still-common viewpoint based on reliable accounts of horrible massacres.

The tremendous extent of the Mongol Empire promoted the movement of people and ideas from one end of Eurasia to the other. Specialized skills developed in different parts of the world spread rapidly throughout the Mongol domains. Trade routes improved, markets expanded, and the demand for products grew. Trade on the Silk Road, which had declined with the fall of the Tang Empire (see Chapter 10), revived.

During their period of domination, lasting from 1218 to about 1350 in western Eurasia and to 1368 in China, the Mongols focused on specific economic and strategic interests and usually permitted local cultures to survive and continue to develop. In some regions, local reactions to Mongol domination and unification sowed seeds of regional and ethnic identity that grew extensively in the period of Mongol decline. Societies in regions as widely separated as Russia, Iran, China, Korea, and Japan benefited from the Mongol stimulation of economic and cultural exchange and also found in their opposition to the Mongols new bases for political consolidation and affirmation of cultural difference.

As you read this chapter, ask yourself the following questions:

- What accounts for the magnitude and speed of the Mongol conquests?
- What benefits resulted from the integration of Eurasia in the Mongol Empire?
- How did the effect of Mongol rule on Russia and the lands of Islam differ from its effect on East Asia?
- In what ways did the Ming Empire continue or discontinue Mongol practices?

THE RISE OF THE MONGOLS, 1200–1260

The environment, economic life, cultural institutions, and political traditions of the steppes (prairies) and deserts of Central and Inner Asia contributed to the expansion and contraction of empires. The Mongol Empire owes much of its success to these long-term conditions. Yet the interplay of environment and technology, on the one hand, and specific human actions, on the other, cannot easily be determined. The way of life known as **nomadism** gives rise to imperial expansion only occasionally, and historians disagree about what triggers these episodes. In the case of the Mongols, a precise assessment of the personal contributions of Genghis Khan and his followers remains uncertain.

Temüjin (TEM-uh-jin)   Keraits (keh-rates)
Genghis Khan (GENG-iz KAHN)

Nomadism in Central and Inner Asia

Descriptions of steppe nomads from as early as the Greek writer Herodotus in the sixth century B.C.E. portray them as superb riders, herdsmen, and hunters. Traditional accounts maintain that the Mongols put their infants on goats to accustom them to riding. Moving regularly and efficiently with flocks and herds required firm decision making, and the independence of individual Mongols and their families made this decision making public, with many voices being heard. A council with representatives from powerful families ratified the decisions of the leader, the *khan*. Yet people who disagreed with a decision could strike off on their own. Even during military campaigns, warriors moved with their families and possessions.

Menial work in camps fell to slaves—people who were either captured during warfare or who sought refuge in slavery to escape starvation. Weak groups secured land rights and protection from strong groups by providing them with slaves, livestock, weapons, silk, or cash. More powerful groups, such as Genghis Khan's extended family and descendants, lived almost entirely off tribute, so they spent less time and fewer resources on herding and more on warfare designed to secure greater tribute.

Leading families combined resources and solidified intergroup alliances through arranged marriages and other acts, a process that helped generate political federations. Marriages were arranged in childhood—in Temüjin's case, at the age of eight—and children thus became pawns of diplomacy. Women from prestigious families could wield power in negotiation and management, though they ran the risk of assassination or execution just like men (see Diversity and Dominance: Mongol Politics, Mongol Women).

Families often included believers in two or more religions, most commonly Buddhism, Christianity, or Islam. Virtually all Mongols observed the practices of traditional shamanism, rituals in which special individuals visited and influenced the supernatural world. Whatever their faith, the Mongols believed in world rulership by a khan who, with the aid of his shamans, could speak to and for an ultimate god, represented as Sky or Heaven. This universal ruler transcended particular cultures and dominated them all.

The Mongols were not unfamiliar with agriculture or unwilling to use products grown by farmers, but their ideal was self-sufficiency. Since their wanderings with their herds normally took them far from any farming region, self-sufficiency dictated foods they could provide for themselves—primarily meat and milk—and clothing made from felt, leather, and furs. Women oversaw the breeding and birthing of livestock and the preparation of furs.

Mongol dependency on settled regions related primarily to iron for bridles, stirrups, cart fittings, and weapons. They acquired iron implements in trade and reworked them to suit their purposes. As early as the 600s the Turks, a related pastoral people, had large iron-working stations south of the Altai Mountains in western Mongolia. Neighboring agricultural states tried to limit the export of iron but never succeeded. Indeed, Central Asians developed improved techniques of iron forging, which the agricultural regions then adopted. The Mongols revered iron and the secrets of ironworking. Temüjin means "blacksmith," and several of his prominent followers were the sons of blacksmiths.

Steppe nomads situated near settled areas traded wool, leather, and horses for wood, cotton and cottonseed, silk, vegetables, grain, and tea. An appreciation of the value of permanent settlements for growing grain and cotton, as well as for working iron, led some nomadic groups to establish villages at strategic points, often with the help of migrants from the agricultural regions. The frontier regions east of the Caspian Sea and in northern China thus became economically and culturally diverse. Despite their interdependence, nomads and farmers often came into conflict. On rare occasion such conflicts escalated into full-scale invasions in which the martial prowess of the nomads usually resulted in at least temporary victory.

The Mongol Conquests, 1215–1283

Shortly after his acclamation in 1206 Genghis set out to convince the kingdoms of Eurasia to pay him tribute. Two decades of Mongol aggression followed. By 1209 he had forced the Tanggut rulers of northwest China to submit, and in 1215 he captured the Jin capital of Yanjing, today known as Beijing. He began to attack the west in 1219 with a full-scale invasion of a Central Asian state centered on Khwarezm, an oasis area east of the Caspian Sea. By 1221 he had overwhelmed most of Iran. By this time his conquests had gained such momentum that Genghis did not personally participate in all campaigns, and subordinate generals sometimes led the Mongol armies, which increasingly contained non-Mongol nomads as well.

Genghis Khan died in 1227. His son and successor, the Great Khan Ögödei° (see Figure 12.1), continued to

Ögödei (ERG-uh-day)

C H R O N O L O G Y

	Mongolia and China	Central Asia and Middle East	Russia	Korea, Japan, and Southeast Asia
1200	**1206** Temüjin chosen Genghis Khan of the Mongols			
	1227 Death of Genghis Khan	**1221–1223** First Mongol attacks in Iran	**1221–1223** First Mongol attacks on Russia	
	1227–1241 Reign of Great Khan Ögödei			
	1234 Mongols conquer northern China		**1240** Mongols sack Kiev	
			1242 Alexander Nevskii defeats Teutonic Knights	
		1250 Mamluk regime controls Egypt and Syria		
		1258 Mongols sack Baghdad and kill the caliph		**1258** Mongols conquer Koryo rulers in Korea
	1271 Founding of Yuan Empire	**1260** Mamluks defeat Il-khans at Ain Jalut	**1260** War between Il-khans and Golden Horde	
	1279 Mongol conquest of Southern Song			**1274, 1281** Mongols attack Japan
				1283 Yuan invades Annam
1300		**1295** Il-khan Ghazan converts to Islam		**1293** Yuan attacks Java
			1346 Plague outbreak at Kaffa	**1333–1338** End of Kamakura Shogunate in Japan, beginning of Ashikaga
		1349 End of Il-khan rule		
	1368 Ming Empire founded	**ca. 1350** Egypt infected by plague		
		1370–1405 Reign of Timur		**1392** Founding of Yi kingdom in Korea
1400	**1403–1424** Reign of Yongle	**1402** Timur defeats Ottoman sultan		
	1405–1433 Voyages of Zheng He			
	1449 Mongol attack on Beijing	**1453** Ottomans capture Constantinople	**1462–1505** Ivan III establishes authority as tsar. Moscow emerges as major political center.	**1471–1500** Annam conquers Champa

DIVERSITY AND DOMINANCE

MONGOL POLITICS, MONGOL WOMEN

Women in nomadic societies often enjoy more freedom and wield greater influence than women in villages and towns. The wives or mothers of Mongol rulers traditionally managed state affairs during the interregnum between a ruler's death and the selection of a successor. Princes and heads of ministries treated such regents with great deference and obeyed their commands without question. Since a female regent could not herself succeed to the position of khan, her political machinations usually focused on gaining the succession for a son or other male relative.

The History of the World-Conqueror *by the Iranian historian 'Ata-Malik Juvaini, elegantly written in Persian during the 1250s, combines a glorification of the Mongol rulers with an unflinching picture of the cruelties and devastation inflicted by their conquests. As a Muslim, he explains these events as God's punishment for Muslim sins. But this religious viewpoint does not detract from his frank depiction of the instruments of Mongol domination and the fate of those who tried to resist.*

When [Qa'an, i.e., Ögödei, Genghis Khan's son and successor] was on his hunting ground someone brought him two or three water-melons. None of his attendants had any [money] or garments available, but Möge Khatun [his wife], who was present, had two pearls in her ears like the two bright stars of the Lesser Bear when rendered auspicious by conjunction with the radiant moon. Qa'an ordered these pearls to be given to the man. But as they were very precious she said: "This man does not know their worth and value: it is like giving saffron to a donkey. If he is commanded to come to the *ordu* [residence] tomorrow, he will there receive [money] and clothing." "He is a poor man," said Qa'an, "and cannot bear to wait until tomorrow. And whither should these pearls go? They too will return to us in the end. . . ."

At Qa'an's command she gave the pearls to the poor man, and he went away rejoicing and sold them for a small sum, round about two thousand dinars [Note: this is actually a very large sum]. The buyer was very pleased and thought to himself: "I have acquired two fine jewels fit for a present to the Emperor. He is rarely brought such gifts as these." He ac-

cordingly took the pearls to the Emperor, and at that time Möge Khatun was with him. Qa'an took the pearls and said: "Did we not say they would come back to us?" . . . And he distinguished the bearer with all kinds of favours. . . .

When the decree of God Almighty had been executed and the Monarch of the World . . . . Qa'an had passed away, Güyük, his eldest son, had not returned from the campaign against the Qifchaq, and therefore in accordance with precedent the dispatch of orders and the assembling of the people took place at the door of the *ordu*, or palace of his wife, Möge Khatun, who, in accordance with the Mongol custom, had come to him from his father, Chinggiz-Khan. But since Töregene Khatun was the mother of his eldest sons and was moreover shrewder and more sagacious than Möge Khatun, she sent messages to the princes, i.e. the brothers and nephews of the Qa'an, and told them of what had happened and of the death of Qa'an, and said that until a Khan was appointed by agreement someone would have to be ruler and leader in order that the business of state might not be neglected nor the affairs of the commonweal thrown into confusion; in order, too, that the army and the court might be kept under control and the interests of the people protected.

Chaghatai [another of Genghis's sons] and the other princes sent representatives to say that Töregene Khatun was the mother of the princes who had a right to the Khanate; therefore, until a *quriltai* [family council] was held, it was she that should direct the affairs of the state, and the old ministers should remain in the service of the Court, so that the old and new *yasas* [imperial decrees] might not be changed from what was the law.

Now Töregene Khatun was a very shrewd and capable woman, and her position was greatly strengthened by this unity and concord. And when Möge Khatun shortly followed in the wake of Qa'an [i.e., died], by means of finesse and cunning she obtained control of all the affairs of state and won over the hearts of her relatives by all kind of favours and kindnesses and by the sending of gifts and presents. And for the most part strangers and kindred, family and army inclined towards her, and submitted themselves obediently and gladly to her commands and prohibitions, and came under her sway. . . .

And when Güyük came to his mother, he took no part in affairs of state, and Töregene Khatun still executed the decrees of the Empire although the Khanate was settled upon her son. But when two or three months had passed and the son was somewhat estranged from his mother on account of Fatima [see below], the decree of God the Almighty and Glorious was fulfilled and Töregene passed away. . . .

And at that time there was a woman called Fatima, who had acquired great influence in the service of Töregene Khatun and to whose counsel and capability were entrusted all affairs of state. . . .

At the time of the capture of the place [Mashhad, Iran] in which there lies the Holy Shrine of 'Ali ar-Riza [the eighth Shi'ite Imam], she was carried off into captivity. It so chanced she came to Qara-Qorum [Karakorum], where she was a procuress in the market; and in the arts of shrewdness and cunning the wily Delilah could have been her pupil. During the reign of Qa'an she had constant access to the *ordu* of Töregene Khatun; and when times changed and Chinqai [a high official] withdrew from the scene, she enjoyed even greater favour, and her influence became paramount; so that she became the sharer of intimate confidences and the depository of hidden secrets, and the ministers were debarred from executing business, and she was free to issue commands and prohibitions. And from every side the grandees sought her protection, especially the grandees of Khorasan [where Mashhad is located]. And there also came to her certain of the *sayyids* [i.e., descendants of Muhammad] of the Holy Shrine [the tomb of 'Ali ar-Riza], for she claimed to be of the race of the great *sayyids*.

When Güyük succeeded to the Khanate, a certain native of Samarqand, who was said to be an 'Alid [i.e., descendant of Muhammad], one Shira . . . hinted that Fatima had bewitched Köten [another of Töregene Khatun's sons], which was why he was so indisposed. When Köten returned, the malady from which he was suffering grew worse, and he sent a messenger to his brother Güyük to say that he had been attacked by that illness because of Fatima's magic and that if anything happened to him Güyük should seek retribution from her. Following on this message there came tidings of Köten's death. Chinqai, who was now a person of authority, reminded Güyük of the message, and he sent an envoy to his mother to fetch Fatima. His mother refused to let her go saying that she would bring her herself. He sent again several times, and each time she refused him in a different way. As a result his relations with his mother became very bad, and he sent the man from Samarqand with instructions to bring Fatima by force if his mother should still delay in sending her or find some reason for refusing. It being no longer possible to excuse herself, she agreed to send Fatima; and shortly af-

terwards she passed away. Fatima was brought face to face with Güyük, and was kept naked, and in bonds, and hungry and thirsty for many days and nights; she was plied with all manner of violence, severity, harshness and intimidation; and at last she confessed to the calumny of the slanderous talebearer and avowed her falseness . . . She was rolled up in a sheet of felt and thrown into the river.

And everyone who was connected with her perished also. And messengers were sent to fetch certain persons who had come from the Shrine and claimed to be related to her; and they suffered many annoyances.

This was the year in which Güyük Khan went to join his father, and it was then that 'Ali Khoja of Emil accused Shira of the same crime, namely of bewitching Khoja. He was cast into bonds and chains and remained imprisoned for nearly two years, during which time by reason of all manner of questioning and punishment he despaired of the pleasure of life. And when he recognized and knew of a certainty that this was [his] punishment he resigned himself to death and surrendering his body to the will of Fate and Destiny confessed to a crime which he had not committed. He too was cast into the river, and his wives and children were put to the sword. . . .

[I]n that same year, in a happy and auspicious hour, the Khanate had been settled upon Mengü Qa'an. . . . And when Khoja was brought to the Qa'an, a messenger was sent to 'Ali Khoja, who was one of his courtiers. Some other person brought the same accusation against him, and Mengü-Qa'an ordered him to be beaten from the left and the right until all his limbs were crushed; and so he died. And his wives and children were cast into the baseness of slavery and disgraced and humiliated.

And it is not hidden from the wise and intelligent man, who looks at these matters in the light of understanding and reflects and ponders on them, that the end of treachery and the conclusion of deceit, which spring from evil ways and wicked pretensions, is shameful and the termination thereof unlucky. . . . God preserve us from the like positions and from trespassing into the region of deliberate offenses!

QUESTIONS FOR ANALYSIS

1. How do the stories of Töregene Khatun and Fatima differ in their presentation of female roles?
2. What does the passage indicate concerning the respect of the Mongols for women?
3. What does Güyük's refusal to take over the affairs of state while his mother is still alive imply?

Source: Reprinted by permission of the publisher from 'Ala-ad-Din 'Ata-Malik Juvaini, *The History of the World-Conqueror*, vol. 1, trans. John Andrew Boyle (Cambridge, MA: Harvard University Press, 1958), 211–212, 239–248. Copyright © 1958 by Manchester University Press.

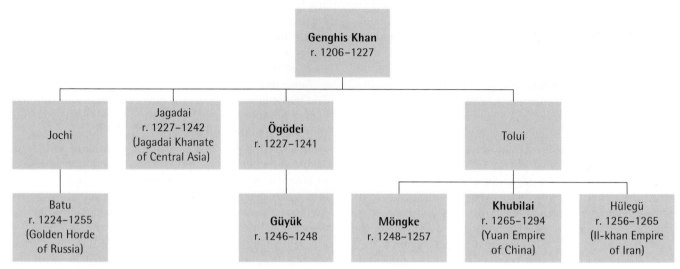

Figure 12.1   Mongol Rulers, 1206–1260   The names of the Great Khans are shown in bold type. Those who founded the regional khanates are listed with their dates of rule.

assault China. He destroyed the Tanggut and then the Jin and put their territories under Mongol governors. In 1236 Genghis's grandson Batu° (d. 1255) attacked Russian territories, took control of all the towns along the Volga° River, and within five years conquered Kievan Russia, Moscow, Poland, and Hungary. Europe would have suffered grave damage in 1241 had not the death of Ögödei compelled the Mongol forces to suspend their campaign. With Genghis's grandson Güyük° installed as the new Great Khan, the conquests resumed. By 1234 the Mongols controlled most of northern China and were threatening the Southern Song. In the Middle East they sacked Baghdad in 1258 and executed the last Abbasid caliph (see Chapter 8).

Although the Mongols' original objective may have been tribute, the scale and success of the conquests created a new historical situation. Ögödei unquestionably sought territorial rule. Between 1240 and 1260 his imperial capital at Karakorum° attracted merchants, ambassadors, missionaries, and adventurers from all over Eurasia. A European who visited in 1246 found the city isolated but well populated and cosmopolitan.

The Mongol Empire remained united until about 1265, as the Great Khan in Mongolia exercised authority over the khans of the Golden Horde in Russia, the khans of the Jagadai domains in Central Asia, and the Il-khans

in Iran (see Map 12.1). After Ögödei's death in 1241 family unity began to unravel. When Khubilai° declared himself Great Khan in 1265, the descendants of Jagadai and other branches of the family refused to accept him. The destruction of Karakorum in the ensuing fighting contributed to Khubilai's transferring his court to the old Jin capital that is now Beijing. In 1271 he declared himself founder of the **Yuan Empire.**

Jagadai's descendants, who continued to dominate Central Asia, had much closer relations with Turkic-speaking nomads than did their kinsmen farther east. This, plus a continuing hatred of Khubilai and the Yuan, contributed to the strengthening of Central Asia as an independent Mongol center and to the adoption of Islam in the western territories.

After the Yuan destroyed the Southern Song (see Chapter 10) in 1279, Mongol troops crossed south of the Red River and attacked Annam—now northern Vietnam. They occupied Hanoi three times and then withdrew after arranging for the payment of tribute. In 1283 Khubilai's forces invaded Champa in what is now southern Vietnam and made it a tribute nation as well. A plan to invade Java by sea failed, as did two invasions of Japan in 1274 and 1281.

In tactical terms, the Mongols did not usually outnumber their enemies, but like all steppe nomads for many centuries, they displayed extraordinary abilities

---

Batu (BAH-too)   **Volga** (VOHL-gah)   **Güyük** (gi-yik)
Karakorum (kah-rah-KOR-um)

Khubilai (KOO-bih-lie)

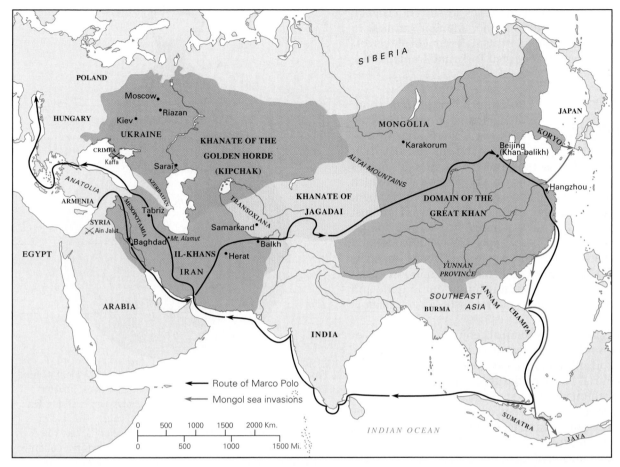

Map 12.1   The Mongol Domains in Eurasia in 1300   After the death of Genghis Khan in 1227, his empire was divided among his sons and grandsons. Son Ögödei succeeded Genghis as Great Khan. Grandson Khubilai expanded the domain of the Great Khan into southern China by 1279. Grandson Hülegü was the first Il-khan in the Middle East. Grandson Batu founded the Khanate of the Golden Horde in southern Russia. Son Jagadai ruled the Jagadai Khanate in Central Asia.

on horseback and utilized superior bows. The Central Asian bow, made strong by laminated layers of wood, leather, and bone, could shoot one-third farther (and was significantly more difficult to pull) than the bows used by their enemies in the settled lands.

Mounted Mongol archers rarely expended all of the five dozen or more arrows they carried in their quivers. As the battle opened, they shot arrows from a distance to decimate enemy marksmen. Then they galloped against the enemy's infantry to fight with sword, lance, javelin, and mace. The Mongol cavalry met its match only at the Battle of Ain Jalut°, where it confronted Mamluk forces whose war techniques shared some of the same traditions (see Chapter 8).

To penetrate fortifications, the Mongols fired flaming arrows and hurled enormous projectiles—sometimes flaming—from catapults. The first Mongol catapults, built on Chinese models, transported easily but had short range and poor accuracy. During western campaigns in Central Asia, the Mongols encountered a catapult design that was half again as powerful as the Chinese model. They used this improved weapon against the cities of Iran and Iraq.

Cities that resisted Mongol attack faced mass slaughter or starvation under siege. Timely surrender brought food, shelter, and protection. The bloodletting the Mongols inflicted on cities such as Balkh° (in present-day northern Afghanistan) spread terror and made it easier

---

Ain Jalut (ine jah-LOOT)

Balkh (bahlk)

for the Mongols to persuade cities to surrender. Each conquered area helped swell the "Mongol" armies. In campaigns in the Middle East a small Mongol elite oversaw armies of recently recruited Turks and Iranians.

Overland Trade and the Plague

Commercial integration under Mongol rule strongly affected both the eastern and western wings of the empire. Like their aristocratic predecessors in Inner Asia, Mongol nobles had the exclusive right to wear silk, almost all of which came from China. Trade under Mongol dominion brought new styles and huge quantities of silk westward, not just for clothing but also for wall hangings and furnishings. Abundant silk fed the luxury trade in the Middle East and Europe. Artistic motifs from Japan and Tibet reached as far as England and Morocco. Porcelain was another eastern luxury product that became important in trade and strongly influenced later cultural tastes in the Islamic world.

Traders from all over Eurasia enjoyed the benefits of Mongol control. Merchants encountered ambassadors, scholars, and missionaries over the long routes to the Mongol courts. Some of the resulting travel literature, like the account of the Venetian Marco Polo° (1254–1324), freely mixed the fantastic with the factual. Stories of fantastic wealth stimulated a European ambition to find easier routes to Asia.

Exchange also held great dangers. In southwestern China **bubonic plague** had festered in Yunnan province since the early Tang period. In the mid-thirteenth century Mongol troops established a garrison in Yunnan whose military and supply traffic provided the means for flea-infested rats to carry the plague into central China, northwestern China, and Central Asia. Marmots and other desert rodents along the routes became infected and passed the disease to dogs and people. The caravan traffic infected the oasis towns. The plague incapacitated the Mongol army during their assault on the city of Kaffa° in Crimea° in 1346. They withdrew, but the plague remained. From Kaffa rats infected by fleas reached Europe and Egypt by ship (see Chapter 14).

Typhus, influenza, and smallpox traveled with the plague. The combination of these and other diseases created what is often called the "great pandemic" of 1347–1352 and spread devastation far in excess of what the Mongols inflicted in war. Peace and trade, not conquest, gave rise to the great pandemic.

Marco Polo (mar-koe POE-loe)   **Kaffa** (KAH-fah)
Crimea (cry-MEE-ah)

Passport   The Mongol Empire facilitated the movement of products, merchants, and diplomats over long distances. Travelers frequently encountered new languages, laws, and customs. The *paisa* (from a Chinese word for "card" or "sign"), with its inscription in Mongolian, proclaimed that the traveler had the ruler's permission to travel through the region. Europeans later adopted the practice, thus making the *paisa* the ancestor of modern passports.   (The Metropolitan Museum of Art, purchase bequest of Dorothy Graham Bennett, 1993 [1993.256]. Photograph 1997 The Metropolitan Museum of Art)

The Mongols and Islam, 1260–1500

From the perspective of Mongol imperial history, the issue of which branches of the family espoused Islam and which did not mostly concerns their political rivalries and their respective quests for allies. From the standpoint of the history of Islam, however, recovery from the political, religious, and physical devastation that culminated in the destruction of the Abbasid caliphate in Baghdad in 1258 attests to the vitality of the faith and the ability of Muslims to overcome adversity. Within fifty years of its darkest hour, Islam had reemerged as a potent ideological and political force.

Mongol Rivalry

By 1260 the **Il-khan°** state, established by Genghis's grandson Hülegü, controlled parts of Armenia and all of Azerbaijan, Mesopotamia, and Iran. The Mongols who had conquered southern Russia settled north of the Caspian Sea and established the capital of their Khanate of the **Golden Horde** (also called the Kipchak° Khanate) at Sarai° on the Volga River. There they established dominance over the indigenous Muslim Turkic population, both settled and pastoral.

Some members of the Mongol imperial family had professed Islam before the Mongol assault on the Middle East, and Turkic Muslims had served the family in various capacities. Indeed, Hülegü himself, though a Buddhist, had a trusted Shi'ite adviser and granted privileges to the Shi'ites. As a whole, however, the Mongols under Hülegü's command came only slowly to Islam.

The passage of time did little to reconcile Islamic doctrines with Mongol ways. Muslims abhorred the Mongols' worship of idols, a fundamental part of shamanism. Furthermore, Mongol law specified slaughtering animals without spilling blood, which involved opening the chest and stopping the heart. This horrified Muslims, who were forbidden to consume blood and slaughtered animals by slitting their throats and draining the blood.

Islam became a point of inter-Mongol tension when Batu's successor as leader of the Golden Horde declared himself a Muslim, swore to avenge the murder of the Abbasid caliph, and laid claim to the Caucasus—the region between the Black and Caspian Seas—which the Il-khans also claimed (see Map 12.2).

Some European leaders believed that if they helped the non-Muslim Il-khans repel the Golden Horde from the Caucasus, the Il-khans would help them relieve Muslim pressure on the crusader states in Syria, Lebanon, and Palestine (see Chapter 8). This resulted in a brief correspondence between the Il-khan court and Pope Nicholas IV (r. 1288–1292) and a diplomatic mission that sent two Christian Turks to western Europe as Il-khan ambassadors in the late 1200s. Many Christian crusaders enlisted in the Il-khan effort, but the pope later excommunicated some for doing so.

The Golden Horde responded by seeking an alliance with the Muslim Mamluks in Egypt (see Chapter 8) against both the crusaders and the Il-khans. These complicated efforts effectively extended the life of the crusader states; the Mamluks did not finish ejecting the crusaders until the fifteenth century.

Before the Europeans' diplomatic efforts could produce a formal alliance, however, a new Il-khan ruler, Ghazan° (1271–1304), declared himself a Muslim in 1295. Conflicting indications of Sunni and Shi'ite affiliation on such things as coins indicate that the Il-khans did not pay too much attention to theological matters. Nor is it clear whether the many Muslim Turkic nomads who served alongside the Mongols in the army were Shi'ite or Sunni.

Islam and the State

Like the Turks before them (see Chapter 8), the Il-khans gradually came to appreciate the traditional urban culture of the Muslim territories they ruled. Though nomads continued to serve in their armies, the Il-khans used tax farming, a fiscal method developed earlier in the Middle East, to extract maximum wealth from their domain. The government sold tax-collecting contracts to small partnerships, mostly consisting of merchants who might also work together to finance caravans, small industries, or military expeditions. The corporations that offered to collect the most revenue for the government won the contracts. They could use whatever methods they chose and could keep anything over the contracted amount.

Initially, the cost of collecting taxes fell, but over the long term, the exorbitant rates the tax farmers charged drove many landowners into debt and servitude. Agricultural productivity declined. The government had difficulty procuring supplies for the soldiers and resorted to taking land to grow its own grain. Like land held by religious trusts, this land paid no taxes. Thus the tax base shrank even as the demands of the army and the Mongol nobility continued to grow.

Ghazan faced many economic problems. Citing the humane values of Islam, he promised to reduce taxes, but the need for revenues kept the decrease from being permanent. He also witnessed the failure of a predecessor's experiment with the Chinese practice of using paper money. Having no previous exposure to paper money, the Il-khan's subjects responded negatively. The economy quickly sank into a depression that lasted beyond the end of the Il-khan state in 1349. High taxes caused widespread popular unrest and resentment. Mongol nobles competed fiercely among themselves for the decreasing revenues, and fighting among Mongol factions destabilized the government.

In the mid-fourteenth century Mongols from the Golden Horde moved through the Caucasus into the

---

Il-khan (IL-con)   **Kipchak** (KIP-chahk)   **Sarai** (sah-RYE)   **Ghazan** (haz-ZAHN)

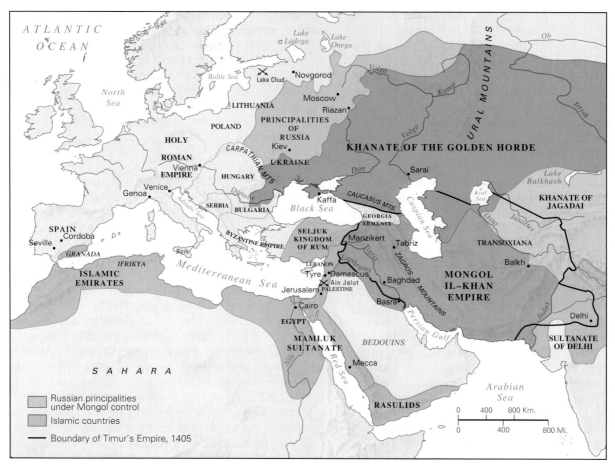

Map 12.2 Western Eurasia in the 1300s   Ghazan's conversion to Islam in 1295 upset the delicate balance of power in Mongol domains. European leaders abandoned their hope of finding an Il-khan ally against the Muslim defenders in Palestine, while an alliance between the Mamluks and the Golden Horde kept the Il-khans from advancing west. This helped the Europeans retain their lands in Palestine and Syria.

western regions of the Il-khan Empire and then into the Il-khan's central territory, Azerbaijan, briefly occupying its major cities. At the same time a new power was emerging to the east, in the Central Asian Khanate of Jagadai (see Map 12.1). The leader **Timur°,** known to Europeans as Tamerlane, skillfully maneuvered himself into command of the Jagadai forces and launched campaigns into western Eurasia, apparently seeing himself as a new Genghis Khan. By ethnic background he was a Turk with only an in-law relationship to the family of the Mongol conqueror. This prevented him from assuming the title *khan*, but not from sacking the Muslim sultanate of Delhi in northern India in 1398 or defeating

the sultan of the rising Ottoman Empire in Anatolia in 1402. By that time he had subdued much of the Middle East, and he was reportedly preparing to march on China when he died in 1405. The Timurids (descendants of Timur) could not hold the empire together, but they laid the groundwork for the establishment in India of a Muslim Mongol-Turkic regime, the Mughals, in the sixteenth century.

Culture and Science in Islamic Eurasia

The Il-khans of Iran and Timurids of Central Asia presided over a brilliant cultural flowering in Iran, Afghanistan, and Central Asia based on the shar-

Timur (tem-EER)

Tomb of Timur in Samarqand   The turquoise tiles that cover the dome are typical of Timurid architectural decoration. Timur's family ornamented his capital with an enormous mosque, three large religious colleges facing one another on three sides of an open plaza, and a lane of brilliantly tiled Timurid family tombs in the midst of a cemetery. Timur brought craftsmen to Samarqand from the lands he conquered to build these magnificent structures.   (Sassoon/Robert Harding Picture Library)

ing of artistic trends, administrative practices, and political ideas between Iran and China, the dominant urban civilizations at opposite ends of the Silk Road. The dominant cultural tendencies of the Il-khan and Timurid periods are Muslim, however. Although Timur died before he could reunite Iran and China, his forcible concentration of Middle Eastern scholars, artists, and craftsmen in his capital, Samarkand, fostered advancement in some specific activities under his descendants.

The historian Juvaini° (d. 1283), the literary figure who noted Genghis Khan's deathbed speech, came from the city of Balkh, which the Mongols had devastated in 1221. His family switched their allegiance to the Mongols, and both Juvaini and his older brother assumed high government posts. The Il-khan Hülegü, seeking to immortalize and justify the Mongol conquest of the Middle East, enthusiastically supported Juvaini's writing. This resulted in the first comprehensive narrative of the rise of the Mongols under Genghis Khan.

Juvaini combined a florid style with historical objectivity—he often criticized the Mongols—and served as an inspiration to **Rashid al-Din°**, Ghazan's prime minister, when he attempted the first history of the world. Rashid al-Din's work included the earliest known general history of Europe, derived from conversations with European monks, and a detailed description of China based on information from an important Chinese Muslim official stationed in Iran. The miniature paintings that accompanied some copies of Rashid al-Din's work included depictions of European and Chinese people and events and reflected the artistic traditions of both cultures. The Chinese techniques of composition helped inaugurate the greatest period of Islamic miniature painting under the Timurids.

Rashid al-Din traveled widely and collaborated with administrators from other parts of the far-flung Mongol dominions. His idea that government should be in accord with the moral principles of the majority of the population buttressed Ghazan's adherence to Islam. Administratively, however, Ghazan did not restrict himself to Muslim precedents but employed financial and monetary techniques that roughly resembled those in use in Russia and China.

Under the Timurids, the tradition of the Il-khan historians continued. After conquering Damascus, Timur himself met there with the greatest historian of the age, Ibn Khaldun° (1332–1406), a Tunisian. In a scene reminiscent of Ghazan's answering Rashid al-Din's questions on the history of the Mongols, Timur and Ibn Khaldun exchanged historical, philosophical, and geographical viewpoints. Like Genghis, Timur saw himself as a world conqueror. At their capitals of Samarkand and Herat (in western Afghanistan), later Timurid rulers sponsored historical writing in both Persian and Turkish.

A Shi'ite scholar named **Nasir al-Din Tusi°** represents the beginning of Mongol interest in the scientific traditions of the Muslim lands. Nasir al-Din may have

Juvaini (joo-VINE-nee)   **Rashid al-Din** (ra-SHEED ad-DEEN)
Ibn Khaldun (ee-bin hal-DOON)
Nasir al-Din Tusi (nah-SEER ad-DEEN TOO-si)

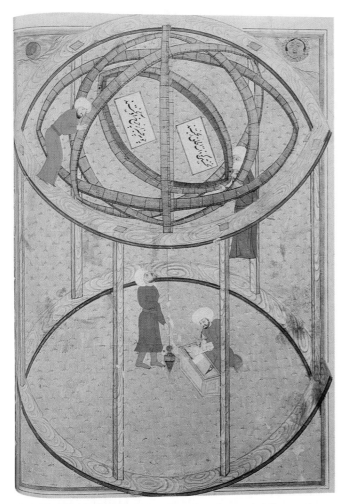

Astronomy and Engineering Observational astronomy went hand in hand not only with mathematics and calendrical science but also with engineering as the construction of platforms, instruments for celestial measurement, and armillary spheres became more sophisticated. This manual in Persian, completed in the 1500s but illustrating activities of the Il-khan period, illustrates the use of a plumb line with an enormous armillary sphere. (Istanbul University Library)

he laid new foundations for algebra and trigonometry. Some followers working at an observatory built for Nasir al-Din at Maragheh°, near the Il-khan capital of Tabriz, used the new mathematical techniques to solve a fundamental problem in classical cosmology.

Islamic scholars had preserved and elaborated on the insights of the Greeks in astronomy and mathematics and adopted the cosmological model of Ptolemy°, which assumed a universe with the earth at its center surrounded by the sun, moon, and planets traveling in concentric circular orbits. However, the motions of these orbiting bodies did not coincide with predictions based on circular orbits. Astronomers and mathematicians had long sought a mathematical explanation for the movements that they observed.

Nasir al-Din proposed a model based on the idea of small circles rotating within a large circle. One of his students reconciled this model with the ancient Greek idea of epicycles (small circles rotating around a point on a larger circle) to explain the movement of the moon around the earth. The mathematical tables and geometric models devised by this student somehow became known to Nicholas Copernicus (1473–1543), a Polish monk and astronomer. Copernicus adopted the lunar model as his own, virtually without revision. He then proposed the model of lunar movement developed under the Il-khans as the proper model for planetary movement as well—but with the planets circling the sun.

Sponsorship of observational astronomy and the making of calendars had engaged the interest of earlier Central Asian rulers, particularly the Uighurs° and the Seljuks. Under the Il-khans, the astronomers of Maragheh excelled in predicting lunar and solar eclipses. Astrolabes, armillary spheres, three-dimensional quadrants, and other instruments acquired new precision.

The remarkably accurate eclipse predictions and tables prepared by Il-khan and Timurid astronomers reached the hostile Mamluk lands in Arabic translation. Byzantine monks took them to Constantinople and translated them into Greek, while Christian scholars working in Muslim Spain translated them into Latin. In India the sultan of Delhi ordered them translated into Sanskrit. The Great Khan Khubilai (see below) summoned a team of Iranians to Beijing to build an observatory for him. Timur's grandson Ulugh Beg° (1394–1449), who mixed science and rule, constructed a great observatory in Samarkand and actively participated in compiling observational tables that were later translated into Latin and used by European astronomers.

joined the entourage of Hülegü during a campaign in 1256 against the Assassins, a Shi'ite religious sect derived from the Fatimid dynasty in Egypt and at odds with his more mainstream Shi'ite views (see Chapter 8). Nasir al-Din wrote on history, poetry, ethics, and religion, but made his most outstanding contributions in mathematics and cosmology. Following Omar Khayyam° (1038?–1131), a poet and mathematician of the Seljuk° period,

---

Omar Khayyam (oh-mar kie-YAM)   **Seljuk** (SEL-jook)

Maragheh (mah-RAH-gah)   **Ptolemy** (TOHL-uh-mee)
Uigur (WEE-ger)   **Ulugh Beg** (oo-loog bek)

A further advance made under Ulugh Beg came from the mathematician Ghiyas al-Din Jamshid al-Kashi°, who noted that Chinese astronomers had long used one ten-thousandth of a day as a unit in calculating the occurrence of a new moon. This seems to have inspired him to employ decimal fractions, by which quantities less than one could be represented by a marker to show place. Al-Kashi's proposed value for *pi* (π) was far more precise than any previously calculated. This innovation arrived in Europe by way of Constantinople, where a Greek translation of al-Kashi's work appeared in the fifteenth century.

REGIONAL RESPONSES IN WESTERN EURASIA

Safe, reliable overland trade throughout Eurasia benefited Mongol ruling centers and commercial cities along the length of the Silk Road. But the countryside, ravaged by conquest, sporadically continuing violence, and heavy taxes, suffered terribly. As Mongol control weakened, regional forces in Russia, eastern Europe, and Anatolia reasserted themselves. All were influenced by Mongol predecessors, and all had to respond to the social and economic changes of the Mongol era. Sometimes this meant collaborating with the Mongols. At other times it meant using local ethnic or religious traditions to resist or roll back Mongol influence.

Russia and Rule from Afar

The Golden Horde established by Genghis's grandson Batu after his defeat of a combined Russian and Kipchak (a Turkic people) army in 1223 started as a unified state but gradually lost its unity as some districts crystallized into smaller khanates. The White Horde, for instance, came to rule much of southeastern Russia in the fifteenth century, and the Crimean khanate on the northern shore of the Black Sea succumbed to Russian invasion only in 1783.

Trade routes east and west across the steppe and north and south along the rivers of Russia and Ukraine conferred importance on certain trading entrepôts, as they had under Kievan Russia (see Chapter 9). The Mongols of the Golden Horde settled at (Old) Sarai, just north of where the Volga flows into the Caspian Sea (see Map 12.1). They ruled their Russian domains to the north and east from afar. To facilitate their control, they granted privileges to the Orthodox Church, which then helped reconcile the Russian people to their distant masters.

The politics of language played a role in subsequent history. Old Church Slavonic, an ecclesiastical language, revived; but Russian steadily acquired greater importance and eventually became the dominant written language. Russian scholars shunned Byzantine Greek, previously the main written tongue, even after the Golden Horde permitted renewed contacts with Constantinople. The Golden Horde enlisted Russian princes to act as their agents, primarily as tax collectors and census takers. Some had to visit the court of the Great Khans at Karakorum to secure the documents upon which their authority was based.

The flow of silver and gold into Mongol hands starved the local economy of precious metal. Like the Il-khans, the khans of the Golden Horde attempted to introduce paper money as a response to the currency shortage. This had little effect in a largely nonmonetary economy, but the experiment left such a vivid memory that the Russian word for money (*denga*°) comes from the Mongolian word for the stamp (*tamga*°) used to create paper currency. But commerce depended more on direct exchange of goods than on currency transactions.

Alexander Nevskii° (ca. 1220–1263), the prince of Novgorod, persuaded some fellow princes to submit to the Mongols. In return, the Mongols favored both Novgorod and the emerging town of Moscow, ruled by Alexander's son Daniel. These towns eclipsed devastated Kiev as political, cultural, and economic centers. This, in turn, drew people northward to open new agricultural land far from the Mongol steppe lands to the southwest. Decentralization continued in the 1300s, with Moscow only very gradually becoming Russia's dominant political center (see Map 12.2).

Russia was deeply affected by the Mongol presence. Bubonic plague became endemic among rodents in the Crimea. Ukraine°, a fertile and well-populated region in the late Kievan period (1000–1230), suffered severe population loss as Mongol armies passed through on campaigns against eastern Europe and raided villages to collect taxes.

Historians debate the Mongol impact on Russia. Some see the destructiveness of the Mongol conquests and the subsequent domination of the khans as isolating

Ghiyas al-Din Jamshid al-Kashi   (gee-YASS ad-DIN jam-SHEED al-KAH-shee)

denga (DENG-ah)   *tamga* (TAHM-gah)   **Nevskii** (nih-EFF-skee)   **Ukraine** (you-CRANE)

Transformation of the Kremlin Like other northern Europeans, the Russians preferred to build in wood, which was easy to handle and comfortable to live in. But they fortified important political centers with stone ramparts. In the 1300s, the city of Moscow emerged as a new capital, and its old wooden palace, the Kremlin, was gradually transformed into a stone structure.   (Novosti)

Russia and parts of eastern Europe from developments to the west. These historians refer to the "Mongol yoke" and hypothesize a sluggish economy and dormant culture under the Mongols.

Others point out that Kiev declined economically well before the Mongols struck and that the Kievan princes had already ceased to mint coins. Moreover, the Russian territories regularly paid their heavy taxes in silver. These payments indicate both economic surpluses and an ability to convert goods into cash. The burdensome taxes stemmed less from the Mongols than from their tax collectors, Russian princes who often exempted their own lands and shifted the load to the peasants.

As for Russia's cultural isolation, skeptics observe that before the Mongol invasion, the powerful and constructive role played by the Orthodox Church oriented Russia primarily toward Byzantium (see Chapter 9). This situation discouraged but did not eliminate contacts with western Europe, which probably would have become stronger after the fall of Constantinople to the Ottomans in 1453 regardless of Mongol influence.

The traditional structure of local government survived Mongol rule, as did the Russian princely families, who continued to battle among themselves for dominance. The Mongols merely added a new player to those struggles.

Ivan° III, the prince of Moscow (r. 1462–1505), established himself as an autocratic ruler in the late 1400s. Before Ivan, the title **tsar** (from "caesar"), of Byzantine origin, applied only to foreign rulers, whether the emperors of Byzantium or the Turkic khans of the steppe. Ivan's use of the title, which began early in his reign, probably represents an effort to establish a basis for legitimate rule with the decline of the Golden Horde and disappearance of the Byzantine Empire.

New States in Eastern Europe and Anatolia

The interplay between religion, political maneuvering, and new expressions of local identity affected Anatolia and parts of Europe confronted with the Mongol challenge as well. Raised in Sicily, the Holy Roman Emperor Frederick II (r. 1212–1250) appreciated Muslim culture and did not recoil from negotiating with Muslim rulers. When the pope threatened to excommunicate him unless he went on a crusade, Frederick nominally regained Jerusalem through a flimsy treaty with the Mamluk sultan in Egypt. This did not satisfy the pope, and the preoccupation of both pope and emperor with their quarrel left Hungary, Poland, and other parts of eastern Europe to deal with the Mongol onslaught on their own. Many princes capitulated and went to (Old) Sarai to offer their submission of Batu.

The Teutonic° Knights, however, resisted. Like the Knights Templar in the Middle East (see Chapter 8), the German-speaking Teutonic Knights had a crusading goal: to Christianize the Slavic and Kipchak populations of northern Europe, whose territories they colonized with thousands of German-speaking settlers. Having an interest in protecting Slav territory from German expansion, Alexander Nevskii cooperated in the Mongol campaigns against the Teutonic Knights and their Finnish allies. The latter suffered a catastrophic setback in 1242,

Ivan (ee-VAHN) **Teutonic** (two-TOHN-ik)

when many broke through ice on Lake Chud (see Map 12.2) and drowned. This destroyed the power of the Knights, and the northern Crusades virtually ceased.

The "Mongol" armies encountered by the Europeans were barely Mongol other than in most command positions. Mongol recruitment and conscription created an international force of Mongols, Turks, Chinese, Iranians, a few Europeans, and at least one Englishman, who had gone to the Middle East as a crusader but joined the Mongols and served in Hungary.

Initial wild theories describing the Mongols as coming from Hell or from the caves where Alexander the Great confined the monsters of antiquity gave way to more sophisticated understanding as European embassies to the Golden Horde, the Il-khan, and the Great Khan in Mongolia reported on Mongol trade routes and the internal structure of Mongol rule. In some quarters terror gave way to awe and even idealization of Mongol wealth and power. Europeans learned about diplomatic passports, coal mining, movable type, high-temperature metallurgy, higher mathematics, gunpowder, and, in the fourteenth century, the casting and use of bronze cannon. Yet with the outbreak of bubonic plague in the late 1340s (see Chapter 14), the memory of Mongol terror helped ignite religious speculation that God might be punishing the Christians of eastern and central Europe with a series of tribulations.

In the fourteenth century several regions, most notably Lithuania° (see Map 12.2), escaped the Mongol grip. When Russia fell to the Mongols and eastern Europe was first invaded, Lithuania had experienced an unprecedented centralization and military strengthening. Like Alexander Nevskii, the Lithuanian leaders maintained their independence by cooperating with the Mongols. In the late 1300s Lithuania capitalized on its privileged position to dominate its neighbors—particularly Poland—and ended the Teutonic Knights' hope of regaining power.

In the Balkans independent and well-organized kingdoms separated themselves from the chaos of the Byzantine Empire and thrived amidst the political uncertainties of the Mongol period. The Serbian king Stephen Dushan (ca. 1308–1355) proved to be the most effective leader. Seizing power from his father in 1331, he took advantage of Byzantine weakness to raise the archbishop of Serbia to the rank of an independent patriarch. In 1346 the patriarch crowned him "tsar and autocrat of the Serbs, Greeks, Bulgarians, and Albanians," a title that fairly represents the wide extent of his rule. As in the case of Timur, however, his kingdom declined after his death

in 1355 and disappeared entirely after a defeat by the Ottomans at the battle of Kosovo in 1389.

The Turkic nomads from whom the rulers of the **Ottoman Empire** descended had come to Anatolia in the same wave of Turkic migrations as the Seljuks (see Chapter 8). Though centered in Iran and preoccupied with quarrels with the Golden Horde, the Il-khans exerted great influence in eastern Anatolia. However, a number of small Turkic principalities emerged farther to the west. The Ottoman principality was situated in the northwest, close to the Sea of Marmara. This not only put them in a position to cross into Europe and take part in the internal dynastic struggles of the declining Byzantine state, but it also attracted Muslim religious warriors who wished to extend the frontiers of Islam in battle with the Christians. Though the Ottoman sultan suffered defeat at the hands of Timur in 1402, this was only a temporary setback. In 1453 Sultan Mehmet II captured Constantinople and brought the Byzantine Empire to an end.

The Ottoman sultans, like the rulers of Russia, Lithuania, and Serbia, seized the political opportunity that arose with the decay of Mongol power. The new and powerful states they created put strong emphasis on religious and linguistic identity, factors that the Mongols themselves did not stress. As we shall see, Mongol rule stimulated similar reactions in the lands of east and southeast Asia.

MONGOL DOMINATION IN CHINA, 1271–1368

After the Mongols conquered northern China in the 1230s, Great Khan Ögödei told a newly recruited Confucian adviser that he planned to turn the heavily populated North China Plain into a pasture for livestock. The adviser reacted calmly but argued that taxing the cities and villages would bring greater wealth. The Great Khan agreed, but he imposed the oppressive tax-farming system in use in the Il-khan Empire, rather than the fixed-rate method traditional to China.

The Chinese suffered under this system during the early years, but Mongol rule under the Yuan Empire, established by Genghis Khan's grandson Khubilai in 1271, also brought benefits: secure routes of transport and communication; exchange of experts and advisers between eastern and western Eurasia; and transmission of information, ideas, and skills.

Lithuania (lith-oo-WAY-nee-ah)

The Yuan Empire, 1279–1368

Just as the Il-khans in Iran and the Golden Horde in Russia came to accept many aspects of Muslim and Christian culture, so the Mongols in China sought to construct a fruitful synthesis of the Mongol and Chinese religious and moral traditions. **Khubilai Khan** gave his oldest son a Chinese name and had Confucianists participate in the boy's education. In public announcements and the crafting of laws, he took Confucian conventions into consideration. Buddhist and Daoist leaders visited the Great Khan and came away believing that they had all but convinced him to accept their beliefs.

The teachings of Buddhist priests from Tibet called **lamas°** became increasingly popular with some Mongol rulers in the 1200s and 1300s. Their idea of a militant universal ruler bringing the whole world under control of the Buddha and thus pushing it nearer to salvation mirrored an ancient Central Asia idea of universal rulership.

Beijing, the Yuan capital, became the center of cultural and economic life. Where Karakorum had been remote from any major settled area, Beijing served as the eastern terminus of the caravan routes that began near Tabriz, the Il-khan capital, and (Old) Sarai, the Golden Horde capital. An imperial horseback courier system utilizing hundreds of stations maintained close communications along routes that were generally policed and safe for travelers. Ambassadors and merchants arriving in Beijing found a city that was much more Chinese in character than its predecessor in Mongolia.

Called Great Capital (Dadu) or City of the Khan (*khan-balikh°*, Marco Polo's "Cambaluc"), Khubilai's capital featured massive Chinese-style walls of rammed earth, a tiny portion of which can still be seen. Khubilai's engineers widened the streets and developed linked lakes and artificial islands at the city's northwest edge to form a closed imperial complex, the Forbidden City. For his summer retreat, Khubilai maintained the palace and parks at Shangdu°, now in Inner Mongolia. This was "Xanadu°" celebrated by the English poet Samuel Taylor Coleridge, its "stately pleasure dome" the hunting preserve where Khubilai and his courtiers practiced riding and shooting.

"China" as we think of it today did not exist before the Mongols. Before they reunified it, China had been divided into three separate states (see Chapter 10). The Tanggut and Jin empires controlled the north, the South-ern Song most of the area south of the Yellow River. These states had different languages, writing systems, forms of government, and elite cultures. The Great Khans destroyed all three and encouraged the restoration or preservation of many features of Chinese government and society, thereby reuniting China in what proved to be a permanent fashion.

By law, Mongols had the highest social ranking. Below them came, in order, Central Asians and Middle Easterners, then northern Chinese, and finally southern Chinese. This apparent racial ranking also reflected a hierarchy of functions, the Mongols being the empire's warriors, the Central Asians and Middle Easterners its census takers and tax collectors. The northern Chinese outranked the southern Chinese because they had come under Mongol control almost two generations earlier.

Though Khubilai included some "Confucians" (under the Yuan, a formal and hereditary status) in government, their position compared poorly with their status as elite officeholders in pre-Mongol times. The Confucians criticized the favoring of merchants, many of whom were from the Middle East or Central Asia, and physicians. They regarded doctors as mere technicians, or even heretical practitioners of Daoist mysticism. The Yuan encouraged medicine and began the long process of integrating Chinese medical and herbal knowledge with western approaches derived from Greco-Roman and Muslim sources.

Like the Il-khan rulers in the Middle East, the Yuan rulers concentrated on counting the population and collecting taxes. They brought Persian, Arab, and Uighur administrators to China to staff the offices of taxation and finance, and Muslim scholars worked at calendar making and astronomy. For census taking and administration, the Mongols organized all of China into provinces. Central appointment of provincial governors, tax collectors, and garrison commanders marked a radical change by systematizing government control in all parts of the country.

The scarcity of contemporary records and the hostility of later Chinese writers make examination of the Yuan economy difficult. Many cities seem to have prospered: in north China by being on the caravan routes; in the interior by being on the Grand Canal; and along the coast by participation in maritime grain shipments from south China. The reintegration of East Asia (though not Japan) with the overland Eurasian trade, which had lapsed with the fall of the Tang (see Chapter 10), stimulated the urban economies.

The privileges and prestige that merchants enjoyed changed urban life and the economy of China. With only

---

lama (LAH-mah) **khan-balikh** (kahn-BAL-ik)
Shangdu (shahng-DOO) **Xanadu** (ZAH-nah-doo)

a limited number of government posts open to the old Chinese elite, great families that had previously spent fortunes on educating sons for government service sought other outlets. Many gentry families chose commerce, despite its lesser prestige. Corporations—investor groups that behaved as single commercial and legal units and shared the risk of doing business—handled most economic activities, starting with financing caravans and expanding into tax farming and lending money to the Mongol aristocracy. Central Asians and Middle Easterners headed most corporations in China in the early Yuan period; but as Chinese bought shares, most corporations acquired mixed membership, or even complete Chinese ownership.

The agricultural base, damaged by war, overtaxation, and the passage of armies, could not satisfy the financial needs of the Mongol aristocracy. Following earlier precedent, the imperial government issued paper money to make up the shortfall. But the massive scale of the Yuan experiment led people to doubt the value of the notes, which were unsecured. Copper coinage partially offset the failure of the paper currency. During the Song, exports of copper to Japan, where the metal was scarce, had caused a severe shortage in China, leading to a rise in value of copper in relation to silver. By cutting off trade with Japan, the Mongols intentionally or unintentionally stabilized the value of copper coins.

Gentry families that had previously prepared their sons for the state examinations moved from their traditional homes in the countryside to engage in urban commerce, and city life began to cater to the tastes of merchants instead of scholars. Specialized shops selling clothing, grape wine, furniture, and religiously butchered meats became common. Teahouses featured sing-song girls, drum singers, operas, and other entertainments previously considered coarse. Writers published works in the style of everyday speech. And the increasing influence of the northern, Mongolian-influenced Chinese language, often called Mandarin in the West, resulted in lasting linguistic change.

Cottage industries linked to the urban economies dotted the countryside, where 90 percent of the people lived. Some villages cultivated mulberry trees and cotton using dams, water wheels, and irrigation systems patterned in part on Middle Eastern models. Treatises on planting, harvesting, threshing, and butchering were published. One technological innovator, Huang Dao Po°, brought knowledge of cotton growing, spinning, and weaving from her native Hainan Island to the fertile Yangzi Delta. Some villagers came to revere such innovators as local gods.

Yet on the whole, the countryside did poorly during the Yuan period. After the initial conquests, the Mongol princes evicted many farmers and subjected the rest to brutal tax collection. As in Iran under the Il-khans, by the time the Yuan shifted to lighter taxes and encouragement of farming at the end of the 1200s, it was too late. Servitude or homelessness had overtaken many farmers. Neglect of dams and dikes caused disastrous flooding, particularly on the Yellow River.

According to Song records from before the Mongol conquest and the Ming census taken after their overthrow—each, of course, possibly subject to inaccuracy or exaggeration—China's population may have shrunk by 40 percent during eighty years of Mongol rule, with many localities in northern China losing up to five-sixths of their inhabitants. Scholars have suggested several causes, not all of them directly associated with Mongol rule: prolonged warfare, privations in the countryside causing people to resort to female infanticide, a southward movement of people fleeing the Mongols, and flooding on the Yellow River. The last helps explain why losses in the north exceeded those in the south and why the population along the Yangzi River markedly increased.

The bubonic plague and its attendant diseases, spread by the population movements, contributed as well. The Mongol incorporation of Yunnan°, a mountainous southwestern province where rodents commonly carried bubonic plague, into the centralized provincial system of government exposed the lowlands to plague (see Map 12.1). Cities seem to have managed outbreaks of disease better than rural areas as the epidemic moved from south to north in the 1300s.

Cultural and Scientific Exchange

Government officials in Yuan China maintained regular contact with their counterparts in Il-khan Iran and pursued similar economic and financial policies. While Chinese silks and porcelains affected elite tastes at the western end of the Silk Road, Il-khan engineering, astronomy, and mathematics reached China and Korea. Just as Chinese painters taught Iranian artists appealing new ways of drawing clouds, rocks, and trees, Muslims from the Middle East oversaw most of the weapons manufacture and engineering projects for

Huang Dao Po (hwahng DOW poh)

Yunnan (YOON-nahn)

Khubilai's armies. Similarly, the Il-khans imported scholars and texts that helped them understand Chinese technological advances, including stabilized sighting tubes for precisely noting the positions of astronomical objects, mechanically driven armillary spheres that showed how the sun, moon, and planets moved in relation to one another, and new techniques for measuring the movement of the moon. And Khubilai brought Iranians to Beijing to construct an observatory and an institute for astronomical studies similar to the Il-khans' facility at Maragheh. He made the state responsible for maintaining and staffing the observatory.

Muslim doctors and Persian medical texts—particularly in anatomy, pharmacology, and ophthalmology—circulated in China during the Yuan. Khubilai, who suffered from alcoholism and gout, accorded high status to doctors. New seeds and formulas from the Middle East stimulated medical practice. The traditional Chinese study of herbs, drugs, and potions came in for renewed interest and publication.

The Fall of the Yuan Empire

In the 1340s power contests broke out among the Mongol princes. Within twenty years farmer rebellions and feuds among the Mongols engulfed the land. Amidst the chaos, a charismatic Chinese leader, Zhu Yuanzhang°, mounted a campaign that destroyed the Yuan Empire and brought China under control of his new empire, the Ming, in 1368. Many Mongols—as well as the Muslims, Jews, and Christians who had come with them—remained in China, some as farmers or shepherds, some as high-ranking scholars and officials. Most of their descendants took Chinese names and became part of the diverse cultural world of China.

Many other Mongols, however, had never moved out of their home territories in Mongolia. Now they welcomed back refugees from the Yuan collapse. Though Turkic peoples were becoming predominant in the steppe region in the west of Central Asia, including territories still ruled by descendants of Genghis Khan, Mongols retained control of Inner Asia, the steppe regions bordering on Mongolia. Their reconcentration in this region fostered a renewed sense of Mongol unity. Some Mongol groups adopted Islam; others favored Tibetan Buddhism. But religious affiliation proved less important than Mongol identity.

The Ming thus fell short of dominating all the Mongols. The Mongols of Inner Asia paid tribute to the Ming only to the extent that doing so facilitated their trade.

The Mongols remained a continuing threat on the northern Ming frontier.

THE EARLY MING EMPIRE, 1368–1500

The history of the **Ming Empire** raises questions about the overall impact of the Mongol era in China. Just as historians of Russia and Iran divide over whether Mongol invasion and political domination retarded or stimulated the pace and direction of political and economic change, so historians of China have differing opinions about the Mongols. Since the Ming reestablished many practices that are seen as purely Chinese, they receive praise from people who ascribe central importance to Chinese traditions. On the other hand, historians who look upon the Mongol era as a pivotal historical moment when communication across the vast interior of Eurasia served to bring east and west together sometimes see the inward-looking Ming as less dynamic and productive than the Yuan.

Ming China on a Mongol Foundation

Zhu Yuanzhang, a former monk, soldier, and bandit, had watched his parents and other family members die of famine and disease, conditions he blamed on Mongol misrule. During the Yuan Empire's chaotic last decades, he vanquished rival rebels and assumed imperial power under the name Hongwu (r. 1368–1398). He ruled a highly centralized, militarily formidable empire.

Hongwu moved the capital to Nanjing° ("southern capital") on the Yangzi River, turning away from the Mongol's Beijing ("northern capital"; see Map 12.3). Though Zhu Yuanzhang the rebel had espoused a radical Buddhist belief in a coming age of salvation, once in power he used Confucianism to depict the emperor as the champion of civilization and virtue, justified in making war on uncivilized "barbarians."

Hongwu choked off the close relations with Central Asia and the Middle East fostered by the Mongols and imposed strict limits on imports and foreign visitors. Silver replaced paper money for tax payments and commerce. These practices, illustrative of an anti-Mongol ideology, proved as economically unhealthy as some of the Yuan economic policies and did not last. Instead, the Ming government gradually came to resemble the Yuan. Ming

---

Zhu Yuanzhang (JOO yuwen-JAHNG)

Nanjing (nahn-JING)

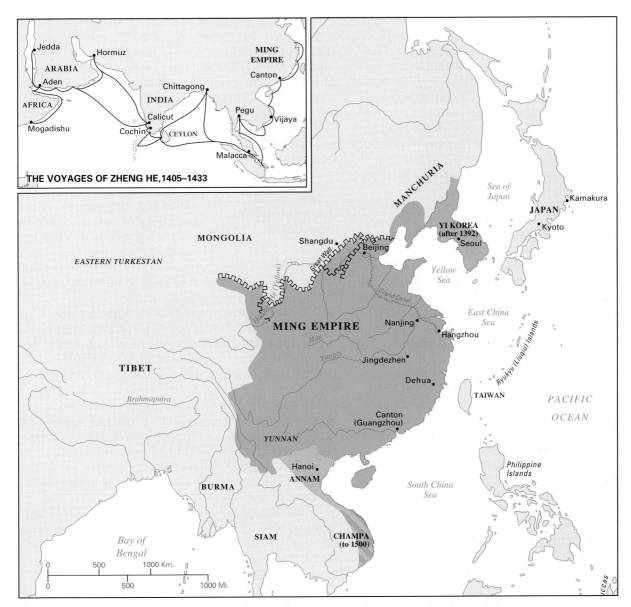

Map 12.3   The Ming Empire and Its Allies, 1368–1500   The Ming Empire controlled China but had a hostile relationship with peoples in Mongolia and Inner Asia who had been under the rule of the Mongol Yuan emperors. Mongol attempts at conquest by seas were continued by the Ming mariner Zheng He. Between 1405 and 1433 he sailed to Southeast Asia and then beyond, to India, the Persian Gulf, and East Africa.

rulers retained the provincial structure and continued to observe the hereditary professional categories of the Yuan period. Muslims made calendars and astronomical calculations at a new observatory at Nanjing, a replica of Khubilai's at Beijing. The Mongol calendar continued in use.

Continuities with the Yuan became more evident after an imperial prince seized power through a coup d'état

to rule as the emperor **Yonglle**° (r. 1403–1424). He returned the capital to Beijing, enlarging and improving Khubilai's imperial complex. The central area—the Forbidden City—acquired its present character, with moats, orange-red outer walls, golden roofs, and marble bridges.

Yongle (yoong-LAW)

Yongle intended this combination fortress, religious site, bureaucratic center, and imperial residential park to overshadow Nanjing, and it survives today as China's most imposing traditional architectural complex.

Yongle also restored commercial links with the Middle East. Because hostile Mongols still controlled much of the caravan route, Yongle explored maritime connections. In Southeast Asia, Annam became a Ming province as the early emperors continued the Mongol program of aggression. This focus on the southern frontier helped inspire the naval expeditions of the trusted imperial eunuch **Zheng He°** from 1405 to 1433.

A Muslim whose father and grandfather had made the pilgrimage to Mecca, Zheng He had a good knowledge of the Middle East; and his religion eased relations with the states of the Indian subcontinent, where he directed his first three voyages. Subsequent expeditions reached Hormuz on the Persian Gulf, sailed the southern coast of Arabia and the Horn of Africa (modern Somalia), and possibly reached as far south as the Strait of Madagascar (see Map 12.3).

On early voyages he visited long-established Chinese merchant communities in Southeast Asia in order to cement their allegiance to the Ming Empire and to collect taxes. When a community on the island of Sumatra resisted, he slaughtered the men to set an example. By pursuing commercial relations with the Middle East and possibly Africa, he also publicized Yongle's reversal of Hongwu's opposition to foreign trade.

The expeditions added some fifty new tributary states to the Ming imperial universe, but trade did not increase as dramatically. Sporadic embassies reached Beijing from rulers in India, the Middle East, Africa, and Southeast Asia. During one visit the ruler of Brunei° died and received a grand burial at the Chinese capital. Occasional expeditions continued until the 1430s, after the death of both Yongle and Zheng He, when they stopped.

Having demonstrated such abilities at long-distance navigation, why did the Chinese not develop seafaring for commercial and military gain? Contemporaries considered the voyages a personal project of Yongle, an upstart ruler who had always sought to prove his worthiness. Building the Forbidden City in Beijing and sponsoring gigantic encyclopedia projects might be taken to reflect a similar motivation. Yongle may also have been emulating Khubilai Khan, who had sent enormous fleets against Japan and Southeast Asia. This would fit with the rumor spread by Yongle's political enemies that he was actually a Mongol.

A less speculative approach to the question starts with the fact that the new commercial opportunities fell short of expectations, despite bringing foreign nations into the Ming orbit. In the meantime, Japanese coastal piracy intensified, and Mongol threats in the north and west grew. The human and financial demands of fortifying the north, redesigning and strengthening Beijing, and outfitting military expeditions against the Mongols ultimately took priority over the quest for maritime empire.

Technology and Population

Although innovation continued in all areas of the Ming economy, advances were less frequent and less significant than under the Song, particularly in agriculture. Agricultural production peaked around the mid-1400s and remained level for more than a century.

The Ming government limited mining, partly to reinforce the value of metal coins and partly to control and tax the industry. Farmers had difficulty obtaining iron and bronze for farm implements. The peace that had followed the Mongol conquest resulted in a decline in techniques for making high-quality bronze and steel, which were especially used for weapons. Central Asian and Middle Eastern technicians rather than Chinese cast the bronze instruments for Khubilai's observatory at Beijing. Japan quickly surpassed China in the production of extremely high-quality steel swords. Copper, iron, and steel became expensive in Ming China, leading to a lessened use of metal.

After the death of Emperor Yongle in 1424, shipbuilding also declined, and few advances occurred in printing, timekeeping, and agricultural technology. New weaving techniques did appear, but technological development in this field had peaked by 1500.

Reactivation of the examination system as a way of recruiting government officials (see Chapter 10) drew large numbers of educated, ambitious men into a renewed study of the Confucian classics. This reduced the vitality of commerce, where they had previously been employed, just as population increase was creating a labor surplus. Records indicating a growth from 60 million at the end of the Yuan period in 1368 to nearly 100 million by 1400 may not be entirely reliable, but rapid population growth encouraged the production of staples—wheat, millet, and barley in the north and rice in the south—at the expense of commercial crops such as cotton that had stimulated many technological innovations under the Song. Staple crops yielded lower profits, which further discouraged capital improvements. New

---

Zheng He (JEHNG HUH)   **Brunei** (broo-NIE)

Ming Porcelain Bowl   High-quality Chinese blue-and-white ware commanded an international market under the Ming Empire. This piece, bearing a Portuguese inscription showing that it was made in 1541 for the Portuguese governor of Malacca, is one of the earliest examples of works made specifically for a European.   (Collection, Junta de Baixo Alentago, Beja, Portugal)

foods, such as sweet potatoes, became available but were little adopted. Population growth in southern and central China caused deforestation and raised the price of wood.

The Mongols that the Ming confronted in the north fought on horseback with simple weapons. The Ming fought back with arrows, scattershot mortars, and explosive canisters. They even used a few cannon, which they knew about from contacts with the Middle East and later with Europeans (see Environment and Technology: From Gunpowder to Guns). Fearing that technological secrets would get into enemy hands, the government censored the chapters on gunpowder and guns in early Ming encyclopedias. Shipyards and ports shut down to avoid contact with Japanese pirates and to prevent Chinese from migrating to Southeast Asia.

A technology gap with Korea and Japan opened up nevertheless. When superior steel was needed, supplies came from Japan. Korea moved ahead of China in the design and production of firearms and ships, in printing techniques, and in the sciences of weather prediction and calendar making. The desire to tap the wealthy Ming market fueled some of these advances.

The Ming Achievement

In the late 1300s and the 1400s the wealth and consumerism of the early Ming stimulated high achievement in literature, the decorative arts, and painting. The Yuan period interest in plain writing had produced some of the world's earliest novels. This type of literature flourished under the Ming. *Water Margin*, which originated in the raucous drum-song performances loosely related to Chinese opera, features dashing Chinese bandits who struggle against Mongol rule, much as Robin Hood and his merry men resisted Norman rule in England. Many authors had a hand in the final print version.

Luo Guanzhong°, one of the authors of *Water Margin*, is also credited with *Romance of the Three Kingdoms*, based on a much older series of stories that in some ways resemble the Arthurian legends. It describes the attempts of an upright but doomed war leader and his followers to restore the Han Empire of ancient times and resist the power of the cynical but brilliant villain. *Romance of the Three Kingdoms* and *Water Margin* expressed much of the militant but joyous pro-China sentiment of the early Ming era and remain among the most appreciated Chinese fictional works.

Probably the best-known product of Ming technological advance was porcelain. The imperial ceramic works at Jingdezhen° experimented with new production techniques and new ways of organizing and rationalizing workers. "Ming ware," a blue-on-white style developed in the 1400s from Indian, Central Asian, and Middle Eastern motifs, became especially prized around the world. Other Ming goods in high demand included furniture, lacquered screens, and silk, all eagerly transported by Chinese and foreign merchants throughout Southeast Asia and the Pacific, India, the Middle East, and East Africa.

Luo Guanzhong (LAW GWAHB-JOONG)
Jingdezhen (JING-deh-JUHN)

ENVIRONMENT + TECHNOLOGY

From Gunpowder to Guns

Long before the invention of guns, gunpowder was used in China and Korea to excavate mines, build canals, and channel irrigation. Alchemists in China used related formulas to make noxious gas pellets to paralyze enemies and expel evil spirits. A more realistic benefit was eliminating disease-carrying insects, a critical aid to the colonization of malarial regions in China and Southeast Asia. The Mongol Empire staged fireworks displays on ceremonial occasions, delighting European visitors to Karakorum who saw them for the first time.

Anecdotal evidence in Chinese records gives credit for the introduction of gunpowder to a Sogdian Buddhist monk of the 500s. The monk described the wondrous alchemical transformation of elements produced by a combination of charcoal and saltpeter. In this connection he also mentioned sulfur. The distillation of naphtha, a light, flammable derivative of oil or coal, seems also to have been first developed in Central Asia, the earliest evidence coming from the Gandhara region (in modern Pakistan).

By the eleventh century, the Chinese had developed flamethrowers powered by burning naphtha, sulfur, or gunpowder in a long tube. These weapons intimidated and injured foot soldiers and horses and also set fire to thatched roofs in hostile villages and, occasionally, the rigging of enemy ships.

In their long struggle against the Mongols, the Song learned to enrich saltpeter to increase the amount of nitrate in gunpowder. This produced forceful explosions rather than jets of fire. Launched from catapults, gunpowder-filled canisters could rupture fortifications and inflict mass casualties. Explosives hurled from a distance could sink or burn ships.

The Song also experimented with firing projectiles from metal gun barrels. The earliest gun barrels were broad and squat and were transported on special wagons to their emplacements. The mouths of the barrels projected saltpeter mixed with scattershot minerals. The Chinese and then the Koreans adapted gunpowder to shooting masses of arrows—sometimes flaming—at enemy fortifications.

In 1280 weapons makers of the Yuan Empire produced the first device featuring a projectile that completely filled the mouth of the cannon and thus concentrated the explosive force. The Yuan used cast bronze for the barrel and iron for the cannonball. The new weapon shot farther and more accurately, and was much more destructive, than the earlier Song devices.

Knowledge of the cannon and cannonball moved westward across Eurasia. By the end of the thirteenth century cannon were being produced in the Middle East. By 1327 small, squat cannon called "bombards" were being used in Europe.

Launching Flaming Arrows   Song soldiers used gunpowder to launch flaming arrows.   (British Library)

CENTRALIZATION AND MILITARISM IN EAST ASIA, 1200–1500

Korea, Japan, and Annam, the other major states of East Asia, were all affected by confrontation with the Mongols, but with differing results. Japan and Annam escaped Mongol conquest but changed in response to the Mongol threat, becoming more effective and expansive regimes with enhanced commitments to independence.

As for Korea, just as the Ming stressed Chinese traditions and identity in the aftermath of Yuan rule, so Mongol domination contributed to revitalized interest in Korea's own language and history. The Mongols conquered Korea after a difficult war, and though Korea suffered socially and economically under Mongol rule, members of the elite associated closely with the Yuan Empire. After the fall of the Yuan, merchants continued the international connections established in the Mongol period, while Korean armies consolidated a new kingdom and fended off pirates.

Korea from the Mongols to the Yi, 1231–1500

In their effort to establish control over all of China, the Mongols searched for coastal areas from which to launch naval expeditions and choke off the sea trade of their adversaries. Korea offered such possibilities. When the Mongols attacked in 1231, the leader of a prominent Korean family assumed the role of military commander and protector of the king (not unlike the shoguns of Japan). His defensive war, which lasted over twenty years, left a ravaged countryside, exhausted armies, and burned treasures, including the renowned nine-story pagoda at Hwangnyong-sa° and the wooden printing blocks of the *Tripitaka*°, a ninth-century masterpiece of printing art. The commander's underlings killed him in 1258. Soon afterward the Koryo° king surrendered to the Mongols and became a subject monarch by linking his family to the Great Khan by marriage.

By the mid-1300s the Koryo kings were of mostly Mongol descent, and they favored Mongol dress, customs, and language. Many lived in Beijing. The kings, their families, and their entourages often traveled between China and Korea, thus exposing Korea to the philosophical and artistic styles of Yuan China: neo-

Confucianism, Chan Buddhism (called *Sŏn* in Korea), and celadon (light green) ceramics.

Mongol control was a stimulus after centuries of comparative isolation. Cotton began to be grown in southern Korea; gunpowder came into use; and the art of calendar making, including eclipse prediction and vector calculation, stimulated astronomical observation and mathematics. Celestial clocks built for the royal observatory at Seoul reflected Central Asian and Islamic influences more than Chinese. Avenues of advancement opened for Korean scholars willing to learn Mongolian, landowners willing to open their lands to falconry and grazing, and merchants servicing the new royal exchanges with Beijing. These developments contributed to the rise of a new landed and educated class.

When the Yuan Empire fell in 1368, the Koryo ruling family remained loyal to the Mongols and had to be forced to recognize the new Ming Empire. In 1392 the **Yi**° established a new kingdom with a capital in Seoul and sought to reestablish a local identity. Like Russia and China after the Mongols, the Yi regime publicly rejected the period of Mongol domination. Yet the Yi government continued to employ Mongol-style land surveys, taxation in kind, and military garrison techniques.

Like the Ming emperors, the Yi kings revived the study of the Confucian classics, an activity that required knowledge of Chinese and showed the dedication of the state to learning. This revival may have led to a key technological breakthrough in printing technology.

Koreans had begun using Chinese woodblock printing in the 700s. This technology worked well in China, where a large number of buyers wanted copies of a comparatively small number of texts. But in Korea, the comparatively few literate men had interests in a wide range of texts. Movable wooden or ceramic type appeared in Korea in the early thirteenth century and may have been invented there. But the texts were frequently inaccurate and difficult to read. In the 1400s Yi printers, working directly with the king, developed a reliable device to anchor the pieces of type to the printing plate: they replaced the old beeswax adhesive with solid copper frames. The legibility of the printed page improved, and high-volume, accurate production became possible. Combined with the phonetic *han'gul*° writing system, this printing technology laid the foundation for a high literacy rate in Korea.

Yi publications told readers how to produce and use fertilizer, transplant rice seedlings, and engineer reservoirs. Building on Eurasian knowledge imported by the Mongols and introduced under the Koryo, Yi scholars

Hwanghnyong-sa (hwahng-NEEYAHNG-sah)
Tripitaka (tri-PIH-tah-kah) **Koryo** (KAW-ree-oh)

Yi (YEE) *han'gul* (HAHN-goor)

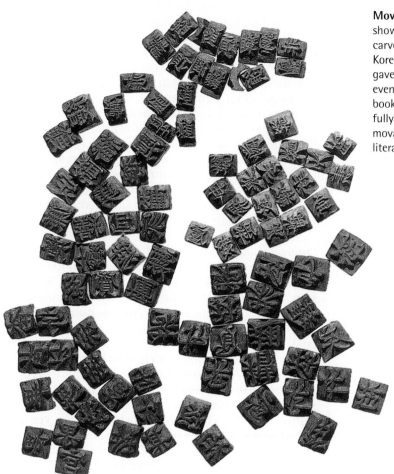

Movable Type   The improvement of cast bronze tiles, each showing a single character, eliminated the need to cast or carve whole pages. Individual tiles—the ones shown are Korean—could be moved from page frame to page frame and gave an even and pleasing appearance. All parts of East Asia eventually adopted this form of printing for cheap, popular books. In the mid-1400s Korea also experimented with a fully phonetic form of writing, which in combination with movable type allowed Koreans unprecedented levels of literacy and access to printed works.   (Courtesy, Yushin Yoo)

developed a meteorological science of their own. They invented or redesigned instruments to measure wind speed and rainfall and perfected a calendar based on minute comparisons of the systems of China and the Islamic world.

In agriculture, farmers expanded the cultivation of cash crops, the reverse of what was happening in Ming China. Cotton, the primary crop, enjoyed such high value that the state accepted it for tax payments. The Yi army used cotton uniforms, and cotton became the favored fabric of the Korean civil elite. With cotton gins and spinning wheels powered by water, Korea advanced more rapidly than China in mechanization and began to export considerable amounts of cotton to China and Japan.

Although both the Yuan and the Ming withheld the formula for gunpowder from the Korean government, Korean officials acquired the information by subterfuge.

By the later 1300s they had mounted cannon on ships that patrolled against pirates and used gunpowder-driven arrow launchers against enemy personnel and the rigging of enemy ships. Combined with skills in armoring ships, these techniques made the small Yi navy a formidable defense force.

Political Transformation in Japan, 1274–1500

Having secured Korea, the Mongols looked toward Japan, a target they could easily reach from Korea and a possible base for controlling China's southern coast. Their first thirty-thousand-man invasion force in 1274 included Mongol cavalry and archers and sailors from Korea and northeastern Asia. Its weaponry included light catapults and incendiary and explosive projectiles of Chinese manufacture. The Mongol forces landed successfully and decimated the Japanese cavalry, but a great storm on Hakata° Bay on the north side of Kyushu° Island (see Map 12.4) prevented the establishment of a beachhead and forced the Mongols to sail back to Korea.

The invasion deeply impressed Japan's leaders and hastened social and political changes that were already under way. Under the Kamakura° Shogunate established in 1185—another powerful family actually exercised control—the shogun, or military leader, distributed land and privileges to his followers. In return they paid him tribute and supplied him with soldiers. This stable, but decentralized, system depended on the balancing of power among regional warlords. Lords in the north and east of Japan's main island were remote from those in the south and west. Beyond devotion to the emperor and the shogun, little united them until the alien and terrifying Mongol threat materialized.

After the return of his fleet, Khubilai sent envoys to Japan demanding submission. Japanese leaders executed them and prepared for war. The shogun took steps to centralize his military government. The effect was to increase the influence of warlords from the south and west of Honshu (Japan's main island) and from the island of Kyushu, because this was where invasion seemed most likely, and they were the local commanders acting under the shogun's orders.

Military planners studied Mongol tactics and retrained and outfitted Japanese warriors for defense against advanced weaponry. Farm laborers drafted from all over the country constructed defensive fortifications at Hakata and other points along the Honshu and Kyushu coasts. This effort demanded, for the first time, a national system to move resources toward western points rather than toward the imperial or shogunal centers to the east.

The Mongols attacked in 1281. They brought 140,000 warriors, including many non-Mongols, as well as thousands of horses, in hundreds of ships. However, the wall the Japanese had built to cut off Hakata Bay from the mainland deprived the Mongol forces of a reliable landing point. Japanese swordsmen rowed out and boarded the Mongol ships lingering offshore. Their superb steel swords shocked the invaders. After a prolonged standoff, a typhoon struck and sank perhaps half of the Mongol ships. The remainder sailed away, never again to harass Japan. The Japanese gave thanks to the "wind of the Gods"—*kamikaze*°—for driving away the Mongols.

Nevertheless, the Mongol threat continued to influence Japanese development. Prior to his death in 1294,

Hakata (HAH-kah-tah)   Kyushu (KYOO-shoo)
Kamakura (kah-mah-KOO-rah)   *kamikaze* (KUM-i-kuh-zee)

Map 12.4   Korea and Japan, 1200–1500   The proximity of Korea and northern China to Japan gave the Mongols the opportunity to launch enormous fleets against the Kamakura Shogunate, which controlled most of the three islands (Honshu, Shikoku, and Kyushu) of central Japan.

Khubilai had in mind a third invasion. His successors did not carry through with it, but the shoguns did not know that the Mongols had given up the idea of conquering Japan. They rebuilt coastal defenses well into the fourteenth century, helping to consolidate the social position of Japan's warrior elite and stimulating the development of a national infrastructure for trade and communication. But the Kamakura Shogunate, based on regionally collected and regionally dispersed revenues, suffered financial strain in trying to pay for centralized road and defense systems.

Between 1333 and 1338 the emperor Go-Daigo broke the centuries-old tradition of imperial seclusion and aloofness from government and tried to reclaim power from the shoguns. This ignited a civil war that destroyed the Kamakura system. In 1338, with the Mongol

Painting by Sesshu Sesshu Toyo (1420–1506) created a distinctive style of ink painting that contrasted with the Chinese styles that predominated earlier in Japan. Benefiting from growing Japanese commerce in the period of the Ashikaga Shogunate, he traveled to China as a youth and studied Chinese techniques. As he developed his style, a market for his art developed among merchant communities and other urban elites. (Collection of the Tokyo National Museum)

threat waning, the **Ashikaga Shogunate°**, took control at the imperial center of Kyoto.

Provincial warlords enjoyed renewed independence. Around their imposing castles, they sponsored the development of market towns, religious institutions, and schools. The application of technologies imported in earlier periods, including water wheels, improved plows, and Champa rice, increased agricul-

---

Ashikaga (ah-shee-KAH-gah)

tural productivity. Growing wealth and relative peace stimulated artistic creativity, mostly reflecting Zen Buddhist beliefs held by the warrior elite. In the simple elegance of architecture and gardens, in the contemplative landscapes of artists like Sesshu Toyo, and in the eerie, stylized performances of the No theater, the unified aesthetic code of Zen became established in the Ashikaga era.

Despite the technological advancement, artistic productivity, and rapid urbanization of this period, competition among warlords and their followers led to regional wars. By the later 1400s these conflicts resulted in the near destruction of the warlords. The great Onin War in 1477 left Kyoto devastated and the Ashikaga Shogunate a central government in name only. Ambitious but low-ranking warriors, some with links to trade with the continent, began to scramble for control of the provinces.

After the fall of the Yuan in 1368 Japan resumed trade with China and Korea. Japan exported raw materials as well as folding fans, invented in Japan during the period of isolation, and swords. Japan's primary imports from China were books and porcelain. The volatile political environment in Japan gave rise to partnerships between warlords and local merchants. All worked to strengthen their own towns and treasuries through overseas commerce or, sometimes, through piracy.

The Emergence of Vietnam, 1200–1500

Before the first Mongol attack in 1257, the states of Annam (northern Vietnam) and Champa (southern Vietnam) had clashed frequently. Annam (once called Dai Viet) looked toward China and had once been subject to the Tang. Chinese political ideas, social philosophies, dress, religion, and language heavily influenced its official culture. Champa related more closely to the trading networks of the Indian Ocean; its official culture was strongly influenced by Indian religion, language, architecture, and dress. Champa's relationship with China depended in part on how close its enemy Annam was to China at any particular time. During the Song period Annam was neither formally subject to China nor particularly threatening to Champa militarily, so Champa inaugurated a trade and tribute relationship with China that spread fast-ripening Champa rice throughout East Asia.

The Mongols exacted submission and tribute from both Annam and Champa until the fall of the Yuan Empire in 1368. Mongol political and military ambitions were mostly focused elsewhere, however, which minimized their impact on politics and culture. The two Vietnamese kingdoms soon resumed their warfare. When Annam moved its army to reinforce its southern border, Ming troops occupied the capital, Hanoi, and installed a puppet government. Almost thirty years elapsed before Annam regained independence and resumed a tributary status. By then the Ming were turning to meet Mongol challenges to their north. In a series of ruthless campaigns, Annam terminated Champa's independence, and by 1500 the ancestor of the modern state of Vietnam, still called Annam, had been born.

The new state still relied on Confucian bureaucratic government and an examination system, but some practices differed from those in China. The Vietnamese legal code, for example, preserved group landowning and decision making within the villages, as well as women's property rights. Both developments probably had roots in an early rural culture based on the growing of rice in wet paddies; by this time the Annamese considered them distinctive features of their own culture.

CONCLUSION

Despite their brutality and devastation, the Mongol conquests brought a degree of unity to the lands between China and Europe that had never before been known. Nomadic mobility and expertise in military technology contributed to communication across vast spaces and initially, at least, an often-callous disregard for the welfare of farmers, as manifested in oppressive tax policies. Trade, on the other hand, received active Mongol stimulation through the protection of routes and encouragement of industrial production. The Mongol regimes were characterized by an unprecedented openness, employing talented people irrespective of their linguistic, ethnic, or religious affiliations. As a consequence, the period of comparative Mongol unity, which lasted less than a century, saw a remarkable exchange of ideas, techniques, and products across the breadth of Eurasia. Chinese gunpowder spurred the development of Ottoman and European cannon; Muslim astronomers introduced new instruments and mathematical techniques to Chinese observatories.

However, rule over dozens of restive peoples could not endure. Where Mongol military enterprise reached its limit of expansion, it stimulated local aspirations for independence. Division and hostility among branches of Genghis Khan's family—between the Yuan in China and the Jagadai in Central Asia or between the Golden Horde in Russia and the Il-khans in Iran—provided opportunities for achieving these aspirations. The Russians gained freedom from Mongol domination in western Eurasia, and the general political disruption and uncertainty of the Mongol era assisted the emergence of the Lithuanian, Serbian, and Ottoman states. In the east, China, Korea, and Annam similarly found renewed political identity in the aftermath of Mongol rule, while Japan fought off two Mongol invasions and transformed its internal political and cultural identity in the process. In every case, the reality or threat of Mongol attack and domination encouraged centralization of government, improvement of military techniques, and renewed stress on local cultural identity. Thus, in retrospect, despite its traditional association with death and destruction, the Mongol period appears as a watershed establishing new connections between widespread parts of Eurasia and leading to the development of strong, assertive, and culturally creative regional states.

■ Key Terms

Mongols	tsar
Genghis Khan	Ottoman Empire
nomadism	Khubilai Khan
Yuan Empire	lama
bubonic plague	Beijing
Il-khan	Ming Empire
Golden Horde	Yongle
Timur	Zheng He
Rashid al-Din	Yi
Nasir al-Din Tusi	kamikaze
Alexander Nevskii	Ashikaga Shogunate

■ Suggested Reading

David Morgan's *The Mongols* (1986) affords an accessible introduction to the Mongol Empire. Morgan and Reuven Amitai-Preiss have also edited a valuable collection of essays, *The Mongol Empire and Its Legacy* (2000). Thomas T. Allsen has written more-specialized studies: *Mongol Imperialism: The Policies of the Grand Qan Möngke in China, Russia, and the Islamic Lands, 1251–1259* (1987); *Commodity and Exchange in the Mongol Empire: A Cultural History of Islamic Textiles* (2002); and *Culture and Conquest in Mongol Eurasia* (2001). Larry Moses and Stephen A. Halkovic, Jr., *Introduction to Mongolian History and Culture* (1985) links early and modern Mongol history and culture. Tim Severin, *In Search of Chinggis Khan* (1992), revisits the paths of Genghis's conquests.

William H. McNeill's *Plagues and Peoples* (1976) outlines the demographic effects of the Mongol conquests, and Joel Mokyr discusses their technological impact in *The Lever of Riches: Technological Creativity and Economic Progress* (1990). Connections between commercial development in Europe and Eurasian trade routes of the Mongol era within a broad theoretical framework inform Janet L. Abu-Lughod's *Before European Hegemony: The World System A.D. 1250–1350* (1989).

The only "primary" document relating to Genghis Khan, *Secret History of the Mongols,* has been reconstructed in Mongolian from Chinese script and has been variously produced in scholarly editions by Igor de Rachewilz and Francis Woodman Cleaves, among others. Paul Kahn produced a readable prose English paraphrase of the work in 1984. Biographies of Genghis Khan include Leo de Hartog, *Genghis Khan, Conqueror of the World* (1989); Michel Hoang, *Genghis Khan,* trans. Ingrid Canfield (1991); and Paul Ratchnevsky, *Genghis Khan: His Life and*

Legacy, trans. and ed. Thomas Nivison Haining (1992), which is most detailed on Genghis's childhood and youth.

On Central Asia after the conquests see S. A. M. Adshead, *Central Asia in World History* (1993). The most recent scholarly study of Timur is Beatrice Manz, *The Rise and Rule of Tamerlane* (1989).

David Christian, *A History of Russia, Central Asia, and Mongolia* (1998), and Charles Halperin, *Russia and the Golden Horde: The Mongol Impact on Medieval Russian History* (1987), provide one-volume accounts of the Mongols in Russia. A more detailed study is John Lister Illingworth Fennell, *The Crisis of Medieval Russia, 1200–1304* (1983). See also Donald Ostrowski, *Muscovy and the Mongols: Cross-Cultural Influences on the Steppe Frontier* (1998). Religion forms the topic of Devin DeWeese, *Islamization and Native Religion in the Golden Horde* (1994). *The Cambridge History of Iran*: Volume 5, *The Saljuq and Mongol Periods,* ed. J. A. Boyle (1968) and Volume 6, *The Timurid and Safavid Periods,* eds. Peter Jackson and Laurence Lockhart (rprt 2001) contain detailed scholarly articles covering the period in Iran and Central Asia.

Translations from the great historians of the Il-khan period include Juvaini, 'Ala al-Din 'Ata Malek, *The History of the World-Conqueror,* trans. John Andrew Boyle (1958), and Rashid al-Din, *The Successors of Genghis Khan,* trans. John Andrew Boyle (1971). The greatest traveler of the time was Ibn Battuta; see C. Defremery and B. R. Sanguinetti, eds., *The Travels of Ibn Battuta, A.D. 1325–1354,* translated with revisions and notes from the Arabic text by H. A. R. Gibb (1994), and Ross E. Dunn, *The Adventures of Ibn Battuta, a Muslim Traveler of the 14th Century* (1986).

On Europe's Mongol encounter see James Chambers, *The Devil's Horsemen: The Mongol Invasion of Europe* (1979). Christopher Dawson, ed., *Mission to Asia* (1955; reprinted 1981), assembles some of the best-known European travel accounts. See also Marco Polo, *The Travels of Marco Polo* (many editions), and the controversial skeptical appraisal of his account in Frances Wood, *Did Marco Polo Really Go to China?* (1995). Morris Rossabi's *Visitor from Xanadu* (1992) deals with the European travels of Rabban Sauma, a Christian Turk.

For China under the Mongols see Morris Rossabi's *Khubilai Khan: His Life and Times* (1988). On the Mongol impact on economy and technology in Yuan and Ming China see Mark Elvin, *The Pattern of the Chinese Past* (1973); Joseph Needham, *Science in Traditional China* (1981). Also see the important interpretation of Ming economic achievement in Andre Gunder Frank, *ReORIENT: Global Economy in the Asian Age* (1998).

The Cambridge History of China, Vol. 8, *The Ming Dynasty 1368–1644,* part 2, ed. Denis Twitchett and Frederick W. Mote (1998), provides scholarly essays about a little studied period. See also Albert Chan, *The Glory and Fall of the Ming Dynasty* (1982), and Edward L. Farmer, *Early Ming Government: The Evolution of Dual Capitals* (1976).

On early Ming literature see Lo Kuan-chung, *Three Kingdoms: A Historical Novel Attributed to Luo Guanzhong,* translated and annotated by Moss Roberts (1991); Pearl Buck's translation of

Water Margin, entitled *All Men Are Brothers,* 2 vols. (1933), and a later translation by J. H. Jackson, *Water Margin, Written by Shih Nai-an* (1937); and Shelley Hsüeh-lun Chang, *History and Legend: Ideas and Images in the Ming Historical Novels* (1990).

Joseph R. Levenson, ed., *European Expansion and the Counter-Example of Asia, 1300–1600* (1967), recounts the Zheng He expeditions. Philip Snow's *The Star Raft* (1988) contains more recent scholarship, while Louise Levathes, *When China Ruled the Seas* (1993) makes for lively reading.

For a general history of Korea in this period see Andrew C. Nahm, *Introduction to Korean History and Culture* (1993); Ki-Baik Lee, *A New History of Korea* (1984); and William E. Henthorn, *Korea: The Mongol Invasions* (1963). On a more specialized topic see Joseph Needham et al., *The Hall of Heavenly Records: Korean Astronomical Instruments and Clocks, 1380–1780* (1986).

For a collection of up-to-date scholarly essays on Japan, see Kozo Yamamura, ed., *The Cambridge History of Japan, Vol. 3: Medieval Japan* (1990). See also John W. Hall and Toyoda Takeshi, eds., *Japan in the Muromachi Age* (1977); H. Paul Varley, trans., *The Onin War: History of Its Origins and Background with a Selective Translation of the Chronicle of Onin* (1967); Yamada Nakaba, *Ghenko, the Mongol Invasion of Japan, with an Introduction by Lord Armstrong* (1916); and the novel *Fûtô* by Inoue Yasushi, translated by James T. Araki as *Wind and Waves* (1989).

■ Notes

1. Quotation adapted from Desmond Martin, *Chingis Khan and His Conquest of North China* (Baltimore: The John Hopkins Press, 1950), 303.

Document-Based Question
The Integration of Mongol Eurasia

Using the following documents, analyze the role of Mongol dominance in the integration of Eurasia.

DOCUMENT 1
Excerpt from Genghis Khan (p. 295)

DOCUMENT 2
Mongol Politics, Mongol Women (Diversity and Dominance, pp. 298–299)

DOCUMENT 3
Map 12.1 The Mongol Domains in Eurasia in 1300 (p. 301)

DOCUMENT 4
Passport (photo, p. 302)

DOCUMENT 5
Astronomy and Engineering (photo, p. 306)

DOCUMENT 6
Movable Type (photo, p. 318)

What passages from Document 3 illustrate the author's view of Mongol domination? How does the author's role as an Iranian historian affect the reliability of the document? What additional types of documents would help you understand the role of Mongol dominance in the integration of Eurasia?

13

Tropical Africa and Asia, 1200–1500

East African Pastoralists Herding large and small livestock has long been a way of life in drier parts of the tropics.

CHAPTER OUTLINE

Tropical Lands and Peoples

New Islamic Empires

Indian Ocean Trade

Social and Cultural Change

DIVERSITY AND DOMINANCE: Personal Styles of Rule in India and Mali

ENVIRONMENT AND TECHNOLOGY: The Indian Ocean Dhow

Sultan Abu Bakr° customarily offered his personal hospitality to every distinguished visitor to his city of Mogadishu, an Indian Ocean port in northeast Africa. In 1331 he provided food and lodging for Muhammad ibn Abdullah ibn Battuta° (1304–1369), a young Muslim scholar from Morocco who had set out to explore the Islamic world. Before beginning his tour of the trading cities of the Red Sea and East Africa, Ibn Battuta had completed a pilgrimage to Mecca and had traveled throughout the Middle East. Subsequent travels took him through Central Asia and India, China and Southeast Asia, Muslim Spain, and sub-Saharan West Africa. Logging some 75,000 miles (120,000 kilometers) in twenty-nine years, Ibn Battuta became the most widely traveled man of his times. For this reason the journals he wrote about his travels provide valuable information about these lands.

Other Muslim princes and merchants welcomed Ibn Battuta as graciously as did the ruler of Mogadishu. Hospitality was a noble virtue among Muslims, and they ignored visitors' physical and cultural differences. Although the Moroccan traveler noted that Sultan Abu Bakr had skin darker than his own and spoke a different native language (Somali), that was of little consequence. They were brothers in faith when they prayed together at Friday services in the Mogadishu mosque, where the sultan greeted his foreign guest in Arabic, the common language of the Islamic world: "You are heartily welcome, and you have honored our land and given us pleasure." When Sultan Abu Bakr and his jurists heard cases after the mosque service, they decided them on the basis of the law code familiar in all the lands of Islam.

Islam was not the only thing that united the diverse peoples of Africa and southern Asia. They also shared a tropical environment itself and a network of land and sea trade routes. The variations in tropical environments led societies to develop different specialties, which stimulated trade among them. Tropical winds governed the trading patterns of the Indian Ocean. Older than Islam, these routes were important

for spreading beliefs and technologies as well as goods. Ibn Battuta made his way down the coast of East Africa in merchants' ships and joined their camel caravans across the Sahara to West Africa. His path to India followed overland trade routes, and a merchant ship carried him on to China.

As you read this chapter, ask yourself the following questions:

- How did environmental differences shape cultural differences in tropical Africa and Asia?

- How did cultural and ecological differences promote trade in specialized goods from one place to another?

- How did trade and other contacts promote state growth and the spread of Islam?

TROPICAL LANDS AND PEOPLES

To obtain food, the people who inhabited the tropical regions of Africa and Asia used methods that had proved successful during generations of experimentation, whether at the desert's edge, in grasslands, or in tropical rain forests. Much of their success lay in learning how to blend human activities with the natural order, but their ability to modify the environment to suit their needs was also evident in irrigation works and mining.

The Tropical Environment

Because of the angle of earth's axis, the sun's rays warm the **tropics** year-round. The equator marks the center of the tropical zone, and the Tropic of Cancer and Tropic of Capricorn mark its outer limits. As Map 13.1 shows, Africa lies almost entirely within the tropics, as do southern Arabia, most of India, and all of the Southeast Asian mainland and islands.

Lacking the hot and cold seasons of temperate lands, the Afro-Asian tropics have their own cycle of rainy and dry seasons caused by changes in wind patterns across the surrounding oceans. Winds from a permanent high-pressure air mass over the South Atlantic deliver heavy rainfall to the western coast of Africa during much of the year. In December and January large

Abu Bakr (a-BOO BAK-uhr) **Ibn Battuta** (IB-uhn ba-TOO-tuh)

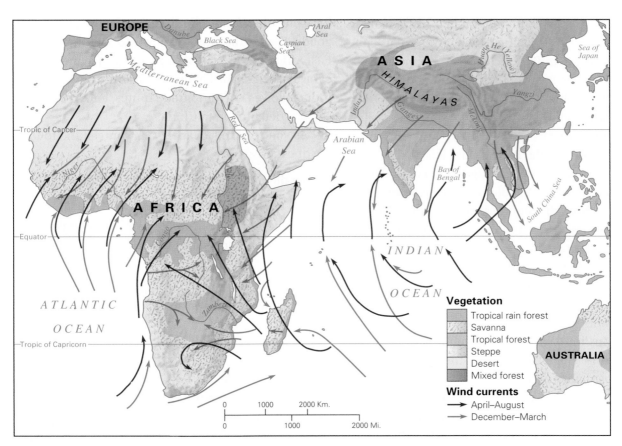

Map 13.1 Africa and the Indian Ocean Basin: Physical Characteristics Seasonal wind patterns control rainfall in the tropics and produce the different tropical vegetation zones to which human societies have adapted over thousands of years. The wind patterns also dominated sea travel in the Indian Ocean.

high-pressure zones over northern Africa and Arabia produce a southward movement of dry air that limits the inland penetration of the moist ocean winds.

In the lands around the Indian Ocean the rainy and dry seasons reflect the influence of alternating winds known as **monsoons.** A gigantic high-pressure zone over the Himalaya° Mountains that is at its peak from December to March produces a strong southward air movement (the northeast monsoon) in the western Indian Ocean. This is southern Asia's dry season. Between April and August a low-pressure zone over India creates a northward movement of air from across the ocean (the southwest monsoon) that brings southern Asia its heaviest rains. This is the wet season.

Areas with the heaviest rainfall—coastal West Africa and west-central Africa, Southeast Asia, and much of India—have dense rain forests. Lighter rains produce other

tropical forests. The English word *jungle* comes from an Indian word for the tangled undergrowth in the tropical forests that once covered most of southern India.

Other parts of the tropics rarely see rain at all. The Sahara, the world's largest desert, stretches across northern Africa. This arid zone continues eastward across Arabia and into northwest India. Another desert zone occupies southwestern Africa. Most of the people of tropical India and Africa live between the deserts and the rain forests in lands that are favored with moderate amounts of moisture during the rainy seasons. These lands range from fairly wet woodlands to the much drier grasslands characteristic of much of East Africa.

Altitude produces other climatic changes. Thin atmospheres at high altitudes hold less heat than atmospheres at lower elevations. Snow covers some of the volcanic mountains of eastern Africa all or part of the year. The snowcapped Himalayas rise so high that they block cold air from moving south, thus giving northern

Himalaya (him-uh-LAY-uh)

CHRONOLOGY

	Tropical Africa	Tropical Asia
1200		**1206** Delhi Sultanate founded in India
	1230s Mali Empire founded	
1300	**1270** Solomonic dynasty in Ethiopia founded	**1298** Delhi Sultanate annexes Gujarat
	1324–1325 Mansa Musa's pilgrimage to Mecca	
1400	**1400s** Great Zimbabwe at its peak	**1398** Timur sacks Delhi, Delhi Sultanate declines
	1433 Tuareg retake Timbuktu, Mali declines	
1500		**1500** Port of Malacca at its peak

India a more tropical climate than its latitude would suggest. The many plateaus of inland Africa and the Deccan° Plateau of central India also make these regions somewhat cooler than the coastal plains.

The mighty rivers that rise in these mountains and plateaus redistribute water far from where it falls. Heavy rains in the highlands of Central Africa and Ethiopia supply the Nile's annual floods that make Egypt bloom in the desert. On its long route to the Atlantic, the Niger River of West Africa arcs northward to the Sahara's edge, providing waters to the trading cities along its banks. In like fashion, the Indus River provides nourishing waters from the Himalayas to arid northwest India. The Ganges° and its tributaries provide valuable moisture to northeastern India during the dry season. Mainland Southeast Asia's great rivers, such as the Mekong, are similarly valuable.

Human Ecosystems

Thinkers in temperate lands once imagined that surviving in the year-round warmth of the tropics was simply a matter of picking wild fruit off trees. In fact, mastering the tropics' many different environments was a long and difficult struggle. A careful observer touring the tropics in 1200 would have noticed that the many differences in societies derived from their particular ecosystems—that is, how people made use of the plants, animals, and other resources of their physical environments.

Domesticated plants and animals had been commonplace long before 1200, but people in some environments found it preferable to rely primarily on wild food that they obtained by hunting, fishing, and gathering. The small size of the ancient Pygmy° people in the dense forests of Central Africa permitted them to pursue their prey through dense undergrowth. Hunting also continued as a way of life in the upper altitudes of the Himalayas and in some desert environments. According to a Portuguese expedition in 1497, the people along the arid coast of southwestern Africa were well fed from a diet of "the flesh of seals, whales, and gazelles, and the roots of wild plants." Fishing was common along all the major lakes and rivers as well as in the oceans. The boating skills of ocean fishermen in East Africa, India, and Southeast Asia often led them to engage in ocean trade.

Tending herds of domesticated animals was common in areas too arid for agriculture. Unencumbered by bulky personal possessions and elaborate dwellings, they used their knowledge of local water and rain patterns to find adequate grazing for their animals in all but the severest droughts. Pastoralists consumed milk from their herds and traded hides and meat to neighboring farmers for grain and vegetables. The arid and semiarid lands of northeastern Africa and Arabia were home to the world's largest concentration of pastoralists. Like Ibn Battuta's host at Mogadishu, some Somali were urban dwellers, but most grazed their herds of goats and camels in the desert hinterland of the Horn of Africa. The western Sahara sustained

---

Deccan (de-KAN)   **Ganges** (GAN-jeez)

Pygmy (PIG-mee)

herds of sheep and camels belonging to the Tuareg°, whose intimate knowledge of the desert also made them invaluable as guides to caravans, such as the one **Ibn Battuta** joined on the two-month journey across the desert. Along the Sahara's southern edge the cattle-herding Fulani° people gradually extended their range during this period. By 1500 they had spread throughout the western and central Sudan. Pastoralists in southern Africa sold meat to early Portuguese visitors.

By 1200 most Africans had been making their livelihood through agriculture for many centuries. Favorable soils and rainfall made farming even more dominant in South and Southeast Asia. High yields from intensive cultivation supported dense populations in Asia. In 1200 over 100 million people may have lived in South and Southeast Asia, more than four-fifths of them on the fertile Indian mainland. Though a little less than the population of China, this was triple the number of people living in all of Africa at that time and nearly double the number of people in Europe.

India's lush vegetation led one Middle Eastern writer to call it "the most agreeable abode on earth . . . its delightful plains resemble the garden of Paradise."[1] Rice cultivation dominated in the fertile Ganges plain of northeast India, in mainland Southeast Asia, and in southern China. Farmers in drier areas grew grains—such as wheat, sorghum, millet, and ensete—and legumes such as peas and beans, whose ripening cycle matched the pattern of the rainy and dry seasons. Tubers and tree crops characterized farming in rain-forest clearings.

Many useful domesticated plants and animals spread around the tropics. By 1200 Bantu-speaking farmers (see Chapter 7) had introduced grains and tubers from West Africa throughout the southern half of the continent. Bananas, brought to southern Africa centuries earlier by mariners from Southeast Asia, had become the staple food for people farming the rich soils around the Great Lakes of East Africa. Yams and cocoyams of Asian origin had spread across equatorial Africa. Asian cattle breeds grazed contentedly in pastures throughout Africa, and coffee of Ethiopian origin would shortly become a common drink in the Middle East.

Water Systems and Irrigation

In most parts of sub-Saharan Africa and many parts of Southeast Asia until quite recent times, the basic form of cultivation was extensive rather than intensive. Instead of enriching fields with manure and vegetable compost so they could be cultivated year after year, farmers abandoned fields every few years when the natural fertility of the soil was exhausted, and they cleared new fields. Ashes from the brush, grasses, and tree limbs that were cut down and burned gave the new fields a significant boost in fertility. Even though a great deal of work was needed to clear the fields initially, modern research suggests that such shifting cultivation was an efficient use of labor in areas where soils were not naturally rich in nutrients.

In other parts of the tropics, environmental necessity and population pressure led to the adoption of more intensive forms of agriculture. A rare area of intensive cultivation in sub-Saharan Africa was the inland delta of the Niger River, where large crops of rice were grown using the river's naturally fertilizing annual floods. The rice was probably sold to the trading cities along the Niger bend.

The uneven distribution of rainfall during the year was one of the great challenges faced by many Asian farmers. Unlike pastoralists who could move their herds to the water, they had to find ways of moving the water to their crops. Farmers in Vietnam, Java, Malaya, and Burma constructed special water-control systems to irrigate their terraced rice paddies. Villagers in southeast India built a series of stone and earthen dams across rivers to store water for gradual release through elaborate irrigation canals. Over many generations these canals were extended to irrigate more and more land. Although the dams and channels covered large areas, they were relatively simple structures that local people could keep working by routine maintenance. Other water-storage and irrigation systems were constructed in other parts of India in this period.

As had been true since the days of the first river-valley civilizations (see Chapter 1), the largest irrigation systems in the tropics were government public works projects. The **Delhi° Sultanate** (1206–1526) introduced extensive new water-control systems in northern India. Ibn Battuta commented appreciatively on one reservoir that supplied the city of Delhi with water. He reported that enterprising farmers planted sugar cane, cucumbers, and melons along the reservoir's rim as the water level fell during the dry season. A sultan in the fourteenth century built a network of irrigation canals in the Ganges plain that were not surpassed in size until the nineteenth century. These irrigation systems made it possible to grow crops throughout the year.

Since the tenth century the Indian Ocean island of Ceylon (modern Sri Lanka°) had been home to the greatest concentration of irrigation reservoirs and canals

---

Tuareg (TWAH-reg)   Fulani (foo-LAH-nee)

Delhi (DEL-ee)   Sri Lanka (sree LAHNG-kuh)

in the world. These facilities enabled the powerful Sinhalese° kingdom in arid northern Ceylon to support a large population. There was another impressive water-works in Southeast Asia, where a system of reservoirs and canals served Cambodia's capital city Angkor°.

These complex systems were vulnerable to disruption. Between 1250 and 1400 the irrigation complex in Ceylon fell into ruin when invaders from South India disrupted the Sinhalese government. The population of Ceylon then suffered from the effects of malaria, a tropical disease spread by mosquitoes breeding in the irrigation canals. The great Cambodian system fell into ruin in the fifteenth century when the government that maintained it collapsed. Neither system was ever rebuilt.

The vulnerability of complex irrigation systems built by powerful governments suggests an instructive contrast. Although village-based irrigation systems could be damaged by invasion and natural calamity, they usually bounced back because they were the product of local initiative, not centralized direction, and they depended on simpler technologies.

Mineral Resources

Throughout the tropics people mined and refined metal-rich ores, which skilled metalworkers turned into tools, weapons, and decorative objects. The more valuable metals, copper and gold, became important in long-distance trade.

Iron was the most abundant and useful of the metals worked in the tropics. Farmers depended on iron hoes, axes, and knives to clear and cultivate their fields and to open up parts of the rain forests of coastal West Africa and Southeast Asia for farming. Iron-tipped spears and arrows improved hunting success. Needles facilitated making clothes and leather goods; nails held timbers together. Indian metalsmiths were renowned for making strong and beautiful swords. In Africa the ability of iron smelters and blacksmiths to transform metal fostered a belief in their magical powers.

Copper and its alloys were of special importance in Africa. In the Copperbelt of southeastern Africa, the refined metal was cast into large X-shaped ingots (metal castings). Local coppersmiths worked these copper ingots into wire and decorative objects. Ibn Battuta described a town in the western Sudan that produced two sizes of copper bars that were used as a currency in place of coins. Skilled artisans in West Africa cast copper and brass (an alloy of copper and zinc) statues and heads that are considered among the masterpieces of world

King and Queen of Ife This copper-alloy work shows the royal couple of the Yoruba kingdom of Ife, the oldest and most sacred of the Yoruba kingdoms of southwestern Nigeria. The casting dates to the period between 1100 and 1500, except for the reconstruction of the male's face, the original of which shattered in 1957 when the road builder who found it accidentally struck it with his pick. (Andre Held, Switzerland)

art. These works were made by the "lost-wax" method, in which molten metal melts a thin layer of wax sandwiched between clay forms, replacing the "lost" wax with hard metal.

Africans exported large quantities of gold across the Sahara, the Red Sea, and the Indian Ocean. Some gold came from stream beds along the upper Niger River and farther south in modern Ghana°. In the hills south of the

Sinhalese (sin-huh-LEEZ) **Angkor** (ANG-kor)

Ghana (GAH-nuh)

Zambezi° River (in modern Zimbabwe°) archaeologists have discovered thousands of mine shafts, dating from 1200, that were sunk up to 100 feet (30 meters) into the ground to get at gold ores. Although panning for gold remained important in the streams descending from the mountains of northern India, the gold and silver mines in India seem to have been exhausted by this period. For that reason, Indians imported considerable quantities of gold from Southeast Asia and Africa for jewelry and temple decoration.

Although they are rarely given credit for it, ordinary farmers, fishermen, herders, metalworkers, and others made possible the rise of powerful states and profitable commercial systems. Caravans could not have crossed the Sahara without the skilled guidance of desert pastoralists. The seafaring skills of the coastal fishermen underlay the trade of the Indian Ocean. Cities and empires rested on the food, labors, and taxes of these unsung heroes.

NEW ISLAMIC EMPIRES

The empires of Mali in West Africa and Delhi in South Asia were the largest and richest tropical states of the period between 1200 and 1500. Both utilized Islamic administrative and military systems introduced from the Islamic heartland, but in other ways these two Muslim sultanates were very different. **Mali** was founded by an indigenous African dynasty that had earlier adopted Islam through the peaceful influence of Muslim merchants and scholars. In contrast, the Delhi Sultanate was founded and ruled by invading Turkish and Afghan Muslims. Mali's wealth depended heavily on its participation in the trans-Saharan trade, but long-distance trade played only a minor role in Delhi.

Mali in the Western Sudan

The consolidation of the Middle East and North Africa under Muslim rule during the seventh and eighth centuries (see Chapter 8) greatly stimulated exchanges along the routes that crossed the Sahara. In the centuries that followed, the faith of Muhammad gradually spread to the lands south of the desert, which the Arabs called the *bilad al-sudan*°, "land of the blacks."

The role of force in spreading Islam south of the Sahara was limited. Muslim Berbers invading out of the

desert in 1076 caused the collapse of Ghana, the empire that preceded Mali in the western Sudan (see Chapter 7), but their conquest did little to spread Islam. To the east, the Muslim attacks that destroyed the Christian Nubian kingdoms on the upper Nile in the late thirteenth century opened that area to Muslim influences, but Christian Ethiopia successfully withstood Muslim advances. Instead, the usual pattern for the spread of Islam south of the Sahara was through gradual and peaceful conversion. The expansion of commercial contacts in the western Sudan and on the East African coast greatly promoted the process of conversion. African converts found the teachings of Islam meaningful, and rulers and merchants found that the administrative, legal, and economic aspects of Islamic traditions suited their interests. The first sub-Saharan African ruler to adopt the new faith was in Takrur° in the far western Sudan, about 1030.

Shortly after 1200 Takrur expanded in importance under King Sumanguru°. Then in about 1240 Sundiata°, the upstart leader of the Malinke° people, handed Sumanguru a major defeat. Even though both leaders were Muslims, the Malinke epic sagas recall their battles as the clash of two powerful magicians, suggesting how much older beliefs shaped popular thought. The sagas say that Sumanguru was able to appear and disappear at will, assume dozens of shapes, and catch arrows in midflight. Sundiata defeated Sumanguru's much larger forces through superior military maneuvers and by successfully wounding his adversary with a special arrow that robbed him of his magical powers. This victory was followed by others that created Sundiata's Mali empire (see Map 13.2).

Like Ghana before it, Mali depended on a well-developed agricultural base and control of the lucrative regional and trans-Saharan trade routes. But Mali differed from Ghana in two ways. First, it was much larger. Mali controlled not only the core trading area of the upper Niger but the gold fields of the Niger headwaters to the southwest as well. Second, from the beginning its rulers were Muslims who fostered the spread of Islam among the political and trading elite of the empire. Control of the important gold and copper trades and contacts with North African Muslim traders gave Mali and its rulers unprecedented prosperity. The pilgrimage to Mecca of the ruler **Mansa Kankan Musa**° (r. 1312–1337), in fulfillment of his personal duty as a Muslim, also gave him an opportunity to display Mali's exceptional wealth. As befitted a powerful ruler, he

---

Zambezi (zam-BEE-zee) Zimbabwe (zim-BAHB-way)
bilad al-sudan (bih-LAD uhs–soo-DAN)

Takrur (TAHK-roor) Sumanguru (soo-muhn-GOO-roo)
Sundiata (soon-JAH-tuh) Malinke (muh-LING-kay)
Mansa Kankan Musa (MAHN-suh KAHN-kahn MOO-suh)

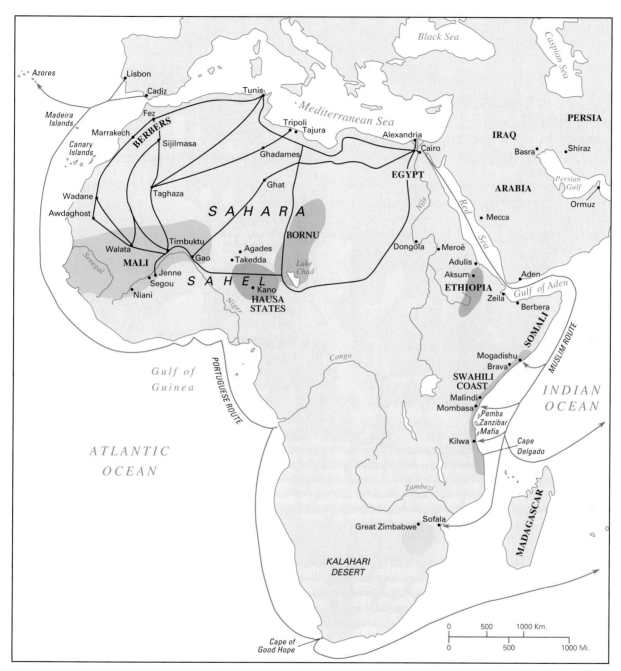

Map 13.2   Africa, 1200–1500   Many African states had beneficial links to the trade that crossed the Sahara and the Indian Ocean. Before 1500, sub-Saharan Africa's external ties were primarily with the Islamic world.

Map of the Western Sudan (1375)   A Jewish geographer on the Mediterranean island of Majorca drew this lavish map in 1375, incorporating all that was known in Europe about the rest of the world. This portion of the Catalan Atlas shows a North African trader approaching the king of Mali, who holds a gold nugget in one hand and a golden scepter in the other. A caption identifies the black ruler as Mansa Musa, "the richest and noblest king in all the land."   (Bibliothèque Nationale de France)

departed in 1324 with a large entourage. Besides his senior wife and 500 of her ladies in waiting and their slaves, according to one account, there were also 60,000 porters and a vast caravan of camels carrying supplies and provisions. For purchases and gifts he took eighty packages of gold each weighing 122 ounces (3.8 kilograms). In addition, 500 slaves each carried a golden staff. Mansa Musa was so lavish with his gifts when the entourage passed through Cairo that the value of gold there remained depressed for years.

After his return from the pilgrimage in 1325, Mansa Musa was eager to promote the religious and cultural influence of Islam in his empire. He built new mosques and opened Quranic schools in the cities along the Niger bend. When Ibn Battuta visited Mali from 1352 to 1354, during the reign of Mansa Musa's successor Mansa

Suleiman° (r. 1341–1360), he praised the Malians for their faithful recitation of Islamic prayers and for their zeal in teaching children the Quran.

Ibn Battuta also had high praise for Mali's government. He reported that "complete and general safety" prevailed in the vast territories ruled by Suleiman and that foreign travelers had no reason to fear being robbed by thieves or having their goods confiscated if they died. (For Ibn Battuta's account of the sultan's court and his subjects' respect see Diversity and Dominance: Personal Styles of Rule in India and Mali.)

Two centuries after Sundiata founded the empire, Mali began to disintegrate. When Mansa Suleiman's successors proved to be less able rulers, rebellions broke out

---

Mansa Suleiman (MAHN-suh SOO-lay-mahn)

among the diverse peoples who had been subjected to Malinke rule. Avid for Mali's wealth, other groups attacked from without. The desert Tuareg retook their city of Timbuktu° in 1433. By 1500 the rulers of Mali had dominion over little more than the Malinke heartland.

The cities of the upper Niger survived Mali's collapse, but some of the western Sudan's former trade and intellectual life moved east to other African states in the central Sudan. Shortly after 1450 the rulers of several of the Hausa city-states adopted Islam as their official religion. The Hausa states were also able to increase their importance as manufacturing and trading centers, becoming famous for their cotton textiles and leatherworking. Also expanding in the late fifteenth century was the central Sudanic state of Kanem-Bornu°. It was descended from the ancient kingdom of Kanem, whose rulers had accepted Islam in about 1085. At its peak about 1250, Kanem had absorbed the state of Bornu south and west of Lake Chad and gained control of important trade routes crossing the Sahara. As Kanem-Bornu's armies conquered new territories in the late fifteenth century, they also spread the rule of Islam.

The Delhi Sultanate in India

The arrival of Islam in India was more violent than in West Africa. Having long before lost the defensive unity of the Gupta Empire (see Chapter 6), the divided states of northwest India were subject to raids by Afghan warlords beginning in the early eleventh century. Motivated by a wish to spread their Islamic faith and by a desire for plunder, the raiders looted Hindu and Buddhist temples of their gold and jewels, kidnapped women for their harems, and slew Indian defenders by the thousands.

In the last decades of the twelfth century a new Turkish dynasty mounted a furious assault that succeeded in capturing the important northern Indian cities of Lahore and Delhi. The Muslim warriors could fire powerful crossbows from the backs of their galloping horses thanks to the use of iron stirrups. One partisan Muslim chronicler recorded, "The city [Delhi] and its vicinity was freed from idols and idol-worship, and in the sanctuaries of the images of the [Hindu] Gods, mosques were raised by the worshippers of one God."[2] The invaders' strength was bolstered by a ready supply of Turkish adventurers from Central Asia eager to follow individual leaders and by the unifying force of their common religious faith. Although Indians fought back bravely, their small states,

Salt Making in the Central Sahara   For many centuries, people have extracted salt from the saline soils of places like Tegguida N'Tisent. Spring water is poured into shallow pits to dissolve the salt. The desert sun soon evaporates the water, leaving pure salt behind.   (Afrique Photo, Cliché Naud, Paris)

often at war with one another, were unable to present an effective united front.

Between 1206 and 1236, the Muslim invaders extended their rule over the Hindu princes and chiefs in much of northern India. Sultan Iltutmish° (r. 1211–1236) consolidated the conquest of northern India in a series of military expeditions that made his empire the largest state in India (see Map 13.3). He also secured official recognition of the Delhi Sultanate as a Muslim state by the caliph of Baghdad. Although the looting and destruction of temples, enslavement, and massacres continued, especially on the frontiers of the empire, the Muslim invaders gradually underwent a transformation from brutal conquerors to more benign rulers. Muslim commanders accorded protection to the conquered, freeing them from persecution in return for payment of a special tax. Yet Hindus never forgot the intolerance and destruction of their first contacts with the invaders.

Timbuktu (tim-buk-TOO)
Kanem-Bornu (KAH-nuhm–BOR-noo)

Iltutmish (il-TOOT-mish)

DIVERSITY AND DOMINANCE

PERSONAL STYLES OF RULE IN INDIA AND MALI

Ibn Battuta wrote vivid descriptions of the powerful men who dominated the Muslim states he visited. Although his accounts are explicitly about the rulers, they also raise important issues about their relations with their subjects. The following account of Sultan Muhammad ibn Tughluq of Delhi may be read as a treatise on the rights and duties of rulers and ways in which individual personalities shaped diverse governing styles.

Muhammad is a man who, above all others, is fond of making presents and shedding blood. There may always be seen at his gate some poor person becoming rich, or some living one condemned to death. His generous and brave actions, and his cruel and violent deeds, have obtained notoriety among the people. In spite of this, he is the most humble of men, and the one who exhibits the greatest equity. The ceremonies of religion are dear to his ears, and he is very severe in respect of prayer and the punishment which follows its neglect. . . .

When drought prevailed throughout India and Sind, . . . the Sultan gave orders that provisions for six months should be supplied to all the inhabitants of Delhi from the royal granaries. . . . The officers of justice made registers of the people of the different streets, and these being sent up, each person received sufficient provisions to last him for six months.

The Sultan, notwithstanding all I have said about his humility, his justice, his kindness to the poor, and his boundless generosity, was much given to bloodshed. It rarely happened that the corpse of some one who had been killed was not seen at the gate of his palace. I have often seen men killed and their bodies left there. One day I went to his palace and my horse shied. I looked before me, and I saw a white heap on the ground, and when I asked what it was, one of my companions said it was the trunk of a man cut into three pieces. The sovereign punished little faults like great ones, and spared neither the learned, the religious, nor the noble. Every day hundreds of individuals were brought chained into his hall of audience; their hands tied to their necks and their feet bound together. Some of them were killed, and others were tortured, or well beaten . . . .

The Sultan has a brother named Masud Khan, [who] was one of the handsomest fellows I have even seen. The king suspected him of intending to rebel, so he questioned him, and, under fear of the torture, Masud confessed the charge. Indeed, every one who denies charges of this nature, which the Sultan brings against him, is put to the torture, and most people prefer death to being tortured. The Sultan had his brother's head cut off in the palace, and the corpse, according to custom, was left neglected for three days in the same place. The mother of Masud had been stoned two years before in the same place on a charge of debauchery or adultery. . . .

One of the most serious charges against this Sultan is that he forced all the inhabitants of Delhi to leave their homes. [After] the people of Delhi wrote letters full of insults and invectives against [him,] the Sultan . . . decided to ruin Delhi, so he purchased all the houses and inns from the inhabitants, paid them the price, and then ordered them to remove to Daulatabad. . . .

The greater part of the inhabitants departed, but [h]is slaves found two men in the streets: one was paralyzed, the other blind. They were brought before the sovereign, who ordered the paralytic to be shot away from a *manjanik* [catapult], and the blind man to be dragged from Delhi to Daulatabad, a journey of forty days' distance. The poor wretch fell to pieces during the journey, and only one of his legs reached Daulatabad. All of the inhabitants of Delhi left; they abandoned their baggage and their merchandize, and the city remained a perfect desert.

A person in whom I felt confidence assured me that the Sultan mounted one evening upon the roof of his palace, and, casting his eyes over the city of Delhi, in which there was neither fire, smoke, nor light, he said, "Now my heart is satisfied, and my feelings are appeased." . . . When we entered this capital, we found it in the state which has been described. It was empty, abandoned, and had but a small population.

In his description of Mansa Suleiman of Mali in 1353, Ibn Battuta places less emphasis on personality, a difference that may only be due to the fact that he had little personal contact with him. He stresses the huge social distance between the ruler and the ruled, between the master and the slave, and goes on to tell more of the ways in which Islam had altered life in Mali's cities as well as complaining about customs that the introduction of Islam had not changed.

The sultan of Mali is *Mansa* Suleiman, *mansa* meaning sultan, and Suleiman being his proper name. He is miserly, not a man from which one might hope for a rich present. It happened that I spent these two months without seeing him on account of my illness. Later on he held a banquet . . . to which the commanders, doctors, *qadi* and preacher were invited, and I went along with them. . . .

On certain days the sultan holds audiences in the palace yard, where there is a platform under a tree . . . carpeted with silk, [over which] is raised the umbrella, . . . surmounted by a bird in gold, about the size of a falcon. The sultan comes out of a door in a corner of the palace, carrying a bow in his hand and a quiver on his back. On his head he has a golden skullcap, bound with a gold band which has narrow ends shaped like knives, more than a span in length. His usual dress is a velvety red tunic, made of the European fabrics called *mutanfas*. The sultan is preceded by his musicians, who carry gold and silver [two-stringed guitars], and behind him come three hundred armed slaves. He walks in a leisurely fashion, affecting a very slow movement, and even stops and looks round the assembly, then ascends [the platform] in the sedate manner of a preacher ascending a mosque-pulpit. As he takes his seat, the drums, trumpets, and bugles are sounded. Three slaves go at a run to summon the sovereign's deputy and the military commanders, who enter and sit down. . . .

The blacks are of all people the most submissive to their king and the most abject in their behavior before him. They swear by his name, saying *Mansa Suleiman ki* [by Mansa Suleiman's law]. If he summons any of them while he is holding an audience in his pavilion, the person summoned takes off his clothes and puts on worn garments, removes his turban and dons a dirty skullcap and enters with his garments and trousers raised knee-high. He goes forward in an attitude of humility and dejection, and knocks the ground hard with his elbows, then stands with bowed head and bent back listening to what he says. If anyone addresses the king and receives a reply from him, he uncovers his back and throws dust over his head and back, for all the world like a bather splashing himself with water. I used to wonder how it was that they did not blind themselves.

Among the admirable qualities of these people, the following are to be noted:

1. The small number of acts of injustice that one finds there; for the blacks are of all people those who most abhor injustice. The sultan pardons no one who is guilty of it.
2. The complete and general safety one enjoys throughout the land. The traveller has no more reason than the man who stays at home to fear brigands, thieves, or ravishers.
3. The blacks do not confiscate the goods of white men [i.e., North Africans and the Middle Easterners] who die in their country, not even when these consist of big treasure, They deposit them, on the contrary, with a man of confidence among the whites until those who have a right to the goods present themselves and take possession.
4. They make all their prayers punctually; they assiduously attend their meetings of the faithful, and punish their children if these should fail in this. On Fridays, anyone who is late at the mosque will find nowhere to pray, the crowd is so great. . . .
5. The blacks wear fine white garments on Fridays. If by chance a man has no more than one shirt or a soiled tunic, at least he washes it before putting it on to go to public prayer.
6. They zealously learn the Koran by heart. Those children who are neglectful in this are put in chains until they have memorized the Koran by heart. . . .

But these people have some deplorable customs, as for example:

1. Women servants, slave women, and young girls go about quite naked, not even covering their sexual parts. I saw many like this during Ramadan. . . .
2. Women go naked in the sultan's presence, too, without even a veil; his daughters also go about naked. On the twenty-seventh night of Ramadan I saw about a hundred women slaves coming out of the sultan's palace with food and they were naked. Two daughters of the sultan were with them, and these had no veil either, although they had big breasts.
3. The blacks throw dust and cinders on their heads as a sign of good manners and respect.
4. They have buffoons who appear before the sultan when his poets are reciting their praise songs.
5. And then a good number of the blacks eat the flesh of dogs and donkeys.

QUESTIONS FOR ANALYSIS

1. How would the actions of these rulers have enhanced their authority? To what extent do their actions reflect Islamic influences?

2. Although Ibn Battuta tells what the rulers did, can you imagine how one of their subjects would have described his or her perception of the same events and customs?

3. Which parts of Ibn Battuta's descriptions seem to be objective and believable? Which parts are more reflective of his personal values?

Source: The first excerpt is from Henry M. Elliot, *The History of India as Told by Its Own Historians* (London: Trübner and Co., 1869–1871) 3:611–614. The second excerpt is adapted from H. A. R. Gibb, ed., *Selections from the Travels of Ibn Battuta in Asia and Africa, 1325-1354* (London: Cambridge University Press, 1929), pp. 326–328. Copyright © 1929. Reprinted with permission of the Cambridge University Press.

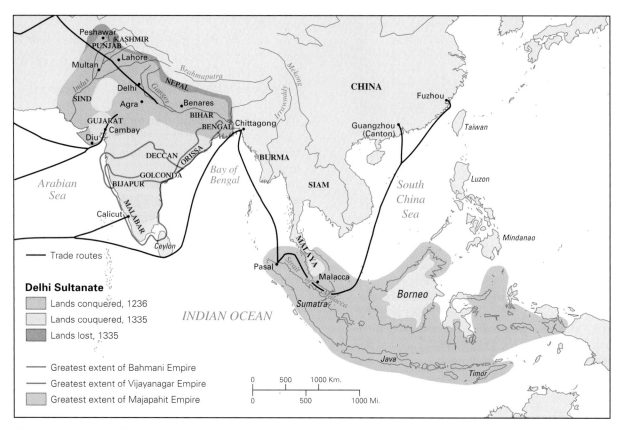

Map 13.3   South and Southeast Asia, 1200–1500   The rise of new empires and the expansion of maritime trade reshaped the lives of many tropical Asians.

To the astonishment of his ministers, Iltutmish passed over his weak and pleasure-seeking sons and designated his beloved and talented daughter Raziya° as his heir. When they questioned the unprecedented idea of a woman ruling a Muslim state, he said, "My sons are devoted to the pleasures of youth: no one of them is qualified to be king. . . . There is no one more competent to guide the State than my daughter.

In the event, her brother—whose great delight was riding his elephant through the bazaar, showering the crowds with coins—ruled ineptly for seven months before the ministers relented and put Raziya (r. 1236–1240) on the throne.

A chronicler who knew her explained why the reign of this able ruler lasted less than four years:

> Sultan Raziya was a great monarch. She was wise, just, and generous, a benefactor to her kingdom, a dispenser of justice, the protector of her subjects, and the leader of her armies. She was endowed with all the qualities befitting a king, but that she was not born of the right sex, and so in the estimation of men all these virtues were worthless. May God have mercy upon her![3]

Doing her best to prove herself a proper king, Raziya dressed like a man and rode at the head of her troops atop an elephant. Nothing, however, could overcome the prejudice against a woman ruler. In the end the Turkish chiefs imprisoned her. Soon after she escaped, she died at the hands of a robber.

After a half-century of stagnation and rebellion, the ruthless but efficient policies of Sultan Ala-ud-din Khalji° (r. 1296–1316) increased his control over the empire's outlying provinces. Successful frontier raids and high taxes kept his treasury full; wage and price controls in Delhi kept down the cost of maintaining a large army; and a network of spies stifled intrigue. When a Mongol threat from the northeast eased, Ala-ud-din's forces extended the sultanate's southern flank, seizing the rich

---

Raziya (rah-ZEE-uh)   **Ala-ud-din Khalji** (uh-LAH–uh-DEEN KAL-jee)

Meenakshi Temple, Madurai, India Some 15,000 pilgrims a day visit the large Hindu temple of Meenakshi (the fish-eyed goddess) in the ancient holy city of Madurai in India's southeastern province of Tamil Nadu. The temple complex dates from at least 1000 C.E., although the elaborately painted statues of these gopuram (gate towers) have been rebuilt and restored many times. The largest gopura rises 150 feet (46 meters) above the ground. (Jean Louis NOU/akg-images)

trading state of **Gujarat**° in 1298. Then troops drove southward, briefly seizing the southern tip of the Indian peninsula.

At the time of Ibn Battuta's visit, Delhi's ruler was Sultan Muhammad ibn Tughluq° (r. 1325–1351), who received his visitor at his palace's celebrated Hall of a Thousand Pillars. The world traveler praised the sultan's piety and generosity, but also recounted his cruelties (see Diversity and Dominance: Personal Styles of Rule in India and Mali). In keeping with these complexities, the sultan resumed a policy of aggressive expansion that enlarged the sultanate to its greatest extent. He balanced that policy with religious toleration intended to win the loyalty of Hindus and other non-Muslims. He even attended Hindu religious festivals. However, his successor Firuz Shah° (r. 1351–1388) alienated powerful Hindus by taxing the Brahmins, preferring to cultivate good relations with the Muslim elite. Muslim chroniclers praised

him for constructing forty mosques, thirty colleges, and a hundred hospitals.

A small minority in a giant land, the Turkish rulers relied on terror more than on toleration to keep their subjects submissive, on harsh military reprisals to put down rebellion, and on pillage and high taxes to sustain the ruling elite in luxury and power. Though little different from most other large states of the time (including Mali) in being more a burden than a benefit to most of its subjects, the sultanate never lost the disadvantage of foreign origins and alien religious identity. Nevertheless, over time, the sultans incorporated some Hindus into their administration. Some members of the ruling elite also married women from prominent Hindu families, though the brides had to become Muslims.

Personal and religious rivalries within the Muslim elite, as well as the discontent of the Hindus, threatened the Delhi Sultanate with disintegration whenever it showed weakness and finally hastened its end. In the mid-fourteenth century Muslim nobles challenged the sultan's dominion and successfully established the

Gujarat (goo-juh-RAHT) Tughluq (toog-LOOK)
Firuz Shah (fuh-ROOZ shah)

Bahmani° kingdom (1347–1482), which controlled the Deccan Plateau. To defend themselves against the southward push of Bahmani armies, the Hindu states of southern India united to form the Vijayanagar° Empire (1336–1565), which at its height controlled the rich trading ports on both coasts and held Ceylon as a tributary state.

The rulers of Vijayanagar and the Bahmani turned a blind eye to religious differences when doing so favored their interests. Bahmani rulers sought to balance devotion to Muslim domination with the practical importance of incorporating the leaders of the majority Hindu population into the government, marrying Hindu wives, and appointing Brahmins to high offices. Vijayanagar rulers hired Muslim cavalry specialists and archers to strengthen their military forces, and they formed an alliance with the Muslim-ruled state of Gujarat.

By 1351, when all of South India was independent of Delhi's rule, much of north India was also in rebellion. In the east, Bengal successfully broke away from the sultanate in 1338, becoming a center of the mystical Sufi tradition of Islam (see Chapter 8). In the west, Gujarat had regained its independence by 1390. The weakening of Delhi's central authority revived Mongol interests in the area. In 1398 the Turko-Mongol leader Timur (see Chapter 12) seized the opportunity to invade and captured the city of Delhi. When his armies withdrew the next year with vast quantities of pillage and tens of thousands of captives, the largest city in southern Asia lay empty and in ruins. The Delhi Sultanate never recovered.

For all its shortcomings, the Delhi Sultanate was important in the development of centralized political authority in India. It established a bureaucracy headed by the sultan, who was aided by a prime minister and provincial governors. There were efforts to improve food production, promote trade and economic growth, and establish a common currency. Despite the many conflicts that Muslim conquest and rule provoked, Islam gradually acquired a permanent place in South Asia.

INDIAN OCEAN TRADE

The maritime network that stretched across the Indian Ocean from the Islamic heartland of Iran and Arabia to Southeast Asia connected to Europe, Africa, and China. The Indian Ocean region was the world's richest maritime trading network and an area of rapid Muslim expansion.

Bahmani (bah MAHN-ee) **Vijayanagar** (vee-juh-yah-NAH-gar)

Monsoon Mariners

The rising prosperity of Asian, European, and African states stimulated the expansion of trade in the Indian Ocean after 1200. Some of the growth was in luxuries for the wealthy—precious metals and jewels, rare spices, fine textiles, and other manufactures. The construction of larger ships also made shipments of bulk cargoes of ordinary cotton textiles, pepper, food grains (rice, wheat, barley), timber, horses, and other goods profitable. When the collapse of the Mongol Empire in the fourteenth century disrupted overland trade routes across Central Asia, the Indian Ocean routes assumed greater strategic importance in tying together the peoples of Eurasia and Africa.

Some goods were transported from one end of this trading network to the other, but few ships or crews made a complete circuit. Instead the Indian Ocean trade was divided into two legs: one from the Middle East across the Arabian Sea to India, and the other from India across the Bay of Bengal to Southeast Asia (see Map 13.4).

The characteristic cargo and passenger ship of the Arabian Sea was the **dhow**° (see Environment and Technology: The Indian Ocean Dhow). Ports on the Malabar coast of southwestern India constructed many of these vessels, which grew from an average capacity of 100 tons in 1200 to 400 tons in 1500. On a typical expedition, a dhow might sail west from India to Arabia and Africa on the northeast monsoon winds (December to March) and return on the southwest monsoons (April to August). Small dhows kept the coast in sight. Relying on the stars to guide them, skilled pilots steered large vessels by the quicker route straight across the water. A large dhow could sail from the Red Sea to mainland Southeast Asia in from two to four months, but few did so. Instead, cargoes and passengers normally sailed eastward to India in junks, which dominated travel in the Bay of Bengal and the South China Sea.

The largest, most technologically advanced, and most seaworthy vessel of this time, the junk had been developed in China. Junks were built from heavy spruce or fir planks held together with enormous nails. The space below the deck was divided into watertight compartments to minimize flooding in case of damage to the ship's hull. According to Ibn Battuta, the largest junks had twelve sails made of bamboo and carried a crew of a thousand men, of whom four hundred were soldiers. A large junk might have up to a hundred passenger cabins and could carry a cargo of over 1,000 tons. Chinese junks dominated China's foreign shipping to Southeast Asia

dhow (dow)

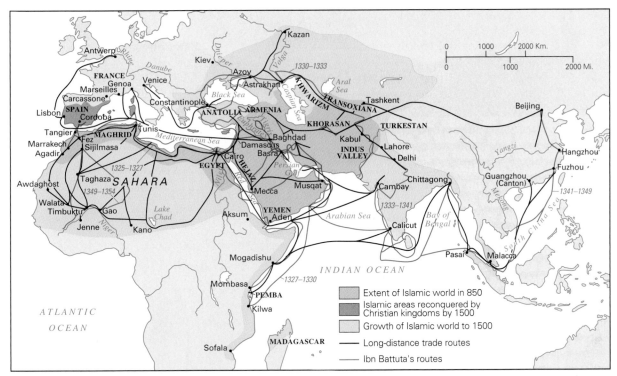

Map 13.4   Arteries of Trade and Travel in the Islamic World, to 1500   Ibn Battuta's journeys across Africa and Asia made use of land and sea routes along which Muslim traders and the Islamic faith had long traveled.

and India, but not all of the junks that plied these waters were Chinese. During the fifteenth century, vessels of this type came from shipyards in Bengal and Southeast Asia and were sailed by local crews.

The trade of the Indian Ocean was decentralized and cooperative. Commercial interests, rather than political authorities, tied several distinct regional networks together (see Map 13.4). Eastern Africa supplied gold from inland areas. Ports around the Arabian peninsula shipped horses and goods from the northern parts of the Middle East, the Mediterranean, and eastern Europe. At the center of the Indian Ocean trade, merchants in the cities of coastal India received goods from east and west, sold some locally, passed others along, and added vast quantities of Indian goods to the trade. The Strait of Malacca°, between the eastern end of the Indian Ocean and the South China Sea, was the meeting point of trade from Southeast Asia, China, and the Indian Ocean. In each region certain ports functioned as giant emporia, consolidating goods from smaller ports

and inland areas for transport across the seas. The operation of this complex trading system can best be understood by looking at some of the regions and their emporia in greater detail.

Africa: The Swahili and Zimbabwe

Trade expanded steadily along the East African coast from about 1250, giving rise to between thirty and forty separate city-states by 1500. As a result of this rising prosperity, new masonry buildings, sometimes three or four stories high, replaced many of the mud and thatch African fishing villages. Archaeology reveals the growing presence of imported glass beads, Chinese porcelain, and other exotic goods. As a result of trading contacts, many loan words from Arabic and Persian enriched the language of the coastal Africans, and the first to write in it used Arabic script. The visitors called these people "Swahili,"° from the Arabic name *sawahil*° *al-sudan*, meaning "shores of the blacks," and the name stuck.

Malacca (meh-LAK-eh)

Swahili (swah-HEE-lee)   *sawahil* (suh-WAH-hil)

The Indian Ocean Dhow

The sailing vessels that crossed the Indian Ocean shared the diversity of that trading area. The name by which we know them, *dhow*, comes from the Swahili language of the East African coast. The planks of teak from which their hulls were constructed were hewn from the tropical forests of South India and Southeast Asia. Their pilots, who navigated by stars at night, used the ancient technique that Arabs had used to find their way across the desert. Some pilots used a magnetic compass, which originated in China.

Dhows came in various sizes and designs, but all had two distinctive features in common. The first was hull construction. The hulls of dhows consisted of planks that were sewn together, not nailed. Cord made of fiber from the husk of coconuts or other materials was passed through rows of holes drilled in the planks. Because cord is weaker than nails, outsiders considered this shipbuilding technique strange. Marco Polo fancifully suggested that it indicated sailors' fear that large ocean magnets would pull any nails out of their ships. More probable explanations are that pliant sewn hulls were cheaper to build than rigid nailed hulls and were less likely to be damaged if the ships ran aground on coral reefs.

The second distinctive feature of dhows was their triangular (lateen) sails made of palm leaves or cotton. The sails were suspended from tall masts and could be turned to catch the wind.

The sewn hull and lateen sails were technologies developed centuries earlier, but there were two innovations between 1200 and 1500. First, a rudder positioned at the stern (rear end) of the ship replaced the large side oar that formerly had controlled steering. Second, shipbuilders increased the size of dhows to accommodate bulkier cargoes.

Dhow This modern model shows the vessel's main features. (National Maritime Museum, London)

Royal Enclosure, Great Zimbabwe   Inside these oval stone walls the rulers of the trading state of Great Zimbabwe lived. Forced to enter the enclosure through a narrow corridor between two high walls, visitors were meant to be awestruck.   (Courtesy of the Department of Information, Rhodesia)

At the time of Ibn Battuta's visit, the southern city of Kilwa had displaced Mogadishu as the **Swahili Coast's** most important commercial center. The traveler declared Kilwa "one of the most beautiful and well-constructed towns in the world." He noted that its dark-skinned inhabitants were devout and pious Muslims, and he took special pains to praise their ruler as a man rich in the traditional Muslim virtues of humility and generosity.

Swahili oral traditions associate the coast's commercial expansion with the arrival of Arab and Iranian merchants, but do not say what had attracted them. In Kilwa's case the answer is gold. By the late fifteenth century the city was exporting a ton of gold a year. The gold was mined by inland Africans much farther south. Much of it came from or passed through a powerful state on the plateau south of the Zambezi River, whose capital city is known as **Great Zimbabwe.** At its peak in about 1400, the city, which occupied 193 acres (78 hectares), may have had 18,000 inhabitants.

Between about 1250 and 1450, local African craftsmen built stone structures for Great Zimbabwe's rulers, priests, and wealthy citizens. The largest structure, a walled enclosure the size and shape of a large football stadium, served as the king's court. Its walls of unmortared stone were up to 17 feet (5 meters) thick and 32 feet (10 meters) high. Inside the walls were many buildings, including a large conical stone tower. The stone ruins of Great Zimbabwe are one of the most famous historical sites in sub-Saharan Africa.

Mixed farming and cattle-herding was Great Zimbabwe's economic base, but, as in Mali, the state's wealth came from long-distance trade. Trade began regionally with copper ingots from the upper Zambezi Valley, salt, and local manufactures. The gold exports into the Indian Ocean in the fourteenth and fifteenth centuries brought Zimbabwe to the peak of its political and economic power. However, historians suspect that the city's residents depleted nearby forests for firewood while their cattle overgrazed surrounding grasslands. The resulting ecological crisis hastened the empire's decline in the fifteenth century.

Arabia: Aden and the Red Sea

The city of **Aden**° had a double advantage in the Indian Ocean trade. Most of the rest of Arabia was desert, but monsoon winds brought Aden enough rainfall to supply drinking water to a large population and to grow grain for export. In addition, Aden's location (see Map 13.2) made it a convenient stopover for trade with India, the Persian Gulf, East Africa, and Egypt. Aden's merchants sorted out the goods from one place and sent them on to another: cotton cloth and beads from India, spices from Southeast Asia, horses from Arabia and Ethiopia, pearls from the Red Sea, luxurious manufactures from Cairo, slaves, gold, and ivory from Ethiopia, and grain, opium, and dyes from Aden's own hinterland.

After visiting Mecca in 1331, Ibn Battuta sailed down the Red Sea to Aden, probably wedged among bales of trade goods. His comments on the great wealth of Aden's leading merchants include a story about the slave of one merchant who paid the fabulous sum of 400 dinars for a ram in order to keep the slave of another merchant from buying it. Instead of punishing the slave for this extravagance, the master freed him as a reward for outdoing his rival. Ninety years later a Chinese Muslim visitor, Ma Huan, found "the country . . . rich, and the people numerous," living in stone residences several stories high.

Common commercial interests generally promoted good relations among the different religions and cultures of this region. For example, in the mid-thirteenth century a wealthy Jew from Aden named Yosef settled in Christian Ethiopia, where he acted as an adviser. South Arabia had been trading with neighboring parts of Africa since before the time of King Solomon of Israel. The dynasty that ruled Ethiopia after 1270 claimed descent from Solomon and from the South Arabian princess Sheba. Solomonic Ethiopia's consolidation was associated with a great increase in trade through the Red Sea port of Zeila°, including slaves, amber, and animal pelts, which went to Aden and on to other destinations.

Friction sometimes arose, however. In the fourteenth century the Sunni Muslim king of Yemen sent materials for the building of a large mosque in Zeila, but the local Somalis (who were Shi'ite Muslims) threw the stones into the sea. The result was a year-long embargo of Zeila ships in Aden. In the late fifteenth century Ethiopia's territorial expansion and efforts to increase control over the trade provoked conflicts with Muslims who ruled the coastal states of the Red Sea.

India: Gujarat and the Malabar Coast

The state of Gujarat in western India prospered as its ports shared in the expanding trade of the Arabian Sea and the rise of the Delhi Sultanate. Blessed with a rich agricultural hinterland and a long coastline, Gujarat attracted new trade after the Mongol capture of Baghdad in 1258 disrupted the northern land routes. Gujarat's forcible incorporation into the Delhi Sultanate in 1298 had mixed results. The state suffered from the violence of the initial conquest and from subsequent military crackdowns, but it also prospered from increased trade with Delhi's wealthy ruling class. Independent again after 1390, Gujarat's Muslim rulers extended their control over neighboring Hindu states and regained their preeminent position in the Indian Ocean trade.

The state derived much of its wealth from its export of cotton textiles and indigo to the Middle East and Europe, largely in return for gold and silver. Gujaratis also dominated the trade from India to the Swahili Coast, selling cotton cloth, carnelian beads, and foodstuffs in exchange for ebony, slaves, ivory, and gold. During the fifteenth century traders expanded their trade from Gujarat eastward to the Strait of Malacca. These Gujarati merchants helped spread the Islamic faith among East Indian traders, some of whom even imported specially carved gravestones from Gujarat.

Unlike Kilwa and Aden, Gujarat was important for its manufactures as well as its commerce. According to the thirteenth-century Venetian traveler Marco Polo, Gujarat's leatherworkers dressed enough skins in a year to fill several ships to Arabia and other places and also made beautiful sleeping mats for export to the Middle East "in red and blue leather, exquisitely inlaid with figures of birds and beasts, and skilfully embroidered with gold and silver wire," as well as leather cushions embroidered in gold. Later observers considered the Gujarati city of Cambay the equal of cities in Flanders and northern Italy (see Chapter 14) in the size, skill, and diversity of its textile industries.

Gujarat's cotton, linen, and silk cloth, as well as its carpets and quilts, found a large market in Europe, Africa, the Middle East, and Southeast Asia. Cambay also was famous for its polished gemstones, gold jewelry, carved ivory, stone beads, and both natural and artificial pearls. At the height of its prosperity in the fifteenth century, this substantial city's well-laid-out streets and open places boasted fine stone houses with tiled roofs. Al-

Aden (AY-den)   **Zeila** (ZEYE-luh)

though most of Gujarat's overseas trade was in the hands of its Muslim residents, members of its Hindu merchant caste profited so much from related commercial activities that their wealth and luxurious lives were the envy of other Indians.

More southerly cities on the Malabar Coast duplicated Gujarat's importance in trade and manufacturing. Calicut° and other coastal cities prospered from their commerce in locally made cotton textiles and locally grown grains and spices, and as clearing-houses for the long-distance trade of the Indian Ocean. The Zamorin° (ruler) of Calicut presided over a loose federation of its Hindu rulers along the Malabar Coast. As in eastern Africa and Arabia, rulers were generally tolerant of other religious and ethnic groups that were important to commercial profits. Most trading activity was in the hands of Muslims, many originally from Iran and Arabia, who intermarried with local Indian Muslims. Jewish merchants also operated from Malabar's trading cities.

Southeast Asia: The Rise of Malacca

At the eastern end of the Indian Ocean, the principal passage into the South China Sea was through the Strait of Malacca between the Malay Peninsula and the island of Sumatra (see Map 13.3). As trade increased in the fourteenth and fifteenth centuries, this commercial choke point became the object of considerable political rivalry. The mainland kingdom of Siam gained control of most of the upper Malay Peninsula, while the Java-based kingdom of Majapahit° extended its dominion over the lower Malay Peninsula and much of Sumatra. Majapahit, however, was not strong enough to suppress a nest of Chinese pirates who had gained control of the Sumatran city of Palembang° and preyed on ships sailing through the strait. In 1407 a fleet sent by the Chinese government smashed the pirates' power and took their chief back to China for trial.

Weakened by internal struggles, Majapahit was unable to take advantage of China's intervention. The chief beneficiary of the safer commerce was the newer port of **Malacca** (or Melaka), which dominated the narrowest part of the strait. Under the leadership of a prince from Palembang, Malacca had quickly grown from an obscure fishing village into an important port by means of a series of astute alliances. Nominally subject to the king of Siam, Malacca also secured an alliance with China that was sealed by the visit of the imperial fleet in 1407. The

Calicut (KAL-ih-cut) Zamorin (ZAH-much-ruhn)
Majapahit (mah-jah-PAH-hit) Palembang (pah-lem-BONG)

conversion of an early ruler from Hinduism to Islam helped promote trade with the Gujarati and other Muslim merchants who dominated so much of the Indian Ocean commerce. Merchants also appreciated Malacca's security and low taxes.

Malacca served as the meeting point for traders from India and China as well as an emporium for Southeast Asian trade: rubies and musk from Burma, tin from Malaya, gold from Sumatra, cloves and nutmeg from the Moluccas (or Spice Islands, as Europeans later dubbed them) to the east. Shortly after 1500, when Malacca was at its height, one resident counted eighty-four languages spoken among the merchants gathered there, who came from as far away as Turkey, Ethiopia, and the Swahili Coast. Four officials administered the large foreign merchant communities: one official for the very numerous Gujaratis, one for other Indians and Burmese, one for Southeast Asians, and one for the Chinese and Japanese. Malacca's wealth and its cosmopolitan residents set the standard for luxury in Malaya for centuries to come.

SOCIAL AND CULTURAL CHANGE

State growth, commercial expansion, and the spread of Islam between 1200 and 1500 led to many changes in the social and cultural life of tropical peoples. The political and commercial elites at the top of society grew more numerous, as did the slaves who served their needs. The spread of Islamic practices and beliefs affected social and cultural life—witness words of Arabic origin like *Sahara, Sudan, Swahili,* and *monsoon*—yet local traditions remained important.

Architecture, Learning, and Religion

Social and cultural changes typically affect cities more than rural areas. As Ibn Battuta observed, wealthy merchants and the ruling elite spent lavishly on new mansions, palaces, and places of worship.

Places of worship from this period exhibit fascinating blends of older traditions and new influences. African Muslims strikingly rendered Middle Eastern mosque designs in local building materials: sun-baked clay and wood in the western Sudan, coral stone on the Swahili Coast. Hindu temple architecture influenced the design of mosques, which sometimes incorporated pieces of older structures. The congregational mosque at Cambay, built in 1325, was assembled out of pillars,

Church of Saint George, Ethiopia King Lalibela, who ruled the Christian kingdom of Ethiopia between about 1180 and 1220, had a series of churches carved out of solid volcanic rock to adorn his kingdom's new capital (also named Lalibela). The church of Saint George, excavated to a depth of 40 feet (13 meters) and hollowed out inside, has the shape of a Greek cross. (S. Sassoon/ Robert Harding Picture Library)

porches, and arches taken from sacked Hindu and Jain° temples. The culmination of a mature Hindu-Muslim architecture was the congregational mosque erected at the Gujarati capital of Ahmadabad° in 1423. It had an open courtyard typical of mosques everywhere, but the surrounding verandas incorporated many typical Gujarati details and architectural conventions.

Even more unusual than these Islamic architectural amalgams were the Christian churches of King Lalibela° of Ethiopia, constructed during the first third of the thirteenth century. As part of his new capital, Lalibela directed Ethiopian sculptors to carve eleven churches out of solid rock, each commemorating a sacred Christian site in Jerusalem. These unique structures carried on an old Ethiopian tradition of rock sculpture, though on a far grander scale.

Mosques, churches, and temples were centers of education as well as prayer. Muslims promoted literacy among their sons (and sometimes their daughters) so

that they could read the religion's classic texts. Ibn Battuta reported seeing several boys in Mali who had been placed in chains until they finished memorizing passages of the Quran. In sub-Saharan Africa the spread of Islam was associated with the spread of literacy, which had previously been confined largely to Christian Ethiopia. Initially, literacy was in Arabic, but in time Arabic characters were used to write local languages.

Islam affected literacy less in India, which had an ancient heritage of writing. Arabic served primarily for religious purposes, while Persian became the language of high culture and was used at court. Eventually, **Urdu**° arose, a Persian-influenced literary form of Hindi written in Arabic characters. Muslims also introduced papermaking in India.

Advanced Muslim scholars studied Islamic law, theology, and administration, as well as works of mathematics, medicine, and science, derived in part from ancient Greek writings. By the sixteenth century in the West African city **Timbuktu,** there were over 150 Quranic

Jain (jine) Ahmadabad (AH-muhd-ah-bahd)
Lalibela (LAH-lee-BEL-uh)

Urdu (ER-doo)

schools, and advanced classes were held in the mosques and homes of the leading clerics. So great was the demand for books that they were the most profitable item to bring from North Africa to Timbuktu. At his death in 1536 one West African scholar, al-Hajj Ahmed of Timbuktu, possessed some seven hundred volumes, an unusually large library for that time. In Southeast Asia, Malacca became a center of Islamic learning from which scholars spread Islam throughout the region. Other important centers of learning developed in Muslim India, particularly in Delhi, the capital.

Even in conquered lands, such as India, Muslim rulers generally did not impose their religion. Example and persuasion by merchants and Sufis proved a more effective way of making converts. Many Muslims were active missionaries for their faith and worked hard to persuade others of its superiority. Islam's influence spread along regional trade routes from the Swahili Coast, in the Sudan, in coastal India, and in Southeast Asia. Commercial transactions could take place between people of different religions, but the common code of morality and law that Islam provided attracted many local merchants.

Marriage also spread Islam. Single Muslim men who journeyed along the trade routes often married local women and raised their children in the Islamic faith. Since Islam permitted a man to have up to four legal wives and many men took concubines as well, some wealthy men had dozens of children. In large elite Muslim households the many servants, both free and enslaved, were also required to be Muslims. Although such conversions were not fully voluntary, individuals could still find personal fulfillment in the Islamic faith.

In India Islamic invasions practically destroyed the last strongholds of long-declining Buddhism. In 1196 invaders overran the great Buddhist center of study at Nalanda° in Bihar° and burned its manuscripts, killing thousands of monks or driving them into exile in Nepal and Tibet. With Buddhism reduced to a minor faith in the land of its birth (see Chapter 7), Islam emerged as India's second most important religion. Hinduism was still India's dominant faith in 1500, but in most of maritime Southeast Asia Islam displaced Hinduism.

Islam also spread among the pastoral Fulani of West Africa and Somali of northeastern Africa, as well as among pastoralists in northwest India. In Bengal Muslim religious figures oversaw the conversion of jungle into farmland and thereby gained many converts among low-caste Hindus who admired the universalism of Islam.

The spread of Islam did not simply mean the replacement of one set of beliefs by another. Islam also adapted to the cultures of the regions it penetrated, developing African, Indian, and Indonesian varieties.

Social and Gender Distinctions

The conquests and commerce brought new wealth to some and new hardships to others. The poor may not have become poorer, but a significant growth in slavery accompanied the rising prosperity of the elite. According to Islamic sources, military campaigns in India reduced hundreds of thousands of Hindu "infidels" to slavery. Delhi overflowed with slaves. Sultan Ala-ud-din owned 50,000; Firuz Shah had 180,000, including 12,000 skilled artisans. Sultan Tughluq sent 100 male slaves and 100 female slaves as a gift to the emperor of China in return for a similar gift. His successor prohibited any more exports of slaves, perhaps because of reduced supplies in the smaller empire.

Mali and Bornu sent slaves across the Sahara to North Africa, including young maidens and eunuchs (castrated males). Ethiopian expansion generated a regular supply of captives for sale to Aden traders at Zeila. About 2.5 million enslaved Africans may have crossed the Sahara and the Red Sea between 1200 and 1500. Other slaves were shipped from the Swahili Coast to India, where Africans played conspicuous roles in the navies, armies, and administrations of some Indian states, especially in the fifteenth century. A few African slaves even found their way to China, where a Chinese source dating from about 1225 says that rich families preferred gatekeepers whose bodies were "black as lacquer."

With "free" labor abundant and cheap, most slaves were trained for special purposes. In some places, skilled trades and military service were dominated by hereditary castes of slaves, some of whom were rich and powerful. Indeed, the earliest rulers of the Delhi Sultanate rose from military slaves. A slave general in the western Sudan named Askia Muhammad seized control of the Songhai Empire (Mali's successor) in 1493. Less fortunate slaves, like the men and women who mined copper in Mali, did hard menial work.

Wealthy households in Asia and Africa employed many slaves as servants. Eunuchs guarded the harems of wealthy Muslims; female slaves were in great demand as household servants, entertainers, and concubines. Some rich men aspired to have a concubine from every part of the world. One of Firuz Shah's nobles was said to have two thousand harem slaves, including women from Turkey and China.

Nalanda (nuh-LAN-duh)   **Bihar** (bee-HAHR)

Indian Woman Spinning, ca. 1500 This drawing of a Muslim woman by an Indian artist shows the influence of Persian styles. The spinning of cotton fiber into thread—women's work—was made much easier by the spinning wheel, which the Muslim invaders introduced. Men then wove the threads into the cotton textiles for which India was celebrated. (British Library, Oriental and Indian Office Library, Or 3299, f. 151)

Sultan Ala-ud-din's campaigns against Gujarat at the end of the thirteenth century yielded a booty of twenty thousand maidens in addition to innumerable younger children of both sexes. The supply of captives became so great that the lowest grade of horse sold for five times as much as an ordinary female slave destined for service, although beautiful young virgins destined for the harems of powerful nobles commanded far higher prices. Some decades later, when Ibn Battuta was given ten girls captured from among the "infidels," he commented: "Female captives [in Delhi] are very cheap because they are dirty and do not know civilized ways. Even the educated ones are cheap." It would seem fairer to say that such slaves were cheap because the large numbers offered for sale had made them so.

Hindu legal digests and commentaries suggest that the position of Hindu women may have improved somewhat overall. The ancient practice of sati°—in which an upper-caste widow threw herself on her husband's funeral pyre—remained a meritorious act strongly ap-

proved by social custom. But Ibn Battuta believed that sati was strictly optional, an interpretation reinforced by the Hindu commentaries that devote considerable attention to the rights of widows.

Indian parents still gave their daughters in marriage before the age of puberty, but consummation of the marriage was supposed to take place only when the young woman was ready. Wives were expected to observe far stricter rules of fidelity and chastity than were their husbands and could be abandoned for many serious breaches. But women often were punished by lighter penalties than men for offenses against law and custom.

A female's status was largely determined by the status of her male master—father, husband, or owner. Women usually were not permitted to play the kind of active roles in commerce, administration, or religion that would have given them scope for personal achievements. Even so, women possessed considerable skills within those areas of activity that social norms allotted to them.

Besides child rearing, one of the most widespread female skills was food preparation. So far, historians have paid little attention to the development of culinary skills, but preparing meals that were healthful and tasty required much training and practice, especially given the limited range of foods available in most places. One kitchen skill that has received greater attention is brewing, perhaps because men were the principal consumers. In many parts of Africa women commonly made beer from grains or bananas. These mildly alcoholic beverages, taken in moderation, were a nutritious source of vitamins and minerals. Socially they were an important part of male rituals of hospitality and relaxation.

Throughout tropical Africa and Asia women did much of the farm work. They also toted home heavy loads of food, firewood, and water for cooking, balanced on their heads. Other common female activities included making clay pots for cooking and storage and making clothing. In India the spinning wheel, introduced by the Muslim invaders, greatly reduced the cost of making yarn for weaving. Spinning was a woman's activity done in the home; the weavers were generally men. Marketing was a common activity among women, especially in West Africa, where they commonly sold agricultural products, pottery, and other craftwork in the markets.

Some free women found their status improved by becoming part of a Muslim household, while many others were forced to become servants and concubines. Adopting Islam did not require accepting all the social customs of the Arab world. Ibn Battuta was appalled that Muslim women in Mali did not completely cover their

sati (suh-TEE)

bodies and veil their faces when appearing in public. He considered their nakedness an offense to women's (and men's) modesty. In another part of Mali he berated a Muslim merchant from Morocco for permitting his wife to sit on a couch and chat with a male friend of hers. The husband replied, "The association of women with men is agreeable to us and part of good manners, to which no suspicion attaches." Ibn Battuta's shock at this "laxity" and his refusal to ever visit the merchant again reveal the patriarchal precepts that were dear to most elite Muslims. So does the fate of Sultan Raziya of Delhi.

CONCLUSION

Tropical Africa and Asia contained nearly 40 percent of the world's population and over a quarter of its habitable land. Between 1200 and 1500 commercial, political, and cultural expansion drew the region's diverse peoples closer together. The Indian Ocean became the world's most important and richest trading area. The Delhi Sultanate brought South Asia its greatest political unity since the decline of the Guptas. In the western Sudan, Mali extended the political and trading role pioneered by Ghana. This growth of trade and empires was closely connected with the enlargement of Islam's presence in the tropical world along with the introduction of greater diversity into Islamic practice.

But if change was an important theme of this period, so too was social and cultural stability. Most tropical Africans and Asians never ventured far outside the rural communities in which their families had lived for generations. Their lives followed the familiar pattern of the seasons, the cycle of religious rituals and festivals, and the stages from childhood to elder status. Custom and necessity defined occupations. Most people engaged in food production by farming, herding, and fishing; some specialized in crafts or religious leadership. Based on the accumulated wisdom about how best to deal with their environment, such village communities were remarkably hardy. They might be ravaged by natural disaster or pillaged by advancing armies, but over time most recovered. Empires and kingdoms rose and fell in these centuries, but the villages endured.

In comparison, social, political, and environmental changes taking place in the Latin West, described in the next chapter, were in many ways more profound and disruptive. They would have great implications for tropical peoples after 1500.

■ Key Terms

tropics	dhow
monsoon	Swahili Coast
Ibn Battuta	Great Zimbabwe
Delhi Sultanate	Aden
Mali	Malacca
Mansa Kankan Musa	Urdu
Gujarat	Timbuktu

■ Suggested Reading

The trading links among the lands around the Indian Ocean have attracted the attention of recent scholars. A fine place to begin is Patricia Risso, *Merchants and Faith: Muslim Commerce and Culture in the Indian Ocean* (1995). More ambitious but perhaps more inclined to overreach the evidence is Janet Abu-Lughod, *Before European Hegemony: The World System, A.D. 1250–1350* (1989), which may usefully be read with K. N. Chaudhuri, *Asia Before Europe: Economy and Civilization of the Indian Ocean from the Rise of Islam to 1750* (1991). Students will find clear summaries of Islam's influences in tropical Asia and Africa in Ira Lapidus, *A History of Islamic Societies*, 2d ed. (2002), part II, and of commercial relations in Philip D. Curtin, *Cross-Cultural Trade in World History* (1984).

Greater detail about tropical lands is found in regional studies. For Southeast Asia see Nicholas Tarling, ed., *The Cambridge History of Southeast Asia*, vol. 1 (1992); John F. Cady, *Southeast Asia: Its Historical Development* (1964); and G. Coedes, *The Indianized States of Southeast Asia*, ed. Walter F. Vella (1968). India is covered comprehensively by R. C. Majumdar, ed., *The History and Culture of the Indian People*, vol. 4, *The Delhi Sultanate*, 2d ed. (1967); with brevity by Stanley Wolpert, *A New History of India*, 6th ed. (1999); and from an intriguing perspective by David Ludden, *A Peasant History of South India* (1985). For advanced topics see Tapan Raychaudhuri and Irfan Habib, eds., *The Cambridge Economic History of India*, vol. 1, *c. 1200–c. 1750* (1982).

A great deal of new scholarship on Africa in this period is summarized in chapters 6 and 7 of Christopher Ehret's *The Civilizations of Africa: A History to 1800* (2002). See also the latter parts of Graham Connah's *African Civilizations: Precolonial Cities and States in Tropical Africa: An Archaeological Perspective* (1987), and, for greater depth, D. T. Niane, ed., *UNESCO General History of Africa*, vol. 4, *Africa from the Twelfth to the Sixteenth Century* (1984), and Roland Oliver, ed., *The Cambridge History of Africa*, vol. 3, *c. 1050 to c. 1600* (1977).

For accounts of slavery and the slave trade see Salim Kidwai, "Sultans, Eunuchs and Domestics: New Forms of Bondage in Medieval India," in *Chains of Servitude: Bondage and Slavery in India*, ed. Utsa Patnaik and Manjari Dingwaney (1985), and the first two chapters of Paul E. Lovejoy, *Transformations in Slavery: A History of Slavery in Africa*, 2d ed. (2000).

Three volumes of Ibn Battuta's writings have been translated by H. A. R. Gibb, *The Travels of Ibn Battuta, A.D. 1325–1354* (1958–1971). Ross E. Dunn, *The Adventures of Ibn Battuta: A Muslim of the 14th Century* (1986), provides a modern retelling of his travels with commentary. For annotated selections see Said Hamdun and Noël King, *Ibn Battuta in Black Africa* (1995).

The most accessible survey of Indian Ocean sea travel is George F. Hourani, *Arab Seafaring*, expanded ed. (1995). For a Muslim Chinese traveler's observations see Ma Huan, *Ying-yai Sheng-lan, "The Overall Survey of the Ocean's Shore" [1433]*, trans. and ed. J. V. G. Mills (1970). Another valuable contemporary account of trade and navigation in the Indian Ocean is G. R. Tibbetts, *Arab Navigation in the Indian Ocean Before the Coming of the Portuguese, Being a Translation of the Kitab al-Fawa'id . . . of Ahmad b. Majidal-Najdi* (1981).

■ Notes

1. Tarikh-i-Wassaf, in Henry M. Elliot, *The History of India as Told by Its Own Historians,* ed. John Dowson (London: Trübner and Co., 1869–1871), 2:28.
2. Hasan Nizami, Taju-l Ma-asir, in Elliot, *The History of India as Told by Its Own Historians,* 2:219.
3. Minhaju-s Siraj, Tabakat-i Nasiri, in Elliot, *The History of India as Told by Its Own Historians,* 2:332–333.

Document-Based Question
Environment and Culture in Tropical Africa, 1200–1500

Using the following documents, analyze the environmental factors that shaped culture in tropical Africa from 1200 to 1500

DOCUMENT 1
East African Pastoralists (p. 324)

DOCUMENT 2
Map 13.1 Africa and the Indian Ocean Basin: Physical Characteristics (p. 326)

DOCUMENT 3
Map 13.2 Africa, 1200–1500 (p. 331)

DOCUMENT 4
Map of the Western Sudan (1375) (photo, p. 332)

DOCUMENT 5
Excerpt from Ibn Battuta on Mansa Suleiman of Mali (Diversity and Dominance, pp. 334–335)

DOCUMENT 6
Royal Enclosure, Great Zimbabwe (photo, p. 341)

DOCUMENT 7
Church of Saint George, Ethiopia (photo, p. 344)

How do Documents 6 and 7 illustrate the human ability to modify the natural environment? What additional types of documents would help you understand the environmental factors that shaped culture in tropical Africa from 1200 to 1500?

14

The Latin West, 1200–1500

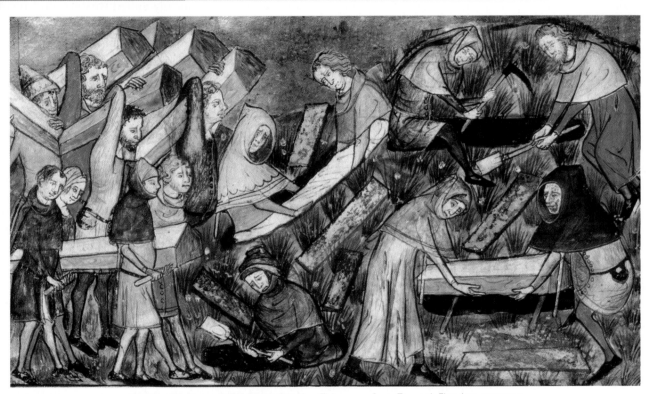

Burying Victims of the Black Death   This scene from Tournai, Flanders, captures
the magnitude of the plague.

In the summer of 1454, a year after the Ottoman Turks had captured the Greek Christian city of Constantinople, Aeneas Sylvius Piccolomini° was trying to stir up support for a crusade to halt the Muslim advances that were engulfing southeastern Europe and that showed no sign of stopping. The man who in four years would become pope doubted that anyone could persuade the rulers of Christian Europe to take up arms together against the Muslims: "Christendom has no head whom all will obey;" he lamented, "neither the pope nor the emperor receives his due."

Aeneas Sylvius had good reason to believe that Latin Christians were more inclined to fight with each other than to join a common front against the Turks. French and English armies had been at war for more than a century. The German emperor presided over dozens of states that were virtually independent of his control. The numerous kingdoms and principalities of Mediterranean Europe had never achieved unity. With only slight exaggeration Aeneas Sylvius complained, "Every city has its own king, and there are as many princes as there are households."

He attributed this lack of unity to Europeans' being so preoccupied with personal welfare and material gain that they would never sacrifice themselves to stop the Turkish armies. During the century since a devastating plague had carried off a third of western Europe's population, people had become cynical about human nature and preoccupied with material things.

Yet despite all these divisions, disasters, and wars, historians now see the period from 1200 to 1500 (Europe's later Middle Ages) as a time of unusual progress. The avarice and greed Aeneas Sylvius lamented were the dark side of the material prosperity that was most evident in the splendid architecture, institutions of higher learning, and cultural achievements of the cities. Frequent wars caused havoc and destruction, but in the long run they promoted the development of more powerful weapons and more unified monarchies.

A European fifty years later would have known that the Turks did not overrun Europe, that a truce in the Anglo-French conflict would hold, and that explorers sent by Portugal and a newly united Spain would extend Europe's reach to other continents. In 1454 Aeneas Sylvius knew only what had been, and the conflicts and calamities of the past made him shudder.

Although their contemporary Muslim and Byzantine neighbors commonly called western Europeans "Franks," western Europeans ordinarily referred to themselves as "Latins." That term underscored their allegiance to the Latin rite of Christianity (and to its patriarch, the pope) as well as the use of the Latin language by their literate members. The **Latin West** deserves special attention because its achievements during this period had profound implications for the future of the world. The region was emerging from the economic and cultural shadow of its Islamic neighbors and, despite grave disruptions caused by plague and warfare, boldly setting out to extend its dominance. Some common elements promoted the Latin West's remarkable resurgence: competition, the pursuit of success, and the effective use of borrowed technology and learning.

As you read this chapter, ask yourself the following questions:

- How well did inhabitants of the Latin West deal with their natural environment?

- How did warfare help rulers in the Latin West acquire the skills, weapons, and determination that enabled them to challenge other parts of the world?

- How did superior technology in the Latin West promote excellence in business, learning, and architecture?

- How much did the region's achievements depend on its own people, and how much on things borrowed from Muslim and Byzantine neighbors?

Aeneas Sylvius Piccolomini (uh-NEE-uhs SIL-vee-uhs pee-kuh-lo-MEE-nee)

C H R O N O L O G Y

	Technology and Environment	Culture	Politics and Society
1200	**1200s** Use of crossbows and longbows becomes widespread; windmills in increased use	**1210s** Religious orders founded: Teutonic Knights, Franciscans, Dominicans **1225–1274** Thomas Aquinas, monk and philosopher **1265–1321** Dante Alighieri, poet **ca. 1267–1337** Giotto, painter	**1200s** Champagne fairs flourish **1204** Fourth Crusade launched **1215** Magna Carta issued
1300	**1300** First mechanical clocks in the West **1315–1317** Great Famine **1347–1351** Black Death **ca. 1350** Growing deforestation	**1300–1500** Rise of universities **1304–1374** Francesco Petrarch, humanist writer **1313–1375** Giovanni Boccaccio, humanist writer **ca. 1340–1400** Geoffrey Chaucer, poet **1389–1464** Cosimo de' Medici, banker **ca. 1390–1441** Jan van Eyck, painter	**1337** Start of Hundred Years War **1381** Wat Tyler's Rebellion
1400	**1400s** Large cannon in use in warfare; hand-held firearms become prominent **ca. 1450** First printing with movable type in the West **1454** Gutenberg Bible printed	**1449–1492** Lorenzo de' Medici, art patron **1452–1519** Leonardo da Vinci, artist **ca. 1466–1536** Erasmus of Rotterdam, humanist **1472–1564** Michelangelo, artist **1492** Explusion of Jews from Spain	**1415** Portuguese take Ceuta **1431** Joan of Arc burned as witch **1453** End of Hundred Years War; Turks take Constantinople **1469** Marriage of Ferdinand of Aragon and Isabella of Castile **1492** Fall of Muslim state of Granada

RURAL GROWTH AND CRISIS

Between 1200 and 1500 the Latin West brought more land under cultivation, adopted new farming techniques, and made greater use of machinery and mechanical forms of energy. Yet for most rural Europeans—more than nine out of ten people were rural—this period was a time of calamity and struggle. Most rural men and women worked hard for meager returns and suffered mightily from the effects of famine, epidemics, warfare, and social exploitation. After the devastation caused from 1347 to 1351 by the plague known as the Black Death, social changes speeded up by peasant revolts released many persons from serfdom and brought some improvements to rural life.

Rural French Peasants Many scenes of peasant life in winter are visible in this small painting by the Flemish Limbourg brothers from the 1410s. Above the snow-covered beehives one man chops firewood, while another drives a donkey loaded with firewood to a little village. At the lower right a woman, blowing on her frozen fingers, heads past the huddled sheep and hungry birds to join other women warming themselves in the cottage (whose outer wall the artists have cut away). (Musée Conde, Chantilly, France/Art Resource, NY)

Peasants and Population

Society was divided by class and gender. In 1200 most western Europeans were serfs, obliged to till the soil on large estates owned by the nobility and the church (see Chapter 9). Each noble household typically rested on the labors of from fifteen to thirty peasant families. The standard of life in the lord's stone castle or manor house stood in sharp contrast to that in the peasant's one-room thatched cottage containing little furniture and no luxuries. Despite numerous religious holidays, peasant cultivators labored long hours, but more than half of the fruits of their labor went to the landowner. Because of these meager returns, serfs were not motivated to introduce extensive improvements in farming practices.

Scenes of rural life show both men and women at work in the fields, although there is no reason to believe that equality of labor meant equality of decision making at home. In the peasant's hut, as elsewhere in medieval Europe, women were subordinate to men. The influential theologian Thomas Aquinas° (1225–1274) spoke for his age when he argued that, although both men and women were created in God's image, there was a sense in which "the image of God is found in man, and not in woman: for man is the beginning and end of woman; as God is the beginning and end of every creature."[1]

Rural poverty was not simply the product of inefficient farming methods and social inequality. It also re-

Aquinas (uh-KWY-nuhs)

sulted from the rapid growth of Europe's population. In 1200 China's population may have surpassed Europe's by two to one; by 1300 the population of each was about 80 million. China's population fell because of the Mongol conquest (see Chapter 12). Why Europe's more than doubled between 1100 and 1345 is uncertain. Some historians believe that the reviving economy may have stimulated the increase. Others argue that warmer-than-usual temperatures reduced the number of deaths from starvation and exposure, while the absence of severe epidemics lessened deaths from disease.

Whatever the causes, more people required more productive ways of farming and new agricultural settlements. One new technique gaining widespread acceptance in northern Europe increased the amount of farmland available for producing crops. Instead of following the custom of leaving half of their land fallow (uncultivated) every year to regain its fertility, some farmers tried a new **three-field system.** They grew crops on two-thirds of their land each year and planted the third field in oats. The oats stored nitrogen and rejuvenated the soil, and they could be used to feed plow horses. In much of Europe, however, farmers continued to let half of their land lie fallow and to use oxen (less efficient but cheaper than horses) to pull their plows.

Population growth also led to the foundation of new agricultural settlements. In the twelfth and thirteenth centuries large numbers of Germans migrated into the fertile lands east of the Elbe River and into the eastern Baltic states. Knights belonging to Latin Christian religious orders slaughtered or drove away native inhabitants who had not yet adopted Christianity. For example, during the thirteenth century, the Order of Teutonic Knights conquered, resettled, and administered a vast area along the eastern Baltic that later became Prussia (see Map 14.3). Other Latin Christians founded new settlements on lands conquered from the Muslims and Byzantines in southern Europe and on Celtic lands in the British Isles.

Draining swamps and clearing forests also brought new land under cultivation. But as population continued to rise, some people had to farm lands that had poor soils or were vulnerable to flooding, frost, or drought. As a result average crop yields declined after 1250, and more people were vulnerable to even slight changes in the food supply resulting from bad weather or the disruptions of war. According to one historian, "By 1300, almost every child born in western Europe faced the probability of extreme hunger at least once or twice during his expected 30 to 35 years of life."[2] One unusually cold spell led to the Great Famine of 1315–1317, which affected much of Europe.

The Black Death and Social Change

The **Black Death** cruelly resolved the problem of overpopulation by killing off a third of western Europeans. This terrible plague spread out of Asia and struck Mongol armies attacking the city of Kaffa° on the Black Sea in 1346 (see Chapter 12). A year later Genoese° traders in Kaffa carried the disease back to Italy and southern France. During the next two years the Black Death spread across Europe, sparing some places and carrying off two-thirds of the populace in others.

The plague's symptoms were ghastly to behold. Most victims developed boils the size of eggs in their groins and armpits, black blotches on their skin, foul body odors, and severe pain. In most cases, death came within a few days. To prevent the plague from spreading, town officials closed their gates to people from infected areas and burned victims' possessions. Such measures helped spare some communities but could not halt the advance of the disease across Europe (see Map 14.1). It is now believed that the Black Death was a combination of two diseases. One was anthrax, a disease that can spread to humans from cattle and sheep. The primary form of the Black Death was bubonic plague, a disease spread by contact with an infected person or from the bites of fleas that infest the fur of certain rats. But even if medieval Europeans had been aware of that route of infection, they could have done little to eliminate the rats, which thrived on urban refuse.

The plague left its mark on the survivors, bringing home how sudden and unexpected death could be. Some people became more religious, giving money to the church or flogging themselves with iron-tipped whips to atone for their sins. Others turned to reckless enjoyment, spending their money on fancy clothes, feasts, and drinking. Whatever their mood, most people soon resumed their daily routines.

Periodic returns of plague made recovery from population losses slow and uneven. By 1400 Europe's population regained the size it had had in 1200. Not until after 1500 did it rise above its preplague level.

In addition to its demographic and psychological effects, the Black Death triggered social changes in western Europe. Skilled and manual laborers who survived demanded higher pay for their services. At first authorities tried to freeze wages at the old levels. Seeing such repressive measures as a plot by the rich, peasants rose up against wealthy nobles and churchmen. During a widespread revolt in France in 1358 known as the Jacquerie,

Kaffa (KAH-fah) **Genoese** (JEN-oh-eez)

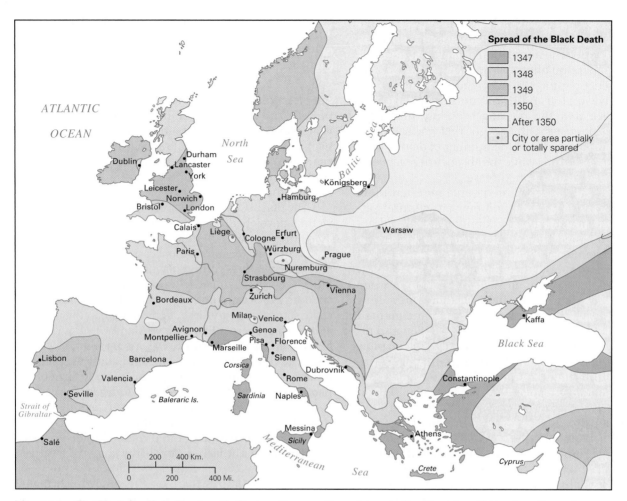

Map 14.1 The Black Death in Fourteenth-Century Europe Spreading out of southwestern China along the routes opened by Mongol expansion, the plague reached the Black Sea port of Kaffa in 1346. This map documents its deadly progress year by year from there into the Mediterranean and north and east across the face of Europe.

peasants looted castles and killed dozens of persons. Urban unrest also took place. In a large revolt led by Wat Tyler in 1381, English peasants invaded London, calling for an end to all forms of serfdom and to most kinds of manorial dues. Angry demonstrators murdered the archbishop of Canterbury and many royal officials. Authorities put down these rebellions with even greater bloodshed and cruelty, but they could not stave off the higher wages and other social changes the rebels demanded.

Serfdom practically disappeared in western Europe as peasants bought their freedom or ran away. Free agricultural laborers used their higher wages to purchase land that they could farm for themselves. Some English landowners who could no longer afford to hire enough fieldworkers used their land to pasture sheep for their wool. Others grew less-labor-intensive crops or made greater use of draft animals and labor-saving tools. Because the plague had not killed wild and domesticated animals, more meat was available for each survivor and more leather for shoes. Thus the welfare of the rural masses generally improved after the Black Death, though the gap between rich and poor remained wide.

In urban areas employers had to raise wages to attract enough workers to replace those killed by the plague. Guilds (see below) found it necessary to reduce the period of apprenticeship. Competition within crafts also became more common. Although the overall econ-

Watermills on the Seine River in Paris Sacks of grain were brought to these mills under the bridge called the Grand Pont to be ground into flour. The water wheels were turned by the river flowing under them. Gears translated the vertical motion of the wheels into the horizontal motion of the millstones. (Bibliothèque Nationale de France)

omy shrank with the decline in population, per capita production actually rose.

Mines and Mills

Mining, metalworking, and the use of mechanical energy expanded so much in the centuries before 1500 that some historians have spoken of an "industrial revolution" in medieval Europe. That may be too strong a term, but the landscape fairly bristled with mechanical devices. Mills powered by water or wind were used to grind grain and flour, saw logs into lumber, crush olives, tan leather, make paper, and perform other useful tasks.

England's many rivers had some fifty-six hundred functioning watermills in 1086. After 1200 such mills spread rapidly across the western European mainland. By the early fourteenth century entrepreneurs had crammed sixty-eight watermills into a one-mile section of the Seine° River in Paris. The flow of the river below turned the simplest **water wheels.** Greater efficiency came from channeling water over the top of the wheel. Dams ensured these wheels a steady flow of water throughout the year. Some watermills in France and England even harnessed the power of ocean tides.

Windmills were common in comparatively dry lands like Spain and in northern Europe, where ice made water wheels useless in winter. Water wheels and windmills had long been common in the Islamic world, but people in the Latin West used these devices on a much larger scale than did people elsewhere.

Wealthy individuals or monasteries built many mills, but because of the expenses involved groups of investors undertook most of the construction. Since nature furnished the energy to run them for free, mills could be very profitable, a fact that often aroused the jealousy of their neighbors. In his *Canterbury Tales* the English poet Geoffrey Chaucer (ca. 1340–1400) captured millers' unsavory reputation (not necessarily deserved) by portraying a miller as "a master-hand at stealing grain" by pushing down on the balance scale with his thumb.[3]

Waterpower also made possible such a great expansion of iron making that some historians say Europe's real Iron Age came in the later Middle Ages, not in antiquity. Water powered the stamping mills that broke up the iron, the trip hammers that pounded it, and the bellows (first documented in the West in 1323) that raised temperatures to the point where the iron was liquid enough to pour into molds. Blast furnaces capable of producing high-quality iron are documented from 1380. The finished products included everything from armor and nails to horseshoes and agricultural tools.

Iron mining expanded in many parts of Europe to meet the demand. In addition, new silver, lead, and copper mines in Austria and Hungary supplied metal for coins, church bells, cannon, and statues. Techniques of deep mining that developed in Central Europe spread farther west in the latter part of the fifteenth century. To keep up with a building boom France quarried more

Seine (sen)

stone during the eleventh, twelfth, and thirteenth centuries than ancient Egypt had done during two millennia for all of its monuments.

The rapid growth of industry changed the landscape significantly. Towns grew outward and new ones were founded; dams and canals changed the flow of rivers; and the countryside was scarred by quarry pits and mines tunneled into hillsides. Pollution sometimes became a serious problem. Urban tanneries (factories that cured and processed leather) dumped acidic wastewater back into streams, where it mixed with human waste and the runoff from slaughterhouses. The first recorded antipollution law was passed by the English Parliament in 1388, although enforcing it was difficult.

One of the most dramatic environmental changes was deforestation. Trees were cut to provide timber for buildings and for ships. Tanneries stripped bark to make acid for tanning leather. Many forests were cleared to make room for farming. The glass and iron industries consumed great quantities of charcoal, made by controlled burning of oak or other hardwood. It is estimated that a single iron furnace could consume all the trees within five-eighths of a mile (1 kilometer) in just forty days. Consequently, the later Middle Ages saw the depletion of many once-dense forests in western Europe.

URBAN REVIVAL

In the tenth century not a single town in the Latin West could compare in wealth and comfort—still less in size—with the cities in the Byzantine Empire and the Islamic caliphates. Yet by the later Middle Ages wealthy commercial centers stood all along the Mediterranean, Baltic, and Atlantic, as well as on major rivers draining into these bodies of water (see Map 14.2). The greatest cities in the East were still larger, but those in the West were undergoing greater commercial, cultural, and administrative changes. Their prosperity was visible in impressive new churches, guild halls, and residences. This urban revival is a measure of the Latin West's recovery from the economic decline that had followed the collapse of the Roman Empire (see Chapter 9) as well as an illustration of how the West's rise was aided by its ties to other parts of the world.

Trading Cities

Most urban growth in the Latin West after 1200 was a result of the continuing growth of trade and manufacturing. Most of the trade was between cities and their hinterlands, but long-distance trade also stimulated urban revival. Cities in northern Italy in particular benefited from maritime trade with the bustling port cities of the eastern Mediterranean and, through them, with the great markets of the Indian Ocean and East Asia. In northern Europe commercial cities in the County of Flanders (roughly today's Belgium) and around the Baltic Sea profited from growing regional networks and from overland and sea routes to the Mediterranean.

Venice's diversion of the Fourth Crusade into an assault in 1204 against the city of Constantinople temporarily removed an impediment to Italian commercial expansion in the eastern Mediterranean. By crippling this Greek Christian stronghold, Venetians were able to seize the strategic island of Crete in the eastern Mediterranean and expand their trading colonies around the Black Sea.

Another boon to Italian trade was the westward expansion of the Mongol Empire, which opened trade routes from the Mediterranean to China (see Chapter 12). In 1271 the young Venetian merchant Marco Polo set out to reach the Mongol court by a long overland trek across Central Asia. There he spent many years serving the emperor Khubilai Khan as an ambassador and as the governor of a Chinese province. Some scholars question the truthfulness of Polo's later account of these adventures and of his treacherous return voyage through the Indian Ocean that finally brought him back to Venice in 1295, after an absence of twenty-four years. Few in Venice could believe Polo's tales of Asian wealth.

Even after the Mongol Empire's decline disrupted the trans-Asian caravan trade in the fourteenth century, Venetian merchants continued to purchase the silks and spices that reached Constantinople, Beirut, and Alexandria. Three times a year galleys (ships powered by some sixty oarsmen each) sailed in convoys of two or three from Venice, bringing back some 2,000 tons of goods. Other merchants began to explore new overland or sea routes.

Venice was not the only Latin city whose trade expanded in the thirteenth century. The sea trade of Genoa on the west coast of northern Italy probably equaled that of Venice. Genoese merchants established colonies on the shores of the eastern Mediterranean and around the Black Sea as well as in the western Mediterranean. In northern Europe an association of trading cities known as the **Hanseatic° League** traded extensively in the Baltic, including the coasts of Prussia, newly conquered by German knights. Their merchants ranged eastward to Novgorod in Russia and westward across the North Sea to London.

Hanseatic (han-see-AT-ik)

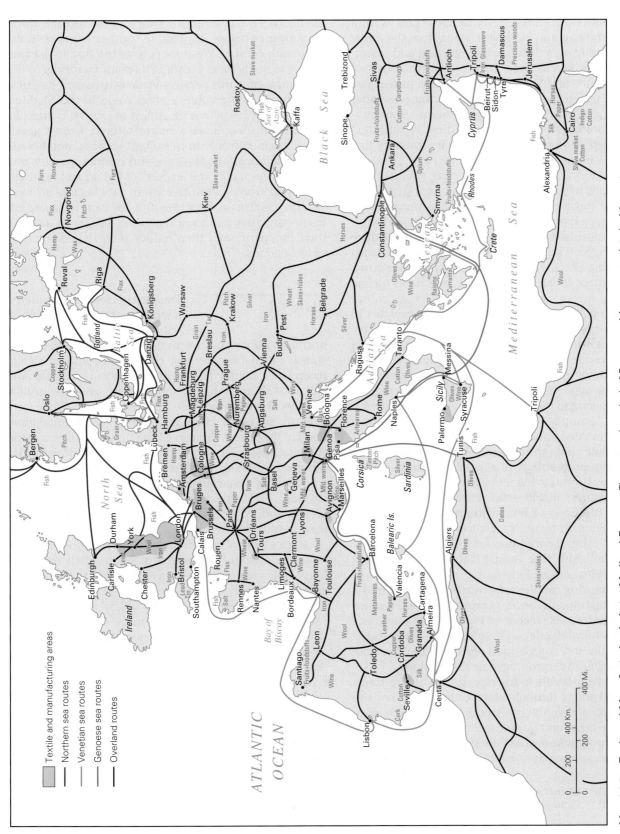

Map 14.2 Trade and Manufacturing in Later Medieval Europe The economic revival of European cities was associated with great expansion of commerce. Notice the concentration of wool and linen textile manufacturing in northern Italy, the Netherlands, and England; the importance of trade in various kinds of foodstuffs; and the slave-exporting markets in Cairo, Kiev, and Rostov.

By the late thirteenth century Genoese galleys from the Mediterranean and Hanseatic ships from the Baltic were converging on a third area, the trading and manufacturing cities in Flanders. In the Flemish towns of Bruges°, Ghent°, and Ypres° skilled artisans turned raw wool from English sheep into a fine cloth that was softer and smoother than the coarse "homespuns" from simple village looms. Dyed in vivid hues, these Flemish textiles appealed to wealthy Europeans who formerly had imported their fine textiles from Asia.

Along the overland route connecting Flanders and northern Italy, important trading fairs developed in the Champagne° region of Burgundy. The Champagne fairs began as regional markets, meeting once or twice a year, where manufactured goods, livestock, and farm produce were exchanged. When Champagne came under the control of the king of France at the end of the twelfth century, royal guarantees of safe conduct to all merchants turned the regional markets into international fairs. A century later fifteen Italian cities had permanent consulates in Champagne to represent the interests of their citizens. The fairs were also important for currency exchange and other financial transactions. During the fourteenth century the volume of trade grew so large that it became cheaper to send Flemish woolens to Italy by sea than to send them overland on pack animals. As a consequence, the fairs of Champagne lost some of their international trade but remained important regional markets.

In the late thirteenth century higher English taxes made it more profitable to turn wool into cloth in England than to export it to Flanders. Raw wool exports from England fell from 35,000 sacks at the beginning of the fourteenth century to 8,000 in the mid-fifteenth. With the aid of Flemish textile specialists and the spinning wheels and other devices they introduced, English exports of wool cloth rose from 4,000 pieces just before 1350 to 54,000 a century later.

Local banking families also turned Florence into a center for high-quality wool making. In 1338 Florence manufactured 80,000 pieces of cloth, while importing only 10,000 from Flanders. These changes in the textile industry show how competition promoted the spread of manufacturing and encouraged new specialties.

The growing textile industries channeled the power of wind and water through gears, pulleys, and belts to drive all sorts of machinery. Flanders, for example, used windmills to clean and thicken woven cloth by beating it in water, a process known as fulling. Another application of mill power was in papermaking. Although papermaking had been common in China and the Muslim world for centuries before it spread to southern Europe in the thirteenth century, Westerners were the first to use machines to do the heavy work in its manufacturing.

In the fifteenth century Venice surpassed its European rivals in the volume of its trade in the Mediterranean as well as across the Alps into Central Europe. Its skilled craftspeople also manufactured luxury goods once obtainable only from eastern sources, notably silk and cotton textiles, glassware and mirrors, jewelry, and paper. At the same time, exports of Italian and northern European woolens to the eastern Mediterranean were also on the rise. In the space of a few centuries western European cities had used the eastern trade to increase their prosperity and then reduce their dependence on eastern goods.

Civic Life

Trading cities in Europe offered people more social freedom than did rural places. Most northern Italian and German cities were independent states, much like the port cities of the Indian Ocean basin (see Chapter 13). Other European cities held special royal charters that exempted them from the authority of local nobles. Because of their autonomy, they were able to adapt to changing market conditions more quickly than were cities in China and the Islamic world that were controlled by imperial authorities. Social mobility was also easier in the Latin West because anyone who lived in a chartered city for over a year might claim freedom. Thus cities became a refuge for all sorts of ambitious individuals, whose labor and talent added to their wealth.

Cities were also home to most of Europe's Jews. The largest population of Jews was in Spain, where earlier Islamic rulers had made them welcome. Many commercial cities elsewhere welcomed Jews for their manufacturing and business skills. Despite the official protection they received from Christian rulers and the church, Jews were subject to violent religious persecutions or expulsions (see Diversity and Dominance: Persecution and Protection of Jews, 1272–1349). Persecution peaked in times of crisis, such as during the Black Death. In the Spanish kingdom of Castile violent attacks on Jews were widespread in 1391 and brought the once vibrant Jewish community in Seville to an end. Terrified Jews left or converted to Christianity, but Christian fanaticism continued to rise over the next century, leading to new attacks on Jews and Jewish converts. In the Latin West only the papal city of Rome left its Jews undisturbed throughout the centuries before 1500.

Bruges (broozh)   **Ghent** (gent [hard *g* as in *get*])
Ypres (EE-pruh)   **Champagne** (sham-PAIN)

Flemish Weavers, Ypres   The spread of textile weaving gave employment to many people in the Netherlands. The city of Ypres in Flanders (now northern Belgium) was an important textile center in the thirteenth century. This drawing from a fourteenth-century manuscript shows a man and a woman weaving cloth on a horizontal loom, while a child makes thread on a spinning wheel.   (Stedelijke Openbare Bibliotheek, Ypres)

Opportunities for individual enterprise in European cities came with many restrictions. In most towns and cities powerful associations known as guilds dominated civic life. A **guild** was an association of craft specialists, such as silversmiths, or of merchants that regulated the business practices of its members and the prices they charged. Guilds also trained apprentices and promoted members' interests with the city government. By denying membership to outsiders and all Jews, guilds perpetuated the interests of the families that already were members. Guilds also perpetuated male dominance of most skilled jobs.

Nevertheless, in a few places women were able to join guilds either on their own or as the wives, widows, or daughters of male guild members. Large numbers of poor women also toiled in nonguild jobs in urban textile industries and in the food and beverage trades, generally receiving lower wages than men. Some women advanced socially through marriage. One of Chaucer's *Canterbury Tales* concerns a woman from Bath, a city in southern England, who became wealthy by marrying a succession of old men for their money (and then two other husbands for love), "aside from other company in youth." Chaucer says she was also a skilled weaver: "In making cloth she showed so great a bent, / She bettered those of Ypres and of Ghent."

By the fifteenth century a new class of wealthy merchant-bankers operated on a vast scale and specialized in money changing, loans, and investments. The merchant-bankers handled the financial transactions of a variety of merchants as well as of ecclesiastical and secular officials. They arranged for the transmission to the pope of funds known as Peter's pence, a collection taken up annually in every church in the Latin West. Their loans supported rulers' wars and lavish courts. Some merchant-bankers even developed their own news services, gathering information on any topic that could affect business.

Florence became a center of new banking services from checking accounts and shareholding companies

DIVERSITY AND DOMINANCE

PERSECUTION AND PROTECTION OF JEWS, 1272–1349

Because they did not belong to the dominant Latin Christian faith, Jews suffered from periodic discrimination and persecution. For the most part, religious and secular authorities tried to curb such anti-Semitism. Jews, after all, were useful citizens who worshipped the same God as their Christian neighbors. Still it was hard to know where to draw the line between justifiable and unjustifiable discrimination. The famous reviser of Catholic theology, St. Thomas Aquinas, made one such distinction in his Summa Theologica *with regard to attempts at forced conversion.*

Now, the practice of the Church never held that the children of Jews should be baptized against the will of their parents. . . . Therefore, it seems dangerous to bring forward this new view, that contrary to the previously established custom of the Church, the children of Jews should be baptized against the will of their parents.

There are two reasons for this position. One stems from danger to faith. For, if children without the use of reason were to receive baptism, then after reaching maturity they could easily be persuaded by their parents to relinquish what they had received in ignorance. This would tend to do harm to the faith.

The second reason is that it is opposed to natural justice . . . it [is] a matter of natural right that a son, before he has the use of reason, is under the care of his father. Hence, it would be against natural justice for the boy, before he has the use of reason, to be removed from the care of his parents, or for anything to be arranged for him against the will of his parents.

The "new view" Aquinas opposed was much in the air, for in 1272 Pope Gregory X issued a decree condemning forced baptism. The pope's decree reviews the history of papal protection given to the Jews, starting with a quotation from Pope Gregory I dating from 598, and decrees two new protections of Jews' legal rights.

Even as it is not allowed to the Jews in their assemblies presumptuously to undertake for themselves more than that which is permitted them by law, even so they ought not to suffer any disadvantage in those [privileges] which have been granted them.

Although they prefer to persist in their stubbornness rather than to recognize the words of their prophets and the mysteries of the Scriptures, and thus to arrive at a knowledge of Christian faith and salvation; nevertheless, inasmuch as they have made an appeal for our protection and help, we therefore admit their petition and offer them the shield of our protection through the clemency of Christian piety. In so doing we follow in the footsteps of our predecessors of happy memory, the popes of Rome—Calixtus, Eugene, Alexander, Clement, Celestine, Innocent, and Honorius.

We decree moreover that no Christian shall compel them or any one of their group to come to baptism unwillingly. But if any one of them shall take refuge of his own accord with Christians, because of conviction, then, after his intention will have been made manifest, he shall be made a Christian without any intrigue. For indeed that person who is known to come to Christian baptism not freely, but unwillingly, is not believed to possess the Christian faith.

Moreover, no Christian shall presume to seize, imprison, wound, torture, mutilate, kill, or inflict violence on them; furthermore no one shall presume, except by judicial action of the authorities of the country, to change the good customs in the land where they live for the purpose of taking their money or goods from them or from others.

In addition, no one shall disturb them in any way during the celebration of their festivals, whether by day or by night, with clubs or stones or anything else. Also no one shall exact any compulsory service of them unless it be that which they have been accustomed to render in previous times.

Inasmuch as the Jews are not able to bear witness against the Christians, we decree furthermore that the testimony of Christians against Jews shall not be valid unless there is among these Christians some Jew who is there for the purpose of offering testimony.

Since it occasionally happens that some Christians lose their Christian children, the Jews are accused by their enemies of secretly carrying off and killing these same Christian children, and of making sacrifices of the heart and blood of these very children. It happens, too, that the parents of these children, or some other Christian enemies of these Jews, secretly hide these very children in order that they may be able to injure these Jews, and in order that they may be able to extort from them a certain amount of money by redeeming them from their straits.

And most falsely do these Christians claim that the Jews have secretly and furtively carried away these children and killed them, and that the Jews offer sacrifice from the heart and the blood of these children, since their law in this matter precisely and expressly forbids Jews to sacrifice, eat, or drink the blood, or eat the flesh of animals having claws. This has been demonstrated many times at our court by Jews converted to the Christian faith: nevertheless very many Jews are often seized and detained unjustly because of this.

We decree, therefore, that Christians need not be obeyed against Jews in such a case or situation of this type, and we order that Jews seized under such a silly pretext be freed from imprisonment, and that they shall not be arrested henceforth on such a miserable pretext, unless—which we do not believe— they be caught in the commission of the crime. We decree that no Christian shall stir up anything against them, but that they should be maintained in that status and position in which they were from the time of our predecessors, from antiquity till now.

We decree, in order to stop the wickedness and avarice of bad men, that no one shall dare to devastate or to destroy a cemetery of the Jews or to dig up human bodies for the sake of getting money [by holding them for ransom]. Moreover, if anyone, after having known the content of this decree, should—which we hope will not happen—attempt audaciously to act contrary to it, then let him suffer punishment in his rank and position, or let him be punished by the penalty of excommunication, unless he makes amends for his boldness by proper recompense. Moreover, we wish that only those Jews who have not attempted to contrive anything toward the destruction of the Christian faith be fortified by the support of such protection. . . .

Despite such decrees violence against Jews might burst out when fears and emotions were running high. This selection is from the official chronicles of the upper-Rhineland towns.

In the year 1349 there occurred the greatest epidemic that ever happened. Death went from one end of the earth to the other, on that side and this side of the [Mediterranean] sea, and it was greater among the Saracens [Muslims] than among the Christians. In some lands everyone died so that no one was left. Ships were also found on the sea laden with wares; the crew had all died and no one guided the ship. The Bishop of Marseilles and priests and monks and more than half of all the people there died with them. In other kingdoms and cities so many people perished that it would be horrible to describe. The pope at Avignon stopped all sessions of court, locked himself in a room, allowed no one to approach him and had a fire burning before him all the time. And from what this epidemic came, all wise teachers and physicians could only say that it was the God's will. And the plague was now here, so it was in other places, and lasted more than a whole year. This epidemic also came to Strasbourg in the summer of the above mentioned year, and it is estimated about sixteen thousand people died.

In the matter of this plague the Jews throughout the world were reviled and accused in all lands of having caused it through the poison which they are said to have put into the water and the wells—that is what they were accused of— and for this reason the Jews were burnt all the way from the Mediterranean into Germany, but not in Avignon, for the pope protected them there.

Nevertheless they tortured a number of Jews in Berne and Zofingen who admitted they had put poison into many wells, and they found the poison in the wells. Thereupon they burnt the Jews in many towns and wrote of this affair to Strasbourg, Freiburg, and Basel in order that they too should burn their Jews. . . . The deputies of the city of Strasbourg were asked what they were going to do with their Jews. They answered and said that they knew no evil of them. Then . . . there was a great indignation and clamor against the deputies from Strasbourg. So finally the Bishop and the lords and the Imperial Cities agreed to do away with the Jews. The result was that they were burnt in many cities, and wherever they were expelled they were caught by the peasants and stabbed to death or drowned. . . .

On Saturday—that was St. Valentine's Day—they burnt the Jews on a wooden platform in their cemetery. There were about two thousand people of them. Those who wanted to baptize themselves were spared. Many small children were taken out of the fire and baptized against the will of their fathers and mothers. And everything that was owed to the Jews was cancelled, and the Jews had to surrender all pledges and notes that they had taken for debts. The council, however, took the cash that the Jews possessed and divided it among the working-men proportionately. The money was indeed the thing that killed the Jews. If they had been poor and if the feudal lords had not been in debt to them, they would not have been burnt.

QUESTIONS FOR ANALYSIS

1. Why do Aquinas and Pope Gregory oppose prejudicial actions against Jews?
2. Why did prejudice increase at the time of the Black Death?
3. What factors account for the differences between the views of Christian leaders and the Christian masses?

Source: First selection reprinted with permission of Pocket Books, an imprint of Simon & Schuster Adult Publishing Group, from *The Pocket Aquinas*, edited with translations by Vernon J. Bourke. Copyright © 1960 by Washington Square Press. Copyright renewed © 1988 by Simon & Schuster Adult Publishing Group. Second selection from Jacob R. Marcus, ed., *The Jew in the Medieval World: A Source Book, 315–1791* (Cincinnati: Union of American Hebrew Congregations, 1938), 152–154, 45–47. Reprinted with permission of the Hebrew Union College Press, Cincinnati.

to improved bookkeeping. In the fifteenth century the Medici° family of Florence operated banks in Italy, Flanders, and London. Medicis also controlled the government of Florence and were important patrons of the arts. By 1500 the greatest banking family in western Europe was the Fuggers° of Augsburg, who had ten times the Medici bank's lending capital. Starting out as cloth merchants under Jacob "the Rich" (1459–1525), the family branched into many other activities, including the trade in Hungarian copper, essential for casting cannon.

Christian bankers had to devise ways to profit indirectly from loans in order to get around the Latin Church's condemnation of usury (charging interest). Some borrowers agreed to repay a loan in another currency at a rate of exchange favorable to the lender. Others added a "gift" in thanks to the lender to the borrowed sum. For example, in 1501 papal officials agreed to repay a loan of 6,000 gold ducats in five months to the Fuggers along with a "gift" of 400 ducats, amounting to an effective interest rate of 16 percent a year. In fact, the return was much smaller since the church failed to repay the loan on time. Because they were not bound by church laws, Jews were important moneylenders.

Despite the money made by some, for most residents of western European cities poverty and squalor were the norm. Even for the wealthy, European cities generally lacked civic amenities, such as public baths and water supply systems, that had existed in the cities of Western antiquity and still survived in cities of the Islamic Middle East.

Gothic Cathedrals

Master builders were in great demand in the thriving cities of late medieval Europe. Cities vied to outdo one another in the magnificence of their guild halls, town halls, and other structures (see Environment and Technology: The Clock). But the architectural wonders of their times were the new **Gothic cathedrals,** which made their appearance in about 1140 in France.

The hallmark of the new cathedrals was the pointed Gothic arch, which replaced the older round Roman arch. External (flying) buttresses stabilized the high, thin stone columns below the arches. This method of construction enabled master builders to push the Gothic cathedrals to great heights and fill the outside walls with giant windows of brilliantly colored stained glass. During the next four centuries, interior heights went ever higher,

Medici (MED-ih-chee) Fuggers (FOOG-uhrz)

Strasbourg Cathedral   Only one of the two spires originally planned for this Gothic cathedral was completed when work ceased in 1439. But the Strasbourg Cathedral was still the tallest masonry structure of medieval Europe. This engraving is from 1630.   (Courtesy of the Trustees of the British Museum)

towers and spires pierced the heavens, and walls dazzled worshippers with religious scenes in stained glass.

The men who designed and built the cathedrals had little or no formal education and limited understanding of the mathematical principles of modern civil engineering. Master masons sometimes miscalculated, and parts of some overly ambitious cathedrals collapsed. For instance, the record-high choir vault of Beauvais Cathedral—154 feet (47 meters) in height—came tumbling down in 1284. But as builders gained experience, they devised new ways to push their steeples heavenward. The spire of the Strasbourg cathedral reached

The Clock

Clocks were a prominent feature of the Latin West in the late medieval period. The Song-era Chinese had built elaborate mechanical clocks centuries earlier (see Chapter 10), but the West was the first part of the world where clocks became a regular part of urban life. Whether mounted in a church steeple or placed on a bridge or tower, mechanical clocks proclaimed Western people's delight with mechanical objects, concern with precision, and display of civic wealth.

The word *clock* comes from a word for bell. The first mechanical clocks that appeared around 1300 in western Europe were simply bells with an automatic mechanical device to strike the correct number of hours. The most elaborate Chinese clock had been powered by falling water, but this was impractical in cold weather. The levers, pulleys, and gears of European clocks were powered by a weight hanging from a rope wound around a cylinder. An "escapement" lever regulated the slow, steady unwinding.

Enthusiasm for building expensive clocks came from various parts of the community. For some time, monks had been using devices to mark the times for prayer.

Employers welcomed chiming clocks to regulate the hours of their employees. Universities used them to mark the beginning and end of classes. Prosperous merchants readily donated money to build a splendid clock that would display their city's wealth. The city of Strasbourg, for example, built a clock in the 1350s that included statues of the Virgin, the Christ Child, and the three Magi; a mechanical rooster; the signs of the zodiac; a perpetual calendar; and an astrolabe—and it could play hymns, too!

By the 1370s and 1380s clocks were common enough for their measured hours to displace the older system that varied the length of the hour in proportion to the length of the day. Previously, for example, the London hour had varied from thirty-eight minutes in winter to eighty-two minutes in summer. By 1500 clocks had numbered faces with hour and minute hands. Small clocks for indoor use were also in vogue. Though not very accurate by today's standards, these clocks were still a great step forward. Some historians consider the clock the most important of the many technological advances of the later Middle Ages because it fostered so many changes during the following centuries.

Early Clock This weight-driven clock dates from 1454. (Bodleian Library Oxford, Ms. Laud Misc. 570, 25v.)

466 feet (142 meters) into the air—as high as a 40-story building. Such heights were unsurpassed until the twentieth century.

Learning, Literature, and the Renaissance

Throughout the Middle Ages people in the Latin West lived amid reminders of the achievements of the Roman Empire. They wrote and worshiped in a version of its language, traveled its roads, and obeyed some of its laws. Even the vestments and robes of medieval popes, kings, and emperors were modeled on the regalia of Roman officials. Yet early medieval Europeans lost touch with much of the learning of Greco-Roman antiquity. More vivid was the biblical world they heard about in the Hebrew and Christian scriptures.

A small revival of classical learning associated with the court of Charlemagne in the ninth century was followed by a larger renaissance (rebirth) in the twelfth century. The growing cities were home to intellectuals, artists, and universities after 1200. In the mid-fourteenth century the pace of intellectual and artistic life quickened in what is often called the **Renaissance,** which began in northern Italy and later spread to northern Europe. Some Italian authors saw the Italian Renaissance as a sharp break with an age of darkness. A more balanced view might reveal this era as the high noon of a day that had been dawning for several centuries.

Universities and Learning

Before 1100 Byzantine and Islamic scholarship generally surpassed scholarship in Latin Europe. When southern Italy was wrested from the Byzantines and Sicily and Toledo from the Muslims in the eleventh century, many manuscripts of Greek and Arabic works came into Western hands and were translated into Latin for readers eager for new ideas. These included philosophical works by Plato and Aristotle°; newly discovered Greek treatises on medicine, mathematics, and geography; and scientific and philosophical writings by medieval Muslims. Latin translations of the Iranian philosopher Ibn Sina° (980–1037), known in the West as Avicenna°, were particularly influential. Jewish scholars contributed significantly to the translation and explication of Arabic and other manuscripts.

Two new religious orders, the Dominicans and the Franciscans, contributed many talented professors to the growing number of new independent colleges after 1200. Some scholars believe that the colleges established in Paris and Oxford in the late twelfth and thirteenth centuries may have been modeled after similar places of study then spreading in the Islamic world—*madrasas,* which provided subsidized housing for poor students and paid the salaries of their teachers. The Latin West, however, was the first part of the world to establish modern **universities,** degree-granting corporations specializing in multidisciplinary research and advanced teaching.

Between 1300 and 1500 sixty new universities joined the twenty existing institutions of higher learning in the Latin West. Students banded together to found some of them; guilds of professors founded others. Teaching guilds, like the guilds overseeing manufacturing and commerce, set the standards for membership in their profession, trained apprentices and masters, and defended their professional interests.

Universities set the curriculum of study for each discipline and instituted comprehensive final examinations for degrees. Students who passed the exams at the end of their apprenticeship received a teaching diploma known as a "license." Students who completed longer training and successfully defended a scholarly treatise became "masters" or "doctors." The colleges of Paris were gradually absorbed into the city's university, but the colleges of Oxford and Cambridge remained independent, self-governing organizations.

Universally recognized degrees, well-trained professors, and exciting new texts promoted the rapid spread of universities in late medieval Europe. Because all university courses were taught in Latin, students and masters could move freely across political and linguistic lines, seeking out the university that offered the courses they wanted and that had the most interesting professors. Universities offered a variety of programs of study but generally were identified with a particular specialty. Bologna° was famous for the study of law; Montpellier and Salerno specialized in medicine; Paris and Oxford excelled in theology.

The prominence of theology partly reflected the fact that many students were destined for ecclesiastical careers, but theology was also seen as "queen of the sciences"—the central discipline that encompassed all knowledge. For this reason thirteenth-century theologians sought to synthesize the newly rediscovered philosophical works of Aristotle, as well as the commentaries of Avicenna, with the revealed truth of the Bible. Their

---

Aristotle (AR-ih-stah-tahl) **Ibn Sina** (IB-uhn SEE-nah)
Avicenna (av-uh-SEN-uh)

Bologna (buh-LOHN-yuh)

daring efforts to synthesize reason and faith were known as **scholasticism**°.

The most notable scholastic work was the *Summa Theologica*°, issued between 1267 and 1273 by Thomas Aquinas, a brilliant Dominican priest who was a professor of theology at the University of Paris. Although Aquinas's exposition of Christian belief organized on Aristotelian principles was later accepted as a masterly demonstration of the reasonableness of Christianity, scholasticism upset many traditional thinkers. Some church authorities even tried to ban Aristotle from the curriculum. There also was much rivalry between the leading Dominican and Franciscan theological scholars over the next two centuries. However, the considerable freedom of medieval universities from both secular and religious authorities eventually enabled the new ideas of accredited scholars to prevail over the fears of church administrators.

Humanists and Printers

The intellectual achievements of the later Middle Ages were not confined to the universities. Talented writers of this era made important contributions to literature and literary scholarship. A new technology in the fifteenth century helped bring works of literature and scholarship to a larger audience.

Dante Alighieri° (1265–1321) completed a long, elegant poem, the *Divine Comedy*, shortly before his death. This supreme expression of medieval preoccupations tells the allegorical story of Dante's journey through the nine circles of hell and the seven terraces of purgatory (a place where the souls not deserving eternal punishment were purged of their sinfulness), followed by his entry into Paradise. His guide through hell and purgatory is the Roman poet Virgil. His guide through Paradise is Beatrice, a woman whom he had loved from afar since childhood and whose death inspired him to write the poem.

The *Divine Comedy* foreshadows some of the literary fashions of the later Italian Renaissance. Like Dante, later Italian writers made use of Greco-Roman classical themes and mythology and sometimes chose to write not in Latin but in the vernacular languages spoken in their regions, in order to reach broader audiences. (Dante used the vernacular spoken in Tuscany°.)

scholasticism (skoh-LAS-tih-sizm)
Summa Theologica (SOOM-uh thee-uh-LOH-jih-kuh)
Dante Alighieri (DAHN-tay ah-lee-GYEH-ree)
Tuscany (TUS-kuh-nee)

The English poet Geoffrey Chaucer was another vernacular writer of this era. Many of his works show the influence of Dante, but he is most famous for the *Canterbury Tales*, the lengthy poem written in the last dozen years of his life. These often humorous and earthy tales, told by fictional pilgrims on their way to the shrine of Thomas à Becket in Canterbury, are cited several times in this chapter because they present a marvelous cross-section of medieval people and attitudes.

Dante also influenced the literary movement of the **humanists** that began in his native Florence in the mid-fourteenth century. The term refers to their interest in the humanities, the classical disciplines of grammar, rhetoric, poetry, history, and ethics. With the brash exaggeration characteristic of new intellectual fashions, humanist writers such as the poet Francesco Petrarch° (1304–1374) and the poet and storyteller Giovanni Boccaccio° (1313–1375) claimed that their new-found admiration for the classical values revived Greco-Roman traditions that for centuries had lain buried under the rubble of the Middle Ages. This idea of a rebirth of learning long dead overlooks the fact that scholars at the monasteries and universities had been recovering and preserving all sorts of Greco-Roman learning for many centuries. Dante (whom the humanists revered) had anticipated humanist interests by a generation.

Yet it is hard to exaggerate the beneficial influences of the humanists as educators, advisers, and reformers. Their greatest influence was in reforming secondary education. Humanists introduced a curriculum centered on the languages and literature of Greco-Roman antiquity, which they felt provided intellectual discipline, moral lessons, and refined tastes. This curriculum dominated secondary education in Europe and the Americas well into the twentieth century. Despite the humanists' influence, theology, law, medicine, and branches of philosophy other than ethics remained prominent in university education during this period. After 1500 humanist influence grew in university education.

Believing the pinnacle of learning, beauty, and wisdom had been reached in antiquity, many humanists tried to duplicate the elegance of classical Latin or Greek. Others followed Dante in composing literary works in vernacular languages. Boccaccio is most famous for his vernacular writings, especially the *Decameron*, an earthy work that has much in common with Chaucer's boisterous tales. Under Petrarch's influence, however, Boccaccio turned to writing in classical Latin, including *De mulieribus claris (Famous Women)*, a chronicle of 106

Franceso Petrarch (fran-CHES-koh PAY-trahrk)
Giovanni Boccaccio (jo-VAH-nee boh-KAH-chee-oh)

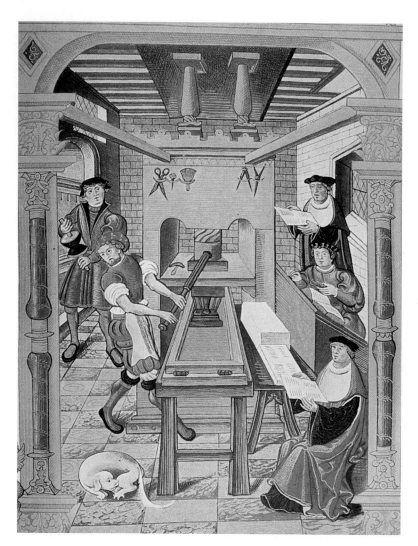

A French Printshop, 1537 A workman operates the "press," quite literally a screw device that presses the paper to the inked type. Other employees examine the printed sheets, each of which holds four pages. When folded, the sheets make a book. (Giraudon/Art Resource, NY)

famous women from Eve to his own day. It was the first collection of women's lives in Western literature.

Once they had mastered classical Latin and Greek, a number of humanist scholars of the fifteenth century worked to restore the original texts of Greco-Roman writers and of the Bible. By comparing many different manuscripts, they eliminated errors introduced by generations of copyists. To aid in this task, Pope Nicholas V (r. 1447–1455) created the Vatican Library, buying scrolls of Greco-Roman writings and paying to have accurate copies and translations made. Working independently, the respected Dutch scholar Erasmus° of Rotterdam (ca. 1466–1536) produced a critical edition of the New Testament in Greek.

Erasmus was able to correct many errors and mistranslations in the Latin text that had been in general use throughout the Middle Ages. In later years this humanist priest and theologian also wrote—in classical Latin—influential moral guides including the *Enchiridion militis christiani* (*The Manual of the Christian Knight*, 1503) and *The Education of a Christian Prince* (1515).

The influence of the humanists was enhanced after 1450 because new printing technology increased the availability of their critical editions of ancient texts, literary works, and moral guides. The Chinese were the first to use carved wood blocks for printing (see Chapter 12), and block-printed playing cards from China were circulating in Europe before 1450. Then, around 1450, three technical improvements revolutionized printing: (1) mov-

---

Erasmus (uh-RAZ-muhs)

The Medici Family   This detail of a mural painting of 1459 by Benozzo Gozzoli depicts the arrival of the Magi at the birthplace of the Christ Child, but the principal figures are important members of the wealthy Medici family of Florence and their entourage in costumes of their day. The bowman on the left suggests how common African servants and slaves became in southern Europe during the Renaissance.   (Art Resource, NY)

able pieces of type consisting of individual letters, (2) new ink suitable for printing on paper, and (3) the **printing press,** a mechanical device that pressed inked type onto sheets of paper.

The man who did most to perfect printing was Johann Gutenberg° (ca. 1394–1468) of Mainz. The Gutenberg Bible of 1454, the first book in the West printed from movable type, was a beautiful and finely crafted work that bore witness to the printer's years of diligent experimentation. As printing spread to Italy and France, humanists worked closely with printers. Erasmus worked for years as an editor and proofreader for the great scholar-printer Aldo Manuzio (1449–1515), whose press in Venice published critical editions of many classical Latin and Greek texts.

By 1500 at least 10 million printed copies had issued forth from presses in 238 towns in western Europe. Though mass-produced paperbacks were still in the future, the printers and humanists had launched a revolution that was already having an effect on students, scholars, and a growing number of literate people who could gain access to ancient texts as well as to unorthodox political and religious tracts.

Johann Gutenberg (yoh-HAHN GOO-ten-burg)

Renaissance Artists

The fourteenth and fifteenth centuries were as distinguished for their masterpieces of painting, sculpture, and architecture as they were for their scholarship. Although artists continued to depict biblical subjects, the spread of Greco-Roman learning led many artists, especially in Italy, to portray Greco-Roman deities and mythical tales. Another popular trend was depicting the scenes of daily life.

However, neither daily life nor classical images were entirely new subjects. Renaissance art, like Renaissance scholarship, owed a major debt to earlier generations. The Florentine painter Giotto° (ca. 1267–1337) had a formidable influence on the major Italian painters of the fifteenth century, who credited him with single-handedly reviving the "lost art of painting." In his religious scenes Giotto replaced the stiff, staring figures of the Byzantine style, which were intended to overawe viewers, with more natural and human portraits with whose emotions of grief and love viewers could identify. Rather than floating on backgrounds of gold leaf, his saints inhabit earthly landscapes.

Giotto (JAW-toh)

Another important contribution to the early Italian Renaissance was a new painting technology from north of the Alps. The Flemish painter Jan van Eyck° (ca. 1390–1441) mixed his pigments with linseed oil instead of the diluted egg yolk of earlier centuries. Oil paints were slower drying and more versatile, and they gave pictures a superior luster. Van Eyck's use of the technique for his own masterfully realistic paintings on religious and domestic themes was quickly copied by talented painters of the Italian Renaissance.

The great Italian Leonardo da Vinci° (1452–1519), for example, used oil paints for his famous *Mona Lisa*. Renaissance artists like Leonardo were masters of many media. His other works include the fresco (painting in wet plaster) *The Last Supper*, bronze sculptures, and imaginative designs for airplanes, submarines, and tanks. Leonardo's younger contemporary Michelangelo° (1472–1564) painted frescoes of biblical scenes on the ceiling of the Sistine Chapel in the Vatican, sculpted statues of David and Moses, and designed the dome for a new Saint Peter's Basilica.

The patronage of wealthy and educated merchants and prelates did much to foster an artistic blossoming in the cities of northern Italy and Flanders. The Florentine banker Cosimo de' Medici (1389–1464), for example, spent immense sums on paintings, sculpture, and public buildings. His grandson Lorenzo (1449–1492), known as "the Magnificent," was even more lavish. The church was also an important source of artistic commissions. Seeking to restore Rome as the capital of the Latin Church, the papacy° launched a building program culminating in the construction of the new Saint Peter's Basilica and a residence for the pope.

These scholarly and artistic achievements exemplify the innovation and striving for excellence of the Late Middle Ages. The new literary themes and artistic styles of this period had lasting influence on Western culture. But the innovations in the organization of universities, in printing, and in oil painting had wider implications, for they were later adopted by cultures all over the world.

POLITICAL AND MILITARY TRANSFORMATIONS

Stronger and more unified states and armies developed in western Europe in parallel with the economic and cultural revivals. In no case were transformations

Jan van Eyck (yahn vahn-IKE)
Leonardo da Vinci (lay-own-AHR-doh dah-VIN-chee)
Michelangelo (my-kuhl-AN-juh-low)   **papacy** (PAY-puh-see)

smooth and steady, and the political changes unfolded somewhat differently in each state (see Map 14.3). During and after the prolonged struggle of the Hundred Years War, French and English monarchs forged closer ties with the nobility, the church, and the merchants. The consolidation of Spain and Portugal was linked to crusades against Muslim states. In Italy and Germany, however, political power remained in the hands of small states and loose alliances.

Monarchs, Nobles, and Clergy

Thirteenth-century states still shared many features of early medieval states (see Chapter 9). Hereditary monarchs occupied the peak of the political pyramid, but their powers were limited by modest treasuries and the rights possessed by others. Below them came the powerful noblemen who controlled vast estates and whose advice and consent were often required on important matters of state. The church, jealous of its traditional rights and independence, was another powerful body within each kingdom. Towns, too, had acquired many rights and privileges. Indeed, the towns in Flanders, the Hanseatic League, and Italy were nearly independent from royal interference.

In theory, nobles were vassals of the reigning monarchs and were obliged to furnish them with armored knights in time of war. In practice, vassals sought to limit the monarch's power and protect their own rights and privileges. The nobles' privileged economic and social position rested on the large estates that had been granted to their ancestors in return for supporting and training knights in armor to serve in a royal army.

In the year 1200 knights were still the backbone of western European fighting forces, but two changes in weaponry were bringing their central military role, and thus the system of estates that supported them, into question. The first involved the humble arrow. Improved crossbows could shoot metal-tipped arrows with such force that they could pierce helmets and light body armor. Professional crossbowmen, hired for wages, became increasingly common and much feared. Indeed, a church council in 1139 outlawed the crossbow as being too deadly for use against Christians. The ban was largely ignored. The second innovation in military technology that weakened the feudal system was the firearm. This Chinese invention, using gunpowder to shoot stone or metal projectiles, further transformed the medieval army.

The church also resisted royal control. In 1302 the outraged Pope Boniface VIII (r. 1294–1303) went so far as to assert that divine law made the papacy superior to

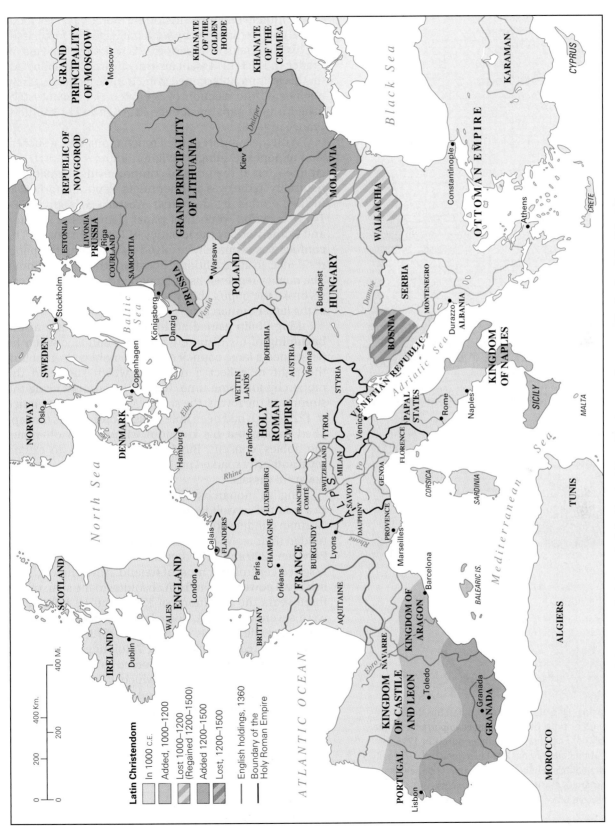

Latin Christendom

- In 1000 C.E.
- Added, 1000–1200
- Lost 1000–1200 (Regained 1200–1500)
- Added 1200–1500
- Lost 1200–1500

— English holdings, 1360

— Boundary of the Holy Roman Empire

Map 14.3   Europe in 1453   This year marked the end of the Hundred Years War between France and England and the fall of the Byzantine capital city of Constantinople to the Ottoman Turks. Muslim advances into southeastern Europe were offset by the Latin Christian reconquests of Islamic holdings in southern Italy and the Iberian Peninsula and by the conversion of Lithuania.

The Magna Carta   One of four extant copies, this document shows the ravages of time, but the symbolic importance of the charter King John of England signed under duress in 1215 for English constitutional history has not been dimished. Originally a guarantee of the baron's feudal rights, it came to be seen as a limit on the monarch's authority over all subjects.   (The National Archives, Public Record Office and Historical Manuscripts Commission)

"every human creature," including monarchs. This theoretical claim of superiority was challenged by force. Issuing his own claim of superiority, King Philip "the Fair" of France (r. 1285–1314) sent an army to arrest the pope. After this treatment hastened Pope Boniface's death, Philip engineered the election of a French pope who established a new papal residence at Avignon° in southern France in 1309.

With the support of the French monarchy, a succession of popes residing in Avignon improved church discipline—but at the price of compromising the papacy's neutrality in the eyes of other rulers. Papal authority was further eroded by the **Great Western Schism** (1378–1415), a period when rival papal claimants at Avignon and Rome vied for the loyalties of Latin Christians. The conflict was eventually resolved by returning the papal residence to its traditional location, the city of Rome. The papacy regained its independence, but the long crisis broke the pope's ability to challenge the rising power of the larger monarchies.

King Philip gained an important advantage at the beginning of his dispute with Pope Boniface when he persuaded a large council of French nobles to grant him the right to collect a new tax, which sustained the monarchy for some time. Earlier, by adroitly using the support of the towns, the saintly King Louis IX of France (r. 1226–1270) had been able to issue ordinances that applied throughout his kingdom without first obtaining the nobles' consent. But later kings' efforts to extend royal authority sparked prolonged resistance by the most powerful vassals.

English monarchs wielded more centralized power as a result of consolidation that had taken place after the Norman conquest of 1066. Anglo-Norman kings also extended their realm by assaults on their Celtic neighbors. Between 1200 and 1400 they incorporated Wales and reasserted control over most of Ireland. Nevertheless, English royal power was far from absolute. In the span of just three years the ambitions of King John (r. 1199–1216) were severely set back. First he was compelled to acknowledge the pope as his overlord (1213). Then he lost his bid to reassert claims to Aquitaine in southern France (1214). Finally he was forced to sign the Magna Carta ("Great Charter," 1215), which affirmed that monarchs were subject to established law, confirmed the independence of the church and the city of London, and guaranteed nobles' hereditary rights.

Separate from the challenges to royal authority by the church and the nobles were the alliances and conflicts generated by the hereditary nature of monarchial

Avignon (ah-vee-NYON)

rule. Monarchs and their vassals entered into strategic marriages with a view to increasing their lands and their wealth. Such marriages showed scant regard for the emotions of the wedded parties or for "national" interests. Besides unhappiness for the parties involved, these marriages often led to conflicts over far-flung inheritances. Although these dynastic struggles and shifting boundaries make European politics seem chaotic in comparison with the empires of Asia, some important changes were emerging from them. Aided by the changing technology of war, monarchs were strengthening their authority and creating more stable (but not entirely fixed) state boundaries within which the nations of western Europe would in time develop. Nobles lost autonomy and dominance on the battlefield but retained their social position and important political roles.

The Hundred Years War, 1337–1453

The long conflict between the king of France and his vassals known as the **Hundred Years War** (1337–1453) was a key example of the transformation in politics and warfare. This long conflict set the power of the French monarchy against the ambitions of his vassals, who included the kings of England (for lands that belonged to their Norman ancestors) and the heads of Flanders, Brittany, and Burgundy. In typical fashion, the conflict grew out of a marriage alliance.

Princess Isabella of France married King Edward II of England (r. 1307–1327) to ensure that this powerful vassal remained loyal to the French monarchy. However, when none of Isabella's three brothers, who served in turn as kings of France, produced a male heir, Isabella's son, King Edward III of England (r. 1327–1377), laid claim to the French throne in 1337. Edward decided to fight for his rights after French courts awarded the throne to a more distant (and more French) cousin. Other vassals joined in a series of battles for the French throne that stretched out over a century.

New military technology shaped the conflict. Early in the war, hired Italian crossbowmen reinforced the French cavalry, but arrows from another late medieval innovation, the English longbow, nearly annihilated the French force. Adopted from the Welsh, the 6-foot (1.8-meter) longbow could shoot farther and more rapidly than the crossbow. Although arrows from longbows could not pierce armor, in concentrated volleys they often found gaps in the knights' defenses or struck their less-well-protected horses. To defend against these weapons, armor became heavier and more encompassing, making it harder for a knight to move. A knight who was pulled off his steed by a foot soldier armed with a pike (hooked pole) was usually unable to get up to defend himself.

Firearms became prominent in later stages of the Hundred Years War. Early cannon were better at spooking the horses than at hitting rapidly moving targets. As cannon grew larger, they proved quite effective in blasting holes through the heavy walls of medieval castles and towns. The first use of such artillery, against the French in the Battle of Agincourt (1415), gave the English an important victory.

A young French peasant woman, Joan of Arc, brought the English gains to a halt. Believing she was acting on God's instructions, she donned a knight's armor and rallied the French troops, which defeated the English in 1429 just as they seemed close to conquering France. Shortly after this victory, Joan had the misfortune of falling into English hands. English churchmen tried her for witchcraft and burned her at the stake in 1431.

In the final battles of the Hundred Years War, French forces used large cannon to demolish the walls of once-secure castles held by the English and their allies. The truce that ended the struggle in 1453 left the French monarchy in firm control.

New Monarchies in France and England

The war proved to be a watershed in the political history of France and England. The **new monarchies** that emerged differed from their medieval predecessors in having greater centralization of power, more fixed "national" boundaries, and stronger representative institutions. English monarchs after 1453 strove to consolidate control within the British Isles, though the Scots strongly defended their independence. French monarchs worked to tame the independence of their powerful noble vassals. Holdings headed by women were especially vulnerable. Mary of Burgundy (1457–1482) was forced to surrender much of her family's vast holdings to the king. Anne of Brittany's forced marriage to the king led to the eventual incorporation of her duchy° into France.

Changes in military technology helped undermine nobles' resistance. Smaller, more mobile cannon developed in the late fifteenth century blasted through their castle walls. More powerful hand-held firearms that could pierce even the heaviest armor hastened the demise of the armored knights. New armies depended less on knights from noble vassals and more on bowmen,

duchy (DUTCH-ee)

pikemen, musketeers, and artillery units paid by the royal treasury.

The new monarchies tried several strategies to pay for their standing armies. Monarchs encouraged noble vassals to make monetary payments in place of military service and levied additional taxes in time of war. For example, Charles VII of France (r. 1422–1461) won the right to impose a land tax on his vassals that enabled him to pay the costs of the last years of war with England. This new tax sustained the royal treasury for the next 350 years.

Taxes on merchants were another important revenue source. The taxes on the English wool trade, begun by King Edward III, paid most of the costs of the Hundred Years War. Some rulers taxed Jewish merchants and extorted large contributions from wealthy towns. Individual merchants sometimes curried royal favor with loans, even though such debts could be difficult or dangerous to collect. For example, the wealthy fifteenth-century French merchant Jacques Coeur° gained many social and financial benefits for himself and his family by lending money to important members of the French court, but he was ruined when his jealous debtors accused him of murder and had his fortune confiscated.

The church was a third source of revenue. The clergy often made voluntary contributions to a war effort. English and French monarchs gained further control of church funds in the fifteenth century by gaining the right to appoint important ecclesiastical officials in their realms. Although reformers complained that this subordinated the church's spiritual mission to political and economic concerns, the monarchs often used state power to enforce religious orthodoxy in their realms more vigorously than the popes had ever been able to do.

The shift in power to the monarchs and away from the nobility and the church did not deprive nobles of social privileges and special access to high administrative and military offices. Moreover, towns, nobles, and clergy found new ways to check royal power in the representative institutions that came into existence in England and France. By 1500 Parliament had become a permanent part of English government: the House of Lords contained all the great nobles and English church officials; the House of Commons represented the towns and the leading citizens of the counties. In France a similar but less effective representative body, the Estates General, represented the church, the nobles, and the towns.

Iberian Unification

The growth of Spain and Portugal into strong, centralized states was also shaped by struggles between kings and vassals, dynastic marriages and mergers, and warfare. But Spain and Portugal's **reconquest** of Iberia from Muslim rule was also a religious crusade. Religious zeal did not rule out personal gain. The Christian knights who gradually pushed the borders of their kingdoms southward expected material rewards. The spoils of victory included irrigated farmland, cities rich in Moorish architecture, and trading ports with access to the Mediterranean and the Atlantic. Serving God, growing rich, and living off the labor of others became a way of life for the Iberian nobility.

The reconquest advanced in waves over several centuries. Christian knights took Toledo in 1085. The Atlantic port of Lisbon fell in 1147 with the aid of English crusaders on their way to capture the Holy Land. It became the new capital of Portugal and the kingdom's leading city, displacing the older capital of Oporto, whose name (meaning "the port") is the root of the word *Portugal*. A Christian victory in 1212 broke the back of Muslim power in Iberia. During the next few decades Portuguese and Castilian forces captured the beautiful and prosperous cities of Cordova (1236) and Seville (1248) and in 1249 drove the Muslims from the southwestern corner of Iberia, known as Algarve° ("the west" in Arabic). Only the small kingdom of Granada hugging the Mediterranean coast remained in Muslim hands.

By incorporating Algarve in 1249, Portugal attained its modern territorial limits. After a long pause to colonize, Christianize, and consolidate this land, Portugal took the Christian crusade to North Africa. In 1415 Portuguese knights seized the port city of Ceuta° in Morocco, where they learned more about the trans-Saharan caravan trade in gold and slaves (see Chapter 13). During the next few decades, Portuguese mariners sailed down the Atlantic coast of Africa seeking access to this rich trade and alliances with rumored African Christians (see Chapter 15).

Although it took the other Iberian kingdoms much longer to complete the reconquest, the struggle served to bring them together and to keep their Christian religious zealotry at a high pitch. The marriage of Princess Isabella of Castile and Prince Ferdinand of Aragon in 1469 led to the permanent union of their kingdoms into Spain a decade later when they inherited their respective thrones. Their conquest of Granada in 1492 secured the final piece of Muslim territory in Iberia for the new kingdom.

Coeur (cur)

Algarve (ahl-GAHRV)   **Ceuta** (say-OO-tuh)

The year 1492 was also memorable because of Ferdinand and Isabella's sponsorship of the voyage led by Christopher Columbus in search of the riches of the Indian Ocean (see Chapter 15). A third event that year also reflected Spain's crusading mentality. Less than three months after Granada's fall, the monarchs ordered all Jews to be expelled from their kingdoms. Efforts to force the remaining Muslims to convert or leave led to a Muslim revolt at the end of 1499 that was not put down until 1501. Portugal also began expelling Jews in 1493, including many thousands who had fled from Spain.

CONCLUSION

From an ecological perspective, the later medieval history of the Latin West is a story of triumphs and disasters. Westerners excelled in harnessing the inanimate forces of nature with their windmills, water wheels, and sails. They mined and refined the mineral wealth of the earth, although localized pollution and deforestation were among the results. But their inability to improve food production and distribution as rapidly as their population grew created a demographic crisis that became a demographic calamity when the Black Death swept through Europe in the mid-fourteenth century.

From a regional perspective, the period witnessed the coming together of the basic features of the modern West. States were of moderate size but had exceptional military capacity honed by frequent wars with one another. The ruling class, convinced that economic strength and political strength were inseparable, promoted the welfare of the urban populations that specialized in trade, manufacturing, and finance—and taxed their profits. Autonomous universities fostered intellectual excellence, and printing diffused the latest advances in knowledge. Art and architecture reached peaks of design and execution that set the standard for subsequent centuries. Perhaps most fundamentally, later medieval Europeans were fascinated by tools and techniques. In commerce, warfare, and industry, new inventions and improved versions of old ones underpinned the region's continuing dynamism.

From a global perspective, these centuries marked the Latin West's change from a region dependent on cultural and commercial flows from the East to a region poised to export its culture and impose its power on other parts of the world. It is one of history's great ironies that many of the tools that the Latin West used to challenge Eastern supremacy had originally been borrowed from the East. Medieval Europe's mills, printing, firearms, and navigational devices owed much to Eastern designs, just as its agriculture, alphabet, and numerals had in earlier times. Western European success depended as much on strong motives for expansion as on adequate means. Long before the first voyages overseas, population pressure, religious zeal, economic motives, and intellectual curiosity had expanded the territory and resources of the Latin West. From the late eleventh century onward such expansion of frontiers was notable in the English conquest of Celtic lands, in the establishment of crusader and commercial outposts in the eastern Mediterranean and Black Seas, in the massive German settlement east of the Elbe River, and in the reconquest of southern Iberia from the Muslims. The early voyages into the Atlantic were an extension of similar motives in a new direction.

■ Key Terms

Latin West	universities
three-field system	scholasticism
Black Death	humanists (Renaissance)
water wheel	printing press
Hanseatic League	Great Western Schism
guild	Hundred Years War
Gothic cathedral	new monarchies
Renaissance (European)	reconquest

■ Suggested Reading

A fine guide to the Latin West (including its ties to eastern Europe, Africa, and the Middle East) is Robert Fossier, ed., *The Cambridge Illustrated History of the Middle Ages*, vol. 3, *1250–1520* (1986). George Holmes, *Europe: Hierarchy and Revolt, 1320–1450*, 2d ed. (2000), and Denys Hay, *Europe in the Fourteenth and Fifteenth Centuries*, 2d ed. (1989), are comprehensive overviews. For the West's economic revival and growth, see Robert S. Lopez, *The Commercial Revolution of the Middle Ages, 950–1350* (1976), and Harry A. Miskimin, *The Economy of Early Renaissance Europe, 1300–1460* (1975). For greater detail see *The New Cambridge Medieval History*, vol. 6, *1300–c.1415*, ed. M. Jones (1998), and vol. 7, *1415–1500*, ed. C. Allmand (1999).

For fascinating primary sources see James Bruce Ross and Mary Martin McLaughlin, eds., *The Portable Medieval Reader* (1977) and *The Portable Renaissance Reader* (1977). *The Notebooks of Leonardo da Vinci*, ed. Pamela Taylor (1960), show this versatile genius at work.

Technological change is surveyed by Arnold Pacey, *The Maze of Ingenuity: Ideas and Idealism in the Development of Technology* (1974); Jean Gimpel, *The Medieval Machine: The Industrial Revolution of the Middle Ages* (1977); and William H. McNeill, *The Pursuit of Power: Technology, Armed Force, and Society Since A.D. 1000* (1982). For a key aspect of the environment see Roland Bechmann, *Trees and Man: The Forest in the Middle Ages* (1990).

Charles Homer Haskins, *The Rise of the Universities* (1923; reprint, 1957), is a brief, lighthearted introduction; more detailed and scholarly is Olef Pedersen, *The First Universities: Studium Generale and the Origins of University Education in Europe* (1998). Johan Huizinga, *The Waning of the Middle Ages* (1924), is the classic account of the "mind" of the fifteenth century. A multitude of works deal with the Renaissance, but few in any broad historical context. Lisa Jardine, *Worldly Goods: A New History of the Renaissance* (1996), is well illustrated and balanced; see also John R. Hale, *The Civilization of Europe in the Renaissance* (1995).

For social history see Georges Duby, *Rural Economy and Country Life in the Medieval West* (1990), for the earlier centuries. George Huppert, *After the Black Death: A Social History of Early Modern Europe* (1986), takes the analysis past 1500. Brief lives of individuals are found in Eileen Power, *Medieval People*, new ed. (1997), and Frances Gies and Joseph Gies, *Women in the Middle Ages* (1978). More systematic are the essays in Mary Erler and Maryanne Kowaleski, eds., *Women and Power in the Middle Ages* (1988). Vita Sackville-West, *Saint Joan of Arc* (1926; reprint, 1991), is a readable introduction to this extraordinary person.

Key events in the Anglo-French dynastic conflict are examined by Christopher Alland, *The Hundred Years War: England and France at War, ca. 1300–ca. 1450* (1988). Joseph F. O'Callaghan, *A History of Medieval Spain* (1975), provides the best one-volume coverage; for more detail see Jocelyn N. Hillgarth, *The Spanish Kingdoms*, 2 vols. (1976, 1978). Barbara W. Tuchman, *A Distant Mirror: The Calamitous 14th Century* (1978), is a popular account of the crises of that era. Norman F. Cantor, *In the Wake of the Plague: The Black Death and the World It Made* (2001), supplies a thorough introduction.

The Latin West's expansion is well treated by Robert Bartlett, *The Making of Europe: Conquest, Colonization, and Cultural Change* (1993); J. R. S. Phillips, *The Medieval Expansion of Europe*, 2d ed. (1998); and P. E. Russell, *Portugal, Spain and the African Atlantic, 1343–1492* (1998).

Francis C. Oakley, *The Western Church in the Later Middle Ages* (1985), is a reliable summary of modern scholarship. Kenneth R. Stow, *Alienated Minority: The Jews of Medieval Latin Europe* (1992), provides a fine survey up through the fourteenth century. For pioneering essays on the Latin West's external ties see Khalil I. Semaan, ed., *Islam and the Medieval West: Aspects of Intercultural Relations* (1980).

■ Notes

1. Quoted in Marina Warner, *Alone of All Her Sex: The Myth and Cult of the Virgin Mary* (New York: Random House, 1983), 179.
2. Harry Miskimin, *The Economy of the Early Renaissance, 1300–1460* (Englewood Cliffs, NJ: Prentice-Hall, 1969), 26–27.
3. Quotations here and later in the chapter are from Geoffrey Chaucer, *The Canterbury Tales*, trans. Nevill Coghill (New York: Penguin Books, 1952), 25, 29, 32.

Document-Based Question
Religion and Society in the Latin West, 1200–1500

Using the following documents, analyze the various ways that religious belief shaped Western European society from 1200 to 1500. Compare and contrast the effects of religious beliefs on men and women.

DOCUMENT 1
Excerpt from theologian Thomas Aquinas (p. 352)

DOCUMENT 2
Persecution and Protection of Jews, 1272–1349 (Diversity and Dominance, pp. 360–361)

DOCUMENT 3
Strasbourg Cathedral (photo, p. 362)

DOCUMENT 4
Early Clock (Environment and Technology, p. 363)

DOCUMENT 5
The Medici Family (photo, p. 367)

DOCUMENT 6
Map 14.3 Europe in 1453 (p. 369)

Which of the texts in Document 2 offers the most realistic view of the state of religious tolerance in late medieval Europe? What additional types of documents would help you understand how religious belief shaped Western European society in this period?

The Maritime Revolution, to 1550

15

Columbus Prepares to Cross the Atlantic, 1492 This later representation shows Columbus with the ships, soldiers, priests, and seamen that were part of Spain's enterprise.

CHAPTER OUTLINE

Global Maritime Expansion Before 1450

European Expansion, 1400–1550

Encounters with Europe, 1450–1550

ENVIRONMENT AND TECHNOLOGY: **Vasco da Gama's Fleet**

DIVERSITY AND DOMINANCE: **Kongo's Christian King**

In 1511 young Ferdinand Magellan sailed from Europe around the southern tip of Africa and eastward across the Indian Ocean as a member of the first Portuguese expedition to explore the East Indies (maritime Southeast Asia). Eight years later, this time in the service of Spain, he headed an expedition that sought to demonstrate the feasibility of reaching the East Indies by sailing westward from Europe. By the middle of 1521 Magellan's expedition had achieved its goal by sailing across the Atlantic, rounding the southern tip of South America, and crossing the Pacific Ocean—but at a high price.

One of the five ships that had set out from Spain in 1519 was wrecked on a reef, and the captain of another deserted and sailed back to Spain. The passage across the vast Pacific took much longer than anticipated, resulting in the deaths of dozens of sailors due to starvation and disease. In the Philippines, Magellan himself was killed on April 27, 1521, while aiding a local king who had promised to become a Christian. Magellan's successor met the same fate a few days later.

To consolidate their dwindling resources, the expedition's survivors burned the least seaworthy of their remaining three ships and transferred the men and supplies from that ship to the smaller *Victoria*, which continued westward across the Indian Ocean, around Africa, and back to Europe. Magellan's flagship, the *Trinidad*, tried unsuccessfully to recross the Pacific to Central America. The *Victoria*'s return to Spain on September 8, 1522, was a crowning example of Europeans' new ability and determination to make themselves masters of the oceans. A century of daring and dangerous voyages backed by the Portuguese crown had opened new routes through the South Atlantic to Africa, Brazil, and the rich trade of the Indian Ocean. Rival voyages sponsored by Spain since 1492 had opened new contacts with the American continents. Now the unexpectedly broad Pacific Ocean had been crossed as well. A maritime revolution was under way that would change the course of history.

That new maritime skill marked the end of an era in which the flow of historical influences tended to move from east to west. Before 1500 most overland and maritime expansion had come from Asia, as had the most useful technologies and the most influential systems of belief. Asia also had been home to the most powerful states and the richest trading networks. The Iberians set out on their voyages of exploration to reach Eastern markets, and their success began a new era in which the West gradually became the world's center of power, wealth, and innovation.

The maritime revolution created many new contacts, alliances, and conflicts. Some ended tragically for individuals like Magellan. Some were disastrous for entire populations: Amerindians, for instance, suffered conquest, colonization, and a rapid decline in numbers. Sometimes the results were mixed: Asians and Africans found both risks and opportunities in their new relations with the visitors from Europe.

As you read this chapter, ask yourself the following questions:

- Why did Portugal and Spain undertake voyages of exploration?

- Why do the voyages of Magellan and other Iberians mark a turning point in world history?

- What were the consequences for the different peoples of the world of the new contacts resulting from these voyages?

GLOBAL MARITIME EXPANSION BEFORE 1450

Since ancient times travel across the salt waters of the world's seas and oceans had been one of the great challenges to people's technological ingenuity. Ships had to be sturdy enough to survive heavy winds and waves, and pilots had to learn how to cross featureless expanses of water to reach their destinations. In time ships, sails, and navigational techniques perfected in the more protected seas were tried on the vast, open oceans.

However complex the solutions and dangerous the voyages, the rewards of sea travel made them worthwhile. Ships could move goods and people more quickly and cheaply than any form of overland travel then possible. Because of its challenges and rewards, sea travel attracted adventurers. To cross the unknown waters, find

C H R O N O L O G Y

	Pacific Ocean	Atlantic Ocean	Indian Ocean
1400	400–1300 Polynesian settlement of Pacific islands	770–1200 Viking voyages 1300s Settlement of Madeira, Azores, Canaries **Early 1300s** Mali voyages 1418–1460 Voyages of Henry the Navigator 1440s Slaves from West Africa 1482 Portuguese at Gold Coast and Kongo 1486 Portuguese at Benin 1488 Bartolomeu Dias reaches Indian Ocean 1492 Columbus reaches Caribbean 1492–1500 Spanish conquer Hispaniola 1493 Columbus returns to Caribbean (second voyage) 1498 Columbus reaches mainland of South America (third voyage)	1405–1433 Voyages of Zheng He 1497–1498 Vasco da Gama reaches India
1500	 1519–1522 Magellan expedition	1500 Cabral reaches Brazil 1513 Ponce de León explores Florida 1519–1520 Cortés conquers Aztec Empire 1531–1533 Pizarro conquers Inca Empire	1505 Portuguese bombard Swahili Coast cities 1510 Portuguese take Goa 1511 Portuguese take Malacca 1515 Portuguese take Hormuz 1535 Portuguese take Dui 1538 Portuguese defeat Ottoman fleet 1539 Portuguese aid Ethiopia

new lands, and open up new trade or settlements was an exciting prospect. For these reasons, some men on every continent had long turned their attention to the sea.

By 1450 much had been accomplished and much remained undone. Daring mariners had discovered and settled most of the islands of the Pacific, the Atlantic, and the Indian Oceans. The greatest success was the trading system that united the peoples around the Indian Ocean. But no individual had yet crossed the Pacific in either direction. Even the narrower Atlantic was a barrier that kept the peoples of the Americas, Europe, and Africa

in ignorance of each other's existence. The inhabitants of Australia were likewise completely cut off from contact with the rest of humanity. All this was about to change.

The Pacific Ocean

The voyages of Polynesian peoples out of sight of land over vast distances across the Pacific Ocean are one of the most impressive feats in maritime history before 1450 (see Map 15.1). Though they left no written records, over several thousand years

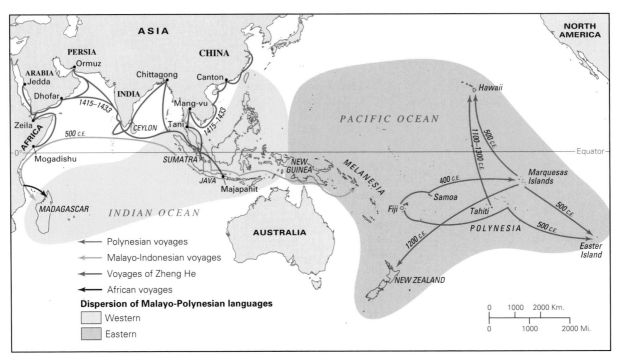

Map 15.1   Exploration and Settlement in the Indian and Pacific Oceans Before 1500   Over many centuries, mariners originating in Southeast Asia gradually colonized the islands of the Pacific and Indian Oceans. The Chinese voyages led by Zheng He in the fifteenth century were lavish official expeditions.

intrepid mariners from the Malay° Peninsula of Southeast Asia explored and settled the island chains of the East Indies and moved onto New Guinea and the smaller islands of Melanesia°. Beginning sometime before the Common Era (C.E.), a new wave of expansion from the area of Fiji brought the first humans to the islands of the central Pacific known as Polynesia. The easternmost of the Marquesas° Islands were reached about 400 C.E.; Easter Island, 2,200 miles (3,540 kilometers) off the coast of South America, was settled a century later. From the Marquesas, Polynesian sailors sailed to the Hawaiian Islands as early as 500 C.E. They settled New Zealand about 1200. Then, between 1100 and 1300, new voyages northward from Tahiti to Hawaii brought more Polynesian settlers across the more than 2,000 nautical miles (4,000 kilometers) to Hawaii.

Until recent decades some historians argued that Polynesians could have reached the eastern Pacific islands only by accident because they lacked navigational devices to plot their way. Others wondered how Polynesians could have overcome the difficulties, illustrated by

Magellan's flagship, *Trinidad*, of sailing eastward across the Pacific. In 1947 one energetic amateur historian of the sea, Thor Heyerdahl°, argued that Easter Island and Hawaii were actually settled from the Americas. He sought to prove his theory by sailing his balsa-wood raft, *Kon Tiki*, westward from Peru.

Although some Amerindian voyagers did use ocean currents to travel northward from Peru to Mexico between 300 and 900 C.E., there is now considerable evidence that the settlement of the islands of the eastern Pacific was the result of planned expansion by Polynesian mariners. The first piece of evidence is the fact that the languages of these islanders are all closely related to the languages of the western Pacific and ultimately to those of Malaya. The second is the finding that accidental voyages could not have brought sufficient numbers of men and women for founding a new colony along with all the plants and domesticated animals that were basic to other Polynesian islands.

In 1976 a Polynesian crew led by Ben Finney used traditional navigational methods to sail an ocean canoe from Hawaii south to Tahiti. The *Hokulea* was a 62-foot-

---

Malay (May-LAY)   **Melanesia** (mel-uh-NEE-zhuh)
Marquesas (mar-KAY-suhs)

Heyerdahl (HIGH-uhr-dahl)

Polynesian Canoes   Pacific Ocean mariners sailing canoes such as these, shown in an eighteenth-century painting, made epic voyages of exploration and settlement. A large platform connects two canoes at the left, providing more room for the members of the expedition, and a sail supplements the paddlers.   ("Tereoboo, King of Owyhee, bringing presents to Captain Cook," D. L. Ref. p. xx 2f. 35. Courtesy, The Dixon Library, State Library of New South Wales)

long (19-meter-long) double canoe patterned after old oceangoing canoes, which sometimes were as long as 120 feet (37 meters). Not only did the *Hokulea* prove seaworthy, but, powered by an inverted triangular sail and steered by paddles (not by a rudder), it was able to sail across the winds at a sharp enough angle to make the difficult voyage, just as ancient mariners must have done. Perhaps even more remarkable, the *Hokulea*'s crew was able to navigate to their destination using only their observation of the currents, stars, and evidence of land.

The Indian Ocean

While Polynesian mariners were settling Pacific islands, other Malayo-Indonesians were sailing westward across the Indian Ocean and colonizing the large island of Madagascar off the southeastern coast of Africa. These voyages continued through the fifteenth century. To this day the inhabitants of Madagascar speak Malayo-Polynesian languages. However, part of the island's population is descended from Africans who had crossed the 300 miles (500 kilometers) from the mainland to Madagascar, most likely in the centuries leading up to 1500.

Other peoples had been using the Indian Ocean for trade since ancient times. The landmasses of Southeast Asia and eastern Africa that enclose the Indian Ocean on each side, and the Indian subcontinent that juts into its middle, provided coasts that seafarers might safely follow and coves for protection. Moreover, seasonal winds known as monsoons are so predictable and steady that navigation using sailing vessels called dhows° was less difficult and dangerous in ancient times than elsewhere.

The rise of medieval Islam gave Indian Ocean trade an important boost. The great Muslim cities of the Middle East provided a demand for valuable commodities. Even more important were the networks of Muslim traders that tied the region together. Muslim traders shared a common language, ethic, and law and actively spread their religion to distant trading cities. By 1400 there were Muslim trading communities all around the Indian Ocean.

The Indian Ocean traders operated largely independently of the empires and states they served, but in East Asia imperial China's rulers were growing more and more interested in these wealthy ports of trade. In 1368

dhow (dow)

Chinese Junk   This modern drawing shows how much larger one of Zheng He's ships was than one of Vasco da Gama's vessels. Watertight interior bulkheads made junks the most seaworthy large ships of the fifteenth century. Sails made of pleated bamboo matting hung from the junk's masts, and a stern rudder provided steering. European ships of exploration, though smaller, were faster and more maneuverable.   (Dugald Stermer)

the Ming dynasty overthrew Mongol rule and began expansionist policies to reestablish China's predominance and prestige abroad.

Having restored Chinese dominance in East Asia, the Ming next moved to establish direct contacts with the peoples around the Indian Ocean. In choosing to send out seven imperial fleets between 1405 and 1433, the Ming may have been motivated partly by curiosity. The fact that most of the ports the fleets visited were important in the Indian Ocean trade suggests that enhancing China's commerce was also a motive. Yet because the expeditions were far larger than needed for exploration or promoting trade, their main purpose probably was to inspire awe of Ming power and achievements.

The Ming expeditions into the Indian Ocean basin were launched on a scale that reflected imperial China's resources and importance. The first consisted of sixty-two specially built "treasure ships," large Chinese junks each about 300 feet long by 150 feet wide (90 by 45 meters). There were also at least a hundred smaller vessels, most of which were larger than the flagship in which Columbus later sailed across the Atlantic. Each treasure ship had nine masts, twelve sails, many decks, and a car-

rying capacity of 3,000 tons (six times the capacity of Columbus's entire fleet). One expedition carried over 27,000 individuals, including infantry and cavalry troops. The ships would have been armed with small cannon, but in most Chinese sea battles arrows from highly accurate crossbows dominated the fighting.

At the command of the expeditions was Admiral **Zheng He°** (1371–1435). A Chinese Muslim with ancestral connections to the Persian Gulf, Zheng was a fitting emissary to the increasingly Muslim-dominated Indian Ocean basin. The expeditions carried other Arabic-speaking Chinese as interpreters.

One of these interpreters kept a journal recording the customs, dress, and beliefs of the people visited, along with the trade, towns, and animals of their countries. He observed exotic animals such as the black panther of Malaya and the tapir of Sumatra; beliefs in legendary "corpse headed barbarians" whose heads left their bodies at night and caused infants to die; the division of coastal Indians into five classes, which correspond to the four Hindu varna and a separate Muslim class; and the fact

Zheng He (jung huh)

that traders in the rich Indian trading port of Calicut° could perform error-free calculations by counting on their fingers and toes rather than using the Chinese abacus. After his return, the interpreter went on tour in China, telling of these exotic places and "how far the majestic virtue of [China's] imperial dynasty extended."[1]

The Chinese "treasure ships" carried rich silks, precious metals, and other valuable goods intended as gifts for distant rulers. In return those rulers sent back gifts of equal or greater value to the Chinese emperor. Although the main purpose of these exchanges was diplomatic, they also stimulated trade between China and its southern neighbors. For that reason they were welcomed by Chinese merchants and manufacturers. Yet commercial profits could not have offset the huge cost of the fleets.

Interest in new contacts was not confined to the Chinese side. In 1415–1416 at least three trading cities on the Swahili° Coast of East Africa sent delegations to China. The delegates from one of them, Malindi, presented the emperor of China with a giraffe, creating quite a stir among the normally reserved imperial officials. Such African delegations may have encouraged more contacts, for the next three of Zheng's voyages were extended to the African coast. Unfortunately, no documents record how Africans and Chinese reacted to each other during these historic meetings between 1417 and 1433. It appears that China's lavish gifts stimulated the Swahili market for silk and porcelain. An increase in Chinese imports of pepper from southern Asian lands also resulted from these expeditions.

Had the Ming court wished to promote trade for the profit of its merchants, Chinese fleets might have continued to play a dominant role in Indian Ocean trade. But some high Chinese officials opposed increased contact with peoples whom they regarded as barbarians with no real contribution to make to China. Such opposition caused a suspension in the voyages from 1424 to 1431, and after the final expedition of 1432 to 1433, no new fleets were sent out. Later Ming emperors focused their attention on internal matters in their vast empire. China's withdrawal left a power vacuum in the Indian Ocean.

The Atlantic Ocean

The greatest mariners of the Atlantic in the early Middle Ages were the Vikings. These northern European raiders and pirates used their small, open ships to attack coastal European settlements for several centuries. They also dis-

covered and settled one island after another in the North Atlantic during these warmer than usual centuries. Like the Polynesians, the Vikings had neither maps nor navigational devices, but they managed to find their way wonderfully well using their knowledge of the heavens and the seas.

The Vikings first settled Iceland in 770. From there some moved to Greenland in 982, and by accident one group sighted North America in 986. Fifteen years later Leif Ericsson established a short-lived Viking settlement on the island of Newfoundland, which he called Vinland. When a colder climate returned after 1200, the northern settlements in Greenland went into decline, and Vinland became only a mysterious place mentioned in Norse sagas.

Some southern Europeans also used the maritime skills they had acquired in the Mediterranean and coastal Atlantic to explore the Atlantic. In 1291 two Vivaldo brothers from Genoa set out to sail through the South Atlantic and around Africa to India. They were never heard of again. Other Genoese and Portuguese expeditions into the Atlantic in the fourteenth century discovered (and settled) the islands of Madeira°, the Azores°, and the Canaries.

There is also written evidence of African voyages of exploration in the Atlantic in this period. The celebrated Syrian geographer al-Umari (1301–1349) relates that when Mansa Kankan Musa°, the ruler of the West African empire of Mali, passed through Egypt on his lavish pilgrimage to Mecca in 1324, he told of voyages to cross the Atlantic undertaken by his predecessor, Mansa Muhammad. Muhammad had sent out four hundred vessels with men and supplies, telling them, "Do not return until you have reached the other side of the ocean or if you have exhausted your food or water." After a long time one canoe returned, reporting that the others had been swept away by a "violent current in the middle of the sea." Muhammad himself then set out at the head of a second, even larger, expedition, from which no one returned.

In addition to sailing up the Pacific coast, early Amerindian voyagers from South America also colonized the West Indies. By the year 1000 Amerindians known as the **Arawak**° had moved up from the small islands of the Lesser Antilles (Barbados, Martinique, and Guadeloupe) into the Greater Antilles (Cuba, Hispaniola, Jamaica, and Puerto Rico) as well as into the Bahamas

Calicut (KAL-ih-kut)   Swahili (swah-HEE-lee)

Madeira (muh-DEER-uh)   Azores (A-zorz)
Mansa Kankan Musa (MAHN-suh KAHN-kahn MOO-suh)
Arawak (AR-uh-wahk)

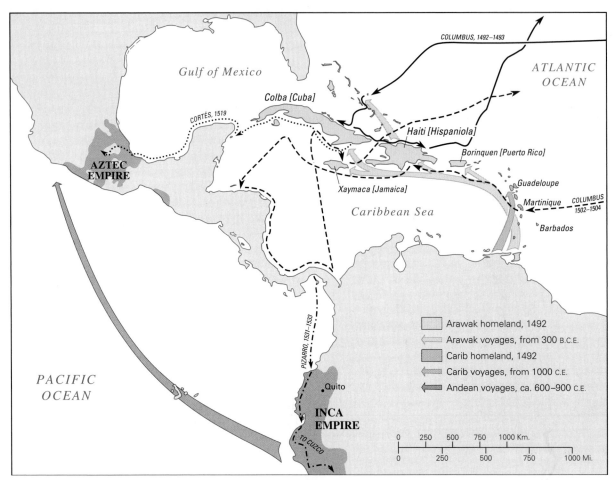

Map 15.2 Middle America to 1533   Early Amerindian voyages from South America brought new settlers to the West Indies and western Mexico. The arrival of Europeans in 1492 soon led to the conquest and depopulation of Amerindians.

(see Map 15.2). The Carib followed the same route in later centuries and by the late fifteenth century had overrun most Arawak settlements in the Lesser Antilles and were raiding parts of the Greater Antilles. From the West Indies Arawak and Carib also undertook voyages to the North American mainland.

EUROPEAN EXPANSION, 1400–1550

The preceding survey shows that maritime expansion occurred in many parts of the world before 1450. The epic sea voyages sponsored by the Iberian kingdoms of Portugal and Spain are of special interest because they began a maritime revolution that profoundly altered the course of world history. The Portuguese and Spanish expeditions ended the isolation of the Americas and increased global interaction. The influence in world affairs of the Iberians and other Europeans who followed them overseas rose steadily in the centuries after 1500.

Iberian overseas expansion was the product of two related phenomena. First, Iberian rulers had strong economic, religious, and political motives to expand their contacts and increase their dominance. Second, improvements in their maritime and military technologies gave them the means to master treacherous and unfamiliar ocean environments, seize control of existing maritime trade routes, and conquer new lands.

Motives for Exploration

Why did Iberian kingdoms decide to sponsor voyages of exploration in the fifteenth century? Part of the answer lies in the individual ambitions and adventurous personalities of these states' leaders. Another part of the answer can be found in long-term tendencies in Europe and the Mediterranean. In many ways these voyages continued four trends evident in the Latin West since about the year 1000: (1) the revival of urban life and trade, (2) a struggle with Islamic powers for dominance of the Mediterranean that mixed religious motives with the desire for trade with distant lands, (3) growing intellectual curiosity about the outside world, and (4) a peculiarly European alliance between merchants and rulers.

The city-states of northern Italy took the lead in all these developments. By 1450 they had well-established trade links to northern Europe, the Indian Ocean, and the Black Sea, and their merchant princes had also sponsored an intellectual and artistic Renaissance. But there were two reasons why Italian states did not take the lead in exploring the Atlantic, even after the expansion of the Ottoman Empire disrupted their trade to the East and led other Christian Europeans to launch new religious wars against the Ottomans in 1396 and 1444. The first was that the trading states of Venice and Genoa preferred to continue the system of alliances with the Muslims that had given their merchants privileged access to the lucrative trade from the East. The second was that the ships of the Mediterranean were ill suited to the more violent weather of the Atlantic. However, many individual Italians played leading roles in the Atlantic explorations.

In contrast, the special history and geography of the Iberian kingdoms led them in a different direction. Part of that special history was centuries of anti-Muslim warfare that dated back to the eighth century, when Muslim forces overran most of Iberia. By about 1250 the Iberian kingdoms of Portugal, Castile, and Aragon had conquered all the Muslim lands in Iberia except the southern kingdom of Granada. United by a dynastic marriage in 1469, Castile and Aragon conquered Granada in 1492. These territories were gradually amalgamated into Spain, sixteenth-century Europe's most powerful state.

Christian militancy continued to be an important motive for both Portugal and Spain in their overseas ventures. But the Iberian rulers and their adventurous subjects were also seeking material returns. With only a modest share of the Mediterranean trade, they were much more willing than the Italians to take risks to find new routes through the Atlantic to the rich trade of Africa and Asia. Moreover, both were participants in the shipbuilding changes and the gunpowder revolution that were under way in Atlantic Europe. Though not centers of Renaissance learning, both were especially open to new geographical knowledge. Finally, both states were blessed with exceptional leaders.

Portuguese Voyages

Portugal's decision to invest significant resources in new exploration rested on well-established Atlantic fishing and a history of anti-Muslim warfare. When the Muslim government of Morocco in northwestern Africa showed weakness in the fifteenth century, the Portuguese went on the attack, beginning with the city of Ceuta° in 1415. This assault combined aspects of a religious crusade, a plundering expedition, and a military tournament in which young Portuguese knights displayed their bravery. The capture of the rich North African city, whose splendid homes, they reported, made those of Portugal look like pigsties, also made the Portuguese better informed about the caravans that brought gold and slaves to Ceuta from the African states south of the Sahara. Despite the capture of several more ports along Morocco's Atlantic coast, the Portuguese were unable to push inland and gain access to the gold trade. So they sought more direct contact with the gold producers by sailing down the African coast.

The attack on Ceuta was led by young Prince Henry (1394–1460), third son of the king of Portugal. Because he devoted the rest of his life to promoting exploration of the South Atlantic, he is known as **Henry the Navigator**. His official biographer emphasized Henry's mixed motives for exploration—converting Africans to Christianity, making contact with existing Christian rulers in Africa, and launching joint crusades with them against the Ottomans. Prince Henry also wished to discover new places and hoped that such new contacts would be profitable. His initial explorations were concerned with Africa. Only later did reaching India become an explicit goal of Portuguese explorers.

Despite being called "the Navigator," Prince Henry himself never ventured much farther from home than North Africa. Instead, he founded a sort of research institute at Sagres° for studying navigation and collecting information about the lands beyond Muslim North Africa. His staff drew on the pioneering efforts of Italian merchants, especially the Genoese, who had learned some of the secrets of the trans-Saharan trade, and of fourteenth-century Jewish cartographers who used information from Arab and European sources to produce remarkably

---

Ceuta (say-OO-tuh)   **Sagres** (SAH-gresh)

accurate sea charts and maps of distant places. Henry also oversaw the collection of new geographical information from sailors and travelers and sent out ships to explore the Atlantic. His ships established permanent contact with the islands of Madeira in 1418 and the Azores in 1439.

Henry devoted resources to solving the technical problems faced by mariners sailing in unknown waters and open seas. His staff studied and improved navigational instruments that had come into Europe from China and the Islamic world. These instruments included the magnetic compass, first developed in China, and the astrolabe, an instrument of Arab or Greek invention that enabled mariners to determine their location at sea by measuring the position of the sun or the stars in the night sky. Even with such instruments, however, voyages still depended on the skill and experience of the navigators.

Another achievement of Portuguese mariners was the design of vessels appropriate for the voyages of exploration. The galleys in use in the Mediterranean were powered by large numbers of oarsmen and were impractical for long ocean voyages. The square sails of the three-masted European ships of the North Atlantic were propelled by friendly winds but could not sail at much of an angle against the wind. The voyages of exploration made use of a new vessel, the **caravel°**. Caravels were small, only one-fifth the size of the largest European ships of their day and of the large Chinese junks. Their size permitted them to enter shallow coastal waters and explore upriver, but they were strong enough to weather ocean storms. When equipped with lateen sails, caravels had great maneuverability and could sail deeply into the wind; when sporting square Atlantic sails, they had great speed. The addition of small cannon made them good fighting ships as well. The caravels' economy, speed, agility, and power justified a contemporary's claim that they were "the best ships that sailed the seas."[2]

To conquer the seas, pioneering captains had to overcome crew's fears that the South Atlantic waters were boiling hot and contained ocean currents that would prevent any ship entering them from ever returning home. It took Prince Henry fourteen years—from 1420 to 1434—to coax an expedition to venture beyond southern Morocco (see Map 15.3). The crew's fears proved unfounded, but the next stretch of coast, 800 miles (1,300 kilometers) of desert, offered little of interest to the explorers. Finally, in 1444 the mariners reached the Senegal River and the well-watered and well-populated lands below the Sahara beginning at what they named "Cape Verde" (Green Cape) because of its vegetation.

In the years that followed, Henry's explorers made an important addition to the maritime revolution by learning how to return speedily to Portugal. Instead of battling the prevailing northeast trade winds and currents back up the coast, they discovered that by sailing northwest into the Atlantic to the latitude of the Azores, ships could pick up prevailing westerly winds that would blow them back to Portugal. The knowledge that ocean winds tend to form large circular patterns helped explorers discover many other ocean routes.

To pay for the research, the ships, and the expeditions during the many decades before the voyages became profitable, Prince Henry drew partly on the income of the Order of Christ, a military religious order of which he was governor. The Order of Christ had inherited the properties and crusading traditions of the Order of Knights Templar, which had disbanded in 1314. The Order of Christ received the exclusive right to promote Christianity in all the lands that were discovered, and the Portuguese emblazoned their ships' sails with the crusaders' red cross.

The first financial return from the voyages came from selling into slavery Africans captured by the Portuguese in raids on the northwest coast of Africa and the Canary Islands during the 1440s. The total number of Africans captured or purchased on voyages exceeded eighty thousand by the end of the century and rose steadily thereafter. However, the gold trade quickly became more important than the slave trade as the Portuguese made contact with the trading networks that flourished in West Africa and reached across the Sahara. By 1457 enough African gold was coming back to Portugal for the kingdom to issue a new gold coin called the *cruzado* (crusade), another reminder of how deeply the Portuguese entwined religious and secular motives.

By the time of Prince Henry's death in 1460, his explorers had established a secure base of operations in the uninhabited Cape Verde Islands and had explored 600 miles (950 kilometers) of coast beyond Cape Verde, as far as what they named Sierra Leone° (Lion Mountain). From there they knew the coast of Africa curved sharply toward the east. It had taken the Portuguese four decades to cover the 1,500 miles (2,400 kilometers) from Lisbon to Sierra Leone; it took only three decades to explore the remaining 4,000 miles (6,400 kilometers) to the southern tip of the African continent.

The Portuguese crown continued to sponsor voyages of exploration, but speedier progress resulted from the growing participation of private commercial interests. In 1469 a prominent Lisbon merchant named

---

caravel (KAR-uh-vel)

Sierra Leone (see- ER-uh lee-OWN)

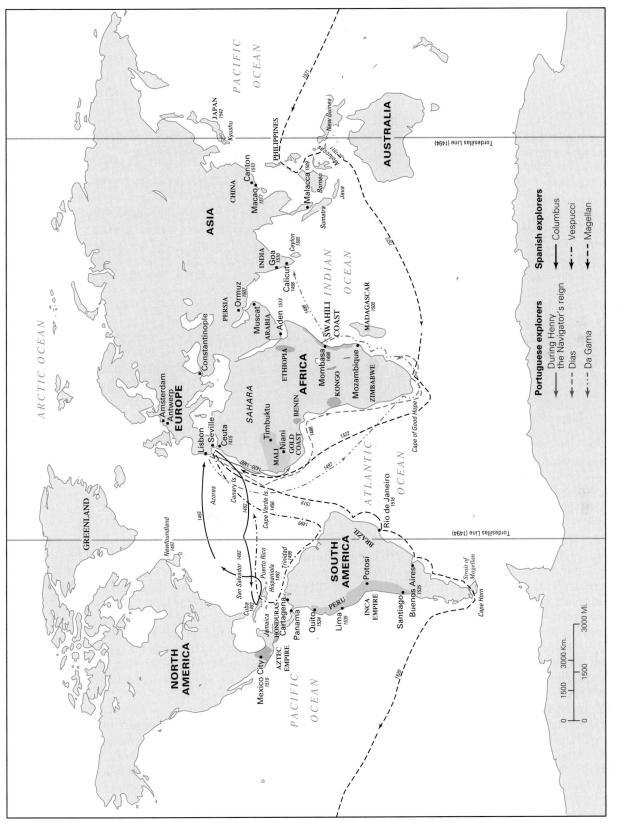

Map 15.3   European Exploration, 1420–1542   Portuguese and Spanish explorers showed the possibility and practicality of intercontinental maritime trade. Before 1540 European trade with Africa and Asia was much more important than that with the Americas,
but after the Spanish conquest of the Aztec and Inca Empires transatlantic trade began to increase. Notice the Tordesillas line, which
in theory separated the Spanish and Portuguese spheres of activity.

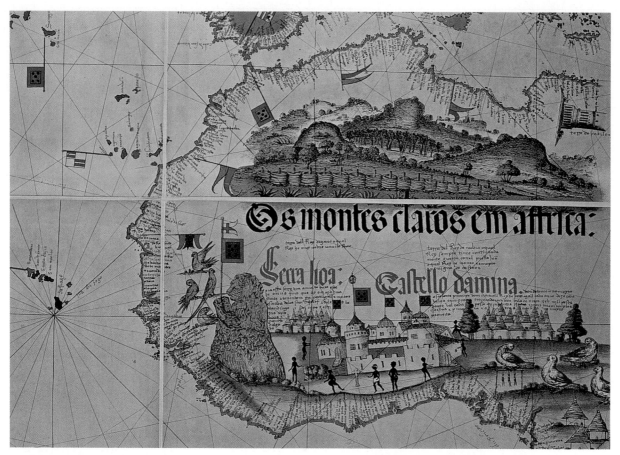

Portuguese Map of Western Africa, 1502 This map shows in great detail a section of African coastline that Portuguese explorers charted and named in the fifteenth century. The cartographer illustrated the African interior, which was almost completely unknown to Europeans, with drawings of birds and views of coastal sights: Sierra Leone (Serra lioa), named for a mountain shaped like a lion, and the Portuguese Castle of the Mine (Castello damina) on the Gold Coast. (akg-images)

Fernão Gomes purchased from the Crown the privilege of exploring 350 miles (550 kilometers) of new coast a year for five years in return for a monopoly on the trade he developed there. During the period of his contract, Gomes discovered the uninhabited island of São Tomé° on the equator; in the next century it became a major source of sugar produced with African slave labor. He also explored what later Europeans called the **Gold Coast**, which became the headquarters of Portugal's West African trade.

The final thrust down the African coast was spurred by the expectation of finding a passage around Africa to the rich trade of the Indian Ocean. In 1488 **Bartolomeu Dias** was the first Portuguese explorer to round the southern tip of Africa and enter the Indian Ocean. In 1497–1498 a Portuguese expedition led by **Vasco da Gama** sailed around Africa and reached India (see Environment and Technology: Vasco da Gama's Fleet). In 1500 ships in an expedition under Pedro Alvares Cabral°, while swinging wide to the west in the South Atlantic to catch the winds that would sweep them around southern Africa and on to India, came on the eastern coast of South America, laying the basis for Portugal's later claim to Brazil. The gamble that Prince Henry had begun eight decades earlier was about to pay off handsomely.

Spanish Voyages

In contrast to the persistence and planning behind Portugal's century-long exploration of the South Atlantic, haste and blind luck lay behind Spain's early discoveries. Throughout most of the fifteenth cen-

São Tomé (sow toh-MAY)

Cabral (kah-BRAHL)

Vasco da Gama's Fleet

The four small ships that sailed for India from Lisbon in June 1497 may seem a puny fleet compared to the sixty-two Chinese vessels that Zheng He had led into the Indian Ocean ninety-five years earlier. But given the fact that China had a hundred times as many people as Portugal, Vasco da Gama's fleet represented at least as great a commitment of resources. In any event, the Portuguese expedition had a far greater impact on the course of history. Having achieved its aim of inspiring awe at China's greatness, the Chinese throne sent out no more expeditions after 1432. Although da Gama's ships seemed more odd than awesome to Indian Ocean observers, that modest fleet began a revolution in global relations.

Portugal spared no expense in ensuring that the fleet would make it to India and back. Craftsmen built extra strength into the hulls to withstand the powerful storms that Dias had encountered in 1488 at the tip of Africa. Small enough to be able to navigate any shallow harbors and rivers they might encounter, the ships were crammed with specially strengthened casks and barrels of water, wine, oil, flour, meat, and vegetables far in excess of what was required even on a voyage that would take the better part of a year. Arms and ammunition were also in abundance.

Three of da Gama's ships were rigged with square sails on two masts for speed and a lateen sail on the third mast. The fourth vessel was a caravel with lateen sails. Each ship carried three sets of sails and plenty of extra rigging so as to be able to repair any damages due to storms. The crusaders' red crosses on the sails signaled one of the expedition's motives.

The captains and crew—Portugal's most talented and experienced—received extra pay and other rewards for their service. Yet there was no expectation that the unprecedented sums spent on this expedition would bring any immediate return. According to a contemporary chronicle, the only immediate return the Portuguese monarch received was

Vasco da Gama's Flagship   This vessel carried the Portuguese captain on his second expedition to India in 1505.   (The Pierpont Morgan Library/Art Resource, NY)

"the knowledge that some part of Ethiopia and the beginning of Lower India had been discovered." However, the scale and care of the preparations suggest that the Portuguese expected the expedition to open up profitable trade to the Indian Ocean. And so it did.

tury, the Spanish kingdoms had been preoccupied with internal affairs: completion of the reconquest of southern Iberia; amalgamation of the various dynasties; and the conversion or expulsion of religious minorities. Only in the last decade of the century were Spanish monarchs ready to turn again to overseas exploration, by which time the Portuguese had already found a new route to the Indian Ocean.

The leader of their overseas mission was **Christopher Columbus** (1451–1506), a Genoese mariner. His four voyages between 1492 and 1502 established the existence of a vast new world across the Atlantic, whose existence few in "old world" Eurasia and Africa had ever suspected. But Columbus refused to accept that he had found unknown continents and peoples, insisting that he had succeeded in his goal of finding a shorter route to the Indian Ocean than the one the Portuguese had found.

As a younger man Columbus had gained considerable experience of the South Atlantic while participating in Portuguese explorations along the African coast, but he had become convinced there was a shorter way to reach the riches of the East than the route around Africa. By his reckoning (based on a serious misreading of a ninth-century Arab authority), the Canaries were a mere 2,400 nautical miles (4,450 kilometers) from Japan. The actual distance was five times as far.

It was not easy for Columbus to find a sponsor willing to underwrite the costs of testing his theory that one could reach Asia by sailing west. Portuguese authorities twice rejected his plan, first in 1485 following a careful study and again in 1488 after Dias had established the feasibility of a route around Africa. Columbus received a more sympathetic hearing in 1486 from Castile's able ruler, Queen Isabella, but no commitment of support. After a four-year study a Castilian commission appointed by Isabella concluded that a westward sea route to the Indies rested on many questionable geographical assumptions, but Columbus's persistence finally won over the queen and her husband, King Ferdinand of Aragon. In 1492 they agreed to fund a modest expedition. Their elation at expelling the Muslims from Granada may have put them in a favorable mood.

Columbus recorded in his log that he and his mostly Spanish crew of ninety men "departed Friday the third day of August of the year 1492," toward "the regions of India." Their mission, the royal contract stated, was "to discover and acquire certain islands and mainland in the Ocean Sea." He carried letters of introduction from the Spanish sovereigns to Eastern rulers, including one to the "Grand Khan" (meaning the Chinese emperor). Also on board was a Jewish convert to Christianity whose knowledge of Arabic was expected to facilitate communication with the peoples of eastern Asia. The expedition traveled in three small ships, the *Santa María*, the *Santa Clara* (nicknamed the *Niña*), and a third vessel now known only by its nickname, the *Pinta*. The *Niña* and the *Pinta* were caravels.

The expedition began well. Other attempts to explore the Atlantic west of the Azores had been impeded by unfavorable headwinds. But on earlier voyages along the African coast, Columbus had learned that he could find west-blowing winds in the latitudes of the Canaries, which is why he chose that southern route. After reaching the Canaries, he had the *Niña's* lateen sails replaced with square sails, for he knew that from then on speed would be more important than maneuverability.

In October 1492 the expedition reached the islands of the Caribbean. Columbus insisted on calling the inhabitants "Indians" because he believed that the islands were part of the East Indies. A second voyage to the Caribbean in 1493 did nothing to change his mind. Even when, two months after Vasco da Gama reached India in 1498, Columbus first sighted the mainland of South America on a third voyage, he stubbornly insisted it was part of Asia. But by then other Europeans were convinced that he had discovered islands and continents previously unknown to the Old World. Amerigo Vespucci's explorations, first on behalf of Spain and then for Portugal, led mapmakers to name the new continents "America" after him, rather than "Columbia" after Columbus.

To prevent disputes arising from their efforts to exploit their new discoveries and to spread Christianity among the people there, Spain and Portugal agreed to split the world between them. Modifying an earlier papal proposal, the Treaty of Tordesillas° of 1494 drew an imaginary line down the middle of the North Atlantic Ocean. Lands east of the line in Africa and southern Asia could be claimed by Portugal; lands to the west in the Americas were reserved for Spain. Cabral's discovery of Brazil, however, gave Portugal a valid claim to the part of South America that bulged east of the line.

But if the Tordesillas line were extended around the earth, where would Spain's and Portugal's spheres of influence divide in the East? Given Europeans' ignorance of the earth's true size in 1494, it was not clear whether the Moluccas°, whose valuable spices had been a goal of the Iberian voyages, were on Portugal's or Spain's side of the line. The missing information concerned the size of the Pacific Ocean. By chance, in 1513 a Spanish adventurer named Vasco Núñez de Balboa° crossed the

---

Tordesillas (tor-duh-SEE-yuhs)   **Moluccas** (muh-LOO-kuhz)
Balboa (bal-BOH-uh)

isthmus (a narrow neck of land) of Panama from the east and sighted the Pacific Ocean on the other side. And the 1519 expedition of **Ferdinand Magellan** (ca. 1480–1521) was designed to complete Columbus's interrupted westward voyage by sailing around the Americas and across the Pacific, whose vast size no European then guessed. The Moluccas turned out to lie well within Portugal's sphere, as Spain formally acknowledged in 1529.

Magellan's voyage laid the basis for Spanish colonization of the Philippine Islands after 1564. Nor did Magellan's death prevent him from being considered the first person to encircle the globe, for a decade earlier he had sailed from Europe to the East Indies as part of an expedition sponsored by his native Portugal. His two voyages took him across the Tordesillas line, through the separate spheres claimed by Portugal and Spain—at least until other Europeans began demanding a share. Of course, in 1500 European claims were largely theoretical. Portugal and Spain had only modest settlements overseas.

Although Columbus failed to find a new route to the East, the consequences of his voyages for European expansion were momentous. Those who followed in his wake laid the basis for Spain's large colonial empires in the Americas and for the empires of other European nations. In turn, these empires promoted, among the four Atlantic continents, the growth of a major new trading network whose importance rivaled and eventually surpassed that of the Indian Ocean network. The more immediately important consequence was Portugal's entry into the Indian Ocean, which quickly led to a major European presence and profit. Both the eastward and the westward voyages of exploration marked a tremendous expansion of Europe's role in world history.

ENCOUNTERS WITH EUROPE, 1450–1550

European actions alone did not determine the consequences of the new contacts that Iberian mariners had opened. The ways in which Africans, Asians, and Amerindians perceived their new visitors and interacted with them also influenced their future relations. Some welcomed the Europeans as potential allies; others viewed them as rivals or enemies. In general, Africans and Asians had little difficulty in recognizing the benefits and dangers that European contacts might bring. However, the long isolation of the Amerindians from the rest of the world added to the strangeness of their encounter

with the Spanish and made them more vulnerable to the unfamiliar diseases that these explorers inadvertently introduced.

Western Africa

Many Africans along the West African coast were eager for trade with the Portuguese. It would give them new markets for their exports and access to imports cheaper than those that reached them through the middlemen of the overland routes to the Mediterranean. This reaction was evident along the Gold Coast of West Africa, first visited by the Portuguese in 1471. Miners in the hinterland had long sold their gold to African traders, who took it to the trading cities along the southern edge of the Sahara, where it was sold to traders who had crossed the desert from North Africa. Recognizing that they might get more favorable terms from the new sea visitors, coastal Africans were ready to negotiate with the royal representative of Portugal who arrived in 1482 seeking permission to erect a trading fort.

The Portuguese noble in charge and his officers (likely including the young Christopher Columbus, who had entered Portuguese service in 1476) were eager to make a proper impression. They dressed in their best clothes, erected and decorated a reception platform, celebrated a Catholic Mass, and signaled the start of negotiations with trumpets, tambourines, and drums. The African king, Caramansa, staged his entrance with equal ceremony, arriving with a large retinue of attendants and musicians. Through an African interpreter, the two leaders exchanged flowery speeches pledging goodwill and mutual benefit. Caramansa then gave his permission for a small trading fort to be built, assured, he said, by the appearance of these royal delegates that they were honorable persons, unlike the "few, foul, and vile" Portuguese visitors of the previous decade.

Neither side made a show of force, but the Africans' upper hand was evident in Caramansa's warning that if the Portuguese failed to be peaceful and honest traders, he and his people would simply move away, depriving their post of food and trade. Trade at the post of Saint George of the Mine (later called Elmina) enriched both sides. From there the Portuguese crown was soon purchasing gold equal to one-tenth of the world's production at the time. In return, Africans received large quantities of goods that Portuguese ships brought from Asia, Europe, and other parts of Africa.

After a century of aggressive expansion, the kingdom of Benin in the Niger Delta was near the peak of its power when it first encountered the Portuguese. Its oba (king) presided over an elaborate bureaucracy from a spacious palace in his large capital city, also known as Benin. In response to a Portuguese visit in 1486, the oba sent an ambassador to Portugal to learn more about the homeland of these strangers. Then he established a royal monopoly on trade with the Portuguese, selling pepper and ivory tusks (to be taken back to Portugal) as well as stone beads, textiles, and prisoners of war (to be resold at Elmina). In return, the Portuguese merchants provided Benin with copper and brass, fine textiles, glass beads, and a horse for the king's royal procession. In the early sixteenth century, as the demand for slaves for the Portuguese sugar plantations on the nearby island of São Tomé grew, the oba first raised the price of slaves and then imposed restrictions that limited their sale.

Early contacts generally involved a mixture of commercial, military, and religious interests. Some African rulers were quick to appreciate that the European firearms could be a useful addition to their spears and arrows in conflicts with their enemies. Because African religions did not presume to have a monopoly on religious knowledge, coastal rulers were also willing to test the value of Christian practices, which the Portuguese eagerly promoted. The rulers of Benin and Kongo, the two largest coastal kingdoms, invited Portuguese missionaries and soldiers to accompany them into battle to test the Christians' religion along with their muskets.

Portuguese efforts to persuade the king and nobles of Benin to accept the Catholic faith ultimately failed. Early kings showed some interest, but after 1538 the rulers declined to receive any more missionaries. They also closed the market in male slaves for the rest of the sixteenth century. Exactly why Benin chose to limit its contacts with the Portuguese is uncertain, but the rulers clearly had the power to control the amount of interaction.

Farther south, on the lower Congo River, relations between the kingdom of Kongo and the Portuguese began similarly but had a very different outcome. Like the oba of Benin, the manikongo° (king of Kongo) sent delegates to Portugal, established a royal monopoly on trade with the Portuguese, and expressed interest in missionary teachings. Deeply impressed with the new religion, the royal family made Catholicism the kingdom's official faith. But Kongo, lacking ivory and pepper, had less to trade than Benin. To acquire the goods brought by Portugal and to pay the costs of the missionaries, it had to sell more and more slaves.

Soon the manikongo began to lose his royal monopoly over the slave trade. In 1526 the Christian manikongo, Afonso I (r. 1506–ca. 1540), wrote to his royal

---

manikongo (mah-NEE-KONG-goh)

Afro-Portuguese Ivory   A skilled ivory carver from the kingdom of Benin probably made this saltcellar. Intended for a European market, it depicts a Portuguese ship on the cover and Portuguese nobles around the base. However European the subject, the craftsmanship is typical of Benin.   (Courtesy of the Trustees of the British Museum)

"brother," the king of Portugal, begging for his help in stopping the trade because unauthorized Kongolese were kidnapping and selling people, even members of good families (see Diversity and Dominance: Kongo's Christian King). Alfonso's appeals for help received no reply from Portugal, whose interests had moved to the Indian Ocean. Some subjects took advantage of the manikongo's weakness to rebel against his authority. After 1540 the major part of the slave trade from this part of Africa moved farther south.

Eastern Africa

Different still were the reactions of the Muslim rulers of the trading coastal states of eastern Africa. As Vasco da Gama's fleet sailed up the coast in 1498, most rulers gave the Portuguese a cool reception, suspicious of the intentions of these visitors who painted crusaders' crosses on their sails. But the ruler of one of the ports, Malindi, saw in the Portuguese an ally who could help him expand the city's trading position and provided da Gama with a pilot to guide him to India. The suspicions of most rulers were justified seven years later when a Portuguese war fleet bombarded and looted most of the coastal cities of eastern Africa in the name of Christ and commerce, though they spared Malindi.

Another eastern African state that saw potential benefit in an alliance with the Portuguese was Christian Ethiopia. In the fourteenth and early fifteenth centuries, Ethiopia faced increasing conflicts with Muslim states along the Red Sea. Emboldened by the rise of the Ottoman Turks, who had conquered Egypt in 1517 and launched a major fleet in the Indian Ocean to counter the Portuguese, the talented warlord of the Muslim state of Adal launched a furious assault on Ethiopia. Adal's decisive victory in 1529 reduced the Christian kingdom to a precarious state. At that point Ethiopia's contacts with the Portuguese became crucial.

For decades, delegations from Portugal and Ethiopia had been exploring a possible alliance between their states based on their mutual adherence to Christianity. A key figure was Queen Helena of Ethiopia, who acted as regent for her young sons after her husband's death in 1478. In 1509 Helena sent a letter to "our very dear and well-beloved brother," the king of Portugal, along with a gift of two tiny crucifixes said to be made of wood from the cross on which Christ had died in Jerusalem. In her letter she proposed an alliance of her land army and Portugal's fleet against the Turks. No such alliance was completed by the time Helena died in 1522. But as Ethiopia's situation grew increasingly desperate, renewed appeals for help were made.

Finally, a small Portuguese force commanded by Vasco da Gama's son Christopher reached Ethiopia in 1539, at a time when what was left of the empire was being held together by another woman ruler. With Portuguese help, the queen rallied the Ethiopians to renew their struggle. Christopher da Gama was captured and tortured to death, but the Muslim forces lost heart when their leader was mortally wounded in a later battle. Portuguese aid helped the Ethiopian kingdom save itself from extinction, but a permanent alliance faltered because Ethiopian rulers refused to transfer their Christian affiliation from the patriarch of Alexandria to the Latin patriarch of Rome (the pope) as the Portuguese wanted.

As these examples illustrate, African encounters with the Portuguese before 1550 varied considerably, as much because of the strategies and leadership of particular African states as because of Portuguese policies. Africans and Portuguese might become royal brothers, bitter opponents, or partners in a mutually profitable trade, but Europeans remained a minor presence in most of Africa in 1550. By then the Portuguese had become far more interested in the Indian Ocean trade.

Indian Ocean States

Vasco da Gama's arrival on the Malabar Coast of India in May 1498 did not make a great impression on the citizens of Calicut. After more than ten months at sea, many members of the crew were in ill health. Da Gama's four small ships were far less imposing than the Chinese fleets of gigantic junks that had called at Calicut sixty-five years earlier and no larger than many of the dhows that filled the harbor of this rich and important trading city. The samorin (ruler) of Calicut and his Muslim officials showed mild interest in the Portuguese as new trading partners, but the gifts da Gama had brought for the samorin evoked derisive laughter. Twelve pieces of fairly ordinary striped cloth, four scarlet hoods, six hats, and six wash basins seemed inferior goods to those accustomed to the luxuries of the Indian Ocean trade. When da Gama tried to defend his gifts as those of an explorer, not a rich merchant, the samorin cut him short, asking whether he had come to discover men or stones: "If he had come to discover men, as he said, why had he brought nothing?"

Coastal rulers soon discovered that the Portuguese had no intention of remaining poor competitors in the rich trade of the Indian Ocean. Upon da Gama's return to Portugal in 1499, the jubilant King Manuel styled himself "Lord of the Conquest, Navigation, and Commerce of Ethiopia, Arabia, Persia, and India," setting forth the ambitious scope of his plans. Previously the Indian Ocean had been an open sea, used by merchants (and pirates) of all the surrounding coasts. Now the Portuguese crown intended to make it Portugal's sea, the private property of the Portuguese alone, which others might use only on Portuguese terms.

The ability of little Portugal to assert control over the Indian Ocean stemmed from the superiority of its ships and weapons over the smaller and lightly armed merchant dhows. In 1505 the Portuguese fleet of eighty-one ships and some seven thousand men bombarded Swahili Coast cities. Next on the list were Indian ports. Goa, on the

Portuguese in India In the sixteenth century Portuguese men moved to the Indian Ocean basin to work as administrators and traders. This Indo-Portuguese drawing from about 1540 shows a Portuguese man speaking to an Indian woman, perhaps making a proposal of marriage. (Ms. 1889, c. 97, Biblioteca Casanateunse Rome. Photo: Humberto Nicoletti Serra)

west coast of India, fell to a well-armed fleet in 1510, becoming the base from which the Portuguese menaced the trading cities of Gujarat° to the north and Calicut and other Malabar Coast cities to the south. The port of Hormuz, controlling the entry to the Persian Gulf, was taken in 1515. Aden, at the entrance to the Red Sea, used its intricate natural defenses to preserve its independence. The addition of the Gujarati port of Diu in 1535 consolidated Portuguese dominance of the western Indian Ocean.

Meanwhile, Portuguese explorers had been reconnoitering the Bay of Bengal and the waters farther east. The independent city of Malacca° on the strait between the Malay Peninsula and Sumatra became the focus of their attention. During the fifteenth century Malacca had become the main entrepôt° (a place where goods are stored or deposited and from which they are distributed) for the trade from China, Japan, India, the Southeast Asian mainland, and the Moluccas. Among the city's more than 100,000 residents an early Portuguese counted

eighty-four different languages, including those of merchants from as far west as Cairo, Ethiopia, and the Swahili Coast of East Africa. Many non-Muslim residents supported letting the Portuguese join this cosmopolitan trading community, perhaps to offset the growing solidarity of Muslim traders. In 1511, however, the Portuguese seized this strategic trading center with a force of a thousand fighting men, including three hundred recruited in southern India.

Force was not always necessary. On the China coast, local officials and merchants interested in profitable new trade with the Portuguese persuaded the imperial government to allow the Portuguese to establish a trading post at Macao° in 1557. Operating from Macao, Portuguese ships nearly monopolized the trade between China and Japan.

In the Indian Ocean, the Portuguese used their control of the major port cities to enforce an even larger trading monopoly. They required all spices, as well as all goods on the major ocean routes such as between Goa

---

Gujarat (goo-juh-RAHT) **Malacca** (muh-LAH-kuh)
entrepôt (ON-truh-poh)

Macao (muh-COW)

and Macao, to be carried in Portuguese ships. In addition, the Portuguese also tried to control and tax other Indian Ocean trade by requiring all merchant ships entering and leaving one of their ports to carry a Portuguese passport and to pay customs duties. Portuguese patrols seized vessels that attempted to avoid these monopolies, confiscated their cargoes, and either killed the captain and crew or sentenced them to forced labor.

Reactions to this power grab varied. Like the emperors of China, the Mughal° emperors of India largely ignored Portugal's maritime intrusions, seeing their interests as maintaining control over their vast land possessions. The Ottomans responded more aggressively. From 1501 to 1509 they supported Egypt's fleet of fifteen thousand men against the Christian intruders. Then, having absorbed Egypt into their empire, the Ottomans sent another large expedition against the Portuguese in 1538. Both expeditions failed because the Ottoman galleys were no match for the faster, better-armed Portuguese vessels in the open ocean. However, the Ottomans retained the advantage in the Red Sea and Persian Gulf, where they had many ports of supply.

The smaller trading states of the region were even less capable of challenging Portuguese domination head on, since their mutual rivalry impeded the formation of any common front. Some chose to cooperate with the Portuguese to maintain their prosperity and security. Others engaged in evasion and resistance. Two examples illustrate the range of responses among Indian Ocean peoples.

The merchants of Calicut put up some of the most sustained local resistance. In retaliation, the Portuguese embargoed all trade with Aden, Calicut's principal trading partner, and centered their trade on the port of Cochin, which had once been a dependency of Calicut. Some Calicut merchants became adept at evading the patrol, but the price of resistance was the shrinking of Calicut's importance as Cochin gradually became the major pepper-exporting port on the Malabar Coast.

The traders and rulers of the state of Gujarat farther north had less success in keeping the Portuguese at bay. At first they resisted Portuguese attempts at monopoly and in 1509 joined Egypt's failed effort to sweep the Portuguese from the Arabian Sea. But in 1535, finding his state at a military disadvantage due to Mughal attacks, the ruler of Gujarat made the fateful decision to allow the Portuguese to build a fort at Diu in return for their support. Once established, the Portuguese gradually extended their control, so that by midcentury they were licensing and taxing all Gujarati ships. Even after the Mughals (who were Muslims) took control of Gujarat in

---

Mughal (MOO-gahl)

1572, the Mughal emperor Akbar permitted the Portuguese to continue their maritime monopoly in return for allowing one ship a year to carry pilgrims to Mecca without paying the Portuguese any fee.

The Portuguese never gained complete control of the Indian Ocean trade, but their domination of key ports and the main trade routes during the sixteenth century brought them considerable profit, which they sent back to Europe in the form of spices and other luxury goods. The effects were dramatic. The Portuguese sold the large quantities of pepper that they exported for less than the price charged by Venice and Genoa for pepper obtained through Egyptian middlemen, thus breaking the Italian cities' monopoly.

In Asia the consequences were equally startling. Asian and East African traders were at the mercy of Portuguese warships, but their individual responses affected their fates. Some were devastated. Others prospered by meeting Portuguese demands or evading their patrols. Because the Portuguese were ocean-based, they had little impact on the Asian and African mainlands, in sharp contrast to what was occurring in the Americas.

The Americas

In the Americas the Spanish established a vast territorial empire, in contrast to the trading empires the Portuguese created in Africa and Asia. This outcome had little to do with differences between the two Iberian kingdoms, except for the fact that the Spanish kingdoms had somewhat greater resources to draw on. The Spanish and Portuguese monarchies had similar motives for expansion and used identical ships and weapons. Rather, the isolation of the Amerindian peoples made their responses to outside contacts different from the responses of peoples in Africa and the Indian Ocean cities. In dealing with the small communities in the Caribbean, the first European settlers resorted to conquest and plunder rather than trade. This practice was later extended to the more powerful Amerindian kingdoms on the American mainland. The spread of deadly new diseases among the Amerindians after 1518 weakened their ability to resist.

The first Amerindians to encounter Columbus were the Arawak of Hispaniola (modern Haiti and the Dominican Republic) in the Greater Antilles and the Bahamas to the north (see Map 15.2). They cultivated maize (corn), cassava (a tuber), sweet potatoes, and hot peppers, as well as cotton and tobacco, and they met their other material needs from the sea and wild plants. Although they were skilled at mining and working gold, the Arawak did not trade gold over long distances as

Africans did, and they had no iron. The Arawak at first extended a cautious welcome to the Spanish but were unprepared to sell them large quantities of gold. Instead, they told Columbus exaggerated stories about gold in other places to persuade him to move on.

When Columbus made his second trip to Hispaniola in 1493, he brought several hundred settlers from southern Iberia who hoped to make their fortune and missionaries who were eager to persuade the Indians to accept Christianity. The settlers stole gold ornaments, confiscated food, and raped women, provoking the Hispaniola Arawak to war in 1495. In this and later conflicts, horses and body armor gave the Spaniards a great advantage. Tens of thousands of Arawak were slaughtered. Those who survived were forced to pay a heavy tax in gold, spun cotton, and food. Any who failed to meet the quotas were condemned to forced labor. Meanwhile, the cattle, pigs, and goats introduced by the settlers devoured the Arawak's food crops, causing deaths from famine and disease. A governor appointed by the Spanish crown in 1502 forced the Arawak remaining on Hispaniola to be laborers under the control of Spanish settlers.

The actions of the Spanish in the Antilles were reflections of Spanish actions and motives during the wars against the Muslims in Spain in the previous centuries: seeking to serve God by defeating nonbelievers and placing them under Christian control—and becoming rich in the process. Individual **conquistadors**° (conquerors) extended that pattern around the Caribbean. Some attacked the Bahamas to get gold and labor as both became scarce on Hispaniola. Many Arawak from the Bahamas were taken to Hispaniola as slaves. Juan Ponce de León (1460–1521), who had participated in the conquest of Muslim Spain and the seizure of Hispaniola, conquered the island of Borinquen (Puerto Rico) in 1508 and explored southeastern Florida in 1513.

An ambitious and ruthless nobleman, **Hernán Cortés**° (1485–1547), led the most audacious expedition to the mainland. Cortés left Cuba in 1519 with six hundred fighting men and most of the island's stock of weapons to assault the Mexican mainland in search of slaves and to establish trade. When the expedition learned of the rich Aztec Empire in central Mexico, Cortés brought to the American mainland, on a massive scale, the exploitation and conquest begun in the reconquest of Muslim Iberia and continued in the Greater Antilles.

The Aztecs themselves had conquered their vast empire only during the previous century, and many of the Amerindians they had subjugated were far from loyal subjects. Many resented the tribute they had to pay the

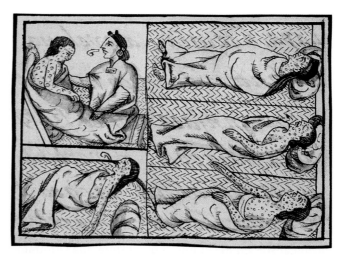

Death from Smallpox This Aztec drawing shows a healer attending smallpox victims. The little puffs coming from their mouths represent speech. (Biblioteca Medicea Laurenziana. Photo: MicroFoto, Florence)

Aztecs, the forced labor, and the large-scale human sacrifices to the Aztec gods. Many subject people saw the Spaniards as powerful human allies against the Aztecs and gave them their support. Like the Caribbean people, the Amerindians of Mexico had no precedent by which to judge these strange visitors.

Aztec accounts suggest that some believed Cortés to be the legendary ruler Quetzalcoatl°, whose return to earth had been prophesied, and treated him with great deference. Another consequence of millennia of isolation was far more significant: the lack of acquired immunity to the diseases of the Old World. Smallpox was the most deadly of the early epidemics that accompanied the Spanish conquistadors. It appeared for the first time on the island of Hispaniola late in 1518. An infected member of the Cortés expedition then transmitted smallpox to Mexico in 1519, where it spread with deadly efficiency.

From his glorious capital city Tenochtitlan°, the Aztec emperor **Moctezuma**° II (r. 1502–1520) sent messengers to greet Cortés and determine whether he was god or man, friend or foe. Cortés advanced steadily toward Tenochtitlan, overcoming Aztec opposition with cavalry charges and steel swords and gaining the support of thousands of Amerindian allies from among the unhappy subjects of the Aztecs. When the Spaniards

---

conquistador (kon-KEY-stuh-dor) Cortés (kor-TEZ)

Quetzalcoatl (ket-zahl-COH-ah-tal)
Tenochtitlan (teh-noch-TIT-lan)
Moctezuma (mock-teh-ZOO-ma)

Coronation of Emperor Moctezuma This painting by an unnamed Aztec artist depicts the Aztec ruler's coronation. Moctezuma, his nose pierced by a bone, receives the crown from a prince in the palace at Tenochtitlan.   (Oronoz)

were near, the emperor went out in a great procession, dressed in all his finery, to welcome Cortés with gifts and flower garlands.

Despite Cortés's initial promise that he came in friendship, Moctezuma quickly found himself a prisoner in his own palace. The Spanish looted his treasury and melted down its golden objects. Soon a battle was raging in and about the capital between the Spaniards (helped by their new Amerindian allies) and the Aztecs and their supporters. Briefly the Aztecs gained the upper hand. They destroyed half of the Spanish force and four thousand of the Spaniards' Amerindian allies, and they sacrificed to their gods fifty-three Spanish prisoners and four horses, displaying their severed heads in rows on pikes. In the battle Moctezuma was killed.

The Spanish survivors retreated from the city and rebuilt their strength. Their successful capture of Tenochtitlan in 1521 was greatly facilitated by the spread of smallpox, which weakened and killed more of the city's defenders than died in the fighting. One source remembered that the disease "spread over the people as a great destruction." The bodies of the afflicted were covered with oozing sores, and large numbers soon died. It is likely that many Amerindians as well as Europeans blamed the devastating spread of this disease on supernatural forces.

After the capital fell, the conquistadors took over other parts of Mexico. Then some Spaniards began eyeing the vast Inca Empire, stretching nearly 3,000 miles (5,000 kilometers) south from the equator and containing half of the population in South America. The Inca had conquered the inhabitants of the Andes Mountains and the Pacific coast of South America during the previous century, and their rule was not fully accepted by all of the peoples they had defeated.

With the vast Pacific Ocean on one side of their realm and the sparsely inhabited Amazon forests on the other, it is not surprising that Inca rulers believed they controlled most of the world worth controlling. Theirs was a great empire with highly productive agriculture, exquisite stone cities (such as the capital, Cuzco), and rich gold and silver mines. The power of the Inca emperor was sustained by beliefs that he was descended from the Sun God and by an efficient system of roads and messengers that kept him informed about major events in the empire. Yet all was not well.

At the end of the 1520s, before even a whisper of news about the Spanish reached the Inca rulers, small-

파운드폭탄 4발 투하… 두 아들과 함께 사망

□심진지 구축… 이틀째 시가戰

령이 대중 앞에 나타나거나 애국심 라크 전후
을 고취하는 노래만을 내보내던 방 의에서는
송마저 중단됐다. 영국 주도

DIVERSITY AND DOMINANCE

KONGO'S CHRISTIAN KING

The new overseas voyages brought conquest to some and opportunities for fruitful borrowings and exchanges to others. The decision of the ruler of the kingdom of Kongo to adopt Christianity in 1491 added cultural diversity to Kongolese society and in some ways strengthened the hand of the king. From then on Kongolese rulers sought to introduce Christian beliefs and rituals while at the same time Africanizing Christianity to make it more intelligible to their subjects. In addition, the kings of Kongo sought a variety of more secular aid from Portugal, including schools and medicine. Trade with the Portuguese introduced new social and political tensions, especially in the case of the export trade in slaves for the Portuguese sugar plantations on the island of São Tomé to the north.

Two letters sent to King João (zhwao) III of Portugal in 1526 illustrate how King Afonso of Kongo saw his kingdom's new relationship with Portugal and the problems that resulted from it. (Afonso adopted that name when he was baptized as a young prince.) After the death of his father in 1506, Afonso successfully claimed the throne and ruled until 1542. His son Henrique became the first Catholic bishop of the Kongo in 1521.

These letters were written in Portuguese and penned by the king's secretary João Teixera (tay-SHER-uh), a Kongo Christian, who, like Afonso, had been educated by Portuguese missionaries.

6 July 1526

To the very powerful and excellent prince Dom João, our brother:

On the 20th of June just past, we received word that a trading ship from your highness had just come to our port of Sonyo. We were greatly pleased by that arrival for it had been many days since a ship had come to our kingdom, for by it we would get news of your highness, which many times we had desired to know, . . . and likewise as there was a great and dire need for wine and flour for the holy sacrament; and of this we had had no great hope for we have the same need frequently. And

that, sir, arises from the great negligence of your highness's officials toward us and toward shipping us those things. . . .

Sir, your highness should know how our kingdom is being lost in so many ways that we will need to provide the needed cure, since this is caused by the excessive license given by your agents and officials to the men and merchants who come to this kingdom to set up shops with goods and many things which have been prohibited by us, and which they spread throughout our kingdoms and domains in such abundance that many of our vassals, whose submission we could once rely on, now act independently so as to get the things in greater abundance than we ourselves; whom we had formerly held content and submissive and under our vassalage and jurisdiction, so it is doing a great harm not only to the service of God, but also to the security and peace of our kingdoms and state.

And we cannot reckon how great the damage is, since every day the mentioned merchants are taking our people, sons of the land and the sons of our noblemen and vassals and our relatives, because the thieves and men of bad conscience grab them so as to have the things and wares of this kingdom that they crave; they grab them and bring them to be sold. In such a manner, sir, has been the corruption and deprivation that our land is becoming completely depopulated, and your highness should not deem this good nor in your service. And to avoid this we need from these kingdoms [of yours] no more than priests and a few people to teach in schools, and no other goods except wine and flour for the holy sacrament, which is why we beg of your highness to help and assist us in this matter. Order your agents to send here neither merchants nor wares, because it is our will that in these kingdoms there should not be any dealing in slaves nor outlet for them, for the reasons stated above. Again we beg your highness's agreement, since otherwise we cannot cure such manifest harm. May Our Lord in His mercy have your highness always under His protection and may you always do the things of His holy service. I kiss your hands many times.

From our city of Kongo. . . .

The King, Dom Afonso

18 October 1526

Very high and very powerful prince King of Portugal, our brother,

Sir, your highness has been so good as to promise us that anything we need we should ask for in our letters, and that everything will be provided. And so that there may be peace and health of our kingdoms, by God's will, in our lifetime. And as there are among us old folks and people who have lived for many days, many and different diseases happen so often that we are pushed to the ultimate extremes. And the same happens to our children, relatives, and people, because this country lacks physicians and surgeons who might know the proper cures for such diseases, as well as pharmacies and drugs to make them better. And for this reason many of those who had been already confirmed and instructed in the things of the holy faith of Our Lord Jesus Christ perish and die. And the rest of the people for the most part cure themselves with herbs and sticks and other ancient methods, so that they live putting all their faith in the these herbs and ceremonies, and die believing that they are saved; and this serves God poorly.

And to avoid such a great error, I think, and inconvenience, since it is from God and from your highness that all the good and the drugs and medicines have come to us for our salvation, we ask your merciful highness to send us two physicians and two pharmacists and one surgeon, so that they may come with their pharmacies and necessary things to be in our kingdoms, for we have extreme need of each and everyone of them. We will be very good and merciful to them, since sent by your highness, their work and coming should be for good. We ask your highness as a great favor to do this for us, because besides being good in itself it is in the service of God as we have said above.

Moreover, sir, in our kingdoms there is another great inconvenience which is of little service to God, and this is that many of our people, out of great desire for the wares and things of your kingdoms, which are brought here by your people, and in order to satisfy their disordered appetite, seize many of our people, freed and exempt men. And many times noblemen and the sons of noblemen, and our relatives are stolen, and they take them to be sold to the white men who are in our kingdoms and take them hidden or by night, so that they are not recognized. And as soon as they are taken by the white men, they are immediately ironed and branded with fire. And when they are carried off to be embarked, if they are caught by our guards, the whites allege that they have bought them and cannot say from whom, so that it is our duty to do justice and to restore to the free their freedom. And so they went away offended.

And to avoid such a great evil we passed a law so that every white man living in our kingdoms and wanting to purchase slaves by whatever means should first inform three of our noblemen and officials of our court on whom we rely in this matter, namely Dom Pedro Manipunzo and Dom Manuel Manissaba, our head bailiff, and Gonçalo Pires, our chief supplier, who should investigate if the said slaves are captives or free men, and, if cleared with them, there will be no further doubt nor embargo and they can be taken and embarked. And if they reach the opposite conclusion, they will lose the aforementioned slaves. Whatever favor and license we give them [the white men] for the sake of your highness in this case is because we know that it is in your service too that these slaves are taken from our kingdom; otherwise we should not consent to this for the reasons stated above that we make known completely to your highness so that no one could say the contrary, as they said in many other cases to your highness, so that the care and remembrance that we and this kingdom have should not be withdrawn. . . .

We kiss your hands of your highness many times.

From our city of Kongo, the 18th day of October,

The King, Dom Afonso

QUESTIONS FOR ANALYSIS

1. What sorts of things does King Afonso desire from the Portuguese?

2. What is he willing and unwilling to do in return?

3. What problem with his own people has the slave trade created and what has King Afonso done about it?

4. Does King Afonso see himself as an equal to King João or his subordinate? Do you agree with that analysis?

Source: From António Brásio, ed., *Monumenta Missionaria Africana: Africa Ocidental (1471-1531)* (Lisbon: Agência Geral do Ultramar, 1952), I:468, 470-471, 488-491. Translated by David Northrup.

pox claimed countless Amerindian lives, perhaps including the Inca emperor in 1530. Even more devastating was the threat awaiting the empire from **Francisco Pizarro°** (ca. 1478– 1541) and his motley band of 180 men, 37 horses, and two cannon.

With limited education and some military experience, Pizarro had come to the Americas in 1502 at the age of twenty-five to seek his fortune. He had participated in the conquest of Hispaniola and in Balboa's expedition across the Isthmus of Panama. By 1520 Pizarro was a wealthy landowner and official in Panama, yet he gambled his fortune on more adventures, exploring the Pacific coast to a point south of the equator, where he learned of the riches of the Inca. With a license from the king of Spain, he set out from Panama in 1531 to conquer them.

In November 1532 Pizarro arranged to meet the new Inca emperor, **Atahualpa°** (r. 1531–1533), near the Andean city of Cajamarca°. With supreme boldness and brutality, Pizarro's small band of armed men seized Atahualpa off a rich litter borne by eighty nobles as it passed through an enclosed courtyard. Though surrounded by an Inca army of at least forty thousand, the Spaniards were able to use their cannon to create confusion while their swords sliced thousands of the emperor's lightly armed retainers and servants to pieces. The strategy to replicate the earlier Spanish conquest of Mexico was working.

Noting the glee with which the Spaniards seized gold, silver, and emeralds, the captive Atahualpa offered them what he thought would satisfy even the greediest among them in exchange for his freedom: a roomful of gold and silver. But when the ransom of 13,400 pounds (6,000 kilograms) of gold and 26,000 pounds (12,000 kilograms) of silver was paid, the Spaniards gave Atahualpa a choice: he could be burned at the stake as a heathen or baptized as a Christian and then strangled. He chose the latter. His death and the Spanish occupation broke the unity of the Inca Empire.

In 1533 the Spaniards took Cuzco and from there set out to conquer and loot the rest of the empire. The defeat of a final rebellion in 1536 spelled the end of Inca rule. Five years later Pizarro himself met a violent death at the hands of Spanish rivals, but the conquest of the mainland continued. Incited by the fabulous wealth of the Aztecs and Inca, conquistadors extended Spanish conquest and exploration in South and North America, dreaming of new treasuries to loot.

Pizarro (pih-ZAHR-oh)   **Atahualpa** (ah-tuh-WAHL-puh)
Cajamarca (kah-hah-MAHR-kah)

Patterns of Dominance

Within fifty years of Columbus's first landing in 1492, the Spanish had located and occupied all of the major population centers of the Americas, and the penetration of the more thinly populated areas was well under way. In no other part of the world was European dominance so complete. Why did the peoples of the Americas suffer a fate so different from that of peoples in Africa and Asia? Why were the Spanish able to erect a vast land empire in the Americas so quickly? Three factors seem crucial.

First, long isolation from the rest of humanity made the inhabitants of the Americas vulnerable to new diseases. The unfamiliar illnesses first devastated the native inhabitants of the Caribbean islands and then spread to the mainland. Contemporaries estimated that between 25 and 50 percent of those infected with smallpox died. Repeated epidemics inhibited Amerindians' ability to regain control. Because evidence is very limited, estimates of the size of the population before Columbus's arrival vary widely, but there is no disputing the fact that the Amerindian population fell sharply during the sixteenth century. The Americas became a "widowed land," open to resettlement from across the Atlantic.

A second major factor was Spain's military superiority. Steel swords, protective armor, and horses gave the Spaniards an advantage over their Amerindian opponents in many battles. Though few in number, muskets and cannon also gave the Spaniards a significant psychological edge. However, it should not be forgotten that the Spanish conquests depended heavily on large numbers of Amerindian allies armed with the same weapons as the people they defeated. Perhaps the Spaniards' most decisive military advantage came from the no-holds-barred fighting techniques they had developed during a long history of warfare at home.

The patterns of domination previously established in reconquest of Iberia were a third factor in Spain's ability to govern its New World empire. The forced labor, forced conversion, and system for administering conquered lands all had their origins in the Iberian reconquest.

The same three factors help explain the quite different outcomes elsewhere. Because of centuries of contacts before 1500, Europeans, Africans, and Asians shared the same Old World diseases. Only small numbers of very isolated peoples in Africa and Asia suffered the demographic calamity that undercut Amerindians' ability to retain control of their lands. The Iberians enjoyed a military advantage at sea, as the conquest of the Indian Ocean trade routes showed, but on land they had no decisive advantage against more numerous indigenous people who were not weakened by disease. Everywhere, Iberian religious zeal to conquer non-Christians went hand in hand with a desire for riches. In Iberia and America conquest brought wealth. But in Africa and Asia, where existing trading networks were already well established, Iberian desire for wealth from trade restrained or negated the impulse to conquer.

CONCLUSION

Historians agree that the century between 1450 and 1550 was a major turning point in world history. It was the beginning of an age to which they have given various names: the "Vasco da Gama epoch," the "Columbian era," the "age of Magellan," or simply the "modern period." During those years European explorers opened new long-distance trade routes across the world's three major oceans, for the first time establishing regular contact among all the continents. By 1550 those who followed them had broadened trading contacts with sub-Saharan Africa, gained mastery of the rich trade routes of the Indian Ocean, and conquered a vast land empire in the Americas.

As dramatic and momentous as these events were, they were not completely unprecedented. The riches of the Indian Ocean trade that brought a gleam to the eye of many Europeans had been developed over many centuries by the trading peoples who inhabited the surrounding lands. European conquests of the Americas were no more rapid or brutal than the earlier Mongol conquests of Eurasia. Even the crossing of the Pacific had been done before, though in stages.

What gave this maritime revolution unprecedented importance had more to do with what happened after 1550 than with what happened earlier. Europeans' overseas empires would endure longer than the Mongols' and would continue to expand for three-and-a-half centuries after 1550. Unlike the Chinese, the Europeans did not turn their backs on the world after an initial burst of exploration. Not content with dominance in the Indian Ocean trade, Europeans opened an Atlantic maritime network that grew to rival the Indian Ocean network in the wealth of its trade. They also pioneered regular trade across the Pacific. The maritime expansion begun in the period from 1450 to 1550 marked the beginning of a new age of growing global interaction.

■ Key Terms

Zheng He	caravel
Arawak	Gold Coast
Henry the Navigator	Bartolomeu Dias

Vasco da Gama	Hernán Cortés
Christopher Columbus	Moctezuma
Ferdinand Magellan	Francisco Pizarro
conquistadors	Atahualpa

■ Suggested Reading

There is no single survey of the different expansions covered by this chapter, but the selections edited by Joseph R. Levenson, *European Expansion and the Counter Example of Asia, 1300–1600* (1967), remain a good introduction to Chinese expansion and Western impressions of China. Janet Abu-Lughod, *Before European Hegemony: The World System, A.D. 1250–1350* (1989), provides a stimulating speculative reassessment of the importance of the Mongols and the Indian Ocean trade in the creation of the modern world system; she summarizes her thesis in the American Historical Association booklet *The World System in the Thirteenth Century: Dead-End or Precursor?* (1993).

The Chinese account of Zheng He's voyages is Ma Huan, *Ying-yai Sheng-lan: "The Overall Survey of the Ocean's Shores"* [1433], ed. and trans. J. V. G. Mills (1970). A reliable guide to Polynesian expansion is Jesse D. Jennings, ed., *The Prehistory of Polynesia* (1979), especially the excellent chapter "Voyaging" by Ben R. Finney, which encapsulates his *Voyage of Rediscovery: A Cultural Odyssey Through Polynesia* (1994). The medieval background to European intercontinental voyages is summarized by Felipe Fernandez-Armesto, *Before Columbus: Exploration and Colonization from the Mediterranean to the Atlantic, 1229–1492* (1987). Tim Severin, *The Brendan Voyage* (2000) vividly recounts a modern retracing of even earlier Irish voyages.

A simple introduction to the technologies of European expansion is Carlo M. Cipolla, *Guns, Sails, and Empires: Technological Innovation and the Early Phases of European Expansion, 1400–1700* (1965; reprint, 1985). More advanced is Roger C. Smith, *Vanguard of Empire: Ships of Exploration in the Age of Columbus* (1993).

The European exploration is well documented and the subject of intense historical investigation. Clear general accounts based on the contemporary records are Boies Penrose, *Travel and Discovery in the Age of the Renaissance, 1420–1620* (1952); J. H. Parry, *The Age of Reconnaissance: Discovery, Exploration, and Settlement, 1450–1650* (1963); and G. V. Scammell, *The World Encompassed: The First European Maritime Empires, c. 800–1650* (1981).

An excellent general introduction to Portuguese exploration is C. R. Boxer, *The Portuguese Seaborne Empire, 1415–1825* (1969). More detail can be found in Bailey W. Diffie and George D. Winius, *Foundations of the Portuguese Empire, 1415–1580* (1977); A. J. R. Russell-Wood, *The Portuguese Empire: A World on the Move* (1998); and Luc Cuyvers, *Into the Rising Sun: The Journey of Vasco da Gama and the Discovery of the Modern World* (1998). John William Blake, ed., *Europeans in West Africa, 1450–1560* (1942), is an excellent two-volume collection of contemporary

Portuguese, Castilian, and English sources. Elaine Sanceau, *The Life of Prester John: A Chronicle of Portuguese Exploration* (1941), is a very readable account of Portuguese relations with Ethiopia. The *Summa Oriental of Tomé Pires: An Account of the East, from the Red Sea to Japan, Written in Malacca and India in 1512–1515*, trans. Armando Cortesão (1944), provides a detailed first-hand account of the Indian Ocean during the Portuguese's first two decades there.

The other Iberian kingdoms' expansion is well summarized by J. H. Parry, *The Spanish Seaborne Empire* (1967). Samuel Eliot Morison's *Admiral of the Ocean Sea: A Life of Christopher Columbus* (1942) is a fine scholarly celebration of the epic mariner, and is also available in an abridged version as *Christopher Columbus, Mariner* (1955). More focused on the shortcomings of Columbus and his Spanish peers is Tzvetan Todorov, *The Conquest of America*, trans. Richard Howard (1985). Marvin Lunenfeld, ed., *1492: Discovery, Invasion, Encounter* (1991), critically examines contemporary sources and interpretations. William D. Phillips and Carla Rhan Phillips, *The Worlds of Christopher Columbus* (1992), examines the mariner and his times in terms of modern concerns. Peggy K. Liss, *Isabel the Queen: Life and Times* (1992), is a sympathetic examination of Queen Isabella of Castile. Detailed individual biographies of all of the individuals in Pizarro's band are the subject of James Lockhart's *Men of Cajamarca: A Social and Biographical Study of the First Conquerors of Peru* (1972). A firsthand account of Magellan's expedition is Antonio Pigafetta, *Magellan's Voyage: A Narrative Account of the First Circumnavigation*, available in a two-volume edition (1969) that includes a facsimile reprint of the manuscript.

Matthew Restall, *Seven Myths of the Spanish Conquests* (2003) uses indigenous sources to challenge traditional interpretations of New World conquests. The trans-Atlantic encounters of Europe and the Americas are described by J. H. Elliott, *The Old World and the New, 1492–1650* (1970). Alfred W. Crosby, *The Columbian Voyages, the Columbian Exchange, and Their Historians* (1987), available as an American Historical Association booklet, provides a brief overview of the first encounters in the Americas and their long-term consequences. The early chapters of Mark A. Burkholder and Lyman L. Johnson, *Colonial Latin America*, 2d ed. (1994), give a clear and balanced account of the Spanish conquest.

The perceptions of the peoples European explorers encountered are not as well documented. David Northrup, *Africa's Discovery of Europe, 1450–1850* (2002) and John Thornton, *Africa and Africans in the Making of the Atlantic World, 1400–1800*, 2d ed. (1998), examine Africans' encounters with Europe and their involvement in the Atlantic economy. *The Broken Spears: The Aztec Account of the Conquest of Mexico*, ed. Miguel Leon-Portilla (1962), presents Amerindian chronicles in a readable package, as does Nathan Wachtel, *The Vision of the Vanquished: The Spanish Conquest of Peru Through Indian Eyes* (1977). Anthony Reid, *Southeast Asia in the Age of Commerce, 1450–1680*, 2 vols. (1988, 1993), deals with events in that region.

■ **Notes**

1. Ma Huan, *Ying-yai Sheng-lan: "The Overall Survey of the Ocean's Shores,"* ed. Feng Ch'eng-Chün, trans. J. V. G. Mills (Cambridge, England: Cambridge University Press, 1970), 180.
2. Alvise da Cadamosto in *The Voyages of Cadamosto and Other Documents*, ed. and trans. G. R. Crone (London: Hakluyt Society, 1937), 2.

Document-Based Question
Cross-Cultural Exchange in the Atlantic World

Using the following documents, characterize cross-cultural contact and exchange between Europeans and other peoples of the Atlantic World during the fifteenth and sixteenth centuries.

DOCUMENT 1
Columbus Prepares to Cross the Atlantic, 1492 (photo, p. 375)

DOCUMENT 2
Map 15.1 European Exploration, 1420–1542 (p. 378)

DOCUMENT 3
Portuguese Map of Western Africa, 1502 (photo, p. 386)

DOCUMENT 4
Excerpt from Christopher Columbus (p. 388)

DOCUMENT 5
Afro-Portuguese Ivory (photo, p. 390)

DOCUMENT 6
Death from Smallpox (photo, p. 394)

DOCUMENT 7
Kongo's Christian King (Diversity and Dominance, pp. 396–397)

How does King Afonso's point of view in Document 7 provide insight into the relationship between Kongo and Portugal? What additional types of documents would help you characterize cross-cultural contact and exchange between Europeans and other peoples of the Atlantic World during the fifteenth and sixteenth centuries?

The Globe Encompassed, 1500–1750

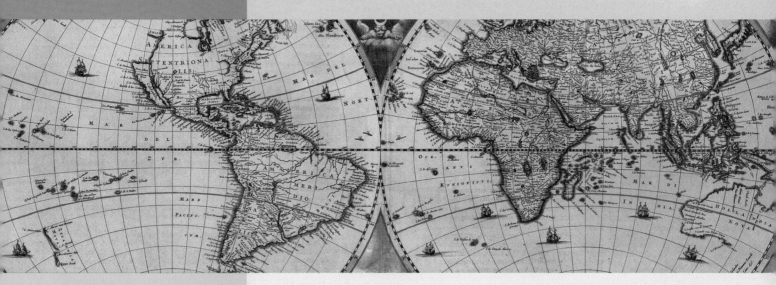

The decades between 1500 and 1750 witnessed a tremendous expansion of commercial, cultural, and biological exchanges around the world. New long-distance sea routes linked Europe with sub-Saharan Africa and the existing maritime networks of the Indian Ocean and East Asia. Spanish and Portuguese voyages ended the isolation of the Americas and created new webs of exchange in the Atlantic and Pacific. Overland expansion of Muslim, Russian, and Chinese empires also increased global interaction.

These expanding contacts had major demographic and cultural consequences. In the Americas, European diseases devastated the Amerindian population, facilitating the establishment of large Spanish, Portuguese, French, and British empires. Europeans introduced enslaved Africans to relieve the labor shortage. Immigrant Africans and Europeans brought new languages, religious practices, music, and forms of personal adornment.

In Asia and Africa, by contrast, the most important changes owed more to internal forces than to European actions. The Portuguese seized control of some important trading ports and networks in the Indian Ocean and pioneered new contacts with China and Japan. In time, the Dutch, French, and English expanded these profitable connections, but in 1750 Europeans were still primarily a maritime force. Asians and Africans generally retained control of their lands and participated freely in overseas trade.

The Islamic world saw the dramatic expansion of the Ottoman Empire in the Middle East and the establishment of the Safavid Empire in Iran and the Mughal Empire in South Asia. In northern Eurasia, Russia and China acquired vast new territories and populations, while a new national government in Japan promoted economic development and stemmed foreign influence.

Ecological change was rapid in areas of rising population and economic activity. Forests were cut down to meet the increasing need for farmland, timber, and fuel. Population growth in parts of Eurasia placed great strain on the environment. On a more positive note, domesticated animals and crops from the Old World transformed agriculture in the Americas, while Amerindian foods such as the potato became staples of the diet of the Old World.

New goods, new wealth, and new tastes from overseas transformed Europe in this period. Global and regional trade promoted urban growth, but conflict was also rife. States spent heavily on warfare in Europe and abroad. The printing press spread new religious and scientific ideas, and challenges to established values and institutions.

By 1750 the balance of power in the world had begun to shift from the East to the West. The Ottoman, Mughal, and Chinese empires had declined in relative strength compared to the much smaller but technologically more sophisticated states of northwestern Europe.

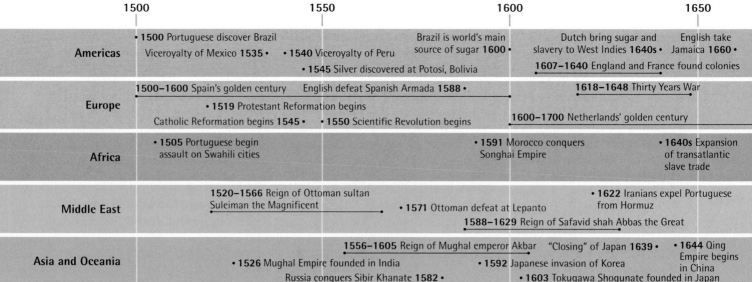

	1500	1550	1600	1650
Americas	• **1500** Portuguese discover Brazil Viceroyalty of Mexico **1535** • • **1540** Viceroyalty of Peru • **1545** Silver discovered at Potosí, Bolivia	Brazil is world's main source of sugar **1600** •	Dutch bring sugar and English take slavery to West Indies **1640s** • Jamaica **1660** • **1607–1640** England and France found colonies	
Europe	**1500–1600** Spain's golden century English defeat Spanish Armada **1588** • • **1519** Protestant Reformation begins Catholic Reformation begins **1545** • • **1550** Scientific Revolution begins		**1618–1648** Thirty Years War **1600–1700** Netherlands' golden century	
Africa	• **1505** Portuguese begin assault on Swahili cities		• **1591** Morocco conquers Songhai Empire	• **1640s** Expansion of transatlantic slave trade
Middle East	**1520–1566** Reign of Ottoman sultan Suleiman the Magnificent		• **1571** Ottoman defeat at Lepanto **1588–1629** Reign of Safavid shah Abbas the Great	• **1622** Iranians expel Portuguese from Hormuz
Asia and Oceania	• **1526** Mughal Empire founded in India Russia conquers Sibir Khanate **1582** •	**1556–1605** Reign of Mughal emperor Akbar • **1592** Japanese invasion of Korea • **1603** Tokugawa Shogunate founded in Japan	"Closing" of Japan **1639** •	• **1644** Qing Empire begins in China

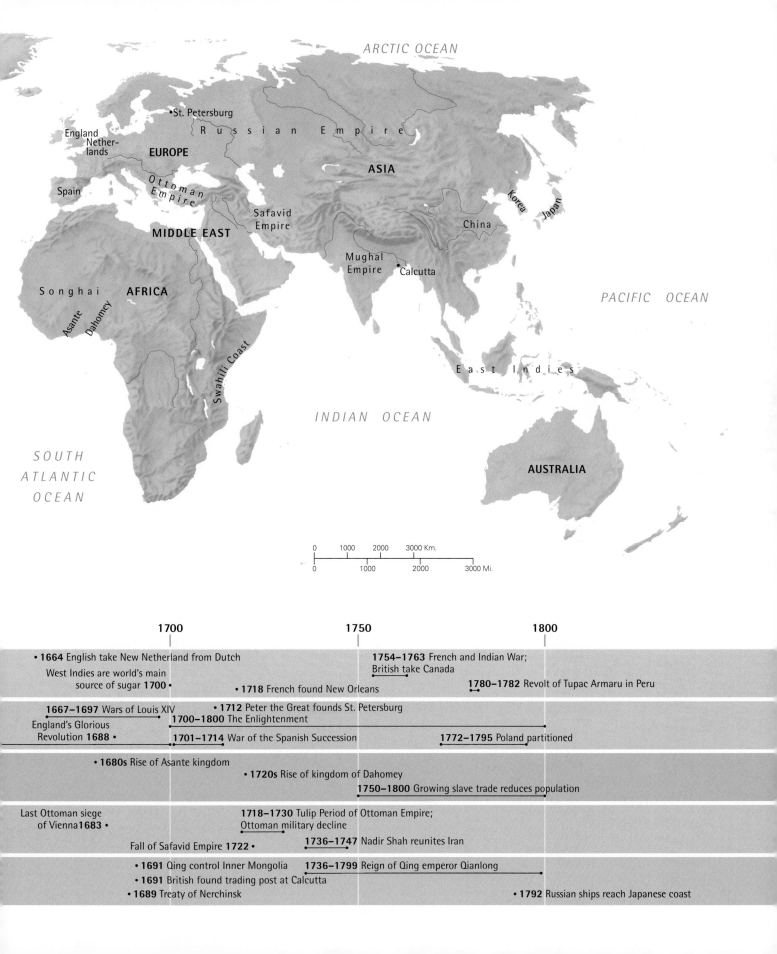

ARCTIC OCEAN

•St. Petersburg

England
Nether-
lands

EUROPE

R u s s i a n   E m p i r e

ASIA

Spain

Ottoman
Empire

Safavid
Empire

Korea

Japan

MIDDLE EAST

China

Songhai

AFRICA

Mughal
Empire

•Calcutta

PACIFIC   OCEAN

Asante

Dahomey

Swahili Coast

East Indies

INDIAN   OCEAN

SOUTH
ATLANTIC
OCEAN

AUSTRALIA

0	1000	2000	3000 Km.
0	1000	2000	3000 Mi.

1700   1750   1800

• **1664** English take New Netherland from Dutch   **1754–1763** French and Indian War;
                                                                         British take Canada
 West Indies are world's main
       source of sugar **1700** •   **1780–1782** Revolt of Tupac Armaru in Peru
                         • **1718** French found New Orleans

 1667–1697 Wars of Louis XIV   • **1712** Peter the Great founds St. Petersburg
 England's Glorious   **1700–1800** The Enlightenment
 Revolution **1688** •   **1701–1714** War of the Spanish Succession   **1772–1795** Poland partitioned

      • **1680s** Rise of Asante kingdom
                    • **1720s** Rise of kingdom of Dahomey
                                1750–1800 Growing slave trade reduces population

 Last Ottoman siege   **1718–1730** Tulip Period of Ottoman Empire;
 of Vienna **1683** •   Ottoman military decline
                              1736–1747 Nadir Shah reunites Iran
      Fall of Safavid Empire **1722** •

      • **1691** Qing control Inner Mongolia   **1736–1799** Reign of Qing emperor Qianlong
      • **1691** British found trading post at Calcutta
   • **1689** Treaty of Nerchinsk   • **1792** Russian ships reach Japanese coast

16 Transformations in Europe, 1500–1750

Winter in Flanders, 1565 This January scene by the Flemish artist Pieter Bruegel, the Elder, shows many everyday activities.

CHAPTER OUTLINE

Culture and Ideas

Social and Economic Life

Political Innovations

ENVIRONMENT AND TECHNOLOGY: **Mapping the World**

DIVERSITY AND DOMINANCE: **Political Craft and Craftiness**

As he neared the end of his life in 1575, the French scholar and humanist Loys Le Roy° reflected on the times in which he lived. It was, he believed, a golden age for Europe, and he ticked off the names of more than 130 scholars and translators, writers and poets, artists and sculptors, and explorers and philosophers whose work over the preceding two centuries had restored the standards of ancient learning. Later ages would call this scholarly and artistic revival the European **Renaissance.**

In addition, Le Roy enumerated a series of technological innovations that he believed had also transformed his age: printing, the marine compass, and cannonry. He put printing first because its rapid spread across Europe had done so much to communicate the literary and scholarly revival. The marine compass had made possible the sea voyages that now connected Europe directly to Africa and Asia and had led to the discovery and conquest of the Americas.

Le Roy gave third place to firearms because they had transformed warfare. Cannon and more recently devised hand-held weapons had swept before them all older military instruments. His enthusiasm for this transformation was dampened by the demonstrated capacity of firearms to cause devastation and ruin. Among the other evils of his age Le Roy enumerated syphilis and the spread of religious heresies and sects.

Reading Loys Le Roy's analysis more than four centuries later, one is struck not only by the acuity of his judgment and the beauty and clarity of his prose, but also by the astonishing geographical and historical range of his understanding. He credits both ancient and modern Greeks and Italians for their cultural contributions, the Germans for their role in perfecting printing and cannonry, and the Spanish for their overseas voyages. But his frame of reference is not confined to Europe. He cites the mathematical skills of ancient Egyptians; the military conquests of Mongols, Turks, and Persians (Iranians); Arabs' contributions to science and medicine; and China's contributions to the development of printing.

The global framework of Le Roy's analysis led him to conclude that he was living at a turning point in world history. For long centuries, he argued, the military might of the Mongols and Turks had threatened the peoples of Europe, and Safavid Iran and Mamluk Egypt had surpassed any European land in riches. Now the West was in the ascendancy. Europeans' military might equaled that of their Middle Eastern neighbors. They were amassing new wealth from Asian trade and American silver. Most of all, the explosion of learning and knowledge had given Europe intellectual equality and perhaps superiority. Le Roy noted perceptively that while printing presses were in use all across Europe, the Islamic world has closed itself off to the benefits of this new technology, refusing to allow presses to be set up and even forbidding the entry of Arabic works about their lands printed in Europe.

As you read this chapter ask yourself these questions:

- How perceptive was Loys Le Roy about his own age and its place in world history?

- How much did learning, printing, and firearms define early modern Europe? (The marine compass was considered in Chapter 15.)

- Would someone from a lower social station in Europe share Le Roy's optimism about their era?

CULTURE AND IDEAS

One place to observe the conflict and continuity of early modern Europe is in the world of ideas. Theological controversies broke the religious unity of the Latin Church and contributed to violent wars. A huge witch scare showed the power of Christian beliefs about the Devil and traditional folklore about malevolent powers. The influence of classical ideas from Greco-Roman antiquity increased among better-educated people, but some thinkers challenged the authority of the ancients. Their new models of the motion of the planets encouraged others to challenge traditional social and political systems, with important implications for the period after 1750. Each of these events has its own causes, but the technology of the printing press enhanced the impact of all.

Loys Le Roy (lwa-EES le-RWAH)

Martin Luther   This detail of a painting by Lucas Cranach (1547) shows the Reformer preaching in his hometown church at Wittenberg.   (Church of St. Marien, Wittenberg, Germany/The Bridgeman Art Library, New York and London)

Religious Reformation

In 1500 the **papacy,** the central government of Latin Christianity, was simultaneously gaining stature and suffering from corruption and dissent. Larger donations and tax receipts let popes fund ambitious construction projects in Rome, their capital city. During the sixteenth century Rome gained fifty-four new churches and other buildings, which showcased the artistic Renaissance then under way. However, the church's wealth and power also attracted ambitious men, some of whose personal lives became the source of scandal.

The jewel of the building projects was the magnificent new Saint Peter's Basilica in Rome. The unprecedented size and splendor of this church were intended to glorify God, display the skill of Renaissance artists and builders, and enhance the standing of the papacy. Such a project required refined tastes and vast sums of money.

The skillful overseer of the design and financing of the new Saint Peter's was Pope Leo X (r. 1513–1521), a member of the wealthy Medici° family of Florence, famous for its patronage of the arts. Pope Leo's artistic taste was superb and his personal life free from scandal, but he was more a man of action than a spiritual leader. One technique that he used to raise funds for the basilica was to authorize an **indulgence**—a forgiveness of the punishment due for past sins, granted by church authorities as a reward for a pious act such as making a pilgrimage, saying a particular prayer, or making a donation to a religious cause.

A young professor of sacred scripture, Martin Luther (1483–1546), objected to the way the new indulgence was preached. As the result of a powerful religious experience, Luther had forsaken money and marriage for a monastic life of prayer, self-denial, and study. He found personal consolation in his own religious quest in passage in Saint Paul's Epistle to the Romans that argued that salvation came not from "doing certain things" but from religious faith. That passage also led Luther to object to the way the indulgence preachers appeared to emphasize giving money more than the faith behind the act. He wrote to Pope Leo, asking him to stop this abuse, and challenged the preachers to a debate on the theology of indulgences.

This theological dispute quickly escalated into a contest between two strong-minded men. Largely ignoring Luther's theological objections, Pope Leo regarded his letter as a challenge to papal power and moved to silence the German monk. During a debate in 1519, a papal representative led Luther into open disagreement with some church doctrines, for which the papacy condemned him. Blocked in his effort to reform the church from within, Luther burned the papal bull (document) of condemnation, rejecting the pope's authority and beginning the movement known as the **Protestant Reformation.**

Accusing those whom he called "Romanists" (Roman Catholics) of relying on "good works," Luther insisted that the only way to salvation was through faith in Jesus Christ. He further declared that Christian belief must be based on the word of God in the Bible and on Christian tradition, not on the authority of the pope, as Catholics held. Eventually his conclusions led him to abandon his monastic prayers and penances and to marry a former nun.

Today Roman Catholics and Lutherans have resolved many of their theological differences, but in the sixteenth century stubbornness on both sides made reconciliation impossible. Moreover, Luther's use of the printing press to promote his ideas won him the support

Medici (MED-ih-chee)

C H R O N O L O G Y

	Politics and Culture	Environment and Technology	Warfare
1500	**1500s** Spain's golden century **1519** Protestant Reformation begins **1540s** Scientific Revolution begins **1545** Catholic Reformation begins **Late 1500s** Witch-hunts increase	**Mid-1500s** Improved windmills and increasing land drainage in Holland **1590s** Dutch develop flyboats; Little Ice Age begins	**1526–1571** Ottoman wars **1546–1555** German Wars of Religion **1562–1598** French Wars of Religion **1566–1648** Netherlands Revolt
1600	**1600s** Holland's golden century	**1600s** Depletion of forests growing **1609** Galileo's astronomical telescope **1682** Canal du Midi completed	**1618–1648** Thirty Years War **1642–1648** English Civil War **1652–1678** Anglo-Dutch Wars **1667–1697** Wars of Louis XIV **1683–1697** Ottoman wars
1700	**1700s** The Enlightenment begins	**1750** English mine nearly 5 million tons of coal a year **1755** Lisbon earthquake	**1700–1721** Great Northern War **1701–1714** War of the Spanish Succession

of powerful Germans, who responded to his nationalist portrayal of the dispute as an effort of an Italian pope to beautify his city with German funds.

Inspired by Luther's denunciation of the ostentation and corruption of church leaders, other leaders called for a return to authentic Christian practices and beliefs. John Calvin (1509–1564), a well-educated Frenchman who turned from the study of law to theology after experiencing a religious conversion, became a highly influential Protestant leader. As a young man, Calvin published *The Institutes of the Christian Religion*, a masterful synthesis of Christian teachings, in 1535. Much of the *Institutes* was traditional medieval theology, but Calvin's teaching differed from that of Roman Catholics and Lutherans in two respects. First, while agreeing with Luther's emphasis on faith over works, Calvin denied that even human faith could merit salvation. Salvation, said Calvin, was a gift God gave to those He "predestined" for salvation. Second, Calvin went farther than Luther in curtailing the power of a clerical hierarchy and in simplifying religious rituals. Calvinist congregations elected their own governing committees and in time cre-

ated regional and national synods (councils) to regulate doctrinal issues. Calvinists also displayed simplicity in dress, life, and worship. In an age of ornate garments, they wore simple black clothes, avoided ostentatious living, and worshiped in churches devoid of statues, most musical instruments, stained-glass windows, incense, and vestments.

The Reformers appealed to genuine religious sentiments, but their successes and failures were also due to political circumstances (discussed below) and the social agendas that motivated people to join them. It was no coincidence that Lutheranism had its greatest appeal to German speakers and linguistically related Scandinavians. Peasants and urban laborers sometimes defied their masters by adopting a different faith. Protestants were no more inclined than Roman Catholics to question male dominance in the church and the family, but most Protestants rejected the medieval tradition of celibate priests and nuns and advocated Christian marriage for all adults.

Shaken by the intensity of the Protestant Reformers' appeal, the Catholic Church undertook its own reforms.

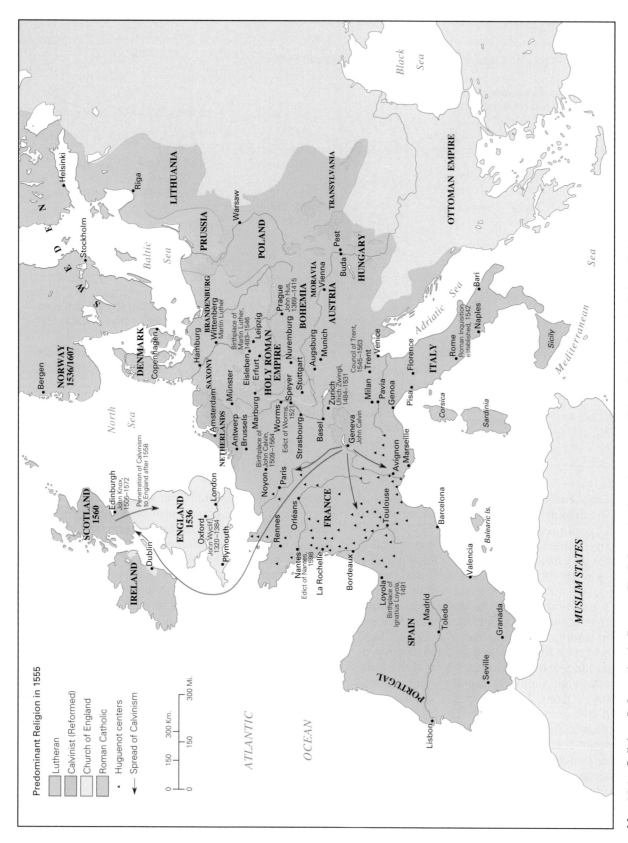

Map 16.1   Religious Reformation in Europe   The Reformation brought greater religious freedom but also led to religious conflict and persecution. In many places the Reformation accelerated the trend toward state control of religion and added religious differences to the motives for wars among Europeans.

Death to Witches   This woodcut from 1574 depicts three women convicted of witchcraft being burned alive in Baden, Switzerland. The well dressed townsmen look on stolidly.   (Zentralbibliothek Zurich)

A council that met at the city of Trent, in northern Italy, in three sessions between 1545 and 1563 painstakingly distinguished proper Catholic doctrines from Protestant "errors." The council also reaffirmed the supremacy of the pope and called for a number of reforms, including requiring each bishop to reside in his diocese and each diocese to have a theological seminary to train priests. Also important to this **Catholic Reformation** were the activities of a new religious order—the Society of Jesus, or "Jesuits," that Ignatius of Loyola (1491–1556), a Spanish nobleman, founded in 1540. Well-educated Jesuits helped stem the Protestant tide and win back some adherents by their teaching and preaching (see Map 16.1). Other Jesuits became important missionaries overseas (see Chapters 17 and 20).

Given the complexity of the issues and the intensity of the emotions that the Protestant Reformation stirred, it is not surprising that violence often flared up. Both sides persecuted and sometimes executed those of differing views. Bitter "wars of religion," fought over a mixture of religious and secular issues, continued in parts of western Europe until 1648.

Traditional Thinking and Witch-Hunts

Religious differences among Protestants and between them and Catholics continued to generate animosity long after the first generation of reformers, but from a global perspective European Christians still had much in common both in their theology and in the local folk customs and pre-Christian beliefs that remained powerful everywhere in Europe. The widespread **witch-hunts** that Protestants and Catholics undertook in early modern Europe are a dramatic illustration of those common beliefs and cultural heritage.

Prevailing European ideas about the natural world blended two distinct traditions. One was the folklore about magic and forest spirits passed down orally from pre-Christian times. The second was the biblical teachings of the Christian and Jewish scriptures, heard by all in church and read by growing numbers in vernacular translations. In the minds of most people, Christian teachings about miracles, saints, and devils mixed with folklore.

Like people in other parts of the world, most early modern Europeans believed that natural events could have supernatural causes. When crops failed or domestic animals died unexpectedly, many people blamed unseen spirits. People also attributed human triumphs and tragedies to supernatural causes. When an earthquake destroyed much of Lisbon, Portugal's capital city, in November 1755, for example, both educated and uneducated people saw the event as a punishment sent by God. A Jesuit charged it "scandalous to pretend that the earthquake was just a natural event." An English Protestant leader agreed, comparing Lisbon's fate with that of Sodom, the city that God destroyed because of the sinfulness of its citizens, according to the Hebrew Bible.

The extraordinary fear of the power of witches that swept across northern Europe in the late sixteenth and seventeenth centuries was powerful testimony to belief in the spiritual causes of natural events. It is estimated that secular and church authorities tried over a hundred thousand people—some three-fourths of them women—for practicing witchcraft. Some were acquitted; some recanted; but more than half were executed—most in Protestant lands. Torture and badgering questions persuaded many accused witches to confess to casting spells and to describe in vivid detail their encounters with the Devil and their attendance at nighttime assemblies of witches.

The trial records make it clear that both the accusers and the accused believed that it was possible for angry and jealous individuals to use evil magic and the power of the Devil to cause people and domestic animals to sicken and die or to cause crops to wither in the fields.

Researchers think that at least some of those accused in early modern Europe may really have tried to use witchcraft to harm their enemies. However, it was the Reformation's focus on the Devil—the enemy of God—as the source of evil that made such malevolence so serious a crime and may have helped revive older fears of witchcraft.

Modern historians also argue that many accusations against widows and independent-minded women drew on the widespread belief that women not directly under the control of fathers or husbands were likely to turn to evil. The fact that such women had important roles in tending animals and the sick and in childbirth also made them suspects if death occurred. In parts of the world where belief in witchcraft is still strong, witch-hunts arise at times of social stress, and people who are marginalized by poverty and by the suspicions of others often relish the celebrity that public confession brings. Self-confessed "witches" may even find release from the guilt they feel for wishing evil on their neighbors.

No single reason can explain the rise in witchcraft accusations and fears in early modern Europe, but, for both the accusers and the accused, there are plausible connections between the witch-hunts and rising social tensions, rural poverty, and environmental strains. Far from being a bizarre aberration, witch-hunts reflected the larger social climate of early modern Europe.

The Scientific Revolution

Among the educated, the writings of Greco-Roman antiquity and the Bible were more trusted guides to the natural world than was folklore. The Renaissance had recovered many manuscripts of ancient writers, some of which were printed and widely circulated. The greatest authority on physics was Aristotle, a Greek philosopher who taught that everything on earth was reducible to four elements. The surface of the earth was composed of the two heavy elements, earth and water. The atmosphere was made up of two lighter elements, air and fire, which floated above the ground. Higher still were the sun, moon, planets, and stars, which, according to Aristotelian physics, were so light and pure that they floated in crystalline spheres. This division between the ponderous, heavy earth and the airy, celestial bodies accorded perfectly with the commonsense perception that all heavenly bodies revolved around the earth.

The prevailing conception of the universe was also influenced by the tradition derived from the ancient Greek mathematician Pythagoras, who proved the validity of the famous theorem that still bears his name: in a right triangle, the square of the hypotenuse is equal to the sum of the squares of the other two sides ($a^2 + b^2 = c^2$). Pythagoreans attributed to mystical properties the ability of simple mathematical equations to describe physical objects. They attached special significance to the simplest (to them perfect) geometrical shapes: the circle (a point rotated around another point) and the sphere (a circle rotated on its axis). They believed that celestial objects were perfect spheres orbiting the earth in perfectly circular orbits.

In the sixteenth century, however, the careful observations and mathematical calculations of some daring and imaginative European investigators began to challenge these prevailing conceptions of the physical world. These pioneers of the **Scientific Revolution** demonstrated that the workings of the universe could be explained by natural causes.

Over the centuries, observers of the nighttime skies had plotted the movements of the heavenly bodies, and mathematicians had worked to fit these observations into the prevailing theories of circular orbits. To make all the evidence fit, they had come up with eighty different spheres and some ingenious theories to explain the many seemingly irregular movements. Pondering these complications, a Polish monk and mathematician named Nicholas Copernicus (1473–1543) came up with a mathematically simpler solution: switching the center of the different orbits from the earth to the sun would reduce the number of spheres that were needed.

Copernicus did not challenge the idea that the sun, moon, and planets were light, perfect spheres or that they moved in circular orbits. But his placement of the sun, not the earth, at the center of things began a revolution in understanding about the structure of the heavens and about the central place of humans in the universe. To escape the anticipated controversies, Copernicus delayed the publication of his heliocentric (sun-centered) theory until the end of his life.

Other astronomers, including the Danish Tycho Brahe (1546–1601) and his German assistant Johannes Kepler (1571–1630), strengthened and improved on Copernicus's model, showing that planets actually move in elliptical, not circular orbits. The most brilliant of the Copernicans was the Italian Galileo Galilei° (1564–1642). In 1609 Galileo built a telescope through which he took a closer look at the heavens. Able to magnify distant objects thirty times beyond the power of the naked eye, Galileo saw that heavenly bodies were not the perfectly smooth spheres of the Aristotelians. The moon, he reported in *The Starry Messenger* (1610), had mountains and valleys; the sun had spots; other planets had their own moons. In other words, the earth was not alone in being heavy and changeable.

Galileo Galilei (gal-uh-LAY-oh gal-uh-LAY-ee)

Galileus Galileus   Florentinus

Superior   licentia
J 6   2 4.

Eques Octauius Leone   Roman' pictor fecit

Galileo in 1624   This engraving by Ottavio Leone shows the Italian scientist in full vigor at age sixty.   (British Museum)

At first, the Copernican universe found more critics than supporters because it so directly challenged not just popular ideas but also the intellectual synthesis of classical and biblical authorities. How, demanded Aristotle's defenders, could the heavy earth move without producing vibrations that would shake the planet apart? Is the Bible wrong, asked the theologians, when the Book of Joshua says that, by God's command, "the sun [not the earth] stood still . . . for about a whole day" to give the ancient Israelites victory in their conquest of Palestine? If Aristotle's physics was wrong, worried other traditionalists, would not the theological synthesis built on other parts of his philosophy be open to question?

Intellectual and religious leaders encouraged political authorities to suppress the new ideas. Most Protestant leaders, following the lead of Martin Luther, condemned the heliocentric universe as contrary to the Bible. Catholic authorities waited longer to act. After all, both Copernicus and Galileo were Roman Catholics. Copernicus had dedicated his book to the pope, and in 1582 another pope, Gregory XIII, had used the latest astronomical findings to issue a new and more accurate calendar (still used today). Galileo ingeniously argued that the conflict between scripture and science was only apparent: the word of God revealed in the Bible was expressed in the imperfect language of ordinary people, but in nature God's truth was revealed more perfectly in a language that could be learned by careful observation and scientific reasoning.

Unfortunately, Galileo also ridiculed those who were slow to accept his findings, charging that Copernican ideas were "mocked and hooted at by an infinite multitude . . . of fools." Smarting under Galileo's stinging sarcasm, some Jesuits and other critics got his ideas condemned by the Roman Inquisition in 1616, which put *The Starry Messenger* on the Index of Forbidden Books and prohibited Galileo from publishing further on the subject. (In 1992 the Catholic Church officially retracted its condemnation of Galileo.)

Despite official opposition, printed books spread the new scientific ideas among scholars across Europe. In England, Robert Boyle (1627–1691) used experimental methods and a trial-and-error approach to examine the inner workings of chemistry. Through the Royal Society, chartered in London in 1662 to promote knowledge of the natural world, Boyle and others became enthusiastic missionaries of mechanical science and fierce opponents of the Aristotelians.

Meanwhile, English mathematician Isaac Newton (1642–1727) was carrying Galileo's demonstration that the heavens and earth share a common physics to its logical conclusion. Newton formulated a set of mathematical laws that all physical objects obeyed. It was the force of gravity—not angels—that governed the elliptical orbits of heavenly bodies. It was gravitation (and the resistance of air) that caused cannonballs to fall back to earth. From 1703 until his death Newton served as president of the Royal Society, using his prestige to promote the new science that came to bear his name.

As the condemnation of Galileo demonstrates, in 1700 most religious and intellectual leaders viewed the new science with suspicion or outright hostility because of the unwanted challenge it posed to established ways of thought. Yet all the principal pioneers of the Scientific Revolution were convinced that scientific discoveries and revealed religion were not in conflict. At the peak of his fame Newton promoted a series of lectures devoted to proving the validity of Christianity. However, by showing that the Aristotelians and biblical writers held ideas about the natural world that were naive and unfactual, these pioneers opened the door to others who used reason to challenge a broader range of unquestioned traditions and superstitions. The world of ideas was forever changed.

The Early Enlightenment

The advances in scientific thought inspired a few brave souls to question the reasonableness of everything from agricultural methods to laws, religion, and social hierarchies. The belief that human reason could discover the laws that governed social behavior and were just as scientific as the laws that governed physics energized a movement known as the **Enlightenment.** Like the Scientific Revolution, this movement was the work of a few "enlightened" individuals, who often faced bitter opposition from the political, intellectual, and religious establishment. Leading Enlightenment thinkers became accustomed to having their books burned or banned and spent long periods in exile to escape being imprisoned.

Influences besides the Scientific Revolution affected the Enlightenment. The Reformation had aroused many to champion one creed or another, but partisan bickering and bloodshed led others to doubt the superiority of any theological position and to recommend toleration of all religions. The killing of suspected witches also shocked many thoughtful people. The leading French thinker Voltaire (1694–1778) declared: "No opinion is worth burning your neighbor for."

Accounts of cultures in other parts of the world also led some European thinkers to question assumptions about the superiority of European political institutions, moral standards, and religious beliefs. Reports of Amerindian life, though romanticized, led some to conclude that those whom they had called savages were in many ways nobler than European Christians. Matteo Ricci, a Jesuit missionary to China whose journals made a strong impression in Europe, contrasted the lack of territorial ambition of the Chinese with the constant warfare in the West and attributed the difference to the fact that China was wisely ruled by educated men whom he called "Philosophers."

Although many circumstances shaped "enlightened" thinking, the new scientific methods and discoveries provided the clearest model for changing European society. Voltaire posed the issues in these terms: "it would be very peculiar that all nature, all the planets, should obey eternal laws" but a human being, "in contempt of these laws, could act as he pleased solely according to his caprice." The English poet Alexander Pope (1688–1774) made a similar point in verse: "Nature and Nature's laws lay hidden in night;/God said, 'Let Newton be' and all was light."

The Enlightenment was more a frame of mind than a coherent movement. Individuals who embraced it drew inspiration from different sources and promoted different agendas. By 1750 its proponents were clearer about what they disliked than about what new institutions should be created. Some "enlightened" thinkers thought society could be made to function with the mechanical orderliness of planets spinning in their orbits. Nearly all were optimistic that—at least in the long run—human beliefs and institutions could be improved. This belief in progress would help foster political and social revolutions after 1750, as Chapter 21 recounts.

Despite the enthusiasm the Enlightenment aroused in some circles, it was decidedly unpopular with many absolutist rulers and with most clergymen. Europe in 1750 was neither enlightened nor scientific. It was a place where political and religious divisions, growing literacy, and the printing press made possible the survival of the new ideas that profoundly changed life in future centuries.

SOCIAL AND ECONOMIC LIFE

From a distance European society seemed quite rigid. At the top of the social pyramid a small number of noble families had privileged access to high offices in the church, government, and military and enjoyed many special privileges, including exemption from taxation. A big step below them were the classes of merchants and professionals, who had acquired wealth but no legal privileges. At the base of the pyramid were the masses, mostly rural peasants and landless laborers, who were exploited by everyone above them. The subordination of women to men seemed equally rigid.

This model of European society is certainly not wrong, but even contemporaries knew that it was too simple. A study of English society in 1688, for example, distinguished twenty-five different social categories and pointed up the shocking inequality among them. It argued that less than half the population contributed to increasing the wealth of the kingdom, while the rest—the majority—were too poor and unskilled to make any substantial contribution.

Some social mobility did occur, particularly in the middle. The principal engine of social change was the economy, and the places where social change occurred most readily were the cities. A secondary means of change was education—for those who could get it.

The Bourgeoisie

Europe's growing cities were the products of a changing economy. In 1500 Paris was the only northern European city with over 100,000 inhabitants. By 1700 both Paris and London had populations over 500,000, and twenty other European cities contained over 60,000 people.

The wealth of the cities came from manufacturing and finance, but especially from trade, both within Europe and overseas. The French called the urban class that dominated these activities the **bourgeoisie**° (burghers, town dwellers). Members of the bourgeoisie devoted long hours to their businesses and poured much of their profits back into them or into new ventures. Even so, they had enough money to live comfortably in large houses with many servants. In the seventeenth and eighteenth centuries wealthier urban classes could buy exotic luxuries imported from the far corners of the earth—Caribbean and Brazilian sugar and rum, Mexican chocolate, Virginia tobacco, North American furs, East Indian cotton textiles and spices, and Chinese tea.

The Netherlands provided many good examples of bourgeois enterprise in the seventeenth century. Manufacturers and skilled craftsmen turned out a variety of goods in the factories and workshops of many cities and towns in the province of Holland. The highly successful Dutch textile industry concentrated on the profitable weaving, finishing, and printing of cloth, leaving the spinning to low-paid workers elsewhere. Along with fine woolens and linens the Dutch were successfully making cheaper textiles for mass markets. Other factories in Holland refined West Indian sugar, brewed beer from Baltic grain, cut Virginia tobacco, and made imitations of Chinese ceramics (see Environment and Technology: East Asian Porcelain in Chapter 20). Free from the censorship imposed by political and religious authorities in neighboring countries, Holland's printers published books in many languages, including manuals with the latest advances in machinery, metallurgy, agriculture, and other technical areas. For a small province barely above sea level, lacking timber and other natural resources, this was a remarkable achievement.

Burgeoning from a fishing village to a metropolis of some 200,000 by 1700, Amsterdam was Holland's largest city and Europe's major port. The bourgeoisie there and in other cities had developed huge commercial fleets that dominated sea trade in Europe and overseas. Dutch ships carried over 80 percent of the trade between Spain and northern Europe, even while Spain and the Netherlands were at war. By one estimate, the Dutch conducted more than half of all the oceangoing commercial shipping in the world in the seventeenth century (for details see Chapters 19 and 20).

Amsterdam also served as Europe's financial center. Seventeenth-century Dutch banks had such a reputation for security that wealthy individuals and governments from all over western Europe entrusted them with their money. The banks in turn invested these funds in

---

bourgeoisie (boor-zwah-ZEE)

The Fishwife, 1572   Women were essential partners in most Dutch family businesses. This scene by the Dutch artist Adriaen van Ostade shows a woman preparing fish for retail sale. (Rijksmuseum–Amsterdam)

real estate, loaned money to factory owners and governments, and provided capital for big business operations overseas.

The expansion of maritime trade led to new designs for merchant ships. In this, too, the Dutch played a dominant role. Using timber imported from northern Europe, shipyards in Dutch ports built their own vast fleets and other ships for export. Especially successful was the *fluit*, or "flyboat," a large-capacity cargo ship developed in the 1590s. It was inexpensive to build and required only a small crew. Another successful type of merchant ship, the heavily armed "East Indiaman," helped the Dutch establish their supremacy in the Indian Ocean. The Dutch also excelled at mapmaking (see Environment and Technology: Mapping the World).

Like merchants in the Islamic world, Europe's merchants relied on family and ethnic networks. In addition to families of local origin, many northern European cities contained merchant colonies from Venice, Florence, Genoa, and other Italian cities. In Amsterdam and Hamburg lived Jewish merchants who had fled religious persecution in Iberia. Other Jewish communities expanded out of eastern Europe into the German states, especially after the Thirty Years War. Armenian merchants from Iran were moving into the Mediterranean and became important in Russia in the seventeenth century.

Mapping the World

In 1602 in China the Jesuit missionary Matteo Ricci printed an elaborate map of the world. Working from maps produced in Europe and incorporating the latest knowledge gathered by European maritime explorers, Ricci introduced two changes to make the map more appealing to his Chinese hosts. He labeled it in Chinese characters, and he split his map down the middle of the Atlantic so that China lay in the center. This version pleased Chinese elite, who considered China the "Middle Kingdom" surrounded by lesser states. A copy of Ricci's map in six large panels adorned the emperor's Beijing palace.

The stunningly beautiful maps and globes of sixteenth-century Europe were the most complete, detailed, and useful representations of the earth that any society had ever produced. The best mapmaker of the century was Gerhard Kremer, who is remembered as Mercator (the merchant) because his maps were so useful to European ocean traders. By incorporating the latest discoveries and scientific measurements,

Mercator could depict the outlines of the major continents in painstaking detail, even if their interiors were still largely unknown to outsiders.

To represent the spherical globe on a flat map, Mercator drew the lines of longitude as parallel lines. Because such lines actually meet at the poles, Mercator's projection greatly exaggerated the size of every landmass and body of water distant from the equator. However, Mercator's rendering offered a very practical advantage: sailors could plot their course by drawing a straight line between their point of departure and their destination. Because of this useful feature, the Mercator projection of the world remained in common use until quite recently. To some extent, its popularity came from the exaggerated size this projection gave to Europe. Like the Chinese, Europeans liked to think of themselves as at the center of things. Europeans also understood their true geographical position better than people in any other part of the world.

Dutch World Map, 1641   It is easy to see why the Chinese would not have liked to see their empire at the far right edge of this widely printed map. Besides the distortions caused by the Mercator projection, geographical ignorance exaggerates the size of North America and Antarctica.   (Courtesy of the Trustees British Museum)

Port of Amsterdam   Ships, barges, and boats of all types are visible in this busy seventeenth-century scene. The large building in the center is the Admiralty House, the headquarters of the Dutch East India Company. (Mansell TimeLife Pictures/Getty Images)

The bourgeoisie sought mutually beneficial alliances with European monarchs, who welcomed economic growth as a means of increasing state revenues. The Dutch government pioneered chartering **joint-stock companies,** giving the Dutch East and West India Companies monopolies over trade to the East and West Indies. France and England chartered companies of their own. The companies then sold shares to individuals to raise large sums for overseas enterprises while spreading the risks (and profits) among many investors (see Chapter 18). Investors could buy and sell shares in specialized financial markets called **stock exchanges,** an Italian innovation transferred to the cities of northwestern Europe in the sixteenth century. The greatest stock market in the seventeenth and eighteenth centuries was the Amsterdam Exchange, founded in 1530. Large insurance companies also emerged in this period, and insuring long voyages against loss became a standard practice after 1700.

Governments also undertook large projects to improve water transport. The Dutch built numerous canals for transport and to drain the lowlands for agriculture. Other governments also financed canals, which included elaborate systems of locks to raise barges up over hills. One of the most important was the 150–mile (240–kilometer) Canal du Midi in France, built by the French government between 1661 and 1682 to link the Atlantic and the Mediterranean. By the seventeenth century

rulers sought the talents of successful businessmen as administrators. Jean Baptiste Colbert° (1619–1683), Louis XIV's able minister of finance, was a notable example.

After 1650 the Dutch faced growing competition from the English, who were developing their own close association of business and government. With government support, the English merchant fleet doubled between 1660 and 1700, and foreign trade rose by 50 percent. As a result, state revenue from customs duties tripled. In a series of wars (1652–1678) the English government used its naval might to break Dutch dominance in overseas trade and to extend England's colonial empire.

Some successful members of the bourgeoisie in England and France chose to use their wealth to raise their social status. By retiring from their businesses and buying country estates, they could become members of the **gentry.** These landowners affected the lifestyle of the old aristocracy. The gentry loaned money to impoverished peasants and to members of the nobility and in time increased their ownership of land. Some families sought aristocratic husbands for their daughters. The old nobility found such alliances attractive because of the large dowries that the bourgeoisie provided. In France a family could gain the exemption from taxation by living in gentility for three generations or, more quickly, by purchasing a title from the king.

Colbert (kohl-BEAR)

Peasants and Laborers

At the other end of society things were bad, but they had been worse. Serfdom, which bound men and women to land owned by a local lord, had been in deep decline since the great plague of the mid-fourteenth century. The institution did not return in western Europe as the population recovered, but competition for work exerted a downward pressure on wages. However, the development of large estates raising grain for the cities led to the rise of serfdom in eastern Europe for the first time. There was also a decline in slavery, which had briefly expanded in southern Europe around 1500 as the result of the Atlantic slave trade from sub-Saharan Africa. After 1600, however, Europeans shipped nearly all African slaves to the Americas.

There is much truth in the argument that western Europe continued to depend on unfree labor but kept it at a distance rather than at home. In any event, legal freedom did little to make a peasant's life safer and more secure. The techniques and efficiency of European agriculture had improved little since 1300. As a result, bad years brought famine; good ones provided only small surpluses. Indeed, the condition of the average person in western Europe may have worsened between 1500 and 1750 as the result of prolonged warfare, environmental problems, and adverse economic conditions. In addition, Europeans felt the adverse effects of a century of relatively cool climate that began in the 1590s. During this **Little Ice Age** average temperatures fell only a few degrees, but the effects were startling.

By 1700 high-yielding new crops from the Americas were helping the rural poor avoid starvation. Once grown only as hedges against famine, potatoes and maize (corn) became staples for the rural poor in the eighteenth century. Potatoes sustained life in northeastern and Central Europe and in Ireland, while poor peasants in Italy subsisted on maize. The irony is that all of these lands were major exporters of wheat, but most of those who planted and harvested it could not afford to eat it.

Instead, the grain was put on carts, barges, and ships and carried to the cities of Western Europe. Other fleets brought wine from southern to northern Europe. Parisians downed 100,000 barrels of wine a year at the end of the seventeenth century. Some of the grain was made into beer, which the poor drank because it was cheaper than wine. In 1750 Parisian breweries brewed 23 million quarts (22 million liters) of beer for local consumption.

Other rural men made a living as miners, lumberjacks, and charcoal makers. The expanding iron industry in England provided work for all three, but the high consumption of wood fuel for this and other purposes caused serious **deforestation.** One early-seventeenth-

century observer lamented: "within man's memory, it was held impossible to have any want of wood in England. But . . . at present, through the great consuming of wood . . . and the neglect of planting of woods, there is a great scarcity of wood throughout the whole kingdom."[1] The managers of the hundreds of ironworks in England tried to meet the shortages by importing timber and charcoal from more heavily forested Scandinavian countries and Russia. Eventually, the high price of wood and charcoal encouraged smelters to use coal as an alternative fuel. England's coal mining increased twelvefold from 210,000 tons in 1550 to 2,500,000 tons in 1700. From 1709 coke—coal refined to remove impurities—gradually replaced charcoal in the smelting of iron. These new demands drove English coal production to nearly 5 million tons a year by 1750.

France was much more forested than England, but increasing deforestation there prompted Colbert to predict that "France will perish for lack of wood." By the late eighteenth century deforestation had become an issue even in Sweden and Russia, where iron production had become a major industry. New laws in France and England designed to protect the forests were largely inspired by fears of shortages for naval vessels, whose keels required high-quality timbers of exceptional size and particular curvature. Although wood consumption remained high, rising prices encouraged some individuals to plant trees for future harvest.

Everywhere in Europe the rural poor felt the depletion of the forests most strongly. For centuries they had depended on woodlands for abundant supplies of wild nuts and berries, free firewood and building materials, and wild game. Modest improvements in food production in some places were overwhelmed by population growth. Rural women had long supplemented household incomes by spinning yarn. From the mid-1600s rising wages in towns led textile manufacturers to farm more and more textile weaving out to rural areas with high underemployment. This provided men and women with enough to survive on, but the piecework paid very little for long hours of tedious labor.

Throughout this period, many rural poor migrated to the towns and cities in hopes of better jobs, but only some were successful. Even in the prosperous Dutch towns, half of the population lived in acute poverty. Authorities estimated that those permanent city residents who were too poor to tax, the "deserving poor," made up 10 to 20 percent of population. That calculation did not include the large numbers of "unworthy poor"—recent migrants from impoverished rural areas, peddlers traveling from place to place, and beggars (many with horrible deformities and sores) who tried to survive on charity. Many young women were forced into prostitution to survive. There were also many criminals, usually organized in gangs, ranging from youthful pickpockets to highway robbers.

The pervasive poverty of rural and urban Europe shocked those who were not hardened to it. In about 1580 the mayor of the French city of Bordeaux° asked a group of visiting Amerindian chiefs what impressed them most about European cities. The chiefs are said to have expressed astonishment at the disparity between the fat, well-fed people and the poor, half-starved men and women in rags. Why, the visitors wondered, did the poor not grab the rich by the throat or set fire to their homes?[2]

In fact, misery provoked many rebellions in early modern Europe. For example, in 1525 peasant rebels in the Alps attacked both nobles and clergy as representatives of the privileged and landowning classes. They had no love for merchants either, whom they denounced for lending at interest and charging high prices. Rebellions multiplied as rural conditions worsened. In southwestern France alone some 450 uprisings occurred between 1590 and 1715, many of them set off by food shortages and tax increases. The exemption of the wealthy from taxation was a frequent source of complaint. A rebellion in southern France in 1670 began when a mob of townswomen attacked the tax collector. It quickly spread to the country, where peasant leaders cried, "Death to the people's oppressors!" Authorities dealt severely with such revolts and executed or maimed their leaders.

Women and the Family

Women's status and work were closely tied to their husbands' and families'. In lands that allowed it, a woman in a royal family might inherit a throne (see Table 16.1, page 423 for examples)—in the absence of a male heir. These rare exceptions do not negate the rule that women everywhere ranked below men, but one should also not forget that her class and wealth defined a woman's position in life more than her sex. The wife or daughter of a rich man, for example, had a much better life than any poor man. In special cases, a single woman might be secure and respected, as in the case of women from good families who might head convents of nuns in Catholic countries. But unmarried women and widows were less well off than their married sisters. A good marriage was thus of great importance.

In contrast to the arranged marriages that prevailed in much of the rest of the world, young men and women in early modern Europe most often chose their own

°**Bordeaux** (bor-DOH)

spouses. Ironically, privileged families were more inclined to control marriage plans than poor ones. Royal and noble families carefully plotted the suitability of their children's marriages in furthering the family's status. Bourgeois parents were less likely to force their children into arranged marriages, but the fact that nearly all found spouses within their social class strongly suggests that the bourgeoisie promoted marriages that furthered their business alliances.

Europeans also married later than people in other lands. The sons and daughters of craftworkers and the poor had to delay marriage until they could afford to live on their own. Young men had to serve long apprenticeships to learn trades. Young women also had to work—helping their parents, as domestic servants, or in some other capacity—to save money for the dowry they were expected to bring into the marriage. A dowry was the money and household goods—the amount varied by social class—that enabled a young couple to begin marriage independent of their parents. The typical groom in western and central Europe could not hope to marry before his late twenties, and his bride would be a few years younger—in contrast to the rest of the world, where people usually married in their teens. Marriage also came late in bourgeois families, in part to allow young men to complete their education.

Besides enabling young people to be independent of their parents, the late age of marriage in early modern Europe also held down the birthrate and thus limited family size. Even so, about one-tenth of the births in a city were to unmarried women, often servants, who generally left their infants on the doorsteps of churches, convents, or rich families. Despite efforts to raise such abandoned children, many perished. Delayed marriage also had links to the existence of public brothels, where young men could satisfy their lusts in cheap and impersonal encounters with unfortunate young women, often newly arrived from impoverished rural villages. Nevertheless, rape was a common occurrence, usually perpetrated by gangs of young men who attacked young women rumored to be free with their favors. Some historians believe that such gang rapes reflected poor young men's jealousy at older men's easier access to women.

Bourgeois parents were very concerned that their children have the education and training necessary for success. They promoted the establishment of municipal schools to provide a solid education, including Latin and perhaps Greek, for their sons, who were then sent abroad to learn modern languages or to a university to earn a law degree. Legal training was useful for conducting business and was a prerequisite for obtaining government judgeships and treasury positions. Daughters were less likely to be groomed for business careers, but wives often helped their husbands as bookkeepers and sometimes inherited businesses.

The fact that most schools barred female students, as did most guild and professions, explains why women were not prominent in the cultural Renaissance, the Reformation, the Scientific Revolution, and the Enlightenment. Yet from a global perspective, women in early modern Europe were more prominent in the creation of culture than were women in most other parts of the world. Recent research has brought to light the existence of a number of successful women who were painters, musicians, and writers. Indeed, the spread of learning, the stress on religious reading, and the growth of business likely meant that Europe led the world in female literacy. In a period when most men were illiterate, the number of literate women was small, and only women in wealthier families might have a good education. From the late 1600s some wealthy French women ran intellectual gatherings in their homes. Many more were prominent letter writers. Galileo's daughter, Maria Celeste Galilei, carried on a detailed correspondence with her father from the confinement of her convent, whose walls she had taken a religious vow never to leave.

POLITICAL INNOVATIONS

The monarchs of early modern Europe occupied the apex of the social order, were arbitrators of the intellectual and religious conflicts of their day, and had important influences on the economic life of their realms. For these reasons an overview of political life incorporates all the events previously described in this chapter. In addition, monarchs' political agendas introduced new elements of conflict and change.

The effort to create a European empire failed, but monarchs succeeded in achieving a higher degree of political centralization within their separate kingdoms. The frequent civil and international conflicts of this era sometimes promoted cooperation, but they often encouraged innovation. Leadership and success passed from Spain to the Netherlands and then to England and France. It is hard to avoid the conclusion that the key political technology was cannonry.

State Development

Political diversity characterized Europe. City-states and principalities abounded, either independently or bound into loose federations, of which the **Holy Roman Empire** of the German heartland was the most notable example.

In western Europe the strong monarchies that had emerged were acquiring national identities. Dreams of a European empire comparable to those of Asia remained strong, although efforts to form one were frustrated.

Dynastic ambitions and historical circumstances combined to favor and then block the creation of a powerful empire in the early sixteenth century. In 1519 electors of the Holy Roman Empire chose Charles V (r. 1519–1556) to be the new emperor. Like his predecessors for three generations, Charles belonged to the powerful **Habsburg°** family of Austria, but he had recently inherited the Spanish thrones of Castile and Aragon. With the vast resources of all these offices behind him (see Map 16.2), Charles hoped to centralize his imperial power and lead a Christian coalition to halt the advance into southeastern Europe of the Ottoman Empire, whose Muslim rulers already controlled most of the Middle East and North Africa.

Charles and his Christian allies eventually halted the Ottomans at the gates of Vienna in 1529, although Ottoman attacks continued on and off until 1697. But Charles's efforts to forge his several possessions into Europe's strongest state failed. King Francis I of France, who had lost to Charles in the election for Holy Roman Emperor, openly supported the Muslim Turks to weaken his rival. In addition, the princes of the Holy Roman Empire's many member states were able to use Luther's religious Reformation to frustrate Charles's efforts to reduce their autonomy. Swayed partly by Luther's appeals to German nationalism, many German princes opposed Charles's defense of Catholic doctrine in the imperial Diet (assembly).

After decades of bitter squabbles turned to open warfare in 1546 (the German Wars of Religion), Charles V finally gave up his efforts at unification, abdicated control of his various possessions to different heirs, and retired to a monastery. By the Peace of Augsburg (1555), he recognized the princes' right to choose whether Catholicism or Lutheranism would prevail in their particular states, and he allowed them to keep the church lands they had seized before 1552. The triumph of religious diversity had derailed Charles's plan for centralizing authority in central Europe and put off German political unification for three centuries.

Meanwhile, the rulers of Spain, France, and England were building a more successful program of political unification based on political centralization and religious unity. The most successful rulers reduced the autonomy of the church and the nobility in their states, while making them part of a unified national structure

---

Habsburg (HABZ-berg)

Map 16.2   The European Empire of Charles V   Charles was Europe's most powerful ruler from 1519 to 1556, but he failed to unify the Christian West. In addition to being the elected head of the Holy Roman Empire, he was the hereditary ruler of the Spanish realms of Castile and Aragon and the possessions of the Austrian Habsburgs in Central Europe. The map does not show his extensive holdings in the Americas and Asia.

with the monarch at its head (see Diversity and Dominance: Political Craft and Craftiness). The cooption of the church in the sixteenth century was stormy, but the outcome was clear. Bringing the nobles and other powerful interests into a centralized political system took longer and led to more diverse outcomes.

Religious Policies

The rulers of Spain and France successfully defended the Catholic tradition against Protestant challenges. Following the pattern used by his predecessors to suppress Jewish and Muslim practices, King Philip II of Spain used an ecclesiastical court, the

우세인 은신 방

운드폭탄 4발 투하… 두 아들과 함께 사망

심진지 구축… 이틀째 시가戰

령이 대중 앞에 나타나거나 애국심
을 고취하는 노래만을 내보내던 방
송마저 중단됐다.

라크 전후
의에서는 전
영국 주도하

DIVERSITY AND DOMINANCE

POLITICAL CRAFT AND CRAFTINESS

Political power was becoming more highly concentrated in early modern Europe, but absolute dominance was more a goal than a reality. Whether subject to constitutional checks or not, rulers were very concerned with creating and maintaining good relations with their more powerful subjects. Their efforts to manipulate public opinion and perceptions have much in common with the efforts of modern politicians to manage their "image."

A diplomat and civil servant in the rich and powerful Italian city-state of Florence, Niccolò Machiavelli, is best known for his book The Prince *(1532). This influential essay on the proper exercise of political power has been interpreted as cynical by some and as supremely practical and realistic by others. Because Machiavelli did not have a high opinion of the intelligence and character of most people, he urged rulers to achieve obedience by fear and deception. But he also suggested that genuine mercy, honesty, and piety may be superior to feigned virtue.*

OF CRUELTY AND CLEMENCY, AND WHETHER IT IS BETTER TO BE LOVED THAN FEARED

. . . It will naturally be answered that it would be desirable to be both the one and the other; but, as it is difficult to be both at the same time, it is much safer to be feared than to be loved, when you have to choose between the two. For it may be said of men in general that they are ungrateful and fickle, dissemblers, avoiders of danger, and greedy of gain. So long as you shower benefits on them, they are all yours; they offer you their blood, their substance, their lives, and their children, provided the necessity for it is far off; but when it is near at hand, then they revolt. And the prince who relies on their words, without having otherwise provided for his security is ruined; for friendships that are won by rewards, not by greatness and nobility of soul, although deserved, yet are not real, and cannot be depended upon in time of adversity.

Besides, men have less hesitation in offending one who makes himself beloved than one who makes himself feared; for love holds by a bond of obligation which, as mankind is bad, is broken on every occasion whenever it is for the interest of the obligated party to break it. But fear holds by the apprehension of punishment, which never leaves men. A prince, however, should make himself feared in such a manner that, if he has not won the affection of his people, he shall at least not incur their hatred. . . .

IN WHAT MANNER PRINCES SHOULD KEEP THEIR FAITH

It must be evident to every one that it is more praiseworthy for a prince always to maintain good faith, and practice integrity rather than craft and deceit. And yet the experience of our own times has shown those princes have achieved great things who made small account of good faith, and who understood by cunning to circumvent the intelligence of others; and that in the end they got the better of those whose actions were dictated by loyalty and good faith. You must know, therefore, that there are two ways of carrying on a struggle; one by law and the other by force. The first is practiced by men, and the other by animals; and as the first is often insufficient, it becomes necessary to resort to the second.

. . . If men were altogether good, this advice would be wrong; but since they are bad and will not keep faith with you, you need not keep faith with them. Nor will a prince ever be short of legitimate excuses to give color to his breaches of faith. Innumerable modern examples could be given of this; and it could easily be shown how many treaties of peace, and how many engagements, have been made null and void by the faithlessness of princes; and he who has best known how to play the fox has ever been the most successful.

But it is necessary that the prince should know how to color this nature well, and how to be a great hypocrite and dissembler. For men are so simple, and yield so much to immediate necessity, that the deceiver will never lack dupes. I will mention one of the most recent examples. [Pope] Alexander VI never did nor ever thought of anything but to deceive, and always found a reason for doing so . . . and yet he was always successful in his deceits, because he knew the weakness of men in that particular.

It is not necessary, however, for a prince to possess all the above-mentioned qualities; but it is essential that he should at least seem to have them. I will even venture to say, that to have and practice them constantly is pernicious, but to seem to have them is useful. For instance, a prince should seem to be merciful, faithful, humane, religious, and upright, and should even be so in reality; but he should have his mind so trained that, when occasion requires it, he may know how to change to the opposite. And it must be understood that a prince, and especially one who has but recently acquired his state, cannot perform all those things which cause men to be esteemed as good; he being obligated, for the sake of maintaining his state, to act contrary to humanity, charity, and religion. And therefore, it is necessary that he should have a versatile mind, capable of changing readily, according as the winds and changes of fortune bid him; and, as has been said above, not to swerve from the good if possible, but to know how to resort to evil if necessity demands it.

A prince then should be very careful never to allow anything to escape his lips that does not abound in the above-mentioned five qualities, so that to see and to hear him he may seem all charity, integrity, and humanity, all uprightness and all piety. And more than all else is it necessary for a prince to seem to possess the last quality; for mankind in general judge more by what they see than by what they feel, every one being capable of the former, and few of the latter. Everybody sees what you seem to be, but few really feel what you are; and those few dare not oppose the opinion of the many, who are protected by the majority of the state; for the actions of all men, and especially those of princes, are judged by the result, where there is no other judge to whom to appeal.

A prince should look mainly to the successful maintenance of his state. For the means which he employs for this will always be counted honorable, and will be praised by everybody; for the common people are always taken in by appearances and by results, and it is the vulgar mass that constitutes the world.

Because, as Machiavelli argued, appearances count for as much in the public arena as realities, it is difficult to judge whether rulers' statements expressed their real feelings and beliefs or what may have been the most expedient to say at the moment. An example is this speech Queen Elizabeth of England made at the end of November 1601 to Parliament after a particularly difficult year. One senior noble had led a rebellion and was subsequently executed. Parliament was pressing for extended privileges. Having gained the throne in 1558 after many difficulties (including a time in prison), the sixty-eight-year-old queen had much experience in the language and wiles of politics and was well aware of the importance of public opinion. Reprinted many times, the speech became famous as "The Golden Speech of Queen Elizabeth."

I do assure you, there is no prince that loveth his subjects better, or whose love can countervail our love. There is no jewel, be it of never so rich a price, which I set before this jewel: I mean your love. For I do esteem it more than any treasure or riches; for that we know how to prize, but love and thanks I count unvaluable.

And, though God has raised me high, yet this I count the glory of my crown, that I have reigned with your loves. This makes me that I do not so much rejoice that God hath made me to be a Queen, as to be Queen over so thankful a people.

Therefore, I have cause to wish nothing more than to content the subjects; and that is the duty I owe. Neither do I desire to live longer days than I may see your prosperity; and that is my only desire.

And as I am that person that still (yet under God) has delivered you, so I trust, by the almighty power of God, that I shall be His instrument to preserve you from every peril, dishonour, shame, tyranny, and oppression. . . .

Of myself I must say this: I was never any greedy scraping grasper, nor a straight, fast-holding prince, nor yet a waster. My heart was never set on worldly goods, but only for my subjects' good. What you bestow on me, I will not hoard it up, but receive it to bestow on you again. Yea, mine own properties I count yours, and to be expended for your good. . . .

To be a king and wear a crown is a thing more glorious to them that see it, than it is pleasing to them that bear it. For myself, I was never so much enticed with the glorious name of king, or royal authority of a queen, as delighted that God made me his instrument to maintain his truth and glory, and to defend this Kingdom (as I said) from peril, dishonour, tyranny and oppression.

There will never Queen sit in my seat with more zeal to my country, care for my subjects, and that sooner with willingness will venture her life for your good and safety than myself. For it is not my desire to live nor reign longer than my life and reign shall be for your good. And though you have had and may have many more princes more mighty and wise sitting in this state, yet you never had or shall have any that will be more careful and loving.

Shall I ascribe anything to myself and my sexly weakness? I were not worthy to live then; and of all, most unworthy of the great mercies I have had from God, who has even yet given me a heart, which never feared foreign of home enemy. I speak to give God the praise . . . That I should speak for any glory, God forbid.

QUESTIONS FOR ANALYSIS

1. Do you find Machiavelli's advice to be cynical or realistic?
2. Describe how a member of Parliament might have responded to Queen Elizabeth's declarations of her concern for the welfare of her people above all else.
3. Can a ruler be sincere and manipulative at the same time?

Source: From *The Historical, Political, and Diplomatic Writings of Niccolo Machiavelli,* trans. Christian E. Detmold (Boston: Houghton, Mifflin and Company, 1891), II: 54–59, and Heywood Townshend, *Historical Collections, or an Exact Account of the Proceedings of the Last Four Parliaments of Q. Elizabeth* (London: Basset, Crooke, and Cademan, 1680), 263–266.

Spanish Inquisition, to bring into line those who resisted his authority. Suspected Protestants, as well as critics of the king, found themselves accused of heresy, an offense punishable by death. Even those who were acquitted of the charge learned not to oppose the king again.

In France the Calvinist opponents of the Valois rulers gained the military advantage in the French Wars of Religion (1562–1598), but in the interest of forging lasting unity, their leader Prince Henry of Navarre then embraced the Catholic faith of the majority of his subjects. In their embrace of a union of church and state, the new Bourbon king, Henry IV, his son King Louis XIII, and his grandson King Louis XIV were as supportive of the Catholic Church as their counterparts in Spain. In 1685 Louis XIV even revoked the Edict of Nantes°, by which his grandfather had granted religious freedom to his Protestant supporters in 1598.

In England King Henry VIII had initially been a strong defender of the papacy against Lutheran criticism. But when Henry failed to obtain a papal annulment of his marriage to Catherine of Aragon, who had not furnished him with a male heir, he challenged the papacy's authority over the church in his kingdom. Henry had the English archbishop of Canterbury annul the marriage in 1533. The breach with Rome was sealed the next year when Parliament made the English monarch head of the Church of England.

Like many Protestant rulers, Henry used his authority to disband monasteries and convents and seize their lands. He gave the lands to his powerful allies and sold some to pay for his new navy. However, under Henry and his successors the new Anglican church moved away from Roman Catholicism in ritual and theology much less than was wanted by English Puritans (Calvinists who wanted to "purify" the Anglican church of Catholic practices and beliefs). In 1603 the first Stuart king, James I, dismissed a Puritan petition to eliminate bishops with the statement "No bishops, no king"—a reminder of the essential role of the church in supporting royal power.

Monarchies in England and France

Over the course of the seventeenth century, the rulers of England and France went through some very intense conflicts with their leading subjects over the limits of royal authority. Religion was never absent as an issue in these struggles, but the different constitutional outcomes they produced were of more significance in the long run.

So as to evade any check on his power, King Charles I of England (see Table 16.1) ruled for eleven years without summoning Parliament, his kingdom's representative body. Lacking Parliament's consent to new taxes, he raised funds by coercing "loans" from wealthy subjects and applying existing tax laws more broadly. Then in 1640 a rebellion in Scotland forced him to summon a Parliament to approve new taxes to pay for an army. Noblemen and churchmen sat in the House of Lords. Representatives from the towns and counties sat in the House of Commons. Before it would authorize new taxes, Parliament insisted on strict guarantees that the king would never again ignore the body's traditional rights. These King Charles refused to grant. When he ordered the arrest of his leading critics in the House of Commons in 1642, he plunged the kingdom into the **English Civil War.**

Charles suffered defeat on the battlefield, but still refused to compromise. In 1649 a "Rump" Parliament purged of his supporters ordered him executed and replaced the monarchy with a republic under the Puritan general Oliver Cromwell. During his rule, Cromwell expanded England's presence overseas and imposed firm control over Ireland and Scotland, but he was as unwilling as the Stuart kings to share power with Parliament. After his death Parliament restored the Stuart line, and for a time it was unclear which side had won the war.

However, when King James II refused to respect Parliament's rights and had his heir baptized a Roman Catholic, the leaders of Parliament forced James into exile in the bloodless Glorious Revolution of 1688. The Bill of Rights of 1689 specified that Parliament had to be called frequently and had to consent to changes in laws and to the raising of an army in peacetime. Another law reaffirmed the official status of the Church of England but extended religious toleration to the Puritans.

A similar struggle in France produced a different outcome. There the Estates General represented the traditional rights of the clergy, the nobility, and the towns (that is, the bourgeoisie). The Estates General was able to assert its rights during the sixteenth-century French Wars of Religion, when the monarchy was weak. But thereafter the Bourbon monarchs generally ruled without having to call it into session. They avoided financial crises by more efficient tax collection and by selling appointments to high government offices. In justification they claimed that the monarch had absolute authority to rule in God's name on earth.

Louis XIV's gigantic new palace at **Versailles**° symbolized the French monarch's triumph over the traditional rights of the nobility, clergy, and towns. Capable of hous-

---

Nantes (nahnt)

Versailles (vuhr-SIGH)

Table 16.1   Rulers in Early Modern Western Europe

Spain	France	England/Great Britain
Habsburg Dynasty	**Valois Dynasty**	**Tudor Dynasty**
Charles I (1516–1556) (Holy Roman Emperor Charles V)	Francis I (1515–1547)	Henry VIII (1509–1547)
	Henry II (1547–1559)	Edward VI (1547–1553)
Philip II (1556–1598)	Francis II (1559–1560)	Mary I (1553–1558)
	Charles IX (1560–1574)	Elizabeth I (1558–1603)
	Henry III (1574–1589)	
	Bourbon Dynasty	**Stuart Dynasty**
Philip III (1598–1621)	Henry IV (1589–1610)[a]	James I (1603–1625)
Philip IV (1621–1665)	Louis XIII (1610–1643)	Charles I (1625–1649)[a, b]
Charles II (1665–1700)	Louis XIV (1643–1715)	(Puritan Republic, 1649–1660)
		Charles II (1660–1685)
		James II (1685–1688)[b]
		William III (1689–1702)
		and Mary II (1689–1694)
Bourbon Dynasty		Anne (1702–1714)
Philip V (1700–1746)		
		Hanoverian Dynasty
	Louis XV (1715–1774)	George I (1714–1727)
Ferdinand VI (1746–1759)		George II (1727–1760)

[a]Died a violent death.   [b]Was overthrown.

ing ten thousand people and surrounded by elaborately landscaped grounds and parks, the palace can be seen as a sort of theme park of royal absolutism. Elaborate ceremonies and banquets centered on the king kept the nobles who lived at Versailles away from plotting rebellion. According to one of them, the duke of Saint-Simon°, "no one was so clever in devising petty distractions" as the king.

The balance of powers in the English model would be widely admired in later times. Until well after 1750 most European rulers admired and imitated the centralized powers and absolutist claims of the French. Some went so far as to build imitations of the Versailles palace. The checks and balances of the English model had a less immediate effect. In his influential *Second Treatise of Civil Government* (1690), the English political philosopher John Locke (1632–1704) disputed monarchial claims to absolute authority by divine right. Rather, he argued, rulers derived their authority from the consent of the governed and, like everyone else, were subject to the law. If monarchs overstepped the law, Locke argued, citizens had not only the right but also the duty to rebel. The later consequences of this idea are considered in Chapter 21.

Saint-Simon (san see-MON)

Warfare and Diplomacy

In addition to the bitter civil wars that pounded the Holy Roman Empire, France, and England, European states engaged in numerous international conflicts. Warfare was almost constant in early modern Europe (see the Chronology at the beginning of the chapter). In their pursuit of power monarchs expended vast sums of money and caused widespread devastation and death. The worst of the international conflicts, the Thirty Years War (1618–1648), caused long-lasting depopulation and economic decline in much of the Holy Roman Empire.

However, the wars also produced dramatic improvements in the skill of European armed forces and in their weaponry that arguably made them the most powerful in the world. The numbers of men in arms increased steadily throughout the early modern period. French forces, for example grew from about 150,000 in 1630 to 400,000 by the early eighteenth century. Even smaller European states built up impressive armies. Sweden, with under a million people, had one of the finest and best-armed military forces in seventeenth-century Europe. Though the country had fewer than 2 million inhabitants in 1700, Prussia's splendid army made it one of Europe's major powers.

Versailles, 1722 This painting by P.-D. Martin shows the east expanse of buildings and courtyards that make up the palace complex built by King Louis XIV. (Giraudon/Art Resource, NY)

Larger armies required more effective command structures. In the words of a modern historian, European armies "evolved . . . the equivalent of a central nervous system, capable of activating technologically differentiated claws and teeth."[3] New signaling techniques improved control of battlefield maneuvers. Frequent marching drills trained troops to obey orders instantly and gave them a close sense of comradeship. To defend themselves cities built new fortifications able to withstand cannon bombardments. Each state tried to outdo its rivals by improvements in military hardware, but battles between evenly matched armies often ended in stalemates that prolonged the wars. Victory increasingly depended on naval superiority.

Only England did not maintain a standing army in peacetime, but England's rise as a sea power had begun under King Henry VIII, who spent heavily on ships and promoted a domestic iron-smelting industry to supply cannon. The Royal Navy also copied innovative ship de-signs from the Dutch in the second half of the seventeenth century. By the early eighteenth century the Royal Navy surpassed the rival French fleet in numbers. By then, England had merged with Scotland to become Great Britain, annexed Ireland, and built a North American empire.

Although France was Europe's most powerful state, Louis XIV's efforts to expand its borders and dominance were increasingly frustrated by coalitions of the other great powers. In a series of eighteenth-century wars beginning with the War of the Spanish Succession (1701–1714), the combination of Britain's naval strength and the land armies of its Austrian and Prussian allies was able to block French expansionist efforts and prevent the Bourbons from uniting the thrones of France and Spain.

This defeat of the French monarchy's empire-building efforts illustrated the principle of **balance of power** in international relations: the major European states formed

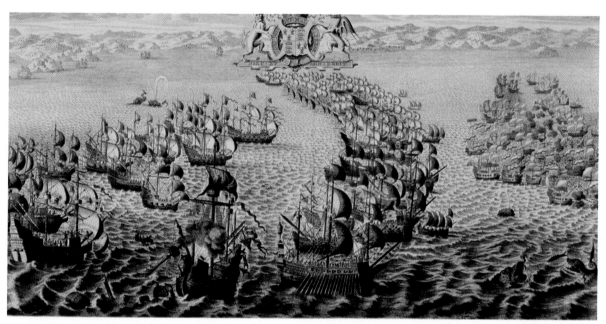

The Spanish Armada   This drawing for a tapestry shows the great warships of the Spanish fleet lined up to face the smaller but faster vessels of the British navy. The ship with oars in the foreground is a galley.   (Eileen Tweedy/The Art Archive)

temporary alliances to prevent any one state from becoming too powerful. Russia emerged as a major power in Europe after its modernized armies defeated Sweden in the Great Northern War (1700–1721). During the next two centuries, though adhering to four different branches of Christianity, the great powers of Europe—Catholic France, Anglican Britain, Catholic Austria, Lutheran Prussia, and Orthodox Russia (see Map 16.3)—maintained an effective balance of power in Europe by shifting their alliances for geopolitical rather than religious reasons. These pragmatic alliances were the first successful efforts at international peacekeeping.

Paying the Piper

To pay the extremely heavy military costs of their wars, European rulers had to increase their revenues. The most successful of them after 1600 promoted mutually beneficial alliances with the rising commercial elite. Both sides understood that trade thrived where government taxation and regulation were not excessive, where courts enforced contracts and collected debts, and where military power stood ready to protect overseas expansion by force when necessary.

Spain, sixteenth-century Europe's mightiest state, illustrates how the financial drains of an aggressive military policy and the failure to promote economic development could lead to decline. Expensive wars against the Ot-

tomans, northern European Protestants, and rebellious Dutch subjects caused the treasury to default on its debts four times during the reign of King Philip II. Moreover, the Spanish rulers' concerns for religious uniformity and traditional aristocratic privilege further undermined the country's economy. In the name of religious uniformity they expelled Jewish merchants, persecuted Protestant dissenters, and forced tens of thousands of skilled farmers and artisans into exile because of their Muslim ancestry. In the name of aristocratic privilege the 3 percent of the population that controlled 97 percent of the land in 1600 was exempt from taxation, while high sales taxes discouraged manufacturing.

For a time, vast imports of silver and gold bullion from Spain's American colonies filled the government treasury. These bullion shipments also contributed to severe inflation (rising prices), worst in Spain but bad throughout the rest of western Europe as well. A Spanish saying captured the problem: American silver was like rain on the roof—it poured down and washed away. Huge debts for foreign wars drained bullion from Spain to its creditors. More wealth flowed out to purchase manufactured goods and even food in the seventeenth century.

The rise of the Netherlands as an economic power stemmed from opposite policies. The Spanish crown had acquired these resource-poor but commercially successful provinces as part of Charles V's inheritance. But King Philip II's decision to impose Spain's ruinously heavy

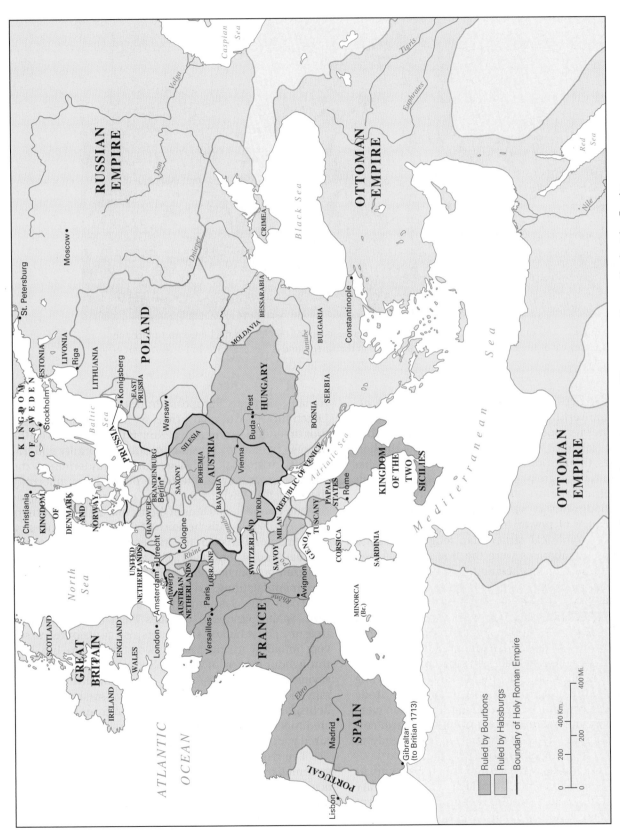

Map 16.3 **Europe in 1740** By the middle of the eighteenth century the great powers of Europe were France, the Austrian Empire, Great Britain, Prussia, and Russia. Spain, the Holy Roman Empire, and the Ottoman Empire were far weaker in 1740 than they had been two centuries earlier.

sales tax and enforce Catholic orthodoxy drove the Dutch to revolt in 1566 and again in 1572. If successful, those measures would have discouraged business and driven away the Calvinists, Jews, and others who were essential to Dutch prosperity. The Dutch fought with skill and ingenuity, raising and training an army and a navy that were among the most effective in Europe. By 1609 Spain was forced to agree to a truce that recognized the autonomy of the northern part of the Netherlands. In 1648, after eight decades of warfare, the independence of these seven United Provinces of the Free Netherlands (their full name) became final.

Rather than being ruined by the long war, the United Netherlands emerged as the dominant commercial power in Europe and the world's greatest trading nation. During the seventeenth century, the wealth of the Netherlands multiplied. This economic success owed much to a decentralized government. During the long struggle against Spain, the provinces united around the prince of Orange, their sovereign, who served as commander-in-chief of the armed forces. But in economic matters each province was free to pursue its own interests. The maritime province of Holland grew rich by favoring commercial interests.

After 1650 the Dutch faced growing competition from the English, who were developing their own close association of business and government. In a series of wars (1652–1678) England used its naval might to break Dutch dominance in overseas trade and to extend its own colonial empire. With government support, the English merchant fleet doubled between 1660 and 1700, and foreign trade rose by 50 percent. As a result, state revenue from customs duties tripled. During the eighteenth century Britain's trading position strengthened still more.

The debts run up by the Anglo-Dutch Wars helped persuade the English monarchy to greatly enlarge the government's role in managing the economy. The outcome has been called a "financial revolution." The government increased revenues by taxing the formerly exempt landed estates of the aristocrats and by collecting taxes directly. Previously, private individuals known as tax farmers had advanced the government a fixed sum of money; in return they could keep whatever money they were able to collect from taxpayers. To secure cash quickly for warfare and other emergencies and to reduce the burden of debts from earlier wars, England also followed the Dutch lead in creating a central bank, from which the government was able to obtain long-term loans at low rates.

The French government was also developing its national economy, especially under Colbert. He streamlined tax collection, promoted French manufacturing and shipping by imposing taxes on foreign goods, and improved transportation within France itself. Yet the power of the wealthy aristocrats kept the French government from following England's lead in taxing wealthy landowners, collecting taxes directly, and securing low-cost loans. Nor did France succeed in managing its debt as efficiently as England. (The role of governments in promoting overseas trade is further discussed in Chapter 18.)

CONCLUSION

European historians have used the word *revolution* to describe many different changes taking place in Europe between 1500 and 1750. The expansion of trade has been called a commercial revolution, the reform of state spending a financial revolution, and the changes in weapons and warfare a military revolution. We have also encountered a scientific revolution and the religious revolution of the Reformation.

These important changes in government, economy, society, and thought were parts of a dynamic process that began in the later Middle Ages and led to even bigger industrial and political revolutions before the eighteenth century was over. Yet the years from 1500 to 1750 were not simply—perhaps not even primarily—an age of progress for Europe. For many, the ferocious competition of European armies, merchants, and ideas was a wrenching experience. The growth of powerful states extracted a terrible price in death, destruction, and misery. The Reformation brought greater individual choice in religion but widespread religious persecution as well. Individual women rose or fell with their social class, but few gained equality with men. The expanding economy benefited members of the emerging merchant elite and their political allies, but most Europeans became worse off as prices rose faster than wages. New scientific and enlightened ideas ignited new controversies long before they yielded any tangible benefits.

The historical significance of this period of European history is clearer when viewed in a global context. What stands out are the powerful and efficient European armies, economies, and governments, which larger states elsewhere in the world feared, envied, and sometimes imitated. From a global perspective, the balance of political and economic power was shifting slowly, but inexorably, in the Europeans' favor. In 1500 the Ottomans threatened Europe. By 1750, as the remaining chapters of Part Five detail, Europeans had brought the world's seas and a growing part of its land and people under their control. No single group of Europeans accomplished this. The Dutch eclipsed the pioneering Portuguese and Spanish; then the English and French bested the Dutch. Competition, too, was a factor in European success.

Other changes in Europe during this period had no great overseas significance at the time. The new ideas of the Scientific Revolution and the Enlightenment were still of minor importance. Their full effects in furthering Europeans' global dominion were felt after 1750, as Parts Six and Seven explore.

■ Key Terms

Renaissance (European)	stock exchange
papacy	gentry
indulgence	Little Ice Age
Protestant Reformation	deforestation
Catholic Reformation	Holy Roman Empire
witch-hunt	Habsburg
Scientific Revolution	English Civil War
Enlightenment	Versailles
bourgeoisie	balance of power
joint-stock company	

■ Suggested Reading

Overviews of this period include Euan Cameron, ed., *Early Modern Europe* (1999); H. G. Koenigsberger, *Early Modern Europe: Fifteen Hundred to Seventeen Eighty-Nine* (1987); and Joseph Bergin, *The Short Oxford History of Europe: The Seventeenth Century* (2001). Global perspectives can be found in Fernand Braudel, *Civilization and Capitalism, 15th–18th Century*, trans. Siân Reynolds, 3 vols. (1979), and Immanuel Wallerstein, *The Modern World-System*, vol. 2, *Mercantilism and the Consolidation of the European World-Economy, 1600–1750* (1980).

Technological and environmental changes are the focus of Geoffrey Parker, *Military Revolution: Military Innovation and the Rise of the West, 1500–1800*, 2d ed. (1996); William H. McNeill, *The Pursuit of Power: Technology, Armed Force, and Society Since A.D. 1000* (1982); Robert Greenhalgh Albion, *Forests and Sea Power: The Timber Problem of the Royal Navy, 1652–1862* (1965); Emmanuel Le Roy Ladurie, *Times of Feast, Times of Famine: A History of Climate Since the Year 1000*, trans. Barbara Bray (1971); and Brian Fagan, *The Little Ice Age: How Climate Made History, 1300–1850* (1988). Robert C. Allen, *Enclosure and the Yeoman: The Agricultural Development of the South Midlands, 1450–1850* (1992), focuses on England.

Steven Stapin, *The Scientific Revolution* (1998), and Hugh Kearney, *Science and Change, 1500–1700* (1971) are accessible introductions. Thomas S. Kuhn, *The Structure of Scientific Revolution*, 3d ed. (1996), and A. R. Hall, *The Scientific Revolution, 1500–1800:*

The Formation of the Modern Scientific Attitude, 2d ed. (1962), are classic studies. Carolyn Merchant, *The Death of Nature: Women, Ecology and the Scientific Revolution* (1980), tries to combine several broad perspectives. *The Sciences in Enlightened Europe*, ed. W. Clark, J. Golinski, and S. Schaffer (1999), examines particular topics in a sophisticated way. Dorinda Outram, *The Enlightenment* (1995), provides a recent summary of research.

Excellent introductions to social and economic life are George Huppert, *After the Black Death: A Social History of Early Modern Europe* (1986), and Carlo M. Cipolla, *Before the Industrial Revolution: European Society and Economy, 1000–1700*, 2d ed. (1980). Peter Burke, *Popular Culture in Early Modern Europe* (1978), offers a broad treatment of nonelite perspectives, as does Robert Jütte, *Poverty and Deviance in Early Modern Europe* (1994). For more economic detail see Robert S. DuPlessis, *Transitions to Capitalism in Early Modern Europe* (1997); Myron P. Gutmann, *Toward the Modern Economy: Early Industry in Europe, 1500–1800* (1988); and Carlo M. Cipolla, ed., *The Fontana Economic History of Europe*, vol. 2, *The Sixteenth and Seventeenth Centuries* (1974).

Topics of women's history are examined by Merry Wiesner, *Women and Gender in Early Modern Europe*, 2d ed. (2000); Bonie S. Anderson and Judith Zinsser, *A History of Their Own: Women in Europe*, vol. II, rev. ed. (2000); and Monica Chojnacka and Merry E. Wiesner-Hanks, *Ages of Woman, Ages of Man* (2002). An excellent place to begin examining the complex subject of witchcraft is Brian Levack, *The Witch-Hunt in Early Modern Europe*, 2d ed. (1995); other up-to-date perspectives can be found in J. Barry, M. Hester, and G. Roberts, eds., *Witchcraft in Early Modern Europe: Studies in Culture and Belief* (1998), and Carlo Ginzburg, *The Night Battles: Witchcraft and Agrarian Cults in the Sixteenth and Seventeenth Centuries*, trans. John and Anne Tedechi (1983).

Good single-country surveys are J. A. Sharpe, *Early Modern England: A Social History*, 2d ed. (1997); Emmanuel Le Roy Ladurie, *The Royal French State, 1460–1610* (1994), and *The Ancien Régime: A History of France, 1610–1774* (1998); Jonathan Israel, *The Dutch Republic: Its Rise, Greatness and Fall, 1477–1806* (1995); and James Casey, *Early Modern Spain: A Social History* (1999).

■ Notes

1. Quoted by Carlo M. Cipolla, "Introduction," *The Fontana Economic History of Europe*, vol. 2, *The Sixteenth and Seventeenth Centuries* (Glasgow: Collins/Fontana Books, 1974), 11–12.
2. Michel de Montaigne, *Essais* (1588), ch. 31, "Des Cannibales."
3. William H. McNeill, *The Pursuit of Power: Technology, Armed Force, and Society Since A.D. 1000* (Chicago: University of Chicago Press, 1982), 124.

Document-Based Question
Political Change in Early Modern Western Europe

Using the following documents, analyze the ideas that shaped political change in early modern Western Europe.

DOCUMENT 1
Map 16.1 Religious Reformation in Europe (p. 408)

DOCUMENT 2
Two excerpts from Voltaire (p. 412)

DOCUMENT 3
Excerpt from Alexander Pope (p. 412)

DOCUMENT 4
Port of Amsterdam (photo, p. 415)

DOCUMENT 5
Political Craft and Craftiness (Diversity and Dominance, pp. 420–421)

DOCUMENT 6
Versailles, 1722 (photo, p. 424)

DOCUMENT 7
The Spanish Armada (photo, p. 425)

How do Documents 4 through 7 illustrate the increasing importance of public opinion in early modern Western Europe? What additional types of documents would help you understand the ideas that shaped political change in this era?

17 The Diversity of American Colonial Societies, 1530–1770

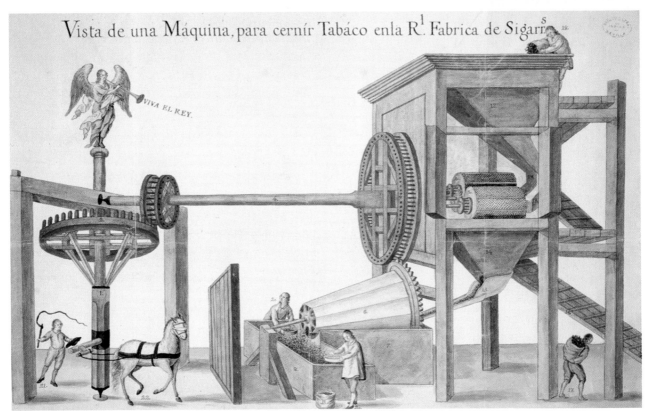

Vista de una Máquina, para cernír Tabáco enla R¹ Fabrica de Sigarr...

VIVA EL REY.

Tobacco Factory Machinery in Colonial Mexico City   The tobacco factory in eighteenth-century Mexico City used a horse-driven mechanical shredder to produce snuff and cigarette tobacco.

CHAPTER OUTLINE

The Columbian Exchange

Spanish America and Brazil

English and French Colonies in North America

Colonial Expansion and Conflict

ENVIRONMENT AND TECHNOLOGY: The Silver Refinery at Potosí, Bolivia, 1700

DIVERSITY AND DOMINANCE: Race and Ethnicity in the Spanish Colonies: Negotiating Hierarchy

Shulush Homa—an eighteenth-century Choctaw leader called "Red Shoes" by the English—faced a dilemma. For years he had befriended the French who had moved into the lower Mississippi Valley, protecting their outlying settlements from other indigenous groups and producing a steady flow of deerskins for trade. In return he received guns and gifts as well as honors previously given only to chiefs. Though born a commoner, he had parlayed his skillful politicking with the French—and the shrewd distribution of the gifts he received—to enhance his position in Choctaw society. Then his fortunes turned. In the course of yet another war between England and France, the English cut off French shipping. Faced with followers unhappy over his sudden inability to supply French guns, Red Shoes decided to make a deal with the English. Unfortunately, the new tactic backfired. His former allies, the French, put a price on his head, which was soon collected. His murder in 1747 launched a Choctaw civil war, a conflict that left French settlements unprotected and the Choctaw people weakened.

The story of Red Shoes reveals a number of themes from the period of European colonization of the Americas. First, although the wars, epidemics, and territorial loss associated with European settlement threatened Amerindians, many adapted the new technologies and new political possibilities to their own purposes and thrived—at least for a time. In the end, though, the best that they could achieve was a holding action. The people of the Old World were coming to dominate the people of the New.

Second, after centuries of isolation, the Americas were being drawn into global events, influenced by the political and economic demands of Europe. The influx of Europeans and Africans resulted in a vast biological and cultural transformation, as the introduction of new plants, animals, diseases, peoples, and technologies fundamentally altered the natural environment of the Western Hemisphere. This was not a one-way transfer, however. The technologies and resources of the New World contributed to profound changes in the Old. Staple crops introduced from the Americas provided highly nutritious foods that helped fuel a population spurt in Europe, Asia, and Africa. As we saw in Chapter 16, riches and products funneled from the Americas changed economic, social, and political relations in Europe.

Third, the fluidity of the Choctaw's political situation reflects the complexity of colonial society, where Amerindians, Europeans, and Africans all contributed to the creation of new cultures. Although similar processes took place throughout the Americas, the particulars varied from place to place, creating a diverse range of cultures. The society that arose in each colony reflected the colony's mix of native peoples, its connections to the slave trade, and the characteristics of the European society establishing the colony. As the colonies matured, new concepts of identity developed, and those living in the Americas began to see themselves as distinct.

As you read this chapter, ask yourself the following questions:

- How did the development of European colonies in the Americas alter the natural environment?

- What were the most important differences in the colonial political institutions and economies created by Spain, Portugal, England, and France?

- How important was forced labor to the European colonies?

THE COLUMBIAN EXCHANGE

The term **Columbian Exchange** refers to the transfer of peoples, animals, plants, and diseases between the New and Old Worlds. The European invasion and settlement of the Western Hemisphere opened a long era of biological and technological transfers that altered American environments. Within a century of first settlement, the domesticated livestock and major agricultural crops of the Old World (the known world before Columbus's voyage) had spread over much of the Americas, and the New World's useful staple crops had enriched the agricultures of Europe, Asia, and Africa. Old World diseases that entered the Americas with European immigrants and African slaves devastated indigenous populations. These dramatic population changes weakened native peoples' capacity for resistance and facilitated the transfer of plants, animals, and related technologies. As a result, the colonies of Spain, Portugal, England, and France became vast arenas of cultural and social experimentation.

Demographic Changes

Because of their long isolation from other continents (see Chapter 15), the peoples of the New World lacked immunity to diseases introduced from the Old World. As a result, death rates among Amerindian peoples during the epidemics of the early colonial period were very high. The lack of reliable data has frustrated efforts to measure the deadly impact of these diseases. Scholars disagree about the size of the precontact population but generally agree that, after contact, Old World diseases overwhelmed native populations. According to one estimate, in the century that followed the triumph of Hernán Cortés in 1521, the indigenous population of central Mexico fell from a high somewhere between 13 million and 25 million to approximately 700,000. In this same period nearly 75 percent of the Maya population disappeared. In the region of the Inca Empire, population fell from about 9 million to approximately 600,000. Brazil's native population was similarly ravaged, falling from 2.5 million to under a million within a century of the arrival of the Portuguese. The most conservative estimates of population loss begin with smaller precontact populations but accept that epidemics had a catastrophic effect.

Smallpox, which arrived in the Caribbean in 1518, was the most deadly of the early epidemics. In Mexico and Central America, 50 percent or more of the Amerindian population died during the first wave of smallpox epidemics. The disease then spread to South America with equally devastating effects. Measles arrived in the New World in the 1530s and was followed by diphtheria, typhus, influenza, and, perhaps, pulmonary plague. Mortality was often greatest when two or more diseases struck at the same time. Between 1520 and 1521 influenza, in combination with other ailments, attacked the Cakchiquel of Guatemala. Their chronicle recalls:

> Great was the stench of the dead. After our fathers and grandfathers succumbed, half the people fled to the fields. The dogs and vultures devoured the bodies. . . . So it was that we became orphans, oh my sons! . . . We were born to die![1]

By the mid-seventeenth century malaria and yellow fever were also present in tropical regions. The deadliest form of malaria arrived with the African slave trade. It ravaged the already reduced native populations and af-

flicted European immigrants as well. Most scholars believe that yellow fever was also brought from Africa, but new research suggests that the disease was present before the conquest in the tropical low country near present-day Veracruz on the Gulf of Mexico. Whatever its origins, yellow fever killed Europeans in the Caribbean Basin and in other tropical regions nearly as efficiently as smallpox had earlier extinguished Amerindians.

The development of English and French colonies in North America in the seventeenth century led to similar patterns of contagion and mortality. In 1616 and 1617 epidemics nearly exterminated many of New England's indigenous groups. French fur traders transmitted measles, smallpox, and other diseases as far as Hudson Bay and the Great Lakes. Although there is very little evidence that Europeans consciously used disease as a tool of empire, the deadly results of contact clearly undermined the ability of native peoples to resist settlement.

Transfer of Plants and Animals

Even as epidemics swept through the indigenous population, the New and the Old Worlds were participating in a vast exchange of plants and animals that radically altered diet and lifestyles in both regions. All the staples of southern European agriculture—such as wheat, olives, grapes, and garden vegetables—were being grown in the Americas in a remarkably short time after contact. African and Asian crops—such as rice, bananas, coconuts, breadfruit, and sugar cane—were soon introduced as well. Native peoples remained loyal to their traditional staples but added many Old World plants to their diet. Citrus fruits, melons, figs, and sugar as well as onions, radishes, and salad greens all found a place in Amerindian cuisines.

In return the Americas offered the Old World an abundance of useful plants. The New World staples—maize, potatoes, and manioc—revolutionized agriculture and diet in parts of Europe, Africa, and Asia (see Environment and Technology: Amerindian Foods in Africa, in Chapter 18). Many experts assert that the rapid growth of world population after 1700 resulted in large measure from the spread of these useful crops, which provided more calories per acre than did any Old World staples other than rice. Beans, squash, tomatoes, sweet potatoes, peanuts, chilies, and chocolate also gained widespread acceptance in the Old World. In addition, the New World provided the Old with plants that provided dyes, medicinal plants, varieties of cotton, and tobacco.

The introduction of European livestock had a dramatic impact on New World environments and cultures.

C H R O N O L O G Y

	Spanish America	Brazil	British America	French America
1500	**1518** Smallpox arrives in Caribbean **1535** Creation of Viceroyalty of New Spain **1540s** Creation of Viceroyalty of Peru **1542** New Laws attempt to improve treatment of Amerindians **1545** Silver discovered at Potosí, Bolivia	**1540–1600** Era of Amerindian slavery **After 1540** Sugar begins to dominate the economy		**1524–1554** Jacques Cartier's voyages to explore Newfoundland and Gulf of St. Lawrence
1600	**1625** Population of Potosí reaches 120,000	**By 1620** African slave trade provides majority of plantation workers	**1583** Unsuccessful effort to establish colony on Newfoundland **1607** Jamestown founded **1620** Plymouth founded **1660** Slave population in Virginia begins period of rapid growth **1664** English take New York from Dutch	**1608** Quebec founded
1700	**1700** Last Habsburg ruler of Spain dies **1713** First Bourbon ruler of Spain crowned **1770s and 1780s** Amerindian revolts in Andean region	**1750–1777** Reforms of marquis de Pombal	**1754–1763** French and Indian War	**1699** Louisiana founded **1760** English take Canada

Faced with few natural predators, cattle, pigs, horses, and sheep, as well as pests like rats and rabbits, multiplied rapidly in the open spaces of the Americas. On the vast plains of present-day southern Brazil, Uruguay, and Argentina, herds of wild cattle and horses exceeded 50 million by 1700. Large herds of both animals also appeared in northern Mexico and what became the southwest of the United States.

Where Old World livestock spread most rapidly, environmental changes were most dramatic. Many priests and colonial officials noted the destructive impact of marauding livestock on Amerindian agriculturists. The first viceroy of Mexico, Antonio de Mendoza, wrote to the Spanish king: "May your Lordship realize that if cattle are allowed, the Indians will be destroyed." Sheep, which grazed grasses close to the ground, were also an environ-

mental threat. Yet the viceroy's stark choice misrepresented the complex response of indigenous peoples to these new animals.

Wild cattle on the plains of South America, northern Mexico, and Texas provided indigenous peoples with abundant supplies of meat and hides. In the present-day southwestern United States, the Navajo became sheepherders and expert weavers of woolen cloth. Even in the centers of European settlement, individual Amerindians turned European animals to their own advantage by becoming muleteers, cowboys, and sheepherders.

No animal had a more striking effect on the cultures of native peoples than the horse, which increased the efficiency of hunters and the military capacity of warriors on the plains. The horse permitted the Apache, Sioux, Blackfoot, Comanche, Assiniboine, and others to more

The Columbian Exchange   After the conquest, the introduction of plants and animals from the Old World dramatically altered the American environment. Here an Amerindian woman is seen milking a cow. Livestock sometimes destroyed the fields of native peoples, but cattle, sheep, pigs, and goats also provided food, leather, and wool.   (From Martinez Compañon, *Trujillo del Perú*, V.II, E 79. Photo: Imaging services, Harvard College Library)

efficiently hunt the vast herds of buffalo in North America. The horse also revolutionized the cultures of the Araucanian (or Mapuche) and Pampas peoples in South America.

SPANISH AMERICA AND BRAZIL

The frontiers of conquest and settlement expanded rapidly. Within one hundred years of Columbus's first voyage to the Western Hemisphere, the Spanish Empire in America included most of the islands of the Caribbean, Mexico, the American southwest, Central

America, the Caribbean and Pacific coasts of South America, the Andean highlands, and the vast plains of the Rio de la Plata region (a region that includes the modern nations of Argentina, Uruguay, and Paraguay). Portuguese settlement in the New World developed more slowly. But before the end of the sixteenth century, Portugal occupied most of the Brazilian coast.

Early settlers from Spain and Portugal sought to create colonial societies based on the institutions and customs of their homelands. They viewed society as a vertical hierarchy of estates (classes of society), as uniformly Catholic, and as an arrangement of patriarchal extended-family networks. They quickly moved to establish the religious, social, and administrative institutions that were familiar to them.

Despite the imposition of foreign institutions and the massive loss of life caused by epidemics in the sixteenth century, indigenous peoples exercised a powerful influence on the development of colonial societies. Aztec and Inca elite families sought to protect their traditional privileges and rights through marriage or less formal alliances with the Spanish settlers. They also often used colonial courts to defend their claims to land. In Spanish and Portuguese colonies, indigenous military allies and laborers proved crucial to the development of European settlements. Nearly everywhere, Amerindian religious beliefs and practices survived beneath the surface of an imposed Christianity. Amerindian languages, cuisines, medical practices, and agricultural techniques also survived the conquest and influenced the development of Latin American culture.

The African slave trade added a third cultural stream to colonial Latin American society. At first, African slaves were concentrated in plantation regions of Brazil and the Caribbean (see Chapter 18), but by the end of the colonial era, Africans and their descendants were living throughout Latin America, enriching colonial societies with their traditional agricultural practices, music, religious beliefs, cuisine, and social customs.

State and Church

The Spanish crown moved quickly to curb the independent power of the conquistadors and to establish royal authority over both the defeated native populations and the rising tide of European settlers. Created in 1524, the **Council of the Indies** in Spain supervised all government, ecclesiastical, and commercial activity in the Spanish colonies. Geography and technology, however, limited the Council's real power. Local officials could not be controlled too closely, because a ship needed more than two hundred days to make a roundtrip voyage from Spain to Veracruz,

Saint Martín de Porres (1579–1639) Martín de Porres was the illegitimate son of a Spanish nobleman and his black servant. Eventually recognized by his father, he entered the Dominican Order in Lima, Peru. Known for his generosity, he experienced visions and gained the ability to heal the sick. As was common in colonial religious art, the artist celebrates Martín de Porres's spirituality while representing him doing the type of work assumed most suitable for a person of mixed descent.   (Private Collection)

Mexico, and additional months of travel were required to reach Lima, Peru.

The highest-ranking Spanish officials in the colonies, the viceroys of New Spain and Peru, enjoyed broad power because of their distance from Spain. But the two viceroyalties in their jurisdiction were also vast territories with geographic obstacles to communication. Created in 1535, the Viceroyalty of New Spain, with its capital in Mexico City, included Mexico, the southwest of what is now the United States, Central America, and the islands of the Caribbean. The Viceroyalty of Peru, with its capital in Lima, was formed in the 1540s to govern Span-

ish South America (see Map 17.1). Each viceroyalty was divided into a number of judicial and administrative districts. Until the seventeenth century, almost all of the officials appointed to high positions in Spain's colonial bureaucracy were born in Spain. Eventually, economic mismanagement in Spain forced the Crown to sell appointments to these positions; as a result, local-born members of the colonial elite gained many offices.

In the sixteenth century Portugal concentrated its resources and energies on Asia and Africa. Because early settlers found neither mineral wealth nor rich native empires in Brazil, the Portuguese king hesitated to set up expensive mechanisms of colonial government in the New World. Seeking to promote settlement but limit costs, the king in effect sublet administrative responsibilities in Brazil to court favorites by granting twelve hereditary captaincies in the 1530s. After mismanagement and inadequate investment doomed this experiment, the king appointed a governor-general in 1549 and made Salvador, in the northern province of Bahia, Brazil's capital. In 1720 the first viceroy of Brazil was named.

The government institutions of the Spanish and Portuguese colonies had a more uniform character and were much more extensive and costly than those later established in North America by France and Great Britain. Taxes paid in Spanish America by the silver and gold mines and in Brazil by the sugar plantations and, after 1690, gold mines funded large and intrusive colonial bureaucracies. These institutions made the colonies more responsive to the initiatives of Spain and Portugal, but they also thwarted local economic initiative and political experimentation.

In both Spanish America and Brazil the Catholic Church became the primary agent for the introduction and transmission of Christian belief as well as European language and culture. It undertook the conversion of Amerindians, ministered to the spiritual needs of European settlers, and promoted intellectual life through the introduction of the printing press and formal education.

Spain and Portugal justified their American conquests by assuming an obligation to convert native populations to Christianity. This religious objective was sometimes forgotten, and some members of the clergy were themselves exploiters of native populations. Nevertheless, the effort to convert America's native peoples expanded Christianity on a scale similar to its earlier expansion in Europe at the time of Constantine in the fourth century. In New Spain alone hundreds of thousands of conversions and baptisms were achieved within a few years of the conquest.

The Catholic clergy sought to achieve their evangelical ends by first converting members of the Amerindian elites, in the hope that they could persuade others to

NEW
FRANCE

Mississippi

ENGLISH COLONIES
(Independence declared, 1776)

ATLANTIC
OCEAN

Colorado

Effective frontier
of Spanish settlement

Silver

Silver

COAHUILA

Rio Grande

FLORIDA
(Ceded to England, 1763–1783)

Gulf of Mexico

VICEROYALTY OF NEW SPAIN
(1535)

Silver

BAJÍO LEÓN Silver

Guadalajara •

Mexico City •   • Veracruz

Silver

Havana

Sugar cane
Beef
Tobacco

HAITI [SAINT DOMINGUE]
(Ceded to France, 1697)

Sugar cane
Indigo

Beef   Sugar cane

Sugar cane   PUERTO RICO

Cacao

BRITISH
HONDURAS

SANTO DOMINGO

JAMAICA
(Conquered by England, 1655)

Sugar cane

Sugar
cane
Cochineal

Cochineal
Cacao
Indigo

• Guatemala

Silver

*Caribbean
Sea*

Pearls

Sugar cane

Caracas

Cacao

Gold
Suárez

Magdalena

• Bogotá

GUIANA

VICEROYALTY OF
NEW GRANADA
(Separated from
Viceroyalty of Peru,
1717, 1739)

Quito •

ANDES

Amazon

Forest
products

PACIFIC
OCEAN

VICEROYALTY
OF PERU
(1590s)

Sugar cane

VICEROYALTY
OF BRAZIL
(1720)

Pernambuco

Sugar
cane

Lima •

• Cuzco

Sugar
cane

• La Paz

Cacao

Salvador

Chuquisaca
• (La Plata; Sucre)
Silver • Potosí

Diamonds
Gold

São Paulo •

Yerba
Tobacco

ANDES

Rio de Janeiro
(Capital, 1763)

Paraná

Spanish colonies

Viceroyalty of New Spain

Viceroyalty of New Granada

Viceroyalty of Peru and Audiencia of Chile

Viceroyalty of Río de la Plata

Portuguese colonies

Viceroyalty of Brazil

VICEROYALTY OF
LA PLATA
(Separated from
Viceroyalty of Peru,
1776)

Wheat

Santiago •

Buenos Aires •

Beef and
hides

Montevideo

Beef and
hides

AUDIENCIA
OF CHILE
(Retained by
Viceroyalty of Peru,
1776)

Claimed but
not settled by Spain

0   500   1000 Km.

0   500   1000 Mi.

Islas Malvinas
(Falkland Islands)

Cape Horn

Map 17.1   Colonial Latin America in the Eighteenth Century   Spain and Portugal controlled most of the Western Hemisphere in the eighteenth century. In the sixteenth century they had created new administrative jurisdictions—viceroyalties—to defend their respective colonies against European rivals. Taxes assessed on colonial products helped pay for this extension of governmental authority.

follow their example. Franciscan missionaries in Mexico hoped to train members of the indigenous elite for the clergy. These idealistic efforts had to be abandoned when church authorities discovered that many converts were secretly observing old beliefs and rituals. The trial and punishment of two converted Aztec nobles for heresy in the 1530s highlighted this problem. Three decades later, Spanish clergy resorted to torture, executions, and the destruction of native manuscripts to eradicate traditional beliefs and rituals among the Maya. Repelled by these events, the church hierarchy ended both the violent repression of native religious practice and efforts to recruit an Amerindian clergy.

Despite its failures, the Catholic clergy did provide native peoples with some protections against the abuse and exploitation of Spanish settlers. The priest **Bartolomé de Las Casas** (1474–1566) was the most influential defender of the Amerindians in the early colonial period. He arrived in Hispaniola in 1502 as a settler and initially lived off the forced labor of Amerindians. Deeply moved by the deaths of so many Amerindians and by the misdeeds of the Spanish, Las Casas gave up this way of life and entered the Dominican Order, later becoming the first bishop of Chiapas, in southern Mexico. For the remainder of his long life Las Casas served as the most important advocate for native peoples, writing a number of books that detailed their mistreatment by the Spanish. His most important achievement was the enactment of the New Laws of 1542—reform legislation that outlawed the enslavement of Amerindians and limited other forms of forced labor.

European clergy arrived in the colonies with the intention of transmitting Catholic Christian belief and ritual without alteration. But the large size of Amerindian populations and their geographic dispersal over a vast landscape thwarted this objective. Linguistic and cultural differences among native peoples also inhibited missionary efforts. These problems frustrated Catholic missionaries and sometimes led to repression and cruelty. The limited success of evangelization permitted the appearance of what must be seen as an Amerindian Christianity that blended Catholic Christian beliefs with important elements of traditional native cosmology and ritual. Most commonly, indigenous beliefs and rituals came to be embedded in the celebration of saints' days or Catholic rituals associated with the Virgin Mary. The Catholic clergy and most European settlers viewed this evolving mixture as the work of the Devil or as evidence of Amerindian inferiority. Instead, it was one component of the process of cultural borrowing and innovation that contributed to a distinct and original Latin American culture.

After 1600 the terrible loss of Amerindian population caused by epidemics and growing signs of resistance to conversion led the Catholic Church to redirect most of its resources from native regions in the countryside to growing colonial cities and towns with large European populations. One important outcome of this altered mission was the founding of universities and secondary schools and the stimulation of urban intellectual life. Over time, the church became the richest institution in the Spanish colonies, controlling ranches, plantations, and vineyards as well as serving as the society's banker.

Colonial Economies

The silver mines of Peru and Mexico and the sugar plantations of Brazil dominated the economic development of colonial Latin America. The mineral wealth of the New World fueled the early development of European capitalism and funded Europe's greatly expanded trade with Asia. Profits produced in these economic centers also promoted the growth of colonial cities, concentrated scarce investment capital and labor resources, and stimulated the development of livestock raising and agriculture in neighboring rural areas (see Map 17.1). Once established, this colonial dependence on mineral and agricultural exports left an enduring social and economic legacy in Latin America.

Gold worth millions of pesos was extracted from mines in Latin America, but silver mines in the Spanish colonies generated the most wealth and therefore exercised the greatest economic influence. The first important silver strikes occurred in Mexico in the 1530s and 1540s. In 1545 the single richest silver deposit in the Americas was discovered at **Potosí°**, in what is now Bolivia, and until 1680 the silver production of Bolivia and Peru dominated the Spanish colonial economy. After this date Mexican silver production greatly surpassed that of the Andean region.

A large labor force was needed to mine silver. The metal was extracted from deep shafts, and the refining process was complex. Silver mines supported farming, livestock raising, and even textile production, which in turn promoted urbanization and the elaboration of regional commercial relations. Silver mining also greatly altered the environment.

At first, silver was extracted from ore by smelting: the ore was crushed in giant stamping mills, then packed with charcoal in a furnace and fired. Within a short time, the wasteful use of forest resources for fuel destroyed forests near the mining centers. Faced with rising fuel costs, Mexican miners developed an efficient method of chemical extraction that relied on mixing mercury with

Potosí (poh-toh-SEE)

A Silver Refinery at Potosí, Bolivia, 1700

The silver refineries of Spanish America were among the largest and most heavily capitalized industrial enterprises in the Western Hemisphere during the colonial period. By the middle of the seventeenth century the mines of Potosí, Bolivia, had attracted a population of more than 120,000.

The accompanying illustration shows a typical refinery (ingenio). Aqueducts carried water from large reservoirs on nearby mountainsides to the refineries. The water wheel shown on the right drove two sets of vertical stamps that crushed ore. Each iron-shod stamp was about the size and weight of a telephone pole. Crushed ore was sorted, dried, and mixed with mercury and other catalysts to extract the silver. The amalgam was then separated by a combination of washing and heating. The end result was a nearly pure ingot of silver that was later assayed and taxed at the mint.

Silver production carried a high environmental cost. Forests were cut to provide fuel and the timbers needed to shore up mine shafts and construct stamping mills and other machinery. Unwanted base metals produced in the refining process poisoned the soil. In addition, the need for tens of thousands of horses, mules, and oxen to drive machinery and transport material led to overgrazing and widespread erosion.

A Bolivian Silver Refinery, 1700   The silver refineries of Spanish America were among the largest industrial establishments in the Western Hemisphere.   (From *In Quest of Mineral Wealth: Aboriginal and Colonial Mining and Metallurgy in Spanish America*, edited by Alan K. Craig and Robert C. West, 1994. Vol. 33 of *Geoscience and Man.* Courtesy, Geoscience Publications)

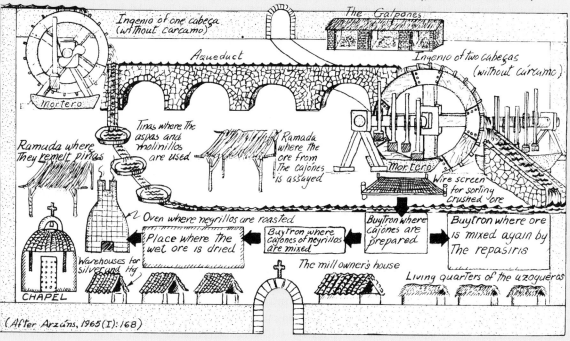

the silver ore (see Environment and Technology: The Silver Refinery at Potosí, Bolivia, 1700). Silver yields and profits increased with the use of mercury amalgamation, but this process, too, had severe environmental costs. Mercury was a poison, and its use contaminated the environment and sickened the Amerindian work force.

From the time of Columbus, indigenous populations had been compelled to provide labor for European settlers in the Americas. Until the 1540s in Spanish colonies, Amerindian peoples were divided among the settlers and were forced to provide them with labor or with textiles, food, or other goods. This form of forced labor was called the **encomienda°**. As epidemics and mistreatment led to the decline in Amerindian population, reforms such as the New Laws sought to eliminate the encomienda. The discovery of silver in both Peru and Mexico, however, led to new forms of compulsory labor. In the mining region of Mexico, Amerindian populations had been greatly reduced by epidemic diseases. Therefore, from early in the colonial period, Mexican silver miners relied on free-wage laborers. Peru's Amerindian population survived in larger numbers, allowing the Spanish to impose a form of labor called the mita°. Under this system, one-seventh of adult male Amerindians were compelled to work for six months each year in mines, farms, or textile factories. The most dangerous working conditions existed in the silver mines, where workers were forced to carry heavy bags of ore up fragile ladders to the surface.

This colonial institution was a corrupted version of the Inca-era mit'a, which had been both a labor tax that supported elites and a reciprocal labor obligation that allowed kin groups to produce surpluses of essential goods that provided for the elderly and incapacitated. In the Spanish mita, few Amerindian workers could survive on their wages. Wives and children were commonly forced to join the work force to help meet expenses. Even those who remained behind in the village were forced to send food and cash to support mita workers.

As the Amerindian population fell with each new epidemic, some of Peru's villages were forced to shorten the period between mita obligations. Instead of serving every seven years, many men were forced to return to mines after only a year or two. Unwilling to accept mita service and the other tax burdens imposed on Amerindian villages, large numbers of Amerindians abandoned traditional agriculture and moved permanently to Spanish mines and farms as wage laborers. The long-term result of these individual decisions weakened Amerindian village life and promoted the assimilation of Amerindians into Spanish-speaking Catholic colonial society.

Before the settlement of Brazil, the Portuguese had already developed sugar plantations that depended on slave labor on the Atlantic islands of Madeira, the Azores, the Cape Verdes, and São Tomé. Because of the success of these early experiences, they were able to quickly transfer this profitable form of agriculture to Brazil. After 1550 sugar production expanded rapidly in the northern provinces of Pernambuco and Bahia. By the seventeenth century, sugar dominated the Brazilian economy.

The sugar plantations of colonial Brazil always depended on slave labor. At first the Portuguese sugar

planters enslaved Amerindians captured in war or seized from their villages. They used Amerindian men as field hands, although in this indigenous culture women had primary responsibility for agriculture. Any effort to resist or flee led to harsh punishments. Thousands of Amerindian slaves died during the epidemics that raged across Brazil in the sixteenth and seventeenth centuries. This terrible loss of Amerindian life and the rising profits of the sugar planters led to the development of an internal slave trade dominated by settlers from the southern region of São Paulo. To supply the rising labor needs of the sugar plantations of the northeast, slave raiders pushed into the interior, even attacking Amerindian populations in neighboring Spanish colonies. Many of the most prominent slavers were the sons of Portuguese fathers and Amerindian mothers.

Amerindian slaves remained an important source of labor and slave raiding a significant business in frontier regions into the eighteenth century. But sugar planters eventually came to rely more on African than Amerindian slaves. Although African slaves at first cost much more than Amerindian slaves, planters found them to be more productive and more resistant to disease. As profits from the plantations increased, imports of African slaves rose from an average of two thousand per year in the late sixteenth century to approximately seven thousand per year a century later, outstripping the immigration of free Portuguese settlers. Between 1650 and 1750, for example, more than three African slaves arrived in Brazil for every free immigrant from Europe.

Within Spanish America, the mining centers of Mexico and Peru eventually exercised global economic influence. American silver increased the European money supply, promoting commercial expansion and, later, industrialization. Large amounts of silver also flowed across the Pacific to the Spanish colony of the Philippines, where it was exchanged for Asian spices, silks, and pottery. Spain tried to limit this trade, but the desire for Asian goods in the colonies was so strong that there was large-scale trade in contraband goods.

The rich mines of Peru, Bolivia, and Mexico stimulated urban population growth as well as commercial links with distant agricultural and textile producers. The population of the city of Potosí, high in the Andes, reached 120,000 inhabitants by 1625. This rich mining town became the center of a vast regional market that depended on Chilean wheat, Argentine livestock, and Ecuadorian textiles.

The sugar plantations of Brazil played a similar role in integrating the economy of the south Atlantic region. The ports of Salvador and Rio de Janeiro in Brazil exchanged sugar, tobacco, and reexported slaves from Brazil for yerba (Paraguayan tea), hides, livestock, and

encomienda (in-co-mee-EN-dah)   mita (MEE-tah)

Brazilian Sugar Plantation Sugar was the most important agricultural product exported from Europe's Western Hemisphere colonies. The African slave trade was developed in large measure to supply the labor needs of sugar plantations and refineries in the Americas. Brazil's economy was dominated by sugar and slavery in the colonial period. In this illustration slaves unload sugar cane from a cart before crushing it in the horizontal mill to extract the juice to process into molasses and sugar. (From Johann Mority Rugendas, Viagem Pitoresca Atraves di Brasil (São Paolo: Livraria Martins Editora, 1954). Harvard College Library Imaging Services)

silver produced in neighboring Spanish colonies. Portugal's increasing openness to British trade also allowed Brazil to become a conduit for an illegal trade between Spanish colonies and Europe. At the end of the seventeenth century the discovery of gold in Brazil helped overcome this large region's currency shortage and promoted further economic integration.

Both Spain and Portugal attempted to control the trade of their American colonies. Spain's efforts were more ambitious, granting first Seville and then Cádiz monopoly trade rights. Similar monopoly privileges were then awarded to the merchant guilds of Lima, Peru, and Mexico City. Because ships returning to Spain with silver and gold were often attacked by foreign naval forces and pirates, Spain came to rely on convoys escorted by warships to supply the colonies and return with silver and gold. By 1650 Portugal had instituted a similar system of monopoly trade and fleets. The combination of monopoly commerce and convoy systems protected shipping and facilitated the collection of taxes, but these measures also slowed the flow of European goods to the colonies and kept prices high. Frustrated by these restraints, colonial populations established illegal commercial relations with the English, French, and Dutch. By the middle of the seventeenth century a majority of European imports were arriving in Latin America illegally.

Society in Colonial Latin America

With the exception of some early viceroys, few members of Spain's great noble families came to the New World. *Hidalgos*°—lesser nobles—were well represented, as were Spanish merchants, artisans, miners, priests, and lawyers. Small numbers of criminals, beggars, and prostitutes also found their way to the colonies. This flow of immigrants from Spain was never large, and Spanish settlers were always a tiny minority in a colonial society numerically dominated by Amerindians and rapidly growing populations of Africans, **creoles** (whites born in America to European parents), and people of mixed ancestry (see Diversity and Dominance: Race and Ethnicity in the Spanish Colonies: Negotiating Hierarchy).

Conquistadors and early settlers who received from the Crown grants of labor and tribute goods (encomienda) from Amerindian communities as rewards for service to Spain dominated colonial society in early Spanish America. These encomenderos sought to create a hereditary social and political class comparable to the nobles of Europe. But their systematic abuse of Amerindian communities and the catastrophic loss of Amerindian life during the epidemics of the sixteenth century undermined their position. They also confronted the

hidalgos (ee-DAHL-goes)

growing power of colonial viceroys, judges, and bishops appointed by the king.

By the end of the sixteenth century, the elite of Spanish America included both European immigrants and creoles. Europeans dominated the highest levels of the church and government as well as commerce. Creoles commonly controlled colonial agriculture and mining. Wealthy creole families with extensive holdings in land and mines often sought to increase their family prestige by arranging for their daughters to marry successful Spanish merchants and officials. Often richer in reputation than in wealth, immigrants from Spain welcomed the opportunity to forge these connections. Although tensions between Spaniards and creoles were inevitable, most elite families included members of both groups.

Before the Europeans arrived in the Americas, the native peoples were members of a large number of distinct cultural and linguistic groups. Cultural diversity and class distinctions were present even in the highly centralized Aztec and Inca empires. The loss of life provoked by the European conquest undermined this rich social and cultural complexity, and the imposition of Catholic Christianity further eroded ethnic boundaries among native peoples. Colonial administrators and settlers broadly applied the racial label "Indian," which facilitated the imposition of special taxes and labor obligations while at the same time erasing long-standing class and ethnic differences.

Amerindian elites struggled to survive in the new political and economic environments created by military defeat and European settlement. Crucial to this survival was the maintenance of hereditary land rights and continued authority over indigenous commoners. Some elite families sought to protect their positions by forging links with conquistadors and early settlers through marriage or less formal relations. As a result, indigenous and colonial elite families were often tied together by kinship, particularly in the sixteenth century. Both self-interest and a desire to protect their communities led them to quickly gain familiarity with colonial legal systems and establish political alliances with judges and other members of the colonial administrative classes. In many cases they were successful. For example, in New Spain many representatives of the indigenous elite gained both recognition of their nobility and new hereditary land rights from Spanish authorities. As this successful minority of elite families solidified their position in the new order, they became essential intermediaries between the indigenous masses and colonial administrators, collecting Spanish taxes and organizing the labor of their dependents for colonial enterprises.

Indigenous commoners suffered the heaviest burdens. Tribute payments, forced labor obligations, and the loss of traditional land rights were common. European domination dramatically changed the indigenous world. The old connections between peoples and places were weakened or, in some cases, lost. Religious life, marriage practices, diet, and material culture were altered profoundly. The survivors of these terrible shocks learned to adapt to the new colonial environment. They embraced some elements of the dominant colonial culture and its technologies. They found ways to enter the market economies of the cities. They learned to produce new products, such as raising sheep and growing wheat. Most importantly, they learned new forms of resistance, like using colonial courts to protect community lands or to resist the abuses of corrupt officials.

Thousands of blacks participated in the conquest and settlement of Spanish America. The majority were European-born Catholic slaves who came to the New World with their masters. Some free blacks immigrated voluntarily. More than four hundred blacks, most of them slaves, participated in the conquest of Peru and Chile. In the fluid social environment of the conquest era, many slaves gained their freedom. Some simply fled from their masters. Juan Valiente escaped his master in Mexico, participated in Francisco Pizarro's conquest of the Inca Empire, and later became one of the most prominent early settlers of Chile, where he was granted Amerindian laborers in an encomienda.

The status of the black population of colonial Latin America declined with the opening of a direct slave trade with Africa (for details, see Chapter 18). Africans were culturally different from the Afro-Iberian slaves and freedmen who accompanied the conquerors. Afro-Iberians commonly had deep roots in Spain or Portugal; their language was Spanish or Portuguese; and their religion was Catholicism. African slaves had different languages, religious beliefs, and cultural practices, and these differences were viewed by settlers as signs of inferiority, ultimately serving as a justification for slavery. By 1600 people with black ancestry were barred from positions in church and government as well as from many skilled crafts.

The rich mosaic of African identities was retained in colonial Latin America. Enslaved members of many cultural groups struggled to retain their languages, religious beliefs, and marriage customs. But in regions with large slave majorities, these cultural and linguistic barriers often divided slaves and made resistance more difficult. Over time, elements from many African traditions blended and mixed with European (and in some cases Amerindian) language and beliefs to forge distinct local cultures. The rapid growth of an American-born slave population accelerated this process of cultural change.

령이 대중 앞에 나타나거나 애국심
을 고취하는 노래만을 내보내던 방
송마저 중단됐다.

라크 전후
의에서는
영국 주도

파운드폭탄 4발 투하… 두 아들과 함께 사망
국심진지 구축… 이틀째 시가戰

DIVERSITY AND DOMINANCE

RACE AND ETHNICITY IN THE SPANISH COLONIES: NEGOTIATING HIERARCHY

Many European visitors to colonial Latin America were interested in the mixing of Europeans, Amerindians, and Africans in the colonies. Many also commented on the treatment of slaves. The passages that follow allow us to examine two colonial societies.

The first selection was written by two young Spanish naval officers and scientists, Jorge Juan and Antonio de Ulloa, who arrived in the colonies in 1735 as members of a scientific expedition. They visited the major cities of the Pacific coast of South America and traveled across some of the most difficult terrain in the hemisphere. In addition to their scientific chores, they described architecture, local customs, and the social order. In this section they describe the ethnic mix in Quito, now the capital of Ecuador.

The second selection was published in Lima under the pseudonym Concolorcorvo around 1776. We now know that the author was Alonso Carrío de la Vandera. Born in Spain, he traveled to the colonies as a young man. He served in many minor bureaucratic positions, one of which was the inspection of the postal route between Buenos Aires and Lima. Carrío turned his long and often uncomfortable trip into an insightful, and sometimes highly critical, examination of colonial society. The selection that follows describes Córdoba, Argentina.

Juan and Ulloa and Carrío seem perplexed by colonial efforts to create and enforce a racial taxonomy that stipulated and named every possible mixture of European, Amerindian, and African, noting the vanity and social presumptions of the dominant white population. We are fortunate to have these contemporary descriptions of the diversity of colonial society, but it is important to remember that these authors were clearly rooted in their time and confident in the superiority of Europe. Although they noted many of the abuses of Amerindian, mixed, and African populations while puncturing the pretensions of the colonial elites, they were also quick to assume the inferiority of the nonwhite population.

QUITO

This city is very populous, and has, among its inhabitants, some families of high rank and distinction; though their number is but small considering its extent, the poorer class bearing here too great a proportion. The former are the descendants either of the original conquerors, or of presidents, auditors, or other persons of character [high rank], who at different times came over from Spain invested with some lucrative post, and have still preserved their luster, both of wealth and descent, by intermarriages, without intermixing with meaner families though famous for their riches. The commonalty may be divided into four classes; Spaniards or Whites, Mestizos, Indians or Natives, and Negroes, with their progeny. These last are not proportionally so numerous as in the other parts of the Indies; occasioned by it being something inconvenient to bring Negroes to Quito, and the different kinds of agriculture being generally performed by Indians.

The name of Spaniard here has a different meaning from that of Chapitone [sic] or European, as properly signifying a person descended from a Spaniard without a mixture of blood. Many Mestizos, from the advantage of a fresh complexion, appear to be Spaniards more than those who are so in reality; and from only this fortuitous advantage are accounted as such. The Whites, according to this construction of the word, may be considered as one sixth part of the inhabitants.

The Mestizos are the descendants of Spaniards and Indians, and are to be considered here in the same different degrees between the Negroes and Whites, as before at Carthagena [sic]; but with this difference, that at Quito the degrees of Mestizos are not carried so far back; for, even in the second or third generations, when they acquire the European color, they are considered as Spaniards. The complexion of the Mestizos is swarthy and reddish, but not of that red common in the fair Mulattos. This is the first degree, or the immediate issue of a Spaniard and Indian. Some are, however, equally tawny with the Indians themselves, though they are distinguished from them by their beards: while others, on the contrary, have so fine a complexion that they might pass for Whites, were it not for some signs which betray them, when viewed attentively. Among these, the most remarkable is the lowness of the forehead, which often leaves but a small space between their hair and eye-brows; at the same time the hair grows remarkably forward on the temples, extending to the lower part of the ear. Besides, the hair itself is harsh, lank, coarse, and very black; their nose very small, thin, and has a little rising on the middle, from whence it forms a small curve, terminating in a point, bending towards the upper lip. These marks, besides some dark spots on the body, are so constant and invariable, as to make it very difficult to conceal the fallacy of their complexion. The Mestizos may be reckoned a third part of the inhabitants.

The next class is the Indians, who form about another third; and the others, who are about one sixth, are the Castes [mixed]. These four classes, according to the most authentic accounts taken from the parish register, amount to between 50 and 60,000 persons, of all ages, sexes, and ranks. If among these classes the Spaniards, as is natural to think, are the most eminent for riches, rank, and power, it must at the same time be owned, however melancholy the truth may appear, they are in proportion the most poor, miserable and distressed; for they refuse to apply themselves to any mechanic business, considering it as a disgrace to that quality they so highly value themselves upon, which consists in not being black, brown, or of a copper color. The Mestizos, whose pride is regulated by prudence, readily apply themselves to arts and trades, but chose those of the greatest repute, as painting, sculpture, and the like, leaving the meaner sort to the Indians.

CÓRDOBA

There was not a person who would give me even an estimate of the number of residents comprising this city, because neither the secular nor the ecclesiastical council has a register, and I know not how these colonists prove the ancient and distinguished nobility of which they boast; it may be that each family has its genealogical history in reserve. In my computation, there must be within the city and its limited common lands around 500 to 600 residents, but in the principal houses there are a very large number of slaves, most of them Creoles [native born] of all conceivable classes, because in this city and in all of Tucumán there is no leniency about granting freedom to any of them. They are easily supported since the principal aliment, meat, is of such moderate price, and there is a custom of dressing them only in ordinary cloth which is made at home by the slaves themselves, shoes being very rare. They aid their masters in many profitable ways and under this system do not think of freedom, thus exposing themselves to a sorrowful end, as is happening in Lima.

As I was passing through Córdoba, they were selling 2,000 Negroes, all Creoles from Temporalidades [property confiscated from the Jesuit order in 1767], from just the two farms of the [Jesuit] colleges of this city. I have seen the lists, for each one has its own, and they proceed by families numbering from two to eleven, all pure Negroes and Creoles back to the fourth generation, because the priests used to sell all of those born with a mixture of Spanish, mulatto, or Indian blood. Among this multitude of Negroes were many musicians and many other crafts; they proceeded with the sale by families. I was assured that the nuns of Santa Teresa alone had a group of 300 slaves of both sexes, to whom they give

their just ration of meat and dress in the coarse cloth which they make, while these good nuns content themselves with what is left from other ministrations. The number attached to other religious establishments is much smaller, but there is a private home which has 30 or 40, the majority of whom are engaged in various gainful activities. The result is a large number of excellent washerwomen whose accomplishments are valued so highly that they never mend their outer skirts in order that the whiteness of their undergarments may be seen. They do the laundry in the river, in water up to the waist, saying vaingloriously that she who is not soaked cannot wash well. They make ponchos [hand-woven capes], rugs, sashes, and sundries, and especially decorated leather cases which the men sell for 8 reales each, because the hides have no outlet due to the great distance to the port; the same thing happens on the banks of the Tercero and Cuarto rivers, where they are sold at 2 reales and frequently for less.

The principal men of the city wear very expensive clothes, but this is not true of the women, who are an exception in both Americas and even in the entire world, because they dress decorously in clothing of little cost. They are very tenacious in preserving the customs of their ancestors. They do not permit slaves, or even freedmen who have a mixture of Negro blood, to wear any cloth other than that made in this country, which is quite coarse. I was told recently that a certain bedecked mulatto [woman] who appeared in Córdoba was sent word by the ladies of the city that she should dress according to her station, but since she paid no attention to this reproach, they endured her negligence until one of the ladies, summoning her to her home under some other pretext, had the servants undress her, whip her, burn her finery before her eyes, and dress her in the clothes befitting her class; despite the fact that the [victim] was not lacking in persons to defend her, she disappeared lest the tragedy be repeated.

QUESTIONS FOR ANALYSIS

1. What do the authors of these selections seem to think about the white elites of the colonies? Are there similarities in the ways that Juan and Ulloa and Carrío describe the mixed population of Quito and the slave population of Córdoba?

2. Are there differences in the way that the authors characterize the relationship between color and class?

3. What does the humiliation of the mixed-race woman in Córdoba tell us about ideas of race and class in the Spanish colony?

Sources: Jorge Juan and Antonio de Ulloa, *A Voyage to South America,* The John Adams translation (abridged), Introduction by Irving A. Leonard (New York: Alfred A. Knopf, 1964), 135–137, copyright © 1964 by Alfred A. Knopf, Inc. Used by permission of Alfred A. Knopf, a division of Random House, Inc.; Concolorcorvo, *El Lazarillo, A Guide for Inexperienced Travelers between Buenos Aires and Lima,* 1773, translated by Walter D. Kline, (Bloomington: Indiana University Press, 1965), 78–80. Used with permission of Indiana University Press.

Slave resistance took many forms, including sabotage, malingering, running away, and rebellion. Although many slave rebellions occurred, colonial authorities were always able to reestablish control. Groups of runaway slaves, however, were sometimes able to defend themselves for years. In both Spanish America and Brazil, communities of runaways (called quilombos° in Brazil and palenques° in Spanish colonies) were common. The largest quilombo was Palmares, where thousands of slaves defended themselves against Brazilian authorities for sixty years until they were finally overrun in 1694.

Slaves were skilled artisans, musicians, servants, artists, cowboys, and even soldiers. However, the vast majority worked in agriculture. Conditions for slaves were worst on the sugar plantations of Brazil and the Caribbean, where harsh discipline, brutal punishments, and backbreaking labor were common. Because planters preferred to buy male slaves, there was always a gender imbalance on plantations. As a result, neither the traditional marriage and family patterns of Africa nor those of Europe developed. The disease environment of the tropics, as well as the poor housing, diet, hygiene, and medical care offered to slaves, also weakened slave families.

The colonial development of Brazil was distinguished from that of Spanish America by the absence of rich and powerful indigenous civilizations such as those of the Aztecs and Inca and by lower levels of European immigration. Nevertheless, Portuguese immigrants came to exercise the same domination in Brazil as the Spanish exercised in their colonies. The growth of cities and the creation of imperial institutions eventually duplicated in outline the social structures found in Spanish America, but with an important difference. By the early seventeenth century, Africans and their American-born descendants were the largest racial group in Brazil. As a result, Brazilian colonial society (unlike Spanish Mexico and Peru) was influenced more by African culture than by Amerindian culture.

Both Spanish and Portuguese law provided for manumission, the granting of freedom to individual slaves. The majority of those gaining their liberty had saved money and purchased their own freedom. This was easiest to do in cities, where slave artisans and market women had the opportunity to earn and save money. Only a tiny minority of owners freed slaves without demanding compensation. Household servants were the most likely beneficiaries of this form of manumission. Only about 1 percent of the slave population gained freedom each year through manumission. However, because slave women received the majority of manumissions and because children born subse-

Painting of Castas   This is an example of a common genre of colonial Spanish American painting. In the eighteenth century there was increased interest in ethnic mixing, and wealthy colonials as well as some Europeans commissioned sets of paintings that showed mixed families. The paintings commonly also indicated what the artist believed was an appropriate class setting. In this painting a richly dressed Spaniard is depicted with his Amerindian wife dressed in European clothing. Notice that the painter has the mestiza daughter look to her European father for guidance.   (Private Collection. Photographer: Camilo Garza/Fotocam, Monterrey, Mexico)

quently were considered free, the free black population grew rapidly.

Within a century of settlement, groups of mixed descent were in the majority in many regions. There were few marriages between Amerindian women and European men, but less formal relationships were common. Few European or creole fathers recognized their mixed offspring, who were called **mestizos**°. Nevertheless, this rapidly expanding group came to occupy a middle position in colonial society, dominating urban artisan trades and small-scale agriculture and ranching. In frontier re-

---

quilombos (key-LOM-bos)   **palenques** (pah-LEN-kays)

mestizo (mess-TEE-zoh)

gions many members of the elite were mestizos, some proudly asserting their descent from the Amerindian elite. The African slave trade also led to the appearance of new American ethnicities. Individuals of mixed European and African descent—called **mulattos**—came to occupy intermediate position in the tropics similar to the social position of mestizos in Mesoamerica and the Andean region. In Spanish Mexico and Peru and in Brazil, mixtures of Amerindians and Africans were also common.

All these mixed-descent groups were called castas° in Spanish America. Castas dominated small-scale retailing and construction trades in cities. In the countryside, many small ranchers and farmers as well as wage laborers were castas. Members of mixed groups who gained high status or significant wealth generally spoke Spanish or Portuguese, observed the requirements of Catholicism, and, whenever possible, lived the life of Europeans in their residence, dress, and diet.

ENGLISH AND FRENCH COLONIES IN NORTH AMERICA

The North American colonial empires of England and France and the colonies of Spain and Portugal had many characteristics in common (see Map 17.1). The governments of England and France hoped to find easily extracted forms of wealth or great indigenous empires like those of the Aztecs or Inca. Like the Spanish and Portuguese, English and French settlers responded to native peoples with a mixture of diplomacy and violence. African slaves proved crucial to the development of all four colonial economies.

Important differences, however, distinguished North American colonial development from the Latin American model. The English and French colonies were developed nearly a century after Cortés's conquest of Mexico and initial Portuguese settlement in Brazil. The intervening period witnessed significant economic and demographic growth in Europe. It also witnessed the Protestant Reformation, which helped propel English and French settlement in the Americas. By the time England and France secured a foothold in the Americas, the regions of the world were also more interconnected by trade. Distracted by ventures elsewhere and by increasing military confrontation in Europe, neither England nor France imitated the large and expensive colonial bureaucracies established by Spain and Portugal. As a result, private companies and individual proprietors played a much

larger role in the development of English and French colonies. Particularly in the English colonies, this practice led to greater regional variety in economic activity, political institutions and culture, and social structure than was evident in the colonies of Spain and Portugal.

Early English Experiments

England's first efforts to gain a foothold in the Americas produced more failures than successes. The first attempt was made by a group of West Country gentry and merchants led by Sir Humphrey Gilbert. Their effort in 1583 to establish a colony in Newfoundland, off the coast of Canada, quickly failed. After Gilbert's death in 1584, his half-brother, Sir Walter Raleigh, organized private financing for a new colonization scheme. A year later 108 men attempted a settlement on Roanoke Island, off the coast of present-day North Carolina. Afflicted with poor leadership, undersupplied, and threatened by Amerindian groups, the colony was abandoned within a year. Another effort to settle Roanoke was made in 1587. Because the Spanish Armada was threatening England, no relief expedition was sent to Roanoke until 1590. When help finally arrived, there was no sign of the 117 men, women, and children who had attempted settlement. Raleigh's colonial experiment was abandoned.

In the seventeenth century England renewed its effort to establish colonies in North America. England continued to rely on private capital to finance settlement and continued to hope that the colonies would become sources of high-value products such as silk, citrus, and wine. New efforts to establish American colonies were also influenced by English experience in colonizing Ireland after 1566. In Ireland land had been confiscated, cleared of its native population, and offered for sale to English investors. The city of London, English guilds, and wealthy private investors all purchased Irish "plantations" and then recruited "settlers." By 1650 investors had sent nearly 150,000 English and Scottish immigrants to Ireland. Indeed, Ireland attracted six times as many colonists in the early seventeenth century as did New England.

The South

London investors, organized as the privately funded Virginia Company, took up the challenge of colonizing Virginia in 1606. A year later 144 settlers disembarked at Jamestown, an island 30 miles (48 kilometers) up the James River in the Chesapeake Bay region. Additional settlers arrived in 1609. The investors and settlers hoped for immediate profits, but

castas (CAZ-tahs)

these unrealistic dreams were soon dashed. Although the location was easily defended, it was a swampy and unhealthy place; in the first fifteen years nearly 80 percent of all settlers in Jamestown died from disease or Amerindian attacks. There was no mineral wealth, no passage to Asia, and no docile and exploitable native population. By concentrating their energies on the illusion of easy wealth, settlers failed to grow enough food and were saved on more than one occasion by the generosity of neighboring Amerindian peoples.

In 1624 the English crown was forced to dissolve the Virginia Company because of its mismanagement of the colony. Freed from the company's commitment to Jamestown's unhealthy environment, colonists pushed deeper into the interior, developing a sustainable economy based on furs, timber, and, increasingly, tobacco. The profits from tobacco soon attracted new immigrants and new capital. Along the shoreline of Chesapeake Bay and the rivers that fed it, settlers spread out, developing plantations and farms. Colonial Virginia's population remained dispersed. In Latin America large and powerful cities dominated by viceroys and royal courts and networks of secondary towns flourished. In contrast, no city of any significant size developed in colonial Virginia.

Colonists in Latin America had developed systems of forced labor to develop the region's resources. Encomienda, mita, and slavery were all imposed on indigenous peoples, and later the African slave trade compelled the migration of millions of additional forced laborers to the colonies of Spain and Portugal. The English settlement of the Chesapeake Bay region added a new system of compulsory labor to the American landscape: **indentured servants.** Ethnically indistinguishable from free settlers, indentured servants eventually accounted for approximately 80 percent of all English immigrants to Virginia and the neighboring colony of Maryland. A young man or woman unable to pay for transportation to the New World accepted an indenture (contract) that bound him or her to a term ranging from four to seven years of labor in return for passage and, at the end of the contract, a small parcel of land, some tools, and clothes.

During the seventeenth century approximately fifteen hundred indentured servants, mostly male, arrived each year (see Chapter 18 for details on the indentured labor system). Planters were less likely to lose money if they purchased the cheaper limited contracts of indentured servants instead of purchasing African slaves during the period when both groups suffered high mortality rates. As life expectancy in the colony improved, planters began to purchase more slaves. They calculated that greater profits could be secured by paying the higher initial cost of slaves owned for life than by purchasing the contracts of indentured servants bound for short peri-

ods of time. As a result, Virginia's slave population grew rapidly from 950 in 1660 to 120,000 by 1756.

By the 1660s many of the elements of the mature colony were in place in Virginia. Colonial government was administered by a Crown-appointed governor and his council, as well as by representatives of towns meeting together as the **House of Burgesses.** When these representatives began to meet alone as a deliberative body, they initiated a form of democratic representation that distinguished the English colonies of North America from the colonies of other European powers. Ironically, this expansion in colonial liberties and political rights occurred along with the dramatic increase in the colony's slave population. The intertwined evolution of American freedom and American slavery gave England's southern colonies a unique and conflicted political character that endured even after independence.

At the same time, the English colonists were expanding settlements in the South. The Carolinas at first prospered from the profits of the fur trade. Fur traders pushed into the interior, eventually threatening the French trading networks based in New Orleans and Mobile. Native peoples eventually provided over 100,000 deerskins annually to this profitable commerce. The environmental and cultural costs of the fur trade were little appreciated at the time. As Amerindian peoples hunted more intensely, the natural balance of animals and plants was disrupted in southern forests. The profits of the fur trade altered Amerindian culture as well, leading villages to place less emphasis on subsistence hunting and fishing and traditional agriculture. Amerindian life was profoundly altered by deepening dependencies on European products, including firearms, metal tools, textiles, and alcohol.

Although increasingly brought into the commerce and culture of the Carolina colony, indigenous peoples were being weakened by epidemics, alcoholism, and a rising tide of ethnic conflicts generated by competition for hunting grounds. Conflicts among indigenous peoples—who now had firearms—became more deadly. Many Amerindians captured in these wars were sold as slaves to local colonists, who used them as agricultural workers or exported them to the sugar plantations of the Caribbean islands. Dissatisfied with the terms of trade imposed by fur traders and angered by this slave trade, Amerindians launched attacks on English settlements in the early 1700s. Their defeat by colonial military forces inevitably led to new seizures of Amerindian land by European settlers.

The northern part of the Carolinas had been settled from Virginia and followed that colony's mixed economy of tobacco and forest products. Slavery expanded slowly in this region. Charleston and the interior of South Carolina followed a different path. Settled first by planters from the Caribbean island of Barbados in 1670, this colony soon developed an economy based on plantations and slavery in imitation of the colonies of the Caribbean and Brazil. In 1729 North and South Carolina became separate colonies.

Despite an unhealthy climate, the prosperous rice and indigo plantations near Charleston attracted a diverse array of immigrants and an increasing flow of African slaves. African slaves were present from the founding of Charleston. They were instrumental in introducing irrigated rice agriculture along the coastal lowlands and in developing indigo (a plant that produced a blue dye) plantations at higher elevations away from the coast. Slaves were often given significant responsibilities. As one planter sending two slaves and their families to a frontier region put it: "[They] are likely young people, well acquainted with Rice & every kind of plantation business, and in short [are] capable of the management of a plantation themselves."[2]

As profits from rice and indigo rose, the importation of African slaves created a black majority in South Carolina. African languages, as well as African religious beliefs and diet, strongly influenced this unique colonial culture. Gullah, a dialect with African and English roots, evolved as the common idiom of the Carolina coast. African slaves were more likely than American-born slaves to rebel or run away. Africans played a major role in South Carolina's largest slave uprising, the Stono Rebellion of 1739. After a group of about twenty slaves, many of them African Catholics who sought to flee south to Spanish Florida, seized firearms, about a hundred slaves from nearby plantations joined them. The colonial militia soon defeated the rebels and executed many of them, but the rebellion shocked slave owners throughout England's southern colonies and led to greater repression.

Colonial South Carolina was the most hierarchical society in British North America. Planters controlled the economy and political life. The richest families maintained impressive households in Charleston, the largest city in the southern colonies, as well as on their plantations in the countryside. Small farmers, cattlemen, artisans, merchants, and fur traders held an intermediate but clearly subordinate social position. Native peoples remained influential participants in colonial society through commercial contacts and alliances, but they were increasingly marginalized. As had occurred in colonial Latin America, the growth of a large mixed population blurred racial and cultural boundaries. On the frontier, the children of white men and Amerindian women held an important place in the fur trade. In the plantation regions and Charleston, the offspring of white men and black women often held preferred positions within the slave work force or, if they had been freed, as carpenters, blacksmiths, or in other skilled trades.

New England

The colonization of New England by two separate groups of Protestant dissenters, Pilgrims and Puritans, put the settlement of this region on a different course. The **Pilgrims,** who came first, wished to break completely with the Church of England, which they believed was still essentially Catholic. Unwilling to confront the power of the established church and the monarch, they sought an opportunity to pursue their spiritual ends in a new land. As a result, in 1620 approximately one hundred settlers—men, women, and children—established the colony of Plymouth on the coast of present-day Massachusetts. Although nearly half of the settlers died during the first winter, the colony survived. Plymouth benefited from strong leadership and the discipline and cooperative nature of the settlers. Nevertheless, this experiment in creating a church-directed community failed. The religious enthusiasm and purpose that at first sustained the Pilgrims was dissipated by new immigrants who did not share the founders' religious beliefs, and by geographic dispersal to new towns. In 1691 Plymouth was absorbed into the larger Massachusetts Bay Colony of the Puritans.

The **Puritans** wished to "purify" the Church of England, not break with it. They wanted to abolish its hierarchy of bishops and priests, free it from governmental interference, and limit membership to people who shared their beliefs. Subjected to increased discrimination in England for their efforts to transform the church, large numbers of Puritans began emigrating from England in 1630.

The Puritan leaders of the Massachusetts Bay Company—the joint-stock company that had received a royal charter to finance the Massachusetts Bay Colony—carried the company charter, which spelled out company rights and obligations as well as the direction of company government, with them from England to Massachusetts. By bringing the charter, they limited Crown efforts to control them; the Crown could revoke but not alter the terms of the charter. By 1643 more than twenty thousand Puritans had settled in the Bay Colony.

Immigration to Massachusetts differed from immigration to the Chesapeake and to South Carolina. Most newcomers to Massachusetts arrived with their families. Whereas 84 percent of Virginia's white population in 1625 was male, Massachusetts had a normal gender balance in its population almost from the beginning. It was also the healthiest of England's colonies. The result was a rapid natural increase in population. The population of

The Home of Sir William Johnson, British Superintendent for Indian Affairs, Northern District As the colonial era drew to a close, the British attempted to limit the cost of colonial defense by negotiating land settlements between native peoples and settlers. These agreements were doomed by the growing tide of western migration. William Johnson (1715–1774) maintained a fragile peace along the northern frontier by building strong personal relations with influential leaders of the Mohawk and other members of the Iroquois Confederacy. His home in present-day Johnstown, New York, shows the mixed nature of the frontier—the relative opulence of the main house offset by the two defensive blockhouses built for protection. ("Johnson Hall," by E. L. Henry. Courtesy, Albany Institute of History and Art)

Massachusetts quickly became more "American" than the population of the colonies to the south or in the Caribbean, whose survival depended on a steady flow of new English immigrants to counter high mortality rates. Massachusetts also was more homogeneous and less hierarchical than the southern colonies.

Political institutions evolved out of the terms of the company charter. A governor was elected, along with a council of magistrates drawn from the board of directors of the Massachusetts Bay Company. Disagreements between this council and elected representatives of the towns led, by 1650, to the creation of a lower legislative house that selected its own speaker and began to develop procedures and rules similar to those of the House of Commons in England. The result was greater autonomy and greater local political involvement than in the colonies of Latin America.

Economically, Massachusetts differed dramatically from the southern colonies. Agriculture met basic needs, but poor soils and harsh climate offered no opportunity to develop cash crops like tobacco or rice. To pay for im-

ported tools, textiles, and other essentials, the colonists needed to discover some profit-making niche in the growing Atlantic market. Fur, timber and other forest products, and fish provided the initial economic foundation, but New England's economic well-being soon depended on providing commercial and shipping services in a dynamic and far-flung commercial arena that included the southern colonies, the smaller Caribbean islands, Africa, and Europe.

In Spanish and Portuguese America, heavily capitalized monopolies (companies or individuals given exclusive economic privileges) dominated international trade. In New England, by contrast, merchants survived by discovering smaller but more sustainable profits in diversified trade across the Atlantic. The colony's commercial success rested on market intelligence, flexibility, and streamlined organization. The success of this development strategy is demonstrated by urban population growth. With sixteen thousand inhabitants in 1740, Boston, the capital of Massachusetts Bay Colony, was the largest city in British North America. This coin-

wealth and status and with the most uniformly British and Protestant population in the Americas.

The Middle Atlantic Region

Much of the future success of English-speaking America was rooted in the rapid economic development and remarkable cultural diversity that appeared in the Middle Atlantic colonies. In 1624 the Dutch West India Company established the colony of New Netherland and located its capital on Manhattan Island. The colony was poorly managed and underfinanced from the start, but its location commanded the potentially profitable and strategically important Hudson River. Dutch merchants established trading relationships with the **Iroquois Confederacy**—an alliance among the Mohawk, Oneida, Onondaga, Cayuga, and Seneca peoples—and with other native peoples that gave them access to the rich fur trade of Canada. When confronted by an English military expedition in 1664, the Dutch surrendered without a fight. James, duke of York and later King James II of England, became proprietor of the colony, which was renamed New York.

New York was characterized by tumultuous politics and corrupt public administration. The colony's success was guaranteed in large measure by the development of New York City as a commercial and shipping center. Located at the mouth of the Hudson River, the city played an essential role in connecting the region's grain farmers to the booming markets of the Caribbean and southern Europe. By the early eighteenth century New York Colony had a diverse population that included English colonists; Dutch, German, and Swedish settlers; and a large slave community.

Pennsylvania began as a proprietary colony and as a refuge for Quakers, a persecuted religious minority. In 1682 William Penn secured an enormous grant of territory (nearly the size of England) because the English king Charles II was indebted to Penn's father. As proprietor (owner) of the land, Penn had sole right to establish a government, subject only to the requirement that he provide for an assembly of freemen.

Penn quickly lost control of the colony's political life, but the colony enjoyed remarkable success. By 1700 Pennsylvania had a population of more than 21,000, and Philadelphia, its capital, soon passed Boston to become the largest city in the British colonies. Healthy climate, excellent land, relatively peaceful relations with native peoples (prompted by Penn's emphasis on negotiation rather than warfare), and access through Philadelphia to good markets led to rapid economic and demographic growth in the colony.

Canadian Fur Trader The fur trade provided the economic foundation of early Canadian settlement. The trade depended on a mix of native and European skills and resources. Fur traders were cultural intermediaries. They transmitted European technologies and products like firearms and machine-made textiles to native peoples, and native technologies and products, like the canoe and furs, to European settlements. Many fur traders were the sons of native women and nearly all were fluent in native languages. (National Archives of Canada)

cided with the decline of New England's once-large indigenous population, which had been dramatically reduced by a combination of epidemics and brutal military campaigns.

Lacking a profitable agricultural export like tobacco, New England did not develop the extreme social stratification of the southern plantation colonies. Slaves and indentured servants were present, but in very small numbers. New England was ruled by the richest colonists and shared the racial attitudes of the southern colonies, but it also was the colonial society with fewest differences in

Both Pennsylvania and South Carolina were grain-exporting colonies, but they were very different societies. South Carolina's rice plantations required large numbers of slaves. In Pennsylvania free workers, including a large number of German families, produced the bulk of the colony's grain crops on family farms. As a result, Pennsylvania's economic expansion in the late seventeenth century occurred without reproducing South Carolina's hierarchical and repressive social order. By the early eighteenth century, however, the prosperous city of Philadelphia did have a large population of black slaves and freedmen. Many were servants in the homes of wealthy merchants, but the fast-growing economy offered many opportunities in skilled trades as well.

French America

Patterns of French settlement more closely resembled those of Spain and Portugal than of England. The French were committed to missionary activity among Amerindian peoples and emphasized the extraction of natural resources—furs rather than minerals. The navigator and promoter Jacques Cartier first stirred France's interest in North America. In three voyages between 1524 and 1542, he explored the region of Newfoundland and the Gulf of St. Lawrence. A contemporary of Cortés and Pizarro, Cartier also hoped to find mineral wealth, but the stones he brought back to France turned out to be quartz and iron pyrite, "fool's gold."

The French waited more than fifty years before establishing settlements in North America. Coming to Canada after spending years in the West Indies, Samuel de Champlain founded the colony of **New France** at Quebec°, on the banks of the St. Lawrence River, in 1608. This location provided ready access to Amerindian trade routes, but it also compelled French settlers to take sides in the region's ongoing warfare. Champlain allied New France with the Huron and Algonquin peoples, traditional enemies of the powerful Iroquois Confederacy. Although French firearms and armor at first tipped the balance of power to France's native allies, the members of the Iroquois Confederacy proved to be resourceful and persistent enemies.

The European market for fur, especially beaver, fueled French settlement. Young Frenchmen were sent to live among native peoples to master their languages and customs. These **coureurs de bois°**, or runners of the woods, often began families with indigenous women, and they and their children, who were called métis°, helped direct the fur trade, guiding French expansion to the west and south. Amerindians actively participated in the trade because they quickly came to depend on the goods they received in exchange for furs—firearms, metal tools and utensils, textiles, and alcohol. This change in the material culture of the native peoples led to overhunting, which rapidly transformed the environment and led to the depletion of beaver and deer populations. It also increased competition among native peoples for hunting grounds, thus promoting warfare.

The proliferation of firearms made indigenous warfare more deadly. The Iroquois Confederacy responded to the increased military strength of France's Algonquin allies by forging commercial and military links with Dutch and later English settlements in the Hudson River Valley. Well armed by the Dutch and English, the Iroquois Confederacy nearly eradicated the Huron in 1649 and inflicted a series of humiliating defeats on the French. At the high point of their power in the early 1680s, Iroquois hunters and military forces gained control of much of the Great Lakes region and the Ohio River Valley. A large French military expedition and a relentless attack focused on Iroquois villages and agriculture finally checked Iroquois power in 1701.

Spain had effectively limited the spread of firearms in its colonies. But the fur trade, together with the growing military rivalry between Algonquin and Iroquois peoples and their respective French and English allies, led to the rapid spread of firearms in North America. Use of firearms in hunting and warfare moved west and south, reaching indigenous plains cultures that had previously adopted the horse introduced by the Spanish. This intersection of horse and gun frontiers in the early eighteenth century dramatically increased the military power and hunting efficiency of the Sioux, Comanche, Cheyenne, and other indigenous peoples, and slowed the pace of European settlement in the North American west.

In French Canada, the Jesuits led the effort to convert native peoples to Christianity. Building on earlier evangelical efforts in Brazil and Paraguay, French Catholic missionaries mastered native languages, created boarding schools for young boys and girls, and set up model agricultural communities for converted Amerindians. The Jesuits' greatest successes coincided with a destructive wave of epidemics and renewed warfare among native peoples in the 1630s. Eventually, churches were established throughout Huron and Algonquin territories. Nevertheless, local culture persisted. In 1688 a French nun who had devoted her life to instructing Amerindian girls expressed the frustration of many missionaries with the resilience of indigenous culture:

We have observed that of a hundred that have passed through our hands we have scarcely civilized one. . . .

Quebec (kwuh-BEC)   **coureurs de bois** (koo-RUHR day BWA)
métis (may-TEES)

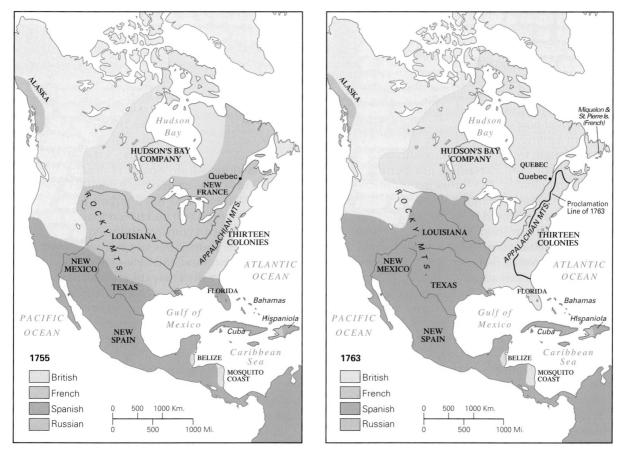

Map 17.2   European Claims in North America, 1755–1763   The results of the French and Indian War dramatically altered the map of North America. France's losses precipitated conflicts between Amerindian peoples and the rapidly expanding population of the British colonies.

When we are least expecting it, they clamber over our wall and go off to run with their kinsmen in the woods, finding more to please them there than in all the amenities of our French house.[3]

As epidemics undermined conversion efforts in mission settlements and evidence of indigenous resistance to conversion mounted, the church redirected some of its resources from the evangelical effort to the larger French settlements, founding schools, hospitals, and churches.

Responsibility for finding settlers and supervising the colonial economy was first granted to a monopoly company chartered in France. Even though the fur trade flourished, population growth was slow. Founded at about the same time as French Canada, Virginia had twenty times more European residents by 1627. After the establishment of royal authority in the 1660s, Canada's French population increased but remained at only seven thousand in 1673. Although improved fiscal manage-

ment and more effective colonial government did promote a limited agricultural expansion, the fur trade remained important. It is clear that Canada's small settler population and the fur trade's dependence on the voluntary participation of Amerindians allowed indigenous peoples to retain greater independence and more control over their traditional lands than was possible in the colonies of Spain, Portugal, or England. Unlike these colonial regimes, which sought to transform ancient ways of life or force the transfer of native lands, the French were compelled to treat indigenous peoples as allies and trading partners. This permitted indigenous peoples to more gradually adapt to new religious, technological, and market realities.

Despite Canada's small population, limited resources, and increasing vulnerability to attack by the English and their indigenous allies, the French aggressively expanded to the west and south. Louisiana was founded in 1699, but by 1708 there were fewer than three hundred soldiers, settlers, and slaves in the territory. Like Canada, Louisiana depended on the fur trade, exporting more than fifty thousand deerskins in 1726. Also as in Canada, Amerindians, driven by a desire for European goods, eagerly embraced this trade. In 1753 a French official reported a Choctaw leader as saying, "[The French] were the first . . . who made [us] subject to the different needs that [we] can no longer now do without."[4]

France's North American colonies were threatened by a series of wars fought by France and England and by the population growth and increasing prosperity of neighboring English colonies. The "French and Indian War" (which led to a broader conflict, the Seven Years War, 1756–1763), however, proved to be the final contest for North American empire (see Map 17.2). England committed a larger military force to the struggle and, despite early defeats, took the French capital of Quebec in 1759. Although resistance continued briefly, French forces in Canada surrendered in 1760. The peace agreement forced France to yield Canada to the English and cede Louisiana to Spain. The differences between French and English colonial realities were suggested by the petition of one Canadian indigenous leader to a British officer after the French surrender. "[W]e learn that our lands are to be given away not only to trade thereon but also to them in full title to various [English] individuals. . . . We have always been a free nation, and now we will become slaves, which would be very difficult to accept after having enjoyed our liberty so long."[5] With the loss of Canada the French concentrated their efforts on their sugar-producing colonies in the Caribbean (see Chapter 18).

COLONIAL EXPANSION AND CONFLICT

In the last decades of the seventeenth century, all of the European colonies in the Americas began to experience a long period of economic and demographic expansion. The imperial powers responded by strengthening their administrative and economic controls in the colonies. They also sought to force colonial populations to pay a larger share of the costs of administration and defense. These efforts at reform and restructuring coincided with a series of imperial wars fought along Atlantic trade routes and in the Americas. France's loss of its North American colonies was one of the most important results of these struggles. Equally significant, colonial populations throughout the Americas became more aware of separate national identities

and more aggressive in asserting local interests against the will of distant monarchs.

Imperial Reform in Spanish America and Brazil

Spain's Habsburg dynasty ended when the Spanish king Charles II died without an heir in 1700 (see Table 16.1, page 423). After thirteen years of conflict involving the major European powers and factions within Spain, Philip of Bourbon, grandson of Louis XIV of France, gained the Spanish throne. Under Philip V and his Bourbon heirs, Spain's colonial administration and tax collection were reorganized. Spain's reliance on convoys protected by naval vessels was abolished; more colonial ports were permitted to trade with Spain; and intercolonial trade was expanded. Spain also created new commercial monopolies to produce tobacco, some alcoholic beverages, and chocolate. The Spanish navy was strengthened, and trade in contraband was more effectively policed.

For most of the Spanish Empire, the eighteenth century was a period of remarkable economic expansion associated with population growth. Amerindian populations began to recover from the early epidemics; the flow of Spanish immigrants increased; and the slave trade to the plantation colonies was expanded. Mining, the heart of the Spanish colonial economy, increased as silver production in Mexico and Peru rose steadily into the 1780s. Agricultural exports also expanded: tobacco, dyes, hides, chocolate, cotton, and sugar joined the flow of goods to Europe.

But these reforms carried unforeseen consequences that threatened the survival of the Spanish Empire. Despite expanded silver production, the economic growth of the eighteenth century was led by the previously minor agricultural and grazing economies of Cuba, the Rio de la Plata region, Venezuela, Chile, and Central America. These export economies were less able than the mining economies of Mexico and Peru to weather breaks in trade caused by imperial wars. Each such disruption forced landowning elites in Cuba and the other regions to turn to alternative, often illegal, trade with English, French, or Dutch merchants. By the 1790s the wealthiest and most influential sectors of Spain's colonial society had come to view the Spanish Empire as an impediment to prosperity and growth.

Bourbon political and fiscal reforms also contributed to a growing sense of colonial grievance by limiting creoles' access to colonial offices and by imposing new taxes and monopolies on colonial production. Consumer and producer resentment, for example, led to rioting when

Market in Rio de Janeiro
In many of the cities of colonial Latin America female slaves and black free women dominated retail markets. In this scene from late colonial Brazil Afro-Brazilian women sell a variety of foods and crafts. (Sir Henry Chamberlain, Views and Costumes of the City and Neighborhoods of Rio de Janeiro, London, 1822)

the Spanish established monopolies on tobacco, cacao (chocolate), and brandy. Because these reforms produced a more intrusive and expensive colonial government that interfered with established business practices, many colonists saw the changes as an abuse of the informal constitution that had long governed the empire. Only in the Bourbon effort to expand colonial militias in the face of English threats did creoles find opportunity for improved status and greater responsibility.

In addition to tax rebellions and urban riots, colonial policies also provoked Amerindian uprisings. Most spectacular was the rebellion initiated in 1780 by the Peruvian Amerindian leader José Gabriel Condorcanqui. Once in rebellion, he took the name of his Inca ancestor Tupac Amaru°, who had been executed as a rebel in 1572. **Tupac Amaru II** was well connected in Spanish colonial society. He had been educated by the Jesuits and was actively involved in trade with the silver mines at Potosí. Despite these connections, he still resented the abuse of Amerindian villagers.

Historians still debate the objectives of this rebellion. Tupac Amaru's own pronouncements did not clearly state whether he sought to end local injustices or overthrow Spanish rule. It appears that a local Spanish judge

who challenged Tupac Amaru's hereditary rights provided the initial provocation, but that Tupac Amaru was ultimately driven by the conviction that colonial authorities were oppressing the indigenous people. As thousands joined him, he dared to contemplate the overthrow of Spanish rule.

Amerindian communities suffering under the mita and tribute obligations provided the majority of Tupac Amaru's army. He also received some support from creoles, mestizos, and slaves. After his capture, he was brutally executed, as were his wife and fifteen other family members and allies. Even after his execution, Amerindian rebels continued the struggle for more than two years. By the time Spanish authority was firmly reestablished, more than 100,000 lives had been lost and enormous amounts of property destroyed.

Brazil experienced a similar period of expansion and reform after 1700. Portugal created new administrative positions and gave monopoly companies exclusive rights to little-developed regions. Here, too, a more intrusive colonial government led to rebellions and plots, including open warfare in 1707 between "sons of the soil" and "outsiders" in São Paulo. The most aggressive period of reform occurred during the ministry of the marquis of Pombal (1750–1777). The Pombal reforms were made possible by an economic expansion fueled by

Tupac Amaru (TOO-pack a-MAH-roo)

the discovery of gold in the 1690s and diamonds after 1720 as well as by the development of markets for coffee and cotton. This new wealth paid for the importation of nearly 2 million African slaves. In Spanish America, a reinvigorated Crown sought to eliminate contraband trade. Portugal, however, had fallen into the economic orbit of England, and Brazil's new prosperity fueled a new wave of English imports.

Reform and Reorganization in British America

England's efforts to reform and reorganize its North American colonies began earlier than the Bourbon initiative in Spanish America. After the period of Cromwell's Puritan Republic (see Chapter 16), the restored Stuart king, Charles II, undertook an ambitious campaign to establish greater Crown control over the colonies. Between 1651 and 1673 a series of Navigation Acts sought to severely limit colonial trading and colonial production that competed directly with English manufacturers. James II also attempted to increase royal control over colonial political life. Royal governments replaced original colonial charters as in Massachusetts and proprietorships as in the Carolinas. Because the New England colonies were viewed as centers of smuggling, the king temporarily suspended their elected assemblies. At the same time, he appointed colonial governors and granted them new fiscal and legislative powers.

James II's overthrow in the Glorious Revolution of 1688 ended this confrontation, but not before colonists were provoked to resist and, in some cases, rebel. They overthrew the governors of New York and Massachusetts and removed the Catholic proprietor of Maryland. William and Mary restored relative peace, but these conflicts alerted the colonists to the potential for aggression by the English government. Colonial politics would remain confrontational until the American Revolution.

During the eighteenth century the English colonies experienced renewed economic growth and attracted a new wave of European immigration, but social divisions were increasingly evident. The colonial population in 1770 was more urban, more clearly divided by class and race, and more vulnerable to economic downturns. Crises were provoked when imperial wars with France and Spain disrupted trade in the Atlantic, increased tax burdens, forced military mobilizations, and provoked frontier conflicts with the Amerindians. On the eve of the American Revolution, England defeated France and weakened Spain. The cost, however, was great. Administrative, military, and tax policies imposed to gain empirewide victory alienated much of the American colonial population.

CONCLUSION

The New World colonial empires of Spain, Portugal, France, and England had many characteristics in common. All subjugated Amerindian peoples and introduced large numbers of enslaved Africans. Within all four empires forests were cut down, virgin soils were turned with the plow, and Old World animals and plants were introduced. Colonists in all four applied the technologies of the Old World to the resources of the New, producing wealth and exploiting the commercial possibilities of the emerging Atlantic market.

Each of the New World empires also reflected the distinctive cultural and institutional heritages of its colonizing power. Mineral wealth allowed Spain to develop the most centralized empire. Political and economic power was concentrated in the great capital cities of Mexico City and Lima. Portugal and France pursued objectives similar to Spain's in their colonies. However, neither Brazil's agricultural economy nor France's Canadian fur trade produced the financial resources that made possible the centralized control achieved by Spain. Nevertheless, all three of these Catholic powers were able to impose and enforce significant levels of religious and cultural uniformity, relative to the British.

Greater cultural and religious diversity characterized British North America. Colonists were drawn from throughout the British Isles and included participants in all of Britain's numerous religious traditions. They were joined by German, Swedish, Dutch, and French Protestant immigrants. British colonial government varied somewhat from colony to colony and was more responsive to local interests. Thus colonists in British North America were better able than those in the areas controlled by Spain, Portugal, and France to respond to changing economic and political circumstances. Most importantly, the British colonies attracted many more European immigrants than did the other New World colonies. Between 1580 and 1760 French colonies received 60,000 immigrants, Brazil 523,000, and the Spanish colonies 678,000. Within a shorter period—between 1600 and 1760—the British settlements welcomed 746,000. Population in British North America—free and slave combined—reached an extraordinary 2.5 million by 1775.

By the eighteenth century, colonial societies across the Americas had matured as wealth increased, populations grew, and contacts with the rest of the world became more common (see Chapter 18). Colonial elites were more confident of their ability to define and defend local interests. Colonists in general were increasingly aware of their unique and distinctive cultural identities and willing to defend American experience and practice in the face of European presumptions of superiority. Moreover, influential groups in all the colonies were drawn toward the liberating ideas of Europe's Enlightenment. In the open and less inhibited spaces of the Western Hemisphere, these ideas (as Chapter 21 examines) soon provided a potent intellectual basis for opposing the continuation of empire.

■ Key Terms

Columbian Exchange	indentured servant
Council of the Indies	House of Burgesses
Bartolomé de Las Casas	Pilgrims
Potosí	Puritans
encomienda	Iroquois Confederacy
creoles	New France
mestizo	coureurs de bois
mulatto	Tupac Amaru II

■ Suggested Reading

Alfred W. Crosby, Jr., is justifiably the best-known student of the Columbian Exchange. See his *The Columbian Exchange: Biological and Cultural Consequences of 1492* (1972) and *Ecological Imperialism* (1986). William H. McNeill, *Plagues and Peoples* (1976), puts the discussion of the American exchange in a world history context. Elinor G. K. Melville, *A Plague of Sheep: Environmental Consequences of the Spanish Conquest of Mexico* (1994), is the most important recent contribution to this field.

Colonial Latin America, 4th ed. (2001), by Mark A. Burkholder and Lyman L. Johnson, provides a good introduction to colonial Latin American history. *Early Latin America* (1983) by James Lockhart and Stuart B. Schwartz and *Spain and Portugal in the New World, 1492–1700* (1984) by Lyle N. McAlister are both useful introductions as well.

The specialized historical literature on the American colonial empires is extensive and deep. A sampling of useful works follows. For the early colonial period see Inga Clendinnen, *Ambivalent Conquests* (1987); James Lockhart, *The Nahuas After the Conquest* (1992); and John Hemming, *Red Gold: The Conquest of the Brazilian Indians* (1978). Nancy M. Farriss, *Maya Society Under Spanish Rule: The Collective Enterprise of Survival* (1984), is also one of the most important books on colonial Spanish America. For the Catholic Church see William Taylor, *Magistrates of the Sacred: Priests and Parishioners in Eighteenth-Century Mexico* (1996). Lyman L. Johnson and Sonya Lipsett-Rivera, eds., *The Faces of Honor* (1999), provides a good introduction to the culture of honor. For the place of women see Asunción Lavrin, ed., *Sexuality and Marriage in Colonial Latin America* (1989). On issues of class R. Douglas Cope, *The Limits of Racial Domination* (1994), is recom-

mended. On the slave trade Herbert S. Klein, *The Middle Passage* (1978), and Philip D. Curtin, *The Atlantic Slave Trade: A Census* (1969), are indispensable. Frederick P. Bowser, *The African Slave in Colonial Peru, 1524–1650* (1973); Mary C. Karasch, *Slave Life and Culture in Rio de Janeiro, 1808–1850* (1986); and Stuart B. Schwartz, *Sugar Plantations in the Formation of Brazilian Society: Bahia, 1550–1835* (1985), are excellent introductions to the African experience in two very different Latin American societies.

Among the useful general studies of the British colonies are Charles M. Andrews, *The Colonial Period of American History: The Settlements*, 3 vols. (1934–1937); David Hackett Fischer, *Albion's Seed: Four British Folkways in America* (1989); and Gary B. Nash, *Red, White, and Black: The Peoples of Early America*, 2d ed. (1982). On the economy see John J. McCusker and Russell R. Menard, *The Economy of British America, 1607–1789* (1979). For slavery see David Brion Davis, *The Problem of Slavery in Western Culture* (1966); Allan Kulikoff, *Tobacco and Slaves: The Development of Southern Cultures in the Chesapeake, 1680–1800* (1986); and Peter H. Wood, *Black Majority: Negroes in Colonial South Carolina from 1670 Through the Stono Rebellion* (1974). Two very useful works on the relations between Europeans and Indians are James Merrill, *The Indians' New World: Catawbas and Their Neighbors from European Contact Through the Era of Removal* (1989); and Daniel H. Usner, Jr., *Indians, Settlers, and Slaves in a Frontier Exchange Economy: The Lower Mississippi Valley Before 1783* (1992).

For late colonial politics see Gary B. Nash, *Urban Crucible: Social Change, Political Consciousness, and the Origins of the American Revolution* (1979); Bernard Bailyn, *The Origins of American Politics* (1986); Jack P. Greene, *The Quest for Power: The Lower Houses of Assembly in the Southern Royal Colonies* (1963); and Richard Bushman, *King and People in Provincial Massachusetts* (1985). On immigration see Bernard Bailyn, *The Peopling of British North America* (1986).

On French North America, William J. Eccles, *France in America*, rev. ed. (1990), is an excellent overview; see also his *The Canadian Frontier, 1534–1760* (1969). G. F. G. Stanley, *New France, 1701–1760* (1968), is also an important resource. R. Cole Harris, *The Seigneurial System in Canada: A Geographical Study* (1966), provides an excellent analysis of the topic. Harold Innis, *The Fur Trade in Canada: An Introduction to Canadian Economic History* (1927), remains indispensable. Also of value are Cornelius Jaenen, *The Role of the Church in New France* (1976), Carole Blackburn, *Harvest of Souls: The Jesuit Missions and Colonialism in North America, 1632–1650* (2000); and Alison L. Prentice, *Canadian Women: A History* (1988).

■ Notes

1. Quoted in Alfred W. Crosby, Jr., *The Columbian Exchange: Biological and Cultural Consequences of 1492* (Westport, CT: Greenwood, 1972), 58.
2. Ibid.

3. Quoted in R. Douglas Francis, Richard Jones, and Donald B. Smith, *Origins: Canadian History to Confederation* (Toronto: Holt, Rinehart, and Winston of Canada, 1992), 52.

4. Quoted in Daniel H. Usner, Jr., *Indians, Settlers and Slaves in a Frontier Exchange Economy: The Lower Mississippi Valley Before 1783*, Institute of Early American History and Culture Series (Chapel Hill: University of North Carolina Press, 1992), 96.

5. Quoted in Cornelius J. Jaenen, "French and Native Peoples in New France," in J. M. Bumsted, *Interpreting Canada's Past*, vol. 1, 2d ed. (Toronto: Oxford University Press, 1993), 73.

Document-Based Question

Diversity in American Colonial Societies

Using the following documents, analyze the influence of race, ethnicity, and gender in the development of social and cultural diversity in American colonial societies before 1770.

DOCUMENT 1
Saint Martín de Porres (1579–1639) (photo p. 435)

DOCUMENT 2
Brazilian Sugar Plantation (photo, p. 440)

DOCUMENT 3
Race and Ethnicity in the Spanish Colonies: Negotiating Hierarchy (Diversity and Dominance, pp. 442–443)

DOCUMENT 4
Painting of Castas (photo, p. 444)

DOCUMENT 5
The Home of Sir William Johnson, British Superintendent for Indian Affairs, Northern District (photo, p. 448)

DOCUMENT 6
Excerpt from a French nun (pp. 450–451)

DOCUMENT 7
Quote from Choctaw leader (p. 452)

DOCUMENT 8
Excerpt from Canadian indigenous leader (p. 452)

DOCUMENT 9
Market in Rio de Janeiro (photo, p. 453)

Which documents seem to provide an idealized or sanitized representation of American colonial society? What additional types of documents would help you analyze the development of social and cultural diversity in American colonial societies before 1770?

18

The Atlantic System and Africa, 1550–1800

Caribbean Sugar Mill The wind mill crushes sugar cane whose juice is boiled down in the smoking building next door.

CHAPTER OUTLINE

Plantations in the West Indies

Plantation Life in the Eighteenth Century

Creating the Atlantic Economy

Africa, the Atlantic, and Islam

ENVIRONMENT AND TECHNOLOGY: Amerindian Foods in Africa

DIVERSITY AND DOMINANCE: Slavery in West Africa and the Americas

In 1694 the English ship *Hannibal* called at the West African port of Whydah° to purchase slaves. The king of Whydah welcomed Captain Thomas Phillips and others of the ship's officers and invited them to his residence. Phillips gave the African ruler the rich presents required for Europeans to trade there and negotiated an agreement on the prices for slaves.

The ship's doctor carefully inspected the naked captives to be sure they were of sound body, young, and free of disease. After their purchase, the slaves were branded with an H (for *Hannibal*) to establish ownership. Once they were loaded on the ship, the crew put shackles on the men to prevent their escape. Phillips recorded that the shackles were removed once the ship was out of sight of land and the risk of a slave revolt had passed. In all, the *Hannibal* purchased 692 slaves, of whom about a third were women and girls.

This was not a private venture. The *Hannibal* had been hired by the **Royal African Company** (RAC), an association of English investors that in 1672 had received a charter from the English monarchy giving them exclusive rights to trade along the Atlantic coast of Africa. Besides slaves, the RAC purchased ivory and other products.

Under the terms of their agreement, the RAC would pay the owners of the *Hannibal* £10.50 for each slave brought to Barbados—but only for those delivered alive. To keep the slaves healthy, Captain Phillips had the crew feed them twice a day on boiled corn meal and beans brought from Europe flavored with hot peppers and palm oil purchased in Africa. Each slave received a pint (half a liter) of water with every meal. In addition, the slaves were made to "jump and dance for an hour or two to our bagpipe, harp, and fiddle" every evening to keep them fit. Despite the incentives and precautions for keeping the cargo alive, deaths were common among the hundreds of people crammed into every corner of a slave ship. The *Hannibal*'s experience was worse than most, losing 320 slaves and 14 crew members during the seven-week

voyage to Barbados. One hundred slaves came down with smallpox, an infection one must have brought on board. Only a dozen died of that disease, but, the captain lamented, "what the small-pox spar'd, the flux [dysentery] swept off, to our great regret, after all our pains and care to give them their messes [meals] in due order and season, keeping their lodgings as clean as possible, and enduring so much misery and stench so long among a parcel of creatures nastier than swine." One wonders what one of the Africans might have written about the nasty creatures who put them in these conditions.

The *Hannibal*'s high losses, nearly double the average losses of an English slaver during the passage to Barbados in the last quarter of the seventeenth century, destroyed the profitability of the voyage. The 372 Africans who were landed alive netted the RAC about £7,000, but the purchase price of 692 slaves at Whydah and the costs of their transportation on the *Hannibal* amounted to about £10,800.

As the *Hannibal*'s experience suggests, the Atlantic slave trade took a devastating toll in African lives and was far from a sure-fire money maker for European investors. Nevertheless, the slave trade and plantation slavery were crucial pieces of a booming new **Atlantic system** that moved goods and wealth, as well as people and cultures, around the Atlantic.

As you read this chapter, ask yourself the following questions:

- How did the Atlantic system affect Europe, Africa, and the Americas?

- How and why did European businessmen, with the help of their governments, put this trading system together?

- How and why did the West Indies and other places in the Americas become centers of African population and culture?

- How did sub-Saharan Africa's expanding contacts in the Atlantic compare with its contacts with the Islamic world?

Whydah (WEE-duh)

	West Indies	Atlantic	Africa
1500	**ca. 1500** Spanish settlers introduce sugar-cane cultivation	**1530** Amsterdam Exchange opens	**1500–1700** Gold trade predominates
			1591 Morocco conquers Songhai
1600	**1620s and 1630s** English and French colonies in Caribbean	**1621** Dutch West India Company chartered	**1638** Dutch take Elmina
	1640s Dutch bring sugar plantation system from Brazil		
	1655 English take Jamaica		
	1670s French occupy western half of Hispaniola	**1660s** English Navigation Acts	
		1672 Royal African Company chartered	**1680s** Rise of Asante
		1698 French *Exclusif*	
1700	**1700** West Indies surpass Brazil in sugar production	**1700 to present** Atlantic system flourishing	**1700–1830** Slave trade predominates
			1720s Rise of Dahomey
			1730 Oyo makes Dahomey pay tribute
	1760 Tacky's rebellion in Jamaica		
	1795 Jamaican Maroon rebellion		

PLANTATIONS IN THE WEST INDIES

The West Indies was the first place in the Americas reached by Columbus and the first part of the Americas where native populations collapsed. It took a long time to repopulate these islands from abroad and forge new economic links between them and other parts of the Atlantic. But after 1650 sugar plantations, African slaves, and European capital made these islands a major center of the Atlantic economy.

Colonization Before 1650

Spanish settlers introduced sugar-cane cultivation into the West Indies shortly after 1500, but these colonies soon fell into neglect as attention shifted to colonizing the American mainland. After 1600 the West Indies revived as a focus of colonization, this time by northern Europeans interested in growing tobacco and other crops. In the 1620s and 1630s English colonization societies founded

small European settlements on Montserrat°, Barbados°, and other Caribbean islands, while the French colonized Martinique°, Guadeloupe°, and some other islands. Because of greater support from their government, the English colonies prospered first, largely by growing tobacco for export.

This New World leaf, long used by Amerindians for recreation and medicine, was finding a new market among seventeenth-century Europeans. Despite the opposition of individuals like King James I of England, who condemned tobacco smoke as "dangerous to the eye, hateful to the nose, harmful to the brain, and dangerous to the lungs," the habit spread. By 1614 tobacco was reportedly being sold in seven thousand shops in and around London, and some English businessmen were dreaming of a tobacco trade as valuable as Spain's silver fleets.

Turning such pipe dreams into reality was not easy. Diseases, hurricanes, and attacks by the Carib and the Spanish scourged the early French and English West

Montserrat (mont-suh-RAHT)   **Barbados** (bahr-BAY-dohs)
Martinique (mahr-tee-NEEK)   **Guadeloupe** (gwah-duh-LOOP)

Indies colonists. They also suffered from shortages of supplies from Europe and shortages of labor sufficient to clear and plant virgin land with tobacco. Two changes improved the colonies' prospects. One was the formation of **chartered companies.** To promote national claims without government expense, France and England gave groups of private investors monopolies over trade to their West Indies colonies in exchange for the payment of annual fees. The other change was that the companies began to provide free passage to the colonies for poor Europeans. These indentured servants paid off their debt by working three or four years for the established colonists (see Chapter 17).

Under this system the French and English population on several tobacco islands grew rapidly in the 1630s and 1640s. By the middle of the century, however, the Caribbean colonies were in crisis because of stiff competition from milder Virginia-grown tobacco, also cultivated by indentured servants. The cultivation of sugar cane, introduced in the 1640s by Dutch investors expelled from Brazil, provided a way out of this crisis. In the process, the labor force changed from mostly European to mostly African.

The Portuguese had introduced sugar cultivation into Brazil from islands along the African coast after 1550 and had soon introduced enslaved African labor as well (see Chapter 17). By 1600 Brazil was the Atlantic world's greatest sugar producer. Some Dutch merchants invested in Brazilian sugar plantations so that they might profit from transporting the sugar across the Atlantic and distributing it in Europe. However, in the first half of the seventeenth century the Dutch were fighting for their independence from the Spanish crown, which then ruled Portugal and Brazil. As part of that struggle, the Dutch government chartered the **Dutch West India Company** in 1621 to carry the conflict to Spain's overseas possessions.

Not just a disguised form of the Dutch navy, the Dutch West India Company was a private trading company. Its investors expected the company's profits to cover its expenses and pay them dividends. After the capture of a Spanish treasure fleet in 1628, the company used some of the windfall to pay its stockholders a huge dividend and the rest to finance an assault on Brazil's valuable sugar-producing areas. By 1635 the Dutch company controlled 1,000 miles (1,600 kilometers) of northeastern Brazil's coast. Over the next fifteen years the new Dutch owners improved the efficiency of the Brazilian sugar industry, and the company prospered by supplying the plantations with enslaved Africans and European goods and carrying the sugar back to Europe.

Like its assault on Brazil, the Dutch West India Company's entry into the African slave trade combined eco-

nomic and political motives. It seized the important West African trading station of Elmina from the Portuguese in 1638 and took their port of Luanda° on the Angolan coast in 1641. From these coasts the Dutch shipped slaves to Brazil and the West Indies. Although the Portuguese were able to drive the Dutch out of Angola after a few years, Elmina remained the Dutch West India Company's headquarters in West Africa.

Once free of Spanish rule in 1640, the Portuguese crown turned its attention to reconquering Brazil. By 1654 Portuguese armies had driven the last of the Dutch sugar planters from Brazil. Some of the expelled planters transplanted their capital and knowledge of sugar production to small Caribbean colonies, which the Dutch had founded earlier as trading bases with Spanish colonies; others introduced the Brazilian system into English and French Caribbean islands. This was a momentous turning point in the history of the Atlantic economy.

Sugar and Slaves

The Dutch infusion of expertise and money revived the French colonies of Guadeloupe and Martinique, but the English colony of Barbados best illustrates the dramatic transformation that sugar brought to the seventeenth-century Caribbean. In 1640 Barbados's economy depended largely on tobacco, mostly grown by European settlers, both free and indentured. By the 1680s sugar had become the colony's principal crop, and enslaved Africans were three times as numerous as Europeans. Exporting up to 15,000 tons of sugar a year, Barbados had become the wealthiest and most populous of England's American colonies. By 1700 the West Indies had surpassed Brazil as the world's principal source of sugar.

The expansion of sugar plantations in the West Indies required a sharp increase in the volume of the slave trade from Africa (see Figure 18.1). During the first half of the seventeenth century about ten thousand slaves a year had arrived from Africa. Most were destined for Brazil and the mainland Spanish colonies. In the second half of the century the trade averaged twenty thousand slaves a year. More than half were intended for the English, French, and Dutch West Indies and most of the rest for Brazil. A century later the volume of the Atlantic slave trade was three times larger.

The shift in favor of African slaves was a product of many factors. Recent scholarship has cast doubt on the once-common assertion that Africans were more suited than Europeans to field labor, since newly arrived Africans

Luanda (loo-AHN-duh)

Figure 18.1   Transatlantic Slave Trade from Africa, 1551–1850

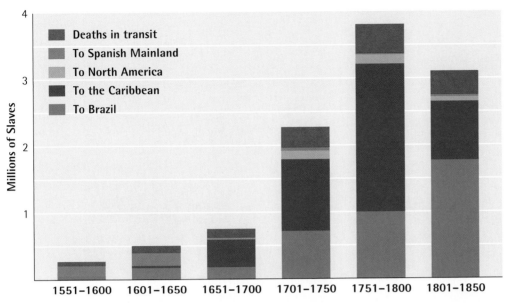

Source: Data from David Eltis, "The Volume and Structure of the Transatlantic Slave Trade: A Reassessment," *William and Mary Quarterly*, 3d Series, 58 (2001), tables II and III.

and Europeans both died in large numbers in the American tropics. Africans' slightly higher survival rate was not decisive because mortality was about the same among later generations of blacks and whites born in the West Indies and acclimated to its diseases.

The West Indian historian Eric Williams also refuted the idea that the rise of African slave labor was primarily motivated by prejudice. Citing the West Indian colonies' prior use of enslaved Amerindians and indentured Europeans, along with European convicts and prisoners of war, he argued that "Slavery was not born of racism: rather, racism was the consequence of slavery."[1] Williams suggested that the shift was due to the lower cost of African labor.

Yet slaves were far from cheap. Cash-short tobacco planters in the seventeenth century preferred indentured Europeans because they cost half as much as African slaves. Poor European men and women were willing to work for little in order to get to the Americas, where they could acquire their own land cheaply at the end of their terms of service. However, as the cultivation of sugar spread after 1750, rich speculators drove the price of land in the West Indies so high that end-of-term indentured servants could not afford to buy it. As a result, poor Europeans chose to indenture themselves in the mainland North American colonies, where cheap land was still available. Rather than raise wages to attract European laborers, Caribbean sugar planters switched to slaves.

Rising sugar prices helped the West Indian sugar planters afford the higher cost of African slaves. The fact that the average slave lived seven years, while the typical indentured labor contract was for only three or four years, also made slaves a better investment. The planters could rely on the Dutch and other traders to supply them with enough new slaves to meet the demands of the expanding plantations. Rising demand for slaves (see Figure 18.1) drove their sale price up steadily during the eighteenth century. These high labor costs were one more factor favoring large plantations over smaller operations.

PLANTATION LIFE IN THE EIGHTEENTH CENTURY

To find more land for sugar plantations, France and England founded new Caribbean colonies. In 1655 the English had wrested the island of Jamaica from the Spanish (see Map 17.1). The French seized the western half of the large Spanish island of Hispaniola in the 1670s. During the eighteenth century this new French colony of Saint Domingue° (present-day Haiti) became the greatest producer of sugar in the Atlantic world,

Saint Domingue (san doh-MANGH)

Plantation Scene, Antigua, British West Indies   The sugar made at the mill in the background was sealed in barrels and loaded on carts that oxen and horses drew to the beach. By means of a succession of vessels the barrels were taken to the ship that hauled the cargo to Europe. The importance of African labor is evident from the fact that only one white person appears in the painting. (Courtesy of the John Carter Brown Library at Brown University)

while Jamaica surpassed Barbados as England's most important sugar colony. The technological, environmental, and social transformation of these island colonies illustrates the power of the new Atlantic system.

Technology and Environment

The cultivation of sugar cane was fairly straightforward. From fourteen to eighteen months after planting, the canes were ready to be cut. The roots continued to produce new shoots that could be harvested about every nine months. Only simple tools were needed: spades for planting, hoes to control the weeds, and sharp machetes to cut the canes. What made the sugar plantation a complex investment was that it had to be a factory as well as a farm. Freshly cut canes needed to be crushed within a few hours to extract the sugary sap. Thus, for maximum efficiency, each plantation needed its own expensive crushing and processing equipment.

At the heart of the sugar works was the mill where canes were crushed between sets of heavy rollers. Small mills could be turned by animal or human power, but larger, more efficient mills needed more sophisticated sources of power. Eighteenth-century Barbados went in heavily for windmills, and the French sugar islands and Jamaica used costly water-powered mills, often fed by elaborate aqueducts.

From the mill, lead-lined wooden troughs carried the cane juice to a series of large copper kettles in the boiling shed, where the excess water boiled off, leaving a thick syrup. Workers poured the syrup into conical molds in the drying shed. The sugar crystals that formed in the molds were packed in wooden barrels for shipment to Europe. The dark molasses that drained off was made into rum in yet another building, or it was barreled for export.

To make the operation more efficient and profitable, investors gradually increased the size of the typical West Indian plantation from around 100 acres (40 hectares) in the seventeenth century to at least twice that size in the eighteenth century. Some plantations were even larger. In 1774 Jamaica's 680 sugar plantations averaged 441 acres (178 hectares) each; some spread over 2,000 acres

(800 hectares). Jamaica specialized so heavily in sugar production that the island had to import most of its food. Saint Domingue had a comparable number of plantations of smaller average size but generally higher productivity. The French colony was also more diverse in its economy. Although sugar production was paramount, some planters raised provisions for local consumption and crops such as coffee and cacao for export.

In some ways the mature sugar plantation was environmentally responsible. The crushing mill was powered by water, wind, or animals, not fossil fuels. The boilers were largely fueled by burning the crushed canes, and the fields were fertilized by manure from the cattle. In two respects, however, the plantation was very damaging to the environment: soil exhaustion and deforestation.

Repeated cultivation of a single crop removes more nutrients from the soil than animal fertilizer and fallow periods can restore. Instead of rotating sugar with other crops in order to restore the nutrients naturally, planters found it more profitable to clear new lands when yields declined too much in the old fields. When land close to the sea was exhausted, planters moved on to new islands. Many of the English who first settled Jamaica were from Barbados, and the pioneer planters on Saint Domingue came from older French sugar colonies. In the second half of the eighteenth century, Jamaican sugar production began to fall behind that of Saint Domingue, which still had access to virgin land. Thus the plantations of this period were not a stable form of agriculture but rather gradually laid waste to the landscape.

Deforestation, the second form of environmental damage, continued a trend begun in the sixteenth century. The Spanish had cut down some forests in the Caribbean to make pastures for the cattle they introduced. Sugar cultivation rapidly accelerated land clearing. Forests near the coast were the first to disappear, and by the end of the eighteenth century only land in the interior of the islands retained dense forests.

Combined with soil exhaustion and deforestation, other changes profoundly altered the ecology balance of the West Indies. By the eighteenth century nearly all of the domesticated animals and cultivated plants in the Caribbean were ones that Europeans had introduced. The Spanish had brought cattle, pigs, and horses, all of which multiplied so rapidly that no new imports had been necessary after 1503. They had also introduced new plants. Of these, bananas and plantain from the Canary Islands were a valuable addition to the food supply, and sugar and rice formed the basis of plantation agriculture, along with native tobacco. Other food crops arrived with the slaves from Africa, including okra, black-eyed peas, yams, grains such as millet and sorghum, and mangoes. Many of these new animals and plants were useful additions to the islands,

but they crowded out indigenous species. New World foods also found their way to Africa (see Environment and Technology: Amerindian Foods in Africa).

The most tragic and dramatic transformation in the West Indies occurred in the human population. Chapter 15 detailed how the indigenous Arawak peoples of the large islands were wiped out by disease and abuse within fifty years of Columbus's first voyage. As the plantation economy spread, the Carib surviving on the smaller islands were also pushed to the point of extinction. Far earlier and more completely than in any mainland colony, the West Indies were repeopled from across the Atlantic—first from Europe and then from Africa.

Slaves' Lives

During the eighteenth century West Indian plantation colonies were the world's most polarized societies. On most islands 90 percent or more of the inhabitants were slaves. Power resided in the hands of a **plantocracy,** a small number of very rich men who owned most of the slaves and most of the land. Between the slaves and the masters might be found only a few others—some estate managers and government officials and, in the French islands, small farmers, both white and black. Thus it is only a slight simplification to describe eighteenth-century Caribbean society as being made up of a large, abject class of slaves and a small, powerful class of masters.

The profitability of a Caribbean plantation depended on extracting as much work as possible from the slaves. Their long workday might stretch to eighteen hours or more when the cane harvest and milling were in full swing. Sugar plantations achieved exceptional productivity through the threat and use of force. As Table 18.1 shows (see page 465), on a typical Jamaican plantation about 80 percent of the slaves actively engaged in productive tasks; the only exceptions were infants, the seriously ill, and the very old. Everyone on the plantation, except those disabled by age or infirmity, had an assigned task.

Table 18.1 also illustrates how slave labor was organized by age, sex, and ability. As in other Caribbean colonies, only 2 or 3 percent of the slaves were house servants. About 70 percent of the able-bodied slaves worked in the fields, generally in one of three labor gangs. A "great gang," made up of the strongest slaves in the prime of life, did the heaviest work, such as breaking up the soil at the beginning of the planting season. A second gang of youths, elders, and less fit slaves did somewhat lighter work. A "grass gang," composed of children under the supervision of an elderly slave, was responsible for weeding and other simple work, such as collecting grass

Amerindian Foods in Africa

The migration of European plants and animals across the Atlantic to the New World was one side of the Columbian Exchange (see Chapter 17). The Andean potato, for example, became a staple crop of the poor in Europe, and cassava (a Brazilian plant cultivated for its edible roots) and maize (corn) moved across the Atlantic to Africa.

Maize was a high-yielding grain that could produce much more food per acre than many grains indigenous to Africa. The varieties of maize that spread to Africa were not modern high-bred "sweet corn" but starchier types found in white and yellow corn meal. Cassava—not well known to modern North Americans except perhaps in the form of tapioca—became the most important New World food in Africa. Truly a marvel, cassava had the highest yield of calories per acre of any staple food and thrived even in poor soils and during droughts. Both the leaves and the root could be eaten. Ground into meal, the root could be made into a bread that would keep for up to six months, or it could be fermented into a beverage.

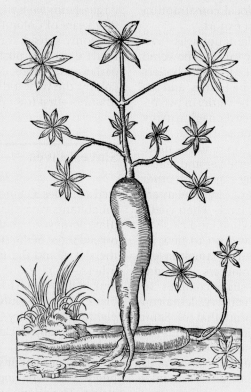

Cassava Plant   Both the leaves and the starchy root of the cassava plant could be eaten.   (Engraving from André Thevet, *Les Singularitez de la France Antarctique*. Paris: Maurice de la Porte, 1557. Courtesy of the James Bell Library, University of Minnesota)

Cassava and maize were probably accidentally introduced into Africa by Portuguese ships from Brazil that discarded leftover supplies after reaching Angola. It did not take long for local Africans to recognize the food value of these new crops, especially in drought-prone areas. As the principal farmers in Central Africa, women must have played an important role in learning how to cultivate, harvest, and prepare these foods. By the eighteenth century Lunda rulers hundreds of miles from the Angolan coast were actively promoting the cultivation of maize and cassava on their royal estates in order to provide a more secure food supply.

Some historians of Africa believe that in the inland areas these Amerindian food crops provided the nutritional base for a population increase that partially offset losses due to the Atlantic slave trade. By supplementing the range of food crops available and by enabling populations to increase in once lightly settled or famine-prone areas, cassava and maize, along with peanuts and other New World legumes, permanently altered Africans' environmental prospects.

---

for the animals. Women formed the majority of the field laborers, even in the great gang. Nursing mothers took their babies with them to the fields. Slaves too old for field labor tended the toddlers.

Because slave ships brought twice as many males as females from Africa, men outnumbered women on Caribbean plantations. As Table 18.1 shows, a little over half of the adult males were employed in nongang work. Some tended the livestock, including the mules and oxen that did the heavy carrying work; others were skilled tradesmen, such as blacksmiths and carpenters. The most important artisan slave was the head boiler, who oversaw the delicate process of reducing the cane sap to crystallized sugar and molasses.

Skilled slaves received rewards of food and clothing or time off for good work, but the most common reason for working hard was to escape punishment. A slave gang was headed by a privileged male slave, appropriately called the **"driver,"** whose job was to ensure that the gang completed its work. Since production quotas

Table 18.1　Slave Occupations on a Jamaican Sugar Plantation, 1788

Occupations and Conditions	Men	Women	Boys and Girls	Total
Field laborers	62	78		140
Tradesmen	29			29
Field drivers	4			4
Field cooks		4		4
Mule-, cattle-, and stablemen	12			12
Watchmen	18			18
Nurse		1		1
Midwife		1		1
Domestics and gardeners		5	3	8
Grass-gang			20	20
Total employed	**125**	**89**	**23**	**237**
Infants			23	23
Invalids (18 with yaws)				32
Absent on roads				5
Superannuated [elderly]				7
Overall total				**304**

Source: Adapted from "Edward Long to William Pitt," in Michael Craton, James Walvin, and David Wright, eds., *Slavery, Abolition, and Emancipation* (London: Longman, 1976), 103. © Michael Craton, James Walvin, and David Wright, reprinted by permission of Pearson Education Limited.

Punishment for Slaves　In addition to whipping and other cruel punishments, slave owners devised other ways to shame and intimidate slaves into obedience. This metal face mask prevented the wearer from eating or drinking.　(By permission of the Syndics of Cambridge University Library)

were high, slaves toiled in the fields from sunup to sunset, except for meal breaks. Those who fell behind due to fatigue or illness soon felt the sting of the whip. Openly rebellious slaves who refused to work, disobeyed orders, or tried to escape were punished with flogging, confinement in irons, or mutilation. Sometimes slaves were punished with an "iron muzzle," which covered their faces and kept them from eating and drinking.

Even though slaves did not work in the fields on Sunday, it was no day of rest, for they had to farm their own provisioning grounds, maintain their dwellings, and do other chores, such as washing and mending their rough clothes. Sunday markets, where slaves sold small amounts of produce or animals they had raised to get a little spending money, were common in the British West Indies.

Except for occasional holidays—including the Christmas-week revels in the British West Indies—there was little time for recreation and relaxation. Slaves might sing in the fields, but singing was simply a way to distract themselves from their fatigue and the monotony of the work. There was certainly no time for schooling, nor was there willingness to educate slaves beyond skills useful to the plantation.

Time for family life was also inadequate. Although the large proportion of young adults in plantation colonies ought to have had a high rate of natural increase, the opposite occurred. Poor nutrition and overwork lowered fertility. A woman who did become pregnant found it difficult to carry a child to term while continuing heavy fieldwork or to ensure her infant's survival. As a result of these conditions along with disease and accidents from dangerous mill equipment, deaths heavily outnumbered births on West Indian plantations (see Table 18.2). Life expectancy for slaves in nineteenth-century Brazil was only 23 years of age for males and 25.5 years for females. The figures were probably similar for the eighteenth-century Caribbean. A callous opinion, common among slave owners in the Caribbean and in parts of Brazil, held that it was cheaper to import a youthful new slave from Africa than to raise one to the same age on a plantation.

The harsh conditions of plantation life played a major role in shortening slaves' lives, but the greatest killer

Table 18.2 Birth and Death on a Jamaican Sugar Plantation, 1779–1785

Year	Born			Died		Proportion of Deaths
	Males	Females	Purchased	Males	Females	
1779	5	2	6	7	5	1 in 26
1780	4	3	–	3	2	1 in 62
1781	2	3	–	4	2	1 in 52
1782	1	3	9	4	5	1 in 35
1783	3	3	–	8	10	1 in 17
1784	2	1	12	9	10	1 in 17
1785	2	3	–	0	3	1 in 99
Total	19	18	27	35	37	
	Born 37			Died 72		

Source: From "Edward Long to William Pitt," in Michael Craton, James Walvin, and David Wright, eds., *Slavery, Abolition, and Emancipation* (London: Longman, 1976), 105. © Michael Craton, James Walvin, and David Wright, reprinted by permission of Pearson Education Limited.

was disease. The very young were carried off by dysentery caused by contaminated food and water. Slaves newly arrived from Africa went through the period of adjustment to a new environment known as **seasoning,** during which one-third, on average, died of unfamiliar diseases. Slaves also suffered from diseases brought with them, including malaria. On the plantation profiled in Table 18.1, for example, more than half of the slaves incapacitated by illness had yaws, a painful and debilitating skin disease common in Africa. As a consequence, only slave populations in the healthier temperate zones of North America experienced natural increase; those in tropical Brazil and the Caribbean had a negative rate of growth.

Such high mortality greatly added to the volume of the Atlantic slave trade, since plantations had to purchase new slaves every year or two just to replace those who died (see Table 18.2). The additional imports of slaves to permit the expansion of the sugar plantations meant that the majority of slaves on most West Indian plantations were African-born. As a result, African religious beliefs, patterns of speech, styles of dress and adornment, and music were prominent parts of West Indian life.

Given the harsh conditions of their lives, it is not surprising that slaves in the West Indies often sought to regain the freedom into which most had been born. Individual slaves often ran away, hoping to elude the men and dogs who would track them. Sometimes large groups of plantation slaves rose in rebellion against their bondage and abuse. For example, a large rebellion in Ja-

maica in 1760 was led by a slave named Tacky, who had been a chief on the Gold Coast of Africa. One night his followers broke into a fort and armed themselves. Joined by slaves from nearby plantations, they stormed several plantations, setting them on fire and killing the planter families. Tacky died in the fighting that followed, and three other rebel leaders stoically endured cruel deaths by torture that were meant to deter others from rebellion.

Because they believed rebellions were usually led by slaves with the strongest African heritage, European planters tried to curtail African cultural traditions. They required slaves to learn the colonial language and discouraged the use of African languages by deliberately mixing slaves from different parts of Africa. In French and Portuguese colonies, slaves were encouraged to adopt Catholic religious practices, though African deities and beliefs also survived. In the British West Indies, where only Quaker slave owners encouraged Christianity among their slaves before 1800, African herbal medicine remained strong, as did African beliefs concerning nature spirits and witchcraft.

Free Whites and Free Blacks

The lives of the small minority of free people were very different from the lives of slaves. In the French colony of Saint Domingue, which had nearly half of the slaves in the Caribbean in the eighteenth century, free people fell into three distinct groups. At the top of free society were the wealthy owners of large sugar plantations (the *grands*

The Unknown Maroon of Saint-Domingue This modern sculpture by Albert Mangonès celebrates the brave but perilous life of a runaway slave, who is shown drinking water from a seashell. (Albert Mangonès, "The Unknown Maroon of Saint-Domingue." From Richard Price, *Maroon Societies*, Johns Hopkins University Press. Reproduced with permission.)

One source estimated that a planter had to invest nearly £20,000 ($100,000) to acquire even a medium-size Jamaican plantation of 600 acres (240 hectares) in 1774. A third of this money went for land on which to grow sugar and food crops, pasture animals, and cut timber and firewood. A quarter of the expense was for the sugar works and other equipment. The largest expense was to purchase 200 slaves at about £40 ($200) each. In comparison, the wage of an English rural laborer at this time was about £10 ($50) a year (one-fourth the price of a slave), and the annual incomes in 1760 of the ten wealthiest noble families in Britain averaged only £20,000 each.

Reputedly the richest Englishmen of this time, West Indian planters often translated their wealth into political power and social prestige. The richest planters put their plantations under the direction of managers and lived in Britain, often on rural estates that once had been the preserve of country gentlemen. Between 1730 and 1775 seventy of these absentee planters secured election to the British Parliament, where they formed an influential voting bloc. Those who resided in the West Indies had political power as well, for the British plantocracy controlled the colonial assemblies.

Most Europeans in plantation colonies were single males. Many of them took advantage of slave women for sexual favors or took slave mistresses. A slave owner who fathered a child by a female slave often gave both mother and child their freedom. In some colonies such **manumission** (a legal grant of freedom to an individual slave) produced a significant free black population. By the late eighteenth century free blacks were more numerous than slaves in most of the Spanish colonies. They made up almost 30 percent of the black population of Brazil, and they existed in significant numbers in the French colonies. Free blacks were far less common in the British colonies and the United States, where manumission was rare.

As in Brazil (see Chapter 17), escaped slaves constituted another part of the free black population. In the Caribbean runaways were known as **maroons.** Maroon communities were especially numerous in the mountainous interiors of Jamaica and Hispaniola as well as in the island parts of the Guianas°. Jamaican maroons, after withstanding several attacks by the colony's militia, signed a treaty in 1739 that recognized their independence in return for their cooperation in stopping new runaways and suppressing slave revolts. Similar treaties with the large maroon population in the Dutch colony of Surinam (Dutch Guiana) recognized their possession of large inland regions.

blancs°, or "great whites"), who dominated the economy and society of the island. Second came less-well-off Europeans (*petits blancs*°, or "little whites"). Most of them raised provisions for local consumption and crops such as coffee, indigo, and cotton for export, relying on their own and slave labor. Third came the free blacks. Though nearly as numerous as the free whites and engaged in similar occupations, they ranked below whites socially. A few free blacks became wealthy enough to own their own slaves.

The dominance of the plantocracy was even greater in British colonies. Whereas sugar constituted about half of Saint Domingue's exports, in Jamaica the figure was over 80 percent. Such concentration on sugar cane left much less room for small cultivators, white or black, and confined most landholding to a few larger owners. At midcentury three-quarters of the farmland in Jamaica belonged to individuals who owned 1,000 acres (400 hectares) or more.

---

grands blancs (grawn blawnk)   **petits blancs** (pay-TEE blawnk)

Guianas (guy-AHN-uhs)

CREATING THE ATLANTIC ECONOMY

At once archaic in their cruel system of slavery and oddly modern in their specialization in a single product, the West Indian plantation colonies were the bittersweet fruits of a new Atlantic trading system. Changes in the type and number of ships crossing the Atlantic illustrate the rise of this new system. The Atlantic trade of the sixteenth century calls to mind the treasure fleet, an annual convoy of from twenty to sixty ships laden with silver and gold bullion from Spanish America. Two different vessels typify the far more numerous Atlantic voyages of the late seventeenth and eighteenth centuries. One was the sugar ship, returning to Europe from the West Indies or Brazil crammed with barrels of brown sugar destined for further refinement. At the end of the seventeenth century an average of 266 sugar ships sailed every year just from the small island of Barbados. The second type of vessel was the slave ship. At the trade's peak between 1760 and 1800, some 300 ships, crammed with an average of 250 African captives each, crossed the Atlantic to the Americas each year.

Many separate pieces went into the creation of the new Atlantic economy. Besides the plantation system itself, three other elements merit further investigation: new economic institutions, new partnerships between private investors and governments in Europe, and new working relationships between European and African merchants. The new trading system is a prime example of how European capitalist relationships were reshaping the world.

Capitalism and Mercantilism

The Spanish and Portuguese voyages of exploration in the fifteenth and sixteenth centuries were government ventures, and both countries tried to keep their overseas trade and colonies royal monopolies (see Chapters 15 and 17). Monopoly control, however, proved both expensive and inefficient. The success of the Atlantic economy in the seventeenth and eighteenth centuries owed much to private enterprise, which made trading venues more efficient and profitable. European private investors were attracted by the profits they could make from an established and growing trading and colonial system, but their successful participation in the Atlantic economy depended on new institutions and a significant measure of government protection that reduced the likelihood of catastrophic loss.

Two European innovations enabled private investors to fund the rapid growth of the Atlantic economy. One was the ability to manage large financial resources through mechanisms that modern historians have labeled **capitalism.** The essence of early modern capitalism was a system of large financial institutions—banks, stock exchanges, and chartered trading companies—that enabled wealthy investors to reduce risks and increase profits. Originally developed for business dealings within Europe, the capitalist system expanded overseas in the seventeenth century, when slow economic growth in Europe led many investors to seek greater profits abroad.

Banks were a central capitalist institution. By the early seventeenth century Dutch banks had developed such a reputation for security that individuals and governments from all over western Europe entrusted them with large sums of money. To make a profit, the banks invested these funds in real estate, local industries, loans to governments, and overseas trade.

Individuals seeking returns higher than the low rate of interest paid by banks could purchase shares in a joint-stock company, a sixteenth-century forerunner of the modern corporation. Shares were bought and sold in specialized financial markets called stock exchanges. The Amsterdam Exchange, founded in 1530, became the greatest stock market in the seventeenth and eighteenth centuries. To reduce risks in overseas trading, merchants and trading companies bought insurance on their ships and cargoes from specialized companies that agreed to cover losses.

The capitalism of these centuries was buttressed by **mercantilism,** policies adopted by European states to promote their citizens' overseas trade and accumulate capital in the form of precious metals, especially gold and silver. Mercantilist policies strongly discouraged citizens from trading with foreign merchants and used armed force when necessary to secure exclusive relations.

Chartered companies were one of the first examples of mercantilist capitalism. A charter issued by the government of the Netherlands in 1602 gave the Dutch East India Company a legal monopoly over all Dutch trade in the Indian Ocean. This privilege encouraged private investors to buy shares in the company. They were amply rewarded when Dutch East India Company captured control of long-distance trade routes in the Indian Ocean from the Portuguese (see Chapter 19). As we have seen, a sister firm, the Dutch West India Company, was chartered in 1621 to engage in the Atlantic trade and to seize sugar-producing areas in Brazil and African slaving ports from the Portuguese.

Such successes inspired other governments to set up their own chartered companies. In 1672 a royal charter placed all English trade with West Africa in the hands of a new Royal African Company, which established its headquarters at Cape Coast Castle, just east of Elmina on the Gold Coast. The French government also played an active role in chartering companies and promoting overseas trade and colonization. Jean Baptiste Colbert°, King Louis XIV's minister of finance from 1661 to 1683, chartered French East India and French West India Companies to reduce French colonies' dependence on Dutch and English traders.

French and English governments also used military force in pursuit of commercial dominance, especially to break the trading advantage of the Dutch in the Americas. Restrictions on Dutch access to French and English colonies provoked a series of wars with the Netherlands between 1652 and 1678 (see Chapter 17), during which the larger English and French navies defeated the Dutch and drove the Dutch West India Company into bankruptcy.

With Dutch competition in the Atlantic reduced, the French and English governments moved to revoke the monopoly privileges of their chartered companies. England opened trade in Africa to any English subject in 1698 on the grounds that ending monopolies would be "highly beneficial and advantageous to this kingdom." It was hoped that such competition would also cut the cost of slaves to West Indian planters, though the demand for slaves soon drove the prices up again.

Such new mercantilist policies fostered competition among a nation's own citizens, while using high tariffs and restrictions to exclude foreigners. In the 1660s England had passed a series of Navigation Acts that confined trade with its colonies to English ships and cargoes. The French called their mercantilist legislation, first codified in 1698, the *Exclusif*°, highlighting its exclusionary intentions. Other mercantilist laws defended manufacturing and processing interests in Europe against competition from colonies, imposing prohibitively high taxes on any manufactured goods and refined sugar imported from the colonies.

As a result of such mercantilist measures, the Atlantic became Britain, France, and Portugal's most important overseas trading area in the eighteenth century. Britain's imports from its West Indian colonies in this period accounted for over one-fifth of the value of total British imports. The French West Indian colonies played an even larger role in France's overseas trade. Only the Dutch, closed out of much of the American trade, found Asian trade of greater importance (see Chapter 19). Profits from the Atlantic economy, in turn, promoted further economic expansion and increased the revenues of European governments.

Colbert (kōhl-BEAR)   *Exclusif* (ek-skloo-SEEF)

The Atlantic Circuit

At the heart of this trading system was a clockwise network of sea routes known as the **Atlantic Circuit** (see Map 18.1). It began in Europe, ran south to Africa, turned west across the Atlantic Ocean to the Americas, and then swept back to Europe. Like Asian sailors in the Indian Ocean, Atlantic mariners depended on the prevailing winds and currents to propel their ships. What drove the ships as much as the winds and currents was the desire for the profits that each leg of the circuit was expected to produce.

The first leg, from Europe to Africa, carried European manufactures—notably metal bars, hardware, and guns—as well as great quantities of cotton textiles brought from India. Some of these goods were traded for West African gold, timber, and other products, which were taken back to Europe. More goods went to purchase slaves, who were transported across the Atlantic to the plantation colonies in the part of the Atlantic Circuit known as the **Middle Passage.** On the third leg, plantation goods from the colonies returned to Europe. Each leg carried goods from where they were abundant and relatively cheap to where they were scarce and therefore more valuable. Thus, in theory, each leg of the Atlantic Circuit could earn much more than its costs, and a ship that completed all three legs could return a handsome profit to its owners. In practice, shipwrecks, deaths, piracy, and other risks could turn profit into loss.

The three-sided Atlantic Circuit is only the simplest model of Atlantic trade. Many other trading voyages supplemented the basic circuit. Cargo ships made long voyages from Europe to the Indian Ocean, passed southward through the Atlantic with quantities of African gold and American silver, and returned with the cotton textiles necessary to the African trade. Other sea routes brought the West Indies manufactured goods from Europe or foodstuffs and lumber from New England. In addition, some Rhode Island and Massachusetts merchants participated in a "Triangular Trade" that carried rum to West Africa, slaves to the West Indies, and molasses and rum back to New England. There was also a considerable two-way trade between Brazil and Angola that exchanged Brazilian liquor and other goods for slaves. On another route, Brazil and Portugal exchanged sugar and gold for European imports.

European interests dominated the Atlantic system. The manufacturers who supplied the trade goods and the investors who provided the capital were all based in Europe, but so too were the principal consumers of the plantation products. Before the seventeenth century, sugar had been rare and fairly expensive in western Europe. By 1700 annual consumption of sugar in England had risen to about 4 pounds (nearly 2 kilograms) per

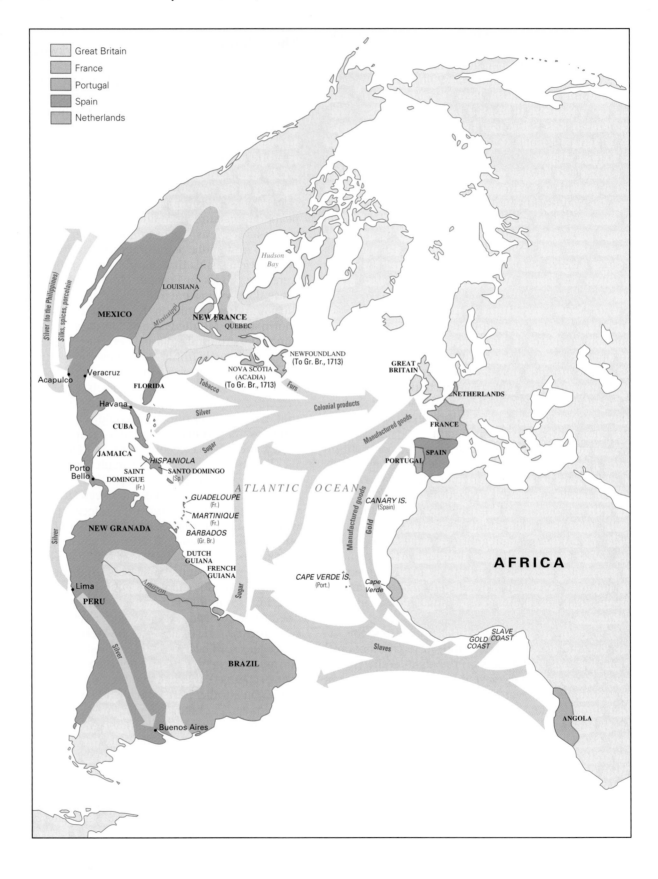

Great Britain
France
Portugal
Spain
Netherlands

Silver (to the Philippines)
Silks, spices, porcelain

LOUISIANA

Hudson
Bay

MEXICO

NEW FRANCE
QUEBEC

NEWFOUNDLAND
(To Gr. Br., 1713)

GREAT
BRITAIN

Acapulco
Veracruz

FLORIDA

NOVA SCOTIA
(ACADIA)
(To Gr. Br., 1713)

Tobacco

Furs

NETHERLANDS

Colonial products

FRANCE

Havana

Silver

CUBA

Sugar

Manufactured goods

SPAIN

JAMAICA

HISPANIOLA

PORTUGAL

Porto
Bello

SAINT
DOMINGUE
(Fr.)

SANTO DOMINGO
(Sp.)

ATLANTIC OCEAN

GUADELOUPE
(Fr.)

CANARY IS.
(Spain)

Manufactured goods

MARTINIQUE
(Fr.)

NEW GRANADA

BARBADOS
(Gr. Br.)

Gold

AFRICA

DUTCH
GUIANA
FRENCH
GUIANA

Lima

CAPE VERDE IS.
(Port.)

Cape
Verde

PERU

Amazon

Sugar

Silver

SLAVE
COAST

GOLD
COAST

Slaves

BRAZIL

Silver

ANGOLA

Buenos Aires

Mississippi

Slave Ship   This model of the English vessel *Brookes* shows the specially built section of the hold where enslaved Africans were packed together during the Middle Passage. Girls, boys, and women were confined separately.   (Wilberforce House Museum, Hull, Humberside, UK/The Bridgeman Art Library, London and New York)

person. Rising western European prosperity and declining sugar prices promoted additional consumption, starting with the upper classes and working its way down the social ladder. People spooned sugar into popular new beverages imported from overseas—tea, coffee, and chocolate—to overcome the beverages' natural bitterness. By 1750 annual sugar consumption in Britain had doubled, and it doubled again to about 18 pounds (8 kilograms) per person by the early nineteenth century (well below the American average of about 100 pounds [45 kilograms] a year in 1960).

The flow of sugar to Europe depended on another key component of the Atlantic trading system: the flow of slaves from Africa (see Map 18.2). The rising volume of the Middle Passage also measures the Atlantic system's expansion. During the first 150 years after the European discovery of the Americas, some 800,000 Africans had begun the journey across the Atlantic. During the boom in sugar production between 1650 and 1800, the slave trade amounted to nearly 7.5 million. Of the survivors,

Map 18.1   The Atlantic Economy   By 1700 the volume of maritime exchanges among the Atlantic continents had begun to rival the trade of the Indian Ocean basin. Notice the trade in consumer products, slave labor, precious metals, and other goods. Silver trade to East Asia laid the basis for a Pacific Ocean economy.

over half landed in the West Indies and nearly a third in Brazil. Plantations in North America imported another 5 percent, and the rest went to other parts of Spanish America (see Figure 18.1).

In these peak decades, the transportation of slaves from Africa was a highly specialized trade, although it regularly attracted some amateur traders hoping to make a quick profit. Most slaves were carried in ships that had been specially built or modified for the slave trade by the construction between the ships' decks of additional platforms on which the human cargo was packed as tightly as possible.

Seventeenth-century mercantilist policies placed much of the Atlantic slave trade in the hands of chartered companies. During their existence the Dutch West India Company and the English Royal African Company each carried about 100,000 slaves across the Atlantic. In the eighteenth century private English traders from Liverpool and Bristol controlled about 40 percent of the slave trade. The French, operating out of Nantes and Bordeaux, handled about half as much, but the Dutch hung on to only 6 percent. The Portuguese supplying Brazil and other places had nearly 30 percent of the Atlantic slave trade, in contrast to the 3 percent carried in North American ships.

To make a profit, European slave traders had to buy slaves in Africa for less than the cost of the goods they traded in return. Then they had to deliver as many

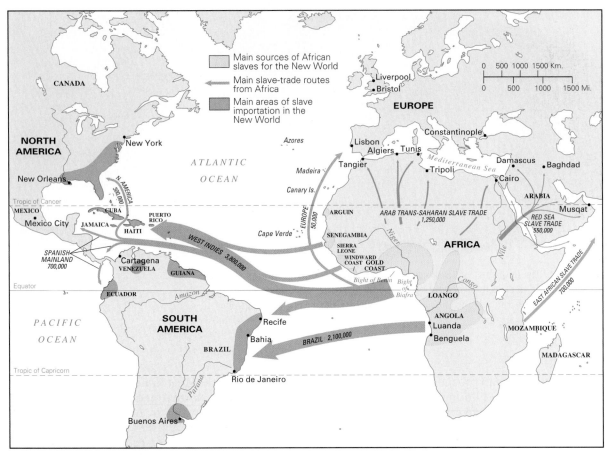

Map 18.2 The African Slave Trade, 1500–1800 After 1500 a vast new trade in slaves from sub-Saharan Africa to the Americas joined the ongoing slave trade to the Islamic states of North Africa, the Middle East, and India. The West Indies were the major destination of the Atlantic slave trade, followed by Brazil.

healthy slaves as possible across the Atlantic for resale in the plantation colonies. The treacherous voyage to the Americas lasted from six to ten weeks. Some ships completed it with all of their slaves alive, but large, even catastrophic, losses of life were common (see Figure 18.1). On average, however, slave transporters succeeded in lowering mortality during the Middle Passage from about 23 percent on voyages before 1700 to half that in the last half of the eighteenth century.

Some deaths resulted from the efforts of the captives to escape. As on the voyage of the *Hannibal* recounted at the beginning of the chapter, male slaves were shackled together to prevent them from trying to escape while they were still in sight of land. Because some still managed to jump overboard in pairs, slave ships were outfitted with special netting around the outside. Some slaves developed deep psychological depression, known to

contemporaries as "fixed melancholy." Crews force-fed slaves who refused to eat, but some successfully willed themselves to death.

When opportunities presented themselves (nearness to land, illness among the crew), some enslaved Africans tried to overpower their captors. To inhibit such mutinies, African men were confined below deck during most of the voyage, except at mealtimes when they were brought up in small groups under close supervision. In any event, "mutinies" were rarely successful and were put down with brutality that occasioned further losses of life.

Other deaths during the Middle Passage were due to ill treatment. Although it was in the interests of the captain and crew to deliver their slave cargo in good condition, whippings, beatings, and even executions were used to maintain order or force captives to take nourishment. Moreover, the dangers and brutalities of the slave trade were so notorious that many ordinary seamen shunned such work. As a consequence, cruel and brutal officers and crews abounded on slave ships.

Although examples of unspeakable cruelties are common in the records, most deaths in the Middle Passage were the result of disease rather than abuse, as the voyage of the *Hannibal* illustrated. Dysentery spread by contaminated food and water caused many deaths. Other slaves died of contagious diseases such as smallpox carried by persons whose infections were not detected during medical examinations prior to boarding. Such maladies spread quickly in the crowded and unsanitary confines of the ships, claiming the lives of many slaves already physically weakened and mentally traumatized by their ordeals.

Crew members in close contact with the slaves were exposed to the same epidemics and also died in great numbers. Moreover, sailors often fell victim to tropical diseases, such as malaria, to which Africans had acquired resistance. It is a measure of the callousness of the age, as well as the cheapness of European labor, that over the course of a round-trip voyage from Europe the proportion of crew deaths could be as high as the slave deaths.

AFRICA, THE ATLANTIC, AND ISLAM

The Atlantic system took a terrible toll in African lives both during the Middle Passage and under the harsh conditions of plantation slavery. Many other Africans died while being marched to African coastal ports for sale overseas. The overall effects on Africa of these losses and of other aspects of the slave trade have been the subject of considerable historical debate. It is clear that the trade's impact depended on the intensity and terms of different African regions' involvement.

Any assessment of the Atlantic system's effects in Africa must also take into consideration the fact that some Africans profited from the trade by capturing and selling slaves. They chained the slaves together or bound them to forked sticks for the march to the coast, then bartered them to the European slavers for trade goods. The effects on the enslaver were different from the effects on the enslaved. Finally, a broader understanding of the Atlantic system's effects in sub-Saharan Africa comes from comparisons with the effects of Islamic contacts.

The Gold Coast and the Slave Coast

As Chapter 15 showed, early European visitors to Africa's Atlantic coast were interested more in trading than in colonizing or controlling the continent. As the Africa trade mushroomed after 1650, this pattern continued. African kings and merchants sold slaves and goods at many new coastal sites, but the growing slave trade did not lead to substantial European colonization.

The transition to slave trading was not sudden. Even as slaves were becoming Atlantic Africa's most valuable export, goods such as gold, ivory, and timber remained a significant part of the total trade. For example, during its eight decades of operation from 1672 to 1752, the Royal African Company made 40 percent of its profits from dealings in gold, ivory, and forest products. In some parts of West Africa, such nonslave exports remained predominant even at the peak of the trade.

African merchants were very discriminating about what merchandise they received in return for slaves or goods. A European ship that arrived with goods of low quality or not suited to local tastes found it hard to purchase a cargo at a profitable price. European guidebooks to the African trade carefully noted the color and shape of beads, the pattern of textiles, the type of guns, and the sort of metals that were in demand on each section of the coast. In the early eighteenth century the people of Sierra Leone had a strong preference for large iron kettles; brass pans were preferred on the Gold Coast; and iron and copper bars were in demand in the Niger Delta, where smiths turned them into useful objects (see Map 18.3).

Although preferences for merchandise varied, Africans' greatest demands were for textiles, hardware, and guns. Of the goods the Royal African Company traded in West Africa in the 1680s, over 60 percent were Indian and European textiles and 30 percent were hardware and weaponry. Beads and other jewelry made up 3 percent. The rest consisted of cowrie shells that were used as money. In the eighteenth century, tobacco and rum from the Americas became welcome imports.

Both Europeans and Africans attempted to drive the best bargain for themselves and sometimes engaged in deceitful practices. The strength of the African bargaining position, however, may be inferred from the fact that as the demand for slaves rose, so too did their price in Africa. In the course of the eighteenth century the goods needed to purchase a slave on the Gold Coast doubled and in some places tripled or quadrupled.

West Africans' trading strengths were reinforced by African governments on the Gold and Slave Coasts that made Europeans observe African trading customs and

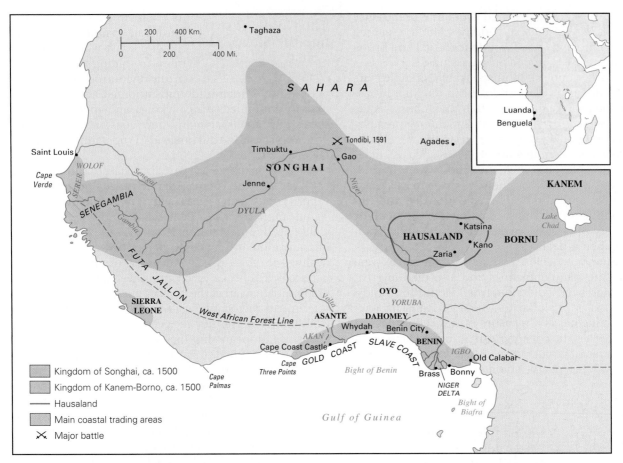

Map 18.3   West African States and Trade, 1500–1800   The Atlantic and the trans-Saharan trade brought West Africans new goods and promoted the rise of powerful states and trading communities. The Moroccan invasion of Songhai and Portuguese colonization of the Angolan ports of Luanda and Benguela showed the political dangers of such relations.

prevented them from taking control of African territory. Rivalry among European nations, each of which established its own trading "castles" along the Gold Coast, also reduced Europeans' bargaining strength. In 1700 the head of the Dutch East India Company in West Africa, Willem Bosman°, bemoaned the fact that, to stay competitive against the other European traders, his company had to include large quantities of muskets and gunpowder in the goods it exchanged, thereby adding to Africans' military power.

Bosman also related that before being allowed to buy slaves at Whydah on the Slave Coast, his agents first had to pay the king a substantial customs duty and then pay a premium price for whatever slaves the king had to sell. By

African standards, Whydah was a rather small kingdom controlling only that port and its immediate hinterland. In 1727 it was annexed by the larger kingdom of Dahomey°, which maintained a strong trading position with Europeans at the coast. Dahomey's rise in the 1720s depended heavily on the firearms that the slave trade supplied for its well-trained armies of men and women.

In the cases of two of Dahomey's neighbors, the connections between state growth and the Atlantic trade were more complex. One was the inland Oyo° kingdom to the northeast. Oyo cavalry overran Dahomey in 1730 and forced it to pay an annual tribute to keep its independence. The other was the newer kingdom of Asante°,

---

Willem Bosman (VIL-uhm boos-MAHN)

Dahomey (dah-HOH-mee)   **Oyo** (aw-YOH)
Asante (uh-SHAN-tee)

west of Dahomey along the Gold Coast, which expanded rapidly after 1680. Both Oyo and Asante participated in the Atlantic trade, but neither kingdom was as dependent on it as Dahomey. Overseas trade formed a relatively modest part of the economies of these large and populous states and was balanced by their extensive overland trade with their northern neighbors and with states across the Sahara. Like the great medieval empires of the western Sudan, Oyo and Asante were stimulated by external trade but not controlled by it.

How did African kings and merchants obtain slaves for sale? Bosman dismissed misconceptions prevailing in Europe in his day. "Not a few in our country," he wrote to a friend in 1700, "fondly imagine that parents here sell their children, men their wives, and one brother the other. But those who think so, do deceive themselves; for this never happens on any other account but that of necessity, or some great crime; but most of the slaves that are offered to us are prisoners of war, which are sold by the victors as their booty."[2] Other accounts agree that prisoners taken in war were the greatest source of slaves for the Atlantic trade, but it is difficult to say how often capturing slaves for export was the main cause of warfare. "Here and there," conclude two respected historians of Africa, "there are indications that captives taken in the later and more peripheral stages of these wars were exported overseas, but it would seem that the main impetus of conquest was only incidentally concerned with the slave-trade in any external direction."[3]

An early-nineteenth-century king of Asante had a similar view: "I cannot make war to catch slaves in the bush, like a thief. My ancestors never did so. But if I fight a king, and kill him when he is insolent, then certainly I must have his gold, and his slaves, and his people are mine too. Do not the white kings act like this?"[4] English rulers had indeed sentenced seventeenth-century Scottish and Irish prisoners to forced labor in the West Indies. One may imagine that the African and the European prisoners did not share their kings' view that such actions were legitimate.

The Bight of Biafra and Angola

In the eighteenth century the slave trade expanded eastward to the Bight° of Biafra. In contrast to the Gold and Slave Coasts, where strong kingdoms predominated, the densely populated interior of the Bight of Biafra contained no large states. Even so, the powerful merchant princes of the coastal ports made European traders give

them rich presents. Because of the absence of sizable states, there were no large-scale wars and consequently few prisoners of war. Instead, kidnapping was the major source of slaves.

Through a network of markets and inland routes, some inland African merchants supplied European slave traders at the coast with debtors, victims of kidnapping, and convicted criminals. The largest inland traders of the Bight of Biafra were the Aro of Arochukwu, who used their control of a famous religious oracle to enhance their prestige. The Aro cemented their business links with powerful inland families and the coastal merchants through gifts and marriage alliances.

As the volume of the Atlantic trade along the Bight of Biafra expanded in the late eighteenth century, some inland markets evolved into giant fairs with different sections specializing in slaves and imported goods. In the 1780s an English ship's doctor reported that slaves were "bought by the black traders at fairs, which are held for that purpose, at a distance of upwards of two hundred miles from the sea coast." He reported seeing between twelve hundred and fifteen hundred enslaved men and women arriving at the coast from a single fair.[5]

The local context of the Atlantic trade was different south of the Congo estuary at Angola, the greatest source of slaves for the Atlantic trade (see Map 18.2). This was also the one place along the Atlantic coast where a single European nation, Portugal, controlled a significant amount of territory. Except when overrun by the Dutch for a time in the seventeenth century, Portuguese residents of the main coastal ports of Luanda and Benguela° served as middlemen between the caravans that arrived from the far interior and the ships that crossed from Brazil. From the coastal cities Afro-Portuguese traders guided large caravans of trade goods inland to exchange for slaves at special markets. Some markets met in the shadow of Portuguese frontier forts; powerful African kings controlled others.

Many of the slaves sold at these markets were prisoners of war captured by expanding African states. By the late eighteenth century slaves sold from Angolan ports were prisoners of wars fought as far as 600 to 800 miles (1,000 to 1,300 kilometers) inland. Many were victims of wars of expansion fought by the giant federation of Lunda kingdoms. As elsewhere in Africa, such prisoners usually seem to have been a byproduct of African wars rather than the purpose for which the wars were fought.

Research has linked other enslavement with environmental crises in the hinterland of Angola.[6] During

Bight (bite)

Benguela (ben-GWAY-luh)

Queen Nzinga of Angola, 1622   This formidable African woman went to great lengths to maintain her royal dignity when negotiating a treaty for her brother with the Portuguese governor of Luanda. To avoid having to stand in his presence, she had one of her women bend herself into a human seat. Nzinga later ruled in her own name and revolted against the Portuguese with the aid of Dutch and African allies.   (Jean-Loup Charmet)

the eighteenth century these southern grasslands periodically suffered severe droughts, which drove famished refugees to better-watered areas. Powerful African leaders gained control of such refugees in return for supplying them with food and water. These leaders built up their followings by assimilating refugee children, along with adult women, who were valued as food producers and for reproduction. However, they often sold into the Atlantic trade the adult male refugees, who were more likely than the women and children to escape or challenge the ruler's authority. Rising Angolan leaders parceled out the Indian textiles, weapons, and alcohol they received in return for such slaves as gifts to attract new followers and to cement the loyalty of their established allies.

The most successful of these inland Angolan leaders became heads of powerful new states that stabilized areas devastated by war and drought and repopulated them with the refugees and prisoners they retained. The slave frontier then moved farther inland. This cruel system worked to the benefit of a few African rulers and merchants at the expense of the many thousands of Africans who were sent to death or perpetual bondage in the Americas.

Although the organization of the Atlantic trade in Africa varied, it was based on a partnership between European and African elites. To obtain foreign textiles, metals, and weapons, African rulers and merchants sold slaves and many products. Most of the exported slaves were prisoners taken in wars associated with African state growth. But strong African states also helped offset the Europeans' economic advantage and hindered them from taking control of African territory. Even in the absence of strong states, powerful African merchant communities everywhere dominated the movement of goods and people. The Africans who gained from these exchanges were the rich and powerful few. Many more Africans were losers in the exchanges.

Africa's European and Islamic Contacts

The ways in which sub-Saharan Africans were establishing new contacts with Europe paralleled their much older pattern of relations with the Islamic world. There were striking similarities and differences in Africans' political, commercial, and cultural interactions with these two external influences between 1500 and 1800.

Traders Approaching Timbuktu   As they had done for centuries, traders brought their wares to this ancient desert-edge city. Timbuktu's mosques tower above the ordinary dwellings of the fabled city.   (The Art Archive)

During the three and a half centuries of contact up to 1800, Africans ceded very little territory to Europeans. Local African rulers kept close tabs on the European trading posts they permitted along the Gold and Slave Coasts and collected lucrative rents and fees from the traders who came there. Aside from some uninhabited islands off the Atlantic coast, Europeans established colonial beachheads in only two places. One was the Portuguese colony of Angola; the other was the Dutch East India Company's Cape Colony at the southern tip of the continent, which was tied to the Indian Ocean trade, not to the Atlantic trade. Unlike Angola, the Cape Colony did not export slaves; rather, most of the 25,750 slaves in its population in 1793 were imported from Madagascar, South Asia, and the East Indies.

North Africa had become a permanent part of the Islamic world in the first century of Islamic expansion. Sub-Saharan Africans had learned of Muslim beliefs and practices more gradually from the traders who crossed the Sahara from North Africa or who sailed from the Middle East to the Swahili trading cities of East Africa. However, the geography, trading skills, and military prowess of sub-Saharan Africans had kept them from

being conquered by expansive Middle Eastern empires. During the sixteenth century all of North Africa except Morocco was annexed to the new Ottoman Islamic empire, and Ethiopia lost extensive territory to other Muslim conquerors, but until 1590 the Sahara was an effective buttress against invasion.

The great **Songhai°** Empire of West Africa was pushing its dominion into the Sahara from the south. Like its predecessor Mali, Songhai drew its wealth from the trans-Saharan trade and was ruled by an indigenous Muslim dynasty (see Map 18.3). However, Songhai's rulers faced a challenge from the northwestern kingdom of Morocco, whose Muslim rulers sent a military expedition of four thousand men and ten thousand camels across the desert. Half the men perished on their way across the desert. Songhai's army of forty thousand cavalry and foot soldiers faced the survivors in 1591, but could not withstand the Moroccans' twenty-five hundred muskets. Although Morocco was never able to annex the western Sudan, for the next two centuries the occupying troops extracted a massive tribute of slaves

Songhai (song-GAH-ee)

우세인 은신어
파운드폭탄 4발 투하… 두 아들과 함께 사망
실진지 구축… 이틀째 시가戰
령이 대중 앞에 나타나거나 애국심
을 고취하는 노래만을 내보내던 방
송마저 중단했다.
라크 전후
의에서는
영국 주도

DIVERSITY AND DOMINANCE

SLAVERY IN WEST AFRICA AND THE AMERICAS

Social diversity was common in Africa and the domination of masters over slaves was a feature of many societies. Ahmad Baba (1556–1627) was an outstanding Islamic scholar in the city of Timbuktu. He came from an old Muslim family of the city. In about 1615 he replied to some questions that had been sent to him. His answers reveal a great deal about the official and unofficial condition of slavery in the Sudan of West Africa, especially in the Hausa states of Kano and Katsina (see Map 18.3).

You asked: What have you to say concerning the slaves imported from the lands of the Sudan whose people are acknowledged to be Muslims, such as Bornu, . . . Kano, Goa, Songhay, Katsina and others among whom Islam is widespread? Is it permissible to possess them [as slaves] or not?

Know—may God grant us and you success—that these lands, as you have stated are Muslim. . . . But close to each of them are lands in which are unbelievers whom the Muslim inhabitants of these lands raid. Some of these unbelievers are under the Muslims' protection and pay them [taxes]. . . . Sometimes there is war between the Muslim sultans of some of these lands and one attacks the other, taking as many prisoners as he can and selling the captive though he is a free-born Muslim. . . . This is a common practice among them in Hausaland; Katsina raids Kano, as do others, though their language is one and their situations parallel; the only difference they recognize among themselves is that so-and-so is a born Muslim and so-and-so is a born unbeliever. . . .

Whoever is taken prisoner in a state of unbelief may become someone's property, whoever he is, as opposed to those who have become Muslims of their own free will . . . and may not be possessed at all.

A little over a century later another African provided information about enslavement practices in the Western Sudan. Ayuba Suleiman Diallo (ah-YOO-bah SOO-lay-mahn JAH-loh) (1701–?) of the state of Bondu some 200 miles from the Gambia River was enslaved and transported to Maryland, where he was a slave from 1731 to 1733. When an Englishman learned of Ayuba's literacy in Arabic, he recorded his life story, anglicizing his name to Job Solomon. According to the account, slaves in Bondu did much of the hard work, while men of Ayuba's class were free to devote themselves to the study of Islamic texts.

In February, 1730, Job's father hearing of an English ship at Gambia River, sent him, with two servants to attend him, to sell two Negroes, and to buy paper, and some other necessaries; but desired him not to venture over the river, because the country of the Mandingoes, who are enemies to the people of Futa, lies on the other side. Job not agreeing with Captain Pike (who commanded the ship, lying then at Gambia, in the service of Captain Henry Hunt, brother to Mr. William Hunt, merchant, in Little Tower-street, London) sent back the two servants to acquaint his father with it, and to let him know that he intended to go no farther. Accordingly . . . he crossed the River Gambia, and disposed of his Negroes for some cows. As he was returning home, he stopped for some refreshment at the house of an old acquaintance; and the weather being hot, he hung up his arms in the house, while he refreshed himself. . . . It happened that a company of the Mandingoes, . . . passing by at that time, and observing him unarmed, rushed in, to the number of seven or eight at once, at a back door, and pinioned Job, before he could get his arms, together with his interpreter, who is a slave in Maryland still. They then shaved their heads and beards, which Job and his man resented as the highest indignity; tho' the Mandingoes meant no more by it, than to make them appear like slaves taken in war. On the 27th of February, 1730, they carried them to Captain Pike at Gambia, who purchased them; and on the first of March they were put on board. Soon after Job found means to acquaint Captain Pike that he was the same person that came to trade with him a few days before, and after what manner he had been taken. Upon this Captain Pike gave him free leave to redeem himself and his man; and Job sent to an acquaintance of his father's, near Gambia, who promised to send to Job's father, to inform him of what had happened, that he might take some course to have him set at liberty. But it being a fortnight's [two weeks'] journey between that friend's house and his father's, and the ship sailing in about a week after, Job was brought with the rest of the slaves to Annapolis in Maryland, and delivered to Mr. Vachell Denton. . . .

Mr. Vachell Denton sold Job to one Mr. Tolsey in Kent Island in Maryland, who put him to work in making tobacco; but he was soon convinced that Job had never been used to such labour. He every day showed more and more uneasiness under this exercise, and at last grew sick, being no way able to bear it; so his master was obliged to find easier work for him, and therefore put him to tend the cattle. Job would often leave the cattle, and withdraw into the woods to pray; but a white boy frequently watched him, and whilst he was at his devotion would mock him and throw dirt in his face. This very much disturbed Job, and added considerably to his other misfortunes; all which were increased by his ignorance of the English language, which prevented his complaining, or telling his case to any person about him. Grown in some measure desperate, by reason of his present hardships, he resolved to travel at a venture; thinking he might possibly be taken up by some master, who would use him better, or otherwise meet with some lucky accident, to divert or abate his grief. Accordingly, he travelled thro' the woods, till he came to the County of Kent, upon Delaware Bay. . . . There is a law in force, throughout the [mid-Atlantic] colonies . . . as far as Boston in New England, viz. that any Negroe, or white servant who is not known in the county, or has no pass, may be secured by any person, and kept in the common [jail], till the master of such servant shall fetch him. Therefore Job being able to give no account of himself, was put in prison there.

This happened about the beginning of June 1731, when I, who was attending the courts there, and heard of Job, went with several gentlemen to the [jailer's] house, being a tavern, and desired to see him. He was brought into the tavern to us, but could not speak one word of English. Upon our talking and making signs to him, he wrote a line to two before us, and when he read it, pronounced the words Allah and Mahommed; by which, and his refusing a glass of wine we offered him, we perceived he was a Mahometan [Muslim], but could not imagine of what country he was, or how he got thither; for by his affable carriage, and the easy composure of his countenance, we could perceive he was no common slave.

When Job had been some time confined, an old Negroe man, who lived in that neighborhood, and could speak the Jalloff [Wolof] language, which Job also understood, went to him, and conversed with him. By this Negroe the keeper was informed to whom Job belonged, and what was the cause of his leaving his master. The keeper thereupon wrote to his master, who soon after fetched him home, and was much kinder to him than before; allowing him place to pray in, and in some other conveniences, in order to make his slavery as easy as possible. Yet slavery and confinement was by no means agreeable to Job, who had never been used to it; he therefore wrote a letter in Arabick to his father, acquainting him with his misfortunes, hoping he might yet find means to redeem him. . . . It happened that this letter was seen by James Oglethorpe, Esq. [founder of the colony of Georgia and

Ayuba Suleiman Diallo (1701–??)   (British Library)

director of the Royal African Company]; who, according to his usual goodness and generosity, took compassion on Job, and [bought him from his master]; his master being very willing to part with him, as finding him no ways fit for his business.

*I*n spring 1733 Job's benefactors took him to England, teaching him passable English during the voyage, and introduced him to the English gentry. Job attracted such attention that local men took up a collection to buy his freedom and pay his debts, and introduced him at the royal court. In 1735 Job returned to Gambia in a Royal African Company ship, richly clothed and accompanied by many gifts.

QUESTIONS FOR ANALYSIS

1. Since Ahmad Baba points out that Islamic law permitted a Muslim to raid and enslave non-Muslims, do you think that the non-Mulsim Mandinka (Mandingos) would have considered it justifiable to enslave Ayuba, since he was a Muslim?

2. What aspects of Ayuba Suleiman's experiences of enslavement were normal, and which unusual?

3. How different might Ayuba's experiences of slavery have been had he been sold to Jamaica rather than Maryland?

4. How strictly was the ban against enslaving Muslims observed in Hausaland?

Source: Thomas Hodgkin, ed., *Nigerian Perspectives: An Historical Anthology,* 2d ed. (London: Oxford University Press, 1975), 154–156; Thomas Bluett, *Some Memoirs of the Life of Job, the Son of Solomon the High Priest of Boonda in Africa* (London: Richard Ford, 1734), 16–24.

and goods from the local population and collected tolls from passing merchants.

Morocco's destruction of Songhai weakened the trans-Saharan trade in the western Sudan. The **Hausa** trading cities in the central Sudan soon attracted most of the caravans bringing textiles, hardware, and weapons across the Sahara. The goods the Hausa imported and distributed through their trading networks were similar to those coastal African traders commanded from the Atlantic trade, except for the absence of alcohol (which was prohibited to Muslims). The goods they sent back in return also resembled the major African exports into the Atlantic: gold and slaves. One unique export to the north was the caffeine-rich kola nut, a stimulant that was much in demand among Muslims in North Africa. The Hausa also exported cotton textiles and leather goods.

Few statistics of the slave trade to the Islamic north exist, but the size of the trade seems to have been substantial, if smaller than the transatlantic trade at its peak. Between 1600 and 1800, by one estimate, about 850,000 slaves trudged across the desert's various routes (see Map 18.2). A nearly equal number of slaves from sub-Saharan Africa entered the Islamic Middle East and India by way of the Red Sea and the Indian Ocean.

In contrast to the plantation slavery of the Americas, most African slaves in the Islamic world were soldiers and servants. In the late seventeenth and eighteenth centuries Morocco's rulers employed an army of 150,000 African slaves obtained from the south, whose loyalty they trusted more than the loyalty of recruits from their own lands. Other slaves worked for Moroccans on sugar plantations, as servants, and as artisans. Unlike the case in the Americas, the majority of African slaves in the Islamic world were women who served wealthy households as concubines, servants, and entertainers. The trans-Saharan slave trade also included a much higher proportion of children than did the Atlantic trade, including eunuchs meant for eventual service as harem guards. It is estimated that only one in ten of these boys survived the surgical removal of their genitals.

The central Sudanese kingdom of **Bornu** illustrates several aspects of trans-Saharan contacts. Ruled by the same dynasty since the ninth century, this Muslim state had grown and expanded in the sixteenth century as the result of guns imported from the Ottoman Empire. Bornu retained many captives from its wars or sold them as slaves to the north in return for the firearms and horses that underpinned the kingdom's military power. One Bornu king, Mai Ali, conspicuously displayed his kingdom's new power and wealth while on four pilgrimages to Mecca between 1642 and 1667. On the last, an enormous entourage of slaves—said to number fifteen thousand—accompanied him.

Like Christians of this period, Muslims saw no moral impediment to owning or trading in slaves. Indeed, Islam considered enslaving "pagans" to be a meritorious act because it brought them into the faith. Although Islam forbade the enslavement of Muslims, Muslim rulers in Bornu, Hausaland, and elsewhere were not strict observers of that rule (see Diversity and Dominance: Slavery in West Africa and the Americas).

Sub-Saharan Africans had much longer exposure to Islamic cultural influences than to European cultural influences. Scholars and merchants learned to use the Arabic language to communicate with visiting North Africans and to read the Quran. Islamic beliefs and practices as well as Islamic legal and administrative systems were influential in African trading cities on the southern edge of the Sahara and on the Swahili coast. In some places Islam had extended its influence among rural people, but in 1750 it was still very much an urban religion.

European cultural influence in Africa was even more limited. Some coastal Africans had shown an interest in Western Christianity during the first century of contact with the Portuguese, but in the 1700s only Angola had a significant number of Christians. Coastal African traders found it useful to learn one or more European languages, but African languages dominated inland trade routes. A few African merchants sent their sons to Europe to learn European ways. One of these young men, Philip Quaque°, who was educated in England, was ordained as a priest in the Church of England and became the official chaplain of the Cape Coast Castle from 1766 until his death in 1816. A few other Africans learned to write in a European language, such as the Old Calabar trader Antera Duke who kept a diary in English in the late eighteenth century.

Overall, how different and similar were the material effects of Islam and Europe in sub-Saharan Africa by 1800? The evidence is incomplete, but some assessment is possible with regard to population and possessions.

Although both foreign Muslims and Europeans obtained slaves from sub-Saharan Africa, there was a significant difference in the numbers they obtained. Between 1550 and 1800 some 8 million Africans were exported into the Atlantic trade, compared to perhaps 2 million in the Islamic trade to North Africa and the Middle East. What effect did these losses have on Africa's population? Scholars who have looked deeply into the question generally agree on three points: (1) even at the

Quaque (KWAH-kay)

peak of the trade in the 1700s sub-Saharan Africa's overall population remained very large; (2) localities that contributed heavily to the slave trade, such as the lands behind the Slave Coast, suffered acute losses; (3) the ability of a population to recover from losses was related to the proportion of fertile women who were shipped away. The fact that Africans sold fewer women than men into the larger Atlantic trade somewhat reduced its long-term effects.

Many other factors played a role. Angola, for example, supplied more slaves over a longer period than any other part of Africa, but the trade drew upon different parts of a vast and densely populated hinterland. Moreover, the periodic population losses due to famine in this region may have been reduced by the increasing cultivation of high-yielding food plants from the Americas (see Environment and Technology: Amerindian Foods in Africa).

The impact of the goods received in sub-Saharan Africa from these trades is another topic of research. Africans were very particular about what they received, and their experience made them very adept at assessing the quality of different goods. Economic historians have questioned the older idea that the imports of textiles and metals undermined African weavers and metalworkers. First, they point out that on a per capita basis the volume of these imports was too small to have idled many African artisans. Second, the imports are more likely to have supplemented rather than replaced local production. The goods received in sub-Saharan Africa were intended for consumption and thus did not serve to develop the economy. Likewise, the sugar, tea, and chocolate Europeans consumed did little to promote economic development in Europe. However, both African and European merchants profited from trading these consumer goods. Because they directed the whole Atlantic system, Europeans gained far more wealth than Africans.

Historians disagree in their assessment of how deeply European capitalism dominated Africa before 1800, but Europeans clearly had much less political and economic impact in Africa than in the West Indies or on the mainland of the Americas. Still, it is significant that Western capitalism was expanding rapidly in the seventeenth century, while the Ottoman Empire, the dominant state of the Middle East, was entering a period of economic and political decline (see Chapter 19). The tide of influence in Africa was thus running in the Europeans' direction.

CONCLUSION

The new Atlantic trading system had great importance in and momentous implications for world history. In the first phase of their expansion Europeans had conquered and colonized the Americas and captured major Indian Ocean trade routes. The development of the Atlantic system showed their ability to move beyond the conquest and capture of existing systems to create a major new trading system that could transform a region almost beyond recognition.

The West Indies felt the transforming power of capitalism more profoundly than did any other place outside Europe in this period. The establishment of sugar plantation societies was not just a matter of replacing native vegetation with alien plants and native peoples with Europeans and Africans. More fundamentally, it made these once-isolated islands part of a dynamic trading system controlled from Europe. To be sure, the West Indies was not the only place affected. Parts of northern Brazil were touched as deeply by the sugar revolution, and other parts of the Americas were yielding to the power of European colonization and capitalism.

Africa played an essential role in the Atlantic system, importing trade goods and exporting slaves to the Americas. Africa, however, was less dominated by the Atlantic system than were Europe's American colonies. Africans remained in control of their continent and interacted culturally and politically with the Islamic world more than with the Atlantic.

Historians have seen the Atlantic system as a model of the kind of highly interactive economy that became global in later centuries. For that reason the Atlantic system was a milestone in a much larger historical process, but not a monument to be admired. Its transformations were destructive as well as creative, producing victims as well as victors. Yet one cannot ignore that the system's awesome power came from its ability to create wealth. As the next chapter describes, southern Asia and the Indian Ocean basin were also beginning to feel the effects of Europeans' rising power.

■ Key Terms

Royal African Company	maroon
Atlantic system	capitalism
chartered company	mercantilism
Dutch West India Company	Atlantic Circuit
plantocracy	Middle Passage
driver	Songhai
seasoning	Hausa
manumission	Bornu

■ Suggested Reading

The global context of early modern capitalism is examined by Immanuel Wallerstein, *The Modern World-System,* 3 vols. (1974–1989); by Fernand Braudel, *Civilization and Capitalism, 15th–18th Century,* 3 vols. (1982–1984); and in two volumes of scholarly papers edited by James D. Tracy, *The Rise of Merchant Empires* (1990) and *The Political Economy of Merchant Empires* (1991). Especially relevant are the chapters in *The Rise of Merchant Empires* by Herbert S. Klein, summarizing scholarship on the Middle Passage, and by Ralph A. Austen, on the trans-Saharan caravan trade between 1500 and 1800.

The best general introductions to the Atlantic system are Philip D. Curtin, *The Rise and Fall of the Plantation Complex* (1990); David Ellis, *The Rise of African Slavery in the Americas* (2000); and Robin Blackburn, *The Making of New World Slavery* (1997). Recent scholarly articles on subjects considered in this chapter are available in *The Atlantic Slave Trade: Effects on Economies, Societies, and Peoples in Africa, the Americas and Europe,* ed. Joseph E. Inikori and Stanley L. Engerman (1992); in *Slavery and the Rise of the Atlantic System,* ed. Barbara L. Solow (1991); and in *Africans in Bondage: Studies in Slavery and the Slave Trade,* ed. Paul Lovejoy (1986). Pieter Emmer has edited a valuable collection of articles on *The Dutch in the Atlantic Economy, 1580–1880: Trade, Slavery, and Emancipation* (1998).

Herbert S. Klein's *The Atlantic Slave Trade* (1999) provides a brief overview of research on that subject. A useful collection of debates is David Northrup, ed., *The Atlantic Slave Trade,* 2d ed. (2002). Hugh Thomas's *The Slave Trade: The Story of the Atlantic Slave Trade, 1440–1870* (1999) and Basil Davidson's *The Atlantic Slave Trade,* rev. ed. (1980) are other useful historical narratives. More global in its conception is Patrick Manning, *Slave Trades, 1500–1800: Globalization of Forced Labor* (1996).

The connections of African communities to the Atlantic are explored by David Northrup, *Africa's Discovery of Europe, 1450–1850* (2002); John Thornton, *Africa and Africans in the Making of the Atlantic World, 1400–1800,* 2d ed. (1998); and the authors of *Captive Passage: The Transatlantic Slave Trade and the Making of the Americas* (2002). Still valuable are Margaret E. Crahan and Franklin W. Knight, eds., *Africa and the Caribbean: The Legacies of a Link* (1979), and Richard Price, ed., *Maroon Societies: Rebel Slave Communities in the Americas,* 2d ed. (1979).

Herbert S. Klein's *African Slavery in Latin America and the Caribbean* (1986) is an exceptionally fine synthesis of recent research on New World slavery. The larger context of Caribbean history is skillfully surveyed by Eric Williams, *From Columbus to Castro: The History of the Caribbean* (1984), and more simply surveyed by William Claypole and John Robottom, *Caribbean Story,* vol. 1, *Foundations,* 2d ed. (1990). A useful collection of sources and readings is Stanley Engerman, Seymour Drescher, and Robert Paquette, eds., *Slavery* (2001).

Roland Oliver and Anthony Atmore, *The African Middle Ages, 1400–1800,* 2d ed. (2003), summarize African history in this period. Students can pursue specific topics in more detail in Richard Gray, ed., *The Cambridge History of Africa,* vol. 4 (1975), and B. A. Ogot, ed., *UNESCO General History of Africa,* vol. 5 (1992). For recent research on slavery and the African, Atlantic, and Muslim slave trades with Africa, see Paul Lovejoy, *Transformations in Slavery: A History of Slavery in Africa,* 2d ed. (2000); Claire C. Robertson and Martin A. Klein, eds., *Women and Slavery in Africa* (1983); and Patrick Manning, *Slavery and African Life: Occidental, Oriental, and African Slave Trades* (1990). See also Philip D. Curtin, ed., *Africa Remembered: Narratives by West Africans from the Era of the Slave Trade* (1968, 1997).

Those interested in Islam's cultural and commercial contacts with sub-Saharan Africa will find useful information in James L. A. Webb, Jr., *Desert Frontier: Ecological and Economic Change Along the Western Sahel, 1600–1850* (1995); Elizabeth Savage, ed., *The Human Commodity: Perspectives on the Trans-Saharan Slave Trade* (1992); and J. Spencer Trimingham, *The Influence of Islam upon Africa* (1968).

■ Notes

1. Eric Williams, *Capitalism and Slavery* (Charlotte: University of North Carolina Press, 1944), 7.
2. Willem Bosman, *A New and Accurate Description of Guinea, etc.* (London, 1705), quoted in David Northrup, ed., *The Atlantic Slave Trade* (Lexington, MA: D. C. Heath, 1994), 72.
3. Roland Oliver and Anthony Atmore, *The African Middle Ages, 1400–1800* (Cambridge, England: Cambridge University Press, 1981), 100.
4. King Osei Bonsu, quoted in Northrup, ed., *The Atlantic Slave Trade,* 93.
5. Alexander Falconbridge, *Account of the Slave Trade on the Coast of Africa* (London: J. Phillips, 1788), 12.
6. Joseph C. Miller, "The Significance of Drought, Disease, and Famine in the Agriculturally Marginal Zones of West-Central Africa," *Journal of African History* 23 (1982), 17–61.

Document-Based Question
The Economics of Atlantic Slavery

Using the following documents, analyze the economic factors that contributed to the expansion of slavery and the slave trade in the Atlantic World from 1550 to 1800.

DOCUMENT 1
Caribbean Sugar Mill (photo, p. 457)

DOCUMENT 2
Figure 18.1 Transatlantic Slave Trade from Africa, 1551–1850 (p. 461)

DOCUMENT 3
Plantation Scene, Antigua, British West Indies (photo, p. 462)

DOCUMENT 4
Table 18.1 Slave Occupations on a Jamaican Sugar Plantation, 1788 (p. 465)

DOCUMENT 5
Table 18.2 Birth and Death on a Jamaican Sugar Plantation, 1779–1785 (p. 466)

DOCUMENT 6
Map 18.1 The Atlantic Economy (p. 470)

DOCUMENT 7
Slave Ship (photo, p. 471)

DOCUMENT 8
Map 18.2 The African Slave Trade, 1500–1800 (p. 472)

DOCUMENT 9
Excerpt on Ayuba Suleiman Diallo (Diversity and Dominance, pp. 478–479)

How do the data in Documents 2, 4, and 5 affect your analysis of the remaining documents? What additional types of documents would help you analyze the economic factors that contributed to the expansion of slavery and the slave trade in the Atlantic World from 1550 to 1800?

19

Southwest Asia and the Indian Ocean, 1500–1750

Building a Palace   This miniature painting from the reign of the Mughal emperor Akbar illustrates the building techniques of seventeenth-century India.

CHAPTER OUTLINE

The Ottoman Empire, to 1750

The Safavid Empire, 1502–1722

The Mughal Empire, 1526–1761

Trade Empires in the Indian Ocean, 1600–1729

DIVERSITY AND DOMINANCE: Islamic Law and Ottoman Rule

ENVIRONMENT AND TECHNOLOGY: Metal Currency and Inflation

Anthony Jenkinson, merchant-adventurer for the Muscovy Company, which was founded in 1555 to develop trade with Russia, became the first Englishman to set foot in Iran. In 1561 he sailed to Archangel in Russia's frigid north, and from there found his way down the Volga River and across the Caspian Sea. The local ruler he met in northwestern Iran was an object of wonder:

> richly appareled with long garments of silk, and cloth of gold, embroidered with pearls of stone; upon his head was a *tolipane* [headdress shaped like a tulip] with a sharp end pointing upwards half a yard long, of rich cloth of gold, wrapped about with a piece of India silk of twenty yards long, wrought in gold richly enameled, and set with precious stones; his earrings had pendants of gold a handful long, with two rubies of great value, set in the ends thereof.

Moving on to Qazvin°, Iran's capital, Jenkinson met the shah, whom the English referred to as the "Great Sophie" (apparently from Safavi°, the name of the ruling family). "In lighting from my horse at the Court gate, before my feet touched the ground, a pair of the Sophie's own shoes . . . were put upon my feet, for without the same shoes I might not be suffered to tread upon his holy ground."[1] Finding no one capable of reading a letter he carried from Queen Elizabeth, written in Latin, English, Hebrew, and Italian, he nevertheless managed to propose trade between England and Iran. The shah, who was in the midst of negotiations with the Ottoman sultan to end a half-century of hostilities, rejected the idea of diverting Iranian silk from Ottoman markets.

Though Jenkinson and later merchants discovered that Central Asia's bazaars were only meagerly supplied with goods, the idea of bypassing the Ottomans in the eastern Mediterranean and trading directly with Iran through Russia remained tempting. The Ottomans, too, dreamed of outflanking Safavid Iran. In 1569 an Ottoman army unsuccessfully tried to dig a 40-mile (64-kilometer) canal between the Don

Qazvin (kaz-VEEN)   Safavi (SAH-fah-vee)

River, which opened into the Black Sea, and the Volga, which flowed into the Caspian. Putting Ottoman ships in the Caspian would have facilitated an attack on Iran from the north.

Russia, then ruled by Tsar Ivan IV (r. 1533–1584), known as Ivan the Terrible or Awesome, stood in the Ottoman path. Ivan transformed his principality from a second-rate power into the sultan's primary competitor in Central Asia. In the river-crossed steppe, where Turkic nomads had long enjoyed uncontested sway, Slavic Christian Cossacks from the region of the Don and Dnieper Rivers used armed wagon trains and river craft fitted with small cannon to push southward and establish a Russian presence.

A contest for trade with or control of Central Asia, and beyond that with the Muslim Mughal empire in India, grew out of the centrality conferred on the region by three centuries of Mongol and Turkic conquest. Nevertheless, changes in the organization of world trade were sapping the vitality of the Silk Road, and power was shifting to European seafaring empires linking the Atlantic with the Indian Ocean. For all their naval power in the Mediterranean, neither the Ottomans, the Safavid shahs in Iran, nor the Mughal emperors of India deployed more than a token navy in the southern seas.

As you read this chapter, ask yourself the following questions:

- What were the advantages and disadvantages of a land empire as opposed to a maritime empire?
- What role did religion play in political alliances and rivalries and in the formation of states?
- How did trading patterns change between 1500 and 1750?
- How did imperial rulers maintain dominance over their diverse populations?

THE OTTOMAN EMPIRE, TO 1750

The most long-lived of the post-Mongol Muslim empires, the **Ottoman Empire** grew from a tiny nucleus in 1300 to encompass most of southeastern Europe by the late fifteenth century. Mamluk Syria and Egypt succumbed in the early sixteenth century, leaving the Ottomans with the largest Muslim empire since the original Islamic caliphate in the seventh century. However, the empire resembled the new centralized monarchies of France and Spain (see Chapter 16) more than any medieval model.

Enduring more than five centuries until 1922, the Ottoman Empire survived several periods of wrenching change, some caused by internal problems, others by the growing power of European adversaries. These periods of change reveal the problems faced by huge, land-based empires around the world.

Expansion and Frontiers

At first a tiny state in north-western Anatolia built by Turkish nomad horsemen, zealous Muslim warriors, and a few Christian converts to Islam (see Map 19.1), the empire grew because of three factors: (1) the shrewdness of its founder Osman (from which the name "Ottoman" comes) and his descendants, (2) control of a strategic link between Europe and Asia at Gallipoli° on the Dardanelles strait, and (3) the creation of an army that took advantage of the traditional skills of the Turkish cavalryman and new military possibilities presented by gunpowder and Christian prisoners of war.

At first, Ottoman armies concentrated on Christian enemies in Greece and the Balkans, conquering a strong Serbian kingdom at the Battle of Kosovo° (in present-day Yugoslavia) in 1389. Much of southeastern Europe and Anatolia was under the control of the sultans by 1402, when Bayazid° I, "the Thunderbolt," confronted Timur's challenge from Central Asia. After Timur defeated and captured Bayazid at the Battle of Ankara (1402), a generation of civil war followed, until Mehmed° I reunified the sultanate.

During a century and a half of fighting for territory both east and west of Constantinople, the sultans repeatedly eyed the heavily fortified capital of the slowly dying Byzantine Empire. In 1453 Sultan Mehmed II, "the Conqueror," laid siege to Constantinople, using enormous cannon to bash in the city's walls, dragging warships over a high hill from the Bosporus strait to the city's inner harbor to avoid its sea defenses, and finally penetrating the city's land walls through a series of infantry assaults. The fall of Constantinople—henceforth commonly known as Istanbul—brought over eleven hundred

years of Byzantine rule to an end and made the Ottomans seem invincible.

In 1514, at the Battle of Chaldiran (in Armenia), Selim° I, "the Inexorable," ended a potential threat on his eastern frontier from the new and expansive realm of the Safavid shah in Iran (see below). Although warfare between the two recurred, the general border between the Ottomans and their eastern neighbor dates to this battle. Iraq became a contested and repeatedly ravaged frontier zone.

When Selim conquered the Mamluk Sultanate of Egypt and Syria in 1516 and 1517, the Red Sea became the Ottomans' southern frontier. In the west, the rulers of the major port cities of Algeria and Tunisia, some of them Greek or Italian converts to Islam, voluntarily joined the empire in the early sixteenth century, thereby strengthening its Mediterranean fleets.

The son of Selim I, **Suleiman° the Magnificent** (r. 1520–1566), known to his subjects as Suleiman Kanuni, "the Lawgiver," commanded the greatest Ottoman assault on Christian Europe. Suleiman seemed unstoppable as he conquered Belgrade in 1521, expelled the Knights of the Hospital of St. John from the island of Rhodes the following year, and laid siege to Vienna in 1529. Only the lateness of the season and the need to retreat before the onset of winter saved Vienna's overmatched Christian garrison. In later centuries, Ottoman historians looked back on Suleiman's reign as a golden age when the imperial system worked to perfection.

While Ottoman armies pressed deeper and deeper into eastern Europe, the sultans also sought to control the Mediterranean. Between 1453 and 1502 the Ottomans fought the opening rounds of a two-century war with Venice, the most powerful of Italy's commercial city-states. From the Fourth Crusade of 1204 onward, Venice had assembled a profitable maritime empire that included major islands such as Crete and Cyprus along with strategic coastal strongpoints in Greece. Venice thereby became more than just a trading nation. Its island sugar plantations, exploiting cheap slave labor, competed favorably with Egypt in the international trade of the fifteenth century. With their rivals the Genoese, who traded through the strategic island of Chios, the Venetians stifled Ottoman maritime activities in the Aegean Sea.

The initial fighting left Venice with reduced military power and subject to an annual tribute payment, but it controlled its lucrative islands for another century. The Ottomans, like the Chinese, were willing to let other nations carry trade to and from their ports; they preferred trade of this sort as long as the other nations acknowl-

---

Gallipoli (gah-LIP-po-lee) Kosovo (KO-so-vo)
Bayazid (BAY-yah-zeed) Mehmed (MEH-met)

Selim (seh-LEEM) Suleiman (SOO-lay-man)

C H R O N O L O G Y			
	Ottoman Empire	**Safavid Empire**	**Mughal Empire**	**Europeans in the Indian Ocean States**

	Ottoman Empire	Safavid Empire	Mughal Empire	Europeans in the Indian Ocean States
1500		**1502–1524** Shah Ismail establishes Safavid rule in Iran		**1511** Portuguese seize Malacca from local Malay ruler
	1514 Selim I defeats Safavid shah at Chaldiran; conquers Egypt and Syria (1516–1517)	**1514** Defeat by Ottomans at Chaldiran limits Safavid growth		
	1520–1566 Reign of Suleiman the Magnificent; peak of Ottoman Empire		**1526** Babur defeats last sultan of Delhi at Panipat	
	1529 First Ottoman siege of Vienna		**1539** Death of Nanak, founder of Sikh religion	
			1556–1605 Akbar rules in Agra; peak of Mughal Empire	**1565** Spanish establish their first fort in the Philippines
	1571 Ottoman naval defeat at Lepanto	**1587–1629** Reign of Shah Abbas the Great; peak of Safavid Empire		
1600				**1600** English East India company founded
				1602 Dutch East India Company founded
	1610 End of Anatolian revolts	**1622** Iranians oust Portuguese from Hormuz after 108 years		**1606** Dutch reach Australia
				1641 Dutch seize Malacca from Portuguese
			1658–1707 Aurangzeb imposes conservative Islamic regime	**1650** Omani Arabs capture Musqat from Portuguese
			1690 British found city of Calcutta	
1700				**1698** Omani Arabs seize Mombasa from Portuguese
	1718–1730 Tulip Period; military decline apparent to Austria and Russia	**1722** Afghan invaders topple last Safavid shah		
		1736–1747 Nadir Shah temporarily reunites Iran; invades India (1739)	**1739** Iranians under Nadir Shah sack Delhi	**1742** Expansion of French Power in India

edged Ottoman authority. It never occurred to them that a sea empire held together by flimsy ships could rival a great land empire fielding an army of a hundred thousand.

In the south Muslims of the Red Sea and Indian Ocean region customarily traded by way of Egypt and Syria. In the early sixteenth century merchants from southern India and Sumatra sent emissaries to Istanbul requesting naval support against the Portuguese. The Ottomans responded vigorously to Portuguese threats close to their territories, such as at Aden at the southern entrance to the Red Sea, but their efforts farther afield fell short of stopping the Portuguese.

So long as eastern luxury products still flowed to Ottoman markets, why commit major resources to

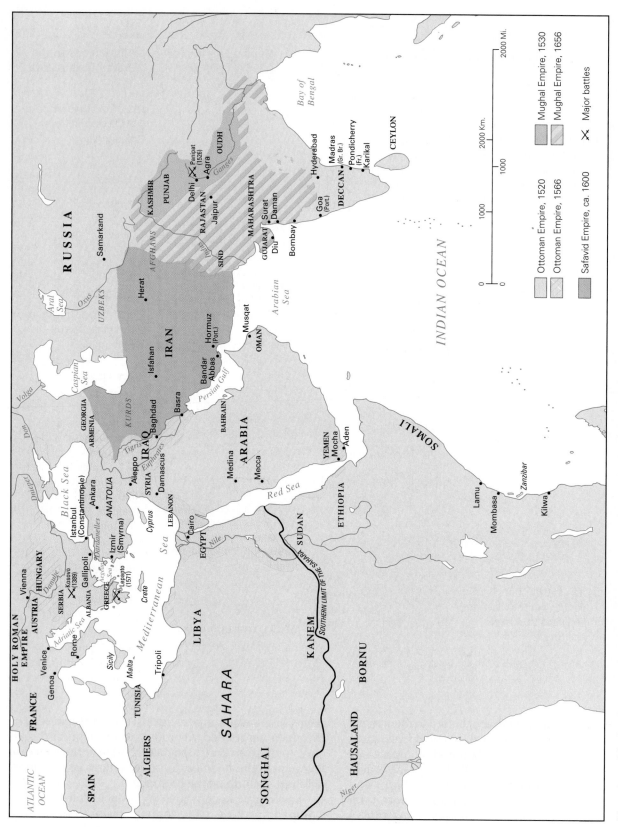

Map 19.1 Muslim Empires in the Sixteenth and Seventeenth Centuries Iran, a Shi'ite state flanked by Sunni Ottomans on the west and Sunni Mughals on the east, had the least exposure to European influences. Ottoman expansion across the southern Mediterranean Sea intensified European fears of Islam. The areas of strongest Mughal control dictated that Islam's spread into southeast Asia would be heavily influenced by merchants and religious figures from Gujarat instead of from eastern India.

Aya Sofya Mosque in Istanbul   Orginally a Byzantine cathedral, Aya Sofya (in Greek, Hagia Sophia) was transformed into a mosque after 1453, and four minarets were added. It then became a model for subsequent Ottoman mosques. To the right behind it is the Bosporus strait dividing Europe and Asia, to the left the Golden Horn inlet separating the old city of Istanbul from the newer parts. The gate to the Ottoman sultan's palace is to the right of the mosque. The pointed tower to the left of the dome is part of the palace.   (Robert Frerck/Woodfin Camp & Associates)

subduing an enemy whose main threat was a demand that merchant vessels, mostly belonging to non-Ottoman Muslims, buy protection from Portuguese attack? Portuguese power was territorially limited to fortified coastal points, such as Hormuz at the entrance to the Persian Gulf, Goa in western India, and Malacca in Malaya (see Chapter 15). The Ottomans did send a small naval force to Indonesia, but they never acted consistently or aggressively in the Indian Ocean.

Central Institutions

Heirs of the military traditions of Central Asia, the Ottoman army originally consisted of lightly armored mounted warriors skilled at shooting short bows made of compressed layers of bone, wood, and leather. The conquest of Christian territories in the Balkans in the late fourteenth century, however, gave the Ottomans access to a new military resource: Christian prisoners of war induced to serve as military slaves.

Slave soldiery had a long history in Islamic lands. The Mamluk Sultanate of Egypt and Syria was built on that practice. The Mamluks, however, acquired their new blood from slave markets in Central Asia and the Caucasus. Enslaving Christian prisoners, an action of questionable legality in Islamic law, was an Ottoman innovation. Converted to Islam, these "new troops," called yeni cheri in Turkish and **"Janissary"°** in English, gave the Ottomans great military flexibility.

Christians by upbringing, the Janissaries had no misgivings about fighting against Turks and Muslims when the sultans attacked in western Asia. Not coming from a culture of horse nomads, they readily accepted the idea of fighting on foot and learning to use guns, which were then still too heavy and awkward for a horseman to load and fire. The Janissaries lived in barracks and trained all year round. Until the mid-sixteenth century, they were barred from holding jobs or marrying.

Selection for Janissary training changed early in the fifteenth century. The new system, called the **devshirme°** (literally "selection"), imposed a regular levy of male children on Christian villages in the Balkans and occasionally elsewhere. Devshirme children were placed with Turkish families to learn their language before commencing military training. The most promising of them received their education at the sultan's palace in Istanbul, where they studied Islam and what we might call the liberal arts in addition to military matters. This regime, sophisticated for its time, produced not only the Janissary soldiers but

---

Janissary (JAN-nih-say-ree)   **devshirme** (dev-sheer-MEH)

also, from among the few who received special training in the inner service of the palace, senior military commanders and heads of government departments up to the rank of grand vizier.

The Ottoman Empire became cosmopolitan in character. The sophisticated court language, Osmanli° (the Turkish form of Ottoman), shared basic grammar and vocabulary with the Turkish spoken by Anatolia's nomads and villagers, but Arabic and Persian elements made it as distinct from that language as the Latin of educated Europeans was from the various Latin-derived Romance languages. People who served in the military or the bureaucracy and conversed in Osmanli belonged to the askeri°, or "military," class, which made them exempt from taxes and dependent on the sultan for their well-being. The mass of the population, whether Muslims, Christians, or Jews—Jews flooded into Ottoman territory after their expulsion from Spain in 1492 (see Chapter 16)—constituted the raya°, literally "flock of sheep."

By the beginning of the reign of Sultan Suleiman, the Ottoman Empire was the most powerful and best-organized state in Europe and the Islamic world. Its military balanced mounted archers, primarily Turks supported by grants of land in return for military service, with Janissaries—Turkified Albanians, Serbs, and Macedonians paid from the central treasury and trained in the most advanced weaponry. Greek, Turkish, Algerian, and Tunisian sailors manned the galley-equipped navy, usually under the command of an admiral from one of the North African ports.

The balance of the Ottoman land forces brought success to Ottoman arms in recurrent wars with the Safavids, who were much slower to adopt firearms, and in the inexorable conquest of the Balkans. In naval matters, a major expedition against Malta that would have given the Ottomans a foothold in the western Mediterranean failed in 1565. Combined Christian forces also achieved a massive naval victory at the Battle of Lepanto, off Greece, in 1571. In a year's time, however, the sultan had replaced all of the galleys sunk in that battle.

Under the land-grant system, resident cavalrymen administered most rural areas in Anatolia and the Balkans. They maintained order, collected taxes, and reported for each summer's campaign with their horses, retainers, and supplies, all paid for from the taxes they collected. When not campaigning, they stayed at home. Some historians maintain that these cavalrymen, who did not own their land, had little interest in encouraging production or introducing new technologies; but since a

Ottoman Glassmakers on Parade Celebrations of the circumcisions of the sultan's sons featured parades organized by the craft guilds of Istanbul. This float features glassmaking, a common craft in Islamic realms. The most elaborate glasswork included oil lamps for mosques and colored glass for the small stained-glass windows below mosque domes. (Topkapi Saray Museum)

militarily able son usually succeeded his father, the grant holders did have some interest in productivity.

The Ottoman conception of the world saw the sultan providing justice for his raya and the military protecting them. In return, the raya paid the taxes that supported both the sultan and the military. In reality, the central government, like most large territorial governments in premodern times, seldom intersected the lives of most subjects. Arab, Turkish, and Balkan townsfolk sought justice in religious law courts and depended on local notables and religious leaders to represent them before Ottoman provincial officials. Balkan regions such as Albania and Bosnia had large numbers of converts, and Islam gradually became the majority religion. Thus the law of Islam (the Shari'a°), as interpreted by local ulama° (religious scholars), conditioned urban institutions and social life (see Diversity and Dominance: Islamic Law and Ottoman Rule). Local customs prevailed among non-Muslims and in many rural areas. Non-Muslims also looked to their own religious leaders for guidance in family and spiritual matters.

Osmanli (os-MAHN-lee) **askeri** (AS-keh-ree) **raya** (RAH-yah)   **Shari'a** (sha-REE-ah) **ulama** (oo-leh-MAH)

Crisis of the Military State, 1585–1650

As military technology evolved, cannon and lighter-weight firearms played an ever-larger role on the battlefield. Accordingly, the size of the Janissary corps—and its cost to the government—grew steadily, and the role of the Turkish cavalry, which continued to disdain firearms, diminished. In the mid-sixteenth century, to fill state coffers and pay the Janissaries, the sultan started reducing the number of landholding cavalrymen. Revenues previously spent on their living expenses and military equipment went directly into the imperial treasury. Some of the displaced cavalrymen, armed and unhappy, became a restive element in rural Anatolia.

In the late sixteenth century, inflation caused by a flood of cheap silver from the New World (see Environment and Technology: Metal Currency and Inflation), affected many of the remaining landholders, who collected taxes according to legally fixed rates. Some saw their purchasing power decline so much that they could not report for military service. This delinquency played into the hands of the government, which wanted to reduce the cavalry and increase the Janissary corps. As the central government recovered control of the land, more and more cavalrymen joined the ranks of dispossessed troopers. Students and professors in madrasas (religious colleges) similarly found it impossible to live on fixed stipends from madrasa endowments.

Constrained by religious law from fundamentally reforming the tax system, the government levied emergency surtaxes to obtain enough funds to pay the Janissaries and bureaucrats. For additional military strength, particularly in wars with Iran, the government reinforced the Janissaries with partially trained, salaried soldiers hired for the duration of a campaign. Once the summer campaign season ended, these soldiers found themselves out of work and short on cash.

This complicated situation resulted in revolts that devastated Anatolia between 1590 and 1610. Former landholding cavalrymen, short-term soldiers released at the end of a campaign, peasants overburdened by emergency taxes, and even impoverished students of religion formed bands of marauders. Anatolia experienced the worst of the rebellions and suffered greatly from emigration and loss of agricultural production. Banditry, made worse by the government's inability to stem the spread of muskets among the general public, beset other parts of the empire as well.

In the meantime, the Janissaries took advantage of their growing influence to gain relief from prohibitions on marrying and engaging in business. Janissaries who involved themselves in commerce lessened the burden on the state budget. Married Janissaries who enrolled sons or relatives in the corps made it possible in the seventeenth century for the government to save state funds by abolishing the devshirme system with its traveling selection officers. However, the increase in the total number of Janissaries and their steady deterioration as a military force more than offset these savings.

Economic Change and Growing Weakness, 1650–1750

A very different Ottoman Empire emerged from this period of crisis. The sultan once had led armies. Now he mostly resided in his palace and had little experience of the real world. This manner of living resulted from a gradually developed policy of keeping the sultan's male relatives confined to the palace to prevent them from plotting coups or meddling in politics. The sultan's mother and the chief eunuch overseeing the private quarters of the palace thus became important arbiters of royal favor, and even of succession to the sultanate, while the chief administrators—the grand viziers—oversaw the affairs of government. (Ottoman historians draw special attention to the negative influence of women in the palace after the time of Suleiman, but to some degree they reflect stereotypical male, and Muslim, fears about women in politics.)

The devshirme had been discontinued, and the Janissaries had taken advantage of their increased power and privileges to make membership in their corps hereditary. Together with several other newly prominent infantry regiments, they involved themselves in crafts and trading, both in Istanbul and in provincial capitals such as Cairo, Aleppo, and Baghdad. This activity took a toll on their military skills, but they continued to be a powerful faction in urban politics that the sultans could neither ignore nor reform.

Land grants in return for military service also disappeared. Tax farming arose in their place. Tax farmers paid specific taxes, such as customs duties, in advance in return for the privilege of collecting greater amounts from the actual taxpayers. In one instance, two tax farmers advanced the government 18 million akches° (small silver coins) for the customs duties of the Aegean port of Izmir° and collected a total of 19,169,203 akches, for a profit of 6.5 percent.

Rural administration, already disrupted by the rebellions, suffered from the transition to tax farms. The military landholders had kept order on their lands to maintain their incomes. Tax farmers seldom lived on the land, and their tax collection rights could vary from year to year. The imperial government, therefore, faced

akches (ahk-CHEH)   Izmir (IZ-meer)

DIVERSITY AND DOMINANCE

ISLAMIC LAW AND OTTOMAN RULE

Ebu's-Su'ud was the Mufti of Istanbul from 1545 to 1574, serving under the sultans Suleiman the Magnificent (1520–1566) and his son Selim II (1566–1574). Originally one of many city-based religious scholars giving opinions on matters of law, the mufti of Istanbul by Ebu's-Su'ud's time had become the top religious official in the empire and the personal adviser to the sultan on religious and legal matters. The position would later acquire the title Shaikh al-Islam.

Historians debate the degree of independence these muftis had. Since the ruler, as a Muslim, was subject to the Shari'a, the mufti could theoretically veto his policies. On important matters, however, the mufti more often seemed to come up with the answer that best suited the sultan who appointed him. This bias is not apparent in more mundane areas of the law.

The collection of Ebu's-Su'ud's fatwas, or legal opinions, from which the examples below are drawn shows the range of matters that came to his attention. They are also an excellent source for understanding the problems of his time, the relationship between Islamic law and imperial governance, and the means by which the state asserted its dominance over the common people. Some opinions respond directly to questions posed by the sultan. Others are hypothetical, using the names Zeyd, 'Amr, and Hind the way police today use John Doe and Jane Doe. While qadis, or Islamic judges, made findings of fact in specific cases on trial, muftis issued only opinions on matters of law. A qadi as well as a plaintiff or defendant might ask a question of a mufti. Later jurists consulted collections of fatwas for precedents, but the fatwas had no permanent binding power.

On the plan of Selim II to attack the Venetians in Crete in 1570   A land was previously in the realm of Islam. After a while, the abject infidels overran it, destroyed the colleges and mosques, and left them vacant. They filled the pulpits and the galleries with the tokens of infidelity and error, intending to insult the religion of Islam with all kinds of vile deeds, and by spreading their ugly acts to all corners of the earth.

His Excellency the Sultan, the Refuge of Religion, has, as zeal for Islam requires, determined to take the aforementioned land from the possession of the shameful infidels and to annex it to the realm of Islam.

When peace was previously concluded with the other lands in the possession of the said infidels, the aforenamed land was included. An explanation is sought as to whether, in accordance with the Pure shari'a, this is an impediment to the Sultan's determining to break the treaty.

Answer: There is no possibility that it could ever be an impediment. For the Sultan of the People of Islam (may God glorify his victories) to make peace with the infidels is legal only when there is a benefit to all Muslims. When there is no benefit, peace is never legal. When a benefit has been seen, and it is then observed to be more beneficial to break it, then to break it becomes absolutely obligatory and binding.

His Excellency [Muhammad] the Apostle of God (may God bless him and give him peace) made a ten-year truce with the Meccan infidels in the sixth year of the Hegira. His Excellency 'Ali (may God ennoble his face) wrote a document that was corroborated and confirmed. Then, in the following year, it was considered more beneficial to break it and, in the eighth year of the Hegira, [the Prophet] attacked [the Meccans], and conquered Mecca the Mighty.

On war against the Shi'ite Muslim Safavids of Iran   Is it licit according to the shari'a to fight the followers of the Safavids? Is the person who kills them a holy warrior, and the person who dies at their hands a martyr?

Answer: Yes, it is a great holy war and a glorious martyrdom.

Assuming that it is licit to fight them, is this simply because of their rebellion and enmity against the [Ottoman] Sultan of the People of Islam, because they drew the sword against the troops of Islam, or what?

Answer: They are both rebels and, from many points of view, infidels.

Can the children of Safavid subjects captured in the Nakhichevan campaign be enslaved?
Answer: No.

The followers of the Safavids are killed by order of the Sultan. If it turns out that some of the prisoners, young and old, are [Christian] Armenian[s], are they set free?

Answer: Yes. So long as the Armenians have not joined the Safavid troops in attacking and fighting against the troops of Islam, it is illegal to take them prisoner.

On the Holy Land   Are all the Arab realms Holy Land, or does it have specific boundaries, and what is the difference between the Holy Land and other lands?

Answer: Syria is certainly called the Holy Land. Jerusalem, Aleppo and its surroundings, and Damascus belong to it.

On land-grants   What lands are private property, and what lands are held by feudal tenure [i.e., assignment in exchange for military service]?

Answer: Plots of land within towns are private property. Their owners may sell them, donate them or convert them to trust. When [the owner] dies, [the land] passes to all the heirs. Lands held by feudal tenure are cultivated lands around villages, whose occupants bear the burden of their services and pay a portion of their [produce in tax]. They cannot sell the land, donate it or convert it to trust. When they die, if they have sons, these have the use [of the land]. Otherwise, the cavalryman gives [it to someone else] by *tapu* [title deed].

On the consumption of coffee   Zeyd drinks coffee to aid concentration or digestion. Is this licit?

Answer: How can anyone consume this reprehensible [substance], which dissolute men drink when engaged in games and debauchery?

The Sultan, the Refuge of Religion, has on many occasions banned coffee-houses. However, a group of ruffians take no notice, but keep coffee-houses for a living. In order to draw the crowds, they take on unbearded apprentices, and have ready instruments of entertainment and play, such as chess and backgammon. The city's rakes, rogues and vagabond boys gather there to consume opium and hashish. On top of this, they drink coffee and, when they are high, engage in games and false sciences, and neglect the prescribed prayers. In law, what should happen to a judge who is able to prevent the said coffee-sellers and drinkers, but does not do so?

Answer: Those who perpetrate these ugly deeds should be prevented and deterred by severe chastisement and long imprisonment. Judges who neglect to deter them should be dismissed.

On matters of theft   How are thieves to be "carefully examined"?

Answer: His Excellency 'Ali (may God ennoble his face) appointed Imam Shuraih as judge. It so happened that, at that time, several people took a Muslim's son to another district. The boy disappeared and, when the people came back, the missing boy's father brought them before Judge Shuraih. [When he brought] a claim [against them on account of the

loss of his son], they denied it, saying: "No harm came to him from us." Judge Shuraih thought deeply and was perplexed.

When the man told his tale to His Excellency 'Ali, [the latter] summoned Judge Shuraih and questioned him. When Shuraih said; "Nothing came to light by the shari'a," ['Ali] summoned all the people who had taken the man's son, separated them from one another, and questioned them separately. For each of their stopping places, he asked: "What was the boy wearing in that place? What did you eat? And where did he disappear?" In short, he made each of them give a detailed account, and when their words contradicted each other, each of their statements was written down separately. Then he brought them all together, and when the contradictions became apparent, they were no longer able to deny [their guilt] and confessed to what had happened.

This kind of ingenuity is a requirement of the case.

[This fatwa appears to justify investigation of crimes by the state instead of by the qadi. Judging from court records, which contain very few criminal cases, it seems likely that in practice, many criminal cases were dealt with outside the jurisdiction of the qadi's court.]

Zeyd takes 'Amr's donkey without his knowledge and sells it. Is he a thief?

Answer: His hand is not cut off.

Zeyd mounts 'Amr's horse as a courier and loses it. Is compensation necessary?

Answer: Yes

In which case: What if Zeyd has a Sultanic decree [authorising him] to take horses for courier service?

Answer: Compensation is required in any case. He was not commanded to lose [the horse]. Even if he were commanded, it is the person who loses it who is liable.

On homicides   Zeyd enters Hind's house and tries to have intercourse forcibly. Since Hind can repel him by no other means, she strikes and wounds him with an axe. If Zeyd dies of the wound, is Hind liable for anything?

Answer: She has performed an act of Holy War.

QUESTIONS FOR ANALYSIS

1. **What do these fatwas indicate with regard to the balance between practical legal reasoning and religious dictates?**

2. **How much was the Ottoman government constrained by the Shari'a?**

3. **What can be learned about day-to-day life from materials of this sort?**

Source: Excerpts from Colin Imber, *Ebu's-Su'ud: The Islamic Legal Tradition* (Stanford, CA: University Press, 1997), 84–88, 93–94, 223–226, 250, 257. Copyright © 1997 Colin Imber, originating publisher Edinburg University Press. Used with permission of Stanford University Press, www.sup.org.

Metal Currency and Inflation

Inflation occurs when the quantity of goods and services available for purchase remains stable while the quantity of money in circulation increases. With more money in their pockets, people are willing to pay more to get what they want. Prices go up, and what people think of as the value of money goes down.

Today, with paper money and electronic banking, governments try to control inflation by regulating the printing of money or by other means. Prior to the nineteenth century, money consisted of silver and gold coins, and governments did not keep track of how much money was in circulation. As long as the annual production of gold and silver mines was quite small, inflation was not a worry. In the sixteenth and seventeenth centuries, however, precious metal poured into Spain from silver and gold mines in the New World, but there was no increase in the availability of goods and services. The resulting inflation triggered a "price revolution" in Europe—a general tripling of prices between 1500 and 1650. In Paris in 1650 the price of wheat and hay was fifteen times higher than the price had been in 1500.

This wave of inflation worked its way east, contributing to social disorder in the Ottoman Empire. European traders had more money available than Ottoman merchants and could outbid them for scarce commodities. Lacking silver and gold mines, the Ot-

toman government reduced the amount of precious metal in Ottoman coins. This made the problem worse. Hit hardest were people who had fixed incomes. Cavalrymen holding land grants worth a set amount each year were unable to equip themselves for military campaigns. Students living on fixed scholarships went begging.

Safavid Iran needed silver and gold to pay for imports from Mughal India, which imported few Iranian goods. Iranians sold silk to the Ottoman Empire for silver and gold, worsening the Ottoman situation, and then passed the precious metal on to India. Everyday life in Iran depended on barter or locally minted copper coinage, both more resistant to inflation. Copper for coins was sometimes imported from China.

Though no one then grasped the connection between silver production in Mexico and the trade balance between Iran and India, the world of the sixteenth and seventeenth centuries was becoming more closely linked economically than it had ever been before.

Set of Coin Dies The lower die, called the anvil die, was set in a piece of wood. A blank disk of gold, silver or copper was placed on top of it. The hammer die was placed on top of the blank and struck with a hammer to force the coin's image onto it. (Courtesy, Israel Museum, Jerusalem)

greater administrative burdens and came to rely heavily on powerful provincial governors or on wealthy men who purchased lifelong tax collection rights that prompted them to behave more or less as private landowners.

Rural disorder and decline in administrative control sometimes opened the way for new economic opportunities. The port of Izmir, known to Europeans by the ancient name "Smyrna," had a population of around two thousand in 1580. By 1650 the population had increased to between thirty thousand and forty thousand. Along with refugees from the Anatolian uprisings and from European pirate attacks along the coast came European merchants and large colonies of Armenians, Greeks, and

Jews. A French traveler in 1621 wrote: "At present, Izmir has a great traffic in wool, beeswax, cotton, and silk, which the Armenians bring there instead of going to Aleppo . . . because they do not pay as many dues."[2]

Izmir transformed itself between 1580 and 1650 from a small Muslim Turkish town into a multiethnic, multireligious, multilinguistic entrepôt because of the Ottoman government's inability to control trade and the slowly growing dominance of European traders in the Indian Ocean. Spices from the East, though still traded in Aleppo and other long-established Ottoman centers, were not to be found in Izmir. Aside from Iranian silk brought in by caravan, European traders at Izmir purchased local agricultural products—dried fruits, sesame seeds, nuts, and olive oil. As a consequence, local farmers who previously had grown grain for subsistence shifted their plantings more and more to cotton and other cash crops, including, after its introduction in the 1590s, tobacco, which quickly became popular in the Ottoman Empire despite government prohibitions. In this way, the agricultural economy of western Anatolia, the Balkans, and the Mediterranean coast—the Ottoman lands most accessible to Europe (see Map 19.1)—became enmeshed in a growing European commercial network.

At the same time, military power slowly ebbed. The ill-trained Janissaries sometimes resorted to hiring substitutes to go on campaign, and the sultans relied on partially trained seasonal recruits and on armies raised by the governors of frontier provinces. By the middle of the eighteenth century it was obvious to the Austrians and Russians that the Ottoman Empire was weakening. On the eastern front, however, Ottoman exhaustion after many wars was matched by the demise in 1722 of their perennial adversary, the Safavid state of Iran.

The Ottoman Empire lacked both the wealth and the inclination to match European economic advances. Overland trade from the east dwindled as political disorder in Safavid Iran cut deeply into Iranian silk production (see below). Coffee from the highlands of Yemen, a product that rose from obscurity in the fifteenth century to become the rage first in the Ottoman Empire and then in Europe, traditionally reached the market by way of Egypt. By 1770, however, Muslim merchants trading in the Yemeni port of Mocha° (literally "the coffee place") paid 15 percent in duties and fees. But European traders, benefiting from long-standing trade agreements with the sultans, paid little more than 3 percent.

Such trade agreements, called capitulations, led to European domination of Ottoman seaborne trade. Nevertheless, the Europeans did not control strategic ports in the Mediterranean comparable to Malacca in the Indian Ocean and Hormuz on the Persian Gulf, so their economic power stopped short of colonial settlement or direct control in Ottoman territories.

A few astute Ottoman statesmen observed the growing disarray of the empire and advised the sultans to reestablish the land-grant and devshirme systems of Suleiman's reign. Most people, however, could not perceive the downward course of imperial power, much less the reasons behind it. Ottoman historians named the period between 1718 and 1730 the **"Tulip Period"** because of the craze for high-priced tulip bulbs that swept Ottoman ruling circles. The craze echoed a Dutch tulip

mania that had begun in the mid-sixteenth century, when the flower was introduced into Holland from Istanbul, and had peaked in 1636 with particularly rare bulbs going for 2,500 florins apiece—the value of twenty-two oxen. Far from seeing Europe as the enemy that would eventually dismantle the empire, the Istanbul elite experimented with European clothing and furniture styles and purchased printed books from the empire's first (and short-lived) press.

In 1730, however, the gala soirees, at which guests watched turtles with candles on their backs wander in the dark through massive tulip beds, gave way to a conservative Janissary revolt with strong religious overtones. Sultan Ahmed III abdicated, and the leader of the revolt, Patrona Halil°, an Albanian former seaman and stoker of the public baths, swaggered around the capital for several months dictating government policies before he was seized and executed.

The Patrona Halil rebellion confirmed the perceptions of a few that the Ottoman Empire was facing severe difficulties. Yet decay at the center spelled benefit elsewhere. In the provinces, ambitious and competent governors, wealthy landholders, urban notables, and nomad chieftains took advantage of the central government's weakness. By the middle of the eighteenth century groups of Mamluks had regained a dominant position in Egypt, and Janissary commanders had become virtually independent rulers in Baghdad. In central Arabia a conservative Sunni movement inspired by Muhammad ibn Abd al-Wahhab began a remarkable rise beyond the reach of Ottoman power. Although no region declared full independence, the sultan's power was slipping away to the advantage of a broad array of lower officials and upstart chieftains in all parts of the empire while the Ottoman economy was reorienting itself toward Europe.

THE SAFAVID EMPIRE, 1502–1722

The **Safavid Empire** of Iran (see Map 19.1) resembled its longtime Ottoman foe in many ways: it initially used land grants to support its all-important cavalry; its population spoke several languages; it focused on land rather than sea power; and urban notables, nomadic chieftains, and religious scholars served as intermediaries between the people and the government. Certain other qualities, such as a royal tradition rooted in pre-Islamic

Mocha (MOH-kuh)

Patrona Halil (pa-TROH-nuh ha-LEEL)

Safavid Shah with Attendants and Musicians   This painting by Ali-Quli Jubbadar, a European convert to Islam working for the Safavid armory, reflects Western influences. Notice the use of light and shadow to model faces and the costume of the attendant to the shah's right. The shah's waterpipe indicates the spread of tobacco, a New World crop, to the Middle East.   (Courtesy of Oriental Institute, Academy of Sciences, Leningrad. Reproduced from Album of Persian and Indian Miniatures [Moscow, 1962], ill. no. 98)

legends and adoption of Shi'ism, continue to the present day to set Iran off from its neighbors.

The Rise of the Safavids

Timur had been a great conqueror, but his children and grandchildren contented themselves with modest realms in Afghanistan and Central Asia, while a number of would-be rulers vied for control elsewhere. In Iran itself, the ultimate victor in a complicated struggle for power among Turkish chieftains was a boy of Kurdish, Iranian, and Greek ancestry named Ismail°, the hereditary leader of a militant Sufi brotherhood called the "Safaviya" for his ancestor Safi al-Din. In 1502, at age sixteen, Ismail proclaimed himself shah of Iran. At around the same time, he declared that henceforward his realm would practice **Shi'ite Islam** and revere the family of Muhammad's son-in-law Ali. He called on his subjects to abandon their Sunni beliefs.

Most of the members of the Safaviya spoke Turkish and belonged to nomadic groups known as qizilbash°, or "redheads," because of their distinctive turbans. Many considered Ismail god incarnate and fought ferociously on his behalf. If Ismail wished his state to be Shi'ite, his word was law to the qizilbash. The Iranian subject population, however, resisted. Neighboring lands gave asylum to Sunni refugees whose preaching and intriguing helped stoke the fires that kept Ismail (d. 1524) and his son Tahmasp° (d. 1576) engaged in war after war. It took a century and a series of brutal persecutions to make Iran an overwhelmingly Shi'ite land. The transformation also involved the importation of Arab Shi'ite scholars from Lebanon and Bahrain to institute Shi'ite religious education at a high level.

Society and Religion

Although Ismail's reasons for compelling Iran's conversion are unknown, the effect was to create a deep chasm between Iran and its neighbors, all of which were Sunni. Iran's distinctiveness had been long in the making, however. Persian, written in the Arabic script from the tenth century onward, had emerged as the second language of Islam. By 1500 an immense library of legal and theological writings; epic, lyric, and mystic poetry; histories; and drama and fiction had come into being. Iranian scholars and writers normally read Arabic as well as Persian and sprinkled their writings with Arabic phrases, but their Arab counterparts were much less inclined to learn Persian. Even handwriting styles differed, Iranians preferring highly cursive forms of the Arabic script.

This divergence between the two language areas had intensified after 1258 when the Mongols destroyed Baghdad, the capital of the Islamic caliphate, and thereby diminished the importance of Arabic-speaking Iraq. Syria and Egypt, under Mamluk rule, had become the heart-

Ismail (IS-ma-eel)   **qizilbash** (KIH-zil-bahsh)

Tahmasp (tah-MAHSP)

land of the Arab world, while Iran developed largely on its own, building extensive contacts with India, whose Muslim rulers favored the Persian language.

Where cultural styles had radiated in all directions from Baghdad during the heyday of the Islamic caliphate in the seventh through ninth centuries, now Iraq separated an Arab zone from a Persian zone. The post-Mongol period saw an immense burst of artistic creativity and innovation in Iran, Afghanistan, and Central Asia. Painted and molded tiles and tile mosaics, often in vivid turquoise blue, became the standard exterior decoration of mosques in Iran. Architects in Syria and Egypt never used them. The Persian poets Hafez (1319–1389?) and Sa'di (1215–1291) raised morally instructive and mystical-allegorical verse to a peak of perfection. Arabic poetry languished.

The Turks, who steadily came to dominate the political scene from Bengal to Istanbul, generally preferred Persian as a vehicle for literary and religious expression. The Mamluks in Egypt and Syria, however, showed greatest respect for Arabic. The Turkish language, which had a vigorous tradition of folk poetry, developed only slowly, primarily in the Ottoman Empire, as a language of literature and administration. Ironically, Ismail Safavi was a noted religious poet in the Turkish language of his qizilbash followers, while his mortal adversary, the Ottoman Selim I (r. 1512–1520), composed elegant poetry in Persian.

To be sure, Islam itself provided a tradition that crossed ethnic and linguistic borders. Mosque architecture differed, but Iranians, Arabs, and Turks, as well as Muslims in India, all had mosques. They also had madrasas that trained the ulama to sustain and interpret the Shari'a as the all-encompassing law of Islam. Yet local understandings of the common tradition differed substantially.

Each Sufi brotherhood had distinctive rituals and concepts of mystical union with God, but Iran stood out as the land where Sufism most often fused with militant political objectives. The Safaviya was not the first brotherhood to deploy armies and use the point of a sword to promote love of God. The later Safavid shahs, however, banned (somewhat ineffectively) all Sufi orders from their domain.

Even prior to Shah Ismail's imposition of Shi'ism, therefore, Iran had become a distinctive society. Nevertheless, the impact of Shi'ism was significant. Shi'ite doctrine says that all temporal rulers, regardless of title, are temporary stand-ins for the **"Hidden Imam,"** the twelfth descendant of Ali, who was the prophet Muhammad's cousin and son-in-law. Shi'ites believe that leadership of the Muslim community rests solely with divinely appointed Imams from Ali's family, that the twelfth descen-dant (the Hidden Imam) disappeared as a child in the ninth century, and that the Shi'ite community will lack a proper religious authority until he returns. Some Shi'ite scholars concluded that the faithful should calmly accept the world as it was and wait quietly for the Hidden Imam's return. Others maintained that they themselves should play a stronger role in political affairs because they were best qualified to know the Hidden Imam's wishes. These two positions, which still play a role in Iranian Shi'ism, tended to enhance the self-image of the ulama as independent of imperial authority and slowed the trend of religious scholars' becoming subordinate government functionaries, as happened with many Ottoman ulama.

Shi'ism also affected the psychological life of the people. Commemoration of the martyrdom of Imam Husayn (d. 680), Ali's son and the third Imam, during the first two weeks of every lunar year regularized an emotional outpouring with no parallel in Sunni lands. Day after day for two weeks (as they do today) preachers recited the woeful tale to crowds of weeping believers, and chanting and self-flagellating men paraded past crowds of reverent onlookers in elaborate street processions, often organized by craft guilds. Passion plays in which Husayn and his family are mercilessly killed by the Sunni caliph's general became a unique form of Iranian public theater.

Of course, Shi'ites elsewhere observed some of the same rites of mourning for Imam Husayn, particularly in the Shi'ite pilgrimage cities of Karbala and Najaf° in Ottoman Iraq. But Iran, with over 90 percent of its population professing Shi'ism, felt the impact of these rites most strongly. Over time, the subjects of the Safavid shahs came to feel more than ever a people apart, even though many of them had been Shi'ite for only two or three generations.

A Tale of Two Cities: Isfahan and Istanbul

Isfahan° became Iran's capital in 1598 by decree of **Shah Abbas I** (r. 1587–1629). Outwardly, Istanbul and Isfahan looked quite different. Built on seven hills on the south side of the narrow Golden Horn inlet, Istanbul boasted a skyline punctuated by the gray stone domes and thin, pointed minarets of the great imperial mosques. Their design derived from Hagia Sophia, the Byzantine cathedral converted to a mosque and renamed Aya Sofya° after 1453. By contrast, the mosques surrounding the royal plaza in Isfahan featured brightly tiled domes rising to gentle peaks and unobtrusive minarets. High walls surrounded the sultan's palace in

---

Najaf (NAH-jaf)   **Isfahan** (is-fah-HAHN)
Aya Sofya (AH-yah SOAF-yah)

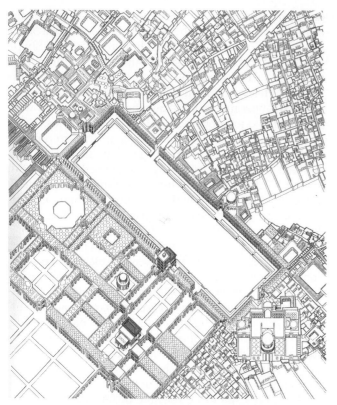

Royal Square in Isfahan   Built by the order Shah Abbas over a period of twenty years starting in 1598, the open space is as long as five football fields (555 by 172 yards). At the upper left end of the square in this drawing is the entrance to the covered bazaar, at the bottom the immense Royal Mosque. The left hand side adjoins the Shah's palace and state administrative office. A multi-story pavilion for reviewing troops and receiving guests overlooks the square across from the smaller domed personal mosque of the Shah.   [Reproduced with permission from Klaus Herdeg, *Formal Structure in Islamic Architecture of Iran and Turkestan* (New York: Rizzoli, 1990)]

Istanbul. Shah Abbas focused Isfahan on the giant royal plaza, which was large enough for his army to play polo, and he used an airy palace overlooking the plaza to receive dignitaries and review his troops. This public image contributed to Shah Abbas' being called "the Great."

The harbor of Istanbul, the primary Ottoman seaport, teemed with sailing ships and smaller craft, many of them belonging to a colony of European merchants perched on a hilltop on the north side of the Golden Horn. Isfahan, far from the sea, only occasionally received European visitors. Along with Jews and Hindus, a colony of Armenian Christians brought in by Shah Abbas who settled in a suburb of the city handled most of its trade.

Beneath these superficial differences, the two capitals had much in common. Wheeled vehicles were scarce in hilly Istanbul and nonexistent in Isfahan, which was within the broad zone where camels supplanted wheeled transport after the rise of the Arab caravan cities in the pre-Islamic centuries. In size and layout both cities favored walking and, aside from the royal plaza in Isfahan, lacked the open spaces common in contemporary European cities. Away from the major mosque complexes, streets were narrow and irregular. Houses crowded against each other in dead-end lanes. Residents enjoyed the privacy of interior courtyards. Artisans and merchants organized themselves into guilds that had strong social and religious as well as economic bonds. The shops of the guilds adjoined each other in the markets.

Women seldom appeared in public, even in Istanbul's mazelike covered market or in Isfahan's long, serpentine bazaar. At home, the women's quarters—called anderun°, or "interior," in Iran and harem, or "forbidden area," in Istanbul—were separate from the public rooms where the men of the family received visitors. Low cushions, charcoal braziers for warmth, carpets, and small tables constituted most of the furnishings. In Iran and the Arab provinces, shelves and niches for books could be cut into thick, mud-brick walls. Residences in Istanbul were usually built of wood. Glazed tile in geometric or floral patterns covered the walls of wealthy men's reception areas.

The private side of family life has left few traces, but it is apparent that women's society—consisting of wives, children, female servants, and sometimes one or more eunuchs (castrated male servants)—had some connections with the outside world. Ottoman court records reveal that women using male agents bought and sold urban real estate, often dealing with inherited shares of their fathers' estates. Some even established religious endowments for pious purposes. The fact that Islamic law, unlike most European codes, permitted a wife to retain her property after marriage gave some women a stake in the general economy and a degree of independence from their spouses. Women also appeared in other types of court cases, where they often testified for themselves, for Islamic courts did not recognize the role of attorney. Although comparable Safavid court records do not survive, historians assume that a parallel situation prevailed in Iran.

European travelers commented on the veiling of women outside the home, but miniature paintings indicate that ordinary female garb consisted of a long, ample dress with a scarf or long shawl pulled tight over the forehead to conceal the hair. Lightweight trousers, either close-fitting or baggy, were worn under the dress. This mode of dress differed little from that of men. Poor men wore light trousers, a long shirt, a jacket, and a brimless

°**anderun** (an-deh-ROON)

Istanbul Family on the Way to a Bath House   Public baths, an important feature of Islamic cities, set different hours for men and women. Young boys, such as the lad in the turban shown here, went with their mothers and sisters. Notice that the children wear the same styles as the adults.   (Osterreichische Nationalbibliothek)

cap or turban. Wealthier men wore ankle-length caftans, often closely fitted around the chest, over their trousers. The norm for both sexes was complete coverage of arms, legs, and hair.

Men monopolized public life. Poetry and art, both somewhat more elegantly developed in Isfahan than in Istanbul, centered as much on the charms of beardless boys as of pretty maidens. Despite religious disapproval of homosexuality, attachments to adolescent boys were neither unusual nor hidden. Women on city streets included non-Muslims, the aged, the very poor, and slaves. Miniature paintings frequently depict female dancers, musicians, and even acrobats in attitudes and costumes that range from decorous to decidedly erotic.

Despite social similarities, the overall flavors of Isfahan and Istanbul were not the same. Isfahan had a prosperous Armenian quarter across the river from the city's center, but it was not a truly cosmopolitan capital. Like other rulers of extensive land empires, Shah Abbas located his capital toward the center of his domain, within comparatively easy reach of any threatened frontier. Istanbul, in contrast, was a great seaport and crossroads located on the straits separating the sultan's European and Asian possessions. People of all sorts lived or spent time in Istanbul—Venetians, Genoese, Arabs, Turks, Greeks, Armenians, Albanians, Serbs, Jews, Bulgarians, and more. In this respect, Istanbul conveyed the cosmopolitan character of major seaports from London to Can-

ton (Guangzhou) and belied the fact that its prosperity rested on the vast reach of the sultan's territories rather than on the voyages of its merchants.

Economic Crisis and Political Collapse

The silk fabrics of northern Iran, monopolized by the shahs, provided the mainstay of the Safavid Empire's foreign trade. However, the manufacture that eventually became most powerfully associated with Iran was the deep-pile carpet made by knotting colored yarns around stretched warp threads. Different cities produced distinctive carpet designs. Women and girls did much of the actual knotting work.

Carpets with geometrical or arabesque designs appear in Timurid miniature paintings, but no knotted "Persian rug" survives from the pre-Safavid era. One of the earliest dated carpets was produced in 1522 to adorn the tomb of Shaikh Safi al-Din, the fourteenth-century founder of the Safaviya. This use indicates the high value accorded these products within Iran. One German visitor to Isfahan remarked: "The most striking adornment of the banqueting hall was to my mind the carpets laid out over all three rostra [platforms to sit on for eating] in a most extravagant fashion, mostly woolen rugs from Kirman with animal patterns and woven of the finest wool."[3]

Overall, Iran's manufacturing sector was neither large nor notably productive. Most of the shah's subjects, whether Iranians, Turks, Kurds, or Arabs, lived by subsistence farming or herding. Neither area of activity recorded significant technological advances during the Safavid period. The shahs granted large sections of the country to the qizilbash nomads in return for mounted warriors for the army. Nomad groups held these lands in common, however, and did not subdivide them into individual landholdings as in the Ottoman Empire. Thus, many people in rural areas lived according to the will of a nomad chieftain who had little interest in building the agricultural economy.

The Safavids, like the Ottomans, had difficulty finding the money to pay troops armed with firearms. This crisis occurred somewhat later in Iran because of its greater distance from Europe. By the end of the sixteenth century, it was evident that a more systematic adoption of cannon and firearms in the Safavid Empire would be needed to hold off the Ottomans and the Uzbeks° (Turkish rulers who had succeeded the Timurids on Iran's Central Asian frontier; see Map 19.1). Like the Ottoman cavalry a century earlier, however, the nomad warriors refused to trade in their bows for firearms. Shah Abbas

Uzbeks (UHZ-bex)

responded by establishing a slave corps of year-round soldiers and arming them with guns.

The Christian converts to Islam who initially provided the manpower for the new corps came mostly from captives taken in raids on Georgia in the Caucasus°. Some became powerful members of the court. They formed a counterweight to the nomad chiefs just as the Janissaries had earlier challenged the landholding Turkish cavalry in the Ottoman Empire. The strong hand of Shah Abbas kept the inevitable rivalries and intrigues between the factions under control. His successors showed less skill.

In the late sixteenth century the inflation caused by cheap silver spread into Iran; then overland trade through Safavid territory declined because of mismanagement of the silk monopoly after Shah Abbas's death in 1629. As a result, the country faced the unsolvable problem of finding money to pay the army and bureaucracy. Trying to remove the nomads from their lands to regain control of taxes proved more difficult and more disruptive militarily than the piecemeal dismantling of the land-grant system in the Ottoman Empire. Demands from the central government caused the nomads, who were still a potent military force, to withdraw to their mountain pastures until the pressure subsided. By 1722 the government had become so weak and commanded so little support from the nomadic groups that an army of marauding Afghans was able to capture Isfahan and effectively end Safavid rule.

Despite Iran's long coastline, the Safavids never possessed a navy. The Portuguese seized the strategic Persian Gulf island of Hormuz in 1517 and were expelled only in 1622, when the English ferried Iranian soldiers to the attack. Entirely land-oriented, the shahs relied on the English and Dutch for naval support and never considered confronting them at sea. Nadir Shah, a general who emerged from the confusion of the Safavid fall to reunify Iran briefly between 1736 and 1747, purchased some naval vessels from the English and used them in the Persian Gulf. But his navy decayed after his death, and Iran did not have a navy again until the twentieth century.

THE MUGHAL EMPIRE, 1526–1761

As a land of Hindus ruled by a Muslim minority, the realm of the Mughal° sultans of India differed substantially from the empires of the Ottomans and Safavids. To be sure, the Ottoman provinces in the Balkans, except for Albania and Bosnia, remained mostly Christian; but the remainder of the Ottoman Empire was overwhelmingly Muslim with small Christian and Jewish minorities. The Ottoman sultans made much of their control of Mecca and Medina and resulting supervision of the annual pilgrimage caravans just as the Safavids fostered pilgrimages to a shrine in Mashhad in northeastern Iran for their overwhelmingly Shi'ite subjects.

India, in contrast, lay far from the Islamic homelands (see Map 19.1). Muslim dominion in northern India began with repeated military campaigns in the early eleventh century, and the Mughals had to contend with the Hindus' long-standing resentment of the destruction of their culture. Unlike the Balkan peoples who had struggled to maintain their separate identities in relation to the Byzantines, the crusaders, and one another before arrival of the Turks, the peoples of the Indian subcontinent had used centuries of freedom from foreign intrusion to forge a distinctive Hindu civilization that could not easily accommodate the worldview of Islam. Thus, the Mughals faced the challenge not just of conquering and organizing a large territorial state but also of finding a formula for Hindu-Muslim coexistence.

Political Foundations

Babur° (1483–1530), the founder of the **Mughal Empire,** descended from Timur. Though Mughal means "Mongol" in Persian, the Timurids were of Turkic rather than Mongol origin. Timur's marriage to a descendant of Genghis Khan had earned him the Mongol designation "son-in-law," but like the Ottomans, his family did not enjoy the political legitimacy that came with Genghisid descent experienced by lesser rulers in Central Asia and in the Crimea north of the Black Sea.

Invading from Central Asia, Babur defeated the last Muslim sultan of Delhi at the Battle of Panipat in 1526. Even though this victory marked the birth of a brilliant and powerful state in India, Babur's descendants continued to think of Central Asia as their true home, from time to time expressing intentions of recapturing Samarkand and referring to its Uzbek ruler—a genuine descendant of Genghis Khan—as a governor rather than an independent sovereign.

India proved to be the primary theater of Mughal accomplishment, however. Babur's grandson **Akbar** (r. 1556–1605), a brilliant but mercurial man whose illiteracy

---

Caucasus (CAW-kuh-suhs)   Mughal (MOH-guhl)

Babur (BAH-bur)

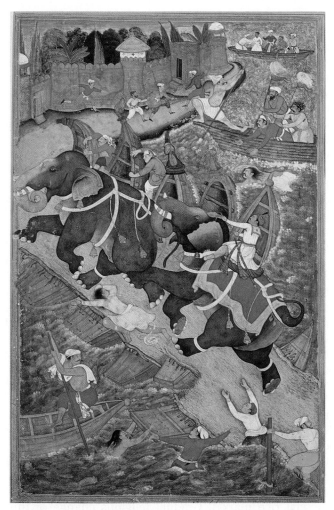

Elephants Breaking Bridge of Boats   This illustration of an incident in the life of Akbar illustrates the ability of Mughal miniature painters to depict unconventional action scenes. Because the flow of rivers in India and the Middle East varied greatly from dry season to wet season, boat bridges were much more common than permanent constructions.   (Victoria and Albert Museum, London/Bridgeman Art Library)

holders to revenue assignments. As in the other Islamic empires, the central government kept careful track of these nonhereditary grants.

With a population of 100 million, a thriving trading economy based on cotton cloth, and a generally efficient administration, India under Akbar enjoyed great prosperity in the sixteenth century. Akbar and his successors faced few external threats and experienced generally peaceful conditions in their northern Indian heartland. Nevertheless, they were capable of squandering immense amounts of blood and treasure fighting Hindu kings and rebels in the Deccan region or Afghans on their western frontier (see Map 19.1).

Foreign trade boomed at the port of Surat in the northwest, which also served as an embarkation point for pilgrims headed for Mecca. Like the Safavids, the Mughals had no navy or merchant ships. The government saw the Europeans—now primarily Dutch and English, the Portuguese having lost most of their Indian ports—less as enemies than as shipmasters whose naval support could be procured as needed in return for trading privileges. It never questioned the wisdom of selling Indian cottons for European coin—no one understood how cheap silver had become in Europe—and shipping them off to European customers in English and Dutch vessels.

Hindus and Muslims

India had not been dominated by a single ruler since the time of Harsha Vardhana (r. 606–647). Muslim destruction of Hindu cultural monuments, the expansion of Muslim territory, and the practice, until Akbar's time, of enslaving prisoners of war and compelling them to convert to Islam horrified the Hindus. But the politically divided Hindus did not put up a combined resistance. The Mughal state, in contrast, inherited traditions of unified imperial rule from both the Islamic caliphate and the more recent examples of Genghis Khan and Timur.

Those Mongol-based traditions did not necessarily mean religious intolerance. Seventy percent of the mansabdars° (officials holding land grants) appointed under Akbar were Muslim soldiers born outside India, but 15 percent were Hindus, mostly warriors from the north called **Rajputs°**. One of them rose to be a powerful revenue minister. Their status as mansabdars confirmed the policy of religious accommodation adopted by Akbar and his successors.

Akbar, the most illustrious Mughal ruler, differed

betrayed his upbringing in the wilds of Afghanistan, established the central administration of the expanding state. Under him and his three successors—the last of whom died in 1707—all but the southern tip of India fell under Mughal rule, administered first from Agra and then from Delhi°.

Akbar granted land revenues to military officers and government officials in return for their service. Ranks called **mansabs°,** some high and some low, entitled their

---

Delhi (DEL-ee)   **mansabs** (MAN-sabz)

mansabdars (man-sab-DAHRZ)   **Rajputs** (RAHJ-putz)

from his Ottoman and Safavid counterparts—Suleiman the Magnificent and Shah Abbas the Great—in his striving for social harmony and not just for more territory and revenue. He succeeded to the throne at age thirteen, and his actions were dominated at first by a regent and then by his strong-minded childhood nurse. On reaching twenty, Akbar took command of the government. He married a Hindu Rajput princess, whose name is not recorded, and welcomed her father and brother to the court in Agra.

Other rulers might have used such a marriage as a means of humiliating a subject group, but Akbar signaled his desire for Muslim-Hindu reconciliation. A year later he rescinded the head tax that Muslim rulers traditionally levied on tolerated non-Muslims. This measure was more symbolic than real because the tax had not been regularly collected, but the gesture helped cement the allegiance of the Rajputs.

Akbar longed for an heir. Much to his relief, his Rajput wife gave birth to a son in 1569, ensuring that future rulers would have both Muslim and Hindu ancestry.

Akbar ruled that in legal disputes between two Hindus, decisions would be made according to village custom or Hindu law as interpreted by local Hindu scholars. Muslims followed Shari'a law. Akbar made himself the legal court of last resort in a 1579 declaration that he was God's infallible earthly representative. Thus, appeals could be made to Akbar personally, a possibility not usually present in Islamic jurisprudence.

He also made himself the center of a new "Divine Faith" incorporating Muslim, Hindu, Zoroastrian, Sikh°, and Christian beliefs. Sufi ideas attracted him and permeated the religious rituals he instituted at his court. To promote serious consideration of his religious principles, he monitored, from a high catwalk, debates among scholars of all religions assembled in his private octagonal audience chamber. When courtiers uttered the Muslim exclamation "Allahu Akbar"—"God is great"—its second grammatical meaning, "God is Akbar," was not lost on them. Akbar's religious views did not survive him, but the court culture he fostered, reflecting a mixture of Muslim and Hindu traditions, flourished until his zealous great-grandson Aurangzeb° (r. 1658–1707) reinstituted many restrictions on Hindus.

Mughal and Rajput miniature portraits of political figures and depictions of scantily clad women brought frowns to the faces of pious Muslims, who deplored the representation of human beings in art. Most of the leading painters were Hindus. In literature, in addition to the florid style of Persian verse favored at court, a new taste developed for poetry and prose in the popular language of the Delhi region. The modern descendant of this language is called Urdu in Pakistan, from the Turkish word *ordu*, meaning "army" (in India it is called Hindi).

Akbar's policy of toleration does not explain the pattern of conversion in Mughal India, most of which was to Sunni Islam. Some scholars maintain that most converts came from the lowest Hindu social groups, or castes, who hoped to improve their lot in life, but little data confirm this theory. Others argue that Sufi brotherhoods, which developed strongly in India, led the way in converting people to Islam, but this proposition has not been proved. The most heavily Muslim regions developed in the valley of the Indus River and in Bengal. The Indus center dates from the isolated establishment of Muslim rule there as early as the eighth century.

A careful study of local records and traditions from east Bengal indicates that the eastward movement of the delta of the Ganges River, caused by silting, and the spread of rice cultivation into forest clearings played the primary role in conversions to Islam there. Mansabdars (mostly Muslims) with land grants in east Bengal contracted with local entrepreneurs to collect a labor force, cut down the forest, and establish rice paddies. Though some entrepreneurs were Hindu, most were non-Sufi Muslim religious figures. The latter centered their farming communities on mosques and shrines, using religion as a social cement. Most natives of the region were accustomed to worshiping local forest deities rather than the main Hindu gods. So the shift to Islam represented a move to a more sophisticated, literate culture appropriate to their new status as farmers producing for the commercial rice market. Gradual religious change of this kind often produced Muslim communities whose social customs differed little from those in neighboring non-Muslim communities. In east Bengal, common Muslim institutions, such as madrasas, the ulama, and law courts, were little in evidence.

The emergence of **Sikhism** in the Punjab region of northwest India constituted another change in Indian religious life in the Mughal period. Nanak (1469–1539), the religion's first guru (spiritual teacher), stressed meditation as a means of seeking enlightenment and drew upon both Muslim and Hindu imagery in his teachings. His followers formed a single community without differences of caste. However, after Aurangzeb ordered the ninth guru beheaded in 1675 for refusing to convert to Islam, the tenth guru dedicated himself to avenging his father's death and reorganized his followers into "the army of the pure," a religious order dedicated to defending Sikh beliefs. These devotees signaled their faith by leaving their hair uncut beneath a turban; carrying a comb, a steel bracelet, and a sword or dagger; and wear-

---

Sikh (sick)   **Aurangzeb** (ow-rang-ZEB)

ing military-style breeches. By the eighteenth century, the Mughals were encountering fierce opposition from the Sikhs as well as from Hindu guerrilla forces in the rugged and ravine-scarred province of Maharashtra on India's west coast.

Central Decay and Regional Challenges, 1707–1761

Mughal power did not long survive Aurangzeb's death in 1707. Some historians consider the land-grant system a central element in the rapid decline of imperial authority, but other factors played a role as well. Aurangzeb failed to effectively integrate new Mughal territories in southern India into the imperial structure, and a number of strong regional powers challenged Mughal military supremacy. The Marathas proved a formidable enemy as they carved out a swath of territory across India's middle, and Sikhs, Hindu Rajputs, and Muslim Afghans exerted intense pressure from the northwest. A climax came in 1739 when Nadir Shah, the general who had seized power in Iran after the fall of the Safavids, invaded the subcontinent and sacked Delhi, which Akbar's grandson had rebuilt and beautified as the Mughal capital some decades before. He carried off to Iran, as part of the booty, the priceless, jewel-encrusted "peacock throne," symbol of Mughal grandeur. The later Mughals found another throne to sit on; but their empire, which survived in name to 1857, was finished.

In 1723 Nizam al-Mulk°, the powerful vizier of the Mughal sultan, gave up on the central government and established his own nearly independent state at Hyderabad in the eastern Deccan. Other officials bearing the title nawab° (from Arabic *na'ib* meaning "deputy" and Anglicized as "nabob") became similarly independent in Bengal and Oudh° in the northeast, as did the Marathas farther west. In the northwest, simultaneous Iranian and Mughal weakness allowed the Afghans to establish an independent kingdom.

Some of these regional powers and smaller princely states flourished with the removal of the sultan's heavy hand. Linguistic and religious communities, freed from the religious intolerance instituted during the reign of Aurangzeb, similarly enjoyed greater opportunity for political expression. However, this disintegration of central power favored the intrusion of European adventurers.

Joseph François Dupleix° took over the presidency of the east coast French stronghold of Pondicherry° in

1741 and began a new phase of European involvement in India. He captured the English trading center of Madras and used his small contingent of European and European-trained Indian troops to become a power broker in southern India. Though offered the title nawab, Dupleix preferred to operate behind the scenes, using Indian princes as puppets. His career ended in 1754 when he was called home. Deeply involved in European wars, the French government declined to pursue further adventures in India. Dupleix's departure cleared the way for the British, whose ventures in India are described in Chapter 24.

TRADE EMPIRES IN THE INDIAN OCEAN, 1600–1729

It is no coincidence that the Mughal, Safavid, and Ottoman Empires declined simultaneously in the seventeenth and eighteenth centuries. Complex changes in military technology and in the world economy, along with the increasing difficulty of basing an extensive land empire on military forces paid through land grants, affected them all adversely. The opposite held for seafaring countries intent on turning trade networks into maritime empires. Improvements in ship design, navigation accuracy, and the use of cannon gave an ever-increasing edge to European powers competing with local seafaring peoples. Moreover, the development of joint-stock companies, in which many merchants pooled their capital, provided a flexible and efficient financial instrument for exploiting new possibilities. The English East India Company was founded in 1600, the Dutch East India Company in 1602.

Although the Ottomans, Safavids, and Mughals did not effectively contest the growth of Portuguese and then Dutch, English, and French maritime power, the majority of non-European shipbuilders, captains, sailors, and traders were Muslim. Groups of Armenian, Jewish, and Hindu traders were also active, but they remained almost as aloof from the Europeans as the Muslims did. The presence in every port of Muslims following the same legal traditions and practicing their faith in similar ways cemented the Muslims' trading network. Islam, from its very outset in the life and preaching of Muhammad (570–632), had favored trade and traders. Unlike Hinduism, it was a proselytizing religion, a factor that encouraged the growth of coastal Muslim communities as local non-Muslims associated with Muslim commercial activities converted and intermarried with Muslims from abroad.

Nizam al-Mulk (nee-ZAHM al-MULK)   nawab (NAH-wab)
Oudh (OW-ad)   Dupleix (doo-PLAY)
Pondicherry (pon-dir-CHEH-ree)

Although European missionaries, particularly the Jesuits, tried to extend Christianity into Asia and Africa (see Chapters 15 and 20), most Europeans, the Portuguese excepted, did not treat local converts or the offspring of mixed marriages as full members of their communities. Islam was generally more welcoming. As a consequence, Islam spread extensively into East Africa and Southeast Asia during precisely the time of rapid European commercial expansion. Even without the support of the Muslim land empires, Islam became a source of resistance to growing European domination.

Muslims in the East Indies

Historians disagree about the chronology and manner of Islam's spread in Southeast Asia. Arab traders appeared in southern China as early as the eighth century, so Muslims probably reached the East Indies at a similarly early date. Nevertheless, the dominance of Indian cultural influences in the area for several centuries thereafter indicates that early Muslim visitors had little impact on local beliefs. Clearer indications of conversion and the formation of Muslim communities date from roughly the fourteenth century, with the strongest overseas linkage being to the port of Cambay in India (see Map 19.2) rather than to the Arab world. Islam first took root in port cities and in some royal courts and spread inland only slowly, possibly transmitted by itinerant Sufis.

Although appeals to the Ottoman sultan for support against the Europeans ultimately proved futile, Islam strengthened resistance to Portuguese, Spanish, and Dutch intruders. When the Spaniards conquered the Philippines during the decades following the establishment of their first fort in 1565, they encountered Muslims on the southern island of Mindanao° and the nearby Sulu archipelago. They called them "Moros," the Spanish term for their old enemies, the Muslims of North Africa. In the ensuing Moro wars, the Spaniards portrayed the Moros as greedy pirates who raided non-Muslim territories for slaves. In fact, they were political, religious, and commercial competitors whose perseverance enabled them to establish the Sulu Empire based in the southern Philippines, one of the strongest states in Southeast Asia from 1768 to 1848.

Other local kingdoms that looked on Islam as a force to counter the aggressive Christianity of the Europeans included the actively proselytizing Brunei° Sultanate in northern Borneo and the **Acheh° Sultanate** in northern Sumatra. At its peak in the early seventeenth century,

Acheh succeeded Malacca as the main center of Islamic expansion in Southeast Asia. It prospered by trading pepper for cotton cloth from Gujarat in India. Acheh declined after the Dutch seized Malacca from Portugal in 1641.

How well Islam was understood in these Muslim kingdoms is open to question. In Acheh, for example, a series of women ruled between 1641 and 1699. This practice ended when local Muslim scholars obtained a ruling from scholars in Mecca and Medina that Islam did not approve of female rulers. After this ruling scholarly understandings of Islam gained greater prominence in the East Indies.

Historians have looked at merchants, Sufi preachers, or both as the first propagators of Islam in Southeast Asia. The scholarly vision of Islam, however, took root in the sixteenth century by way of pilgrims returning from years of study in Mecca and Medina. Islam promoted the dissemination of writing in the region. Some of the returning pilgrims wrote in Arabic, others in Malay or Javanese. As Islam continued to spread, adat ("custom"), a form of Islam rooted in pre-Muslim religious and social practices, retained its preeminence in rural areas over practices centered on the Shari'a, the religious law. But the royal courts in the port cities began to heed the views of the pilgrim teachers. Though different in many ways, both varieties of Islam provided believers with a firm basis of identification in the face of the growing European presence. Christian missionaries gained most of their converts in regions that had not yet converted to Islam, such as the northern Philippines.

Muslims in East Africa

Muslim rulers also governed the East African ports that the Portuguese began to visit in the fifteenth century, though they were not allied politically (see Map 19.2). People living in the millet and rice lands of the Swahili Coast—from the Arabic sawahil° meaning "coasts"—had little contact with those in the dry hinterlands. Throughout this period, the East African lakes region and the highlands of Kenya witnessed unprecedented migration and relocation of peoples because of drought conditions that persisted from the late sixteenth through most of the seventeenth century.

Cooperation among the trading ports of Kilwa, Mombasa, and Malindi was hindered by the thick bush country that separated the cultivated tracts of coastal land and by the fact that the ports competed with one another in the export of ivory; ambergris° (a whale

---

Mindanao (min-duh-NOW)   **Brunei** (BROO-nie)
Acheh (AH-cheh)

sawahil (suh-WAH-hil)   **ambergris** (AM-ber-grees)

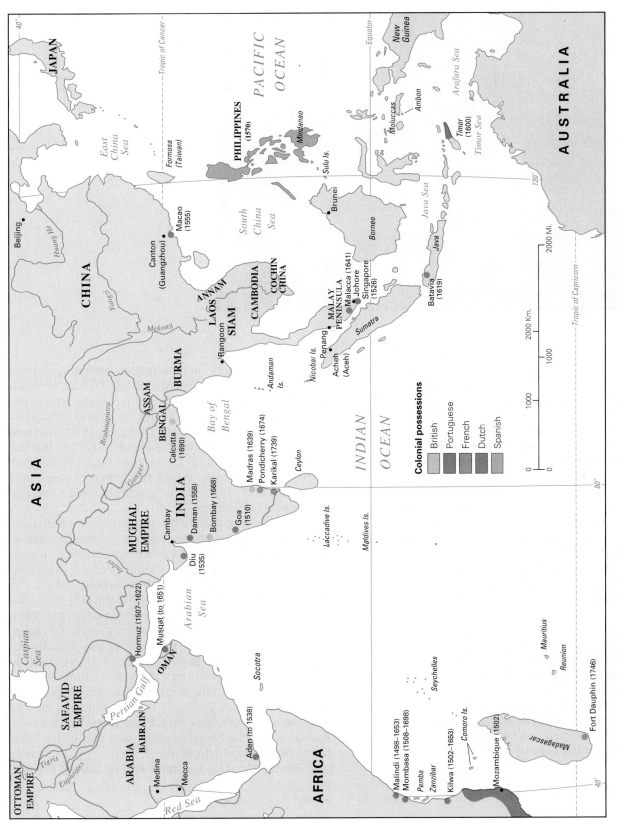

Map 19.2 European Colonization in the Indian Ocean to 1750 Since Portuguese explorers were the first Europeans to reach India by rounding Africa, Portugal gained a strong foothold in both areas. Rival Spain was barred from colonizing the region by the Treaty of Tordesillas in 1494, which limited Spanish efforts to lands west of a line drawn through the mid-Atlantic Ocean. The line carried around the globe provided justification of Spanish colonization in the Philippines. French, British, and Dutch colonies date from after 1600, when joint-stock companies provided a new stimulus for overseas commerce.

Colonial possessions

British
Portuguese
French
Dutch
Spanish

Portuguese Fort Guarding Musqat Harbor Musqat in Oman and Aden in Yemen, the best harbors in southern Arabia, were targets for imperial navies trying to establish dominance in the Indian Ocean. Musqat's harbor is small and circular, with one narrow entrance overlooked by this fortress. The palace of the sultan of Oman is still located at the opposite end of the harbor. (Robert Harding Picture Library)

byproduct used in perfumes); and forest products such as beeswax, copal tree resin, and wood. Kilwa also exported gold. In the eighteenth century slave trading, primarily to Arabian ports but also to India, increased in importance. Because Europeans—the only peoples who kept consistent records of slave-trading activities—played a minor role in this slave trade, few records have survived to indicate its extent. Perhaps the best estimate is that 2.1 million slaves were exported between 1500 and 1890, a little over 12.5 percent of the total traffic in African slaves during that period (see Chapter 18).

The Portuguese conquered all the coastal ports from Mozambique northward except Malindi, with whose ruler Portugal cooperated. A Portuguese description of the ruler names some of the cloth and metal goods that Malindi imported, as well as some local manufactures:

> The King wore a robe of damask trimmed with green satin and a rich [cap]. He was seated on two cushioned chairs of bronze, beneath a rough sunshade of crimson satin attached to a pole. An old man, who attended him as a page, carried a short sword in a silver sheath. There were many players on [horns], and two trumpets of ivory richly carved and of the size of a man, which were blown through a hole in the side, and made sweet harmony with the [horns].[4]

Initially, the Portuguese favored the port of Malindi, which caused the decline of Kilwa and Mombasa. Re-

peatedly plagued by local rebellion, Portuguese power suffered severe blows when the Arabs of **Oman** in southeastern Arabia captured their south Arabian stronghold at Musqat (1650) and then went on to seize Mombasa (1698), which had become the Portuguese capital in East Africa. The Portuguese briefly retook Mombasa but lost control permanently in 1729. From then on, the Portuguese had to content themselves with Mozambique in East Africa and a few remaining ports in India (Goa) and farther east (Macao and Timor).

The Omanis created a maritime empire of their own, one that worked in greater cooperation with the African populations. The Bantu language of the coast, broadened by the absorption of Arabic, Persian, and Portuguese loanwords, developed into **Swahili°,** which was spoken throughout the region. Arabs and other Muslims who settled in the region intermarried with local families, giving rise to a mixed population that played an important role in developing a distinctive Swahili culture.

Islam also spread in the southern Sudan in this period, particularly in the dry areas away from the Nile River. This growth coincided with a waning of Ethiopian power as a result of Portugal's stifling of trade in the Red Sea. Yet no significant contact developed between the emerging Muslim Swahili culture and that of the Muslims in the Sudan to the north.

The Dutch played a major role in driving the Por-

Swahili (swah-HEE-lee)

tuguese from their possessions in the East Indies. They were better organized than the Portuguese through the Dutch East India Company. Just as the Portuguese had tried to dominate the trade in spices, so the Dutch concentrated at first on the spice-producing islands of Southeast Asia. The Portuguese had seized Malacca, a strategic town on the narrow strait at the end of the Malay Peninsula, from a local Malay ruler in 1511 (see Chapter 15). The Dutch took it away from them in 1641, leaving Portugal little foothold in the East Indies except the islands of Ambon° and Timor (see Map 19.2).

Although the United Netherlands was one of the least autocratic countries of Europe, the governors-general appointed by the Dutch East India Company deployed almost unlimited powers in their efforts to maintain their trade monopoly. They could even order the execution of their own employees for "smuggling"—that is, trading on their own. Under strong governors-general, the Dutch fought a series of wars against Acheh and other local kingdoms on Sumatra and Java. In 1628 and 1629 their new capital at **Batavia,** now the city of Jakarta on Java, was besieged by a fleet of fifty ships belonging to the sultan of Mataram°, a Javanese kingdom. The Dutch held out with difficulty and eventually prevailed when the sultan was unable to get effective help from the English.

Suppressing local rulers, however, was not enough to control the spice trade once other European countries adopted Dutch methods, learned more about where goods might be acquired, and started to send more ships to Southeast Asia. In the course of the eighteenth century, therefore, the Dutch gradually turned from being middlemen between Southeast Asian producers and European buyers to producing crops in areas they controlled, notably in Java. Javanese teak forests yielded high-quality lumber, and coffee, transplanted from Yemen, grew well in the western hilly regions. In this new phase of colonial export production, Batavia developed from being the headquarters town of a far-flung enterprise to being the administrative capital of a conquered land.

Beyond the East Indies, the Dutch utilized their discovery of a band of powerful eastward-blowing winds (called the "Roaring Forties" because they blow throughout the year between 40 and 50 degrees south latitude) to reach Australia in 1606. In 1642 and 1643 Abel Tasman became the first European to set foot on Tasmania and New Zealand and to sail around Australia, signaling European involvement in that region (see Chapter 24).

CONCLUSION

Asians and Africans ruled by the Ottoman and Mughal sultans and the Safavid shahs did not perceive that a major shift in world economic and political alignments was under way by the late seventeenth century. The rulers focused their efforts on conquering more and more land, sometimes at the expense of Christian Europe and Hindu India, but also at one another's expense, since the Sunni-Shi'ite division justified Iranian attacks on its neighbors and vice versa.

To be sure, more and more trade was being carried in European vessels, particularly after the advent of joint-stock companies in 1600; and Europeans had enclaves in a handful of port cities and islands. But the age-old tradition of Asia was that imperial wealth came from control of broad expanses of agricultural land. Except for state monopolies, such as Iranian silk, governments did not greatly concern themselves with what farmers did. They relied mostly on land taxes, usually indirectly collected via holders of land grants or tax farmers, rather than on customs duties or control of markets to fill the government coffers.

With ever-increasing military expenditures, these taxes fell short of the rulers' needs. Few people realized, however, that this problem was basic to the entire economic system rather than a temporary revenue shortfall. Imperial courtiers pursued their luxurious ways; poetry and the arts continued to flourish; and the quality of manufacturing and craft production remained generally high. Eighteenth-century European observers, luxuriating in the prosperity gained from their ever-increasing control of the Indian Ocean, marveled no less at the riches and industry of these eastern lands than at the fundamental weakness of their political and military systems.

■ Key Terms

Ottoman Empire	Mughal Empire
Suleiman the Magnificent	Akbar
Janissary	mansabs
devshirme	Rajputs
Tulip Period	Sikhism
Safavid Empire	Acheh Sultanate
Shi'ite Islam	Oman
Hidden Imam	Swahili
Shah Abbas I	Batavia

Ambon (am-BOHN)   **Mataram** (MAH-tah-ram)

■ Suggested Reading

The best comprehensive and comparative account of the post-Mongol Islamic land empires, with an emphasis on social history, is Ira Lapidus, *A History of Islamic Societies* (1988). For a work of similar scope concentrating on intellectual history see Marshall G. S. Hodgson, *The Venture of Islam*, vol. 3, *The Gunpowder Empires and Modern Times* (1974).

On the Ottoman Empire in its prime see Colin Imber, *The Ottoman Empire, 1300–1650: The Structure of Power* (2002). Daniel Goffman, *The Ottoman Empire and Early Modern Europe* (2002), compares the Ottomans with contemporary European kingdoms. Jason Goodwin, *Lords of the Horizons: A History of the Ottoman Empire* (1999), offers a brief journalistic account. Ottoman origins are well covered in Cemal Kafadar, *Between Two Worlds* (1995). For a collection of articles on nonpolitical matters see Halil Inalcik and Donald Quataert, eds., *An Economic and Social History of the Ottoman Empire, 1300–1914* (1994). For a sociological analysis of change in the seventeenth century see Karen Barkey, *Bandits and Bureaucrats* (1994).

Some specialized studies of cities and regions give a sense of the major changes in Ottoman society and economy after the sixteenth century: Daniel Goffman, *Izmir and the Levantine World, 1550–1650* (1990); Abraham Marcus, *The Middle East on the Eve of Modernity: Aleppo in the Eighteenth Century* (1989); Bruce McGowan, *Economic Life in the Ottoman Empire: Taxation, Trade, and the Struggle for Land, 1600–1800* (1981); and Dina Rizk Khoury, *State and Provincial Society in the Ottoman Empire: Mosul, 1540–1834* (1997).

Articles in Benjamin Braude and Bernard Lewis, eds., *Christians and Jews in the Ottoman Empire: The Functioning of a Plural Society* (1982), deal with questions relating to religious minorities. Leslie Pierce skillfully treats the role of women in the governance of the empire in *The Imperial Harem: Women and Sovereignty in the Ottoman Empire* (1993). Ralph S. Hattox, *Coffee and Coffeehouses: The Origins of a Social Beverage in the Medieval Near East* (1988), is an excellent contribution to Ottoman social history.

The most comprehensive treatment of the history of Safavid Iran is in the articles in Peter Jackson and Laurence Lockhart, eds., *The Cambridge History of Iran*, vol. 6, *The Timurid and Safavid Periods* (1986). The articles by Hans Roemer in this volume provide solid political narratives of the pre-Safavid and Safavid periods. Roger Savory's important article on the structure of the Safavid state is available in a more extensive form in his *Iran Under the Safavids* (1980).

For the artistic side of Safavid history, abundantly illustrated, see Anthony Welch, *Shah Abbas and the Arts of Isfahan* (1973). Said Amir Arjomand, *The Shadow of God and the Hidden Imam: Religion, Political Order, and Societal Change in Shiite Iran from the Beginning to 1890* (1984), contains the best analysis of the complicated relationship between Shi'ism and monarchy. For Safavid economic history see Willem Floor, *A Fiscal History of Iran in the Safavid and Qajar Periods, 1500–1925* (1998); and Rudoph Matthee, *The Politics of Trade in Safavid Iran: Silk for Silver, 1600–1730* (1999).

A highly readable work that situates the Mughal Empire within the overall history of the subcontinent is Stanley Wolpert, *A New History of India*, 6th ed. (1999). For a broad treatment of the entire development of Islamic society in India with emphasis on the Mughal period, see S. M. Ikram, *History of Muslim Civilization in India and Pakistan* (1989). Wheeler Thackston has made a lively translation of Babur's autobiography in *The Baburnama: Memoirs of Babur, Prince and Emperor* (1996). For a comprehensive history of the Mughals see John F. Richards, *The Mughal Empire* (1993). See also Richard Foltz, *Mughal India and Central Asia* (1999). Irfan Habib has edited an extensive collection of articles on the Mughal Empire in its prime entitled *Akbar and His India* (1997). For the history of the Sikhs see W. H. McLeod, *The Sikhs: History, Religion, and Society* (1989). Two specialized works on the economic and trading history of India are Ashin Das Gupta and M. N. Pearson, eds., *India and the Indian Ocean, 1500–1800* (1987), and Stephen Frederic Dale, *Indian Merchants and Eurasian Trade, 1600–1750* (1994).

The history of East Africa in this period is not well documented, but B. A. Ogot, ed., *UNESCO General History of Africa*, vol. 5, *Africa from the Sixteenth to the Eighteenth Century* (1992), provides a useful collection of articles. See also Tom Spear, *The Swahili* (1984), and James de Vere Allen, *Swahili Origins* (1993).

For a brief, general introduction to the relations between the Muslim land empires and the development of Indian Ocean trade, see Patricia Risso, *Merchants and Faith: Muslim Commerce and Culture in the Indian Ocean* (1995). Esmond Bradley Martin and Chryssee Perry Martin have written a popular and well-illustrated work on the western Indian Ocean entitled *Cargoes of the East: The Ports, Trade and Culture of the Arabian Seas and Western Indian Ocean* (1978). C. R. Boxer, *The Dutch Seaborne Empire, 1600–1800* (1973), is a classic account of all aspects of Dutch maritime expansion.

■ Notes

1. Quoted in Sarah Searight, *The British in the Middle East* (New York: Atheneum 1970), 36.
2. Daniel Goffman, *Izmir and the Levantine World, 1550–1650* (Seattle: University of Washington Press, 1990), 52.
3. Quoted in Peter Jackson and Laurence Lockhart, eds., *The Cambridge History of Iran*, vol. 6, *The Timurid and Safavid Periods* (New York: Cambridge University Press, 1986), 703.
4. Esmond Bradley Martin and Chryssee Perry Martin, *Cargoes of the East: The Ports, Trade and Culture of the Arabian Seas and Western Indian Ocean* (1978), 17.

Document-Based Question

Islam and Society in the Ottoman Empire

Using the following documents, analyze the various ways that Islam shaped the development of society in the Ottoman Empire from 1500 to 1750.

DOCUMENT 1
Aya Sofya Mosque in Istanbul (photo, p. 489)

DOCUMENT 2
Ottoman Glassmakers on Parade (photo, p. 490)

DOCUMENT 3
Islamic Law and Ottoman Rule (Diversity and Dominance, pp. 492–493)

DOCUMENT 4
Istanbul Family on the Way to a Bath House (photo, p. 499)

How does Ebu's-su'ud's position as the mufti of Istanbul influence his interpretation of Islamic law? What additional types of documents would help you analyze the various ways Islam shaped the development of society in the Ottoman Empire from 1500 to 1750?

20

Northern Eurasia, 1500–1800

Russian Ambassadors to Holland Display Their Furs, 1576   Representatives from Muscovy impressed the court of King Maximilian II of Bohemia with their sable coats and caps.

L i Zicheng° was an apprentice ironworker in a barren northern Chinese province. His dreams for the future were dashed when, in a desperate effort to save money, the Hanli emperor ordered the elimination of Li's job and those of many other government employees. The savings went to fund more troops to defend the capital city of Beijing° against attacks by **Manchu** armies from Manchuria in the northeast. By 1630 Li Zicheng had found work as a soldier, but he and his fellow soldiers mutinied when the government failed to provide them with needed supplies. A natural leader, Li soon headed a group of several thousand Chinese rebels. In 1635 he and other rebel leaders were strong enough to control much of north central China.

Wedged between the armies of the Manchu pressing from the north and the rebels to the southwest, the Ming government grew ever weaker. Taking advantage of the weakness, Li Zicheng's forces began to move toward Beijing. Along the way they captured towns and conscripted young men into their army. The rebels also won popular support with promises to end the abuses of the Ming and restore peace and prosperity. In April 1644 Li's armies were able to take over Beijing without a fight. The last Ming emperor hanged himself in the palace garden, bringing to an end the dynasty that had ruled China since 1368.

The rebels' success was short-lived. Believing there was more to fear from uneducated, violent men like Li, the Ming general Wu Sangui joined forces with the Manchu. Wu may have been influenced by the fact that Li had captured one of the general's favorite concubines and taken her for himself. Together Wu and the Manchu retook Beijing in June. Li's forces scattered, and a year later he was dead, either a suicide or beaten to death by peasants whose food he tried to steal.[1]

Meanwhile, the Manchu were making it clear that they intended to be the new masters of China. They installed their young sovereign as the new emperor and over the next two decades hunted down the last of the Ming loyalists and heirs to the throne.

China was not the only state in Northern Eurasia facing uprisings from within and foreign threats. In the period from 1500 to 1800 Japan and Russia experienced turbulence as they underwent massive political change and economic growth. Besides challenges from nearby neighbors, the three also faced new contacts and challenges from the commercially and militarily powerful European states.

As you read this chapter, ask yourself the following questions:

- How did Japan, China, and Russia respond to internal social, economic, and political pressures?

- How did China and Russia deal with military challenges from their immediate neighbors?

- How did Japan, China, and Russia differ in the ways they reacted to western European commercial and cultural contacts?

JAPANESE REUNIFICATION

L ike China and Russia in the centuries between 1500 and 1800, Japan experienced three major changes: internal and external military conflicts, political growth and strengthening, and expanded commercial and cultural contacts. Along with its culturally homogenous population and natural boundaries, Japan's smaller size made the process of political unification shorter than in the great empires of China and Russia. Japan also differed in its responses to new contacts with western Europeans.

Civil War and the Invasion of Korea, 1500–1603

In the twelfth century Japan's imperial unity had disintegrated, and the country fell under the rule of numerous warlords known as **daimyo**°. Each of the daimyo had his own castle town, a small bureaucracy, and an army of warriors, the **samurai**°. Daimyo pledged a loose allegiance to the hereditary commander of the armies, the shogun, as well as to the Japanese emperor residing in the capital city of Kyoto°. The emperor and shogun were symbols of national unity but lacked political power.

Warfare among the different daimyo was common. In the late 1500s Japan experienced a prolonged civil war

---

Li Zicheng (lee ZUH-cheng)   Beijing (bay-JING)

daimyo (DIE-mee-oh)   **samurai** (SAH-moo-rye)
Kyoto (KYOH-toh)

that brought the separate Japanese islands under powerful warlords. The most successful of these warlords was Hideyoshi°. In 1592, buoyed with his success in Japan, the supremely confident Hideyoshi launched an invasion of the Asian mainland with 160,000 men. His apparent intention was not just to conquer the Korean peninsula but to make himself emperor of China as well.

The Korean and Japanese languages are closely related, but the dominant influence on Korean culture had long been China. Korea generally accepted a subordinate relationship with its giant neighbor and paid tribute to the Chinese dynasty in power. In many ways the Yi dynasty that ruled Korea from 1392 to 1910 was a model Confucian state. Although Korea had developed its own system of writing in 1443 and made extensive use of printing with movable type from the fifteenth century, most printing continued to use Chinese characters.

Against Hideyoshi's invaders the Koreans employed all the technological and military skill for which the Yi period was renowned. Ingenious covered warships, or "turtle boats," intercepted a portion of the Japanese fleet. The mentally unstable Hideyoshi countered with brutal punitive measures. The Koreans and their Chinese allies could not stop the Japanese conquest of the peninsula and into the Chinese province of Manchuria. However, after Hideyoshi's death in 1598, the other Japanese military leaders withdrew their forces, and the Japanese government made peace in 1606.

Korea was severely devastated by the invasion. In the confusion after the Japanese withdrawal, the Korean *yangban* (nobility) and lesser royals were able to lay claim to so much tax-paying land that royal revenues may have fallen by two-thirds. But the most dramatic consequences of the Japanese invasion were in China. The battles in Manchuria weakened Chinese garrisons there, permitting Manchu opposition to consolidate. Manchu forces invaded Korea in the 1620s and eventually compelled the Yi to become a tributary state. As already related, the Manchu would be in possession of Beijing, China's capital, by 1644.

The Tokugawa Shogunate, to 1800

After Hideyoshi's demise, Japanese leaders brought the civil wars to an end, and in 1603 they established a more centralized government. A new shogun, Tokugawa Ieyasu° (1543–1616), had gained the upper hand in the conflict and established a new military government known as the **Tokugawa Shogunate.**

The shoguns created a new administrative capital at Edo° (now Tokyo). Trade along the well-maintained road between Edo and the imperial capital of Kyoto promoted the development of the Japanese economy and the formation of other trading centers (see Map 25.3).

Although the Tokugawa Shogunate gave Japan more political unity than the islands had seen in centuries, the regional lords, the daimyo, still had a great deal of power and autonomy. Ieyasu and his successor shoguns had to work hard to keep this decentralized political system from disintegrating.

In some ways, economic integration was more a feature of Tokugawa Japan than was political centralization. Because Tokugawa shoguns required the daimyo to visit Edo frequently, good roads and maritime transport linked the city to the castle towns on three of the four main islands of Japan. Commercial traffic also developed along these routes. The shogun paid the lords in rice, and the lords paid their followers in rice. To meet their personal expenses, recipients of rice had to convert much of it into cash. This transaction stimulated the development of rice exchanges at Edo and at Osaka°, where merchants speculated in rice prices. By the late seventeenth century Edo was one of the largest cities in the world, with nearly a million inhabitants.

The domestic peace of the Tokugawa era forced the warrior class to adapt itself to the growing bureaucratic needs of the state. As the samurai became better educated, more attuned to the tastes of the civil elite, and more interested in conspicuous consumption, they became important customers for merchants dealing in silks, *sake*° (rice wine), fans, porcelain, lacquer ware, books, and moneylending. The state attempted—unsuccessfully—to curb the independence of the merchants when the economic well-being of the samurai was threatened, particularly when rice prices went too low or interest rates on loans were too high.

The 1600s and 1700s were centuries of high achievement in artisanship, and Japanese skills in steel making, pottery, and lacquer ware were joined by excellence in the production and decoration of porcelain (see Environment and Technology: East Asian Porcelain), thanks in no small part to Korean experts brought back to Japan after the invasion of 1592. In the early 1600s manufacturers and merchants amassed enormous family fortunes. Several of the most important industrial and financial companies—for instance, the Mitsui° companies—had their origins in sake breweries of the early Tokugawa period, then branched out into manufacturing, finance, and transport.

Hideyoshi (HEE-duh-YOH-shee)
Tokugawa Ieyasu (TOH-koo-GAH-wah ee-ay-YAH-soo)

Edo (ED-oh)   Osaka (OH-sah-kah)   sake (SAH-kay)
Mitsui (MIT-soo-ee)

CHRONOLOGY

	Korea and Japan	China and Central Asia	Russia
1500		1517 Portuguese embassy to China	
	1543 First Portuguese contacts		1547 Ivan IV tsar
	1592 Japanese invasion of Korea		1582 Russians conquer Khanate of Sibir
1600	1603 Tokugawa Shogunate formed	1601 Matteo Ricci allowed to reside in Beijing	1613–1645 Rule of Mikhail, the first Romanov tsar
	1633–1639 Edicts close down trade with Europe	1644 Qing conquest of Beijing	
		1662–1722 Rule of Emperor Kangxi	1649 Subordination of serfs complete
		1689 Treaty of Nerchinsk with Russia	1689–1725 Rule of Peter the Great
1700	1702 Trial of the Forty-Seven Ronin	1691 Qing control of Inner Mongolia	1712 St. Petersburg becomes Russia's capital
		1736–1795 Rule of Emperor Qianlong	1762–1796 Rule of Catherine the Great
	1792 Russian ships first spotted off the coast of Japan		1799 Alaska becomes a Russian colony

Wealthy merchant families usually cultivated close alliances with their regional daimyo and, if possible, with the shogun himself. In this way they could weaken the strict control of merchant activity that was an official part of Tokugawa policy. By the end of the 1700s the merchant families of Tokugawa Japan held the key to future modernization and the development of heavy industry, particularly in the prosperous provinces.

Japan and the Europeans

Direct contacts with Europeans from the mid-sixteenth century presented Japan with new opportunities and problems. The first major impact was on Japanese military technology. Within thirty years of the arrival of the first Portuguese in 1543, the daimyo were fighting with Western-style firearms, copied and improved upon by Japanese armorers. Japan's civil conflicts of the late sixteenth century launched the first East Asian "gunpowder revolution."

The Japanese also welcomed new trade with merchants from distant Portugal, Spain, the Netherlands, and England, but the government closely regulated their activities. Aside from the brief boom in porcelain exports in the seventeenth century, few Japanese goods went to Europe, and not much from Europe found a market in Japan. The Japanese sold the Dutch copper and silver, which the Dutch exchanged in China for silks that they then resold in Japan. The Japanese, of course, had their own trade with China.

Portuguese and Spanish merchant ships also brought Catholic missionaries. One of the first, Francis Xavier, went to India in the mid-sixteenth century looking for converts and later traveled throughout Southeast and East Asia. He spent two years in Japan and died in 1552, hoping to gain entry to China.

Japanese responses were decidedly mixed to Xavier and other Jesuits (members of the Catholic religious order the Society of Jesus). Large numbers of ordinary Japanese found the new faith deeply meaningful, but

ENVIRONMENT + TECHNOLOGY

East Asian Porcelain

By the 1400s artisans in China, Korea, and Japan were all producing high-quality pottery with lustrous surface glazes. The best quality, intended for the homes of the wealthy and powerful, was made of pure white clay and covered with a hard translucent glaze. Artisans often added intricate decorations in cobalt blue and other colors. Cheaper pottery found a huge market in East Asia.

Such pottery was also exported to Southeast Asia, the Indian Ocean, and the Middle East. Little found its way to Europe before 1600, but imports soared once the Dutch established trading bases in East Asia. Europeans called the high-quality ware "porcelain." Blue and white designs were especially popular.

One of the great centers of Chinese production was at the large artisan factory at Jingdezhen (JING-deh-JUHN). No sooner had the Dutch tapped into this source than the civil wars and Manchu conquests disrupted production in the middle 1600s. Desperate for a substitute source, the Dutch turned to porcelain from Japanese producers at Arita and Imari, near Nagasaki. Despite Japan's restriction of European trade, the Dutch East India Company transported some 190,000 pieces of Japanese ceramic ware to the Netherlands between 1653 and 1682.

In addition to a wide range of Asian designs, Chinese and Japanese artisans made all sorts of porcelain for the European market. These included purely decorative pottery birds, vases, and pots as well as utilitarian vessels and dishes intended for table use. The serving dish illustrated here came from dinnerware sets the Japanese made especially for the Dutch East India Company. The VOC logo at the center represents the first letters of the company's name in Dutch. It is surrounded by Asian design motifs.

After the return of peace in China, the VOC imported tens of thousands of Chinese porcelain pieces a year. The Chinese artisans sometimes produced imitations of Japanese designs that had become popular in Europe. Meanwhile, the Dutch were experimenting with making their own imitations of East Asian porcelain, right down to the Asian motifs and colors that had become so fashionable in Europe.

Japanese Export Porcelain Part of a larger set made for the Dutch East India Company (Photograph courtesy Peabody Essex Museum, #83830).

members of the Japanese elite were inclined to oppose it as disruptive and foreign. By 1580 more than 100,000 Japanese had become Christians, and one daimyo gave Jesuit missionaries the port city of Nagasaki°. In 1613 Date Masamune°, the fierce and independent daimyo of northern Honshu°, sent his own embassy to the Vatican, by way of the Philippines (where there were significant communities of Japanese merchants and pirates) and Mexico City. Some daimyo converts ordered their subjects to become Christians as well. Other Japanese were won over by the Jesuit, Dominican, and Franciscan missionaries.

By the early seventeenth century there were some 300,000 Japanese Christians and a few newly ordained Japanese priests. But these extraordinary events could not stand apart from the fractious politics of the day and suspicions about the larger intentions of the Europeans and their well-armed ships. The new shogunate in Edo became the center of hostility to Christianity. In 1614 a decree charging the Christians with seeking to overthrow true doctrine, change the government, and seize

Nagasaki (NAH-guh-SAHK-kee) **Date Masamune** (DAH-tay mah-suh-MOO-nay) **Honshu** (HOHN-shoo)

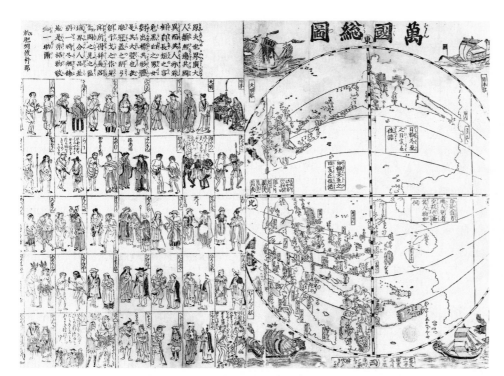

Comprehensive Map of the Myriad Nations Thanks to the "Dutch studies" scholars and to overseas contacts, many Japanese were well informed about the cultures, technologies, and political systems of various parts of the world. This combination map and ethnographic text of 1671 enthusiastically explores the differences among the many peoples living or traveling in Asia. The map of the Pacific hemisphere has the north pole on the left and the south pole on the extreme right of the drawing. (British Museum/ Fotomas Index)

the land ordered the movement eliminated. Some missionaries left Japan, but others took their movement underground. The government began its persecutions in earnest in 1617, and the beheadings, crucifixions, and forced recantations over the next several decades destroyed almost the entire Christian community.

A series of decrees issued between 1633 and 1639 went much farther, ordering an end to European trade as the price to be paid for eliminating Christian influences. Europeans who entered illegally faced the death penalty. A new government office made sure Christianity did not reemerge; people were required to produce certificates from Buddhist temples attesting to their religious orthodoxy and thus their loyalty to the regime.

The closing of Japan to European influence was not total. A few Dutch were permitted to reside on a small artificial island in Nagasaki's harbor, and a few Japanese were licensed to supply their needs. The information these intermediaries acquired about European weapons technology, shipbuilding, mathematics and astronomy, anatomy and medicine, and geography was known as "Dutch studies."

The Tokugawa government also placed restrictions on the number of Chinese ships that could trade in Japan, but these were harder to enforce. Regional lords in northern and southern Japan not only pursued overseas trade and piracy but also claimed dominion over islands between Japan and Korea to the east and between Japan and Taiwan to the south, including present-day Okinawa.

Despite such evasions, the larger lesson is the substantial success of the new shogunate in exercising its authority.

Elite Decline and Social Crisis

During the 1700s population growth put a great strain on the well-developed lands of central Japan. In more remote provinces, where the lords promoted new settlements and agricultural expansion, the rate of economic growth far outstripped the growth rate in central Japan.

Also destabilizing the Tokugawa government in the 1700s was the shogunate's inability to stabilize rice prices and halt the economic decline of the samurai. To finance their living, the samurai had to convert their rice to cash in the market. The Tokugawa government realized that the rice brokers might easily enrich themselves at the expense of the samurai if the price of rice and the rate of interest were not strictly controlled. Laws designed to regulate both had been passed early in the Tokugawa period, and laws requiring moneylenders to forgive samurai debts were added later. But these laws were not always enforced, sometimes because neither the lords nor the samurai wished them to be. By the early 1700s members of both groups were dependent on the willingness of merchants to provide credit.

The Tokugawa shoguns sought to protect the samurai from decline while curbing the growing power of the

Woodblock Print of the "Forty-Seven Ronin" Story The saga of the forty-seven ronin and the avenging of their fallen leader has fascinated the Japanese public since the event occurred in 1702. This watercolor from the Tokugawa period shows the leaders of the group pausing on the snowy banks of the Sumida River in Edo (Tokyo) before storming their enemy's residence. (Jean-Pierre Hauchecorne Collection)

merchant class. Their legitimacy rested on their ability to reward and protect the interests of the lords and samurai who had supported the Tokugawa conquest. But the Tokugawa government, like the governments of China, Korea, and Vietnam, accepted the Confucian idea that agriculture should be the basis of state wealth and that merchants should occupy lowly positions in society because of their reputed lack of moral character.

Governments throughout East Asia used Confucian philosophy to attempt to limit the influence and power of merchants. The Tokugawa government, however, was at a special disadvantage. Its decentralized system limited its ability to regulate merchant activities and actually stimulated the growth of commercial activities. From the founding of the Tokugawa Shogunate in 1603 until 1800, the economy grew faster than the population. Household amenities and cultural resources that in China were found only in the cities were common in the Japanese countryside. Despite official disapproval, merchants and

others involved in the growing economy enjoyed relative freedom and influence in eighteenth-century Japan. They produced a vivid culture of their own, fostering the development of *kabuki* theater, colorful woodblock prints and silk-screened fabrics, and restaurants.

The ideological and social crisis of Tokugawa Japan's transformation from a military to a civil society is captured in the "Forty-Seven Ronin°" incident of 1701–1703. A senior minister provoked a young daimyo into drawing his sword at the shogun's court. For this offense the young lord was sentenced to commit *seppuku°*, the ritual suicide of the samurai. His own followers then became *ronin*, "masterless samurai," obliged by the traditional code of the warrior to avenge their deceased master. They broke into the house of the senior minister who had provoked their own lord, and they killed him and others in his household. Then they withdrew to a temple in Edo and notified the shogun of what they had done out of loyalty to their lord and to avenge his death.

A legal debate began in the shogun's government. To deny the righteousness of the ronin would be to deny samurai values. But to approve their actions would create social chaos, undermine laws against murder, and deny the shogunal government the right to try cases of samurai violence. The shogun ruled that the ronin had to die but would be permitted to die honorably by committing *seppuku*. Traditional samurai values had to surrender to the supremacy of law. The purity of purpose of the ronin is still celebrated in Japan, but since then Japanese writers, historians, and teachers have recognized that the self-sacrifice of the ronin for the sake of upholding civil law was necessary.

The Tokugawa Shogunate put into place a political and economic system that fostered innovation, but the government itself could not exploit it. Thus, during the Tokugawa period the government remained quite traditional while other segments of society developed new methods of productivity and management.

THE LATER MING AND EARLY QING EMPIRES

Like Japan, China after 1500 experienced civil and foreign wars, an important change in government, and new trading and cultural relations with Europe and its neighbors. The internal and external forces at work in China were different in detail and operated on a much larger scale, but they led in similar directions. By 1800

ronin (ROH-neen)   **seppuku** (SEP-poo-koo)

China had a greatly enhanced empire, an expanding economy, and growing doubts about the importance of European trade and Christianity.

The Ming Empire, 1500–1644

The brilliant economic and cultural achievements of the early **Ming Empire** continued during the 1500s. Ming manufacturers had transformed the global economy with their techniques for the assembly-line production of porcelain. An international market eager for Ming porcelain, as well as for silk and lacquered furniture, stimulated the commercial development of East Asia, the Indian Ocean, and Europe. But this golden age was followed by many decades of political weakness, warfare, and rural woes until a new dynasty, the Qing° from Manchuria, guided China back to peace and prosperity.

The Europeans whose ships began to seek out new contacts with China in the early sixteenth century left many accounts of their impressions. Like others before them, they were astonished at Ming China's imperial power, exquisite manufactures, and vast population. European merchants bought such large quantities of the high-grade blue-on-white porcelain commonly used by China's upper classes that in English all fine dishes became known simply as "china."

The growing integration of China into the world economy stimulated rapid growth in the silk, cotton, and porcelain industries. Agricultural regions that supplied raw materials to these industries and food for the expanding urban populations also prospered. In exchange for Chinese porcelain and textiles, tens of thousands of tons of silver from Japan and Latin America flooded into China in the century before 1640. The influx of silver led many Chinese to substitute payments in silver for various land taxes, labor obligations, and other kinds of dues.

Ming cities had long been culturally and commercially vibrant. Many large landowners and absentee landlords lived in the cities, as did officials, artists, and rich merchants who had purchased ranks or prepared their sons for the examinations. The elite classes had created a brilliant culture in which novels, operas, poetry, porcelain, and painting were all closely interwoven. Owners of small businesses catering to the urban elites could make money through printing, tailoring, running restaurants, or selling paper, ink, ink-stones, and writing brushes. The imperial government operated factories for the production of ceramics and silks. Enormous government complexes at Jingdezhen and elsewhere invented assembly-line techniques and produced large quantities of high-quality ceramics for sale in China and abroad.

Despite these achievements, serious problems were developing that left the Ming Empire economically exhausted, politically deteriorating, and technologically lagging behind both its East Asian neighbors and some European countries. Some of these problems were the result of natural disasters associated with climate change and disease. There is evidence that the climate changes known as the Little Ice Age in seventeenth-century Europe affected the climate in China as well. Annual temperatures dropped, reached a low point about 1645, and remained low until the early 1700s. The resulting agricultural distress and famine fueled large uprisings that speeded the end of the Ming Empire. The devastation caused by these uprisings and the spread of epidemic disease resulted in steep declines in local populations.

Along with many benefits, the rapid growth in the trading economy also led to such problems as rapid urban growth and business speculation. Some provinces suffered from price inflation that the flood of silver caused. In contrast to the growing involvement of European governments in promoting economic growth, the Ming government showed little interest in developing the economy and pursued some policies that were inimical to it. Despite the fact that paper currency had failed to find general acceptance as far back as the 1350s, Ming governments persisted in issuing new paper money and promoting copper coins, even after abundant supplies of silver had won the approval of the markets. Corruption was also a serious government problem. By the end of the Ming period the factories were plagued by disorder and inefficiency. The situation became so bad during the late sixteenth and seventeenth centuries that workers held strikes with increasing frequency. During a labor protest at Jingdezhen in 1601, workers threw themselves into the kilns to protest working conditions.

Yet the urban and industrial sectors of later Ming society fared much better than the rural, agricultural sector. After a period of economic growth and recovery from the population decline of the thirteenth century, the rural Ming economy did not maintain strong growth. After the beginning of the sixteenth century, China had knowledge, gained from European traders, of new crops from Africa and America. But they were introduced very slowly, and neither rice-growing regions in southern China nor wheat-growing regions in northern China experienced a meaningful increase in productivity under the later Ming. After 1500 economic depression in the countryside, combined with recurring epidemics in central and southern China, kept rural population growth in check.

Qing (ching)

Ming Collapse and the Rise of the Qing

Rising environmental, economic, and administrative problems weakened the Ming Empire but did not cause its fall. That was the result of growing rebellion within and the rising power of the Manchu outside the borders.

Insecure boundaries are an indication of the later Ming Empire's difficulties. The Ming had long been under pressure from the powerful Mongol federations of the north and west. In the late 1500s large numbers of Mongols were unified by their devotion to the Dalai Lama°, or universal teacher, of Tibetan Buddhism, whom they regarded as their spiritual leader. Building on this spiritual unity, a brilliant leader named Galdan restored Mongolia as a regional military power around 1600. The Manchu, an agriculturally based people who controlled the region north of Korea, grew stronger in the northeast.

In the southwest, there were repeated uprisings among native peoples crowded by the immigration of Chinese farmers. Pirates, many Japanese, based in Okinawa and Taiwan frequently looted the southeastern coastal towns. Ming military resources, concentrated against the Mongols and the Manchu in the north, could not be deployed to defend the coasts. As a result, many southern Chinese migrated to Southeast Asia to profit from the sea-trading networks of the Indian Ocean.

As the previous section related, the Japanese invasion of 1592 to 1598 set the Ming collapse in motion. To stop the Japanese the Ming brought Manchu troops into an international force and eventually paid a high price for that invitation. Weakened by the strain of repelling the Japanese, Chinese defenses in the northeast could not stop the advance of Manchu troops, who had already brought Korea under their sway.

Taking advantage of this situation, as the opening of this chapter related, the Chinese rebel leader Li Zicheng advanced and captured Beijing. With the emperor dead by his own hand and the imperial family in flight, a Ming general invited Manchu leaders to help his forces take Beijing from the rebels. The Manchu did so in the summer of 1644. Rather than restoring the Ming, they claimed China for their own and began a forty-year conquest of the rest of the Ming territories (see Diversity and Dominance: Gendered Violence: The Yangzhou Massacre). By the end of the century, the Manchu had gained control of south China and incorporated the island of Taiwan into imperial China for the first time (see Map 20.1). They also conquered parts of Mongolia and Central Asia.

A Manchu family headed the new **Qing Empire,** and Manchu generals commanded the military forces. But Manchu were a very small portion of the population, and one of several minority populations. The overwhelming majority of Qing officials, soldiers, merchants, and farmers were ethnic Chinese. Like other successful invaders of China, the Qing soon adopted Chinese institutions and policies.

Trading Companies and Missionaries

For the European mariners who braved the long voyages to Asia, the China trade was second in importance only to the spice trade of southern Asia. China's vast population and manufacturing skills drew a steady supply of ships from western Europe, but enthusiasm for the trade developed more slowly, especially at the imperial court.

A Portuguese ship reached China at the end of 1513, but was not permitted to trade. A formal Portuguese embassy in 1517 got bogged down in Chinese protocol and procrastination, and China expelled the Portuguese in 1522. Finally, in 1557 the Portuguese gained the right to trade from a base in Macao°. Spain's Asian trade was conducted from Manila in the Philippines, which served as the terminus of trans-Pacific trade routes from South America. For a time, the Spanish and the Dutch both maintained outposts for trade with China and Japan on the island of Taiwan, but in 1662 they were forced to concede control over the island to the Qing, who incorporated Taiwan for the first time as a part of China.

By then, the Dutch East India Company (VOC) had displaced the Portuguese as the major European trader in the Indian Ocean and, despite the setback on Taiwan, was establishing itself as the main European trader in East Asia. VOC representatives courted official favor in China by acknowledging the moral superiority of the emperor. They performed the ritual kowtow (in which the visitor knocked his head on the floor while crawling toward the throne) to the Ming emperor.

Catholic missionaries accompanied the Portuguese and Spanish merchants to China, just as they did to Japan. While the Franciscans and Dominicans sought to replicate the conversion efforts at the bottom of society that had worked so well in Japan, the Jesuits concentrated their efforts among China's intellectual and political elite. In this they were far more successful than they had been in Japan—at least until the eighteenth century.

The outstanding Jesuit of late Ming China, Matteo Ricci° (1552–1610), became expert in the Chinese language and an accomplished scholar of the Confucian

Dalai Lama (DAH-lie LAH-mah)

Macao (muh-KOW)   **Matteo Ricci** (mah-TAY-oh REE-chee)

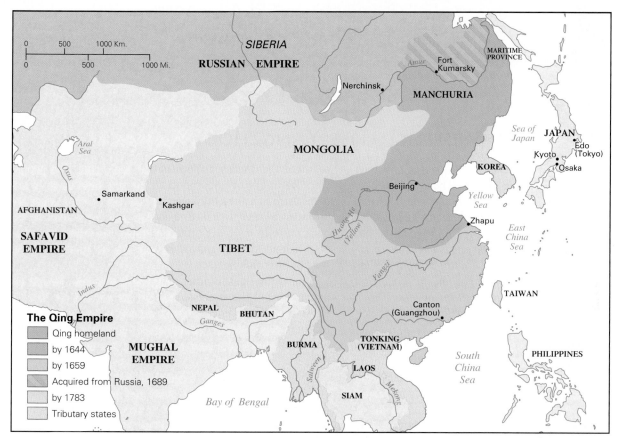

Map 20.1   The Qing Empire, 1644–1783   The Qing Empire began in Manchuria and captured north China in 1644. Between 1644 and 1783 the Qing conquered all the former Ming territories and added Taiwan, the lower Amur River basin, Inner Mongolia, eastern Turkestan, and Tibet. The resulting state was more than twice the size of the Ming Empire.

classics. Under Ricci's leadership, the Jesuits sought to adapt Catholic Christianity to Chinese cultural traditions while enhancing their status by introducing the Chinese to the latest science and technology from Europe. From 1601 Ricci was allowed to reside in Beijing on an imperial stipend as a Western scholar. Later Jesuits headed the office of astronomy that issued the official calendar.

Emperor Kangxi (r. 1662–1722)

The seventeenth and eighteenth centuries—particularly the reigns of the **Kangxi°** (r. 1662–1722) and Qianlong° (r. 1736–1796) emperors—were a period of great economic, military, and cultural achievement in China. The early Qing emperors wished to foster economic and demographic recovery in China. They repaired the roads

Kangxi (KAHNG-shee)   Qianlong (chee-YEN-loong)

and waterworks, lowered transit taxes, mandated comparatively low rents and interest rates, and established economic incentives for resettlement of the areas devastated during the peasant rebellions of the late Ming period. Foreign trade was encouraged. Vietnam, Burma, and Nepal sent regular embassies to the Qing tribute court and carried the latest Chinese fashions back home. Overland routes of communication from Korea to Central Asia were revived, and through its conquests the Qing Empire gained access to the superior horses of Afghanistan.

The early Qing conquest of Beijing and north China was carried out under the leadership of a group of Manchu aristocrats who dominated the first Qing emperor based in China and were regents for his young son, who was declared emperor in 1662. This child-emperor, Kangxi, spent several years doing political battle with his regents, and in 1669 he gained real as well as formal control of the government by executing his chief regent.

우세인 은신처
팡운드폭탄 4발 투하… 두 아들과 함께 사망
심진지 구축… 이틀째 시가戰
령이 대중 앞에 나타나거나 애국심
을 고취하는 노래만을 내보내던 방
송마저 중단됐다.
라크 전후
의에서는
영국 주도

DIVERSITY AND DOMINANCE

GENDERED VIOLENCE: THE YANGZHOU MASSACRE

After the fall of Beijing to the Manchu, the rest of China felt the dominance of the conquerors. The Qing were not eager for reminders of their brutal takeover to circulate. This rare eyewitness account, which survived because it was smuggled out of China, reveals not just the violence of the conquest but also the diversity of its impact on men and women.

The account begins in 1645 as rumors of approaching Manchu soldiers spread through Yangzhou, an important city near the juncture of the Yangzi River and the Grand Canal, and the soldiers charged with its defense begin to flee.

Crowds of barefoot and disheveled refugees were flocking into the city. When questioned, they were too distraught to reply. At that point dozens of mounted soldiers in confused waves came surging south looking as though they had given up all hope. Along them appeared a man who turned out to be the commandant himself. It seems he had intended to leave by the east gate but could not because the enemy soldiers outside the wall were drawing too near; he was therefore forced to cut across this part of town to reach the south gate. This is how we first learned for sure that the enemy troops would enter the city. . . .

My house backed against the city wall, and peeping through the chinks in my window, I saw the soldiers on the wall marching south then west, solemn and in step. Although the rain was beating down, it did not seem to disturb them. This reassured me because I gathered that they were well disciplined units.

. . . For a long time no one came. I retreated again to the back window and found that the regiment on the wall had broken ranks; some soldiers were walking about, others standing still.

All of a sudden I saw some soldiers escorting a group of women dressed in Yangzhou fashion. This was my first real shock. Back in the house, I said to my wife, "Should things go badly when the soldiers enter the city, you may need to end your life."

"Yes," she replied, "Whatever silver we have you should keep. I think we women can stop thinking about life in this world." She gave me all the silver, unable to control her crying. . . .

Soon my younger brother arrived, then my two older brothers. We discussed the situation and I said, "The people who live in our neighborhood are all rich merchants. It will be disastrous if they think we are rich too." I then urged my brothers to brave the rain and quickly take the women by the back route to my older brother's house. His home was situated behind Mr. He's graveyard and was surrounded by the huts of poor families. . . .

Finally, my eldest brother reappeared and said, "People are being killed in the streets! What are we waiting for here? It doesn't matter so much whether we live or die, as long as we brothers stay together." Immediately I gathered together our ancestral tablets and went with him to our second brother's house. . . .

The cunning soldiers, suspecting that many people were still hidden, tried to entice them out by posting a placard promising clemency. About fifty to sixty people, half of them women, emerged. My elder brother said, "We four by ourselves will never survive if we run into these vicious soldiers, so we had better join the crowd. Since there are so many of them, escape will be easier. Even if things do not turn out well, as long as we are together, we will have no cause for regret." In our bewilderment we could think of no other way to save our lives. Thus agreed, we went to join the group.

The leaders were three Manchu soldiers. They searched my brothers and found all the silver they were carrying, but left me untouched. At that point some women appeared, two of whom called out to me. I recognized them as the concubines of my friend Mr. Zhu Shu and stopped them anxiously. They were disheveled and partly naked, their feet bare and covered with mud up to the ankles. One was holding a girl whom the soldiers hit with a whip and threw into the mud. Then we were immediately driven on. One soldier, sword in hand, took the lead; another drove us from behind with a long spear; and a third walked along on our right and left flanks alternately, making sure no one escaped. In groups of twenty or thirty we were herded along like sheep and cattle. If we faltered we were struck, and some people were even killed on the spot. The women were tied together with long chains around their necks, like a clumsy string of pearls. Stumbling at every step, they were soon covered with mud. Here and there on the ground lay babies, trampled by people or horses. Blood and gore soaked the fields, which were filled with the sound of sobbing. We passed gutters and ponds piled high with corpses; the blood had turned the water to a deep greenish-red color and filled the ponds to the brim.

. . . We then entered the house of [a] merchant, . . . which had been taken over by the three soldiers. Another soldier was already there. He had seized several attractive women and was rifling their trunks for fancy silks, which he piled in a heap. Seeing the three soldiers arrive, he laughed and pushed several dozen of us into the back hall. The women he led into a side chamber. . . .

The three soldiers stripped the women of their wet clothing all the way to their underwear, then ordered the seamstress to measure them and give them new garments. The women, thus coerced, had to expose themselves and stand naked. What shame they endured! Once they had changed, the soldiers grabbed them and forced them to join them in eating and drinking, then did whatever they pleased with them, without any regard for decency.

[The narrator escapes and hides atop a wooden canopy over a bed.] Later on a soldier brought a woman in and wanted her to sleep with him in the bed below me. Despite her refusal he forced her to yield. "This is too near the street. It is not a good place to stay," the woman said. I was almost discovered, but after a time the soldier departed with the woman. . . . [The narrator flees again and is reunited with his wife and relatives.]

At length, however, there came a soldier of the "Wolf Men" tribe, a vicious-looking man with a head like a mouse and eyes like a hawk. He attempted to abduct my wife. She was obliged to creep forward on all fours, pleading as she had with the others, but to no avail. When he insisted that she stand up, she rolled on the ground and refused. He then beat her so savagely with the flat of his sword that the blood flowed out in streams, totally soaking her clothes. Because my wife had once admonished me, "If I am unlucky I will die no matter what; do not plead for me as a husband or you will get caught too," I acted as if I did not know she was being beaten and hid far away in the grass, convinced she was about to die. Yet the depraved soldier did not stop there; he grabbed her by the hair, cursed her, struck her cruelly, and then dragged her away by the leg. . . . Just then they ran into a body of mounted soldiers. One of them said a few words to the soldier in Manchu. At this he dropped my wife and departed with them. Barely able to crawl back, she let out a loud sob, every part of her body injured. . . .

Unexpectedly there appeared a handsome looking man of less than thirty, a double-edged sword hung by his side, dressed in Manchu-style hat, red coat, and a pair of black boots. His follower, in a yellow jacket, was also very gallant in appearance. Immediately behind them were several residents of Yangzhou. The young man in red, inspecting me closely, said, "I would judge from your appearance that you are not one of these people. Tell me honestly, what class of person are you?"

I remembered that some people had obtained pardons and others had lost their lives the moment they said that they were poor scholars. So I did not dare come out at once with the truth and instead concocted a story. He pointed to my wife and son and asked who they were, and I told him the truth. "Tomorrow the prince will order that all swords be sheathed and all, of you will be spared," he said and then commanded his followers to give us some clothes and an ingot of silver. He also asked me, "How many days have you been without food?"

"Five days," I replied.

"Then come with me," he commanded. Although we only half trusted him, we were afraid to disobey. He led us to a well-stocked house, full of rice, fish, and other provisions. "Treat these four people well," he said to a woman in the house and then left. . . .

The next day was [April 30]. Killing and pillaging continued, although not on the previous scale. Still the mansions of the rich were thoroughly looted, and almost all the teenage girls were abducted. . . . every grain of rice, every inch of silk now entered these tigers' mouths. The resulting devastation is beyond description.

[May 2]. Civil administration was established in all the prefectures and counties; proclamations were issued aimed at calming the people, and monks from each temple were ordered to burn corpses. The temples themselves were clogged with women who had taken refuge, many of whom had died of fright or starvation. The "List of Corpses Burned" records more than eight hundred thousand, and this list does not include those who jumped into wells, threw themselves into the river, hanged themselves, were burned to death inside houses, or were carried away by the soldiers. . . .

When this calamity began there had been eight of us: my two elder brothers, my younger brother, my elder brother's wife, their son, my wife, my son, and myself. Now only three of us survived for sure, though the fate of my wife's brother and sister-in-law was not yet known. . . .

From the 25th of the fourth month to the 5th of the fifth month was a period of ten days. I have described here only what I actually experienced or saw with my own eyes; I have not recorded anything I picked up from rumor or hearsay.

QUESTIONS FOR ANALYSIS

1. What accounts for the soldiers' brutal treatment of the women.
2. What did different women do to protect themselves?
3. Having conquered, what did the Manchu do to restore order?

Source: Reprinted with permission of the Free Press, a division of Simon and Schuster Adult Publishing Group, from *Chinese Civilization: A Sourcebook,* Second Edition, edited by Patricia Buckley Ebrey. Copyright © 1993 by Patricia Buckley Ebrey.

Emperor Kangxi   In a portrait from about 1690, the young Manchu ruler is portrayed as a refined scholar in the Confucian tradition. He was a scholar and had great intellectual curiosity, but this portrait would not suggest that he was also capable of leading troops in battle.   (The Palace Museum, Beijing)

Kangxi was then sixteen. He was an intellectual prodigy who mastered classical Chinese, Manchu, and Mongolian at an early age and memorized the Chinese classics. His reign, lasting until his death in 1722, was marked not only by great expansion of the empire but by great stability as well.

The Qing rulers were as anxious as the Ming to consolidate their northern frontiers, especially as they feared an alliance between Galdan's Mongol state and the expanding Russian presence along the **Amur° River.** In the 1680s the Kangxi sent forces to attack the wooden forts on the northern bank of the Amur that hardy Russian scouts had built. Neither empire sent large forces into the Amur territories, and the contest was partly a struggle for the goodwill of the local Evenk and Dagur

Amur (AH-moor)

peoples. The Qing emperor emphasized the importance of treading lightly in the struggle and well understood the principles of espionage:

> Upon reaching the lands of the Evenks and the Dagurs you will send to announce that you have come to hunt deer. Meanwhile, keep a careful record of the distance and go, while hunting, along the northern bank of the Amur until you come by the shortest route to the town of Russian settlement at Albazin. Thoroughly reconnoiter its location and situation. I don't think the Russians will take a chance on attacking you. If they offer you food, accept it and show your gratitude. If they do attack you, don't fight back. In that case, lead your people and withdraw into our own territories. For I have a plan of my own.[2]

That delicacy gives a false impression of the intensity of the struggle between these two great empires. Qing forces twice attacked Albazin. The Qing were worried about Russian alliances with other frontier peoples, while Russia wished to protect its access to the furs, timber, and metals concentrated in Siberia, Manchuria, and Yakutsk. The Qing and Russians were also rivals for control of northern Asia's Pacific coast. Continued conflict would benefit neither side. In 1689 the Qing and Russian Empires negotiated the Treaty of Nerchinsk, using Jesuit missionaries as interpreters. The treaty fixed the border along the Amur River and regulated trade across it. Although this was a thinly settled area, the treaty proved important since the frontier it demarcated has long endured.

The next step was to settle the Mongolian frontier. Kangxi personally led troops in the great campaigns that defeated Galdan and brought Inner Mongolia under Qing control by 1691.

Kangxi was distinguished by his openness to new ideas and technologies from different regions. Unlike the rulers of Japan, who drove Christian missionaries out, he welcomed Jesuit advisers and put them in important offices. Jesuits helped create maps in the European style as practical guides to newly conquered regions and as symbols of Qing dominance. Kangxi considered introducing the European calendar, but protests from the Confucian elite were so strong that the plan was dropped. The emperor frequently discussed scientific and philosophical issues with the Jesuits. When he fell ill with malaria in the 1690s, Jesuit medical expertise (in this case, the use of quinine) aided his recovery. Kangxi also ordered the creation of illustrated books in Manchu detailing European anatomical and pharmaceutical knowledge.

To gain converts among the Chinese elite, the Jesuits made important compromises in their religious teaching. The most important was their toleration of Confucian ancestor worship. The matter caused great controversy

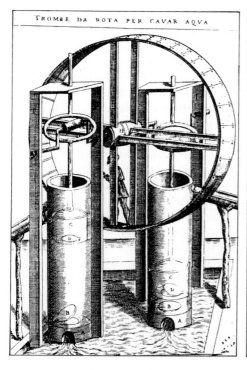

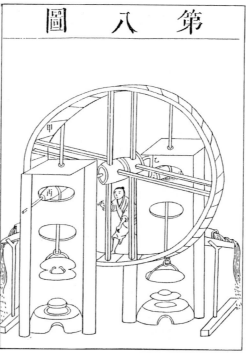

From the Jesuit Library at Beijing Jesuits such as Matteo Ricci were willing to share books on technology and science with Chinese scholars. But without firsthand experience it was impossible for Chinese translators to convey how the devices actually worked. Here, a man walking in a wheel drives a shaft that changes the pressure inside two pumps. In the Chinese translation of the drawing, the mechanisms were all lost. (Left: From Zonca, *Trombe da Rota per Cavar Aqua* [1607]. Right: "Diagram Number Eight" from *Qi tushuo* [*Illustrations on Energy*] [1627]. Both courtesy of Joseph Needham, *Science and Civilization in China*, vol. 4)

between the Jesuits and their Catholic rivals in China, the Franciscans and Dominicans, and also between the Jesuits and the pope. In 1690 the disagreement reached a high pitch. Kangxi wrote to Rome supporting the Jesuit position. Further disagreement with a papal legate to China led Kangxi to order the expulsion of all missionaries who refused to sign a certificate accepting his position. Most of the Jesuits signed, but relations with the imperial court were irreparably harmed. Jesuit presence in China declined in the eighteenth century, and later Qing emperors persecuted Christians rather than naming them to high offices.

Chinese Influences on Europe

The exchange of information between the Qing and the Europeans that Kangxi had fostered was never one-way. When the Jesuits informed the Qing court on matters of anatomy, for instance, the Qing were able to demonstrate an early form of inoculation, called "variolation," that had been used to stem the spread of smallpox after the Qing conquest of Beijing. The technique helped inspire the development of other vaccines later in Europe.

Similarly, Jesuit writings about the intellectual and cultural achievements of China excited admiration in Europe. The wealthy and the aspiring middle classes of

Europe demanded Chinese things—or things that looked to Europeans as if they could be Chinese. Not only silk, porcelain, and tea were avidly sought, but also cloisonné jewelry, tableware and decorative items, lacquered and jeweled room dividers, painted fans, and carved jade and ivory (which originated in Africa and was finished in China). One of the most striking Chinese influences on European interior life in this period was wallpaper—an adaptation of the Chinese practice of covering walls with enormous loose-hanging watercolors or calligraphy scrolls. By the mid-1700s special workshops throughout China were producing wallpaper and other consumer items according to the specifications of European merchants. The items were shipped to Canton for export to Europe.

In political philosophy, too, the Europeans felt they had something to learn from the early Qing emperors. In the late 1770s poems supposedly written by Emperor Qianlong were translated into French and disseminated through the intellectual circles of western Europe. These works depicted the Qing emperors as benevolent despots who campaigned against superstition and ignorance, curbed the excesses of the aristocracy, and patronized science and the arts. European intellectuals who were questioning their own political systems found the image of a practical, secular, compassionate ruler intriguing. The French thinker Voltaire proclaimed the

Qing emperors model philosopher-kings and advocated such rulership as a protection against the growth of aristocratic privilege.

Tea and Diplomacy

The Qing were eager to expand China's economic influence but were determined to control the trade very strictly. To make trade easier to tax and to limit piracy and smuggling, the Qing permitted only one market point for each foreign sector. Thus Europeans were permitted to trade only at Canton.

This system worked well enough for European traders until the late 1700s, when Britain became worried about its massive trade deficit with China. From bases in India and Singapore, British traders moved eastward to China and eventually displaced the Dutch as China's leading European trading partner. The directors of the East India Company (EIC) believed that China's technological achievements and gigantic potential markets made it the key to limitless profit. China had tea, rhubarb, porcelain, and silk to offer. By the early 1700s the EIC dominated European trading in Canton.

Tea from China had spread overland on Eurasian routes in medieval and early modern times to become a prized import in Russia, Central Asia, and the Middle East, all of which know it by its northern Chinese name, *cha*—as do the Portuguese. Other western Europeans acquired tea from the sea routes and thus know it by its name in the Fujian province of coastal China and Taiwan: *te*. In much of Europe, tea competed with chocolate and coffee as a fashionable drink by the mid-1600s.

Great fortunes were being made in the tea trade, but the English had not found a product to sell to China. They believed that China was a vast unexploited market, with hundreds of millions of potential consumers of lamp oil made from whale blubber, cotton grown in India or the American South, or guns manufactured in London or Connecticut. Particularly after the loss of the thirteen American colonies, Britain feared that its markets would diminish, and the EIC and other British merchants believed that only the Qing trade system—the "Canton system," as the British called it—stood in the way of opening new paths for commerce.

The British government also worried about Britain's massive trade deficit with China. Because the Qing Empire rarely bought anything from Britain, British silver poured into China to pay for imported tea and other products. The Qing government, whose revenues were declining in the later 1700s while its expenses rose, needed the silver. But in Britain the imbalance of payments stirred anxiety and anger over the restrictions that the Qing placed on imported foreign goods. To make matters worse, the East India Company had managed its worldwide holdings badly, and as it teetered on bankruptcy, its attempts to manipulate Parliament became increasingly intrusive. In 1792 the British government dispatched Lord George Macartney, a well-connected peer with practical experience in Russia and India, to China. Including scientists, artists, and translators as well as guards and diplomats, the **Macartney mission** showed Britain's great interest in the Qing Empire as well as the EIC's desire to revise the trade system.

China was not familiar with the European system of ambassadors, and Macartney struggled to portray himself in Chinese terms as a "tribute emissary" come to salute the Qianlong emperor's eightieth birthday. He steadfastly refused to perform the kowtow to the emperor, but did agree to bow on one knee as he would to his own monarch, King George III. The Qianlong emperor received Macartney courteously in September 1793, but refused to alter the Canton trading system, open new ports of trade, or allow the British to establish a permanent mission in Beijing. The Qing had no interest in changing a system that provided revenue to the imperial family and lessened serious piracy problems. Qianlong sent a letter to King George explaining that China had no need to increase its foreign trade, had no use for Britain's ingenious devices and manufacturers, and set no value on closer diplomatic ties.

Dutch, French, and Russian embassies soon attempted to achieve what Macartney had failed to do. When they also failed, European frustration with the Qing mounted. The great European admiration for China faded, and China was considered despotic, self-satisfied, and unrealistic. Political solutions seemed impossible because the Qing court would not communicate with foreign envoys or observe the simplest rules of the diplomatic system familiar to Europeans. In Macartney's view, China was like a venerable old warship, well maintained and splendid to look at, but obsolete and no longer up to the task.

Population and Social Stress

The Chinese who escorted Macartney and his entourage in 1792–1793 took them through China's prosperous cities and productive farmland. The visitors did not see evidence of the economic and environmental decline that had begun to affect China in the last decades of the 1700s. The population explosion had intensified demand for rice and wheat, for land to be opened for the planting of crops imported from Africa and the Americas, and for more thorough exploitation of land already in use.

East Meets West In a large procession, sixteen men carry the seated Qianlong emperor to a meeting with the English ambassador Lord Macartney at the emperor's extensive summer palace on 14 September 1793. The British are on the right. (British Museum, Department of Prints and Drawings)

In the peaceful decades of Qing rule, China's population had grown to three times its size in 1500. If one accepts an estimate of some 350 million in the late 1700s, China had twice the population of all of Europe. Despite the efficiency of Chinese agriculture and the gradual adoption of New World crops such as corn and sweet potatoes, population growth led to social and environmental problems. More people meant less land per person for farming. Increased demand for building materials and firewood sharply reduced China's remaining woodlands. Deforestation, in turn, accelerated wind and water erosion and increased the danger of flooding. Dams and dikes were not maintained, and silted-up river channels were not dredged. By the end of the eighteenth century parts of the thousand-year-old Grand Canal linking the rivers of north and south China were nearly unusable, and the towns that bordered it were starved for commerce.

The result was misery in many parts of interior China. Some districts responded by increasing production of cash crops such as tea, cotton, and silk that were tied to the export market. Some peasants sought seasonal jobs in better-off agricultural areas or worked in low-status jobs such as barge puller, charcoal burner, or night soil carrier. Many drifted to the cities to make their way by begging, prostitution, or theft. In central and southwestern China, where serious floods had impoverished many farmers, rebellions became endemic. Often joining in revolt were various indigenous peoples, who were largely concentrated in the less fertile lands in the south and in the northern and western borderlands of the empire (see Map 20.2).

The Qing government was not up to controlling its vast empire. The Qing Empire was twice the size of the Ming geographically, but employed about the same number of officials. The government's dependence on working alliances with local elites had led to widespread corruption and shrinking government revenues. As was the case with other empires, the Qing's spectacular rise had ended, and decline had set in.

THE RUSSIAN EMPIRE

From modest beginnings in 1500, Russia expanded rapidly during the next three centuries to create an empire that stretched from eastern Europe across northern Asia and into North America. Russia also became one of the major powers of Europe by 1750, with armies capable of mounting challenges to its Asian and European neighbors.

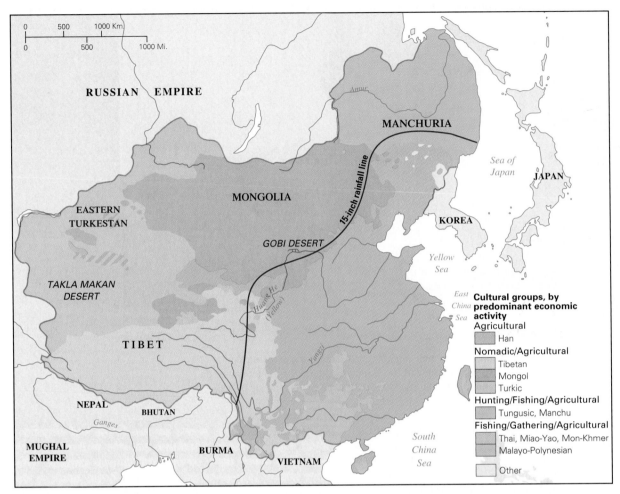

Map 20.2   Climate and Diversity in the Qing Empire   The Qing Empire encompassed different environmental zones, and the climate differences corresponded to population density and cultural divisions. Wetter regions to the east of the 15-inch rainfall line also contained the most densely populated 20 percent of Qing land. The drier, less densely populated 80 percent of the empire was home to the greatest portion of peoples who spoke languages other than Chinese. Many were nomads, fishermen, hunters, and farmers who raised crops other than rice.

The Drive Across Northern Asia

The Russians were a branch of the Slavic peoples of eastern Europe, and most were Orthodox Christians like the Greeks. During the centuries just before 1500, their history had been dominated by Asian rule. The Mongol Khanate of the Golden Horde had ruled the Russians and their neighbors from the 1240s until 1480.

Under the Golden Horde Moscow became the most important Russian city and the center of political power. Moscow lay in the forest that stretched across northern Eurasia, in contrast to the treeless steppe (plains) fa-

vored by Mongol horsemen for pasture. The princes of **Muscovy°**, the territory surrounding the city of Moscow, led the movement against the Golden Horde and ruthlessly annexed the great territories of the neighboring Russian state of Novgorod in 1478.

Once free from Mongol domination, the princes of Moscovy set out on conquests that in time made them masters of the old dominions of the Golden Horde and then of a far greater empire. Prince Ivan IV (r. 1533–1584) pushed the conquests south and east, expanding Rus-

Muscovy (MUSS-koe-vee)

sia's borders far to the east through the conquest of the Khanates of Kazan and Astrakhan and the northern Caucasus region (see Map 20.3).

At the end of the sixteenth century, Russians ruled the largest state in Europe and large territories on the Asian side of the **Ural Mountains** as well. Since 1547 the Russian ruler used the title **tsar°** (from the Roman imperial title "caesar"), the term Russians had used for the rulers of the Mongol Empire. The Russian church promoted the idea of Moscow as the "third Rome," successor to the Roman Empire's second capital, Constantinople, which had fallen to the Ottoman Turks in 1453. But such foreign titles were a thin veneer over a very Russian pattern of expansion.

These claims to greatness were also exaggerated: in 1600 the Russian Empire was poor, backward, and landlocked. Only the northern city of Arkangelsk was connected by water to the rest of the world—when its harbor was not frozen. The independent Crimean peoples to the south were powerful enough to sack Moscow in 1571. Beyond them, the still vigorous Ottoman Empire controlled the shores of the Black Sea, while the Safavid rulers of Iran dominated the trade routes of southern Central Asia. The powerful kingdoms of Sweden and Poland-Lithuania to the west turned back Russian forces trying to gain access to the warmer waters of the Baltic Sea and pummeled them badly.

A path of less resistance lay to the east across **Siberia,** and it had much to recommend it. Many Russians felt more at home in the forested northern part of Siberia than on the open steppes, and the thinly inhabited region teemed with valuable resources. Most prominent of these resources was the soft, dense fur that forest animals grew to survive the long winter cold. Like their counterparts in Canada (see Chapter 17), hardy Russian pioneers in Siberia made a living from animal pelts. The merchants from western Europe and other lands who came to buy these furs in Moscow provided the tsars with revenues and access to European technology.

Early Russian exploration of Siberia was not the work of the state but of the Strogonovs, a wealthy Russian trading family. The small bands of hunting and fishing peoples who inhabited this cold and desolate region had no way of resisting the armed adventurers hired by the Strogonovs. Their troops attacked the only political power in the region, the Khanate of Sibir, and they used their rifles to destroy the khanate in 1582. Taking advantage of rivers to move through the almost impenetrable forests, Russian fur trappers reached the Pacific during the seventeenth century and soon crossed over into

Alaska. Russian political control followed at a much slower pace. In the seventeenth century Siberia was a frontier zone with widely scattered forts, not a province under full control. Native Siberian peoples continued to resist Russian control fiercely, and the Russians had to placate local leaders with gifts and acknowledge their rights and authority. From the early seventeenth century the tsar also used Siberia as a penal colony for criminals and political prisoners.

The trade in furs and forest products helped ease Russian isolation and fund further conquests. The eastward expansion of the Russian state took second place during the seventeenth century to the tsars' efforts to build political and military power and establish control over the more numerous peoples of Siberia and the steppe.

In the 1640s Russian settlers had begun to move into the valley of the Amur River east of Mongolia in order to grow grain. The government's wooden forts aroused the concerns of the Ming about yet another threat on their northern frontier. As seen already, by the time the Qing were in a position to deal with the Russian presence, the worrisome threat of Galdan's Mongol military power had arisen. Equally concerned about the Mongols, the Russians were pleased to work out a frontier agreement with China. The 1689 Treaty of Nerchinsk recognized Russian claims west of Mongolia but required the Russians to withdraw their settlements east. Moreover, the negotiations showed China's recognition of Russia as an important and powerful neighbor.

Russian Society and Politics to 1725

Russian expansion produced far-reaching demographic changes and more gradual changes in the relations of the tsar with the elite classes. A third transformation was in the freedom and mobility of the Russian peasantry.

As the empire expanded, it incorporated people with different languages, religious beliefs, and ethnic identities. The emerging Russian Empire included peoples who spoke Asian languages and who were not Christians. Language differences were not hard to overcome, but religious and other cultural differences often caused tensions, especially when differences were manipulated for political purposes. Orthodox missionaries made great efforts to turn people in Siberia into Christians, in much the same way that Catholic missionaries did in Canada. But among the more populous steppe peoples, Islam eventually replaced Christianity as the dominant religion. More fundamental than language, ethnicity, or religion were the differences in how people made their living. Russians tended to live as

tsar (zahr)

The Russian Empire
- Russia in 1533
- Added by 1598
- Added by 1721
- Added by 1796
- ■ Fort

Map 20.3 The Expansion of Russia, 1500–1800   Sweden and Poland initially blocked Russian expansion in Europe, while the Ottoman Empire blocked the southwest. In the sixteenth century, Russia began to expand east, toward Siberia and the Pacific Ocean. By the end of the rule of Catherine the Great in 1796, Russia encompassed all of northern and northeastern Eurasia.

farmers, hunters, builders, scribes, or merchants, while those newly incorporated into the empire were mostly herders, caravan workers, and soldiers.

As people mixed, individual and group identities could become quite complex. Even among Russian speakers who were members of the Russian Orthodox Church there was wide diversity of identity. The **Cossacks** are a revealing example. The name probably came from a Turkic word for a warrior or mercenary soldier and referred to bands of people living on the steppes between Moscovy and the Caspian and Black Seas. In practice, Cossacks became highly diverse in their origins and beliefs. What mattered was that they belonged to close-knit bands, were superb riders and fighters, and were feared by both the villagers and the legal authorities. Cossacks made temporary allegiances with many rulers but were most loyal to their bands and to whoever was currently paying for their military services.

Many Cossacks were important allies in the expansion of the Russian Empire. They formed the majority of the soldiers and early settlers employed by the Strogonovs in the penetration of Siberia. Most historians believe that Cossacks founded all the major towns of Russian Siberia. They also manned the Russian camps on the Amur River. The Cossacks west of the Urals performed distinctive service for Russia in defending against Swedish and Ottoman incursions, but they also resisted any efforts to undermine their own political autonomy. Those in the rich and populous lands of the Ukraine, for example, rebelled when the tsar agreed to a division of their lands with Poland-Lithuania in 1667.

In the early seventeenth century Swedish and Polish forces briefly occupied Moscow on separate occasions. In the midst of this "Time of Troubles" the old line of Muscovite rulers was finally deposed, and the Russian aristocracy—the boyars°—allowed one of their own, Mikhail Romanov°, to become tsar (r. 1613–1645). The early Romanov rulers saw a close connection between the consolidation of their own authority and successful competition with neighboring powers. They tended to represent conflicts between Slavic Russians and Turkic peoples of Central Asia as being between Christians and "infidels" or between the civilized and the "barbaric." Despite this rhetoric, it is important to understand that these cultural groups were defined less by blood ties than by the way in which they lived.

The political and economic transformations of the Russian Empire had serious repercussions for the peasants who tilled the land in European Russia. As centralized power rose, the freedom of the peasants fell. The

process was longer and more complex than the rise of slavery in the Americas. The Moscovy rulers and early tsars rewarded their loyal nobles with grants of land that included obligations of the local peasants to work for these lords. Law and custom permitted peasants to change masters during a two-week period each year, which encouraged lords to treat their peasants well, but the rising commercialization of agriculture also raised the value of these labor obligations.

The long periods of civil and foreign warfare in the late sixteenth and early seventeenth centuries caused such disruption and economic decline that many peasants fled to the Cossacks or across the Urals to escape. Some who couldn't flee sold themselves into slavery to ensure a steady supply of food. When peace returned, landlords sought to recover these runaway peasants and bind them more firmly to their land. A law change in 1649 completed the transformation of peasants into **serfs** by eliminating the period when they could change masters and removing limitations on the length of the period during which runaways could be forced to return to their masters.

Like slavery, serfdom was a hereditary status, but in theory the serf was tied to a piece of land, not owned by a master. In practice, the difference between serfdom and slavery grew finer as the laws regulating selfdom became stricter. By 1723 all Russian slaves were transformed into serfs. In the Russian census of 1795, serfs made up over half the population of Russia. The serfs were under the control of landowners who made up only 2 percent of Russia's population, similar to the size of the slave-owning class in the Caribbean.

Peter the Great

The greatest of the Romanovs was Tsar **Peter the Great** (r. 1689–1725), who made major changes to reduce Russia's isolation and increase the empire's size and power. Tsar Peter is remembered for his efforts to turn Russia away from its Asian cultural connections and toward what he deemed the civilization of the West. In fact, he accelerated trends under way for some time. By the time he ascended the throne, there were hundreds of foreign merchants in Moscow; western European soldiers had trained a major part of the army in new weapons and techniques; and Italian architects had made an impression on the city's churches and palaces. It was on this substantial base that Peter erected a more rapid transformation of Russia.

Peter matured quickly both physically and mentally. In his youth the government was in the hands of his half-sister Sophia, who was regent on behalf of him and her sickly brother Ivan. Living on an estate near the foreigners' quarter outside Moscow, Peter learned what he could

---

boyar (BOY-ar)
Romanov (ROH-man-off or roh-MAN-off)

of life outside Russia and busied himself with gaining practical skills in blacksmithing, carpentry, shipbuilding, and the arts of war. He organized his own military drill unit among other young men. When Princess Sophia tried to take complete control of the government in 1689, Peter rallied enough support to send her to a monastery, secure the abdication of Ivan, and take charge of Russia. He was still in his teens.

Peter concerned himself with Russia's expansion and modernization. To secure a warm-water port on the Black Sea, he constructed a small but formidable navy that could blockade Ottoman ports. Describing his wars with the Ottoman Empire as a new crusade to liberate Constantinople from the Muslim sultans, Peter also saw himself as the legal protector of Orthodox Christians living under Ottoman rule. Peter's forces had seized the port of Azov in 1696, but the fortress was lost again in 1713, and Russian expansion southward was blocked for the rest of Peter's reign.

In the winter of 1697–1698, after his Black Sea campaign, Peter traveled in disguise across Europe to discover how western European societies were becoming so powerful and wealthy. The young tsar paid special attention to ships and weapons, even working for a time as a ship's carpenter in the Netherlands. With great insight, he perceived that western European success owed as much to trade and toleration as to technology. Trade generated the money to spend on weapons, while toleration attracted talented persons fleeing persecution. Upon his return to Russia, Peter resolved to expand and reform his vast and backward empire.

In the long and costly Great Northern War (1700–1721), his modernized armies broke Swedish control of the Baltic Sea, establishing more direct contacts between Russia and Europe. Peter's victory forced the European powers to recognize Russia as a major power for the first time.

On land captured from Sweden at the eastern end of the Baltic, Peter built St. Petersburg, a new city that was to be his window on the West. In 1712 the city became Russia's capital. To demonstrate Russia's new sophistication, Peter ordered architects to build St. Petersburg's houses and public buildings in the baroque style then fashionable in France.

Peter also pushed the Russian elite to imitate western European fashions. He personally shaved off his noblemen's long beards to conform to Western styles and ordered them to wear Western clothing. To end the traditional seclusion of upper-class Russian women, Peter required officials, officers, and merchants to bring their wives to the social gatherings he organized in the capital. He also directed the nobles to educate their children.

Another of Peter's strategies was to reorganize Rus-

Peter the Great This portrait from his time as a student in Holland in 1697 shows Peter as ruggedly masculine and practical, quite unlike most royal portraits of the day that posed rulers in foppish elegance and haughty majesty. Peter was a popular military leader as well as an autocratic ruler. (Collection, Countess Bobrinskoy/Michael Holford)

sian government along the lines of the powerful German state of Prussia. To break the power of the boyars he sharply reduced their traditional roles in government and the army. The old boyar council of Moscow was replaced by a group of advisers in St. Petersburg whom the tsar appointed. Members of the traditional nobility continued to serve as generals and admirals, but officers in Peter's modern, professional army and navy were promoted according to merit, not birth.

The goal of Peter's westernization strategy was to strengthen the Russian state and increase the power of the tsar. A decree of 1716 proclaimed that the tsar "is not obliged to answer to anyone in the world for his doings, but possesses power and authority over his kingdom and land, to rule them at his will and pleasure as a Christian ruler." Under this expansive definition of his role, Peter brought the Russian Orthodox Church more firmly under state control, built factories and iron and copper foundries to provide munitions and supplies for the military, and increased the burdens of taxes and forced labor on the serfs. Peter was an absolutist ruler of the sort then popular in western Europe, and he had no more intention of improving the conditions of the serfs, on whose labors the production of basic foodstuffs depended, than did the European slave owners of the Americas.

The Fontanka Canal in St. Petersburg in 1753   The Russian capital continued to grow as a commercial and administrative center. As in Amsterdam, canals were the city's major arteries. On the right is a new summer palace built by Peter's successor.   (Engraving, after M. I. Makhaiev, from the official series of 1753, British Museum)

Consolidation of the Empire

Russia's eastward expansion also continued under Peter the Great and his successors. The frontier settlement with China and Qianlong's quashing of Inner Mongolia in 1689 freed Russians to concentrate on the northern Pacific. The Pacific northeast was colonized, and in 1741 an expedition led by Captain Vitus Bering crossed the strait (later named for him) into North America. In 1799 a Russian company of merchants received a monopoly over the Alaskan fur trade, and its agents were soon active along the entire northwestern coast of North America.

Far more important than these immense territories in the cold and thinly populated north were the populous agricultural lands to the west acquired during the reign of Catherine the Great (r. 1762–1796). A successful war with the Ottoman Empire gave Russia control of the rich north shore of the Black Sea by 1783. As a result of three successive partitions of the once powerful kingdom of Poland between 1772 and 1795, Russia's frontiers advanced 600 miles (nearly 1,000 km.) to the west (see Map 20.3). When Catherine died, the Russian Empire extended from Poland in the west to Alaska in the east, from the Barents Sea in the north to the Black Sea in the south.

Catherine also made important additions to Peter's policies of promoting industry and building a canal system to improve trade. Besides furs, the Russians had also become major exporters of gold, iron, and timber. Catherine implemented administrative reforms and showed a special talent for diplomacy. Through her promotion of the ideas of the Enlightenment, she expanded Peter's policies of westernizing the Russian elite.

COMPARATIVE PERSPECTIVES

Looked at separately, the histories of Japan, China, and Russia seem to have relatively little in common. Contacts with each other and with other parts of the world appear far less important than forces within each state. However, when examined comparatively these separate histories reveal similarities and differences that help explain the global dynamics of this period and the larger historical patterns of which it is a part.

Political Comparisons

China and Russia are examples of the phenomenal flourishing of empires in Eurasia between 1500 and 1800. Already a vast empire under the Ming, China doubled in size under the Qing, mostly through westward expansion into less densely populated areas. In expanding from a modestly sized principality into the world's largest land empire, Russia added rich and well-populated lands to the west and south and far larger but less populous lands to the east. Russia and China were land based, just like the Ottoman and Mughal Empires, with the strengths and problems of administrative control and tax collection that size entailed.

Although western Europe is often seen as particularly imperialist in the centuries after 1500, only Spain's empire merits comparison with Russia's in the speed of its growth, its land size, and its presence on three continents. The more typical western European empires of this era, the new seaborne trading empires of the Portuguese, Dutch, French, and English, had much less territory, far tighter administration, and a much more global sweep.

Japan was different. Though nominally headed by an emperor, Japan's size and ethnic homogeneity do not support calling it an empire in the same breath with China and Russia. Tokugawa Japan was similar in size and population to France, the most powerful state of western Europe, but its political system was much more decentralized. Japan's efforts to add colonies on the East Asian mainland had failed.

China had once led the world in military innovation (including the first uses of gunpowder), but the modern "gunpowder revolution" of the fifteenth and sixteenth centuries was centered in the Ottoman Empire and western European states. Although the centuries after 1500 were full of successful military operations, Chinese armies continued to depend on superior numbers and tactics for their success, rather than on new technology. As in the past, infantrymen armed with guns served alongside others armed with bows and arrows, swords, and spears.

The military forces of Japan and Russia underwent more innovative changes than those of China, in part through Western contacts. In the course of its sixteenth-century wars of unification, Japan produced its own gunpowder revolution but thereafter lacked the motivation and the means to stay abreast of the world's most advanced military technology. By the eighteenth century Russia had made greater progress in catching up with its European neighbors, but its armies still relied more on their size than on the sophistication of their weapons.

Naval power provides the greatest military contrast among the three. Eighteenth-century Russia constructed modern fleets of warships in the Baltic and the Black Seas, but neither China nor Japan developed navies commensurate with their size and coastlines. China's defenses against pirates and other sea invaders were left to its maritime provinces, whose small war junks were armed with only a half-dozen cannon. Japan's naval capacity was similarly decentralized. In 1792, when Russian ships exploring the North Pacific turned toward the Japanese coast, the local daimyo used his own forces to chase them away. All Japanese daimyo understood that they would be on their own if foreign incursions increased.

Cultural, Social, and Economic Comparisons

The expansion of China and Russia incorporated not just new lands but also diverse new peoples. Both empires pursued policies that tolerated diversity along with policies to promote cultural assimilation. In contrast, Japan remained more culturally homogeneous, and the government reacted with great intolerance to the growing influence of converts to western Christianity.

Chinese society had long been diverse, and its geographical, occupational, linguistic, and religious differences grew as the Qing expanded (see Map 20.2). China had also long used Confucian models, imperial customs, and a common system of writing to transcend such differences. These techniques were most effective in assimilating elites. It is striking how quickly and thoroughly the Manchu conquerors adopted Chinese imperial ways of thinking and acting as well as of dressing, speaking, and writing.

Kangxi's reign is a notable example of how tolerant the Chinese elite could be of new ideas from the Jesuits and other sources. Yet it is important to note that the Jesuits' success owed much to their portraying themselves as supporters of Confucian values and learning. Although Chinese converts to Catholicism were instrumental in introducing European techniques of crop production and engineering, influential members of China's government were highly suspicious of the loyalties of these converts, persecuted them, and eventually moved to prohibit or severely limit missionary activity.

Russia likewise approached its new peoples with a mixture of pragmatic tolerance and a propensity for seeing Russian ways and beliefs as superior. Religion was a particular sore point. With the support of the tsars, Russian Orthodox missionaries encouraged conversion of Siberian peoples. In the new lands of Eastern Europe, Orthodoxy was a common bond for some new subjects, but the Roman Catholic Poles incorporated in the late 1700s would soon suffer greatly for their divergent beliefs and practices. The Russian language was strongly promoted. Russia was also notable for its absorption of new ideas and styles from western Europe, especially under the leadership of its eighteenth-century rulers, although even among the elite, these influences often overlay Russian cultural traditions in a very superficial way

Social structures in China and Russia were as hierarchical and oppressive as in the Islamic states of southern Asia, and in the case of Russia have invited comparisons with the slave plantation societies of the Americas. Rulers were nearly absolute in their powers in theory, though more limited in practice by the size of their empires and by layers of bureaucracy and corruption.

Forced labor remained common in the Russian and Chinese Empires. Serfdom grew more brutal and widespread in Russia in the seventeenth and eighteenth centuries, although the expansion of the frontier eastward across Siberia also opened an escape route for many peasants and serfs. Some Chinese peasants also improved their lot by moving to new territories, but population growth increased overall misery in the eighteenth century. China was also notable for the size of its popular insurrections, especially the one that toppled the Ming.

In striking contrast to the rising importance of commercial interests in the West, private merchants in China and Japan occupied more precarious positions. Confucian thought ranked merchants below peasants in their contributions to society. In Japan a line between maritime traders and pirates would be very difficult to draw, and Chinese sea trade was not much different. Governments conducted diplomatic and strategic missions but had no interest in encouraging overseas voyages or colonies. Instead both Japan and China moved to restrict overseas trade. In the end, commercial contacts were far more important to Europe than to East Asia.

CONCLUSION

As the world has grown more interconnected, it has become increasingly difficult to sort out the degree to which major historical changes were due to forces within a society or to outside forces acting upon it. The histories of Japan, China, and Russia between 1500 and 1800 reveal how internal forces operated separately from external ones and the degree to which they were intertwined.

The formation of the Tokugawa in Japan is a clear example of a society changing from within. The decisions

of government to suppress the Christianity that some Japanese had adopted from European missionaries and to severely curtail commercial and intellectual contacts with distant Europe illustrate how readily even the smallest of the three states could control its dealings with outsiders.

China's history illustrates a more complex interplay of internal and external forces. In the world's most populous state, the already faltering Ming dynasty was greatly weakened by Hideyoshi's Japanese invasion through Korea, overthrown by Li Zicheng's rebels from within, and replaced by the conquering armies of the Manchu from across the northern frontier. The Qing's settlement of the Amur frontier with Russia illustrates how diplomacy and compromise could serve mutual interests. Finally, the Chinese added new European customers to already extensive internal and external markets and developed both positive and problematic cultural relations with the Jesuits and some other Europeans. From a Chinese perspective, European contacts could be useful but were neither essential nor of great importance.

The internal and external factors in Russia's history are the hardest to sort out. Especially problematic is assessing the rising importance of the West in light of Russia's growing trade in that direction, Russia's emergence as a European Great Power, and the stated policies of both Peter the Great and Catherine the Great to westernize their people. Clearly, Western influences were very important, but just as clearly their importance can easily be exaggerated. The impetus for Muscovy's expansion came out of its own history and domination by the Mongols. Trade with western Europe was not the center of the Russian economy. Tsar Peter was primarily interested in imitating Western technology, not in the full range of Western culture. The Russian church was quite hostile to the Catholics and Protestants to their west, whom it regarded as heretics. Peter the Great banned the Jesuits from Russia, considering them a subversive and backward influence.

Looking at each country separately and from within, the influence of western Europeans seems clearly inferior to a host of internal and regional influences. Yet when one looks at what happened in Japan, China, and Russia in the decades after 1800, it is hard to avoid the conclusion that their relationship with the West was a common factor that, when combined with unresolved internal problems, would have a tremendous impact on the course of their history. Qianlong might tell Macartney and the British that he had no use for expanded contacts, but the sentiment was not mutual. As the next part details, after the increasingly powerful Western societies got over dealing with their own internal problems, they would be back, and they would be impossible to dismiss or resist.

■ Key Terms

Manchu	Macartney Mission
daimyo	Muscovy
samurai	Ural Mountains
Tokugawa Shogunate	tsar
Ming Empire	Siberia
Qing Empire	Cossacks
Kangxi	serfs
Amur River	Peter the Great

■ Suggested Reading

A fascinating place to begin is with John E. Wills, Jr., *1688: A Global History* (2001), Part III, "Three Worlds Apart: Russia, China, and Japan."

On Japan in this period see Andrew Gordon, *A Modern History of Japan: From Tokugawa Times to the Present* (2003); *The Cambridge History of Japan*, vol. 4: *Early Modern Japan,* ed. John Whitney Hall (1991); Chie Nakane and Shinzaburo Oishi, *Tokugawa Japan: The Social and Economic Antecedents of Modern Japan,* trans. Conrad Totman (1990); and Tessa Morris-Suzuki, *The Technological Transformation of Japan from the Seventeenth to the Twenty-First Century* (1994). Mary Elizabeth Berry, *Hideyoshi* (1982), is an account of the reunification of Japan at the end of the sixteenth century and the invasion of Korea. See also Michael Cooper, ed., *They Came to Japan: An Anthology of European Reports on Japan, 1543–1640* (1965).

For China during the transition from the Ming to Qing periods, see Jonathan D. Spence, *The Search for Modern China* (1990); James W. Tong, *Disorder Under Heaven: Collective Violence in the Ming Dynasty* (1991); Frederic Wakeman, *The Great Enterprise* (1985); and Lynn Struve, *Voices from the Ming-Qing Cataclysm: In Tiger's Jaws* (1993). The latest work on the late Ming is summarized in *The Cambridge History of China*, vol. 8, *The Ming Dynasty, 1368–1644, Part 2* (1998). On the history of the Manchu and of the Qing Empire see Evelyn Sakakida Rawski, *The Last Emperors* (1999), and Pamela Kyle Crossley, *The Manchus* (1997).

On Chinese society generally in this period, see two classic (though slightly dated) works by Ping-ti Ho, *The Ladder of Success in Imperial China: Aspects of Social Mobility, 1368–1911* (1962), and *Studies in the Population of China 1368–1953* (1959); and see the general study by Susan Naquin and Evelyn S. Rawski, *Chinese Society in the Eighteenth Century* (1987). On the two greatest of the Qing emperors and their times, see Jonathan D. Spence, *Emperor of China; Self Portrait of K'ang Hsi, 1654–1722* (1974). For a more scholarly treatment see Lawrence D. Kessler, *K'ang-hsi and the Consolidation of Ch'ing Rule, 1661–1684* (1976); Jonathan D. Spence, *Ts'ao Yin and the K'ang-hsi Emperor: Bondservant and Master* (1966); and Harold Kahn, *Monarchy in the Emperor's Eyes: Image and Reality in the Ch'ien-lung Reign* (1971).

On the Qing trade systems see John E. Wills, *Embassies and Illusions: Dutch and Portuguese Envoys to K'ang-hsi, 1666–1687* (1984), and Craig Clunas, *Chinese Export Art and Design* (1987).

There is a great deal published on the Macartney mission, much of it originating in the diaries and memoirs of the participants. See the exhaustively detailed Alain Peyrefitte, *The Immobile Empire,* trans. Jon Rothschild (1992). For a more theoretical discussion see James L. Hevia, *Cherishing Men from Afar: Qing Guest Ritual and the Macartney Embassy of 1793* (1995).

On early modern Russian history, see Robert O. Crummey, *Aristocrats and Servitors: The Boyar Elite in Russia, 1613–1689* (1983), and Andreas Kappeler, *The Russian Empire: A Multiethnic History* (2001). Western perceptions of Russia are examined in Marshall T. Poe, *"A People Born to Slavery": Russia in Early Modern European Ethnography* (2000), and Lloyd E. Berry and Robert O. Crummey, ed., *Rude and Barbarous Kingdom: Russia in the Accounts of Sixteenth-Century English Voyagers* (1968). Among the best-known recent books on Tsar Peter are Matthew Smith Anderson, *Peter the Great,* 2d ed. (1995); Robert K. Massie, *Peter the Great: His Life and World* (1980); and Lindsey Hughes, *Russia in the Age of Peter the Great: 1682–1725* (1998). For Russian naval development and Russian influence in the Pacific and in America, see Glynn Barratt, *Russia in Pacific Waters, 1715–1825: A Survey of the Origins of Russia's Naval Presence in the North and South Pacific* (1981), and Howard I. Kushner, *Conflict on the Northwest Coast: American-Russian Rivalry in the Pacific Northwest, 1790–1867* (1975).

For Jesuits in East Asia in the sixteenth and seventeenth centuries, see Michael Cooper, S.J., *Rodrigues the Interpreter: An Early Jesuit in Japan and China* (1974); David E. Mungello, *Curious Land: Jesuit Accommodation and the Origins of Sinology* (1985); and Jonathan D. Spence, *The Memory Palace of Matteo Ricci* (1984). Still useful are C. R. Boxer, *The Christian Century in Japan, 1549–1650* (1951), and Cornelius Wessels, *Early Jesuit Travellers in Central Asia, 1603–1721* (1924). On European images of and interactions with China connected to the Jesuits, see the relevant portions of Jonathan D. Spence, *The Chan's Great Continent: China in Western Minds* (1998); Joanna Waley-Cohen, *The Sextants of Beijing: Global Currents in Chinese History* (1999); and David E. Mungello, *The Great Encounter of China and the West, 1500–1800* (1999).

On the East India companies see John E. Wills, *Pepper, Guns, and Parleys: The Dutch East India Company and China, 1662–1681* (1974); Dianne Lewis, *Jan Compagnie in the Straits of Malacca, 1641–1795* (1995); and John Keay, *The Honourable Company: A History of the English East India Company* (1991). On the development of global commerce in tea, coffee, and cocoa, see the relevant chapters in Roy Porter and Mikulås Teich, *Drugs and Narcotics in History* (1995).

■ Notes

1. Adapted from Jonathan D. Spence, *The Search for Modern China* (New York: W. W. Norton, 1990), 21–25.
2. Adapted from G. V. Melikhov, "Manzhou Penetration into the Basin of the Upper Amur in the 1680s," in S. L. Tikhvinshii, ed., *Manzhou Rule in China* (Moscow: Progress Publishers, 1983).

Document-Based Question
Cultural Interaction in Northern Eurasia, 1500–1800

Using the following documents, analyze the modes of cultural interaction in Northern Eurasia from 1500 to 1800. Consider trade, diplomacy, intellectual activity, and conquest as part of your response.

DOCUMENT 1
Russian Ambassadors to Holland Display Their Furs, 1576 (photo, p. 510)

DOCUMENT 2
East Asian Porcelain (Environment and Technology, p. 514)

DOCUMENT 3
Map 20.1 The Qing Empire, 1644–1783 (p. 519)

DOCUMENT 4
Gendered Violence: The Yangzhou Massacre (Diversity and Dominance, pp. 520–521)

DOCUMENT 5
From the Jesuit Library at Beijing (photo, p. 523)

DOCUMENT 6
East Meets West (photo, p. 525)

DOCUMENT 7
Map 20.3 The Expansion of Russia, 1500–1800 (p. 528)

DOCUMENT 8
The Fontanka Canal in St. Petersburg in 1753 (photo, p. 531)

What accounts for the different treatment of men and women evident in Document 4? What additional types of documents would help you understand the modes of cultural interaction in Northern Eurasia from 1500 to 1800?

Revolutions Reshape the World, 1750–1870

Between 1750 and 1870, nearly every part of the world experienced dramatic political, economic, and social change. The beginnings of industrialization, the American and French Revolutions, and the revolutions for independence in Latin America transformed political and economic life in Europe and the Americas. The most powerful nations challenged existing borders and ethnic boundaries. European nations expanded into Africa, Asia, and the Middle East while Russia and the United States acquired vast new territories.

The American, French, and Latin American revolutions created new political institutions and unleashed the forces of nationalism and social reform. The Industrial Revolution introduced new technologies and patterns of work that made industrial societies wealthier, more fluid socially, and militarily more powerful. Western intellectual life became more secular as the practical benefits of science and technology became evident. Reformers led successful efforts to abolish the Atlantic slave trade and, later, slavery itself in the Western Hemisphere. Efforts to expand voting rights and improve the status of women also gained support in Europe and the Americas.

European empires in the Western Hemisphere were largely dismantled by 1825. But the Industrial Revolution led to a new wave of economic and imperial expansion. France conquered the North African state of Algeria, while Great Britain expanded its colonial rule in India and established new colonies in Australia and New Zealand. Of these, India alone had a larger population than that of all the colonies Europe had lost in the Americas.

Throughout Africa, European economic influence greatly expanded, deepening the region's connection to the Atlantic economy and generating new political forces. Some African states were invigorated by this era of intensified cultural exchange, creating new institutions and developing new products for export. The Ottoman Empire and the Qing Empire were also deeply influenced by Western expansionism. Both empires met this challenge by implementing reform programs that preserved traditional structures while adopting elements of Western technology and organization. The Ottoman court introduced reforms in education, the military, and law and created the first constitution in an Islamic state. The Qing Empire survived the period of European expansion, but a series of military defeats and a prolonged civil war severely weakened the authority of the central government. Russia lagged behind Western Europe in transforming its economy and political institutions, but military weakness and internal reform pressures led to modernization efforts, including the abolition of serfdom.

The economic, political, and social revolutions that began in the mid-eighteenth century shook the foundations of European culture and led to the expansion of Western power around the globe. Some of the nations of Asia, Africa, and Latin America resisted foreign intrusions by reforming and strengthening their own institutions, forms of production, and military technologies. Others pushed for more radical change, adopting Western commercial policies, industrial technologies, and government institutions. But after 1870, all these states would face even more aggressive Western imperialism, which few of them were able to resist.

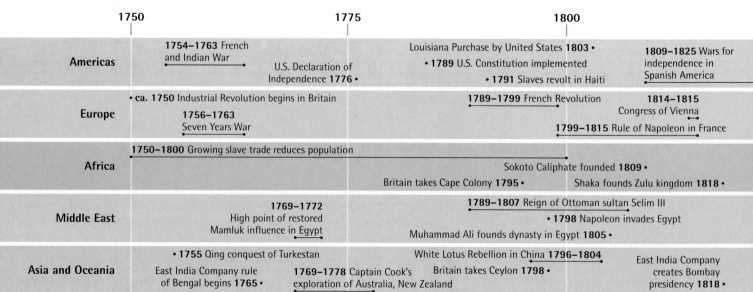

	1750	1775	1800	
Americas	1754–1763 French and Indian War	U.S. Declaration of Independence **1776** •	Louisiana Purchase by United States **1803** • • **1789** U.S. Constitution implemented • **1791** Slaves revolt in Haiti	**1809–1825** Wars for independence in Spanish America
Europe	• **ca. 1750** Industrial Revolution begins in Britain **1756–1763** Seven Years War		**1789–1799** French Revolution **1799–1815** Rule of Napoleon in France	**1814–1815** Congress of Vienna
Africa	**1750–1800** Growing slave trade reduces population	Britain takes Cape Colony **1795** •	Sokoto Caliphate founded **1809** • Shaka founds Zulu kingdom **1818** •	
Middle East	**1769–1772** High point of restored Mamluk influence in Egypt		**1789–1807** Reign of Ottoman sultan Selim III • **1798** Napoleon invades Egypt Muhammad Ali founds dynasty in Egypt **1805** •	
Asia and Oceania	• **1755** Qing conquest of Turkestan East India Company rule of Bengal begins **1765** •	**1769–1778** Captain Cook's exploration of Australia, New Zealand	White Lotus Rebellion in China **1796–1804** Britain takes Ceylon **1798** •	East India Company creates Bombay presidency **1818** •

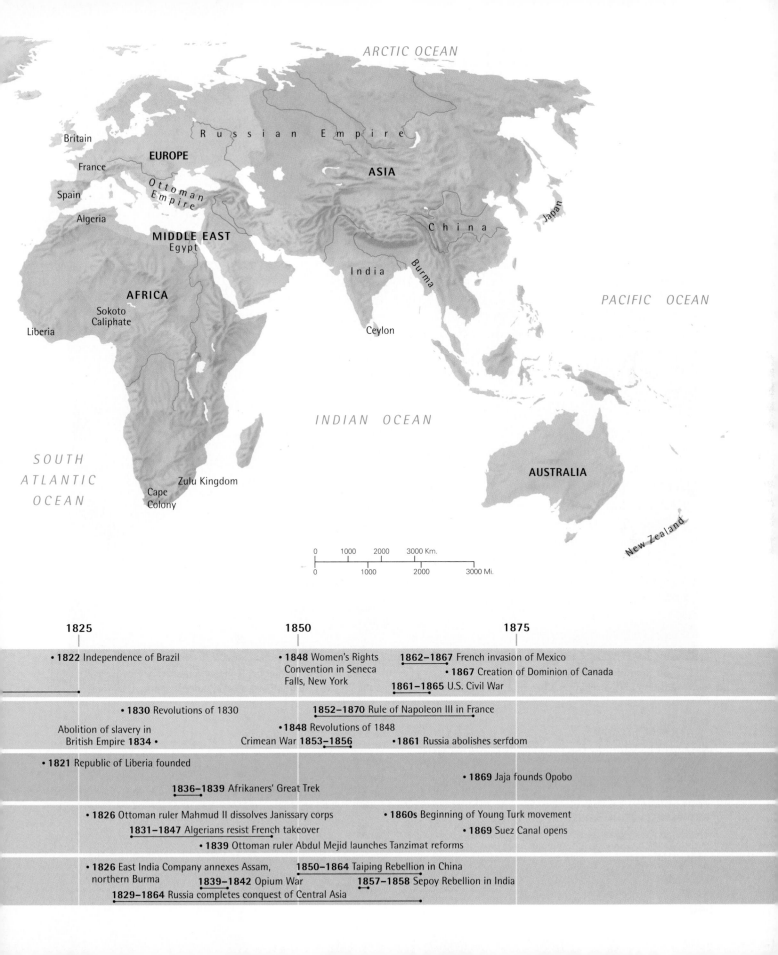

ARCTIC OCEAN

Britain

EUROPE

France

R u s s i a n   E m p i r e

ASIA

Spain

Ottoman
Empire

Algeria

MIDDLE EAST

Egypt

C h i n a

Japan

AFRICA

I n d i a

Burma

PACIFIC   OCEAN

Sokoto
Caliphate

Liberia

Ceylon

INDIAN OCEAN

SOUTH
ATLANTIC
OCEAN

Zulu Kingdom

AUSTRALIA

Cape
Colony

New Zealand

| 0 | 1000 | 2000 | 3000 Km. |
| 0 | 1000 | 2000 | 3000 Mi. |

1825   **1850**   **1875**

• **1822** Independence of Brazil

• **1848** Women's Rights
Convention in Seneca
Falls, New York

1862–1867 French invasion of Mexico

• **1867** Creation of Dominion of Canada

1861–1865 U.S. Civil War

• **1830** Revolutions of 1830

1852–1870 Rule of Napoleon III in France

Abolition of slavery in
British Empire **1834** •

• **1848** Revolutions of 1848

Crimean War **1853–1856**

• **1861** Russia abolishes serfdom

• **1821** Republic of Liberia founded

• **1869** Jaja founds Opobo

1836–1839 Afrikaners' Great Trek

• **1826** Ottoman ruler Mahmud II dissolves Janissary corps

• **1860s** Beginning of Young Turk movement

1831–1847 Algerians resist French takeover

• **1869** Suez Canal opens

• **1839** Ottoman ruler Abdul Mejid launches Tanzimat reforms

• **1826** East India Company annexes Assam,
northern Burma

1850–1864 Taiping Rebellion in China

1839–1842 Opium War

1857–1858 Sepoy Rebellion in India

1829–1864 Russia completes conquest of Central Asia

21 Revolutionary Changes in the Atlantic World, 1750–1850

Burning of Cap Français, St. Domingue in 1793   In 1791, the slaves of St. Domingue, France's richest colony, began a rebellion that, after years of struggle, ended slavery and created the Western Hemisphere's second independent nation, Haiti.

CHAPTER OUTLINE

Prelude to Revolution: The Eighteenth-Century Crisis

The American Revolution, 1775–1800

The French Revolution, 1789–1815

Revolution Spreads, Conservatives Respond, 1789–1850

ENVIRONMENT AND TECHNOLOGY: The Pencil

DIVERSITY AND DOMINANCE: Robespierre and Wollstonecraft Defend and Explain the Terror

On the evening of August 14, 1791, more than two hundred slaves and black freedmen met in secret in the plantation district of northern Saint Domingue° (present-day Haiti) to set the date for an armed uprising against local slave owners. Although the delegates agreed to delay the attack for a week, violence began almost immediately. During the following decade, slavery was abolished; military forces from Britain and France were defeated; and Haiti achieved independence.

The meeting was provoked by news and rumors about revolutionary events in France that had spread through the island's slave community. Events in France had also divided the island's white population into competing camps of royalists (supporters of France's King Louis XVI) and republicans (who sought an end to monarchy). The free mixed-race population initially gained some political rights from the French Assembly but was then forced to rebel when the local slave-owning elite reacted violently.

A black freedman named François Dominique Toussaint eventually became leader of the insurrection. He proved to be one of the most remarkable representatives of the revolutionary era, later taking the name Toussaint L'Ouverture°. He organized the rebels into a potent military force, negotiated with the island's royalist and republican factions and with representatives of Great Britain and France, and wrote his nation's first constitution. Commonly portrayed as a fiend by slave owners throughout the Western Hemisphere, to the slaves Toussaint became a towering symbol of resistance to oppression.

The Haitian slave rebellion was an important episode in the long and painful political and cultural transformation of the modern Western world. Economic expansion and the growth of trade were creating unprecedented wealth. The first stage of the Industrial Revolution (see Chapter 22) increased manufacturing productivity and led to greater global interdependence, new patterns of consumerism, and altered social structures. At the same time, intellectuals were questioning the traditional place of monarchy and religion in society. An increasingly powerful class of merchants, professionals, and manufacturers created by the emerging economy provided an audience for these new intellectual currents and began to press for a larger political role.

This revolutionary era turned the Western world "upside down." The *ancien régime*°, the French term for Europe's old order, rested on medieval principles: politics dominated by powerful monarchs, intellectual and cultural life dominated by religion, and economics dominated by a hereditary agricultural elite. In the West's new order, politics was opened to vastly greater participation; science and secular inquiry took the place of religion in intellectual life; and economies were increasingly opened to competition.

This radical transformation did not take place without false starts and temporary setbacks. Imperial powers resisted the loss of colonies; monarchs and nobles struggled to retain their ancient privileges; and the church fought against the claims of science. Revolutionary steps forward were often matched by reactionary steps backward. The liberal and nationalist ideals of the eighteenth-century revolutionary movements were only imperfectly realized in Europe and the Americas in the nineteenth century. Despite setbacks, belief in national self-determination and universal suffrage and a passion for social justice continued to animate reformers into the twentieth century.

As you read this chapter, ask yourself the following questions:

- How did imperial wars among European powers provoke revolution?

- In what ways were the revolutions, expanded literacy, and new political ideas linked?

- How did revolution in one country help incite revolution elsewhere?

- Why were the revolutions in France and Haiti more violent than the American Revolution?

Saint Domingue (san doe-MANG) **Toussaint L'Ouverture** (too-SAN loo-ver-CHORE)

ancien régime (ahn-see-EN ray-ZHEEM)

PRELUDE TO REVOLUTION: THE EIGHTEENTH-CENTURY CRISIS

In large measure, the cost of wars fought among Europe's major powers over colonies and trade precipitated the revolutionary era that began in 1775 with the American Revolution. Britain, France, and Spain were the central actors in these global struggles, but other imperial powers were affected as well. Unpopular and costly wars had been fought earlier and paid for with new taxes. But changes in the Western intellectual and political environments led to a much more critical response. Any effort to extend the power of a monarch or impose new taxes now raised questions about the rights of individuals and the authority of political institutions.

Colonial Wars and Fiscal Crises

The rivalry among European powers intensified in the early 1600s when the newly independent Netherlands began an assault on the American and Asian colonies of Spain and Portugal. The Dutch attacked Spanish treasure fleets in the Caribbean and Pacific and seized parts of Portugal's colonial empire in Brazil and Angola. Europe's other emerging sea power, Great Britain, also attacked Spanish fleets and seaports in the Americas. By the end of the seventeenth century expanding British sea power had checked Dutch commercial and colonial ambitions and ended the Dutch monopoly of the African slave trade.

As Dutch power ebbed, Britain and France began a long struggle for political preeminence in western Europe and for territory and trade outlets in the Americas and Asia. Both the geographic scale and the expense of this conflict expanded during the eighteenth century. Nearly all of Europe's great powers were engaged in the War of the Spanish Succession (1701–1714). In 1739 a war between Britain and Spain over smuggling in the Americas quickly broadened into a generalized European conflict, the War of the Austrian Succession (1740–1748). Conflict between French and English settlers in North America then helped ignite a long war that altered the colonial balance of power. War began along the American frontier between French and British forces and their Amerindian allies. Known as the French and Indian War, this conflict helped lead to a wider struggle, the Seven Years War (1756–1763). British victory led to undisputed control of North America east of the Mississippi River while also forcing France to surrender most of its holdings in India.

The enormous costs of these conflicts distinguished them from earlier wars. Traditional taxes collected in traditional ways no longer covered the obligations of governments. For example, at the end of the Seven Years War in 1763, Britain's war debt reached £137 million. Britain's total budget before the war had averaged only £8 million. With the legacy of war debt, Britain's interest payments alone came to exceed £5 million. Even as European economies expanded because of increased trade and the early stages of the Industrial Revolution, fiscal crises overtook one European government after another. In an intellectual environment transformed by the Enlightenment, the need for new revenues provoked debate and confrontation within a vastly expanded and more critical public.

The Enlightenment and the Old Order

The complex and diverse intellectual movement called the **Enlightenment** applied the methods and questions of the Scientific Revolution of the seventeenth century to the study of human society. Dazzled by Copernicus's ability to explain the structure of the solar system and Newton's representation of the law of gravity, European intellectuals began to apply the logical tools of scientific inquiry to other questions. Some labored to systematize knowledge or organize reference materials. For example, Carolus Linnaeus° (a Swedish botanist known by the Latin form of his name) sought to categorize all living organisms, and Samuel Johnson published a comprehensive English dictionary with over forty thousand definitions. In France Denis Diderot° worked with other Enlightenment thinkers to create a compendium of human knowledge, the thirty-five-volume *Encyclopédie*.

Other thinkers pursued lines of inquiry that challenged long-established religious and political institutions. Some argued that if scientists could understand the laws of nature, then surely similar forms of disciplined investigation might reveal laws of human nature. Others wondered whether society and government might be better regulated and more productive if guided by science rather than by hereditary rulers and the church. These new perspectives and the intellectual optimism that fed them were to help guide the revolutionary movements of the late eighteenth century.

The English political philosopher John Locke (1632–1704) argued in 1690 that governments were created to

---

Carolus Linnaeus (kar-ROLL-uhs lin-NEE-uhs)   **Denis Diderot** (duh-nee DEE-duh-roe)

C H R O N O L O G Y

	The Americas	Europe
1750		
	1754–1763 French and Indian War	**1756–1763** Seven Years War
	1770 Boston Massacre	
1775	**1776** American Declaration of Independence	
	1778 United States alliance with France	**1778** Death of Voltaire and Rousseau
	1781 British surrender at Yorktown	
	1783 Treaty of Paris ends American Revolution	
		1789 Storming of Bastille begins French Revolution; Declaration of Rights of Man and Citizen in France
	1791 Slaves revolt in Saint Domingue (Haiti)	**1793–1794** Reign of Terror in France
	1798 Toussaint L'Ouverture defeats British in Haiti	**1795–1799** The Directory rules France
1800		**1799** Napoleon overthrows the Directory
	1804 Haitians defeat French invasion and declare independence	**1804** Napoleon crowns himself emperor
		1814 Napoleon abdicates; Congress of Vienna opens
		1815 Napoleon defeated at Waterloo
		1830 Greece gains independence; revolution in France overthrows Charles X
		1848 Revolutions in France, Austria, Germany, Hungary, and Italy

protect life, liberty, and property and that the people had a right to rebel when a monarch violated these natural rights. Locke's closely reasoned theory began with the assumption that individual rights were the foundation of civil government. In *The Social Contract*, published in 1762, the French-Swiss intellectual Jean-Jacques Rousseau° (1712–1778) asserted that the will of the people was sacred and that the legitimacy of the monarch depended on the consent of the people. Although both men believed that government rested on the will of the people rather than on divine will, Locke emphasized the importance of individual rights, and Rousseau envisioned the people acting collectively because of their shared historical experience.

All Enlightenment thinkers were not radicals like Rousseau. There was never a uniform program for political and social reform, and the era's intellectuals often disagreed about principles and objectives. The Enlightenment is commonly associated with hostility toward religion and monarchy, but few European intellectuals openly expressed republican or atheist sentiments. The church was most commonly attacked when it attempted to censor ideas or ban books. Critics of monarchial au-

thority were as likely to point out violations of ancient custom as to suggest democratic alternatives. Even Voltaire, one of the Enlightenment's most critical intellects and great celebrities, believed that Europe's monarchs were likely agents of political and economic reform and even wrote favorably of China's Qing° emperors.

Indeed, sympathetic members of the nobility and reforming European monarchs such as Charles III of Spain (r. 1759–1788), Catherine the Great of Russia (r. 1762–1796), Joseph II of Austria (r. 1780–1790), and Frederick the Great of Prussia (r. 1740–1786) actively sponsored and promoted the dissemination of new ideas, providing patronage for many intellectuals. They recognized that elements of the Enlightenment critique of the ancien régime buttressed their own efforts to expand royal authority at the expense of religious institutions, the nobility, and regional autonomy. Goals such as the development of national bureaucracies staffed by civil servants selected on merit, the creation of national legal systems, and the modernization of tax systems united many of Europe's monarchs and intellectuals. Monarchs also understood that the era's passion for science and technology held the potential of fattening

---

Jean-Jacques Rousseau (zhah-zhock roo-SOE)

Qing (ching)

The Pencil

From early times Europeans had used sharp points, lead, and other implements to sketch, make marks, and write brief notes. At the end of the seventeenth century a source of high-quality graphite was discovered at Borrowdale in northwestern England. Borrowdale graphite gained acceptance among artists, artisans, and merchants. At first, pure graphite was simply wrapped in string. By the eighteenth century, pieces of graphite were being encased in wooden sheaths and resembled modern pencils. Widespread use of this useful tool was retarded by the limited supply of high-quality graphite from the English mines.

The English crown periodically closed the Borrowdale mines or restricted production to keep prices high and maintain adequate supplies for future needs. As a result, artisans in other European nations developed alternatives that used lower-quality graphite or, most commonly, graphite mixed with sulfur and glues.

The major breakthrough occurred in 1793 in France when war with England ruptured trade links. The government of revolutionary France responded to the shortage of graphite by assigning a thirty-nine-year-old scientist, Nicolas-Jacques Conté, to find an alternative. Conté had earlier promoted the military use of balloons and conducted experiments with hydrogen. He had also used graphite alloys in the development of crucibles for melting metal.

Within a short period, Conté produced a graphite that is the basis for most lead pencils today. He mixed finely ground graphite with potter's clay and water. The resulting paste was dried in a long mold, sealed in a ceramic box, and fired in an oven. The graphite strips were then placed in wooden cases. Although some believed the Conté pencils were inferior to the pencils made from Borrowdale graphite, Conté produced

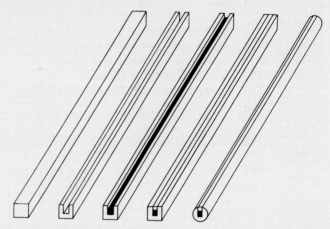

Pencils Wartime necessity led to invention of the modern pencil in France. (Drawing by Fred Avent for Henry Petroski. Reproduced by permission)

a very serviceable pencil that could be produced in uniform quality and unlimited amounts.

Summarizing the achievement of Conté in *The Pencil*, Henry Petroski wrote: "The laboratory is really the modern workshop. And modern engineering results when the scientific method is united with experience with the tools and products of craftsmen. . . . Modern engineering, in spirit if not in name, would come to play a more and more active role in turning the craft tradition into modern technology, with its base of research and development."

Source: This discussion depends on Henry Petroski, *The Pencil: A History of Design and Circumstance* (New York: Knopf, 1990); the quotation is from pp. 50–78. Drawing by Fred Avent for Henry Petroski. Reproduced by permission.

national treasuries and improving economic performance (see Environment and Technology: The Pencil). Periodicals disseminating new technologies often gained the patronage of these reforming monarchs.

Though willing to embrace reform proposals when they served royal interests, Europe's monarchs moved quickly to suppress or ban radical ideas that promoted republicanism or directly attacked religion. However, too many channels of communication were open to per-

mit a thoroughgoing suppression of ideas. In fact, censorship tended to enhance intellectual reputations, and persecuted intellectuals generally found patronage in the courts of foreign rivals.

Many of the major intellectuals of the Enlightenment maintained extensive correspondence with each other as well as with political leaders. This communication led to numerous firsthand contacts among the intellectuals of different nations and helped create a coherent assault on what was typically called ignorance—beliefs and values associated with the ancien régime. Rousseau, for example, briefly sought refuge in Britain, where the Scottish philosopher David Hume befriended him. Similarly, Voltaire sought patronage and protection in England and later in Prussia.

Women were instrumental in the dissemination of the new ideas. In England educated middle-class women purchased and discussed the books and pamphlets of the era. Some were important contributors to intellectual life as writers and commentators, raising by example and in argument the issue of the rights of women. In Paris wealthy women made their homes centers of debate, intellectual speculation, and free inquiry. Their salons brought together philosophers, social critics, artists, and members of the aristocracy and commercial elite. Unlike their contemporaries in England, the women of the Parisian salons used their social standing more to direct the conversations of men than to give vent to their own opinions.

The intellectual ferment of the era deeply influenced the expanding middle class in Europe and the Western Hemisphere. Members of this class were eager consumers of books and the inexpensive newspapers and journals that were widely available. This broadening of the intellectual audience overwhelmed traditional institutions of censorship. Scientific discoveries, new technologies, and controversial work on human nature and politics also were discussed in the thousands of coffeehouses and teashops opening in major cities and market towns.

Many European intellectuals were interested in the Americas. Some Europeans continued to dismiss the New World as barbaric and inferior, but others used idealized accounts of the New World to support their critiques of European society. These thinkers looked to Britain's North American colonies for confirmation of their belief that human nature unconstrained by the corrupted practices of Europe's old order would quickly produce material abundance and social justice. More than any other American, the writer and inventor **Benjamin Franklin** came to symbolize both the natural genius and the vast potential of America.

Born in 1706 in Boston, the young Franklin was apprenticed to his older brother, a printer. At seventeen he ran away to Philadelphia, where he succeeded as a printer and publisher and was best known for his *Poor Richard's Almanac*. By age forty-two he was a wealthy man. He retired from active business to pursue writing, science, and public affairs. In Philadelphia Franklin was instrumental in the creation of the organizations that later became the Philadelphia Free Library, the Amer-

ican Philosophical Society, and the University of Pennsylvania.

Franklin's contributions were both practical and theoretical. He was the inventor of bifocal glasses, the lightning rod, and an efficient wood-burning stove. In 1751 he published a scientific work, *Experiments and Observations on Electricity*, that established his intellectual reputation in Europe. Intellectuals heralded the book as proof that the simple and unsophisticated world of America was a particularly hospitable environment for genius.

Franklin was also an important political figure. He served Pennsylvania as a delegate to the Albany (New York) Congress in 1754, which sought to coordinate colonial defense against attacks by the French and their Amerindian allies. Later he was a Pennsylvania delegate to the Continental Congress that issued the Declaration of Independence in 1776. His service in England as colonial lobbyist and later as the Continental Congress's ambassador to Paris allowed him to cultivate his European reputation. Franklin's wide achievement, witty conversation, and careful self-promotion make him a symbol of the era. In him the Enlightenment's most radical project, the freeing of human potential from the inhibitions of inherited privilege, found its most agreeable confirmation.

As Franklin's career demonstrates, the Western Hemisphere shared in the debates of Europe. New ideas penetrated the curricula of many colonial universities and appeared in periodicals and books published in the New World. As scientific method was applied to economic and political questions, colonial writers, scholars, and artists on both sides of the Atlantic were drawn into a debate that eventually was to lead to the rejection of colonialism itself. This radicalization of the colonial intellectual community was provoked by the European monarchies' efforts to reform colonial policies. As European authorities swept away colonial institutions and long-established political practices without consultation, colonial residents had to acknowledge that their status as colonies meant perpetual subordination to European rulers. Among people compelled to recognize this structural dependence and inferiority, the idea that government authority ultimately rested on the consent of the governed was potentially explosive.

In Europe and the colonies, many intellectuals resisted the Enlightenment, seeing it as a dangerous assault on the authority of the church and monarchy. This Counter Enlightenment was most influential in France and other Catholic nations. Its adherents argued the importance of faith to human happiness and social well-being. They also emphasized duty and obligation to the community of believers in opposition to the concern for

Beer Street (1751) This engraving by William Hogarth shows an idealized London street scene where beer drinking is associated with manly strength, good humor, and prosperity. The self-satisfied corpulent figure in the left foreground has been reading a copy of the king's speech to Parliament. We can imagine him offering a running commentary to his drinking companions as he reads. (The Art Archive)

individual rights and individual fulfillment common in the works of the Enlightenment. Most importantly for the politics of the era, they rejected their enemies' enthusiasm for change and utopianism, reminding their readers of human fallibility and the importance of history. While the central ideas of the Enlightenment gained strength across the nineteenth century, the Counter Enlightenment provided the ideological roots of both conservatism and popular antidemocratic movements.

Folk Cultures and Popular Protest

While intellectuals and the reforming royal courts of Europe debated the rational and secular enthusiasms of the Enlightenment, most people in Western society remained loyal to competing cultural values grounded in the preindustrial past. These regionally distinct folk cultures were framed by the memory of shared local historical experience and nourished by religious practices encouraging emotional release. They emphasized the obligations that people had to each other and local, rather than national, loyalties. Though never formally articulated, these cultural traditions composed a coherent expression of the mutual rights and obligations connecting the people and their rulers. Rulers who violated the constraints of these understandings were likely to face violent opposition.

In the eighteenth century, European monarchs sought to increase their authority and to centralize power by reforming tax collection, judicial practice, and public administration. Although monarchs viewed these changes as reforms, the common people often saw them as violations of sacred customs and sometimes expressed their outrage in bread riots, tax protests, and attacks on royal officials. These violent actions were not efforts to overturn traditional authority but were instead efforts to preserve custom and precedent. In Spain and the Spanish colonies, for example, protesting mobs commonly asserted the apparently contradictory slogan "Long live the King. Death to bad government." They expressed loyalty to and love for their monarch while at the same time assaulting his officials and preventing the implementation of changes to long-established customs.

Folk cultures were threatened by other kinds of reform as well. Rationalist reformers of the Enlightenment sought to bring order and discipline to the citizenry by banning or by altering the numerous popular cultural traditions—such as harvest festivals, religious holidays, and country fairs—that enlivened the drudgery of everyday life. These events were popular celebrations of sexuality and individuality as well as opportunities for masked and costumed celebrants to mock the greed, pretension, and foolishness of government officials, the wealthy, and the clergy. Hard drinking, gambling, and blood sports like cockfighting and bearbaiting were popular in this preindustrial mass culture. Because these customs were viewed as corrupt and decadent by reformers influenced by the Enlightenment, governments undertook efforts to substitute civic rituals, patriotic anniversaries, and institutions of self-improvement. These challenges to custom—like the efforts at political reform—often provoked protests, rebellions, and riots.

The efforts of ordinary men and women to resist the growth of government power and the imposition of new cultural forms provide an important political undercurrent to much of the revolutionary agitation and conflict between 1750 and 1850. Spontaneous popular uprisings and protests punctuated nearly every effort at reform in the eighteenth century. But these popular actions gained revolutionary potential only when they coincided with ideological divisions and conflicts within the governing class itself. In America and France the old order was swept away when the protests and rebellions of the rural and urban poor coincided with the appearance of revolutionary leaders who followed Enlightenment ideals in efforts to create secular republican states. Likewise, the slave rebellion in Saint Domingue (Haiti) achieved revolutionary potential when it attracted the support of black freedmen and disaffected poor whites radicalized by news of the French Revolution.

THE AMERICAN REVOLUTION, 1775–1800

In British North America, clumsy efforts to reform colonial tax policy to cover rising defense expenditures and to diminish the power of elected colonial legislatures outraged a populace accustomed to greater local auton-

omy. Once begun, the American Revolution ushered in a century-long process of political and cultural transformation in Europe and the Americas. By the end of this revolutionary century the authority of monarchs had been swept away or limited by constitutions, and religion had lost its dominating place in Western intellectual life. Moreover, the medieval idea of a social order determined by birth had been replaced by a capitalist vision that emphasized competition and social mobility.

Frontiers and Taxes

After defeating the French in 1763, the British government faced two related problems in its North American colonies. As settlers pushed west into Amerindian lands, the government saw the likelihood of renewed conflict and rising military expenses. Already burdened with heavy debts from the French and Indian War, Britain tried to limit settler pressure on Amerindian lands and get colonists to shoulder more of the costs of imperial defense and colonial administration.

In the Great Lakes region the British tried to contain costs by reducing the prices paid for furs and refusing to honor the French practice of giving gifts and paying rent for frontier forts to Amerindian communities that had become dependent on European trade goods, especially firearms, gunpowder, textiles, and alcohol. When the British forced down the trade value of furs, Amerindians had to hunt more aggressively to get the volume of commodities they required, putting new pressures on the environment and endangering some species. The situation got worse as settlers and white trappers pushed across the Appalachians to compete with indigenous hunters.

At the end of the Seven Years War (see Chapter 17), Pontiac, an Ottawa chief, led a broad alliance of native peoples that drove the British military from western outposts and raided settled areas of Virginia and Pennsylvania. Although this Amerindian alliance was defeated within a year, the potential for new violence existed all along the frontier.

The British government's panicked reaction was the Proclamation of 1763, which sought to establish an effective western limit for settlement, throwing into question the claims of thousands of established farmers without effectively protecting Amerindian land. No one was satisfied. In 1774 the British government annexed disputed western territory to the province of Quebec, thus denying eastern colonies the authority to distribute additional lands.

Frontier issues increased hostility and suspicion between the British government and many of the colonists but did not directly lead to a breach. However, when the British government sought relief from the cost of imperial wars with a campaign of fiscal reforms and new taxes, it sparked a political confrontation that would lead to rebellion. New commercial regulations increased the cost of foreign molasses and endangered New England's profitable trade with Spanish and French Caribbean sugar colonies. The colonial practice of issuing paper money, a custom made necessary by the colonies' chronic balance-of-payments deficits, was outlawed. Colonial legislatures formally protested these measures, and angry colonists organized boycotts of British goods.

The Stamp Act of 1765, which imposed a tax, to be paid in scarce coin, on all legal documents, newspapers, pamphlets, and nearly all other printed material, proved incendiary. Propertied colonists, including holders of high office and members of the colonial elite, now assumed leading roles in protests, using fiery political language that identified Britain's rulers as "parricides" and "tyrants." Women from many of the most prominent colonial families organized boycotts of British goods. The production of homespun textiles by colonial women now became a patriotic enterprise. A young girl in Boston proclaimed that she was a "daughter of liberty" because she had learned to spin.[1] Organizations such as the Sons of Liberty held public meetings, intimidated royal officials, and developed committees to enforce the boycotts. The combination of violent protest and trade boycott forced the repeal of the Stamp Act, but new taxes and duties were soon imposed, and Parliament sent British troops to quell urban riots. One indignant woman later sent her poignant perception of this injustice to a British officer:

> [T]he most ignorant peasant knows, and [it] is clear to the weakest capacity, that no man has the right to take their money without their consent. The supposition is ridiculous and absurd, as none but highwaymen and robbers attempt it. Can you, my friend, reconcile it with your own good sense, that a body of men in Great Britain, who have little intercourse with America . . . shall invest themselves with a power to command our lives and properties [?][2]

New colonial boycotts cut the importation of British goods by two-thirds. Angry colonists also destroyed property and bullied or attacked royal officials. British authorities reacted by threatening traditional liberties, even dissolving the colonial legislature of Massachusetts, and by dispatching two regiments of soldiers to reestablish control of Boston's streets. Support for a

The Tarring and Feathering of a British Official, 1774 This illustration from a British periodical shows the unfortunate John Malcomb, commissioner of customs at Boston. By the mid-1770s British periodicals were focusing public opinion on mob violence and the breakdown of public order in the colonies. British critics of colonial political protests viewed the demand for liberty as little more than an excuse for mob violence. (The Granger Collection, New York)

complete break with Britain grew after March 5, 1770, when a British force fired on an angry Boston crowd, killing five civilians. This "Boston Massacre," which seemed to expose the naked force on which colonial rule rested, radicalized public opinion throughout the colonies.

Parliament attempted to calm public opinion by repealing some taxes and duties, but then stumbled into another crisis by granting a monopoly for importing tea to the colonies to the British East India Company, raising anew the constitutional issue of Parliament's right to tax the colonies. The crisis came to a head when protesters dumped tea worth £10,000 into Boston harbor. Britain responded by appointing a military man, Thomas Gage, as governor of Massachusetts and by closing the port of Boston. Public order in Boston now depended on British troops, and public administration was in the hands of a general. This militarization of colonial government in Boston undermined Britain's constitutional authority and made a military test of strength inevitable.

The Course of Revolution, 1775–1783

As the crisis mounted, patriot leaders created new governing bodies that made laws, appointed justices, and even took control of colonial militias, thus effectively deposing many British governors, judges, and customs officers. Simultaneously, radical leaders organized crowds to intimidate loyalists—people who were pro-British—and organized women to enforce boycotts of British goods.

When representatives elected to the Continental Congress met in Philadelphia in 1775, patriot militia had met British troops at Lexington and Concord, Massachusetts (see Map 21.1), and blood had already been shed. Events were propelling the colonies toward revolution. Congress assumed the powers of government, creating a currency and organizing an army led by **George Washington** (1732–1799), a Virginia planter who had served in the French and Indian War.

Popular support for independence was given a hard edge by the angry rhetoric of thousands of street-corner speakers and the inflammatory pamphlet *Common Sense*, written by Thomas Paine, a recent immigrant from England. Paine's pamphlet sold 120,000 copies. On July 4, 1776, Congress approved the Declaration of Independence, the document that proved to be the most enduring statement of the revolutionary era's ideology:

> We hold these truths to be self evident: That all men are created equal; that they are endowed by their creator with certain unalienable rights; that among these are life, liberty and the pursuit of happiness; that, to secure these rights, governments are instituted among men, deriving their just powers from the consent of the governed.

The Declaration's affirmation of popular sovereignty and individual rights would influence the language of revolution and popular protest around the world.

Hoping to shore up British authority, Great Britain sent additional military forces to pacify the colonies. By 1778 British land forces numbered 50,000 and were supported by 30,000 German mercenaries. This military commitment proved futile. Despite the existence of a large loyalist community, the British army found it difficult to control the countryside. Although British forces won most of the battles, Washington slowly built a competent Continental army as well as the civilian support networks that provided supplies and financial resources.

The real problem for the British government was its inability to discover a compromise solution that would satisfy colonial grievances. Half-hearted efforts to resolve the bitter conflict over taxes failed, and a later offer to roll back the clock and reestablish the administrative arrangements of 1763 made little headway. Overconfidence and poor leadership prevented the British from finding a political solution before revolutionary institutions were in place and the armies engaged. By allowing confrontation to occur, the British government lost the opportunity to mobilize and give direction to the large numbers of loyalists and pacifists in the colonies.

Along the Canadian border, both sides solicited Amerindians as potential allies and feared them as potential enemies. For over a hundred years, members of the powerful Iroquois Confederacy—Mohawk, Oneida, Onondaga, Cayuga, Seneca, and (after 1722) Tuscarora—had protected their traditional lands with a combination of diplomacy and warfare, playing a role in all the colonial wars of the eighteenth century. Just as the American Revolution forced neighbors and families to join the rebels or remain loyal, it divided the Iroquois, who fought on both sides.

The Mohawk proved to be the most valuable British allies among the Iroquois. Their loyalist leader **Joseph Brant** (Thayendanegea°) organized Britain's most potent fighting force along the Canadian border. His raids along the northern frontier earned him the title "Monster" Brant, but he was actually a man who moved easily between European and Amerindian cultures. Educated by missionaries, he was fluent in English and helped translate Protestant religious tracts into Mohawk. He was tied to many of the wealthiest loyalist families through his sister, formerly the mistress of Sir William Johnson, Britain's superintendent of Indian affairs for North America. Brant had traveled to London, had an audience with George III, (r. 1760–1820) and had been embraced by London's aristocratic society.

The defeat in late 1777 of Britain's general John Burgoyne by General Horatio Gates at Saratoga, New York, put the future of the Mohawk at risk. This victory, which gave heart to patriot forces that had recently suffered a string of defeats, led to destructive attacks on Iroquois villages. Brant's supporters fought on to the end of the war, but patriot victories along the frontier curtailed their political and military power. Brant eventually joined the loyalist exodus to Canada. For these Ameri-

Thayendanegea (ta YEHN dah NEY geh ah)

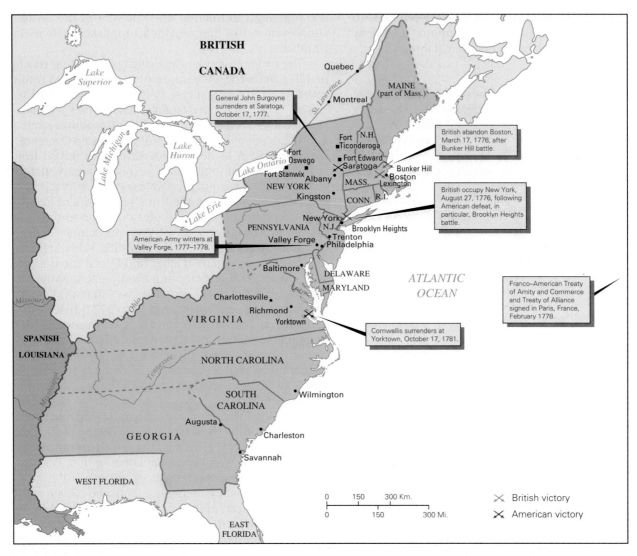

Map 21.1 The American Revolutionary War The British army won most of the major battles, and British troops held most of the major cities. Even so, the American revolutionaries eventually won a comprehensive military and political victory.

cans the revolution did not mean the protection of life and property.

The British defeat at Saratoga also convinced France to enter the war as an ally of the United States in 1778. French military help proved crucial, supplying American forces and forcing the British to defend their colonies in the Caribbean. The French contribution was most clear in the final decisive battle, fought at Yorktown, Virginia (see Map 21.1). With the American army supported by French soldiers and a French fleet, General Charles Cornwallis surrendered to Washington as

the British military band played "The World Turned Upside-Down."

This victory effectively ended the war. The Continental Congress sent representatives to the peace conference that followed with instructions to work in tandem with the French. Believing that France was more concerned with containing British power than with guaranteeing a strong United States, America's peace delegation chose to negotiate directly with Britain and gained a generous settlement. The Treaty of Paris (1783) granted unconditional independence and established generous boundaries for the former colonies. In return the United States promised to repay prewar debts due to British merchants and to allow loyalists to recover property confiscated by patriot forces. In the end, loyalists were poorly treated, and thousands of them decided to leave for Canada.

The Construction of Republican Institutions, to 1800

Even before the Declaration of Independence, many colonies had created new governments independent of British colonial authorities. After independence leaders in each of the new states (as the former colonies were called) summoned constitutional conventions to draft formal charters and submitted the results to voters for ratification. Europeans were fascinated by the drafting of written constitutions and by the formal ratification of these constitutions by a vote of the people. Many of these documents were quickly translated and published in Europe. Remembering conflicts between royal governors and colonial legislatures, the authors of state constitutions placed severe limits on executive authority but granted legislatures greater powers than in colonial times. Many state constitutions also included bills of rights to provide further protection against government tyranny.

An effective constitution for the new national government was developed with difficulty. The Second Continental Congress sent the Articles of Confederation—the first constitution of the United States—to the states for approval in 1777, but it was not accepted by all the states until 1781. It created a one-house legislature in which each state was granted a single vote. A simple majority of the thirteen states was sufficient to pass minor legislation, but nine votes were necessary for declaring war, imposing taxes, and coining or borrowing money. Executive power was exercised by committees, not by a president. Given the intended weakness of this government, it is remarkable that it successfully organized the human and material resources to defeat Great Britain.

With the coming of peace, many of the most powerful political figures in the United States recognized that the Confederation was unable to enforce unpopular requirements of the peace treaty such as the recognition of loyalist property claims, the payment of prewar debts, and even the payment of military salaries and pensions to veterans. In September 1786 Virginia invited the other states to discuss the government's failure to deal with trade issues. This led to a call for a new convention to meet in Philadelphia nine months later. A rebellion led by Revolutionary War veterans in western Massachusetts gave the assembling delegates a sense of urgency.

The **Constitutional Convention,** which began meeting in May 1787, achieved a nonviolent second American Revolution. The delegates pushed aside the announced purpose of the convention—"to render the constitution of the federal government adequate to the exigencies of the union"—and secretly undertook the creation of a new constitution. George Washington was elected presiding officer. His reputation and popularity provided a solid foundation on which the delegates could contemplate an alternative political model.

Debate focused on representation, electoral procedures, executive powers, and the relationship between the federal government and the states. Compromise solutions included distribution of political power among the executive, legislative, and judicial branches and the division of authority between the federal government and the states. The final compromise provided for a two-house legislature: the lower house (the House of Representatives) to be elected directly by voters and the upper house (the Senate) to be elected by state legislatures. The chief executive—the president—was to be elected indirectly by "electors" selected by ballot in the states.

Although the U.S. Constitution created the most democratic government of the era, only a minority of the adult population was given full rights. In some northern states where large numbers of free blacks had fought with patriot forces, there was some hostility to the continuation of slavery, but southern leaders were able to protect the institution. Although slaves were denied participation in the political process, slave states were permitted to count three-fifths of the slave population in the calculations that determined the number of congressional representatives, thus multiplying the political power of the slave-owning class. Southern delegates also gained a twenty-year continuation of the slave trade to 1808 and a fugitive slave clause that required all states to return runaway slaves to their masters.

Women were powerfully affected by their participation in revolutionary politics and by the changes in the economy brought on by the break with Britain. They had led prewar boycotts and had organized relief and charitable organizations during the war. Some had served in the military as nurses, and a smaller number had joined the ranks disguised as men. Nevertheless, they were denied political rights in the new republic. Only New Jersey did not specifically bar women from voting, granting the right to vote to all free residents who met modest property-holding requirements. As a result, women and

African-Americans who met property requirements were able to vote in New Jersey until 1807, when lawmakers eliminated this right.

The French Revolution, 1789–1815

The French Revolution undermined traditional monarchy as well as the power of the Catholic Church and the hereditary aristocracy but, unlike the American Revolution, did not create an enduring form of representative democracy. The colonial revolution in North America, however, did not confront so directly the entrenched privileges of an established church, monarchy, and aristocracy, and the American Revolution produced no symbolic drama comparable to the public beheading of the French king Louis XVI in early 1793. Among its achievements, the French Revolution expanded mass participation in political life and radicalized the democratic tradition inherited from the English and American experiences. But in the end, the passions unleashed by revolutionary events in France could not be sustained, and popular demagogues and the dictatorship of Napoleon stalled democratic reform.

French Society and Fiscal Crisis

French society was divided into three groups. The clergy, called the First Estate, numbered about 130,000 in a nation of 28 million. The Catholic Church owned about 10 percent of the nation's land and extracted substantial amounts of wealth from the economy in the form of tithes and ecclesiastical fees. Despite its substantial wealth, the church was exempted from nearly all taxes. The clergy was organized hierarchically, and members of the hereditary nobility held almost all the upper positions in the church.

The 300,000 members of the nobility, the Second Estate, controlled about 30 percent of the land and retained ancient rights on much of the rest. Nobles held the vast majority of high administrative, judicial, military, and church positions. Though traditionally barred from some types of commercial activity, nobles were important participants in wholesale trade, banking, manufacturing, and mining. Like the clergy, this estate was hierarchical: important differences in wealth, power, and outlook separated the higher from the lower nobility. The nobility was also a highly permeable class: the Second Estate in the eighteenth century saw an enormous infusion of

Parisian Stocking Mender   The poor lived very difficult lives. This woman uses a discarded wine barrel as a shop where she mends socks.   (Private collection)

wealthy commoners who purchased administrative and judicial offices that conferred noble status.

The Third Estate included everyone else, from wealthy financier to homeless beggar. The bourgeoisie°, or middle class, grew rapidly in the eighteenth century. There were three times as many members of this class in 1774, when Louis XVI took the throne, as there had been in 1715, at the end of Louis XIV's reign. Commerce, finance, and manufacturing accounted for much of the wealth of the Third Estate. Wealthy commoners also owned nearly a third of the nation's land. This literate and socially ambitious class supported an expanding publishing industry, subsidized the fine arts, and purchased many of the extravagant new homes being built in Paris and other cities.

bourgeoisie (boor-zwah-ZEE)

Peasants accounted for 80 percent of the French population. Artisans and other skilled workers, small shopkeepers and peddlers, and small landowners held a more privileged position in society. They owned some property and lived decently when crops were good and prices stable. By 1780 poor harvests had increased their cost of living and led to a decline in consumer demand for their products. They were rich enough to fear the loss of their property and status, well educated enough to be aware of the growing criticism of the king, but too poor and marginalized to influence policy.

The nation's poor were a large, growing, and troublesome sector. The poverty and vulnerability of peasant families forced younger children to seek seasonal work away from home and led many to crime and beggary. That raids by roving vagabonds threatened isolated farms was one measure of this social dislocation. In Paris and other French cities the vile living conditions and unhealthy diet of the working poor were startling to visitors from other European nations. Urban streets swarmed with beggars and prostitutes. Paris alone had 25,000 prostitutes in 1760. The wretchedness of the French poor is perhaps best indicated by the growing problem of child abandonment. On the eve of the French Revolution at least 40,000 children a year were given up by their parents. The convenient fiction was that these children would be adopted; in reality the majority died of neglect.

Unable to afford decent housing, obtain steady employment, or protect their children, the poor periodically erupted in violent protest and rage. In the countryside violence was often the reaction when the nobility or clergy increased dues and fees. In towns and cities an increase in the price of bread often provided the spark, for bread prices largely determined the quality of life of the poor. These explosive episodes, however, were not revolutionary in character. The remedies sought were conventional and immediate rather than structural and long-term. That was to change when the Crown tried to solve its fiscal crisis.

The expenses of the War of the Austrian Succession began the crisis. Louis XV (r. 1715–1774) first tried to impose new taxes on the nobility and on other groups that in the past had enjoyed exemptions. This effort failed in the face of widespread protest and the refusal of the Parlement of Paris, a court that heard appeals from local courts throughout France, to register the new tax. The crisis deepened when debts from the Seven Years War compelled the king to impose emergency fiscal measures. Again, the king met resistance from the Parlement of Paris. In 1768 frustrated authorities exiled the members of that Parlement and pushed through a series of unpopular fiscal measures. When the twenty-two-year-old Louis XVI assumed the throne in 1774, he attempted to gain popular support by recalling the exiled members of the Parlement of Paris, but he soon learned that provincial parlements had also come to see themselves as having a constitutional power to check any growth in monarchial authority.

In 1774 Louis's chief financial adviser warned that the government could barely afford to operate; as he put it, "the first gunshot [act of war] will drive the state to bankruptcy." Despite this warning, the French took on the heavy burden of supporting the American Revolution, delaying collapse by borrowing enormous sums and disguising the growing debt in misleading fiscal accounts. By the end of the war with Britain, more than half of France's national budget was required to service the resulting debt. It soon became clear that fiscal reforms and new taxes, not new loans, were necessary.

In 1787 the desperate king called an Assembly of Notables to approve a radical and comprehensive reform of the economy and fiscal policy. Despite the fact that the members of this assembly were selected by the king's advisers from the high nobility, the judiciary, and the clergy, it proved unwilling to act as a rubber stamp for the proposed reforms or new taxes. Instead, these representatives of France's most privileged classes sought to protect their interests by questioning the competence of the king and his ministers to supervise the nation's affairs.

Protest Turns to Revolution, 1789–1792

In frustration, the king dismissed the Notables and attempted to implement some reforms on his own, but his effort was met by an increasingly hostile judiciary and by popular demonstrations. Because the king was unable to extract needed tax concessions from the French elite, he was forced to call the **Estates General,** the French national legislature, which had not met since 1614. The narrow self-interest and greed of the rich—who would not tolerate an increase in their taxes—rather than the grinding poverty of the common people had created the conditions for political revolution.

In late 1788 and early 1789 members of the three estates came together throughout the nation to discuss grievances and elect representatives who would meet at Versailles°. The Third Estate's representatives were mostly men of property, but there was anger directed against the king's ministers and an inclination to move France toward constitutional monarchy with an elected

Versailles (vuhr-SIGH)

Parisians Storm the Bastille   This depiction of the storming of the Bastille on July 14, 1789, was painted by an artist who witnessed the epochal event still celebrated by the French as a national holiday.   (Photos12.com-ARJ)

legislature. Many nobles and members of the clergy sympathized with the reform agenda of the Third Estate, but deep internal divisions over procedural and policy issues limited the power of the First and the Second Estates.

Traditionally, the three estates met separately, and a positive vote by two of the three was required for action. Tradition, however, was quickly overturned when the Third Estate refused to conduct business until the king ordered the other two estates to sit with it in a single body. During a six-week period of stalemate, many parish priests from the First Estate began to meet with the commoners. When this expanded Third Estate declared itself the **National Assembly,** the king and his advisers recognized that the reformers intended to force them to accept a constitutional monarchy.

After being locked out of their meeting place, the Third Estate appropriated an indoor tennis court and pledged to write a constitution. The Oath of the Tennis Court ended Louis's vain hope that he could limit the

agenda to fiscal reform. The king's effort to solve the nation's fiscal crisis was being connected in unpredictable ways to the central ideas of the era: the people were sovereign, and the legitimacy of political institutions and individual rulers ultimately depended on their carrying out the people's will. Louis prepared for a confrontation with the National Assembly by moving military forces to Versailles. Before he could act, the people of Paris intervened.

A succession of bad harvests beginning in 1785 had propelled bread prices upward throughout France and provoked an economic depression as demand for nonessential goods collapsed. By the time the Estates General met, nearly a third of the Parisian work force was unemployed. Hunger and anger marched hand in hand through working-class neighborhoods.

When the people of Paris heard that the king was massing troops in Versailles to arrest the representatives, crowds of common people began to seize arms and mobilize. On July 14, 1789, a crowd searching for military supplies attacked the Bastille, a medieval fortress used as a prison. The futile defense of the Bastille° cost ninety-eight lives before its garrison surrendered. Enraged, the attackers hacked the commander to death and then paraded through the city with his head and that of Paris's chief magistrate stuck on pikes.

These events coincided with uprisings by peasants in the country. Peasants sacked manor houses and destroyed documents that recorded their traditional obligations. They refused to pay taxes and dues to landowners and seized common lands. Forced to recognize the fury raging through rural areas, the National Assembly voted to end traditional obligations and to reform the tax system. Having forced acceptance of their narrow agenda, the peasants ceased their revolt.

These popular uprisings strengthened the hand of the National Assembly in its dealings with the king. One manifestation of this altered relationship was passage of the **Declaration of the Rights of Man.** There were clear similarities between the language of this declaration and the U.S. Declaration of Independence. Indeed, Thomas Jefferson, who had written the American document, was U.S. ambassador to Paris and offered his opinion to those drafting the French statement. The French declaration, however, was more sweeping in its language than the American. Among the enumerated natural rights were "liberty, property, security, and resistance to oppression." The Declaration of the Rights of Man also guaranteed free expression of ideas, equality before the law, and representative government.

While delegates debated political issues in Versailles, the economic crisis worsened in Paris. Women employed in the garment industry and in small-scale retail businesses were particularly hard hit. Because the working women of Paris faced high food prices everyday as they struggled to feed their families, their anger had a hard edge. Public markets became political arenas where the urban poor met daily in angry assembly. Here the revolutionary link between the material deprivation of the French poor and the political aspirations of the French bourgeoisie was forged.

On October 5, market women organized a crowd of thousands to march the 12 miles (19 kilometers) to Versailles. Once there, they forced their way into the National Assembly to demand action from the frightened representatives: "the point is that we want bread." The crowd then entered the royal apartments, killed some of the king's guards, and searched for Queen Marie Antoinette°, whom they loathed as a symbol of extrava-

Bastille (bass-TEEL)   **Antoinette** (ann twah-NET)

gance. Eventually, the crowd demanded that the royal family return to Paris. Preceded by the heads of two aristocrats carried on pikes and hauling away the palace's supply of flour, the triumphant crowd escorted the royal family to Paris.

With the king's ability to resist democratic change overcome by the Paris crowd, the National Assembly achieved a radically restructured French society in the next two years. It passed a new constitution that dramatically limited monarchial power and abolished the nobility as a hereditary class. Economic reforms swept away monopolies and trade barriers within France. The Legislative Assembly (the new constitution's name for the National Assembly) seized church lands to use as collateral for a new paper currency, and priests—who were to be elected—were put on the state payroll. When the government tried to force priests to take a loyalty oath, however, many Catholics joined a growing counterrevolutionary movement.

At first, many European monarchs had welcomed the weakening of the French king, but by 1791 Austria and Prussia threatened to intervene in support of the monarchy. The Legislative Assembly responded by declaring war. Although the war went badly at first for French forces, people across France responded patriotically to foreign invasions, forming huge new volunteer armies and mobilizing national resources to meet the challenge. By the end of 1792 French armies had gained a stalemate with the foreign forces.

The Terror, 1793–1794

In this period of national crisis and foreign threat, the French Revolution entered its most radical phase. A failed effort by the king and queen to escape from Paris and find foreign allies cost the king any remaining popular support. As foreign armies crossed into France, his behavior was increasingly viewed as treasonous. On August 10, 1792, a crowd similar to the one that had marched on Versailles invaded his palace in Paris and forced the king to seek protection in the Legislative Assembly. The Assembly suspended the king, ordered his imprisonment, and called for the formation of a new National Convention to be elected by the vote of all men.

Rumors of counterrevolutionary plots kept working-class neighborhoods in an uproar. In September mobs surged through the city's prisons, killing nearly half the prisoners. Swept along by popular passion, the newly elected National Convention convicted Louis XVI of treason, sentencing him to death and proclaiming France a republic. The guillotine ended the king's life in January

Playing Cards from the French Revolution Even playing cards could be used to attack the aristocracy and Catholic Church. In this pack of cards, "Equality" and "Liberty" replaced kings and queens. (Jean-Loup Charmet/The Bridgeman Art Library)

1793. Invented in the spirit of the era as a more humane way to execute the condemned, this machine was to become the bloody symbol of the revolution. These events helped by February 1793 to precipitate a wider war with France now confronting nearly all of Europe's major powers.

The National Convention—the new legislature of the new First Republic of France—convened in September. Almost all of its members were from the middle class, and nearly all were **Jacobins°**—the most uncompromising democrats. Deep political differences, however, separated moderate Jacobins—called "Girondists°," after a region in southern France—and radicals known as "the Mountain." Members of the Mountain—so named because their seats were on the highest level in the assembly hall—were more sympathetic than the Girondists to the demands of the Parisian working class and more impatient with parliamentary procedure and constitutional constraints on government action. The Mountain came to be dominated by **Maximilien Robespierre°,** a young, little-known lawyer from the provinces who had been influenced by Rousseau's ideas.

With the French economy still in crisis and Paris suffering from inflation, high unemployment, and scarcity, Robespierre used the popular press and political clubs to forge an alliance with the volatile Parisian working class. His growing strength in the streets allowed him to purge the National Convention of his enemies and to restructure the government. Executive power was placed in the hands of the newly formed Committee of Public Safety, which created special courts to seek out and punish domestic enemies.

Among the groups that lost ground were the active feminists of the Parisian middle class and the working-class women who had sought the right to bear arms in defense of the Revolution. These women had provided decisive leadership at crucial times, helping propel the Revolution toward widened suffrage and a more democratic structure. Armed women had actively participated in every confrontation with conservative forces. It is ironic that the National Convention—the revolutionary era's most radical legislative body, elected by universal male suffrage—chose to repress the militant feminist forces that had prepared the ground for its creation.

Faced with rebellion in the provinces and foreign invasion, Robespierre and his allies unleashed a period of repression called the Reign of Terror (1793–1794) (see Diversity and Dominance: Robespierre and Wollstonecraft Defend and Explain the Terror). During the Terror, approximately 40,000 people were executed or died in prison, and another 300,000 were imprisoned. New actions against the clergy were also approved, including the provocative measure of forcing priests to marry. Even time was subject to revolutionary change. A new republican calendar created twelve thirty-day months divided into ten-day weeks. Sunday, with its Christian meanings, disappeared from the calendar.

By spring 1794 the Revolution was secure from foreign and domestic enemies, but repression, now institutionalized, continued. Among the victims were some who had been Robespierre's closest political collaborators during the early stage of the Terror. The execution of these former allies prepared the way for Robespierre's own fall by undermining the sense of invulnerability that had secured the loyalty of his remaining partisans in the National Convention. After French victories eliminated the immediate foreign threat, conservatives in the

---

Jacobin (JAK-uh-bin)   **Girondist** (juh-RON-dist)   **Robespierre** (ROBES-pee-air)

Convention felt secure enough to vote for the arrest of Robespierre on July 27, 1794. Over the next two days, Robespierre and nearly a hundred of his remaining allies were executed by guillotine.

Reaction and Dictatorship, 1795–1815

Purged of Robespierre's collaborators, the Convention began to undo the radical reforms. It removed many of the emergency economic controls that had been holding down prices and protecting the working class. Gone also was toleration for violent popular demonstrations. When the Paris working class rose in protest in 1795, the Convention approved the use of overwhelming military force. Another retreat from radical objectives was signaled when the Catholic Church was permitted to regain much of its former influence. The church's confiscated wealth, however, was not returned. A more conservative constitution was also ratified. It protected property, established a voting process that reduced the power of the masses, and created a new executive authority, the Directory. Once installed in power, however, the Directory proved unable to end the foreign wars or solve domestic economic problems.

After losing the election of 1797 the Directory suspended the results. The republican phase of the Revolution was clearly dead. Legitimacy was now based on coercive power rather than on elections. Two years later, **Napoleon Bonaparte** (1769–1821), a brilliant young general in the French army, seized power. Just as the American and French Revolutions had been the start of the modern democratic tradition, the military intervention that brought Napoleon to power in 1799 marked the advent of another modern form of government: popular authoritarianism.

The American and French Revolutions had resulted in part from conflicts over representation. If the people were sovereign, what institutions best expressed popular will? In the United States the answer was to expand the electorate and institute representative government. The French Revolution had taken a different direction with the Reign of Terror. Interventions on the floor of the National Convention by market women and soldiers, the presence of common people at revolutionary tribunals and at public executions, and expanded military service were all forms of political communication that temporarily satisfied the French people's desire to influence their government. Napoleon tamed these forms of political expression to organize Europe's first popular dictatorship. He succeeded because his military reputation promised order to a society exhausted by a decade of crisis, turmoil, and bloodshed.

In contrast to the National Convention, Napoleon proved capable of realizing France's dream of dominating Europe and providing effective protection for persons and property at home. Negotiations with the Catholic Church led to the Concordat of 1801. This agreement gave French Catholics the right to freely practice their religion, and it recognized the French government's authority to nominate bishops and retain priests on the state payroll. In his comprehensive rewriting of French law, the Civil Code of 1804, Napoleon won the support of the peasantry and of the middle class by asserting two basic principles inherited from the moderate first stage of the French Revolution: equality in law and protection of property. Even some members of the nobility became supporters after Napoleon declared himself emperor and France an empire in 1804. However, the discrimination against women that had begun during the Terror was extended by the Napoleonic Civil Code. Women were denied basic political rights and were able to participate in the economy only with the guidance and supervision of their fathers and husbands.

While providing personal security, the Napoleonic system denied or restricted many individual rights. Free speech and free expression were limited. Criticism of the government, viewed as subversive, was proscribed, and most opposition newspapers disappeared. Spies and informers directed by the minister of police enforced these limits to political freedom. Thousands of the regime's enemies and critics were questioned or detained in the name of domestic tranquility.

Ultimately, the Napoleonic system depended on the success of French arms and French diplomacy (see Map 21.2). From Napoleon's assumption of power until his fall, no single European state could defeat the French military. Even powerful alliances like that of Austria and Prussia were brushed aside with humiliating defeats and forced to become allies of France. Only Britain, protected by its powerful navy, remained able to thwart Napoleon's plans to dominate Europe. His effort to mobilize forces for an invasion of Britain failed in late 1805 when the British navy defeated the French and allied Spanish fleets off the coast of Spain at the Battle of Trafalgar.

Desiring to again extend French power to the Americas, Napoleon invaded Portugal in 1807 and Spain in 1808. French armies soon became tied down in a costly conflict with Spanish and Portuguese patriots who had forged an alliance with the only available European power, Great Britain. Frustrated by events on the Iberian Peninsula and faced with a faltering economy, Napoleon made the fateful decision to invade Russia. In June 1812

ROBESPIERRE AND WOLLSTONECRAFT DEFEND AND EXPLAIN THE TERROR

Many Europeans who had initially been sympathetic to the French Revolution were repelled by the Terror. In 1793 and 1794 while France was at war with Austria, Prussia, Great Britain, Holland, and Spain about 2,600 people were executed in Paris, including the king and queen, members of the nobility, and Catholic clergy. The public nature of the judicial procedures and executions outraged many. Critics of the Revolution asked if these excesses were not worse than those committed by the French monarchy. Others defended the violence as necessary, arguing that the Terror had been provoked by enemies of the Revolution or was the consequence of earlier injustices.

The following two opinions date from 1794. Maximilien Robespierre was the head of the Committee of Public Safety, the effective head of the revolutionary government. Robespierre was a provincial lawyer who rose to power in Paris as the Revolution was radicalized. In the statement that follows he is unrepentant, arguing that violence was necessary in the defense of liberty. He made this statement on the eve of his political demise; in 1794 he was driven from power and executed by the revolutionary movement he had helped create.

Mary Wollstonecraft, an English intellectual and advocate for women's rights who was living in Paris at the time of the execution of Louis XVI, was troubled by the violence, and her discussion of these events is more an apology than a defense. She had published her famous A Vindication of the Rights of Woman *in 1792, after which she left for Paris. Wollstonecraft left Paris after war broke out between France and Britain. She remained an important force in European intellectual life until her death from complications of childbirth in 1797.*

MAXIMILIEN ROBESPIERRE, "ON THE MORAL AND POLITICAL PRINCIPLES OF DOMESTIC POLICY"

[L]et us deduce a great truth: the characteristic of popular government is confidence in the people and severity towards itself.

The whole development of our theory would end here if you had only to pilot the vessel of the Republic through calm waters; but the tempest roars, and the revolution imposes on you another task.

This great purity of the French revolution's basis, the very sublimity of its objective, is precisely what causes both our strength and our weakness. Our strength, because it gives to us truth's ascendancy over imposture, and the rights of the public interest over private interests; our weakness, because it rallies all vicious men against us, all those who in their hearts contemplated despoiling the people and all those who intend to let it be despoiled with impunity, both those who have rejected freedom as a personal calamity and those who have embraced the revolution as a career and the Republic as prey. Hence the defection of so many ambitious or greedy men who since the point of departure have abandoned us along the way because they did not begin the journey with the same destination in view. The two opposing spirits that have been represented in a struggle to rule nature might be said to be fighting in this great period of human history to fix irrevocably the world's destinies, and France is the scene of this fearful combat. Without, all the tyrants encircle you; within, all tyranny's friends conspire; they will conspire until hope is wrested from crime. We must smother the internal and external enemies of the Republic or perish with it; now in this situation, the first maxim of your policy ought to be to lead the people by reason and the people's enemies by terror.

If the spring of popular government in time of peace is virtue, the springs of popular government in revolution are at once virtue and terror: virtue, without which terror is fatal; terror, without which virtue is powerless. Terror is nothing other than justice, prompt, severe, inflexible; it is therefore an emanation of virtue; it is not so much a special principle as it is a consequence of the general principle of democracy applied to our country's most urgent needs.

It has been said that terror is the principle of despotic government. Does your government therefore resemble despotism? Yes, as the sword that gleams in the hands of the heroes of liberty resembles that with which the henchmen of tyranny are armed. Let the despot govern by terror his brutalized subjects; he is right, as a despot. Subdue by terror the enemies of liberty, and you will be right, as founders of the Republic. The government of the revolution is liberty's despotism against tyranny. Is force made only to protect crime? And is the thunderbolt not destined to strike the heads of the proud?

. . . Society owes protection only to peaceable citizens; the only citizens in the Republic are the republicans. For it, the royalists, the conspirators are only strangers or, rather, enemies. This terrible war waged by liberty against tyranny-is it not indivisible? Are the enemies within not the allies of the enemies without? The assassins who tear our country apart, the intriguers who buy the consciences that hold the people's mandate; the traitors who sell them; the mercenary pamphleteers hired to dishonor the people's cause, to kill public virtue, to stir up the fire of civil discord, and to prepare political counterrevolution by moral counterrevolution—are all those men less guilty or less dangerous than the tyrants whom they serve?

MARY WOLLSTONECRAFT, "AN HISTORICAL AND MORAL VIEW OF THE ORIGIN AND PROGRESS OF THE FRENCH REVOLUTION"

Weeping scarcely conscious that I weep, O France! Over the vestiges of thy former oppression, which, separating man from man with a fence of iron, sophisticated [complicated] all, and made many completely wretched; I tremble, lest I should meet some unfortunate being, fleeing from the despotism of licentious freedom, hearing the snap of the guillotine at his heels, merely because he was once noble, or has afforded an asylum to those whose only crime is their name—and, if my pen almost bound with eagerness to record the day that leveled the Bastille [an abbey used as a prison before the Revolution] with the dust, making the towers of despair tremble to their base, the recollection that still the abbey is appropriated to hold the victims of revenge and suspicion [she means that the Bastille remained a prison for those awaiting revolutionary justice]. . . .

Excuse for the Ferocity of the Parisians The deprivation of natural, equal, civil, and political rights reduced the most cunning the lower orders to practice fraud, and the rest to habits of stealing, audacious robberies, and murders. And why? Because the rich and poor were separated into bands of tyrants and slaves, and the retaliation of slaves is always terrible. In short, every sacred feeling, moral and divine, has been obliterated, and the dignity of man sullied, by a system of policy and jurisprudence as repugnant to reason as at variance with humanity.

The only excuse that can be made for the ferocity of the Parisians is then simply to observe that they had not any

confidence in the laws, which they had always found to be merely cobwebs to catch small flies [the poor]. Accustomed to be punished themselves for every trifle, and often for only being in the way of the rich, or their parasites, when, in fact, had the Parisians seen the execution of a noble, or priest, though convicted of crimes beyond the daring of vulgar minds? When justice, or the law, is so partial, the day of retribution will come with the red sky of vengeance, to confound the innocent with the guilty. The mob were barbarous beyond the tiger's cruelty.

. . .

Let us cast our eyes over the history of man, and we shall scarcely find a page that is not tarnished by some foul deed or bloody transaction. Let us examine the catalogue of the vices of men in a savage state, and contrast them with those of men civilized; we shall find that a barbarian, considered as a moral being, is an angel, compared with the refined villain of artificial life. Let us investigate the causes which have produced this degeneracy, and we shall discover that they are those unjust plans of government which have been formed by peculiar circumstances in every part of the globe.

Then let us coolly and impartially contemplate the improvements which are gaining ground in the formation of principles of policy; and I flatter myself it will be allowed by every humane and considerate being that a political system more simple than has hitherto existed would effectually check those aspiring follies, which, by imitation, leading to vice, have banished from governments the very shadow of justice and magnanimity.

Thus had France grown up and sickened on the corruption of a state diseased. . . . it is only the philosophical eye, which looks into the nature and weighs the consequences of human actions, that will be able to discern the cause, which has produced so many dreadful effects.

QUESTIONS FOR ANALYSIS

1. Why does Robespierre believe that revolution cannot tolerate diversity of opinion? Are his reasons convincing?
2. How does Robespierre distinguish the terror of despots from the terror of liberty?
3. How does Wollstonecraft explain the "ferocity" of the Parisians?
4. What does Wollstonecraft believe will come from this period of violence?

Sources: Maximilien Robespierre, "On the Moral and Political Principles of Domestic Policy," February 5, 1794, *Modern History Sourcebook: Robespierre: Terror and Virtue, 1794, http://www.fordham.edu/halsall/mod/robespierre-terror.html;* Mary Wollstonecraft, "An Historical and Moral View of the Origin and Progress of the French Revolution," *A Mary Wollstonecraft Reader,* ed. Barbara H. Solomon and Paula S. Berggren (New York: New American Library, 1983), 374–375, 382–383.

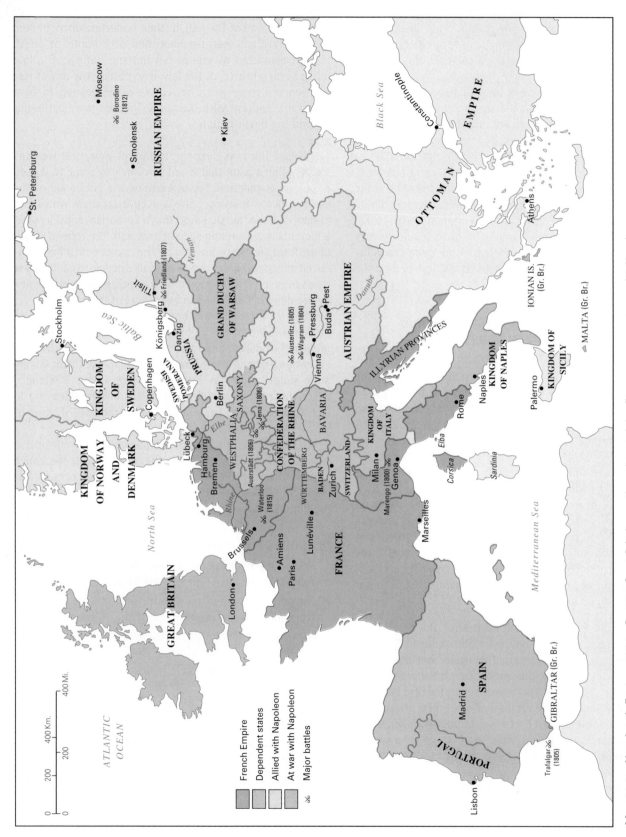

Map 21.2 Napoleon's Europe, 1810 By 1810 Great Britain was the only remaining European power at war with Napoleon. Because of the loss of the French fleet at the Battle of Trafalgar in 1805, Napoleon was unable to threaten Britain with invasion, and Britain was able to actively assist the resistance movements in Spain and Portugal, thereby helping weaken French power.

he began his campaign with the largest army ever assembled in Europe, approximately 600,000 men. After fighting an inconclusive battle at Borodino, Napoleon pressed on to Moscow. Five weeks after occupying Moscow, he was forced to retreat by Russian patriots who set the city on fire and by approaching armies. During the retreat, the brutal Russian winter and attacks by Russian forces destroyed his army. A broken and battered fragment of 30,000 men returned home to France.

After the debacle in Russia, Austria and Prussia deserted Napoleon and entered an alliance with England and Russia. Unable to defend Paris, Napoleon was forced to abdicate the French throne in April 1814. The allies exiled Napoleon to the island of Elba off the coast of Italy and restored the French monarchy. The next year Napoleon escaped from Elba and returned to France. But his moment had passed. He was defeated by an allied army at Waterloo, in Belgium, after only one hundred days in power. His final exile was on the distant island of St. Helena in the South Atlantic, where he died in 1821.

REVOLUTION SPREADS, CONSERVATIVES RESPOND, 1789–1850

Even as the dictatorship of Napoleon eliminated the democratic legacy of the French Revolution, revolutionary ideology was spreading and taking hold in Europe and the Americas. In Europe the French Revolution promoted nationalism and republicanism. In the Americas the legacies of the American and French Revolutions led to a new round of struggles for independence. News of revolutionary events in France destabilized the colonial regime in Saint Domingue (present-day Haiti), a small French colony on the western half of the island of Hispaniola, and resulted in the first successful slave rebellion. In Europe, however, the spread of revolutionary fervor was checked by reaction as monarchs formed an alliance to protect themselves from further revolutionary outbreaks.

The Haitian Revolution, 1789–1804

In 1789 the French colony of Saint Domingue was among the richest European colonies in the Americas. Its plantations produced sugar, cotton, indigo, and coffee. The colony produced two-thirds of France's tropical imports and generated nearly one-third of all French foreign trade. This impressive wealth depended on a brutal slave regime. Saint Domingue's harsh punishments and poor living conditions were notorious throughout the Caribbean. The colony's high mortality and low fertility rates created an insatiable demand for African slaves. As a result, in 1790 the majority of the colony's 500,000 slaves were African-born.

In 1789, when news of the calling of France's Estates General arrived on the island, wealthy white planters sent a delegation to Paris charged with seeking more home rule and greater economic freedom for Saint Domingue. The free mixed-race population, the **gens de couleur°,** also sent representatives. These nonwhite delegates were mostly drawn from the large class of slave-owning small planters and urban merchants. They focused on ending race discrimination and achieving political equality with whites. They did not seek freedom for slaves; the most prosperous gens de couleur were slave owners themselves. As the French Revolution became more radical, the gens de couleur forged an alliance with sympathetic French radicals, who came to identify the colony's wealthy planters as royalists and aristocrats.

The political turmoil in France weakened the ability of colonial administrators to maintain order. The authority of colonial officials was no longer clear, and the very legitimacy of slavery was being challenged in France. In the vacuum that resulted, rich planters, poor whites, and the gens de couleur pursued their narrow interests, engendering an increasingly bitter and confrontational struggle. Given the slaves' hatred of the brutal regime that oppressed them and the accumulated grievances of the free people of color, there was no way to limit the violence once the control of the slave owners slipped. When Vincent Ogé°, leader of the gens de couleur mission to France, returned to Saint Domingue in 1790 to organize a military force, the planters captured, tortured, and executed him. This cruelty was soon repaid in kind.

By 1791 whites, led by the planter elite, and the gens de couleur were engaged in open warfare. This breach between the two groups of slave owners gave the slaves an opening. A slave rebellion began on the plantations of the north and spread throughout the colony (see Map 21.3). Plantations were destroyed, masters and overseers killed, and crops burned. An emerging rebel leadership that combined elements of African political culture with revolutionary ideology from France mobilized and directed the rebelling slaves.

The rebellious slaves eventually gained the upper hand under the leadership of **François Dominique Toussaint L'Ouverture,** a former domestic slave, who created a disciplined military force. Toussaint was politically

---

gens de couleur (zhahn deh koo-LUHR)   **Ogé** (oh-ZHAY)

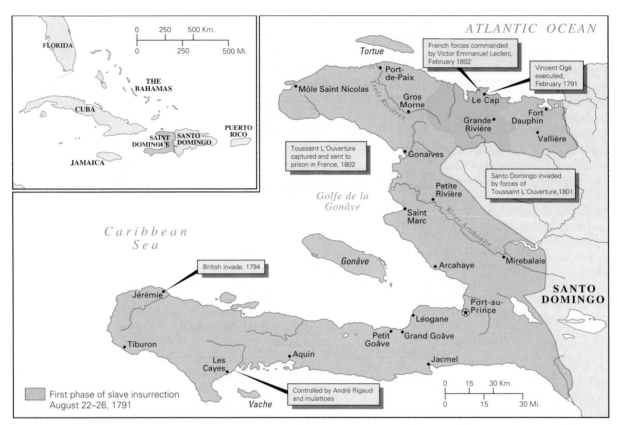

Map 21.3 The Haitian Revolution On their way to achieving an end to slavery and gaining national independence, the Haitian revolutionaries were forced to defeat British and French military interventions as well as the local authority of the slave masters.

strengthened in 1794 when the radical National Convention in Paris abolished slavery in all French possessions. He overcame his rivals in Saint Domingue, defeated a British expeditionary force in 1798, and then led an invasion of the neighboring Spanish colony of Santo Domingo, freeing the slaves there. Toussaint continued to assert his loyalty to France but gave the French government no effective role in local affairs.

As reaction overtook revolution in France, both the abolition of slavery and Toussaint's political position were threatened. When the Directory contemplated the reestablishment of slavery, Toussaint protested:

> Do they think that men who have been able to enjoy the blessing of liberty will calmly see it snatched away? They supported their chains only so long as they did not know any condition of life more happy than slavery. But today when they have left it, if they had a thousand lives they would sacrifice them all rather than be forced into slavery again.[3]

In 1802 Napoleon sent a large military force to Saint Domingue to reestablish both French colonial authority and slavery (see Map 21.3). At first the French forces were successful. Toussaint was captured and sent to France, where he died in prison. Eventually, however, the loss of thousands of lives to yellow fever and the resistance of the revolutionaries turned the tide. Visible in the resistance to the French were small numbers of armed women. During the early stages of the Haitian Revolution, very few slave women had taken up arms, although many had aided Toussaint's forces in support roles. But after a decade of struggle and violence, more Haitian women were politically aware and willing to join the armed resistance. In 1804 Toussaint's successors declared independence, and the free republic of Haiti joined the United States as the second independent nation in the Western Hemisphere. But independence and emancipation were achieved at a terrible price. Tens of thousands had died; the economy was destroyed; and public administration was corrupted by more than a decade of vio-

Haiti's Former Slaves Defend Their Freedom   In this representation, a veteran army sent by Napoleon to reassert French control in Haiti battles with Haitian forces in a tropical forest. The combination of Haitian resistance and yellow fever defeated the French invasion.   (Bettmann/Corbis)

lence. Political violence and economic stagnation were to trouble Haiti throughout the nineteenth century.

The Congress of Vienna and Conservative Retrenchment, 1815–1820

From 1814 to 1815 representatives of Britain, Russia, Austria, and Prussia met as the **Congress of Vienna** to reestablish political order in Europe. While they were meeting, Napoleon escaped from Elba, then was defeated at Waterloo. The French Revolution and Napoleon's imperial ambitions had threatened the very survival of Europe's old order. Ancient monarchies had been overturned and dynasties replaced with interlopers. Long-established political institutions had been tossed aside, and long-recognized international borders had been ignored. The very existence of the nobility and church had been put at risk. Under the leadership of the Austrian foreign minister, Prince Klemens von Metternich° (1773–1859), the allies worked together in Vienna

Metternich (MET-uhr-nik)

to create a comprehensive peace settlement that they hoped would safeguard the conservative order.

The central objective of the Congress of Vienna was to roll back the clock in France. Because the participants believed that a strong and stable France was the best guarantee of future peace, the French monarchy was reestablished, and France's 1792 borders were recognized. Most of the continental European powers received some territorial gains, for Metternich sought to offset French strength with a balance of power. In addition, Austria, Russia, and Prussia formed a separate alliance to more actively confront the revolutionary and nationalist energies that the French Revolution had unleashed. In 1820 this "Holy Alliance" acted decisively to defeat liberal revolutions in Spain and Italy. By repressing republican and nationalist ideas in universities and the press, the Holy Alliance also attempted to meet the potential challenge posed by subversive ideas. Metternich's program of conservative retrenchment succeeded in the short term, but powerful ideas associated with liberalism and nationalism remained a vital part of European political life throughout the nineteenth century.

Nationalism, Reform, and Revolution, 1821–1850

Despite the power of the conservative monarchs, popular support for national self-determination and democratic reform grew throughout Europe. Greece had been under Ottoman control since the fifteenth century. In 1821 Greek patriots launched an independence movement. Metternich and other conservatives opposed Greek independence, but European artists and writers enamored with the cultural legacy of ancient Greece rallied political support for intervention. After years of struggle, Russia, France, and Great Britain forced the Ottoman Empire to recognize Greek independence in 1830.

Louis XVIII, brother of the executed Louis XVI, had been placed on the throne of France by the victorious allies in 1814. He ruled as a constitutional monarch until his death in 1824 and was followed to the throne by his brother Charles X. Charles attempted to rule in the prerevolutionary style of his ancestors, repudiating the constitution in 1830. Unwilling to accept this reactionary challenge, the people of Paris rose up and forced Charles to abdicate. His successor was his cousin Louis Philippe° (r. 1830–1848), who accepted the reestablished constitution and extended voting privileges.

At the same time democratic reform movements appeared in both the United States and Great Britain. In the United States after 1790 the original thirteen states were joined by new states with constitutions granting voting rights to most free males. After the War of 1812 the right to vote was expanded in the older states as well. This broadening of the franchise led to the election of the populist president Andrew Jackson in 1828 (see Chapter 23).

However, revolutionary violence in France made the British aristocracy and the conservative Tory Party fearful of expanded democracy and mass movements of any kind. In 1815 the British government passed the Corn Laws, which limited the importation of foreign grains. The laws favored the profits of wealthy landowners who produced grain at the expense of the poor who were forced to pay more for their bread. When poor consumers organized to overturn these laws, the government outlawed most public meetings, using troops to crush protest in Manchester. Reacting against these policies, reformers gained the passage of laws that increased the power of the House of Commons, redistributed votes from agricultural to industrial districts, and increased the number of voters by nearly 50 percent. Although the most radical demands of these reformers, called

Chartists, were defeated, new labor and economic reforms addressing the grievances of workers were passed (see Chapter 22).

Despite the achievement of Greek independence and limited political reform in France and Great Britain, conservatives continued to hold the upper hand in Europe. Finally, in 1848 the desire for democratic reform and national self-determination and the frustrations of urban workers led to upheavals across Europe. The **Revolutions of 1848** began in Paris, where members of the middle class and workers united to overthrow the regime of Louis Philippe and create the Second French Republic. Adult men were given voting rights; slavery was abolished in French colonies; the death penalty was ended; and a ten-hour workday was legislated for Paris. But Parisian workers' demands for programs to reduce unemployment and prices provoked conflicts with the middle class, which wanted to protect property rights. When workers rose up against the government, French troops were called out to crush them. Desiring the reestablishment of order, the French elected Louis Napoleon, nephew of the former emperor, president in December 1848. Three years later, he overturned the constitution as a result of popular plebiscite and, after ruling briefly as dictator, became Emperor Napoleon III. He remained in power until 1871.

Reformers in Hungary, Italy, Bohemia, and elsewhere pressed for greater national self-determination in 1848. When the Austrian monarchy did not meet their demands, students and workers in Vienna took to the streets to force political reforms similar to those sought in Paris. With revolution spreading throughout the Austrian Empire, Metternich, the symbol of reaction, fled Vienna in disguise. Little lasting change occurred, however, because the new Austrian emperor, Franz Joseph (r. 1848–1916) was able to use Russian military assistance and loyal Austrian troops to reestablish central authority.

Middle-class reformers and workers in Berlin joined forces in an attempt to compel the Prussian king to accept a liberal constitution and seek unification of the German states. But the Constituent Assembly called to write a constitution and arrange for national integration became entangled in diplomatic conflicts with Austria and Denmark. As a result, Frederick William IV (r. 1840–1861) was able to reassert his authority, thwarting both constitutional reform and unification.

Despite their heroism on the barricades of Paris, Vienna, Rome, and Berlin, the revolutionaries of 1848 failed to gain either their nationalist or their republican objectives. Monarchs retained the support not only of aristocrats but also of professional militaries, largely re-

---

Louis Philippe (loo-EE-fee-LEEP)

The Revolution of 1830 in Belgium   After the 1830 uprising that overturned the restored monarchy in France, Belgians rose up to declare their independence from Holland. In Poland and Italy, similar uprisings combining nationalism and a desire for self-governance failed. This painting by Baron Gustaf Wappers romantically illustrates the popular nature of the Belgian uprising by bringing to the barricades men, women, and children drawn from both the middle and the working classes.   (Musées royaux des Beaux-Arts de Belgique, Brussels)

cruited from among peasants who had little sympathy for urban workers. Revolutionary coalitions, in contrast, were fragile and lacked clear objectives. Workers' demands for higher wages, lower prices, and labor reform often drove their middle-class allies into the arms of the reactionaries.

CONCLUSION

This era of revolution was, in large measure, the product of a long period of costly warfare among the imperial nations of Europe. Using taxes and institutions inherited from the past, England and France found it increasingly difficult to fund distant wars in the Americas or in Asia. Royal governments attempting to impose new taxes met with angry resistance. The spread of literacy and the greater availability of books helped create a European culture more open to reform or the revolutionary change of existing institutions. The ideas of Locke and Rousseau guided critics of monarchy toward a new political culture of elections and representative institutions. Each new development served as example and provocation for new revolutionary acts. French officers who took part in the American Revolution helped ignite the French Revolution. Black freemen from Haiti traveled to France to seek their rights and returned to spread revolutionary passions. Each revolution had its own character. The revolutions in France and Haiti proved to be more violent and destructive than the American Revolution. Revolutionaries in France and Haiti, facing a more strongly entrenched and more powerful opposition and greater social inequalities, responded with greater violence.

The conservative retrenchment that followed the defeat of Napoleon succeeded in the short term. Monarchy, multinational empires, and the established church retained their hold on the loyalty of millions of Europeans and could count on the support of many of Europe's wealthiest and most powerful individuals. But liberalism and nationalism continued to stir revolutionary sentiment. The contest between adherents of the old order and partisans of change was to continue well into the nineteenth century. In the end, the nation-state, the Enlightenment legacy of rational inquiry, broadened political participation, and secular intellectual culture prevailed. This outcome was determined in large measure by the old order's inability to satisfy the new social classes that appeared with the emerging industrial economy. The material transformation produced by industrial capitalism could not be contained in the narrow confines of a hereditary social system, nor could the rapid expansion of scientific learning be contained within the doctrines of traditional religion.

The revolutions of the late eighteenth century began the transformation of Western society, but they did not complete it. Only a minority gained full political rights. Women did not achieve full political rights until the twentieth century. Democratic institutions, as in revolutionary France, often failed. Moreover, as Chapter 23 discusses, slavery endured in the Americas past the mid-1800s, despite the revolutionary era's enthusiasm for individual liberty.

■ Key Terms

Enlightenment
Benjamin Franklin
George Washington
Joseph Brant
Constitutional Convention
Estates General
National Assembly
Declaration of the Rights of Man
Jacobins
Maximilien Robespierre
Napoleon Bonaparte
gens de couleur
François Dominique Toussaint L'Ouverture
Congress of Vienna
Revolutions of 1848

■ Suggested Reading

The American Revolution has received a great amount of attention from scholars. Colin Bonwick, *The American Revolution* (1991), and Edward Countryman, *The American Revolution* (1985), provide excellent introductions. Edmund S. Morgan, *The Challenge of the American Revolution* (1976), remains a major work of interpretation. Gordon S. Wood, *The Radicalism of the American Revolution* (1992), is a brilliant examination of the ideological and cultural meanings of the Revolution. A contrarian view is offered by Francis Jennings, *The Creation of America Through Revolution to Empire* (2003). See also William Howard Adams, *The Paris Years of Thomas Jefferson* (1997). Lance Banning, *The Sacred Fire of Liberty: James Madison and the Founding of the Federal Republic* (1995), is a convincing revision of the story of Madison and his era. For the role of women in the American Revolution see Linda K. Kerber, *Women of the Republic: Intellect and Ideology in Revolutionary America* (1980), and Mary Beth Norton, *Liberty's Daughters: The Revolutionary Experience of American Women, 1750–1800* (1980). Also recommended is Norton's *Founding Mothers and Fathers: Gendered Power and the Forming of American Society* (1996). Among the many works that deal with African-Americans and Amerindians during the era, see Sylvia Frey, *Water from Rock: Black Resistance in a Revolutionary Age* (1991); Barbara Graymont, *The Iroquois in the American Revolution* (1972); and William N. Fenton, *The Great Law and the Longhouse: A Political History of the Iroquois Confederacy* (1998).

For intellectual life in the era of the French Revolution see Anne Goldgar, *Impolite Learning: Conduct and Community in the Republic of Letters, 1680–1750* (1995); Dena Goodman, *The Republic of Letters: A Cultural History of the Enlightenment* (1994); and James Swenson, *On Jean-Jacques Rousseau Considered as One of the First Authors of the Revolution* (2002). For the Counter Enlightenment see Darrin M. McMahon, *Enemies of the Enlightenment, The French Counter-Enlightenment and the Making of Modernity* (2001). For the "underside" of this era see the discussion of "folk culture" in *Shaping History: Ordinary People in European Politics, 1500–1700* (1998), by Wayne Te Brake. François Furet, *Interpreting the French Revolution* (1981), breaks with interpretations that emphasize class and ideology. Georges Lefebve, *The Coming of the French Revolution*, trans. R. R. Palmer (1947), presents the classic class-based analysis. George Rudé, *The Crowd in History: Popular Disturbances in France and England* (1981), remains the best introduction to the role of mass protest in the period. Lynn Hunt, *The Family Romance of the French Revolution* (1992), examines the gender content of revolutionary politics. For the role of women see Joan Landes, *Women and the Public Sphere in the Age of the French Revolution* (1988), and the recently published *The Women of Paris and Their French Revolution* (1998) by Dominique Godineau. Felix Markham, *Napoleon* (1963), and Robert B. Holtman, *The Napoleonic Revolution* (1967), provide reliable summaries of the period.

The Haitian Revolution has received less extensive coverage than the revolutions in the United States and France. C. L. R.

James, *The Black Jacobins*, 2d ed. (1963), is the classic study. Anna J. Cooper, *Slavery and the French Revolutionists, 1788–1805* (1988), also provides an overview of this important topic. Carolyn E. Fick, *The Making of Haiti: The Saint Domingue Revolution from Below* (1990), is the best recent synthesis. David P. Geggus, *Slavery, War, and Revolution* (1982), examines the British role in the revolutionary period. See also David Barry Gaspar and David Patrick Geggus, eds., *A Turbulent Time: The French Revolution and the Greater Caribbean* (1997).

For the revolutions of 1830 and 1848 see Arthur J. May's brief survey in *The Age of Metternich, 1814–48*, rev. ed. (1963). Henry Kissinger's *A World Restored* (1957) remains among the most interesting discussions of the Congress of Vienna. Eric Hobsbawm's *The Age of Revolution* (1962) provides a clear analysis of the class issues that appeared during this era. Paul Robertson's *Revolutions of 1848: A Social History* (1960) remains a valuable introduction. See also Peter Stearns and Herrick Chapman, *European Society in Upheaval* (1991). For the development of European social reform movements see Albert Lindemann, *History of European Socialism* (1983).

For national events in Hungary see István Deák's examination of Hungary, *The Lawful Revolution: Louis Kossuth and the Hungarians, 1848–49* (1979). On Germany see Theodore S. Hamerow, *Restoration, Revolution, and Reaction, 1815–1871* (1966). For French events see Roger Price, *A Social History of Nineteenth-Century France* (1987). Barbara Taylor, *Eve and the New Jerusalem: Socialism and Feminism in the Nineteenth Century* (1983), analyzes connections between workers' and women's rights issues in England.

◼ Notes

1. Quoted in Ray Raphael, *A People's History of the American Revolution* (New York: Perenial, 2001), 142.
2. Ibid., 141.
3. Quoted in C. L. R. James, *The Black Jacobins*, 2d ed., (New York: Vintage Books, 1963), 196.

Document-Based Question
Revolutionary Ideas in the Americas and France

Using the following documents, analyze the ideas of the American, French, and Haitian revolutions and the ways people responded to those ideas.

Document 1
Excerpt from American colonist (p. 548)

Document 2
The Tarring and Feathering of a British Official, 1774 (photo, p. 548)

Document 3
Excerpt from the Declaration of Independence (p. 549)

Document 4
Parisians Storm the Bastille (photo, p. 554)

Document 5
Playing Cards from the French Revolution (photo, p. 556)

Document 6
Robespierre and Wollstonecraft Defend and Explain the Terror (Diversity and Dominance, pp. 558–559)

Document 7
Quote from Toussaint L'Ouverture (p. 562)

Document 8
Haiti's Former Slaves Defend Their Freedom (photo, p. 563)

In Document 6, what factors shaped the two different reactions to the same events? What additional types of documents would help you understand the ideas of the American, French, and Haitian revolutions and the ways people responded to those ideas?

22 The Early Industrial Revolution, 1760–1851

Mr. Watt's Engine This drawing shows the functioning parts of a Watt engine used to pump water from a mine: the boiler, cylinder Q, condenser N, rocking horse, and pump S.

CHAPTER OUTLINE

From 1765 until the 1790s a small group of men calling themselves the Lunar Society met once a month in Birmingham, England. They gathered on nights when the moon was full, so they could find their way home in the dark. Among them were the pottery manufacturer Josiah Wedgwood, the engine designer James Watt, the chemist Joseph Priestley, the iron manufacturer Matthew Boulton, and the naturalist Erasmus Darwin. They did not leave a record of what they discussed, but the fact that businessmen, craftsmen, and scientists had interests in common was something new in the history of the world. Though members of very different professions, they were willing to exchange ideas and discoveries in an atmosphere of experimentation and innovation. They invited experts in industry, science, and engineering to speak at their meetings in order to obtain the latest information in their fields.

Meanwhile, similar societies throughout Britain were creating a vogue for science and were giving the word *progress* a new meaning: "change for the better." By focusing on the practical application of knowledge, groups like the Lunar Society laid the groundwork for the economic and social transformations that historians call the **Industrial Revolution.** This revolution involved dramatic innovations in manufacturing, mining, transportation, and communications and equally rapid changes in society and commerce. New relationships between social groups created an environment that was conducive to technical innovation and economic growth. New technologies and new social and economic arrangements allowed the industrializing countries—first Britain, then western Europe and the United States—to unleash massive increases in production and productivity, exploit the world's natural resources as never before, and transform the environment and human life in unprecedented ways.

The distribution of power and wealth generated by the Industrial Revolution was very uneven, for industrialization widened the gap between rich and poor. The people who owned and controlled the innovations amassed wealth and power over nature and over other people. Some of them lived lives of spectacular luxury. Workers, including children, worked long hours in dangerous factories and lived crowded together in unsanitary tenements.

The effect of the Industrial Revolution around the world was also very uneven. The first countries to industrialize grew rich and powerful. In Egypt and India, the economic and military power of the European countries stifled the tentative beginnings of industrialization. Regions that had little or no industry were easily taken advantage of. The disparity between the industrial and the developing countries that exists today has its origins in the early nineteenth century.

As you read this chapter, ask yourself the following questions:

- What caused the Industrial Revolution?

- What were the key innovations that increased productivity and drove industrialization?

- What was the impact of these changes on the society and environment of the industrializing countries?

- How did the Industrial Revolution affect the relations between the industrialized and the nonindustrialized parts of the world?

CAUSES OF THE INDUSTRIAL REVOLUTION

What caused the Industrial Revolution, and why did it begin in England in the late eighteenth century? These are two of the great questions of history. The basic preconditions of this momentous event seem to have been economic development propelled by population growth, an agricultural revolution, the expansion of trade, and an openness to innovation.

Population Growth

The population of Europe rose in the eighteenth century—slowly at first, faster after 1780, then even faster in the early nineteenth century. The fastest growth took place in England and Wales. Population there rose from 5.5 million in 1688 to 9 million in 1801 and 18 million by 1851—increases never before experienced in European history.

The growth of population resulted from more widespread resistance to disease and more reliable food supplies, thanks to the new crops that originated in the Americas (see Chapter 16). More dependable food supplies and better job opportunities led people to marry at earlier ages and have more children. A high birthrate meant a large percentage of children in the general population. In the early nineteenth century some 40 percent of the population of Britain was under fifteen years of age. This high proportion of youths explains both the vitality of the British people in that period and the widespread use of child labor. People also migrated at an unprecedented rate—from the countryside to the cities, from Ireland to England, and, more generally, from Europe to the Americas. Thanks to immigration, the population of the United States rose from 4 million in 1791 to 9.6 million in 1820 and 31.5 million in 1860—faster growth than in any other part of the world at the time.

The Agricultural Revolution

Innovations in manufacturing could only have taken place alongside a simultaneous revolution in farming that provided food for city dwellers and forced poorer peasants off the land. This **agricultural revolution** had begun long before the eighteenth century. One important aspect was the acceptance of the potato, introduced from South America in the sixteenth century. In the cool and humid regions of Europe from Ireland to Russia, potatoes yielded two or three times more food per acre than did the wheat, rye, and oats they replaced. Maize (American corn) was grown across Europe from northern Iberia to the Balkans. Turnips, legumes, and clover did not deplete the soil and could be fed to cattle, which were sources of milk and meat. Manure from cattle in turn fertilized the soil for other crops.

The security of small-scale tenant farmers and sharecroppers depended on traditional methods and rural customs such as collecting plants left over in the fields after the harvest, pasturing their animals on common village lands, and gathering firewood in common woods. Only prosperous landowners with secure titles to their land could afford to bear the risk of trying new methods and new crops. Rich landowners therefore "enclosed" the land—that is, consolidated their holdings—and got Parliament to give them title to the commons that in the past had been open to all. Once in control of the land, they could drain and improve the soil, breed better livestock, and introduce crop rotation. This "enclosure movement" turned tenants and sharecroppers into landless farm laborers. Many moved to the cities to seek work; others became homeless migrants and vagrants; and still others emigrated to Canada, Australia, and the United States.

In eastern Europe, as in Britain, large estates predominated, and aristocratic landowners used such improvements to increase their wealth and political influence. In western Europe enclosure was hampered by the fact that the law gave secure property rights to numerous small farmers.

Trade and Inventiveness

In most of Europe the increasing demand that accompanied the growth of population was met by increasing production in traditional ways. Roads were improved so stagecoaches could travel faster. Royal manufacturers trained additional craftsmen to produce fine china, silks, and carpets by hand. In rural areas much production was carried out through cottage industries. Merchants delivered fibers, leather, and other raw materials to craftspeople (often farmers in the off-season) and picked up the finished products. The growth of the population and food supply was accompanied by the growth of trade. Most of it was local trade in traditional goods and services. But a growing share consisted of simple goods that even middle-class people could afford: sugar, tea, cotton textiles, iron hardware, pottery. Products from other parts of the world like tea and sugar required extensive networks of shipping and finance.

As the story of the Lunar Society demonstrates, scientific discoveries, commercial enterprise, and technical skills became closely connected. Technology and innovation fascinated educated people throughout Europe and eastern North America. The French *Encyclopédie* contained thousands of articles and illustrations of crafts and manufacturing (see Diversity and Dominance: Adam Smith and the Division of Labor). The French and British governments sent expeditions around the world to collect plants that could profitably be grown in their colonies. They also offered prizes to anyone who could find a method of determining the longitude of a ship at sea to avoid the shipwrecks that had cost the lives of thousands of sailors. The American Benjamin Franklin, like many others, experimented with electricity. In France, the Montgolfier brothers invented a hot-air balloon. Claude Chappe° created the first semaphore telegraph. French artillery officers proposed making guns with interchangeable parts. The American Eli Whitney and his associate John Hall invented machine tools, that

Chappe (SHAPP)

C H R O N O L O G Y

	Technology	Economy, Society, and Politics
1750		
	1759 Josiah Wedgwood opens pottery factory	
	1764 Spinning jenny	
	1769 Richard Arkwright's water frame; James Watt patents steam engine	**1776** Adam Smith's *Wealth of Nations*
	1779 First iron bridge	**1776–1783** American Revolution
	1785 Boulton and Watt sell steam engines; Samuel Crompton's mule	**1789–1799** French Revolution
	1793 Eli Whitney's cotton gin	
1800	**1800** Alessandro Volta's battery	
	1807 Robert Fulton's *Clermont*	**1804–1815** Napoleonic Wars
	1820s Construction of Erie Canal	**1820s** U.S. cotton industry begins
	1829 *Rocket,* first steam-powered locomotive	**1833** Factory Act in Britain
	1837 Wheatstone and Cooke's telegraph	**1834** German Zollverein; Robert Owen's Grand National Consolidated Trade Union
	1838 First ships steam across the Atlantic	
	1840 *Nemesis* sails to China	**1846** Repeal of British Corn Laws
	1843 Samuel Morse's Baltimore-to-Washington telegraph	**1847–1848** Irish famine
		1848 Collapse of Chartist movement; Revolutions in Europe
1850	**1851** Crystal Palace opens in London	**1854** First cotton mill in India

is, machines capable of making other machines. These machines greatly increased the productivity of manufacturing.

Britain and Continental Europe

Economic growth was evident throughout the North Atlantic area, yet industrialization did not take place everywhere at once. To understand why, we must look at the peculiar role of Great Britain. Britain enjoyed a rising standard of living during the eighteenth century, thanks to good harvests, a growing population, and a booming overseas trade. Britain was the world's leading exporter of tools, guns, hardware, clocks, and other craft goods (see Map 22.1). Its mining and metal industries employed engineers willing to experiment with new ideas. It had the largest merchant marine and produced more ships, naval supplies, and navigation instruments than other countries.

Until the mid-eighteenth century the British were better known for their cheap imitations than for their innovations or quality products. But they put inventions into practice more quickly than other people, as the engineer John Farey told a parliamentary committee in 1829: "The prevailing talent of English and Scotch people is to apply new ideas to use and to bring such applications to perfection, but they do not imagine as much as foreigners" (see Environment and Technology: The Origin of Graphs).

Before 1790 Britain had a more fluid society than did the rest of Europe. The English royal court was less ostentatious than the courts of France, Spain, and Austria. Its aristocracy was less powerful, and the lines separating the social classes were not as sharply drawn. Political power was not as centralized as on the European continent, and the government employed fewer bureaucrats and officials. Members of the gentry, and even some aristocrats, married into merchant families. Intermarriage among the families of petty merchants, yeoman farmers, and town craftsmen was common. Guilds, which resisted innovation, were relatively weak. Ancestry remained important, but wealth also commanded respect. A businessman with enough money could buy a landed estate,

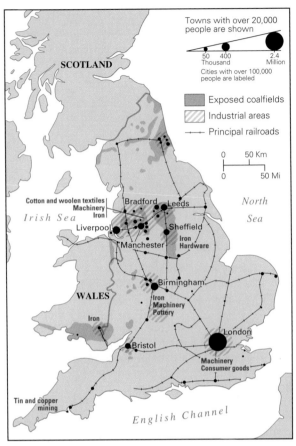

Map 22.1 The Industrial Revolution in Britain, ca. 1850
The first industries arose in northern and western England. These regions had abundant coal and iron-ore deposits for the iron industry and moist climate and fast-flowing rivers, factors imporant for the cotton textile industry.

a seat in Parliament, and the social status that accompanied them.

At a time when transportation by land was very costly, Great Britain had good water transportation thanks to its indented coastline, navigable rivers, and growing network of canals. It had a unified internal market with none of the duties and tolls that goods had to pay every few miles in France. This encouraged regional specialization, such as tin mining in Cornwall and cotton manufacturing in Lancashire, and a growing trade between regions.

Britain was highly commercial; more people were involved in production for export and in trade and finance than in any other major country. It was especially active in overseas trade with the Americas, West Africa, the Middle East, and India. It had financial and insur-

ance institutions able to support growing business enterprises and a patent system that offered inventors the hope of rich rewards. The example of men who became wealthy and respected for their inventions—such as Richard Arkwright, the cotton magnate, and James Watt, the steam engine designer—stimulated others.

In the eighteenth century, the economies of continental Europe also underwent a dynamic expansion, thanks to the efforts of individual entrepreneurs and investors. Yet growth was still hampered by high transportation costs, misguided government regulations, and rigid social structures. The Low Countries were laced with canals, but the terrain elsewhere in Europe made canal building costly and difficult. The ruling monarchies made some attempts to import British techniques and organize factory production, but they all foundered for lack of markets or management skills. From 1789 to 1815 Europe was scarred by revolutions and wars. War created opportunities for suppliers of weapons, uniforms, and horses produced by traditional methods. But the interruption of trade between Britain and continental Europe slowed the diffusion of new techniques, and the insecurity of countries at war discouraged businessmen from investing in factories and machinery.

The political revolutions swept away the restrictions of the old regimes. After 1815 the economies of western Europe were ready to begin industrializing. Industrialization took hold in Belgium and northern France, as businessmen visited Britain to observe the changes and spy out industrial secrets. In spite of British laws forbidding the emigration of skilled workers and the export of textile machinery, many workers slipped through. By the 1820s several thousand Britons were at work on the continent of Europe setting up machines, training workers in the new methods, and even starting their own businesses.

Acutely aware of Britain's head start and the need to stimulate their own industries, European governments took action. They created technical schools. They eliminated internal tariff barriers, tolls, and other hindrances to trade. They encouraged the formation of joint-stock companies and banks to channel private savings into industrial investments. On the European continent, as in Britain, cotton cloth was the first industry. The mills of France, Belgium, and the German states served local markets but could not compete abroad with the more advanced British industry. By 1830 the political climate in western Europe was as favorable to business as Britain's had been a half-century earlier.

Abundant coal and iron-ore deposits determined the concentration of industries in a swath of territories running from northern France through Belgium and the

The Origin of Graphs

Not all technologies involve hardware. There are also information technologies, such as graphs, the visual representation of numerical tables. We see graphs so often in textbooks, magazines, and newspapers that we take them for granted. But they too have a history.

Scientists in France and England created the first graphs in the seventeenth century to illustrate natural phenomena. Some represented tables of data, such as the movements of stars and atmospheric pressure. Until the late eighteenth century few people outside of scientific circles knew or cared about such graphs. This changed with the growing public interest in economic data, population statistics, and other secular subjects that were so much a part of the Enlightenment.

The first person to publish graphs of interest to the general public was William Playfair (1729–1823), an Englishman who started his career as a draftsman for the engine manufacturing firm of Boulton and Watt. In 1786 he published *The Commercial and Political Atlas,* a book that was widely read and went though several editions. All but one of the forty-four graphs in it were line graphs with the vertical axis showing economic data and the horizontal axis representing time. Playfair explained to skeptical readers how a line could represent money:

> This method has struck several persons as being fallacious, because geometrical measurement has not any relation to money or to time; yet here it is made to represent both. The most familiar and simple answer to this objection is by giving an example. Suppose the money received by a man in trade were all in guineas, and that every evening he made a single pile of all the guineas received during the day, each pile would represent a day, and its height would be proportioned to the receipts of that day; so that by this plain operation, time, proportion, and amount *would all be physically combined.*
>
> Lineal arithmetic then, it may be averred, is nothing more than those piles of guineas represented on paper, and on a small scale, in which an inch (suppose) represents the thickness of five millions of guineas, as in geography it does the breadth of a river, or any other extent of country.

As for why it was necessary to show economic data in the form of a graph, Playfair explained:

> Men of high rank, or active business, can only pay attention to general outlines; nor is attention to particulars of use, any further than they give a general information; it is hoped that, with the Assistance of these Charts, such information will be got, without the fatigue and trouble of studying the particulars of which it is composed.

Today, graphs are an indispensable means of conveying information in business and finance, in the sciences, and in government. We need graphs because they give us information quickly and efficiently, "without the fatigue and trouble of studying the particulars."

Source: William Playfair, *The Commercial and Political Atlas,* 3rd ed. (London: J. Wallis, 1801), ix, xiv–xv.

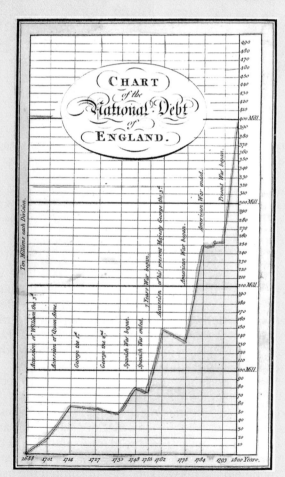

Line Graph of National Debt of England 1803
This graph by William Playfair is designed to shock the viewer by showing the national debt of Britain skyrocketing out of control, especially during the country's many wars. (British Library)

Ruhr district of western Germany to Silesia in Prussia (now part of Poland). By the 1850s France, Belgium, and the German states were in the midst of an industrial boom like that of Britain, based on iron, cotton, steam engines, and railroads.

THE TECHNOLOGICAL REVOLUTION

Five innovations spurred industrialization: (1) mass production through the division of labor, (2) new machines and mechanization, (3) a great increase in the manufacture of iron, (4) the steam engine and the changes it made possible in industry and transportation, and (5) the electric telegraph. China had achieved the first three of these during the Song dynasty (960–1279), but had not developed the steam engine or electricity. The continued success of Western industrialization depended heavily on these new forms of energy.

Mass Production: Pottery

The pottery industry offers a good example of **mass production,** the making of many identical items by breaking the process into simple repetitive tasks. East Asian potters had long known how to make fine glazed porcelain, or "china," but the high cost of transporting it to Europe before the mid-eighteenth century meant that only the wealthy could afford fine Chinese porcelain. Middle-class people used pewter tableware, and the poor ate from wooden or earthenware bowls. Several royal manufactures—Meissen° in Saxony, Delft in Holland, and Sèvres° in France—produced exquisite handmade products for the courts and aristocracy, but their products were much too expensive for mass consumption. Meanwhile, more and more Europeans acquired a taste for Chinese tea as well as for cocoa and coffee, and they wanted porcelain that would not spoil the flavor of hot beverages. This demand created opportunities for inventive entrepreneurs.

Like other countries, Britain had many small pottery workshops where craftsmen made a few plates and cups at a time. Much of this activity took place in a part of the Midlands that possessed good clay, coal for firing, and lead for glazing. There **Josiah Wedgwood,** the son of a potter, started his own pottery business in 1759. He had a scientific bent and invented the pyrometer, a device to measure the extremely high temperatures that are found

Meissen (MY-sen)   Sèvres (SEV-ruh)

Wedgwood's Potteries   In Staffordshire, England, Josiah Wedgwood established a factory to mass-produce beautiful and inexpensive china. The bottle-shaped buildings are kilns in which thousands of pieces of china could be fired at one time. Kilns, factories, and housing were all mixed together in pottery towns, and smoke from burning coal filled the air.   (Mary Evans Picture Library)

in kilns during the firing of pottery, for which he was elected a member of the Royal Society. Today the name Wedgwood is associated with expensive, highly decorated china. But Wedgwood's most important contribution lay in producing ordinary porcelain cheaply by means of the **division of labor** (see Diversity and Dominance: Adam Smith and the Division of Labor).

Wedgwood subdivided the work into highly specialized and repetitive tasks, such as unloading the clay, mixing it, pressing flat pieces, dipping the pieces in glaze, putting handles on cups, packing kilns, and carrying things from one part of his plant to another. To prevent interruptions in production, he instituted strict discipline among his workers. He substituted the use of molds for the potter's wheel wherever possible, a change that not only saved labor but also created identical plates and bowls that could be stacked. He invested in toll roads and canals so that special pottery clay found in southwestern England could be economically shipped to his factories in the Midlands.

Wedgwood's interest in applying technology to manufacturing was sparked by his membership in the Lunar Society. In 1782 the naturalist Erasmus Darwin encouraged him to purchase a steam engine from Boulton and Watt, the firm founded by two other members of the society. The engine that Wedgwood bought to mix clay and grind flint was one of the first to be installed in a factory.

These were radical departures from the age-old methods of craftsmanship. But the division of labor and new machinery allowed Wedgwood to lower the cost of his products while improving their quality, and to offer his wares for sale at lower prices. His factory grew far larger than his competitors' factories and employed several hundred workers. His salesmen traveled throughout England touting his goods, and his products were sold on the European continent as well.

Mechanization: The Cotton Industry

The cotton industry, the largest industry in this period, illustrates the role of **mechanization,** the use of machines to do work previously done by hand. Cotton cloth had long been the most common fabric in China, India, and the Middle East, where it was spun and woven by hand. The cotton plant did not grow in Europe, but the cloth was so much cooler, softer, and cleaner than wool that wealthy Europeans developed a liking for the costly import. When the powerful English woolen industry persuaded Parliament to forbid the import of cotton cloth into England, that prohibition stimulated attempts to import cotton fiber and make the cloth locally. Here was an opportunity for enterprising inventors to reduce costs with labor-saving machinery.

To turn inventions into successful businesses, inventors had to link up with entrepreneurs or become businessmen themselves. Making a working prototype often took years, even decades, and many inventions led to dead ends. History remembers the successful, but even they struggled against great odds.

Beginning in the 1760s a series of inventions revolutionized the spinning of cotton thread. The first was the spinning jenny, invented in 1764, which mechanically drew out the cotton fibers and twisted them into thread. The jenny was simple, cheap to build, and easy for one person to operate. Early models spun six or seven threads at once, later ones up to eighty. The thread, however, was soft and irregular and could be used only in combination with linen, a strong yarn derived from the flax plant.

In 1769 **Richard Arkwright** invented another spinning machine, the water frame, which produced thread strong enough to be used without linen. Arkwright was both a gifted inventor and a successful businessman. His machine was larger and more complex than the jenny and required a source of power such as a water wheel, hence the name "water frame." To obtain the necessary energy he installed dozens of machines in a building next to a fast-flowing river. The resemblance to a flour mill gave such enterprises the name cotton mill.

In 1785 Samuel Crompton patented a machine that combined the best features of the jenny and the water frame. This device, called a mule, produced a strong thread that was thin enough to be used to make a better type of cotton cloth called muslin. The mule could make a finer, more even thread than could any human being, and at a lower cost. At last British industry could undersell high-quality handmade cotton cloth from India, and British cotton output increased tenfold between 1770 and 1790.

The boom in thread production and the soaring demand for cloth created bottlenecks in weaving, stimulating inventors to mechanize the rest of textile manufacturing. The first power loom was introduced in 1784 but was not perfected until after 1815. Other inventions of the period included carding machines, chlorine bleach, and cylindrical presses to print designs on fabric. By the 1830s large English textile mills powered by steam engines were performing all the steps necessary to turn raw cotton into printed cloth. This was a far cry from the cottage industries of the previous century.

Mechanization offered two advantages: (1) increased productivity for the manufacturer and (2) lower prices for the consumer. Whereas in India it took five hundred hours to spin a pound of cotton, the mule of 1790 could do so in three person-hours, and the self-acting mule— an improved version introduced in 1830—required only eighty minutes. Cotton mills needed very few skilled workers, and managers often hired children to tend the spinning machines. The same was true of power looms, which gradually replaced handloom weaving: the number of power looms rose from 2,400 in 1813 to 500,000 by 1850. Meanwhile, the price of cloth fell by 90 percent between 1782 and 1812 and kept on dropping.

The industrialization of Britain made cotton America's most valuable crop. In the 1790s most of Britain's cotton came from India, as the United States produced a mere 750 tons (729 metric tons), mostly from South Carolina. In 1793 the American Eli Whitney patented his cotton gin, a simple device that separated the bolls or seed pods from the fiber and made cotton growing economical. This invention permitted the spread of cotton

파운드폭탄 4발 투하… 두 아들과 함께 사망 ?

, 우세인 은신처 ??

령이 대중 앞에 나타나거나 애국심
을 고취하는 노래만을 내보내던 방
송마저 중단됐다.

라크 전후 대
의에서는 전
영국 주도로

DIVERSITY AND DOMINANCE

ADAM SMITH AND THE DIVISION OF LABOR

Adam Smith (1723–1790), a Scottish social philosopher, is famous for one book, An Inquiry into the Nature and Causes of the Wealth of Nations, *which was first published in 1776 and has been reprinted many times and translated into many languages. It was the first work to explain the economy of a nation as a system. In it, Smith criticized the notion, common in the eighteenth century, that a nation's wealth was synonymous with the amount of gold and silver in the government's coffers. Instead, he defined wealth as the amount of goods and services produced by a nation's people. By this definition, labor and its products are an essential element in a nation's prosperity.*

In the passage that follows, Smith discusses the increase in productivity (to use a modern term) that results from dividing a craft into separate tasks, each of which is performed over and over by one worker. He contrasts two methods of making pins. In one a team of workers divided up the job of making pins and produced a great many every day; in the other pin-workers "wrought separately and independently" and produced very few pins per day. It is clear that the division of labor produces more pins per worker per day. But who benefits? Left unsaid is that a pin factory had to be owned and operated by a manufacturer who hired workers and assigned a task to each one. Thus did industrialization reduce the diversity of self-employed craftsmen by replacing them with a system of dominance.

The illustration shows a pin-makers' workshop in late eighteenth-century France. Each worker is performing a specific task on a few pins at once, and all the energy comes from human muscles. These are the characteristics of a proto-industrial workshop.

To take an example, therefore, from a very trifling manufacture—but one in which the division of labour has been very often taken notice of—the trade of the pin-maker: a workman not educated to this business (which the division of labour has rendered a distinct trade), nor acquainted with the use of machinery employed in it (to the invention of which the same division of labour has probably given occasion), could scarce, perhaps, with his utmost industry, make one pin in a day, and certainly could not make twenty. But in the way in which this business is now carried on, not only the whole work is a peculiar trade, but it is divided into a number of branches, of which the greater part are likewise peculiar trades. One man draws out the wire, another straights it, a third cuts it, a fourth points it, a fifth grinds it at the top for receiving the head; to make the head requires two or three distinct operations, to put it on, is a peculiar business, to whiten the pins is another; it is even a trade by itself to put them into the paper; and the important business of making a pin is, in this manner, divided into about eighteen distinct operations, which, in some manufactories, are all performed by distinct hands, though in others the same man will sometimes perform two or three of them. I have seen a small manufactory of this kind where ten men only were employed, and where some of them, conse-

farming into Georgia, then into Alabama, Mississippi, and Louisiana, and finally as far west as Texas. By the late 1850s the southern states were producing a million tons of cotton a year, five-sixths of the world's total.

With the help of British craftsmen who introduced jennies, mules, and power looms, Americans developed their own cotton industry in the 1820s. By 1840 the United States had twelve hundred cotton mills, two-thirds of them in New England, that served the booming domestic market.

The Iron Industry

Iron making also was transformed during the Industrial Revolution. Throughout Eurasia and Africa, iron had been in use for thousands of years for tools, swords and other weapons, and household items such as knives, pots, hinges, and locks. In the eleventh century, during the Song period, Chinese forges had produced cast iron in large quantities. Production declined after the Song, but iron continued to be common and inexpensive in China. Wherever iron was pro-

A Pin-Makers Workshop   The man in the middle (Figure 2) is pulling wire off a spindle (G) and through a series of posts (HK in Figure 17). This ensures that the wire will be perfectly straight. The worker seated on the lower right (Figure 3) takes the long pieces of straightened wire and cuts them into shorter lengths. The man in the lower left-hand corner (Figure 5) sharpens twelve to fifteen wires at a time by holding them against a grindstone turned by the worker in Figure 6. Figure 16 shows a close-up of this operation. The men in Figures 7 and 8 put the finishing touches on the points. The one in Figure 4 cuts the sharpened pins using the tool shown in Figures 21. Other operations—such as forming the wire to the proper thickness, cleaning and coating it with tin, attaching the heads—are depicted in other engravings in the same encyclopedia.   (Division of Rare and Manuscript Collections, Cornell University Library).

quently, performed two or three distinct operations. But though they were very poor, and therefore but indifferently accommodated with the necessary machinery, they could, when they exerted themselves, make among them about twelve pounds of pins in a day. There are in a pound upwards of four thousand pins of a middling size. Those ten persons, therefore, could make among them upwards of forty-eight thousand pins in a day. Each person, therefore, making a tenth part of forty-eight thousand pins, might be considered as making four thousand eight hundred pins a day. But if they had all wrought separately and independently, and without any of them having been educated to this peculiar business, they certainly could not each of them have made twenty, perhaps not one pin in a day; that is, certainly, not the two hundred and fortieth, perhaps not the four thousand eight hundredth part of what they are at present capable of performing, in consequence of a proper division and combination of their different operations.

QUESTIONS FOR ANALYSIS

1. Why does dividing the job of pin-making into ten or more operations result in the production of more pins per worker? How much more productive are these workers than if each one made complete pins from start to finish?

2. How closely does the picture of a pin-maker's workshop illustrate Smith's verbal description?

3. What disadvantage would there be to working in a pin manufacture where the job was divided as in Smith's example, compared to making entire pins from start to finish?

4. What other examples can you think of, from Adam Smith's day or from more recent times, of the advantages of the division of labor?

Source: Adam Smith, *An Inquiry into the Nature and Causes of the Wealth of Nations,* ed. Edward Gibbon Wakefield (London: Charles Knight & Co., 1843), 7–9.

duced, however, deforestation eventually drove up the cost of charcoal (used for smelting) and restricted output. Furthermore, iron had to be repeatedly heated and hammered to drive out impurities, a difficult and costly process. Because of limited wood supplies and the high cost of skilled labor, iron was a rare and valuable metal outside China before the eighteenth century.

A first breakthrough occurred in 1709 when Abraham Darby discovered that coke (coal from which the impurities have been cooked out) could be used in place

of charcoal. The resulting metal was of lower quality than charcoal-smelted iron but much cheaper to produce, for coal was plentiful. Just as importantly, in 1784 Henry Cort found a way to remove some of the impurities in coke-iron by puddling—stirring the molten iron with long rods. Cort's process made it possible to turn high-sulfur English coal into coke to produce wrought iron (a soft and malleable form of iron) very cheaply. By 1790 four-fifths of Britain's iron was made with coke, while other countries still used charcoal. Coke-iron was cheaper and

Pit Head of a Coal Mine This is a small coal mine. In the center of this picture stands a Newcomen engine used to pump water. The work of hauling coal out of the mine was still done by horses and mules. The smoke coming out of the smokestack is a trademark of the early industrial era. (National Museums and Galleries on Merseyside, Walker Art Gallery [WAG 659])

less destructive of forests, and it allowed a great expansion in the size of individual blast furnaces, substantially reducing the cost of iron. There seemed almost no limit to the quantity of iron that could be produced with coke. Britain's iron production began rising fast, from 17,000 tons in 1740 to 3 million tons in 1844, as much as in the rest of the world put together.

In turn, there seemed no limit to the amount of iron that an industrializing society would purchase or to the novel applications for this cheap and useful material. In 1779 the iron manufacturer Abraham Darby III (grandson of the first Abraham Darby) built a bridge of iron across the Severn River. In 1851 Londoners marveled at the **Crystal Palace,** a huge greenhouse made entirely of iron and glass and large enough to enclose the tallest trees.

The availability of cheap iron made the mass production of objects such as guns, hardware, and tools appealing. However, fitting together the parts of these products required a great deal of labor. To reduce labor costs, manufacturers turned to the idea of interchangeable parts. This idea originated in the eighteenth century when French army officers attempted, without success, to persuade gun makers to produce precisely identical parts. Craftsmen continued to use traditional methods to make gun parts that had to be fitted together by hand. By the mid-nineteenth century, however, interchangeable-parts manufacturing had been adopted in the manufacture of firearms, farm equipment, and sewing machines. At the Crystal Palace exhibition of 1851, Euro-

peans called it the "American system of manufactures." In the next hundred years the use of machinery to mass-produce consumer items was to become the hallmark of American industry.

The Steam Engine

In the history of the world, there had been a number of periods of great technological inventiveness and economic growth. But in all previous cases, the dynamism eventually faltered for various reasons, such as the Mongol invasions that overthrew the Song dynasty in China and the Abassid Caliphate (750–1258) in the Middle East.

The Industrial Revolution that began in the eighteenth century, in contrast, has never slowed down but has instead only accelerated. One reason has been increased interactions between scientists, technicians, and businesspeople. Another has been access to an inexhaustible source of cheap energy, namely fossil fuels.

The first machine to transform fossil fuel into mechanical energy was the **steam engine,** a substitute for human and animal power as well as for wind and water power. Although the mechanization of manufacturing was very important, the steam engine was what set the Industrial Revolution apart from all previous periods of growth and innovation.

Before the eighteenth century, many activities had been limited by the lack of energy. For example, deep

Transatlantic Steamship Race   In 1838, two ships equipped with steam engines, the *Sirius* and the *Great Western,* steamed from England to New York. Although the *Sirius* left a few days earlier, the *Great Western*—shown here arriving in New York harbor—almost caught up with it, arriving just four hours after the *Sirius.* This race inaugurated regular transatlantic steamship service.   (Courtesy of the Mariners' Museum, Newport News, VA)

mines filled with water faster than horses could pump it out. Scientists understood the concept of atmospheric pressure and had created experimental devices to turn heat into motion, but they had not found a way to put those devices to practical use. Then, between 1702 and 1712 Thomas Newcomen developed the first practical steam engine, a crude but effective device. One engine could pump water out of mines as fast as four horses, and it could run day and night without getting tired.

The Newcomen engine's voracious appetite for fuel mattered little in coal mines, where fuel was cheap, but made the engine too costly for other uses. In 1764 **James Watt,** a maker of scientific instruments at Glasgow University in Scotland, was asked to repair the university's model Newcomen engine. Watt realized that the engine wasted fuel because the cylinder had to be alternately heated and cooled. He developed a separate condenser— a vessel into which the steam was allowed to escape after it had done its work, leaving the cylinder always hot and the condenser always cold. Watt patented his idea in 1769. He enlisted the help of the iron manufacturer Matthew Boulton to turn his invention into a commercial product. Their first engines were sold to pump water out of copper and tin mines, where fuel was too costly for Newcomen engines. In 1781 Watt invented the sun-and-planet gear, which turned the back-and-forth action of the piston into rotary motion. This allowed steam en-

gines to power machinery in flour and cotton mills, pottery manufactures, and other industries. Watt's steam engine was the most celebrated invention of the eighteenth century. Because there seemed almost no limit to the amount of coal in the ground, steam-generated energy appeared to be an inexhaustible source of power, and steam engines could be used where animal, wind, and water power were lacking.

Inspired by the success of Watt's engine, inventors in France in 1783, in the United States in 1787, and in England in 1788 put steam engines on boats. The need to travel great distances in the United States explains why the first commercially successful steamboat was Robert Fulton's *North River,* which steamed up and down the Hudson River between New York City and Albany, New York, in 1807.

Soon steamboats were launched on other American rivers, especially the Ohio and the Mississippi, gateways to the Midwest. In the 1820s the Erie Canal linked the Atlantic seaboard with the Great Lakes and opened Ohio, Indiana, and Illinois to European settlement. Steamboats proliferated west of the Appalachian Mountains; by 1830 some three hundred plied the Mississippi and its tributaries. To counter the competition from New York State, Pennsylvania built a thousand miles of canals by 1840. The United States was fast becoming a nation that moved by water.

Oceangoing steam-powered ships were much more difficult to build than river boats, for the first steam engines used so much coal that no ship could carry more than a few days' supply. The *Savannah*, which crossed the Atlantic in 1819, was a sailing ship with an auxiliary steam engine that was used for only ninety hours of its twenty-nine-day trip. Engineers soon developed more efficient engines, and in 1838 two steamers, the *Great Western* and the *Sirius*, crossed the Atlantic on steam power alone. Elsewhere, sailing ships held their own until late in the century. World trade was growing so fast that there was enough business for ships of every kind.

Railroads

On land as on water, the problem was not imagining uses for steam-powered vehicles but building ones that worked, for steam engines were too heavy and weak to pull any weight. After Watt's patent expired in 1800, inventors experimented with lighter, more powerful high-pressure engines—an idea Watt had rejected as too dangerous. In 1804 the engineer Richard Trevithick built an engine that consumed twelve times less coal than Newcomen's and three times less than Watt's. With it, he built several steam-powered vehicles able to travel on roads or rails.

By the 1820s England had many railways on which horses pulled heavy wagons. On one of them, the Stockton and Darlington Railway, chief engineer George Stephenson began using steam locomotives in 1825. Four years later the owners of the Liverpool and Manchester Railway organized a contest between steam-powered locomotives and horse-drawn wagons. Stephenson and his son Robert easily won the contest with their locomotive *Rocket*, which pulled a 20-ton train at up to 30 miles (48 kilometers) per hour. After that triumph, a railroad-building mania that lasted for twenty years swept Britain. The first lines linked towns and mines with the nearest harbor or waterway. In the late 1830s passenger traffic soared, and entrepreneurs built lines between the major cities and then to small towns as well. Railroads were far cheaper, faster, and more comfortable than stagecoaches, and millions of people got in the habit of traveling.

In the United States entrepreneurs built railroads as quickly and cheaply as possible with an eye to fast profits, not long-term durability. By the 1840s, 6,000 miles (10,000 kilometers) of track connected and radiated westward from Boston, New York, Philadelphia, and Baltimore. The boom of the 1840s was dwarfed by the mania of the 1850s, when 21,000 miles (34,000 kilometers) of new track were laid, much of it westward across the Ap-

The De Witt Clinton Locomotive, 1835–1840   The De Witt Clinton was the first steam locomotive built in the United States. The high smokestack let the hot cinders cool so they would not set fire to nearby trees, an important consideration at a time when eastern North America was still covered with forest. The three passenger cars are clearly horse carriages fitted with railroad wheel.   (Corbis)

palachians to Memphis, St. Louis, and Chicago. After 1856 the trip from New York to Chicago, which had once taken three weeks by boat and on horseback, could be made in forty-eight hours. More than anything else, it was the railroads that opened up the Midwest, turning the vast prairie into wheat fields and pasture for cattle to feed the industrial cities of the eastern United States.

Railways triggered the industrialization of Europe (see Map 22.2). Belgium, independent since 1830, quickly copied the British railways. In France and Prussia, the state planned and supervised railroad construction from the start. This delayed construction until the mid-1840s. When it began, however, it had an even greater impact than in Britain, for it not only satisfied the long-standing need for transportation, but also stimulated the iron, machinery, and construction industries.

Communication over Wires

After the Italian scientist Alessandro Volta invented the battery in 1800, making it possible to produce an electric current, many inventors tried to apply electricity to communication. The first practical **electric telegraph** systems were developed almost simultaneously in England and Amer-

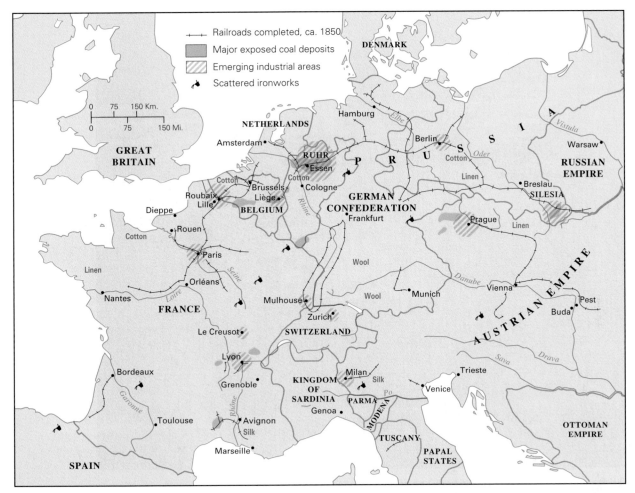

Map 22.2   Industrialization in Europe, ca. 1850   In 1850 industrialization was in its early stages on the European continent. The first industrial regions were comparatively close to England and possessed rich coal deposits: Belgium and the Ruhr district of Germany. Politics determined the location of railroads. Notice the star-shaped French network of rail lines emanating from Paris and the lines linking the different parts of the German Confederation.

ica. In 1837 in England Charles Wheatstone and William Cooke introduced a five-wire telegraph that remained in use until the early twentieth century. That same year, the American Samuel Morse introduced a code of dots and dashes that could be transmitted with a single wire; in 1843 he erected a telegraph line between Washington and Baltimore.

The railroad companies were among the first users of the new electric telegraph. They allowed telegraph companies to string wires along the tracks in exchange for the right to send telegrams from station to station announcing the departure and arrival of trains. Such messages made railroads much safer as well as more efficient.

By the late 1840s telegraph wires were being strung throughout the eastern United States and western Europe. In 1851 the first submarine telegraph cable was laid across the English Channel from England to France; it was the beginning of a network that eventually connected the entire globe. The world was rapidly shrinking, to the applause of Europeans and Americans for whom speed was a clear measure of progress. No longer were communications limited to the speed of a sailing ship, a galloping horse, or a fast-moving train.

Overcrowded London   The French artist Gustave Doré depicted the tenements of industrial London where workers and their families lived. This drawing shows crowded and unsanitary row houses, each one room wide, with tiny back yards, and a train steaming across a viaduct overhead.   (Prints Division, New York Public Library, Astor, Lenox, and Tilden Foundations)

THE IMPACT OF THE EARLY INDUSTRIAL REVOLUTION

The Industrial Revolution led to profound changes in society, politics, and the economy. At first, the changes were local. While some people became wealthy and built beautiful mansions, others lived in slum neighborhoods with polluted water and smoke-filled air. By the mid-nineteenth century, the worst local effects were being alleviated and cities became cleaner and healthier. Replacing them on a national scale were more complex problems: business cycles, labor conflicts, and the transformation of entire regions into industrial landscapes. At the international and global level, industrialization empowered the nations of western Europe and North America at the expense of the rest of the world.

The New Industrial Cities

The most dramatic environmental changes brought about by industrialization occurred in the towns. Never before had towns grown so fast. London, one of the largest cities in Europe in 1700 with 500,000 inhabitants, grew to 959,000 by 1800 and to 2,363,000 by 1850; it was then the largest city the world had ever known. Smaller towns grew even faster. Manchester, a small town of 20,000 in 1758, reached 400,000 a century later, a twentyfold increase. Liverpool grew sixfold in sixty years, from 82,000 in 1801 to 472,000 in 1861. New York City, already 100,000 strong in 1815, reached 600,000 (including Brooklyn) in 1850. European cities also grew, but more slowly; their fastest growth occurred after 1850 with increasing industrialization. In some areas, towns merged and formed megalopolises, such as Greater London, the English Midlands, central Belgium, and the Ruhr district of western Germany.

Industrialization made some people very prosperous. A great deal of this new wealth went into the building of fine homes, churches, museums, and theaters in wealthy neighborhoods in London, Berlin, and New York. Much of the beauty of London dates from the time of the Industrial Revolution. Yet, by all accounts, the industrial cities grew much too fast, and much of the growth occurred in the poorest neighborhoods. As poor migrants streamed in from the countryside, developers built cheap, shoddy row houses for them to rent. These tenements were dangerously overcrowded. Often, several families had to live in one small room.

Sudden population growth, overcrowding, and inadequate municipal services conspired to make urban problems more serious than in earlier times. Town dwellers recently arrived from the country brought country ways with them. People threw their sewage and trash out the windows to be washed down the gutters in the streets. The poor kept pigs and chickens; the rich kept horses; and pedestrians stepped into the street at their own risk. Factories and workers' housing were mixed together. Air pollution from burning coal, a problem since the sixteenth century, got steadily worse. Londoners in particular breathed dense and noxious coal smoke. People drank water drawn from wells and rivers contaminated by sewage and industrial runoff. The River Irwell, which ran through Manchester, was, in the words of one visitor, "considerably less a river than a flood of liquid manure."[1]

"Every day that I live," wrote an American visitor to Manchester, "I thank Heaven that I am not a poor man with a family in England."[2] In his poem "Milton," William Blake (1757–1827) expressed the revulsion of sensitive people at the spoliation of England's "mountains green" and "pleasant pastures":

> And did the Countenance Divine
> Shine forth upon our clouded hills?
> And was Jerusalem builded here
> Among these dark Satanic Mills?

Railroads invaded the towns, bringing noise and smoke into densely populated neighborhoods. Railroad companies built their stations as close to the heart of cities as they could. On the outskirts of cities, railroad yards, sidings, and repair shops covered acres of land,

Paris Apartment at Night   This cutaway drawing in a French magazine shows the vertical segregation by social class that prevailed in the 1840s. The lower level is occupied by the concierge and her family. The first floor belongs to a wealthy family throwing a party for high-society friends. Middle-class people living on the next floor seem annoyed by the noise coming from below. Above them, a thief has entered an artist's studio. A poor seamstress and her child live in the garret under the roof. When elevators were introduced in the late nineteenth century, people of different income levels became segregated by neighborhoods instead of by floors.   (Bibliothèque nationale de France)

surrounded by miles of warehouses and workers' housing. Farther out, far from the dangerous and polluted cities where their factories were located, newly rich industrialists created an environment halfway between country homes and townhouses: the first suburbs.

Under these conditions, diseases proliferated. To the long list of preindustrial urban diseases such as smallpox, dysentery, and tuberculosis, industrialization added new ailments. Rickets, a bone disease caused by lack of sunshine, became endemic in dark and smoky industrial cities. Steamships brought cholera from India, causing great epidemics that struck poor neighborhoods especially hard. In the 1850s, when the average life expectancy in England was forty years, it was only twenty-four years in Manchester, and around seventeen years in Manchester's poorest neighborhoods, because of high rates of infant mortality. Observers of nineteenth-century industrial cities documented the horrors of slum life in vivid detail. Their shocking reports led to municipal reforms, such as garbage removal, water and sewage systems, and parks and schools. These measures began to alleviate the ills of urban life after the mid-nineteenth century.

Rural Environments

Long before the Industrial Revolution began, practically no wilderness areas were left in Britain and very few in western Europe. Almost every piece of land was covered with fields, forests, or pastures shaped by human activity, or by towns; yet humans continued to alter the environment. The most serious problem was deforestation. As they had been doing for centuries, people cut timber to build ships and houses, to heat homes, and to manufacture bricks, iron, glass, beer, bread, and many other items (see Chapter 16).

Americans transformed their environment even faster than Europeans. In North America, the Canadian and American governments seized land from the Indians and made it available at low cost to white farmers and logging companies. After shipbuilding and construction had depleted the British forests in the early nineteenth century, Britain relied heavily on imports of Canadian lumber. East of the Appalachian Mountains, settlers viewed forests not as a valuable resource but as a hindrance to development. In their haste to "open up the West," pioneers felled trees and burned them, built houses and abandoned them, and moved on. The cultivation of cotton in the southern United States was especially harmful. Planters cut down forests, grew cotton for a few years until it depleted the soil, then moved west, abandoning the land to scrub pines. This was slash-and-burn agriculture on an industrial scale.

At that time, America seemed immune to human depredations. Americans thought of nature as an obstacle to be overcome and dominated. This mindset persisted long after the entire continent was occupied and the environment truly endangered.

Paradoxically, in some ways industrialization relieved pressures on the environment in Europe. Raw materials once grown on the land—such as wood, hay, and wool—were replaced by materials found underground, like iron ore and coal, or obtained overseas, like cotton. While Russia, Sweden, the United States, and other forested countries continued to smelt iron with charcoal, the British and western Europeans substituted coke made from coal. As the population increased and land grew scarcer, the cost of growing feed for horses rose, creating incentives to find new, less land-hungry means of transportation. Likewise, as iron became cheaper and wood more expensive, ships and many other objects formerly made of wood began to be made of iron.

To contemporaries, the most obvious changes in rural life were brought about by the new transportation systems. In the eighteenth century France had a national network of quality roads, which Napoleon extended into Italy and Germany. In Britain local governments' neglect of the roads that served long-distance traffic led to the formation of private enterprises—"Turnpike Trusts"—that built numerous toll roads. For heavy goods, horse-drawn wagons were costly even on good roads because of the need to feed the horses. The growing volume of heavy freight triggered canal-building booms in Britain, France, and the Low Countries in the late eighteenth century. Some canals, like the duke of Bridgewater's canal in England, connected coal mines to towns or navigable rivers. Others linked navigable rivers and created national transportation networks.

Canals were marvels of construction, with deep cuts, tunnels, and even aqueducts that carried barges over rivers. They also were a sort of school where engineers learned skills they were able to apply to the next great transportation system: the railroads. They laid track across rolling country by cutting deeply into hillsides and erecting daringly long bridges of stone and iron across valleys. Lesser lines snaked their way to small towns hidden in remote valleys. Soon, clanking trains pulled by puffing, smoke-belching locomotives were invading long-isolated districts.

Thus, in the century after industrialization began, the landscape of industrializing countries was transformed more rapidly than ever before. But the ecological changes, like the technological and economic changes that caused them, were only beginning.

Working Conditions

Industrialization offered new opportunities to the enterprising. Carpenters, metalworkers, and machinists were in great demand. Since industrial machines were fairly simple, some workers became engineers or went into business for themselves. The boldest in England moved to the European continent, the Americas, or India, using their skills to establish new industries.

The successful, however, were a minority. Most industrial jobs were unskilled, repetitive, and boring. Factory work did not vary with the seasons or the time of day but began and ended by the clock. Workdays were long; there were few breaks; and foremen watched constantly. Workers who performed one simple task over and over had little sense of achievement or connection to the final product. Industrial accidents were common and could ruin a family. Unlike even the poorest preindustrial farmer or artisan, factory workers had no control over their tools, jobs, or working hours.

Industrial work, by definition, was physically removed from the home. This had a major impact on women and family life. Women workers were concentrated in textile mills, partly because of ancient traditions, partly because textile work required less strength than metalworking, construction, or hauling. On average, women earned one-third to one-half as much as men. Young unmarried women worked to support themselves or to save for marriage. Married women took factory jobs when their husbands were unable to support the family. Mothers of infants faced a hard choice: whether to leave their babies with wet-nurses at great expense and danger or bring them to the factory and keep them drugged. Rather than working together as family units, husbands and wives increasingly worked in different places.

In the early years of industrialization, even where factory work was available, it was never the main occupation of working women. Most young women who sought paid employment became domestic servants in spite of the low pay, drudgery, and risk of sexual abuse by male employers. Women with small children tried hard to find work they could do at home, such as laundry, sewing, embroidery, millinery, or taking in lodgers.

Even with both parents working, poor families found it hard to make ends meet. As in preindustrial societies, parents thought children should contribute to their upkeep as soon as they were able to. The first generation of workers brought children as young as five or six with them to the factories and mines; they had little choice, since there were no public schools or daycare centers. Employers encouraged the practice and even hired orphans. They preferred children because they were cheaper and more docile than adults and were better able to tie broken threads or crawl under machines to sweep the dust.

In Arkwright's cotton mills two-thirds of the workers were children. In another mill 17 percent were under ten years of age, and 53 percent were between ten and seventeen; they worked fourteen to sixteen hours a day and

"Love Conquers Fear" This is a sentimental Victorian drawing of children in a textile mill. Child labor was common in the first half of the nineteenth century, and workers were exposed to dangerous machines and moving belts, as well as to dust and dirt. (British Library)

were beaten if they made mistakes or fell asleep. Mine operators used children to pull coal carts along the low passageways from the coal face to the mine shaft. In the mid-nineteenth century, when the British government began restricting child labor, mill owners increasingly recruited adult immigrants from Ireland.

American industry began on a somewhat different note than the British. In the early nineteenth century Americans still remembered their revolutionary ideals. When Francis Cabot Lowell built a cotton mill in Massachusetts, he hired the unmarried daughters of New England farmers, promising them decent wages and housing in dormitories under careful moral supervision. Other manufacturers eager to combine profits with morality followed his example. Soon the profit motive won out, and manufacturers imposed longer hours, harsher working conditions, and lower wages. The young women protested: "As our fathers resisted with blood the lordly avarice of the British ministry, so we, their daughters, never will wear the yoke which has been prepared for us."[3] When they went on strike, the mill owners replaced them with Irish immigrant women willing to accept lower pay and worse conditions.

While the cotton boom enriched planters, merchants, and manufacturers, African-Americans paid for it with their freedom. In the 1790s, 700,000 slaves of African descent lived in the United States. The rising demand for cotton and the British and American prohibition of the African slave trade in 1808 caused an increase in the price of slaves. As the "Cotton Kingdom" expanded, the number of slaves rose through natural increase and the reluctance of slave owners to free their slaves. By 1850 there were 3.2 million slaves in the United States, 60 percent of whom grew cotton. Similarly, Europe's and North America's surging demand for tea and coffee prolonged slavery in the sugar plantations of the West Indies and caused it to spread to the coffee-growing regions of southern Brazil. In the British West Indies slavery was abolished in 1833, but elsewhere in the Americas it persisted for another thirty to fifty years.

Slavery was not, as white American southerners maintained, a "peculiar institution"—a consequence of biological differences, biblical injunctions, or African traditions. Slavery was just as much part and parcel of the Industrial Revolution as child labor in Britain, the clothes that people wore, and the beverages they drank.

Changes in Society

Industrialization accentuated the polarization of society and income disparities. In his novel *Sybil; or, The Two Nations*, the British politician Benjamin Disraeli° (1804–1881) spoke of "Two nations between whom there is no intercourse and no sympathy, who are as ignorant of each other's habits, thoughts, and feelings as if they were dwellers in different zones, or inhabitants of different planets . . . the rich and the poor."

In Britain the worst-off were those who clung to an obsolete skill or craft. The cotton-spinning boom of the 1790s briefly brought prosperity to weavers. Their high wages and low productivity, however, induced inventors to develop power looms. As a result, by 1811 the wages of handloom weavers had fallen by a third; by 1832, by two-thirds. Even by working longer hours, they could not escape destitution.

Disraeli (diz-RAY-lee)

In the industrial regions of Britain and continental Europe, the wages and standard of living of factory workers did not decline steadily like those of handloom weavers; they fluctuated wildly. During the war years of 1792 to 1815, the price of food, on which the poor spent most of their income, rose faster than wages. The result was widespread hardship. Then, in the 1820s real wages and public health began to improve. Industrial production grew at over 3 percent a year, pulling the rest of the economy along. Prices fell and wages rose. Even the poor could afford comfortable, washable cotton clothes and underwear.

Improvement, however, was not steady. One reason was the effect of **business cycles**—recurrent swings from economic hard times to recovery and growth, then back to hard times. When demand fell, businesses contracted or closed, and workers found themselves unemployed. Most had few or no savings, and no government at the time provided unemployment insurance. Hard times returned in the "hungry forties." In 1847–1848 the potato crop failed in Ireland. One-quarter of the Irish population died in the resulting famine, and another quarter emigrated to England and North America. On the European continent the negative effects of economic downturns were tempered by the existence of small family farms to which urban workers could return when they were laid off.

Only in the 1850s did the benefits of industrialization—cheaper food, clothing, and utensils—begin to improve workers' standard of living. The real beneficiary of the early Industrial Revolution was the middle class. In Britain landowning gentry and merchants had long shared wealth and influence. In the late eighteenth century a new group arose: entrepreneurs whose money came from manufacturing. Most, like Arkwright and Wedgwood, were the sons of middling shopkeepers, craftsmen, or farmers. Their enterprises were usually self-financed, for little capital was needed to start a cotton-spinning or machine-building business. Many tried and some succeeded, largely by plowing their profits back into the business. A generation later, in the nineteenth century, some newly rich industrialists bought their way into high society. The same happened in western Europe after 1815.

Before the Industrial Revolution, wives of merchants had often participated in the family business; widows occasionally managed sizable businesses on their own. With industrialization came a "cult of domesticity" to justify removing middle-class women from contact with the business world. Instead, they became responsible for the home, the servants, the education of children, and the family's social life (see Chapter 26).

Middle-class people who attributed their success, often correctly, to their own efforts and virtues believed in individual responsibility: if some people could succeed through hard work, thrift, and temperance, then those who did not succeed had no one but themselves to blame. Many workers, however, were newly arrived from rural districts and earned too little to save for the long stretches of unemployment they experienced. The squalor and misery of life in factory towns led to a noticeable increase in drunkenness on paydays. While the life of the poor remained hard, the well-to-do attributed their own success to sobriety, industriousness, thrift, and responsibility. The moral position of the middle-class mingled condemnation with concern, coupled with feelings of helplessness in the face of terrible social problems, such as drunkenness, prostitution, and child abandonment.

NEW ECONOMIC AND POLITICAL IDEAS

Changes as profound as the Industrial Revolution triggered political ferment and ideological conflict. So many other momentous events took place during those years—the American Revolution (1776–1783), the French Revolution (1789–1799), the Napoleonic Wars (1804–1815), the reactions and revolts that periodically swept over Europe after 1815—that we cannot neatly separate out the consequences of industrialization from the rest. But it is clear that by undermining social traditions and causing a growing gap between rich and poor, the Industrial Revolution strengthened the ideas of laissez faire° and socialism and sparked workers' protests.

Laissez Faire and Its Critics

The most celebrated exponent of **laissez faire** ("let them do") was Adam Smith (1723–1790), a Scottish economist. In *The Wealth of Nations* (1776) Smith argued that if individuals were allowed to seek personal gain, the effect, as though guided by an "invisible hand," would be to increase the general welfare. The government should refrain from interfering in business, except to protect private property; it should even allow duty-free trade with foreign countries. By advocating free-market capitalism, Smith was challenging the prevailing economic doctrine of earlier centuries, **mercantilism,** which argued that governments should regulate trade in order to maximize their hoard of precious metals (see Chapter 18).

Persuaded by Adam Smith's arguments, governments dismantled many of their regulations in the decades after 1815. Britain even lowered its import duties, though other countries kept theirs. Nonetheless, it was obvious that industrialization was not improving the general welfare but was instead causing widespread misery. Two other thinkers, Thomas Malthus (1766–1834) and David Ricardo (1772–1832), attempted to explain the poverty they saw without challenging the basic premises of laissez faire. The cause of the workers' plight, Malthus and Ricardo said, was the population boom, which outstripped the food supply and led to falling wages. The workers' poverty, they claimed, was as much a result of "natural law" as the wealth of successful businessmen, and the only way the working class could avoid mass famine was to delay marriage and practice self-restraint and sexual abstinence.

Laissez faire provided an ideological justification for a special kind of capitalism: banks, stock markets, and chartered companies allowed investors to obtain profits with reasonable risks but with much less government control and interference than in the past. In particular, removing guild and other restrictions allowed businesses to employ women and children and keep wages low.

Businesspeople in Britain eagerly adopted laissez-faire ideas that justified their activities and kept the government at bay. But not everyone accepted the grim conclusions of the "dismal science," as economics was then known. The British philosopher Jeremy Bentham (1748–1832) believed that it was possible to maximize "the greatest happiness of the greatest number," if only a Parliament of enlightened reformers would study the social problems of the day and pass appropriate legislation.

The German economist Friedrich List (1789–1846) rejected laissez faire and free trade as a British trick "to make the rest of the world, like the Hindus, its serfs in all industrial and commercial relations." To protect their "infant industries" from British competition, he argued, the German states had to eliminate tariff barriers between them but erect high barriers against imports from Britain. On the European continent, List's ideas were as influential as those of Smith and Ricardo and led in 1834 to the formation of the Zollverein,° a customs union of most of the German states.

laissez faire (LAY-say fair)

Zollverein (TSOLL-feh-rine)

Positivists and Utopian Socialists

Bentham optimistically advocated gradual improvements. In contrast, three French social thinkers, moved by sincere concern for the poor, offered a radically new vision of a just civilization. Espousing a philosophy called **positivism,** the count of Saint-Simon (1760–1825) and his disciple Auguste Comte° (1798–1857) argued that the scientific method could solve social as well as technical problems. They recommended that the poor, guided by scientists and artists, form workers' communities under the protection of benevolent business leaders. These ideas found no following among workers, but they attracted the enthusiastic support of bankers and entrepreneurs, for whom positivism provided a rationale for investing in railroads, canals, and other symbols of modernity. The third French thinker, Charles Fourier° (1768–1837), loathed capitalists and imagined an ideal society in which groups of sixteen hundred workers would live in dormitories and work together on the land and in workshops where music, wine, and pastries would soften the hardships of labor. Critics called his ideas **utopian° socialism,** from the Greek word *utopia* meaning "nowhere." Fourier's ideas are now considered a curiosity, but positivism resonates to this day among liberal thinkers, especially in Latin America.

The person who came closest to creating a utopian community was the Englishman Robert Owen (1771–1858), a successful cotton manufacturer who believed that industry could provide prosperity for all. Conscience-stricken by the plight of British workers, Owen took over the management of New Lanark, a mill town south of Glasgow. He improved the housing and added schools, a church, and other amenities. He also testified in Parliament against child labor and for government inspection of working conditions, angering his fellow industrialists, but helping bring about long-overdue reforms.

Protests and Reforms

Workers benefited little from the ideas of these middle-class philosophers. Instead, they resisted the harsh working conditions in their own ways. They changed jobs frequently. They were often absent, especially on Mondays. When they were not closely watched, the quality of their work was likely to be poor.

Periodically, workers rioted or went on strike, especially when food prices were high and when downturns in the business cycle left many unemployed. In some places, craftsmen broke into factories and destroyed the machines that threatened their livelihoods. Such acts of resistance did nothing to change the nature of industrial work. Not until workers learned to act together could they hope to have much influence.

Gradually, workers formed benevolent societies and organizations to demand universal male suffrage and shorter workdays. In 1834 Robert Owen organized the Grand National Consolidated Trade Union to lobby for an eight-hour workday; it quickly gained half a million members but collapsed a few months later in the face of government prosecution of trade-union activities. A new movement called Chartism arose soon thereafter. It was led by the London cabinetmaker William Lovett and the Irish landlord Fergus O'Connor and appealed to miners and industrial workers. It demanded universal male suffrage, equal electoral districts, the secret ballot, salaries for members of Parliament, and annual elections. It gathered 1.3 million signatures on a petition, but Parliament rejected it. Chartism collapsed in 1848, but left a legacy of labor organizing.

Eventually, mass movements persuaded political leaders to look into the abuses of industrial life, despite the prevailing laissez-faire philosophy. In the 1820s and 1830s the British Parliament began investigating conditions in factories and mines. The Factory Act of 1833 prohibited the employment of children younger than nine in textile mills. It also limited the working hours of children between the ages of nine and thirteen to eight hours a day and of fourteen- to eighteen-year-olds to twelve hours. The Mines Act of 1842 prohibited the employment of women and boys under age ten underground. Several decades passed before the government appointed enough inspectors to enforce the new laws.

Most important was the struggle over the Corn Laws—tariffs on imported grain. Their repeal in 1846, in the name of "free trade," was designed to lower the cost of food for workers and thereby allow employers to pay lower wages. A victory for laissez faire, the repeal also represented a victory for the rising class of manufacturers and other employers over the conservative landowners who had long dominated politics and whose harvests faced competition from cheaper imported food.

The British learned to seek reform through accommodation. On the European continent, in contrast, the revolutions of 1848 revealed widespread discontent with repressive governments but failed to soften the hardships of industrialization (see Chapter 26).

Comte (COME-tuh)   **Fourier** (FOOR-yeh)   **utopian** (you-TOE-pee-uhn)

INDUSTRIALIZATION AND THE NONINDUSTRIAL WORLD

The spread of the Industrial Revolution in the early nineteenth century transformed the relations of western Europe and North America with the rest of the world. For most of the world, trade with the industrial countries meant exporting raw materials, not locally made handicraft products. China was defeated and humiliated by the products of industrial manufacture. In Egypt and India cheap industrial imports, backed by the power of Great Britain, delayed industrialization for a century or more. In these three cases, we can discern the outlines of the Western domination that has characterized the history of the world since the late nineteenth century.

In January 1840 a shipyard in Britain launched a radically new ship. The *Nemesis* had an iron hull, a flat bottom that allowed it to navigate in shallow waters, and a steam engine to power it upriver and against the wind. The ship was heavily armed. In November it arrived off the coast of China. Though ships from Europe had been sailing to China for three hundred years, the *Nemesis* was the first steam-powered iron gunboat seen in Asian waters. A Chinese observer noted: "Iron is employed to make it strong. The hull is painted black, weaver's shuttle fashion. On each side is a wheel, which by the use of coal fire is made to revolve as fast as a running horse. . . . At the vessel's head is a Marine God, and at the head, stern, and sides are cannon, which give it a terrific appearance. Steam vessels are a wonderful invention of foreigners, and are calculated to offer delight to many."[4]

Instead of offering delight, the *Nemesis* and other steam-powered warships that soon joined it steamed up the Chinese rivers, bombarded forts and cities, and transported troops and supplies from place to place along the coast and up rivers far more quickly than Chinese soldiers could move on foot. With this new weapon, Britain, a small island nation half a world away, was able to defeat the largest and most populated country in the world (see Chapter 25).

Egypt, strongly influenced by European ideas since the French invasion of 1798, began to industrialize in the early nineteenth century. The driving force was its ruler, Muhammad Ali (1769–1849), a man who was to play a major role not only in the history of Egypt but in the Middle East and East Africa as well (see Chapter 24). He wanted to build up the Egyptian economy and military in order to become less dependent on the Ottoman sul-

Steam Tractor in India   Power machinery was introduced into India because of the abundance of skilled low-cost labor. In this scene, a steam tractor fords a shallow stream to the delight of onlookers. The towerlike construction on the right is probably a pier for a railroad bridge.   (Billie Love Historical Society)

tan, his nominal overlord. To do so, he imported advisers and technicians from Europe and built cotton mills, foundries, shipyards, weapons factories, and other industrial enterprises. To pay for all this, he made the peasants grow wheat and cotton, which the government bought at a low price and exported at a profit. He also imposed high tariffs on imported goods in order to force the pace of industrialization.

Muhammad Ali's efforts fell afoul of the British, who did not want a powerful country threatening to interrupt the flow of travelers and mail across Egypt, the shortest route between Europe and India. When Egypt went to war against the Ottoman Empire in 1839, Britain intervened and forced Muhammad Ali to eliminate all import duties in the name of free trade. Unprotected, Egypt's fledgling industries could not compete with the flood of cheap British products. Thereafter, Egypt exported raw cotton, imported manufactured goods, and became, in effect, an economic dependency of Britain.

Until the late eighteenth century, India had been the world's largest producer and exporter of cotton textiles, handmade by skilled spinners and weavers. The British

East India Company took over large parts of India just as the Industrial Revolution was beginning in Britain (see Chapter 24 and Map 24.2). It allowed cheap British factory-made yarn and cloth to flood the Indian market duty-free, putting spinners and later handloom weavers out of work. Unlike Britain, India had no factories to which displaced handicraft workers could turn for work. Most of them became landless peasants, eking out a precarious living.

Like other tropical regions, India became an exporter of raw materials and an importer of British industrial goods. To hasten the process, British entrepreneurs and colonial officials introduced railroads into the subcontinent. The construction of India's railroad network began in the mid-1850s, along with coal mining to fuel the locomotives and the installation of telegraph lines to connect the major cities.

Some Indian entrepreneurs saw opportunities in the atmosphere of change that the British created. In 1854 the Bombay merchant Cowasjee Nanabhoy Davar imported an engineer, four skilled workers, and several textile machines from Britain and started India's first textile mill. This was the beginning of India's mechanized cotton industry. Despite many gifted entrepreneurs, India's industrialization proceeded at a snail's pace, for the government was in British hands and the British did nothing to encourage Indian industry.

The cases of Egypt, India, and China show how the demands of Western nations and the military advantage that industrialization gave them led them to interfere in the internal affairs of nonindustrial societies. As we shall see in Chapter 27, this was the start of a new age of Western dominance.

CONCLUSION

The great change we call the Industrial Revolution began in Great Britain, a society that was open to innovation, commercial enterprise, and the cross-fertilization of science, technology, and business. New machines and processes in the cotton and iron industries were instrumental in launching the Industrial Revolution, but what made industrialization an ongoing phenomenon was a new source of energy, the steam engine.

In the period from 1760 to 1851 the new technologies of the Industrial Revolution greatly increased humans' power over nature. Goods could be manufactured in vast quantities at low cost. People and messages could travel at unprecedented speeds. Most important, hu-

mans gained access to the energy stored in coal and used it to power machinery and propel ships and trains faster than vehicles had ever traveled before. With their new-found power, humans turned woodland into farmland, dug canals and laid tracks, bridged rivers and cut through mountains, and covered the countryside with towns and cities.

The ability to command nature, far from benefiting everyone, increased the disparities between individuals and societies. Industrialization brought forth entrepreneurs—whether in the mills of England or on plantations in the American South—with enormous power over their employees or slaves, a power that they found easy and profitable to abuse. Some people acquired great wealth, while others lived in poverty and squalor. While middle-class women were restricted to caring for their homes and children, many working-class women had to leave home to earn wages in factories or as domestic servants. These changes in work and family life provoked intense debates among intellectuals. Some defended the disparities in the name of laissez faire; others criticized the injustices that industrialization brought. Society was slow to bring these abuses under control.

By the 1850s the Industrial Revolution had spread from Britain to western Europe and the United States, and its impact was being felt around the world. To make a product that was sold on every continent, the British cotton industry used African slaves, American land, British machines, and Irish workers. As we shall see in Chapter 23, industrialization brought even greater changes to the Americas than it did to the Eastern Hemisphere.

■ Key Terms

Industrial Revolution
agricultural revolution
mass production
Josiah Wedgwood
division of labor
mechanization
Richard Arkwright
Crystal Palace
steam engine
James Watt
electric telegraph
business cycles
laissez faire
mercantilism
positivism
utopian socialism

■ Suggested Reading

General works on the history of technology give pride of place to industrialization. For an optimistic overview see Joel Mokyr, *The Lever of Riches: Technological Creativity and Economic Progress* (1990). Other important recent works include James McClellan III and Harold Dorn, *Science and Technology in World History* (1999); David Landes, *The Wealth and Poverty of Nations* (1998); and Ian Inkster, *Technology and Industrialization: Historical Case Studies and International Perspectives* (1998).

There is a rich literature on the British industrial revolution, beginning with T. S. Ashton's classic *The Industrial Revolution, 1760–1830*, published in 1948 and often reprinted. The interactions between scientists, technologists, and businessmen are described in Jenny Uglow, *The Lunar Men: Five Friends Whose Curiosity Changed the World* (2002), but see also Joel Mokyr, *The Gifts of Athena: Historical Origins of the Knowledge Economy* (2002). The importance of the steam engine is the theme of Jack Goldstone, "Efflorescences and Economic Growth in World History: Rethinking the 'Rise of the West' and the Industrial Revolution," in *Journal of World History* (Fall 2002).

The impact of industrialization on workers is the theme of E. P. Thompson's classic work *The Making of the English Working Class* (1963), but see also E. R. Pike, *"Hard Times": Human Documents of the Industrial Revolution* (1966). The role of women is most ably revealed in Lynn Y. Weiner, *From Working Girl to Working Mother: The Female Labor Force in the United States, 1820–1980* (1985), and in Louise Tilly and Joan Scott, *Women, Work, and Family* (1978).

European industrialization is the subject of J. Goodman and K. Honeyman, *Gainful Pursuits: The Making of Industrial Eu-rope: 1600–1914* (1988); John Harris, *Industrial Espionage and Technology Transfer: Britain and France in the Eighteenth Century* (1998); and David Landes, *The Unbound Prometheus: Technological Change and Industrial Development in Western Europe from 1750 to the Present* (1972). On the beginnings of American industrialization see David Jeremy, *Artisans, Entrepreneurs and Machines: Essays on the Early Anglo-American Textile Industry, 1770–1840* (1998).

On the environmental impact of industrialization see Richard Wilkinson, *Poverty and Progress: An Ecological Perspective on Economic Development* (1973), and Richard Tucker and John Richards, *Global Deforestation in the Nineteenth-Century World Economy* (1983).

The first book to treat industrialization as a global phenomenon is Peter Stearns, *The Industrial Revolution in World History* (1993); see also Louise Tilly's important article "Connections" in *American Historical Review* (February 1994).

■ Notes

1. Quoted in Lewis Mumford, *The City in History* (New York: Harcourt Brace, 1961), 460.
2. Quoted in F. Roy Willis, *Western Civilization: An Urban Perspective*, vol. II (Lexington, MA: D.C. Heath, 1973), 675.
3. Alice Kessler-Harris, *Women Have Always Worked: A Historical Overview* (Old Westbury, New York: The Feminist Press, 1981), 59.
4. *Nautical Magazine* 12 (1843): 346.

Document-Based Question
Early Industrialization in Western Europe

Using the following documents, analyze the social, economic, and environmental effects of early industrialization in Western Europe.

DOCUMENT 1
Map 22.1 The Industrial Revolution in Britain, ca. 1850 (p. 572)

DOCUMENT 2
Adam Smith and the Division of Labor (Diversity and Dominance, pp. 576–577)

DOCUMENT 3
Pit Head of a Coal Mine (photo, p. 578)

DOCUMENT 4
Map 22.2 Industrialization in Europe, ca. 1850 (p. 581)

DOCUMENT 5
Overcrowded London (photo, p. 582)

DOCUMENT 6
Excerpt from poem by Blake (p. 583)

DOCUMENT 7
Paris Apartment at Night (photo, p. 583)

DOCUMENT 8
"Love Conquers Fear" (photo, p. 585)

What does Adam Smith omit from his discussion of the division of labor in Document 2? What additional types of documents would help you understand the effects of early industrialization in Western Europe?

23 Nation Building and Economic Transformation in the Americas, 1800–1890

The Train Station in Orizaba, Mexico, 1877 In the last decades of the nineteenth century Mexico's political leaders actively promoted economic development. The railroad became the symbol of this ideal.

CHAPTER OUTLINE

Between 1836 and 1848 Mexico lost 50 percent of its territory to the United States. In the political crisis that followed, reformers, called liberals, fought conservatives for control of the nation. The liberal Benito Juárez° dominated this era as a war leader and a symbol of Mexican nationalism. Many have compared him to his contemporary, Abraham Lincoln. Juárez began his life in poverty. An Amerindian orphan, he became a lawyer and political reformer. He helped drive the dictator Antonio López de Santa Anna from power in 1854 and helped lead efforts to reduce the power of the Catholic Church and the military. He later served as chief justice of the Supreme Court and as president.

When conservatives rebelled against the Constitution of 1857, Juárez assumed the presidency and led liberal forces to victory. Mexico's conservatives turned to Napoleon III of France, who sent an army that suspended the constitution and imposed Archduke Maximilian of Habsburg, brother of Emperor Franz Joseph of Austria, as emperor. But the French army could not defeat Juárez, and Mexican resistance was eventually supported by U.S. diplomatic pressure. When the French left, Maximilian was captured and executed. This victory over a powerful foreign enemy redeemed a nation that had earlier been humiliated by the United States. But the creation of democracy proved more elusive than the protection of Mexican sovereignty. Despite the Mexican constitution's prohibition of presidential reelection, Juárez would serve as president until his death in 1872.

Despite cycles of political violence like that experienced by Mexico, the nineteenth century witnessed a radical transformation of the Western Hemisphere. Spurred by the American and French revolutions (see Chapter 21) and encouraged by nationalism and the ideal of political freedom, most of the region's nations achieved independence, although Mexico and others faced foreign interventions.

Throughout the nineteenth century the new nations in the Western Hemisphere wrestled with the difficult questions that independence raised. If colonies could reject submission to imperial powers, could not regions with distinct cultures, social structures, and economies refuse to accept the political authority of the newly formed nation-states? How could nations born in revolution accept the political strictures of written constitutions—even those they wrote themselves? How could the ideals of liberty and freedom expressed in those constitutions be reconciled with the denial of rights to Amerindians, slaves, recent immigrants, and women?

While trying to resolve these political questions, the new nations also attempted to promote economic growth. But colonial economic development, with its emphasis on agricultural and mining exports, inhibited efforts to promote diversification and industrialization, just as the legacy of class and racial division thwarted the realization of political ideals.

As you read this chapter, ask yourself the following questions:

- What were the causes of the revolutions for independence in Latin America?

- What major political challenges did Western Hemisphere nations face in the nineteenth century?

- How did abolitionism, the movement for women's rights, and immigration change the nations of the Western Hemisphere?

- How did industrialization and new agricultural technologies affect the environment?

INDEPENDENCE IN LATIN AMERICA, 1800–1830

As the eighteenth century drew to a close, Spain and Portugal held vast colonial possessions in the Western Hemisphere, although their power had declined relative to that of their British and French rivals. Both Iberian empires had reformed their colonial administration and strengthened their military forces in the eighteenth century. Despite these efforts, the same economic and political forces that had undermined British

---

Benito Juárez (beh-NEE-toh WAH-rez)

rule in the colonies that became the United States were present in Spanish America and Brazil.

Roots of Revolution, to 1810

The great works of the Enlightenment as well as revolutionary documents like the Declaration of Independence and the Declaration of the Rights of Man circulated widely in Latin America by 1800, but very few colonial residents desired to follow the examples of the American and French Revolutions (see Chapter 21). Local-born members of Latin America's elites and middle classes were frustrated by the political and economic power of colonial officials and angered by high taxes and imperial monopolies. But it was events in Europe that first pushed the colonies towards independence. Napoleon's decision to invade Portugal (1807) and Spain (1808), not revolutionary ideas, created the crisis of legitimacy that undermined the authority of colonial officials, and ignited Latin America's struggle for independence.

In 1808 as a French army neared Lisbon, the royal family of Portugal fled to Brazil. King John VI maintained his court there for over a decade. In Spain, in contrast, Napoleon forced King Ferdinand VII to abdicate and placed his own brother, Joseph Bonaparte, on the throne. Spanish patriots fighting against the French created a new political body, the Junta° Central, to administer the areas they controlled. Most Spaniards viewed the Junta as a temporary patriotic institution created to govern Spain while the king remained a French prisoner. The Junta, however, claimed the right to exercise the king's powers over Spain's colonies, and this claim provoked a crisis.

Large numbers of colonial residents in Spanish America, perhaps a majority, favored obedience to the Junta Central. A vocal minority, which included many wealthy and powerful individuals, objected. The dissenters argued that they were subjects of the king, not dependents of the Spanish nation. They wanted to create local juntas and govern their own affairs until Ferdinand regained the throne. Spanish loyalists in the colonies resisted this tentative assertion of local autonomy and thus provoked armed uprisings. In late 1808 and 1809 popular movements overthrew Spanish colonial officials in Venezuela, Mexico, and Alto Peru (modern Bolivia) and created local juntas. In each case, Spanish officials quickly reasserted control and punished the leaders. Their harsh repression, however, further polarized public opinion in the colonies and gave rise to a greater sense of a separate American nationality. By 1810 Spanish colonial authorities were facing a new round of revolutions more clearly focused on the achievement of independence.

Spanish South America, 1810–1825

In Caracas (the capital city of modern Venezuela) a revolutionary Junta led by creoles (colonial-born whites) declared independence in 1811. Although this group espoused popular sovereignty and representative democracy, its leaders were large landowners who defended slavery and opposed full citizenship for the black and mixed-race majority. Their aim was to expand their own privileges by eliminating Spaniards from the upper levels of Venezuela's government and from the church. The junta's narrow agenda spurred loyalists in the colonial administration and church hierarchy to rally thousands of free blacks and slaves to defend the Spanish Empire. Faced with this determined resistance, the revolutionary movement placed overwhelming political authority in the hands of its military leader **Simón Bolívar°** (1783–1830), who later became the preeminent leader of the independence movement in Spanish South America.

The son of wealthy Venezuelan planters, Bolívar had studied both the classics and the works of the Enlightenment. He used the force of his personality to mobilize political support and to hold the loyalty of his troops. Defeated on many occasions, Bolívar successfully adapted his objectives and policies to attract new allies and build coalitions. Although initially opposed to the abolition of slavery, for example, he agreed to support emancipation in order to draw slaves and freemen to his cause and to gain supplies from Haiti. Bolívar was also capable of using harsh methods to ensure victory. Attempting to force resident Spaniards to join the rebellion in 1813 he proclaimed: "Any Spaniard who does not . . . work against tyranny in behalf of this just cause will be considered an enemy and punished; as a traitor to the nation, he will inevitably be shot by a firing squad."[1]

Between 1813 and 1817 military advantage shifted back and forth between the patriots and loyalists. Bolívar's ultimate success was aided by his decision to enlist demobilized English veterans of the Napoleonic Wars and by a military revolt in Spain in 1820. The English veterans, hardened by combat, helped improve the battlefield performance of Bolívar's army. The revolt in Spain forced Ferdinand VII—restored to the throne in 1814 after the defeat of Napoleon—to accept a constitution that

---

Junta (HUN-tah)

Simón Bolívar (see-MOAN bow-LEE-varh)

C H R O N O L O G Y

	United States and Canada	Mexico and Central America	South America
	1789 U.S. Constitution ratified		
1800	**1803** Louisiana Purchase		
			1808 Portuguese royal family arrives in Brazil
	1812–1815 War of 1812	**1810–1821** Mexican movement for independence	**1808–1809** Revolutions for independence begin in Spanish South America
1825			**1822** Brazil gains independence
	1836 Texas gains independence from Mexico		
	1845 Texas admitted as a state	**1846–1848** War between Mexico and the United States	
		1847–1870 Caste War	
1850	**1848** Women's Rights Convention in Seneca Falls, New York	**1857** Mexico's new constitution limits power of Catholic church and military	**1850** Brazilian slave trade ends
	1861–1865 Civil War	**1862–1867** French invade Mexico	**1865–1870** Argentina, Uruguay, and Brazil wage war against Paraguay
	1867 Creation of Dominion of Canada	**1867** Emperor Maximilian executed	**1870s** Governments of Argentina and Chile begin final campaigns against indigenous peoples
1875	**1876** Sioux and allies defeat U.S. Army in Battle of Little Bighorn		
	1879 Thomas Edison develops incandescent lamp		**1879–1881** Chile wages war against Peru and Bolivia; telegraph, barbed wire, and refrigeration introduced in Argentina
	1890 "Jim Crow" laws enforce segregation in South		**1888** Abolition of slavery in Brazil
	1890s United States becomes world's leading steel producer		

limited the powers of both the monarch and the church. Colonial loyalists who for a decade had fought to maintain the authority of monarch and church viewed those reforms as unacceptably liberal.

With the king's supporters divided, momentum swung to the patriots. After liberating present-day Venezuela, Colombia, and Ecuador, Bolívar's army occupied the area that is now Peru and Bolivia (named for Bolívar). Finally defeating the last Spanish armies in 1824, Bolívar and his closest supporters attempted to draw the former Spanish colonies into a formal confederation. The first step was to forge Venezuela, Colombia, and Ecuador into the single nation of Gran Colombia (see Map 23.1). With Bolívar's encouragement, Peru and Bolivia also experimented with unification. Despite his prestige, however, all of these initiatives had failed by 1830.

Buenos Aires (the capital city of modern Argentina) was the second important center of revolutionary activity in Spanish South America. In Buenos Aires news of Ferdinand VII's abdication led to the creation of a junta organized by militia commanders, merchants, and ranchers, which overthrew the viceroy in 1810. To deflect the opposition of loyalists and Spanish colonial officials, the junta claimed loyalty to the imprisoned king. After Ferdinand regained the Spanish throne, however, junta

OREGON
COUNTRY
(Joint U.S.-British
occupation)

BRITISH NORTH AMERICA
(Gr. Br.)

Mississippi

UNITED STATES

Colorado

Rio Grande

MEXICO
1821

San
Antonio

ATLANTIC
OCEAN

Gulf of Mexico

Havana

BAHAMA IS.
(Gr. Br.)

Mexico City

Veracruz

CUBA
(Spain)

HAITI 1804

PUERTO RICO (Spain)

BRITISH
HONDURAS (Gr. Br.)

JAMAICA (Gr. Br.)

GUATEMALA
Guatemala City

*Caribbean
Sea*

UNITED PROVINCES OF
CENTRAL AMERICA
1823—1839

Panama

Caracas

TRINIDAD (Gr. Br.)

VENEZUELA

BR. GUIANA (Gr. Br.)

DUTCH GUIANA (Neth.)

Magdalena

Socorro

Bogotá

FRENCH GUIANA (France)

GRAN COLOMBIA
1819—1830

*Galápagos
Islands*

Quito

ECUADOR

Amazon

EMPIRE OF BRAZIL
1822

PERU
1824

Lima

PACIFIC
OCEAN

Salvador

BOLIVIA
1825

La Paz

Sucre

Paraná

PARAGUAY
1811

São Paulo

Rio de Janeiro

CHILE
1817

UNITED
PROVINCES OF
THE RÍO DE
LA PLATA
1816

URUGUAY
1828

Valparaíso

Santiago

ARGENTINA

Buenos Aires

Bahía
Blanca

Montevideo

1811 Year independence gained

Colony

0   500   1000 Km.

0   500   1000 Mi.

PATAGONIA
(Disputed between
Argentina and Chile)

*Islas Malvinas
(Falkland Islands)*

Map 23.1   **Latin America by 1830**   By 1830 patriot forces had overturned the Spanish and Portuguese Empires of the Western Hemisphere. Regional conflicts, local wars, and foreign interventions challenged the survival of many of these new nations following independence.

Padre Hidalgo   The first stage of Mexico's revolution for independence was led by Padre Miguel Hidalgo y Costilla, who rallied the rural masses of central Mexico to his cause. His defeat, trial, and execution made him one of Mexico's most important political martyrs.   (Schaalkwijk/Art Resource, NY)

leaders dropped this pretense. In 1816 they declared independence as the United Provinces of the Río de la Plata.

Patriot leaders in Buenos Aires at first sought to retain control over the territory of the Viceroyalty of Río de la Plata, which had been created in 1776 and included modern Argentina, Uruguay, Paraguay, and Bolivia. But Spanish loyalists in Uruguay and Bolivia and a separatist movement in Paraguay defeated these ambitions. Even within the territory of Argentina, the government in Buenos Aires was unable to control regional rivalries and political differences. As a result, the region rapidly descended into political chaos.

A weak succession of juntas, collective presidencies, and dictators soon lost control over much of the interior of Argentina. However, in 1817 the government in Buenos Aires did manage to support a mixed force of Chileans and Argentines led by José de San Martín° (1778–1850), who crossed the Andes Mountains to attack Spanish military forces in Chile and Peru. During this campaign San Martín's most effective troops were former slaves, who had gained their freedom by enlisting in the army, and gauchos, the cowboys of the Argentine pampas (prairies). After gaining victory in Chile San Martín pushed on to Peru in 1820, but failed to gain a clear victory there. The violent and destructive uprising of Tupac Amaru II in 1780 had traumatized the Andean region and made colonists fearful that support for independence might unleash another Amerindian uprising (see Chapter 17). Unable to make progress, San Martín surrendered command of patriot forces in Peru to Simón Bolívar, who overcame final Spanish resistance in 1824.

Mexico, 1810–1823

In 1810 Mexico was Spain's wealthiest and most populous colony. Its silver mines were the richest in the world, and the colony's capital, Mexico City, was larger than any city in Spain. Mexico also had the largest population of Spanish immigrants among the colonies. Spaniards dominated the government, church, and economy. When news of Napoleon's invasion of Spain reached Mexico, conser-

vative Spaniards in Mexico City overthrew the local viceroy because he was too sympathetic to the creoles. This action by Spanish loyalists underlined the new reality: with the king of Spain removed from his throne by the French, colonial authority now rested on brute force.

The first stage of the revolution against Spain occurred in central Mexico. In this region wealthy ranchers and farmers had aggressively forced many Amerindian communities from their traditional agricultural lands. Crop failures and epidemics further afflicted the region's rural poor. Miners and the urban poor faced higher food prices and rising unemployment. With the power of colonial authorities weakened by events in Spain, anger and fear spread through towns and villages in central Mexico.

On September 16, 1810, **Miguel Hidalgo y Costilla°,** parish priest of the small town of Dolores, rang the

---

José de San Martín (hoe-SAY deh san mar-TEEN)

Miguel Hidalgo y Costilla (mee-GEHL ee-DAHL-go ee cos-TEA-ah)

church bells, attracting thousands. In a fiery speech he urged the crowd to rise up against the oppression of Spanish officials. Tens of thousands of the rural and urban poor joined his movement. They lacked military discipline and adequate weapons but knew who their oppressors were, spontaneously attacking the ranches and mines that had been exploiting them. Many Spaniards and colonial-born whites were murdered or assaulted. At first wealthy Mexicans were sympathetic to Hidalgo's objectives, but they eventually supported Spanish authorities when they recognized the threat that the angry masses following Hidalgo posed to them. The military tide quickly turned against Hidalgo and he was captured, tried, and executed in 1811.

The revolution continued under the leadership of another priest, **José María Morelos°**, a former student of Hidalgo's. A more adept military and political leader than his mentor, Morelos created a formidable fighting force and, in 1813, convened a congress that declared independence and drafted a constitution. Despite these achievements, loyalist forces also proved too strong for Morelos. He was defeated and executed in 1815.

Although small numbers of insurgents continued to wage war against Spanish forces, colonial rule seemed secure in 1820. However, news of the military revolt in Spain unsettled the conservative groups and church officials who had defended Spanish rule against Hidalgo and Morelos. In 1821 Colonel Agustín de Iturbide° and other loyalist commanders forged an alliance with remaining insurgents and declared Mexico's independence. The conservative origins of Mexico's transition to independence were highlighted by the decision to create a monarchial form of government and crown Iturbide as emperor. In early 1823, however, the army overthrew Iturbide and Mexico became a republic.

Brazil, to 1831

The arrival of the Portuguese royal family in Brazil in 1808 helped maintain the loyalty of the colonial elite and stimulate the local economy. After the defeat of Napoleon in Europe, the Portuguese government called for King John VI to return to Portugal. He at first resisted this pressure. Then in 1820 the military uprising in Spain provoked a sympathetic liberal revolt in Portugal, and the Portuguese military garrison in Rio de Janeiro forced the king to permit the creation of juntas. John recognized that he needed to take dramatic ac-

tion to protect his throne. In 1821 he returned to Portugal. Hoping to protect his claims to Brazil, he left his son Pedro in Brazil as regent.

By 1820 the Spanish colonies along Brazil's borders had experienced ten years of revolution and civil war, and some, like Argentina and Paraguay, had gained independence. Unable to ignore these struggles, some Brazilians began to reevaluate Brazil's relationship with Portugal. Many Brazilians resented their homeland's economic subordination to Portugal. The arrogance of Portuguese soldiers and bureaucrats led others to talk openly of independence. Rumors circulated that Portuguese troops were being sent to discipline Brazil and force the regent Pedro to join his father in Lisbon.

Unwilling to return to Portugal and committed to maintaining his family's hold on Brazil, Pedro aligned himself with the rising tide of independence sentiment. In 1822 he declared Brazilian independence. Pedro's decision launched Brazil into a unique political trajectory. Unlike its neighbors, which became constitutional republics, Brazil gained independence as a constitutional monarchy with Pedro I, heir to the throne of Portugal, as emperor.

Pedro I was committed to both monarchy and many liberal principles. He directed the writing of the constitution of 1824, which provided for an elected assembly and granted numerous protections for political opposition. But he made powerful enemies by attempting to protect the Portuguese who remained in Brazil from arbitrary arrest and seizure of their property. More dangerously still, he opposed slavery in a nation dominated by a slave-owning class. In 1823 Pedro I anonymously published an article that characterized slavery as a "cancer eating away at Brazil" (see Diversity and Dominance: The Afro-Brazilian Experience, 1828). Despite opposition, in 1830 he concluded a treaty with Great Britain to end Brazilian participation in the slave trade. The political elite of Brazil's slave-owning regions opposed the treaty and for nearly two decades worked tirelessly to prevent enforcement. Pedro also continued his father's costly commitment of military forces to control neighboring Uruguay. As military losses and costs rose, the Brazilian public grew impatient. A small but vocal minority that opposed the monarchy and sought the creation of a democracy used these issues to rally public opinion against the emperor.

Confronted by street demonstrations and violence between Brazilians and Portuguese, Pedro I abdicated the throne in 1831 in favor of his five-year-old son Pedro II. After a nine-year regency, Pedro II assumed full powers as emperor of Brazil. He reigned until he was overthrown by republicans in 1889.

José María Morelos (hoe-SAY mah-REE-ah moh-RAY-los)
Agustín de Iturbide (ah-goos-TEEN deh ee-tur-BEE-deh)

THE PROBLEM OF ORDER, 1825–1890

All the newly independent nations of the Western Hemisphere had difficulties establishing stable political institutions. The idea of popular sovereignty found broad support across the hemisphere. As a result, written constitutions and elected assemblies were put in place, often before the actual achievement of independence. Even in the hemisphere's two monarchies, Mexico and Brazil, the emperors sought to legitimize their rule by accepting constitutional limits on their authority and by the creation of representative assemblies. Nevertheless, widespread support for constitutional order and for representative government failed to prevent bitter factional conflict, regionalism, and the appearance of charismatic political leaders and military uprisings.

Constitutional Experiments

In reaction to the arbitrary and tyrannical authority of colonial rulers, revolutionary leaders in both the United States and Latin America espoused constitutionalism. They believed that the careful description of political powers in written constitutions offered the best protection for individual rights and liberties. In practice, however, many new constitutions proved unworkable. In the United States George Washington, James Madison, and other leaders became dissatisfied with the nation's first constitution, the Articles of Confederation. They led the effort to write a new constitution, which was put into effect in 1789. In Latin America few constitutions survived the rough-and-tumble of national politics. Between 1811 and 1833 Venezuela and Chile ratified and then rejected a combined total of nine constitutions.

Important differences in colonial political experience influenced later political developments in the Americas. The ratification of a new constitution in the United States was the culmination of a long historical process that had begun with the development of English constitutional law and continued under colonial charters. Many more residents of the British North American colonies had had the experience of voting and holding political office than did people in Portuguese and Spanish colonies. The British colonies provided opportunities for holding elective offices in town governments and colonial legislatures, and, by the time of independence, citizens had grown accustomed to elections, political parties, and factions. In contrast, constitutional government and elections were only briefly experienced in Spanish America between 1812 and 1814—while Ferdinand VII was a prisoner of Napoleon—and this short period was disrupted by the early stages of the revolutions for independence. Brazil had almost no experience with popular politics before independence. Despite these differences in experience and constitutional forms, every new republic in the Americas initially limited the right to vote to free men of property.

Democratic passions and the desire for effective self-rule led to significant political reform in the Americas, even in some of the region's remaining colonies. British Canada was divided into separate colonies and territories, each with a separate and distinct government. Political life in each colony was dominated by a provincial governor and appointed advisory councils drawn from the local elite. Elected assemblies existed within each province, but they exercised limited power. Agitation to end oligarchic rule and make government responsive to the will of the assemblies led to armed rebellion in 1837. In the 1840s Britain responded by establishing responsible government in each of the Canadian provinces, allowing limited self-rule. By the 1860s regional political leaders interested in promoting economic development realized that railroads and other internal improvements required a government with a "national" character. Both the U.S. Civil War and raids from U.S. territory into Canada by Irish nationalists attempting to force an end to British control of Ireland gave the reform movement a sense of urgency and focused attention on the need to protect the border. Negotiations led to the **Confederation of 1867,** which included the provinces of Ontario, Quebec, New Brunswick, and Nova Scotia. The Confederation that created the new Dominion of Canada with a central government in Ottawa (see Map 23.2) was hailed by one observer as the "birthday of a new nationality."[2] The path to effective constitutional government was rockier to the south. Because neither Spain nor Portugal had permitted anything like the elected legislatures and municipal governments of colonial North America, the drafters of Latin American constitutions were less constrained by practical political experience. As a result, many of the new Latin American nations experimented with untested political institutions. For example, Simón Bolívar, who wrote the first constitutions of five South American republics, included in Bolivia's constitution a fourth branch of government that had "jurisdiction over the youth, the hearts of men, public spirit, good customs, and republican ethics."

Most Latin American nations found it difficult to define the political role of the Catholic Church after independence. In the colonial period the Catholic Church

DIVERSITY AND DOMINANCE

THE AFRO-BRAZILIAN EXPERIENCE, 1828

Brazil was the most important destination for the Atlantic slave trade. From the sixteenth century to the 1850s more than 2 million African slaves were imported by Brazil, roughly twice the number of free European immigrants who arrived in the same period. Beginning in the 1820s Great Britain, Brazil's main trading partner, began to press for an end to the slave trade. British visitors to Brazil became an important source of critical information for those who sought to end the trade.

The following opinions were provided by a British clergyman, Robert Walsh, who traveled widely in Brazil in 1828 and 1829. Walsh's account reflects the racial attitudes of his time, but his testimony is valuable because of his ability to recognize the complex and sometime unexpected ways that slaves and black freedmen were integrated into Brazilian society.

[At the Alfandega, or custom house,] . . . for the first time I saw the Negro population under circumstances so striking to a stranger. The whole labour of bearing and moving burdens is performed by these people, and the state in which they appear is revolting to humanity. Here were a number of beings entirely naked, with the exception of a covering of dirty rags tied about their waists. Their skins, from constant exposure to the weather, had become hard, crusty, and seamed, resembling the coarse black covering of some beast, or like that of an elephant, a wrinkled hide scattered with scanty hairs. On contemplating their persons, you saw them with a physical organization resembling beings of a grade below the rank of man . . . . Some of these beings were yoked to drays, on which they dragged heavy burdens. Some were chained by the necks and legs, and moved with loads thus encumbered. Some followed each other in ranks, with heavy weights on their heads, chattering the most inarticulate and dismal cadence as they moved along. Some were munching young sugar-canes, like beasts of burden eating green provender [animal feed], and some were seen near water, lying on the bare ground among filth and offal, coiled up like dogs, and seeming to expect or require no more comfort or accommodation, exhibiting a state and conformation so unhuman, that they not only seemed, but actually were, far below the inferior animals around them. Horses and mules were not employed in this way; they were used only for pleasure, and not for labour. They were seen in the same streets, pampered, spirited, and richly caparisoned, enjoying a state far superior to the negroes, and appearing to look down on the fettered and burdened wretches they were passing, as on beings of an inferior rank in the creation to themselves. . . .

The first impression of all this on my mind, was to shake the conviction I had always felt, of the wrong and hardship inflicted on our black fellow creatures, and that they were only in that state which God and nature had assigned them; that they were the lowest grade of human existence, and the link that connected it with the brute, and that the gradation was so insensible, and their natures so intermingled, that it was impossible to tell where one had terminated and the other commenced; and that it was not surprising that people who contemplated them every day, so formed, so employed, and so degraded, should forget their claims to that rank in the scale of beings in which modern philanthropists are so anxious to place them. I did not at the moment myself recollect, that the white man, made a slave on the coast of Africa, suffers not only a similar mental but physical deterioration from hardships and emaciation, and becomes in time the dull and deformed beast I now saw yoked to a burden.

A few hours only were necessary to correct my first impressions of the negro population, by seeing them under a different aspect. We were attracted by the sound of military music, and found it proceeded from a regiment drawn up in one of the streets. Their colonel had just died, and they attended to form a procession to celebrate his obsequies. They were all of different shades of black, but the majority were negroes. Their equipment was excellent; they wore dark jackets, white pantaloons, and black leather caps and belts, all which, with their arms, were in high order. Their band produced sweet and agreeable music, of the leader's own composition, and the men went through some evolutions with regularity and dexterity. They were only a militia regiment, yet were as well appointed and disciplined as one of our regiments of the line. Here then was the first step in that gradation by which the black population of this country ascend in the scale of humanity; he advances from the state below that of a beast of burden into a military rank, and he shows himself as capable of discipline and improvement as a human being of any other colour.

Our attention was next attracted by negro men and women bearing about a variety of articles for sale; some in baskets, some on boards and cases carried on their heads. They belonged to a class of small shopkeepers, many of whom vend their wares at home, but the greater number send them about in this way, as in itinerant shops. A few of these people were still in a state of bondage, and brought a certain sum every evening to their owners, as the produce of their daily labour. But a large proportion, I was informed, were free, and exercised this little calling on their own account. They were all very neat and clean in their persons, and had a decorum and sense of respectability about them, superior to whites of the same class and calling. All their articles were good in their kind, and neatly kept, and they sold them with simplicity and confidence, neither wishing to take advantage of others, nor suspecting that it would be taken of themselves. I bought some confectionary from one of the females, and I was struck with the modesty and propriety of her manner; she was a young mother, and had with her a neatly dressed child, of which she seemed very fond. I gave it a little comfit [candy covered nut], and it turned up its dusky countenance to her and then to me, taking my sweetmeat, and at the same time kissing my hand. As yet unacquainted with the coin of the country, I had none that was current about me, and was leaving the articles; but the poor young woman pressed them on me with a ready confidence, repeating in broken Portuguese, outo tempo, I am sorry to say, the "other time" never came, for I could not recognize her person afterwards to discharge her little debt, though I went to the same place for the purpose.

It soon began to grow dark, and I was attracted by a number of persons bearing large lighted wax tapers, like torches, gathering before a house. As I passed by, one was put into my hand by a man who seemed in some authority, and I was requested to fall into a procession that was forming. It was the preparation for a funeral, and on such occasions, I learned that they always request the attendance of a passing stranger, and feel hurt if they are refused. I joined the party, and proceeded with them to a neighbouring church. When we entered we ranged ourselves on each side of a platform which stood near the choir, on which was laid an open coffin, covered with pink silk and gold borders. The funeral service was chanted by a choir of priests, one of whom was a negro, a large comely man, whose jet black visage formed a strong and striking contrast to his white vestments. He seemed to perform his part with a decorum and sense of solemnity, which I did not observe in his brethren. After scattering flowers on the coffin, and fumigating it with incense, they retired, the procession dispersed, and we returned on board. I had been but a few hours on shore, for the first time, and I saw an African negro under four aspects of society; and it appeared to me, that in every one his character depended on the state in which he was placed, and the estimation in which he was held. As a despised slave, he was far lower than other animals of burthen that surrounded him; more miserable in his look, more revolting in his nakedness, more distorted in his person, and apparently more deficient in intellect than the horses and mules that passed him by. Advanced to the grade of a soldier, he was clean and neat in his person, amenable to discipline, expert at his exercises, and showed the port [sic.] and being of a white man similarly placed. As a citizen, he was remarkable for the respectability of his appearance, and the decorum of his manners in the rank assigned him; and as a priest, standing in the house of God, appointed to instruct society on their most important interests, and in a grade in which moral and intellectual fitness is required, and a certain degree of superiority is expected, he seemed even more devout in his impressions, and more correct in his manners, than his white associates. I came, therefore, to the irresistible conclusion in my mind, that colour was an accident affecting the surface of a man, and having no more to do with his qualities than his clothes—that God had equally created an African in the image of his person, and equally given him an immortal soul; and that an European had no pretext but his own cupidity, for impiously thrusting his fellow man from that rank in the creation which the Almighty had assigned him, and degrading him below the lot of the brute beasts that perish.

QUESTIONS FOR ANALYSIS

1. What was the author's first impression of the Brazilian slave population?
2. How does slavery dehumanize slaves?
3. What does the author later observe that changes this opinion?
4. What circumstances or opportunities permitted Brazil's free blacks to improve their lives?

Source: Robert Edgar Conrad, *Children of God's Fire, A Documentary History of Black Slavery in Brazil* (Princeton, NJ: Princeton University Press, 1983), 216–220. Reprinted by permission of the author.

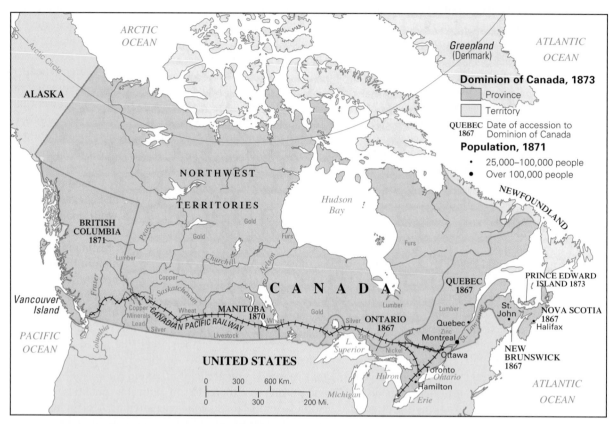

Map 23.2 Dominion of Canada, 1873 Although independence was not yet achieved and settlement remained concentrated along the U.S. border, Canada had established effective political and economic control over its western territories by 1873.

was a religious monopoly that controlled all levels of education, and dominated intellectual life. Many early constitutions aimed to reduce this power by making education secular and by permitting the practice of other religions. The church reacted by organizing its allies and financing conservative political movements. In Mexico, Colombia, Chile, and Argentina conflicts between liberals who sought the separation of church and state and supporters of the church's traditional powers dominated political life until late in the nineteenth century.

Limiting the power of the military proved to be another significant stumbling block to the creation of constitutional governments in Latin America. The wars for independence elevated the prestige of military leaders. When the wars were over, Bolívar and other military commanders seldom proved willing to subordinate themselves to civilian authorities. At the same time, frustrated by the often-chaotic workings of constitutional democracy, few citizens were willing to support civilian politicians in any contest with the military. As a result,

many Latin American militaries successfully resisted civilian control. Brazil, ruled by Emperor Pedro I, was the principal exception to this pattern.

Personalist Leaders

Successful patriot leaders in both the United States and Latin America gained mass followings during the wars for independence. They recruited and mobilized popular support by using patriotic symbols and by carefully associating their actions with national objectives. After independence, many patriot military leaders were able to use their personal followings to gain national political leadership. George Washington's ability to dominate the political scene in the early republican United States anticipated the later political ascendancy of revolutionary heroes such as Iturbide in Mexico and Bolívar in Gran Colombia. In each case, military reputation provided the foundation for personal political power. Washington was distinguished from most other early leaders by his willingness to surrender power. More commonly, **personalist leaders** relied on their ability to mobilize and direct the masses of these new nations rather than on the authority of constitutions and laws. Their model was Napoleon, who rose from the French army to become emperor, not James Madison, the primary author of the U.S. Constitution. In Latin America, a personalist leader who gained and held political power without constitutional sanction was called a *caudillo*°.

Latin America's slow development of stable political institutions made personalist politics more influential than they were in the United States. Nevertheless, charismatic politicians in the United States such as Andrew Jackson did sometimes challenge constitutional limits to their authority, as did the *caudillos* of Latin America.

Throughout the Western Hemisphere charismatic military men played key roles in attracting mass support for independence movements that were commonly dominated by colonial elites. Although this popular support was often decisive in the struggle for independence, the first constitutions of nearly all the American republics excluded large numbers of poor citizens from full political participation. But nearly everywhere in the Americas marginalized groups found populist leaders to articulate their concerns and challenge limits on their participation. Using informal means, these leaders sought to influence the selection of officeholders and to place their concerns in the public arena. Despite their success in overturning the deference-based politics of the colonial past, this populist political style at times threatened constitutional order and led to dictatorship.

Powerful personal followings allowed **Andrew Jackson** of the United States and **José Antonio Páez**° of Venezuela to challenge constitutional limits to their authority. During the independence wars in Venezuela and Colombia, Páez (1790–1873) organized and led Bolívar's most successful cavalry force. Like most of his followers, Páez was uneducated and poor, but his physical strength, courage, and guile made him a natural guerrilla leader and helped him build a powerful political base in Venezuela. Páez described his authority in the following manner: "[The soldiers] resolved to confer on me the supreme command and blindly to obey my will, confident . . . that I was the only one who could save them."[3] Able to count on the personal loyalty of his followers, Páez was seldom willing to accept the constitutional authority of a distant president.

After defeating the Spanish armies, Bolívar pursued his dream of forging a permanent union of former Spanish colonies modeled on the federal system of the United States. But he underestimated the strength of nationalist sentiment unleashed during the independence wars. Páez and other Venezuelan leaders resisted the surrender of their hard-won power to Bolívar's Gran Colombian government in distant Bogotá (the capital city of modern Colombia). When Bolívar's authority was challenged by political opponents in 1829 Páez declared Venezuela's independence. Merciless to his enemies and indulgent with his followers, Páez ruled the country as president or dictator for the next eighteen years. Despite implementing an economic program favorable to the elite, Páez remained popular with the masses by skillfully manipulating popular political symbols. Even as his personal wealth grew through land acquisitions and commerce, Páez took care to present himself as a common man.

Andrew Jackson (1767–1845) was the first U.S. president born in humble circumstances. A self-made man who eventually acquired substantial property and owned over a hundred slaves, Jackson was extremely popular among frontier residents, urban workers, and small farmers. Although he was notorious for his untidy personal life as well as for dueling, his courage, individualism, and willingness to challenge authority helped attain political success as judge, general, congressman, senator, and president.

During his military career, Jackson proved to be impatient with civilian authorities. Widely known because of his victories over the Creek and Seminole peoples, he was elevated to the pinnacle of American politics by his celebrated defeat of the British at the Battle of New Orleans in 1815 and by his seizure of Florida from the Spanish in 1818. In 1824 he received a plurality of the popular votes cast for the presidency, but he failed to win a majority of the electoral votes and was denied the presidency when the House of Representatives chose John Quincy Adams.

Jackson's followers viewed his landslide election victory in 1828 and reelection in 1832 as the triumph of democracy over the entrenched aristocracy. In office Jackson challenged constitutional limits on his authority, substantially increasing presidential power at the expense of Congress and the Supreme Court. Like Páez, Jackson was able to dominate national politics by blending a populist political style that celebrated the virtues and cultural enthusiasms of common people with support for policies that promoted the economic interests of some of the nation's most powerful propertied groups.

Personalist leaders were common in both Latin America and the United States, but Latin America's

---

caudillo (kouh-DEE-yoh)   **José Antonio Páez** (hoe-SAY an-TOE-nee-oh PAH-ays) weaker constitutional tradition, more limited protection of property rights, lower literacy levels, and less-developed communications systems provided fewer checks on the ambitions of popular politicians. The Constitution of the United States was never suspended, and no national election result in the United States was ever successfully overturned by violence. Latin America's personalist leaders, however, often ignored constitutional restraints on their authority, and election results seldom determined access to presidential power. As a result, by 1900 every Latin American nation had experienced periods of dictatorship.

The Threat of Regionalism

After independence, new national governments were generally weaker than the colonial governments they replaced. In debates over tariffs, tax and monetary policies, and, in many nations, slavery and the slave trade, regional elites often were willing to lead secessionist movements or to provoke civil war rather than accept laws that threatened their interests. Some of the hemisphere's newly independent nations did not survive these struggles; others lost territories to aggressive neighbors.

In Spanish America all of the postindependence efforts to forge large multistate federations failed. Central America and Mexico had been united in the Viceroyalty of New Spain and briefly maintained their colonial-era administrative ties following independence in 1821. After the overthrow of Iturbide's imperial rule in Mexico in 1823, however, regional politicians split with Mexico and created the independent Republic of Central America. Regional rivalries and civil wars during the 1820s and 1830s forced the breakup of that entity as well and led to the creation of five separate nations. Bolívar attempted to maintain the colonial unity of Venezuela, Colombia, and Ecuador by creating the nation of Gran Colombia with a capital in Bogotá. But even before his death in 1830 Venezuela and Ecuador had become independent states.

During colonial times Argentina, Uruguay, Paraguay, and Bolivia had been united in a single viceroyalty with its capital in Buenos Aires. With the defeat of Spain, political leaders in Paraguay, Uruguay, and Bolivia declared their independence from Buenos Aires. Argentina, the area that remained after this breakup, was itself nearly overwhelmed by these powerful centrifugal forces. After independence, Argentina's liberals took power in Buenos Aires. They sought a strong central government to promote secular education, free trade, and immigration from Europe. Conservatives dominated the interior provinces. They supported the

Catholic Church's traditional control of education as well as the protection of local textile and winemaking industries from European imports. In 1819, when political leaders in Buenos Aires imposed a national constitution that ignored these concerns, the conservatives of the interior rose in rebellion.

After a decade of civil war and rebellions a powerful local *caudillo*, Juan Manuel de Rosas°, came to power. For more than two decades he dominated Argentina, running the nation as if it were his private domain. The economy expanded under Rosas, but his use of intimidation, mob violence, and assassination created many enemies. In 1852 an alliance of foreign and domestic enemies overthrew him, but a new cycle of provincial rivalry and civil war prevented the creation of a strong central government until 1861.

Regionalism threatened the United States as well. The defense of state and regional interests played an important role in the framing of the U.S. Constitution. Many important constitutional provisions represented compromises forged among competing state and regional leaders. The creation of a Senate with equal representation from each state, for example, was an attempt to calm small states, which feared they might be dominated by larger states. The formula for representation in the House of Representatives was also an effort to compromise the divisions between slave and free states. Yet, despite these constitutional compromises, the nation was still threatened by regional rivalries.

Slavery increasingly divided the nation into two separate and competitive societies. A rising tide of immigration to the northern states in the 1830s and 1840s began to move the center of political power in the House of Representatives away from the south. Many southern leaders sought to protect slavery by expanding it to new territories. They supported the Louisiana Purchase in 1803 (see Map 23.3), an agreement with France that transferred to the United States a vast territory extending from the Gulf of Mexico to Canada. Southern leaders also supported statehood for Texas and war with Mexico (discussed later in the chapter).

The territorial acquisitions proved a mixed blessing to the defenders of slavery because they forced a national debate about slavery itself. Should slavery be allowed to expand into new territories? Could slavery be protected if new territories eligible for statehood were overwhelmingly free?

In 1860 Abraham Lincoln (1809–1865), who was committed to checking the spread of slavery, was elected president of the United States. In response, the planter elite in the southern states chose the dangerous course

Juan Manuel de Rosas (huan man-WELL deh ROH-sas)

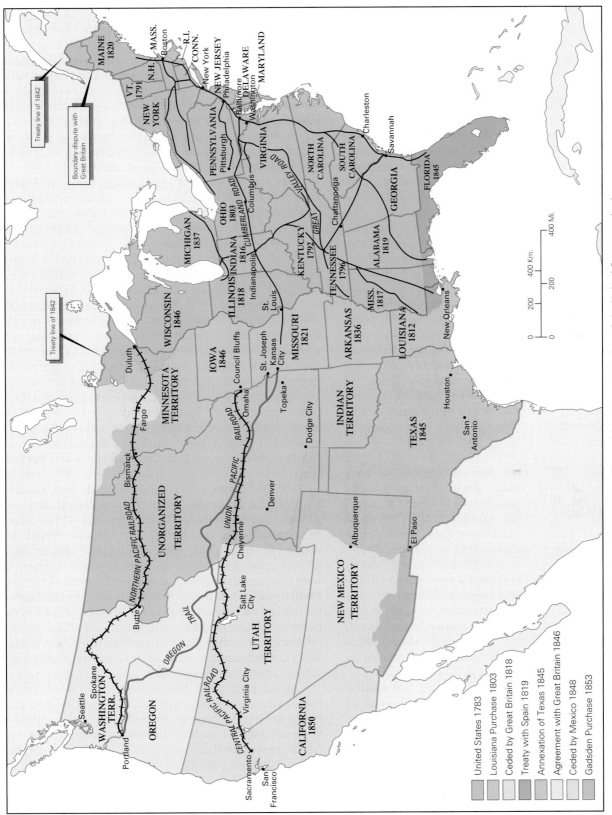

Map 23.3 Territorial Growth of the United States, 1783–1853 The rapid western expansion of the United States resulted from aggressive diplomacy and warfare against Mexico and Amerindian peoples. Railroad development helped integrate the trans-Mississippi west and promote economic expansion.

Treaty line of 1842

Boundary dispute with Great Britain

Treaty line of 1842

MAINE 1820

MASS.

R.I.

CONN.

N.H.

VT. 1791

NEW YORK

New York

NEW JERSEY

Philadelphia

DELAWARE

MARYLAND

Boston

Baltimore

Washington

PENNSYLVANIA

Pittsburgh

VIRGINIA

Charleston

Savannah

NORTH CAROLINA

SOUTH CAROLINA

GEORGIA

FLORIDA 1845

CUMBERLAND ROAD

GREAT VALLEY ROAD

OHIO 1803

Columbus

MICHIGAN 1837

INDIANA 1816

Indianapolis

ILLINOIS 1818

KENTUCKY 1792

TENNESSEE 1796

Chattanooga

ALABAMA 1819

MISS. 1817

LOUISIANA 1812

New Orleans

WISCONSIN 1846

IOWA 1846

St. Louis

MISSOURI 1821

ARKANSAS 1836

MINNESOTA TERRITORY

Duluth

Fargo

Bismarck

Council Bluffs

Omaha

St. Joseph

Kansas City

Topeka

INDIAN TERRITORY

Dodge City

Houston

San Antonio

TEXAS 1845

UNORGANIZED TERRITORY

NORTHERN PACIFIC RAILROAD

UNION PACIFIC RAILROAD

Butte

Denver

Cheyenne

Salt Lake City

NEW MEXICO TERRITORY

Albuquerque

El Paso

OREGON TRAIL

UTAH TERRITORY

Virginia City

CENTRAL PACIFIC RAILROAD

CALIFORNIA 1850

Sacramento

San Francisco

Portland

Seattle

Spokane

WASHINGTON TERR.

OREGON

400 Mi.

400 Km.

200

200

0

0

United States 1783

Louisiana Purchase 1803

Ceded by Great Britain 1818

Treaty with Spain 1819

Annexation of Texas 1845

Agreement with Great Britain 1846

Ceded by Mexico 1848

Gadsden Purchase 1853

of secession from the federal Union. The seceding states formed a new government, the Confederate States of America, known as the Confederacy. Lincoln was able to preserve the Union, but his victory was purchased at an enormous cost. The U.S. Civil War (1861–1865), waged by southern Confederate forces and northern Union (U.S.) forces, was the most destructive conflict in the history of the Western Hemisphere. More than 600,000 lives were lost before the Confederacy surrendered in 1865. The Union victory led to the abolition of slavery. It also transferred national political power to a northern elite committed to industrial expansion and federal support for the construction of railroads and other internal improvements.

The Confederate States of America was better prepared politically and economically for independence than were the successful secessionist movements that broke up Gran Colombia and other Spanish American federations. Nevertheless, the Confederacy failed, in part because of poor timing. The new nations of the Western Hemisphere were most vulnerable during the early years of their existence; indeed, all the successful secessions occurred within the first decades following independence. In the case of the United States, southern secession was defeated by an experienced national government legitimated and strengthened by more than seven decades of relative stability reinforced by dramatic economic and population growth.

Foreign Interventions and Regional Wars

In the nineteenth century wars often determined national borders, access to natural resources, and control of markets in the Western Hemisphere. Even after the achievement of independence, some Western Hemisphere nations, like Mexico, had to defend themselves against Europe's great powers. Contested national borders and regional rivalries also led to wars between Western Hemisphere nations. By the end of the nineteenth century the United States, Brazil, Argentina, and Chile had successfully waged wars against their neighbors and established themselves as regional powers.

Within thirty years of independence the United States fought a second war with England—the War of 1812 (1812–1815). The weakness of the new republic was symbolized by the burning of the White House and Capitol by British troops in 1814. This humiliation was soon overcome, however, and by the end of the nineteenth century the United States was the hemisphere's greatest military power. Its war against Spain in 1898–1899 cre-

ated an American empire that reached from the Philippines in the Pacific Ocean to Puerto Rico in the Caribbean Sea (see Chapter 27).

Europe also challenged the sovereignty of Latin American nations. During the first decades after independence Argentina faced British and French naval blockades, and British naval forces systematically violated Brazil's territorial waters to stop the importation of slaves. Mexico faced more serious threats to its sovereignty, defeating a weak Spanish invasion in 1829 and a French assault on the city of Veracruz in 1838.

Mexico also faced a grave threat from the United States. In the 1820s Mexico had encouraged Americans to immigrate to Texas, which at that time was part of Mexico. By the early 1830s Americans outnumbered Mexican nationals in Texas by four to one and were aggressively challenging Mexican laws such as the prohibition of slavery. In 1835 political turmoil in Mexico led to a rebellion in Texas by an alliance of Mexican liberals and American settlers. Mexico was defeated in a brief war, and in 1836 Texas gained its independence. In 1845 the United States made Texas a state, provoking war with Mexico a year later. American forces eventually captured Mexico City, and a punitive peace treaty was imposed in 1848. Compounding the loss of Texas in 1837, the treaty of 1848 forced Mexico to cede vast territories to the United States, including present-day New Mexico, Arizona, and California. In return Mexico received $15 million. When gold was discovered in California in 1848, the magnitude of Mexico's loss became clear.

With the very survival of the nation at stake, Mexico's liberals took power and imposed sweeping reforms that provoked a civil war with the conservatives (1858–1861). As mentioned in the chapter opening, the French invaded Mexico in 1862, using unpaid government debts as an excuse. Mexico's conservatives allied themselves with the French invaders, and the president of Mexico, **Benito Juárez,** was forced to flee Mexico City. The French then installed the Austrian Habsburg Maximilian as emperor of Mexico. Juárez organized an effective military resistance and after years of warfare drove the French army out of Mexico in 1867. After capturing Maximilian, Juárez ordered his execution.

As was clear in the Mexican-American War, wars between Western Hemisphere nations could lead to dramatic territorial changes. In two wars with neighbors Chile established itself as the leading military and economic power on the west coast of South America. Between 1836 and 1839 Chile defeated the Confederation of Peru and Bolivia. In 1879 Chilean and British investors in nitrate mines located in the Atacama Desert, a dis-

Benito Juárez's Triumph over the French   Benito Juárez overcame humble origins to lead the overthrow of Emperor Maximilian and the defeat of French imperialism. He remains a powerful symbol of secularism and republican virtue in Mexico. In this 1948 mural by José Clemente Orozco, Juárez's face dominates a scene of struggle that pits Mexican patriots against the allied forces of the Catholic Church, Mexican conservatives, and foreign invaders. The artist also celebrates the struggle of Mexico's Amerindians and mestizos against the white elite.   (Museo Nacional de Historia/CENIDIAP-INBA)

puted border region, provoked a new war with Peru and Bolivia (War of the Pacific). The Chilean army and navy won a crushing victory in 1881, forcing Bolivia to cede its only outlet to the sea and Peru to yield the rich mining districts.

Argentina and Brazil fought over control of Uruguay in the 1820s, but a military stalemate eventually forced them to recognize Uruguayan independence. In 1865 Argentina and Uruguay joined Brazil to wage war against Paraguay (War of the Triple Alliance, or Paraguayan War). After five years of warfare the Paraguayan dictator Francisco Solano López° and more than 20 percent of the population of Paraguay had died. Paraguay suffered military occupation, lost territory to the victors, and was forced to open its markets to foreign trade.

Francisco Solano López (fran-CEES-co so-LAN-oh LOH-pehz)

Native Peoples and the Nation-State

Both diplomacy and military action shaped relations between the Western Hemisphere's new nation-states and the indigenous peoples living within them. During late colonial times, to avoid armed conflict and to limit the costs of frontier defense, Spanish, Portuguese, and British imperial governments attempted to restrict the expansion of settlements into territories already occupied by Amerindians. With independence, the colonial powers' role as mediator for and protector of native peoples ended.

Still-independent Amerindian peoples posed a significant military challenge to many Western Hemisphere republics. Weakened by civil wars and constitutional crises, many of the new nations were less able to maintain frontier peace than the colonial governments had been. After independence Amerindian peoples in Argentina, the United States, Chile, and Mexico succeeded

Navajo Leaders Gathered in Washington to Negotiate   As settlers, ranchers, and miners pushed west in the nineteenth century, leaders of Amerindian peoples were forced to negotiate territorial concessions with representatives of the U.S. government. In order to impress Amerindian peoples with the wealth and power of the United States, many of their leaders were invited to Washington, D.C. This photo shows Navajo leaders and their Anglo translators in Washington, D.C., in 1874.   (#5851 Frank McNill Collection, State Records Center & Archives, Sante Fe, NM)

in pushing back some frontier settlements. But despite these early victories, by the end of the 1880s native military resistance was finally overcome in both North and South America.

After the American Revolution, the rapid expansion of agricultural settlements threatened native peoples in North America. Between 1790 and 1810 tens of thousands of settlers entered territories guaranteed to Amerindians in treaties with the United States. More than 200,000 white settlers were present in Ohio alone by 1810. Indigenous leaders responded by seeking the support of British officials in Canada and by forging broad indigenous alliances. American forces decisively defeated one such Amerindian alliance in 1794 at the Battle of Fallen Timbers in Ohio. After 1800 two Shawnee leaders, the brothers **Tecumseh**° and Prophet (Tenskwatawa), created a larger and better-

organized alliance among Amerindian peoples in the Ohio River Valley and gained some support from Great Britain. In 1811 American military forces attacked and destroyed the ritual center of the alliance, Prophet Town. The final blow came during the War of 1812 when Tecumseh, fighting alongside his British allies, was killed in battle.

In the 1820s white settlers forced native peoples living in Ohio, southern Indiana and Illinois, southwestern Michigan, most of Missouri, central Alabama, and southern Mississippi to cede their land. The 1828 presidential election of Andrew Jackson, a veteran of wars against native peoples, brought matters to a head. In 1830 Congress passed the Indian Removal Act, forcing the resettlement of the Cherokee, Creek, Choctaw, and other eastern peoples to land west of the Mississippi River. The removal was carried out in the 1830s, and nearly half of the forced migrants died on this journey, known as the Trail of Tears.

Tecumseh (teh-CUM-sah)

Amerindians living on the Great Plains offered formidable resistance to the expansion of white settlement. By the time substantial numbers of white buffalo hunters, cattlemen, and settlers reached the American west, indigenous peoples were skilled users of horses and firearms. These technologies had transformed the cultures of the Sioux, Comanche, Pawnee, Kiowa, and other Plains peoples. The improved efficiency of the buffalo hunt reduced their dependence on agriculture. As a result, women, whose primary responsibility had been raising crops, lost prestige and social power to male hunters. Living arrangements also changed as the single-family tepees of migratory buffalo hunters replaced the multigenerational lodges of the traditional farming economy.

During the U.S. Civil War, native peoples experienced a disruption of their trade with Eastern merchants and the suspension of payments pledged by previous treaties. After the war ever more settlers pushed onto the plains. Buffalo herds were hunted to near extinction for their hides, and land was lost to farmers and ranchers. During nearly four decades of armed conflict with the United States Army, Amerindian peoples were forced to give up their land and their traditional ways. The Comanche, who had dominated the southern plains during the period of Spanish and Mexican rule, were forced by the U.S. government to cede most of their land in Texas in 1865. The Sioux and their allies resisted. In 1876 they overwhelmed General George Armstrong Custer and the Seventh Cavalry in the Battle of Little Bighorn (in the southern part of the present-day state of Montana). But finally the Sioux were also forced to accept reservation life. Military campaigns in the 1870s and 1880s then broke the resistance of the Apache.

The indigenous peoples of Argentina and Chile experienced a similar trajectory of adaptation, resistance, and defeat. Herds of wild cattle provided indigenous peoples with a limitless food supply, and horses and metal weapons increased their military capacities. Thus, for a while, the native peoples of Argentina and Chile effectively checked the southern expansion of agriculture and ranching. Amerindian raiders operated within 100 miles (160 kilometers) of Buenos Aires into the 1860s. Unable to defeat these resourceful enemies, the governments of Argentina and Chile relied on an elaborate system of gift giving and prisoner exchanges to maintain peace on the frontier. By the 1860s, however, population increase, political stability, and military modernization allowed Argentina and Chile to take the offensive.

In the 1870s the government of Argentina used overwhelming military force to crush native resistance. Thousands of Amerindians were killed, and survivors were driven onto marginal land. In Chile the story was the same. When civil war and an economic depression weakened the Chilean government at the end of the 1850s, the Mapuches° (called "Araucanians" by the Spanish) attempted to push back frontier settlements. Despite early successes the Mapuches were defeated in the 1870s by modern weaponry. In Chile, as in Argentina and the United States, government authorities justified military campaigns against native peoples by demonizing them. Newspaper editorials and the speeches of politicians portrayed Amerindians as brutal and cruel, and as obstacles to progress. In April 1859 a Chilean newspaper commented:

> The necessity, not only to punish the Araucanian race, but also to make it impotent to harm us, is well recognized . . . as the only way to rid the country of a million evils. It is well understood that they are odious and prejudicial guests in Chile . . . conciliatory measures have accomplished nothing with this stupid race—the infamy and disgrace of the Chilean nation.[4]

Political divisions and civil wars within the new nations sometimes provided an opportunity for long-pacified native peoples to rebel. In the Yucatán region of Mexico, the owners of henequen (the agave plant that produces fiber used for twine) and sugar plantations had forced many Maya° communities off their traditional agricultural lands, reducing thousands to peonage. This same regional elite declared itself independent of the government in Mexico City that was convulsed by civil war in the late 1830s. The Mexican government was unable to reestablish control because it faced the greater threat of invasion by the United States. Seeing their oppressors divided, the Maya rebelled in 1847. This well-organized and popular uprising, known as the **Caste War,** nearly returned the Yucatán to Maya rule. Grievances accumulated over more than three hundred years led to great violence and property destruction. The Maya were not defeated until the war with the United States ended. Even then Maya rebels retreated to unoccupied territories and created an independent state, which they called the "Empire of the Cross." Organized around a mix of traditional beliefs and Christian symbols, this indigenous state resisted Mexican forces to 1870. A few defiant Maya strongholds survived until 1901.

Mapuches (mah-POO-chez)
Maya (MY-ah)

THE CHALLENGE OF SOCIAL AND ECONOMIC CHANGE

During the nineteenth century the newly independent nations of the Western Hemisphere struggled to realize the Enlightenment ideals of freedom and individual liberty that had helped ignite the revolutions for independence. The achievement of these objectives was slowed by the persistence of slavery and other oppressive colonial-era institutions. Cultural and racial diversity also presented obstacles to reform. Nevertheless, by century's end reform movements in many of the hemisphere's nations had succeeded in ending the slave trade, abolishing slavery, expanding voting rights, and assimilating immigrants from Asia and Europe.

Increased industrialization and greater involvement in the evolving world economy challenged the region's political stability and social arrangements. A small number of nations embraced industrialization, but most Western Hemisphere economies became increasingly dependent on the export of agricultural goods and minerals during the nineteenth century. While the industrializing nations of the hemisphere became richer than the nations that remained exporters of raw materials, all the region's economies became more vulnerable and volatile as a result of greater participation in international markets. Like contemporary movements for social reform, efforts to assert national economic control produced powerful new political forces.

The Abolition of Slavery

In both the United States and Latin America strong antislavery sentiments were expressed during the struggles for independence. Revolutionary leaders of nearly all the new nations of the Western Hemisphere asserted ideals of universal freedom and citizenship that contrasted sharply with the reality of slavery. Men and women who wanted to outlaw slavery were called **abolitionists.** Despite their efforts, slavery survived in much of the hemisphere until the 1850s. In regions where the export of plantation products was most important—such as the United States, Brazil, and Cuba—the abolition of slavery was achieved with great difficulty.

In the United States slavery was weakened by abolition in some northern states and by the termination of the African slave trade in 1808. But this progress was stalled by the profitable expansion of cotton agriculture after the War of 1812. In Spanish America tens of thousands of slaves gained freedom by joining revolutionary armies during the wars for independence. After independence, most Spanish American republics prohibited the slave trade. Counteracting that trend was the growing international demand for sugar and coffee, products traditionally produced on plantations by slaves. As prices rose for plantation products in the first half of the nineteenth century, Brazil and Cuba (the island remained a Spanish colony until 1899) increased their imports of slaves.

During the long struggle to end slavery in the United States, American abolitionists argued that slavery offended both morality and the universal rights asserted in the Declaration of Independence. Abolitionist Theodore Weld articulated the religious objection to slavery in 1834:

> No condition of birth, no shade of color, no mere misfortune of circumstance, can annul the birth-right charter, which God has bequeathed to every being upon whom he has stamped his own image, by making him a free *moral agent* [emphasis in original], and that he who robs his fellow man of this tramples upon right, subverts justice, outrages humanity . . . and sacrilegiously assumes the prerogative of God.[5]

Two groups denied full rights of citizenship under the Constitution, women and free African-Americans, played important roles in the abolition of slavery. Women served on the executive committee of the American Anti-Slavery Society and produced some of the most effective propaganda against slavery. Eventually, thousands of women joined the abolitionist cause, where they provided leadership and were effective speakers and propagandists. When social conservatives attacked this highly visible public role, many women abolitionists responded by becoming public advocates of female suffrage as well.

Frederick Douglass, a former slave, became one of the most effective abolitionist speakers and writers. Other, more radical black leaders pushed the abolitionist movement to accept the inevitability of violence. They saw civil war or slave insurrection as necessary for ending slavery. In 1843 Henry Highland Garnet stirred the National Colored Convention when he demanded, "Brethren, arise, arise, arise! . . . Let every slave in the land do this and the days of slavery are numbered."[6] In the 1850s the growing electoral strength of the newly formed Republican Party forced a confrontation between slave and free states. After the election of Abraham Lincoln in 1860, the first of the eleven southern states that formed the Confederacy seceded from the Union. During the Civil War pressure for emancipation rose as tens of thousands of black freemen and escaped slaves joined the Union army. Hundreds of thousands of other slaves fled their masters' plantations and farms for the protection of advancing northern armies. In 1863, in the midst of the Civil War and two years after the abolition of serfdom in Russia (see Chapter 25), President Lincoln began the abolition of slavery by issuing the Emancipation Proclamation, which ended slavery in rebel states not occupied by the Union army. Final abolition was accomplished after the war, in 1865, by the Thirteenth Amendment to the Constitution. By the 1880s, however, most African-Americans lived in harsh conditions as sharecroppers, and by the end of the century nearly all southern states had instituted "Jim Crow" laws that segregated blacks in public transportation, jobs, and schools. This coincided with increased racial violence that saw an average of fifty blacks lynched each year.

In Brazil slavery survived for more than two decades after it was abolished in the United States. Progress toward abolition was not only slower but also depended on foreign pressure. In 1830 Brazil signed a treaty with the British ending the slave trade. Despite this agreement, Brazil illegally imported over a half-million more African slaves before the British navy finally forced compliance in the 1850s. In the 1850s and 1860s the Brazilian emperor, Pedro II, and many liberals worked to abolish slavery, but their desire to find a form of gradual emancipation acceptable to slave owners slowed progress.

During the war with Paraguay (1865–1870) large numbers of slaves joined the Brazilian army in exchange for freedom. Their loyalty and heroism undermined the military's support for slavery. Educated Brazilians increasingly viewed slavery as an obstacle to economic development and an impediment to democratic reform. In the 1870s, as abolitionist sentiment grew, reformers forced the passage of laws providing for the gradual emancipation of slaves. When political support for slavery weakened in the 1880s, growing numbers of slaves forced the issue by fleeing from bondage. By then army leaders were resisting demands to capture and return runaway slaves. Legislation abolishing slavery finally was passed by the Brazilian parliament and accepted by the emperor in 1888.

The plantations of the Caribbean region received almost 40 percent of all African slaves shipped to the New World. Throughout the region tiny white minorities lived surrounded by slave and free colored majorities. At the end of the eighteenth century the slave rebellion in Saint Domingue (see Chapter 21) spread terror among slave owners across the Caribbean. Because of fear that any effort to overthrow colonial rule might unleash new slave rebellions, there was little enthusiasm among free

A Former Brazilian Slave Returns from Military Service   The heroic participation of black freemen and slaves in the Paraguayan War (1865–1870) led many Brazilians to advocate the abolition of slavery. The original caption for this drawing reads: "On his return from the war in Paraguay: Full of glory, covered with laurels, after having spilled his blood in defense of the fatherland and to free a people from slavery, the volunteer sees his own mother bound and whipped! Awful reality!"   (Courtesy, Fundacao Biblioteca Nacional, Brazil)

settlers in Caribbean colonies for independence. Nor did local support for abolition appear among white settlers or free colored populations. Thus abolition in most Caribbean colonies commonly resulted from political decisions made in Europe by colonial powers.

Nevertheless, like slaves in Brazil, the United States, and Spanish America, slaves in the Caribbean helped propel the movement toward abolition by rebelling, running away, and resisting in more subtle ways. Although initially unsuccessful, the rebellions that threatened other French Caribbean colonies after the Haitian Revolution (1789–1804)) weakened France's support for slavery. Jamaica and other British colonies also experienced rebellions and saw the spread of communities of runaways. In Spanish Cuba as well, slave resistance forced increases in expenditures for police forces in the nineteenth century.

After 1800 the profitability of sugar plantations in the British West Indian colonies declined with increased competition from Cuba, and a coalition of labor groups, Protestant dissenters, and free traders in Britain pushed for the abolition of slavery. Britain, the major participant in the eighteenth-century expansion of slavery in the Americas, ended its participation in the slave trade in 1807. It then negotiated a series of treaties with Spain, Brazil, and other importers of slaves to eliminate the slave trade to the Americas. Once these treaties were in place, British naval forces acted to force compliance.

Slavery in British colonies was abolished in 1833. However, the law compelled "freed" slaves to remain with former masters as "apprentices." Abuses by planters and resistance to apprenticeship by former slaves led to complete abolition in 1838. A decade later slavery in the French Caribbean was abolished after upheavals in France led to the overthrow of the government of Louis Philippe (see Chapter 21). The abolition of slavery in the Dutch Empire in 1863 freed 33,000 slaves in Surinam and 12,000 in the Antilles. Slave owners were compensated for their loss, and the freedmen of Surinam were required to provide ten years of compensated labor to their former owners.

In the Caribbean, slavery lasted longest in Cuba and Puerto Rico, Spain's remaining colonies. Britain's use of diplomatic pressure and naval force to limit the arrival of African slaves weakened slavery after 1820. More important, however, was the growth of support for abolition in these colonies. Both Cuba and Puerto Rico had larger white and free colored populations than did the Caribbean colonies of Britain and France. As a result, there was less fear in Cuba and Puerto Rico that abolition would lead to the political ascendancy of former slaves (as had occurred in Haiti). In Puerto Rico, where slaves numbered approximately thirty thousand, local reformers secured the abolition of slavery in 1873. In the midst of a decade-long war to defeat forces seeking the independence of Cuba, the Spanish government gradually moved toward abolition. Initially, slave children born after September 18, 1868, were freed but obligated to work for their former masters for eighteen years. In 1880 all other slaves were freed on the condition that they serve their masters for eight additional years. Finally, in 1886 these conditions were eliminated; slavery was abolished; and Cuban patriots forged the multiracial alliance that was to initiate a war for Cuban independence in 1895 (see Chapter 27).

Immigration

During the colonial period free Europeans were a minority among immigrants to the Western Hemisphere. Between 1500 and 1760 African slaves entering the Western Hemisphere outnumbered European immigrants by nearly two to one. Another 4 million or so African slaves were imported before the effective end of the slave trade at the end of the 1850s. As the African slave trade came to an end, the arrival of millions of immigrants from Europe and Asia contributed to the further transformation of the Western Hemisphere. This nineteenth-century wave of immigration fostered rapid economic growth and the occupation of frontier regions in the United States, Canada, Argentina, Chile, and Brazil. It also promoted urbanization. By century's end nearly all of the hemisphere's fastest-growing cities (Buenos Aires, Chicago, New York, and São Paulo, for example) had large immigrant populations.

Europe provided the majority of immigrants to the Western Hemisphere during the nineteenth century. For much of the century they came primarily from western Europe, but after 1870 most came from southern and eastern Europe. The scale of immigration increased dramatically in the second half of the century. The United States received approximately 600,000 European immigrants in the 1830s, 1.5 million in the 1840s, and then 2.5 million per decade until 1880. In the 1890s an astonishing total of 5.2 million immigrants arrived. This helped push the national population from 39 million in 1871 to 63 million in 1891, an increase of 62 percent. Most of the immigrants ended up in cities. Chicago, for example, grew from 444,000 in 1870 to 1.7 million in 1900.

European immigration to Latin America also increased dramatically after 1880. Combined immigration to Argentina and Brazil rose from just under 130,000 in the 1860s to 1.7 million in the 1890s. By 1910, 30 percent of the Argentine population was foreign-born, more than twice the proportion in the U.S. population. Argentina was an extremely attractive destination for European immigrants, receiving more than twice as many immigrants as Canada between 1870 and 1930. Even so, immigration to Canada increased tenfold during this period.

Asian immigration to the Western Hemisphere increased after 1850. Between 1849 and 1875 approximately 100,000 Chinese immigrants arrived in Peru and another 120,000 entered Cuba. Canada attracted about 50,000 Chinese in the second half of the century. The United States, however, was the primary North American destination for Chinese immigrants, receiving 300,000 between 1854 and 1882. India also contributed to the social transformation of the Western Hemisphere, sending more than a half-million immigrants to the Caribbean region. British Guiana alone received 238,000 immigrants, mostly indentured laborers, from the Asian subcontinent.

Despite the obvious economic benefits that accompanied this inflow of people, hostility to immigration mounted in many nations. Nativist political movements

Chinese Funeral in Vancouver, Canada In the 1890s Vancouver was an important Western Hemisphere destination for Chinese immigrants. This photo shows how an important element of traditional Chinese culture thrived among the storefronts and streetcar lines of the late-Victorian Canadian city. (Vancouver Public Library, Special Collections, VPL1234)

argued that large numbers of foreigners could not be successfully integrated into national political cultures. By the end of the century fear and prejudice led many governments in the Western Hemisphere to limit immigration or to distinguish between "desirable" and "undesirable" immigrants, commonly favoring Europeans over Asians.

Asians faced more obstacles to immigration than did Europeans and were more often victims of violence and extreme forms of discrimination in the New World. In the 1870s and 1880s anti-Chinese riots erupted in many western cities in the United States. Congress responded to this wave of racism by passing the Chinese Exclusion Act in 1882, which eliminated most Chinese immigration. In 1886 fears that Canada was being threatened by "inferior races" led to the imposition of a head tax that made immigration to Canada more difficult for Chinese families. During this same period strong anti-Chinese prejudice surfaced in Peru, Mexico, and Cuba. Japanese immigrants in Brazil and East Indians in the English-speaking Caribbean faced similar prejudice.

Immigrants from Europe also faced prejudice and discrimination. In the United States, Italians were commonly portrayed as criminals or anarchists. In Argentina, social scientists attempted to prove that Italian immigrants were more violent and less honest than the native-born population. Immigrants from Spain were widely stereotyped in Argentina as miserly and dishonest. Eastern European Jews seeking to escape pogroms and discrimination at home found themselves barred from many educational institutions and professional careers in both the United States and Latin America. Negative stereotypes were invented for Irish, German, Swedish, Polish, and Middle Eastern immigrants as well. The perceived grievances used to justify these common prejudices were remarkably similar from Canada to Argentina. Immigrants, it was argued, threatened the well-being of native-born workers by accepting low wages, and they threatened national culture by resisting assimilation.

Many intellectuals and political leaders wondered if the evolving mix of culturally diverse populations could sustain a common citizenship. As a result, efforts were directed toward compelling immigrants to assimilate. Schools became cultural battlegrounds where language, cultural values, and patriotic feelings were transmitted to the children of immigrants. Across the hemisphere, school curricula were revised to promote national culture. Ignoring Canada's large French-speaking population, an English-speaking Canadian reformer commented on recent immigration: "If Canada is to become in a real sense a nation, if our people are to become one people, we must have one language."[7] Fear and prejudice were among the emotions promoting the singing of patriotic songs, the veneration of national flags and other symbols, and the writing of national histories that emphasized patriotism and civic virtue. Nearly everywhere in the Americas schools worked to create homogeneous national cultures.

American Cultures

Despite discrimination, immigrants continued to stream into the Western Hemisphere, introducing new languages, living arrangements, technologies, and work customs. Immigrants altered the politics of many of the hemisphere's nations as they sought to influence government policies. Where immigrants arrived in the greatest numbers, they put enormous pressure on housing, schools, and social welfare services. To compensate for their isolation from home, language, and culture, immigrants often created ethnically based mutual aid societies, sports and leisure clubs, and neighborhoods. Ethnic organizations and districts provided valuable social and economic support for recent arrivals while sometimes worsening the fears of the native-born that immigration posed a threat to national culture.

Immigrants were changed by their experiences in their adopted nations and by programs that forced them to accept new cultural values through education or, in some cases, service in the military. Similar efforts to forge national cultures were put in place in Europe by modernizing governments at the same time. The modification of the language, customs, values, and behaviors of a group as a result of contact with people from another culture is called **acculturation.**

Immigrants and their children, in turn, made their mark on the cultures of their adopted nations in the Americas. They learned the language spoken in their adopted countries as fast as possible in order to improve their earning capacity. At the same time, words and phrases from their languages entered the vocabularies of the host nations. Languages as diverse as Yiddish and Italian strongly influenced American English, Argentine Spanish, and Brazilian Portuguese. Dietary practices introduced from Europe and Asia altered the cuisine of nearly every American nation. In turn, immigrants commonly added native foods to their diets, especially the hemisphere's abundant and relatively cheap meats.

Throughout the hemisphere culture and popular music changed as well. For example, the Argentine tango, based on African-Argentine rhythms, was transformed by new instrumentation and orchestral arrangements brought by Italian immigrants. Mexican ballads blended

Arrest of Labor Activist in Buenos Aires The labor movement in Buenos Aires grew in numbers and became more radical with the arrival of tens of thousands of Italian and Spanish immigrants. Fearful of socialist and anarchist unions, the government of Argentina used an expanded police force to break strikes by arresting labor leaders. (Archivo General de la Nación, Buenos Aires)

with English folk music in the U.S. southwest, and Italian operas played to packed houses in Buenos Aires. Sports, games of chance, and fashion also experienced this process of borrowing and exchange.

Union movements and electoral politics in the hemisphere also felt the influence of new arrivals who aggressively sought to influence government and improve working conditions. The labor movements of Mexico, Argentina, and the United States, in particular, were influenced by the anarchist and socialist beliefs of European immigrants. Mutual benevolent societies and less-formal ethnic associations pooled resources to help immigrants open businesses, aid the immigration of relatives, or bury family members. They also established links with political movements, sometimes exchanging votes for favors.

Women's Rights and the Struggle for Social Justice

The abolition of slavery in the Western Hemisphere did not end racial discrimination or provide full political rights for every citizen. Not only blacks but also women, new immigrants, and native peoples in nearly every Western Hemisphere nation suffered the effects of political and economic discrimination. During the second half of the nineteenth century reformers struggled to remove these limits on citizenship while also addressing the welfare needs of workers and the poor.

In 1848 a group of women angered by their exclusion from an international antislavery meeting issued a call for a meeting to discuss women's rights. The **Women's Rights Convention** at Seneca Falls, New York, issued a statement that said, in part, "We hold these truths to be self-evident: that all men and women are equal." While moderates focused on the issues of greater economic independence and full legal rights, increasing numbers of women demanded the right to vote. Others lobbied to provide better conditions for women working outside the home, especially in textile factories. Sarah Grimké responded to criticism of women's activism:

This has been the language of man since he laid aside the whip as a means to keep woman in subjection. He spares her body, but the war he has waged against her mind, her heart, and her soul, has been no less destructive to her as a moral being. How monstrous is the doctrine that woman is to be dependent on man![8]

Progress toward equality between men and women was equally slow in Canada and Latin America. Canada's first women doctors received their training in the United States because no woman was able to receive a medical degree in Canada until 1895. Full enfranchisement occurred in Canada in the twentieth century, but Canadian women did gain the right to vote in some provincial and municipal elections before 1900. Like women in the United States, Canadian women provided leadership in temperance, child welfare, and labor reform movements.

Argentina and Uruguay were among the first Latin American nations to provide public education for women. Both nations introduced coeducation in the 1870s. Chilean women gained access to some careers in medicine and law in the 1870s. In Argentina the first woman doctor graduated from medical school in 1899. In Brazil, where many women were active in the abolitionist movement, four women graduated in medicine by 1882. Throughout the hemisphere more rapid progress was achieved in lower-status careers that threatened male economic power less directly, and by the end of the century women dominated elementary school teaching throughout the Western Hemisphere.

From Canada to Argentina and Chile, the majority of working-class women had no direct involvement in these reform movements, but they succeeded in transforming gender relations in their daily lives. By the end of the nineteenth century, large numbers of poor women worked outside the home on farms, in markets, and, increasingly, in factories. Many bore full responsibility for providing for their children. Whether men thought women should remain in the home or not, by the end of the century women were unambiguously present in the economy (see also Chapter 26).

Throughout the hemisphere there was little progress toward eliminating racial discrimination. Blacks were denied the vote throughout the southern United States. They also were subjected to the indignity of segregation—consigned to separate schools, hotels, restaurants, seats in public transportation, and even water fountains. Racial discrimination against men and women of African descent was also common in Latin America, though seldom spelled out in legal codes. Unlike the southern states of the United States, Latin American nations did not insist on formal racial segregation or permit lynching. Nor did they enforce a strict color line. Many men and women of mixed background were able to enter the skilled working class or middle class. Latin Americans tended to view racial identity across a continuum of physical characteristics rather than in the narrow terms of black and white that defined race relations in the United States.

The abolition of slavery in Latin America did not lead to an end to racial discrimination. Some of the participants in the abolition struggles later organized to promote racial integration. They demanded access to education, the right to vote, and greater economic opportunity, pointing out the economic and political costs of denying full rights to all citizens. Their success depended on effective political organization and on forging alliances with sympathetic white politicians. Black intellectuals also struggled to overturn racist stereotypes. In Brazil, Argentina, and Cuba, as in the United States, political and literary magazines celebrating black cultural achievement became powerful weapons in the struggle against racial discrimination. Although men and women of African descent continued to experience prejudice and discrimination everywhere in the Americas, successful men and women of mixed descent in Latin America confronted fewer obstacles to their advancement than did similar groups in the United States.

Development and Under-development

The Atlantic economy experienced three periods of economic contraction during the nineteenth century, but nearly all the nations of the Western Hemisphere were richer in 1900 than in 1800. The Industrial Revolution, worldwide population growth, and an increasingly integrated world market stimulated economic expansion (see Environment and Technology: Constructing the Port of Buenos Aires, Argentina). Wheat, corn, wool, meats, and nonprecious minerals joined the region's earlier exports of silver, sugar, dyes, coffee, and cotton. During the nineteenth century the United States was the only Western Hemisphere nation to industrialize, but nearly every government promoted new economic activities. Governments and private enterprises invested in roads, railroads, canals, and telegraphs to better serve distant markets. Most governments adopted tariff and monetary policies to foster economic diversification and growth. Despite these efforts, by 1900 only three Western Hemisphere nations—the United States, Canada, and Argentina—achieved individual income levels similar to those of western Europe. All three nations had open land, temperate climates, diverse resources, and large inflows of immigrants.

New demands for copper, zinc, lead, coal, and tin unleashed by the Industrial Revolution led to mining booms in the western United States, Mexico, and Chile. Unlike the small-scale and often short-term gold- and silver-mining operations of the colonial era, the mining companies of the late nineteenth century were heavily capitalized international corporations that could bully governments and buy political favors. During this period, European and North American corporations owned most new mining enterprises in Latin America. Petroleum development, which occurred at the end of the century in Mexico and elsewhere, would follow this pattern as well (see the discussion of the Mexican economy during the Díaz dictatorship in Chapter 30).

New technology accelerated economic integration, but the high cost of this technology often increased dependence on foreign capital. Many governments promoted railroads by granting tax benefits, free land, and monopoly rights to both domestic and foreign investors. By 1890 vast areas of the Great Plains in the United States, the Canadian prairie, the Argentine pampas, and parts of northern Mexico were producing grain and livestock for foreign markets opened by the development of railroads. Steamships also lowered the cost of transportation to distant markets, and the telegraph stimulated expansion by speeding information about the demand for and availability of products.

The simultaneous acquisition of several new technologies multiplied the effects of individual technologies. In Argentina the railroad, the telegraph, barbed wire, and refrigeration all appeared in the 1870s and 1880s. Although Argentina had had abundant livestock herds since the colonial period, the distance from Europe's markets prevented Argentine cattle raisers from exporting fresh meat or live animals. Technology overcame these obstacles. The combination of railroads and the telegraph lowered freight costs and improved information about markets. Steamships shortened trans-Atlantic crossings. Refrigerated ships made it possible to sell meat in the markets of Europe. As land values rose and livestock breeding improved, new investments were protected by barbed wire, the first inexpensive fencing available on the nearly treeless plains.

Growing interdependence and increased competition produced deep structural differences among Western Hemisphere economies by 1900. Two distinct economic tracks became clearly visible. One led to industrialization and prosperity, what is now called **development.** The other continued colonial dependence on exporting raw materials and on low-wage industries, now commonly called **underdevelopment.** By 1900 material prosperity was greater and economic development more diversified in English-speaking North America than in the nations of Latin America. With a temperate climate, vast fertile prairies, and an influx of European immigrants, Argentina was the only Latin American nation to approach the prosperity of the United States and Canada.

The Introduction of New Technologies Changes the Mining Industry   Powerful hydraulic technologies were introduced in western mining sites in the United States. This early photo shows how high-power water jets could transform the natural environment. (Colorado Historical Society)

Changes in the performance of international markets helped determine the trajectory of Western Hemisphere economies as new nations promoted economic development. When the United States gained independence the world capitalist economy was in a period of rapid growth. With a large merchant fleet, a diversified economy that included some manufacturing, and adequate banking and insurance services, the United States benefited from the expansion of the world economy. Rapid population growth due in large measure to immigration, high levels of individual wealth, widespread landownership, and relatively high literacy rates also fostered rapid economic development in the United States. The rapid expansion of railroad mileage suggests this success. In 1865 the United States had the longest network in the world. By 1915 it had multiplied eleven-fold (see Map 23.4). Steel production grew rapidly as well, with the United States overtaking Britain and Germany in the 1890s. One cost of the nation's industrialization

was the vastly expanded power of monopolies, like Standard Oil, over political life.

Canada's struggle for greater political autonomy led to the Confederation of 1867, which coincided with a second period of global economic expansion. Canada also benefited from a special trading relationship with Britain, the world's preeminent industrial nation, and from a rising tide of immigrants after 1850. Nevertheless, some regions within each of these prosperous North American nations—Canada's Maritime Provinces and the southern part of the United States, for example—demonstrated the same patterns of underdevelopment found in Latin America.

Latin American nations gained independence in the 1820s, when the global economy was contracting due to the end of the Napoleonic Wars and market saturation provoked by the early stages of European industrialization. In the colonial period Spain and Portugal had promoted the production of agricultural and mining

ENVIRONMENT + TECHNOLOGY

Constructing the Port of Buenos Aires, Argentina

Located on the banks of the Río de la Plata, Buenos Aires had been a major commercial center and port since the late eighteenth century. But Buenos Aires was not a natural harbor. Because of the shallowness of the river, the largest oceangoing ships were forced to anchor hundreds of yards offshore while goods and passengers were unloaded by small boats or by specially built ox carts with huge wheels. Smaller vessels docked at a river port to the city's south.

By the 1880s the Argentine economy was being transformed by the growing demands of European consumers for meat and grain. As exports surged and land values exploded, the wages of Argentines rose, and the nation became a favored destination for European immigrants. Argentina was becoming the wealthiest nation in Latin America.

The nation's political and economic elites decided that future growth required the modernization and expansion of port facilities. Two competing plans were debated. The first emphasized the incremental expansion and dredging of the river port. This was supported by local engineers and political groups suspicious of foreign economic interests. The second, and ultimately successful, plan involved dredging a port and deep-water channel from the low mud flats near the city center. This plan was more expensive, relying on British engineering firms, British banks, and British technology. It was supported by Argentine economic interests most closely tied to the European export trade and by national political leaders who believed progress and prosperity required the imitation of European models. Already the British were the nation's primary creditors as well as leaders in the development of the nation's railroads, streetcar lines, and gas works in Buenos Aires.

The photograph below shows the construction of Puerto Madero, the new port of Buenos Aires, in the 1890s. The work force was almost entirely recruited from recent immigrants. The engineering staff was dominated by British experts. Most of the profits were culled by the local elite through real estate deals and commissions associated with construction. Puerto Madero, named after its local promoter, was opened in stages beginning in 1890. Cost overruns and corruption stretched out completion to 1898. By 1910 arrivals and departures reached thirty thousand ships and 18 million tons. But the project was poorly designed, and "improvements" were still being made in the 1920s.

Why had the government of Argentina chosen the costliest and most difficult design? Argentine politicians were seduced by the idea of modernity; they chose the most complex and technologically sophisticated solution to the port problem. And they believed that British engineering and British capital were guarantees of modernity. The new port facilities did facilitate a boom in exports and imports, and the huge public works budget did provide incomes for thousands of laborers. However, debts, design flaws, and the increased influence of foreign capital in Argentina left a legacy of problems that Argentina would be forced to deal with in the future. (See the discussion of Juan Perón in Chapter 30.)

Excavation of Port of Buenos Aires, Argentina   Relying on foreign capital and engineering, the government of Argentina improved the port to facilitate the nation's rapidly expanding export economy.   (Courtesy, Hack Hoffenburg, South American Resources)

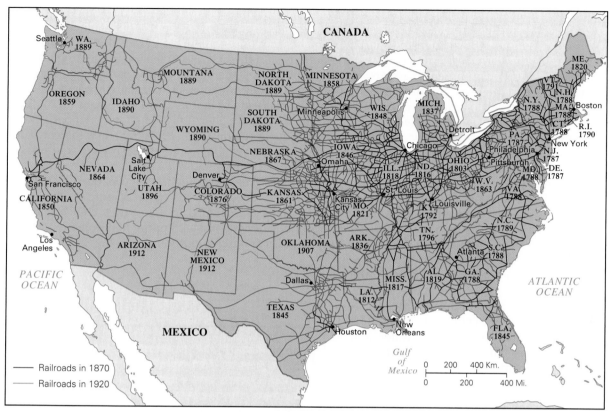

Map 23.4   The Expansion of the United States, 1850–1920.   The settlement of western territories and their admission as states depended on migration, the exploitation of natural resources and important new technologies like railroads and telegraphs that facilitated economic and political integration.

exports. After independence those raw-material exports faced increased competition. Although these sectors experienced periods of great prosperity in the nineteenth century, they also faced stiff competition and falling prices as new regions began production or new products captured markets. Sugar, coffee, nitrates, and copper all followed this pattern.

The history of the specialized Latin American economies, subject to periodic problems of oversupply and low prices, was one of boom and bust. Many Latin American governments sought to promote exports in the face of increased competition and falling prices by resisting union activity and demands for higher wages and by opening domestic markets to foreign manufactures. Resulting low wages and an abundance of foreign manufactured goods, in turn, undermined efforts to promote industrialization in Latin America.

Weak governments, political instability, and, in some cases, civil war also slowed Latin American economic development. A comparative examination of Western Hemisphere economic history makes clear that stable

and reliable public administration is a necessary part of the development process. Because Latin America was dependent on capital and technology from abroad, Great Britain and, by the end of the century, the United States were often able to impose unfavorable trade conditions or even intervene militarily to protect investments. The combined impact of these domestic and international impediments to development became clear when Mexico, Chile, and Argentina failed to achieve high levels of domestic investment in manufacturing late in the nineteenth century, despite a rapid accumulation of wealth derived from traditional exports.

Altered Environments

Population growth, economic expansion, new technologies, and the introduction of plants and animals to new regions dramatically altered the environment of the Western Hemisphere. Cuba's planters cut down many of the island's forests in the early nineteenth century to expand sugar production. Growing demand for meat led ranchers to expand livestock-raising into fragile environments in Argentina, Uruguay, southern Brazil, and the southwestern United States. Other forms of commercial agriculture also threatened the environment. Farmers in South Carolina and Georgia gained a short-term increase in cotton production by abandoning crop rotation after 1870, but this practice quickly led to soil exhaustion and erosion. The use of steel plows on North American prairies and Argentine pampas eliminated many native grasses and increased the threat of soil erosion. Coffee planters in Brazil exhausted soil fertility with a destructive cycle of overplanting followed by expansion onto forest reserves cleared by cutting and burning. Similarly massive transfers of land from public to private ownership occurred in Argentina and Brazil in order to promote livestock-raising and agriculture.

Rapid urbanization also put heavy pressure on the environment. New York, Chicago, Rio de Janeiro, Buenos Aires, and Mexico City were among the world's fastest-growing cities in the nineteenth century. Governments strained to provide adequate sewers, clean water, and garbage disposal. Timber companies clear-cut large areas of Michigan, Wisconsin, and the Appalachian Mountains to provide lumber for railroad ties and frame houses, pulp for paper, and fuel for locomotives and foundries. Under the Timber and Stone Act of 1878, the U.S. government sold more than 3.5 million additional acres (1.4 million hectares) of public land to individual and corporations at low cost by 1900. At the same time, the forest industries of British Honduras (now Belize), Nicaragua, and Guatemala grew rapidly in response to demand in Europe and North America for tropical hardwoods like mahogany. As forest throughout the hemisphere was cleared, animal habitats and native plant species disappeared.

The scale of mining operation grew in Nevada, Montana, and California, accelerating erosion and pollution. Similar results occurred in other mining areas. The expansion of nitrate mining and, later, open-pit copper mining in Chile scarred and polluted the environment. The state of Minas Gerais° in Brazil experienced a series of mining booms that began with gold in the late seventeenth century and continued with iron ore in the nineteenth. By the end of the nineteenth century its red soil was ripped open, its forests were depleted, and erosion was uncontrolled. Similar devastation afflicted parts of Bolivia and Mexico.

Efforts to meet increasing domestic demand for food and housing and to satisfy foreign demands for exports led to environmental degradation but also contributed significantly to the growth of the world economy and to regional prosperity. By the end of the nineteenth century small-scale conservation efforts were under way in many nations, and the first national parks and nature reserves had been created. In the United States large areas remained undeveloped. A few particularly beautiful areas were preserved in a national park system. In 1872 Yellowstone in Wyoming became the first national park. President Theodore Roosevelt (1901–1909) and the naturalist John Muir played major roles in preserving large areas of the western states. In Canada the first national park was created at Banff in 1885 and was expanded from 10 to 260 square miles (26 to 673 square kilometers) two years later. However, when confronted by a choice between economic growth and environmental protection, all the hemisphere's nations embraced growth.

CONCLUSION

The nineteenth century witnessed enormous changes in the Western Hemisphere. Except in Canada, many Caribbean islands, and a handful of mainland colonies like Surinam, the Guyanas, and Belize, colonial controls were removed by century's end. The powerful new political ideas of the Enlightenment and an increased sense of national identity contributed to the desire for independence and self-rule. The success of the American and Haitian Revolutions began the assault on the colonial order, transforming the hemisphere's politics. Napoleon's invasion of Portugal and Spain then helped initiate the movement toward independence in Latin America.

Once colonial rule was overturned, the creation of stable and effective governments proved difficult. Powerful personalist leaders resisted the constraints imposed by constitutions. National governments often confronted divisive regional political movements. From Argentina in the south to the United States in the north, regional political rivalries provoked civil wars that challenged the very survival of the new nations. Foreign military interventions and wars with native peoples also consumed resources and determined national boundaries. The effort to fulfill the promise of universal citizenship led to struggles to end slavery, extend civil and political rights to women and minorities, and absorb new immigrants. These objectives were only partially achieved.

Industrialization had a transforming effect on the hemisphere as well. Wealth, political power, and population were increasingly concentrated in urban areas. In most countries, bankers and manufacturers, rather than farmers and plantation owners, directed national des-

---

Minas Gerais (ME-nas JER-aize)

tinies. The United States, the most industrialized nation in the Americas, played an aggressive economic role in the region's affairs and used its growing military power as well. Industrialization altered the natural environment in dramatic ways. Modern factories consumed huge amounts of raw materials and energy. Copper mines in Chile and Mexico, Cuban sugar plantations, Brazilian coffee plantations, and Canadian lumber companies all left their mark on the natural environment, and all had ties to markets in the United States. The concentration of people in cities in the United States and Latin America put pressure on water supplies, sewage treatment, and food supplies.

By 1900, however, the hemisphere's national governments were much stronger than they had been at independence. Latin America lagged behind the United States and Canada in institutionalizing democratic political reforms, but Latin American nations in 1900 were stronger and more open than they had been in 1850. By 1900 all the hemisphere's nations also were better able to meet the threats of foreign intervention and regionalism. Among the benefits resulting from the increased strength of national governments were the abolition of slavery and the extension of political rights to formerly excluded citizens.

Serious challenges remained. Amerindian peoples were forced to resettle on reservations, were excluded from national political life, and, in some countries, remained burdened with special tribute and tax obligations. Women began to enter occupations previously reserved to men but still lacked full citizenship rights. The baneful legacy of slavery and colonial racial stratification remained a barrier to many men and women. The benefits of economic growth were not equitably distributed among the nations of the Western Hemisphere or within individual nations. In 1900 nearly every American nation was wealthier, better educated, more democratic, and more populous than at independence. But these nations were also more vulnerable to distant economic forces, more profoundly split between haves and have-nots, and more clearly divided into a rich north and a poorer south.

■ Key Terms

Simón Bolívar

Miguel Hidalgo y Costilla

José María Morelos

Confederation of 1867

personalist leaders

Andrew Jackson

José Antonio Páez

Benito Juárez

Tecumseh

Caste War

abolitionists

acculturation

Women's Rights Convention

development

underdevelopment

■ Suggested Reading

For the independence era in Latin America see John Lynch, *The Spanish American Revolutions, 1808–1826*, 2d ed. (1986); Jay Kinsbruner, *Independence in Spanish America* (1994); and A. J. R. Russell-Wood, ed., *From Colony to Nation: Essays on the Independence of Brazil* (1976).

The postindependence political and economic struggles in Latin America can be traced in David Bushnell and Neil Macaulay, *The Emergence of Latin America in the Nineteenth Century* (1988). Tulio Halperin-Donghi, *The Contemporary History of Latin America* (1993), and E. Bradford Burns, *The Poverty of Progress: Latin America in the Nineteenth Century* (1980), argue in different ways that Latin America's economic and social problems originated in unfavorable trade relationships with more-developed nations. See also an excellent collection of essays, Leslie Bethell, ed., *The Cambridge History of Latin America*, vol. 3, *From Independence to c. 1870* (1985).

There is an enormous literature on politics and nation building in the United States and Canada. Among the many worthy studies of the United States are John Lauritz Larson, *Internal Improvement: National Public Works and the Promise of Popular Government in the Early United States* (2001); William J. Cooper, *The South and the Politics of Slavery, 1828–1856* (1978); Kenneth M. Stampp, *America in 1857* (1991); and Lawrence Frederick Kohl, *The Politics of Individualism: Parties and the American Character in the Jacksonian Era* (1989). For Canada see J. M. S. Careless, *The Union of the Canadas: The Growth of Canadian Institutions, 1841–1857* (1967); Ged Martin, ed., *The Causes of Canadian Confederation* (1990); and Arthur I. Silver, *The French-Canadian Idea of Confederation, 1864–1900* (1982).

The social and cultural issues raised in this chapter are also the subject of a vast literature. For an excellent history of the immigration era see Walter Nugent, *Crossing: The Great Transatlantic Migrations, 1870–1914* (1992). See also Gunther Barth, *Bitter Strength: A History of Chinese in the United States, 1850–1870* (1964), and Nicolás Sánchez-Albornoz, *The Population of Latin America: A History* (1974).

On the issue of slavery see David Brion Davis, *Slavery and Human Progress* (1984), and George M. Frederickson, *The Black Image in the White Mind: The Debate on Afro-American Character and Destiny, 1817–1914* (1971). Among the many fine studies of abolition see Benjamin Quarles, *Black Abolitionists* (1969), and John Stauffer, *The Black Hearts of Men* (2001). For the women's rights movement see Ellen C. Du Bois, *Feminism and Suffrage: The Emergence of an Independent Woman's Movement in the Nineteenth Century* (1984), and Lori D. Ginzberg, *Women and the Work of Benevolence: Morality, Politics, and Class in the Nineteenth-Century United States* (1990). Among numerous excellent studies of Indian policies see Robert M. Utley, *The Indian Frontier of the American West, 1846–1890* (1984), and the recent *Andrew Jackson and His Indian Wars* (2001) by Robert V. Remini. On those topics for Canada see J. R. Miller, *Skyscrapers Hide the Heavens: A History of Indian White Relations in Canada* (1989); Olive Patricia Dickason, *Canada's First Nations* (1993); and Alison Prentice, *Canadian Women: A History* (1988).

For abolition in Latin America and the Caribbean see Rebecca Scott, *Slave Emancipation in Cuba: The Transition to Free Labor, 1860–1899* (1985); Robert Conrad, *The Destruction of Brazilian Slavery, 1850–1888* (1973); and William A. Green, *British Slave Emancipation: The Sugar Colonies and the Great Experiment, 1830–1865* (1973). An introduction to the place of women in Latin American society is found in Francesca Miller, *Latin American Women and the Search for Social Justice* (1991), and Jane Jaquette, ed., *The Women's Movement in Latin America* (1989). See also David Barry Gaspar and Darlene Clark Hine, eds., *More Than Chattel: Black Women and Slavery in the Americas* (1996).

An introduction to environmental consequence of North American development is provided by William Cronon, *Nature's Metropolis: Chicago and the Great West* (1991); Joseph M. Petulla, *American Environmental History* (1973); and Donald Worster, *Rivers of Empire: Water, Aridity, and the Growth of the American West* (1985). For Brazil see Warren Dean, *With Broadax and Firebrand: The Destruction of the Brazilian Atlantic Forest* (1995); and for Argentina, Uruguay, and Chile, Alfred Crosby, *Ecological Imperialism: The Biological Expansion of Europe, 900–1900* (1986).

■ Notes

1. Quoted in Lyman L. Johnson, "Spanish American Independence and Its Consequences," in *Problems in Modern Latin American History: A Reader,* ed. John Charles Chasteen and Joseph S. Tulchin (Wilmington, DE: Scholarly Resources, 1994), 21.
2. Quoted in Margaret Conrad, Alvin Finkel, and Cornelius Jaenen, *History of the Canadian Peoples,* vol. 1 (Toronto: Copp Clark Pittman Ltd., 1993), 606–607.
3. José Antonio Páez, *Autobiografía del General José Antonio Páez,* vol. 1 (New York: Hallety Breen, 1869), 83.
4. Quoted in Brian Loveman, *Chile: The Legacy of Hispanic Capitalism* (New York: Oxford University Press, 1979), 170.
5. Quoted in Bernard Bailyn, David Brion Davis, David Herbert Donald, John L. Thomas, Robert H. Wiebe, and Gordon S. Wood, *The Great Republic: A History of the American People* (Lexington, MA: D. C. Heath, 1981), 398.
6. Quoted in Mary Beth Norton, et al, *A People and a Nation. A History of the United States,* 6th ed. (Boston, MA: Houghton Mifflin Company, 2001), 284.
7. J. S. Woodsworth in 1909, quoted in R. Douglas Francis, Richard Jones, and Donald B. Smith, *Destinies: Canadian History Since Confederation,* 2d ed. (Toronto: Holt, Rinehart and Winston, 1992), 141.
8. Sarah Grimké, "Reply to the Massachusetts Clergy," in Nancy Woloch, ed., *Early American Women: A Documentary History, 1600–1900* (Belmont, CA: Wadsworth, 1992), 343.

Document-Based Question
Race and Ethnicity in the Americas, 1800–1890

Using the following documents, analyze the effect of race and ethnicity on the political and economic development of the Americas during the nineteenth century.

DOCUMENT 1
Padre Hidalgo (photo, p. 597)

DOCUMENT 2
The Afro-Brazilian Experience, 1828 (Diversity and Dominance, pp. 600–601)

DOCUMENT 3
Benito Juárez's Triumph over the French (photo, p. 607)

DOCUMENT 4
Navajo Leaders Gathered in Washington to Negotiate (photo, p. 608)

DOCUMENT 5
Quote from Chilean newspaper (p. 609)

DOCUMENT 6
A Former Brazilian Slave Returns from Military Service (photo, p. 611)

DOCUMENT 7
Chinese Funeral in Vancouver, Canada (photo, p. 613)

DOCUMENT 8
Quote from Canadian reformer (pp. 613–614)

What kinds of bias are evident in Documents 2, 5, and 8? What additional documents would help you understand the effect of race and ethnicity on the political and economic development of the Americas during the nineteenth century?

Africa, India, and the New British Empire, 1750–1870

Indian Railroad Station, 1866 British India built the largest network of railroads in Asia. People of every social class traveled by train.

In 1782 Tipu Sultan inherited the throne of the state of Mysore°, which his father had made the most powerful state in South India. The ambitious and talented new ruler also inherited a healthy distrust of the territorial ambitions of Great Britain's East India Company. In 1785, before the company could invade Mysore, Tipu Sultan launched his own attack. He then sent an embassy to France in 1788, seeking an alliance against Britain. Neither of these ventures was immediately successful.

Not until a decade later did the French agree to a loose alliance with Tipu Sultan as part of their plan to challenge Britain's colonial and commercial supremacy in the Indian Ocean. General Napoleon Bonaparte invaded Egypt in 1798 to threaten British trade routes to India and hoped to use the alliance with Tipu Sultan to drive the British out of India. The French invasion of Egypt went well enough at first, but a British naval blockade and the ravages of disease crippled the French force. When the French withdrew, another military adventurer, Muhammad Ali, commander of the Ottoman army in Egypt, took advantage of the situation to revitalize Egypt and expand its rule.

Meanwhile, Tipu's struggle with the East India Company was going badly. A military defeat in 1792 forced him to surrender most of his coastal lands. Despite the loose alliance with France, he was unable to stop further British advances. Tipu lost his life in 1799 while defending his capital against a British assault. Mysore was divided between the British and their Indian allies.

As these events illustrate, talented local leaders and European powers were all vying to expand their influence in South Asia and Africa between 1750 and 1870. Midway through that period, it was by no means clear who would gain the upper hand. Britain and France were as likely to fight each other as they were to fight an Asian or African state. In 1800 the two nations were engaged in their third major war for overseas supremacy since 1750. By 1870, however, Britain had gained a decisive advantage over France.

The new British Empire in the East included the subcontinent of India, settler colonies in Australia and New Zealand, and a growing network of trading outposts. By 1870 Britain had completed the campaign to replace the overseas slave trade from Africa with "legitimate" trade and had spearheaded new Asian and South Pacific labor migrations into a rejuvenated string of tropical colonies.

As you read this chapter, ask yourself the following questions:

- Why were the British able to gain decisive advantages in distant lands?

- Why were Asians and Africans so divided, some choosing to cooperate with the Europeans and others resisting their advances?

- How important an advantage were Britain's weapons, ships, and economic motives?

- How much of the outcome was the result of advance planning, and how much was due to particular individuals or to chance?

- By 1870, how much had the British and the different peoples of Africa and Asia gained or lost?

CHANGES AND EXCHANGES IN AFRICA

In the century before 1870 Africa underwent dynamic political changes and a great expansion of foreign trade. Indigenous African leaders as well as Middle Eastern and European imperialists built powerful new states and expanded old ones. As the continent's external slave trades to the Americas and to Islamic lands died slowly under British pressure, trade in goods such as palm oil, ivory, timber, and gold grew sharply. In return Africans imported large quantities of machine-made textiles and firearms. These complex changes are best understood by looking at African regions separately.

Mysore (my-SORE)

C H R O N O L O G Y

	Empire	Africa	India
1750			**1756** Black Hole of Calcutta
	1763 End of Seven Years War		**1765** East India Company (EIC) rule of Bengal begins
	1769–1778 Captain James Cook explores New Zealand and eastern Australia		
	1795 End of Dutch East India Company	**1795** Britain takes Cape Colony	
		1798 Napoleon invades Egypt	**1798** Britain annexes Ceylon
1800			**1799** EIC defeats Mysore
		1805 Muhammad Ali seizes Egypt	
	1808 Britain outlaws slave trade	**1808** Britain takes over Sierra Leone	
		1809 Sokoto Caliphate founded	
		1818 Shaka founds Zulu kingdom	**1818** EIC creates Bombay Presidency
		1821 Foundation of Republic of Liberia; Egypt takes control of Sudan	**1826** EIC annexes Assam and northern Burma
			1828 Brahmo Samaj founded
	1834 Britain abolishes slavery	**1831–1847** Algerians resist French takeover	**1834** Indentured labor migrations begin
		1836–1839 Afrikaners' Great Trek	
1850		**1840** Omani sultan moves capital to Zanzibar	
	1867 End of Atlantic slave trade	**1869** Jaja founds Opobo	**1857–1858** Sepoy Rebellion leads to end of EIC rule and Mughal rule
	1877 Queen Victoria becomes Empress of India	**1889** Menelik unites modern Ethiopia	**1885** First Indian National Congress

New Africa States

Internal forces produced clusters of new states in two parts of sub-Saharan Africa between 1750 and 1870. In southern Africa changes in warfare gave rise to a powerful Zulu kingdom and other new states. In inland West Africa Islamic reformers created the gigantic Sokoto° Caliphate and companion states (see Map 24.1).

For many centuries the Nguni° peoples had pursued a life based on cattle and agriculture in the fertile coastlands of southeastern Africa (in modern South Africa). Small independent chiefdoms suited their political needs until a serious drought hit the region at the beginning of the nineteenth century. Out of the conflict for grazing and farming lands, an upstart military genius named Shaka (r. 1818–1828) created the **Zulu** kingdom in 1818. Strict military drill and close-combat warfare featuring ox-hide shields and lethal stabbing spears made the Zulu the most powerful and most feared fighters in southern Africa.

Shaka expanded his kingdom by raiding his African neighbors, seizing their cattle, and capturing their women and children. Breakaway military bands spread this system of warfare and state building inland to the high plateau country, across the Limpopo River (in modern Zimbabwe°), and as far north as Lake Victoria. As the power and population of these new kingdoms increased, so too did the number of displaced and demoralized refugees around them.

To protect themselves from the Zulu, some neighboring Africans created their own states. The Swazi kingdom consolidated north of the Zulu, and the kingdom of

Sokoto (SOH-kuh-toh)   **Nguni** (ng-GOO-nee)

Zimbabwe (zim-BAH-bway)

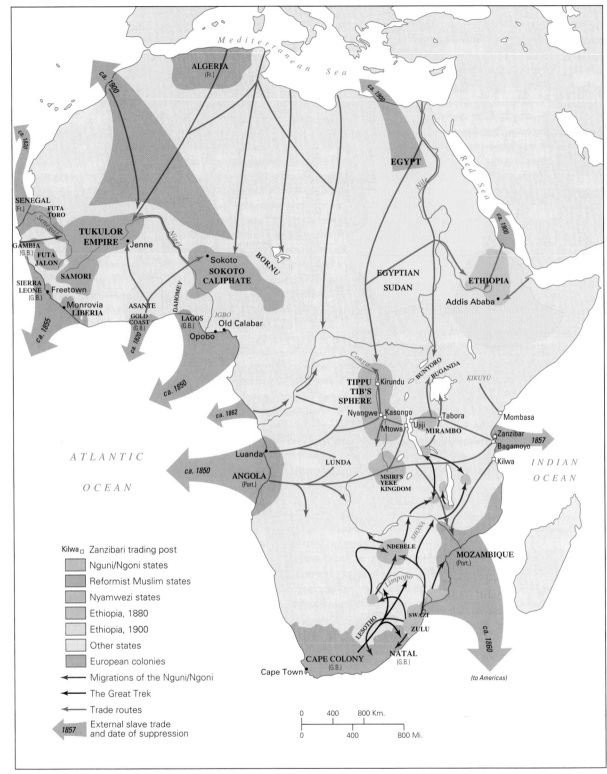

Map 24.1   Africa in the Nineteenth Century   Expanding internal and overseas trade drew much of Africa into global networks, but foreign colonies in 1870 were largely confined to Algeria and southern Africa. Growing trade, Islamic reform movements, and other internal forces created important new states throughout the continent.

Lesotho° grew by attracting refugees to strongholds in southern Africa's highest mountains. Both Lesotho and Swaziland survive as independent states to this day.

Although Shaka ruled for little more than a decade, he succeeded in creating a new national identity as well as a new kingdom. He grouped all the young people in his domains by age into regiments. Regiment members lived together and immersed themselves in learning Zulu lore and customs, including fighting methods for the males. A British trader named Henry Francis Fynn expressed his "astonishment at the order and discipline" he found everywhere in the Zulu kingdom. He witnessed public festivals of loyalty to Shaka at which regiments of young men and women numbering in the tens of thousands danced around the king for hours. Parades showed off the king's enormous herds of cattle, a Zulu measure of wealth.

Meanwhile, Islamic reform movements were creating another cluster of powerful states in the savannas of West Africa. Islam had been a force in the politics and cities of this region for centuries, but it had made only slow progress among most rural people. As a consequence, most Muslim rulers had found it prudent to tolerate the older religious practices of their rural subjects. In the 1770s local Muslim scholars began preaching the need for a vigorous reform of Islamic practices. They condemned the accommodations Muslim rulers had made with older traditions and called for a forcible conquest of rural "pagans." The reformers followed a classic Muslim pattern: a *jihad* (holy war) added new lands, where governments enforced Islamic laws and promoted the religion's spread among conquered people.

The largest of the new Muslim reform movements occurred in the Hausa° states (in what is now northern Nigeria) under the leadership of Usuman dan Fodio° (1745–1817), a Muslim cleric of the Fulani° people. He charged that the Hausa kings, despite their official profession of Islam, were "undoubtedly unbelievers . . . because they practice polytheistic rituals and turn people away from the path of God."Distressed by the lapses of a former pupil, the king of Gobir, Usuman issued a call in 1804 for a jihad to overthrow him. Muslims unhappy with their social or religious position spread the movement to other Hausa states. The successful armies united the conquered Hausa states and neighboring areas under a caliph (sultan) who ruled from the city of Sokoto. The **Sokoto Caliphate** (1809–1906) was the largest state

Lesotho (luh-SOO-too)   Hausa (HOW-suh)
Usuman dan Fodio (OO-soo-mahn dahn FOH-dee-oh)
Fulani (foo-LAH-nee)

Zulu in Battle Dress, 1838   Elaborate costumes helped impress opponents with the Zulu's strength. Shown here are long-handled spears and thick leather shields. The stabbing spear is not shown. (Killie Campbell Africana Library. Photo: Jane Taylor/Sonia Halliday)

in West Africa since the fall of Songhai in the sixteenth century.

As in earlier centuries, these new Muslim states became centers of Islamic learning and reform. Schools for training boys in Quranic subjects spread rapidly, and the great library at Sokoto attracted many scholars. Although officials permitted non-Muslims within the empire to follow their religions in exchange for paying a special tax, they suppressed public performances of dances and ceremonies associated with traditional religions. During the jihads, many who resisted the expansion of Muslim rule were killed, enslaved, or forced to convert.

Sokoto's leaders sold some captives into the Atlantic slave trade and many more into the trans-Saharan slave trade, which carried ten thousand slaves a year, mostly women and children, across the desert to North Africa and the Middle East. Slavery also increased greatly within the Sokoto Caliphate and other new Muslim states. It is estimated that by 1865 there were more slaves in the Sokoto Caliphate than in any remaining slave-holding state in the Americas.[1] Most of the enslaved persons raised food, making possible the seclusion of free women in their homes in accordance with reformed Muslim practice.

Modernization in Egypt and Ethiopia

While new states were arising elsewhere, in northeastern Africa the ancient states of Egypt and Ethiopia were undergoing growth and **modernization.** Napoleon's invading army had withdrawn from Egypt by 1801, but the shock of this display of European strength and Egyptian weakness was long-lasting. The successor to Napoleon's rule was **Muhammad Ali** (1769– 1849), who eliminated his rivals and ruled Egypt from 1805 to 1848. He began the political, social, and economic reforms that created modern Egypt.

Muhammad Ali's central aim was to give Egypt sufficient military strength to prevent another European conquest, but he was pragmatic enough to make use of European experts and techniques to achieve that goal. His reforms transformed Egyptian landholding, increased agricultural production, and created a modern administration and army. To train candidates for the army and administration, Muhammad Ali set up a European-style state school system and opened a military college at Aswan°. To pay for these ventures and for the European experts and equipment he imported, he required Egyptian peasants to cultivate cotton and other crops for export.

In the 1830s Muhammad Ali headed the strongest state in the Islamic world and the first to employ Western methods and technology for modernization. The process was far from blind imitation of the West. Rather, the technical expertise of the West was combined with Islamic religious and cultural traditions. For example, the Egyptian printing industry, begun to provide Arabic translations of technical manuals, turned out critical editions of Islamic classics and promoted a revival of Arabic writing and literature later in the century.

By the end of Muhammad Ali's reign in 1848, the modernization of Egypt was well underway. The population had nearly doubled; trade with Europe had expanded by almost 600 percent; and a new class of educated Egyptians had begun to replace the old ruling aristocracy. Egyptians were replacing many of the foreign experts, and the fledgling program of industrialization was providing the country with its own textiles, paper, weapons, and military uniforms. The demands on peasant families for labor and military service, however, were acutely disruptive.

Ali's grandson Ismail° (r. 1863–1879) placed even more emphasis on westernizing Egypt. "My country is no longer in Africa," Ismail declared, "it is in Europe."[2] His efforts increased the number of European advisers in Egypt—and Egypt's debts to French and British banks. In the first decade of his reign, revenues increased thirty-fold and exports doubled (largely because of a huge increase in cotton exports during the American Civil War). By 1870 Egypt had a network of new irrigation canals, 800 miles (1,300 kilometers) of railroads, a modern postal service, and the dazzling new capital city of Cairo. When the market for Egyptian cotton collapsed after the American Civil War, however, Egypt's debts to British and French investors led to the country's partial occupation.

From the middle of the century, state building and reform also were underway in the ancient kingdom of Ethiopia, whose rulers had been Christian for fifteen hundred years. Weakened by internal divisions and the pressures of its Muslim neighbors, Ethiopia was a shadow of what it had been in the sixteenth century, but under Emperor Téwodros° II (r. 1833–1868) and his successor Yohannes° IV (r. 1872–1889) most highland regions were brought back under imperial rule. The only large part of ancient Ethiopia that remained outside Emperor Yohannes's rule was the Shoa kingdom, ruled by King Menelik° from 1865. When Menelik succeeded Yohannes as emperor in 1889, the merger of their separate realms created the modern boundaries of Ethiopia.

Beginning in the 1840s Ethiopian rulers purchased modern weapons from European sources and created strong armies loyal to the ruler. Emperor Téwodros also encouraged the manufacture of weapons locally. With the aid of Protestant missionaries his craftsmen even constructed a giant cannon capable of firing a half-ton shell. However, his efforts to coerce more technical aid by holding some British officials captive backfired when the British invaded instead. As the British forces advanced, Téwodros committed suicide to avoid being taken prisoner. Satisfied that their honor was avenged, the British withdrew. Later Ethiopian emperors kept up the program of reform and modernization.

Aswan (AS-wahn)

Ismail (is-MAH-eel) **Téwodros** (tay-WOH-druhs)
Yohannes (yoh-HAHN-nehs) **Menelik** (MEN-uh-lik)

Téwodros's Mighty Cannon   Like other modernizers in the nineteenth century, Emperor Téwodros of Ethiopia sought to reform his military forces. In 1861 he forced resident European missionaries and craftsmen to build guns and cannon, including this 7-ton behemoth nicknamed "Sebastapol" after the Black Sea port that had been the center of the Crimean War. It took five hundred men to haul the cannon across Ethiopia's hilly terrain.   (From Hormuzd Rassam, *Narrative of the British Mission to Theodore, King of Abyssinia, II*, London 1869, John Murray)

European Penetration

More lasting than Britain's punitive invasion of Ethiopia was France's conquest of Algeria, a move that anticipated the general European "scramble" for Africa after 1870. Equally pregnant with future meaning was the Europeans' exploration of the inland parts of Africa in the middle decades of the century.

Long an exporter of grain and olive oil to France, the North African state of Algeria had even supplied Napoleon with grain for his 1798 invasion of Egypt. The failure of French governments to repay this debt led to many disputes between Algeria and France and eventually to a severing of diplomatic relations in 1827 after the ruler of Algeria, annoyed with the French ambassador, allegedly struck him with a fly whisk. Three years later an unpopular French government, hoping to stir French nationalism with an easy overseas victory, attacked Algeria on the pretext of avenging this insult.

The invasion of 1830 proved a costly mistake. The French government was soon overthrown, but the war in Algeria dragged on for eighteen years. The attack by an alien Christian power united the Algerians behind 'Abd al-Qadir°, a gifted and resourceful Muslim holy man. To achieve victory, the French built up an army of over 100,000 that broke Algerian resistance by destroying farm animals and crops and massacring villagers by the tens of thousands. After 'Abd al-Qadir was captured and exiled in 1847, the resistance movement fragmented, but the French occupiers faced resistance in the mountains for another thirty years. Poor European settlers,

'Abd al-Qadir (AHB-dahl-KAH-deer)

who rushed in to take possession of Algeria's rich coast-lands, numbered 130,000 by 1871.

Meanwhile, a more peaceful European intrusion was penetrating Africa's geographical secrets. Small expeditions of adventurous explorers, using their own funds or financed by private geographical societies, were seeking to uncover the mysteries of inner Africa that had eluded Europeans for four centuries. Besides discovering more about the course of Africa's mighty rivers, these explorers wished to assess the continent's mineral wealth or convert the African millions to Christianity.

Many of the explorers were concerned with tracing the course of Africa's great rivers. Explorers learned in 1795 that the Niger River in West Africa flowed from west to east (not the other way, as had often been supposed) and in 1830 that the great morass of small streams entering the Gulf of Guinea was in fact the Niger Delta.

The north-flowing Nile, whose annual floods made Egypt bloom, similarly attracted explorers bent on finding the headwaters of the world's longest river. In 1770 Lake Tana in Ethiopia was established as a major source, and in 1861–1862 Lake Victoria (named for the British sovereign) was found to be the other main source.

In contrast to the heavily financed expeditions with hundreds of African porters that searched the Nile, the Scottish missionary David Livingstone (1813–1873) organized modest treks through southern and Central Africa. The missionary doctor's primary goal was to scout out locations for Christian missions, but he was also highly influential in tracing the course of the Zambezi River between 1853 and 1856. He named its greatest waterfall for the British monarch Queen Victoria. Livingstone also traced the course of the upper Congo River, where in 1871 he was met by the Welsh-American journalist Henry Morton Stanley (1841–1904) on a publicity-motivated search for the "lost" missionary doctor. On an expedition from 1874 to 1877, Stanley descended the Congo River to its mouth.

One of the most remarkable features of the explorers' experiences in Africa was their ability to move unmolested from place to place. The strangers were seldom harmed without provocation. Stanley preferred large expeditions that fought their way across the continent, but Livingstone's modest expeditions, which posed no threat to anyone, regularly received warm hospitality.

Abolition and Legitimate Trade

No sooner was the mouth of the Niger River discovered than eager entrepreneurs began to send expeditions up the river to scout out its potential for trade. Along much of coastal West Africa, commercial relations with Europeans remained dominant between 1750 and 1870. The value of trade between Africa and the other Atlantic continents more than doubled between the 1730s and the 1780s, then doubled again by 1870.[3] Before about 1825 the slave trade accounted for most of that increase, but thereafter African exports of vegetable oils, gold, ivory, and other goods drove overseas trade to new heights.

Europeans played a critical role in these changes in Africa's overseas trade. The Atlantic trade had arisen to serve the needs of the first European empires, and its transformation was linked to the ideas and industrial needs of Britain's new economy and empire.

One step in the Atlantic slave trade's extinction was the successful slave revolt in Saint Domingue in the 1790s (see Chapter 21). It ended slavery in the largest plantation colony in the West Indies, and elsewhere in the Americas it inspired slave revolts that were brutally repressed. As news of the slave revolts and their repression spread, humanitarians and religious reformers called for an end to the trade. Since it was widely believed that African-born slaves were more likely to rebel than were persons born into slavery, support for abolition of the slave trade was found even among Americans wanting to preserve slavery. In 1808 both Great Britain and the United States made carrying and importing slaves from Africa illegal for their citizens. Most other Western countries followed suit by 1850, but few enforced abolition with the vigor of the British.

Once the world's greatest slave traders, the British became the most aggressive abolitionists. Britain sent a naval patrol to enforce the ban along the African coast and negotiated treaties allowing the patrol to search other nations' vessels suspected of carrying slaves. During the half-century after 1815, Britain spent some $60 million (£12 million) to end the slave trade, a sum equal to the profits British slave traders had made in the fifty years before 1808.

Although British patrols captured 1,635 slave ships and liberated over 160,000 enslaved Africans, the trade proved difficult to stop. Cuba and Brazil continued to import huge numbers of slaves, which drove prices up and persuaded some African rulers and merchants to continue to sell slaves and to help foreign slavers evade the British patrols. After British patrols quashed the slave trade along the Gold Coast, the powerful king of Asante° even tried to persuade a British official in 1820 that reopening the trade would be to their mutual profit. Because the slave trade moved to other parts of Africa, the trans-Atlantic slave trade did not end until 1867.

Asante (uh-SHAHN-tee)

The demand for slaves in the Americas claimed the lives and endangered the safety of untold numbers of Africans, but the trade also satisfied other Africans' desires for the cloth, metals, and other goods that European traders brought in return. To continue their access to those imports, Africans expanded their **"legitimate" trade** (exports other than slaves). They revived old exports or developed new ones as the Atlantic slave trade was shut down. On the Gold Coast, for example, annual exports of gold climbed to nearly 25,000 ounces (750 kilograms) in the 1840s and 1850s, compared to 10,000 ounces (300 kilograms) in the 1790s.

The most successful of the new exports from West Africa was palm oil, a vegetable oil used by British manufacturers for soap, candles, and lubricants. Though still a major source of slaves until the mid-1830s, the trading states of the Niger Delta simultaneously emerged as the premier exporters of palm oil. In inland forests men climbed tall oil palms and cut down large palm-nut clusters, which women pounded to extract the thick oil. Coastal African traders bought the palm oil at inland markets and delivered it to European ships at the coast.

The dramatic increase in palm-oil exports—from a few hundred tons at the beginning of the century to tens of thousands of tons by midcentury—did not require any new technology, but it did alter the social structure of the coastal trading communities. Coastal traders grew rich and used their wealth to buy large numbers of male slaves to paddle the giant dugout canoes that transported palm oil from inland markets along the narrow delta creeks to the trading ports. Niger Delta slavery could be as harsh and brutal as slavery on New World plantations, but it offered some male and female slaves a chance to gain wealth and power. Some female slaves who married big traders exercised great authority over junior members of trading households. Male slaves who supervised canoe fleets were well compensated, and a few even became wealthy enough to take over the leadership of the coastal "canoe houses" (companies). The most famous, known as "Jaja" (ca. 1821–1891), rose from canoe slave to become the head of a major canoe house. In 1869, to escape discrimination by free-born Africans, he founded the new port of Opobo, which he ruled as king. In the 1870s Jaja of Opobo was the greatest palm-oil trader in the Niger Delta.

Another effect of the suppression of the slave trade was the spread of Western cultural influences in West Africa. To serve as a base for their anti-slave-trade naval squadron, the British had taken over the small colony of Sierra Leone° in 1808. Over the next several years,

130,000 men, women, and children taken from "captured" vessels were liberated in Sierra Leone. Christian missionaries helped settle these impoverished and dispirited **recaptives** in and around Freetown, the capital. In time the mission churches and schools made many willing converts among such men and women.

Sierra Leone's schools also produced a number of distinguished graduates. For example, Samuel Adjai

King Jaja of Opobo This talented man rose from slavery in the Niger Delta port of Bonny to head one of the town's major palm-oil trading firms, the Anna Pepple House, in 1863. Six years later, Jaja founded and ruled his own trading port of Opobo. (Reproduced from *West Africa: An Introduction to Its History*, by Michael Crowder, by courtesy of the publishers, Addison Wesley Longman)

Sierra Leone (see-ER-uh lee-OWN)

Crowther (1808–1891), freed as a youth from a slave ship by the British squadron in 1821, became the first Anglican bishop in West Africa in 1864, administering a pioneering diocese along the lower Niger River. James Africanus Horton (1835–1882), the son of slaves liberated in Sierra Leone, became a doctor and the author of many studies of West Africa.

Other Western cultural influences came from people of African birth or descent returning to their ancestral homeland. In 1821, to the south of Sierra Leone, free black Americans began a settlement that grew into the Republic of Liberia, a place of liberty at a time when slavery was legal and flourishing in the United States. After their emancipation in 1865 other African-Americans moved to Liberia. Emma White, a literate black woman from Kentucky, moved from Liberia to Opobo in 1875, where King Jaja employed her to write his commercial correspondence and run a school for his children. Edward Wilmot Blyden (1832–1912), born in the Danish West Indies and proud of his West African parentage, emigrated to Liberia in 1851 and became a professor of Greek and Latin (and later Arabic) at the fledgling Liberia College. Free blacks from Brazil and Cuba chartered ships to return to their West African homelands, bringing Roman Catholicism, architectural motifs, and clothing fashions from the New World. Although the number of Africans exposed to Western culture in 1870 was still small, this influence grew rapidly.

Secondary Empires in Eastern Africa

When British patrols hampered the slave trade in West Africa, slavers moved southward and then around the tip of southern Africa to eastern Africa. There the Atlantic slave trade joined an existing trade in slaves to the Islamic world that also was expanding. Two-thirds of the 1.2 million slaves exported from eastern Africa in the nineteenth century went to markets in North Africa and the Middle East; the other third went to plantations in the Americas and to European-controlled Indian Ocean islands.

Slavery also became more prominent within eastern Africa itself. Between 1800 and 1873 Arab and Swahili° owners of clove plantations along the coast purchased some 700,000 slaves from inland eastern Africa to do the labor-intensive work of harvesting this spice. The plantations were on Zanzibar Island and in neighboring territories belonging to the Sultanate of Oman, an Arabian kingdom on the Persian Gulf that had been expanding its control over the East African coast since 1698. The sultan had even moved his court to Zanzibar in 1840 to take better advantage of the burgeoning trade in cloves. Zanzibar also was an important center of slaves and ivory. Most of the ivory was shipped to India, where much of it was carved into decorative objects for European markets.

Ivory caravans came to the coast from hundreds of miles inland under the direction of African and Arab merchants. Some of these merchants brought large personal empires under their control by using capital they had borrowed from Indian bankers and modern firearms they had bought from Europeans and Americans. Some trading empires were created by inland Nyamwezi° traders, who worked closely with the indigenous Swahili and Arabs in Zanzibar to develop the long-distance caravan routes.

The largest of these personal empires, along the upper Congo River, was created by Tippu Tip (ca. 1830–1905), a trader from Zanzibar, who was Swahili and Nyamwezi on his father's side and Omani Arab on his mother's. Livingstone, Stanley, and other explorers who received Tippu Tip's gracious hospitality in the remote center of the continent praised their host's intelligence and refinement. On an 1876 visit, for example, Stanley recorded in his journal that Tippu Tip was "a remarkable man," a "picture of energy and strength" with "a fine intelligent face: almost courtier-like in his manner."

Tippu Tip also composed a detailed memoir of his adventures in the heart of Africa, written in the Swahili language of the coast. In it he mocked innocent African villagers for believing that his gunshots were thunder. As the memoir and other sources make clear, modern rifles not only felled countless elephants for their ivory tusks but also inflicted widespread devastation and misery on the people of this isolated area.

One can blame Tippu Tip and other Zanzibari traders, along with their master, the sultan of Oman, for the pillage and havoc in the once-peaceful center of Africa. However, the circle of responsibility was broader. Europeans supplied the weapons and were major consumers of ivory and cloves. For this reason histories have referred to the states carved out of eastern Africa by the sultans of Oman, Tippu Tip, and others as "secondary empires," in contrast to the empire that Britain was establishing directly. At the same time, British officials pressured the sultan of Oman into halting the Indian Ocean slave trade from Zanzibar in 1857 and ending the import of slaves into Zanzibar in 1873.

Swahili (swah-HEE-lee)

Nyamwezi (nn-nyahm-WAY-zee)

Egypt's expansion southward during the nineteenth century can also be considered a secondary empire. Muhammad Ali had pioneered the conquest of the upper Nile, in 1821 establishing a major base at Khartoum° that became the capital of Egyptian Sudan. A major reason for his invasion of Sudan was to secure slaves for his army so that more Egyptian peasants could be left free to grow cotton for export. From the 1840s unscrupulous traders of many origins, leading forces armed with European weapons, pushed south to the modern frontiers of Uganda and Zaire in search of cattle, ivory, and slaves. They set one African community against another and reaped profit from the devastation they sowed.

INDIA UNDER BRITISH RULE

The people of South Asia felt the impact of European commercial, cultural, and colonial expansion more immediately and profoundly than did the people of Africa. While Europeans were laying claim to only small parts of Africa between 1750 and 1870, nearly all of India (with three times the population of all of Africa) came under Britain's direct or indirect rule. During the 250 years after the founding of East India Company in 1600, British interests commandeered the colonies and trade of the Dutch, fought off French and Indian challenges, and picked up the pieces of the decaying Mughal° Empire. By 1763 the French were stymied; in 1795 the Dutch East India Company was dissolved; and in 1858 the last Mughal emperor was dethroned, leaving the vast subcontinent in British hands.

Company Men

As Mughal power weakened in the eighteenth century, Europeans were not the first outsiders to make a move. In 1739 Iranian armies defeated the Mughal forces, sacked Delhi, and returned home with vast amounts of booty. Indian states also took advantage of Mughal weakness to assert their independence. By midcentury, the Maratha° Confederation, a coalition of states in central India, controlled more land than the Mughals did (see Map 24.2). Also ruling their own powerful states were the **nawabs**° (a term used for Muslim princes who were deputies of the Mughal emperor, though in name only): the nawab of

Khartoum (khar-TOOM)   **Mughal** (MOO-guhl)
Maratha (muh-RAH-tuh)   **nawab** (NAH-wab)

Bengal in the northeast; the nawab of Arcot in the southeast, Haidar Ali (1722–1782)—the father of Tipu Sultan and ruler of the southwestern state of Mysore; and many others.

British, Dutch, and French companies were also eager to expand their profitable trade into India in the eighteenth century. Such far-flung European trading companies were speculative and risky ventures in 1750. Their success depended on hard-drinking and ambitious young "company men," who used hard bargaining, and hard fighting when necessary, to persuade Indian rulers to allow them to establish trading posts at strategic points along the coast. To protect their fortified warehouses from attack by other Europeans or by native states, the companies hired and trained Indian troops known as **sepoys**°. In divided India these private armies came to hold the balance of power.

In 1691 Great Britain's East India Company (EIC) had convinced the nawab of the large state of Bengal in northeast India to let the company establish a fortified outpost at the fishing port of Calcutta. A new nawab, pressing claims for additional tribute from the prospering port, overran the fort in 1756 and imprisoned a group of EIC men in a cell so small that many died of suffocation. To avenge their deaths in this "Black Hole of Calcutta," a large EIC force from Madras, led by the young Robert Clive, overthrew the nawab. The weak Mughal emperor was persuaded to acknowledge the East India Company's right to rule Bengal in 1765. Fed by the tax revenues of Bengal as well as by profits from trade, the EIC was on its way. Calcutta grew into a city of 250,000 by 1788.

In southern India, Clive had used EIC forces from Madras to secure victory for the British Indian candidate for nawab of Arcot during the Seven Years War (1756–1763), thereby gaining an advantage over French traders who had supported the loser. The defeat of Tipu Sultan of Mysore at the end of the century (described at the start of the chapter) secured south India for the company and prevented a French resurgence.

Along with Calcutta and Madras, the third major center of British power in India was Bombay, on the western coast. There, after a long series of contests with Maratha Confederation rulers, the East India Company gained a decisive advantage in 1818, annexing large territories to form the core of what was called the "Bombay Presidency." Some states were taken over completely, as Bengal had been, but very many others remained in the hands of local princes who accepted the political control of the company.

sepoy (SEE-poy)

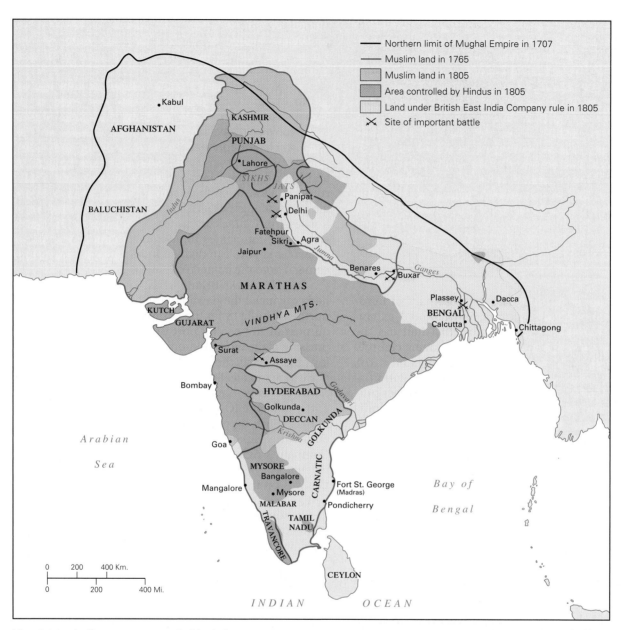

Map 24.2   India, 1707–1805   As Mughal power weakened during the eighteenth century, other Indian states and the East India Company expanded their territories.

**Raj and
Rebellion,
1818–1857**

In 1818 the East India Company controlled an Empire with more people than in all of western Europe and fifty times the population of the colonies the British had lost in North America. One thrust of **British raj** (reign) was to remake India on a British model through administrative and social reform, economic development, and the introduction of new technology. But at the same time the company men—like the Mughals before them—had to temper their interference with Indian social and religious customs lest they provoke rebellion or lose the support of their Indian princely allies. For this reason and because of the complexity of the task of ruling such a vast empire, there were many inconsistencies in Britain's policies toward India.

The main policy was to create a powerful and efficient system of government. British rule before 1850 relied heavily on military power—170 sepoy regiments and 16 European regiments. Another policy very much in the interests of India's new rulers was to disarm approximately 2 million warriors who had served India's many states and turn them to civilian tasks, mostly cultivation. A third policy was to give freer rein to Christian missionaries eager to convert and uplift India's masses. Few converts were made, but the missionaries kept up steady pressure for social reforms.

Another key British policy was to substitute ownership of private property for India's complex and overlapping patterns of landholding. In Bengal this reform worked to the advantage of large landowners, but in Mysore the peasantry gained. Private ownership made it easier for the state to collect the taxes that were needed to pay for administration, the army, and economic reform.

Such policies of "westernization, Anglicization, and modernization," as they have been called, were only one side of British rule. The other side was the bolstering of "traditions"—both real and newly invented. In the name of tradition the Indian princes who ruled nearly half of British India were frequently endowed by their British overlords with greater power and splendor and longer tenure than their predecessors had ever had. Hindu and Muslim holy men were able to expand their "traditional" power over property and people far beyond what had been the case in earlier times. Princes, holy men, and other Indians frequently used claims of tradition to resist British rule as well as to turn it to their advantage. The British rulers themselves invented many "traditions"—including elaborate parades and displays—half borrowed from European royal pomp, half freely improvised from Mughal ceremonies.

The British and Indian elites danced sometimes in close partnership, sometimes in apparent opposition. But the ordinary people of India suffered. Women of every status, members of subordinate Hindu castes, the "untouchables" and "tribals" outside the caste system, and the poor generally experienced less benefit from the British reforms and much new oppression from the taxes and "traditions" that exalted their superiors' status.

The transformation of British India's economy was also doubled-edged. On the one hand, British raj created many new jobs as a result of the growth of internal and external trade and the expansion of agricultural production, such as in opium in Bengal—largely for export to China (see Chapter 25)—coffee in Ceylon (an island off the tip of India), and tea in Assam (a state in northeastern India). On the other hand, competition from cheap cotton goods produced in Britain's industrial mills drove many Indians out of the handicraft textile industry. In the eighteenth century India had been the world's greatest exporter of cotton textiles; in the nineteenth century India increasingly shipped raw cotton fiber to Britain.

Even the beneficial economic changes introduced under Britain rule were disruptive, and there were no safety nets for the needy. Displaced ruling elites, disgruntled religious traditionalists, and the economically dispossessed fomented almost constant local rebellions during the first half of the nineteenth century. British rulers readily handled these isolated uprisings, but they were more concerned about the continuing loyalty of Indian sepoys in the East India Company's army. The EIC employed 200,000 sepoys in 1857, along with 38,000 British officers. Armed with the latest rifles and disciplined in fighting methods, the sepoys had a potential for successful rebellion that other groups lacked.

In fact, discontent was growing among Indian soldiers. In the early decades of EIC rule, most sepoys came from Bengal, one of the first states the company had annexed. The Bengali sepoys resented the active recruitment of other ethnic groups into the army after 1848, such as Sikhs° from Punjab and Gurkhas from Nepal. Many high-caste Hindus objected to a new law in 1856 requiring new recruits to be available for service overseas in the growing Indian Ocean empire, for their religion prohibited ocean travel. The replacement of the standard military musket by the far more accurate Enfield rifle in 1857 also caused problems. Soldiers were ordered to use their teeth to tear open the ammunition cartridges, which were greased with animal fat. Hindus were offended by this order if the fat came from cattle, which they considered sacred. Muslims were offended if the fat came from pigs, which they considered unclean.

Although the cartridge-opening procedure was quickly changed, the initial discontent grew into rebellion by Hindu sepoys in May 1857. British troubles mushroomed when Muslim sepoys, peasants, and discontented elites joined in. The rebels asserted old traditions to challenge British authority: sepoy officers in Delhi proclaimed their loyalty to the Mughal emperor; others rallied behind the Maratha leader Nana Sahib. The rebellion was put down by March 1858, but it shook this piecemeal empire to its core.

Historians have attached different names and meanings to the events of 1857 and 1858. Concentrating on

Sikh (seek)

the technical fact that the uprising was an unlawful action by soldiers, nineteenth-century British historians labeled it the **"Sepoy Rebellion"** or the "Mutiny," and these names are still commonly used. Seeing in these events the beginnings of the later movement for independence, some modern Indian historians have termed it the "Revolution of 1857." In reality, it was much more than a simple mutiny, because it involved more than soldiers, but it was not yet a nationalist revolution, for the rebels' sense of a common Indian national identity was weak.

Political Reform and Industrial Impact

Whatever it is called, the rebellion of 1857–1858 was a turning point in the history of modern India. Some say it marks the beginning of modern India. In its wake Indians gained a new centralized government, entered a period of rapid economic growth, and began to develop a new national consciousness.

The changes in government were immediate. In 1858 Britain eliminated the last traces of Mughal and Company rule. In their place, a new secretary of state for India in London oversaw Indian policy, and a new government-general in Delhi acted as the British monarch's viceroy on the spot. A proclamation by Queen Victoria in November 1858 guaranteed all Indians equal protection of the law and the freedom to practice their religions and social customs; it also assured Indian princes that so long as they were loyal to the queen British India would respect their control of territories and "their rights, dignity and honour."[4]

British rule continued to emphasize both tradition and reform after 1857. At the top, the British viceroys lived in enormous palaces amid hundreds of servants and gaudy displays of luxury meant to convince Indians that the British viceroys were legitimate successors to the Mughal emperors. They treated the quasi-independent Indian princes with elaborate ceremonial courtesy and maintained them in splendor. When Queen Victoria was proclaimed "Empress of India" in 1877 and periodically thereafter, the viceroys put on great pageants known as **durbars.** The most elaborate was the durbar at Delhi in 1902–1903 to celebrate the coronation of King Edward VII, at which Viceroy Lord Curzon honored himself with a 101-gun salute and a parade of 34,000 troops in front of 50 princes and 173,000 visitors (see Diversity and Dominance: Ceremonials of Imperial Domination).

Behind the pomp and glitter, a powerful and efficient bureaucracy controlled the Indian masses. Members of the elite **Indian Civil Service** (ICS), mostly graduates of Oxford and Cambridge Universities, held the senior administrative and judicial posts. Numbering only a thousand at the end of the nineteenth century, these men visited the villages in their districts, heard lawsuits and complaints, and passed judgments. Beneath them were a far greater number of Indian officials and employees. Recruitment into the ICS was by open examinations. In theory any British subject could take these exams. But they were given in England, so in practice the system worked to exclude Indians. In 1870 only one Indian was a member of the ICS. Subsequent reforms by Viceroy Lord Lytton led to fifty-seven Indian appointments by 1887, but there the process stalled.

The key reason qualified Indians were denied entry into the upper administration of their country was the racist contempt most British officials felt for the people they ruled. When he became commander-in-chief of the Indian army in 1892, Lord Kitchener declared:

> It is this consciousness of the inherent superiority of the European which had won for us India. However well educated and clever a native may be, and however brave he may have proved himself, I believe that no rank we can bestow on him would cause him to be considered an equal of the British officer.

A second transformation of India after 1857 resulted from involvement with industrial Britain. The government invested millions of pounds sterling in harbors, cities, irrigation canals, and other public works. British interests felled forests to make way for tea plantations, persuaded Indian farmers to grow cotton and jute for export, and created great irrigation systems to alleviate the famines that periodically decimated whole provinces. As a result, India's trade expanded rapidly.

Most of the exports were agricultural commodities for processing elsewhere: cotton fiber, opium, tea, silk, and sugar. In return India imported manufactured goods from Britain, including the flood of machine-made cotton textiles that severely undercut Indian hand-loom weavers. The effects on individual Indians varied enormously. Some women found new jobs, though at very low pay, on plantations or in the growing cities, where prostitution flourished. Others struggled to hold families together or ran away from abusive husbands. Everywhere in India poverty remained the norm.

The Indian government also promoted the introduction of new technologies into India not long after their appearance in Britain. Earlier in the century there were steamboats on the rivers and a massive program of canal building for irrigation. Beginning in the 1840s a

Delhi Durbar, January 1, 1903 The parade of Indian princes on ornately decorated elephants and accompanied by retainers fostered their sense of belonging to the vast empire of India that British rule had created. The durbar was meant to evoke the glories of India's earlier empires, but many of the details and ceremonies were nineteenth-century creations. (British Empire and Commonwealth Museum, Bristol, UK/The Bridgeman Art Library)

railroad boom (paid for out of government revenues) gave India its first national transportation network, followed shortly by telegraph lines. Indeed, in 1870 India had the greatest rail network in Asia and the fifth largest in the world. Originally designed to serve British commerce, the railroads were owned by British companies, constructed with British rails and equipment, and paid dividends to British investors. Ninety-nine percent of the railroad employees were Indians, but Europeans occupied all the top positions—"like a thin film of oil on top of a glass of water, resting upon but hardly mixing with [those] below," as one official report put it.

Although some Indians opposed the railroads at first because the trains mixed people of different castes, faiths, and sexes, the Indian people took to rail travel with great enthusiasm. Indians rode trains on business, on pilgrimage, and in search of work. In 1870 over 18 million passengers traveled along the network's 4,775 miles (7,685 kilometers) of track, and

more than a half-million messages were sent up and down the 14,000 miles (22,500 kilometers) of telegraph wire. By 1900 India's trains were carrying 188 million passengers a year.

But the freer movement of Indian pilgrims and the flood of poor Indians into the cities also promoted the spread of cholera°, a disease transmitted through water contaminated by human feces. Cholera deaths rose rapidly during the nineteenth century, and eventually the disease spread to Europe. In many Indian minds *kala mari* ("the black death") was a divine punishment for failing to prevent the British takeover. This chastisement also fell heavily on British residents, who died in large numbers. In 1867 officials demonstrated the close connection between cholera and pilgrims who bathed in and drank from sacred pools and rivers. The installation of a new sewerage system (1865) and a filtered water

---

cholera (KAHL-uhr-uh)

우세인 은신처
파운드폭탄 4발 투하… 두 아들과 함께 사망
진지 구축… 이틀째 시가戰
령이 대중 앞에 나타나거나 애국심
을 고취하는 노래만을 내보내던 방
송마저 중단했다.
라크 전후
의에서는
영국 주도

DIVERSITY AND DOMINANCE

CEREMONIALS OF IMPERIAL DOMINATION

This letter to Queen Victoria from Edward Robert Bulwer-Lytton, the Earl of Lytton and the viceroy of India, describes the elaborate durbar that the government of India staged in 1876 in anticipation of her being named "Empress of India." It highlights the effects these ceremonies had on the Indian princes who governed many parts of India as agents ("feudatories") of the British or as independent rulers.

British India's power rested on the threat of military force, but the letter points up how much it also depended on cultivating the allegiance of powerful Indian rulers. For their part, as the letter suggests, such rulers were impressed with such displays of majesty and organization and found much to be gained from granting the British their support.

The day before yesterday (December 23), I arrived, with Lady Lytton and all my staff at Delhi....I was received at the [railroad] station by all the native chiefs and princes, and, ... after shaking hands..., I immediately mounted my elephant, accompanied by Lady Lytton, our two little girls following us on another elephant. The procession through Delhi to the camp ... lasted upwards of three hours.... The streets were lined for many miles with troops; those of the native princes being brigaded with those of your Majesty. The crowd along the way, behind the troops, was dense, and apparently enthusiastic; the windows, walls, and housetops being thronged with natives, who salaamed, and Europeans, who cheered as we passed along....

My reception by the native princes at the station was most cordial. The Maharaja of Jeypore informed Sir John Strachey that India had never seen such a gathering as this, in which not only all the great native princes (many of whom have never met before), but also chiefs and envoys from Khelat, Burmah, Siam, and the remotest parts of the East, are assembled to do homage to your Majesty....

On Tuesday (December 26) from 10 A.M. till past 7 P.M., I was, without a moment's intermission, occupied in receiving visits from native chiefs, and bestowing on those entitled to them the banners, medals, and other honours given by your Majesty. The durbar, which lasted all day and long after dark, was most successful.... Your Majesty's portrait, which was placed over the Viceregal throne in the great durbar tent,

was thought by all to be an excellent likeness of your Majesty. The native chiefs examined it with special interest.

On Wednesday, the 27th, I received visits from native chiefs, as before, from 10 A.M. til 1 P.M., and from 1:30 P.M. to 7:30 P.M., was passed in returning visits. I forgot to mention that on Tuesday and Wednesday evenings I gave great State dinners to the Governors of Bombay and Madras. Every subsequent evening of my stay at Delhi was similarly occupied by state banquets and receptions [for officials, foreign dignitaries, and] many distinguished natives. After dinner on Thursday, I held a levee [reception], which lasted till one o'clock at night, and is said to have been attended by 2,500 persons—the largest, I believe, ever held by any Viceroy or Governor-General in India. . . .

The satisfactory and cordial assurances received from [the ruler of] Kashmir are, perhaps, less important, because his loyalty was previously assumed. But your Majesty will, perhaps, allow me to mention, in connection with the name of this prince, one little circumstance which appears to me very illustrative of the effect which the assemblage has had on him and others. In the first interviews which took place months ago between myself and Kashmir, which resulted in my securing his assent to the appointment of a British officer at Gilgit, I noticed that, though perfectly courteous, he was extremely mistrustful of the British Government and myself. He seemed to think that every word I had said to him must have a hidden meaning against which he was bound to be on his guard. During our negotiations he carefully kept all his councillors round him, and he referred to them before answering any question I put to him, and, although he finally agreed to my proposals, he did so with obvious reluctance and suspicion, after taking a night to think them over. On the day following the Imperial assemblage, I had another private interview with Kashmir for the settlement of some further details. His whole manner and language on this last occasion were strikingly different. [He said:] "I am now convinced that you mean nothing that is not for the good of me and mine. Our interests are identical with those of the empire. Give me your orders and they shall be obeyed."

I have already mentioned to your Majesty that one of the sons of Kashmir acted as my page at the assemblage. I can truly affirm that all the native princes, great and small, with whom I was previously acquainted vied with each other in doing honor to the occasion, and I sincerely believe that this great gathering has also enabled me to establish the most cordial and confidential personal relations with a great many others whom I then met for the first time.

...If the vast number of persons collected together at Delhi, and all almost entirely under canvas, be fairly taken into consideration—a number alluding the highest executive officers of your Majesty's administration from every part of India, each with his own personal staff; all the members of my own Council, with their wives and families, who were entertained as the Viceroy's personal guests; all the representatives of the Press, native and European; upwards of 15,000 British troops, besides about 450 native princes and nobles, each with a following of from 2 to 500 attendants; the foreign ambassadors with their suites; the foreign consuls; a large number of the rudest and most unmanageable transfrontier chieftains with their horses and camels, &c.; and then an incalculably large concourse of private persons attracted by curiosity from every corner of the country—I say if all this be fairly remembered, no candid person will, I think, deny that to bring together, lodge, and feed so vast a crowd without a single case of sickness, or a single accident due to defective arrangements, without a moment's confusion or an hour's failure in the provision of supplies, and then to have sent them all away satisfied and loud in their expressions of gratitude for the munificent hospitality with which they had been entertained (at an expenditure of public money scrupulously moderate), was an achievement highly creditable to all concerned in carrying it out. Sir Dinkur Rao (Sindiah's great Minister) said to one of my colleagues: "If any man would understand why it is that the English are, and must necessarily remain, the masters of India, he need only go up to the Flagstaff Tower, and look down upon this marvellous camp. Let him notice the method, the order, the cleanliness, the discipline, the perfection of its whole organisation, and he will recognise in it at once the epitome of every title to command and govern which one race can possess over others." This anecdote reminds me of another which may perhaps please your Majesty. [The ruler of] Holkar said to me when I took leave of him: "India has been till now a vast heap of stones, some of them big, some of them small. Now the house is built, and from roof to basement each stone of it is in the right place."

The Khan of Khelat and his wild Sirdars were, I think, the chief objects of curiosity and interest to our Europeans....
On the Khan himself and all his Sirdars, the assemblage seems to have made an impression more profound even than I had anticipated. Less than a year ago they were all at war with each other, but they have left Delhi with mutual embraces, and a very salutary conviction that the Power they witnessed there is resolved that they shall henceforth keep the peace and not disturb its frontiers with their squabbles.

The Khan asked to have a banner given to him. It was explained to His Highness that banners were only given to your Majesty's feudatories, and that he, being an independent prince, could not receive one without compromising his independence. He replied: "But I am a feudatory of the Empress, a feudatory quite as loyal and obedient as any other. I don't want to be an independent prince, and I do want to have my banner like all the rest. Pray let me have it."

I anticipate an excellent effect by and by from the impressions which the yet wilder envoys and Sirdars of Chitral and Yassin will carry with them from Delhi, and propagate throughout that important part of our frontier where the very existence of the British Government has hitherto been almost unrealised, except as that of a very weak power, popularly supposed in Kafristan to be exceedingly afraid of Russia. Two Burmese noblemen, from the remotest part of Burmah, said to me: "The King of Burmah fancies he is the greatest prince upon earth. When we go back, we shall tell all his people that he is nobody. Never since the world began has there been in it such a power as we have witnessed here." These Burmese are writing a journal or memoir of their impressions and experiences at Delhi, of which they have promised me a copy. I have no doubt it will be very curious and amusing. Kashmir and some other native princes have expressed a wish to present your Majesty with an imperial crown of great value; but as each insists upon it that the crown shall be exclusively his own gift, I have discouraged an idea which, if carried out, would embarrass your Majesty with the gift of half a dozen different crowns, and probably provoke bitter heart-burnings amongst the donors. The Rajpootana Chiefs talk of erecting a marble statue of the Empress on the spot where the assemblage was held; native noblemen have already intimated and several to me their intention of building bridges, or other public works, and founding charities, to be called after your Majesty in commemoration of the event.

QUESTIONS FOR ANALYSIS

1. What is significant about the fact that Lord Lytton and his family arrived in Delhi by train and then chose to move through the city on elephants?

2. What impression did the viceroy intend to create in the minds of the Indian dignitaries by assembling so many of them together and bestowing banners, medals, and honors on them?

3. What might account for some Indians' remarkable changes of attitude toward the viceroy and the empire? How differently might a member of the Indian middle class or an unemployed weaver have reacted?

Source: Lady Betty Balfour, *The History of Lord Lytton's Indian Administration, 1876 to 1880* (London: Longmans, Green, and Co., 1899), 116–125.

supply (1869) in Calcutta dramatically reduced cholera deaths there. Similar measures in Bombay and Madras also led to great reductions, but most Indians lived in small villages where famine and lack of sanitation kept cholera deaths high. In 1900 an extraordinary four out of every thousand residents of British India died of cholera. Sanitary improvements lowered the rate later in the twentieth century.

Rising Indian Nationalism

Ironically, both the successes and the failures of British India stimulated the development of Indian nationalism. Stung by the inability of the rebellion of 1857 to overthrow British rule, some thoughtful Indians began to argue that the only way for Indians to regain control of their destiny was to reduce their country's social and ethnic divisions and promote Pan-Indian nationalism.

Individuals such as Rammohun Roy (1772–1833) had promoted development along these lines a generation earlier. A Western-educated Bengali from a Brahmin family, Roy was a successful administrator for the East India Company and a thoughtful student of comparative religion. His Brahmo Samaj° (Divine Society), founded in 1828, attracted Indians who sought to reconcile the values they found in the West with the ancient religious traditions of India. They supported efforts to reform some Hindu customs, including the restrictions on widows and the practice of child marriage. They advocated reforming the caste system, encouraged a monotheistic form of Hinduism, and urged a return to the founding principles of the Upanishads, ancient sacred writings of Hinduism.

Roy and his supporters had backed earlier British efforts to reform or ban some practices they found repugnant. Widow burning (*sati*°) was outlawed in 1829 and slavery in 1843. Reformers sought to correct other abuses of women: prohibitions against widows remarrying were revoked in 1856, and female infanticide was made a crime in 1870.

Although Brahmo Samaj remained an influential movement after the rebellion of 1857, many Indian intellectuals turned to Western secular values and nationalism as the way to reclaim India for its people. In this process the spread of Western education played an important role. Roy had studied both Indian and Western subjects, mastering ten languages in the process, and helped found the Hindu College in Calcutta in 1816. Other Western-curriculum schools quickly followed, in-

cluding Bethune College in Calcutta, the first secular school for Indian women, in 1849. European and American missionaries played a prominent role in the spread of Western education. In 1870 there were 790,000 Indians in over 24,000 elementary and secondary schools, and India's three universities (established in 1857) awarded 345 degrees. Graduates of these schools articulated a new Pan-Indian nationalism that transcended regional and religious differences.

Rammohun Roy   This romanic portrait of the Indian reformer emphasizes his scholarly accomplishments and India's traditional architecture and natural beauty.   (Bristol City Museum and Art Gallery, UK/The Bridgemen Art Library)

Bramo Samaj (BRAH-moh suh-MAHJ)   **sati** (suh-TEE)

Many of the new nationalists came from the Indian middle class, which had prospered from the increase of trade and manufacturing. Such educated and ambitious people were angered by the obstacles that British rules and prejudices put in the way of their advancement. Hoping to increase their influence and improve their employment opportunities in the Indian government, they convened the first **Indian National Congress** in 1885. The members sought a larger role for Indians in the Civil Service. They also called for reductions in military expenditures, which consumed 40 percent of the government's budget, so that more could be spent on alleviating the poverty of the Indian masses. The Indian National Congress promoted unity among the country's many religions and social groups, but most early members were upper-caste Western-educated Hindus and Parsis (members of a Zoroastrian religious sect descended from Persians). The Congress effectively voiced the opinions of elite Indians, but until it attracted the support of the masses, it could not hope to challenge British rule.

BRITAIN'S EASTERN EMPIRE

In 1750 Britain's empire was centered on slave-based plantation and settler colonies in the Americas. A century later its main focus was on commercial networks and colonies in the East. In 1750 the French and Dutch were also serious contenders for global dominion. A century later they had been eclipsed by the British colossus that was straddling the world.

Several distinct changes facilitated the expansion and transformation of Britain's overseas empire. A string of military victories pushed aside other rivals for overseas trade and colonies; new policies favored free trade over mercantilism; and changes in shipbuilding techniques increased the speed and volume of maritime commerce. Linked to these changes were new European settlements in southern Africa, Australia, and New Zealand and the growth of a new long-distance trade in indentured labor.

Colonies and Commerce

As the story of Tipu Sultan told at the beginning of this chapter illustrates, France was still a serious rival for dominion in the Indian Ocean at the end of the eighteenth century. However, defeats in the wars of the French Revolution (see Chapter 21) ended Napoleon's dream of restoring French dominance overseas. The wars also dismantled much of the Netherlands' Indian Ocean empire. When French armies occupied the Netherlands, the Dutch ruler, who had fled to Britain in January 1795, authorized the British to take over Dutch possessions overseas in order to keep them out of French hands. During 1795 and 1796 British forces quickly occupied the Cape Colony at the tip of southern Africa, the strategic Dutch port of Malacca on the strait between the Indian Ocean and the South China Sea, and the island of Ceylon (see Map 24.3).

Then the British occupied Dutch Guiana° and Trinidad in the southern Caribbean. In 1811 they even seized the island of Java, the center of the Netherlands' East Indian empire. British forces had also attacked French possessions, gaining control of the islands of Mauritius° and Réunion in the southwestern Indian Ocean. At the end of the Napoleonic Wars in 1814, Britain returned Java to the Dutch and Réunion to the French but kept the Cape Colony, British Guiana (once part of Dutch Guiana), Trinidad, Ceylon, Malacca, and Mauritius.

The Cape Colony was valuable because of Cape Town's strategic importance as a supply station for ships making the long voyages between Britain and India. With the port city came some twenty thousand descendants of earlier Dutch and French settlers who occupied far-flung farms and ranches in its hinterland. Despite their European origins, these people thought of themselves as permanent residents of Africa and were beginning to refer to themselves as "Afrikaners°" ("Africans" in their dialect of Dutch). British governors prohibited any expansion of the white settler frontier because such expansion invariably led to wars with indigenous Africans. This decision, along with the imposition of laws protecting African rights within Cape Colony (including the emancipation of slaves in 1834), alienated many Afrikaners.

Between 1836 and 1839 parties of Afrikaners embarked on a "Great Trek," leaving British-ruled Cape Colony for the fertile high *veld* (plateau) to the north that two decades of Zulu wars had depopulated. The Great Trek led to the foundation of three new settler colonies in southern Africa by 1850: the Afrikaners' Orange Free State and Transvaal on the high veld and the British colony of Natal on the Indian Ocean coast. Although firearms enabled the settlers to win some important battles against the Zulu and other Africans, they were still a tiny minority surrounded by the populous and powerful independent African kingdoms that had grown up at the beginning of the century. A few thousand British settlers came to Natal and the Cape Colony by midcentury, but

---

Guiana (ghee-AH-nuh)   **Mauritius** (moh-RIHS-uhs)   **Afrikaner** (af-rih-KAHN-uhr)

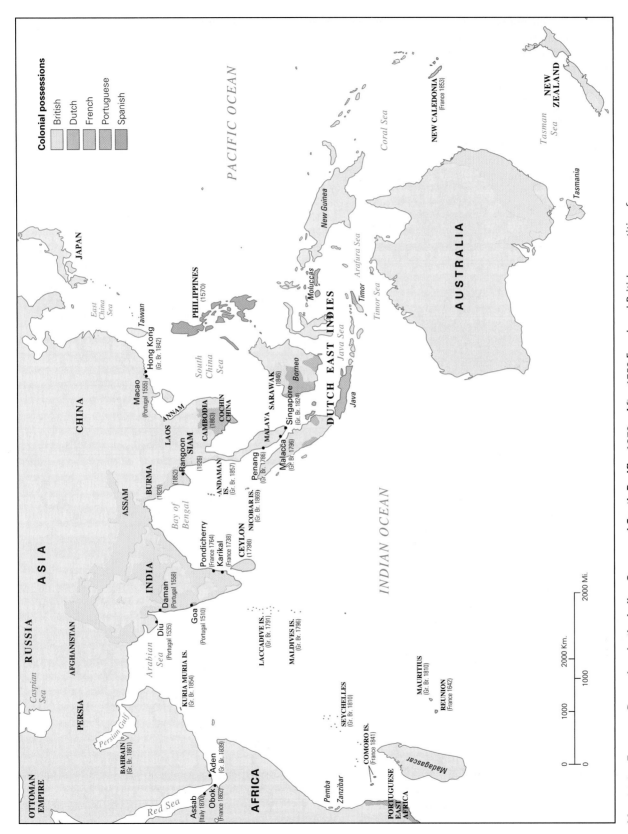

Map 24.3   European Possessions in the Indian Ocean and South Pacific, 1870   After 1750 French and British competition for new territories generally expanded the European presence established earlier by the Portuguese, Spanish, and Dutch. By 1870 the British controlled much of India, were settling Australia and New Zealand, and possessed important trading enclaves throughout the region.

these colonies were important to Britain only as stop-overs for shipping between Britain and British India.

Meanwhile, another strategic British outpost was being established in Southeast Asia. One prong of the advance was led by Thomas Stamford Raffles, who had governed Java during the period of British occupation from 1811 to 1814. After Java's return to the Dutch, Raffles helped the British East India Company establish a new free port at Singapore in 1824, on the site of a small Malay fishing village with a superb harbor. By attracting British merchants and Chinese businessmen and laborers, Singapore soon became the center of trade and shipping between the Indian Ocean and China. Along with Malacca and other possessions on the strait, Singapore formed the "Straits Settlements," which British India administered until 1867.

Further British expansion in Malaya (now Malaysia) did not occur until after 1874, but it came more quickly in neighboring Burma. Burma had emerged as a powerful kingdom by 1750, with plans for expansion. In 1785 Burma tried to annex neighboring territories of Siam (now Thailand) to the east, but a coalition of Thai leaders thwarted Burmese advances by 1802. Burma next attacked Assam to the west, but this action led to war with British India, which was concerned for the security of its own frontier with Assam. After a two-year war, India annexed Assam in 1826 and occupied two coastal provinces of northern Burma. As rice and timber trade from these provinces grew important, the occupation became permanent, and in 1852 British India annexed the port of Rangoon and the rest of coastal Burma.

Imperial Policies and Shipping

Through such piecemeal acquisitions, by 1870 Britain had added several dozen colonies to the twenty-six colonies it had in 1792, after the loss of the thirteen in North America (see Chapter 21). Nevertheless, historians usually portray Britain in this period as a reluctant empire builder, its leaders unwilling to acquire new outposts that could prove difficult and expensive to administer. This apparent contradiction is resolved by the recognition that the underlying goal of most British imperial expansion during these decades was trade rather than territory. Most of the new colonies were meant to serve as ports in the growing network of shipping that encircled the globe or as centers of production and distribution for those networks.

This new commercial expansion was closely tied to the needs of Britain's growing industrial economy and reflected a new philosophy of overseas trade. Rather than rebuilding the closed, mercantilist network of trade

Great Trek Aided by African Servants   The ox-drawn wagons of the Afrikaners struggled over the Drakensberg Mountains to the high plains in an effort to escape British control.   (Hulton Getty/ Liaison)

with its colonies, Britain sought to trade freely with all parts of the world. Free trade was also a wise policy in light of the independence of so many former colonies in the Americas (see Chapter 23).

Whether colonized or not, more and more African, Asian, and Pacific lands were being drawn into the commercial networks created by British expansion and industrialization. As was pointed out earlier, uncolonized parts of West Asia became major exporters to Britain of vegetable oils for industrial and domestic use and forest products for dyes and construction, while areas of eastern Africa free of European control exported ivory that ended up as piano keys and decorations in the elegant homes of the industrial middle class. From the far corners of the world came coffee, cocoa, and tea (along with sugar to sweeten them) for the tables of the new industrial classes in Britain and other parts of Europe, and indigo dyes and cotton fibers for their expanding textile factories.

In return, the factories of the industrialized nations supplied manufactured goods at very attractive prices. By the mid-nineteenth century a major part of their textile production was destined for overseas markets. Sales of cotton cloth to Africa increased 950 percent from the 1820s to the 1860s. British trade to India grew 350 percent between 1841 and 1870, while India's exports increased 400 percent. Trade with other regions also expanded rapidly. In most cases such trade benefited both sides, but there is no question that the industrial nations were the dominant partners.

A second impetus to global commercial expansion was the technological revolution in the construction of oceangoing ships under way in the nineteenth century. The middle decades of the century were the golden age of the sailing ship. Using iron to fasten timbers together permitted shipbuilders to construct much larger vessels. Merchant ships in the eighteenth century rarely exceeded 300 tons, but after 1850 swift American-built **clipper ships** of 2,000 tons were commonplace in the British merchant fleet. Huge canvas sails hung from tall masts made the streamlined clippers faster than earlier vessels. Ships from the East Indies or India had taken six months to reach Europe in the seventeenth century; after 1850 the new ships could complete the voyage in half that time.

This increase in size and speed lowered shipping costs and further stimulated maritime trade. The growth in size and numbers of ships increased the tonnage of British merchant shipping by 400 percent between 1778 and 1860. To extend the life of such ships in tropical lands, clippers intended for Eastern service generally were built of teak and other tropical hardwoods from new British colonies in South and Southeast Asia. Although tropical forests began to be cleared for rice and sugar plantations as well as for timbers, the effects on the environment and people of Southeast Asia came primarily after 1870.

Colonization of Australia and New Zealand

The development of new ships and shipping contributed to a third form of British rule in the once-remote South Pacific. British settlers displaced indigenous populations in the new colonies of Australia and New Zealand, just as they had done in North America. This differs from India, where Britain ruled numerous indigenous populations, and Singapore and Cape Town, which were outposts of a commercial empire.

Portuguese mariners had sighted the continent of Australia in the early seventeenth century, but it was too remote to be of much interest to Europeans. However, after the English adventurer Captain James Cook systematically explored New Zealand and the fertile eastern coast of Australia between 1769 and 1778, expanding

shipping networks brought in growing numbers of visitors and settlers.

At the time of Cook's visits Australia was the home of about 650,000 hunting-and-gathering people, whose Melanesian° ancestors had settled there some forty thousand years earlier. The two islands of New Zealand, lying 1,000 miles (1,600 kilometers) southeast of Australia, were inhabited by about 250,000 Maori°, who practiced hunting, fishing, and simple forms of agriculture, which their Polynesian ancestors had introduced around 1200 C.E. Because of their long isolation from the rest of humanity, the populations of Australia and New Zealand were as vulnerable as the Amerindians had been to unfamiliar diseases introduced by new overseas contacts. In the 1890s only 93,000 aboriginal Australians and 42,000 Maori survived. By then, British settler populations outnumbered and dominated the indigenous peoples.

The first permanent British settlers in Australia were 736 convicts, of whom 188 were women, sent into exile from British prisons in 1788. Over the next few decades, Australian penal colonies grew slowly and had only slight contact with the indigenous population, whom the British called "Aborigines." However, the discovery of gold in 1851 brought a flood of free European settlers (and some Chinese) and hastened the end of the penal colonies. When the gold rush subsided, government subsidies enabled tens of thousands of British settlers to settle "down under." Improved sailing ships made possible a voyage halfway around the world, although it still took more than three months to reach Australia from Britain. By 1860 Australia had a million immigrants, and the settler population doubled during the next fifteen years.

British settlers were drawn more slowly to New Zealand. Some of the first were temporary residents along the coast who slaughtered seals and exported seal pelts to Western countries to be made into men's felt hats. A single ship in 1806 took away sixty thousand sealskins. By the early 1820s overhunting had nearly exterminated the seal population. Special ships also hunted sperm whales extensively near New Zealand for their oil, used for lubrication, soap, and lamps; ambergris°, an ingredient in perfume; and bone, used in women's corsets (see Environment and Technology: Whaling). Military action that overcame Maori resistance, a brief gold rush, and the availability of faster ships and subsidized passages attracted more British immigrants after 1860. The colony especially courted women immigrants to offset

---

Melanesian (mel-uh-NEE-zhuhn)   **Maori** (MOW-ree [*ow* as in *cow*])   **ambergris** (AM-ber-grees)

ENVIRONMENT + TECHNOLOGY

Whaling

The rapid expansion of whaling aptly illustrates the growing power of technology over nature in this period. Many contemporaries, like many people today, were sickened by the killing of the planet's largest living mammals. American novelist Herman Melville captured the conflicting sentiments in his epic whaling story, *Moby Dick* (1851). One of his characters enthusiastically explains why the grisly and dangerous business existed:

> But, though the world scorns us as whale hunters, yet does it unwittingly pay us the profoundest homage; yea, an all abounding adoration! for almost all the tapers, lamps, and candles that burn around the globe, burn, as before so many shrines, to our glory!

Melville's character overstates the degree to which whale oil dominated illumination and does not mention its many other industrial uses. Neither does he describe the commercial importance of whalebone (baleen). For a time its use in corsets allowed fashionable women to achieve the hourglass shape that fashion dictated. Whalebone's use for umbrella stays, carriage springs, fishing rods, suitcase frames, combs, brushes, and many other items made it the plastic of its day.

New manufacturing technologies went hand in hand with new hunting technologies. The revolution in ship design enabled whalers from Europe and North America to extend the hunt into the southern oceans off New Zealand. By the nineteenth century whaling ships were armed with guns that shot a steel harpoon armed with vicious barbs deep into the whale. In the 1840s explosive charges on harpoon heads ensured the whale's immediate death. Yet, as this engraving of an expedition off New Zealand shows, flinging small harpoons from rowboats in the open sea continued to be part of the dangerous work.

Another century of extensive hunting devastated many whale species before international agreements finally limited the killing of these giant sea creatures.

South Pacific Whaling One boat was swamped, but the hunters killed the huge whale. (The Granger Collection, New York)

Asian Laborers in British Guiana
The manager of the sugar estate reposes on the near end of the gallery of his house with the proprietor's attorney. At the other end of the gallery European overseers review the plantation's record books. In the yard cups of lifeblood are being drained from bound Chinese and Indian laborers. This allegorical drawing by a Chinese laborer represents the exploitation of Asian laborers by Europeans. (Boston Athenaeum)

the preponderance of single men. By the early 1880s fertile agricultural lands of this most distant frontier of the British Empire had a settler population of 500,000.

Britain encouraged the settlers in Australia and New Zealand to become self-governing, following the 1867 model that had formed the giant Dominion of Canada out of the very diverse and thinly settled colonies of British North America. In 1901 a unified Australia emerged from the federation of six separate colonies. New Zealand became a self-governing dominion in 1907.

Britain's policies toward its settler colonies in Canada and the South Pacific reflected a desire to avoid the conflicts that had led to the American Revolution in the eighteenth century. By gradually turning over governing power to the colonies' inhabitants, Britain accomplished three things. It satisfied the settlers' desire for greater control over their own territories; it muted demands for independence; and it made the colonial governments responsible for most of their own expenses. Indigenous peoples were outvoted by the settlers or even excluded from voting.

North American patterns also shaped the indigenous peoples' fate. An 1897 Australian law segregated the remaining Aborigines onto reservations, where they lacked the rights of Australian citizenship. The requirement that voters had to be able to read and write English kept Maori from voting in early New Zealand elections, but four seats in the lower house of the legislature were reserved for Maori from 1867.

In other ways the new settler colonies were more progressive. Australia developed very powerful trade unions, which improved the welfare of skilled and semi-skilled urban white male workers, promoted democratic values, and exercised considerable political clout. In New Zealand, where sheep raising was the main occupation, populist and progressive sentiments promoted the availability of land for the common person. Australia and New Zealand were also among the first states in the world to grant women the right to vote, beginning in 1894.

New Labor Migrations

Europeans were not the only people to transplant themselves overseas in the mid-nineteenth century. Between 1834 and 1870 many thousands of Indians, Chinese, and Africans responded to labor recruiters, especially to work overseas on sugar plantations. In the half-century after 1870 tens of thousands of Asians and Pacific Islanders made similar voyages.

In part these migrations were linked to the end of slavery. After their emancipation in British colonies in 1834, the freed men and women were no longer willing to put in the long hours they had been forced to work as slaves. When given full freedom of movement in 1839, many left the plantations. To compete successfully with sugar plantations in Cuba, Brazil, and the French Caribbean that were still using slave labor, British colonies had to recruit new laborers.

India's impoverished people seemed one obvious alternative. After planters on Mauritius successfully introduced Indian laborers, the Indian labor trade moved to the British Caribbean in 1838. In 1841 the British government also allowed Caribbean planters to recruit Africans whom British patrols had rescued from slave ships and liberated in Sierra Leone and elsewhere. By 1870 nearly 40,000 Africans had settled in British colonies, along with over a half-million Indians and over 18,000 Chinese. After the French and Dutch abolished slavery in 1848, their colonies also recruited over 150,000 new laborers from Asia and Africa.

Slavery was not abolished in Cuba until 1886, but the rising cost of slaves led the burgeoning sugar plantations to recruit 138,000 new laborers from China between 1847 and 1873. Indentured labor recruits also became the mainstay of new sugar plantations in places that had never known slave labor. After 1850 American planters in Hawaii recruited labor from China and Japan; British planters in Natal recruited from India; and those in Queensland (in northeastern Australia) relied on laborers from neighboring South Pacific islands.

Larger, faster ships made transporting laborers halfway around the world affordable, though voyages from Asia to the Caribbean still took an average of three months. Despite close regulation and supervision of shipboard conditions, the crowded accommodations encouraged the spread of cholera and other contagious diseases that took many migrants' lives.

All of these laborers served under **contracts of indenture,** which bound them to work for a specified period (usually from five to seven years) in return for free passage to their overseas destination. They were paid a small salary and were provided with housing, clothing, and medical care. Indian indentured laborers also received the right to a free passage home if they worked a second five-year contract. British Caribbean colonies required forty women to be recruited for every hundred men as a way to promote family life. So many Indians chose to stay in Mauritius, Trinidad, British Guiana, and Fiji that they constituted a third or more of the to-tal population of these colonies by the early twentieth century.

Although many early recruits from China and the Pacific Islands were kidnapped or otherwise coerced into leaving their homes, in most cases the new indentured migrants had much in common with contemporary emigrants from Europe (described in Chapter 22). Both groups chose to leave their homelands in hopes of improving their economic and social conditions. Both earned modest salaries. Many saved to bring money back when they returned home, or they used their earnings to buy land or to start a business in their new countries, where large numbers chose to remain. One major difference was that people recruited as indentured laborers were generally so much poorer than emigrants from Europe that they had to accept lower-paying jobs in less desirable areas because they could not pay their own way. However, it is also true that many European immigrants into distant places like Australia and New Zealand had their passages subsidized but did not have to sign a contract of indenture. This shows that racial and cultural preferences, not just economics, shaped the flow of labor into European colonies.

A person's decision to accept an indentured labor contract could also be shaped by political circumstances. In India disruption brought by British colonial policies and the suppression of the 1857 rebellion contributed significantly to people's desire to emigrate. Poverty, famine, and warfare had not been strangers in precolonial India. Nor were these causes of emigration absent in China and Japan (see Chapter 25).

The indentured labor trade reflected the unequal commercial and industrial power of the West, but it was not an entirely one-sided creation. The men and women who signed indentured contracts were trying to improve their lives by emigrating, and many succeeded. Whether for good or ill, more and more of the world's peoples saw their lives being influenced by the existence of Western colonies, Western ships, and Western markets.

CONCLUSION

What is the global significance of these complex political and economic changes in southern Asia, Africa, and the South Pacific? One perspective stresses the continuing exploitation of the weak by the strong, of African, Asian, and Pacific peoples by aggressive Europeans. In this view, the emergence of Britain as a dominant power in the Indian Ocean basin and South Pacific continues the European expansion that the

Portuguese and the Spanish pioneered and the Dutch took over. Likewise, Britain's control over the densely populated lands of South and Southeast Asia and over the less populated lands of Australia and New Zealand can be seen as a continuation of the conquest and colonization of the Americas.

From another perspective what was most important about this period was not the political and military strength of the Europeans but their growing domination of the world's commerce, especially through long-distance ocean shipping. In this view, like other Europeans, the British were drawn to Africa and southern Asia by a desire to obtain new materials.

However, Britain's commercial expansion in the nineteenth century was also the product of Easterners' demand for industrial manufactures. The growing exchanges could be mutually beneficial. African and Asian consumers found industrially produced goods far cheaper and sometimes better than the handicrafts they replaced or supplemented. Industrialization created new markets for African and Asian goods, as in the case of the vegetable-oil trade in West Africa or cotton in Egypt and India. There were also negative impacts, as in the case of the weavers of India and the damage to species of seals and whales.

Europeans' military and commercial strength did not reduce Africa, Asia, and the Pacific to mere appendages of Europe. While the balance of power shifted in the Europeans' favor between 1750 and 1870, other cultures were still vibrant and local initiatives often dominant. Islamic reform movements and the rise of the Zulu nation had greater significance for their respective regions of Africa than did Western forces. Despite some ominous concessions to European power, Southeast Asians were still largely in control of their own destinies. Even in India, most people's lives and beliefs showed more continuity with the past than the change due to British rule.

Finally, it must not be imagined that Asians and Africans were powerless in dealing with European expansion. The Indian princes who extracted concessions from the British in return for their cooperation and the Indians who rebelled against the raj both forced the system to accommodate their needs. Moreover, some Asians and Africans were beginning to use European education, technology, and methods to transform their own societies. Leaders in Egypt, India, and other lands, like those in Russia, the Ottoman Empire, China, and Japan—the subject of Chapter 25—were learning to challenge the power of the West on its own terms. In 1870 no one could say how long and how difficult that learning process would be, but Africans and Asians would continue to shape their own futures.

■ Key Terms

Zulu

Sokoto Caliphate

modernization

Muhammad Ali

"legitimate" trade

recaptives

nawab

sepoy

British raj

Sepoy Rebellion

durbar

Indian Civil Service

Indian National Congress

clipper ship

contract of indenture

■ Suggested Reading

Volumes 2 and 3 of *The Oxford History of the British Empire,* ed. William Roger Louis, (1998, 1999), are the most up-to-date global surveys of this period. Less Anglocentric in their interpretations are Immanuel Wallerstein's *The Modern World-System III: The Second Era of Great Expansion of the Capitalist World-Economy, 1730–1840s* (1989) and William Wodruff's *Impact of Western Man: A Study of Europe's Role in the World Economy, 1750–1960* (1982). Atlantic relations are well handled by David Eltis, *Economic Growth and the Ending of the Transatlantic Slave Trade* (1987). For the Indian Ocean basin see Sugata Bose, *The Indian Ocean Rim: An Inter-Regional Arena in the Age of Global Empire* (2003).

Roland Oliver and Anthony Atmore provide a brief introduction to Africa in *Africa Since 1800,* 4th ed. (1994). More advanced works are J. F. Ade Ajayi, ed., *UNESCO General History of Africa,* vol. 6, *Africa in the Nineteenth Century until the 1880s* (1989), and John E. Flint, ed., *The Cambridge History of Africa,* vol. 5, *From c. 1790 to c. 1870* (1976). Although specialized literature has refined some of their interpretations, the following are excellent introductions to their subjects: J. D. Omer-Cooper, *The Zulu Aftermath* (1966); Murray Last, *The Sokoto Caliphate* (1967); A. G. Hopkins, *An Economic History of West Africa* (1973); Robert W. July, *The Origins of Modern African Thought* (1967); and Robert I. Rotberg, ed., *Africa and Its Explorers: Motives, Methods, and Impact* (1970). For eastern and northeastern Africa see Norman R. Bennett, *Arab Versus European: War and Diplomacy in Nineteenth Century East Central Africa* (1985); P. J. Vatikiotis, *The History of Modern Egypt: From Muhammad Ali to Mubarak,* 4th ed. (1991); and, for the negative social impact of Egyptian modernization, Judith Tucker, "Decline of the Family Economy in Mid-Nineteenth-Century Egypt," *Arab Studies Quarterly 1* (1979): 245–271.

Very readable introductions to India in this period are Sugata Bose and Ayeshia Jalal, *Modern South India* (1998); Burton Stein, *A History of India* (1998); and Stanley Wolpert, *A New History of India*, 6th ed. (1999). More advanced treatments in the "New Cambridge History of India" series are P. J. Marshall, *Bengal: The British Bridgehead: Eastern India, 1740–1828* (1988); C. A. Bayly, *Indian Society and the Making of the British Empire* (1988); Sugata Bose, *Peasant Labour and Colonial Capital: Rural Bengal Since 1700* (1993); and Kenneth W. Jones, *Socio-Religious Reform Movements in British India* (1989). Environmental and technological perspectives on India are offered in the appropriate parts of Daniel Headrick, *The Tentacles of Progress: Technology Transfer in the Age of Imperialism, 1850–1940* (1988); Mashav Gadgil and Ramachandra Guha, *This Fissured Land: An Ecological History of India* (1992). For Tipu Sultan see Kate Brittlebank, *Tipu Sultan's Search for Legitimacy: Islam and Kingship in a Hindu Domain* (1997).

A good introduction to the complexities of Southeast Asian history is D. R. SarDesai, *Southeast Asia: Past and Present*, 2nd ed. (1989). More detail can be found in the appropriate chapters of Nicholas Tarling, ed., *The Cambridge History of South East Asia*, 2 vols. (1992). The second and third volumes of *The Oxford History of Australia*, ed. Geoffrey Bolton (1992, 1988), deal with the period covered by this chapter. A very readable multicultural and gendered perspective is provided by *Images of Australia*, ed. Gillian Whitlock and David Carter (1992). *The Oxford Illustrated History of New Zealand*, ed. Keith Sinclair (1990), provides a wide-ranging introduction to that nation.

For summaries of recent scholarship on the indentured labor trade see David Northrup, *Indentured Labor in the Age of Imperialism, 1834–1922* (1995), and Robin Cohen, ed., *The Cambridge Survey of World Migration*, part 3, "Asian Indentured and Colonial Migration" (1995).

An outstanding analysis of British whaling is Gordon Jackson's *The British Whaling Trade* (1978). Edouard A. Stackpole's *Whales & Destiny: The Rivalry Between America, France, and Britain for Control of the Southern Whale Fishery, 1785–1825* (1972) is more anecdotal.

■ Notes

1. Paul E. Lovejoy and Jan S. Hogendorn, *Slow Death for Slavery: The Course of Abolition in Northern Nigeria, 1897–1936* (New York: Cambridge University Press, 1993).
2. Quoted in P. J. Vatikiotis, *The History of Modern Egypt: From Muhammad Ali to Mubarak*, 4th ed. (Baltimore: Johns Hopkins University Press, 1991), 74.
3. David Eltis, "Precolonial Western Africa and the Atlantic Economy," in *Slavery and the Rise of the Atlantic Economy*, ed. Barbara Solow (New York: Cambridge University Press, 1991), table 1.
4. Quoted by Bernard S. Cohn, "Representing Authority in Victorian India," in *The Invention of Tradition*, ed. Eric Hobsbawm and Terence Ranger (Cambridge, England: Cambridge University Press, 1983), 165.

Document-Based Question
British Rule in India

Using the following documents, evaluate the nonmilitary methods used by Britain to assert its authority in India from 1750 to 1870.

DOCUMENT 1
Indian Railroad Station, 1866 (photo, p. 623)

DOCUMENT 2
Map 24.2 India, 1707–1805 (p. 634)

DOCUMENT 3
Quote from Lord Kitchener (p. 636)

DOCUMENT 4
Delhi Durbar, January 1, 1903 (photo, p. 637)

DOCUMENT 5
Ceremonials of Imperial Domination (Diversity and Dominance, pp. 638–639)

DOCUMENT 6
Rammohun Roy (photo, p. 640)

Is Document 5 a reliable account of the 1876 durbar? What additional types of documents would confirm (or refute) the reliability of Document 5?

25 Land Empires in the Age of Imperialism, 1800–1870

Muhammad Ali Meets with European Representatives in 1839 This meeting came after the European powers brought the expansive portion of the Egyptian governor's meteoric career to an end.

CHAPTER OUTLINE

The Ottoman Empire

The Russian Empire

The Qing Empire

DIVERSITY AND DOMINANCE: **The French Occupation of Egypt**

ENVIRONMENT AND TECHNOLOGY: **The Web of War**

When the emperor of the Qing° (the last empire to rule China) died in 1799, the imperial court received a shock. For decades officials had known that the emperor was indulging his handsome young favorite, Heshen°, allowing him extraordinary privileges and power. Senior bureaucrats hated Heshen, suspecting him of overseeing a widespread network of corruption. They believed he had been scheming to prolong the inconclusive wars against the native Miao° peoples of southwest China in the late 1700s. Glowing reports of successes against the rebels had poured into the capital, and enormous sums of government money had flowed to the battlefields. But there was no adequate accounting for the funds, and the war persisted.

After the emperor's death, Heshen's enemies ordered his arrest. When they searched his mansion, they discovered a magnificent hoard of silk, furs, porcelain, furniture, and gold and silver. His personal cash alone exceeded what remained in the imperial treasury. The new emperor ordered Heshen to commit suicide with a rope of gold silk. The government seized Heshen's fortune, but the financial damage could not be undone. The declining agricultural base could not replenish the state coffers, and much of the income that did flow in was squandered by an increasingly corrupt bureaucracy. In the 1800s the Qing Empire faced increasing challenges from Europe and the United States with an empty treasury, a stagnant economy, and a troubled society.

The Qing Empire's problems were not unique. They were common to all the land-based empires of Eurasia, where old and inefficient ways of governing put states at risk. The international climate was increasingly dominated by industrializing European economies drawing on the wealth of their overseas colonies. During the early 1800s rapid population growth and slow agricultural growth affected much of Eurasia. Earlier military expansion had stretched the resources of imperial treasuries (see Chapter 20), leav-

ing the land-based empires vulnerable to European military pressure. Responses to this pressure varied, with reform and adaptation gaining headway in some lands and tradition being reasserted in others. In the long run, attempts to meet western Europe's economic and political demands produced financial indebtedness to France, Britain, and other Western powers.

This chapter contrasts the experiences of the Qing Empire with the Russian and Ottoman Empires, with a particular look at the Ottomans' semi-independent province of Egypt. While the Qing opted for resistance, the others made varying attempts to adapt and reform. Russia eventually became part of Europe and shared in many aspects of European culture, while the Ottomans and the Qing became subject to ever greater imperialist pressure. These different responses raise the question of the role of culture in shaping western Europe's relations with the rest of the world in the nineteenth century.

As you read this chapter, ask yourself the following questions:

- Why did the Ottoman and Qing Empires find themselves on the defensive in their encounters with Europeans in the 1800s?

- By what strategies did the land-based empires try to adapt to nineteenth-century economic and political conditions?

- How did the Russian Empire maintain its status as both a European power and a great Asian land empire?

THE OTTOMAN EMPIRE

During the eighteenth century the central government of the Ottoman Empire lost much of its power to provincial governors, military commanders, ethnic leaders, and bandit chiefs. In several parts of the empire local officials and large landholders tried to increase their independence and divert imperial funds into their own coffers.

Qing (ching)   **Heshen** (huh-shun)   **Miao** (mee-ow)

A kingdom in Arabia led by the Saud family, and following the puritanical and fundamentalist religious views of an eighteenth-century leader named Muhammad ibn Abd al-Wahhab°, took control of the holy cities of Mecca and Medina and deprived the sultan of the honor of organizing the annual pilgrimage. In Egypt the Mamluk slave-soldiers purchased as boys in Georgia and nearby parts of the Caucasus and educated for war reasserted their influence. Between 1260 and 1517, when they were defeated by the Ottomans, Egypt's sultans had come from the ranks of the Mamluks. Now Ottoman weakness allowed the Mamluk factions to reemerge as local military forces.

For the sultans, hopes of escaping still further decline were few. The inefficient Janissary corps wielded great political power in Istanbul. It used this power to force Sultan Selim III to abandon efforts to train a modern, European-style army at the end of the eighteenth century. This situation unexpectedly changed when France invaded Egypt.

Egypt and the Napoleonic Example, 1798–1840

Napoleon Bonaparte and an invasion force of 36,000 men and four hundred ships invaded Egypt in May 1798 (see Diversity and Dominance: The French Occupation of Egypt). The French quickly defeated the Mamluk forces that for several decades had dominated the country under the loose jurisdiction of the Ottoman sultan in Istanbul. Fifteen months later, after being stopped by Ottoman land and British naval forces in an attempted invasion of Syria, Napoleon secretly left Cairo and returned to France. Three months later he seized power and made himself emperor.

Back in Egypt, his generals tried to administer a country that they only poorly understood. Cut off from France by British ships in the Mediterranean, they had little hope of remaining in power and agreed to withdraw in 1801. For the second time in three years, a collapse of military power produced a power vacuum in Egypt. The winner of the ensuing contest was **Muhammad Ali°,** the commander of a contingent of Albanian soldiers sent by the sultan to restore imperial control. By 1805 he had taken the place of the official Ottoman governor, and by 1811 he had dispossessed the Mamluks of their lands and privileges.

Muhammad ibn Abd al-Wahhab (Moo-HAH-muhd ib-uhn ab-dahl-wa HAHB)
Muhammad Ali (moo-HAM-mad AH-lee)

Muhammad Ali's rise to power coincided with the meteoric career of Emperor Napoleon I. It is not surprising, therefore, that he adopted many French practices in rebuilding the Egyptian state. Militarily, he dutifully sent an army against the Saudi kingdom in Arabia to reclaim Mecca and Medina for the sultan. Losses during the successful war greatly reduced his contingent of Albanians, leaving him free to construct a new army. Instead of relying on picked groups of warriors like the Mamluks, Muhammad Ali instituted the French practice of conscription. For the first time since the days of the pharaohs, Egyptian peasants were compelled to become soldiers.

He also established special schools for training artillery and cavalry officers, army surgeons, military bandmasters, and others. The curricula of these schools featured European skills and sciences, and Muhammad Ali began to send promising young Turks and Circassians (an ethnic group from the Caucasus), the only people permitted to serve as military officers, to France for education. In 1824 he started a gazette devoted to official affairs, the first newspaper in the Islamic world.

To outfit his new army Muhammad Ali built all sorts of factories. These did not prove efficient enough to survive, but they showed a determination to achieve independence and parity with the European powers.

Money for these enterprises came from confiscation of lands belonging to Muslim religious institutions, under the pretext that the French occupation had canceled religious trusts established in earlier centuries, and from forcing farmers to sell their crops to the government at fixed prices. Muhammad Ali resold some of the produce abroad, making great profits as long as the Napoleonic wars kept European prices for wheat at a high level.

In the 1830s Muhammad Ali's son Ibrahim invaded Syria and instituted some of the changes already underway in Egypt. The improved quality of the new Egyptian army had been proven during the Greek war of independence (see below), when Ibrahim had commanded an expeditionary force to help the sultan. In response, the sultan embarked on building his own new army in 1826. The two armies met in 1839 when Ibrahim attacked northward into Anatolia. The Egyptian army was victorious, and Istanbul would surely have fallen if not for European intervention.

In 1841 European pressure, highlighted by British naval bombardment of coastal cities in Egyptian-controlled Syria, forced Muhammad Ali to withdraw to the present-day border between Egypt and Israel. The great powers imposed severe limitations on his army and navy and forced him to dissolve his economic mo-

CHRONOLOGY

	Ottoman Empire	Russian Empire	Qing Empire
1800	**1805–1849** Muhammad Ali governs Egypt **1808–1839** Rule of Mahmud II **1826** Janissary corps dissolved **1829** Greek independence	**1801–1825** Reign of Alexander I **1812** Napoleon's retreat from Moscow **1825** Decembrist revolt **1825–1855** Reign of Nicholas I	**1794–1804** White Lotus Rebellion
1850	**1839** Abdul Mejid begins Tanzimat reforms **1853–1856** Crimean War **1876** First constitution by an Islamic government	**1853–1856** Crimean War **1855–1881** Reign of Alexander II **1861** Emancipation of the serfs	**1839–1842** Opium War **1850–1864** Taiping Rebellion **1856–1860** Arrow War **1860** Sack of Beijing **1862–1875** Reign of Tongzhi

nopolies and allow Europeans to undertake business ventures in Egypt.

Muhammad Ali remained Egypt's ruler, under the suzerainty of the sultan, until his death in 1849; and his family continued to rule the country until 1952. But his dream of making Egypt a mighty country capable of standing up to Europe faded. What survived was the example he had set for the sultans in Istanbul.

Ottoman Reform and the European Model, 1807–1853

At the end of the eighteenth century Sultan Selim° III (r. 1789–1807), an intelligent and forward-looking ruler who stayed well informed about events in Europe, introduced reforms to create European-style military units, bring provincial governors under the control of the central government, and standardize taxation and land tenure. The rise in government expenditures to implement the reforms was supposed to be offset by taxes on selected items, primarily tobacco and coffee.

These reforms failed for political, more than economic, reasons. The most violent and persistent opposition came from the **Janissaries°**. Originally Christian boys taken from their homes in the Balkans, converted to Islam, and required to serve for life in the Ottoman army, in the eighteenth century the Janissaries became a

Selim (seh-LEEM)   Janissaries (JAN-nih-say-rees)

significant political force in Istanbul and in provincial capitals like Baghdad. Their interest in preserving special economic privileges made them resist the creation of new military units.

At times, the disapproval of the Janissaries produced military uprisings. An early example occurred in the Balkans, in the Ottoman territory of **Serbia,** where Janissaries acted as provincial governors. Their control in Serbia was intensely resented by the local residents, particularly Orthodox Christians who claimed that the Janissaries abused them. In response to the charges, Selim threatened to reassign the Janissaries to the Ottoman capital at Istanbul. Suspecting that the sultan's threat signaled the beginning of the end of their political power, in 1805 the Janissaries revolted against Selim and massacred Christians in Serbia. Selim was unable to reestablish central Ottoman rule over Serbia. Instead, the Ottoman court had to rely on the ruler of Bosnia, another Balkan province, who joined his troops with the peasants of Serbia to suppress the Janissary uprising. The threat of Russian intervention prevented the Ottomans from disarming the victorious Serbians, so Serbia became effectively independent.

Other opponents of reform included ulama, or Muslim religious scholars, who distrusted the secularization of law and taxation that Selim proposed. In the face of widespread rejection of his reforms, Selim suspended his program in 1806. Nevertheless, a massive military uprising occurred at Istanbul, and the sultan was deposed and imprisoned. Reform forces rallied and recaptured

운드폭탄 4발 투하… 두 아들과 함께 사망 가
심진지 구축… 이틀째 시가戰

령이 대중 앞에 나타나거나 애국심
을 고취하는 노래만을 내보내던 방
송마저 중단됐다.

라크 전후 대책
의에서는 전후
영국 주도로

DIVERSITY AND DOMINANCE

THE FRENCH OCCUPATION OF EGYPT

Napoleon's invasion of Egypt in 1798 strikingly illustrates the techniques of dominance employed by the French imperial power and the means of resistance available to noncombatant Egyptian intellectuals in reasserting their cultural diversity and independence. Abd al-Rahman al-Jabarti (1753–1826), from whose writings the first four passages are drawn, came from a family of ulama, or Muslim religious scholars. His three works concerning the French occupation, which lasted until 1801, provide the best Egyptian account of that period. The selections below start with the first half of Napoleon's first proclamation to the Egyptian people, which was published in Arabic at the time of the invasion and is quoted here from al-Jabarti's text.

In the Name of God the Compassionate the Merciful: There is no god but God. He has not begotten a son, and does not share in His Kingship.

On behalf of the French Republic, which is founded upon the principles of liberty and equality, the Commander-in-Chief of the French armies, the great head-general Bonaparte, hereby declares to all inhabitants of Egyptian lands that the Sanjaqid rulers of Egypt [i.e., the Mamluk commanders] have persisted far too long in their maltreatment and humiliation of the French nation and have unjustly subjected French merchants to all manner of abuse and extortion. The hour of their punishment has now come.

It is a great pity that this group of slave fighters [Mamluks], caught in the mountains of Abkhazia and Georgia, have for such a long time perpetrated so much corruption in the fairest of all lands on the face of the globe. Now, the omnipotent Lord of the Universe has ordained their demise.

O people of Egypt, should they say to you that I have only come hither to defile your religion, this is but an utter lie that you must not believe. Say to my accusers that I have only come to rescue your rights from the hands of tyrants, and that I am a better servant of God—may He be praised and exalted—and that I revere His Prophet Muhammad and the grand Koran more than the group of slave fighters do.

Tell them also that all people stand equally before God and that reason, virtue, and knowledge comprise the only distinguishing qualities among them. Now, what do the group of slave fighters possess of reason, virtue, and knowledge that would distinguish them from the rest of the people and qualify them exclusively to benefit from everything that is desirable in this worldly life?

The most fertile of all agricultural lands, the prettiest concubines, the best horses, and most attractive residences, all are appropriated exclusively by them. If the land of Egypt was ever conferred upon this group of slave fighters exclusively, let them show us the document that God has written for them: of course, the Lord of the Universe acts with compassion and equity toward mankind. With His help—may He be Exalted—from this day on no Egyptian shall be excluded from high positions nor barred from acquiring high ranks, and men of reason, virtue and learning from among them will administer the affairs, and as a result the welfare of the entire Muslim community (*umma*) shall improve.

The following passages provide examples of al-Jabarti's line-by-line commentary on the proclamation and two examples of his more general comments on the French and on French rule.

Explanation of the wretched proclamation composed of incoherent words and vulgar phrases:

By saying, "in the Name of God the Compassionate the Merciful: There is no god but God. He has not begotten a son, and does not share in His Kingship" [the French] implicitly claim in three propositions that they concur with the three religions [Islam, Christianity, and Judaism] whereas in truth they falsify all three and indeed any other [viable] doctrine. They concur with the Muslims in opening [the statement] with the name of God and in rejecting His begetting a son or sharing in His Kingship. They differ from them in not professing the two essential Articles of Faith: refusing to recognize Prophet Muhammad, and rebuffing the essential teachings of Islam in word and deed. They concur with the Christians in most of what they say and do, but diverge over the question of Trinity, in their rejection of the vocation [of Christ], and furthermore in rebuffing their beliefs and rituals, killing the priests, and desecrating places of worship. They concur with the Jews in believing in one God, as the Jews also do not believe in the Trinity but hold on to anthropomorphism. [The French Republicans] do not share in the religious beliefs and practices of the Jews either. Apparently they do not follow any particular religion and do not adhere to a set of specific rituals: each of them fathoms a religion as it suits his own reason. The rest of the [people of France] are Christians but keep it hidden, and there are some real Jews among them as well. However, even those who may follow a religion, when they come to Egypt, they concur with the agents of the Republic in their insistence upon leading the Egyptians astray.

Their saying "On behalf of the French Republic, etc." implies that the proclamation comes from the Republic or their people directly, because unlike other nations they have no overlord or sovereign whom they unanimously appoint, and who has exclusive authority to speak on their behalf. It is now six years since they revolted against their sovereign and murdered him. Subsequently, the people agreed not to have a single ruler but rather to put the affairs of the government, provincial issues, legislation and administration, into the hands of men of discretion and reason among themselves. They chose and appointed men in a hierarchy: a head of the entire army followed in rank by generals and military commanders each in charge of groups of a thousand, two hundred, or ten men. They similarly appointed administrators and advisers by observing their essential equality and non-supremacy of one over the others, in the same way that people are created equally in essence. This constitutes the foundation and touchstone of their system, and this is what "founded upon the principles of liberty and equality" means. The reference to "liberty" implies that unlike the slaves and [the slave fighters ruling over Egypt] they are not anybody's slaves; the meaning of "equality" has already been explained.

[On that day the French] started to operate a new court bureau, which they named the Ad hoc Court (*mahkamat al-qadaya*). On this occasion they drafted a decree that included clauses framed in most unacceptable terms that sounded rather repellant to the ear. Six Copts and six Muslim merchants were appointed to the bureau, and the presiding judge and chief of the bureau was the Copt from Malta who used to work as secretary to Ayyub Bey, the notary (*daftardar*). Ad hoc cases involving commercial, civil, inheritance disputes, and other suits were referred to this bureau. [The French] formulated corrupt principles for this institution that were based on heresy, founded in tyranny, and rooted in all sorts of abominable unprecedented rulings (*bid'a al-sayyi'a*).

[The French] devastated the palace of Yusuf Salah al-Din including the cities where sovereigns and sultans held audiences, and they tore down strong foundations and demolished towering columns. They also destroyed mosques, meditation spots (*zawaya*), and shrines of martyrs (*mashahid*). They defaced the Grand Congregational Mosque, built by the venerable Muhammad b. Qalawan al-Malik al-Nasir: wrecked the pulpit, spoiled the mosque's courtyard, looted its lumber, undermined its columns, and razed the well-wrought iron enclosure inside of which the sultan used to pray.

The final passage, which is not in any of al-Jabarti's chronicles, is the full text of an announcement distributed to Napoleon's thirty-six thousand troops on board ship as they headed for Egypt.

Soldiers,—You are about to undertake a conquest the effects of which on civilization and commerce are incalculable. The blow you are about to give to England will be the best aimed, and the most sensibly felt, she can receive until the time arrive when you can give her her death-blow.

We must make some fatiguing marches; we must fight several battles; we shall succeed in all we undertake. The destinies are with us. The Mameluke Beys, who favour exclusively English commerce, whose extortions oppress our merchants , and who tyrannise over the unfortunate inhabitants of the Nile, a few days after our arrival will no longer exist.

The people amongst whom we are going to live are Mahometans. The first article of their faith is this: "there is no God but God, and Mahomet is His prophet." Do not contradict them. Behave to them as you have behaved to the Jews—to the Italians. Pay respect to their muftis [jurists], and their Imaums [sic], as you did to the rabbis and the bishops. Extend to the ceremonies prescribed by the Koran and to the mosques the same toleration which you showed to the synagogues, to the religion of Moses and of Jesus Christ.

The Roman legions protected all religions. You will find here customs different from those of Europe. You must accommodate yourselves to them. The people amongst whom we are to mix differ from us in the treatment of women; but in all countries he who violates is a monster. Pillage enriches only a small number of men; it dishonours us; it destroys our resources; it converts into enemies the people whom it is our interest to have for friends.

The first town we shall come to was built by Alexander. At every step we shall meet with grand recollections, worthy of exciting the emulations of Frenchmen.

Bonaparte

QUESTIONS FOR ANALYSIS

1. Why are the reasons for invading Egypt given to the French soldiers different from those announced to the Egyptians?

2. How do Napoleon and al-Jabarti use religious feeling as a political tool?

3. What do texts like these suggest about the role culture plays in confrontations between imperial powers and imperialized peoples?

Source: First selection from *Abd al-Rahman al-Jabarti's History of Egypt,* ed. Thomas Phillipp and Moshe Perlmann (Stuttgart, 1994), translated by Hossein Kamaly. Second selection from Louis Antoine Fauvelet de Bourrienne, *Memoirs of Napoleon Bonaparte* (1843).

the capital, but not before Selim had been executed. Selim's cousin Sultan Mahmud° II (r.1808–1839) cautiously revived the reform movement. The fate of Selim III had taught the Ottoman court that reform needed to be more systematic and imposed more forcefully, but it took the concrete evidence of the effectiveness of radical reform in Muhammad Ali's Egypt to drive this lesson home. Mahmud II was able to use an insurrection in Greece, and the superior performance of Egyptian forces in the unsuccessful effort to suppress it, as a sign of the weakness of the empire and the pressing need for reform.

Greek independence in 1829 was a complex event that had dramatic international significance. A combination of Greek nationalist organizations and interlopers from Albania formed the independence movement. By the early nineteenth century interest in the classical age of Greece and Rome had intensified European desires to encourage and if possible aid the struggle for independence. Europeans considered the war for Greek independence a campaign to recapture the classical roots of their civilization from Muslim despots, and many—including the "mad, bad and dangerous to know" English poet Lord Byron, who lost his life in the war—went to Greece to fight as volunteers. The Ottomans called on Ibrahim Pasha° of Egypt, the son of Muhammad Ali, to help preserve their rule in Greece; but when the combined squadrons of the British, French, and Russian fleets, under orders to observe but not intervene in the war, made an unauthorized attack that sank the Ottoman fleet at the Battle of Navarino, not even Ibrahim's help could prevent defeat (see Map 25.1).

Europeans trumpeted the victory of the Greeks as a triumph of European civilization over the Ottoman Empire, and Mahmud II agreed that the loss of Greece indicated a profound weakness—he considered it backwardness—in Ottoman military and financial organization. With popular outrage over the military setbacks in Greece strong, the sultan made his move in 1826. First he announced the creation of a new artillery unit, which he had secretly been training. When the Janissaries rose in revolt, he ordered the new unit to bombard the Janissary barracks. The Janissary corps was officially dissolved.

Like Muhammad Ali, Mahmud felt he could not implement major changes without reducing the political power of the religious elite. He visualized restructuring the bureaucracy and the educational and legal systems, where ulama power was strongest. Before such strong measures could be undertaken, however, Ibrahim at-

tacked from Syria in 1839. Battlefield defeat, the decision of the rebuilt Ottoman navy to switch sides and support Egypt, and the death of Mahmud, all in the same year, left the empire completely dependent on the European powers for survival.

Mahmud's reforming ideas received their widest expression in the **Tanzimat**° ("reorganization"), a series of reforms announced by his sixteen-year-old son and successor, Abdul Mejid°, in 1839 and strongly endorsed by the European ambassadors. One proclamation called for public trials and equal protection under the law for all, whether Muslim, Christian, or Jew. It also guaranteed some rights of privacy, equalized the eligibility of men for conscription into the army (a practice copied from Egypt), and provided for a new, formalized method of tax collection that legally ended tax farming in the Ottoman Empire. It took many years and strenuous efforts by reforming bureaucrats, known as the "men of the Tanzimat," to give substance to these reforms. At a theoretical level, however, they opened a new chapter in the history of the Islamic world. European observers praised them for their noble principles and rejection of religious influences in government. Ottoman citizens were more divided; the Christians and Jews, about whom the Europeans showed the greatest concern, were generally more enthusiastic than the Muslims. Many historians see the Tanzimat as the dawn of modern thought and enlightened government in the Middle East. Others point out that removing the religious elite from influence in government also removed the one remaining check on authoritarian rule.

With the passage of time, one legal code after another—commercial, criminal, civil procedure—was introduced to take the place of the corresponding areas of religious legal jurisdiction. All the codes were modeled closely on those of Europe. The sharia, or Islamic law, gradually became restricted to matters of family law such as marriage and inheritance. As the sharia was displaced, job opportunities for the ulama shrank, as did the value of a purely religious education.

Like Muhammad Ali, Sultan Mahmud sent military cadets to France and the German states for training. Military uniforms were modeled on those of France. In the 1830s an Ottoman imperial school of military sciences, later to become Istanbul University, was established at Istanbul. Instructors imported from western Europe taught chemistry, engineering, mathematics, and physics in addition to military history. Reforms in military education became the model for more general educational reforms. In 1838 the first medical school was established

---

Mahmud (MAH-mood)
Ibrahim Pasha (ib-rah-HEEM PAH-shah)

Tanzimat (TAHNZ-ee-MAT)   **Abdul Mejid** (ab-dul meh-JEED)

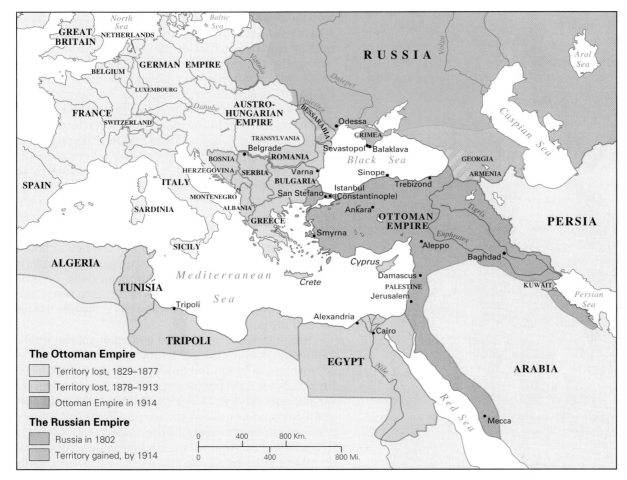

Map 25.1   The Ottoman and Russian Empires, 1829–1914   At its height the Ottoman Empire controlled most of the perimeter of the Mediterranean Sea. But in the 1800s Ottoman territory shrank as many countries gained their independence. The Black Sea, where the Turkish coast was vulnerable to assault, became a weak spot as Russian naval power grew. Russian challenges to the Ottomans at the eastern end of the Black Sea, and to the Persians east and west of the Caspian aroused fears in Europe that Russia was trying to reach the Indian Ocean.

to train army doctors and surgeons. Later, a national system of preparatory schools was created to feed graduates into the military schools. The subjects that were taught and many of the teachers were foreign, so the issue of whether Turkish would be a language of instruction in the new schools was a serious one. Because it was easier to import and use foreign textbooks than to write new ones in Turkish, French became the preferred language in all advanced professional and scientific training. In numerical terms, however, the great majority of students still learned to read and write in Quran schools down to the twentieth century.

In the capital city of Istanbul, the reforms stimulated the growth of a small but cosmopolitan milieu embracing

European language and culture. The first Turkish newspaper, a government gazette modeled on that of Muhammad Ali, appeared in 1831. Other newspapers followed, many written in French. Travel to Europe—particularly to England and France—became more common among wealthy Turks. Interest in importing European military, industrial, and communications technology remained strong through the 1800s.

The Ottoman rulers quickly learned that limited improvements in military technology had unforeseen cultural and social effects. Accepting the European notion that modern weapons and drill required a change in traditional military dress, beards were deemed unhygienic and, in artillery units, a fire hazard. They were restricted,

Change with Tradition Change in the Ottoman armies was gradual, beginning with the introduction of European guns and artillery. To use the new weapons efficiently and safely, the Janissaries were required to modify their dress and beards. Beards were trimmed, and elaborate headgear was reserved for ritual occasions. Traditional military units attempted to retain distinctive dress whenever possible, and one compromise was the brimless cap adapted from the high hats that some Janissaries had traditionally worn. (Courtesy, Turkish Ministry of Culture and Tourism. Photo: Necmettin Kulahci)

along with the wearing of loose trousers and turbans. Military headgear also became controversial. European military caps, which had leather bills on the front to protect against the glare of the sun, were not acceptable because they interfered with Muslim soldiers' touching their foreheads to the ground during daily prayers. The compromise was the brimless cap now called the *fez*, which was adopted by the military and then by Ottoman civil officials in the early years of Mahmud II's reign.

The changes in military dress—so soon after the suppression of the Janissaries—were recognized as an indication of the empire's new orientation. Government ministries that traditionally drew young men from traditional bureaucratic families and trained them for ministerial service were gradually transformed into formal civil services hiring men educated in the new schools. Among self-consciously progressive men, particularly those in government service, European dress became the fashion in the Ottoman cities of the later 1800s. Traditional dress became a symbol of the religious, the rural, and the parochial.

Secularization of the legal code had special implications for the non-Muslim subjects of the Ottomans. Islamic law had required non-Muslims to pay a special head tax that was sometimes explained as a substitute for military service. Under the Tanzimat, the tax was abolished and non-Muslims became liable for military service—unless they bought their way out by paying a new military exemption tax. Under the new law codes, all male subjects had equal access to the courts, while the sphere of operation of the Islamic law courts shrank. Perhaps the biggest enhancement of the status of non-Muslims, however, was the strong and direct concern for their welfare consistently expressed by the European powers. The Ottoman Empire became a rich field of operation for Christian missionaries and European supporters of Jewish community life in the Muslim world.

The public rights and political participation granted during the Tanzimat applied specifically to men. Private life, including everything connected to marriage and divorce, remained within the sphere of religious law, and at no time was there a question of political participation or reformed education for women. Indeed, the reforms may have decreased the influence of women. The political changes ran parallel to economic changes that also narrowed women's opportunities.

The influx of silver from the Americas that had begun in the 1600s increased the monetarization of some sectors of the Ottoman economy, particularly in the cities. Workers were increasingly paid in cash rather than in goods, and businesses associated with banking, finance, and law developed. Competition drove women from the work force. Early industrial labor and the professions were not open to women, and traditional "woman's work" such as weaving was increasingly mechanized and done by men.

Nevertheless, women retained considerable power in the management and disposal of their own property, gained mostly through fixed shares of inheritance, well into the 1800s. After marriage a woman was often pressured to convert her landholdings to cash in order to transfer her personal wealth to her husband's family, with whom she and her husband would reside; but this was not a requirement, since men were legally obligated to support their families single-handedly. Until the 1820s many women retained their say in the distribution of property through the creation of charitable trusts for their sons. Because these trusts were set up in the religious courts, they could be designed to conform to the wishes of family members, and they gave women of wealthy families an opportunity to exercise significant indirect control over property. Then, in the 1820s and 1830s the secularizing reforms of Mahmud II, which did not always produce happy results, transferred jurisdiction over the charitable trusts from religious courts to the state and ended women's control over this form of property. In addition, reforms in the military, higher education, the professions, and commerce all bypassed women.

Street Scene in Cairo   This engraving from Edward William Lane's influential travel book, *Account of the Manners and Customs of the Modern Egyptians Written in Egypt During the Years 1833–1835* conveys the image of narrow lanes and small stores that became stock features of European thinking about Middle Eastern cities.   (From Edward William Lane, *The Manners and Customs of the Modern Egyptians*, London: J. M. D & Co. 1860)

The Crimean War and Its Aftermath, 1853–1877

Since the reign of Peter the Great (r. 1689–1725) the Russian Empire had been attempting to expand southward at the Ottomans' expense (see "Russia and Asia," below). By 1815 Russia had pried the Georgian region of the Caucasus away from the Ottomans, and the threat of Russian intervention had prevented the Ottomans from crushing Serbian independence. Russia seemed poised to exploit Ottoman weakness and acquire the long-sought goal of free access to the Mediterranean Sea. In the eighteenth century Russia had claimed to be the protector of Ottoman subjects of Orthodox Christian faith in Greece and the Balkans. When Muhammad Ali's Egyptian army invaded Syria in 1833, Russia signed a treaty in support of the Ottomans. In return, the sultan recognized an extension of this claim to cover all of the empire's Orthodox subjects. This set the stage for an obscure dispute that resulted in war.

In 1852 the sultan bowed to British and French pressure and named France Protector of the Holy Sepulchre in Jerusalem, a position with certain ecclesiastical privileges. Russia protested, but the sultan held firm. So

Russia invaded Ottoman territories in what is today Romania, and Britain and France went to war as allies of the sultan. The real causes of the war went beyond church quarrels in Jerusalem. Diplomatic maneuvering among European powers over whether the Ottoman Empire should continue to exist and, if not, who should take over its territory lasted until the empire finally disappeared after World War I. The Eastern Question was the simple name given to this complex issue. Though the

Interior of the Ottoman Financial Bureau This engraving from the eighteenth century depicts the governing style of the Ottoman Empire before the era of westernizing reforms. By the end of the Tanzimat period in 1876, government offices and the costumes of officials looked much more like those in contemporary European capitals. (From Ignatius Mouradgea d'Ohsson, *Tableau General de l'Empire Ottoman,* large folio edition, Paris, 1787–1820, pl. 178, following p. 340)

powers had agreed to save the empire from Ibrahim's invasion in 1839, Britain subsequently became very suspicious of Russian ambitions. A number of prominent British politicians were strongly anti-Russian. They feared that Russia would threaten the British hold on India either overland through Central Asia or by placing its navy in the Mediterranean Sea.

Between 1853 and 1856 the **Crimean° War** raged in Romania, on the Black Sea, and on the Crimean peninsula. Britain, France, and the Italian kingdom of Sardinia-Piedmont sided with the Ottomans, allowing Austria to mediate the final outcome. Britain and France trapped the Russian fleet in the Black Sea, where its commanders decided to sink the ships to protect the approaches to Sevastopol, their main base in Crimea. An army largely made up of British and French troops landed and laid siege to the city. A lack of railways and official corruption hampered Russian attempts to supply both its land and its sea forces. On the Romanian front, the Ottomans resisted effectively. At Sevastopol, the Russians were outmatched militarily and suffered badly from disease. Tsar Nicholas died as defeat became apparent, leaving his successor, Alexander II (r. 1855–1881), to sue for peace when Sevastopol finally fell three months later.

A formal alliance among Britain, France, and the Ottoman Empire blocked further Russian expansion into eastern Europe and the Middle East. The terms of peace also gave Britain and France a means of checking each other's colonial ambitions in the Middle East; neither, according to the agreement that ended the war, was entitled to take Ottoman territory for its exclusive use.

Crimean (cry-ME-uhn)

The Crimean War brought significant changes to all the combatants. The tsar and his government, already beset by demands for the reform of serfdom, education, and the military (discussed later), were further discredited. In Britain and France, the conflict was accompanied by massive propaganda campaigns. For the first time newspapers were an important force in mobilizing public support for a war. Press accounts of British participation in the war were often so glamorized that the false impression has lingered ever since that Ottoman troops played a negligible role in the conflict. At the time, however, British and French military commanders noted the massive losses among Turkish troops in particular. The French press, dominant in Istanbul, promoted a sense of unity between Turkish and French society that continued to influence many aspects of Turkish urban culture.

The larger significance of the Crimean War was that it marked the transition from traditional to modern warfare (see Environment and Technology: The Web of War). A high casualty count resulted in part from the clash of mechanized and unmechanized means of killing. All the combatant nations had previously prided themselves on the effective use of highly trained cavalry to smash through the front lines of infantry. Cavalry coexisted with firearms until the early 1800s, primarily because early rifles were awkward to load, vulnerable to explosion, and not very accurate. Swift and expert cavalry could storm infantry lines during the intervals between volleys and even penetrate artillery barrages. In the 1830s and 1840s percussion caps that did away with pouring gunpowder into the barrel of a musket were widely adopted in Europe. In Crimean War battles many cavalry units were destroyed by the rapid and relatively accurate fire of rifles that loaded at the breech rather than down the barrel. That was the fate of the British Light Brigade, which was sent to relieve an Ottoman unit surrounded by Russian troops. Ironically, in the charge of the Light Brigade, the heroic but obsolete horsemen were on the side with the most advanced weaponry. In the long run, despite the pathos of Alfred Lord Tennyson's famous poem, the new military technologies pioneered in the Crimean War, not its heroic events, made the conflict a turning point in the history of war.

After the Crimean War, declining state revenues and increasing integration with European commercial networks created hazardous economic conditions in the Ottoman Empire. The men of the Tanzimat dominated government affairs under Abdul Mejid's successors and continued to secularize Ottoman financial and commercial institutions, modeling them closely on European

counterparts. The Ottoman imperial bank was founded in 1840, and a few years later currency reform pegged the value of Ottoman gold coins to the British pound. Sweeping changes in the 1850s expedited the creation of banks, insurance companies, and legal firms throughout the empire. These and other reforms facilitating trade contributed to a strong demographic shift in the Ottoman Empire between about 1850 and 1880, as many rural people headed to the cities. Within this period many of the major cities of the empire—Istanbul, Damascus, Beirut, Alexandria, Cairo—expanded. A small but influential urban professional class emerged, as did a considerable class of wage laborers. This shift was magnified by an influx into the northern Ottoman territories of refugees from Poland and Hungary, where rivalry between the European powers and the Russian Empire caused political tension and sporadic warfare, and from Georgia and other parts of the Caucasus, where Russian expansion forced many Muslims to emigrate (discussed later).

The Ottoman reforms stimulated commerce and urbanization, but no reform could repair the chronic insolvency of the imperial government. Declining revenues from agricultural yields and widespread corruption damaged Ottoman finances. Some of the corruption was exposed in the early 1840s. From the conclusion of the Crimean War in 1856 on, the Ottoman government became heavily dependent on foreign loans. In return the Ottoman government lowered tariffs to favor European imports, and European banks opened in Ottoman cities. Currency changes allowed more systematic conversion to European currencies. Europeans were allowed to live in their own enclaves in Istanbul and other commercial centers, subject to their own laws and exempt from Ottoman jurisdiction. This status was known as **extraterritoriality.**

As the cities prospered, they became attractive to laborers, and still more people moved from the countryside. But opportunities for wage workers reached a plateau in the bloated cities. Foreign trade brought in large numbers of imports, but—apart from tobacco and the Turkish opium that American traders took to China to compete against the Indian opium of the British—few exports were sent abroad from Anatolia. Together with the growing national debt, these factors aggravated inflationary trends that left urban populations in a precarious position in the mid-1800s. By contrast, Egyptian cotton exports soared during the American Civil War, when American cotton exports plummeted, but the profits benefited Muhammad Ali's descendants, who had become the hereditary governors of Egypt, rather than the Ottoman government. The Suez Canal, which

ENVIRONMENT + TECHNOLOGY

The Web of War

The lethal military technologies of the mid-nineteenth century that were used on battlefields in the United States, Russia, India, and China were rapidly transmitted from one conflict to the next. This dissemination was due not only to the rapid development of communications but also to the existence of a new international network of soldiers who moved from one trouble spot to another, bringing expertise in the use of new techniques.

General Charles Gordon (1833–1885), for instance, was commissioned in the British army in 1852, then served in the Crimean War after Britain entered on the side of the Ottomans. In 1860 he was dispatched to China. He served with British forces during the Arrow War and took part in the sack of Beijing. Afterward, he stayed in China and was seconded to the Qing imperial government until the suppression of the Taipings in 1864, earning himself the nickname "Chinese" Gordon. Gordon later served the Ottoman rulers of Egypt as governor of territory along the Nile. He was killed in Egypt in 1885 while leading his Egyptian troops in defense of the city of Khartoum against an uprising by the Sudanese religious leader, the Mahdi.

Journalism played an important part in the developing web of telegraph communications that sped orders to and from the battlefields. Readers in London could learn details of the drama occurring in the Crimea or in China within a week—or in some cases days—after they occurred. Print and, later, photographic journalism created new "stars" from these war experiences. Charles Gordon was one. Florence Nightingale was another.

In the great wars of the 1800s, the vast majority of deaths resulted from infection or excessive bleeding, not from the wounds themselves. Florence Nightingale (1820–1910), while still a young woman, became interested in hospital management and nursing. She went to Prussia and France to study advanced techniques. Before the outbreak of the Crimean War she was credited with bringing about marked improvement in British health care. When the public reacted to news reports of the suffering in the Crimea, the British government sent Nightingale to the region. Within a year of her arrival the death rate in the military hospitals there dropped from 45 percent to under 5 percent. Her techniques for preventing septicemia and dysentery and for promoting healing therapies were quickly adopted by those working for and with her. On her return to London, Nightingale established institutes for nursing that soon were recognized around the world as leaders. She herself was lionized by the British public and received the Order of Merit in 1907, three years before her death.

The importance of Nightingale's innovations in public hygiene is underscored by the life of her contemporary, Mary Seacole (1805–1881). A Jamaican woman who volunteered to nurse British troops in the Crimean War, Seacole was repeatedly excluded from nursing service by British authorities. She eventually went to Crimea and used her own funds to run a hospital there, bankrupting herself in the process. The drama of the Crimean War moved the British public to support Seacole after her sacrifices were publicized. She was awarded medals by the British, French, and Turkish governments and today is recognized with her contemporary Florence Nightingale as an innovative field nurse and a champion of public hygiene in peacetime.

With Florence Nightingale in Crimea Readers could read about war dramas in telegraphed copy and see them in vivid illustrations. (The Granger Collection, New York)

was partly financed by cotton profits, opened in 1869, and Cairo was redesigned and beautified. Eventually overexpenditure on such projects plunged Egypt into the same debt crisis that plagued the empire as a whole.

In the 1860s and 1870s reform groups demanded a constitution and entertained the possibility of a law permitting all men to vote. Spokesmen for the Muslim majority expressed dismay at the possibility that the Ottoman Empire would no longer be a Muslim society. Muslims were also suspicious of the motives of Christians, many of whom enjoyed close relations with European powers. Memories of attempts by Russia and France to interfere in Ottoman affairs for the benefit of Christians seemed to some to warrant hostility toward Christians in Ottoman territories.

The decline of Ottoman power and prosperity had a strong impact on a group of well-educated young urban men who aspired to wealth and influence. They believed that the empire's rulers and the Tanzimat officials who worked for them would be forced to—or would be willing to—allow the continued domination of the empire's political, economic, and cultural life by Europeans. Though lacking a sophisticated organization, these **Young Ottomans** (who are sometimes called Young Turks, though that term properly applies to a later movement) promoted a mixture of liberal ideas derived from Europe, national pride in Ottoman independence, and modernist views of Islam. Prominent Young Ottomans helped draft a constitution that was promulgated in 1876 by a new and as yet untried sultan, Abdul Hamid II. This apparent triumph of liberal reform was short-lived. With war against Russia again threatening in the Balkans in 1877, Abdul Hamid suspended the constitution and the parliament that had been elected that year. He ruthlessly opposed further political reforms, but the Tanzimat programs of extending modern schooling, utilizing European military practices and advisers, and making the government bureaucracy more orderly continued during his reign.

THE RUSSIAN EMPIRE

Awareness of western Europe among Russia's elite began with the reign of Peter the Great (r. 1689–1725), but knowledge of the French language, considered by Russians to be the language of European culture, spread only slowly among the aristocracy in the second half of the eighteenth century. In 1812, when Napoleon's march on Moscow ended in a disastrous retreat brought on more by what a later tsar called "Generals January and February" than by Russian military action, the European image of Russia changed. Just as Napoleon's withdrawal from Egypt paved the way for the brief emergence of Muhammad Ali's Egypt as a major power, so his withdrawal from Russia conferred status on another autocrat. Conservative Europeans still saw Russia as an alien, backward, and oppressive land, but they acknowledged its immensity and potential power and included Tsar Alexander I (r. 1801–1825) as a major partner in efforts to restore order and suppress revolutionary tendencies throughout Europe. Like Muhammad Ali, Alexander attempted reforms in the hope of strengthening his regime. Unlike Muhammad Ali, acceptance by the other European monarchs saved a rising Russia from being strangled in its cradle.

In several important respects Russia resembled the Ottoman Empire more than the conservative kingdoms of Europe whose autocratic practices it so staunchly supported. Socially dominated by nobles whose country estates were worked by unfree serfs, Russia had almost no middle class. Industry was still at the threshold of development by the standards of the rapidly industrializing European powers, though it was somewhat more dynamic than Ottoman industry. And the absolute power of the tsar was unchallenged. Like Egypt and the Ottoman Empire, Russia engaged in reforms from the top down under Alexander I, but when his conservative brother Nicholas I (r. 1825–1855) succeeded to the throne, iron discipline and suspicion of modern ideas took priority over reform.

Russia and Europe

In 1700 only 3 percent of the Russian people lived in cities, two-thirds of them in Moscow alone. By the middle of the nineteenth century the town population had grown tenfold, though it still accounted for only 6 percent of the population because the territories of the tsars had grown greatly through wars and colonization (see Chapter 20). Since mining and small-scale industry can be carried out in small communities, urbanization is only a general indicator of modern economic developments. These figures do demonstrate, however, that, like the Ottoman Empire, Russia was an overwhelmingly agricultural land. Moreover, Russian transportation was even worse than that of the Ottomans, since many of the latter's major cities were seaports. Both empires encompassed peoples speaking many different languages.

Well-engineered roads did not begin to appear until 1817, and steam navigation commenced on the Volga in 1843. Tsar Nicholas I built the first railroad in Russia

Raising of the Alexander Monument in St. Petersburg   The death of Alexander I in 1825 brought to power his conservative brother Nicholas I. Yet Alexander remained a heroic figure for his resistance to Napoleon. This monument in Winter Palace Square was erected in 1829.   (Novosti Photo Library)

from St. Petersburg, the capital, to his summer palace in 1837. A few years later his commitment to strict discipline led him to insist that the trunk line from St. Petersburg to Moscow run in a perfectly straight line. American engineers, among them the father of the painter James McNeill Whistler, who learned to paint in St. Petersburg, oversaw the laying of track and built locomotive workshops. This slow start in modern transportation compares better with that of Egypt, where work on the first railroad began in 1851, than with France, which saw railroad building soar during the 1840s. Industrialization projects depended heavily on foreign expertise. British engineers set up the textile mills that gave wool and cotton a prominent place among Russia's industries.

Until the late nineteenth century the Russian government's interest in industry was limited and hesitant. To be successful, an industrial revolution required large numbers of educated and independent-minded artisans and entrepreneurs. Suspicious of Western ideas, especially anything smacking of liberalism, socialism, or revolution, Nicholas feared the spread of literacy and

modern education beyond the minimum needed to train the officer corps and the bureaucracy. Rather than run the risk of allowing the development of a middle class and a working class that might challenge his control, Nicholas I kept the peasants in serfdom and preferred to import most industrial goods and pay for them with exports of grain and timber.

Like Egypt and the Ottoman Empire, Russia aspired to Western-style economic development. But fear of political change caused the country to fall farther behind western Europe, economically and technologically, than it had been a half-century before. When France and Britain entered the Crimean War, they faced a Russian army equipped with obsolete weapons and bogged down by lack of transportation. At a time when European engineers were making major breakthroughs in fast loading of cannon through an opening at the breech end, muzzle-loading artillery remained the Russian standard.

Despite these deficiencies in technology and its institutional supports, in some ways Russia bore a closer resemblance to other European countries than the Ottoman Empire did. From the point of view of the French and the British, the Cyrillic alphabet and the Russian Orthodox form of Christianity seemed foreign, but they were not nearly as foreign as the Arabic alphabet and the Muslim faith of the Turks, Arabs, Persians, and Muslim Indians. Britain and France feared Russia as a rival for power in eastern Europe and the eastern Mediterranean lands, but they increasingly accepted Tsar Nicholas's view of the Ottoman Empire as "the sick man of Europe," capable of surviving only so long as the European powers found it a useful buffer state.

From the Russian point of view, kinship with western Europe was of questionable value. Westernizers, like the men of the Tanzimat in the Ottoman Empire, put their trust in technical advances and governmental reform. Opposing them were intellectuals known as **Slavophiles,** who in some respects resembled the Young Ottomans and considered the Orthodox faith, the solidity of peasant life, and the tsar's absolute rule to be the proper bases of Russian civilization. After Russia's humiliating defeat in the Crimea, the Slavophile tendency gave rise to **Pan-Slavism,** a militant political doctrine advocating unity of all the Slavic peoples, including those living under Austrian and Ottoman rule.

On the diplomatic front, the tsar's inclusion among the great powers of Europe contrasted sharply with the sultan's exclusion. However, this did not prevent the development of a powerful sense of Russophobia in the west. Britain in particular saw Russia as a geostrategic threat and despised the continuing subjection of the serfs, who were granted their freedom by Tsar Alexander II only in 1861, twenty-eight years after the British had abolished slavery. The passions generated by the Crimean War and its outcome affected the relations of Russia, Europe, and the Ottoman Empire for the remainder of the nineteenth century.

Russia and Asia

The Russian drive to the east in the eighteenth century brought the tsar's empire to the Pacific Ocean and the frontiers of China (see Map 20.1) by century's end. In the nineteenth century Russian expansionism continued with a drive to the south. The growing inferiority of the Russian military in comparison with the European powers did not affect these Asian battlefronts, since the peoples they faced were even less industrialized and technologically advanced than Russians. In 1860 Russia established a military outpost on the Pacific coast that would eventually grow into the great naval port of Vladivostok, today Russia's most southerly city. In Central Asia the steppe lands of the Kazakh nomads came under Russian control early in the century, setting the stage for a confrontation with three Uzbek states farther south. They succumbed to Russian pressure and military action one by one, beginning in 1865, giving rise to the new province of Turkestan, with its capital at Tashkent in present-day Uzbekistan. In the region of the Caucasus Mountains, the third area of southward expansion, Russia first took over Christian Georgia (1786), Muslim Azerbaijan° (1801), and Christian Armenia (1813) before embarking on the conquest of the many small principalities, each with its own language or languages, in the heart of the mountains. Between 1829 and 1864 Dagestan, Chechnya°, Abkhazia°, and other regions that were to gain political prominence only after the breakup of the Soviet Union at the end of the twentieth century became parts of the Russian Empire.

The drive to the south intensified political friction with Russia's new neighbors: Qing China and Japan in the east, Iran on the Central Asian and Caucasus frontiers, and the Ottoman Empire at the eastern end of the Black Sea. In the latter two instances, a flow of Muslim refugees from the territories newly absorbed by Russia increased anti-Russian feelings, but in some cases also brought talented people into Iran and the Ottoman lands. Armenian, Azerbaijani, and Bukharan exiles who had been exposed to Russian administration and education brought new ideas to Iran in the later decades of the century, and a massive migration of Crimean Turks and Circassians from Russia's Caucasian territories affected the demography of the Ottoman Empire, which resettled some of the immigrants as far away as Syria and Jordan and others as buffer populations on the Russian frontiers.

In a broader political perspective, the Russian drive to the south added a new element to the Eastern Question. Many British statesmen and strategists reckoned that a warlike Russia would press on until it had conquered all the lands separating it from British India, a prospect that made them shudder, given India's enormous contribution to Britain's prosperity. The competition that ensued over which power would control southern Central Asia resulted in a standoff in Afghanistan, which became a buffer zone under the control of neither, and direct competition in Iran, where both powers sought to gain an economic and political advantage while preserving the independence of the Qajar dynasty of shahs.

Azerbaijan (ah-zer-by-JAHN)   **Chechnya** (CHECH-nee-yah)
Abkhazia (ab-KAH-zee-yah)

Cultural Trends

Unlike Egypt and the Ottoman Empire, which began to send students to Europe for training only in the nineteenth century, Russia had been in cultural contact with western Europe since the time of Peter the Great (r. 1689–1725). Members of the Russian court knew western languages, and the tsars employed officials and advisers from western countries. Peter had also enlisted the well-educated Ukrainian clerics who headed the Russian Orthodox Church to help spread a western spirit of education. As a result, Alexander I's reforms met a more positive reception than those of Muhammad Ali and Mahmud II.

While Muhammad Ali put his efforts into building a modern army and an economic system to support it, the reforms of Sultan Mahmud II and Alexander promised more on paper than they brought about in practice. Both monarchs hoped to create better organized and more efficient government bureaus, but it took many years to develop a sufficient pool of trained bureaucrats to make the reforms effective. Alexander's Council of State worked better than the new ministerial system he devised. The council coordinated ministry affairs and deliberated over new legislation. As for the ministries, Alexander learned a lesson from Napoleon's military organization. He made each minister theoretically responsible for a strict hierarchy of officers below him, and ordered them to report directly to him as commander-in-chief. But this system remained largely ineffective, as did the provincial advisory councils that were designed to extend the new governing ideas into outlying areas.

Ironically, much of the opposition to these reforms came from well-established families that were not at all unfriendly to western ideas. Their fear was that the new government bureaucrats, who often came from humbler social origins, would act as agents of imperial despotism. This fear was realized during the conservative reign of Nicholas I in the same way that the Tanzimat-inspired bureaucracy of the Ottoman Empire served the despotic purposes of Sultan Abdul al-Hamid II after 1877. In both cases, historians have noted that administrative reforms made by earlier rulers began to take hold under conservative despots, though more because of accumulating momentum and training than because of those rulers' policies.

Individuals favoring more liberal reforms, including military officers who had served in western Europe, intellectuals who read western political tracts, and members of Masonic lodges who exchanged views with Freemasons in the west, formed secret societies of opposition. Some placed their highest priority on freeing the serfs; others advocated a constitution and a republican form of government. When Alexander I died in December 1825, confusion over who was to succeed him encouraged a group of reform-minded army officers to try to take over the government and provoke an uprising. The so-called **Decembrist revolt** failed, and many of the participants were severely punished. These events ensured that the new tsar, Nicholas I, would pay little heed to calls for reform over the next thirty years.

Though the great powers meeting in Paris to settle the Crimean War in 1856 compelled the Ottoman sultan to issue new reform decrees improving the status of non-Muslim subjects, Russia faced a heavier penalty, being forced to return land to the Ottomans in both Europe and Asia. This humiliation contributed to the determination of Nicholas's son and successor, Alexander II, to institute major new reforms to reinvigorate the country. The greatest of his reforms was the emancipation of the serfs in 1861 and the conferral on them of property rights to prevent them from simply becoming hired laborers of big landowners (see Chapter 26). He also authorized new joint stock companies, projected a railroad network to tie the country together, and modernized the legal and administrative arms of government.

Intellectual and cultural trends that began to germinate under Alexander I, and continued to grow under Nicholas, flourished under Alexander II. More and more people became involved in intellectual, artistic, and professional life. Under Alexander I education expanded both at the preparatory and university levels, though Alexander imposed curbs on liberal thought in his later years. Most prominent intellectuals received some amount of instruction at Moscow University, and some attended German universities. Universities also appeared in provincial cities like Kharkov and Kazan. Student clubs, along with Masonic lodges, became places for discussing new ideas.

Nicholas continued his brother's crackdown on liberal education in the universities, but he encouraged professional and scientific training. By the end of his reign Russian scholars and scientists were achieving recognition for their contributions to European thought. Scholarly careers attracted many young men from clerical families, and this helped stimulate reforms in religious education. Perhaps because political activism was prohibited, clubs, salons, and organizations promoting scientific and scholarly activities became more and more numerous. The ideas of Alexander Herzen (1812–1870), a Russian intellectual working abroad who praised traditional peasant assemblies as the heart of Russia, encouraged socialist and Slavophile thinking and gave rise, under Alexander II, to the *narodniki*, a political movement dedicated to making Russia a land of peasant communes. Feodor Dostoyevsky° (1821–1881) and Count Leo Tolstoy (1828–1910), both of whom began to publish their major novels during the reign of Alexander II, aired these and other reforming ideas in the debates of the characters they created.

Just as the Tanzimat reforms of the Ottoman Empire preceded the emergence of the Young Ottomans as a new and assertive political and intellectual force in the second half of the nineteenth century, so the initially ineffective bureaucratic reforms of Alexander I set in motion cultural currents that would make Russia a dynamic center of intellectual, artistic, and political life under his nephew Alexander II. Thus Russia belonged to two different spheres of development. It entered the nineteenth century as a recognized political force in European politics, but in other ways it had a greater resemblance to the Ottoman Empire. Rulers in both empires instituted reforms, overcame opposition, and increased the power of their governments. These activities also stimulated intellectual and political trends that would ultimately work against the absolute rule of tsar and sultan. Yet Russia would eventually develop much closer relations with western Europe and become an arena for every sort of European intellectual, artistic, and political tendency, while the Ottoman Empire would ultimately succumb to European imperialism.

THE QING EMPIRE

In 1800 the Qing Empire faced many of the crises the Ottomans had encountered, but no early reform movement of the kind initiated by Sultan Selim III emerged in China. The reasons are not difficult to understand. The Qing Empire, created by the Manchus, had skillfully countered Russian strategic and diplomatic moves in the 1600s. Instead of a Napoleon threatening them with invasion, the Qing rulers enjoyed the admiration of Jesuit priests who likened them to enlightened philosopher-kings. In 1793, however, a British attempt to establish diplomatic and trade relations—the Macartney mission—turned European opinion against China (see Chapter 20).

For their part, the Qing rulers and bureaucrats faced serious crises of a depressingly familiar sort: rebellions

Feodor Dostoyevsky (FE-oh-dor doh-stoh-YEHV-skee)

by displaced indigenous peoples and the poor, and protests against the injustice of the local magistrates. They dealt with these problems in the usual way, by suppressing rebels and dismissing incompetent or untrustworthy officials, and paid little attention to contacts with far-off Europeans. Complaints from European merchants at Canton, who chafed against the restrictions of the "Canton system" by which the Qing limited and controlled foreign trade, were brushed off.

Economic and Social Disorder, 1800–1839

Early Qing successes and territorial expansion sowed the seeds of the domestic and political chaos of the later period. The Qing conquest in the 1600s brought stability to central China after decades of rebellion and agricultural shortages. The new emperors encouraged the recovery of farmland, the opening of previously uncultivated areas, and the restoration and expansion of the road and canal systems. The result was a great expansion of the agricultural base together with a doubling of the population between about 1650 and 1800. Enormous numbers of farmers, merchants, and day laborers migrated in search of less crowded conditions, and a permanent floating population of the unemployed and homeless emerged. By 1800 population strain on the land had caused serious environmental damage in some parts of central and western China.

While farmers tried to cope with agricultural deterioration, other groups vented grievances against the government: Minority peoples in central and southwestern China complained about being driven off their lands during the boom of the 1700s; Mongols resented appropriation of their grazing lands and the displacement of their traditional elites. In some regions, village vigilante organizations took over policing and governing functions from Qing officials who had lost control. Growing numbers of people mistrusted the government, suspecting that all officials were corrupt. The growing presence of foreign merchants and missionaries in Canton and in the Portuguese colony of Macao aggravated discontent in neighboring districts.

In some parts of China the Qing were hated as foreign conquerors and were suspected of sympathy with the Europeans. Indeed, the White Lotus Rebellion (1794–1804)—partly inspired by a messianic ideology that predicted the restoration of the Chinese Ming dynasty and the coming of the Buddha—raged across central China and was not suppressed until 1804. It initiated a series of internal conflicts that continued through the

1800s. Ignited by deepening social instabilities, these movements were sometimes intensified by local ethnic conflicts and by unapproved religions. The ability of some village militias to defend themselves and attack others intensified the conflicts, though the same techniques proved useful to southern coastal populations attempting to fend off British invasion.

The Opium War and Its Aftermath, 1839–1850

Unlike the Ottomans, the Qing believed that the Europeans were remote and only casually interested in trade. They knew little of the enormous fortunes being made in the early 1800s by European and American merchants smuggling opium into China. They did not know that silver gained in this illegal trade was helping finance the industrial transformation of England and the United States. But Qing officials slowly became aware of British colonies in India that grew and exported opium, and of the major naval base at Singapore through which British opium reached East Asia.

For more than a century, British officials had been frustrated by the trade deficit caused by the British demand for tea and the Qing refusal to facilitate the importation of any British product. In the early 1700s a few European merchants and their Chinese partners were importing small quantities of opium. In 1729 the first Qing law banning opium imports was promulgated. By 1800, however, opium smuggling had swelled the annual import level to as many as four thousand chests. British merchants had pioneered this extremely profitable trade; Chinese merchants likewise profited from distributing the drugs. A price war in the early 1820s stemming from competition between British and American importers raised demand so sharply that as many as thirty thousand chests were being imported by the 1830s. Addiction spread to people at all levels of Qing society, including very high-ranking officials. The Qing emperor and his officials debated whether to legalize and tax opium or to enforce the existing ban more strictly. Having decided to root out the use and importation of opium, in 1839 they sent a high official to Canton to deal with the matter.

Britain considered the ban on opium importation an intolerable limitation on trade, a direct threat to Britain's economic health, and a cause for war. British naval and marine forces arrived at the south China coast in late 1839. The power of modern naval forces dawned on the Qing slowly. Indeed, Qing strategists did not learn to dis-

tinguish a naval invasion from piracy until the Opium War was nearly ended.

The **Opium War** (1839–1842) broke out when negotiations between the Qing official and British representatives reached a stalemate. The war exposed the fact that the traditional, hereditary soldiers of the Qing Empire—the **Bannermen**—were, like the Janissaries of the Ottoman Empire, hopelessly obsolete. As in the Crimean War, the British excelled at sea, where they deployed superior technology. British ships landed marines who pillaged coastal cities and then sailed to new destinations (see Map 25.2). The Qing had no imperial navy, and until they were able to engage the British in prolonged fighting on land, they were unable to defend themselves against British attacks. Even in the land engagements, Qing resources proved woefully inadequate. The British could quickly transport their forces by sea along the coast; Qing troops moved primarily on foot. Moving Qing reinforcements from central to eastern China took more than three months, and when the defense forces arrived, they were exhausted and basically without weapons.

The Bannermen used the few muskets the Qing had imported during the 1700s. The weapons were matchlocks, which required the soldiers to ignite the load of gunpowder in them by hand. Firing the weapons was dangerous, and the canisters of gunpowder that each musketeer carried on his belt were likely to explode if a fire broke out nearby—a frequent occurrence in encounters with British artillery. Most of the Bannermen, however, had no guns and fought with swords, knives, spears, and clubs. Soldiers under British command—many of them were Indians—carried percussion-cap rifles, which were far quicker, safer, and more accurate than the matchlocks. In addition, the long-range British artillery could be moved from place to place and proved deadly in the cities and villages of eastern China.

Qing commanders thought that British gunboats rode so low in the water that they could not sail up the Chinese rivers. Hence, evacuating the coasts, they believed, would protect the country from the British threat. But the British deployed new gunboats for shallow waters and moved without difficulty up the Yangzi River.

When the invaders approached Nanjing, the former Ming capital, the Qing decided to negotiate. In 1842 the terms of the **Treaty of Nanking** (the British name for Nanjing) dismantled the old Canton system. The number of **treaty ports**—cities opened to foreign residents—increased from one (Canton) to five (Canton, Xiamen, Fuzhou, Ningbo, and Shanghai°), and the island of Hong

---

Shanghai (shahng-hie)

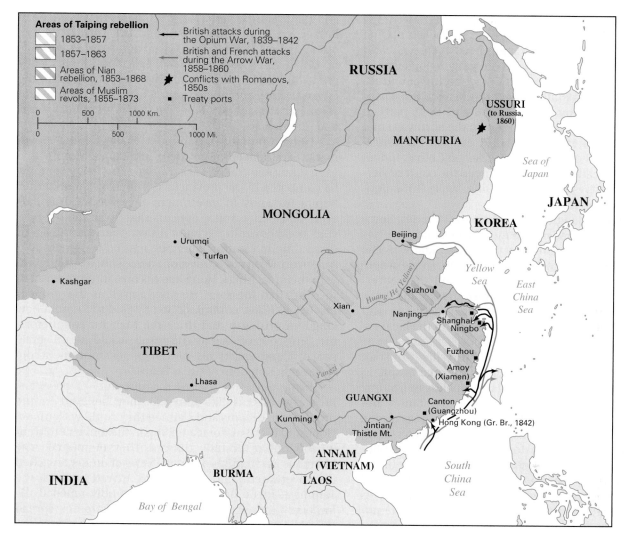

Map 25.2   Conflicts in the Qing Empire, 1839–1870   In both the Opium War of 1839–1842 and the Arrow War of 1856–1860, the seacoasts saw most of the action. Since the Qing had no imperial navy, the well-armed British ships encountered little resistance as they shelled the southern coasts. In inland conflicts, such as the Taiping Rebellion, the opposing armies were massive and slow moving. Battles on land were often prolonged attempts by one side to starve out the other side before making a major assault.

Kong became a permanent British colony. British residents in China gained extraterritorial rights. The Qing government agreed to set a low tariff of 5 percent on imports and to pay Britain an indemnity of 21 million ounces of silver as a penalty for having started the war. A supplementary treaty the following year guaranteed **most-favored-nation status** to Britain; any privileges that China granted to another country would be automatically extended to Britain as well. This provision effectively prevented the colonization of China, because giving land to one country would have necessitated giving it to all.

With each round of treaties came a new round of privileges for foreigners. In 1860 a new treaty legalized their right to import opium. Later, French treaties established the rights of foreign missionaries to travel extensively in the Chinese countryside and preach their religion. The number of treaty ports grew, too; by 1900 they numbered more than ninety.

The treaty system and the principle of extraterritoriality resulted in the colonization of small pockets of Qing territory, where foreign merchants lived at ease. Greater territorial losses resulted when outlying regions gained independence or were ceded to neighboring countries. Districts north and south of the Amur River in the northeast fell to Russia by treaty in 1858 and 1860; parts of modern Kazakhstan and Kirgizstan in the northwest met the same fate in 1864. From 1865 onward the British gradually gained control of territories on China's Indian frontier. In the late 1800s France forced the court of Vietnam to end its vassalage to the Qing, while Britain encouraged Tibetan independence.

In Canton, Shanghai, and other coastal cities, Europeans and Americans maintained offices and factories that employed local Chinese as menial laborers. The foreigners built comfortable housing in zones where Chinese were not permitted to live, and they entertained themselves in exclusive restaurants and bars. Around the foreign establishments, gambling and prostitution offered employment to part of the local urban population.

Whether in town or in the countryside, Christian missionaries whose congregations sponsored hospitals, shelters, and soup kitchens or gave stipends to Chinese who attended church enjoyed a good reputation. But just as often the missionaries themselves were regarded as another evil. They seemed to subvert Confucian beliefs by condemning ancestor worship, pressuring poor families to put their children into orphanages, or fulminating against foot-binding. The growing numbers of foreigners, and their growing privileges, became targets of resentment for a deeply dissatisfied, daily more impoverished, and increasingly militarized society.

The Taiping Rebellion, 1850–1864

The inflammatory mixture of social unhappiness and foreign intrusion exploded in the great civil war usually called the **Taiping° Rebellion.** In Guangxi, where the Taiping movement originated, entrenched social problems had been generating disorders for half a century. Agriculture in the region was unstable, and many people made their living from arduous and despised trades such as disposing of human waste, making charcoal, and mining. Ethnic divisions complicated economic distress. The lowliest trades frequently involved a minority group, the Hakkas, and tensions between them

and the majority were rising. Problems may have been intensified by the sharp rises and falls in the trade of opium, which flooded the coastal and riverine portions of China after 1842, then collapsed as domestically grown opium began to dominate the market. Also, the area was close enough to Canton to feel the cultural and economic impact of the growing number of Europeans and Americans.

Hong Xiuquan°, the founder of the Taiping movement, experienced all of these influences. Hong came from a humble Hakka background. After years of study, he competed in the provincial Confucian examinations, hoping for a post in government. He failed the examinations repeatedly, and it appears that he suffered a nervous breakdown in his late thirties. Afterward he spent some time in Canton, where he met both Chinese and American Protestant missionaries, who inspired him with their teachings. Hong had his own interpretation of the Christian message. He saw himself as the younger brother of Jesus, commissioned by God to found a new kingdom on Earth and drive the Manchu conquerors, the Qing, out of China. The result would be universal peace. Hong called his new religious movement the "Heavenly Kingdom of Great Peace."

Hong quickly attracted a community of believers, primarily Hakkas like himself. They believed in the prophecy of dreams and claimed they could walk on air. Hong and his rivals for leadership in the movement went in and out of ecstatic trances. They denounced the Manchus as creatures of Satan. News of the sect reached the government, and Qing troops arrived to arrest the Taiping leaders. But the Taipings soundly repelled the imperial troops. Local loyalty to the Taipings spread quickly; their numbers multiplied; and they began to enlarge their domain.

The Taipings relied at first on Hakka sympathy and the charismatic appeal of their religious doctrine to attract followers. But as their numbers and power grew, they altered their methods of preaching and governing. They replaced the anti-Chinese appeals used to enlist Hakkas with anti-Manchu rhetoric designed to enlist Chinese. They forced captured villages to join their movement. Once people were absorbed, the Taipings strictly monitored their activities. They segregated men and women and organized them into work and military teams. Women were forbidden to bind their feet (the Hakkas had never practiced foot-binding) and participated fully in farming and labor. Brigades of women soldiers took to the field against Qing forces.

Taiping (tie-PING)

Hong Xiuquan (hoong shee-OH-chew-an)

As the movement grew, it began to move toward eastern and northern China (see Map 25.2). Panic preceded the Taipings. Villagers feared being forced into Taiping units, and Confucian elites recoiled in horror from the bizarre ideology of foreign gods, totalitarian rule, and walking, working, warring women. But the huge numbers the Taipings were able to muster overwhelmed attempts at local defense. The tremendous growth in the number of Taiping followers required the movement to establish a permanent base. When the rebel army conquered Nanjing in 1853, the Taiping leaders decided to settle there and make it the capital of the new "Heavenly Kingdom of Great Peace."

Qing forces attempting to defend north China became more successful as problems of organization and growing numbers slowed Taiping momentum. Increasing Qing military success resulted mainly from the flexibility of the imperial military commanders in the face of an unprecedented challenge. In addition, the military commanders received strong backing from a group of civilian provincial governors who had studied the techniques developed by local militia forces for self-defense. Certain provincial governors combined their knowledge of civilian self-defense and local terrain with more efficient organization and the use of modern weaponry. The result was the formation of new military units, in which many of the Bannermen voluntarily served under civilian governors. The Qing court agreed to special taxes to fund the new armies and acknowledged the new combined leadership of the civilian and professional force.

When the Taipings settled into Nanjing, the new Qing armies surrounded the city, hoping to starve out the rebels. The Taipings, however, had provisioned and fortified themselves well. They also had the services of several brilliant young military commanders, who mobilized enormous campaigns in nearby parts of eastern China, scavenging supplies and attempting to break the encirclement of Nanjing. For more than a decade the Taiping leadership remained ensconced at Nanjing, and the "Heavenly Kingdom" endured.

In 1856 Britain and France, freed from their preoccupation with the Crimean War, turned their attention to China. European and American missionaries had visited Nanjing, curious to see what their fellow Christians were up to. Their reports were discouraging. Hong Xiuquan and the other leaders appeared to lead lives of indulgence and abandon, and more than one missionary accused them of homosexual practices. Relieved of the possible accusation of quashing a pious Christian movement, the British and French surveyed the situation. Though the Taipings were not going to topple the Qing,

rebellious Nian ("Bands") in northern China added a new threat in the 1850s. A series of simultaneous large insurrections might indeed destroy the empire. Moreover, since the Qing had not observed all the provisions of the treaties signed after the Opium War, Britain and France were now considering renewing war on the Qing themselves.

In 1856 the British and French launched a series of swift, brutal coastal attacks—a second opium war, called the Arrow War (1856–1860)—which culminated in a British and French invasion of Beijing and the sacking of the Summer Palace in 1860. A new round of treaties punished the Qing for not enacting all the provisions of the Treaty of Nanking. Having secured their principal objective, the British and French forces joined the Qing campaign against the Taipings. Attempts to coordinate the international forces were sometimes riotous and sometimes tragic, but the injection of European weaponry and money helped quell both the Taiping and the Nian rebellions during the 1860s.

The Taiping Rebellion ranks as the world's bloodiest civil war and the greatest armed conflict before the twentieth century. Estimates of deaths range from 20 million to 30 million. The loss of life came primarily from starvation and disease, for most engagements consisted of surrounding fortified cities and waiting until the enemy forces died, surrendered, or were so weakened that they could be easily defeated. Many sieges continued for months, and after starving for a year under the occupation of the rebels, people within some cities had to starve for another year under the occupation of the imperial forces. Reports of people eating grass, leather, hemp, and human flesh were widespread. The dead were rarely buried properly, and epidemic disease was common.

The area of early Taiping fighting was close to the regions of southwest China in which bubonic plague had been lingering for centuries. When the rebellion was suppressed, many Taiping followers sought safety in the highlands of Laos and Vietnam, which soon showed infestation by plague. Within a few years the disease reached Hong Kong. From there it spread to Singapore, San Francisco, Calcutta, and London. In the late 1800s there was intense apprehension over the possibility of a worldwide outbreak, and Chinese immigrants were regarded as likely carriers. This fear became a contributing factor in the passage of discriminatory immigration bans on Chinese in the United States in 1882.

The Taiping Rebellion devastated the agricultural centers of China. Many of the most intensely cultivated regions of central and eastern China were depopulated and laid barren. Some were still uninhabited decades

Nanjing Encircled   For a decade the Taipings held the city of Nanjing as their capital. For years Qing and international troops attempted to break the Taiping hold. By the summer of 1864, Qing forces had built tunnels leading to the foundations of Nanjing's city walls and had planted explosives. The detonation of the explosives signaled the final Qing assault on the rebel capital. As shown here, the common people of the city, along with their starving livestock, were caught in the cross-fire. Many of the Taiping leaders escaped the debacle at Nanjing, but nearly all were hunted down and executed.   (Roger-Viollet/Getty Images)

later, and major portions of the country did not recover until the twentieth century.

Cities, too, were hard hit. Shanghai, a treaty port of modest size before the rebellion, saw its population multiplied many times by the arrival of refugees from war-blasted neighboring provinces. The city then endured months of siege by the Taipings. Major cultural centers in eastern China lost masterpieces of art and architecture; imperial libraries were burned or their collections exposed to the weather; and the printing blocks used to make books were destroyed. While the empire faced the mountainous challenge of dealing with the material and cultural destruction of the war, it also was burdened by a

major ecological disaster in the north. The Yellow River changed course in 1855, destroying the southern part of impoverished Shandong province with flood and initiating decades of drought along the former riverbed in northern Shandong.

Decentralization at the End of the Qing Empire, 1864–1875

The Qing government emerged from the 1850s with no hope of achieving solvency. The corruption of the 1700s, attempts in the very early 1800s to restore waterworks and roads, and de-

We Have Got the Maxim Gun   These two representatives of the Qing Empire visited northern England after the Taiping Rebellion to examine and, if possible, purchase new weapons. They posed for a photograph after watching the famous Maxim gun, one of the first machine guns, shoot a tree in half.   (Peter Newark's Military Pictures)

clining yields from land taxes had bankrupted the treasury. By 1850, before the Taiping Rebellion, Qing government expenditures were ten times revenues. The indemnities demanded by Europeans after the Opium and Arrow Wars foreclosed any hope that the Qing would get out of debt. Vast stretches of formerly productive rice land were devastated, and the population was dispersed. Refugees pleaded for relief, and the imperial, volunteer, foreign, and mercenary troops that had suppressed the Taipings demanded unpaid wages.

Britain and France became active participants in the period of recovery that followed the rebellion. To insure repayment of the debt to Britain, Robert Hart was installed as inspector-general of a newly created Imperial Maritime Customs Service. Britain and the Qing split the

revenues he collected. Britons and Americans worked for the Qing government as advisers and ambassadors, attempting to smooth communications between the Qing, Europe, and the United States.

The real work of the recovery, however, was managed by provincial governors who had come to the forefront in the struggle against the Taipings. To prosecute the war, they had won the right to levy their own taxes, raise their own troops, and run their own bureaucracies. These special powers were not entirely canceled when the war ended. Chief among these governors was Zeng Guofan°, who oversaw programs to restore agriculture, communications, education, and publishing, as well as

---

Zeng Guofan (zung gwoh-FAN)

Cixi's Allies   In the 1860s and 1870s, Cixi was a supporter of reform. In later years she was widely regarded as corrupt and self-centered and as an obstacle to reform. Her greatest allies were the court eunuchs. Introduced to palace life in early China as managers of the imperial harems, eunuchs became powerful political parties at court. The first Qing emperors refused to allow the eunuchs any political influence, but by Cixi's time the eunuchs once again were a political factor.   (Freer Gallery, Smithsonian Institution)

efforts to reform the military and industrialize armaments manufacture.

Like many provincial governors, Zeng preferred to look to the United States rather than to Britain for models and aid. He hired American advisers to run his weapons factories, shipyards, and military academies. He sponsored a daring program in which promising Chinese boys were sent to Hartford, Connecticut, a center of missionary activity, to learn English, science, mathematics, engineering, and history. They returned to China to assume some of the positions previously held by foreign advisers. Though Zeng was never an advocate of participation in public life by women, his Confucian convictions taught him that educated mothers were more than ever a necessity. He not only encouraged but partly over-

saw the advanced classical education of his own daughters. Zeng's death in 1872 deprived the empire of a major force for reform.

The period of recovery marked a fundamental structural change in the Qing Empire. Although the emperors after 1850 were ineffective rulers, a coalition of aristocrats supported the reform and recovery programs. Without their legitimization of the new powers of provincial governors like Zeng Guofan, the empire might have evaporated within a generation. A crucial member of this alliance was Cixi°, who was known as the "Empress Dowager" after the 1880s. Later observers, both Chinese and foreign, reviled her as a monster of corrup-

Cixi (tsuh-shee)

tion and arrogance. But in the 1860s and 1870s Cixi supported the provincial governors, some of whom became so powerful that they were managing Qing foreign policy as well as domestic affairs.

No longer a conquest regime dominated by a Manchu military caste and its Chinese civilian appointees, the empire came under the control of a group of reformist aristocrats and military men, independently powerful civilian governors, and a small number of foreign advisers. The Qing lacked strong, central, unified leadership and could not recover their powers of taxation, legislation, and military command once they had been granted to the provincial governors. From the 1860s forward, the Qing Empire disintegrated into a number of large power zones in which provincial governors handed over leadership to their protégés in a pattern that the Qing court eventually could only ritually legitimate.

CONCLUSION

Most of the subjects of the Ottoman, Russian, and Qing rulers did not think of European pressure or competition as determining factors in their lives during the first half of the nineteenth century. They continued to live according to the social and economic institutions they inherited from previous generations. By the 1870s, however, the challenge of Europe had become widely realized. The Crimean War, where European allies achieved a hollow victory for the Ottomans and then pressured the sultan for more reforms, confirmed both Ottoman and Russian military weakness. The Opium War did the same for China. Though all three empires faced similar problems of reform and military rebuilding, Russia enjoyed a comparative advantage in being less appealing to rapacious European merchants and strategists concerned with protecting overseas empires.

The policies adopted by the three imperial governments responded both to traditional concerns and to European demands. The sultans gave first priority to strengthening the central government to prevent territorial losses that began when Serbia, Egypt, and Greece became fully or partially independent. The Qing emperors confronted population growth and agricultural decline that resulted in massive rebellions. The tsars focused on continued territorial expansion. However, each faced different European pressures. In China, the Europeans and Americans wanted trade rights. In the Ottoman Empire, Britain, France, and Russia wanted equality for Christians and freedom from naval and commercial competition in the eastern Mediterranean. In Russia, moral demands for the abolition of serfdom accompanied British determination to stop territorial advances in Asia that might threaten India.

Repeated crises in all three empires would eventually result in the fall of the Qing, Romanov, and Ottoman dynasties in the first two decades of the twentieth century, but in 1870 it was still unclear whether the traditional land empires of Asia would be capable of weathering the storm. One thing that had become clear, however, at least to European eyes, was that Russia was part of Europe, while the other two empires were fundamentally alien. This judgment was based partly on religion, partly on the enthusiasm of westernizing Russian artists and intellectuals for European cultural trends, and partly on the role Russia had played in defeating Napoleon at the beginning of the century, a role that brought the tsars into the highest councils of royal decision making in Europe.

■ Key Terms

Muhammad Ali
Janissaries
Serbia
Tanzimat
Crimean War
extraterritoriality
Young Ottomans
Slavophile
Pan-Slavism
Decembrist revolt
Opium War
Bannermen
Treaty of Nanking
treaty ports
most-favored-nation status
Taiping Rebellion

■ Suggested Reading

For widely available general histories of the Ottoman Empire see Stanford Shaw, *History of the Ottoman Empire and Modern Turkey* (1976–1977), and J. P. D. B. Kinross, *The Ottoman Centuries: The Rise and Fall of the Turkish Empire* (1977).

On the economy and society of the nineteenth-century Ottoman Empire see Huri Islamoglu-Inan, ed., *The Ottoman Empire and the World-Economy* (1987); Resat Kasaba, *The Ottoman Empire and the World Economy: The Nineteenth Century* (1988); Sevket Pamuk, *The Ottoman Empire and European Capitalism, 1820–1913: Trade, Investment, and Production* (1987); Kemal H. Karpat, *Ottoman Population, 1830–1914: Demographic and Social Characteristics* (1985); and Carter V. Findley, *Bureaucratic Reform in the Ottoman Empire: The Sublime Porte, 1789–1922*

(1980). On the reform program and the emergence of national concepts see also Selim Deringil, *The Well-Protected Domains: Ideology and the Legitimation of Power in the Ottoman Empire, 1876–1909* (1998).

Marc Raeff, *Understanding Imperial Russia* (1984), sets nineteenth-century Russian developments in a broad context and challenges many standard ideas. Andreas Kappeler, *The Russian Multi-Ethnic Empire* (2001), and Mark Bassin, *Imperial Visions: Nationalist Imagination and Geographical Expansion in the Russian Far East, 1840–1865* (1999), address Russian expansion and the problems inherent in diversity of population. On economic matters see W. L. Blackwell, *The Beginnings of Russian Industrialization, 1800–1860* (1968). Daniel Field, *The End of Serfdom: Nobility and Bureaucracy in Russia, 1855–1861* (1976), addresses the primary problem besetting Russian society during this period. On the intellectual debates see M. Malia, *Alexander Herzen and the Birth of Russian Socialism* (1961), and Andrzej Walicki, *The Slavophile Controversy* (1975).

On the Qing Empire of the nineteenth century see Pamela Kyle Crossley, *Orphan Warriors: Three Manchu Generations and the End of the Qing World* (1990), and for a more detailed political history see Mary C. Wright, *The Last Stand of Chinese Conservatism: The T'ung-chih Restoration, 1862–1874* (1971). There is a very large literature on both the Opium War and the Taiping Rebellion, including reprinted editions of contemporary observers. For general histories of the Opium War see Peter Ward Fay, *The Opium War, 1840–1842: Barbarians in the Celestial Empire in the Early Part of the Nineteenth Century and the War by Which They Forced Her Gates Ajar* (1975); Christopher Hibbert, *The Dragon Wakes: China and the West, 1793–1911* (1970); and the classic study by Chang Hsin-pao, *Commissioner Lin and the Opium War* (1964). For a recent, more monographic study on Qing political thought in the period of the Opium War see James M. Polachek, *The Inner Opium War* (1992). On the Taiping Rebellion, enduring sources are S. Y. Têng, *The Taiping Rebellion and the Western Powers: A Comprehensive Survey* (1971), and C. A. Curwen, *Taiping Rebel: The Deposition of Li Hsiuch'eng* (1976); see also Caleb Carr, *The Devil Soldier: The Story of Frederick Townsend Ward* (1992). The most recent study is Jonathan D. Spence, *God's Chinese Son: The Taiping Heavenly Kingdom of Hong Xiuquan* (1996).

Document-Based Question
Europe and the Ottoman Empire

Using the following documents, compare and contrast the perceptions of Europeans and Ottoman subjects of one another.

DOCUMENT 1
Muhammad Ali Meets with European Representatives in 1839 (photo, p. 650)

DOCUMENT 2
The French Occupation of Egypt (Diversity and Dominance, pp. 654–655)

DOCUMENT 3
Map 25.1 The Ottoman and Russian Empires, 1829–1914 (p. 657)

DOCUMENT 4
Change with Tradition (photo, p. 658)

DOCUMENT 5
Street Scene in Cairo (photo, p. 659)

In Document 2, how did Napoleon and al-Jabarti tailor their statements to suit their different audiences? What additional types of documents would help you evaluate the effectiveness of their statements?

Global Diversity and Dominance, 1850–1945

In 1850, despite centuries of global contacts, the world still embraced a huge diversity of societies and cultures and of independent states. During the century that followed, much of the world came to be dominated by a few European nations, along with the United States and Japan.

After 1870, the industrializing nations used their newfound power to dominate Africa, South and Southeast Asia, and the Pacific in a wave of conquest we call the New Imperialism. Their domination was more than military or economic, for their agents—soldiers, administrators, missionaries, teachers, and merchants—tried to convert their new subjects to their own cultures, business practices, and ways of life. They were partly successful, as the spread of Western religions, languages, clothing, and political ideas testifies.

By 1900, Europe had been largely at peace for almost a century. As memories of war faded, the rise of nationalism and the awesome power of modern armies and navies made national rivalries dangerously inflammable. Germany, a latecomer to national unity, found its imperial ambitions frustrated by the earlier conquests of France, Britain, and Russia. Mounting tensions between the great powers led to the devastating Great War of 1914–1918. Far from settling issues, this war destabilized the victors as much as the vanquished. Russia and China erupted in revolution. The collapse of the Ottoman Empire led to the emergence of modern Turkey, while its Arab provinces were taken over by France and Britain. In the 1920s, the European powers struggled to maintain a precarious peace.

By the 1930s, the political and economic system they had crafted after the Great War fell apart. While the capitalist nations fell into a deep economic depression that their governments seemed helpless to stop, the Soviet Union industrialized at breakneck speed. Social disruption in Germany and Japan brought to power extremist politicians who sought to solve their countries' economic woes and political grievances by military conquest. Nationalism and industrial warfare assumed their most hideous forms in World War II, leading to the massacre of millions of innocent people and the destruction of countless cities.

World War II weakened European control of their overseas empires. Leaders of liberation movements in Asia, Latin America, and Africa were inspired by Western ideas of nationalism and communism and by the desire to acquire the benefits of industrialization. After decades of struggle India gained its independence in 1947. Two years later, Chinese communists led by Mao Zedong overthrew a government they viewed as subservient to the West. In Latin America, leaders turned to nationalist economic and social policies. Of all the once great powers, only the United States and the Soviet Union remained to compete for global dominance. In the face of their military and economic might, other nations continued to assert the diversity of their cultures and political aspirations.

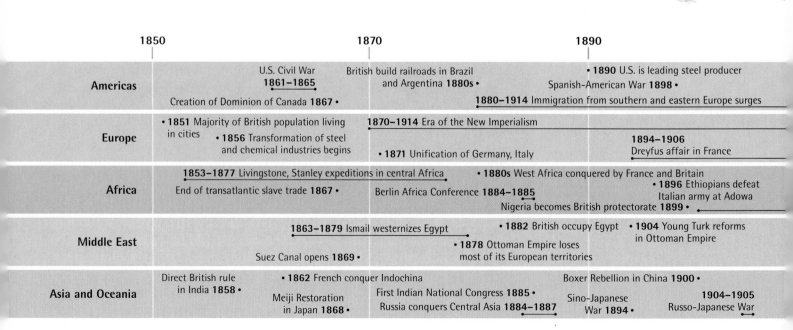

	1850	1870	1890
Americas	U.S. Civil War **1861–1865** Creation of Dominion of Canada **1867** •	British build railroads in Brazil and Argentina **1880s** •	• **1890** U.S. is leading steel producer Spanish-American War **1898** • **1880–1914** Immigration from southern and eastern Europe surges
Europe	• **1851** Majority of British population living in cities • **1856** Transformation of steel and chemical industries begins	**1870–1914** Era of the New Imperialism • **1871** Unification of Germany, Italy	**1894–1906** Dreyfus affair in France
Africa	**1853–1877** Livingstone, Stanley expeditions in central Africa End of transatlantic slave trade **1867** •	• **1880s** West Africa conquered by France and Britain Berlin Africa Conference **1884–1885** Nigeria becomes British protectorate **1899** •	• **1896** Ethiopians defeat Italian army at Adowa
Middle East	**1863–1879** Ismail westernizes Egypt Suez Canal opens **1869** •	• **1882** British occupy Egypt • **1878** Ottoman Empire loses most of its European territories	• **1904** Young Turk reforms in Ottoman Empire
Asia and Oceania	Direct British rule in India **1858** • • **1862** French conquer Indochina Meiji Restoration in Japan **1868** •	First Indian National Congress **1885** • Russia conquers Central Asia **1884–1887**	Boxer Rebellion in China **1900** • Sino-Japanese War **1894** • **1904–1905** Russo-Japanese War

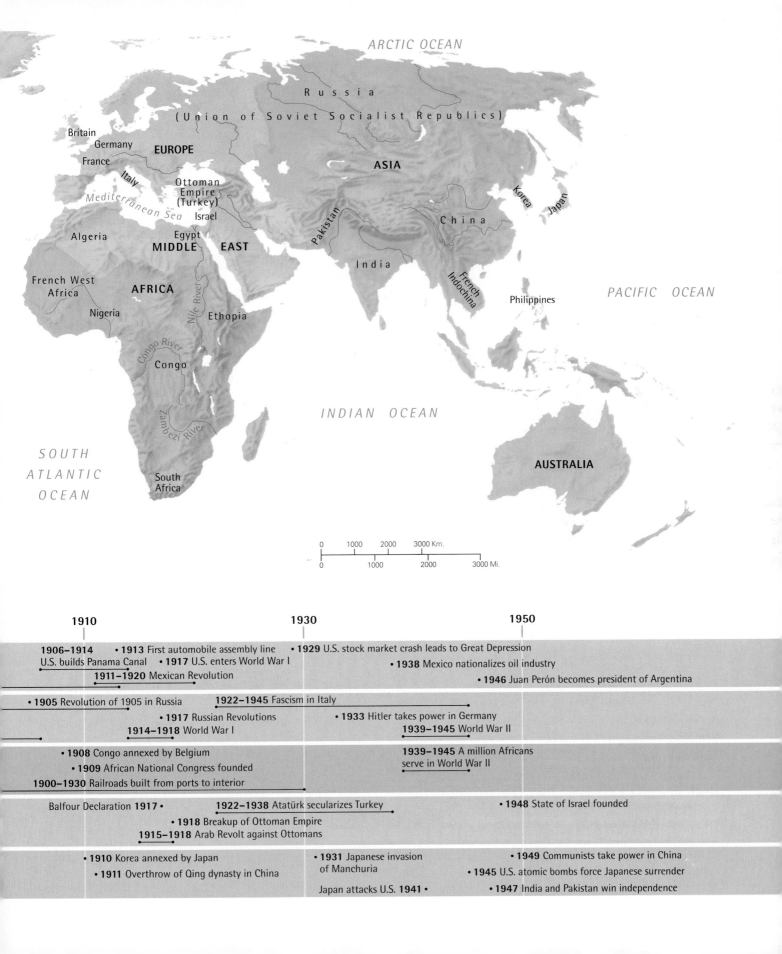

ARCTIC OCEAN

Russia
(Union of Soviet Socialist Republics)

Britain
Germany
EUROPE
France
Italy
Ottoman
Empire
(Turkey)
Israel
ASIA
Korea
Japan
Pakistan
China
Mediterranean Sea
Algeria
Egypt
MIDDLE   EAST
India
French
Indochina
Philippines
PACIFIC OCEAN
French West
Africa
AFRICA
Nigeria
Ethopia
Nile River
Congo River
Congo
INDIAN OCEAN
Zambezi River
SOUTH
ATLANTIC
OCEAN
AUSTRALIA
South
Africa

0   1000   2000   3000 Km.
0   1000   2000   3000 Mi.

1910	1930	1950

1906–1914 • **1913** First automobile assembly line
U.S. builds Panama Canal • **1917** U.S. enters World War I
1911–1920 Mexican Revolution

• **1929** U.S. stock market crash leads to Great Depression
• **1938** Mexico nationalizes oil industry
• **1946** Juan Perón becomes president of Argentina

• **1905** Revolution of 1905 in Russia   **1922–1945** Fascism in Italy
• **1917** Russian Revolutions
1914–1918 World War I
• **1933** Hitler takes power in Germany
1939–1945 World War II

• **1908** Congo annexed by Belgium
• **1909** African National Congress founded
1900–1930 Railroads built from ports to interior
1939–1945 A million Africans
serve in World War II

Balfour Declaration **1917** •   **1922–1938** Atatürk secularizes Turkey
• **1918** Breakup of Ottoman Empire
1915–1918 Arab Revolt against Ottomans
• **1948** State of Israel founded

• **1910** Korea annexed by Japan
• **1911** Overthrow of Qing dynasty in China
• **1931** Japanese invasion
of Manchuria
Japan attacks U.S. **1941** •
• **1949** Communists take power in China
• **1945** U.S. atomic bombs force Japanese surrender
• **1947** India and Pakistan win independence

26 The New Power Balance, 1850–1900

Silk Factory in Japan   Silk manufacture, Japan's best known industry, began to be mechanized in the 1870s. In this factory, as in most textile mills, the workers were women.

On January 18, 1871, in the Hall of Mirrors of the palace of Versailles, King Wilhelm I of Prussia was proclaimed emperor of Germany before a crowd of officers and other German rulers. This ceremony marked the unification of many small German states into one nation. In the center stood Prussian chancellor Otto von Bismarck°, the man most responsible for the creation of a united Germany. A few years earlier, he had declared: "The great issues of the day will be decided not by speeches and votes of the majority— that was the great mistake of 1848 and 1849—but by iron and blood." Indeed it was "blood"—that is, victories on the battlefield—rather than popular participation that had led to the unification of Germany. The "iron" was not only weapons but, more importantly, the industries that produced weapons. Thus, after 1871, nationalism, once a dream of revolutionaries and romantics, became ever more closely associated with military force and with industry.

In the late nineteenth century a very small number of states, known as "great powers," dominated the world. Great Britain, France, and Russia had been recognized as great powers long before the industrial age. Russia began industrializing in the late nineteenth century, as did Germany, the United States, and Japan. The rise of the United States was covered in Chapter 23; in this chapter we will turn to the other great powers of the age. In the next chapter, which deals with the era of the "New Imperialism" (1870–1914), we will see how these nations used their power to establish colonial empires in Asia and Africa and to control Latin America. Together, Chapters 26 and 27 describe an era in which a handful of wealthy industrialized nations imposed on the other peoples of the world a domination more powerful than any experienced before or since.

As you read this chapter, ask yourself the following questions:

- What new technologies and industries appeared between 1850 and 1900, and how did they affect the world economy?

Otto von Bismarck (UTT-oh fun BIS-mark)

- How did the societies of the industrial countries change during this period?

- How was nationalism transformed from a revolutionary to a conservative ideology?

- How did China and Japan respond to the challenge of the Western powers?

NEW TECHNOLOGIES AND THE WORLD ECONOMY

The Industrial Revolution marked the beginning of a massive transformation of the world. In the nineteenth century the technologies discussed in Chapter 22—textile mills, railroads, steamships, the telegraph, and others—spread from Britain to other parts of the world. By 1890 Germany and the United States had surpassed Great Britain as the world's leading industrial powers. Small companies, like those that flourished in Britain, were overshadowed by large corporations, some owned by wealthy capitalists, others (especially in Russia and Japan) by governments.

Industrialization did not consist only of familiar technologies spreading to new areas, but also of entirely new technologies that revolutionized everyday life and transformed the world economy. The motive force behind this second phase of industrialization consisted of deliberate combinations of business entrepreneurship, engineering, and science, especially physics and chemistry. The first Industrial Revolution that you read about in Chapter 22 also involved the interactions of science, crafts, and business through the friendships of people with different interests, as in the Lunar Society. By the mid-nineteenth century this potent combination was institutionalized in the creation of engineering schools and research laboratories, first in Germany and then in the United States. Electricity and the steel and chemical industries were the first results of this new force. Let us turn first to the diffusion of earlier technologies, and then to the newer industries of the late nineteenth century.

Railroads

By the mid-nineteenth century, steam engines had become the prime mover of industry and commerce. Nowhere was this more evident than in the spread of **railroads.** By 1850 the first railroads had proved so successful that every industrializing country, and many that aspired to become industrial, began to build lines. The next fifty years saw a tremendous expansion of the world's rail networks. After a rapid spurt of building new lines, British railroad mileage leveled off at around 20,000 miles (over 32,000 kilometers) in the 1870s. France and Germany built networks longer than Britain's, as did Canada and Russia. When Japan began building its railway network in the 1870s, it imported several hundred engineers from the United States and Britain, then replaced them with newly trained Japanese engineers in the 1880s. By the early twentieth century, rail lines reached every city and province in Japan (see Map 26.3).

The largest rail network by far was in the United States. At the end of its Civil War in 1865 the United States already had 35,000 miles (over 56,000 kilometers) of track, three times as much as Britain. By 1915 the American network reached 390,000 miles (around 628,000 kilometers), more than the next seven longest networks combined.

Railroads were not confined to the industrialized nations; they could be constructed almost anywhere they would be of value to business or government. That included regions with abundant raw materials or agricultural products, like South Africa, Mexico, and Argentina, and densely populated countries like Egypt. The British built the fourth largest rail network in the world in India in order to reinforce their presence and develop trade with their largest colony. Before the opening of the Panama Canal in 1915, a railroad across the isthmus carried freight between the Atlantic and Pacific Oceans.

Railroads consumed huge amounts of land. Many old cities doubled in size to accommodate railroad stations, sidings, tracks, warehouses, and repair shops. In the countryside, railroads required bridges, tunnels, and embankments. Railroads also consumed vast quantities of timber for ties to hold the rails and for bridges, often using up whole forests for miles on either side of the tracks. Throughout the world, they opened new land to agriculture, mining, and other human exploitation of natural resources, whether for the benefit of the local inhabitants, as in Europe and North America, or for a distant power, as in the colonial empires.

Steamships and Telegraph Cables

Steam-powered ships dated back to the 1830s but were initially too costly for anything but first-class passenger traffic. Then, by midcentury, a series of developments radically transformed ocean shipping. First iron, then steel, replaced the wood that had been used for hulls since shipbuilding began. Propellers replaced paddle wheels.

Engineers built more powerful and fuel-efficient engines. By the turn of the century a marine engine could convert the heat produced by burning a single sheet of paper into the power to move one ton over half a mile. The average size of freighters increased from 200 tons in 1850 to 7,500 tons in 1900. Coaling stations and ports able to handle large ships were built around the world. Most of all, the Suez Canal, constructed in 1869, shortened the distance between Europe and Asia and triggered a massive switch from sail power to steam (see Chapter 27).

The steamers of the turn of the century were so costly they had to be used as efficiently as possible. As the world's fleet of merchant ships grew from 9 million tons in 1850 to 35 million tons in 1910, new organizations developed to make the best use of them. One such organization was the shipping line, a company that offered fast, punctual, and reliable service on a fixed schedule. Passengers, mail, and perishable freight traveled on scheduled liners. Most ships, however, were tramp freighters that voyaged from one port to another under orders from their company headquarters in Europe or North America.

To control their ships around the globe, shipping companies used a new medium of communications: **submarine telegraph cables** laid on the ocean floor. Cables were laid across the Atlantic in 1866, to India in 1870, to China, Japan, and Australia in 1871 and 1872, to Latin America in 1872 and 1873, to East and South Africa in 1879, and to West Africa in 1886. By the turn of the century cables connected every country and almost every inhabited island. As cables became the indispensable tools of modern shipping and business, the public and the press extolled the "annihilation of time and space."

The Steel and Chemical Industries

Steel is a special form of iron, both hard and elastic. Until the nineteenth century it could be made only by skilled blacksmiths in very small quantities at a very high cost and was reserved for swords, knives, axes, and watch springs. Then came a series of inventions that made steel the cheapest and most versatile metal ever known. In the 1850s William Kelly, a Kentucky iron master, discovered that air forced through molten pig iron by powerful pumps turned the iron into steel without additional fuel. In 1856 the Englishman Henry Bessemer improved Kelly's method, producing steel at one-tenth the cost of earlier methods. Other new processes permitted steel to be made from scrap iron, an increasingly important raw material, and from the phosphoric iron ores common in western Europe. As a result,

C H R O N O L O G Y

	Europe and United States	East Asia
1850	1851 Majority of British population living in cities	
	1856 Bessemer converter; first synthetic dye	1853–1854 Commodore Matthew Perry visits Japan
	1859 Charles Darwin, *On the Origin of Species*	
	1861 Emancipation of serfs (Russia)	
	1866 Alfred Nobel develops dynamite	1862–1908 Rule of Dowager Empress Cixi (China)
	1867 Karl Marx, *Das Kapital*	
1870	1860–1870 Unification of Italy	1868 Meiji Restoration begins modernization drive in Japan
	1871 Unification of Germany	
	1875 Social Democratic Party founded in Germany	
	1879 Thomas Edison develops incandescent lamp	
	1882 Married Women's Property Act (Britain)	
1890	1894–1906 Dreyfus affair (France)	1894 Sino-Japanese War
	1905 Revolution of 1905 (Russia)	1900 Boxer Uprising (China)
		1904–1905 Russo-Japanese War
		1910 Japan annexes Korea

world steel production rose from a half-million tons in 1870 to 28 million in 1900, of which the United States produced 10 million, Germany 8 million, and Britain 4.9 million. Steel became cheap and abundant enough to make rails, bridges, ships, and even "tin" cans meant to be used once and thrown away.

The chemical industry followed a similar pattern. Until the late eighteenth century chemicals were produced by trial and error in small workshops. By the early nineteenth century soda, sulfuric acid, and chlorine bleach (used in the cotton industry) were manufactured on a large scale, especially in Britain. In 1856 the Englishman William Perkin created the first synthetic dye, aniline purple, from coal tar; the next few years were known in Europe as the "mauve decade" from the pale purple color of fashionable women's clothes. Industry began mass-producing other organic chemicals—compounds containing carbon atoms. Toward the end of the century German chemists synthesized red, violet, blue, brown, and black dyes as well. These bright, long-lasting colors were cheaper to manufacture and could be produced in much greater quantities than natural dyes. They delighted consumers but ruined the natural-dye producers in tropical countries, such as the indigo plantations of India.

Chemistry also made important advances in the manufacture of explosives. The first of these, nitroglycerin, was so dangerous that it exploded when shaken. In 1866 the Swedish scientist Alfred Nobel found a way to turn nitroglycerin into a stable solid—dynamite. This and other new explosives were useful in mining and were critical in the construction of railroads and canals, including the all-important Suez Canal. They also enabled the armies and navies of the great powers to arm themselves with increasingly accurate and powerful rifles and cannon.

The growing complexity of industrial chemistry made it one of the first fields where science and technology interacted on a daily basis. This development gave a great advantage to Germany, which had the most advanced engineering schools and scientific institutes of the time. While the British government paid little attention to science and engineering, the German government funded research and encouraged cooperation between universities and industries. By the end of the nineteenth century, Germany was the world's leading producer of dyes, drugs, synthetic fertilizers, ammonia, and nitrates used in making explosives.

Industrialization affected entire regions such as the English Midlands, the German Ruhr, and parts of Pennsylvania in the United States. The new steel mills were hungry consumers of coal, iron ore, limestone, and other raw materials that were extracted from the ground. They took up as much space as whole towns, belched smoke and particulates, and left behind huge hills of slag and other waste products. Railroad locomotives and other steam engines polluted the air with coal smoke. The dyestuff and other chemical industries left behind toxic wastes that were usually dumped into nearby rivers. This phase of industrialization, unrestrained by

Paris Lit Up by Electricity, 1900   The electric light bulb was invented in the United States and Britain, but Paris made such extensive use of the new technology that it was nicknamed "City of Lights." To mark the Paris Exposition of 1900, the Eiffel Tower and all the surrounding buildings were illuminated with strings of light bulbs while powerful spotlights swept the sky.   (Courtesy, Civiche Raccolte d'Art Applicata ed Incisioni (Raccolte Bertarelli) Photo: Foto Saporetti)

environmental regulations, caused considerable damage to nature and to the health of nearby inhabitants.

Electricity

No innovation of the late nineteenth century changed people's lives as radically as **electricity.** At first, producing electric current was so costly that it was used only for electroplating and telegraphy. In 1831 the Englishman Michael Faraday° showed that the motion of a copper wire through a magnetic field induced an electric current in the wire. Based on his discovery, inventors in the 1870s devised efficient generators that turned mechanical energy into electric current. As an energy source, electricity was more flexible and much easier to use than water power or the stationary steam engine, which had powered industrialization until then. This opened the way to a host of new applications.

Arc lamps lit up public squares, theaters, and stores. For a while, homes continued to rely on gas lamps, which produced a softer light. Then in 1879 in the United States **Thomas Edison** developed an incandescent lamp well suited to lighting small rooms. In 1882 Edison created the world's first electrical distribution network in New York City. By the turn of the century electric lighting was rapidly replacing dim and smelly gas lamps in the cities of Europe and North America.

Other uses of electricity quickly appeared. Electric streetcars and, later, subways helped reduce the traffic jams that clogged the large cities of Europe and North America. Electric motors replaced steam engines and power belts, increasing productivity and improving workers' safety. As demand for electricity grew, engineers learned to use waterpower to produce electricity, and hydroelectric plants were built. The plant at Niagara Falls, on the border between Ontario, Canada, and New York State, produced an incredible 11,000 horsepower when it opened in 1895.

World Trade and Finance

World trade expanded tenfold between 1850 and 1913. Europe imported wheat from the United States and India, wool from Australia, and beef from Argentina, and exported coal, railroad equipment, textiles, and machinery to Asia and the Americas. Because steamships were much more efficient than sailing ships, the cost of freight dropped between 50 and 95 percent, making it worthwhile to ship even cheap and heavy products over very long distances. The advantage that steamers had over sailing ships was

---

Faraday (FAIR-ah-day)

especially pronounced close to industrial countries that produced coal, such as Britain and the United States. On seas and oceans to which coal had to be shipped halfway around the world, such as the Pacific Ocean, sailing ships retained a competitive advantage until the early twentieth century.

The growth of world trade transformed the economies of different parts of the world in different ways. The economics of western Europe and North America, the first to industrialize, grew more diversified and prosperous. Industries mass produced consumer goods for a growing number of middle-class and even working-class customers: soap, canned and packaged foods, ready-made clothes, household items, and small luxuries like cosmetics and engravings.

Capitalist economies, however, were prey to sudden swings in the business cycle—booms followed by deep depressions in which workers lost their jobs and investors their fortunes. For example, because of the close connections among the industrial economies, the collapse of a bank in Austria in 1873 triggered a depression that spread to the United States, causing mass unemployment. Worldwide recessions occurred in the mid-1880s and mid-1890s as well.

In the late 1870s and early 1880s Germany, the United States, and other late-industrializing Western nations raised tariffs to protect their industries from British competition. Yet trade barriers could not insulate them from the business cycle, for money continued to flow almost unhindered around the world. One of the main causes of the growing interdependence of the global economy was the financial power of Great Britain. Long after German and American industries surpassed the British, Britain continued to dominate the flow of trade, finance, and information. In 1900 two-thirds of the world's submarine cables were British or passed through Britain. Over half of the world's shipping was British owned. Britain invested one-fourth of its national wealth overseas, much of it in the United States and Argentina. British money financed many of the railroads, harbors, mines, and other big projects outside Europe. While other currencies fluctuated, the pound sterling was as good as gold, and nine-tenths of international transactions used sterling.

Nonindustrial areas also were tied to the world economy as never before. They were more vulnerable to changes in price and demand than were the industrialized nations, for many of them produced raw materials that could be replaced by synthetic substitutes (like dyestuffs) or alternative sources of supply (like coffee from Brazil). Electricity created a huge demand for copper, tying Chile, Montana, and southern Africa to the

world economy as never before. Even products in constant demand, like Cuban sugar or Bolivian tin, were subject to wild swings in price on the world market. Nevertheless, until World War I, the value of exports from the tropical countries generally kept up with the growth of their populations.

SOCIAL CHANGES

The technological and economic changes of the late nineteenth century sparked profound social changes in the industrial nations. A fast-growing population swelled cities to unprecedented size, and millions of Europeans emigrated to the Americas. Strained relations between industrial employers and workers spawned labor movements and new forms of radical politics. Women found their lives dramatically altered, both in the home and in the public sphere.

Population and Migrations

The population of Europe grew faster from 1850 to 1914 than ever before or since, almost doubling from 265 million to 468 million. In non-European countries with predominantly white populations—the United States, Canada, Australia, New Zealand, and Argentina—the increase was even greater because of the inflow of Europeans. There were many reasons for the mass migrations of this period: the Irish famine of 1847–1848; the persecution of Jews in Russia; poverty and population growth in Italy, Spain, Poland, and Scandinavia; and the cultural ties between Great Britain and English-speaking countries overseas. Equally important was the availability of cheap and rapid steamships and railroads serving travelers at both ends (see Environment and Technology: Railroads and Immigration). Between 1850 and 1900, on average, 400,000 Europeans migrated overseas every year; between 1900 and 1914 the flood rose to over 1 million a year. From 1850 to 1910 the population of the United States and Canada rose from 25 million to 98 million, nearly a fourfold increase. The proportion of people of European ancestry in the world's population rose from one-fifth to one-third.

Why did the number of Europeans and their descendants overseas jump so dramatically? Much of the increase came from a drop in the death rate, as epidemics and starvation became less common. The Irish famine was the last peacetime famine in European history. As farmers plowed up the plains of North America and

ENVIRONMENT + TECHNOLOGY

Railroads and Immigration

Why did so many Europeans emigrate to North America in the late nineteenth and early twentieth centuries? The quick answer is that they wanted to. Millions of people longed to escape the poverty or tyranny of their home countries and start new lives in a land of freedom and opportunity. Personal desire alone, however, does not account for the migrations. After all, poverty and tyranny existed long before the late nineteenth century. Two other factors helped determine when and where people migrated: whether they were allowed to migrate, and whether they were able to.

In the nineteenth century Asians were recruited to build railroads and work on farms. But from the 1890s on, the United States and Canada closed their doors to non-Europeans, so regardless of what they wanted, they could not move to North America. In contrast, emigrants from Europe were admitted until after the First World War.

The ability to travel was a result of improvements in transportation. Until the 1890s most immigrants came from Ireland, England, or Germany—countries with good rail transportation to their own harbors and low steamship fares to North America. As rail lines were extended into eastern and southern Europe, more and more immigrants came from Italy, Austria-Hungary, and Russia.

Similarly, until the 1870s most European immigrants to North America settled on the east coast. Then, as the railroads pushed west, more of them settled on farms in the central and western parts of the continent. The power of railroads moved people as much as their desires did.

Emigrant Waiting Room   The opening of the western region of the United States attracted settlers from the east coast and from Europe. These migrants are waiting for a train to take them to the Black Hills of Dakota during one of the gold rushes of the late nineteenth century.   (Library of Congress)

planted wheat, much of which was shipped to Europe, food supplies increased faster than the population. Fertilizers boosted crop yields, and canning and refrigeration made food abundant year-round. The diet of Europeans and North Americans improved as meat, fruit, vegetables, and oils became part of the daily fare of city dwellers in winter as well as in summer.

Asians also migrated in large numbers during this period, often as indentured laborers recruited to work on plantations, in mines, and on railroads. Indians went mainly to Africa, Southeast Asia, and other tropical colonies of Great Britain. Chinese emigrated to Southeast Asia and the East Indies. Indian and Chinese workers were brought to the Caribbean to work in the sugar plantations after the emancipation of African slaves. Japanese migrated to Brazil and other parts of Latin America. Many Chinese, as well as Japanese and Filipinos, went to Hawaii and California, where they encountered growing hostility from European-Americans.

Urbanization and Urban Environments

In 1851 Britain became the first nation with a majority of its population living in towns and cities. By 1914, 80 percent of its population was urban, as were 60 percent of the German and 45 percent of the French populations. Cities grew to unprecedented size. London grew from 2.7 million in 1850 to 6.6 million in 1900. New York, a small town of 64,000 people in 1800, reached 3.4 million by 1900, a fiftyfold increase. Population growth and the building of railroads and industries allowed cities to invade the countryside, swallowing nearby towns and villages. In 1800 New York had covered only the southernmost quarter of Manhattan Island, some 3 square miles (nearly 8 square kilometers); by 1900 it covered 150 square miles (390 square kilometers). London in 1800 measured about 4 square miles (about 10 square kilometers); by 1900 it covered twenty times more area. In the English Midlands, in the German Ruhr, and around Tokyo Bay, towns fused into one another, filling in the fields and woods that once had separated them.

As cities grew, they changed in character. Newly built railroads not only brought goods into the cities on a predictable schedule but also allowed people to live farther apart. At first, only the well-to-do could afford to commute by train; by the end of the century, electric streetcars and subways allowed working-class people to live miles from their workplaces.

In preindustrial and early industrial cities, the poor crowded together in tenements; sanitation was bad; water often was contaminated with sewage; and darkness made life dangerous. New urban technologies and the growing powers and responsibilities of governments transformed city life for all but the poorest residents. The most important change was the installation of pipes to bring in clean water and to carry away sewage. First gas lighting and then electric lighting made cities safer and more pleasant at night. By the turn of the twentieth century municipal governments provided police and fire protection, sanitation and garbage removal, building and health inspection, schools, parks, and other amenities unheard of a century earlier.

As sanitation improved, epidemics became rare. For the first time, urban death rates fell below birthrates. The decline in infant mortality was especially significant. Confident that their children would survive infancy, couples began to limit the number of children they had, and ancient scourges like infanticide and child abandonment became less frequent. By the beginning of the twentieth century middle-class and even working-class couples began using contraceptives.

To accommodate the growing population, builders created new neighborhoods, from crowded tenements for the poor to opulent mansions for the newly rich. In the United States planners laid out new cities, such as Chicago, on rectangular grids, and middle-class families moved to new developments on the edges of cities. In Paris older neighborhoods with narrow crooked streets and rickety tenements were torn down to make room for broad boulevards and modern apartment buildings. Brilliantly lit by gas and electricity, Paris became the "city of lights," a model for city planners from New Delhi to Buenos Aires. The rich continued to live in inner cities that contained the monuments, churches, and palaces of preindustrial times, while workers moved to the outskirts.

Lower population densities and better transportation divided cities into industrial, commercial, and residential zones occupied by different social classes. Improvements such as water and sewerage, electricity, and streetcars always benefited the wealthy first, then the middle class, and finally the working class. In the complex of urban life, businesses of all kinds arose, and the professions—engineering, accounting, research, journalism, and the law, among others—took on increased importance. The new middle class exhibited its wealth in fine houses with servants and in elegant entertainment.

In fast-growing cities such as London, New York, or Chicago, newcomers arrived so quickly that housing construction and municipal services could not keep up. Immigrants who saved their money to reunite their families could not afford costly municipal services. As a result, the poorest neighborhoods remained as overcrowded,

Separate Spheres in Great Britain In the Victorian Age, men and women of the middle and upper classes led largely separate lives. In *Aunt Emily's Visit* (1845), we see women and children at home, tended by a servant. *The Royal Exchange*, meanwhile, was a place for men to transact business. (Mary Evans Picture Library)

unhealthy, and dangerous as they had been since the early decades of industrialization.

While urban environments improved in many ways, air quality worsened. Coal, burned to power steam engines and heat buildings, polluted the air, creating unpleasant and sometimes dangerous "pea-soup" fog and coating everything with a film of grimy dust. The thousands of horses that pulled the carts and carriages covered the streets with their wastes, causing a terrible stench. The introduction of electricity helped alleviate some of these environmental problems. Electric motors and lamps did not pollute the air. Power plants were built at a distance from cities. As electric trains and streetcars began replacing horse-drawn trolleys and coal-burning locomotives, cities became cleaner and healthier. However, most of the environmental benefits of electricity were to come in the twentieth century.

Middle-Class Women's "Separate Sphere"

In English-speaking countries the period from about 1850 to 1901 is known as the **"Victorian Age."** The expression refers not only to the reign of Queen Victoria of England (r. 1837–1901) but also to rules of behavior and to an ideology surrounding the family and the relations between men and women. The Victorians contrasted the masculine ideals of strength and courage with the feminine virtues of beauty and kindness, and they idealized the home as a peaceful and loving refuge from the dog-eat-dog world of competitive capitalism.

Victorian morality claimed to be universal, yet it best fit upper- and middle-class European families. Men and women were thought to belong in **"separate spheres."** Successful businessmen spent their time at work or relaxing in men's clubs. They put their wives in charge of rearing the children, running the household, and spending the family money to enhance the family's social status.

Before electric appliances, maintaining a middle-class home involved enormous amounts of work. Not only were families larger, but middle-class couples entertained often and lavishly. Carrying out these tasks required servants. A family's status and the activities and lifestyle of the "mistress of the house" depended on the availability of servants to help with household tasks. Only families that employed at least one full-time servant were considered middle class.

Toward the turn of the century modern technology began to transform middle-class homes. Plumbing eliminated the pump and the outhouse. Central heating replaced fireplaces, stoves, trips to the basement for coal, and endless dusting. Gas and electricity lit houses and cooked food without soot, smoke, and ashes. In the early twentieth century wealthy families acquired the first vacuum cleaners and washing machines. These technological advances did not mean less housework for women. As families acquired new household technologies, they raised their standards of cleanliness, thus demanding just as much labor as before.

The most important duty of middle-class women was raising children. Unlike the rich of previous eras who handed their children over to wet nurses and tutors, Victorian mothers nursed their own babies and show-

Emmeline Pankhurst Under Arrest The leader of the British women's suffrage movement frequently called attention to her cause by breaking the law to protest discrimination against women. Here she is being arrested and carried off to jail by the police. (Mary Evans Picture Library)

Most professional careers were closed to women. Until late in the century few universities granted degrees to women. In the United States higher education was available to women only at elite colleges in the East and teachers' colleges in the Midwest. European women had fewer opportunities. Before 1914 very few women became doctors, lawyers, or professional musicians.

The first profession open to women was teaching, due to laws calling for universal compulsory education. By 1911, for instance, 73 percent of all teachers in England were women. They were considered well suited to teaching young children and girls—an extension of the duties of Victorian mothers. Teaching, however, was judged suitable only for single women. A married woman was expected to get pregnant right away and to stay home taking care of her own children rather than the children of other people.

A home life, no matter how busy, did not satisfy all middle-class women. Some became volunteer nurses or social workers, receiving little or no pay. Others organized to fight prostitution, alcohol, and child labor. By the turn of the century a few were challenging male domination of politics and the law. Women suffragists, led in Britain by Emmeline Pankhurst and in the United States by Elizabeth Cady Stanton and Susan B. Anthony, demanded the right to vote. By 1914 U.S. women had won the right to vote in twelve states. British women did not vote until 1918.

Working-Class Women

In the new industrial cities, men and women no longer worked together at home or in the fields. The separation of work and home affected women's lives even more than men's lives. Women formed a majority of the workers in the textile industries and in domestic service. Yet working-class women needed to keep homes and raise children as well as earn their living. As a result, they led lives of toil and pain, considerably harder than the lives of their menfolk. Parents expected girls as young as ten to contribute to the household. Many became domestic servants, commonly working sixteen or more hours a day, six-and-a-half days a week, for little more than room and board. Their living quarters, usually in attics or basements, contrasted with the luxurious quarters of their masters. Without appliances, much of their work was physically hard: hauling coal and water up stairs, washing laundry by hand.

Female servants were vulnerable to sexual abuse by their masters or their masters' sons. A well-known case is that of Helene Demuth, who worked for Karl and Jenny Marx all her life. At age thirty-one she bore a son by Karl

ered their children with love and attention. Even those who could afford nannies and governesses remained personally involved in their children's education. Girls received an education very different from that of boys. While boys were being prepared for the business world or the professions, girls were taught such skills as embroidery, drawing, and music, which offered no monetary reward or professional preparation but enhanced their social graces and marriage prospects.

Victorian morality frowned on careers for middle-class women. Young women could work until they got married, but only in genteel places like stores and offices, never in factories. When the typewriter and telephone were introduced into the business world in the 1880s, businessmen found that they could get better work at lower wages from educated young women than from men, and operating these machines was typecast as women's work.

Marx and put him with foster parents rather than leave the family. She was more fortunate than most; the majority of families fired servants who got pregnant, rather than embarrass the master of the house.

Young women often preferred factory work to domestic service. Here, too, Victorian society practiced a strict division of labor by gender. Men worked in construction, iron and steel, heavy machinery, or on railroads; women worked in textiles and the clothing trades, extensions of traditional women's household work. Appalled by the abuses of women and children in the early years of industrialization, most industrial countries passed protective legislation limiting the hours or forbidding the employment of women in the hardest and most dangerous occupations, such as mining and foundry work. Such legislation limited abuses but also reinforced gender divisions in industry, keeping women in low-paid, subordinate positions. Denied access to the better-paid jobs of foremen or machine repairmen, female factory workers earned between one-third and two-thirds of men's wages.

Married women with children were expected to stay home, even if their husbands did not make enough to support the family. Most working-class married women had double responsibilities within the home: not only the work of child-rearing and housework but also that of contributing to the family's income. Families who had room to spare, even a bed or a corner in the kitchen, took in boarders. Many women did piecework such as sewing dresses, making hats or gloves, or weaving baskets. The hardest and worst-paid work was washing other people's clothes. Many women worked at home ten to twelve hours a day and enlisted the help of their small children, perpetuating practices long outlawed in factories. Since electric lighting and indoor plumbing cost more than most working-class families could afford, even ordinary household duties like cooking and washing remained heavy burdens.

SOCIALISM AND LABOR MOVEMENTS

Industrialization combined with the revolutionary ideas of the late eighteenth century to produce two kinds of movements calling for further changes: socialism and labor unions. **Socialism** was an ideology developed by radical thinkers who questioned the sanctity of private property and argued in support of industrial workers against their employers. **Labor unions** were organizations formed by industrial workers to defend their

interests in negotiations with employers. The socialist and labor movements were never identical. Most of the time they were allies; occasionally they were rivals.

Marx and Socialism

Socialism began as an intellectual movement. By far the best-known socialist was **Karl Marx** (1818–1883), a German journalist and writer who spent most of his life in England and collaborated with another socialist, Friedrich Engels (1820–1895), author of *The Condition of the Working Class in England in 1844* (1845). Together, they combined German philosophy, French revolutionary ideas, and knowledge of British industrial conditions.

Marx expressed his ideas succinctly in the *Communist Manifesto* (1848) (see Diversity and Dominance: Marx and Engels on Global Trade and the Bourgeoisie) and in great detail in *Das Kapital°* (1867). He saw history as a long series of conflicts between social classes, the latest being between property owners (the bourgeoisie) and workers (the proletariat). He argued that the capitalist system allowed the bourgeoisie to extract the "surplus value" of workers' labor—that is, the difference between their wages and the value of the goods they manufactured. He saw business enterprises becoming larger and more monopolistic and workers growing more numerous and impoverished with every downturn in the business cycle. He concluded that this conflict would inevitably lead to a revolution and the overthrow of the bourgeoisie, after which the workers would establish a communist society without classes.

What Marx called "scientific socialism" provided an intellectual framework for the growing dissatisfaction with raw industrial capitalism. In the late nineteenth century business tycoons spent money lavishly on mansions, yachts, private railroad cars, and other displays of wealth that contrasted sharply with the poverty of the workers. Even though industrial workers were not becoming poorer as Marx believed, the class struggle between workers and employers was brutally real. What Marx did was to offer a persuasive explanation of the causes of this contrast and the antagonisms it bred.

Marx was not just a philosopher; he also had a direct impact on politics. In 1864 he helped found the International Working Man's Association (later known as the First International), a movement he hoped would bring about the overthrow of the bourgeoisie. However, it attracted more intellectuals than workers. Workers found

Das Kapital (DUSS cop-ee-TALL)

other means of redressing their grievances, such as the vote and labor unions.

Labor Movements

Since the beginning of the nineteenth century, workers had united to create "friendly societies" for mutual assistance in times of illness, unemployment, or disability. Anticombination laws, however, forbade workers to strike. These laws were abolished in Britain in the 1850s and in the rest of Europe in subsequent decades. Labor unions sought not only better wages but also improved working conditions and insurance against illness, accidents, disability, and old age. They grew slowly because they required a permanent staff and a great deal of money to sustain their members during strikes. By the end of the century British labor unions counted 2 million members, and German and American unions had 1 million members each.

Just as labor unions strove to enable workers to share in the benefits of a capitalist economy, so did electoral politics persuade workers to become part of the existing political system instead of seeking to overthrow it. The nineteenth century saw a gradual extension of the right to vote throughout Europe and North America. Universal male suffrage became law in the United States in 1870, in France and Germany in 1871, in Britain in 1885, and in the rest of Europe soon thereafter. Because there were so many newly enfranchised workers, universal male suffrage meant that socialist politicians could expect to capture many seats in their nations' parliaments. Unlike Marx, who predicted that workers would seize power through revolution, the socialists expected workers to use their voting power to obtain concessions from government and eventually even to form a government.

The classic case of socialist electoral politics is the Social Democratic Party of Germany. Founded in 1875 with a revolutionary socialist program, within two years it won a half-million votes and several seats in the Reichstag° (the lower house of the German parliament). Through superb organizing efforts and important concessions wrung from the government, the party grew fast, garnering 4.2 million votes in 1912 and winning more seats in the Reichstag than any other party. In pursuit of electoral success, the Social Democrats became more reformist and less radical. By joining the electoral process, they abandoned the idea of violent revolution.

Working-class women, burdened with both job and family responsibilities, found little time for politics and were not welcome in the male-dominated trade unions

Reichstag (RIKES-tog)

or radical political parties. A few radical women, such as the German socialist Rosa Luxemburg and Emma Goldman in the United States, an **anarchist** who believed in the abolition of all governments, became famous but did not have a large following. It was never easy to reconcile the demands of workers and those of women. In 1889 the German socialist Clara Zetkin wrote: "Just as the male worker is subjected by the capitalist, so is the woman by the man, and she will always remain in subjugation until she is economically independent. Work is the indispensable condition for economic independence." Six years later, she recognized that the liberation of women would have to await a change in the position of the working class as a whole: "The proletarian woman cannot attain her highest ideal through a movement for the equality of the female sex, she attains salvation only through the fight for the emancipation of labor."[1]

NATIONALISM AND THE UNIFICATION OF GERMANY AND ITALY

The most influential idea of the nineteenth century was **nationalism.** The French revolutionaries had defined people, who had previously been considered the subjects of a sovereign, as the citizens of a *nation*—a concept identified with a territory, the state that ruled it, and the culture of its people.

Language and National Identity Before 1871

Language was usually the crucial element in creating a feeling of national unity. It was important both as a way to unite the people of a nation and as the means of persuasion by which political leaders could inspire their followers. Language was the tool of the new generation of political activists, most of them lawyers, teachers, students, and journalists. Yet language and citizenship seldom coincided.

The fit between France and the French language was closer than in most large countries, though some French-speakers lived outside of France and some French people spoke other languages. Italian- and German-speaking people, however, were divided among many small states. Living in the Austrian Empire were peoples who spoke German, Czech, Slovak, Hungarian, Polish, and other languages. Even where people spoke a common language, they could be divided by religion or

DIVERSITY AND DOMINANCE

MARX AND ENGELS ON GLOBAL TRADE AND THE BOURGEOISIE

In 1848 the German philosophers Karl Marx (1818–1883) and Friedrich Engels (1820–1895), who were living in England at the time, published a small book called Manifesto of the Communist Party. *In it, they tried to explain why owners of manufactures and business—the "bourgeoisie"—had become the wealthiest and most powerful class of people in industrializing countries like Britain, and why urban and industrial workers—the "proletariat"—lived in poverty. In their view, the dominance of the European commercial and industrial bourgeoisie was in the process of destroying the diversity of human cultures, reducing all classes in Europe and all cultures to the status of proletarians selling their labor.*

In the Manifesto, *Marx and Engels did not limit themselves to publicizing social inequities. They also called for a social revolution in which the workers would overthrow the bourgeoisie and establish a new society without private property or government. Their* Manifesto *was soon translated into many languages and became the best-known expression of radical communist ideology.*

Whatever one may think of their call to revolution, Marx and Engels's analysis of class relations has had a lasting impact on social historians. Their ideas are especially interesting from the perspective of global history because of the way in which they connect the rise of the bourgeois with world trade and industrial technology. The following paragraphs explain these connections.

The history of all hitherto existing society is the history of class struggles.

Freeman and slave, patrician and plebeian, lord and serf, guild-master and journeyman, in a word, oppressor and oppressed, stood in constant opposition to one another, carried on an uninterrupted, now hidden, now open fight, a fight that each time ended, either in a revolutionary re-constitution of society at large, or in the common ruin of the contending classes.

In the earlier epochs of history, we find almost everywhere a complicated arrangement of society into various orders, a manifold gradation of social rank. In ancient Rome we have patricians, knights, plebeians, slaves; in the middle ages, feudal lords, vassals, guild-masters, journeymen, apprentices, serfs; in almost all of these classes, again, subordinate gradations.

The modern bourgeois society that has sprouted from the ruins of feudal society, has not done away with class antagonisms. It has but established new classes, new conditions of oppression, new forms of struggle in place of the old ones.

Our epoch, the epoch of the bourgeoisie, possesses, however, this distinctive feature; it has simplified the class antagonisms. Society as a whole is more and more splitting up into two great hostile camps, into two great classes directly facing each other: Bourgeoisie and Proletariat.

From the serfs of the middle ages sprang the chartered burghers of the earliest towns. From these burgesses the first elements of the bourgeoisie were developed.

The discovery of America, the rounding of the Cape, opened up fresh ground for the rising bourgeoisie. The East-Indian and Chinese markets, the colonization of America, trade with the colonies, the increase in the means of exchange and in commodities generally, gave to commerce, to navigation, to industry, an impulse never before known, and thereby, to the revolutionary element in the tottering feudal society, a rapid development.

The feudal system of industry, under which industrial production was monopolised by close guilds, now no longer sufficed for the growing wants of the new markets. The manufacturing system took its place. The guild-masters were pushed on one side by the manufacturing middle-class; division of labour between the different corporate guilds vanished in the face of division of labour in each single workshop.

Meantime the markets kept ever growing, the demand, ever rising. Even manufacture no longer sufficed. Thereupon, steam and machinery revolutionised industrial production. The place of manufacture was taken by the giant, Modern Industry, the place of the industrial middle-class, by industrial millionaires, the leaders of whole industrial armies, the modern bourgeois.

Modern industry has established the world-market, for which the discovery of America paved the way. This market has given an immense importance to commerce, to navigation, to communication by land. This development has, in its turn, reacted on the extension of industry; and in proportion

692

as industry, commerce, navigation, railways extended, in the same proportion the bourgeoisie developed, increased its capital, and pushed into the background every class handed down from the Middle Ages.

We see, therefore, how the modern bourgeoisie is itself the product of a long course of development, of a series of revolutions in the modes of production and of exchange. . . .

[T]he bourgeoisie has at last, since the establishment of Modern Industry and of the world-market, conquered for itself, in the modern representative State, exclusive political sway. The executive of the modern State is but a committee for managing the common affairs of the whole bourgeoisie.

The bourgeoisie, historically, has played a most revolutionary part. . . .

It has been the first to shew what man's activity can bring about. It has accomplished wonders far surpassing Egyptian pyramids, Roman aqueducts, and Gothic cathedrals; it has conducted expeditions that put in the shade all former Exoduses of nations and crusades.

The bourgeoisie cannot exist without constantly revolutionising the instruments of production, and thereby the relations of production, and with them the whole relations of society. Conservation of the old modes of production in unaltered form, was, on the contrary, the first condition of existence for all earlier industrial classes. Constant revolutionising of production, uninterrupted disturbance of all social conditions, everlasting uncertainty and agitation distinguish the bourgeois epoch from all earlier ones. All fixed, fast-frozen relations, with their train of ancient and venerable prejudices and opinions, are swept away, all new-formed ones become antiquated before they can ossify. All that is solid melts into air, all that is holy is profaned, and man is at last compelled to face with sober senses, his real conditions of life, and his relations with his kind.

The need of a constantly expanding market for its products chases the bourgeoisie over the whole surface of the globe. It must nestle everywhere, settle everywhere, establish connexions everywhere.

The bourgeoisie has through its exploitation of the world-market given a cosmopolitan character to production and consumption in every country. To the great chagrin of Reactionists, it has drawn from under the feet of industry the national ground on which it stood. All old-fashioned national industries have been destroyed or are daily being destroyed. They are dislodged by new industries, whose introduction becomes a life or death question for all civilised nations, by industries that no longer work up indigenous raw material, but raw material drawn from the remotest zones; industries whose products are consumed, not only at home, but in every quarter of the globe. In place of the old wants, satisfied by the productions of the country, we find new wants, requiring for their satisfaction the products of distant lands and climes. In place of the old local and national seclusion

and self-sufficiency, we have intercourse in every direction, universal inter-dependence of nations. And as in material, so also in intellectual production. The intellectual creations of individual nations become common property. National one-sidedness and narrow-mindedness become more and more impossible, and from the numerous national and local literatures there arises a world-literature.

The bourgeoisie, by the rapid improvement of all instruments of production, by the immensely facilitated means of communication, draws all, even the most barbarian, nations into civilisation. The cheap prices of its commodities are the heavy artillery with which it batters down all Chinese walls, with which it forces the barbarians' intensely obstinate hatred of foreigners to capitulate. It compels all nations, on pain of extinction, to adopt the bourgeois mode of production; it compels them to introduce what it calls civilisation into their midst, i.e., to become bourgeois themselves. In a word, it creates a world after its own image.

The bourgeoisie has subjected the country to the rule of the towns. It has created enormous cities, has greatly increased the urban population as compared with the rural, and has thus rescued a considerable part of the population from the idiocy of rural life. Just as it has made the country dependent on the towns, so it has made barbarian and semi-barbarian countries dependent on the civilised ones, nations of peasants on nations of bourgeois, the East on the West. . . .

The bourgeoisie, during its rule of scarce one hundred years, has created more massive and more colossal productive forces than have all preceding generations together. Subjection of Nature's forces to man, machinery, application of chemistry to industry and agriculture, steam-navigation, railways, electric telegraphs, clearing of whole continents for cultivation, canalization of rivers, whole populations conjured out of the ground—what earlier century had even a presentiment that such productive forces slumbered in the lap of social labour?

QUESTIONS FOR ANALYSIS

1. How did the growth of world trade since the European discovery of America affect relations between social classes in Europe?

2. What effect did the growth of trade and industry have on products, intellectual creations, and consumer tastes around the world?

3. Why does Marx think the bourgeoisie requires constant changes in technology and social relations? How well does that description fit the world you live in?

4. Can you think of recent examples of the Western bourgeoisie's creating "a world after its own image"?

Source: Karl Marx and Frederick Engels, *Manifesto of the Communist Party,* Authorized English Translation: Edited and Annotated by Frederick Engels (Chicago: Charles H. Kerr & Company, 1906), 12–20.

institutions. The Irish, though English-speaking, were mostly Catholic, whereas the English were primarily Protestant; and in the United States, different economic systems and the issue of slavery divided the south from the north.

The idea of redrawing the boundaries of states to accommodate linguistic, religious, or cultural differences was revolutionary. In Italy and Germany it led to the forging of large new states out of many small ones in 1871. In central and eastern Europe, nationalism threatened to break up large states into smaller ones.

Until the 1860s nationalism was associated with **liberalism,** the revolutionary middle-class ideology that emerged from the French Revolution, asserted the sovereignty of the people, and demanded constitutional government, a national parliament, and freedom of expression. The most famous nationalist of the early nineteenth century was the Italian liberal Giuseppe Mazzini° (1805–1872), the leader of the failed revolution of 1848 in Italy. Mazzini not only sought to unify the Italian peninsula into one nation but also associated with likeminded revolutionaries elsewhere to bring nationhood and liberty to all peoples oppressed by tyrants and foreigners. Although the governments of Russia, Prussia, and Austria censored the new ideas, they could not be quashed. To staff bureaucracies and police forces to maintain law and order, even conservative regimes required educated personnel, and education meant universities, the seedbeds of new ideas transmitted by a national language.

Although the revolutions of 1848 failed except in France, the strength of the revolutionary movements convinced conservatives that governments could not forever keep their citizens out of politics, and that mass politics, if properly managed, could strengthen rather than weaken the state. A new generation of conservative political leaders learned how to preserve the social status quo through public education, universal military service, and colonial conquests, all of which built a sense of national unity.

The Unification of Italy, 1860–1870

The Austrian statesman Prince Metternich had famously described Italy as "a geographical expression." By midcentury, however, popular sentiment was building throughout Italy for unification. Opposing it were Pope Pius IX, who abhorred everything modern, and Austria, which controlled two Italian provinces, Lombardy and Venetia (see Map 26.1). The prime minister of the Kingdom of Piedmont-Sardinia, Count Camillo Benso di Cavour, saw the rivalry between France and Austria as an opportunity to unify Italy. He secretly formed an alliance with France, then instigated a war with Austria in 1858. The war was followed by uprisings throughout northern and central Italy in favor of joining Piedmont-Sardinia, a moderate constitutional monarchy under King Victor Emmanuel.

If the conservative, top-down approach to unification prevailed in the north, a more radical approach was still possible in the south. In 1860 the fiery revolutionary **Giuseppe Garibaldi°** and a small band of followers landed in Sicily and then in southern Italy, overthrew the Kingdom of the Two Sicilies, and prepared to found a democratic republic. The royalist Cavour, however, took advantage of the unsettled situation to sideline Garibaldi and expand Piedmont-Sardinia into a new Kingdom of Italy. Unification was completed with the addition of Venetia in 1866 and the Papal States in 1870. The process of unification illustrates the shift of nationalism from a radical democratic idea to a conservative method of building popular support for a strong centralized government, even an aristocratic and monarchical one.

The Unification of Germany, 1866–1871

Because the most widely spoken language in nineteenth-century Europe was German, the unification of most German-speaking people into a single state in 1871 had momentous consequences for the world. Until the 1860s the region of Central Europe where people spoke German (the former Holy Roman Empire) consisted of Prussia, the western half of the Austrian Empire, and numerous smaller states (see Map 26.2). Some German nationalists wanted to unite all Germans under the Austrian throne. Others wanted to exclude Austria with its many non-Germanic peoples and unite all other German-speaking areas under Prussia. The divisions were also religious: Austria and southwestern Germany were Catholic; Prussia and the northeast were Lutheran. The Prussian state had two advantages: (1) the newly developed industries of the Rhineland, and (2) the first European army to make use of railroads, telegraphs, breechloading rifles, steel artillery, and other products of modern industry.

During the reign of King Wilhelm I (r. 1861–1888) Prussia was ruled by the brilliant and authoritarian aris-

---

Giuseppe Mazzini (jew-SEP-pay mots-EE-nee)

Giuseppe Garibaldi (jew-SEP-pay gary-BAHL-dee)

Map 26.1   Unification of Italy, 1859–1870   The unification of Italy was achieved by the expansion of the kingdom of Piedmont-Sardinia, with the help of France.

tocrat, Chancellor **Otto von Bismarck** (1815–1898). Bismarck was determined to use Prussian industry and German nationalism to make his state the dominant power in Germany. In 1866 Prussia attacked and defeated Austria. To everyone's surprise, Prussia took no Austrian ter-

ritory. Instead, Prussia and some smaller states formed the North German Confederation, the nucleus of a future Germany. Then in 1870, confident that Austria would not hinder him, Bismarck took advantage of French Emperor Napoleon III's hostility to the North

Wilhelm I Proclaimed Emperor of Germany On January 18, 1871, Prussia and the smaller states of Germany united to form the German Reich (empire). King Wilhelm I of Prussia was proclaimed kaiser (emperor) as his chancellor, Otto von Bismarck (in a white jacket), and dozens of generals and lesser princes cheered. The ceremony took place in the Great Hall of Mirrors in the palace of Versailles, near Paris, to mark Prussia's stunning victory over France. (Bismarck Museum, Friedrichsruh)

German Confederation to start a war with France. Prussian armies, joined by troops from southern as well as northern Germany, used their superior firepower and tactics to achieve a quick victory. "Blood and iron" were the foundation of the new German Empire.

The spoils of victory included a large indemnity and two provinces of France bordering on Germany: Alsace and Lorraine. The French paid the indemnity easily enough but resented the loss of their provinces. To the Germans, this region was German because a majority of its inhabitants spoke German. To the French, it was French because it had been so when the nation of France was forged in the Revolution and because most of its inhabitants considered themselves French. These two conflicting definitions of nationalism kept enmity between France and Germany smoldering for decades. In this case, nationalism turned out to be a divisive rather than a unifying force.

Nationalism After 1871

The Franco-Prussian War of 1870–1871 changed the political climate of Europe. France became more liberal. The kingdom of Italy completed the unification of the peninsula. Germany, Austria-Hungary (as the Austrian Empire had renamed itself in 1867), and Russia remained conservative and used nationalism to maintain the status quo.

Nationalism and parliamentary elections made politicians of all parties appeal to public opinion. They were greatly aided by the press, especially cheap daily newspapers that sought to increase circulation by publishing sensational articles about overseas conquests and foreign threats. As governments increasingly came to recognize the advantages of an educated population in the competition between states, they opened public schools in every town and admitted women into public-

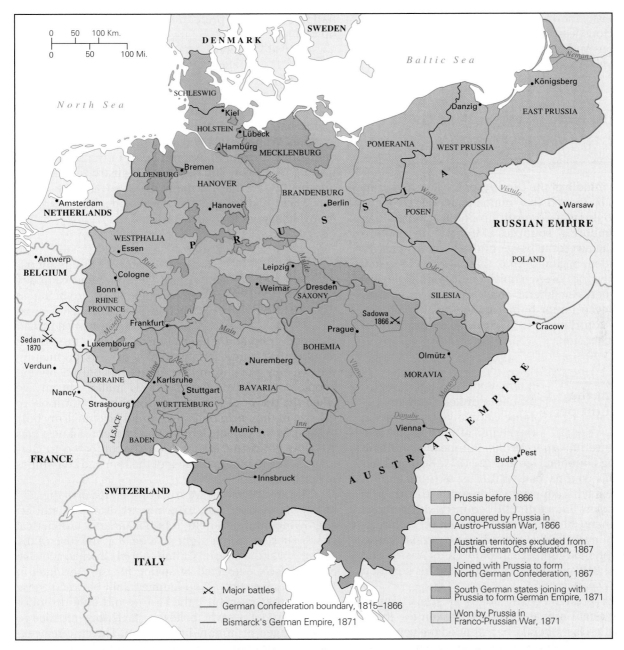

Map 26.2   The Unification of Germany, 1866–1871   Germany was united after a series of short, successful wars by the kingdom of Prussia against Austria in 1866 and against France in 1871.

service jobs for the first time. The spread of literacy allowed politicians and journalists to appeal to the emotions of the poor, diverting their anger from their employers to foreigners and their votes from socialist to nationalist parties.

In many countries the dominant group used nationalism to justify imposing its language, religion, or cus-

toms on minority populations. The Russian Empire attempted to "Russify" its diverse ethnic populations. The Spanish government made the Spanish language compulsory in the schools, newspapers, and courts of its Basque- and Catalan-speaking provinces. Immigrants to the United States were expected to learn English to safeguard national unity.

Nationalism soon spread. By the 1880s signs of national consciousness appeared in Egypt, Japan, India, and other non-Western countries, inspiring anti-Western and anticolonial movements.

THE GREAT POWERS OF EUROPE, 1871–1900

After the middle of the century, politicians and journalists discovered that minor incidents involving foreigners could be used to stir up popular indignation against neighboring countries. Military officers, impressed by the awesome power of the weapons that industry provided, began to think that the weapons were invincible. Rivalries over colonial territories, ideological differences between liberal and conservative governments, and even minor border incidents or trade disagreements contributed to a growing atmosphere of international tension.

Germany at the Center of Europe

International relations revolved around a united Germany because Germany was located in the center of Europe and had the most powerful army on the European continent. After creating a unified Germany in 1871, Bismarck declared that his country had no further territorial ambitions, and he put his effort into maintaining the peace in Europe. To isolate France, the only country with a grudge against Germany, he forged a loose coalition with Austria-Hungary and Russia, the other two conservative powers. Despite the competing ambitions of Austria and Russia in the Balkans, he was able to keep his coalition together for twenty years.

Bismarck proved equally adept at strengthening German national unity at home. To weaken the influence of middle-class liberals, he extended the vote to all adult men, thereby allowing Socialists to win seats in the *Reichstag* or parliament. By imposing high tariffs on manufactured goods and wheat, he gained the support of both the wealthy industrialists of the Rhineland and the great landowners of eastern Germany, traditional rivals for power. Though he repressed labor unions, he gained the acquiescence of industrial workers by introducing social legislation—medical, unemployment, and disability insurance and old-age pensions—long before other industrial countries. His government supported public and technical education. Under his leadership, the German people developed a strong sense of national unity and pride in their industrial and military power.

In 1888 Wilhelm I was succeeded by his grandson Wilhelm II (r. 1888–1918), an insecure and arrogant man who tried to gain respect by using bullying tactics. Within two years he had dismissed Chancellor Bismarck and surrounded himself with yes men. Whereas Bismarck had shown little interest in acquiring colonies overseas, Wilhelm II talked about his "global policy" and demanded a colonial empire. Ruler of the nation with the mightiest army and the largest industrial economy in Europe, he felt that Germany deserved "a place in the sun." His intemperate speeches made him seem far more belligerent than he really was.

The Liberal Powers: France and Great Britain

France, once the dominant nation in Europe, had difficulty reconciling itself to being in second place. Though a prosperous country with flourishing agriculture and a large colonial empire, the French republic had some serious weaknesses. Its population was scarcely growing; in 1911 France had only 39 million people compared to Germany's 64 million. In an age when the power of nations was roughly proportional to the size of their armies, France could field an army only two-thirds the size of Germany's. Another weakness was the slow growth of French industry compared to Germany's, due in part to the loss of the iron and coal mines of Lorraine.

The French people were deeply divided over the very nature of the state: some were monarchists and Catholic; a growing number held republican and anticlerical views. These divisions came to a head at the turn of the century over the case of Captain Alfred Dreyfus, a Jewish officer falsely convicted of spying for the Germans in 1894. French society, even families, split between those who felt that reopening the case would only dishonor the army and those who believed that letting injustice go unchallenged dishonored the nation. The case reawakened the dormant anti-Semitism in French society. Not until 1906, after twelve painful years, was Dreyfus exonerated. Yet if French political life seemed fragile and frequently in crisis, a long tradition of popular participation in politics and a strong sense of nationhood, reinforced by a fine system of public education, gave the French people a deeper cohesion than appeared on the surface.

Great Britain had a long experience with parliamentary elections and competing parties. The British government alternated smoothly between the Liberal and Conservative Parties, and the income gap between rich

The Doss House   Late-nineteenth-century cities showed more physical than social improvements. This painting by Makovsky of a street in St. Petersburg contrasts the broad avenue and impressive new buildings with the poverty of the crowd.   (The State Russian Museum/Smithsonian Institution Traveling Exhibit)

and poor gradually narrowed. Nevertheless, Britain had problems that grew more apparent as time went on. One problem was Irish resentment of English rule. Nationalism had strengthened the allegiance of the English, Scots, and Welsh to the British crown and state. But the Irish, excluded because they were Catholic and predominantly poor, saw the British as a foreign occupying force.

Another problem was the British economy. Once the workshop of the world, Great Britain had fallen behind the United States and Germany in such important industries as iron and steel, chemicals, electricity, and textiles. Even in shipbuilding and shipping, Britain's traditional specialties, Germany was catching up.

Also, Britain was preoccupied with its enormous and fast-growing empire. A source of wealth for investors and the envy of other imperialist nations, the empire was also a constant drain on Britain's finances. The revolt of 1857 against British rule in India (see Chapter 24) was crushed with difficulty and kept British politicians worried thereafter. The empire required Britain to station several costly fleets of warships throughout the world.

For most of the nineteenth century Britain turned its back on Europe and pursued a policy of "splendid isolation." Only in 1854 did it intervene militarily in Europe, joining France in the Crimean War of 1854–1856 against Russia (see Chapter 25). Britain's preoccupation with India and the shipping routes through the Mediterranean led British statesmen to exaggerate the Russian threat to the Ottoman Empire and to the Central Asian approaches to India. Periodic "Russian scares" and Britain's age-old rivalry with France for overseas colonies diverted the attention of British politicians away from the rise of a large, powerful, united Germany.

The Conservative Powers: Russia and Austria-Hungary

The forces of nationalism weakened rather than strengthened Russia and Austria-Hungary. Their populations were far more divided, socially and ethnically, than were the German, French, or British peoples.

Nationalism was most divisive in south-central Europe, where many different language groups lived in close proximity. In 1867 the Austrian Empire renamed itself the Austro-Hungarian Empire to appease its Hungarian critics. Its attempts to promote the cultures of its Slavic-speaking minorities did little to gain their political allegiance. The Austro-Hungarian Empire still thought of itself as a great power, but instead of seeking conquests in Asia or Africa, it attempted to dominate the Balkans. This strategy irritated Russia, which thought of itself as the protector of Slavic peoples everywhere. The Austrian annexation of the former Turkish province of Bosnia-Herzegovina in 1908 worsened relations between the Austro-Hungarian and Russian Empires. As we will see in Chapter 28, festering quarrels over the Balkans—the "tinderbox of Europe"—eventually pushed Europe into war.

Ethnic diversity also contributed to the instability of imperial Russia. The Polish people, never reconciled to being annexed by Russia in the eighteenth century, rebelled in 1830 and 1863–1864. The tsarist empire also included Finland, Estonia, Latvia, Lithuania, and Ukraine, the very mixed peoples of the Caucasus, and the Muslim population of Central Asia conquered between 1865 and 1881. Furthermore, Russia had the largest Jewish population in Europe, despite the harshness of its anti-Semitic laws and periodic *pogroms* (massacres), which prompted many Jews to flee to America. All in all, only 45 percent of the peoples of the tsarist empire spoke Russian. This meant that Russian nationalism and the state's attempts to impose the Russian language on its subjects were divisive instead of unifying forces.

In 1861 the moderate conservative Tsar Alexander II (r. 1855–1881) emancipated the peasants from serfdom. He did so partly out of a genuine desire to strengthen the bonds between the monarchy and the Russian people, and partly to promote industrialization by enlarging the labor pool. That half-hearted measure, however, did not create a modern society on the western European model. It only turned serfs into communal farmers with few skills and little capital. Though technically "emancipated," the great majority of Russians had little education, few legal rights, and no say in the government. After Alexander's assassination in 1881, his successors Alexander III (r. 1881–1894) and Nicholas II (r. 1894–1917) reluctantly permitted half-hearted attempts at social change. Although the Russian government employed many bureaucrats and policemen, its commercial middle class was small and had little influence. Industrialization consisted largely of state-sponsored projects, such as railroads, iron foundries, and armament factories, and led to social unrest among urban workers. Wealthy landowning aristocrats continued to dominate the Russian court and administration and succeeded in blocking most reforms.

The weaknesses in Russia's society and government became glaringly obvious during a war with Japan in 1904 and 1905. The fighting in the Russo-Japanese War took place in Manchuria, a province in northern China far from European Russia. The Russian army, which received all its supplies by means of the inefficient Trans-Siberian Railway, was soon defeated by the better trained and equipped Japanese. The Russian navy, after a long journey around Europe, Africa, and Asia, was met and sunk by the Japanese fleet at the Battle of Tsushima Strait in 1905.

The shock of defeat caused a popular uprising, the Revolution of 1905, that forced Tsar Nicholas II to grant a constitution and an elected Duma (parliament). But as soon as he was able to rebuild the army and the police, he reverted to the traditional despotism of his forefathers. Small groups of radical intellectuals, angered by the contrast between the wealth of the elite and the poverty of the common people, began plotting the violent overthrow of the tsarist autocracy.

JAPAN JOINS THE GREAT POWERS, 1865–1905

Since the seventeenth century Europeans had come to regard their continent as the center of the universe and their states as the only great powers in the world. The rest of the world was either ignored or used as bargaining chips in the game of power politics. The late nineteenth century marked the high point of European power and arrogance, as the nations of Europe, in a frenzy known as the "New Imperialism," rushed to gobble up the last remaining unclaimed pieces of the world, as we will see in Chapter 27.

Yet at that very moment two nations outside Europe were becoming great powers. One of them, the United States, was inhabited mainly by people of European origin. As we saw in Chapter 23, its rise to great-power status had been predicted early in the nineteenth century by astute observers like the French statesman Alexis de Tocqueville. The other one, Japan, seemed so distant and exotic in 1850 that no European had guessed that it would join the ranks of the great powers.

China, Japan, and the Western Powers, to 1867

After 1850 China and Japan—the two largest countries in East Asia—felt the influence of the Western powers as never before, but their responses were completely opposite. China resisted Western influence and became weaker, while Japan transformed itself into a major industrial and military power. One reason for this difference was the Western powers' heavy involvement in China and the distance to Japan, the nation most remote from Europe by ship. More important was the difference between the Chinese and Japanese elites' attitudes toward foreign cultures.

China had been devastated by the Taiping° Rebellion that raged from 1850 to 1864 (see Chapter 25). The French and British took advantage of China's weakness to demand treaty ports where they could trade at will. The British took over China's customs and allowed the free import of opium until 1917. A Chinese "self-strengthening movement" tried in vain to bring about significant reforms by reducing government expenditures and eliminating corruption. The **Empress Dowager Cixi**° (r. 1862–1908), who had once encouraged the construction of shipyards, arsenals, and telegraph lines, opposed railways and other foreign technologies that could carry foreign influences to the interior. Government officials, who did not dare resist the Westerners outright, secretly encouraged crowds to attack and destroy the intrusive devices. They were able to slow the foreign intrusion, but in doing so, they denied themselves the best means of defense against foreign pressure.

In Japan a completely different political organization was in place. The emperor was revered but had no power. Instead, Japan was governed by the Tokugawa shogunate—a secular government under a military leader, or *shogun*, that had come to power in 1600 (see Chapter 20). Local lords, called *daimyos*, were permitted to control their lands and populations with very little interference from the shogunate.

When threatened from outside, this system showed many weaknesses. It did not permit the coordination of resources necessary to resist a major invasion. Shoguns attempted to minimize exposure to foreign powers. In the early 1600s they prohibited foreigners from entering Japan and Japanese from going abroad. The penalties for breaking these laws was death, but many Japanese ignored them anyway. The most flagrant violators were powerful lords in southern Japan who ran large and very successful pirate or black-market operations. In their entrepreneurial activities these lords benefited from the decentralization of the shogunal political system. But when a genuine foreign threat was suggested—as when, in 1792, Russian and British ships were spotted off the Japanese coast—the local lords realized that Japan was too weak and decentralized to resist a foreign invasion.

As a result, a few of the regional lords began to develop their own reformed armies, arsenals, and shipyards.

By the 1800s Satsuma° and Choshu,° two large domains in southern Japan, had become wealthy and ambitious. They enjoyed high rates of revenue and population growth. Their remoteness from the capital Edo (now Tokyo) and their economic vigor also fostered a strong sense of local self-reliance.

In 1853 the American Commodore Matthew C. Perry arrived off the coast of Japan with a fleet of steam-powered warships that the Japanese called "black ships." He demanded that Japan open its ports to trade and allow American ships to refuel and take on supplies during their voyages between China and California. He promised to return a year later to receive the Japanese answer.

Perry's demands sparked a crisis in the shogunate. After consultation with the provincial daimyos, the shogun's advisers advocated capitulation to Perry. They pointed to China's humiliating defeats in the Opium and Arrow Wars. In 1854, when Perry returned, representatives of the shogun indicated their willingness to sign the Treaty of Kanagawa,° modeled on the unequal treaties between China and the Western powers. Angry and disappointed, some provincial governors began to encourage an underground movement calling for the destruction of the Tokugawa regime and the banning of foreigners from Japan.

Tensions between the shogunate and some provincial leaders, particularly in Choshu and Satsuma, increased in the early 1860s. When British and French ships shelled the southwestern coasts in 1864 to protest the treatment of foreigners, the action enraged the provincial samurai who rejected the Treaty of Kanagawa and resented the shogunate's inability to protect the country. Young, ambitious, educated men who faced mediocre prospects under the rigid Tokugawa class system emerged as provincial leaders. In 1867 the Choshu leaders Yamagata Aritomo and Ito Hirobumi finally realized that they should stop warring with their rival province, Satsuma, and join forces to lead a rebellion against the shogunate.

The Meiji Restoration and the Modernization of Japan, 1868–1894

The civil war was intense but brief. In 1868 provincial rebels overthrew the Tokugawa Shogunate and declared the young emperor Mutsuhito° (r. 1868–1912) "restored." The new leaders called their regime the

---

Taiping (tie-PING)   Cixi (TSUH-shee)

Satsuma (SAT-soo-mah)   Choshu (CHOE-shoo)
Kanagawa (KAH-nah-GAH-wah)   Mutsuhito (moo-tsoo-HE-toe)

Arrivals from the East   In 1853 Commodore Matthew Perry's ships surprised the Tokugawa Shogunate by appearing not in Kyushu or southern Honshu, where European ships previously had been spotted, but at Uraga on the coast of eastern Honshu. The Japanese soon learned that Perry had come not from the south but across the Pacific from the east. The novelty of the threat unsettled the provincial leaders, who were largely responsible for their own defense. In this print done after the Meiji Restoration, the traditionally dressed local samurai go out to confront the mysterious "black ships."   (Courtesy of the Trustees of the British Museum)

"Meiji° Restoration," after Mutsuhito's reign name (*Meiji* means "enlightened rule"). The "Meiji oligarchs," as the new rulers were known, were extraordinarily talented and far-sighted. Determined to protect their country from Western imperialism, they encouraged its transformation into "a rich country with a strong army" with world-class industries. Though imposed from above, the Meiji Restoration marked as profound a change as the French Revolution.

The oligarchs were under no illusion that they could fend off the Westerners without changing their institutions and their society. In the Charter Oath issued in 1868, the young emperor included a prophetic phrase: "Knowledge shall be sought throughout the world and thus shall be strengthened the foundation of the impe-

rial polity." It was to be the motto of a new Japan, which embraced all foreign ideas, institutions, and techniques that could strengthen the nation. The literacy rate in Japan was the highest in Asia at the time, and the oligarchs shrewdly exploited it in their introduction of new educational systems, a conscript army, and new communications. The government was able to establish heavy industry through the use of judicious deficit financing without extensive foreign debt, thanks to decades of experimentation with industrial development and financing in the provinces in the earlier 1800s. With a conscript army and a revamped educational system, the oligarchs attempted to create a new citizenry that was literate and competent but also loyal and obedient.

The Meiji leaders copied the government structure of imperial Germany. They modeled the new Japanese navy on the British and the army on the Prussian. They

Meiji (MAY-gee)

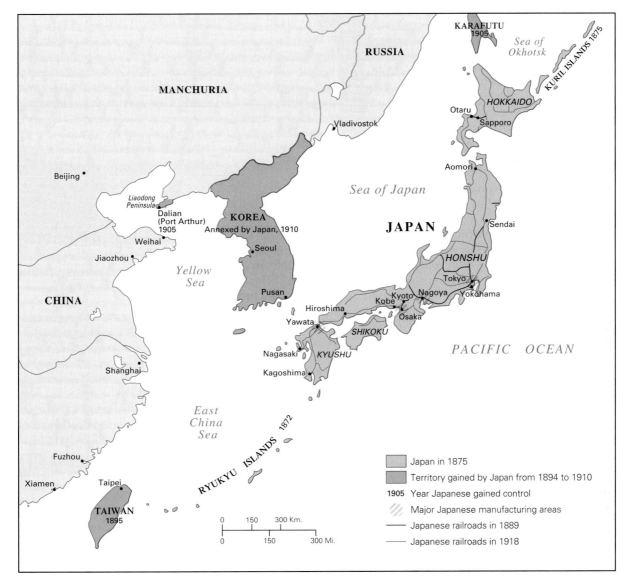

Map 26.3   Expansion and Modernization of Japan, 1868–1918   As Japan acquired modern industry, it followed the example of the European powers in seeking overseas colonies. Its colonial empire grew at the expense of its neighbors: Taiwan was taken from China in 1895; Karafutu (Sakhalin) from Russia in 1905; and all of Korea became a colony in 1910.

introduced Western-style postal and telegraph services, railroads and harbors, banking, clocks, and calendars. To learn the secrets of Western strength, they sent hundreds of students to Britain, Germany, and the United States. They even encouraged foreign clothing styles and pastimes.

The government was especially interested in Western technology. It opened vocational, technical, and agricultural schools and founded four imperial universi-

ties. It brought in foreign experts to advise on medicine, science, and engineering. At the newly created Imperial College of Engineering, an Englishman, William Ayrton, became the first professor of electrical engineering anywhere in the world. His students later went on to found major corporations and government research institutes.

To encourage industrialization, the government set up state-owned enterprises to manufacture cloth and inexpensive consumer goods for sale abroad. The first

Japanese industries, some of which had been founded in the early nineteenth century, exploited their workers ruthlessly, just as the first industries in Europe and America had done. Peasant families, squeezed by rising taxes and rents, were forced to send their daughters to work in textile mills. In 1881, to pay off its debts, the government sold these enterprises to private investors, mainly large *zaibatsu*°, or conglomerates. It encouraged individual technological innovation. Thus the carpenter Toyoda Sakichi founded the Toyoda Loom Works (now Toyota Motor Company) in 1906; ten years later he patented the world's most advanced automatic loom.

The Birth of Japanese Imperialism, 1894–1905

The motive for the transformation of Japan was defensive—to protect the nation from the Western powers—but the methods that strengthened Japan against the imperial ambitions of others could also be used to carry out its own conquests. Japan's path to imperialism was laid out by **Yamagata Aritomo,** a leader of the Meiji oligarchs. He believed that to be independent Japan had to define a "sphere of influence" that included Korea, Manchuria, and part of China (see Map 26.3). If other countries controlled this sphere, Japan would be at risk. To protect this sphere of influence, Yamagata insisted, Japan must sustain a vigorous program of military industrialization, culminating in the building of battleships.

Meanwhile, as Japan grew stronger, China was growing weaker. In 1894 the two nations went to war over Japanese encroachments in Korea. The Sino-Japanese War lasted less than six months, and forced China to evacuate Korea, cede Taiwan and the Liaodong° Peninsula, and pay a heavy indemnity. France, Germany, Britain, Russia, and the United States, upset at seeing a newcomer join the ranks of the imperialists, made Japan give up Liaodong in the name of the "territorial integrity" of China. In exchange for their "protection," the Western powers then made China grant them territorial and trade concessions, including ninety treaty ports.

In 1900 Chinese officials around the Empress Dowager Cixi encouraged a series of antiforeign riots known as the Boxer Uprising. Military forces from the European powers, Japan, and the United States put down the riots and occupied Beijing. Emboldened by China's obvious weakness, Japan and Russia competed for possession of the mineral-rich Chinese province of Manchuria.

zaibatsu (zye-BOT-soo)   Liaodong (li-AH-oh-dong)

Japan's participation in the suppression of the Boxer Uprising demonstrated its military power in East Asia. In 1905 Japan surprised the world by defeating Russia in the Russo-Japanese War. By the Treaty of Portsmouth that ended the war, Japan established a protectorate over Korea. In spite of Western attempts to restrict it to the role of junior partner, Japan continued to increase its influence. It gained control of southern Manchuria, with its industries and railroads. In 1910 it finally annexed Korea, joining the ranks of the world's colonial powers.

CONCLUSION

After World War I broke out in 1914, many people, especially in Europe, looked back on the period from 1850 to 1914 as a golden age. For some, and in certain ways, it was. Industrialization was a powerful torrent changing Europe, North America, and East Asia. While other technologies like shipping and railroads increased their global reach, new ones—electricity, the steel and chemical industries, and the global telegraph network—contributed to the enrichment and empowerment of the industrial nations. Memories of the great scourges—famines, wars, and epidemics—faded. Clean water, electric lights, and railways began to improve the lives of city dwellers, even the poor. Goods from distant lands, even travel to other continents, came within the reach of millions.

European society seemed to be heading toward better organization and greater security. Municipal services made city life less dangerous and chaotic. Through labor unions, workers achieved some measure of recognition and security. By the turn of the century, liberal political reforms had taken hold in western Europe and seemed about to triumph in Russia as well. Morality and legislation aimed at providing security for women and families, though equality between the sexes was still beyond reach.

The framework for all these changes was the nation-state. The world economy, international politics, even cultural and social issues revolved around a handful of countries—the great powers—that believed they controlled the destiny of the world. These included the most powerful European nations of the previous century, as well as three newcomers—Germany, the United States, and Japan—that were to play important roles in the future.

The strength of the dominant countries rested not only on their industries and trade, but also on the enthusiasm of their peoples for the national cause. The feeling of unity and identity that we call nationalism was a two-edged sword, for it could also be divisive for multiethnic states like Russia and Austria-Hungary, and even Great Britain. It was also a Western concept that did not spread easily to other cultures. Thus Japan and China reacted very differently to the Western intrusion. China, long in contact with the West, was ruled by a conservative elite that associated modern technology with Western interference and resisted both. Japan, after a period of turmoil, accepted not only Western technology but also the nationalist and expansionist ideology of the West.

The success of the great powers rested on their ability to extract resources from nature and from other societies, especially in Asia, Africa, and Latin America. In a global context, the counterpart of the rise of the great powers is the story of imperialism and colonialism. To complete our understanding of the period before 1914, let us turn now to the relations between the great powers and the rest of the world.

■ Key Terms

railroads
submarine telegraph cables
steel
electricity
Thomas Edison
Victorian Age
"separate spheres"
socialism
labor unions
Karl Marx
anarchist
nationalism
liberalism
Giuseppe Garibaldi
Otto von Bismarck
Empress Dowager Cixi
Meiji Restoration
Yamagata Aritomo

■ Suggested Reading

More has been written on the great powers in the late nineteenth century than on any previous period in their histories. The following are some interesting recent works and a few classics.

Industrialization is the subject of Peter Stearns, *The Industrial Revolution in World History* (1993), and David Landes, *The Unbound Prometheus: Technological Change and Industrial Development in Western Europe from 1750 to the Present* (1969). Two interesting works on nationalism are E. J. Hobsbawm, *Nation and Nationalism Since 1780* (1990), and Benedict Anderson, *Imagined Communities: Reflections on the Origin and Spread of Nationalism* (1991).

Barrington Moore, *The Social Origins of Dictatorship and Democracy* (1966), is a classic essay on European society. On European women see Renate Bridenthal, Susan Mosher Stuard, and Merry E. Wiesner, eds., *Becoming Visible: Women in European History*, 3d ed. (1998); Patricia Branca, *Silent Sisterhood: Middle-Class Women in the Victorian Home* (1975); Louise Tilly and Joan Scott, *Women, Work, and Family* (1987); and Theresa McBride, *The Domestic Revolution: The Modernization of Household Service in England and France, 1820–1920* (1976). The history of family life is told in Beatrice Gottlieb, *The Family in the Western World from the Black Death to the Industrial Age* (1993). Albert Lindemann, *A History of European Socialism* (1983), covers the labor movements as well.

There are many excellent histories of individual countries. On Germany in the nineteenth century see David Blackbourne, *The Long Nineteenth Century: A History of Germany, 1780–1918* (1998), and Gordon A. Craig, *Germany, 1866–1945* (1980). The standard works on Bismarck and the unification of Germany are Otto Pflanze, *Bismarck and the Development of Germany* (1990), and Lothar Gall, *Bismarck, the White Revolutionary* (1986). On Britain see Donald Read, *The Age of Urban Democracy: England, 1868–1914* (1994), and David Thomson, *England in the Nineteenth Century, 1815–1914* (1978). On France Eugen Weber, *Peasants into Frenchmen* (1976), and Roger Price, *A Social History of Nineteenth-Century France* (1987), are especially recommended. For Austria see Alan Sked, *The Decline and Fall of the Habsburg Empire, 1815–1918* (1989). Two good introductions to Russian history are Hans Rogger, *Russia in the Age of Modernization and Revolution, 1881–1917* (1983), and Gregory L. Freeze, ed., *Russia: A History* (1997).

There are several interesting books on Japan, in particular Peter Duus, *The Rise of Modern Japan*, 2d ed. (1998), and Tessa Morris-Suzuki, *The Technological Transformation of Japan* (1994). Two fine books that cover the history of modern China: John King Fairbank, *The Great Chinese Revolution, 1800–1985* (1987), and Jonathan D. Spence, *The Search for Modern China* (1990).

■ Notes

1. Quoted in Bonnie S. Anderson and Judith P. Zinsser, *A History of Their Own: Women in Europe from Prehistory to the Present*, vol. 2 (New York: Harper & Row, 1988), 372, 387.

Document-Based Question
Class and Gender in the Late Nineteenth Century

Using the following documents, analyze the changing perceptions of class and gender in industrialized nations in the late nineteenth century.

DOCUMENT 1
Silk Factory in Japan (photo, p. 680)

DOCUMENT 2
Emigrant Waiting Room (Environment and Technology, p. 686)

DOCUMENT 3
Separate Spheres in Great Britain (photo, p. 688)

DOCUMENT 4
Emmeline Pankhurst Under Arrest (photo, p. 689)

DOCUMENT 5
Marx and Engels on Global Trade and the Bourgeoisie (Diversity and Dominance, pp. 692–693)

DOCUMENT 6
The Doss House (photo, p. 699)

How would Marx and Engels view Documents 1, 2, and 6? What additional types of documents would help you understand changing perceptions of class and gender in the late nineteenth century?

27

The New Imperialism, 1869–1914

Opening the Suez Canal When the canal opened in 1869, thousands of dignitaries and ordinary people gathered to watch the ships go by.

In 1869 Ismail°, the khedive° (ruler) of Egypt, invited all the Christian princes of Europe and all the Muslim princes of Asia and Africa—except the Ottoman sultan, his nominal overlord—to celebrate the inauguration of the greatest construction project of the century: the **Suez Canal.** Among the sixteen hundred dignitaries from the Middle East and Europe who assembled at Port Said° were Emperor Francis Joseph of Austria-Hungary and Empress Eugénie of France. A French journalist wrote:

> This multitude, coming from all parts of the world, presented the most varied and singular spectacle. All races were represented. . . . We saw, coming to attend this festival of civilization, men of the Orient wearing clothes of dazzling colors, chiefs of African tribes wrapped in their great coats, Circassians in war costumes, officers of the British army of India with their shakos [hats] wrapped in muslin, Hungarian magnates wearing their national costumes.[1]

Ismail used the occasion to emphasize the harmony and cooperation between the peoples of Africa, Asia, and Europe and to show that Egypt was not only independent but was also an equal of the great powers. To bless the inauguration, Ismail had invited clergy of the Muslim, Orthodox, and Catholic faiths. A reporter noted: "The Khedive . . . wished to symbolize thereby the unity of men and their brotherhood before God, without distinction of religion; it was the first time that the Orient had seen such a meeting of faiths to celebrate and bless together a great event and a great work."[2]

The canal was a great success, but not in the way Ismail intended. Ships using it could travel between Europe and India in less than two weeks—much less time than the month or longer consumed by sailing around Africa and across the Indian Ocean. By lowering freight costs, the canal stimulated shipping and the construction of steamships, giving an advantage to nations that had heavy industry and a large maritime trade over land-based empires and countries with few merchant ships. Great Britain, which long opposed construction of the canal for fear that it might fall into enemy hands, benefited more than any other nation. France, which provided half the capital and most of the engineers, came in a distant second, for it had less trade with Asia than Britain did. Egypt, which contributed the other half of the money and most of the labor, was the loser. Instead of making Egypt powerful and independent, the Suez Canal provided the excuse for a British invasion and occupation of Egypt.

Far from inaugurating an era of harmony among the peoples of three continents and three faiths, the canal triggered a wave of European domination over Africa and Asia. Between 1869 and 1914 Germany, France, Britain, Russia, Japan, and the United States used industrial technology to impose their will on the nonindustrial parts of the world. Historians use the expression **New Imperialism** to describe this exercise of power.

As you read this chapter, ask yourself the following questions:

- What motivated the industrial nations to conquer new territories, and what means did they use?

- Why were some parts of the world annexed to the new empires, while others became economic dependencies of the great powers?

- How did the environment change in the lands subjected to the New Imperialism?

THE NEW IMPERIALISM: MOTIVES AND METHODS

Europe had a long tradition of imperialism reaching back to the twelfth-century Crusades against the Arabs, and the United States greatly expanded its territory after achieving independence in 1783 (see Map 23.3). During the first two-thirds of the nineteenth century the European powers continued to increase their influence overseas (see Chapter 24). The New Imperial-

---

Ismail (is-mah-EEL) **khedive** (kuh-DEEV) **Port Said** (port sah-EED)

C H R O N O L O G Y		
The Scramble for Africa	**Asia and Western Dominance**	**Imperialism in Latin America**

	The Scramble for Africa	Asia and Western Dominance	Imperialism in Latin America
1870	**1869** Opening of the Suez Canal **1874** Warfare between the British and the Asante (Gold Coast) **1877–1879** Warfare between the British and the Xhosa and between the British and the Zulu (South Africa) **1882** British forces occupy Egypt **1884–1885** Berlin Conference; Leopold II obtains Congo Free State	**1862–1895** French conquer Indochina **1865–1876** Russian forces advance into Central Asia **1878** United States obtains Pago Pago Harbor (Samoa) **1885** Britain completes conquest of Burma **1887** United States obtains Pearl Harbor (Hawaii)	**1870–1910** Railroad building boom; British companies in Argentina and Brazil; U.S. companies in Mexico.
1890	**1896** Ethiopians defeat Italian army at Adowa; warfare between the British and the Asante **1898** Battle of Omdurman	**1894–1895** China defeated in Sino-Japanese War **1895** France completes conquest of Indochina **1898** United States annexes Hawaii and purchases Philippines from Spain	**1895–1898** Cubans revolt against Spanish rule **1898** Spanish-American War; United States annexes Puerto Rico and Guam
	1899–1902 South African War between Afrikaners and the British **1902** First Aswan Dam completed (Egypt)	**1899–1902** U.S. forces conquer and occupy Philippines **1903** Russia completes Trans-Siberian Railway **1904–1905** Russia defeated in Russo-Japanese War	**1901** United States imposes Platt Amendment on Cuba **1903** United States backs secession of Panama from Colombia **1904–1907, 1916** U.S. troops occupy Dominican Republic **1904–1914** United States builds Panama Canal
1910	**1908** Belgium annexes Congo		**1912** U.S. troops occupy Nicaragua and Honduras

ism was characterized by an explosion of territorial conquests even more rapid than the Spanish conquests of the sixteenth century. Between 1869 and 1914, in a land grab of unprecedented speed, Europeans seized territories in Africa and Central Asia, and both Europeans and Americans took territories in Southeast Asia and the Pacific. Approximately 10 million square miles (26 million square kilometers) and 150 million people fell under the rule of Europe and the United States in this period.

The New Imperialism was more than a land grab. The imperial powers used economic and technological means to reorganize dependent regions and bring them into the world economy as suppliers of foodstuffs and raw materials and as consumers of industrial products. In Africa and other parts of the world, this was done by conquest and colonial administration. In the Latin American republics the same result was achieved indirectly. Even though they remained politically independent, they became economic dependencies of the United States and Europe.

What inspired Europeans and Americans to venture overseas and impose their will on other societies? There is no simple answer to this question. Economic, cultural, and political motives were involved in all cases.

Political Motives

The great powers of the late nineteenth century, as well as less powerful countries like Italy, Portugal, and Belgium, were competitive and hypersensitive about their status. French leaders, humiliated by their defeat by Prussia in 1871 (see Chapter 26), sought to reestablish their nation's prestige through territorial acquisitions overseas. Great Britain, already in possession of the world's largest and richest empire, felt the need to protect India, its "jewel in the crown," by acquiring colonies in East Africa and Southeast Asia. German Chancellor Otto von Bismarck had little interest in acquiring colonies, but many Germans believed that a country as important as theirs required an impressive empire overseas.

Political motives were not limited to statesmen in the capital cities. Colonial governors, even officers posted to the farthest colonial outposts, practiced their own diplomacy. They often decided on their own to claim a piece of land before some rival got it. Armies fighting frontier wars found it easier to defeat their neighbors than to make peace with them. In response to border skirmishes with neighboring states, colonial agents were likely to send in troops, take over their neighbors' territories, and then inform their home governments. Governments felt obligated to back up their men-on-the-spot in order not to lose face. The great powers of Europe acquired much of West Africa, Southeast Asia, and the Pacific islands in this manner.

Cultural Motives

The late nineteenth century saw a Christian revival in Europe and North America, as both Catholics and Protestants founded new missionary societies. Their purpose was not only religious—to convert nonbelievers, whom they regarded as "heathen"—but also cultural in a broader sense. They sought to export their own norms of "civilized" behavior: they were determined to abolish slavery in Africa and bring Western education, medicine, hygiene, and monogamous marriage to all the world's peoples.

Among those attracted by religious work overseas were many women who joined missionary societies to become teachers and nurses, positions of greater authority than they could hope to find at home. Although they did not challenge colonialism directly, their influence often helped soften the harshness of colonial rule—for example, by calling attention to issues of maternity and women's health. Mary Slessor, a British missionary who lived for forty years among the people of southeastern Nigeria, campaigned against slavery, human sacrifice, and the killing of twins and, generally, for women's rights. In India missionaries denounced the customs of child marriages and *sati* (the burning of widows on their husbands' funeral pyres). Such views often clashed with the customs of the people among whom they settled.

The sense of moral duty and cultural superiority was not limited to missionaries. Many Europeans and Americans equated technological innovations with "progress" and "change for the better." They believed that Western technology proved the superiority of Western ideas, customs, and culture. This attitude included the idea that non-Western peoples could achieve, through education, the same cultural level as Europeans and Americans. More harmful were racist ideas that relegated non-Europeans to a status of permanent inferiority. Racists assigned different stages of biological development to peoples of different races and cultures. They divided humankind into several races based on physical appearance and ranked these races in a hierarchy that ranged from "civilized" at the highest level down through "semi-barbarous," "barbarian," and finally, at the bottom, "savage." Caucasians—whites—were always at the top of this ranking. Such ideas were often presented as an excuse for permanent rule over Africans and Asians.

Imperialism first interested small groups of explorers, clergy, and businessmen but soon attracted people from other walks of life. Young men, finding few opportunities for adventure and glory at home in an era of peace, sought them overseas as the Spanish conquistadors had done over three centuries earlier. At first, European people and parliaments were indifferent or hostile to overseas adventures, but a few easy victories in the 1880s helped to overcome their reluctance. The United States was fully preoccupied with its westward expansion until the 1880s, but in the 1890s popular attention shifted to lands outside U.S. borders. Newspapers, which achieved wide readership in the second half of the nineteenth century, discovered that they could boost circulation with reports of wars and conquests. By the 1890s imperialism was a popular cause; it was the overseas extension of the nationalism propelling the power politics of the time.

Economic Motives

The industrialization of Europe and North America stimulated the demand for minerals—copper for electrical wiring, tin for canning, chrome and manganese for the steel industry, coal for steam engines, and, most of all, gold and diamonds. The demand for such industrial crops as cot-

Pears Soap Is Best This advertisement appeared in the *Illustrated London News* in 1887. In identifying a brand of soap as "the formula for British conquest," it credited British manufactured products with the power to overawe spear-wielding indigenous warriors. (*Illustrated London News* Picture Library)

ton and rubber and for stimulants such as sugar, coffee, tea, and tobacco also grew. These products were found in the tropics, but never in sufficient quantities.

An economic depression lasting from the mid-1870s to the mid-1890s caused European merchants, manufacturers, and shippers to seek protection against foreign competition (see below). They argued that their respective countries needed secure sources of tropical raw materials and protected markets for their industries. Declining business opportunities at home prompted entrepreneurs and investors to look for profits from mines, plantations, and railroads in Asia, Africa, and Latin America. Since investment in countries so different from their own was extremely risky, businessmen sought the backing of their governments, preferably with soldiers.

These reasons explain why Europeans and Americans wished to expand their influence over other societies in the late nineteenth and early twentieth centuries. Yet motives do not adequately explain the events of that time. It was possible to conquer a piece of Africa, convert the "heathen," and start a plantation because of the sudden increase in the power that industrial peoples could wield over nonindustrial peoples and over the forces of nature. Technological advances explain both the motives and the outcome of the New Imperialism.

The Tools of the Imperialists

To succeed, empire builders needed the means to achieve their objectives at a reasonable cost. These means were provided by the Industrial Revolution (see Chapter 22). In the early part of the nineteenth century technological innovations began to tip the balance of power in favor of Europe.

Europeans had dominated the oceans since about 1500, and their naval power increased still more with the introduction of steamships. The first steamer reached India in 1825 and was soon followed by regular mail service in the 1830s. The long voyage around Africa was at first too costly for cargo steamers, for coal had to be shipped from England. The building of the Suez Canal and the development of increasingly efficient engines solved this problem and led to a boom in shipping to the Indian Ocean and East Asia. Whenever fighting broke out, passenger liners were requisitioned as troopships, giving European forces greater mobility than Asians and Africans. Their advantage was enhanced even more by the development of a global network of submarine telegraph cables connecting Europe with North America in the 1860s, with Latin America and Asia in the 1870s, with Africa in the 1880s, and finally across the Pacific in 1904.

Until the middle of the nineteenth century, western Europeans were much weaker on land than at sea. Thereafter, Europeans used gunboats with considerable success in China, Burma, Indochina, and the Congo Basin. Although gunboats opened the major river basins to European penetration, the invaders often found themselves hampered by other natural obstacles. *Falciparum* malaria, found only in Africa, was so deadly to Europeans that few explorers survived before the 1850s. In 1854 a British doctor discovered that the drug quinine, taken regularly during one's stay in Africa, could prevent the disease. This and a few sanitary precautions reduced the annual death rate among whites in West Africa from between 250 and 750 per thousand in the early nineteenth century to between 50 and 100 per thousand after

The Battle of Omdurman In the late nineteenth century, most battles between European (or European-led) troops and African forces were one-sided encounters because of the disparity in the opponents' firearms and tactics. The Battle of Omdurman in Sudan in 1898 is a dramatic example. The forces of the Mahdi, some on horseback, were armed with spears and single-shot muskets. The British troops and their Egyptian allies, lined up in the foreground, used repeating rifles and machine guns able to shoot much farther than the Sudanese weapons. As a result, there were many Sudanese casualties but very few British or Egyptian. (The Art Archive)

1850. This reduction was sufficient to open the continent to merchants, officials, and missionaries.

Muzzle-loading smoothbore muskets had been used in Europe, Asia, and the Americas since the late seventeenth century, and by the early nineteenth century they were also common in much of Africa. The development of new and much deadlier firearms in the 1860s and 1870s shifted the balance of power on land between Westerners and other peoples. One of these was the breechloader, which could be fired accurately ten times as fast as, and five or six times farther than, a musket. By the 1870s all armies in Europe and the United States had switched to these new rifles. Two more innovations appeared in the 1880s: smokeless powder, which did not foul the gun or reveal the soldier's position, and repeating rifles, which could shoot fifteen rounds in fifteen sec-

onds. In the 1890s European and American armies began using machine guns, which could fire eleven bullets per second.

In the course of the century Asians and Africans also acquired better firearms, mostly old weapons that European armies had discarded. As European firearms improved, the firepower gap widened, making colonial conquests easier than ever before. By the 1880s and 1890s European-led forces of a few hundred could defeat non-European armies of thousands. Against the latest weapons, African and Asian soldiers armed with muskets or, in some cases, with spears did not stand a chance, no matter how numerous and courageous they were.

A classic example is the **Battle of Omdurman** in Sudan. On September 2, 1898, forty thousand Sudanese attacked an Anglo-Egyptian expedition that had come up the Nile on six steamers and four other boats. General Horatio Kitchener's troops had twenty machine guns and four artillery pieces; the Sudanese were equipped with muskets and spears. Within a few hours eleven thousand Sudanese and forty-eight British lay dead. Winston Churchill, the future British prime minister, witnessed the battle and called it

> The most signal triumph ever gained by the arms of science over barbarians. Within the space of five hours the strongest and best-armed savage army yet arrayed against a modern European Power had been destroyed and dispersed, with hardly any difficulty, comparatively small risk, and insignificant loss to the victors.[3]

Colonial Agents and Administration

Once colonial agents took over a territory, their home government expected them to cover their own costs and, if possible, return some profit to the home country. The system of administering and exploiting colonies for the benefit of the home country is known as **colonialism.** In some cases, such as along the West African coast or in Indochina, there was already a considerable trade that could be taxed. In other places profits could come only from investments and a thorough reorganization of the indigenous societies. In applying modern scientific and industrial methods to their colonies, colonialists started the transformation of Asian and African societies and landscapes that has continued to our day.

Legal experts and academics emphasized the differences between various systems of colonial government and debated whether colonies eventually should be assimilated into the ruling nation, associated in a federation, or allowed to rule themselves. Colonies that were protectorates retained their traditional governments, even their monarchs, but had a European "resident" or "consul-general" to "advise" them. Other colonies were directly administered by a European governor. In fact, the impact of colonial rule depended much more on economic and social conditions than on narrow legal distinctions.

One important factor was the presence or absence of European settlers. In Canada, Australia, and New Zealand, whites were already in the majority by 1869, and their colonial "mother-country," Britain, encouraged them to elect parliaments and rule themselves. Where European settlers were numerous but still a minority of the population, as in Algeria and South Africa, settlers and the home country struggled for control over the indigenous population. In colonies with few white settlers, the European governors ruled autocratically.

In the early years of the New Imperialism, colonial administrations consisted of a governor and his staff, a few troops to keep order, and a small number of tax collectors and magistrates. Nowhere could colonialism operate without the cooperation of indigenous elites, because no colony was wealthy enough to pay the salaries of more than a handful of European officials. In most cases the colonial governors exercised power through traditional rulers willing to cooperate, as in the Princely States of India (see Chapter 24). In addition, colonial governments educated a few local youths for "modern" jobs as clerks, nurses, policemen, customs inspectors, and the like. Thus colonialism relied on two rival indigenous elites.

European and American women seldom took part in the early stages of colonial expansion. As conquest gave way to peaceful colonialism and as steamships and railroads made travel less difficult, colonial officials and settlers began bringing their wives to the colonies. By the 1880s the British Women's Emigration Association was recruiting single women to go out to the colonies to marry British settlers. As one of its founders, Ellen Joyce, explained, "The possibility of the settler marrying his own countrywoman is of imperial as well as family importance."

The arrival of white women in Asia and Africa led to increasing racial segregation. Sylvia Leith-Ross, wife of a colonial officer in Nigeria, explained: "When you are alone, among thousands of unknown, unpredictable people, dazed by unaccustomed sights and sounds, bemused by strange ways of life and thought, you need to remember who you are, where you come from, what your standards are." Many colonial wives found themselves in command of numerous servants and expected to follow the complex etiquette of colonial entertainment in support of their husbands' official positions. Occasionally they found opportunities to exercise personal initiatives, usually charitable work involving indigenous women and children. However well meaning, their efforts were always subordinate to the work of men.

THE SCRAMBLE FOR AFRICA

Until the 1870s African history was largely shaped by internal forces and local initiatives (see Chapter 24). Outside Algeria and southern Africa, only a handful of Europeans had ever visited the interior of Africa, and European countries possessed only small enclaves on the coasts. As late as 1879 Africans ruled more than 90 percent of the continent. Then, within a decade, Africa was invaded and divided among the European powers in a movement often referred to as the **"scramble" for Africa** (see Map 27.1). This invasion affected all regions of the continent. Let us look at the most significant cases, beginning with Egypt, the wealthiest and most populated part of the continent.

Egypt

Ironically, European involvement in Egypt resulted from Egypt's attempt to free itself from Ottoman Turkish rule. Throughout the mid-nineteenth century the khedives of Egypt had tried to modernize their armed forces; build canals, harbors, railroads, and other public works; and reorient agriculture toward export crops, especially cotton (see Chapters 22 and 24). Their interest in the Suez Canal was also part of this policy. Khedive Ismail even tried to make Egypt the center of an empire reaching south into Sudan and Ethiopia.

These ambitions cost vast sums of money, which the khedives borrowed from European creditors at high interest rates. By 1876 Egypt's foreign debt had risen to £100 million sterling, and the interest payments alone consumed one-third of its foreign export earnings. To avoid bankruptcy the Egyptian government sold its shares in the Suez Canal to Great Britain and accepted four foreign "commissioners of the debt" to oversee its finances. French and British bankers, still not satisfied, lobbied their governments to secure the loans by stronger measures. In 1878 the two governments obliged Ismail to appoint a Frenchman as minister of public works and a Briton as minister of finance. When high taxes caused hardship and popular discontent, the French and British persuaded the Ottoman sultan to depose Ismail. This foreign intervention provoked a military uprising under Egyptian army colonel Arabi Pasha, which threatened the Suez Canal.

Fearing for their investments, the British sent an army into Egypt in 1882. They intended to occupy Egypt for only a year or two. But theirs was a seaborne empire that depended on secure communications between Britain and India. So important was the Suez Canal to their maritime supremacy that they stayed for seventy years. During those years the British ruled Egypt "indirectly"—that is, they maintained the Egyptian government and the fiction of Egyptian sovereignty but retained real power in their own hands.

Eager to develop Egyptian agriculture, especially cotton production, the British brought in engineers and contractors to build the first dam across the Nile, at Aswan in upper Egypt. When completed in 1902, it was

Map 27.1 Africa in 1878 and 1914 In 1878 the European colonial presence was limited to a few coastal enclaves, plus portions of Algeria and South Africa. By 1914, Europeans had taken over all of Africa except Ethiopia and Liberia.

one of the largest dams in the world. It captured the annual Nile flood and released its waters throughout the year, allowing farmers to grow two, sometimes three, crops a year. This doubled the effective acreage compared with the basin system of irrigation practiced since the time of the pharaohs, in which the annual floodwaters of the Nile were retained by low dikes around the fields.

The economic development of Egypt by the British enriched a small elite of landowners and merchants, many of them foreigners. Egyptian peasants got little relief from the heavy taxes collected to pay for their country's crushing foreign debt and the expenses of the British army of occupation. Western ways that conflicted with the teachings of Islam—such as the drinking of alcohol and the relative freedom of women—offended Muslim religious leaders. Most Egyptians found British rule more onerous than that of the Ottomans. By the 1890s Egyptian politicians and intellectuals were demanding that the British leave, to no avail.

Western and Equatorial Africa

While the British were taking over Egypt, the French were planning to extend their empire into the interior of West Africa. Starting from the coast of Senegal, which had been in French hands for centuries, they hoped to build a railroad from the upper Senegal River to the upper Niger in order to open the interior to French merchants. This in turn led the French military to undertake the conquest of western Sudan.

Meanwhile, the actions of three individuals, rather than a government, brought about the occupation of the Congo Basin, an enormous forested region in the heart of equatorial Africa (see Map 27.1). In 1879 the American journalist **Henry Morton Stanley,** who had explored the area, persuaded **King Leopold II** of Belgium to invest his personal fortune in "opening up" equatorial Africa. With Leopold's money, Stanley returned to Africa from 1879 to 1884 to establish trading posts along the southern bank of the Congo River. At the same time, **Savorgnan de Brazza,** an Italian officer serving in the French army, obtained from an African ruler living on the opposite bank a treaty that placed the area under the "protection" of France.

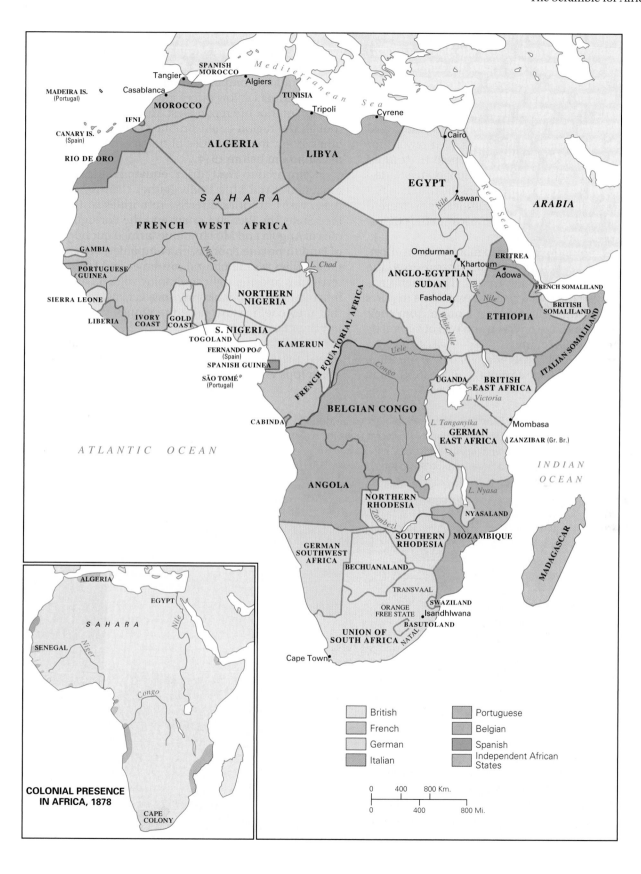

MADEIRA IS.
(Portugal)

SPANISH MOROCCO
Tangier
Casablanca
Algiers
TUNISIA
Tripoli
Cyrene

CANARY IS.
(Spain)

IFNI

MOROCCO

Mediterranean Sea

Cairo

RIO DE ORO

ALGERIA

LIBYA

EGYPT

Red Sea

Nile

Aswan

ARABIA

SAHARA

FRENCH   WEST   AFRICA

GAMBIA

PORTUGUESE
GUINEA

SIERRA LEONE

LIBERIA

IVORY
COAST

GOLD
COAST

Niger

L. Chad

NORTHERN
NIGERIA

S. NIGERIA

TOGOLAND

FERNANDO PO
(Spain)

SPANISH GUINEA

SÃO TOMÉ
(Portugal)

KAMERUN

FRENCH EQUATORIAL AFRICA

Uele

Congo

Omdurman

Khartoum

ANGLO-EGYPTIAN
SUDAN

Fashoda

White Nile

Blue Nile

ERITREA

Adowa

FRENCH SOMALILAND

BRITISH
SOMALILAND

ETHIOPIA

ITALIAN SOMALILAND

UGANDA

BRITISH
EAST
AFRICA

L. Victoria

ATLANTIC OCEAN

CABINDA

BELGIAN CONGO

ANGOLA

L. Tanganyika

GERMAN
EAST AFRICA

Mombasa

ZANZIBAR (Gr. Br.)

INDIAN
OCEAN

NORTHERN
RHODESIA

Zambezi

L. Nyasa

NYASALAND

GERMAN
SOUTHWEST
AFRICA

SOUTHERN
RHODESIA

MOZAMBIQUE

MADAGASCAR

BECHUANALAND

TRANSVAAL

ORANGE
FREE STATE

SWAZILAND

Isandhlwana

BASUTOLAND

NATAL

UNION OF
SOUTH AFRICA

Cape Town

**COLONIAL PRESENCE
IN AFRICA, 1878**

ALGERIA

EGYPT

SAHARA

Nile

SENEGAL

Niger

Congo

CAPE
COLONY

	British		Portuguese
	French		Belgian
	German		Spanish
	Italian		Independent African States

0   400   800 Km.

0   400   800 Mi.

These events sparked a flurry of diplomatic activity. German chancellor Bismarck called the **Berlin Conference** on Africa of 1884 and 1885. There the major powers agreed that henceforth "effective occupation" would replace the former trading relations between Africans and Europeans. This meant that every country with colonial ambitions had to send troops into Africa and participate in the division of the spoils. As a reward for triggering the "scramble" for Africa, Leopold II acquired a personal domain under the name "Congo Free State," while France and Portugal took most of the rest of equatorial Africa. In this manner, the European powers and King Leopold managed to divide Africa among themselves, at least on paper.

"Effective occupation" required many years of effort. In the interior of West Africa, Muslim rulers resisted the French invasion for up to thirty years. The French advance encouraged the Germans to stake claims to parts of the region and the British to move north from their coastal enclaves, until the entire region was occupied by Britain, France, and Germany.

Because West Africa had long had a flourishing trade, the new rulers took advantage of existing trade networks, taxing merchants and farmers, investing the profits in railroads and harbors, and paying dividends to European stockholders. In the Gold Coast (now Ghana) British trading companies bought the cocoa grown by African farmers at low prices and resold it for large profits. The interior of French West Africa lagged behind. Although the region could produce cotton, peanuts, and other crops, the difficulties of transportation limited its development before 1914.

Compared to West Africa, equatorial Africa had few inhabitants and little trade. Rather than try to govern these vast territories directly, authorities in the Congo Free State, the French Congo, and the Portuguese colonies of Angola and Mozambique farmed out huge pieces of land to private concession companies, offering them monopolies on the natural resources and trade of their territories and the right to employ soldiers and tax the inhabitants. The inhabitants, however, had no cash crops that they could sell to raise the money they needed to pay their taxes.

Freed from outside supervision, the companies forced the African inhabitants at gunpoint to produce cash crops and carry them, on their heads or backs, to

A Steamboat for the Congo River Soon after the Congo Basin was occupied by Europeans, the new colonial rulers realized they needed to improve transportation. Since access from the sea was blocked by rapids on the lower Congo River, steamboats had to be brought in sections, hauled from the coast by thousands of Congolese over very difficult terrain. This picture shows the pieces arriving at Stanley Pool, ready to be reassembled. (From H. M. Stanley, *The Congo*, vol. 2, London, 1885)

the nearest railroad or navigable river. The worst abuses took place in the Congo Free State, where a rubber boom lasting from 1895 to 1905 made it profitable for private companies to coerce Africans to collect latex from vines that grew in the forests. One Congolese refugee told the British consul Roger Casement who investigated the atrocities:

> We begged the white men to leave us alone, saying we could get no more rubber, but the white men and their soldiers said: "Go. You are only beasts yourselves, you are only *nyama* (meat)." We tried, always going further into the forest, and when we failed and our rubber was short, the soldiers came to our towns and killed us. Many were shot, some had their ears cut off; others were tied up with ropes around their necks and bodies and taken away.[4]

After 1906 the British press began publicizing the horrors. The public outcry that followed, coinciding with the end of the rubber boom, convinced the Belgian government to take over Leopold's private empire in 1908.

Southern Africa

The history of southern Africa between 1869 and 1914 differs from that of the rest of the continent in several important respects. One was that the land had long attracted settlers. African pastoralists and farmers had inhabited the region for centuries. **Afrikaners,** descendants of Dutch settlers on the Cape of Good Hope, moved inland throughout the nineteenth century; British prospectors and settlers arrived later in the century; and, finally, Indians were brought over by the British and stayed.

Southern Africa attracted European settlers because of its good pastures and farmland and its phenomenal deposits of diamonds, gold, and copper, as well as coal and iron ore. This was the new El Dorado that imperialists had dreamed of since the heyday of the Spanish Empire in Peru and Mexico in the sixteenth century.

The discovery of diamonds at Kimberley in 1868 lured thousands of European prospectors as well as Africans looking for work. It also attracted the interest of Great Britain, colonial ruler of the Cape Colony, which annexed the diamond area in 1871, thereby angering the Afrikaners. Once in the interior, the British defeated the Xhosa° people in 1877 and 1878. Then in 1879 they confronted the Zulu, militarily the most powerful of the African peoples in the region.

The Zulu, led by their king Cetshwayo°, resented their encirclement by Afrikaners and British. A growing sense of nationalism and their proud military tradition led them into a war with the British in 1879. At first they held their own, defeating the British at Isandhlwana°, but a few months later they were defeated. Cetshwayo was captured and sent into exile, and the Zulu lands were given to white ranchers. Yet throughout those bitter times, the Zulu's sense of nationhood remained strong.

Relations between the British and the Afrikaners, already tense as a result of British encroachment, took a turn for the worse when gold was discovered in the Afrikaner republic of Transvaal° in 1886. In the gold rush that ensued, the British soon outnumbered the Afrikaners.

Britain's invasion of southern Africa was driven in part by the ambition of **Cecil Rhodes** (1853–1902), who once declared that he would "annex the stars" if he could. Rhodes made his fortune in the Kimberley diamond fields, founding De Beers Consolidated, a company that has dominated the world's diamond trade ever since. He then turned to politics. He encouraged a concession company, the British South Africa Company, to push north into Central Africa, where he named two new colonies after himself: Southern Rhodesia (now Zimbabwe) and Northern Rhodesia (now Zambia). The Ndebele° and Shona peoples, who inhabited the region, resisted this invasion, but the machine guns of the British finally defeated them.

British attempts to annex the two Afrikaner republics, Transvaal and Orange Free State, and the inflow of English-speaking whites into the gold- and diamond-mining areas led to the South African War, which lasted from 1899 to 1902. At first the Afrikaners had the upper hand, for they were highly motivated, possessed modern rifles, and knew the land. In 1901, however, Great Britain brought in 450,000 troops and crushed the Afrikaner armies. Ironically, the Afrikaners' defeat in 1902 led to their ultimate victory. Wary of costly commitments overseas, the British government expected European settlers in Africa to manage their own affairs, as they were doing in Canada, Australia, and New Zealand. Thus, in 1910 the European settlers created the Union of South Africa, in which the Afrikaners eventually emerged as the ruling element.

Unlike Canada, Australia, and New Zealand, South Africa had a majority of indigenous inhabitants and substantial numbers of Indians and "Cape Coloureds" (people of mixed ancestry). Yet the Europeans were both numerous enough to demand self-rule and powerful enough to deny the vote and other civil rights to the

---

Xhosa (KOH-sah)   **Cetshwayo** (set-SHWAH-yo)

Isandhlwana (ee-sawn-dull-WAH-nuh)   **Transvaal** (trans-VAHL)
Ndebele (en-duh-BELL-ay)

majority. In 1913 the South African parliament passed the Natives Land Act, assigning Africans to reservations and forbidding them to own land elsewhere. This and other racial policies turned South Africa into a land of segregation, oppression, and bitter divisions.

Political and Social Consequences

At the time of the European invasion, Africa contained a wide variety of societies. Some parts of the continent had long-established kingdoms with aristocracies or commercial towns dominated by a merchant class. In other places agricultural peoples lived in villages without any outside government. Still elsewhere pastoral nomads were organized along military lines. In some remote areas people lived from hunting and gathering. Not surprisingly, these societies responded in very different ways to the European invasion.

Some peoples welcomed the invaders as allies against local enemies. Once colonial rule was established, they sought work in government service or in European firms and sent their children to mission schools. In exchange, they were often the first to receive benefits such as clinics and roads.

Others, especially peoples with a pastoral or a warrior tradition, fought tenaciously. Examples abound, from the Zulu and Ndebele of southern Africa to the pastoral Herero° people of Southwest Africa (now Namibia), who rose up against German invaders in 1904; in repressing their uprising, the Germans exterminated two-thirds of them. In the Sahel, a belt of grasslands south of the Sahara, charismatic leaders rose up in the name of a purified Islam, gathered a following of warriors, and led them on part-religious, part empire-building campaigns called *jihads*. These leaders included Samori Toure in western Sudan (now Mali), Rabih in the Chad basin, and the Mahdi° in eastern Sudan. All of them eventually came into conflict with European-led military expeditions and were defeated.

Some commercial states with long histories of contact with Europeans also fought back. The kingdom of **Asante°** in the Gold Coast rose up in 1874, 1896, and 1900 before it was finally overwhelmed. In the Niger Delta, the ancient city of Benin, rich with artistic treasures, resisted colonial control until 1897, when a British "punitive expedition" set it on fire and carted its works of art off to Europe.

One resistance movement succeeded, to the astonishment of Europeans and Africans alike. When **Menelik** became emperor of Ethiopia in 1889 (see Chapter 24), his country was threatened by Sudanese Muslims to the west and by France and Italy, which controlled the coast of the Red Sea to the east. For many years, Ethiopia had been purchasing weapons. By the Treaty of Wichelle (1889), Italy agreed to sell more weapons to Ethiopia. Six years later, when Italians attempted to establish a protectorate over Ethiopia, they found the Ethiopians armed with thousands of rifles and even a few machine guns and artillery pieces. Although Italy sent twenty thousand troops to attack Ethiopia, in 1896 they were defeated at Adowa° by a larger and better-trained Ethiopian army.

Most Africans neither joined nor fought the European invaders but tried to continue living as before. They found this increasingly difficult because colonial rule disrupted every traditional society. The presence of colonial officials meant that rights to land, commercial transactions, and legal disputes were handled very differently, and that traditional rulers lost all authority, except where Europeans used them as local administrators.

Changes in landholding were especially disruptive, for most Africans were farmers or herders for whom access to land was a necessity. In areas with a high population density, such as Egypt and West Africa, colonial rulers left peasants in place, encouraged them to grow cash crops, and collected taxes on the harvest. Elsewhere, the new rulers declared any land that was not farmed to be "waste" or "vacant" and gave it to private concession companies or to European planters and ranchers. In Kenya, Northern Rhodesia, and South Africa, Europeans found the land and climate to their liking, in contrast to other parts of Africa, where soldiers, officials, missionaries, or traders stayed only a few years. White settlers forced Africans to become squatters, sharecroppers, or ranch hands on land they had farmed for generations. In South Africa they forced many Africans off their lands and onto "reserves," much like the nomadic peoples of North America, Russia, and Australia (see Chapter 23).

Although the colonial rulers harbored designs on the land, they were even more interested in African labor. They did not want to pay wages high enough to attract workers voluntarily. Instead, they imposed various taxes, such as the hut tax and the head tax, which Africans had to pay regardless of their income. To find the money, Africans had little choice but to accept whatever work the Europeans offered. In this way Africans were recruited to work on plantations, railroads, and other modern enterprises. In the South African mines Africans were paid, on average, one-tenth as much as Europeans.

Herero (hair-AIR-oh)   **Mahdi** (MAH-dee)
Asante (uh-SAWN-tay)

Adowa (AH-do-ah)

Victorious Ethiopians Among the states of Africa, Ethiopia alone was able to defend itself against European imperialism. In the 1880s, hemmed in by Italian advances to its east and north and by British advances to its south and west, Ethiopia purchased modern weapons and trained its army to use them. Thus prepared, the Ethiopians defeated an Italian invasion at Adowa in 1896. These Ethiopian army officers wore their most elaborate finery to pose for a photograph after their victory. (National Archives)

Some Africans came to the cities and mining camps seeking a better life than they had on the land. Many migrated great distances and stayed away for years at a time. Most migrant workers were men who left their wives and children behind in villages and on reserves. In some cases the authorities did not allow them to bring their families and settle permanently in the towns. This caused great hardship for African women, who had to grow food for their families during the men's absences and care for sick and aged workers. Long separations between spouses also led to an increase in prostitution and to the spread of sexually transmitted diseases.

Some African women welcomed colonial rule, for it brought an end to fighting and slave raiding, but others were led into captivity (see Diversity and Dominance: Two Africans Recall the Arrival of the Europeans). A few succeeded in becoming wealthy traders or owners of livestock. On the whole, however, African women benefited less than men from the economic changes that colonialism introduced. In areas where the colonial rulers replaced communal property (traditional in most of Africa) with private property, property rights were assigned to the head of the household—that is, to the man. Almost all the jobs open to Africans, even those considered "women's work" in Europe, such as nursing and domestic service, were reserved for men.

Cultural Responses

More Africans came into contact with missionaries than with any other Europeans. Missionaries, both men and women, opened schools to teach reading, writing, and arithmetic to village children. Boys were taught crafts such as carpentry and blacksmithing, while girls learned domestic skills such as cooking, laundry, and child care.

Along with basic skills, the first generation of Africans educated in mission schools acquired Western ideas of justice and progress. Samuel Ajayi Crowther, a Yoruba rescued from slavery as a boy and educated in mission schools in Sierra Leone, went on to become an Anglican minister and, in 1864, the first African bishop. Crowther thought that Africa needed European assistance in achieving both spiritual and economic development:

> Africa has neither knowledge nor skill . . . to bring out her vast resources for her own improvement. . . . Therefore to claim Africa for the Africans alone, is to claim for her the right of a continued ignorance. . . . For it is certain, unless help [comes] from without, a nation can never rise above its present state.[5]

After the first generation, many of the teachers in mission schools were African, themselves the products of a mission education. They discovered that Christian ideals clashed with the reality of colonial exploitation. One convert wrote in 1911:

DIVERSITY AND DOMINANCE

TWO AFRICANS RECALL THE ARRIVAL OF THE EUROPEANS

We know a great deal about the arrival of the Europeans into the interior of Africa from the perspective of the conquerors, but very little about how the events were experienced by Africans. Here are two accounts by African women, one from northern Nigeria whose land was occupied by the British, the other from the Congo Free State, a colony of King Leopold II of Belgium. They show not only how Africans experienced European colonial dominance, but also the great diversity of experiences of Africans.

BABA OF KARO, A NIGERIAN WOMAN, REMEMBERS HER CHILDHOOD

When I was a maiden the Europeans first arrived. Ever since we were quite small the *malams* had been saying that the Europeans would come with a thing called a train, they would come with a thing called a motor-car, in them you would go and come back in a trice. They would stop wars, they would repair the world, they would stop oppression and lawlessness, we should live at peace with them. We used to go and sit quietly and listen to the prophecies. They would come, fine handsome people, they would not kill anyone, they would not oppress anyone, they would bring all their strange things. . . .

I remember when a European came to Karo on a horse, and some of his foot soldiers went into the town. Everyone came out to look at them, but in Zerewa they didn't see the European. Everyone at Karo ran away—"There's a European, there's a European!" He came from Zaria with a few black men, two on horses and four on foot. We were inside the town. Later on we heard that they were there in Zaria in crowds, clearing spaces and building houses. One of my younger "sisters" was at Karo, she was pregnant, and when she saw the European she ran away and shut the door.

At that time Yusufu was the king of Kano. He did not like the Europeans, he did not wish them, he would not sign their treaty. Then he say that perforce he would have to agree, so he did. We Habe wanted them to come, it was the Fulani who did not like it. When the Europeans came the Habe saw that if you worked for them they paid you for it, they didn't say, like the Fulani, "Commoner, give me this! Commoner, bring

me that!" Yes, the Habe wanted them; they saw no harm in them. From Zaria they came to Rogo, they were building their big road to Kano City. They called out the people and said they were to come and make the road, if there were trees in the way they cut them down. The Europeans paid them with goods, they collected the villagers together and each man brought his large hoe. Money was not much use to them, so the Europeans paid them with food and other things.

The Europeans said that there were to be no more slaves; if someone said "Slave!" you could complain to the *alkali* who would punish the master who said it, the judge said, "That is what the Europeans have decreed." The first order said that any slave, if he was younger than you, was your younger brother, if he was older than you was your elder brother—they were all brothers of their master's family. No one used the word "slave" any more. When slavery was stopped, nothing much happened at our *rinji* except that some slaves whom we had bought in the market ran away. Our own father went to his farm and worked, he and his son took up their large hoes; they loaned out their spare farms. Tsoho our father and Kadiri my brother with whom I live now and Babambo worked, they farmed guineacorn and millet and groundnuts and everything; before this they had supervised the slaves' work—now they did their own. When the midday food was ready, the women of the compound would give us children the food, one of us drew water, and off we went to the farm to take the men their food at the foot of a tree; I was about eight or nine at that time, I think. . . .

In the old days if the chief liked the look of your daughter he would take her and put her in his house; you could do nothing about it. Now they don't do that.

ILANGA, A CONGOLESE WOMAN, RECOUNTS HER CAPTURE BY AGENTS OF THE CONGO FREE STATE

Our village is called Waniendo, after our chief Niendo. . . . It is a large village near a small stream, and surrounded by large fields of *mohago* (cassava) and *muhindu* (maize) and other foods, for we all worked hard at our plantations, and always had plenty to eat. The men always worked in the fields clearing the ground, or went hunting, . . . We never had war in our country, and the men had not many arms except knives; but our chief Niendo had a gun, which he had bought long ago from another chief for forty-three beads, but he had no powder or caps, and only carried it when he went on a journey.

... we were all busy in the fields hoeing our plantations, for it was the rainy season, and the weeds sprang quickly up, when a runner came to the village saying that a large band of men was coming, that they all wore red caps and blue cloth, and carried guns and long knives, and that many white men were with them, the chief of whom was *Kibalanga* (Michaux). Niendo at once called all the chief men to his house, while the drums were beaten to summon the people to the village. A long consultation was held, and finally we were all told to go quietly to the fields and bring in ground-nuts, plantains, and cassava for the warriors who were coming, and goats and fowl for the white men. The women all went with baskets and filled them, and put them in the road, which was blocked up, so many were there. Niendo then commanded everyone to go and sit quietly in the houses until he gave other orders. This we did, everyone remaining quietly seated while Niendo went up the road with the head men to meet the white chief. We did not know what to think, for most of us feared that so many armed men coming boded evil; but Niendo thought that, by giving presents of much food, he would induce the strangers to pass on without harming us. And so it proved, for the soldiers took the baskets, and were then ordered by the white men to move off through the village. Many of the soldiers looked into the houses and shouted at us words we did not understand. We were glad when they were all gone, for we were much in fear of the white men and the strange warriors, who are known to all the people as being great fighters, bringing war wherever they go. . . .

When the white men and their warriors had gone, we went again to our work, and were hoping that they would not return; but this they did in a very short time. As before, we brought in great heaps of food; but this time *Kibalanga* did not move away directly, but camped near our village, and his soldiers came and stole all our fowl and goats and tore up our cassava; but we did not mind as long as they did not harm us. The next morning it was reported that the white men were going away; but soon after the sun rose over the hill, a large band of soldiers came into the village, and we all went into the houses and sat down. We were not long seated when the soldiers came rushing in shouting, and threatening Niendo with their guns. They rushed into the houses and dragged the people out. Three or four came to our house and caught hold of me, also my husband Oleka and my sister Katinga. We were dragged into the road, and were tied together with cords about our necks, so that we could not escape. We were all crying, for now we knew that we were to be taken away to be slaves. The soldiers beat us with the iron sticks from their guns, and compelled us to march to the camp of *Kibalanga*, who ordered the women to be tied up

separately, ten to each cord, and the men in the same way. When we were all collected—and there were many from other villages whom we now saw, and many from Waniendo—the soldiers brought baskets of food for us to carry, in some of which was smoked human flesh (*niama na nitu*).

We then set off marching very quickly. My sister Katinga had her baby in her arms, and was not compelled to carry a basket; but my husband Oleka was made to carry a goat. We marched until the afternoon, when we camped near a stream, where we were glad to drink, for we were much athirst. We had nothing to eat, for the soldiers would give us nothing, so we lay upon the ground, and at night went to sleep. The next day we continued the march, and when we camped at noon were given some maize and plantains, which were gathered near a village from which the people had run away. So it continued each day until the fifth day, when the soldiers took my sister's baby and threw it in the grass, leaving it to die, and made her carry some cooking pots which they found in the deserted village. On the sixth day we became very weak from lack of food and from constant marching and sleeping in the damp grass, and my husband, who marched behind us with the goat, could not stand up longer, and so he sat down beside the path and refused to walk more. The soldiers beat him, but still he refused to move. Then one of them struck him on the head with the end of his gun, and he fell upon the ground. One of the soldiers caught the goat, while two or three others stuck the long knives they put on the ends of their guns into my husband. I saw the blood spurt out, and then saw him no more, for we passed over the brow of a hill and he was out of sight. Many of the young men were killed the same way, and many babies thrown into the grass to die. A few escaped; but we were so well guarded that it was almost impossible.

After marching ten days we came to the great water (Lualaba) and were taken in canoes across to the white men's town at Nyangwe. Here we stayed for six or seven days, and were then put in canoes and sent down the river; . . . but on the way we could get nothing to eat, and were glad to rest here, where there are good houses and plenty of food; and we hope we will not be sent away.

QUESTIONS FOR ANALYSIS

1. How do Baba and Ilanga recall their existence before the Europeans came?

2. What did they expect when they first heard of the arrival of Europeans? Instead, what happened to them, their relatives, and their towns?

3. How do you explain the difference between these two accounts?

Source: From M. F. Smith, ed., *Baba of Karo: A Woman of the Muslim Hausa* (New York: Philosophical Library, 1955), 66–68. Edgar Canisius, *A Campaign Amongst Cannibals* (London: R. A. Everett & Co., 1903), 250–256. Used by permission of the Philosophical Library.

There is too much failure among all Europeans in Nyasaland. The three combined bodies—Missionaries, Government and Companies or gainers of money—do form the same rule to look upon the native with mockery eyes. . . . If we had enough power to communicate ourselves to Europe, we would advise them not to call themselves Christendom, but Europeandom. Therefore the life of the three combined bodies is altogether too cheaty, too thefty, too mockery. Instead of "Give," they say "Take away from." There is too much breakage of God's pure law.[6]

Christian missionaries from Europe and America were not the only ones to bring religious change to Africa. In southern and Central Africa indigenous preachers adapted Christianity to African values and customs and founded new denominations known as "Ethiopian" churches.

Christianity proved successful in converting followers of traditional religions but made no inroads among Muslims. Instead, Islam, long predominant in northern and eastern Africa, spread southward as Muslim teachers established Quranic schools in the villages and founded Muslim brotherhoods. European colonialism unwittingly helped the diffusion of Islam. By building cities and increasing trade, colonial rule permitted Muslims to settle in new areas. As Islam—a universal religion without the taint of colonialism—became increasingly relevant to Africans, the number of Muslims in sub-Saharan Africa probably doubled between 1869 and 1914.

ASIA AND WESTERN DOMINANCE

From 1869 to 1914 the pressure of the industrial powers was felt throughout Asia, the East Indies, and the Pacific islands. As trade with these regions grew in the late nineteenth century, so did their attractiveness to imperialists eager for economic benefits and national prestige.

Europeans had traded along the coasts of Asia and the East Indies since the early sixteenth century. By 1869 Britain already controlled most of India and Burma; Spain occupied the Philippines; and the Netherlands held large parts of the East Indies (now Indonesia). Between 1862 and 1895 France conquered Indochina (now Vietnam, Kampuchea, and Laos). The existence of these Asian colonial possessions had inspired the building of the Suez Canal.

We have already seen the special cases of British imperialism in India (Chapter 24) and of Japanese imperialism in China and Korea (Chapter 26). Here let us look at the impact of the New Imperialism on Central and Southeast Asia, Indonesia, the Philippines, and Hawaii (see Map 27.2)

Central Asia

For over seven centuries Russians had been at the mercy of the nomads of the Eurasian steppe extending from the Black Sea to Manchuria. When the nomadic tribesmen were united, as they were under the Mongol ruler Genghis Khan (r. 1206–1227), they could defeat the Russians; when they were not, the Russians moved into the steppe. This age-old ebb and flow ended when Russia acquired modern rifles and artillery.

Between 1865 and 1876 Russian forces advanced into Central Asia. Nomads like the Kazakhs, who lived east of the Caspian Sea, fought bravely but in vain. The fertile agricultural land of Kazakhstan attracted 200,000 Russian settlers. Although the governments of Tsar Alexander II (r. 1855–1881) and Tsar Alexander III (r. 1881–1894) claimed not to interfere in indigenous customs, they declared communally owned grazing lands "waste" or "vacant" and turned them over to farmers from Russia. By the end of the nineteenth century the nomads were fenced out and reduced to starvation. Echoing the beliefs of other European imperialists, an eminent Russian jurist declared: "International rights cannot be taken into account when dealing with semibarbarous peoples."

South of the Kazakh steppe land were deserts dotted with oases where the fabled cities of Tashkent, Bukhara, and Samarkand served the caravan trade between China and the Middle East. For centuries the peoples of the region had lived under the protection of the Mongols and later the Qing Empire. But by the 1860s and 1870s the Qing Empire was losing control over Central Asia, so it was fairly easy for Russian expeditions to conquer the indigenous peoples. Russia thereby acquired land suitable for cotton, along with a large and growing Muslim population.

Russian rule brought few benefits to the peoples of the Central Asian oases and few real changes. The Russians abolished slavery, built railroads to link the region with Europe, and planted hundreds of thousands of acres of cotton. Unlike the British in India, however, they did not attempt to change the customs, languages, or religious beliefs of their subjects.

Southeast Asia and Indonesia

The peoples of the Southeast Asian peninsula and the Indonesian archipelago had been

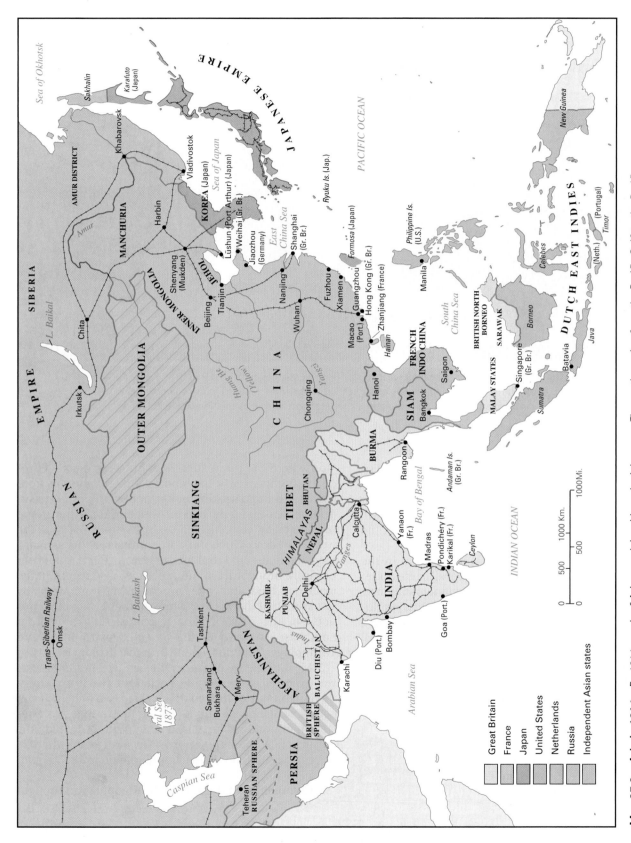

Map 27.2   Asia in 1914   By 1914, much of Asia was claimed by colonial powers. The southern rim, from the Pacific Gulf to the Pacific, was occupied by Great Britain, France, the Netherlands, and the United States. Central Asia had been incorporated into the Russian Empire. Japan, now industrialized, had joined the Western imperialist powers in expanding its territory and influence at the expense of China.

Legend:
- Great Britain
- France
- Japan
- United States
- Netherlands
- Russia
- Independent Asian states

Lim Nee Soon's Plantation   In British Malaya, pineapples and rubber trees were often cultivated together, because pineapples could be grown between the trees during the five or six years it took for the saplings to grow large enough to be tapped. Not all plantation owners were British. In this picture, Lim Nee Soon, known as the "Pineapple King," stands next to a truck that is taking pineapples to his canning factory.   (National Archives of Singapore)

in contact with outsiders—Chinese, Indians, Arabs, Europeans—for centuries. Java and the smaller islands—the fabled Spice Islands (the Moluccas)—had long been subject to Portuguese and later to Dutch domination. Until the mid-nineteenth century, however, most of the region was made up of independent kingdoms.

As in Africa, there is considerable variation in the history of different parts of the region, yet all came under intense imperialist pressure during the nineteenth century. Burma (now Myanmar), nearest India, was gradually taken over by the British in the course of the century, until the last piece was annexed in 1885. Indochina fell under French control piece by piece until it was finally subdued in 1895. Similarly, Malaya (now Malaysia) came under British rule in stages during the 1870s and 1880s. By the early 1900s the Dutch had subdued northern Sumatra, the last part of the Dutch East Indies to be conquered. Only Siam (now Thailand) remained independent, although it lost several border provinces.

Despite their varied political histories, all these regions had features in common. They all had fertile soil, constant warmth, and heavy rains. Furthermore, the peoples of the region had a long tradition of intensive gardening, irrigation, and terracing. In parts of the re-

gion where the population was not very dense, Europeans found it easy to import landless laborers from China and India seeking better opportunities overseas. Another reason for the region's wealth was the transfer of commercially valuable plants from other parts of the world. Tobacco, cinchona° (an antimalarial drug), manioc (an edible root crop), maize (corn), and natural rubber were brought from the Americas; sugar from India; tea from China; and coffee and oil palms from Africa. By 1914 much of the world's supply of these valuable products—in the case of rubber, almost all—came from Southeast Asia and Indonesia (see Environment and Technology: Imperialism and Tropical Ecology).

Most of the wealth of Southeast Asia and Indonesia was exported to Europe and North America. In exchange, the inhabitants of the region received two benefits from colonial rule: peace and a reliable food supply. As a result, their numbers increased at an unprecedented rate. For instance, the population of Java (an island the size of Pennsylvania) doubled from 16 million in 1870 to over 30 million in 1914.

Colonialism and the growth of population brought

cinchona (sin-CHO-nah)

many social changes. The more numerous agricultural and commercial peoples gradually moved into mountainous and forested areas, displacing the earlier inhabitants who practiced hunting and gathering or shifting agriculture. The migrations of the Javanese to Borneo and Sumatra are but one example. Immigrants from China and India (see Chapter 24) changed the ethnic composition and culture of every country in the region. Thus the population of the Malay Peninsula became one-third Malay, one-third Chinese, and one-third Indian.

As in Africa, European missionaries attempted to spread Christianity under the colonial umbrella. Islam, however, was much more successful in gaining new converts, for it had been established in the region for centuries and people did not consider it a religion imposed on them by foreigners.

Education and European ideas had an impact on the political perceptions of the peoples of Southeast Asia and Indonesia. Just as important was their awareness of events in neighboring Asian countries: India, where a nationalist movement arose in the 1880s; China, where modernizers were undermining the authority of the Qing; and especially Japan, whose rapid industrialization culminated in its brilliant victory over Russia in the Russo-Japanese War (1904–1905; see Chapter 26). The spirit of a rising generation was expressed by a young Vietnamese writing soon after the Russo-Japanese War:

> I, . . . an obscure student, having had occasion to study new books and new doctrines, have discovered in a recent history of Japan how they have been able to conquer the impotent Europeans. This is the reason why we have formed an organization. . . . We have selected from young Annamites [Vietnamese] the most energetic, with great capacities for courage, and are sending them to Japan for study. . . . Several years have passed without the French being aware of the movement. . . . Our only aim is to prepare the population for the future.[7]

Hawaii and the Philippines, 1878–1902

By the 1890s the United States had a fast-growing population and industries that produced more manufactured goods than they could sell at home. Merchants and bankers began to look for export markets. The political mood was also expansionist, and many echoed the feelings of the naval strategist Alfred T. Mahan°: "Whether they will or no, Americans must now begin to look outward. The growing production of the country requires it."

Mahan (mah-HAHN)

Some Americans had been looking outward for quite some time, especially across the Pacific to China and Japan. In 1878 the United States obtained the harbor of Pago Pago in Samoa as a coaling and naval station, and in 1887 it secured the use of Pearl Harbor in Hawaii for the same purpose. Six years later American settlers in Hawaii deposed Queen Liliuokalani (1838–1917) and offered the Hawaiian Islands to the United States. At the time President Grover Cleveland (1893–1897) was opposed to annexation, and the settlers had to content themselves with an informal protectorate. By 1898, however, the United States under President William McKinley (1897–1901) had become openly imperialistic, and it annexed Hawaii as a steppingstone to Asia. As the United States became ever more involved in Asian affairs, Hawaii's strategic location brought an inflow of U.S. military personnel, and its fertile land caused planters to import farm laborers from Japan, China, and the Philippines. These immigrants soon outnumbered the native Hawaiians.

While large parts of Asia were falling under colonial domination, the people of the Philippines were chafing under their Spanish rulers. The movement for independence began among young Filipinos studying in Europe. José Rizal, a young doctor working in Spain, was arrested and executed in 1896 for writing patriotic and anticlerical novels. Thereafter, the center of resistance shifted to the Philippines, where **Emilio Aguinaldo,** leader of a secret society, rose in revolt and proclaimed a republic in 1898. The revolutionaries had a good chance of winning independence, for Spain had its hands full with a revolution in Cuba (see below).

Unfortunately for Aguinaldo and his followers, the United States went to war against Spain in April 1898 and quickly overcame Spanish forces in the Philippines and Cuba. President McKinley had not originally intended to acquire the Philippines, but after the Spanish defeat, he realized that a weakened Spain might lose the islands to another imperialist power. Japan, having recently defeated China in the Sino-Japanese War (1894–1895) and annexed Taiwan (see Chapter 26), was eager to expand its empire. So was Germany, which had taken over parts of New Guinea and Samoa and several Pacific archipelagoes during the 1880s. To forestall them, McKinley purchased the Philippines from Spain for $20 million.

The Filipinos were not eager to trade one master for another. For a while, Aguinaldo cooperated with the Americans in the hope of achieving full independence. When his plan was rejected, he rose up again in 1899 and proclaimed the independence of his country. In spite of protests by anti-imperialists in the United States, the U.S. government decided that its global interests outweighed the interests of the Filipino people. In rebel areas, a U.S.

Imperialism and Tropical Ecology

Like all conquerors before them, the European imperialists of the nineteenth century exacted taxes and rents from the peoples they conquered. But they also sent botanists and agricultural experts to their tropical colonies to increase the production of commercial crops, radically changing the landscapes.

The most dramatic effects were brought about by the deliberate introduction of new crops—an acceleration of the Columbian Exchange that had begun in the fifteenth century. In the early nineteenth century tea was transferred from China to India and Ceylon. In the 1850s British and Dutch botanists smuggled seeds of the cinchona tree from the Andes in South America to India and Java. They had to operate in secret because the South American republics, knowing the value of this crop, prohibited the export of seeds. With the seeds, the British and Dutch established cinchona plantations in Ceylon and Java, respectively, to produce quinine, which was essential as an antimalarial drug and a flavoring for tonic water. Similarly, in the 1870s British agents stole seeds of rubber trees from the Amazon rainforest and transferred them to Malaya and Sumatra.

Before these transfers, vast forests covered the highlands of India, Southeast Asia, and Indonesia, precisely the lands where the new plants grew best. So European planters had the forests cut down and replaced with thousands of acres of commercially profitable trees and bushes, all lined up in perfect rows and tended by thousands of indigenous laborers to satisfy the demands of customers in faraway lands. The crops that poured forth from the transformed environments brought great wealth to the European planters and the imperial powers. In 1909 the British botanist John Willis justified the transformation in these terms:

> Whether planting in the tropics will always continue to be under European management is another question, but the northern powers will not permit that the rich and as yet comparatively undeveloped countries of the tropics should be entirely wasted by being devoted merely to the supply of the food and clothing wants of their own people, when they can also supply the wants of the colder zones in so many indispensable products.

This quotation raises important questions about trade versus self-sufficiency. If a region's economy supplies the food and clothing wants of its own people, is its output "entirely wasted"? What is the advantage of trading the prod-

Branch of a Cinchona Tree The bark of the cinchona tree was the source of quinine, the only antimalarial drug known before the 1940s. Quinine made it much safer for Europeans to live in the tropics. (From Bentley & Trimen's Medicinal Plants. Hunt Institute for Botanical Documentation, Carnegie Mellon University)

CINCHONA OFFICINALIS, *Linn.*

ucts of one region (such as the tropics) for those of another (such as the colder zones)? Is this trade an obligation? Should one part of the world (such as the "northern powers") let another refuse to develop and sell its "indispensable products"? Can you think of a case where a powerful country forced a weaker one to trade?

Source: The quotation is from John Christopher Willis, *Agriculture in the Tropics: An Elementary Treatise* (Cambridge: Cambridge University Press, 1909), 38–39.

Emilio Aguinaldo   In 1896, a revolt led by Emilio Aguinaldo attempted to expel Spaniards from the Philippines. When the United States purchased the Philippines from Spain two years later, the Filipino people were not consulted. Aguinaldo continued his campaign, this time against the American occupation forces, until his capture in 1901. In this picture, he appears on horseback, surrounded by some of his troops.   (Corbis)

army of occupation tortured prisoners, burned villages and crops, and forced the inhabitants into "reconcentration camps." Many American soldiers tended to look on Filipinos with the same racial contempt with which Europeans viewed their colonial subjects. By the end of the insurrection in 1902, the war had cost the lives of 5,000 Americans and 200,000 Filipinos.

After the insurrection ended, the United States attempted to soften its rule with public works and economic development projects. New buildings went up in the city of Manila; roads, harbors, and railroads were built; and the Philippine economy was tied ever more closely to that of the United States. In 1907 Filipinos were allowed to elect representatives to a legislative assembly, but ultimate authority remained in the hands of a governor appointed by the president of the United States. In 1916 the Philippines were the first U.S. colony to be promised independence, a promise fulfilled thirty years later.

IMPERIALISM IN LATIN AMERICA

Nations in the Americas followed two divergent paths (see Chapter 23). In Canada and the United States manufacturing industries, powerful corporations, and wealthy financial institutions arose. Latin America and the Caribbean exported raw materials and foodstuffs and imported manufactured goods. The poverty of their people, the preferences of their elites, and the pressures of the world economy made them increasingly dependent on the industrialized countries. Their political systems saved them from outright annexation by the colonial empires. But their natural resources made them attractive targets for manipulation by the industrial powers, including the United States, in a form of economic dependence called **free-trade imperialism.**

In the Western Hemisphere, therefore, the New Imperialism manifested itself not by a "scramble" for territories but in two other ways. In the larger republics of South America, the pressure was mostly financial and economic. In Central America and the Caribbean, it also included military intervention by the United States.

Railroads and the Imperialism of Free Trade

Latin America's economic potential was huge, for the region could produce many agricultural and mineral products in demand in the industrial countries. What was needed was a means of opening the interior to development. Railroads seemed the perfect answer.

Foreign merchants and bankers as well as Latin American landowners and politicians embraced the new technology. Starting in the 1870s almost every country in Latin America acquired railroads, usually connecting mines or agricultural regions with the nearest port rather than linking up the different parts of the interior. Since Latin America did not have any steel or mechanical industries, all the equipment and building material came from Britain or the United States. So did the money to build the networks, the engineers who designed and maintained them, and the managers who ran them.

Argentina, a land of rich soil that produced wheat, beef, and hides, gained the longest and best-developed rail network south of the United States. By 1914, 86 percent of the railroads in Argentina were owned by British

firms; 40 percent of the employees were British; and the official language of the railroads was English, not Spanish. The same was true of mining and industrial enterprises and public utilities throughout Latin America.

In many ways, the situation resembled those of India and Ireland, which also obtained rail networks in exchange for raw materials and agricultural products. The Argentine nationalist Juan Justo saw the parallel:

> English capital has done what English armies could not do. Today our country is tributary to England . . . the gold that the English capitalists take out of Argentina or carry off in the form of products does us no more good than the Irish get from the revenues that the English lords take out of Ireland.[8]

The difference was that the Indians and Irish had little say in the matter because they were under British

Railroads Penetrate South America   The late nineteenth century saw the construction of several railroad networks in South America, often through rugged and dangerous terrain. This photograph shows the opening of a bridge on the Transandine Railroad in Peru. Flags were raised in honor of American construction and British ownership of the railroad.   (Tony Morrison/South American Pictures)

rule. But in Latin America the political elites encouraged foreign companies with generous concessions as the most rapid way to modernize their countries and enrich the property owners. In countries where the majority of the poor were Indians (as in Mexico and Peru) or of African origin (as in Brazil), they were neither consulted nor allowed to benefit from the railroad boom.

American Expansionism and the Spanish-American War, 1898

After 1865 Europeans used their financial power to penetrate Latin America. But they avoided territorial acquisitions for four reasons: (1) they were overextended in Africa and Asia; (2) there was no need, because the Latin American governments provided the political backing for the economic arrangements; (3) the Latin Americans had shown themselves capable of resisting invasions, most recently when Mexico fought off the French in the 1860s (see Chapter 23); and (4) the United States, itself a former colony, claimed to defend the entire Western Hemisphere against all outside intervention. This claim, made in the Monroe Doctrine (1823), did not prevent the United States itself from intervening in Latin American affairs.

The United States had long had interests in Cuba, the closest and richest of the Caribbean islands and a Spanish colony. American businesses had invested great sums of money in Cuba's sugar and tobacco industries, and tens of thousands of Cubans had migrated to the United States. In 1895 the Cuban nationalist José Martí started a revolution against Spanish rule. American newspapers thrilled readers with lurid stories of Spanish atrocities; businessmen worried about their investments; and politicians demanded that the U.S. government help liberate Cuba.

On February 15, 1898, the U.S. battleship *Maine* accidentally blew up in Havana harbor, killing 266 American sailors. The U.S. government immediately blamed Spain and issued an ultimatum that the Spanish evacuate Cuba. Spain agreed to the ultimatum, but the American press and Congress were eager for war, and President McKinley did not restrain them.

The Spanish-American War was over quickly. On May 1, 1898, U.S. warships destroyed the Spanish fleet at Manila in the Philippines. Two months later the United States Navy sank the Spanish Atlantic fleet off Santiago, Cuba. By mid-August Spain was suing for peace. U.S. Secretary of State John Hay called it "a splendid little war." The United States purchased the Philippines from Spain but took over Puerto Rico and Guam as war booty.

The two islands remain American possessions to this day. Cuba became an independent republic, subject, however, to intense interference by the United States.

American Intervention in the Caribbean and Central America, 1901–1914

The nations of the Caribbean and Central America were small and poor, and their governments were corrupt, unstable, and often bankrupt. They seemed to offer an open invitation to foreign interference. A government would borrow money to pay for railroads, harbors, electric power, and other symbols of modernity. When it could not repay the loan, the lending banks in Europe or the United States would ask for assistance from their home governments, which sometimes threatened to intervene. To ward off European intervention, the United States sent in the marines on more than one occasion.

Presidents Theodore Roosevelt (1901–1909), William Taft (1909–1913), and Woodrow Wilson (1913–1921) felt impelled to intervene in the region, though they differed sharply on the proper policy the United States should follow toward the small nations to the south. Roosevelt encouraged regimes friendly to the United States, like Porfirian Mexico; Taft sought to influence them through loans from American banks; and the moralist Wilson tried to impose clean governments through military means.

Having "liberated" Cuba from Spain, the United States forced the Cuban government to accept the Platt Amendment in 1901. The amendment gave the United States the "right to intervene" to maintain order on the island. The United States used this excuse to occupy Cuba militarily from 1906 to 1909, in 1912, and again from 1917 to 1922. In all but name Cuba became an American protectorate. U.S. troops also occupied the Dominican Republic from 1904 to 1907 and again in 1916, Nicaragua and Honduras in 1912, and Haiti in 1915. They brought sanitation and material progress but no political improvements.

The United States was especially forceful in Panama, which was a province of Colombia. Here the issue was not corruption or debts but a more vital interest: the construction of a canal across the isthmus of Panama to speed shipping between the east and west coasts of the United States. In 1878 the Frenchman Ferdinand de Lesseps, builder of the Suez Canal, had obtained a concession from Colombia to construct a canal across the isthmus, which lay in Colombian territory. Financial scandals and yellow fever, however, doomed his project.

When the United States acquired Hawaii and the Philippines, it recognized the strategic value of a canal that would allow warships to move quickly between the Atlantic and Pacific Oceans. The main obstacle was Colombia, whose senate refused to give the United States a piece of its territory. In 1903 the U.S. government supported a Panamanian rebellion against Colombia and quickly recognized the independence of Panama. In exchange, it obtained the right to build a canal and to occupy a zone 5 miles (8 kilometers) wide on either side of it. Work began in 1904, and the **Panama Canal** opened on August 15, 1914.

THE WORLD ECONOMY AND THE GLOBAL ENVIRONMENT

The New Imperialists were not traditional conquerors or empire builders like the Spanish conquistadors. Although their conquests were much larger (see Map 27.3), their aim was not only to extend their power over new territories and peoples but also to control both the natural world and indigenous societies and put them to work more efficiently than had ever been done before. Both their goals and their methods were industrial. A railroad, for example, was an act of faith as well as a means of transportation. They expressed their belief in progress and their good intentions in the clichés of the time: "the conquest of nature," "the annihilation of time and space," "the taming of the wilderness," and "our civilizing mission."

Expansion of the World Economy

For centuries Europe had been a ready market for spices, sugar, silk, and other exotic or tropical products. The Industrial Revolution vastly expanded this demand. Imports of foods and stimulants such as tea, coffee, and cocoa increased substantially during the nineteenth century. The trade in industrial raw materials grew even faster. Some were the products of agriculture, such as cotton, jute for bags, and palm oil for soap and lubricants. Others were minerals such as diamonds, gold, and copper. There also were wild forest products that only later came to be cultivated: timber for buildings and railroad ties, cinchona bark, rubber for rainwear and tires, and gutta-percha° to insulate electric cables.

The growing needs of the industrial world could not be met by the traditional methods of production and transportation of the nonindustrial world. When the U.S. Civil War interrupted the export of cotton to England in the 1860s, the British turned to India. But they found that Indian cotton was ruined by exposure to rain and dust during the long trip on open carts from the interior of the country to the harbors. To prevent the expansion of their industry from being stifled by the technological backwardness of their newly conquered territories, the imperialists made every effort to bring those territories into the mainstream of the world market.

One great change was in transportation. The Suez and Panama Canals cut travel time and lowered freight costs dramatically. Steamships became more numerous, and as their size increased, new, deeper harbors were needed. The Europeans also built railroads throughout the world; India alone had 37,000 miles (nearly 60,000 kilometers) of track by 1915, almost as much as Germany or Russia. Railroads reached into the interior of Latin America, Canada, China, and Australia. In 1903 the Russians completed the Trans-Siberian Railway from Moscow to Vladivostok on the Pacific. Visionaries even made plans for railroads from Europe to India and from Egypt to South Africa.

Transformation of the Global Environment

The economic changes brought by Europeans and Americans also altered environments around the world. The British, whose craving for tea could not be satisfied with the limited exports available from China, introduced tea into the warm, rainy hill country of Ceylon and northeastern India. In those areas and in Java thousands of square miles of tropical rain forests were felled to make way for tea plantations.

Economic botany and agricultural science were applied to every promising plant species. European botanists had long collected and classified exotic plants from around the world. In the nineteenth century they founded botanical gardens in Java, India, Mauritius°, Ceylon, Jamaica, and other tropical colonies. These gardens not only collected local plants but also exchanged plants with other gardens. They were especially active in systematically transferring commercially valuable plant species from one tropical region to another. Cinchona, tobacco, sugar, and other crops were introduced, improved, and vastly expanded in the colonies of Southeast Asia and Indonesia (see Environment and Technology: Imperialism and Tropical Ecology). Cocoa and coffee growing spread over large areas of Brazil and Africa; oil-

---

gutta-percha (gut-tah-PER-cha)

Mauritius (maw-REE-shuss)

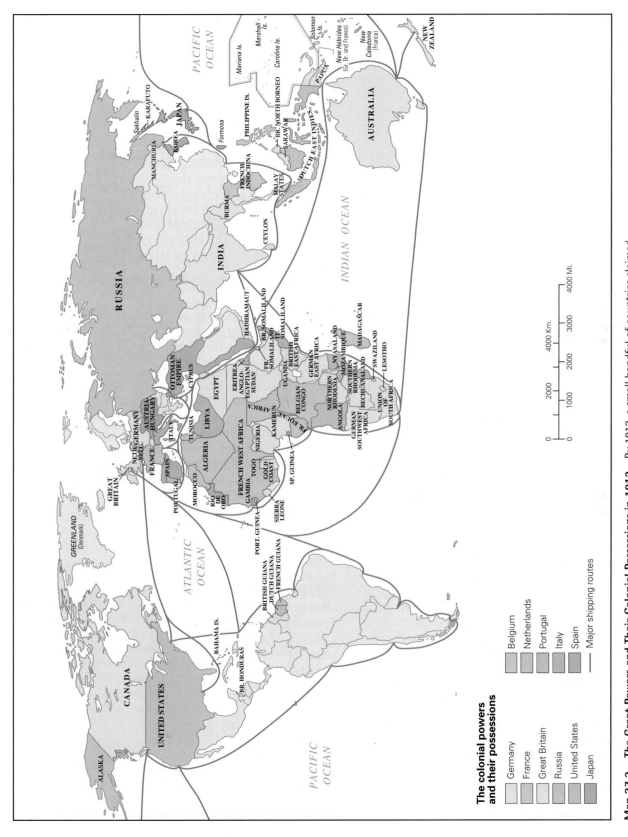

Map 27.3   The Great Powers and Their Colonial Possessions in 1913   By 1913, a small handful of countries claimed sovereignty over more than half the land area of the earth. Global power was closely connected with industries and a merchant marine, rather than with a large territory. This explains why Great Britain, the smallest of the great powers, possessed the largest empire.

The colonial powers and their possessions

- Germany
- France
- Great Britain
- Russia
- United States
- Japan
- Belgium
- Netherlands
- Portugal
- Italy
- Spain
- —— Major shipping routes

palm plantations were established in Nigeria and the Congo Basin. Rubber, used to make waterproof garments and bicycle tires, originally came from the latex of *Hevea* trees growing wild in the Brazilian rain forest. Then, in the 1870s, British agents smuggled seedlings from Brazil to the Royal Botanic Gardens at Kew near London, and from there to the Botanic Garden of Singapore. These plants formed the nucleus of the enormous rubber economy of Southeast Asia.

Throughout the tropics land once covered with forests or devoted to shifting slash-and-burn agriculture was transformed into permanent farms and plantations. Even in areas not developed to export crops, growing populations put pressure on the land. In Java and India farmers felled trees to obtain arable land and firewood. They terraced hillsides, drained swamps, and dug wells.

Irrigation and water control transformed the dry parts of the tropics as well. In the 1830s British engineers in India had restored ancient canals that had fallen into disrepair. Their success led them to build new irrigation canals, turning thousands of previously barren acres into well-watered, densely populated farmland. The migration of European experts spread the newest techniques of irrigation engineering around the world. By the turn of the century irrigation projects were under way wherever rivers flowed through dry lands. In Egypt and Central Asia irrigation brought more acres under cultivation in one forty-year span than in all previous history.

Railroads had voracious appetites for land and resources. They cut into mountains, spanned rivers and canyons with trestles, and covered as much land with their freight yards as whole cities had needed in previous centuries. They also consumed vast quantities of iron, timber for ties, and coal or wood for fuel. Most important of all, railroads brought people and their cities, farms, and industries to areas previously occupied by small, scattered populations.

Prospectors looking for valuable minerals opened the earth to reveal its riches: gold in South Africa, Australia, and Canada; tin in Nigeria, Malaya, and Bolivia; copper in Chile and Central Africa; iron ore in northern India; and much else. Where mines were dug deep inside the earth, the dirt and rocks brought up with the ores formed huge mounds near mine entrances. Open mines dug to obtain ores lying close to the surface created a landscape of lunar craters, and runoff from the minerals poisoned the water for miles around. Refineries that processed the ores fouled the environment with slag heaps and more toxic runoff.

The transformation of the land by human beings, a constant throughout history, accelerated sharply. Only the changes occurring since 1914 can compare with the transformation of the global environment that took place between 1869 and 1914.

CONCLUSION

The industrialization of the late nineteenth century increased the power of Europeans and North Americans over nature and over the peoples of other continents. They used their newfound power to conquer empires.

The opening of the Suez Canal in 1869 was the symbolic beginning of the New Imperialism. It demonstrated the power of modern industry to subdue nature by carving the land. It stimulated shipping and trade between the industrial countries and the tropics. It deepened the involvement of Europeans in the affairs of the Middle East, Africa, and Asia. From that year until 1914, not only the great powers but smaller countries too—even, in some cases, individual Europeans or Americans—had the power to decide the fate of whole countries. The motivation to conquer or control other lands surely helps explain the New Imperialism. But the means at the disposal of the imperialists—that is, the gap that opened between their technologies and forms of organization and those available to Asians, Africans, and Latin Americans—is equally important.

The new technological means and the enhanced motivations of the imperialists resulted in the most rapid conquest of territories in the history of the world. In less than half a century almost all of Africa and large parts of Asia and Oceania were added to the colonial empires, while Latin America, nominally independent, was turned into an economic colony of the industrial powers. In the process of developing the economic potential of their empires, the colonial powers transformed natural environments around the world.

The opening of the Panama Canal in August 1914 confirmed the new powers of the industrializing nations—but with a twist, for it was the United States, a latecomer to the game of imperialism, that created the canal. In that same month, the other imperialist nations turned their weapons against one another and began a life-or-death struggle for supremacy in Europe. That conflict is the subject of the next chapter.

■ Key Terms

Suez Canal	"scramble" for Africa
New Imperialism	Henry Morton Stanley
Battle of Omdurman	King Leopold II
colonialism	Savorgnan de Brazza

Berlin Conference   Menelik
Afrikaners   Emilio Aguinaldo
Cecil Rhodes   free-trade imperialism
Asante   Panama Canal

Suggested Reading

Two good introductions to imperialism are D. K. Fieldhouse, *Colonialism, 1870–1945* (1981), and Scott B. Cook, *Colonial Encounters in the Age of High Imperialism* (1996). The debate on the theories of imperialism is presented in Roger Owen and Robert Sutcliffe, *Studies in the Theory of Imperialism* (1972), and in Winfried Baumgart, *Imperialism* (1982). The British Empire is the subject of Bernard Porter, *The Lion's Share: A Short History of British Imperialism, 1850–1970* (1976).

On Africa in this period see Roland Oliver and Anthony Atmore, *Africa Since 1800*, new ed. (1994); Roland Oliver and G. N. Sanderson, eds., *From 1870 to 1905* (1985), and A. D. Roberts, ed., *From 1905 to 1940* (1986), in *The Cambridge History of Africa*; and A. Adu Boahen, ed., *Africa Under Colonial Domination, 1880–1935* (1985), in *UNESCO General History of Africa*. The European conquest of Africa is recounted in Thomas Pakenham, *The Scramble for Africa* (1991); Bruce Vandervort, *Wars of Imperial Conquest in Africa, 1830–1914* (1998); and Ronald Robinson and John Gallagher, *Africa and the Victorians: The Climax of Imperialism* (1961). Adam Hochschild's *King Leopold's Ghost: A Story of Greed, Terror, and Heroism in Colonial Africa* (1998) is a very readable account of imperialism in the Belgian Congo. The classic novel about the impact of colonial rule on African society is Chinua Achebe's *Things Fall Apart* (1958).

Imperial rivalries in Asia are the subject of Akira Iriye, *Across the Pacific: An Inner History of American-East Asian Relations*, rev. ed. (1992); David Gillard, *The Struggle for Asia, 1828–1914: A Study in British and Russian Imperialism* (1977); and Peter Hopkirk, *The Great Game: The Struggle for Empire in Central Asia* (1994). On other aspects of imperialism in Asia see Clifford Geertz, *Agricultural Involution: The Process of Ecological Change in Indonesia* (1963), especially chapters 4 and 5, and Stanley Karnow, *In Our Image: America's Empire in the Philippines* (1989).

On Latin America in this period see David Bushnell and Neill Macauley, *The Emergence of Latin America in the Nineteenth Century* (1994). Free-trade imperialism is the subject of D. C. M. Platt, *Latin America and British Trade, 1806–1914* (1973). On American expansionism see David Healy, *Drive to Hegemony: The United States in the Caribbean, 1898–1917* (1989), and Walter LaFeber, *The Panama Canal*, rev. ed. (1990).

On race relations in the colonial world see Noel Mostert, *Frontiers: The Epic of South Africa's Creation and the Tragedy of the Xhosa People* (1992), and Robert Huttenback, *Racism and Empire: White Settlers and Colored Immigrants in the British Self-Governing Colonies, 1830–1910* (1976). Gender relations are the subject of Caroline Oliver, *Western Women in Colonial Africa* (1982), and Cheryl Walker, ed., *Women and Gender in Southern Africa to 1945* (1990). David Northrup's *Indentured Labor in the Age of Imperialism, 1834–1922* (1995) discusses migrations and labor. Franz Fanon, *The Wretched of the Earth* (1966), and Albert Memmi, *The Colonizer and the Colonized* (1967), examine colonialism from the point of view of the colonized.

The impact of technology on the New Imperialism is the subject of Daniel R. Headrick, *The Tools of Empire: Technology and European Imperialism in the Nineteenth Century* (1981) and *The Tentacles of Progress: Technology Transfer in the Age of Imperialism, 1850–1940* (1988), and Clarence B. Davis and Kenneth E. Wilburn, Jr., eds., *Railway Imperialism* (1991).

On the economic and demographic transformation of Africa and Asia see Eric Wolf, *Europe and the People Without History* (1982), especially chapters 11 and 12. The impact on the environment is the subject of R. P. Tucker and J. F. Richards, *Deforestation and the Nineteenth-Century World Economy* (1983); Donal McCracken, *Gardens of Empire: Botanical Institutions of the Victorian British Empire* (1997); Lucile H. Brockway, *Science and Colonial Expansion: The Role of the British Royal Botanic Gardens* (1979); and David Arnold and Ramchandra Guha, eds., *Nature, Culture, Imperialism: Essays on the Environmental History of South Asia* (1995). In *Late Victorian Holocausts: El Niño Famines and the Making of the Third World* (2001), Mike Davis argues that imperialism exacerbated the social and demographic effects of famines.

Notes

1. *Journal Officiel* (November 29, 1869), quoted in Georges Douin, *Histoire du Règne du Khédive Ismaïl* (Rome: Reale Societá di Geografia d'Egitto, 1933), 453.
2. E. Desplaces in *Journal de l'Union des Deux Mers* (December 15, 1869), quoted ibid., 453.
3. Winston Churchill, *The River War: An Account of the Reconquest of the Soudan* (New York: Charles Scribner's Sons, 1933), 300.
4. "Correspondence and Report from His Majesty's Consul at Boma respecting the Administration of the Independent State of the Congo," *British Parliamentary Papers, Accounts and Papers*, 1904 (Cd. 1933), lxii, 357.
5. Robert W. July, *A History of the Africa People*, 3d ed. (New York: Charles Scribner's Sons, 1980), 323.
6. George Shepperson and Thomas Price, *Independent African* (Edinburgh: University Press, 1958), 163–164, quoted in Roland Oliver and Anthony Atmore, *Africa Since 1800*, 4th ed. (Cambridge: Cambridge University Press, 1994), 150.
7. Thomas Edson Ennis, *French Policy and Development in Indochina* (Chicago: University of Chicago Press, 1936), 178, quoted in K. M. Panikkar, *Asia and Western Dominance* (New York: Collier, 1969), 167.
8. Quoted in Stanley J. Stein and Barbara H. Stein, *The Colonial Heritage of Latin America* (New York: Oxford University Press, 1970), 151.

Document-Based Question
The African Colonial Experience

Using the following documents, compare and contrast the African and European experience of colonial rule in the late nineteenth and early twentieth centuries.

DOCUMENT 1
Pears Soap Is Best (photo, p. 711)

DOCUMENT 2
Quote from Winston Churchill (p. 713)

DOCUMENT 3
Quote from Ellen Joyce (p. 713)

DOCUMENT 4
Quote from Sylvia Leith-Ross (p. 713)

DOCUMENT 5
Map 27.1 Africa in 1878 and 1914 (p. 715)

DOCUMENT 6
A Steamboat for the Congo River (photo, p. 716)

DOCUMENT 7
Quote from Congolese refugee (p. 717)

DOCUMENT 8
Quote from African bishop Samuel Ajayi Crowther (p. 719)

DOCUMENT 9
Two Africans Recall the Arrival of the Europeans (Diversity and Dominance, pp. 720–721)

DOCUMENT 10
Quote from African convert (p. 722)

How did Africans and Europeans view the colonial enterprise? What additional types of documents would help you understand the African and European experience of colonial rule in the late nineteenth and early twentieth centuries?

28

The Crisis of the Imperial Order, 1900–1929

The Western Front in World War I   In a landscape ravaged by artillery fire, two soldiers dash for cover amid shell holes and the charred remains of a forest.

735

On June 28, 1914, Archduke Franz Ferdinand, heir to the throne of Austria-Hungary, was riding in an open carriage through Sarajevo, capital of Bosnia-Herzegovina, a province Austria had annexed six years earlier. When the carriage stopped momentarily, Gavrilo Princip, member of a pro-Serbian conspiracy, fired his pistol twice, killing the archduke and his wife.

Those shots ignited a war that spread throughout Europe, then became global as the Ottoman Empire fought against Britain in the Middle East and Japan attacked German positions in China. France and Britain involved their empires in the war and brought Africans, Indians, Australians, and Canadians to Europe to fight and labor on the front lines. Finally, in 1917, the United States entered the fray.

The next three chapters tell a story of violence and hope. In this chapter, we will look at the causes of war between the great powers, the consequences of that conflict in Europe, the Middle East, and Russia, and the upheavals in China and Japan. At the same time, we will review the accelerating rate of technological change, which made the first half of the twentieth century so violent and so hopeful. Industrialization continued apace. Entirely new technologies, and the organizations that produced and applied them, made war more dangerous, yet also allowed far more people to live healthier, more comfortable, and more interesting lives than ever before.

As you read this chapter, ask yourself the following questions:

- How did the First World War lead to revolution in Russia and the disintegration of several once-powerful empires?

- What role did the war play in eroding European dominance in the world?

- Why did China and Japan follow such divergent paths in this period?

- How did European and North American society and technology change in the aftermath of the war?

ORIGINS OF THE CRISIS IN EUROPE AND THE MIDDLE EAST

When the twentieth century opened, the world seemed firmly under the control of the great powers that you read about in Chapter 26. The first decade of the twentieth century was a period of relative peace and economic growth in most of the world. Trade boomed. Several new technologies—airplanes, automobiles, radio, and cinema—aroused much excitement. The great powers consolidated their colonial conquests of the previous decades. Their alliances were so evenly matched that they seemed, to observers at the time, likely to maintain peace. The only international war of the period, the Russo-Japanese War (1904–1905), ended quickly with a decisive Japanese victory.

However, two major changes were undermining the apparent stability of the world. In Europe, tensions mounted as Germany, with its growing industrial and military might, challenged Britain at sea and France in Morocco. The Ottoman Empire grew weaker, leaving a dangerous power vacuum. The resulting chaos in the Balkans, the unstable borderlands between a predominantly Christian Europe and a predominantly Muslim Middle East, gradually drew the European powers into a web of hostilities.

The Ottoman Empire and the Balkans

From the fifteenth to the nineteenth centuries the Ottoman Empire was one of the world's richest and most powerful states. By the late nineteenth century, however, it had fallen behind economically, technologically, and militarily, and Europeans referred to it as the "sick man of Europe."

As the Ottoman Empire weakened, it began losing outlying provinces situated closest to Europe. Macedonia rebelled in 1902–1903. In 1908 Austria-Hungary annexed Bosnia. Crete, occupied by European "peacekeepers" since 1898, merged with Greece in 1909. In 1912 Italy conquered Libya, the Ottomans' last foothold in Africa. A year later Albania became independent. In 1912–1913 in rapid succession came two Balkan Wars in which Serbia, Bulgaria, Romania, and Greece chased the Turks out of Europe, except for a small enclave around Constantinople.

The European powers meddled in the internal affairs of the Ottoman Empire, sometimes cooperatively but often as rivals. Russia saw itself as the protector of

C H R O N O L O G Y		
Europe and North America	**Middle East**	**East Asia**
1900		**1900** Boxer Rebellion in China
1904 British-French Entente		**1904–1905** Russo-Japanese War
1907 British-Russian Entente		
1910	**1909** Young Turks overthrow Sultan Abdul Hamid	**1911** Chinese revolutionaries led by Sun Yat-sen overthrow Qing dynasty
1912–1913 Balkan Wars	**1912** Italy conquers Libya, last Ottoman territory in Africa	**1915** Japan presents Twenty-One Demands to China
1914 Assassination of Archduke Franz Ferdinand sparks World War I	**1915** British defeat at Gallipoli	
1916 Battles of Verdun and the Somme	**1916** Arab Revolt in Arabia	
1917 Russian Revolutions; United States enters the war	**1917** Balfour Declaration	
1918 Armistice ends World War I		
1918–1921 Civil war in Russia		**1919** May Fourth Movement in China
1919 Treaty of Versailles	**1919–1922** War between Turkey and Greece	
1920 **1920** First commercial radio broadcast (United States)		
1921 New Economic Policy in Russia		
	1922 Egypt nominally independent	
	1923 Mustafa Kemal proclaims Turkey a republic	
1927 Charles Lindbergh flies alone across the Atlantic		**1927** Guomindang forces occupy Shanghai and expel Communists

the Slavic peoples of the Balkans. France and Britain, posing as protectors of Christian minorities, controlled Ottoman finances, taxes, railroads, mines, and public utilities. Austria-Hungary coveted Ottoman lands inhabited by Slavs, thereby angering the Russians.

In reaction, the Turks began to assert themselves against rebellious minorities and meddling foreigners. Many officers in the army, the most Europeanized segment of Turkish society, blamed Sultan Abdul Hamid II (r. 1876–1909) for the decline of the empire. The group known as "Young Turks" began conspiring to force a constitution on the Sultan. They alienated other anti-Ottoman groups by advocating centralized rule and the Turkification of ethnic minorities.

In 1909 the parliament, dominated by Young Turks, overthrew Abdul Hamid and replaced him with his brother. The new regime began to reform the police, the bureaucracy, and the educational system. At the same time, it cracked down on Greek and Armenian minorities. Galvanized by their defeat in the Balkan Wars, the Turks turned to Germany, the European country that had meddled least in Ottoman affairs, and

hired a German general to modernize their armed forces.

Nationalism, Alliances, and Military Strategy

The assassination of Franz Ferdinand triggered a chain of events over which military and political leaders lost control. The escalation from assassination to global war had causes that went back many years. One was nationalism, which bound citizens to their ethnic group and led them, when called upon, to kill people they viewed as enemies. Another was the system of alliances and military plans that the great powers had devised to protect themselves from their rivals. A third was Germany's yearning to dominate Europe.

Nationalism was deeply rooted in European culture. As we saw in Chapter 26, it united the citizens of France, Britain, and Germany behind their respective governments and gave them tremendous cohesion and strength of purpose. Only the most powerful feelings could inspire millions of men to march obediently into battle and could sustain civilian populations through years of hardship.

Nationalism could also be a dividing force. The large but fragile multinational Russian, Austro-Hungarian, and Ottoman Empires contained numerous ethnic and religious minorities. Having repressed them for centuries, the governments could never count on their full support. The very existence of an independent Serbia threatened Austria-Hungary by stirring up the hopes and resentments of its Slavic populations.

Because of the spread of nationalism, most people viewed war as a crusade for liberty or as long-overdue revenge for past injustices. In the course of the nineteenth century, as memories of the misery and carnage caused by the Napoleonic Wars faded, revulsion against war gradually weakened. The few wars fought in Europe after 1815, such as the Crimean War of 1853–1856 and the Franco-Prussian War of 1871, had been short and caused few casualties or long-term consequences. And in the wars of the New Imperialism (see Chapter 27), Europeans almost always had been victorious at a small cost in money and manpower. The well-to-do began to believe that only war could heal the class divisions in their societies and make workers unite behind their "natural" leaders.

What turned an incident in a small town in the Balkans into a conflict involving all the great powers was the system of alliances that had grown up over the previous decades. At the center of Europe stood Germany, the most heavily industrialized country in Europe. Its army was the best trained and equipped. It challenged Great Britain's naval supremacy by building "dreadnoughts"—heavily armed battleships. It joined Austria-Hungary and Italy in the Triple Alliance in 1882, while France allied itself with Russia. In 1904 Britain joined France in an Entente° ("understanding"), and in 1907 Britain and Russia buried their differences and formed an Entente. Europe was thus divided into two blocs of roughly equal power (see Map 28.1).

The alliance system was cursed by inflexible military planning. In 1914 western and central Europe had highly developed railroad networks but very few motor vehicles. European armies had grown to include millions of soldiers and more millions of reservists. To mobilize these forces and transport them to battle would be an enormous project requiring thousands of trains running on precise schedules. As a result, once under way, a country's mobilization could not be canceled or postponed without causing chaos.

In the years before World War I, military planners in France and Germany had worked out elaborate railroad timetables to mobilize their respective armies in a few days. Other countries were less prepared. Russia, a large country with an underdeveloped rail system, needed several weeks to mobilize its forces. Britain, with a tiny volunteer army, had no mobilization plans, and German planners believed that the British would stay out of a war on the European continent. So that Germany could avoid having to fight France and Russia at the same time, German war plans called for German generals to defeat France in a matter of days, then transport the entire army across Germany to the Russian border by train before Russia could fully mobilize.

On July 28, emboldened by the backing of Germany, Austria-Hungary declared war on Serbia. Diplomats, statesmen, and monarchs sent one another frantic telegrams, but they had lost control of events, for the declaration of war triggered the general mobilization plans of Russia, France, and Germany. On July 29 the Russian government ordered general mobilization to force Austria to back down. On August 1 France honored its treaty obligation to Russia and ordered general mobilization. Minutes later Germany did likewise. Because of the rigid railroad timetables, war was now automatic.

The German plan was to wheel around through neutral Belgium and into northwestern France. The German General Staff expected France to capitulate before the British could get involved. But on August 3, when German troops entered Belgium, Britain demanded their withdrawal. When Germany refused, Britain declared war on Germany.

THE "GREAT WAR" AND THE RUSSIAN REVOLUTIONS, 1914–1918

Throughout Europe, people greeted the outbreak of war with parades and flags, expecting a quick victory. German troops marched off to the front shouting "To Paris!" Spectators in France encouraged marching French troops with shouts of "Send me the Kaiser's moustache!" The British poet Rupert Brooke began a poem with the line "Now God be thanked Who has matched us with His hour." The German sociologist Max Weber wrote: "This war, with all its ghastliness, is nevertheless grand and wonderful. It is worth experiencing." When the war began, very few imagined that their side might not win, and no one foresaw that everyone would lose.

In Russia the effect of the war was especially devastating, for it destroyed the old society, opened the door to revolution and civil war, and introduced a radical new

---

Entente (on-TONT)

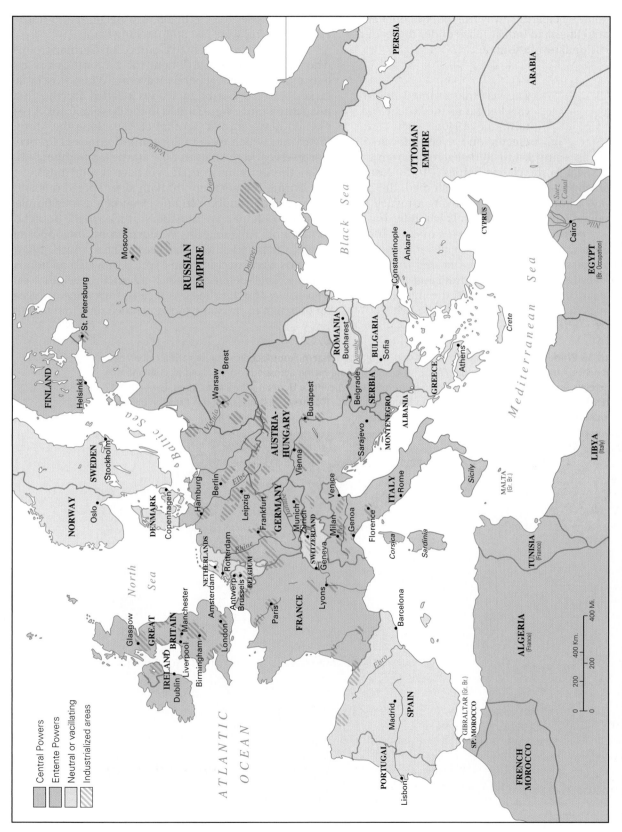

Map 28.1　Europe in 1913　On the eve of World War I, Europe was divided between two great alliance systems—the Central Powers (Germany, Austria-Hungary, and Italy) and the Entente (France, Great Britain, and Russia)—and their respective colonial empires. These alliances were not stable. When war broke out, the Central Powers lost Italy but gained the Ottoman Empire.

Central Powers
Entente Powers
Neutral or vacillating
Industrialized areas

political system. By clearing away the old, the upheaval of war prepared Russia to industrialize under the leadership of professional revolutionaries.

Stalemate, 1914–1917

The war that erupted in 1914 was known as the "Great War" until the 1940s, when a far greater one overshadowed it. Its form came as a surprise to all belligerents, from the generals on down. In the classic battles—from Alexander's to Napoleon's—that every officer studied, the advantage always went to the fastest-moving army led by the boldest general. In 1914 the generals' carefully drawn plans went awry from the start. Believing that a spirited attack would always prevail, French generals hurled their troops, dressed in bright blue-and-red uniforms, against the well-defended German border and suffered a crushing defeat. In battle after battle the much larger German armies defeated the French and the British. By early September the Germans held Belgium and northern France and were fast approaching Paris.

German victory seemed assured. But German troops, who had marched and fought for a month, were exhausted, and their generals wavered. When Russia attacked eastern Germany, troops needed for the final push into France were shifted to the Russian front. A gap opened between two German armies along the Marne River, into which General Joseph Joffre moved France's last reserves. At the Battle of the Marne (September 5–12, 1914), the Germans were thrown back several miles.

During the next month, both sides spread out until they formed an unbroken line extending over 300 miles (some 500 kilometers) from the North Sea to the border of Switzerland. All along this **Western Front,** the opposing troops prepared their defenses. Their most potent weapons were machine guns, which provided an almost impenetrable defense against advancing infantry but were useless for the offensive because they were too heavy for one man to carry and took too much time to set up.

Trench Warfare in World War I   German and Allied soldiers on the Western Front faced each other from elaborate networks of trenches. Attacking meant jumping out of the trenches and racing across a no-man's land of mud and barbed wire. Here we see Princess Patricia's Canadian Light Infantry repelling a German attack near Ypres, in northern France, in March 1915, using machine guns, rifles, and hand grenades.   (Courtesy, The Princess Patricia's Canadian Light Infantry, Regimental Museum and Archives)

To escape the deadly streams of bullets, soldiers dug holes in the ground, connected the holes to form shallow trenches, then dug communications trenches to the rear. Within weeks, the battlefields were scarred by lines of trenches several feet deep, their tops protected by sandbags and their floors covered with planks. Despite all the work they put into the trenches, the soldiers spent much of the year soaked and covered with mud. Trenches were nothing new. What was extraordinary was that the trenches along the entire Western Front were connected, leaving no gaps through which armies could advance (see Map 28.2). How, then, could either side ever hope to win?

For four years, generals on each side again and again ordered their troops to attack. They knew the casualties would be enormous, but they expected the enemy to run out of young men before their own side did. In battle after battle, thousands of young men on one side climbed out of their trenches, raced across the open fields, and were mowed down by enemy machine-gun fire. Hoping to destroy the machine guns, the attacking force would saturate the entrenched enemy lines with artillery barrages. But this tactic alerted the defenders to an impending attack and allowed them to rush in reinforcements and set up new machine guns.

The year 1916 saw the bloodiest and most futile battles of the war. The Germans attacked French forts at Verdun, losing 281,000 men and causing 315,000 French casualties. In retaliation, the British attacked the Germans at the Somme River and suffered 420,000 casualties—60,000 on the first day alone—while the Germans lost 450,000 and the French 200,000.

Warfare had never been waged this way before. It was mass slaughter in a moonscape of mud, steel, and flesh. Both sides attacked and defended, but neither side could win, for the armies were stalemated by trenches and machine guns. During four years of the bloodiest fighting the world had ever seen, the Western Front moved no more than a few miles one way or another.

At sea, the war was just as inconclusive. As soon as war broke out, the British cut the German overseas telegraph cables, blockaded the coasts of Germany and Austria-Hungary, and set out to capture or sink all enemy ships still at sea. The German High Seas Fleet, built at enormous cost, seldom left port. Only once, in May 1916, did it confront the British Grand Fleet. At the Battle of Jutland, off the coast of Denmark, the two fleets lost roughly equal numbers of ships, and the Germans escaped back to their harbors.

Britain ruled the waves but not the ocean below the surface. In early 1915, in retaliation for the British naval blockade, Germany announced a blockade of Britain by submarines. Unlike surface ships, submarines could not rescue the passengers of a sinking ship or distinguish between neutral and enemy ships. German submarines attacked every vessel they could. One of their victims was the British ocean liner *Lusitania*. The death toll from that attack was 1,198 people, 139 of them Americans. When the United States protested, Germany ceased its submarine campaign, hoping to keep America neutral.

Other than machine guns and submarines, military innovations had only minor effects. Airplanes were used for reconnaissance and engaged in spectacular but inconsequential dogfights above the trenches. Poison gas, introduced on the Western Front in 1915, killed and wounded attacking soldiers as well as their intended victims, adding to the horror of battle. Primitive tanks aided, but did not cause, the collapse of the German army in the last weeks of the war. Although these weapons were of limited effectiveness in World War I, they offered an insight into the future of warfare.

The Home Front and the War Economy

Trench-bound armies demanded ever more weapons, ammunition, and food, so civilians had to work harder, eat less, and pay higher taxes. Textiles, coal, meat, fats, and imported products such as tea and sugar were strictly rationed. Governments gradually imposed stringent controls over all aspects of their economies. Socialists and labor unions participated actively in the war effort, for they found government regulation more to their liking than unfettered free enterprise.

The war economy transformed civilian life. In France and Britain food rations were allocated according to need, improving nutrition among the poor. Unemployment vanished. Thousands of Africans, Indians, and Chinese were recruited for heavy labor in Europe. Employers hired women to fill jobs in steel mills, mines, and munitions plants vacated by men off to war. Some women became streetcar drivers, mail carriers, and police officers. Others found work in the burgeoning government bureaucracies. Many joined auxiliary military services as doctors, nurses, mechanics, and ambulance drivers; after 1917, as the war took its toll of young men, the British government established women's auxiliary units for the army, navy, and air force. Though clearly intended "for the duration only," these positions gave thousands of women a sense of participation in the war effort and a taste of personal and financial independence.

German civilians paid an especially high price for the war, for the British naval blockade severed their

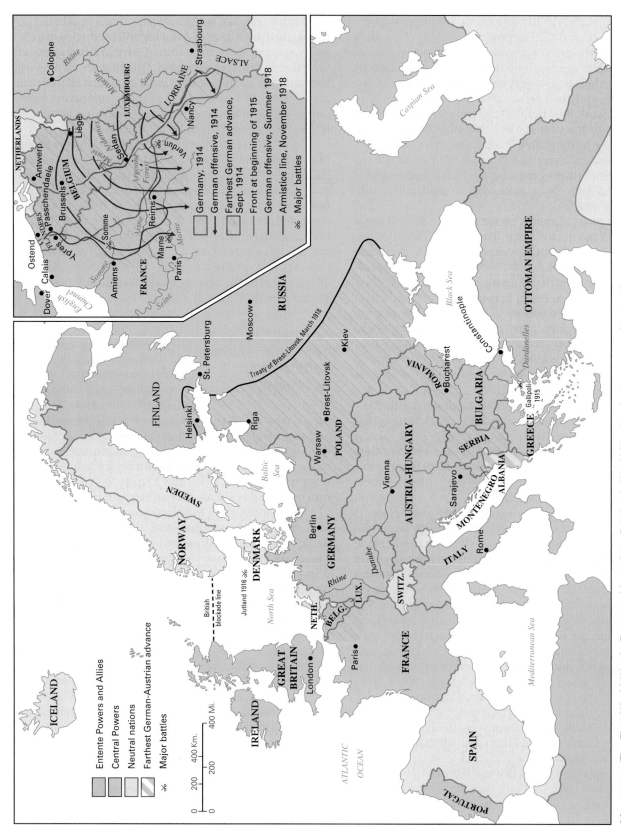

Map 28.2 **The First World War in Europe**   Most of the fighting in World War I took place on two fronts. After an initial surge through Belgium into northern France, the German offensive bogged down for four years along the Western Front. To the East, the German armies conquered a large part of Russia during 1917 and early 1918. Despite spectacular victories in the east, Germany lost the war because its armies collapsed along the strategically important Western Front.

ON HER
THEIR LIVES DEPEND

WOMEN
MUNITION
WORKERS

Enrol at once

Women in World War I Women played a more important role in World War I than in previous wars. As the armies drafted millions of men, employers hired women for essential war work. This poster extolling the importance of women workers in supplying munitions was probably designed to recruit women for factory jobs. (Imperial War Museum)

overseas trade. The German chemical industry developed synthetic explosives and fuel, but synthetic food was not an option. Wheat flour disappeared, replaced first by rye, then by potatoes and turnips, then by acorns and chestnuts, and finally by sawdust. After the failure of the potato crop in 1916 came the "turnip winter," when people had to survive on 1,000 calories per day, half the normal amount that an active adult needed. Women, children, and the elderly were especially hard hit. Soldiers at the front went hungry and raided enemy lines to scavenge food.

When the war began, the British and French overran German Togo on the West African coast. The much

larger German colonies of Southwest Africa and German Cameroon were conquered in 1915. In Tanganyika the Germans remained undefeated until the end of the war.

The war also brought hardships to Europe's African colonies. The Europeans requisitioned foodstuffs, imposed heavy taxes, and forced Africans to grow export crops and sell them at low prices. Many Europeans stationed in Africa joined the war, leaving large areas with little or no European presence. In Nigeria, Libya, Nyasaland (now Malawi), and other colonies, the combination of increased demands on Africans and fewer European officials led to uprisings that lasted for several years.

Over a million Africans served in the various armies, and perhaps three times that number were drafted as porters to carry army equipment. Faced with a shortage of young Frenchmen, France drafted Africans into its army, where many fought side by side with Europeans. The Senegalese Blaise Diagne°, the first African elected to France's Chamber of Deputies in 1914, campaigned for African support of the war effort. Put in charge of recruiting African soldiers, he insisted on equal rights for African and European soldiers and an extension of the franchise to educated Africans. These demands were only partially met.

One country grew rich during the war: the United States. For two and a half years the United States stayed technically neutral—that is, it did not fight but did a roaring business supplying France and Britain. When the United States entered the war in 1917 businesses engaging in war production made spectacular profits. Civilians were exhorted to help the war effort by investing their savings in war bonds and growing food in backyard "victory gardens." Facing labor shortages, employers hired women and African-Americans. Employment opportunities created by the war played a major role in the migration of black Americans from the rural south to the cities of the north.

The Ottoman Empire at War

On August 2, 1914, the Turks signed a secret alliance with Germany. In November they joined the fighting, hoping to gain land at Russia's expense. But the campaign in the Caucasus proved disastrous for both armies and for the civilian populations as well. The Turks deported the Armenians, whom they suspected of being pro-Russian, from their homelands in eastern Anatolia to Syria and other parts of the Ottoman Empire. During the forced march across the mountains in the winter, hundreds of thousands of Armenians died of hunger and exposure.

Blaise Diagne (blez dee-AHN-yuh)

This massacre was a precedent for even ghastlier tragedies still to come.

The Turks also closed the Dardanelles, the strait between the Mediterranean and Black Seas (see Map 28.2). Seeing little hope of victory on the Western Front, British officials tried to open the Dardanelles by landing troops on the nearby Gallipoli Peninsula in 1915. Turkish troops pushed the invaders back into the sea.

Having failed at the Dardanelles, the British tried to subvert the Ottoman Empire from within by promising the emir (prince) of Mecca, Hussein ibn Ali, a kingdom of his own if he would lead an Arab revolt against the Turks. In 1916 Hussein rose up and was proclaimed king of Hejaz° (western Arabia). His son **Faisal**° led an Arab army in support of the British advance from Egypt into Palestine and Syria. The Arab Revolt of 1916 did not affect the struggle in Europe, but it did contribute to the defeat of the Ottoman Empire.

The British made promises to Jews as well as Arabs. For centuries, Jewish minorities had lived in eastern and central Europe, where they developed a thriving culture despite frequent persecutions. By the early twentieth century a nationalist movement called Zionism, led by **Theodore Herzl,** arose among those who wanted to return to their ancestral homeland in Palestine. The concept of a Jewish homeland appealed to many Europeans, Jews and gentiles alike, as a humanitarian solution to the problem of anti-Semitism.

By 1917 Chaim Weizmann°, leader of the British Zionists, had persuaded several British politicians that a Jewish homeland in Palestine should be carved out of the Ottoman Empire and placed under British protection, thereby strengthening the Allied cause (as the Entente was now called). In November, as British armies were advancing on Jerusalem, Foreign Secretary Sir Arthur Balfour wrote:

> His Majesty's Government view with favor the establishment in Palestine of a national home for the Jewish people and will use their best endeavours to facilitate the achievement of that object, it being clearly understood that nothing shall be done which may prejudice the civil and religious rights of existing non-Jewish communities in Palestine.

The British did not foresee that this statement, known as the **Balfour Declaration,** would lead to conflicts between Palestinians and Jewish settlers.

Britain also sent troops to southern Mesopotamia to secure the oil pipeline from Iran. Then they moved north, taking Baghdad in early 1917. The officers for the Mesopotamian campaign were British, but most of the troops and equipment came from India. Most Indians, like other colonial subjects of Britain, supported the war effort despite the hardships it caused. Their involvement in the war bolstered the movement for Indian independence (see Chapter 30).

Double Revolution in Russia, 1917

At the beginning of the war Russia had the largest army in the world, but its generals were incompetent, supplies were lacking, and soldiers were poorly trained and equipped. In August 1914 two Russian armies invaded eastern Germany but were thrown back. The Russians defeated the Austro-Hungarian army several times, only to be defeated in turn by the Germans.

In 1916, after a string of defeats, the Russian army ran out of ammunition and other essential supplies. Soldiers were ordered into battle unarmed and told to pick up the rifles of fallen comrades. With so many men in the army, railroads broke down for lack of fuel and parts, and crops rotted in the fields. Civilians faced shortages and widespread hunger. In the cities food and fuel became scarce. During the bitterly cold winter of 1916–1917 factory workers and housewives had to line up in front of grocery stores before dawn to get food. The court of Tsar° Nicholas II, however, remained as extravagant and corrupt as ever.

In early March 1917 (February by the old Russian calendar) food ran out in Petrograd (St. Petersburg), the capital. Housewives and women factory workers staged mass demonstrations. Soldiers mutinied and joined striking workers to form soviets (councils) to take over factories and barracks. A few days later the tsar abdicated, and leaders of the parliamentary parties, led by Alexander Kerensky, formed a Provisional Government. Thus began what Russians called the "February Revolution."

Revolutionary groups formerly hunted by the tsar's police came out of hiding. Most numerous were the Social Revolutionaries, who advocated the redistribution of land to the peasants. The Social Democrats, a Marxist party, were divided into two factions: Mensheviks and Bolsheviks. The Mensheviks advocated electoral politics and reform in the tradition of European socialists and had a large following among intellectuals and factory workers. The **Bolsheviks,** their rivals, were a small but tightly disciplined group of radicals obedient to the will of their leader, **Vladimir Lenin** (1870–1924).

Lenin, the son of a government official, became a revolutionary in his teens when his older brother was ex-

---

Hejaz (HEE-jaz)   **Faisal** (fie-SAHL)   **Chaim Weizmann** (hi-um VITES-mun)

tsar (zahr)

ecuted for plotting to kill the tsar. He spent years in exile, first in Siberia and later in Switzerland, where he devoted his full attention to organizing his followers. He professed Marx's ideas about class conflict (see Chapter 26), but he never visited a factory or a farm. His goal was to create a party that would lead the revolution rather than wait for it. He explained: "Classes are led by parties and parties are led by individuals. . . . The will of a class is sometimes fulfilled by a dictator."

In early April 1917 the German government, hoping to destabilize Russia, allowed Lenin to travel from Switzerland to Russia in a sealed railway car. As soon as he arrived in Petrograd, he announced his program: immediate peace, all power to the soviets, and transfers of land to the peasants and factories to the workers. This plan proved immensely popular among soldiers and workers exhausted by the war.

The next few months witnessed a tug-of-war between the Provisional Government and the various revolutionary factions in Petrograd. When Kerensky ordered another offensive against the Germans, Russian soldiers began to desert by the hundreds of thousands, throwing away their rifles and walking back to their villages. As the Germans advanced, Russian resistance melted, and the government lost the little support it had.

Meanwhile, the Bolsheviks were gaining support among the workers of Petrograd and the soldiers and sailors stationed there. On November 6, 1917 (October 24 in the Russian calendar), they rose up and took over the city, calling their action the "October Revolution." Their sudden move surprised rival revolutionary groups that believed that a "socialist" revolution could happen only after many years of "bourgeois" rule. Lenin, however, was more interested in power than in the fine points of Marxist doctrine. He overthrew the Provisional Government and arrested Mensheviks, Social Revolutionaries, and other rivals.

Seizing Petrograd was only the first step, for the rest of Russia was in chaos. The Bolsheviks nationalized all private land and ordered the peasants to hand over their crops without compensation. The peasants, having seized their landlords' estates, resisted. In the cities the Bolsheviks took over the factories and drafted the workers into compulsory labor brigades. To enforce his rule Lenin created the Cheka, a secret police force with powers to arrest and execute opponents.

The Bolsheviks also sued for peace with Germany and Austria-Hungary. By the Treaty of Brest-Litovsk, signed on March 3, 1918, Russia lost territories containing a third of its population and wealth. Poland, Finland, and the Baltic states (Estonia, Latvia, and Lithuania) became independent republics. Russian colonies in Central Asia and the Caucasus broke away temporarily.

The End of the War in Western Europe, 1917–1918

Like many other Americans, President **Woodrow Wilson** wanted to stay out of the European conflict. For nearly three years he kept the United States neutral and tried to persuade the belligerents to compromise. But in late 1916 German leaders decided to starve the British into submission by using submarines to sink merchant ships carrying food supplies to Great Britain. The Germans knew that unrestricted submarine warfare was likely to bring the United States into the war, but they were willing to gamble that Britain and France would collapse before the United States could send enough troops to help them.

The submarine campaign resumed on February 1, 1917, and the German gamble failed. The British organized their merchant ships into convoys protected by destroyers, and on April 6 President Wilson asked the United States Congress to declare war on Germany.

On the Western Front, the two sides were so evenly matched in 1917 that the war seemed unlikely to end until one side or the other ran out of young men. Losing hope of winning, soldiers began to mutiny. In May 1917, before the arrival of U.S. forces, fifty-four of one hundred French divisions along the Western Front refused to attack. At Caporetto, Italian troops were so demoralized that 275,000 were taken prisoner.

Between March and August 1918 General Erich von Ludendorff launched a series of surprise attacks that broke through the front at several places and pushed to within 40 miles (64 kilometers) of Paris. But victory eluded him. Meanwhile, every month was bringing another 250,000 American troops to the front. In August the Allies counterattacked, and the Germans began a retreat that could not be halted, for German soldiers, many of them sick with the flu, had lost the will to fight.

In late October Ludendorff resigned, and sailors in the German fleet mutinied. Two weeks later Kaiser Wilhelm fled to Holland as a new German government signed an armistice. On November 11 at 11 A.M. the guns on the Western Front went silent.

PEACE AND DISLOCATION IN EUROPE, 1919–1929

The Great War lasted four years. It took almost twice as long for Europe to recover. Millions of people had died or been disabled; political tensions and resentments lingered; and national economies remained depressed until the mid-1920s. In the late 1920s peace and prosperity finally seemed assured, but this hope proved to be illusory.

The Impact of the War

The war left more dead and wounded and more physical destruction than any previous conflict. It is estimated that between 8 million and 10 million people died, almost all of them young men. Perhaps twice that many returned home wounded, gassed, or shell-shocked, many of them injured for life. Among the dead were about 2 million Germans, 1.7 million Russians, and 1.7 million Frenchmen. Austria-Hungary lost 1.5 million, the British Empire a million, Italy 460,000, and the United States 115,000.

Besides ending over 8 million lives, the war dislocated whole populations, creating millions of refugees. War and revolution forced almost 2 million Russians, 750,000 Germans, and 400,000 Hungarians to flee their homes. War led to the expulsion of hundreds of thousands of Greeks from Anatolia and Turks from Greece.

Many refugees found shelter in France, which welcomed 1.5 million people to bolster its declining population. The preferred destination, however, was the United States, the most prosperous country in the world. About 800,000 immigrants succeeded in reaching the United States before immigration laws passed in 1921 and 1924 closed the door to eastern and southern Europeans. Canada, Australia, and New Zealand adopted similar restrictions on immigration. The Latin American republics welcomed European refugees, but their economies were hard hit by the drop in the prices of their main exports, and their poverty discouraged potential immigrants.

One unexpected byproduct of the war was the great influenza epidemic of 1918–1919, which started among soldiers heading for the Western Front. This was no ordinary flu but a virulent strain that infected almost everyone on earth and killed one person in every forty. It caused the largest number of deaths in so short a time in the history of the world. Half a million Americans perished in the epidemic—five times as many as died in the war. Worldwide, some 20 million people died.

The war also caused serious damage to the environment. No place was ever so completely devastated as the scar across France and Belgium known as the Western Front. The fighting ravaged forests and demolished towns. The earth was gouged by trenches, pitted with craters, and littered with ammunition, broken weapons, chunks of concrete, and the bones of countless soldiers. After the war, it took a decade to clear away the debris, rebuild the towns, and create dozens of military cemeteries with neat rows of crosses stretching for miles. To this day, farmers plow up fragments of old weapons and ammunition, and every so often a long-buried shell explodes. The war also hastened the buildup of industry, with mines, factories, and railroad tracks.

The Peace Treaties

In early 1919 delegates of the victorious powers met in Paris. The defeated powers were kept out until the treaties were ready for signing. Russia, in the throes of civil war, was not invited.

From the start, three men dominated the Paris Peace Conference: U.S. president Wilson, British prime minister David Lloyd George, and French premier Georges Clemenceau°. They ignored the Italians, who had joined the Allies in 1915. They paid even less attention to the delegates of smaller European nations and none at all to non-European nationalities. They rejected the Japanese proposal that all races be treated equally. They ignored the Pan-African Congress organized by the African-American W. E. B. Du Bois to call attention to the concerns of African peoples around the world. They also ignored the ten thousand other delegates of various nationalities that did not represent sovereign states—the Arab leader Faisal, the Zionist Chaim Weizmann, and several Armenian delegations—who came to Paris to lobby for their causes. They were, in the words of Britain's Foreign Secretary Balfour, "three all-powerful, all-ignorant men, sitting there and carving up continents" (see Map 28.3).

Each had his own agenda. Wilson, a high-minded idealist, wanted to apply the principle of self-determination to European affairs, by which he meant creating nations that reflected ethnic or linguistic divisions. He proposed a **League of Nations,** a world organization to safeguard the peace and foster international cooperation. His idealism clashed with the more hard-headed and self-serving nationalism of the Europeans. To satisfy his constituents, Lloyd George insisted that Germany pay a heavy indemnity. Clemenceau wanted Germany to give Alsace and Lorraine (a part of France before 1871) and the industrial Saar region to France and demanded that the Rhineland be detached from Germany to form a buffer state.

The result was a series of compromises that satisfied no one. The European powers formed a League of Nations, but the United States Congress, reflecting the isolationist feelings of the American people, refused to let the United States join. France recovered Alsace and Lorraine but was unable to detach the Rhineland and had to

---

Georges Clemenceau (zhorzh cluh-mon-SO)

Map 28.3   Territorial Changes in Europe After World War I   Although the heaviest fighting took place in western Europe, the territorial changes there were relatively minor; the two provinces taken by Germany in 1871, Alsace and Lorraine, were returned to France. In eastern Europe, in contrast, the changes were enormous. The disintegration of the Austria-Hungary Empire and the defeat of Russia allowed a belt of new countries to arise, stretching from Finland in the north to Yugoslavia in the south.

content itself with vague promises of British and American protection if Germany ever rebuilt its army. Britain acquired new territories in Africa and the Middle East but was greatly weakened by human losses and the disruption of its trade.

On June 28, 1919, the German delegates reluctantly signed the **Treaty of Versailles°**. Germany was forbidden to have an air force and was permitted only a token army

Versailles (vuhr-SIGH)

and navy. It gave up large parts of its eastern territory to a newly reconstituted Poland. The Allies made Germany promise to pay reparations to compensate the victors for their losses, but they did not set a figure or a period of time for payment. A "guilt clause," which was to rankle for years to come, obliged the Germans to accept "responsibility for causing all the loss and damage" of the war. The Treaty of Versailles left Germany humiliated but largely intact and potentially the most powerful nation in Europe. Establishing a peace neither of punishment nor of reconciliation, the treaty was one of the great failures in history.

Meanwhile, the Austro-Hungarian Empire had fallen apart. In the Treaty of Saint-Germain° (1920) Austria and Hungary each lost three-quarters of its territory. New countries appeared in the lands lost by Russia, Germany, and Austria-Hungary: Poland, resurrected after over a century; Czechoslovakia, created from the northern third of Austria-Hungary; and Yugoslavia, combining Serbia and the former south Slav provinces of Austria-Hungary. The new boundaries coincided with the major linguistic groups of eastern Europe, but they all contained disaffected minorities. These small nations were safe only as long as Germany and Russia lay defeated and prostrate.

Russian Civil War and the New Economic Policy

The end of the Great War did not bring peace to all of Europe. Fighting continued in Russia for another three years. The Bolshevik Revolution had provoked Allied intervention. French troops occupied Odessa in the south; the British and Americans landed in Archangel and Murmansk in the north; and the Japanese occupied Vladivostok in the far east. Liberated Czech prisoners of war briefly seized the Trans-Siberian Railway.

Also, in December 1918, civil war broke out in Russia. The Communists—as the Bolsheviks called themselves after March 1918—held central Russia, but all the surrounding provinces rose up against them. Counterrevolutionary armies led by former tsarist officers obtained weapons and supplies from the Allies. For three years the two sides fought each other. They burned farms and confiscated crops, causing a famine that claimed 3 million victims, more than had died in Russia in seven years of fighting. By 1921 the Communists had defeated most of their enemies, for the anti-Bolshevik forces were never united, and the peasants feared that a tsarist victory would mean the return of their landlords. The Communists' victory was also due to the superior discipline of their Red Army and the military genius of their army commander, Leon Trotsky.

Finland, the Baltic states, and Poland remained independent, but the Red Army reconquered other parts of the tsar's empire one by one. In December 1920 Ukrainian Communists declared the independence of a Soviet Republic of Ukraine, which merged with Russia in 1922 to create the Union of Soviet Socialist Republics (USSR), or Soviet Union. The provinces of the Russian Empire in

the Caucasus and Central Asia had also declared their independence in 1918. Although the Bolsheviks staunchly supported anticolonialist movements in Africa and Asia, they opposed what they called "feudalism" in the former Russian colonies. They were also eager to control the oil fields in both regions. In 1920–1921 the Red Army reconquered the Caucasus and replaced the indigenous leaders with Russians. In 1922 the new Soviet republics of Georgia, Armenia, and Azerbaijan joined the USSR. In this way the Bolsheviks rid Russia of the taint of tsarist colonialism but retained control over lands and peoples that had been part of the tsar's empire.

Years of warfare, revolution, and mismanagement ruined the Russian economy. By 1921 it had declined to one-sixth of its prewar level. Factories and railroads had shut down for lack of fuel, raw materials, and parts. Farmland had been devastated and livestock killed, causing hunger in the cities. Finding himself master of a country in ruin, Lenin decided to release the economy from party and government control. In March 1921 he announced The **New Economic Policy** (N.E.P.). It allowed peasants to own land and sell their crops, private merchants to trade, and private workshops to produce goods and sell them on the free market. Only the biggest businesses, such as banks, railroads, and factories, remained under government ownership.

The relaxation of controls had an immediate effect. Production began to climb, and food and other goods became available. In the cities food remained scarce because farmers used their crops to feed their livestock rather than sell them. But the N.E.P. reflected no change in the ultimate goals of the Communist Party. It merely provided breathing space, what Lenin called "two steps back to advance one step forward." The Communists had every intention of creating a modern industrial economy without private property, under party guidance. This meant investing in heavy industry and electrification and moving farmers to the cities to work in the new industries. It also meant providing food for the urban workers without spending scarce resources to purchase it from the peasants. In other words, it meant making the peasants, the great majority of the Soviet people, pay for the industrialization of Russia. This turned them into bitter enemies of the Communists.

When Lenin died in January 1924 his associates jockeyed for power. The leading contenders were Leon Trotsky, commander of the Red Army, and Joseph Stalin, general secretary of the Communist Party. Trotsky had the support of many "Old Bolsheviks" who had joined the party before the Revolution. Having spent years in exile, he saw the revolution as a spark that would ignite a world revolution of the working class.

Saint-Germain (san-zhair-MEN)

Lenin the Orator   The leader of the Bolshevik revolutionaries was a spellbinding orator. Here Lenin is addressing Red Army soldiers in Sverdlov Square, Moscow, in 1920. At the time, the Bolsheviks were mopping up the last of the anti-Bolshevik forces and were fully engaged in a war with Poland. The fate of the Revolution depended on the fighting spirit of the Red Army soldiers and on their loyalty to Lenin. (David King Collection)

Stalin, the only leading Communist who had never lived abroad, insisted that socialism could survive "in one country."

Stalin filled the party bureaucracy with individuals loyal to himself. In 1926–1927 he had Trotsky expelled for "deviation from the party line." In January 1929 he forced Trotsky to flee the country. Then, as absolute master of the party, he prepared to industrialize the Soviet Union at breakneck speed.

An Ephemeral Peace

The 1920s were a decade of apparent progress hiding irreconcilable tensions. Conservatives in Britain and France longed for a return to the stability of the prewar era—the hierarchy of social classes, prosperous world trade, and European dominance over the rest of the world. All over the rest of the world, people's hopes had been raised by the rhetoric of the war, then dashed by its outcome. In Europe, Germans felt cheated out of a victory that had seemed within their grasp, and Italians were disappointed that their sacrifices had not been rewarded at Versailles with large territorial gains. In the Middle East and Asia, Arabs and Indians longed for independence; the Chinese looked for social justice and a lessening of foreign intrusion; and the Japanese hoped to expand their influence in China. In Russia, the Communists were eager to consolidate their power and export their revolution to the rest of the world.

The decade after the end of the war can be divided into two distinct periods: five years of painful recovery and readjustment (1919–1923), followed by six years of growing peace and prosperity (1924–1929). In 1923 Germany suspended reparations payments. In retaliation for the French occupation of the Ruhr, the German government began printing money recklessly, causing the most severe inflation the world had ever seen. Soon German money was worth so little that it took a wheelbarrow full of it to buy a loaf of bread. As Germany teetered on the brink of civil war, radical nationalists called for revenge and tried to overthrow the government. Finally, the German government issued a new currency and promised to resume reparations payments, and the French agreed to withdraw their troops from the Ruhr.

Beginning in 1924 the world enjoyed a few years of calm and prosperity. After the end of the German crisis of 1923, the western European nations became less confrontational, and Germany joined the League of Nations. The vexed issue of reparations also seemed to vanish, as Germany borrowed money from New York banks to make its payments to France and Britain, which used the money to repay their wartime loans from the United States. This triangular flow of money, based on credit, stimulated the rapid recovery of the European economies. France began rebuilding its war-torn northern zone; Germany recovered from its hyperinflation; and a boom began in the United States that was to last for five years.

While their economies flourished, governments grew more cautious and businesslike. Even the Communists, after Lenin's death, seemed to give up their attempts to spread revolution abroad. Yet neither Germany nor the Soviet Union accepted its borders with the small nations that had arisen between them. In 1922 they signed a secret pact allowing the German army to conduct maneuvers in Russia (in violation of the Versailles treaty) in exchange for German help in building up Russian industry and military potential.

The League of Nations proved adept at resolving numerous technical issues pertaining to health, labor relations, and postal and telegraph communications. But the League could carry out its main function, preserving the peace, only when the great powers (Britain, France, and Italy) were in agreement. Without U.S. participation, sanctions against states that violated League rules carried little weight.

CHINA AND JAPAN: CONTRASTING DESTINIES

China and Japan share a common civilization, and both were subject to Western pressures, but their modern histories have been completely opposite. China clung much longer than Japan to a traditional social structure and economy, then collapsed into chaos and revolution. Japan experienced reform from above (see Chapter 26), acquiring industry and a powerful military, which it used to take advantage of China's weakness. Their different reactions to the pressures of the West put these two great nations on a collision course.

Social and Economic Change

China's population—about 400 million in 1900—was the largest of any country in the world and growing fast. But China had little new land to put into cultivation. In 1900 peasant plots averaged between 1 and 4 acres (less than 2 hectares) apiece, half as large as they had been two generations earlier. Farming methods had not changed in centuries. Landlords and tax collectors took more than half of the harvest. Most Chinese worked incessantly, survived on a diet of grain and vegetables, and spent their lives in fear of floods, bandits, and tax collectors.

Constant labor was needed to prevent the Yellow River from bursting its dikes and flooding the low-lying fields and villages on either side. In times of war and civil disorder, when flood-control precautions were neglected, disasters ensued. Between 1913 and 1938 the river burst its dikes seventeen times, each time killing thousands of people and making millions homeless.

Japan had few natural resources and very little arable land on which to grow food for its rising population. It did not suffer from devastating floods like China, but it was subject to other natural calamities. Typhoons regularly hit its southern regions. Earthquakes periodically shook the country, which lies on the great ring of tectonic fault lines that surround the Pacific Ocean. The Kanto earthquake of 1923 destroyed all of Yokohama and half of Tokyo and killed as many as 200,000 people.

Above the peasantry, Chinese society was divided into many groups and strata. Landowners lived off the rents of their tenants. Officials, chosen through an elaborate examination system, enriched themselves from taxes and the government's monopolies on salt, iron, and other products. Wealthy merchants handled China's growing import-export trade in collaboration with foreign companies. Shanghai, China's financial and commercial center, was famous for its wealthy foreigners and its opium addicts, prostitutes, and gangsters.

Although foreign trade represented only a small part of China's economy, contact with the outside world had a tremendous impact on Chinese politics. Young men living in the treaty ports saw no chance for advancement in the old system of examinations and official positions. Some learned foreign ideas in Christian mission schools or abroad. The contrast between the squalor in which most urban residents lived and the luxury of the foreigners' enclaves in the treaty ports sharpened the resentment of educated Chinese.

Japan's population reached 60 million in 1925 and was increasing by a million a year. The crash program of industrialization begun in 1868 by the Meiji oligarchs (see Chapter 26) accelerated during the First World War, when Japan exported textiles, consumer goods, and munitions. In the war years, its economy grew four times as fast as western Europe's, eight times faster than China's.

In the 1880s electrification was still in its infancy, so Japan became competitive very early on. Blessed with a rainy climate and many fast-flowing rivers, Japan quickly expanded its hydroelectric capacity. By the mid-1930s, 89 percent of Japanese households had electric lights, compared with 68 percent of U.S. and 44 percent of British households.

Economic growth aggravated social tensions. The *narikin* ("new rich") affected Western ways and lifestyles that clashed with the austerity of earlier times. In the big

Japanese prosperity depended on foreign trade and imperialism in Asia. The country exported silk and light manufactures and imported almost all its fuel, raw materials, and machine tools, and even some of its food. Though less at the mercy of the weather than China, Japan was much more vulnerable to swings in the world economy.

Revolution and War, 1900–1918

In 1900 China's Empress Dowager Cixi°, who had seized power in a palace coup two years earlier, encouraged a secret society, the Righteous Fists, or Boxers, to rise up and expel all the foreigners from China. When the Boxers threatened the foreign legation in Beijing, an international force from the Western powers and Japan captured the city and forced China to pay a huge indemnity. Shocked by these events, many Chinese students became convinced that China needed a revolution to get rid of the Qing dynasty and modernize their country. In Shanghai dissidents published works that would have been forbidden elsewhere in China.

When Cixi died in 1908, the Revolutionary Alliance led by **Sun Yat-sen**° (Sun Zhongshan, 1867–1925) prepared to take over. Sun had spent much of his life in Japan, England, and the United States, plotting the overthrow of the Qing dynasty. His ideas were a mixture of nationalism, socialism, and Confucian philosophy. His patriotism, his powerful ambition, and his tenacious spirit attracted a large following.

The military thwarted Sun's plans. After China's defeat in the war with Japan in 1895, the government had agreed to equip the army with modern rifles and machine guns. The combination of traditional regional autonomy with modern tactics and equipment led to the creation of local armies beholden to local generals known as warlords, rather than to the central government. When a regional army mutinied in October 1911, **Yuan Shikai**°, the most powerful of the regional generals, refused to defend the Qing. A revolutionary assembly at Nanjing elected Sun president of China in December 1911, and the last Qing ruler, the boy-emperor Puyi, abdicated the throne. But Sun had no military forces at his command. To avoid a clash with the army, he resigned after a few weeks, and a new national assembly elected Yuan president of the new Chinese republic.

Yuan was an able military leader, but he had no political program. When Sun reorganized his followers into a political party called **Guomindang**° (National

The Bund, Shanghai Shanghai was the most important port and industrial city in China. This picture shows the Bund, or waterfront, where ocean-going ships docked and where Chinese and foreign merchants did business. Many of the people you see in the picture were stevedores, who loaded and unloaded ships, and drivers of rickshaws or man-powered taxis.   (Corbis)

cities *mobos* (modern boys) and *mogas* (modern girls) shocked traditionalists with their foreign ways: dancing together, wearing short skirts and tight pants, and behaving like Americans. Students who flirted with dangerous thoughts were called "Marx boys."

The main beneficiaries of prosperity were the *zaibatsu*°, or conglomerates, four of which—Mitsubishi, Sumitomo, Yasuda, and Mitsui—controlled most of Japan's industry and commerce. Farmers, who constituted half of the population, remained poor; in desperation some sold their daughters to textile mills or into domestic service, where young women formed the bulk of the labor force. Labor unions were weak and repressed by the police.

---

zaibatsu (zie-BOT-soo)

Cixi (TSUH-shee)   **Sun Yat-sen** (soon yot-SEN)
Yuan Shikai (you-AHN she-KIE)   **Guomindang** (gwo-min-dong)

People's Party), Yuan quashed every attempt at creating a Western-style government and harassed Sun's followers. Victory in the first round of the struggle to create a new China went to the military.

The Japanese were quick to join the Allied side in World War I. They saw the war as an opportunity to advance their interests while the Europeans were occupied elsewhere. The war created an economic boom, as the Japanese suddenly found their products in greater demand. But it also created hardships for workers, who rioted when the cost of rice rose faster than their wages.

The Japanese soon conquered the German colonies in the northern Pacific and on the coast of China, then turned their attention to the rest of China. In 1915 Japan presented China with Twenty-One Demands, which would have turned it into a virtual protectorate. Britain and the United States persuaded Japan to soften the demands but could not prevent it from keeping the German coastal enclaves and extracting railroad and mining concessions at China's expense. In protest, anti-Japanese riots and boycotts broke out throughout China. Thus began a bitter struggle between the two countries that was to last for thirty years.

Chinese Warlords and the Guomindang, 1919–1929

At the Paris Peace Conference, the great powers accepted Japan's seizure of the German enclaves in China. To many educated Chinese, this decision was a cruel insult. On May 4, 1919, students demonstrated in front of the Forbidden City of Beijing. Despite a government ban, the May Fourth Movement spread to other parts of China. A new generation was growing up to challenge the old officials, the regional generals, and the foreigners.

China's regional generals—the warlords—still supported their armies through plunder and arbitrary taxation. They frightened off trade and investment in railroads, industry, and agricultural improvement. While neglecting the dikes and canals on which the livelihood of Chinese farmers depended, they fought one another and protected the gangsters who ran the opium trade. During the warlord era only the treaty ports prospered, while the rest of China grew poorer and weaker.

Sun Yat-sen tried to make a comeback in Canton (Guangzhou) in the early 1920s. Though not a Communist, he was impressed with the efficiency of Lenin's revolutionary tactics and let a Soviet adviser reorganize the Guomindang along Leninist lines. He also welcomed members of the newly created Chinese Communist Party into the Guomindang.

When Sun died in 1925 the leadership of his party passed to Jiang Jieshi, known in the West as **Chiang Kai-shek°** (1887–1975). An officer and director of the military academy, Chiang trained several hundred young officers who remained loyal to him thereafter. In 1927 he determined to crush the regional warlords. As his army moved north from its base in Canton, he briefly formed an alliance with the Communists. Once his troops had occupied Shanghai, however, he allied himself with local gangsters to crush the labor unions and decimate the Communists, whom he considered a threat. He then defeated or co-opted most of the other warlords and established a dictatorship.

Chiang's government issued ambitious plans to build railroads, develop agriculture and industry, and modernize China from the top down. However, his followers were neither competent administrators like the Japanese officials of the Meiji Restoration nor ruthless modernizers like the Russian Bolsheviks. Instead, the government attracted thousands of opportunists whose goals were to "become officials and get rich" by taxing and plundering businesses. In the countryside tax collectors and landowners squeezed the peasants ever harder, even in times of natural disasters. What little money reached the government's coffers went to the military. For twenty years after the fall of the Qing, China remained mired in poverty, subject to corrupt officials and the whims of nature.

The New Middle East

Having contributed to the Allied victory, the Arab peoples expected to have a say in the outcome of the Great War. But the victorious French and British planned to treat the Middle East like a territory open to colonial rule. The result was a legacy of instability that has persisted to this day.

The Mandate System

At the Paris Peace Conference France, Britain, Italy, and Japan proposed to divide the former German colonies and the territories of the Ottoman Empire among themselves, but their ambitions clashed with President Wilson's ideal of national self-determination. Eventually, the victors arrived at a compromise solution called the **mandate system:** colonial rulers would administer the territories but would be accountable to the League of Nations for "the

Chiang Kai-shek (chang kie-shek)

material and moral well-being and the social progress of the inhabitants."

Class C Mandates—those with the smallest populations—were treated as colonies by their conquerors. South Africa replaced Germany in Southwest Africa (now Namibia). Britain, Australia, New Zealand, and Japan took over the German islands in the Pacific. Class B Mandates, larger than Class C but still underdeveloped, were to be ruled for the benefit of their inhabitants under League of Nations supervision. They were to receive autonomy at some unspecified time in the future. Most of Germany's African colonies fell into this category.

The Arab-speaking territories of the old Ottoman Empire were Class A Mandates. The League of Nations declared that they had "reached a state of development where their existence as independent nations can be provisionally recognized subject to the rendering of administrative advice and assistance by a Mandatory, until such time as they are able to stand alone." Arabs interpreted this ambiguous wording as a promise of independence. Britain and France sent troops into the region "for the benefit of its inhabitants." Palestine (now Israel), Transjordan (now Jordan), and Iraq (formerly Mesopotamia) became British mandates; France claimed Syria and Lebanon (see Map 28.4). (See Diversity and Dominance: The Middle East After World War I.)

The Rise of Modern Turkey

At the end of the war, as the Ottoman Empire teetered on the brink of collapse, France, Britain, and Italy saw an opportunity to expand their empires, and Greece eyed those parts of Anatolia inhabited by Greeks. In 1919 French, British, Italian, and Greek forces occupied Constantinople and parts of Anatolia. By the Treaty of Sèvres (1920) the Allies made the sultan give up most of his lands.

In 1919 Mustafa Kemal, a hero of the Gallipoli campaign, had formed a nationalist government in central Anatolia with the backing of fellow army officers. In 1922, after a short but fierce war against invading Greeks, his armies reconquered Anatolia and the area around Constantinople. The victorious Turks forced hundreds of thousands of Greeks from their ancestral homes in Anatolia. In response the Greek government expelled all Muslims from Greece. The ethnic diversity that had prevailed in the region for centuries ended.

As a war hero and proclaimed savior of his country, Kemal was able to impose wrenching changes on his people faster than any other reformer would have dared. An outspoken modernizer, he was eager to bring Turkey

Mustafa Kemal Atatürk After World War I, Mustafa Kemal was determined to modernize Turkey on the western model. Here he is shown wearing a European-style suit and teaching the Latin alphabet. (Stock Montage)

closer to Europe as quickly as possible. He abolished the sultanate, declared Turkey a secular republic, and introduced European laws. In a radical break with Islamic tradition, he suppressed Muslim courts, schools, and religious orders and replaced the Arabic alphabet with the Latin alphabet.

Kemal attempted to westernize the traditional Turkish family. Women received civil equality, including the right to vote and to be elected to the national assembly. Kemal forbade polygamy and instituted civil marriage and divorce. He even changed people's clothing, strongly discouraging women from veiling their faces, and replaced the fez, until then the traditional Turkish men's hat, with the European brimmed hat. He ordered everyone to take a family name, choosing the name Atatürk ("father of the Turks") for himself. His reforms spread quickly in the cities; but in rural areas, where Islamic traditions remained strong, people resisted them for a long time.

DIVERSITY AND DOMINANCE

THE MIDDLE EAST AFTER WORLD WAR I

During the First World War, Entente forces invaded the Arab provinces of the Ottoman Empire and occupied Palestine, Mesopotamia, and Syria. This raised the question of what to do with these territories after the war. Would they be returned to the Ottoman Empire? Would they simply be added to the colonial empires of Britain and France? Or would they become independent Arab states?

The following documents illustrate the diversity of opinions among various groups planning the postwar settlement: Great Britain concerned with defeating Germany and maintaining its empire; the United States, basing its policies on lofty principles; and Arab delegates from the Middle East, seeking self-determination.

In the early twentieth century, in response to the rise of anti-Semitism in Europe, a movement called Zionism had arisen among European Jews. Zionists, led by Theodore Herzl, hoped for a return to Israel, the ancestral homeland of the Jewish people. For two thousand years this land had been a province of various empires—the Roman, Byzantine, Arab, and Ottoman—and was inhabited by Arabic-speaking people who practiced the Islamic religion.

During the war the British government eagerly sought the support of the American Jewish community to balance the hostility of Irish-Americans and German-Americans toward the British war effort. It was therefore receptive to the idea of establishing a Jewish homeland in Palestine. The British government therefore found itself torn between two contradictory impulses, both motivated by the short-term need to win the war, but not without thought of the more distant future. The result was a policy statement, sent by Foreign Secretary Arthur James Balfour to Baron Rothschild, a prominent supporter of the Zionist movement in England. This statement, called the "Balfour Declaration," has haunted the Middle East ever since.

THE BALFOUR DECLARATION OF 1917

Foreign Office
November 2nd, 1917

Dear Lord Rothschild:

I have much pleasure in conveying to you, on behalf of His Majesty's Government, the following declaration of sympathy with Jewish Zionist aspirations which have been submitted to, and approved by, the Cabinet:

His Majesty's Government view with favor the establishment in Palestine of a national home for the Jewish people, and will use their best endeavors to facilitate the achievement of this object, it being clearly understood that nothing shall be done which may prejudice the civil and religious rights of existing non-Jewish communities in Palestine, or the rights and political status enjoyed by Jews in any other country.

I should be grateful if you would bring this declaration to the knowledge of the Zionist Federation.

Yours,
Arthur James Balfour

On January 8, 1918, the American president Woodrow Wilson issued his famous Fourteen Points proposal to end the war. Much of his speech was devoted to European affairs or to international relations in general, but two of his fourteen points were understood as referring to the Arab world.

WOODROW WILSON'S FOURTEEN POINTS

We entered this war because violations of right had occurred which touches us to the quick and made the life of our own people impossible unless they were corrected and the world secured once for all against their recurrence. What we demand in this war, therefore, is nothing peculiar to ourselves. It is that the world be made fit and safe to live in; and particularly that it be made safe for every peace-loving nation which, like our own, wishes to live its own life, determine its own institutions, be assured of justice and fair dealing by the other peoples of the world as against force and selfish aggression. All the peoples of the world are in effect partners in this interest, and for our own part we see very clearly that unless justice be done to others it will not be done to us. The programme of the world's peace, therefore, is our programme; and that programme, the only possible programme, as we see it, is this:

V. A free, open-minded, and absolutely impartial adjustment of all colonial claims, based upon a strict observance of the principle that in determining all such questions of sovereignty the interests of the populations concerned must have equal weight with the equitable claims of the government whose title is to be determined.

XII. The Turkish portions of the present Ottoman Empire should be assured a secure sovereignty, but the other nationalities which are now under Turkish rule should be assured an undoubted security of life and an absolutely unmolested opportunity of autonomous development. . . .

When the war ended, the victorious Allies assembled in Paris to determine, among other things, the fate of the former Arab provinces of the Ottoman Empire. This was a matter of grave concern to both Zionists and leaders of the Arab populations. Arab leaders, in particular, had reason to doubt the intentions of the great powers, especially Britain and France. When the Allies decided to create mandates in the Arab territories on the grounds that the Arab peoples were not ready for independence, Arab leaders expressed their misgivings, as the following statement shows:

MEMORANDUM OF THE GENERAL SYRIAN CONGRESS, JULY 2, 1919

We the undersigned members of the General Syrian Congress, meeting in Damascus on Wednesday, July 2nd, 1919, made up of representatives from the three Zones, viz., The Southern, Eastern, and Western, provided with credentials and authorizations by the inhabitants of our various districts, Moslems, Christians, and Jews, have agreed upon the following statement of the desires of the people of the country who have elected us. . . .

1. We ask absolutely complete political independence for Syria. . . .
2. We ask that the government of this Syrian country should be a democratic civil constitutional Monarchy on broad decentralization principles, safeguarding the rights of minorities, and that the King be the Emir Feisal, who carried on a glorious struggle in the cause of our liberation and merited our full confidence and entire reliance.
3. Considering the fact that the Arabs inhabiting the Syrian area are not naturally less gifted than other more advanced races and that they are by no means less developed than the Bulgarians, Serbians, Greeks, and Roumanians at the beginning of their independence, we protest against Article 22 of the Covenant of the League of Nations, placing us among the nations in their middle stage of development which stand in need of a mandatory power.
4. In the event of the rejection of the Peace Conference of this just protest for certain considerations that we

may not understand, we, relying on the declarations of President Wilson that his object in waging war was to put an end to the ambition of conquest and colonization, we can only regard the mandate mentioned in the Covenant of the League of Nations as equivalent to the rendering of economical and technical assistance that does not prejudice our complete independence. And desiring that our country should not fall a prey to colonization and believing that the American Nation is furthest from any thought of colonization and has no political ambition in our country, we will seek the technical and economic assistance from the United States of America, provided that such assistance does not exceed 20 years.

5. In the event of America not finding herself in a position to accept our desire for assistance, we will seek this assistance from Great Britain, also provided that such does not prejudice our complete independence and unity of our country and that the duration of such assistance does not exceed that mentioned in the previous article.
6. We do not acknowledge any right claimed by the French Government in any part whatever of our Syrian country and refuse that she should assist us or have a hand in our country under any circumstances and in any place.
7. We opposed the pretensions of the Zionists to create a Jewish commonwealth in the southern part of Syria, known as Palestine, and oppose Zionist migration to any part of our country; for we do not acknowledge their title but consider them a grave peril to our people from the national, economical, and political points of view. Our Jewish compatriots shall enjoy our common rights and assume our common responsibilities.

QUESTIONS FOR ANALYSIS

1. Was there a contradiction between Balfour's proposal to establish "a national home for the Jewish people" and the promise "that nothing shall be done which may prejudice the civil and religious rights of existing non-Jewish communities in Palestine"? If so, why did he make two contradictory promises?
2. How would Woodrow Wilson's statements about "the interests of the populations concerned" and "an absolutely unmolested opportunity of autonomous development" apply to Palestine?
3. Why did the delegates to the Syrian General Congress object to the plan to create mandates in the former Ottoman provinces? What alternatives did they offer?
4. Why did the delegates object to the creation of a Jewish commonwealth?

Source: The Balfour Declaration, *The Times* (London), November 9, 1917. Memorandum of the General Syrian Congress, *Foreign Relations of the United States: Paris Peace Conference*, vol. 12 (Washington, DC: Government Printing Office, 1919), 780–781.

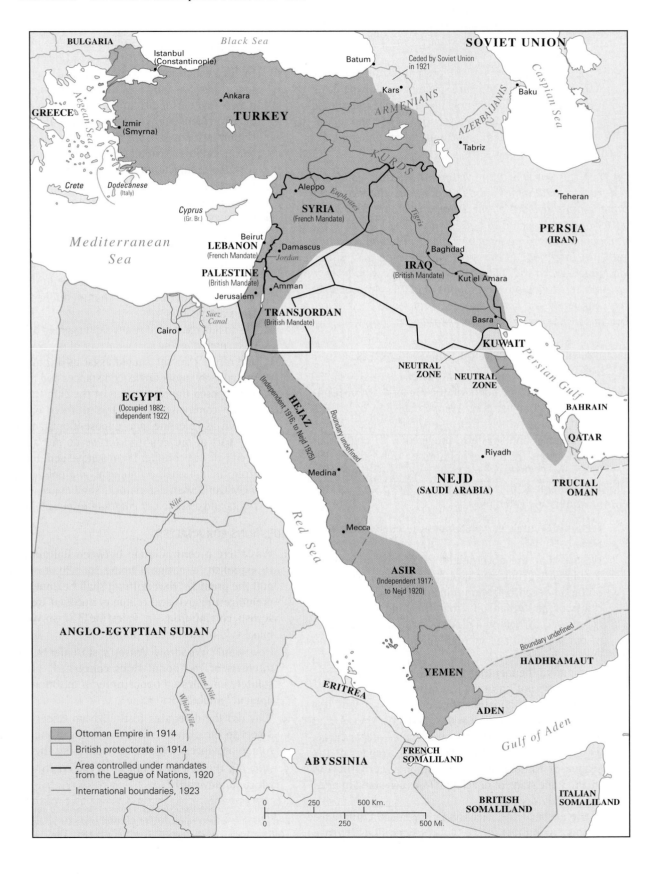

Map 28.4   Territorial Changes in the Middle East After World War I   The defeat and dismemberment of the Ottoman Empire at the end of World War I resulted in an entirely new political map of the region. The Turkish Republic inherited Anatolia and a small piece of the Balkans, while the Ottoman Empire's Arab provinces were divided between France and Great Britain as "Class A Mandates." The French acquired Syria and Lebanon, and the British got Palestine (now Israel), Transjordan (now Jordan), and Iraq. Only Iran and Egypt remained as they had been.

Arab Lands and the Question of Palestine

Among the Arab people, the thinly disguised colonialism of the mandate system set off protests and rebellions not only in the mandated territories, but even as far away as Morocco. Arabs viewed the European presence not as "liberation" from Ottoman "oppression," but as foreign occupation.

After World War I Middle Eastern society underwent dramatic changes. Nomads disappeared from the deserts as trucks replaced camel caravans. The rural population grew fast, and many landless peasants migrated to the swelling cities. The population of the region is estimated to have increased by 50 percent between 1914 and 1939, while that of large cities such as Constantinople, Baghdad, and Cairo doubled.

The urban and mercantile middle class, encouraged by the transformation of Turkey, adopted Western ideas, customs, and styles of housing and clothing. Some families sent their sons to European secular or mission schools, then to Western colleges in Cairo and Beirut or universities abroad, to prepare for jobs in government and business. Among the educated elite were a few women who became schoolteachers or nurses. There were great variations, ranging from Lebanon, with its strong French influence, to Arabia and Iran, which retained their cultural traditions.

The region in closest contact with Europe was the Maghrib—Algeria, Tunisia, and Morocco—which the French army considered its private domain. Alongside the old native quarters, the French built modern neighborhoods inhabited mainly by Europeans (see Environment and Technology: Cities Old and New). France had occupied Algeria since 1830 and had encouraged European immigration. The settlers owned the best lands and monopolized government jobs and businesses, while Arabs and Berbers remained poor and suffered intense discrimination. Nationalism was only beginning to appear before World War II, and the settlers quickly blocked attempts at reform.

The British attempted to control the Middle East with a mixture of bribery and intimidation. They helped Faisal, leader of the Arab Revolt, become king of Syria. When the French ousted him, the British made him king of Iraq. They used bombers to quell rural insurrections in Iraq. In 1931 they reached an agreement with King Faisal's government: official independence for Iraq in exchange for the right to keep two air bases, a military alliance, and an assured flow of petroleum. France, meanwhile, sent thousands of troops to Syria and Lebanon to crush nationalist uprisings.

In Egypt, as in Iraq, the British substituted a phony independence for official colonialism. They declared Egypt independent in 1922 but reserved the right to station troops along the Suez Canal to secure their link with India in the event of war. Most galling to the Wafd (Nationalist) Party was the British attempt to remove Egyptian troops from Sudan, a land many Egyptians considered a colony of Egypt. Britain was successful in keeping Egypt in limbo—neither independent nor a colony—thanks to an alliance with King Farouk and conservative Egyptian politicians who feared both secular and religious radicalism.

Before the war, a Jewish minority lived in Palestine, as in other Arab countries. As soon as Palestine became a British mandate in 1920, Jewish immigrants began arriving from Europe, encouraged by the Balfour Declaration of 1917. Most settled in the cities, but some purchased land to establish *kibbutzim*, communal farms. Their goals were to become self-sufficient and to reestablish their ties to the land of their ancestors. The purchases of land by Jewish agencies angered the indigenous Palestinians, especially tenant farmers who had been evicted to make room for settlers. In 1920–1921 riots erupted between Jews and Arabs. When far more Jewish immigrants arrived than they had anticipated, the British tried to limit immigration, thereby alienating the Jews without mollifying the Arabs. Increasingly, Jews arrived without papers, smuggled in by militant Zionist organizations. In the 1930s the country was torn by strikes and guerrilla warfare that the British could not control. In the process, Britain earned the hatred of both sides and of much of the Arab world as well.

SOCIETY, CULTURE, AND TECHNOLOGY IN THE INDUSTRIALIZED WORLD

With the signing of the peace treaties, the countries that had fought for four years turned their efforts toward building a new future. The war had left a deep imprint on European society and culture. Advances

ENVIRONMENT + TECHNOLOGY

Cities Old and New

Cities do not just grow larger; they change, sometimes radically, in response to culture and technology. The impact of cultural dominance and technological innovations on urban design is evident in these photographs of Cairo.

The European colonial presence was felt more strongly in cities than in the countryside. Cairo, the largest city in the Arab world before the British conquest, grew much larger after 1882. However, the construction of modern quarters for Europeans and wealthy Egyptians had little impact on the older quarters where most Cairenes lived. In the picture of the old quarter of Cairo in 1900 with its narrow streets and open stalls, men wear the burnoose and women cover their faces with a veil. The later picture, taken in 1904, shows Shepheard's hotel, one of the most luxurious hotels in the world, built on a broad avenue in the city's modern quarter.

The picture at left reflects the traditional architecture of hot desert countries: narrow streets, thick whitewashed walls, small windows, and heavy doors, all designed to keep out the heat of the day and protect privacy. The picture below shows the ideas Europeans brought with them about how a city should look. The wide streets and high airy buildings with windows and balconies mimic the urban design of late-nineteenth-century Paris, London, and Rome.

Cairo—Modern and Traditional   The luxurious Shepheard's Hotel (below) was built in the European style on a broad avenue in the new quarter of Cairo. In stark contrast is the street (above) in the old quarter of the city: the street is narrow, the walls of the buildings are thick, and the windows small in order to protect the interiors from the heat of the sun.   (Billie Love Historical Collection)

in science offered astonishing new insights into the mysteries of nature and the universe. New technologies, many of them pioneered in the United States, promised to change the daily lives of millions of people.

Class and Gender

After the war, class distinctions began to fade. Many European aristocrats had died on the battlefields, and with them went their class's long domination of the army, the diplomatic corps, and other elite sectors of society. The United States and Canada had never had as rigidly defined a class structure as European societies or as elaborate a set of traditions and manners. During the war, displays of wealth and privilege seemed unpatriotic. On both sides of the Atlantic, engineers, businessmen, lawyers, and other professionals rose to prominence, increasing the relative importance of the middle class.

The activities of governments had expanded during the war and continued to grow. Governments provided housing, highways, schools, public health facilities, broadcasting, and other services. This growth of government influence created a need for thousands more bureaucrats. Department stores, banks, insurance companies, and other businesses also increased the white-collar work force.

In contrast with the middle class, the working class did not expand. The introduction of new machines and new ways of organizing work, such as the automobile assembly line that Henry Ford devised, increased workers' productivity so that greater outputs could be achieved without a larger labor force.

Women's lives changed more rapidly in the 1920s than in any previous decade. Although the end of the war marked a retreat from wartime job opportunities, some women remained in the work force as wage earners and as salaried professionals. The young and wealthy enjoyed more personal freedoms than their mothers had before the war; they drove cars, played sports, traveled alone, and smoked in public. For others the upheavals of war brought more suffering than liberation. Millions of women had lost their fathers, brothers, sons, husbands, and fiancés in the war or in the great influenza epidemic. After the war the shortage of young men caused many single women to lead lives of loneliness and destitution.

In Europe and North America advocates of women's rights had been demanding the vote for women since the 1890s. New Zealand was the only nation to grant women the vote before the twentieth century. Women in Norway were the first to obtain it in Europe, in 1915. Russian women followed in 1917, and Canadians and Germans in 1918. Britain gave women over age thirty the vote in 1918 and later extended it to younger women. The Nineteenth Amendment to the U.S. Constitution granted suffrage to American women in 1920. Women in Turkey began voting in 1934. Most other countries did not allow women to vote until after 1945.

In dictatorships voting rights for women made no difference, and in democratic countries women tended to vote like their male relatives. In the British elections of 1918—the first to include women—they overwhelmingly voted for the Conservative Party. Everywhere, their influence on politics was less radical than feminists had hoped and conservatives had feared. Even when it did not alter politics and government, however, the right to vote was a potent symbol.

Women were active in many other areas besides the suffrage movement. On both sides of the Atlantic women participated in social reform movements to prevent mistreatment of women and children and of industrial workers. In the United States such reforms were championed by Progressives such as Jane Addams (1860–1935), who founded a settlement house in a poor neighborhood and received the Nobel Peace Prize in 1931. In Europe reformers were generally aligned with Socialist or Labour Parties.

Since 1874 the Women's Christian Temperance Union had campaigned against alcohol and taverns. In the early twentieth century the American Carrie Nation (1846–1911) became famous for destroying saloons and for lectures in the United States and Europe against the evils of liquor. As a result of this campaign the Eighteenth Amendment imposed prohibition in the United States from 1919 until it was revoked by the Twenty-First Amendment fourteen years later.

Among the most controversial, and eventually most effective of the reformers, were those who advocated contraception, such as the American **Margaret Sanger** (1883–1966). Her campaign brought her into conflict with the authorities, who equated birth control with pornography. Finally, in 1923 she was able to found a birth control clinic in New York. In France, however, the government prohibited contraception and abortion in 1920 in an effort to increase the birthrate and make up for the loss of so many young men in the war. Only the Russian communists allowed abortion, for ideological reasons (see Diversity and Dominance: Women, Family Values, and the Russian Revolution in Chapter 29).

Revolution in the Sciences

For two hundred years scientists following in Isaac Newton's footsteps had applied the same laws and equations to astronomical observations and to laboratory experiments. At the end of the nineteenth century, however, a revolution in physics undermined all the old certainties about nature. Physicists discovered that atoms, the building blocks of matter, are not indivisible, but consist of far smaller subatomic particles. In 1900 the German physicist **Max Planck** (1858–1947) found that atoms emit or absorb energy only in discrete amounts, called *quanta*, instead of continuously, as assumed in Newtonian physics. These findings seemed strange enough, but what really undermined Newtonian physics was the general theory of relativity developed by **Albert Einstein** (1879–1955), another German physicist. In 1916 Einstein announced that not only is matter made of insubstantial particles, but that time, space, and mass are not fixed but are relative to one another. Other physicists said that light is made up of either waves or particles, depending on the observer, and that an experiment could determine either the speed or the position of a particle of light, but never both.

To nonscientists it seemed as though theories expressed in arcane mathematical formulas were replacing truth and common sense. Far from being mere speculation, however, the new physics promised to unlock the secrets of matter and provide humans with plentiful—and potentially dangerous—sources of energy.

The new social sciences were even more unsettling than the new physics, for they challenged Victorian morality, middle-class values, and notions of Western superiority. Sigmund Freud (1856–1939), a Viennese physician, developed the technique of psychoanalysis to probe the minds of his patients. He found not only rationality but also hidden layers of emotion and desire repressed by social restraints. "The primitive, savage and evil impulses have not vanished from any individual, but continue their existence, although in a repressed state," he warned. Meanwhile, sociologists and anthropologists had begun the empirical study of societies, both Western and non-Western. Before the war the French sociologist Emile Durkheim (1858–1917) had come to the then-shocking conclusion that "there are no religions that are false. All are true in their own fashion."

If the words *primitive* and *savage* applied to Europeans as well as to other peoples, and if religions were all equally "true," then what remained of the superiority of Western civilization? Cultural relativism, as the new approach to human societies was called, was as unnerving as relativity in physics.

Although these ideas had been expressed before 1914, wartime experiences called into question the West's faith in reason and progress. Some people accepted the new ideas with enthusiasm. Others condemned and rejected them, clinging to the sense of order and faith in progress that had energized European and American culture before the war.

The New Technologies of Modernity

Some Europeans and Americans viewed the sciences with mixed feelings, but the new technologies aroused almost universal excitement. In North America even working-class people could afford some of the new products of scientific research, inventors' ingenuity, and industrial production. Mass consumption lagged in Europe, but science and technology were just as advanced, and public fascination with the latest inventions—the cult of the modern—was just as strong.

Of all the innovations of the time, none attracted public interest as much as airplanes. In 1903 two young American mechanics, **Wilbur and Orville Wright,** built the first aircraft that was heavier than air and could be maneuvered in flight. From that moment on, wherever they appeared, airplanes fascinated people. During the war the exploits of air aces relieved the tedium of news from the front. In the 1920s aviation became a sport and a form of entertainment, and flying daredevils achieved extraordinary fame by pushing their planes to the very limit—and often beyond. Among the most celebrated pilots were three Americans. Amelia Earhart was the first woman to fly across the Atlantic Ocean, and her example encouraged other women to fly. Richard Byrd flew over the North Pole in 1926. The most admired of all was Charles Lindbergh, the first person to fly alone across the Atlantic in 1927. The heroic age of flight lasted until the late 1930s, when aviation became a means of transportation, a business, and a male preserve.

Electricity, produced in industrial quantities since the 1890s (see Chapter 26), began to transform home life. The first home use of electricity was for lighting, thanks to the economical and long-lasting tungsten bulb. Then, having persuaded people to wire their homes, electrical utilities joined manufacturers in advertising electric irons, fans, washing machines, hot plates, and other appliances.

Radio—or wireless telegraphy, as it was called—had served ships and the military during the war as a means of point-to-point telecommunication. After the war, amateurs used surplus radio equipment to talk to one another. The first commercial station began broadcasting in Pittsburgh in 1920. By the end of 1923 six hundred stations were broadcasting news, sports, soap operas, and advertising to homes throughout North America. By 1930, 12 million families owned radio receivers. In Europe radio spread more slowly because governments reserved the airwaves for cultural and official programs and taxed radio owners to pay for the service.

Another medium that spread explosively in the 1920s was film. Motion pictures had begun in France in 1895 and flourished there and elsewhere in Europe, where the dominant concern was to reproduce stage plays. In the United States filmmaking started at almost the same time, but American filmmakers considered it their business to entertain audiences rather than preserve outstanding theatrical performances. In competing for audiences they looked to cinematic innovation, broad humor, and exciting spectacles, in the process developing styles of filmmaking that became immensely popular.

Diversity was a hallmark of the early film industry. After World War I filmmaking took root and flourished in Japan, India, Turkey, Egypt, and a suburb of Los Angeles, California, called Hollywood. American and European movie studios were successful in exporting films, since silent movies presented no language problems. In 1929, out of an estimated 2,100 films produced worldwide, 510 were made in the United States and 750 in Japan. But by then the United States had introduced the first "talking" motion picture, *The Jazz Singer* (1927), which changed all the rules.

The number of Americans who went to see their favorite stars in thrilling adventures and heart-breaking romances rose from 40 million in 1922 to 100 million in 1930, at a time when the population of the country was about 120 million. Europeans had the technology and the art but neither the wealth nor the huge market of the United States. Hollywood studios began the diffusion of American culture that has continued to this day.

Health and hygiene were also part of the cult of modernity. Advances in medicine—some learned in the war—saved many lives. Wounds were regularly disinfected, and x-ray machines helped diagnose fractures. Since the late nineteenth century scientists had known that disease-causing bacteria could be transmitted through contaminated water, spoiled food, or fecal matter. After the war cities built costly water supply and sewage treatment systems. By the 1920s indoor plumbing and flush toilets were becoming common even in working-class neighborhoods.

Interest in cleanliness altered private life. Doctors and home economists bombarded women with warnings and advice on how to banish germs. Soap and appliance manufacturers filled women's magazines with advertisements for products to help housewives keep their family's homes and clothing spotless and their meals fresh and wholesome. The decline in infant mortality and improvements in general health and life ex-

pectancy in this period owe as much to the cult of cleanliness as to advances in medicine.

Technology and the Environment

Two new technologies—the skyscraper and the automobile—transformed the urban environment even more radically than the railroad had done in the nineteenth century. At the end of the nineteenth century architects had begun to design ever-higher buildings using load-bearing steel frames and passenger elevators. Major corporations in Chicago and New York competed to build the most daring buildings in the world, such as New York's fifty-five-story Woolworth Building (1912) and Chicago's thirty-four-story Tribune Tower (1923). A building boom in the late 1920s produced dozens of skyscrapers, culminating with the eighty-six-story, 1,239-foot (377-meter) Empire State Building in New York, completed in 1932.

European cities restricted the height of buildings to protect their architectural heritage; Paris forbade buildings over 56 feet (17 meters) high. In innovative designs, however, European architects led the way. In the 1920s the Swiss architect Charles Edouard Jeanneret (1887–1965), known as Le Corbusier°, outlined a new approach to architecture that featured simplicity of form, absence of surface ornamentation, easy manufacture, and inexpensive materials. Other architects—including the Finn Eero Saarinen, the Germans Ludwig Mies van der Rohe° and Walter Gropius, and the American Frank Lloyd Wright—also contributed their own designs to create what became known as the International Style.

While central business districts were reaching for the sky, outlying areas were spreading far into the countryside, thanks to the automobile. The assembly line pioneered by Henry Ford mass-produced vehicles in ever-greater volume and at falling prices. By 1929 the United States had one car for every five people, five-sixths of the world's automobiles. Far from being blamed for their exhaust emissions, automobiles were praised as the solution to urban pollution. As cars replaced carts and carriages, horses disappeared from city streets, as did tons of manure.

The most important environmental effect of automobiles was suburban sprawl. Middle-class families could now live in single-family homes too spread apart to be served by public transportation. By the late 1920s paved roads rivaled rail networks both in length and in the surface they occupied. As middle- and working-class

Le Corbusier (luh cor-booz-YEH)
Ludwig Mies van der Rohe (LOOD-vig MEES fon der ROW-uh)

The Archetypal Automobile City   As Los Angeles grew from a modest town into a sprawling metropolis, broad avenues, parking lots, and garages were built to accommodate automobiles. By 1929, most families owned a car and streetcar lines had closed for lack of passengers. This photograph shows a street in the downtown business district.   (Ralph Morris Archives/Los Angeles Public Library)

families bought cars, cities acquired rings of automobile suburbs. Los Angeles, the first true automobile city, consisted of suburbs spread over hundreds of square miles and linked together by broad avenues. In sections of the city where streetcar lines went out of business, the automobile, at first a plaything for the wealthy, became a necessity for commuters. Many Americans saw Los Angeles as the portent of a glorious future in which everyone would have a car; only a few foresaw the congestion and pollution that would ensue.

Technological advances also transformed rural environments. Automobile owners quickly developed an interest in "motoring"—driving their vehicles out into the country on weekends or on holiday trips. Farmers began buying cars and light trucks, using them to transport produce as well as passengers. Governments obliged by building new roads and paving old ones to make automobile travel smoother and safer.

Until the 1920s horses remained the predominant source of energy for pulling plows and reapers and powering threshing machines on American farms. Only the wealthiest farmers could afford the slow and costly steam tractors. In 1915 Ford introduced a gasoline-powered tractor, and by the mid-1920s these versatile machines began replacing horses. Larger farms profited most from this innovation, while small farmers sold their land and moved to the cities. Tractors and other expensive equipment hastened the transformation of agriculture from family enterprises to the large agribusinesses of today.

In India, Australia, and the western United States, where there was little virgin rain-watered land left to cultivate, engineers built dams and canals to irrigate dry lands. Dams offered the added advantage of producing electricity, for which there was a booming demand. The immediate benefits of irrigation—land, food, and electricity—far outweighed such distant consequences as salt deposits on irrigated lands and harm to wildlife.

CONCLUSION

In the late 1920s it seemed as though the victors in the Great War might reestablish the prewar prosperity and European dominance of the globe. But the spirit of the 1920s was not real peace; instead it was the eye of a hurricane.

The Great War caused a major realignment among the nations of the world. France and Britain, the two leading colonial powers, emerged economically weakened despite their victory. The war brought defeat and humiliation to Germany but did not reduce its military or industrial potential. It destroyed the old regime and the aristocracy of Russia, leading to civil war and revolution from which the victorious powers sought to isolate themselves. Two other old empires—the Austro-Hungarian and the Ottoman—were divided into many smaller and weaker nations. For a while, the Middle East seemed ripe for a new wave of imperialism. But there and throughout Asia the war unleashed revolutionary nationalist movements that challenged European influence.

Only two countries benefited from the war. Japan took advantage of the European conflict to develop its industries and press its demands on a China weakened by domestic turmoil and social unrest. The United States emerged as the most prosperous and potentially most powerful nation, restrained only by the isolationist sentiments of many Americans.

Modern technology and industrial organization had long been praised in the name of "progress" for their ability to reduce toil and disease and improve living standards. The war showed that they possessed an equally awesome destructive potential. As we shall see in the next chapter, most survivors wanted no repeat of such a nightmare. But a small minority worshiped violence and saw the new weaponry as a means to dominate those who feared conflict and death.

■ Key Terms

Western Front	Sun Yat-sen
Faisal	Yuan Shikai
Theodore Herzl	Guomindang
Balfour Declaration	Chiang Kai-shek
Bolsheviks	mandate system
Vladimir Lenin	Margaret Sanger
Woodrow Wilson	Max Planck
League of Nations	Albert Einstein
Treaty of Versailles	Wilbur and Orville Wright
New Economic Policy	

■ Suggested Reading

Bernadotte Schmitt and Harold C. Bedeler, *The World in the Crucible, 1914–1918* (1984), and John Keegan, *The First World War* (1999), are two engaging overviews of World War I. Imanuel Geiss, *July 1914: The Outbreak of the First World War* (1967), argues that Germany caused the conflict. Barbara Tuchman's *The Guns of August* (1962) and Alexander Solzhenitsyn's *August 1914* (1972) recount the first month of the war in detail. Keegan's *The Face of Battle* (1976) vividly describes the Battle of the Somme from the soldiers' perspective. On the technology of warfare see William H. McNeill, *The Pursuit of Power: Technology, Armed Force, and Society* (1982), and John Ellis, *The Social History of the Machine Gun* (1975). The role of women and the home front is the subject of essays in Margaret Higonnet et al., eds., *Behind the Lines: Gender and the Two World Wars* (1987), and sections of Lynn Weiner, *From Working Girl to Working Mother* (1985). The definitive work on the flu epidemic is Alfred W. Crosby, *America's Forgotten Pandemic: The Influenza of 1918* (1989). Two famous novels about the war are Erich Maria Remarque's *All Quiet on the Western Front* (1928) and Robert

Graves's *Goodbye to All That* (1929). The war in English literature is the subject of Paul Fussell, *The Great War and Modern Memory* (1975).

For the background to the Russian Revolution read Theodore von Laue's *Why Lenin? Why Stalin?* 2d ed. (1971); but see also Richard Pipes, *The Russian Revolution* (1990), and Orlando Figes, *A People's Tragedy: The Russian Revolution, 1891–1924* (1996). The classic eyewitness account of the Revolution is John Reed's *Ten Days That Shook the World* (1919). On gender issues see Wendy Goldman, *Women, the State, and Revolution: Soviet Family Policy and Social Life, 1917–1936* (1993). The best-known novel about the Revolution and civil war is Boris Pasternak's *Doctor Zhivago* (1958).

John Maynard Keynes's *The Economic Consequences of the Peace* (1920) is a classic critique of the Paris Peace Conference. Arno Mayer's *Political Origins of the New Diplomacy, 1917–1918* (1959) analyzes the tensions and failures of great-power politics. The 1920s are discussed in Raymond Sontag's *A Broken World, 1919–1939* (1971).

The best recent book on Japan in the twentieth century is Daikichi Irokawa's *The Age of Hirohito: In Search of Modern Japan* (1995). See also Richard Storry, *A History of Modern Japan* (1982), and Tessa Morris-Suzuki, *The Technological Transformation of Japan* (1994). In the large and fast-growing literature on twentieth-century China, two general introductions are especially useful: John K. Fairbank, *The Great Chinese Revolution, 1800–1985* (1986), and Jonathan Spence, *The Search for Modern China* (1990). On the warlord and Guomindang periods see Lucien Bianco, *Origins of the Chinese Revolution, 1915–1949* (1971).

On the war and its aftermath in the Middle East see David Fromkin, *A Peace to End All Peace* (1989), and M. E. Yapp, *The Near East Since the First World War* (1991). Bernard Lewis, *The Emergence of Modern Turkey* (1968), is a good introduction. On Africa in this period see A. Adu Boahen, ed., *Africa Under Colonial Domination, 1880–1935*, vol. 7 of the *UNESCO General History of Africa* (1985), and A. D. Roberts, ed., *Cambridge History of Africa*, vol. 7, *1905–1940* (1986).

The cultural transformation of Europe is captured in H. Stuart Hughes, *Consciousness and Society: The Reorientation of European Social Thought, 1890–1930* (1958). The towering intellectuals of that era are the subject of Peter Gay, *Freud: A Life for Our Time* (1988), and Abraham Pais, *Subtle Is the Lord: The Science and Life of Albert Einstein* (1982). Three books capture the enthusiastic popular response to technological innovations: David E. Nye, *Electrifying America: Social Meanings of a New Technology* (1990); Peter Fritzsche, *A Nation of Fliers: German Aviation and the Popular Imagination* (1992); and the sweeping overview by Thomas Hughes, *American Genesis: A Century of Invention and Technological Enthusiasm, 1870–1970* (1989). On the role of women is this period, see Ellen DuBois, *Woman Suffrage and Women's Rights* (1998); Sheila Rowbotham, *A Century of Women: The History of Women in Britain and the United States* (1997); and Renate Bridenthal, Claudia Koonz, and Susan Stuard, eds., *Becoming Visible: Women in European History* (1987).

Document-Based Question

Self-Determination in the Middle East after World War I

Using the following documents, assess the success and failure of self-determination in the Middle East after World War I.

DOCUMENT 1
Two quotes from the League of Nations (pp. 752–753)

DOCUMENT 2
Mustafa Kemal Atatürk (photo, p. 753)

DOCUMENT 3
The Middle East After World War I (Diversity and Dominance, pp. 754–755)

DOCUMENT 4
Map 28.4 Territorial Changes in the Middle East After World War I (p. 757)

DOCUMENT 5
Cairo—Modern and Traditional (Environment and Technology, p. 758)

In Document 3, how does the particular purpose of the three authors affect the reliability of their statements? What additional types of documents would help you understand the success and failure of self-determination in the Middle East after World War I?

29

The Collapse
of the Old Order,
1929–1949

German Dive-Bomber over Eastern Europe   A German ME-100 fighter plane attacks a Soviet troop convoy on the Eastern Front.

CHAPTER OUTLINE

The Stalin Revolution

The Depression

The Rise of Fascism

East Asia, 1931–1945

The Second World War

The Character of Warfare

DIVERSITY AND DOMINANCE: Women, Family Values, and the Russian Revolution

ENVIRONMENT AND TECHNOLOGY: Biomedical Technologies

Before the First World War the Italian futurist poet Filippo Marinetti exalted violence as noble and manly: "We want to glorify war, the world's only hygiene—militarism, deed, destroyer of anarchisms, the beautiful ideas that are death-bringing, and the subordination of women." His friend Gabriele d'Annunzio added: "If it is a crime to incite citizens to violence, I shall boast of this crime." Poets are sometimes more prescient than they imagine.

In the nineteenth century the great powers had created a world order with three dimensions. Their constitutional governments were manipulated by politicians—some liberal, some conservative—through appeals to popular nationalism. Internationally, the world order relied on the maintenance of empires, formal or informal, by military or economic means. And the global economy was based on free-market capitalism in which the industrial countries exchanged manufactured goods for the agricultural and mineral products of the nonindustrial world.

After the trauma of World War I the world seemed to return to what U.S. president Warren Harding called "normalcy": prosperity in Europe and America, European colonialism in Asia and Africa, American domination of Latin America, and peace almost everywhere. But the old order, like Humpty Dumpty, could not be put back together again, for its economic underpinnings were fragile and its political support was superficial.

In 1929 the normalcy of the twenties fell apart. Stocks plummeted; businesses went bankrupt; prices fell; factories closed; and workers were laid off. As the Great Depression spread around the world, governments turned against one another in a desperate attempt to protect their people's livelihood. Even wholly agricultural nations and colonies suffered as markets for their exports shriveled.

Most survivors of the war had learned to abhor violence. For a few, however, war and domination became a creed, a goal, and a solution to their problems. The Japanese military tried to save their country from the Depression by conquering China, which erupted in revolution. In Germany the Depression reawakened resentments against the victors of the Great War; people who blamed their troubles on Communists and Jews turned to the Nazis, who promised to save German society by crushing others. In the Soviet Union Stalin used energetic and murderous means to force his country into a Communist version of the Industrial Revolution.

As the old order collapsed, the world was engulfed by a second Great War, far more global and destructive than the first. At the end of World War II much of Europe and East Asia lay in ruins, and millions of destitute refugees sought safety in other lands. The colonial powers were either defeated or so weakened that they could no longer hold onto their empires when Asian and African peoples asserted their desire for independence.

This, then, is the theme of this chapter. As you read it, ask yourself the following questions:

- How did the Soviet Union change under Stalin, and at what cost?
- What caused the Depression, and what effects did it have on the world?
- How did the Depression lead to the Second World War?
- How was the war fought, and why did Japan and Germany lose?

THE STALIN REVOLUTION

During the 1920s other countries ostracized the Soviet Union as it recovered from the Revolutions of 1917 and the civil war that followed (see Chapter 28). After Stalin achieved total mastery over this huge nation in early 1929, he led it through another revolution—an economic and social transformation that turned it into a great industrial and military power and intensified both admiration for and fear of communism throughout the world.

Five-Year Plans

Joseph Stalin (1879–1953) was born Joseph Vissarionovich Dzhugashvili into the family of a poor shoemaker. Before becoming a revolutionary, he

C H R O N O L O G Y		
	Europe and North Africa	**Asia and the Pacific**
1930	**1931** Great Depression reaches Europe	**1931** Japanese forces occupy Manchuria
	1933 Hitler comes to power in Germany	**1934–1935** Mao leads Communists on Long March
1935	**1936** Hitler invades the Rhineland	
		1937 Japanese troops invade China, conquer coastal provinces; Chiang Kai-shek flees to Sichuan
	1939 (Sept. 1) German forces invade Poland	**1937–1938** Japanese troops take Nanjing
1940	**1940 (March–April)** German forces conquer Denmark, Norway, the Netherlands, and Belgium	
	1940 (May–June) German forces conquer France	
	1940 (June–Sept.) Battle of Britain	
	1941 (June 21) German forces invade USSR	**1941 (Dec. 7)** Japanese aircraft bomb Pearl Harbor
	1942–1943 Allies and Germany battle for control of North Africa	**1942 (Jan–March)** Japanese conquer Thailand, Philippines, Malaya
	1943 Soviet victory in Battle of Stalingrad	**1942 (June)** United States Navy defeats Japan at Battle of Midway
	1943–1944 Red Army slowly pushes Wehrmacht back to Germany	
	1944 (June 6) D-day: U.S., British, and Canadian troops land in Normandy	
1945	**1945 (May 7)** Germany surrenders	**1945 (Aug. 6)** United States drops atomic bomb on Hiroshima
		1945 (Aug. 14) Japan surrenders
		1945–1949 Civil war in China
		1949 Communist defeat Guomindang; Mao proclaims People's Republic (Oct. 1)

studied for the priesthood. Under the name "Stalin" (Russian for "man of steel") he played a small part in the Revolutions of 1917. He was a hard-working and skillful administrator who rose within the party bureaucracy and filled its upper ranks with men loyal to himself. By 1927 he had ousted Leon Trotsky, the best-known revolutionary after Lenin, from the party. He then proceeded to squeeze all other rivals out of positions of power, make himself absolute dictator, and transform Soviet society.

Stalin's ambition was to turn the Union of Soviet Socialist Republics (USSR) into an industrial nation. Industrialization was to serve a different purpose in the USSR than in other countries, however. It was not expected to produce consumer goods for a mass market, as in Britain and the United States, or to enrich individuals. Instead, its aim was to increase the power of the Communist Party domestically and the power of the Soviet Union in relation to other countries.

By building up Russia's industry, Stalin was deter-mined to prevent a repetition of the humiliating defeat Russia had suffered at the hands of Germany in 1917. His goal was to quintuple the output of electricity and double that of heavy industry—iron, steel, coal, and machinery—in five years. To do so, he devised the first of a series of **Five-Year Plans,** a system of centralized control copied from the German experience of World War I.

Beginning in October 1928 the Communist Party and government created whole industries and cities from scratch, then trained millions of peasants to work in the new factories, mines, and offices. In every way except actual fighting, Stalin's Russia resembled a nation at war.

Rapid industrialization hastened environmental changes. Hydroelectric dams turned rivers into strings of reservoirs. Roads, canals, and railroad tracks cut the landscape. Forests and grassland were turned into farmland. From an environmental perspective, the outcome of the Five-Year Plans resembled the transformation that had occurred in the United States and Canada a few decades earlier.

Collectivization of Agriculture

Since the Soviet Union was still a predominantly agrarian country, the only way to pay for these massive investments, provide the labor, and feed the millions of new industrial workers was to squeeze the peasantry. Stalin therefore proceeded with the most radical social experiment conceived up to that time: the collectivization of agriculture.

Collectivization meant consolidating small private farms into vast collectives and making the farmers work together in commonly owned fields. Each collective was expected to supply the government with a fixed amount of food and distribute what was left among its members. Machine Tractor Stations leased agricultural machinery to several farms in exchange for the government's share of the crop. Collectives were to become outdoor factories where food was manufactured through the techniques of mass production and the application of machinery. Collectivization was an attempt to replace what Lenin called the peasants' "petty bourgeois" attitudes with an industrial way of life, the only one Communists respected. Collectivization was expected to bring the peasants under government control so they never again could withhold food supplies, as they had done during the Russian civil war of 1918–1921.

When collectivization was announced, the government mounted a massive propaganda campaign and sent party members into the countryside to enlist the farmers' support. At first all seemed to go well, but soon *kulaks*° ("fists"), the better-off peasants, began to resist giving up all their property. When soldiers came to force them into collectives at gunpoint, the kulaks burned their own crops, smashed their own equipment, and slaughtered their own livestock. Within a few months they slaughtered half of the Soviet Union's horses and cattle and two-thirds of the sheep and goats. In retaliation, Stalin ruthlessly ordered the "liquidation of kulaks as a class" and incited the poor peasants to attack their wealthier neighbors. Over 8 million kulaks were arrested. Many were executed. The rest were sent to slave labor camps, where most starved to death.

The peasants who were left had been the least successful before collectivization and proved to be the least competent after. Many were sent to work in factories. The rest were forbidden to leave their farms. With half of their draft animals gone, they could not plant or harvest enough to meet the swelling demands of the cities. Yet government agents took whatever they could find, leav-

The Collectivization of Soviet Agriculture One of the goals of collectivization was to introduce modern farm machinery. This poster shows delighted farmers operating new tractors and threshers. (David King Collection)

ing little or nothing for the farmers themselves. After bad harvests in 1933 and 1934, a famine swept through the countryside, killing some 5 million people, about one in every twenty farmers.

Stalin's second Five-Year Plan, designed to run from 1933 to 1937, was originally intended to increase the output of consumer goods. But when the Nazis took over Germany in 1933 (see below), Stalin changed the plan to emphasize heavy industries that could produce armaments. Between 1927 and 1937 the Soviet output of metals and machines increased fourteen-fold while consumer goods became scarce and food was rationed. After a decade of Stalinism, the Soviet people were more poorly clothed, fed, and housed than they had been during the years of the New Economic Policy.

---

kulaks (COO-lox)

Terror and Opportunities

The 1930s brought both terror and new opportunities to the Soviet people. The forced pace of industrialization, the collectivization of agriculture, and the uprooting of millions of people could be accomplished only under duress. To prevent any possible resistance or rebellion, the NKVD, Stalin's secret police force, created a climate of suspicion and fear. The terror that pervaded the country was a reflection of Stalin's own paranoia, for he distrusted everyone and feared for his life.

As early as 1930 Stalin had hundreds of engineers and technicians arrested on trumped-up charges of counterrevolutionary ideas and sabotage. Three years later, he expelled a million members of the Communist Party—one-third of the membership—on similar charges. He then turned on his most trusted associates.

In December 1934 Sergei Kirov, the party boss of Leningrad (formerly called Petrograd), was assassinated, perhaps on Stalin's orders. Stalin made a public display of mourning Kirov while blaming others for the crime. He then ordered a series of spectacular purge trials in which he accused most of Lenin's associates of "antiparty activities," the worst form of treason. In 1937 he had his eight top generals and many lesser officers charged with treason and executed, leaving the Red Army dangerously weakened. He even executed the head of the dreaded NKVD, which was enforcing the terror. Under torture or psychological pressure, almost all the accused confessed to the "crimes" they were charged with.

While "Old Bolsheviks" and high officials were being put on trial, terror spread steadily downward. The government regularly made demands that people could not meet, so everyone was guilty of breaking some regulation or other. People from all walks of life were arrested, sometimes on mere suspicion or because of a false accusation by a jealous coworker or neighbor, sometimes for expressing a doubt or working too hard or not hard enough, sometimes for being related to someone previously arrested, sometimes for no reason at all. Millions of people were sentenced without trials. At the height of the terror, some 8 million were sent to *gulags*° (labor camps), where perhaps a million died each year of exposure or malnutrition. To its victims the terror seemed capricious and random. Yet it turned a sullen and resentful people into docile hard-working subjects of the party.

In spite of the fear and hardships, many Soviet citizens supported Stalin's regime. Suddenly, with so many people gone and new industries and cities being built everywhere, there were opportunities for those who remained, especially the poor and the young. Women entered careers and jobs previously closed to them, becoming steelworkers, physicians, and office managers; but they retained their household and child-rearing duties, receiving little help from men (see Diversity and Dominance: Women, Family Values, and the Russian Revolution). People who moved to the cities, worked enthusiastically, and asked no questions could hope to rise into the upper ranks of the Communist Party, the military, the government, or the professions—where the privileges and rewards were many.

Stalin's brutal methods helped the Soviet Union industrialize faster than any country had ever done. By the late 1930s the USSR was the world's third largest industrial power, after the United States and Germany. To foreign observers it seemed to be booming with construction projects, production increases, and labor shortages. Even anti-Communist observers admitted that only a planned economy subject to strict government control could avoid the Depression. To millions of Soviet citizens who took pride in the new strength of their country, and to many foreigners who contrasted conditions in the Soviet Union with the unemployment and despair in the West, Stalin's achievement seemed worth any price.

THE DEPRESSION

On October 24, 1929—"Black Thursday"—the New York stock market went into a dive. Within days stocks had lost half their value. The fall continued for three years. Millions of investors lost money, as did the banks and brokers from whom they had borrowed the money. People with savings accounts rushed to make withdrawals, causing thousands of banks to collapse.

Economic Crisis

What began as a stock-market crash soon turned into the deepest and most widespread depression in history. As consumers reduced their purchases, businesses cut production. Companies laid off thousands of workers, throwing them onto public charity. Business and government agencies laid off their female employees, arguing that men had to support families while women worked only for "pin money." Jobless men deserted their families. As farm prices fell, small farmers went bankrupt and lost their land. By mid-1932 the American economy had shrunk by half, and unemployment had risen to an unprecedented 25 percent of the

---

gulag (GOO-log)

령이 대중 앞에 나타나거나 애국심
을 고취하는 노래만을 내보내던 방
송마저 중단됐다.

라크 전후 대
의에서는 전쟁
영국 주도로

DIVERSITY AND DOMINANCE

WOMEN, FAMILY VALUES, AND THE RUSSIAN REVOLUTION

The Bolsheviks were of two minds on the subject of women. Following in the footsteps of Marx, Engels, and other revolutionaries, they were opposed to bourgeois morality and to the oppression of women, especially working-class women, under capitalism, with its attendant evils of prostitution, sexual abuse, and the division of labor. But what to put in its place?

Alexandra Kollontai was the most outspoken of the Bolsheviks on the subject of women's rights and the equality of the sexes. Before and during the Russian Revolution, she advocated the liberation of women, the replacement of housework by communal kitchens and laundries, and divorce on demand. Under socialism, love, sex, and marriage would be entirely equal, reciprocal, and free of economic obligations. Childbearing would be encouraged, but children would be raised communally, rather than individually by their fathers and mothers: "The worker mother ... must remember that there are henceforth only our *children, those of the communist state, the common possession of all workers."*

In a lecture she gave at Sverdlov University in 1921, Kollontai declared:

... it is important to preserve not only the interests of the woman but also the life of the child, and this is to be done by giving the woman the opportunity to combine labour and maternity. Soviet power tries to create a situation where a woman does not have to cling to a man she has learned to loathe only because she has nowhere else to go with her children, and where a woman alone does not have to fear her life and the life of her child. In the labour republic it is not the philanthropists with their humiliating charity but the workers and peasants, fellow-creators of the new society, who hasten to help the working woman and strive to lighten the burden of motherhood. The woman who bears the trials and tribulations of reconstructing the economy on an equal footing with the man, and who participated in the civil war, has a right to demand that in this most important hour of her life, at the moment when she presents society with a new member, the labour republic, the collective, should take upon itself the job of caring for the future of the new citizen. ...

I would like to say a few words about a question which is closely connected with the problem of maternity—the question of abortion, and Soviet Russia's attitude toward it. On 20 November 1920 the labour republic issued a law abolishing the penalties that had been attached to abortion. What is the reason behind this new attitude? Russia after all suffers not from an overproduction of living labour but rather from a lack of it. Russia is thinly, not densely populated. Every unit of labour power is precious. Why then have we declared abortion to be no longer a criminal offence? Hypocrisy and bigotry are alien to proletarian politics. Abortion is a problem connected with the problem of maternity, and likewise derives from the insecure position of women (we are not speaking here of the bourgeois class, where abortion has other reasons—the reluctance to "divide" an inheritance, to suffer the slightest discomfort, to spoil one's figure or miss a few months of the season, etc.)

Abortion exists and flourishes everywhere, and no laws or punitive measures have succeeded in rooting it out. A way round the law is always found. But "secret help" only cripples women; they become a burden on the labour government, and the size of the labour force is reduced. Abortion, when carried out under proper medical conditions, is less harmful and dangerous, and the woman can get back to work quicker. Soviet power realizes that the need for abortion will only disappear on the one hand when Russia has a broad and developed network of institutions protecting motherhood and providing social education, and on the other hand when women understand that *childbirth is a social obligation*; Soviet power has therefore allowed abortion to be performed openly and in clinical conditions.

Besides the large-scale development of motherhood protection, the task of labour Russia is to strengthen in women the healthy instinct of motherhood, to make motherhood and labour for the collective compatible and thus do away with the need for abortion. This is the approach of the labour republic to the question of abortion, which still faces women in the bourgeois countries in all its magnitude. In these countries women are exhausted by the dual burden of hired labour for capital and motherhood. In Soviet Russia the working woman and peasant woman are helping the Communist Party to build a new society and to undermine the old way of life that has enslaved women. As soon as woman is viewed as being essentially a labour unit, the key to the solution of the complex question of maternity can be found. In bourgeois society, where housework complements the system of capitalist economy and private property creates a stable basis for the isolated form of the family, there is no way out for the working woman. The emancipation of women can only be completed when a fundamental transformation of living is effected; and life-styles will change only with the fundamental transformation of all production and the establishment of a communist economy. The revolution in everyday life is unfolding before our very eyes, and in this process the liberation of women is being introduced in practice.

Fifteen years later Joseph Stalin reversed the Soviet policy on abortion.

The published draft of the law prohibiting abortion and providing material assistance to mothers has provoked a lively reaction throughout the country. It is being heatedly discussed by tens of millions of people and there is no doubt that it will serve as a further strengthening of the Soviet family. Parents' responsibility for the education of their children will be increased and a blow will be dealt at the light-hearted, negligent attitude toward marriage.

When we speak of strengthening the Soviet family, we are speaking precisely of the struggle against the survivals of a bourgeois attitude towards marriage, women, and children. So-called "free love" and all disorderly sex life are bourgeois through and through, and have nothing to do with either socialist principles or the ethics and standards of conduct of the Soviet citizens. Socialist doctrine shows this, and it is proved by life itself.

The elite of our country, the best of the Soviet youth, are as a rule also excellent family men who dearly love their children. And vice versa: the man who does not take marriage seriously, and abandons his children to the whims of fate, is usually also a bad worker and a poor member of society.

Fatherhood and motherhood have long been virtues in this country. This can be seen at first glance, without searching enquiry. Go through the parks and streets of Moscow or of any other town in the Soviet Union on a holiday, and you will see not a few young men walking with pink-cheeked, well-fed babies in their arms. . . .

It is impossible even to compare the present state of the family with that which obtained before the Soviet regime—so great has been the improvement towards greater stability and, above all, greater humanity and goodness. The single fact that millions of women have become economically independent and are no longer at the mercy of men's whims, speaks volumes. Compare, for instance, the modern woman collective farmer who sometimes earns more than her husband, with the pre-revolutionary peasant women who completely depended on her husband and was a slave in the household. Has not this fundamentally changed family relations, has it not rationalized and strengthened the family? The very motives for setting up a family, for getting married, have changed for the better, have been cleansed of atavistic and barbaric elements. Marriage has ceased to be matter of sell-and-buy. Nowadays a girl from a collective farm is not given away (or should we say "sold away"?) by her father, for now she is her own mistress, and no one can give her away. She will marry the man she loves. . . .

We alone have all the conditions under which a working woman can fulfill her duties as a citizen and as a mother responsible for the birth and early upbringing of her children.

A woman without children merits our pity, for she does not know the full joy of life. Our Soviet women, full-blooded citizens of the freest country in the world, have been given the bliss of motherhood. We must safeguard the family and raise and rear healthy Soviet heroes!

QUESTIONS FOR ANALYSIS

1. How does Kollontai expect women to be both workers and mothers without depending on a man? How would Soviet society make this possible?

2. Why does Alexandra Kollontai advocate the legalization of abortion in Soviet Russia? Does she view abortion as a permanent right or as a temporary necessity?

3. Why does Stalin characterize a "lighthearted, negligent attitude toward marriage" and "all disorderly sex life" as "bourgeois through and through"?

4. How does Stalin's image of the Soviet family differ from Kollontai's? Are his views a variation of her views, or the opposite?

5. Do the views of Kollontai and Stalin on the role of women represent a diversity of opinions within the Communist Party, or the dominance of one view over others?

Source: First selection from *Selected Writings of Alexandra Kollontai,* translated by Alix Holt (Lawrence Hill Books, 1978). Reprinted with permission. Second selection from Joseph Stalin, *Law on the Abolition of Legal Abortion* (1936).

Two Views of the American Way   In this classic photograph, *Life* magazine photographer Margaret Bourke-White captured the contrast between advertisers' view of the ideal American family and the reality of mass poverty in a land of plenty.   (TimeLife Pictures/Getty Images)

work force. Many observers thought that free-enterprise capitalism was doomed.

In 1930 the U.S. government, hoping to protect American industries from foreign competition, imposed the Smoot-Hawley tariff, the highest import duty in American history. In retaliation, other countries raised their tariffs in a wave of "beggar thy neighbor" protectionism. The result was crippled export industries and shrinking world trade. While global industrial production declined by 36 percent between 1929 and 1932, world trade dropped by a breathtaking 62 percent.

Depression in Industrial Nations

Frightened by the stock-market collapse, the New York banks called in their loans to Germany and Austria. Without American money, Germany and Austria stopped paying reparations to France and Britain, which then could not repay their war loans to America. By 1931 the Depression had spread to Europe. Governments canceled reparations payments and war loans, but it was too late to save the world economy.

Though their economies stagnated, France and Britain weathered the Depression by making their colonial empires purchase their products rather than the products of other countries. Nations that relied on exports to pay for imported food and fuel, in particular Japan and Germany, suffered much more. In Germany unemployment reached 6 million by 1932, twice as high as in Britain. Half the German population lived in poverty. Thousands of teachers and engineers were laid off, and those who kept their jobs saw their salaries cut and their living standards fall. In Japan the burden of the

Depression fell hardest on the farmers and fishermen, who saw their incomes drop sharply.

This massive economic upheaval had profound political repercussions. Nationalists everywhere called for autarchy, or independence from the world economy. Many people in capitalist countries began calling for government intervention in the economy. In the United States Franklin D. Roosevelt was elected president in 1932 on a "New Deal" platform of government programs to stimulate and revitalize the economy. Although the American, British, and French governments intervened in their economies, they remained democratic. In Germany and Japan, as economic grievances worsened long-festering political resentments, radical leaders came to power and turned their nations into military machines, hoping to acquire, by war if necessary, empires large enough to support self-sufficient economies.

Depression in Nonindustrial Regions

The Depression also spread to Asia, Africa, and Latin America, but very unevenly. In 1930 India erected a wall of import duties to protect its infant industries from foreign competition; its living standards stagnated but did not drop. Except for its coastal regions, China was little affected by trade with other countries; as we shall see, its problems were more political than economic.

Countries that depended on exports—sugar from the Caribbean, coffee from Brazil and Colombia, wheat and beef from Argentina, tea from Ceylon and Java, tin from Bolivia, and many other products—were hard hit by the Depression. Malaya, Indochina, and the Dutch East Indies produced most of the world's natural rubber; when automobile production dropped by half in the United States and Europe, so did imports of rubber, devastating their economies. Egypt's economy, dependent on cotton exports, was also affected, and in the resulting political strife, the government became autocratic and unpopular.

Throughout Latin America unemployment and homelessness increased markedly. The industrialization of Argentina and Brazil was set back a decade or more. During the 1920s Cuba had been a playground for Americans who basked in the sun and quaffed liquor forbidden at home by Prohibition; when the Depression hit, the tourists vanished, and with them went Cuba's prosperity. Disenchanted with liberal politics, military officers seized power in several Latin American countries. Consciously imitating dictatorships emerging in Europe, they imposed authoritarian control over their economies, hoping to stimulate local industries and curb imports.

Other than the USSR, only southern Africa boomed during the 1930s. As other prices dropped, gold became relatively more valuable. Copper deposits, found in Northern Rhodesia (now Zambia) and the Belgian Congo, proved to be cheaper to mine than Chilean copper. But this mining boom benefited only a small number of European and white South African mine owners. For Africans it was a mixed blessing; mining provided jobs and cash wages to men while women stayed behind in the villages, farming, herding, and raising children without their husbands' help.

THE RISE OF FASCISM

The Russian Revolution and its Stalinist aftermath frightened property owners in Europe and North America. In the democracies of western Europe and North America, where there was little fear of Communist uprisings or electoral victories, middle- and upper-income voters took refuge in conservative politics. Political institutions in southern and central Europe, in contrast, were frail and lacked popular legitimacy. The war had turned people's hopes of victory to bitter disappointment. Many were bewildered by modernity—with its cities, factories, and department stores—which they blamed on ethnic minorities, especially Jews. In their yearning for a mythical past of family farms and small shops, increasing numbers rejected representative government and sought more dramatic solutions.

Radical politicians quickly learned to apply wartime propaganda techniques to appeal to a confused citizenry, especially young and unemployed men. They promised to use any means necessary to bring back full employment, stop the spread of communism, and achieve the territorial conquests that World War I had denied them. While defending private property from communism, they borrowed the communist model of politics: a single party and a totalitarian state with a powerful secret police that ruled by terror and intimidation.

Mussolini's Italy

The first country to seek radical answers was Italy. World War I, which had never been popular, left thousands of veterans who found neither pride in their victory nor jobs in the postwar economy. Unemployed veterans and violent youths banded together into *fasci di combattimento* (fighting units) to demand action and intimidate politicians. When workers threatened to strike, factory and property owners hired gangs of these *fascisti* to defend them.

Benito Mussolini (1883–1945) had been expelled by the Socialist Party for supporting Italy's entry into the war. A spellbinding orator, he quickly became the leader of the **Fascist Party,** which glorified warfare and the Italian nation. By 1921 the party had 300,000 members, many of whom used violent methods to repress strikes, intimidate voters, and seize municipal governments. A year later Mussolini threatened to march on Rome if he was not appointed prime minister. The government, composed of timid parliamentarians, gave in.

Mussolini proceeded to install Fascist Party members in all government jobs, crush all opposition parties, and jail anyone who criticized him. The party took over the press, public education, and youth activities and gave employers control over their workers. The Fascists lowered living standards but reduced unemployment and provided social security and public services. On the whole, they proved to be neither ruthless radicals nor competent administrators.

What Mussolini and the Fascist movement really excelled at was publicity: bombastic speeches, spectacular parades, and signs everywhere proclaiming "Il Duce° [the Leader] is always right!" Mussolini's genius was to apply the techniques of modern mass communications and advertisement to political life. Movie footage and radio news bulletins galvanized the masses in ways never before done in peacetime. His techniques of whipping up public enthusiasm were not lost on other radicals. By the 1930s fascist movements had appeared in most European countries, as well as in Latin America, China, and Japan. Of all of Mussolini's imitators, none was as sinister as Adolf Hitler.

Hitler the Orator   A masterful public speaker, Adolf Hitler often captivated mass audiences at Nazi Party rallies.   (Getty Images)

Hitler's Germany

Germany had lost the First World War after coming very close to winning. The hyperinflation of 1923 wiped out the savings of middle-class families. Less than ten years later the Depression caused more unemployment and misery than in any other country. Millions of Germans blamed Socialists, Jews, and foreigners for their troubles. Few foresaw that they were about to get a dictatorship dedicated to war and mass murder.

Adolf Hitler (1889–1945) joined the German army in 1914 and was wounded at the front. He later looked back fondly on the clear lines of authority and the camaraderie he had experienced in battle. After the war he used his gifts as an orator to lead a political splinter group called the National Socialist German Workers' Party—**Nazis** for short. While serving a brief jail sentence

he wrote *Mein Kampf*° (*My Struggle*), in which he outlined his goals and beliefs.

When it was published in 1925 *Mein Kampf* attracted little notice. Its ideas seemed so insane that almost no one took it, or its author, seriously. Hitler's ideas went far beyond ordinary nationalism. He believed that Germany should incorporate all German-speaking areas, even those in neighboring countries. He distinguished among a "master race" of Aryans (he meant Germans, Scandinavians, and Britons), a degenerate "Alpine" race of French and Italians, and an inferior race of Russian and eastern European Slavs, fit only to be slaves of the master race. He reserved his most intense hatred for Jews, on whom

---

Il Duce (eel DOO-chay)   *Mein Kampf* (mine compf)

he blamed every disaster that had befallen Germany, especially the defeat of 1918. He glorified violence and looked forward to a future war in which the "master race" would defeat and subjugate all others.

Hitler's first goal was to repeal the humiliation and military restrictions of the Treaty of Versailles. Then he planned to annex all German-speaking territories to a greater Germany, then conquer *Lebensraum*° (room to live) at the expense of Poland and the USSR. Finally, he planned to eliminate all Jews from Europe.

From 1924 to 1930 Hitler's followers remained a tiny minority, for most Germans found his ideas too extreme. But when the Depression hit, the Nazis gained supporters among the unemployed, who believed their promises of jobs for all, and among property owners frightened by the growing popularity of Communists. In March 1933 President Hindenburg called on Hitler to become chancellor of Germany.

Once in office Hitler quickly assumed dictatorial power. He put Nazis in charge of all government agencies, educational institutions, and professional organizations. He banned all other political parties and threw their leaders into concentration camps. The Nazis deprived Jews of their citizenship and civil rights, prohibited them from marrying "Aryans," ousted them from the professions, and confiscated their property. In August 1934 Hitler proclaimed himself *Führer*° ("leader") and called Germany the "Third Reich" (empire)—the third after the Holy Roman Empire of medieval times and the German Empire of 1871 to 1918.

The Nazis' economic and social policies were spectacularly effective. The government undertook massive public works projects. Businesses got contracts to manufacture weapons for the armed forces. Women, who had entered the work force during and after World War I, were urged to return to "Kinder, Kirche, Küche" (children, church, kitchen), releasing jobs for men. By 1936 business was booming; unemployment was at its lowest level since the 1920s; and living standards were rising. Hitler's popularity soared because most Germans believed that their economic well-being outweighed the loss of liberty.

The Road to War, 1933–1939

Hitler's goal was not prosperity or popularity, but conquest. As soon as he came to office, he began to build up the armed forces. Meanwhile, he tested the reactions of the other powers through a series of surprise moves followed by protestations of peace.

Lebensraum (LAY-bens-rowm)   **Führer** (FEW-rer)

In 1933 Hitler withdrew Germany from the League of Nations. Two years later he announced that Germany was going to introduce conscription, build up its army, and create an air force—in violation of the Versailles treaty. Instead of protesting, Britain signed a naval agreement with Germany. The message was clear: neither Britain nor France was willing to risk war by standing up to Germany. The United States, absorbed in its domestic economic problems, reverted to isolationism.

In 1935, emboldened by the weakness of the democracies, Italy invaded Ethiopia, one of only two independent state's in Africa and a member of the League of Nations. The League and the democracies protested but refused to close the Suez Canal to Italian ships or impose an oil embargo. The following year, when Hitler sent troops into the Rhineland on the borders of France and Belgium, the other powers merely protested.

By 1938 Hitler decided that his rearmament plans were far enough advanced that he could afford to escalate his demands. In March Germany invaded Austria. Most Austrians were German-speakers and accepted the annexation of their country without protest. Then came Czechoslovakia, where a German-speaking minority lived along the German border. Hitler first demanded their autonomy from Czech rule, then their annexation to Germany. Throughout the summer he threatened to go to war. At the Munich Conference of September 1938 he met with the leaders of France, Britain, and Italy, who gave him everything he wanted without consulting Czechoslovakia. Once again, Hitler learned that aggression paid off and that the democracies would always give in.

The weakness of the democracies—now called "appeasement"—ran counter to the traditional European balance of power. It had three causes. The first was the deep-seated fear of war among people who had lived through World War I. Unlike the dictators, politicians in the democracies could not ignore their constituents' yearnings for peace. Politicians and most other people believed that the threat of war might go away if they wished for peace fervently enough.

The second cause of appeasement was fear of communism among conservative politicians who were more afraid of Stalin than of Hitler, because Hitler claimed to respect Christianity and private property. Distrust of the Soviet Union prevented them from re-creating the only viable counterweight to Germany: the prewar alliance of Britain, France, and Russia.

The third cause was the very novelty of fascist tactics. Britain's Prime Minister Neville Chamberlain assumed that political leaders (other than the Bolsheviks) were honorable men and that an agreement was as valid as a business contract. Thus, when Hitler promised to incorporate only German-speaking people into Germany and said he had "no further territorial demands," Chamberlain believed him.

After Munich it was too late to stop Hitler, short of war. Germany and Italy signed an alliance called the Axis. In March 1939 Germany invaded what was left of Czechoslovakia. Belatedly realizing that Hitler could not be trusted, France and Britain sought Soviet help. Stalin, however, distrusted the "capitalists" as much as they distrusted him. When Hitler offered to divide Poland between Germany and the Soviet Union, Stalin accepted. The Nazi-Soviet Pact of August 23, 1939, freed Hitler from the fear of a two-front war and gave Stalin time to build up his armies. One week later, on September 1, German forces swept into Poland, and the war was on.

EAST ASIA, 1931–1945

When the Depression hit, China and the United States erected barriers against Japanese imports. The collapse of demand for silk and rice ruined thousands of Japanese farmers; to survive, many sold their daughters into prostitution while their sons flocked to the military. Ultra-nationalists, including young army officers, resented their country's dependence on foreign trade. If only Japan had a colonial empire, they thought, it would not be beholden to the rest of the world. But Europeans and Americans had already taken most potential colonies in Asia. Japan had only Korea, Taiwan, and a railroad in Manchuria. China, however, had not yet been conquered. Japanese nationalists saw the conquest of China, with its vast population and resources, as the solution to their country's problems.

The Manchurian Incident of 1931

Meanwhile, in China the Guomindang° was becoming stronger and preparing to challenge the Japanese presence in Manchuria, a province rich in coal and iron ore. Junior officers in the Japanese army guarding the South Manchurian Railway, frustrated by the caution of their superiors, wanted to take action. In September 1931 an explosion on a railroad track, probably staged, gave them an excuse to conquer the entire province. In Tokyo weak civilian ministers were intimidated by the military. Informed after the fact, they acquiesced to the attack to avoid losing face, but privately one said: "From begin-

ning to end the government has been utterly fooled by the army."

When Chinese students, workers, and housewives boycotted Japanese goods, Japanese troops briefly took over Shanghai, China's major industrial city, and the area around Beijing. Japan thereupon recognized the "independence" of Manchuria under the name "Manchukuo."°

The U.S. government condemned the Japanese conquest. The League of Nations refused to recognize Manchukuo and urged the Japanese to remove their troops from China. Persuaded that the Western powers would not fight, Japan simply resigned from the League.

During the next few years the Japanese built railways and heavy industries in Manchuria and northeastern China and sped up their rearmament. At home, production was diverted to the military, especially to building warships. The government grew more authoritarian, jailing thousands of dissidents. On several occasions, superpatriotic junior officers mutinied or assassinated leading political figures. The mutineers received mild punishments, and generals and admirals sympathetic to their views replaced more moderate civilian politicians.

The Chinese Communists and the Long March

Until the Japanese seized Manchuria, the Chinese government seemed to be consolidating its power and creating conditions for a national recovery. The main challenge to the government of **Chiang Kai-shek**° came from the Communists. The Chinese Communist Party was founded in 1921 by a handful of intellectuals. For several years it lived in the shadow of the Guomindang, kept there by orders of Joseph Stalin, who expected it to subvert the government from within. All its efforts to manipulate the Guomindang and to recruit members among industrial workers came to naught in 1927, when Chiang Kai-shek arrested and executed Communists and labor leaders alike. The few Communists who escaped the mass arrests fled to the remote mountains of Jiangxi°, in southeastern China.

Among them was **Mao Zedong**° (1893–1976), a farmer's son who had left home to study philosophy. He was not a contemplative thinker, but rather a man of action whose first impulse was to call for violent effort: "To be able to leap on horseback and to shoot at the same time; to go from battle to battle; to shake the mountains by one's cries, and the colors of the sky by one's roars of

---

Guomindang (gwo-min-dong)

Manchukuo (man-CHEW-coo-oh)   Chiang Kai-shek (chang kie-shek)   Jiangxi (jang-she)   Mao Zedong (ma-oh zay-dong)

anger." In the early 1920s Mao discovered the works of Karl Marx, joined the Communist Party, and soon became one of its leaders.

In Jiangxi Mao began studying conditions among the peasants, in whom Communists had previously shown no interest. He planned to redistribute land from the wealthier to the poorer peasants, thereby gaining adherents for the coming struggle with the Guomindang army. In this, he was following the example of innumerable leaders of peasant rebellions over the centuries. His goal, however, was not just a nationalist revolution against the traditional government and foreign intervention, but a complete social revolution from the bottom up. Mao's reliance on the peasantry was a radical departure from Marxist-Leninist ideology, which stressed the backwardness of the peasants and pinned its hopes on industrial workers. Mao therefore had to be careful to cloak his pragmatic tactics in Communist rhetoric in order to allay the suspicions of Stalin and his agents.

Mao was also an advocate of women's equality. Radical ideas such as those of Margaret Sanger, the American leader of the birth-control movement, and the feminist play *A Doll's House* by the Norwegian playwright Henrik Ibsen inspired veterans of the May Fourth Movement (see Chapter 28) and young women attending universities and medical or nursing schools. Before 1927 the Communists had organized the women who worked in Shanghai's textile mills, the most exploited of all Chinese workers. Later, in their mountain stronghold in Jiangxi, they organized women farmers, allowed divorce, and banned arranged marriages and footbinding. But they did not admit women to leadership positions, for the party was still run by men whose primary task was warfare.

The Guomindang army pursued the Communists into the mountains, building small forts throughout the countryside. Rather than risk direct confrontations, Mao responded with guerrilla warfare. He harassed the army at its weak points with hit-and-run tactics, relying on the terrain and the support of the peasantry. Government troops often mistreated civilians, but Mao insisted that his soldiers help the peasants, pay a fair price for food and supplies, and treat women with respect.

In spite of their good relations with the peasants of Jiangxi, the Communists gradually found themselves encircled by government forces. In 1934 Mao and his followers decided to break out of the southern mountains and trek to Shaanxi°, an even more remote province in northwestern China. The so-called **Long March** took them 6,000 miles (nearly 9,700 kilometers) in one year,

17 miles (27 kilometers) a day over desolate mountains and through swamps and deserts, pursued by the army and bombed by Chiang's aircraft. Of the 100,000 Communists who left Jiangxi in October 1934, only 4,000 reached Shaanxi a year later (see Map 29.1). Chiang's government thought it was finally rid of the Communists.

The Sino-Japanese War, 1937–1945

In Japan politicians, senior officers, and business leaders disagreed on how to solve their country's economic problems. Some proposed a quick conquest of China; others advocated war with the Soviet Union. While their superiors hesitated, junior officers decided to take matters into their own hands.

On July 7, 1937, Japanese troops attacked Chinese forces near Beijing. As in 1931, the junior officers who ordered the attack quickly obtained the support of their commanders and then, reluctantly, of the government. By November Japanese troops had seized Beijing, Tianjin, Shanghai, and other coastal cities, and the Japanese navy blockaded the entire coast of China.

Once again, the United States and the League of Nations denounced the Japanese atrocities. Yet the Western powers were too preoccupied with events in Europe and with their own economic problems to risk a military confrontation in Asia. When the Japanese sank a U.S. gunboat and shelled a British ship on the Yangzi River, the U.S. and British governments responded only with righteous indignation and pious resolutions.

The Chinese armies were large and fought bravely, but they were poorly led and armed and lost every battle. Japanese planes bombed Hangzhou, Nanjing, and Guangzhou, while soldiers on the ground broke dikes and burned villages, killing thousands of civilians. Within a year Japan controlled the coastal provinces of China and the lower Yangzi and Yellow River Valleys, China's richest and most populated regions (see Map 29.1).

In spite of Japanese organizational and fighting skills, the attack on China did not bring the victory Japan had hoped for. The Chinese people continued to resist, either in the army or, increasingly, with the Communist guerrilla forces. Japan's periodic attempts to turn the tide by conquering one more piece of China only pushed Japan deeper into the quagmire. For the Japanese people, life became harsher and more repressive as taxes rose, food and fuel became scarce, and more and more young men were drafted. Japanese leaders belatedly realized that the war with China was a drain on the Japanese economy and manpower and that their war machine was becoming increasingly dependent on the

---

Shaanxi (SHAWN-she)

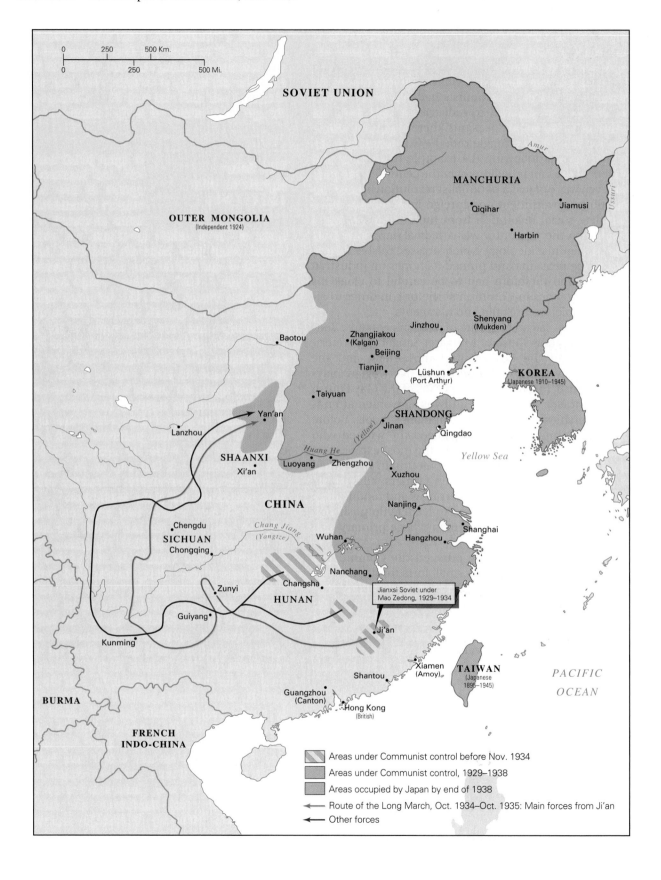

SOVIET UNION

MANCHURIA

Amur

Ussuri

Qiqihar

Jiamusi

OUTER MONGOLIA
(Independent 1924)

Harbin

Baotou

Zhangjiakou
(Kalgan)

Jinzhou

Shenyang
(Mukden)

Beijing

Tianjin

KOREA
(Japanese 1910–1945)

Lüshun
(Port Arthur)

Lanzhou

Yan'an

Taiyuan

SHANDONG

Huang He (Yellow)

Jinan

Qingdao

SHAANXI

Xi'an

Luoyang

Zhengzhou

Yellow Sea

Xuzhou

CHINA

Chengdu

Chang Jiang
(Yangtze)

Nanjing

SICHUAN

Chongqing

Wuhan

Hangzhou

Shanghai

Nanchang

Zunyi

Changsha

Jianxsi Soviet under
Mao Zedong, 1929–1934

Guiyang

HUNAN

Kunming

Ji'an

PACIFIC
OCEAN

BURMA

Shantou

Xiamen
(Amoy)

TAIWAN
(Japanese
1895–1945)

Guangzhou
(Canton)

Hong Kong
(British)

FRENCH
INDO-CHINA

0   250   500 Km.
0   250   500 Mi.

Areas under Communist control before Nov. 1934

Areas under Communist control, 1929–1938

Areas occupied by Japan by end of 1938

Route of the Long March, Oct. 1934–Oct. 1935: Main forces from Ji'an

Other forces

United States for steel and machine tools and for nine-tenths of its oil.

Warfare between the Chinese and Japanese was incredibly violent. In the winter of 1937–1938 Japanese troops took Nanjing, raped 20,000 women, killed 200,000 prisoners and civilians, and looted and burned the city. To slow them down, Chiang ordered the Yellow River dikes blasted open, causing a flood that destroyed four thousand villages, killed 890,000 people, and made 12.5 million homeless. Two years later, when the Communists ordered a massive offensive, the Japanese retaliated with a "kill all, burn all, loot all" campaign, destroying hundreds of villages down to the last person, building, and farm animal.

The Chinese government, led by Chiang Kai-shek, escaped to the mountains of Sichuan in the center of the country. There Chiang built up a huge army, both to fight Japan and to prepare for a future confrontation with the Communists. The army drafted over 3 million men, even though it had only a million rifles and could not provide food or clothing for all its soldiers. The Guomindang raised farmers' taxes, even when famine forced farmers to eat the bark of trees. Such taxes were not enough to support both a large army and the thousands of government officials and hangers-on who had fled to Sichuan. To avoid taxing its wealthy supporters the government printed money, causing inflation, hoarding, and corruption.

From his capital of Yan'an in Shaanxi province, Mao also built up his army and formed a government. Until early 1941 he received a little aid from the Soviet Union; then, after Stalin signed a Soviet-Japanese Neutrality Pact, none at all. Unlike the Guomindang, the Communists listened to the grievances of the peasants, especially the poor, to whom they distributed land confiscated from wealthy landowners. They imposed rigid discipline on their officials and soldiers and tolerated no dissent or criticism from intellectuals. Though they had few weapons, the Communists obtained support and intelligence from farmers in Japanese-occupied territory. They turned military reversals into propaganda victo-ries, presenting themselves as the only group in China that was serious about fighting the Japanese.

THE SECOND WORLD WAR

Many people feared that the Second World War would be a repetition of the First. Instead, it was much bigger in every way. It was fought around the world, from Norway to New Guinea and from Hawaii to Egypt, and on every ocean. It killed far more people than World War I. It was a total war, involving all productive forces and all civilians, and it showed how effectively industry, science, and nationalism could be channeled into mass destruction.

The War of Movement

Defensive maneuvers had dominated in World War I. In World War II motorized weapons gave back the advantage to the offensive. Opposing forces moved fast, their victories hinging as much on the aggressive spirit of their commanders and the military intelligence they obtained as on numbers of troops and firepower.

The Wehrmacht°, or German armed forces, was the first to learn this lesson. It not only had tanks, trucks, and fighter planes but perfected their combined use in a tactic called *Blitzkrieg*° (lightning war): fighter planes scattered enemy troops and disrupted communications, and tanks punctured the enemy's defenses and then, with the help of the infantry, encircled and captured enemy troops. At sea, the navies of both Japan and the United States had developed aircraft carriers that could launch planes against targets hundreds of miles away.

Yet the very size and mobility of the opposing forces made the fighting far different from any the world had ever seen. Instead of engaging in localized battles, armies ranged over vast theaters of operation. Countries were conquered in days or weeks. The belligerents mobilized the economies of entire continents, squeezing them for every possible resource. They tried not only to defeat their enemies' armed forces but—by means of blockades, submarine attacks on shipping, and bombing raids on industrial areas—to damage the economies that supported those armed forces. They thought of civilians not as innocent bystanders but as legitimate targets and, later, as vermin to be exterminated.

Map 29.1   Chinese Communist Movement and the Sino-Japanese War, to 1938   During the 1930s, China was the scene of a three-way war. The Nationalist government attacked and pursued the Communists, who escaped into the mountains of Shaanxi. Meanwhile, Japanese forces, having seized Manchuria in 1931, attacked China in 1937 and quickly conquered its eastern provinces.

Wehrmacht (VAIR-mokt)   **Blitzkrieg** (BLITS-creeg)

War in Europe and North Africa

It took less than a month for the Wehrmacht to conquer Poland. Britain and France declared war on Germany but took no military action. Meanwhile, the Soviet Union invaded eastern Poland and the Baltic republics of Lithuania, Latvia, and Estonia. Although the Poles fought bravely, the Polish infantry and cavalry were no match for German and Russian tanks. During the winter of 1939–1940 Germany and the Western democracies faced each other in what soldiers called a "phony war" and watched as the Soviet Union attacked Finland, which resisted for many months.

In April 1940 Hitler went on the offensive again, conquering Denmark, Norway, the Netherlands, and Belgium in less than two months. In May he attacked France. Although the French army had as many soldiers, tanks, and aircraft as the Wehrmacht, its morale was low and it quickly collapsed. By the end of June Hitler was master of all of Europe between Russia and Spain.

Germany still had to face one enemy: Britain. The British had no army to speak of, but they had other assets: the English Channel, the Royal Navy and Air Force, and a tough new prime minister, Winston Churchill. The Germans knew they could invade Britain only by gaining control of the airspace over the Channel, so they launched a massive air attack—the Battle of Britain—lasting from June through September. The attack failed, however, because the Royal Air Force had better fighters and used radar and code-breaking to detect approaching German planes.

Frustrated in the west, Hitler turned his attention eastward, even though it meant fighting a two-front war. So far he had gotten the utmost cooperation from Stalin, who supplied Germany with grain, oil, and strategic raw materials. Yet he had always wanted to conquer Lebensraum in the east and enslave the Slavic peoples who lived there, and he feared that if he waited, Stalin would build a dangerously strong army. In June 1941 Hitler launched the largest attack in history, with 3 million soldiers and thousands of planes and tanks. Within five months the Wehrmacht conquered the Baltic states, Ukraine, and half of European Russia; captured a million prisoners of war; and stood at the very gates of Moscow and Leningrad. The USSR seemed on the verge of collapse when the weather turned cold, machines froze, and the fighting came to a halt. Like Napoleon, Hitler had ignored the environment of Russia to his peril.

The next spring the Wehrmacht renewed its offensive. It surrounded Leningrad in a siege that was to cost a million lives. Leaving Moscow aside, it turned toward the Caucasus and its oil wells. In August the Germans at-

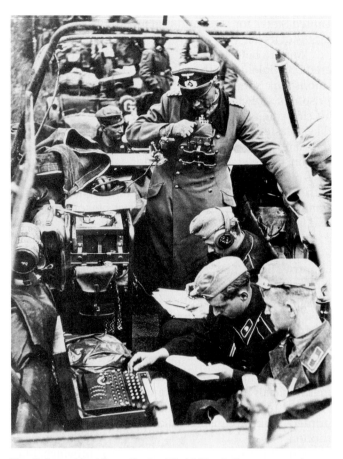

The Enigma Machine During World War II, German armed forces used Enigma machines like the one seen here in the vehicle of a German tank commander. With Enigmas, they could encrypt and decode radio messages, keeping them secret (they believed) from enemy code-breakers. (Brian Johnson)

tacked **Stalingrad** (now Volgagrad), the key to the Volga River and the supply of oil. For months German and Soviet soldiers fought over every street and every house. When winter came the Red Army counterattacked and encircled the city. In February 1943 the remnants of the German army in Stalingrad surrendered. Hitler had lost an army of 200,000 men and his last chance of defeating the Soviet Union and of winning the war (see Map 29.2).

From Europe the war spread to Africa. When France fell in 1940 Mussolini began imagining himself a latter-day Roman emperor and decided that the time had come to realize his imperial ambitions. Italian forces quickly overran British Somaliland, then invaded Egypt. Their victories were ephemeral, however, for when the British counterattacked, Italian resistance crumbled. During 1941 British forces conquered Italian East Africa

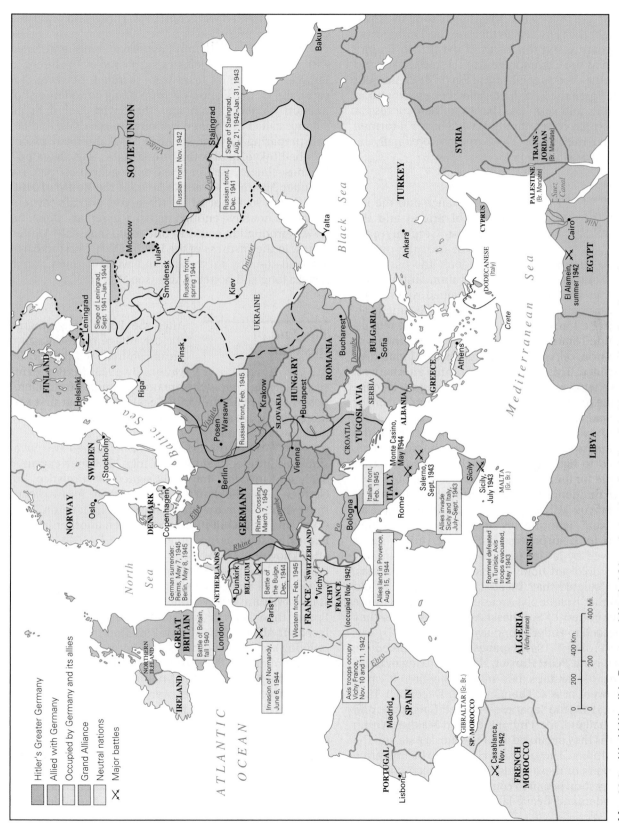

Map 29.2 World War II in Europe and North Africa In a series of quick and decisive campaigns from September 1939 to December 1941, German forces overran much of Europe and North Africa. There followed three years of bitter fighting as the Allies slowly pushed the Germans back. This map shows the maximum extent of Germany's conquests and alliances, as well as the key battles and the front lines at various times.

and invaded Libya as well. The Italian rout in North Africa brought the Germans to their rescue. During 1942 the German army and the forces of the British Empire (now known as the Commonwealth) seesawed back and forth across the deserts of Libya and Egypt. At **El Alamein** in northern Egypt the British prevailed because they had more weapons and supplies. Thanks to their success at breaking German codes, they also were better informed about their enemies' plans. The Germans were finally expelled from Africa in May 1943.

War in Asia and the Pacific

The fall of France and the involvement of Britain and the USSR against Germany presented Japan with the opportunity it had been looking for. Suddenly the European colonies in Southeast Asia, with their abundant oil, rubber, and other strategic materials, seemed ripe for the taking. In September 1940 the French government allowed Japanese forces to occupy Indochina. In retaliation, the United States and Britain stopped shipments of steel, scrap iron, oil, and other products that Japan desperately needed. This left Japan with three alternatives: accept the shame and humiliation of giving up its conquests, as the Americans insisted; face economic ruin; or widen the war. Japan chose war.

Admiral Isoroku Yamamoto, commander of the Japanese fleet, told Prime Minister Fumimaro Konoye: "If I am told to fight regardless of the consequences, I shall run wild for the first six months or a year, but I have utterly no confidence for the second or third year. . . . I hope that you will endeavor to avoid a Japanese-American war." Ignoring his advice, the war cabinet made plans for a surprise attack on the United States Navy, followed by an invasion of Southeast Asia. They knew they could not hope to defeat the United States, but they calculated that the shock of the attack would be so great that isolationist Americans would accept the Japanese conquest of Southeast Asia as readily as they had acquiesced to Hitler's conquests in Europe.

On December 7, 1941, Japanese planes bombed the U.S. naval base at **Pearl Harbor,** Hawaii, sinking or damaging scores of warships, but missing the aircraft carriers, which were at sea. Then, between December 1941 and March 1942, the Japanese bombed Singapore and occupied Thailand, the Philippines, and Malaya. Within a few months they occupied all of Southeast Asia and the Dutch East Indies. The Japanese claimed to be liberating the inhabitants of these lands from European colonialism. But they soon began to confiscate food and raw materials and demand heavy labor from the inhabitants,

whom they treated with contempt. Those who protested were brutally punished.

Japan's dream of an East Asian empire seemed within reach, for its victories surpassed even Hitler's in Europe. Yamamoto's fears were justified, however, because the United States, far from being cowed into submission, joined Britain and the Soviet Union in an alliance called the United Nations (or the Allies) and began preparing for war. In April 1942 American planes bombed Tokyo. In May the United States Navy defeated a Japanese fleet in the Coral Sea, ending Japanese plans to conquer Australia. A month later, at the **Battle of Midway,** Japan lost four of its six largest aircraft carriers. Japan did not have enough industry to replace them, for its war production was only one-tenth that of the United States. In the vastness of the Pacific Ocean aircraft carriers held the key to victory, and without them, Japan faced a long and hopeless war (see Map 29.3).

The End of the War

After the Battle of Stalingrad the advantage on the Eastern Front shifted to the Soviet Union. By 1943 the Red Army was receiving a growing stream of supplies from factories in Russia and the United States. Slowly at first and then with increasing vigor, it pushed the Wehrmacht back toward Germany.

The Western powers, meanwhile, staged two invasions of Europe. Beginning in July 1943 they captured Sicily and invaded Italy. Italy signed an armistice, but German troops held off the Allied advance for two years. In November, at a meeting with Stalin in Teheran, Roosevelt and Churchill promised to open another front in France as soon as possible. On June 6, 1944—forever after known as D-day—156,000 British, American, and Canadian troops landed on the coast of Normandy in western France—the largest shipborne assault ever staged. Within a week the Allies had more troops in France than Germany did, and by September Germany faced an Allied army of over 2 million men with half a million vehicles of all sorts.

Although the Red Army was on the eastern border of Germany, ready for the final push, Hitler transferred part of the Wehrmacht westward. Despite overwhelming odds, Germany held out for almost a year, a result of the fighting qualities of its soldiers and the terror inspired by the Nazi regime, which commanded obedience to the end. In February 1945 the three Allied leaders met again in Yalta on the Black Sea to plan the future of Europe after the war. On May 7, 1945, a week after Hitler committed suicide, German military leaders surrendered.

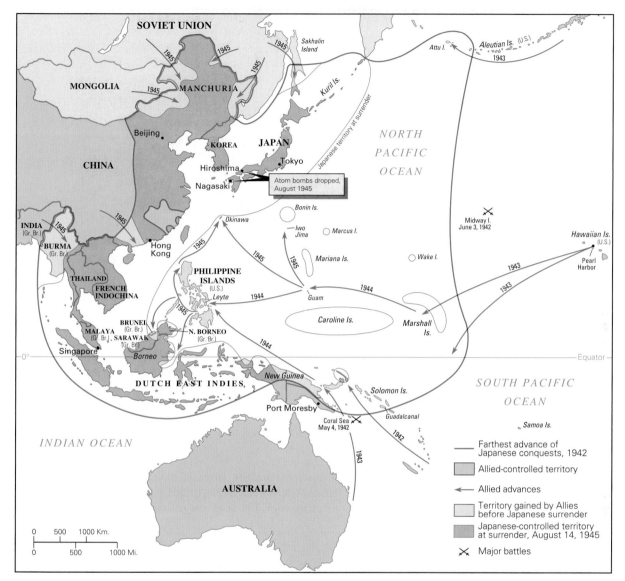

Map 29.3   World War II in Asia and the Pacific   After having conquered much of China between 1937 and 1941, Japanese forces launched a sudden attack on Southeast Asia, Indonesia, and the Pacific in late 1941 and early 1942. American forces slowly reconquered the Pacific islands and the Philippines until August 1945, when the atomic bombing of Hiroshima and Nagasaki forced Japan's surrender.

Japan fought on a while longer, in large part because the United States had aimed most of its war effort at Germany. In the Pacific U.S. forces "leap-frogged" some heavily fortified Japanese island bases in order to capture others closer to Japan itself. By June 1944 U.S. bombers were able to attack Japan. Meanwhile, U.S. submarines sank ever larger numbers of Japanese merchant ships, gradually cutting Japan off from its sources of oil and other raw materials. In 1944 a terrible earthquake devastated the city of Nagoya, compounding the misery of war and bombing raids. After May 1945, with the Japanese air force grounded for lack of fuel, U.S. planes began destroying Japanese shipping, industries, and cities at will.

Even as their homeland was being pounded, the Japanese still held strong positions in Asia. At first, Asian

Hiroshima After the Atomic Bomb On August 6, 1945, an atomic bomb destroyed the city, killing over fifty thousand people. This photo shows the devastation of the city center, where only a few concrete buildings remained standing. (Wide World Photos)

nationalists such as the Indonesian Achmed Sukarno were glad to get rid of the white colonialists and welcomed the Japanese. Yet despite its name, "Greater East Asian Co-Prosperity Sphere," the Japanese occupation was harsh and brutal. By 1945 Asians were eager to see the Japanese leave, but not to welcome back the Europeans. Instead, they looked forward to independence (see Chapters 30 and 31).

On August 6, 1945, the United States dropped an atomic bomb on **Hiroshima,** killing some 80,000 people in a flash and leaving about 120,000 more to die in agony from burns and radiation. Three days later another atomic bomb destroyed Nagasaki. Were these atomic weapons necessary? At the time, Americans believed that the conquest of the Japanese homeland would take more than a year and cost the lives of hundreds of thousands of American soldiers. Although some Japanese were determined to fight to the bitter end, others were willing to surrender if they could retain their emperor. Had the Allies agreed sooner to keep the monarchy, Japan might have surrendered without the nuclear devastation. On August 14 Japan offered to surrender, and

Emperor Hirohito himself gave the order to lay down arms. Two weeks later Japanese leaders signed the terms of surrender. The war was officially over.

Chinese Civil War and Communist Victory

The formal Japanese surrender in September 1945 came as a surprise to the Guomindang. American transport planes flew Guomindang officials and troops to all the cities of China. The United States gave millions of dollars of aid and weapons to the Guomindang, all the while urging "national unity" and a "coalition government" with the Communists. But Chiang used American aid and all other means available to prepare for a civil war. By late 1945 he had an army of 2.7 million, more than twice the size of the Communist forces.

From 1945 to 1949 the contest between the Guomindang and the Communists intensified. Guomindang forces started with more troops and weapons, U.S. support, and control of China's cities. But their behavior

Sale of Gold in the Last Days of the Guomindang   This picture was taken by famed French photojournalist Henri Cartier-Bresson in Shanghai just before the arrival of the Communist-led People's Liberation Army in 1949. It shows people desperate to buy gold before their Guomindang currency becomes worthless.   (Henri Cartier-Bresson/Magnum Photos)

eroded whatever popular support they had. As they moved into formerly Japanese-held territory, they acted like an occupation force. They taxed the people they "liberated" more heavily than the Japanese had, looted businesses, confiscated supplies, and enriched themselves at the expense of the population. To pay its bills Chiang's government printed money so fast that it soon lost all its value, ruining merchants and causing hoarding and shortages. In the countryside the Guomindang's brutality alienated the peasants.

Meanwhile, the Communists obtained Japanese equipment seized by the Soviets in the last weeks of the war and American weapons brought over by deserting Guomindang soldiers. In Manchuria, where they were strongest, they pushed through a radical land reform program, distributing the properties of wealthy landowners among the poorest peasants. In battles against govern-

ment forces, the higher morale and popular support they enjoyed outweighed the heavy equipment of the Guomindang, whose soldiers began deserting by the thousands.

In April 1947, as Chinese Communist forces surrounded Nanjing, the British frigate *Amethyst* sailed up the Yangzi River to evacuate British civilians. Dozens of times since the Opium War of 1839–1842, foreign powers had dispatched warships up the rivers of China to rescue their citizens, enforce their treaty rights, or intimidate the Chinese. Foreign warships deep in the heart of China were the very symbols of its weakness. This time, however, Chinese Communist artillery damaged the *Amethyst* and beat back other British warships sent to its rescue.

By 1949 the Guomindang armies were collapsing everywhere, defeated more by their own greed and ineptness than by the Communists. As the Communists advanced, high-ranking members of the Guomindang fled to Taiwan, protected from the mainland by the United States Navy. On October 1, 1949, Mao Zedong announced the founding of the People's Republic of China.

THE CHARACTER OF WARFARE

The war left an enormous death toll. Recent estimates place the figure at close to 60 million deaths, six to eight times more than in World War I. Over half of the dead were civilian victims of massacres, famines, and bombs. The Soviet Union lost between 20 million and 25 million people, more than any other country. China suffered 15 million deaths; Poland lost some 6 million, of whom half were Jewish; the Jewish people lost another 3 million outside Poland. Over 4 million Germans and over 2 million Japanese died. Great Britain lost 400,000 people, and the United States 300,000. In much of the world, almost every family mourned one or more of its members.

Many parts of the world were flooded with refugees. Some 90 million Chinese fled the Japanese advance. In Europe millions fled from the Nazis or the Red Army or were herded back and forth on government orders. Many refugees never returned to their homes, creating new ethnic mixtures more reminiscent of the New World than of the Old.

One reason for the terrible toll in human lives and suffering was a change in moral values, as belligerents identified not just soldiers but entire peoples as enemies. Some belligerents even labeled their own ethnic minorities as "enemies." Another reason for the devastation was the appearance of new technologies that carried destruction deep into enemy territory, far beyond the traditional battlefields. Let us consider the new technologies of warfare, the changes in morality, and their lethal combination.

The War of Science

As fighting spread around the world, the features that had characterized the early years of the war—the mobilization of manpower and economies and the mobility of the armed forces—grew increasingly powerful. Meanwhile, new aspects of war took on a growing importance. One of these was the impact of science on the technology of warfare. Chemists found ways to make synthetic rubber from coal or oil. Physicists perfected radar, which warned of approaching enemy aircraft and submarines. Cryptanalysts broke enemy codes and were able to penetrate secret military communications. Pharmacologists developed antibiotics that saved the lives of countless wounded soldiers, who in any earlier war would have died of infections (see Environment and Technology: Biomedical Technologies).

Aircraft development was especially striking. As war approached, German, British, and Japanese aircraft manufacturers developed fast, maneuverable fighter planes. U.S. industry produced aircraft of every sort but was especially noted for heavy bombers designed to fly in huge formations and drop tons of bombs on enemy cities. The Japanese developed the Mitsubishi "Zero" fighter plane—light, fast, and agile, but dangerous to fly. Unable to produce heavy planes in large numbers, Germany responded with radically new designs, including the first jet fighters, low-flying buzz bombs, and, finally, V-2 missiles, against which there was no warning or defense.

Military planners no longer dismissed the creations of civilian inventors, as they had done before World War I. Now they expected scientists to furnish secret weapons that could doom the enemy. In October 1939 President Roosevelt received a letter from physicist Albert Einstein, a Jewish refugee from Nazism, warning of the dangers of nuclear power: "There is no doubt that sub-atomic energy is available all around us, and that one day man will release and control its almost infinite power. We cannot prevent him from doing so and can only hope that he will not use it exclusively in blowing up his next door neighbor." Fearing that Germany might develop a nuclear bomb first, Roosevelt placed the vast resources of the U.S. government at the disposal of physicists and engineers, both Americans and refugees from Europe. By 1945 they had built two atomic bombs, each one powerful enough to annihilate an entire city.

Bombing Raids

German bombers damaged Warsaw in 1939 and Rotterdam and London in 1940. Yet Germany lacked a strategic bomber force capable of destroying whole cities. In this area, the British and Americans excelled. Since it was very hard to pinpoint individual buildings, especially at night, the British Air Staff under British Air Chief Marshal Arthur "Bomber" Harris decided that "operations should now be focused on the morale of the enemy civilian population and in particular the industrial workers."

In May 1942, 1,000 British planes dropped incendiary bombs on Cologne, setting fire to most of the old city. Between July 24 and August 2, 1943, 3,330 British and American bombers set fire to Hamburg, killing 50,000 people, mostly women and children. Later raids destroyed Berlin, Dresden, and other German cities. All in

Biomedical Technologies

Life expectancy at birth has nearly doubled in the past 150 years. Even in the poorest countries, life expectancy has risen from forty to sixty or seventy years. The cause of this remarkable change is threefold: clean water, immunizations, and antibiotics.

The realization that drinking water can spread disease came first to Dr. Charles Snow, who noticed the correlation between deaths from cholera and the water from a particular pump in London during an epidemic in 1854. Since then, public health officials have been very conscious of the quality of drinking water, although only wealthy cities can afford to purify and chlorinate water for all their inhabitants.

The practice of immunization goes back to the eighteenth century, when physicians in Turkey and in Europe applied infected pus from a person with smallpox (variolation) or an animal with cowpox (vaccination) to healthy persons to build up their resistance to smallpox. By the end of the nineteenth century it became clear that immunity to many diseases could be conferred by injections of weakened bacteria. Immunizations offer the single most effective way to prevent childhood diseases and thereby increase life expectancy.

Antibiotics are more recent. In 1928 Dr. Alexander Fleming discovered that a certain mold, *Penicillin notatum,* could kill bacteria. Antibiotics were first used in large quantities in the Second World War. Along with two other innovations—synthetic antimalarial drugs and blood transfusions—antibiotics helped cut the fatality of battlefield wounds from 11 percent in World War I to 3 percent in World War II.

The remarkable success of these technologies has led people to consider good health their natural birthright. Unfortunately, the victory over disease is temporary at best. The abuse of antibiotics and of antibacterial products encourages the growth of new strains of old diseases, such as tuberculosis, which can resist all known antibiotics. And although bacterial diseases are no longer as prevalent as they once were, humans are still susceptible to viral afflictions such as influenza and AIDS.

Biotechnology in Action   Campaigns to immunize children against diseases reached even remote villages, as here in Thailand. (Peter Charlesworth/Corbis Saba)

all, the bombing raids against Germany killed 600,000 people—more than half of them women and children—and injured 800,000. If the air strategists had hoped thereby to break the morale of the German people, they failed. German armament production continued to in-

crease until late 1944, and the population remained obedient and hard working. The only effective bombing raids were those directed against oil depots and synthetic fuel plants; by early 1945 they had almost brought the German war effort to a standstill.

Japanese cities were also the targets of American bombing raids. As early as April 1942 sixteen planes launched from an aircraft carrier bombed Tokyo. Later, as American forces captured islands close to Japan, the raids intensified. Their effect was even more devastating than the fire-bombing of German cities, for Japanese cities were made of wood. In March 1945 bombs set Tokyo ablaze, killing 80,000 people and leaving a million homeless. It was a portent of worse destruction to come.

The Holocaust

In World War II, more civilians than soldiers were deliberately put to death. The champions in the art of killing defenseless civilians were the Nazis. Their murders were not the accidental byproducts of some military goal but a calculated policy of exterminating whole races of people.

Their first targets were Jews. Soon after Hitler came to power, he deprived German Jews of their citizenship and legal rights. When eastern Europe fell under Nazi rule, the Nazis herded its large Jewish population into ghettos in the major cities, where many died of starvation and disease. Then, in early 1942, the Nazis decided to carry out Hitler's "final solution to the Jewish problem" by applying modern industrial methods to the slaughter of human beings. German companies built huge extermination camps in eastern Europe, while thousands of ordinary German citizens supported and aided the genocide. Every day trainloads of cattle cars arrived at the camps and disgorged thousands of captives and the corpses of those who had died of starvation or asphyxiation along the way. The strongest survivors were put to work and fed almost nothing until they died. Women, children, the elderly, and the sick were shoved into gas chambers and asphyxiated with poison gas. **Auschwitz,** the biggest camp, was a giant industrial complex designed to kill up to twelve thousand people a day. Most horrifying of all were the tortures inflicted on prisoners selected by Nazi doctors for "medical experiments." This mass extermination, now called the **Holocaust** ("burning"), claimed some 6 million Jewish lives.

Besides the Jews, the Nazis also killed 3 million Polish Catholics—especially professionals, army officers, and the educated—in an effort to reduce the Polish people to slavery. They also exterminated homosexuals, Jehovah's Witnesses, Gypsies, the disabled, and the mentally ill—all in the interests of "racial purity." Whenever a German was killed in an occupied country, the Nazis retaliated by burning a village and all its inhabitants. After the invasion of Russia the Wehrmacht was given orders to execute all captured communists, government

U.S. Army Medics and Holocaust Victims   At the end of World War II, Allied troops entered the Nazi concentration camps, where they found the bodies of thousands of victims of the Holocaust. In this picture, taken at Dachau in southern Germany, two U.S. Army medics are overseeing a truckload of corpses to be taken to a burial site.   (Hulton Deutsch Collection/Corbis)

employees, and officers. They also worked millions of prisoners of war to death or let them die of starvation.

The Home Front in Europe and Asia

In the First World War there had been a clear distinction between the "front" and the "home front." Not so in World War II, where rapid military movements and air power carried the war into people's homes. For the civilian populations of China, Japan, Southeast Asia, and Europe, the war was far more terrifying than their worst nightmares. Armies swept through the land, confiscating food, fuel, and anything else of value. Bombers and heavy artillery pounded cities into rubble, leaving only the skeletons of buildings, while survivors cowered in cellars and scurried like rats. Even when a city was not targeted, air-raid sirens awakened people throughout the night. In countries occupied by the Germans the police arrested civilians, deporting many to die in concentration camps or to work as slave laborers in armaments factories. Millions fled their homes in terror, losing their families and friends. Even in Britain, which was never invaded, children and the elderly were taken from their families for their own safety and sent to live in the countryside.

The war demanded an enormous and sustained effort from all civilians, but more so in some countries than in others. In 1941, even as the Wehrmacht was routing the Red Army, the Soviets dismantled over fifteen hundred factories and rebuilt them in the Ural Mountains and Siberia, where they soon turned out more tanks and artillery than the Axis.

Half of the ships afloat in 1939 were sunk during the war, but the Allied losses were more than made up for by American shipyards, while Axis shipping was reduced to nothing by 1945. The production of aircraft, trucks, tanks, and other materiel showed a similar imbalance. Although the Axis powers made strenuous efforts to increase their production, they could not compete with the vast outpouring of Soviet tanks and American materiel.

The Red Army eventually mobilized 22 million men; Soviet women took over half of all industrial and three-quarters of all agricultural jobs. In the other belligerent countries women also played major roles in the war effort, replacing men in fields, factories, and offices. The Nazis, in contrast, believed that German women should stay home and bear children, and they imported 7 million "guest workers"—a euphemism for war prisoners and captured foreigners.

The Home Front in the United States

The United States flourished during the war. Safe behind their oceans, Americans felt no bombs, saw no enemy soldiers, had almost no civilian casualties, and suffered fewer military casualties than other belligerents. The economy, still depressed in 1939, went into a prolonged boom after 1940. By 1944 the United States was producing twice as much as all the Axis powers combined. Thanks to huge military orders, jobs were plentiful and opportunities beckoned. Bread lines disappeared, and nutrition and health improved. Consumer goods ranging from automobiles to nylon stockings were in short supply, and most Americans saved part of their paychecks, laying the basis for a phenomenal postwar consumer boom. Many Americans later looked back on the conflict as the "good war."

War always exalts such supposedly masculine qualities as physical courage, violence, and domination. These were the official virtues of the Axis powers, but they were highly valued in the United States as well. Yet World War II also did much to weaken the hold of traditional ideas, as employers recruited women and members of racial minorities to work in jobs once reserved for white men. For example, 6 million women entered the labor force during the war, 2.5 million of them in manufacturing jobs previously considered "men's work." In a book entitled *Shipyard Diary of a Woman Welder* (1944), Augusta Clawson recalled her experiences in a shipyard in Oregon:

> The job confirmed my strong conviction—I have stated it before—what exhausts the woman welder is not the work, not the heat, nor the demands upon physical strength. It is the apprehension that arises from inadequate skill and consequent lack of confidence; and this *can* be overcome by the right kind of training. . . . I know I can do it if my machine is correctly set, and I have learned enough of the vagaries of machines to be able to set them. And so, in spite of the discomforts of climbing, heavy equipment, and heat, I enjoyed the work today because *I could do it.*

At the beginning, many men resisted the idea that women, especially mothers of young children, should take jobs that would take them away from their families. As the labor shortage got worse, however, employers and politicians grudgingly admitted that the government ought to help provide day care for the children of working mothers. The entry of women into the labor force proved to be one of the most significant consequences of the war. As one woman put it: "War jobs have uncovered unsuspected abilities in American women. Why lose all these abilities because of a belief that 'a woman's place is in the home'? For some it is, for others not."

The war loosened racial bonds as well, bringing hardships for some and benefits for others. Seeking work in war industries, 1.2 million African-Americans migrated to the north and west. In the southwest Mexican immigrants took jobs in agriculture and war industries. But no new housing was built to accommodate the influx of migrants to the industrial cities, and as a result many suffered from overcrowding and discrimination. Much worse was the fate of 112,000 Japanese-Americans living on the west coast of the United States; they were rounded up and herded into internment camps in the desert until the war was over, ostensibly for fear of spying and sabotage, but actually because of their race.

War and the Environment

During the Depression, construction and industry had slowed to a crawl, reducing environmental stress. The war reversed this trend, sharply accelerating pressures on the environment.

One reason for the change was the fighting itself. Battles scarred the landscape, leaving behind spent ammunition and damaged equipment. Retreating armies flooded large areas of China and the Netherlands. The bombing of cities left ruins that remained visible for a generation or more. Much of the damage eventually was repaired, although the rusted hulls of ships still darken the lagoons of once-pristine coral islands in the Pacific.

The main cause of environmental stress, however, was not the fighting but the economic development that sustained it. The war's half-million aircraft required thousands of air bases, many of them in the Pacific, China, Africa, and other parts of the world that had seldom seen an airplane before. Barracks, shipyards, docks, warehouses, and other military construction sprouted on every continent.

As war industries boomed—the United States increased its industrial production fourfold during the war—so did the demand for raw materials. Mining companies opened new mines and towns in Central Africa to supply strategic minerals. Brazil, Argentina, and other Latin American countries deprived of manufactured imports began building their own steel mills, factories, and shipyards. In India, China, and Europe, timber felling accelerated far beyond the reproduction rate of trees, replacing forests with denuded land. In a few instances the war was good for the environment. For example, submarine warfare made fishing and whaling so dangerous that fish and whale populations had a few years in which to increase.

We must keep the environmental effects of the war in perspective. Except for the destruction of cities, much of the war's impact was simply the result of industrial development only temporarily slowed by the Depression. During the war the damage that military demand caused was tempered by restraints on civilian consumption. From the vantage point of the present, the environmental impact of the war seems quite modest in comparison with the damage inflicted on the earth by the long consumer boom that began in the post–World War II years.

CONCLUSION

Between 1929 and 1949 the old global order—conservative, colonialist, and dominated by Great Britain and France—was shattered by the Depression, the politics of violence, and the most devastating war in history. Stalin transformed the Soviet Union into an industrial giant at enormous human cost. Reacting to the Depression, which weakened the Western democracies, Hitler in Germany and military leaders in Japan prepared for a war of conquest. Though Germany and Japan achieved stunning victories at first, their forces soon faltered in the face of the greater industrial production of the United States and the Soviet Union.

The war was so destructive and spread to so much of the globe because rapidly advancing technology was readily converted from civilian to military production. Machines that had made cars could also manufacture bombers or tanks. Engineers could design factories to kill people with maximum efficiency. The accelerating technology of missiles and nuclear bombs made the entire planet vulnerable to human destruction for the first time in history.

Into the power vacuum left by the collapse of Germany and Japan stepped the two superpowers: the United States and the USSR. When the war ended, U.S. soldiers were stationed in Australia, Japan, and western Europe, and the Red Army occupied all of eastern Europe and parts of northern China. Within months of their victory, these one-time allies became ideological enemies, hovering on the brink of war.

World War I had rearranged the colonial empires. In contrast, the global impact of World War II was drastic and almost immediate, because the war weakened the European colonial powers and because so much of the fighting took place in North Africa, Southeast Asia, and other colonial areas. Within fifteen years of the end of the war almost every European colonial empire had disappeared. As the long era of European domination receded, Asians and Africans began reclaiming their independence.

■ Key Terms

Joseph Stalin	Long March
Five-Year Plans	Stalingrad
Benito Mussolini	El Alamein
Fascist Party	Pearl Harbor
Adolf Hitler	Battle of Midway
Nazi Party	Hiroshima
Chiang Kai-shek	Auschwitz
Mao Zedong	Holocaust

■ Suggested Reading

The literature on the period from 1929–1945 is enormous and growing fast. The following list is but a very brief introduction.

Charles Kindelberger's *The World in Depression, 1929–39* (1973) and Robert McElvaine's *The Great Depression: America, 1929–1941* (1984) provide sophisticated economic analyses of the Depression. A. J. H. Latham's *The Depression and the Developing World, 1914–1939* (1981) gives a global perspective.

The best recent book on Japan in the twentieth century is Daikichi Irokawa's *The Age of Hirohito: In Search of Modern Japan* (1995). On Japanese expansion see W. G. Beasley, *Japanese Imperialism, 1894–1945* (1987). The race to war is covered in Akira Iriye, *The Origins of the Second World War in Asia and the Pacific* (1987); Michael Barnhart, *Japan Prepares for Total War* (1987), is short and well written.

In the large and fast-growing literature on twentieth-century China, two general introductions are especially useful: John K. Fairbank, *The Great Chinese Revolution, 1800–1985* (1986), and Jonathan Spence, *The Search for Modern China* (1990). On the warlord and Guomindang periods see Lucien Bianco, *Origins of the Chinese Revolution, 1915–1949* (1971). The Japanese invasion of China is the subject of Iris Chang, *The Rape of Nanking: The Forgotten Holocaust of World War II* (1997). Jung Chang, *Wild Swans: Three Daughters of China* (1991), is a fascinating account of women's experiences during the Revolution and the Mao era by the daughter of two Communist officials.

Among recent biographies of Stalin, see Dmitrii Volkogonov's *Stalin: Triumph and Tragedy* (1991) and Robert Tucker's *Stalin as Revolutionary, 1879–1929* (1973) and *Stalin in Power: The Revolution from Above, 1928–1941* (1990). On the transformation of the USSR, see Roy Medvedev's *Let History Judge: The Origins and Consequences of Stalinism* (1989) and Stephen Kotkin's *Magnetic Mountain: Stalinism as Civilization* (1995). Stalin's collectivization of agriculture is vividly portrayed in Robert Conquest's *Harvest of Sorrow* (1986); see also Sheila Fitzpatrick's *Stalin's Peasants: Resistance and Survival in the Russian Village After Collectivization* (1994). Conquest's *The Great Terror: A Reassessment* (1990) describes the purges of the 1930s. Alexander Solzhenitsyn, a veteran of Stalin's prisons, explores them in a detailed history, *The Gulag Archipelago, 1918–1956* (3 vols. 1974–1978), and in a short but brilliant novel *One Day in the Life of Ivan Denisovich* (1978).

Alexander De Grand provides an excellent interpretation of fascism in *Italian Fascism: Its Origins and Development*, 2d ed. (1989). William Shirer's *The Rise and Fall of the Third Reich* (1960) is a long but very dramatic eyewitness description of Nazi Germany by a journalist. The dictators are the subject of two fine biographies: Denis Mack Smith's *Mussolini* (1982) and Ian Kershaw's *Hitler* (2001). See also A. J. P. Taylor's controversial classic *The Origins of the Second World War* (1966) and Michael Burleigh's *Third Reich: A New History* (2000).

Two very detailed books on World War II are John Keegan, *The Second World War* (1990), and Gerhard Weinberg, *A World at Arms: A Global History of World War II* (1994). Particular aspects of the war in Europe are covered in Alexander Werth, *Russia at War, 1941–1945* (1965), and Conrad Crane, *Bombs, Cities, and Civilians* (1993). One of the most readable accounts of the war in Asia and the Pacific is Ronald Spector's *Eagle Against the Sun* (1988). Also see Akira Iriye, *Power and Culture: The Japanese-American War, 1941–1945* (1981), and James Hsiung and Steven Levine, eds., *China's Bitter Victory: The War with Japan, 1937–1945* (1992).

The terror of life under Nazi rule is the subject of two powerful memoirs: Anne Frank's *The Diary of a Young Girl* and Eli Wiesel's *Night* (1960). On the Holocaust see Lucy Dawidowicz, *The War Against the Jews, 1933–1945*, 2d ed. (1986); Leni Yahil, *The Holocaust: The Fate of European Jewry* (1990); and Christopher Browning's *Ordinary Men: Reserve Police Battalion 101 and the Final Solution in Poland* (1992).

Among the many books that capture the scientific side of warfare, two are especially recommended: Richard Rhodes's long but fascinating *The Making of the Atomic Bomb* (1986), and F. H. Hinsley and Alan Stripp, eds., *Code Breakers* (1993).

Among the many books on the home front in the United States, the most vivid is Studs Terkel, *"The Good War": An Oral History of World War Two* (1984). Margaret Higonnet et al., eds., *Behind the Lines: Gender and the Two World Wars* (1987), discusses the role of women in the war.

Document-Based Question
The Status of Women in the Mid-Twentieth Century

Using the following documents, analyze how revolution, global depression, and war altered the status of women from 1929 to 1949.

DOCUMENT 1
Quote from Italian poet Filippo Marinetti (p. 766)

DOCUMENT 2
The Collectivization of Soviet Agriculture (photo, p. 768)

DOCUMENT 3
Women, Family Values, and the Russian Revolution (Diversity and Dominance, pp. 770–771)

DOCUMENT 4
Two Views of the American Way (photo, p. 772)

DOCUMENT 5
Nazi slogan: "Kinder, Kirch, Küche" (children, church, kitchen) (p. 775)

DOCUMENT 6
Excerpt from welder Augusta Clawson (p. 789)

DOCUMENT 7
Quote from American woman (p. 789)

What factors shaped Alexandra Kollontai's and Joseph Stalin's point of view in Document 3? What additional types of documents would help you understand changes in the status of women from 1929 to 1949?

Striving for Independence: Africa, India, and Latin America, 1900–1949

30

Rush Hour in Brazil   In Latin American countries, modern conveniences, when first introduced, were often insufficient to meet the demand from eager customers. Here the Sao Januario streetcar in Rio de Janeiro carries twice as may passengers as it was designed for.

CHAPTER OUTLINE

Sub-Saharan Africa, 1900–1945

The Indian Independence Movement, 1905–1947

The Mexican Revolution, 1910–1940

Argentina and Brazil, 1900–1949

DIVERSITY AND DOMINANCE: A Vietnamese Nationalist Denounces French Colonialism

ENVIRONMENT AND TECHNOLOGY: Gandhi and Technology

Emiliano Zapata°, leader of a peasant rebellion in the Mexican Revolution, liked to be photographed on horseback, carrying a sword and a rifle and draped with bandoliers of bullets. Mahatma Gandhi°, who led the independence movement in India, preferred to be seen sitting at a spinning wheel, dressed in a *dhoti*°, the simple loincloth worn by Indian farmers. The images they liked to project and the methods they used could not have been more opposed. Yet their goals were similar: each wanted social justice and a better life for the poor in a country free of foreign domination.

The previous two chapters focused on a world convulsed by war and revolution. The world wars involved Europe, East Asia, the Middle East, and the United States, and they sparked violent revolutions in Russia and China. They accelerated the development of aviation, electronics, nuclear power, and other technologies. Although these momentous events dominate the history of the first half of the twentieth century, parts of the world that were little touched by war also underwent profound changes in this period, partly for internal reasons and partly because of the warfare and revolution in other parts of the world.

In this chapter we examine the changes that took place in sub-Saharan Africa, in India, and in three major countries of Latin America—Mexico, Brazil, and Argentina. These three regions represent three very distinct cultures, yet they had much in common. Africa and India were colonies of Europe, both politically and economically. Though politically independent the Latin American republics were dependent on Europe and the United States for the sale of raw materials and commodities and for imports of manufactured goods, technology, and capital. In all three regions independence movements tried to wrest control from distant foreigners and improve the livelihood of their peoples. Their success was partial at best.

As you read this chapter, ask yourself the following questions:

- How did wars and revolutions in Europe and East Asia affect the countries of the Southern Hemisphere?

- Why did educated Indians and Africans want independence?

- What could Latin Americans do to achieve social justice and economic development? Were these two goals compatible?

SUB-SAHARAN AFRICA, 1900–1945

Of all the continents, Africa was the last to come under European rule (see Chapter 27). The first half of the twentieth century, the time when nationalist movements threatened European rule in Asia (see Diversity and Dominance: A Vietnamese Nationalist Denounces French Colonialism), was Africa's period of classic colonialism. After World War I Britain, France, Belgium, and South Africa divided Germany's African colonies among themselves. In the 1930s Italy invaded Ethiopia. The colonial empires reached their peak shortly before World War II.

Colonial Africa: Economic and Social Changes

Outside of Algeria, Kenya, and South Africa, few Europeans lived in Africa. In 1930 Nigeria, with a population of 20 million, was ruled by 386 British officials and by 8,000 policemen and military, of whom 150 were European. Yet even such a small presence stimulated deep social and economic changes.

Since the turn of the century the colonial powers had built railroads from coastal cities to mines and plantations in the interior, in order to provide raw materials to the industrial world. The economic boom of the interwar years benefited few Africans. Colonial governments took lands that Africans owned communally and sold or leased them to European companies or, in eastern and southern Africa, to white settlers. Large European companies dominated wholesale commerce, while immigrants from various countries—Indians in East Africa, Greeks and Syrians in West Africa—handled much of the retail trade. Airplanes and automobiles were even more alien to the experience of Africans than railroads had been to an earlier generation.

Zapata (sah-PAH-tah)   **Gandhi** (GAHN-dee)   *dhoti* (DOE-tee)

C H R O N O L O G Y

	Africa	India	Latin America
1900	**1900s** Railroads connect ports to the interior		**1876–1910** Porfirio Díaz, dictator of Mexico
		1905 Viceroy Curzon splits Bengal; mass demonstrations	
	1909 African National Congress founded	**1906** Muslims found All-India Muslim League	
		1911 British transfer capital from Calcutta to Delhi	**1911–1919** Mexican Revolution; Emiliano Zapata and Pancho Villa against the Constitutionalists
1920	**1920s** J. E. Casely Hayford organizes political movement in British West Africa	**1919** Amritsar Massacre	**1917** New constitution proclaimed in Mexico
		1929 Gandhi leads March to the Sea	**1928** Plutarco Elías Calles founds Mexico's National Revolutionary Party
		1930s Gandhi calls for independence; he is repeatedly arrested	**1930–1945** Getulio Vargas, dictator of Brazil
			1934–1940 Lázaro Cárdenas, president of Mexico
			1938 Cárdenas nationalizes Mexican oil industry; Vargas proclaims Estado Novo in Brazil
	1939–1945 A million Africans serve in World War II	**1939** British bring India into World War II	**1943** Juan Perón leads military coup in Argentina
1940		**1940** Muhammad Ali Jinnah demands a separate nation for Muslims	**1946** Perón elected president of Argentina
		1947 Partition and independence of India and Pakistan	

Where land was divided into small farms, some Africans benefited from the boom. Farmers in the Gold Coast (now Ghana°) profited from the high price of cocoa, as did palm-oil producers in Nigeria and coffee growers in East Africa. In most of Africa women played a major role in the retail trades, selling pots and pans, cloth, food, and other items in the markets. Many maintained their economic independence and kept their household finances separate from those of their husbands, following a custom that predated the colonial period.

For many Africans economic development meant working in European-owned mines and plantations, often under compulsion. Colonial governments were eager to develop the resources of the territories under their control but could not afford to pay high enough wages to attract workers. Instead, they used their police powers to

force Africans to work under harsh conditions for little or no pay. In the 1920s, when the government of French Equatorial Africa decided to build a railroad from Brazzaville to the Atlantic coast, a distance of 312 miles (502 kilometers), it drafted 127,000 men to carve a roadbed across mountains and through rain forests. For lack of food, clothing, and medical care, 20,000 of them died, an average of 64 deaths per mile of track.

Europeans prided themselves on bringing modern health care to Africa; yet before the 1930s there was too little of it to help the majority of Africans, and other aspects of colonialism actually worsened public health. Migrants to cities, mines, and plantations and soldiers moving from post to post spread syphilis, gonorrhea, tuberculosis, and malaria. Sleeping sickness and smallpox epidemics raged throughout Central Africa. In recruiting men to work, colonial governments depleted rural areas of farmers needed to plant and harvest crops. Forced requisitions of food to feed the workers left the remaining populations

---

Ghana (GAH-nuh)

우**에**안 은잔서
라운드폭탄 4발 투하… 두 아들과 함께 사망 7
실전지 구축… 이틀째 시가戰
령이 대중 앞에 나타나거나 애국심
을 고취하는 노래만을 내보내던 방
송마저 중단됐다.
라크 전후 대
의에서는 전
영국 주도로

DIVERSITY AND DOMINANCE

A VIETNAMESE NATIONALIST DENOUNCES FRENCH COLONIALISM

The regions described in this chapter were not the only ones whose inhabitants chafed at the dominance of the great powers and sought more control over their own national destinies. Movements for independence were a worldwide phenomenon. The tactics that different peoples used to achieve their goals differed widely. Among countries that were formal colonies, the case of India is unique in that its nationalist movement was led by Mahatma Gandhi, a man who subordinated the goal of national independence to his commitment to nonviolent passive resistance. In Mexico, as in China, Russia, and other parts of the world, revolutionary movements were often associated with violent uprisings. French Indochina is a case in point.

Indochina, comprising the countries we now call Vietnam, Kampuchea, and Laos, was conquered piecemeal by the French from 1862 to 1895, but only after overcoming fierce resistance. Thereafter, France modernized the cities and irrigation systems and transformed the country into a leading producer of tea, rice, and natural rubber. This meant transferring large numbers of landless peasants to new plantations and destroying the traditional social structure. To govern Indochina, the French brought in more soldiers and civil administrators than the British had in all of India, a far larger colony. Even though they succeeded in crushing the resistance of the peasants and the old Confucian elites, the French were educating a new elite in the French language. These newly educated youths, inspired by French ideas of liberty and nationhood and by the examples of the Guomindang and the Communist Party in neighboring China, formed the core of two new revolutionary movements.

One movement was the Vietnamese Revolutionary Youth League founded by Ho Chi Minh (1890–1969) in 1925, which later became the Indochinese Communist Party. The other was the Viet Nam Quoc Dan Dang, or Vietnamese Nationalist Party, modeled after Sun Yat-sen's Guomindang, founded in 1927 by a schoolteacher named Nguyen Thai Hoc (1904–1930). This party attracted low-level government employees, soldiers, and small businessmen. At first Nguyen Thai Hoc lobbied the colonial government for reforms, but in vain. Two years later he turned to revolutionary action. In

February 1930 he led an uprising at Yen Bay that the French quickly crushed. He and many of his followers were executed four months later, leaving Ho Chi Minh's Communists as the standard-bearers of nationalist revolution in Vietnam.

While awaiting his execution, Nguyen Thai Hoc wrote the following letter to the French Chamber of Deputies to justify his actions.

Gentlemen:

I, the undersigned, Nguyen Thai Hoc, a Vietnamese citizen, twenty-six years old, chairman and founder of the Vietnamese Nationalist Party, at present arrested and imprisoned at the jail of Yen Bay, Tongking, Indochina, have the great honor to inform you of the following facts:

According to the tenets of justice, everyone has the right to defend his own country when it is invaded by foreigners, and according to the principles of humanity, everyone has the duty to save his compatriots when they are in difficulty or in danger. As for myself, I have assessed the fact that my country has been annexed by you French for more than sixty years. I realize that under your dictatorial yoke, my compatriots have experienced a very hard life, and my people will without doubt be completely annihilated, by the naked principle of natural selection. Therefore, my right and my duty have compelled me to seek every way to defend my country which has been invaded and occupied, and to save my people who are in great danger.

At the beginning, I had thought to cooperate with the French in Indochina in order to serve my compatriots, my country and my people, particularly in the areas of cultural and economic development. As regards economic development, in 1925 I sent a memorandum to Governor General Varenne, describing to him all our aspirations concerning the protection of local industry and commerce in Indochina. I urged strongly in the same letter the creation of a Superior School of Industrial Development in Tongking. In 1926 I again addressed another letter to the then Governor General of Indochina in which I included some explicit suggestions to relieve the hardships of our poor people. In 1927, for a third time, I sent a letter to the Résident Supérieur [provincial administrator] in Tongking, requesting permission to publish a weekly magazine with the aim of safeguarding and encouraging local industry and commerce. With regard to the cultural domain, I sent a letter to the Governor General in 1927, requesting (1) the privilege of opening tuition-free schools for the children of the lower classes, particularly children of workers and peasants; (2) freedom to open popular publishing houses and libraries in industrial centers.

It is absolutely ridiculous that every suggestion has been rejected. My letters were without answer; my plans have not been considered; my requests have been ignored; even the articles that I sent to newspapers have been censored and rejected. From the experience of these rejections, I have come to the conclusion that the French have no sincere intention of helping my country or my people. I also concluded that we have to expel France. For this reason, in 1927, I began to organize a revolutionary party, which I named the Vietnamese Nationalist Party, with the aim of overthrowing the dictatorial and oppressive administration of our country. We aspire to create a Republic of Vietnam, composed of persons sincerely concerned with the happiness of the people. My party is a clandestine organization, and in February 1929, it was uncovered by the security police. Among the members of my party, a great number have been arrested. Fifty-two persons have been condemned to forced labor ranging from two to twenty years. Although many have been detained and many others unjustly condemned, my party has not ceased its activity. Under my guidance, the Party continues to operate and progress towards its aim.

During the Yen Bay uprising someone succeeded in killing some French officers. The authorities accused my party of having organized and perpetrated this revolt. They have accused me of having given the orders for the massacre. In truth, I have never given such orders, and I have presented before the Penal Court of Yen Bay all the evidence showing the inanity of this accusation. Even so, some of the members of my party completely ignorant of that event have been accused of participating in it. The French Indochinese government burned and destroyed their houses. They sent French troops to occupy their villages and stole their rice to divide it among the soldiers. Not just members of my party have been suffering from this injustice—we should rather call this cruelty rather than injustice—but also many simple peasants, interested only in their daily work in the rice fields, living miserable lives like buffaloes and horses, have been compromised in this reprisal. At the present time, in various areas there are tens of thousands of men, women, and children, persons of all ages, who have been massacred. They died either of hunger or exposure because the French Indochinese government burned their homes. I therefore beseech you in tears to redress this injustice which otherwise will annihilate my people, which will stain French honor, and which will belittle all human values.

I have the honor to inform you that I am responsible for all events happening in my country under the leadership of my party from 1927 until the present. You only need to execute me. I beg your indulgence for all the others who at the present time are imprisoned in various jails. I am the only culprit, all the others are innocent. They are innocent because most of them are indeed members of my party, and have joined it only because I have succeeded in convincing them of their duties as citizens of this country, and of the humiliations of a slave with a lost country. Some of them are not even party members. They have been wrongly accused by their enemy or by the security police; or they simply are wrongly accused by their friends who have not been able to bear the tortures inflicted by the security police. I have the honor to repeat once again that you need execute only me. If you are not satisfied with killing one man, I advise you to kill also the members of my family, but I strongly beg your indulgence towards those who are innocent.

Finally, I would like to declare in conclusion: if France wants to stay in peace in Indochina, if France does not want to have increasing troubles with revolutionary movements, she should immediately modify the cruel and inhuman policy now practiced in Indochina. The French should behave like friends to the Vietnamese, instead of being cruel and oppressive masters. They should be attentive to the intellectual and material sufferings of the Vietnamese people, instead of being harsh and tough.

Please, Gentlemen, receive my gratitude.

QUESTIONS FOR ANALYSIS

1. When he first became involved in politics, what were Nguyen Thai Hoc's views of French colonialism?

2. What were his first initiatives, and what response did he get from the French colonial administration?

3. What motivated Nguyen Thai Hoc to organize an uprising, and what was the response of the French?

4. Compare Nguyen Thai Hoc's views and methods and the French response with the situation in India.

Source: Harry Benda and John Larkin, *The World of Southeast Asia* (New York: Harper & Row, 1967), 182–185. Reprinted by permission of the author.

African Farmers in the Gold Coast   African farmers in the Gold Coast (now Ghana) sold their cocoa beans to government agents. The government kept the prices artificially low in order to profit on the transactions. (Popperfoto/Archive Photos)

undernourished and vulnerable to diseases. Not until the 1930s did colonial governments realize the negative consequences of their labor policies and begin to invest in agricultural development and health care for Africans.

In 1900 Ibadan° in Nigeria was the only city in sub-Saharan Africa with more than 100,000 inhabitants; fifty years later, dozens of cities had reached that size, including Nairobi° in Kenya, Johannesburg in South Africa, Lagos in Nigeria, Accra in Gold Coast, and Dakar in Senegal. Africans migrated to cities because they offered hope of jobs and excitement and, for a few, the chance to become wealthy.

However, migrations damaged the family life of those involved, for almost all the migrants were men leaving women in the countryside to farm and raise children. Cities built during the colonial period reflected the colonialists' attitudes with racially segregated housing, clubs, restaurants, hospitals, and other institutions. Patterns of racial discrimination were most rigid in the white-settler colonies of eastern and southern Africa.

Religious and Political Changes

Traditional religious belief could not explain the dislocations that foreign rule, migrations, and sudden economic changes brought to the lives of Africans. Many therefore turned to one of the two universal religions, Christianity and Islam, for guidance.

Christianity was introduced into Africa by Western missionaries, except in Ethiopia, where it was indigenous. It was most successful in the coastal regions of West and South Africa, where the European influence was strongest. A major attraction of the Christian denominations was their mission schools, which taught both craft skills and basic literacy, providing access to employment as minor functionaries, teachers, and shopkeepers. These schools educated a new elite, many of whom learned not only skills and literacy but Western political ideas as well. Many Africans accepted Christianity enthusiastically, reading the suffering of their own peoples into the biblical stories of Moses and the parables of Jesus. The churches trained some of the brighter pupils to become catechists, teachers, and clergymen. A few rose to high positions, such as James Johnson, a Yoruba who became the Anglican bishop of the Niger Delta Pastorate. Independent Christian churches—known as "Ethiopian" churches—associated Christian beliefs with radical ideas of racial equality and participation in politics.

Islam spread inland from the East African coast and southward from the Sahel° toward the West African coast, through the influence and example of Arab and African merchants. Islam also emphasized literacy—in

Ibadan (ee-BAH-dahn)   **Nairobi** (nie-ROE-bee)

Sahel (SAH-hel)

Diamond Mining in Southern Africa   The discovery of diamonds in the Transvaal in 1867 attracted prospectors to the area around Kimberley. The first wave of prospectors consisted of individual "diggers," including a few Africans. By the late 1870s, surface deposits had been exhausted and further mining required complex and costly machinery. After 1889, one company, De Beers Consolidated, owned all the diamond mines. This photograph shows the entrance to a mine shaft and mine workers surrounded by heavy equipment.   (Royal Commonwealth Society. By permission of the Syndics of Cambridge University Library.)

Arabic through Quaranic schools rather than in a European language—and was less disruptive of traditional African customs such as polygamy.

In a few places, such as Dakar in Senegal and Cape Town in South Africa, small numbers of Africans could obtain secondary education. Even smaller numbers went on to college in Europe or America. Though few in number, they became the leaders of political movements. The contrast between the liberal ideas imparted by Western education and the realities of racial discrimination under colonial rule contributed to the rise of nationalism among educated Africans. In Senegal **Blaise Diagne°** agitated for African participation in politics and fair treatment in the French army. In the 1920s J. E.

Diagne (dee-AHN-yuh)

Casely Hayford began organizing a movement for greater autonomy in British West Africa. In South Africa Western-educated lawyers and journalists founded the **African National Congress** in 1909 to defend the interests of Africans. These nationalist movements were inspired by the ideas of Pan-Africanists from America such as W. E. B. Du Bois and Marcus Garvey, who advocated the unity of African peoples around the world, as well as by European ideas of liberty and nationhood. Before World War II, however, they were small and had little influence.

The Second World War (1939–1945) had a profound effect on the peoples of Africa, even those far removed from the theaters of war. The war brought hardships, such as increased forced labor, inflation, and requisitions of raw materials. Yet it also brought hope. During the campaign to oust the Italians from Ethiopia, Emperor **Haile Selassie**° (r. 1930–1974) led his own troops into Addis Ababa, his capital, and reclaimed his title. A million Africans served as soldiers and carriers in Burma, North Africa, and Europe, where many became aware of Africa's role in helping the Allied war effort. They listened to Allied propaganda in favor of European liberation movements and against Nazi racism, and they returned to their countries with new and radical ideas.

The early twentieth century was a relatively peaceful period for sub-Saharan Africa. But this peace—enforced by the European occupiers—masked profound changes that were to transform African life after the Second World War. The building of cities, railroads, and other enterprises brought Africa into the global economy, often at great human cost. Colonialism also brought changes to African culture and religion, hastening the spread of Christianity and Islam. And the foreign occupation awakened political ideas that inspired the next generation of Africans to demand independence (see Chapter 31).

THE INDIAN INDEPENDENCE MOVEMENT, 1905–1947

India was a colony of Great Britain from the late eighteenth to the mid-twentieth centuries. Under British rule the subcontinent acquired many of the trappings of Western-style economic development, such as railroads, harbors, modern cities, and cotton and steel mills, as well as an active and worldly middle class. The economic transformation of the region awakened in this educated middle class a sense of national dignity that demanded political fulfillment. In response, the British gradually granted India a limited amount of political autonomy while maintaining overall control. Religious and communal tensions among the Indian peoples were carefully papered over under British rule. Violent conflicts tore India apart after the withdrawal of the British in 1947 (see Map 30.1).

The Land and the People

Much of India is fertile land, but it is vulnerable to the vagaries of nature, especially droughts caused by the periodic failure of the monsoons. When the rains failed from 1896 to 1900, 2 million people died of starvation.

Despite periodic famines the Indian population grew from 250 million in 1900 to 319 million in 1921 and 389 million in 1941. This growth created pressures in many areas. Landless young men converged on the cities, exceeding the number of jobs available in the slowly expanding industries. To produce timber for construction and railroad ties, and to clear land for tea and rubber plantations, government foresters cut down most of the tropical hardwood forests that had covered the subcontinent in the nineteenth century. In spite of deforestation and extensive irrigation, the amount of land available to peasant families shrank with each successive generation. Economic development—what the British called the "moral and material progress of India"—hardly benefited the average Indian.

Indians were divided into many classes. Peasants, always the great majority, paid rents to the landowner, interest to the village moneylender, and taxes to the government and had little left to improve their land or raise their standard of living. The government protected property owners, from village moneylenders all the way up to the maharajahs,° or ruling princes, who owned huge tracts of land. The cities were crowded with craftsmen, traders, and workers of all sorts, most very poor. Although the British had banned the burning of widows on their husbands' funeral pyres, in other respects women's lives changed little under British rule.

The peoples of India spoke many different languages: Hindi in the north, Tamil in the south, Bengali in the east, Gujerati around Bombay, Urdu in the northwest, and dozens of others. As a result of British rule and increasing trade and travel, English became, like Latin in medieval Europe, the common medium of communication of the Western-educated middle class. This new class of English-speaking government bureaucrats, professionals, and merchants was to play a leading role in the independence movement.

The majority of Indians practiced Hinduism and were subdivided into hundreds of castes, each affiliated with a particular occupation. Hinduism discouraged intermarriage and other social interactions among the castes and with people who were not Hindus. Muslims constituted one-quarter of the people of India but formed a majority in the northwest and in eastern Bengal. Muslim rulers had dominated northern and central India until they were displaced by the British in the eighteenth century. More reluctant than Hindus to learn English, Muslims felt discriminated against by both British and Hindus.

Haile Selassie (HI-lee seh-LASS-ee)

maharajah (mah-huh-RAH-juh)

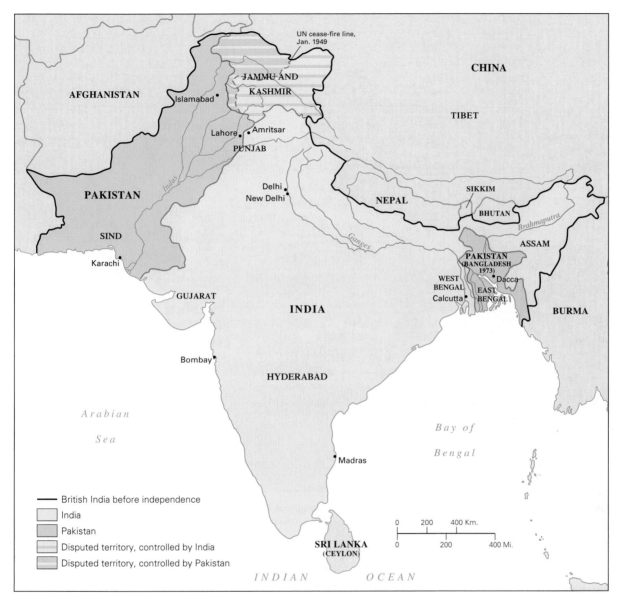

Map 30.1   The Partition of India, 1947   Before the British, India was divided among many states, ethnic groups, and religions. When the British left in 1947, the subcontinent split along religious lines. The predominantly Muslim regions of Sind and Punjab in the northwest and East Bengal in the east formed the new nation of Pakistan. The predominantly Hindu center became the Republic of India. Jammu and Kashmir remained disputed territories and poisoned relations between the two new countries.

British Rule and Indian Nationalism

Colonial India was ruled by a viceroy appointed by the British government and administered by a few thousand members of the Indian Civil Service. These men, imbued with a sense of duty toward their subjects, formed one of the more honest (if not efficient) bureaucracies of all time. Drawn mostly from the English gentry, they liked to think of India as a land of lords and peasants. They believed it was their duty to protect the Indian people from the dangers of industrialization, while defending their own positions from Indian nationalists.

As Europeans they admired modern technology but tried to control its introduction into India so as

Construction Site in Colonial India   British civil engineers were active throughout India building roads, railroads, and canals. Here, a British official supervises Indian workers building a bridge.   (The Billie Love Collection)

to maximize the benefits to Britain and to themselves. For example, they encouraged railroads, harbors, telegraphs, and other communications technologies, as well as irrigation and plantations, because they increased India's foreign trade and strengthened British control. At the same time, they discouraged the cotton and steel industries and limited the training of Indian engineers, ostensibly to spare India the social upheavals that had accompanied the Industrial Revolution in Europe, while protecting British industry from Indian competition.

At the turn of the century the majority of Indians—especially the peasants, landowners, and princes—accepted British rule. But the Europeans' racist attitude toward dark-skinned people increasingly offended Indians who had learned English and absorbed English ideas

of freedom and representative government, only to discover that thinly disguised racial quotas excluded them from the Indian Civil Service, the officer corps, and prestigious country clubs.

In 1885 a small group of English-speaking Hindu professionals founded a political organization called the **Indian National Congress.** For twenty years its members respectfully petitioned the government for access to the higher administrative positions and for a voice in official decisions, but they had little influence outside intellectual circles. Then, in 1905, Viceroy Lord Curzon divided the province of **Bengal** in two to improve the efficiency of its administration. This decision, made without consulting anyone, angered not only educated Indians, who saw it as a way to lessen their influence, but also millions of uneducated Hindu Bengalis, who suddenly found themselves outnumbered by Muslims in East Bengal. Soon Bengal was the scene of demonstrations, boycotts of British goods, and even incidents of violence against the British.

In 1906, while the Hindus of Bengal were protesting the partition of their province, Muslims, fearful of Hindu dominance elsewhere in India, founded the **All-India Muslim League.** Caught in an awkward situation, the government responded by granting Indians a limited franchise based on wealth. Muslims, however, were on average poorer than Hindus, for many poor and low-caste Hindus had converted to Islam to escape caste discrimination. Taking advantage of these religious divisions, the British instituted separate representation and different voting qualifications for Hindus and Muslims. Then, in 1911, the British transferred the capital of India from Calcutta to Delhi°, the former capital of the Mughal° emperors. These changes disturbed Indians of all classes and religions and raised their political consciousness. Politics, once primarily the concern of westernized intellectuals, turned into two mass movements: one by Hindus and one by Muslims.

To maintain their commercial position and prevent social upheavals, the British resisted the idea that India could, or should, industrialize. Their geologists looked for minerals, such as coal or manganese, that British industry required. However, when the only Indian member of the Indian Geological Service, Pramatha Nath Bose, wanted to prospect for iron ore, he had to resign because the government wanted no part of an Indian steel industry that could compete with that of Britain. Bose joined forces with Jamsetji Tata, a Bombay textile magnate who decided to produce steel in spite of British opposition. With the help of German and American engineers and equipment, Tata's son Dorabji opened the first steel mill in India in 1911, in a town called Jamshedpur in honor of his father. Although it produced only a fraction of the steel that India required, Jamshedpur became a powerful symbol of Indian national pride. It prompted Indian nationalists to ask why a country that could produce its own steel needed foreigners to run its government.

During World War I Indians supported Britain enthusiastically; 1.2 million men volunteered for the army, and millions more voluntarily contributed money to the government. Many expected the British to reward their loyalty with political concessions. Others organized to demand concessions and a voice in the government. In 1917, in response to the agitation, the British government announced "the gradual development of self-governing institutions with a view to the progressive realization of responsible government in India as an integral part of the British Empire." This sounded like a promise of self-government, but the timetable was so vague that nationalists denounced it as a devious maneuver to postpone India's independence.

In late 1918 and early 1919 a violent influenza epidemic broke out among soldiers in the war zone of northern France. Within a few months it spread to every country on earth and killed over 20 million people. India was especially hard hit; of the millions who died, two out of three was Indian. This dreadful toll increased the mounting political tensions. Leaders of the Indian National Congress declared that the British reform proposals were too little, too late.

On April 13, 1919, in the city of Amritsar in Punjab, General Reginald Dyer ordered his troops to fire into a peaceful crowd of some 10,000 demonstrators, killing at least 379 and wounding 1,200. Waves of angry demonstrations swept over India, but the government waited six months to appoint a committee to investigate the massacre. After General Dyer retired, the British House of Lords voted to approve his actions, and a fund was raised in appreciation of his services. Indians interpreted these gestures as showing British contempt for their colonial subjects. In the charged atmosphere of the time, the period of gradual accommodation between the British and the Indians came to a close.

Mahatma Gandhi and Militant Nonviolence

For the next twenty years India teetered on the edge of violent uprisings and harsh repression, possibly even war. That it did not succumb was due to **Mohandas K. Gandhi** (1869–1948), a man known to his followers as "Mahatma," the "great soul."

Gandhi began life with every advantage. His family was wealthy enough to send him to England for his education. After his studies he lived in South Africa and practiced law for the small Indian community there. During World War I he returned to India and was one of many Western-educated Hindu intellectuals who joined the Indian National Congress.

Gandhi had some unusual political ideas. Unlike many radical political thinkers of his time, he denounced the popular ideals of power, struggle, and combat. Instead, inspired by both Hindu and Christian concepts, he preached the saintly virtues of *ahimsa*° (nonviolence) and *satyagraha*° (the search for truth). He refused to countenance violence among his followers,

---

Delhi (DEL-ee)   **Mughal** (MOO-guhl)

ahimsa (uh-HIM-sah)   *satyagraha* (suh-TYAH-gruh-huh)

and he called off several demonstrations when they turned violent.

Gandhi had an affinity for the poor that was unusual even among socialist politicians. In 1921 he gave up the Western-style suits worn by lawyers and the fine raiment of wealthy Indians and henceforth wore simple peasant garb: a length of homespun cloth below his waist and a shawl to cover his torso (see Environment and Technology: Gandhi and Technology). He spoke for the farmers and the outcasts, whom he called *harijan*°, "children of God." He attracted ever-larger numbers of followers among the poor and the illiterate, who soon began to revere him; and he transformed the cause of Indian independence from an elite movement of the educated into a mass movement with a quasi-religious aura.

Gandhi was a brilliant political tactician and a master of public relations gestures. In 1929, for instance, he led a few followers on an 80-mile (129-kilometer) walk, camped on a beach, and gathered salt from the sea in a blatant and well-publicized act of civil disregard for the government's monopoly on salt. But he discovered that unleashing the power of popular participation was one thing and controlling its direction was quite another. Within days of his "Walk to the Sea," demonstrations of support broke out all over India, in which the police killed a hundred demonstrators and arrested over sixty thousand.

Many times during the 1930s Gandhi threatened to fast "unto death," and several times he did come close to death, to protest the violence of both the police and his followers and to demand independence. He was repeatedly arrested and spent a total of six years in jail. But every arrest made him more popular. He became a cult figure not only in his own country but also in the Western media. He never won a battle or an election; instead, in the words of historian Percival Spear, he made the British "uncomfortable in their cherished field of moral rectitude," and he gave Indians the feeling that theirs was the ethically superior cause.

India Moves Toward Independence

In the 1920s, slowly and reluctantly, the British began to give in to the pressure of the Indian National Congress and the Muslim League. They handed over control of "national" areas such as education, the economy, and public works. They also gradually admitted more Indians into the Civil Service and the officer corps.

India took its first tentative steps toward industrialization in the years before the First and then the Second World Wars. Indian politicians obtained the right to erect high tariff barriers against imports in order to protect India's infant industries from foreign, even British, competition. Behind these barriers, Indian entrepreneurs built plants to manufacture iron and steel, cement, paper, cotton and jute textiles, sugar, and other products. This early industrialization provided jobs, though not enough to improve the lives of the Indian peasants or urban poor. These manufactures, however, helped create a class of wealthy Indian businessmen. Far from being satisfied by the government's policies, they supported the Indian National Congress and its demands for independence. Though paying homage to Gandhi, they preferred his designated successor as leader of the Indian National Congress, **Jawaharlal Nehru**° (1889–1964). A highly educated nationalist and subtle thinker, Nehru, unlike Gandhi, looked forward to creating a modern industrial India.

Congress politicians won regional elections but continued to be excluded from the viceroy's cabinet, the true center of power. When World War II began in September 1939 Viceroy Lord Linlithgow declared war without consulting a single Indian. The Congress-dominated provincial governments resigned in protest and found that boycotting government office increased their popular support. When the British offered to give India its independence once the war ended, Gandhi called the offer a "postdated cheque on a failing bank" and demanded full independence immediately. His "Quit India" campaign aroused popular demonstrations against the British and provoked a wave of arrests, including his own. Nehru explained: "I would fight Japan sword in hand, but I can only do so as a free man."

The Second World War divided the Indian people. Most Indian soldiers felt they were fighting to defend their country rather than to support the British Empire. As in World War I, Indians contributed heavily to the Allied war effort, supplying 2 million soldiers and enormous amounts of resources, especially the timber needed for emergency construction. A small number of Indians, however, were so anti-British that they joined the Japanese side.

India's subordination to British interests was vividly demonstrated in the famine of 1943 in Bengal. Unlike previous famines, this one was caused not by drought but by the Japanese conquest of Burma, which cut off supplies of Burmese rice that normally went to Bengal. Although food was available elsewhere in India, the

---

harijan (HAH-ree-jahn)

Nehru (NAY-roo)

Gandhi and Technology

In the twentieth century all political leaders but one embraced modern industrial technology. That one exception is Gandhi.

After deciding to wear only handmade cloth, Gandhi made a bonfire of imported factory-made cloth and began spending half an hour every day spinning yarn on a simple spinning wheel, a task he called a "sacrament." The spinning wheel became the symbol of his movement. Any Indian who wished to come before him had to dress in handwoven cloth.

Gandhi had several reasons for reviving this ancient craft. One was his revulsion against "the incessant search for material comforts," an evil to which he thought Europeans were "becoming slaves." Not only had materialism corrupted the people of the West, it had also caused massive unemployment in India. In particular, he blamed the impoverishment of the Indian people on the cotton industries of England and Japan, which had ruined the traditional cotton manufacturing by which India had once supplied all her own needs.

Gandhi looked back to a time before India became a colony of Britian, when "our women spun fine yarns in their own cottages, and supplemented the earnings of their husbands." The spinning wheel, he believed, was "presented to the nation for giving occupation to the millions who had, at least four months of the year, nothing to do." Not only would a return to the spinning wheel provide employment to millions of Indians, it would also become a symbol of "national consciousness and a contribution by every individual to a definite constructive national work."

Nevertheless, Gandhi was a shrewd politician who understood the usefulness of modern devices for mobilizing the masses and organizing his followers. He wore a watch and used the telephone and the printing press to keep in touch with his followers. When he traveled by train, he rode third class—but in a third-class railroad car of his own. His goal was the independence of his country, and he pursued it with every nonviolent means he could find.

Gandhi's ideas challenge us to rethink the purpose of technology. Was he opposed on principle to all modern devices? Was he an opportunist who used those devices that served his political ends and rejected those that did not? Or did he have a higher principle that accounts for his willingness to use the telephone and the railroad but not factory-made cloth?

Source: Quotations from Louis Fischer, *Gandhi: His Life and Message for the World* (New York: New American Library, 1954), 82–83.

Gandhi at the Spinning Wheel Mahatma Gandhi chose the spinning wheel as his symbol because it represented the traditional activity of millions of rural Indians whose livelihoods were threatened by industrialization. (Margaret Bourke-White, *LIFE Magazine* © Time Warner Inc.)

The Partition of India   When India became independent, Muslims fled from Hindu regions, and Hindus fled from Muslims. Margaret Bourke-White photographed a long line of refugees, with their cows, carts, and belongings, trudging down a country road toward safety.   (Margaret Bourke-White, *LIFE Magazine* © Time Inc.)

British army had requisitioned the railroads to transport troops and equipment in preparation for a Japanese invasion. As a result, supplies ran short in Bengal and surrounding areas, while speculators hoarded whatever they could find. Some 2 million people starved to death before the army was ordered to supply food.

Partition and Independence

When the war ended, Britain's new Labour Party government prepared for Indian independence, but deep suspicions between Hindus and Muslims complicated the process. The break between the two communities had started in 1937, when the Indian National Congress won provincial elections and refused to share power with the Muslim League. In 1940 the leader of the League, **Muhammad Ali Jinnah**° (1876–1948) demanded what many Muslims had been dreaming of for years: a country of their own, to be called Pakistan (from "Punjab-Afghans-Kashmir-Sind" plus the Persian suffix -*stan* meaning "kingdom").

Jinnah (jee-NAH)

As independence approached, talks between Jinnah and Nehru broke down and battle lines were drawn. Violent rioting between Hindus and Muslims broke out in Bengal and Bihar. Gandhi's appeals for tolerance and cooperation fell on deaf ears. In despair, he retreated to his home near Ahmedabad. The British made frantic proposals to keep India united, but their authority was waning fast.

By early 1947 the Indian National Congress had accepted the idea of a partition of India into two states, one secular but dominated by Hindus, the other Muslim. In June Lord Mountbatten, the last viceroy, decided that independence must come immediately. On August 15 British India gave way to a new India and Pakistan. The Indian National Congress, led by Nehru, formed the first government of India; Jinnah and the Muslim League established a government for the provinces that made up Pakistan.

The rejoicing over independence was marred by violent outbreaks between Muslims and Hindus. In protest against the mounting chaos, Gandhi refused to attend the independence day celebration. Throughout the land, Muslim and Hindu neighbors turned on one another, and armed members of one faith hunted down people of the other faith. For centuries Hindus and Muslims had intermingled throughout most of India. Now, leaving most of their possessions behind, Hindus fled from predominantly Muslim areas, and Muslims fled from Hindu areas. Trainloads of desperate refugees of one faith were attacked and massacred by members of the other or were left stranded in the middle of deserts. Within a few months some 12 million people had abandoned their ancestral homes and a half-million lay dead. In January 1948 Gandhi died too, gunned down by an angry Hindu refugee.

After the sectarian massacres and flights of refugees, few Hindus remained in Pakistan, and Muslims were a minority in all but one state of India. That state was Kashmir, a strategically important region in the foothills of the Himalayas. India annexed Kashmir because the local maharajah was Hindu and because the state held the headwaters of the rivers that irrigated millions of acres of farmland in the northwestern part of the subcontinent. The majority of the inhabitants of Kashmir were Muslims, however, and would probably have joined Pakistan if they had been allowed to vote on the matter. The consequence of the partition and of Kashmir in particular was to turn India and Pakistan into bitter enemies that have fought several wars in the past half-century.

THE MEXICAN REVOLUTION, 1910–1940

In the nineteenth century Latin America achieved independence from Spain and Portugal but did not industrialize. Throughout much of the century most Latin American republics suffered from ideological divisions, unstable governments, and violent upheavals. By trading their raw materials and agricultural products for foreign manufactured goods and capital investments, they became economically dependent on the wealthier countries to the north, especially on the United States and Great Britain. Their societies, far from fulfilling the promises of their independence, remained deeply split between wealthy landowners and desperately poor peasants.

Mexico, Brazil, and Argentina contained well over half of Latin America's land, population, and wealth, and their relations with other countries and their economies were quite similar. Mexico, however, underwent a traumatic social revolution, while Argentina and Brazil evolved more peaceably.

Mexico in 1910

Few countries in Latin America suffered as many foreign invasions and interventions as Mexico. A Mexican saying observed wryly: "Poor Mexico: so far from God, so close to the United States." In Mexico the chasm between rich and poor was so deep that only a revolution could move the country toward prosperity and democracy.

Mexico was the Latin American country most influenced by the Spanish during three centuries of colonial rule. After independence in 1821 it suffered from a half-century of political turmoil. At the beginning of the twentieth century Mexican society was divided into rich and poor and into persons of Spanish, Indian, and mixed ancestry. A few very wealthy families of Spanish origin, less than 1 percent of the population, owned 85 percent of Mexico's land, mostly in huge *haciendas* (estates). Closely tied to this elite were the handful of American and British companies that controlled most of Mexico's railroads, silver mines, plantations, and other productive enterprises. At the other end of the social scale were Indians, many of whom did not speak Spanish. *Mestizos°*, people of mixed Indian and European ancestry, were only slightly better off; most of them were peasants who worked on the haciendas or farmed small communal plots near their ancestral villages.

The urban middle class was small and had little political influence. Few professional and government positions were open to them, and foreigners owned most businesses. Industrial workers also were few in number; the only significant groups were textile workers in the port of Veracruz on the Gulf of Mexico and railroad workers spread throughout the country.

During the colonial period, the Spanish government had made halfhearted efforts to defend Indians and mestizos from the land-grabbing tactics of the haciendas. After independence in 1821 wealthy Mexican families and American companies used bribery and force to acquire millions of acres of good agricultural land from villages in southern Mexico. Peasants lost not only their fields but also their access to firewood and pasture for their animals. Sugar, cotton, and other commercial crops replaced corn and beans, and peasants had little choice but to work on haciendas. To survive, they had to buy food and other necessities on credit from the landowner's store; eventually, they fell permanently into debt. Sometimes whole communities were forced to relocate.

In the 1880s American investors purchased from the Mexican government dubious claims to more than

---

mestizo (mess-TEE-zoh)

2.5 million acres (1 million hectares) traditionally held by the Yaqui people of Sonora, in northern Mexico. When the Yaqui resisted the expropriation of their lands, they were brutally repressed by the Mexican army.

Northern Mexicans had no peasant tradition of communal ownership, for the northern half of the country was too dry for farming, unlike the tropical and densely populated south. The north was a region of silver mines and cattle ranches, some of them enormous. It was thinly populated by cowboys and miners. The harshness of their lives and vast inequities in the distribution of income made northern Mexicans as resentful as people in the south.

Despite many upheavals in Mexico in the nineteenth century, in 1910 the government seemed in control. For thirty-four years General Porfirio Díaz° (1830–1915) had ruled Mexico under the motto "Liberty, Order, Progress." To Díaz "liberty" meant freedom for rich hacienda owners and foreign investors to acquire more land. The government imposed "order" through rigged elections and a policy of *pan o palo* (bread or the stick)—that is, bribes for Díaz's supporters and summary justice for those who opposed him. "Progress" meant mainly the importing of foreign capital, machinery, and technicians to take advantage of Mexico's labor, soil, and natural resources.

During the Díaz years (1876–1910) Mexico City—with paved streets, streetcar lines, electric street lighting, and public parks—became a showplace, and new telegraph and railroad lines connected cities and towns throughout Mexico. But this material progress benefited only a handful of well-connected businessmen. The boom in railroads, agriculture, and mining at the turn of the century actually caused a decline in the average Mexican's standard of living.

Though a mestizo himself, Díaz discriminated against the nonwhite majority of Mexicans. He and his supporters tried to eradicate what they saw as Mexico's embarrassingly rustic traditions. On many middle- and upper-class tables French cuisine replaced traditional Mexican dishes. The wealthy replaced sombreros and ponchos with European garments. Though bullfighting and cockfighting remained popular, the well-to-do preferred horse racing and soccer. To the educated middle class—the only group with a strong sense of Mexican nationhood—this devaluation of Mexican culture became a symbol of the Díaz regime's failure to defend national interests against foreign influences.

Revolution and Civil War, 1911–1920

Many Mexicans feared or anticipated a popular uprising after Díaz. Unlike the independence movement in India, the Mexican Revolution was not the work of one party with a well-defined ideology. Instead, it developed haphazardly, led by a series of ambitious but limited leaders, each representing a different segment of Mexican society.

The first was Francisco I. Madero (1873–1913), the son of a wealthy landowning and mining family, educated in the United States. When minor uprisings broke out in 1911, the government collapsed and Díaz fled into exile. The Madero presidency was welcomed by some, but aroused opposition from peasant leaders like **Emiliano Zapata** (1879–1919). In 1913, after two years as president, Madero was overthrown and murdered by one of his former supporters, General Victoriano Huerta. Woodrow Wilson (1856–1924), president of the United States, showed his displeasure by sending the United States Marines to occupy Veracruz.

The inequities of Mexican society and foreign intervention in Mexico's affairs angered Mexico's middle class and industrial workers. They found leaders in Venustiano Carranza, a landowner, and in Alvaro Obregón°, a schoolteacher. Calling themselves Constitutionalists, Carranza and Obregón organized private armies and succeeded in overthrowing Huerta in 1914. By then, the revolution had spread to the countryside.

As early as 1911 Zapata, an Indian farmer, had led a revolt against the haciendas in the mountains of Morelos, south of Mexico City (see Map 30.2). His soldiers were peasants, some of them women, mounted on horseback and armed with pistols and rifles. For several years they periodically came down from the mountains, burned hacienda buildings, and returned land to the Indian villages to which it had once belonged.

Another leader appeared in Chihuahua, a northern state where seventeen individuals owned two-fifths of the land and 95 percent of the people had no land at all. Starting in 1913 **Francisco "Pancho" Villa** (1877–1923), a former ranch hand, mule driver, and bandit, organized an army of three thousand men, most of them cowboys. They too seized land from the large haciendas, not to rebuild traditional communities as in southern Mexico but to create family ranches.

Zapata and Villa were part agrarian rebels, part social revolutionaries. They enjoyed tremendous popular support but could never rise above their regional and peasant origins and lead a national revolution. The Con-

---

Díaz (DEE-as)

Obregón (oh-bray-GAWN)

Emiliano Zapata   Zapata, the leader of a peasant rebellion in southern Mexico during the Mexican Revolution, stands in full revolutionary regalia: sword, rifles, bandoleers, boots, and sombrero.   (Brown Brothers)

stitutionalists had fewer soldiers than Zapata and Villa; but they held the major cities, controlled the country's exports of oil, and used the proceeds of oil sales to buy modern weapons. Fighting continued for years, and gradually the Constitutionalists took over most of Mexico. In 1919 they defeated and killed Zapata; Villa was assassinated four years later. An estimated 2 million people lost their lives in the civil war, and much of Mexico lay in ruins.

During their struggle to win support against Zapata and Villa, the Constitutionalists adopted many of their rivals' agrarian reforms, such as restoring communal lands to the Indians of Morelos. The Constitutionalists also proposed social programs designed to appeal to workers and the middle class. The Constitution of 1917 promised universal suffrage and a one-term presidency; state-run education to free the poor from the hold of the Catholic Church; the end of debt peonage; restrictions on foreign ownership of property; and laws specifying minimum wages and maximum hours to protect laborers. Although these reforms were too costly to implement right away, they had important symbolic significance, for they enshrined the dignity of Mexicans and the equality of Indians, mestizos, and whites, as well as of peasants and city people.

The Revolution Institutionalized, 1920–1940

In the early 1920s, after a decade of violence that exhausted all classes, the Mexican Revolution lost momentum. Only in Morelos did peasants receive land, and President Obregón and his closest associates made all the important decisions. Nevertheless, the Revolution changed the social makeup of the governing class. For the first time in Mexico's history, representatives of rural communities, unionized workers, and public employees were admitted to the inner circle.

In the arts the Mexican Revolution sparked a surge of creativity. The political murals of José Clemente Orozco and Diego Rivera and the paintings of Frida Kahlo focused on social themes, showing peasants, workers, and soldiers in scenes from the Revolution.

In 1928 Obregón was assassinated. His successor, Plutarco Elías Calles°, founded the National Revolutionary Party, or PNR (the abbreviation of its name in Spanish). The PNR was a forum where all the pressure groups and vested interests—labor, peasants, businessmen, landowners, the military, and others—worked out compromises. The establishment of the PNR gave the Mexican Revolution a second wind.

Lázaro Cárdenas°, chosen by Calles to be president in 1934, brought peasants' and workers' organizations into the party, renamed it the Mexican Revolutionary Party (PRM), and removed the generals from government positions. Then he set to work implementing the reforms promised in the Constitution of 1917. Cárdenas redistributed 44 million acres (17.6 million hectares) to peasant communes. He closed church-run schools, replacing them with government schools. He nationalized the railroads and numerous other businesses.

Calles (KAH-yace)
Lázaro Cárdenas (LAH-sah-roe KAHR-dih-nahs)

Map 30.2   The Mexican Revolution   The Mexican Revolution began in two distinct regions of the country. One was the mountainous and densely populated area south of Mexico City, particularly Morelos, homeland of Emiliano Zapata. The other was the dry and thinly populated ranch country of the north, such as Chihuahua, home of Pancho Villa. The fighting that ensued crisscrossed the country along the main railroad lines, shown on the map.

Cárdenas's most dramatic move was the expropriation of foreign-owned oil companies. In the early 1920s Mexico was the world's leading producer of oil, but a handful of American and British companies exported almost all of it. In 1938 Cárdenas seized the foreign-owned oil industry, more as a matter of national pride than of economics. The oil companies expected the governments of the United States and Great Britain to come to their rescue, perhaps with military force. But Mexico and the United States chose to resolve the issue through negotiation, and Mexico retained control of its oil industry.

When Cárdenas's term ended in 1940, Mexico, like India, was still a land of poor farmers with a small industrial base. The Revolution had brought great changes, however. The political system was free of both chaos and dictatorships. A small group of wealthy people no longer monopolized land and other resources. The military was

tamed; the Catholic Church no longer controlled education; and the nationalization of oil had demonstrated Mexico's independence from foreign corporations and military intervention.

What did the Mexican Revolution accomplish? It did not fulfill the democratic promise of Madero's campaign, for it brought to power a party that monopolized the government for eighty years. However it allowed far more sectors of the population to participate in politics and made sure no president stayed in office more than six years. The Revolution also promised far-reaching social reforms, such as free education, higher wages and more security for workers, and the redistribution of land to the peasants. These long-delayed reforms began to be implemented during the Cárdenas administration. They fell short of the ideals expressed by the revolutionaries, but they laid the foundation for the later industrialization of Mexico.

***The Agitator,* a Mural by Diego Rivera**   Diego Rivera (1886–1957) was politically committed to the Mexican Revolution and widely admired as an artist. This mural, painted at the National Agricultural School at Chapingo near Mexico City, shows a political agitator addressing peasants and workers. With one hand, the speaker points to miners laboring in a silver mine; with the other, to a hammer and sickle.   (Universidad Autonoma de Chapingo/ CENIDIAP-INBA)

ARGENTINA AND BRAZIL, 1900–1949

On the surface, Argentina and Brazil seem very different. Argentina is Spanish-speaking, temperate in climate, and populated almost exclusively by people of European origin. Brazil is tropical and Portuguese-speaking, and its inhabitants are of mixed European and African origin, with a substantial Indian minority. Yet in the twentieth century their economic, political, and technological experiences were remarkably similar.

The Transformation of Argentina

Most of Argentina consists of *pampas*°, flat, fertile land that is easy to till, much like the prairies of the midwestern United States and Canada. Throughout the nineteenth century Argentina's economy was based on two exports: the hides of longhorn creole cattle and the wool of merino sheep, which roamed the pampas in huge herds. Centuries earlier, Europeans had haphazardly introduced the animals and the grasses they ate. Natural selection had made the animals tough and hardy.

At the end of the nineteenth century railroads and refrigerator ships, which allowed the safe transportation of meat, changed not only the composition of Argentina's exports but also the way they were produced—in other words, the land itself. European consumers preferred the soft flesh of Lincoln sheep and Hereford cattle to the tough sinewy meat of creole cattle and merino sheep. The valuable Lincolns and Herefords could not be allowed to roam and graze on the pampas. They were carefully bred and received a diet of alfalfa and oats. To safeguard them, the pampas had to be divided, plowed, cultivated, and fenced with barbed wire to keep out predators and other unwelcome animals. Once fenced, the land could be used to produce wheat as well as beef and mutton. Within a few years grasslands that had stretched to the horizon were transformed into farmland. Like the North American midwest, the pampas became one of the world's great producers of wheat and meat.

Argentina's government represented the interests of the *oligarquía*°, a very small group of wealthy landowners. Members of this elite controlled enormous haciendas

pampas (POM-pus)

oligarquía (oh-lee-gar-KEE-ah)

where they raised cattle and sheep and grew wheat for export. They also owned fine homes in Buenos Aires°, a city that was built to look like Paris. They traveled frequently to Europe and spent so lavishly that the French coined the superlative "rich as an Argentine." They showed little interest in any business other than farming, however, and were content to let foreign companies, mainly British, build Argentina's railroads, processing plants, and public utilities. In exchange for its agricultural exports Argentina imported almost all its manufactured goods from Europe and the United States. So important were British interests in the Argentinean economy that English, not Spanish, was used on the railroads, and the biggest department store in Buenos Aires was a branch of Harrods of London.

Brazil and Argentina, to 1929

Before the First World War Brazil produced most of the world's coffee and cacao, grown on vast estates, and natural rubber, gathered by Indians from rubber trees growing wild in the Amazon rain forest. Brazil's elite was made up of coffee and cacao planters and rubber exporters. Like their Argentinean counterparts, they spent their money lavishly, building palaces in Rio de Janeiro° and one of the world's most beautiful opera house in Manaus°, deep in the Amazon. They had little interest in other forms of development; let British companies build railroads, harbors, and other infrastructure; and imported most manufactured goods. At the time this seemed to allow each country to do what it did best. If the British did not grow coffee, why should Brazil build locomotives?

Both Argentina and Brazil had small but outspoken middle classes that demanded a share in government and looked to Europe as a model. Beneath each middle class were the poor. In Argentina these were mainly Spanish and Italian immigrants who had ended up as landless farm laborers or workers in urban packing plants. In Brazil there was a large class of sharecroppers and plantation workers, many of them descendants of slaves.

Rubber exports collapsed after 1912, replaced by cheaper plantation rubber from Southeast Asia. The outbreak of war in 1914 put an end to imports from Europe as Britain and France focused all their industries on war production and Germany was cut off entirely. The disruption of the old trade patterns weakened the landown-

ing class. In Argentina the urban middle class obtained the secret ballot and universal male suffrage in 1916 and elected a liberal politician, **Hipólito Irigoyen°**, as president. To a certain extent, the United States replaced the European countries as suppliers of machinery and consumers of coffee. European immigrants built factories to manufacture textiles and household goods. Desperate for money to pay for the war, Great Britain sold many of its railroad, streetcar, and other companies to the governments of Argentina and Brazil.

In contrast to Mexico, the postwar years were a period of prosperity in South America. Trade with Europe resumed; prices for agricultural exports remained high; and both Argentina and Brazil used profits accumulated during the war to industrialize and improve their transportation systems and public utilities. Yet it was also a time of social turmoil, as workers and middle-class professionals demanded social reforms and a larger voice in politics. In Argentina students' and workers' demonstrations were brutally crushed. In Brazil junior officers rose up several times against the government, calling for universal suffrage, social reforms, and freedom for labor unions. Though they accomplished little, they laid the groundwork for later reformist movements. In neither country did the urban middle class take power away from the wealthy landowners. Instead, the two classes shared power at the expense of both the landless peasants and the urban workers.

Yet as Argentina and Brazil were moving forward, new technologies again left them dependent on the advanced industrial countries. Brazilians are justly proud that the first person to fly an airplane outside the United States was Alberto Santos-Dumont, a Brazilian. He did so in 1906 in France, where he lived most of his life and had access to engine manufacturers and technical assistance. Aviation reached Latin America after World War I, when European and American companies such as Aéropostale and Pan American Airways introduced airmail service between cities and linked Latin America with the United States and Europe.

Before and during World War I radio, then called "wireless telegraphy," was used not for broadcasting but for point-to-point communications. Transmitters powerful enough to send messages across oceans or continents were extraordinarily complex and expensive: their antennas covered many acres; they used as much electricity as a small town; and they cost tens of thousands of pounds sterling (millions of dollars in today's money).

Right after the war, the major powers scrambled to build powerful transmitters on every continent to com-

---

Buenos Aires (BWAY-nihs AIR-eze)   **Rio de Janeiro** (REE-oh day zhuh-NAIR-oh)   **Manaus** (meh-NOWSE)

Hipólito Irigoyen (ee-POH-lee-toe ee-ree-GO-yen)

pete with the telegraph cable companies and to take advantage of the boom in international business and news reporting. At the time, no Latin American country possessed the knowledge or funds to build its own transmitters. In 1919, therefore, President Irigoyen of Argentina granted a radio concession to a German firm. France and Britain protested this decision, and eventually four powerful radio companies—one British, one French, one German, and one American—formed a cartel to control all radio communications in Latin America. This cartel set up a national radio company in each Latin American republic, installing a prominent local politician as its president, but the cartel held all the stock and therefore received all the profits. Thus, even as Brazil and Argentina were taking over their railroads and older industries, the major industrial countries controlled the diffusion of the newer aviation and radio technologies.

The Depression and the Vargas Regime in Brazil

The Depression hit Latin America as hard as it hit Europe and the United States; in many ways, it marks a more important turning point for the region than either of the world wars. As long-term customers cut back their orders, the value of agricultural and mineral exports fell by two-thirds between 1929 and 1932. Argentina and Brazil could no longer afford to import manufactured goods. An imploding economy also undermined their shaky political systems. Like European countries, Argentina and Brazil veered toward authoritarian regimes that promised to solve their economic problems.

In 1930 **Getulio Vargas°** (1883–1953), a state governor, staged a coup and proclaimed himself president of Brazil. He proved to be a masterful politician. He wrote a new constitution that broadened the franchise and limited the president to one term. He raised import duties and promoted national firms and state-owned enterprises, culminating in the construction of the Volta Redonda steel mill in the 1930s. By 1936 industrial production had doubled, especially in textiles and small manufactures. Under his guidance, Brazil was on its way to becoming an industrial country. Vargas's policy, called **import-substitution industrialization,** became a model for other Latin American countries as they attempted to break away from neocolonial dependency.

The industrialization of Brazil brought all the familiar environmental consequences. Powerful new machines allowed the reopening of old mines and the digging of new ones. Cities grew as poor peasants looking for work arrived from the countryside. Around the older neighborhoods of Rio de Janeiro and São Paulo°, the poor turned steep hillsides and vacant lands into immense *favelas°* (slums) of makeshift shacks.

The countryside also was transformed. Scrubland was turned into pasture, and new acreage was planted in wheat, corn, and sugar cane. Even the Amazon rain forest—half of the land area of Brazil—was affected. In 1930 American industrialist Henry Ford invested $8 million to clear land along the Tapajós River and prepare it to become the site of the world's largest rubber plantation. Ford encountered opposition from Brazilian workers and politicians; the rubber trees proved vulnerable to diseases; and he had to abandon the project—but not before leaving 3 million acres (1.2 million hectares) denuded of trees. The ecological changes of the Vargas era, however, were but a tiny forerunner of the degradation of the Brazilian environment that was to take place later in the century.

Vargas instituted many reforms favorable to urban workers, such as labor unions, pension plans, and disability insurance, but he refused to take any measures that might help the millions of landless peasants or harm the interests of the great landowners. Although the Brazilian economy recovered from the Depression, the benefits of recovery were so unequally distributed that communist and fascist movements demanded even more radical changes.

In 1938, prohibited by his own constitution from being reelected, Vargas staged another coup, abolished the constitution, and instituted the Estado Novo°, or "New State," with himself as supreme leader. He abolished political parties, jailed opposition leaders, and turned Brazil into a fascist state. When the Second World War broke out, however, Vargas aligned Brazil with the United States and contributed troops and ships to the Allied war effort.

Despite his economic achievements, Vargas harmed Brazil. By running roughshod over laws, constitutions, and rights, he infected not only Brazil but all of South America with the temptations of political violence. It is ironic, but not surprising, that Vargas was overthrown in 1945 by a military coup.

Argentina After 1930

Economically, the Depression hurt Argentina almost as badly as it hurt Brazil. Politically, however, the consequences were

---

Getulio Vargas (jay-TOO-lee-oh VAR-gus)

São Paulo (sow PAL-oh)   *favela* (feh-VEL-luh)   **Estado Novo** (esh-TAH-doe NO-vo)

The Peróns in Front of the TZ Hotel   In 1945, Juan Perón, the dictator of Argentina, married the actress Eva Duarte. Her charms and gifts as an orator attracted the support of the labor unions to the Perón regime. The Peróns are shown riding through Buenos Aires following Perón's second inauguration on June 4, 1952. Eva died a month later, reportedly of cancer. (Bettemann/Corbis)

delayed for many years. In 1930 General José Uriburu° overthrew the popularly elected President Irigoyen. The Uriburu government represented the large landowners and big business interests. For thirteen years the generals and the oligarquía ruled, doing nothing to lessen the poverty of the workers or the frustrations of the middle class. When World War II broke out, Argentina sympathized with the Axis but remained officially neutral.

In 1943 another military revolt flared, this one among junior officers angry at conservative politicians. It was led by Colonel **Juan Perón**° (1895–1974). The intentions of the rebels were clear:

> Civilians will never understand the greatness of our ideal; we shall therefore have to eliminate them from the government and give them the only mission which corresponds to them: work and obedience.[1]

Once in power the officers took over the highest positions in government and business and began to lavish money on military equipment and their own salaries. Their goal, inspired by Nazi victories, was nothing less than the conquest of South America.

As the war turned against the Nazis, the officers saw their popularity collapse. Perón, however, had other plans. Inspired by his charismatic wife **Eva Duarte Perón**° (1919–1952), he appealed to the urban workers. Eva Perón became the champion of the *descamisados*°, or "shirtless ones," and campaigned tirelessly for social benefits and for the cause of women and children. With his wife's help, Perón won the presidency in 1946 and created a populist dictatorship in imitation of the Vargas regime in Brazil.

Like Brazil, Argentina industrialized rapidly under state sponsorship. Perón spent lavishly on social welfare projects as well as on the military, depleting the capital that Argentina had earned during the war. Though a skillful demagogue who played off the army against the navy and both against the labor unions, Perón could not create a stable government out of the chaos of coups and conspiracies. He had to back down from a plan to make Eva his vice president. When she died in 1952, he lost his political skills (or perhaps they were hers), and soon thereafter he was overthrown in yet another military coup.

José Uriburu (hoe-SAY oo-ree-BOO-roo)   **Juan Perón** (hoo-AHN pair-OWN)

Eva Duarte Perón (AY-vuy doo-AR-tay pair-OWN)   *descamisados* (des-cah-mee-SAH-dohs)

Mexico, Argentina, and Brazil: A Comparison

Until 1910 Mexico, Argentina, and Brazil shared a common history and similar cultures. In the first half of the twentieth century their economies followed parallel trajectories, based on unequal relations with the industrialized countries of Europe and North America. All three countries—indeed, all of Latin America—struggled with the failure of neocolonial economics to improve the lives of the middle class, let alone the peasants. And when the Depression hit, all three turned to state intervention and import-substitution industrialization. Like all industrializing countries, they did so by mining, farming, ranching, cutting down forests, and irrigating land, all at the expense of the natural environment.

Yet their political histories diverged radically. Mexico underwent a traumatic and profound social revolution. Argentina and Brazil, meanwhile, languished under conservative regimes devoted to the interests of wealthy landowners, sporadically interrupted by military coups and populist demagogues. Mexicans, thanks to their experience of revolution, developed an acute sense of their national identity and civic pride in their history—pride largely missing in South America. Despite shortcomings, Mexico seriously committed itself to education, land reform, social justice, and political stability as national goals, not merely as the campaign platform of a populist dictator.

CONCLUSION

Sub-Saharan Africa, India, and Latin America lay outside the theaters of war that engulfed most of the Northern Hemisphere, but they were deeply affected by global events and by the demands of the industrial powers. Sub-Saharan Africa and India were still under colonial rule, and their political life revolved around the yearnings of their elites for political independence and their masses for social justice. Mexico, Argentina, and Brazil were politically independent, but their economies, like those of Africa and India, were closely tied to the economies of the industrial nations with which they traded. Their deeply polarized societies and the stresses caused by their dependence on the industrial countries clashed with the expectations of ever larger numbers of their peoples.

In Mexico these stresses brought about a long and violent revolution, out of which Mexicans forged a lasting sense of national identity. Argentina and Brazil moved toward greater economic independence, but the price was social unrest, militarism, and dictatorship. In India the conflict between growing expectations and the reality of colonial rule produced both a movement for independence and an ethnic split that tore the nation apart. In sub-Saharan Africa demands for national self-determination and economic development were only beginning to be voiced by 1949 and did not come to fruition until the second half of the century.

Nationalism and the yearning for social justice were the two most powerful forces for change in the early twentieth century. These ideas originated in the industrialized countries but resonated in the independent countries of Latin America as well as in colonial regions such as the Indian subcontinent and sub-Saharan Africa. However, they did not always unite people against their colonial rulers or foreign oppressors; instead, they often divided them along social, ethnic, or religious lines. Western-educated elites looked to industrialization as a means of modernizing their country and ensuring their position in it, while peasants and urban workers supported nationalist and revolutionary movements in the hope of improving their lives. Often these goals were not compatible.

■ Key Terms

Blaise Diagne

African National Congress

Haile Selassie

Indian National Congress

Bengal

All-India Muslim League

Mohandas K. (Mahatma) Gandhi

Jawaharlal Nehru

Muhammad Ali Jinnah

Emiliano Zapata

Francisco "Pancho" Villa

Lázaro Cárdenas

Hipólito Irigoyen

Getulio Vargas

import-substitution industrialization

Juan Perón

Eva Duarte Perón

■ Suggested Reading

On Africa under colonial rule the classic overview is Melville Herskovits, *The Human Factor in Changing Africa* (1958). Two excellent general introductions are Roland Oliver and Anthony Atmore, *Africa Since 1800*, 4th ed. (1994), and A. E. Afigbo et al.,

The Making of Modern Africa, vol. 2, *The Twentieth Century* (1986). More detailed and challenging are *UNESCO General History of Africa*, vols. 7 and 8; *The Cambridge History of Africa*, vols. 7 and 8; and Adu Boahen, *African Perspectives on Colonialism* (1987). Outstanding novels about Africa in the colonial era include Chinua Achebe, *Arrow of God* (1964); Buchi Emecheta, *The Joys of Motherhood* (1980); and Peter Abraham, *Mine Boy* (1946).

For a general introduction to Indian history see Sumit Sarkar, *Modern India, 1885–1947* (1983), and Percival Spear, *India: A Modern History*, rev. ed. (1972). On the influenza epidemic of 1918–1919 see Alfred W. Crosby, *America's Forgotten Pandemic: The Influenza of 1918* (1989). The Indian independence movement has received a great deal of attention. Judith M. Brown's most recent book on Gandhi is *Gandhi: Prisoner of Hope* (1989). *Gandhi's Truth: On the Origin of Militant Nonviolence* (1969) by noted psychoanalyst Erik Erikson is also recommended. Two collections of memoirs of the last decades of British rule are worth looking at: Charles Allen, ed., *Plain Tales of the Raj: Image of British India in the Twentieth Century* (1975), and Zareer Masani, ed., *Indian Tales of the Raj* (1988). The transition from colonialism to partition and independence is the subject of the very readable *Freedom at Midnight* (1975) by Larry Collins and Dominique Lapierre. The environment is discussed in M. Gadgil and R. Guha, *This Fissured Land: An Ecological History of India* (1993).

Thomas Skidmore and Peter Smith, *Modern Latin America*, 3d ed. (1992), offers the best brief introduction. Two fine general overviews of modern Mexican history are Enrique Krauze, *Mexico: Biography of Power: A History of Modern Mexico, 1810–1996* (1997), and Colin MacLachlan and William Beezley, *El Gran Pueblo: A History of Greater Mexico* (1994). On the Mexican Revolution, two recent books are essential: Alan Knight, *The Mexican Revolution*, 2 vols. (1986), and John M. Hart, *Revolutionary Mexico: The Coming and Process of the Mexican Revolution* (1987). But see also two classics by sympathetic Americans: Frank Tannenbaum, *Peace by Revolution: Mexico After 1910* (1933), and Robert E. Quirk, *The Mexican Revolution, 1914–1915* (1960). Mexico's most celebrated revolutionary is the subject of Manuel Machado, *Centaur of the North: Francisco Villa, the Mexican Revolution, and Northern Mexico* (1988). Mariano Azuela, *The Underdogs* (1988), is an interesting fictional account of this period. The standard work on Brazil is E. Bradford Burns, *A History of Brazil*, 3d ed. (1993). On the environmental history of Brazil, see Warren Dean, *Brazil and the Struggle for Rubber: A Study in Environmental History* (1987). The history of modern Argentina is ably treated in David Rock, *Argentina, 1517–1987: From Spanish Colonization to Alfonsín* (1987). Mark Jefferson, *Peopling the Argentine Pampas* (1971), and Jeremy Adelman, *Frontier Development: Land, Labour and Capital on the Wheatlands of Argentina and Canada, 1890–1914* (1994), describe the transformation of the Argentinean environment.

■ Notes

1. George Blanksten, *Perón's Argentina* (Chicago: University of Chicago Press, 1953), 37.

Document-Based Question
Nationalism and the Struggle for Independence, 1900–1949

Using the following documents, assess the role of nationalism in the struggles for independence in Vietnam and India from 1900 to 1949

DOCUMENT 1
A Vietnamese Nationalist Denounces French Colonialism (Diversity and Dominance, pp. 796–797)

DOCUMENT 2
Map 30.1 The Partition of India, 1947 (p. 801)

DOCUMENT 3
Quote from Jawarharlal Nehru (p. 804)

DOCUMENT 4
Quotes from Mahatma Gandhi (Environment and Technology, p. 805)

DOCUMENT 5
The Partition of India (photo, p. 806)

What factors affect the reliability of Document 1? What additional types of documents would help you understand the role of nationalism in the struggles for independence in Vietnam and India from 1900 to 1949?

PART EIGHT

Perils and Promises of a Global Community, 1945 to the Present

The years after World War II brought many promising changes to an increasingly interconnected world. Major efforts were made to promote peace and international cooperation, and most countries agreed to human rights standards to be enforced through the United Nations. Colonized peoples in Asia and Africa gained their independence, and expanding global trade offered the hope of economic growth. However, these decades also saw major threats to peace, prosperity, and the environment.

A Cold War of rhetoric and frayed nerves between communist and anti-communist states disrupted dreams of a new era of international peace and cooperation. The Iron Curtain divided Soviet-dominated eastern Europe from American-supported western Europe. Regional wars in Korea and Vietnam pitted the United States and its allies against communist regimes. Cold War rivalries sometimes provided a windfall of aid for new states but also intensified civil conflicts in Latin America, Africa, and elsewhere.

Tensions eased in the 1970s, and the United States and the Soviet Union signed agreements to curtail nuclear arms and testing. With the collapse of communism in the Soviet Union in 1991, the Cold War finally ended. The United Nations and other multinational organizations moved to stop the spread of weapons of mass destruction and promote global justice and equality. As the sole remaining superpower, the United States had a unique capacity to act globally and a unique burden of suspicion of its motives.

Economic promises and perils also abounded in the post-war world. The wartime victors experienced rapid economic recovery, as did Germany and Japan, but in less developed lands prosperity came slowly or not at all. Global markets seemed to favor the industrialized nations. After 1975 a number of countries, including China, South Korea, Brazil, and Argentina, made dramatic strides in industrialization. But less developed nations had to struggle, and rapid population growth often offset their economic gains. The divide between rich and poor nations remained—or even widened.

Economic development meant new possibilities and perils for the environment. In the 1960s, the Green Revolution in agriculture greatly increased food supplies in Asia, and in the 1990s genetic engineering advances produced plants that yielded more food and were resistant to disease, drought, and insect damage. But industrial growth added immeasurably to the pollution of water and land. Atmospheric pollution increased exposure to harmful ultraviolet rays and led to increased global temperatures. Over-fishing and over-hunting imperiled many animal species, while thousands of acres of tropical forests were cut or burned for timber and farmland.

Finally, growing global interconnectedness held its own promises and perils. Many welcomed the emergence of English as the global language and the rapid spread of news, money, and ideas via the Internet. Others feared that Western material values and political and economic dominance posed a severe threat to cultural diversity around the world. A dangerous few reacted with violence.

1950 — **1960** — **1970**

Americas
- 1945 United Nations charter signed in San Francisco
- 1946 International Monetary Fund and World Bank founded
- 1952 U.S. tests first hydrogen bomb
- 1962 Cuban missile crisis
- 1959 Cuban Revolution
- 1964 Military takes power in Brazil
- Neil Armstrong walks on moon 1969 •

Europe
- 1948–1952 Marshall Plan helps rebuild western Europe
- 1949 NATO founded
- 1955 Warsaw Pact formed
- Soviet troops crush revolt in Hungary 1956 •
- 1957 Common Market founded
- 1961 Berlin Wall built
- Student uprising in France 1968 •

Africa
- 1948 Apartheid becomes official in South Africa
- Ghana first British colony in West Africa to win independence 1957 •
- 1958 Guinea wins independence from France
- 1960 Nigeria, Congo, Somalia, Togo win independence
- 1963 Kenya independent

Middle East
- 1948 State of Israel founded; first Arab-Israeli War
- 1956 Suez crisis
- 1954–1962 Algerian war for Independence
- Organization of Petroleum Exporting Countries founded 1960 •
- 1967 Six Day Arab-Israeli War

Asia and Oceania
- Communist Revolution in China 1949 •
- 1951–1953 Korean War
- 1954–1975 Vietnam War
- 1949 Indonesia wins independence from Netherlands
- Cultural Revolution in China 1966–1969
- Japan becomes world economic power 1970s •

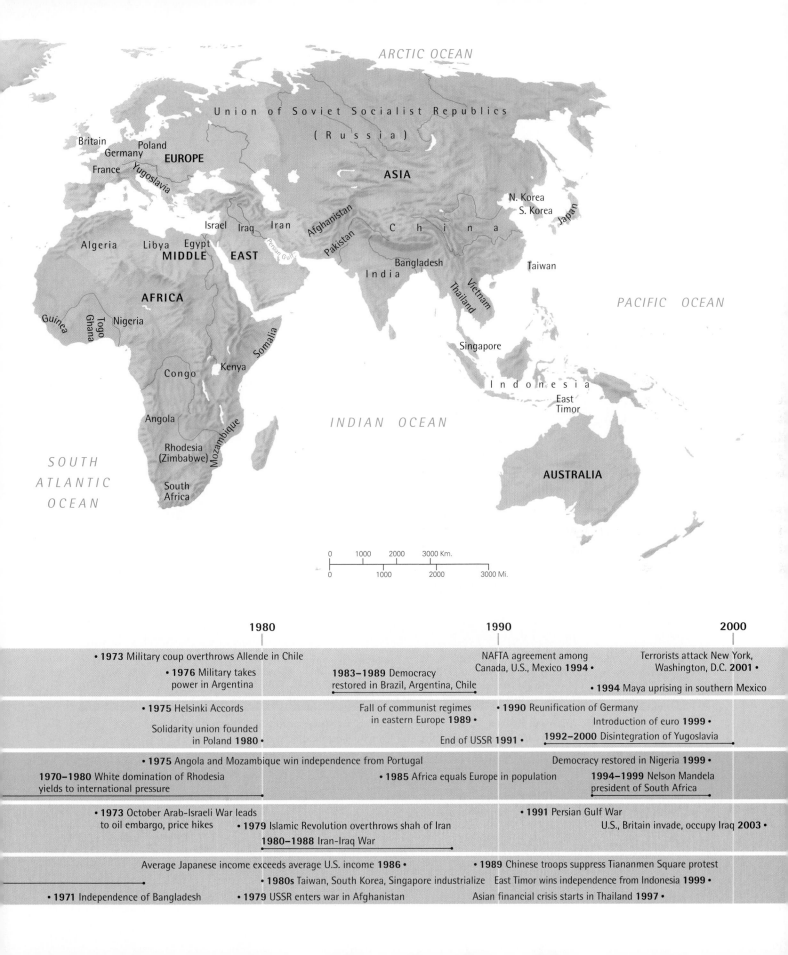

ARCTIC OCEAN

Union of Soviet Socialist Republics
(Russia)

Britain
Poland
Germany   EUROPE
France
Yugoslavia

ASIA

N. Korea
S. Korea
Japan

Israel   Iraq   Iran   Afghanistan
Algeria   Libya   Egypt   Pakistan   C h i n a
MIDDLE   EAST   Persian Gulf
Bangladesh   Taiwan
AFRICA   I n d i a
Vietnam
Guinea   Nigeria   Thailand
Togo   PACIFIC OCEAN
Ghana
Somalia   Singapore
Congo   Kenya
I n d o n e s i a
Angola   East Timor
Mozambique
Rhodesia   INDIAN OCEAN
(Zimbabwe)
SOUTH   AUSTRALIA
ATLANTIC   South
OCEAN   Africa

0   1000   2000   3000 Km.
0   1000   2000   3000 Mi.

1980	1990	2000

• **1973** Military coup overthrows Allende in Chile
NAFTA agreement among
Canada, U.S., Mexico **1994** •
Terrorists attack New York,
Washington, D.C. **2001** •
• **1976** Military takes
power in Argentina
1983–1989 Democracy
restored in Brazil, Argentina, Chile
• **1994** Maya uprising in southern Mexico

• **1975** Helsinki Accords
Fall of communist regimes
in eastern Europe **1989** •
• **1990** Reunification of Germany
Solidarity union founded
in Poland **1980** •
Introduction of euro **1999** •
End of USSR **1991** •
1992–2000 Disintegration of Yugoslavia

• **1975** Angola and Mozambique win independence from Portugal
Democracy restored in Nigeria **1999** •
1970–1980 White domination of Rhodesia
yields to international pressure
• **1985** Africa equals Europe in population
1994–1999 Nelson Mandela
president of South Africa

• **1973** October Arab-Israeli War leads
to oil embargo, price hikes
• **1991** Persian Gulf War
• **1979** Islamic Revolution overthrows shah of Iran
U.S., Britain invade, occupy Iraq **2003** •
1980–1988 Iran-Iraq War

Average Japanese income exceeds average U.S. income **1986** •
• **1989** Chinese troops suppress Tiananmen Square protest
• **1980s** Taiwan, South Korea, Singapore industrialize
East Timor wins independence from Indonesia **1999** •
• **1971** Independence of Bangladesh
• **1979** USSR enters war in Afghanistan
Asian financial crisis starts in Thailand **1997** •

31

The Cold War and Decolonization, 1945–1975

Fidel Castro Arrives in Havana   Castro and his supporters overthrew a brutal dictatorship and began the revolutionary transformation of Cuba. This led to a confrontation with the United States.

CHAPTER OUTLINE

The Cold War

Decolonization and Nation Building

Beyond a Bipolar World

ENVIRONMENT AND TECHNOLOGY: The Green Revolution

DIVERSITY AND DOMINANCE: Race and the Struggle for Justice in South Africa

In 1946, in a speech at Fulton, Missouri, Great Britain's wartime leader Winston Churchill said: "From Stettin in the Baltic to Trieste in the Adriatic, an iron curtain has descended across the Continent. . . . I am convinced there is nothing they [the communists] so much admire as strength, and there is nothing for which they have less respect than weakness, especially military weakness." The phrase **"iron curtain"** became a watchword of the **Cold War,** the state of political tension and military rivalry that was then beginning between the United States and its allies ("running dogs of imperialism," in Chinese communist parlance) and the Soviet Union and its allies ("satellites," in American parlance).

The Atlantic Charter issued by Churchill and President Franklin Roosevelt four months before the United States entered World War II in 1941 and the 1942 declaration signed by twenty-six "United Nations" (Roosevelt's term for the alliance against the Axis) had looked forward to economic cooperation, restoration of sovereignty to nations occupied by the Axis, and above all to a world in which war and territorial conquest were not tolerated. By the time Churchill delivered his "iron curtain" speech, however, Britain's electorate had voted him out of power, Harry S Truman had succeeded to the presidency after Roosevelt's death, Communist Yugoslavia was supporting the communists in Greece, and the Soviet Union was dominating eastern Europe and supporting communist movements in China, Iran, Turkey, and Korea. Although Soviet diplomats joined their former allies in the newly founded United Nations organization, confrontation, not cooperation, was the hallmark of relations between East and West.

The intensity of the Cold War, with its accompanying threat of nuclear destruction, sometimes obscured a postwar phenomenon of more enduring importance. Western domination was greatly reduced in most of Asia, Africa, and Latin America and the colonial empires of the New Imperialism were gradually dismantled. The new generation of national leaders heading the states in these regions sometimes skillfully used Cold War antagonism to their own advantage.

Their real business, however, was nation building, an enterprise charged with almost insurmountable problems and conflicts.

Each region subjected to imperialism had its own history and conditions and followed its own route to independence. Thus the new nations had difficulty finding a collective voice in a world increasingly oriented toward two superpowers, the United States and the Soviet Union. Some sided openly with one or the other. Others banded together in a posture of neutrality and spoke with one voice about their need for economic and technical assistance and the obligation of the wealthy nations to satisfy those needs.

The Cold War military rivalry stimulated extraordinary advances in weaponry and associated technologies, but many new nations faced basic problems of educating their citizens, nurturing industry, and escaping the economic constraints imposed by their former imperialist masters. The environment suffered severe pressures from oil exploration and transport to support the growing economies of the wealthy nations and from deforestation in poor regions challenged by the need for cropland. Neither rich nor poor nations understood the costs associated with these environmental changes.

As you read this chapter, ask yourself the following questions:

- What impact did economic philosophy have on both the Cold War and the decolonization movement?

- How was a third world war averted?

- Was world domination by the superpowers good or bad for the rest of the world?

- How were the experiences of Asia, Africa, and Latin America similar in this period?

THE COLD WAR

The wartime alliance between the United States, Great Britain, and the Soviet Union had been uneasy. Fear of working-class revolution, which the Nazis had played on in their rise to power, was not confined to Germany. For more than a century political and economic leaders committed to free markets and untrammeled capital investment had loathed socialism in its several forms. After World War II the iron curtain in Europe and communist insurgencies in China and elsewhere seemed to confirm the threat of worldwide revolution.

Western leaders quickly came to perceive the Soviet Union as the nerve center of world revolution and as a military power capable of launching a war as destructive and terrible as the one that had recently ended. But particularly after the United States and the countries of western Europe established the **North Atlantic Treaty Organization (NATO)** military alliance in 1949, Soviet leaders felt surrounded by hostile forces just when they were trying to recover from the terrible losses sustained in the war against the Axis. The distrust and suspicion between the two sides played out on a worldwide stage. The United Nations provided the venue for face-to-face debate.

The United Nations

In 1944 representatives from the United States, Great Britain, the Soviet Union, and China drafted proposals that finally bore fruit in the treaty called the United Nations Charter, ratified on October 24, 1945. Like the earlier League of Nations, the **United Nations** had two main bodies: the General Assembly, with representatives from all member states; and the Security Council, with five permanent members—China, France, Great Britain, the United States, and the Soviet Union—and seven rotating members. A full-time bureaucracy headed by a Secretary General carried out the day-to-day business of both bodies. Various agencies focused on specialized international problems—for example, UNICEF (United Nations Children's Emergency Fund), FAO (Food and Agriculture Organization), and UNESCO (United Nations Educational, Scientific and Cultural Organization) (see Environment and Technology: The Green Revolution). Unlike the League of Nations, which required unanimous agreement in both deliberative bodies, the United Nations operated by majority vote, except that the five permanent members of the Security Council had veto power in that chamber.

All signatories to the United Nations Charter renounced war and territorial conquest. Nevertheless, peacekeeping, the sole preserve of the Security Council, became a vexing problem. The permanent members exercised their vetoes to protect their friends and interests. Throughout the Cold War the United Nations was seldom able to forestall or quell international conflicts, though from time to time it sent observers or peacekeeping forces to monitor truces or agreements otherwise arrived at.

The decolonization of Africa and Asia greatly swelled the size of the General Assembly but not of the Security Council. Many of the new nations looked to the United Nations for material assistance and access to a wider political world. While the vetoes of the Security Council's permanent members often stymied actions that even indirectly touched on Cold War concerns, the General Assembly became an arena for opinions on many issues involving decolonization, a movement that the Soviet Union strongly encouraged but the Western colonial powers resisted.

In the early years of the United Nations, General Assembly resolutions carried great weight. An example is a 1947 resolution that sought to divide Palestine into sovereign Jewish and Arab states. Gradually, though, the flood of new members produced a voting majority concerned more with poverty, racial discrimination, and the struggle against imperialism than with the Cold War. As a result, the Western powers increasingly disregarded the General Assembly, in effect allowing the new nations of the world to have their say, but not the means to act collectively.

Capitalism and Communism

In July 1944, with Allied victory a foregone conclusion, economic specialists representing over forty countries met at Bretton Woods, a New Hampshire resort, to devise a new international monetary system. The signatories eventually agreed to fix exchange rates and to create the International Monetary Fund (IMF) and World Bank (formally the International Bank for Reconstruction and Development). The IMF was to use currency reserves from member nations to finance temporary trade deficits, and the **World Bank** was to provide funds for reconstructing Europe and helping needy countries after the war.

The Soviet Union attended the Bretton Woods Conference and signed the agreements, which went into effect in 1946. But deepening suspicion and hostility between the Soviet Union and the United States and Britain undermined cooperation. While the United States held reserves of gold and the rest of the world held reserves of dollars in order to maintain the stability of the monetary system, the Soviet Union established a closed monetary system for itself and the new communist regimes in eastern Europe. Similar differences were found across the economies of the two alliances. In the Western countries, supply and demand determined prices; in the Soviet command economy, government agencies allocated goods and set prices ac-

CHRONOLOGY

	Cold War	Decolonization
1945		
1950	1948–1949 Berlin airlift 1949 NATO formed 1950–1953 Korean War 1952 United States detonates first hydrogen bomb 1954 Jacobo Arbenz overthrown in Guatemala, supported by CIA 1955 Warsaw Pact concluded 1956 Soviet Union suppresses Hungarian revolt 1957 Soviet Union launches first artificial satellite into Earth orbit	1947 Partition of India 1949 Dutch withdraw from Indonesia 1952 Bolivian Revolution 1954 CIA intervention in Guatemala; defeat at Dienbienphu ends French hold on Vietnam 1955 Bandung Conference 1957 Ghana becomes first British colony in Africa to gain independence 1959 Fidel Castro leads revolution in Cuba
1960	1961 East Germany builds Berlin Wall 1961 Bay of Pigs (Cuba) 1962 Cuban missile crisis 1968 Nuclear Non-Proliferation Treaty	1960 Shootings in Sharpeville intensify South African struggle against apartheid; Nigeria becomes independent 1962 Algeria wins independence
1970	1975 Helsinki Accords; end of Vietnam War	1971 Bangladesh secedes from Pakistan

cording to governmental priorities, irrespective of market forces.

Many leaders of newly independent states, having won the struggle against imperialism, preferred the Soviet Union's socialist example to the capitalism of their former colonizers. Thus, the relative success of economies patterned on Eastern or Western models became part of Cold War rivalry. Each side trumpeted economic successes measured by industrial output, changes in per capita income, and productivity gains.

During World War II the U.S. economy finally escaped the lingering effects of the Great Depression (see Chapter 29). Increased military spending and the draft brought full employment and high wages. The wartime conversion of factories from the production of consumer goods had created demand for those goods. With peace, the United States enjoyed prosperity and an international competitive advantage because of massive destruction in Europe.

The economy of western Europe was heavily damaged during World War II, and the early postwar years were bleak in many European countries. With prosperity, the United States was able to support the reconstruction of western Europe. The **Marshall Plan** provided $12.5

billion in aid to friendly European countries between 1948 and 1952. Most of the aid was in the form of food, raw materials, and other goods. By 1961 more than $20 billion in economic aid had been disbursed. European determination backed by American aid spurred recovery, and by 1963 the resurgent European economy had doubled its 1940 output.

Western European governments generally increased their role in economic management during this period. In Great Britain, for example, the Labour Party government of the early 1950s nationalized coal, steel, railroads, and health care. Similarly, the French government nationalized public utilities; the auto, banking, and insurance industries; and parts of the mining industry. These steps provided large infusions of capital for rebuilding and acquiring new technologies.

In 1948 European governments also launched a process of economic cooperation and integration with the creation of the Organization of European Economic Cooperation (OEEC). Cooperative policies were first focused on coal and steel. Often located in disputed border areas, these industries had previously been flash points that led to war. Successes in these crucial areas encouraged some OEEC countries to begin lowering tariffs to

The Green Revolution

Concern about world food supplies grew directly out of serious shortages caused by the devastation and trade disruptions of World War II. The Food and Agriculture Organization of the United Nations, the Rockefeller Foundation, and the Ford Foundation took leading roles in fostering crop research and educating farmers about agricultural techniques. In 1966 the International Rice Research Institute (established in 1960–1962) began distributing seeds for an improved rice variety known as IR-8. Crop yields from this and other new varieties, along with improved farming techniques, were initially so impressive that the term *Green Revolution* was coined to describe a new era in agriculture.

On the heels of the successful new rice strains, new varieties of corn and wheat were introduced. Building on twenty years of Rockefeller-funded research in Mexico, the Centro Internacional de Mejoramiento de Maiz y Trigo (International Center for the Improvement of Maize and Wheat) was established in 1966 under Norman Borlaug, who was awarded the Nobel Peace Prize four years later. This organization distributed short, stiff-strawed varieties of wheat that were resistant to disease and responsive to fertilizer.

By 1970 other centers for research on tropical agriculture had been established in Ibadan, Nigeria, and Cali, Colombia. But the success of the Green Revolution and the growing need for its products called for a more comprehensive effort. The Consultative Group on International Agricultural Research brought together World Bank expertise, private foundations, international organizations, and national foreign aid agencies to undertake worldwide support of efforts to increase food productivity and improve natural resource management. More recently, the optimism that followed these innovations has been muted by the realization that population growth, soil depletion, the costs of irrigation and fertilizer, and the growing concentration of land in the export sector combined to reduce the effects of improved crop technology in poor countries.

Miracle Rice   New strains of so-called "miracle rice" made many nations in South and Southeast Asia self-sufficient in food production after decades of worry that population growth would outstrip agricultural productivity.   (Victor Englebert)

encourage the movement of goods and capital. In 1957 France, West Germany, Italy, the Netherlands, Belgium, and Luxembourg signed a treaty creating the European Economic Community, also known as the Common Market. By the 1970s the Common Market nations had nearly overtaken the United States in industrial production. The economic alliance expanded after 1970, when Great Britain, Denmark, Greece, Ireland, Spain, Portugal, Finland, Sweden, and Austria joined. The enlarged alliance called itself the **European Community (EC).**

Prosperity brought dramatic changes to the societies of western Europe. Average wages increased, unemployment fell, and social welfare benefits were expanded. Governments increased spending on health care, unemployment benefits, old-age pensions, public housing, and grants to poor families with children. The combination of economic growth and income redistribution raised living standards and fueled demand for consumer goods, leading to the development of a mass consumer society. Automobile ownership, for example, grew approximately ninefold between 1950 and 1970.

The Soviet experience was dramatically different. The rapid growth of a powerful Soviet state after 1917 had challenged traditional Western assumptions about economic development and social policy. From the

1920s the Soviet state relied on bureaucratic agencies and political processes to determine the production, distribution, and price of goods. Housing, medical services, retail shops, factories, the land—even musical compositions and literary works—were viewed as collective property and were therefore regulated and administered by the state.

The economies of the Soviet Union and its eastern European allies were just as devastated at the end of the Second World War as those of western Europe. However, the Soviet command economy had enormous natural resources, a large population, and abundant energy at its disposal. Moreover, Soviet planners had made large investments in technical and scientific education, and the Soviet state had developed heavy industry in the 1930s and during the war years. Finally, Soviet leadership was willing to use forced labor on an enormous scale. For example, Bulgaria's postwar free work force of 361,000 was supplemented by 100,000 slave laborers.[1]

As a result, recovery was rapid at first, creating the structural basis for modernization and growth. Then, as the postwar period progressed, bureaucratic control of the economy grew less responsive and efficient at the same time that industrial might came to be more commonly measured by the production of consumer goods

Cold War Confrontation in 1959 U.S. Vice President Richard M. Nixon and Soviet premier Nikita Khrushchev had a heated exchange of views during Nixon's visit to a Moscow trade fair. Two years earlier, the Soviet Union had launched the world's first space satellite. (Seymour Raskin/Magnum Photos, Inc.)

such as television sets and automobiles, rather than by tons of coal and steel. In the 1970s the gap with the West widened. Soviet industry failed to meet domestic demand for clothing, housing, food, automobiles, and consumer electronics, while Soviet agricultural inefficiency compelled increased reliance on food imports.

The socialist nations of eastern Europe were compelled to follow the Soviet economic model, with some national differences. Poland and Hungary, for example, implemented agricultural collectivization more slowly than did Czechoslovakia. Nevertheless, economic planners throughout the region coordinated industrialization and production plans with the Soviet Union. Significant growth occurred in all the socialist economies, but the inefficiencies and failures that plagued the Soviet economy troubled them as well.

Outside Europe, the United States and the Soviet Union competed in providing loans and grants and supplying arms (at bargain prices) to countries willing to align with them. Thus the relative success or failure of capitalism and communism in Europe and the United States was not necessarily the strongest consideration in other parts of the world when the time came to construct new national economies.

West Versus East in Europe and Korea

For Germany, Austria, and Japan, peace brought foreign military occupation and new governments that were initially controlled by the occupiers. When relations with the Western powers cooled at the end of the war, the Soviet Union sought to prevent the reappearance of hostile regimes on its borders. Initially, the Soviet Union seemed willing to accept governments in neighboring states that included a mix of parties as long as they were not hostile to local communist groups or to the Soviets. The nations of central and eastern Europe were deeply split by the legacies of the war, and many were willing to embrace the communists as a hedge against those who had supported fascism or cooperated with the Germans. As relations between the Soviets and the West worsened in the late 1940s, local communists, their strength augmented by Soviet military occupation, gained victories across eastern Europe. Western leaders saw the rapid emergence of communist regimes in Poland, Czechoslovakia, Hungary, Bulgaria, Romania, Yugoslavia, and Albania as a threat.

It took two years for the United States to shift from viewing the Soviet Union as an ally against Germany to seeing it as a worldwide enemy. In the waning days of World War II the United States had seemed amenable to

the Soviet desire for free access to the Bosporus and Dardanelles straits that, under Turkish control, restricted naval deployments from the Black Sea to the Mediterranean. But in July 1947 the **Truman Doctrine** offered military aid to help both Turkey and Greece resist Soviet military pressure and subversion, and in 1951 both were admitted to NATO. NATO's Soviet counterpart, the **Warsaw Pact,** emerged in 1955 in response to the Western powers' decision to allow West Germany to rearm within limits set by NATO (see Map 31.1).

The much-feared and long-prepared-for third great war in Europe did not occur. The Soviet Union tested Western resolve in 1948–1949 by blockading the British, French, and American zones in Berlin (located in Soviet-controlled East Germany). Airlifts of food and fuel defeated the blockade. In 1961 the East German government accentuated Germany's political division by building the Berlin Wall, a structure designed primarily to prevent its citizens from fleeing to the noncommunist western part of the city. In turn, the West tested the East by encouraging a rift between the Soviet Union and Yugoslavia. Western aid and encouragement resulted in Yugoslavia's signing a defensive treaty with Greece and Turkey (but not with NATO) and deciding against joining the Warsaw Pact.

Soviet power set clear limits on how far any eastern European country might stray from Soviet domination. In 1956 Soviet troops crushed an armed anti-Soviet revolt in Hungary. Then in 1968 Soviet troops repressed a peaceful reform effort in Czechoslovakia. The West, a passive onlooker, could only acknowledge that the Soviet Union had the right to intervene in the domestic affairs of any Soviet-bloc nation whenever it wished.

A more explosive crisis erupted in Korea, where the Second World War had left Soviet troops in control north of the thirty-eighth parallel and American troops in control to the south. When no agreement could be reached on holding countrywide elections, communist North Korea and noncommunist South Korea became independent states in 1948. Two years later North Korea invaded South Korea. The United Nations Security Council, in the absence of the Soviet delegation, voted to condemn the invasion and called on members of the United Nations to come to the defense of South Korea. The ensuing **Korean War** lasted until 1953. The United States was the primary ally of South Korea. The People's Republic of China supported North Korea.

The conflict in Korea remained limited to the Korean peninsula because the United States feared that launching attacks into China might prompt China's ally, the Soviet Union, to retaliate, beginning the dreaded third world war. Americans and South Koreans advanced from a toehold in the south to the North Korean–Chinese bor-

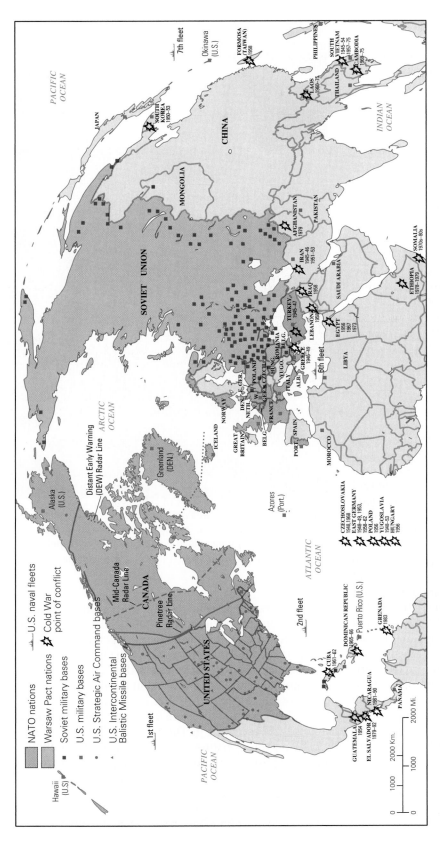

Map 31.1 Cold War Confrontation   A polar projection is shown on this map because Soviet and U.S. strategists planned to attack one another by missile in the polar region; hence the Canadian–American radar lines. Military installations along the southern border of the Soviet Union were directed primarily at China.

der. China sent troops across the border, and the North Koreans and Chinese pushed the Americans and South Koreans back. The fighting then settled into a static war in the mountains along the thirty-eighth parallel. The two sides eventually agreed to a truce along that line; but the cease-fire lines remained fortified, and no peace treaty was concluded. The possibility of renewed warfare between the two Koreas continued well past the end of the Cold War and remains a disturbing possibility today.

Japan benefited from the Korean War in an unexpected way. Massive purchases of supplies by the United States and spending by American servicemen on leave stimulated the Japanese economy similar to the way the Marshall Plan had stimulated Europe's economy.

United States Defeat in Vietnam

The most important postwar communist movement arose in the part of Southeast Asia known as French Indochina. Ho Chi Minh° (1890–1969), who had spent several years in France during World War I, played the pivotal role. Ho had helped form the Communist Party in France. In 1930, after training in Moscow, he returned to Vietnam to found the Indochina Communist Party. He and his supporters took refuge in China during World War II.

At war's end the new French government was determined to keep its prewar colonial possessions. Ho Chi Minh's nationalist coalition, then called the Viet Minh, fought the French with help from the People's Republic of China. After a brutal struggle, the French stronghold of Dienbienphu° fell in 1954, marking the end of France's colonial enterprise. Ho's Viet Minh government took over in the north, and a noncommunist nationalist government ruled in the south.

The United States had given some support to the French. President Dwight D. Eisenhower (1953–1961) and his foreign policy advisers debated long and hard about whether to aid France militarily during the battle for Dienbienphu. They decided not to prop up French colonial rule in Vietnam, perceiving that the European colonial empires were doomed. After winning independence, communist North Vietnam eventually supported a communist guerrilla movement—the Viet Cong—against the noncommunist government of South Vietnam. At issue was the ideological and economic orientation of an independent Vietnam.

President John F. Kennedy (served 1961–1963) and

The Vietnamese People at War   American and South Vietnamese troops burned many villages to deprive the enemy of civilian refuges. This policy undermined support for the South Vietnamese government in the countryside.   (Dana Stone/stockphoto.com)

his advisers decided to support the South Vietnamese government of President Ngo Dinh Diem°. While they knew that the Diem government was corrupt and unpopular, they feared that a communist victory would encourage communist movements throughout Southeast Asia and alter the Cold War balance of power. Kennedy steadily increased the number of American military advisers from 685 to almost 16,000, while secretly encouraging the overthrow of Diem. The execution of Diem following his overthrow instigated a public debate as well as a critical reevaluation within the administration.

Ho Chi Minh (hoe chee min)
Dienbienphu (dee-yen-bee-yen-FOO)

Diem (dee-YEM)

Lyndon Johnson, who became president (served 1963–1969) after Kennedy was assassinated, obtained support from Congress for unlimited expansion of U.S. military deployment after an apparent North Vietnamese attack on two U.S. destroyers in the Gulf of Tonkin. But in South Vietnam there was little support for the nation's new rulers who soon revealed themselves to be just as corrupt and unpopular as the earlier Diem government. Instead, many South Vietnamese were drawn to the heroic nationalist image of North Vietnam's leader Ho Chi Minh who had led the struggles against the Japanese and French. By the end of 1966, 365,000 U.S. troops were engaged in the **Vietnam War,** but they were unable to achieve a comprehensive victory. The Viet Cong guerrillas and their North Vietnamese allies gained significant military credibility in the massive 1968 Tet Offensive. With a battlefield victory unlikely, the antiwar movement in the United States grew and Lyndon Johnson decided to not seek reelection.

In 1973 a treaty between North Vietnam and the United States ended U.S. involvement in the war and promised future elections. Two years later, in violation of the treaty, Viet Cong and North Vietnamese troops overran the South Vietnamese army and captured the southern capital of Saigon, renaming it Ho Chi Minh City. The two parts of Vietnam were reunited in a single state ruled from the north. Over a million Vietnamese and 58,000 Americans had been killed in the war.

President Johnson had begun his administration committed to a broad program of social reforms and civil rights initiatives, called the Great Society. The civil rights campaign in the South led by Martin Luther King, Jr., and others led to a broad examination of issues of social justice and spawned numerous organizations that challenged the status quo. As the commitment of U.S. troops grew, a massive antiwar movement applied the tactics of the civil rights movement to government military policies. Many members of the military and their civilian supporters, on the other hand, were angered by limitations placed on the conduct of operations, despite fears that a wider war would lead to Chinese involvement and possible nuclear confrontation. The rising tide of antiwar rallies, now international in character, and growing economic problems undermined support for Johnson, who declined to seek reelection. By the mid 1970s both antiwar and pro-war groups had drawn lessons from Vietnam, the former seeing any use of military force overseas as dangerous and unnecessarily destructive, and the latter believing that overwhelming force was required in warfare.

The Race for Nuclear Supremacy

Fear of nuclear warfare affected strategic decisions in the Korean and Vietnam Wars. It also affected all other aspects of Cold War confrontation. The devastation of Hiroshima and Nagasaki by atomic weapons (see Chapter 29) had ushered in a new era. Nuclear weapons fed into a logic of total war that was already reaching a peak in Nazi genocide and terror bombing and in massive Allied air raids on large cities. After the Soviet Union exploded its first nuclear device in 1949, fears of a worldwide holocaust grew. Fears increased when the United States exploded a far more powerful weapon, the hydrogen bomb, in 1952 and the Soviet Union followed suit less than a year later. The possibility of the theft of nuclear secrets by Soviet spies fostered paranoia in the United States, and the conviction that the nuclear superpowers were willing to use their terrible weapons if their vital interests were threatened spread despair around the world.

In 1954 President Eisenhower warned Soviet leaders against attacking western Europe. In response to such an attack, he said, the United States would reduce the Soviet Union to "a smoking, radiating ruin at the end of two hours." A few years later the Soviet leader Nikita Khrushchev° made an equally stark promise: "We will bury you." He was referring to economic competition, but Americans interpreted the statement to mean literal burial. Rhetoric aside, both men—and their successors—had the capacity to deliver on their threats, and everyone in the world knew that all-out war with nuclear weapons would produce the greatest global devastation in human history.

Everyone's worst fears seemed about to be realized in 1962 when the Soviet Union deployed nuclear missiles in Cuba. Khrushchev and Cuban president Fidel Castro were reacting to U.S. efforts to overthrow the government of Cuba. When the missiles were discovered, the United States prepared for an invasion of Cuba. Confronted by unyielding diplomatic pressure and military threats, Khrushchev pulled the missiles from Cuba. Subsequently, the United States removed its missiles from Turkey. As frightening as the **Cuban missile crisis** was, the fact that the superpower leaders accepted tactical defeat rather than launch an attack gave reason for hope that nuclear weapons might be contained.

The number, means of delivery, and destructive force of nuclear weapons increased enormously. The bomb dropped on Hiroshima, equal in strength to 12,500 tons of TNT, had destroyed an entire city. By the 1960s explosive yields were measured in megatons (millions of

Khrushchev (KROOSH-chef)

tons) of TNT, and a single missile could contain several weapons of this scale, each of which could be targeted to a different site. When the missiles were placed on submarines, a major component of U.S. nuclear forces, defending against them seemed impossible.

Arms limitation also progressed. In 1963 Great Britain, the United States, and the Soviet Union agreed to ban the testing of nuclear weapons in the atmosphere, in space, and underwater, thus reducing the environmental danger of radioactive fallout. In 1968 the United States and the Soviet Union together proposed a world treaty against further proliferation of nuclear weapons. The Nuclear Non-Proliferation Treaty (NPT) was signed by 137 countries later that year. Not until 1972, however, did the two superpowers truly recognize the futility of squandering their wealth on ever-larger missile forces. They began the arduous and extremely slow process of negotiating weapons limits, a process made even slower by the vested interests of military officers and arms industries in each country—what President Eisenhower had called the "military-industrial complex."

In Europe, the Soviet-American arms race outran the economic ability of atomic powers France and Britain to keep pace. Instead, the European states sought to relax tensions. Between 1972 and 1975 the Conference on Security and Cooperation in Europe (CSCE) brought delegates from thirty-seven European states, the United States, and Canada to Helsinki. The goal of the Soviet Union was European acceptance of the political boundaries of the Warsaw Pact nations. The Helsinki Final Act—commonly known as the **Helsinki Accords**—affirmed that no boundaries should be changed by military force. It also contained formal (but nonbinding) declarations calling for economic, social, and governmental contacts across the iron curtain, and for cooperation in humanitarian fields, a provision that paved the way for dialogue about human rights.

Space exploration was another offshoot of the nuclear arms race. The contest to build larger and more accurate missiles prompted the superpowers to prove their skills in rocketry by launching space satellites. The Soviet Union placed a small Sputnik satellite into orbit around the earth in October 1957. The United States responded with its own satellite three months later. The space race was on, a contest in which accomplishments in space were understood to signify equivalent achievements in the military sphere. Sputnik administered a deep shock to American pride and confidence, but in 1969 two Americans, Neil A. Armstrong and Edwin E. ("Buzz") Aldrin, became the first humans to walk on the moon.

Despite rhetorical Cold War saber-rattling by Soviet and American leaders, the threat of nuclear war forced a measure of restraint on the superpower adversaries. Because fighting each other directly would have risked escalation to the level of nuclear exchange, they carefully avoided crises that might provoke such confrontations. Even when arming third parties to do their fighting by proxy, they set limits on how far such fighting could go. Some of these proxy combatants, however, understood the limitations of the superpowers well enough to manipulate them for their own purposes.

DECOLONIZATION AND NATION BUILDING

After World War I Germany, Austria-Hungary, and the Ottoman Empire lost their empires, and many foreign colonies and dependencies were transferred to the victors, especially to Great Britain and France. Following World War II the victors lost nearly all their imperial possessions. As a result of independence movements in Africa, Asia, and the Americas and growing anti-imperialist movements at home, most of the colonies of Great Britain, France, the Netherlands, Belgium, and the United States were transformed into independent states (see Map 31.2).

Circumstances differed profoundly from place to place. In some Asian countries, where colonial rule was of long standing, newly independent states found themselves in possession of viable industries, communications networks, and education systems. In other countries, notably in Africa, decolonized nations faced dire economic problems and internal disunity that resulted from language and ethnic differences. Political independence had been achieved by most of Latin America in the nineteenth century (see Chapter 21). Following World War II mass political movements in this region focused on the related issue of economic sovereignty—freedom from growing American economic domination.

Despite their differences, a sense of kinship arose among the new and old nations of Latin America, Africa, and Asia. All shared feelings of excitement and rebirth. As the North Americans, Europeans, and Chinese settled into the exhausting deadlock of the Cold War, visions of independence and national growth captivated the rest of the world.

New Nations in South and Southeast Asia

After partition in 1947 the independent states of India and Pakistan were strikingly dissimilar. Muslim Pakistan defined itself according to religion and quickly fell under the control of military leaders. India, a secular republic led by Prime Minister

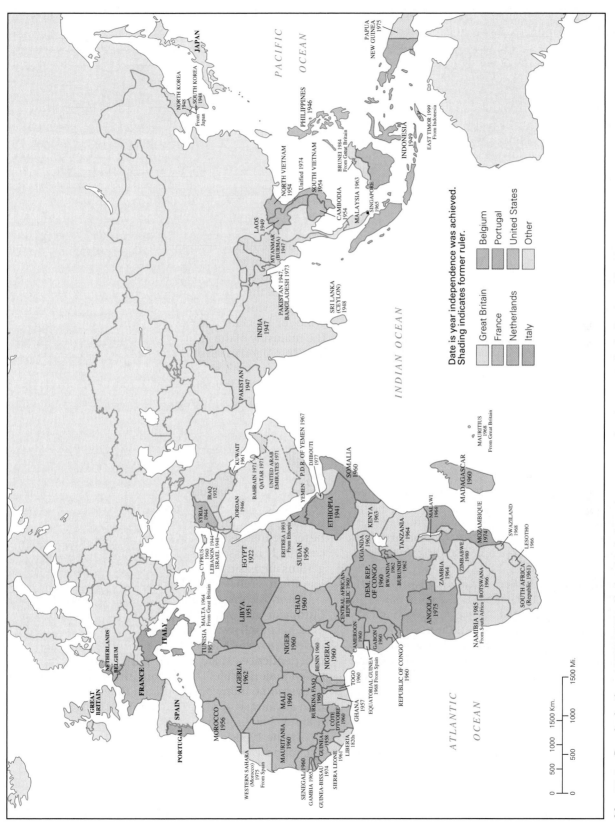

JAPAN

NORTH KOREA
1948
SOUTH KOREA
1948
From Japan

PACIFIC

OCEAN

PAPUA
NEW GUINEA
1975

PHILIPPINES
1946

EAST TIMOR 1999
From Indonesia

INDONESIA
1949

NORTH VIETNAM
1954
Unified 1974
SOUTH VIETNAM
1954

BRUNEI 1984
From Great Britain

CAMBODIA
1954

MALAYSIA 1963

SINGAPORE
1965

LAOS
1949

MYANMAR
(BURMA)
1947

Date is year independence was achieved.
Shading indicates former ruler.

Great Britain		Belgium
France		Portugal
Netherlands		United States
Italy		Other

PAKISTAN 1947,
BANGLADESH 1973

SRI LANKA
(CEYLON)
1948

INDIA
1947

INDIAN OCEAN

PAKISTAN
1947

KUWAIT
1961

BAHRAIN 1971
QATAR 1971
UNITED ARAB
EMIRATES 1971

YEMEN P.D.R. OF YEMEN 1967
DJIBOUTI
1977

MAURITIUS
1968
From Great Britain

IRAQ
1932

SYRIA
1944

JORDAN
1946

CYPRUS 1960
LEBANON 1944
ISRAEL 1948

SOMALIA
1960

MADAGASCAR
1960

ERITREA 1993
From Ethiopia

ETHIOPIA
1941

EGYPT
1922

SUDAN
1956

KENYA
1963

UGANDA
1962

TANZANIA
1964

MALAWI
1964

MOZAMBIQUE
1974

SWAZILAND
1968

LESOTHO
1966

DEM. REP.
OF CONGO
1960

RWANDA
1962
BURUNDI
1962

ZIMBABWE
1980

BOTSWANA
1966

ZAMBIA
1964

TUNISIA
1957

MALTA 1964
From Great Britain

LIBYA
1951

CHAD
1960

CENTRAL AFRICAN
REPUBLIC 1960

ANGOLA
1975

NAMIBIA 1985
From South Africa

SOUTH AFRICA
(Republic 1961)

ITALY

NETHERLANDS
BELGIUM

NIGER
1960

NIGERIA
1960

CAMEROON
1960

GABON
1960

GREAT
BRITAIN

FRANCE

ALGERIA
1962

MALI
1960

BENIN 1960

TOGO
1960

EQUATORIAL GUINEA
1968 From Spain

REPUBLIC OF CONGO
1960

PORTUGAL

SPAIN

MOROCCO
1956

MAURITANIA
1960

BURKINA FASO
1960

COTE
D'IVOIRE
1960

GHANA
1957

WESTERN SAHARA
(Morocco)
1975
From Spain

SENEGAL 1960
GAMBIA 1965
GUINEA-BISSAU
1974
GUINEA
1958

SIERRA LEONE
1961

LIBERIA
1820

ATLANTIC

OCEAN

0	500	1000	1500 Mi.
0	500	1000	1500 Km.

Map 31.2 Decolonization, 1947–1999 Notice that independence came a decade or so earlier in South and Southeast Asia than in Africa. Numerous countries that gained independence after World War II in the Caribbean, in South and Central America, and in the Pacific are not shown.

Jawaharlal Nehru, was much larger and inherited most of the considerable industrial and educational resources the British had developed, along with the larger share of trained civil servants and military officers. Ninety percent of its population was Hindu, most of the rest Muslim.

Adding to the tensions of independence (see Chapter 30) was the decision by the Hindu ruler of the northwestern state known as Jammu and Kashmir, without consulting his overwhelmingly Muslim subjects, to join India. War between India and Pakistan over Kashmir broke out in 1947 and ended with an uneasy truce, only to resume briefly in 1965. Though Kashmir remained a flash point of patriotic feeling, the two countries managed to avoid further warfare.

Despite recurrent predictions that multilingual India might break up into a number of linguistically homogeneous states, most Indians recognized that unity benefited everyone; and the country pursued a generally democratic and socialist line of development. Pakistan, in contrast, did break up. In 1971 its Bengali-speaking eastern section seceded to become the independent country of Bangladesh. Their shared political heritage notwithstanding, India, Pakistan, and Bangladesh grew steadily apart, following markedly different economic, political, religious, and social paths.

As the Japanese had supported anti-British Indian nationalists, so they encouraged the dreams of some anticolonialists in the countries they had occupied in Southeast Asia. Other nationalists, particularly those belonging to communist groups, saw the Japanese as an imperialist enemy; and the harsh character of Japanese occupation eventually alienated most people in the occupied countries. Nevertheless, the defeats the Japanese inflicted on British, French, and Dutch colonial armies set an example of an Asian people standing up to European colonizers.

In the Dutch East Indies, Achmad Sukarno (1901–1970) cooperated with the Japanese in the hope that the Dutch, who had dominated the region economically since the seventeenth century, would never return. After military confrontation, Dutch withdrawal was finally negotiated in 1949, and Sukarno became the dictator of the resource-rich but underdeveloped island nation. He ruled until 1965, when a military coup ousted him and brutally eliminated Indonesia's powerful communist party.

Elsewhere in the region, nationalist movements won independence as well. Britain granted independence to Burma (now Myanmar°) in 1948 and established the Malay Federation the same year. Singapore, once a mem-

ber of the federation, became an independent city-state in 1965. In 1946 the United States kept its promise of postwar independence for the Philippine Islands but retained close economic ties and leases on military bases.

The Struggle for Independence in Africa

The postwar French government was as determined to hold onto Algeria as it was to keep Vietnam. Since invading the country in 1830 France had followed policies very different from those of the British in India. French settlement had been strongly encouraged, and Algeria had been declared an actual part of France rather than a colony. By the mid-1950s, 10 percent of the Algerian population was of French or other European origin. The Algerian economy was strongly oriented toward France. Though Islam, the religion of 90 percent of the people, prohibited the drinking of alcohol, Algerian vineyards produced immense quantities of wine for French tables. Algerian oil and gas fields were the mainstay of the French petroleum industry.

The Algerian revolt in 1954 was pursued with great brutality by both sides. The Algerian revolutionary organization, the Front de Libération National (FLN), was supported by Egypt and other Arab countries acting on the principle that all Arab peoples should be able to choose their own governments. French colonists, however, considered the country rightfully theirs and swore to fight to the bitter end. When Algeria finally won independence in 1962, a flood of angry colonists returned to France. Their departure undermined the Algerian economy because very few Arabs had received technical training or acquired management experience. Despite bitter feelings left by the war, Algeria retained close and seemingly indissoluble economic ties to France, and Algerians increasingly fled unemployment at home by emigrating to France and taking low-level jobs.

In most of sub-Saharan Africa independence from European rule was achieved through negotiation. However, in colonies with significant white settler minorities, African peoples had to resort to armed struggle to gain independence, since settler populations strongly resisted majority rule. Throughout Africa, nationalists had to overcome many obstacles, but they were also able to take advantage of the consequential changes that colonial rule had brought.

In the 1950s and 1960s economic growth and growing support for liberation overcame worries about economic and environmental problems that would develop after independence. In the cities that hosted colonial authorities, educated African nationalists used the languages introduced by colonial governments to help

Myanmar (myahn-MAH)

build multiethnic coalitions within the artificial colonial boundaries. Missionary and colonial schools had produced few high school and college graduates, but graduates of these colonial school systems were often frustrated by obstacles to their advancement and joined the independence movements. Africans who had obtained advanced education in Europe and the United States also played an important role in the struggle for independence as did African veterans of allied armies during World War II.

The networks of roads and railroads built to facilitate colonial exports were used by African truckers and railroad workers to promote Africa's new political consciousness and spread anticolonial ideas. Improvements in medical care and public health had led to rapid population growth. The region's young population enthusiastically embraced the goal of self-rule.

The young politicians who led the nationalist movements devoted their lives to ridding their homelands of foreign occupation. An example is Kwame Nkrumah° (1909–1972), who in 1957 became prime minister of Ghana (formerly the Gold Coast), the first British colony in West Africa to achieve independence. After graduating from a Catholic mission school and a government teacher-training college, Nkrumah spent a decade studying philosophy and theology in the United States, where he absorbed ideas about black pride and independence then being propounded by W. E. B. Du Bois and Marcus Garvey.

During a brief stay in Britain, Nkrumah joined Kenyan nationalist Jomo Kenyatta, a Ph.D. in anthropology, to found an organization devoted to African freedom. In 1947 Nkrumah returned to the Gold Coast to work for independence. The time was right. There was no longer strong public support in Britain for colonialism and, as a result, Britain's political leadership was not enthusiastic about investing resources to hold restive colonies. After Nkrumah's party won a decisive election victory in 1951, the Gold Coast governor released him from prison (where he had been held on "sedition" charges) and appointed him prime minister. Full independence came in 1957. Nkrumah turned out to be more effective as an international spokesman for colonized peoples than as an administrator, and in 1966 a group of army officers ousted him.

After Ghana won independence, Britain quickly granted independence to its other West African colonies, including large and populous Nigeria in 1960. However, white settler opposition in some British colonies in eastern and southern Africa delayed this process. In Kenya a small but influential group of wealthy coffee planters

African Leaders Meet for Conference Prime Minister Jomo Kenyatta of Kenya (right) waves to the crowd before entering the East African Heads of Government Conference held in Nairobi in 1964. With him are President Julius Nyerere (far left) of Tanzania and Dr. Milton Obote (center), president of Uganda. (Bettmann/Corbis)

seized upon a protest movement among the Kikuyu people as proof that Africans were unready for self-government. The settlers called the movement "Mau Mau," a made-up name meant to evoke primitive savagery. When violence between settlers and Mau Mau fighters escalated after 1952, British troops hunted down the Mau Mau leaders and resettled the Kikuyu° in fortified villages to prevent contact with rebel bands. The British also declared a state of emergency, banned all African political protest, and imprisoned Kenyatta and many other nationalists for eight years on charges of being Mau Mau leaders. Released in 1961, Kenyatta negotiated with the British to write a constitution for an independent Kenya. In 1964 he was elected the first president of the Republic of Kenya. He proved to be an effective, though autocratic, ruler. Kenya benefited from greater stability and prosperity than Ghana.

Kwame Nkrumah (KWAH-mee nn-KROO-muh)

Kikuyu (kih-KOO-you)

African leaders in the sub-Saharan French colonies were more reluctant than their counterparts in British colonies to call for full independence. They visualized political change in terms of promises made in 1944 by the Free French movement of General Charles de Gaulle at a conference in Brazzaville, in French Equatorial Africa. Acknowledging the value of his African territorial base, his many African troops, and the food supplied by African farmers, de Gaulle had promised more democratic government and broader suffrage, though not representation in the French National Assembly. He also had promised to abolish forced labor and imprisonment of Africans without charge; to expand French education down to the village level; to improve health services; and to open more administrative positions, though not the top ones, to Africans. The word *independence* was never mentioned at Brazzaville, but the politics of postwar colonial self-government led in that direction.

Most new African politicians who sought election in the colonies of French West Africa were civil servants. Because of the French policy of job rotation, they had typically served in a number of different colonies and thus had a broad outlook. They realized that some colonies—such as Ivory Coast, with coffee and cacao exports, fishing, and hardwood forests—had good economic prospects and others, such as landlocked, desert Niger, did not. Furthermore, they recognized the importance of French public investment in the region—a billion dollars between 1947 and 1956—and their own dependence on civil service salaries, which in places totaled 60 percent of government expenditures. The Malagasy politician Philibert Tsirinana° said at a press conference in 1958: "When I let my heart talk, I am a partisan of total and immediate independence [for Madagascar]; when I make my reason speak, I realize that it is impossible."

When Charles de Gaulle returned to power in France in 1958, at the height of the Algerian war, he warned that a rush to independence would have costs, saying: "One cannot conceive of both an independent territory and a France which continues to aid it." Ultimately, African patriotism prevailed in all of France's West African and Equatorial African colonies. Guinea, under the dynamic leadership of Sékou Touré°, gained full independence in 1958 and the rest in 1960.

Independence in the Belgian Congo was chaotic and violent. Contending political and ethnic groups found external allies; some were aided by Cuba and the Soviet Union, others by the West or by business groups tied to the rich mines. Civil war, the introduction of foreign mercenaries, and the rhetoric of Cold War confrontation roiled the waters and led to heavy loss of life as well as property destruction. In 1965 Mobuto Sese Seko seized the reins in a military coup that included the assassination of Patrice Lumumba, the first prime minister, and held on in one of the region's most corrupt governments until driven from power in 1997.

Decolonization in southern Africa was delayed by the opposition of European settlers, some with deep roots in Africa but many others who were new arrivals after 1945. While the settler minority tried to defend white supremacy, African-led liberation movements were committed to the creation of nonracial societies and majority rule. In the 1960s Africans began guerrilla movements against Portuguese rule in Angola and Mozambique, eventually prompting the Portuguese army to overthrow the undemocratic government of Portugal in 1974. The new Portuguese government granted independence to Angola and Mozambique the following year. In 1980, after a ten-year fight, European settlers in the British colony of Southern Rhodesia accepted African majority rule. The new government changed the country's name, which had honored the memory of the British imperialist Cecil Rhodes, to Zimbabwe, the name of a great stone city built by Africans long before the arrival of European settlers. This left only South Africa and neighboring Namibia in the hands of ruling European minorities.

A succession of South African governments had constructed a state and society based on a policy of racial separation, or *apartheid*°, after World War II. Fourteen percent of the population was descended from Dutch and English settlers. By law, whites controlled the most productive tracts of land, the industrial, mining, and commercial enterprises, and the government. Other laws imposed segregated housing, schools, and jobs on South Asians and people of mixed parentage classified as "nonwhite." The 74 percent of the population made up of indigenous Africans were subjected to far stricter limitations on place of residence, right to travel, and access to jobs and public facilities. African "homelands," somewhat similar to Amerindian reservations in the United States, were created in parts of the country, often far from the more dynamic and prosperous urban and industrial areas. Overcrowded and lacking investment, these restricted "homelands" were very poor and squalid, with few services and fewer opportunities.

The African National Congress (ANC), formed in 1912, and other organizations led the opposition to apartheid (see Diversity and Dominance: Race and the Struggle for Justice in South Africa). After police fired on demonstrators in the African town of Sharpeville in 1960 and banned all peaceful political protest by Africans, an

---

Tsirinana (tsee-REE-nah-nah)　**Sékou Touré** (SAY-koo too-RAY)　　　**apartheid** (uh-PAHRT-ate)

African lawyer named Nelson Mandela (b. 1918) organized guerrilla resistance by the ANC. Mandela was sentenced to life in prison in 1964. The ANC operated from outside the country. The armed struggle against apartheid continued until 1990 (see Chapter 33).

The Quest for Economic Freedom in Latin America

Latin American independence from European rule was achieved more than a hundred years earlier, but European and, by the end of the nineteenth century, American economic domination continued (see Chapters 27 and 30). Chile's copper, Cuba's sugar, Colombia's coffee, and Guatemala's bananas were largely controlled from abroad. The communications networks of several countries were in the hands of ITT (International Telephone and Telegraph Company), a U.S. corporation. From the 1930s, however, support for economic nationalism grew. During the 1930s and 1940s populist political leaders had experimented with programs that would constrain foreign investors or, alternatively, promote local efforts to industrialize (see discussion of Getulio Vargas and Juan Perón in Chapter 30).

In Mexico the revolutionary constitution of 1917 had begun an era of economic nationalism that culminated in the expropriation of foreign oil interests in 1938. Political stability had been achieved under the Institutional Revolutionary Party, or PRI (the abbreviation of its name in Spanish), which controlled the government until the 1990s. Stability allowed Mexico to experience significant economic expansion during the war years, but a yawning gulf between rich and poor, urban and rural, persisted. Although the government dominated important industries like petroleum and restricted foreign investment, rapid population growth, uncontrolled migration to Mexico City and other urban areas, and political corruption challenged efforts to lift the nation's poor. Economic power was concentrated at the top of society, with two thousand elite families benefiting disproportionally from the three hundred foreign and eight hundred Mexican companies that dominated the country. At the other end of the economic scale were the peasants, the 14 percent of the population classified as Indian, and the urban poor.

While Mexico's problems derived only partly from the effects of foreign influence, Guatemala's situation was more representative. Jacobo Arbenz Guzmán, elected in 1951, was typical of Latin American leaders, including Perón of Argentina and Vargas of Brazil (see Chapter 30), who tried to confront powerful foreign interests. An American corporation, the United Fruit Company, was

Guatemala's largest landowner; it also controlled much of the nation's infrastructure, including port facilities and railroads. To suppress banana production and keep prices high, United Fruit kept much of its Guatemalan lands fallow. Arbenz attempted land reform, which would have transferred these fallow lands to the nation's rural poor. The threatened expropriation angered the United Fruit Company. Simultaneously, Arbenz tried to reduce U.S. political influence, raising fears in Washington that he sought closer ties to the Soviet Union. Reacting to the land reform efforts and to reports that Arbenz was becoming friendly to communism, the U.S. Central Intelligence Agency (CIA), in one of its first major overseas operations, sponsored a takeover by the Guatemalan military in 1954. CIA intervention removed Arbenz, but it also condemned Guatemala to decades of governmental instability and growing violence between leftist and rightist elements in society.

In Cuba economic domination by the United States prior to 1960 was overwhelming. U.S. companies effectively controlled sugar production, the nation's most important industry, as well as banking, transportation, tourism, and public utilities. The United States was the most important market for Cuba's exports and the most important source of Cuba's imports. The needs of the U.S. economy largely determined the ebb and flow of Cuban foreign trade. A 1934 treaty had granted preferential treatment (prices higher than world market prices) to Cuban sugar in the American market in return for access to the Cuban market by American manufacturers. Since U.S. companies dominated the sugar business, this was actually a kind of tax imposed on American consumers for the benefit of American corporations. By 1956 sugar accounted for 80 percent of Cuba's exports and 25 percent of Cuba's national income. But demand in the United States dictated keeping only 39 percent of the land owned by the sugar companies in production, while Cuba experienced chronic underemployment. Similarly, immense deposits of nickel in Cuba went untapped because the U.S. government, which owned them, considered them to be a reserve.

Profits went north to the United States or to a small class of wealthy Cubans, many of them, like the owners of the Bacardi rum company, of foreign origin. Between 1951 and 1958 Cuba's economy grew at 1.4 percent per year, less than the rate of population increase. Cuba's government was notoriously corrupt and subservient to the wishes of American interests. In 1953 Fulgencio Batista°, a former military leader and president, illegally returned to power in a coup. Cuban aversion to

Fulgencio Batista (ful-HEHN-see-oh bah-TEES-tah)

우세인 은신처 방

파운드폭탄 4발 투하… 두 아들과 함께 사망 7

심진지 구축… 이틀째 시가戰

령이 대중 앞에 나타나거나 애국심
을 고취하는 노래만을 내보내던 방
송마저 중단됐다.

라크 전후 대
의에서는 전
영국 주도로

DIVERSITY AND DOMINANCE

RACE AND THE STRUGGLE FOR JUSTICE IN SOUTH AFRICA

One of South Africa's martyrs in the struggle against apartheid was Steve Biko (1946–1977), a thinker and activist especially concerned with building pride among Africans and asserting the importance of African cultures. Biko was one of the founders of the Black Consciousness Movement, focusing on the ways in which white settlers had stripped Africans of their freedom. As a result of his activism, he was restricted to his home town in 1973. Between 1975 and 1977 he was arrested and interrogated four times by the police. After his arrest in August 1977 he was severely beaten while in custody. He died days later without having received medical care. His death caused worldwide outrage.

But these are not the people we are concerned with [those who support apartheid]. We are concerned with that curious bunch of nonconformists who explain their participation in negative terms: that bunch of do-gooders that goes under all sorts of names—liberals, leftists etc. These are the people who argue that they are not responsible for white racism and the country's "inhumanity to the black man." These are the people who claim that they too feel the oppression just as acutely as the blacks and therefore should be jointly involved in the black man's struggle for a place under the sun. In short, these are the people who say that they have black souls wrapped up in white skins.

The role of the white liberal in the black man's history in South Africa is a curious one. Very few black organisations were not under white direction. True to their image, the white liberals always knew what was good for the blacks and told them so. The wonder of it all is that the black people have believed in them for so long. It was only at the end of the 50s that the blacks started demanding to be their own guardians.

Nowhere is the arrogance of the liberal ideology demonstrated so well as in their insistence that the problems of the country can only be solved by a bilateral approach involving both black and white. This has, by and large, come to be taken in all seriousness as the modus operandi in South Africa by all those who claim they would like a change in the status quo. Hence the multiracial political organisations and parties and the "nonracial" student organisations, all of which insist on integration not only as an end goal but also as a means.

The integration they talk about is first of all artificial in that it is a response to conscious manoeuvre rather than to the dictates of the inner soul. In other words the people forming the integrated complex have been extracted from various segregated societies with their in built complexes of superiority and inferiority and these continue to manifest themselves even in the "nonracial" setup of the integrated complex. As a result the integration so achieved is a one-way course, with the whites doing all the talking and the blacks the listening. Let me hasten to say that I am not claiming that segregation is necessarily the natural order; however, given the facts of the situation where a group experiences privilege at the expense of others, then it becomes obvious that a hastily arranged integration cannot be the solution to the problem. It is rather like expecting the slave to work together with the slave-master's son to remove all the conditions leading to the former's enslavement.

Secondly, this type of integration as a means is almost always unproductive. The participants waste lots of time in an internal sort of mudslinging designed to prove that A is more of a liberal than B. In other words the lack of common ground for solid identification is all the time manifested in internal strifes [sic] inside the group.

It will not sound anachronistic to anybody genuinely interested in real integration to learn that blacks are asserting themselves in a society where they are being treated as perpetual under-16s. One does not need to plan for or actively encourage real integration. Once the various groups within a given community have asserted themselves to the point that mutual respect has to be shown then you have the ingredients for a true and meaningful integration. At the heart of true integration is the provision for each man, each group to rise and attain the envisioned self. Each group must be able to attain its style of existence without encroaching on or being thwarted by another. Out of this mutual respect for each other and complete freedom of self-determination there will obviously arise a genuine fusion of the life-styles of the various groups. This is true integration.

From this it becomes clear that as long as blacks are suffering from [an] inferiority complex—a result of 300 years of deliberate oppression, denigration and derision—they will be useless as co-architects of a normal society where man is

836

nothing else but man for his own sake. Hence what is necessary as a prelude to anything else that may come is a very strong grass-roots build-up of black consciousness such that blacks can learn to assert themselves and stake their rightful claim.

Thus in adopting the line of a nonracial approach, the liberals are playing their old game. They are claiming a "monopoly on intelligence and moral judgement" and setting the pattern and pace for the realisation of the black man's aspirations. They want to remain in good books with both the black and white worlds. They want to shy away from all forms of "extremisms," condemning "white supremacy" as being just as bad as "Black Power!" They vacillate between the two worlds, verbalising all the complaints of the blacks beautifully while skilfully extracting what suits them from the exclusive pool of white privileges. But ask them for a moment to give a concrete meaningful programme that they intend adopting, then you will see on whose side they really are. Their protests are directed at and appeal to white conscience, everything they do is directed at finally convincing the white electorate that the black man is also a man and that at some future date he should be given a place at the white man's table.

In the following selection Anglican bishop Desmond Tutu (b. 1931) expressed his personal anguish at the death of Steve Biko. He summarized Biko's contributions to the struggle for justice in South Africa. Tutu won the Noble Peace Prize in 1984 and was named archbishop in 1988. From 1995 to 1998 he chaired the Truth and Reconciliation Commission, which investigated atrocities in South Africa during the years of apartheid. He stated that his objective was to create "a democratic and just society without racial divisions."

When we heard the news "Steve Biko is dead" we were struck numb with disbelief. No, it can't be true! No, it must be a horrible nightmare, and we will awake and find that really it is different—that Steve is alive even if it be in detention. But no, dear friends, he is dead and we are still numb with grief, and groan with anguish "Oh God, where are you? Oh God, do you really care—how can you let this happen to us?"

It all seems such a senseless waste of a wonderfully gifted person, struck down in the bloom of youth, a youthful bloom that some wanted to see blighted. What can be the purpose of such wanton destruction? God, do you really love us? What must we do which we have not done, what must we say which we have not said a thousand times over, oh, for so many years—that all we want is what belongs to all God's children, what belongs as an inalienable right—a place in the sun in our own beloved mother country. Oh God, how long can we go on? How long can we go on appealing for a more just ordering of society where we all, black and white together, count not because of some accident of birth or a biological irrelevance—where all of us black and white count because we are human persons, human persons created in your own image.

God called Steve Biko to be his servant in South Africa—to speak up on behalf of God, declaring what the will of this God must be in a situation such as ours, a situation of evil, injustice, oppression and exploitation. God called him to be the founder father of the Black Consciousness Movement against which we have had tirades and fulminations. It is a movement by which God, through Steve, sought to awaken in the Black person a sense of his intrinsic value and worth as a child of God, not needing to apologise for his existential condition as a black person, calling on blacks to glorify and praise God that he had created them black. Steve, with his brilliant mind that always saw to the heart of things, realised that until blacks asserted their humanity and their personhood, there was not the remotest chance for reconciliation in South Africa. For true reconciliation is a deeply personal matter. It can happen only between persons who assert their own personhood, and who acknowledge and respect that of others. You don't get reconciled to your dog, do you? Steve knew and believed fervently that being pro-black was not the same thing as being anti-white. The Black Consciousness Movement is not a "hate white movement," despite all you may have heard to the contrary. He had a far too profound respect for persons as persons, to want to deal with them under readymade, shopsoiled [sic] categories.

All who met him had this tremendous sense of a warm-hearted man, and as a notable acquaintance of his told me, a man who was utterly indestructible, of massive intellect and yet reticent; quite unshakeable in his commitment to principle and to radical change in South Africa by peaceful means; a man of real reconciliation, truly an instrument of God's peace, unshakeable in his commitment to the liberation of all South Africans, black and white, striving for a more just and more open South Africa.

QUESTIONS FOR ANALYSIS

1. What are Steve Biko's charges against white liberals in South Africa?
2. What was the proper role for whites in the antiapartheid movement according to Biko?
3. How does Bishop Tutu's eulogy differ from the political spirit and point of view expressed in Biko's 1970 essay?
4. According to Bishop Tutu, what were Biko's strongest characteristics? Were these characteristics demonstrated in Biko's essay?

Source: First selection from Steve Biko, *I Write What I Like,* ed. by Aelred Stubbs (Harper & Row, 1972). Reprinted with the permission of Bowerdean Publishing Co., Ltd.; second selection from *Crying in the Wilderness: The Struggle for Justice in South Africa,* ed. John Webster (William B. Eerdmans Publishing Co., 1982). Reprinted by permission of the Continuum International Publishing Group.

corruption, repression, and foreign economic domination spread quickly.

A popular rebellion forced Batista to flee the country in 1959. The dictator had been opposed by student groups, labor unions, and supporters of Cuba's traditional parties. The revolution was led by Fidel Castro, a young lawyer who had been jailed and then exiled when a 1953 uprising failed. Castro established his revolutionary base in the countryside and utilized guerrilla tactics. When he and his youthful followers took power, they vowed not to suffer the fate of Arbenz and the Guatemalan reformers. Ernesto ("Che") Guevara°, Castro's chief lieutenant who became the main theorist of communist revolution in Latin America, had been in Guatemala at the time of the CIA coup. He and Castro took for granted that confrontation with the United States was inevitable. As a result, they quickly removed the existing military leadership, executing many Batista supporters and creating a new military.

They also moved rapidly to transform Cuban society. Fidel Castro (b. 1927) gave a number of speeches in the United States in the wake of his victory and was cheered as a heroic enemy of dictatorship and American economic imperialism. Within a year his government redistributed land, lowered urban rents, and raised wages, effectively transferring 15 percent of the national income from the rich to the poor. Within twenty-two months the Castro government seized the property of almost all U.S. corporations in Cuba as well as the wealth of Cuba's elite.

To achieve his revolutionary transformation Castro sought economic support from the Soviet Union. The United States responded by suspending the sugar agreement and seeking to destabilize the Cuban economy. These punitive measures, the nationalization of so much of the economy, and the punishment of Batista supporters caused tens of thousands of Cubans to leave. Initially, most immigrants were from wealthy families and the middle-class, but when the economic failures of the regime eventually became clear, many poor Cubans fled to the United States or to other Latin American nations.

Little evidence supports the view that Castro undertook his revolution to install a communist government, but he certainly sought to break the economic and political power of the United States in Cuba and install dramatic social reforms based on an enhanced role for the state in the economy. With relations between Castro and Washington reaching crisis and Castro openly seeking the support of the Soviet Union, in April 1961 the United States attempted to apply the strategy that had removed Arbenz from power in Guatemala. Some fifteen hundred Cuban exiles trained and armed by the CIA were landed

Che Guevara (chay guh-VAHR-uh)

Cuban Poster of Charismatic Leader Ernesto ("Che") Guevara
A leading theorist of communist revolution in Latin America, Argentine-born Guevara was in Guatemala at the time of the CIA-sponsored coup against Jacobo Arbenz in 1954. He later met and had a strong influence on Fidel Castro. He was killed in 1967 while leading an insurgency in Bolivia. (Christopher Morris/stockphoto.com)

at the Bay of Pigs in an effort to overthrow Castro. The Cuban army defeated the attempted invasion in a matter of days, partly because the new U.S. president, John F. Kennedy, decided to provide less air support than had been planned by the Eisenhower administration.

The failure of the Bay of Pigs tarnished the reputation of the United States and the CIA and gave heart to revolutionaries all over Latin America. The failed overthrow of Castro also helped precipitate the Cuban missile crisis. Fearful of a U.S. invasion, Castro and Khrushchev placed nuclear weapons as well as missiles and bombers in Cuba to forestall the anticipated attack. But the armed revolutionary movements that imitated the tactics, objectives, and even appearance of Cuba's bearded revolutionaries experienced little success. Among the thousands to lose their lives was Che Guevara who was executed after capture in Bolivia in 1967. Nevertheless, Castro had demonstrated that American power could be successfully challenged and that a radical program of economic and social reform could be put in place in the Western Hemisphere.

Challenges of Nation Building

Decolonization occurred on a vast scale. Fifty-one nations signed the United Nations Charter in the closing months of 1945. During the United Nations' first decade twenty-five new members joined, a third of them upon gaining independence. During the next decade forty-six more new members were admitted, nearly all of them former colonial territories.

Each of these nations had to organize and institute some form of government. Comparatively few were able to do so without experiencing coups, rewritten constitutions, or regional rebellions. Leaders did not always agree on the form independence should take. In the absence of established constitutional traditions, leaders frequently tried to impose their own visions by force. Most of the new nations, while trying to establish political stability, also faced severe economic challenges, including foreign ownership and operation of key resources and the need to build infrastructure. Overdependence on world demand for raw materials and on imported manufactured goods persisted in many places long after independence.

Because the achievement of political and economic goals called for educated and skilled personnel, education was another common concern in newly emerging nations. Addressing that concern required more than building and staffing schools. In some countries, leaders had to decide which language to teach and how to inculcate a sense of national unity in students from different—and sometimes historically antagonistic—ethnic, religious, and linguistic groups. Another problem was how to provide satisfying jobs for new graduates, many of whom had high expectations because of their education.

Only rarely were the new nations able to surmount these hurdles. Even the most economically and educationally successful, such as South Korea, suffered from tendencies toward authoritarian rule. Similarly, Costa Rica, a country with a remarkably stable parliamentary regime from 1949 onward and a literacy rate of 90 percent, remained heavily dependent on world prices for agricultural commodities and on importation of manufactured goods.

BEYOND A BIPOLAR WORLD

Although no one doubted the dominating role of the East–West superpower rivalry in world affairs, the newly independent states had concerns that were primarily domestic and regional. Their challenge was to pursue their ends within the bipolar structure of the Cold War—and possibly to take advantage of the East–West rivalry. Where nationalist forces sought to assert political or economic independence, Cold War antagonists provided arms and political support even when the nationalist goals were quite different from those of the superpowers. For other nations, the ruinously expensive superpower arms race opened opportunities to expand industries and exports. In short, the superpowers dominated the world but did not control it. And as time progressed, they dominated it less and less.

The Third World

As one of the most successful leaders of the decolonization movement, Indonesia's President Sukarno was an appropriate figure to host a meeting in 1955 of twenty-nine African and Asian countries at Bandung, Indonesia. The conferees proclaimed solidarity among all peoples fighting against colonial rule. The Bandung Conference marked the beginning of an effort by the many new, poor, mostly non-European nations emerging from colonialism to gain more influence in world affairs by banding together. The terms **nonaligned nations** and **Third World,** which became commonplace in the following years, signaled these countries' collective stance toward the rival sides in the Cold War. If the West, led by the United States, and the East, led by the Soviet Union, represented two worlds locked in mortal struggle, the Third World consisted of everyone else.

Leaders of so-called Third World countries preferred the label *nonaligned,* which signified freedom from membership on either side. However, many leaders in the West noted that the Soviet Union supported national liberation movements and that the nonaligned movement included communist countries such as China and Yugoslavia. As a result, they decided not to take the term *nonaligned* seriously. In a polarized world, they saw Sukarno, Nehru, Nkrumah, and Egypt's Gamal Abd al-Nasir° as stalking horses for a communist takeover of the world. This may also have been the view of some Soviet leaders, since the Soviet Union was quick to offer some of these countries military and financial aid.

For the movement's leaders, however, nonalignment was primarily a way to extract money and support from one or both superpowers. By flirting with the Soviet Union or its ally, the People's Republic of China, a country could get cheap or free weapons, training, and barter agreements that offered an alternative to selling agricultural or mineral products on Western-dominated world markets. The same flirtation might also prompt the

Gamal Abd al-Nasir (gah-MAHL AHB-d al–NAH-suhr)

Bandung Conference, 1955 India's Jawaharlal Nehru (in white hat) was a central figure at the conference held in Indonesia to promote solidarity among nonaligned developing nations. The nonalignment movement failed to achieve the influence that Nehru, Egypt's Nasir, and Indonesia's Sukarno sought. (Wide World Photos)

United States and its allies to proffer grants and loans, cheap or free surplus grain, and investment in industry and infrastructure.

When skillful, nonaligned countries could play the two sides against each other and profit from both. Egypt under Nasir, who had led a military coup against the Egyptian monarchy in 1952, and under Nasir's successor Anwar al-Sadat° after 1970 played the game well. The United States offered to build a dam at Aswan°, on the Nile River, to increase Egypt's electrical generating and irrigation capacity. When Egypt turned to the Soviet Union for arms, the United States reneged on the dam project in 1956. The Soviet Union then picked it up and completed the dam in the 1960s. In 1956 Israel, Great Britain, and France conspired to invade Egypt. Their objective was to overthrow Nasir, regain the Suez Canal (he had recently nationalized it), and secure Israel from any Egyptian threat. The invasion succeeded militarily, but the United States and the Soviet Union both pressured the invaders to withdraw, thus saving Nasir's government. In 1972 Sadat evicted his Soviet military advisers, but a year later he used his Soviet weapons to attack Israel. After he lost that war, he announced his faith in the power of the United States to solve Egypt's political and economic problems.

Numerous other countries adopted similar balancing strategies. In each case, local leaders were trying to develop their nation's economy and assert or preserve their nation's interests. Manipulating the superpowers was a means toward those ends and implied very little about true ideological orientation.

Japan and China

No countries took better advantage of the opportunities presented by the superpowers' preoccupation than did Japan and China. Japan signed a peace treaty with most of its former enemies in 1951 and regained independence from American occupation the following year. Renouncing militarism and its imperialist past (see Chapter 26), Japan remained on the sidelines throughout the Korean War. Its new constitution, written under American supervision in 1946, allowed only a limited self-defense force, banned the deployment of Japanese troops abroad, and gave the vote to women.

The Japanese turned their talents and energies to rebuilding their industries and engaging in world commerce. Peace treaties with countries in Southeast Asia specified reparations payable in the form of goods and services, thus reintroducing Japan to that region as a force for economic development rather than as a military occupier. Nevertheless, bitterness over wartime op-

---

al-Sadat (al-seh-DAT)   **Aswan** (AS-wahn)

pression remained strong, and Japan had to move slowly in developing new regional markets for its manufactured goods. The Cold War isolated Japan and excluded it from most world political issues. It thus provided an exceptionally favorable environment for Japan to develop its economic strength.

Three industries that took advantage of government aid and the newest technologies paved the way for Japan's emergence as an economic superpower after 1975. Electricity was in short supply in 1950; Tokyo itself suffered evening power outages. Projects producing 60 million kilowatts of electricity were completed between 1951 and 1970, almost a third through dams on Japan's many rivers. Between 1960 and 1970 steel production more than quadrupled, reaching 15.7 percent of the total capacity of countries outside the Soviet bloc. The shipbuilding industry produced six times as much tonnage in 1970 as in 1960, almost half the new tonnage produced worldwide outside the Soviet bloc.

While Japan benefited from being outside the Cold War, China was deeply involved in Cold War politics. When Mao Zedong° and the communists defeated the nationalists in 1949 and established the People's Republic of China (PRC), their main ally and source of arms was the Soviet Union. By 1956, however, the PRC and the Soviet Union were beginning to diverge politically, partly in reaction to the Soviet rejection of Stalinism and partly because of China's reluctance to be cast forever in the role of student. Mao had his own notions of communism, focusing strongly on the peasantry, whom the Soviets ignored in favor of the industrial working class.

Mao's Great Leap Forward in 1958 was supposed to vault China into the ranks of world industrial powers by maximizing the use of labor in small-scale, village-level industries and by mass collectivization in agriculture. These policies demonstrated Mao's willingness to carry out massive economic and social projects of his own devising in the face of criticism by the Soviets and by traditional economists. However, these revolutionary reforms failed comprehensively by 1962, leading to an estimated 30 million deaths.

In 1966 Mao instituted another radical nationwide program, the **Cultural Revolution.** Ordering the mass mobilization of Chinese youth into Red Guard units, his goal was to kindle revolutionary fervor in a new generation to ward off the stagnation and bureaucratization he saw in the Soviet Union. But this was also a strategy for increasing Mao's power within the Communist Party. Red Guard units criticized and purged teachers, party officials, and intellectuals for "bourgeois values." The young

Mao Zedong (maow dzuh-dong)

Chinese Red Guards   During the Cultural Revolution young Chinese militants joined the Red Guards, identifying enemies of the Communist Party and Chairman Mao. They also turned on their teachers and sometimes their parents and neighbors, labeling them enemies of the people or members of the bourgeoisie. Here a victim wearing a dunce's cap on which his crimes are written is paraded.   (Wide World Photos)

militants themselves suffered from factionalism, which caused more violence. Executions, beatings, and incarcerations were widespread, leading to a half-million deaths and three million purged by 1971. Finally, Mao admitted that attacks on individuals had gotten out of hand and intervened to reestablish order. The last years of the Cultural Revolution were dominated by radicals led by Mao's wife Jiang Qing°, who focused on restrictions on artistic and intellectual activity.

In the meantime, the rift between the PRC and the Soviet Union had opened so wide that U.S. President Richard Nixon (served 1969–1974), by reputation a

Jiang Qing (jyahn ching)

staunch anticommunist, put out secret diplomatic feelers to revive relations with China. In 1971 the United States agreed to allow the PRC to join the United Nations and occupy China's permanent seat on the Security Council. This decision necessitated the expulsion of the Chinese nationalist government based on the island of Taiwan, which had persistently claimed to be the only legal Chinese authority. The following year, Nixon visited Beijing, initiating a new era of enhanced cooperation between the People's Republic of China and the United States.

The Middle East

The superpowers could not control all dangerous international disputes. Independence had come gradually to the Arab countries of the Middle East. Britain granted Syria and Lebanon independence after World War II. Iraq, Egypt, and Jordan enjoyed nominal independence between the two world wars but remained under indirect British control until the 1950s. Military coups overthrew King Faruq° of Egypt in 1952 and King Faysal° II of Iraq in 1958. King Husayn° of Jordan dismissed his British military commander in 1956 in response to the Suez crisis, but his poor desert country remained dependent on British and later American financial aid.

Overshadowing all Arab politics, however, was the struggle with Israel. British policy on Palestine between the wars oscillated between sentiment favoring Zionist Jews—who emigrated to Palestine, encouraged by the Balfour Declaration—and sentiment for the indigenous Palestinian Arabs, who felt themselves being pushed aside and suspected that the Zionists were aiming at an independent state. As more and more Jews sought a safe haven from persecution by the Nazis, Arabs felt more and more threatened. The Arabs unleashed a guerrilla uprising against the British in 1936, and Jewish groups turned to militant tactics a few years later. Occasionally, Arabs and Jews confronted each other in riots or killings, making it clear that peaceful coexistence in Palestine would be difficult or impossible to achieve.

After the war, under intense pressure to resettle European Jewish refugees, Britain conceded that it saw no way of resolving the dilemma and turned the Palestine problem over to the United Nations. In November 1947 the General Assembly voted in favor of partitioning Palestine into two states, one Jewish and the other Arab. The Jewish community made plans to declare independence, while the Palestinians, who felt that the proposed land division was unfair, reacted with horror and took up

Map 31.3 Middle East Oil and the Arab–Israeli Conflict, 1947–1973 Oil resources were long controlled by private European and American companies. In the 1960s most countries, guided by OPEC, negotiated agreements for sharing control, eventually leading to national ownership. This set the stage for the use of oil as a weapon in the 1973 Arab-Israeli war and for subsequent price increases.

arms. When Israel declared its independence in May 1948, neighboring Arab countries sent armies to help the Palestinians crush the newborn state.

Israel prevailed on all fronts. Some 700,000 Palestinians became refugees, finding shelter in United Nations refugee camps in Jordan, Syria, Lebanon, and the Gaza Strip (a bit of coastal land on the Egyptian-Israeli border). The right of these refugees to return home remains a focal point of Arab politics. In 1967 Israel responded to threatening military moves by Egypt's Nasir by preemptively attacking Egyptian and Syrian air bases. In six days Israel won a smashing victory. When Jordan entered the war, Israel won control of Jerusalem, which it had previously split with Jordan, and the West Bank. Acquiring all of Jerusalem satisfied Jews' deep longing to return to their holiest city, but Palestinians continued to regard Jerusalem as their destined capital, and Muslims in many countries protested Israeli control of the Dome of the Rock, a revered Islamic shrine located in the city. Israel also occupied the Gaza Strip, the strategic Golan Heights in southern Syria, and the entire Sinai Peninsula (see Map 31.3). These acquisitions resulted in a new wave of Palestinian refugees.

The rival claims to Palestine continued to plague Middle Eastern politics. The Palestine Liberation Organization (PLO), headed by Yasir Arafat°, waged guerrilla war against Israel, frequently engaging in acts of terrorism. The militarized Israelis were able to blunt or absorb these attacks and launch counterstrikes that likewise involved assassinations and bombings. Though the United States was a firm friend to Israel and the Soviet Union armed the Arab states, neither superpower saw the struggle between Zionism and Palestinian nationalism as a vital concern—until oil became a political issue.

The phenomenal concentration of oil wealth in the Middle East—Saudi Arabia, Iran, Iraq, Kuwait, Libya, Qatar, Bahrain, and the United Arab Emirates—was not fully realized until after World War II, when demand for oil rose sharply as civilian economies recovered. In 1960, as a world oversupply diminished in the face of rising

---

Faruq (fuh-ROOK) **Faysal** (FIE-suhl) **Husayn** (hoo-SANE)

Arafat (AR-uh-fat)

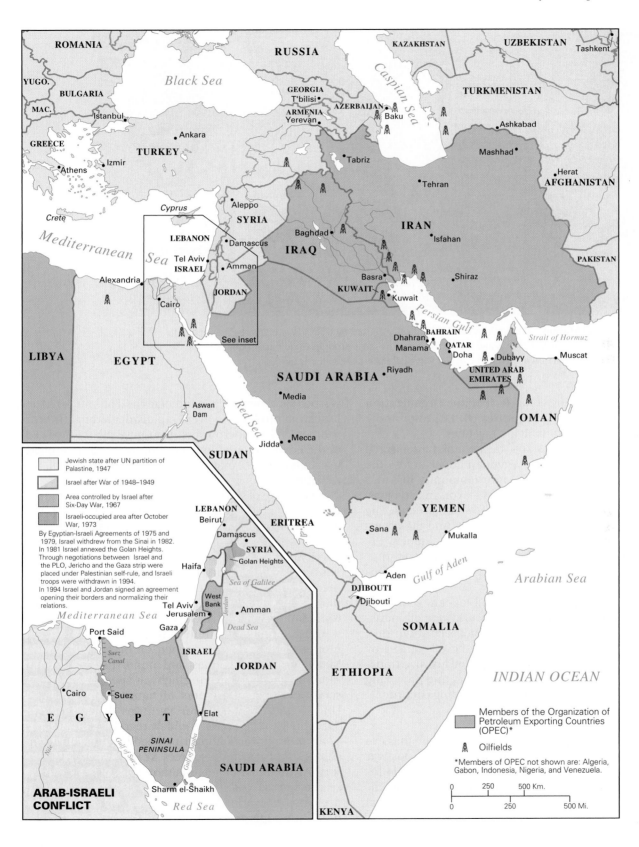

ROMANIA

YUGO.

BULGARIA

MAC.

GREECE

Istanbul

Athens
Izmir

Black Sea

RUSSIA

KAZAKHSTAN

UZBEKISTAN

Tashkent

GEORGIA
T'bilisi

ARMENIA
Yerevan

AZERBAIJAN

Baku

Caspian Sea

TURKMENISTAN

Ashkabad

Ankara

TURKEY

Crete

Mediterranean

Cyprus

Sea

Aleppo

SYRIA

LEBANON

Damascus

Tel Aviv
ISRAEL

Amman

JORDAN

See inset

Tabriz

Mashhad

Herat

AFGHANISTAN

Tehran

IRAN

Isfahan

Baghdad

IRAQ

Basra

Shiraz

PAKISTAN

Alexandria

Cairo

KUWAIT

Kuwait

Persian Gulf

Dhahran
Manama

BAHRAIN

QATAR
Doha

Strait of Hormuz

Dubayy

Muscat

LIBYA

EGYPT

Aswan
Dam

Red Sea

SAUDI ARABIA

Media

Mecca
Jidda

Riyadh

UNITED ARAB
EMIRATES

OMAN

SUDAN

YEMEN

Sana

Mukalla

Aden

Gulf of Aden

Arabian Sea

DJIBOUTI
Djibouti

SOMALIA

ETHIOPIA

INDIAN OCEAN

KENYA

Legend:

- Jewish state after UN partition of Palastine, 1947
- Israel after War of 1948–1949
- Area controlled by Israel after Six-Day War, 1967
- Israeli-occupied area after October War, 1973

By Egyptian-Israeli Agreements of 1975 and 1979, Israel withdrew from the Sinai in 1982. In 1981 Israel annexed the Golan Heights. Through negotiations between Israel and the PLO, Jericho and the Gaza strip were placed under Palestinian self-rule, and Israeli troops were withdrawn in 1994.
In 1994 Israel and Jordan signed an agreement opening their borders and normalizing their relations.

LEBANON
Beirut

Damascus

SYRIA

Haifa
Golan Heights

Sea of Galilee

Mediterranean Sea

West
Bank

Tel Aviv
Jerusalem

Gaza

Dead Sea

Amman

ERITREA

Port Said

*Suez
Canal*

ISRAEL

JORDAN

Cairo

Suez

Elat

E G Y P T

Nile

Gulf of Suez

SINAI
PENINSULA

Gulf of Aqaba

SAUDI ARABIA

Sharm el-Shaikh

Red Sea

**ARAB-ISRAELI
CONFLICT**

Members of the Organization of Petroleum Exporting Countries (OPEC)*

Oilfields

*Members of OPEC not shown are: Algeria, Gabon, Indonesia, Nigeria, and Venezuela.

0   250   500 Km.

0   250   500 Mi.

Oil Crisis at the Gas Station   Dislocations in the oil industry caused by OPEC price increases that began in 1974 produced long lines at gas pumps and local shortages. The crisis brought Middle East politics home to consumers and created a negative stereotype of "oil sheikhs."   (Keza/Liaison/Getty Images)

demand, oil-producing states formed the **Organization of Petroleum Exporting Countries (OPEC)** to promote their collective interest in higher revenues.

Oil politics and the Arab-Israeli conflict intersected in October 1973. A surprise Egyptian attack across the Suez Canal threw the Israelis into temporary disarray. Within days the war turned in Israel's favor, and an Egyptian army was trapped at the canal's southern end. The United States then arranged a cease fire and the disengagement of forces. But before that could happen, the Arab oil-producing countries voted to embargo oil shipments to the United States and the Netherlands as punishment for their support of Israel.

The implications of using oil as an economic weapon profoundly disturbed the worldwide oil industry. Prices rose—along with feelings of insecurity. In 1974 OPEC responded to the turmoil in the oil market by quadrupling prices, setting the stage for massive transfers of wealth to the producing countries and provoking a feeling of crisis throughout the consuming countries.

The Emergence of Environmental Concerns

The Cold War and the massive investments made in postwar economic recovery had focused public and governmental attention on technological innovations and enormous projects such as hydroelectric dams and nuclear power stations. Only a few people warned that untested technologies and all-out drives for industrial productivity were rapidly degrading the environment. The superpowers were particularly negligent of the environmental impact of pesticide and herbicide use, automobile exhaust, industrial waste disposal, and radiation.

The wave of student unrest that swept many parts of the world in 1968 and the early 1970s created a new awareness of environmental issues and a new constituency for environmental action. As the current of youth activism grew, governments in the West began to pass new environmental regulations. Earth Day, a benchmark of the new awareness, was first celebrated in 1970, the year in which the United States established its Environmental Protection Agency.

The problem of finite natural resources became more broadly recognized when oil prices skyrocketed. Making gasoline engines and home heating systems more efficient and lowering highway speed limits to conserve fuel became matters of national debate in the United States, while poorer countries struggled to find the money to import oil. A widely read 1972 study called *The Limits of Growth* forecast a need to cut back on consumption of natural resources in the twenty-first century. As the most dangerous moments of the Cold War seemed to be passing, ecological and environmental problems of worldwide impact vied for public attention with superpower rivalry and Third World nation building.

CONCLUSION

The impact of the Second World War was so immense that for several decades people commonly referred to the time they were living in as the "postwar era," not needing to specify which war they were referring to. The Cold War and the decolonization movement seemed to be logical extensions of World War II. The question of who would control the parts of Europe and Asia liberated from Axis occupation led to Churchill's notion of an iron curtain dividing East and West. The war exhaustion of the European imperialist powers encouraged Asian and African peoples to seek independence and embark on building their own nations.

Intellectuals often framed their understanding of the period in terms of a philosophical struggle between capitalism and socialism dating back to the nineteenth century. But for leaders facing the challenge of governing new nations and creating viable economies, economic philosophy was inextricably intertwined with questions of how to take advantage of the Cold War rivalry between the United States and the Soviet Union.

There is some disagreement among historians about whether the postwar era ended in 1975. The end of the Vietnam War, the beginning of the world oil crisis, and the signing of the Helsinki Accords that brought a measure of agreement among Europeans on both sides of the iron curtain were pivotal events for some countries. But the number of independent countries in the world had grown enormously, and each was in the process of working out its own problems. What marks the mid-1970s as the end of an era, therefore, is not a single event so much as the emergence of new concerns. Young people in particular—the new generation that had no memories of World War II—seemed less concerned with the Cold War and the specter of nuclear annihilation and more interested in newly recognized threats to the world environment and in seeking opportunities for making their way in the world. For those in wealthier nations, this meant taking advantage of economic growth and increasing technological sophistication. For those in the developing world, it meant seeking the education and employment needed for playing active roles in the drama of nation building.

■ Key Terms

iron curtain
Cold War
North Atlantic Treaty Organization (NATO)
United Nations
World Bank
Marshall Plan
European Community
Truman Doctrine
Warsaw Pact
Korean War
Vietnam War
Cuban missile crisis
Helsinki Accords
nonaligned nations
Third World
Cultural Revolution (China)
Organization of Petroleum Exporting Countries (OPEC)

■ Suggested Reading

The period since 1945 has been particularly rich in memoirs by government leaders. Some that are particularly relevant to the Cold War and decolonization are Dean Acheson (U.S. secretary of state under Truman), *Present at the Creation* (1969); Nikita Khrushchev, *Khrushchev Remembers* (1970); and Anthony Eden (British prime minister), *Full Circle* (1960).

Geoffrey Barraclough, *An Introduction to Contemporary History* (1964), is a remarkable early effort at understanding the broad sweep of history during this period. See also David Reynolds, *One World Divisible: A Global History Since 1945* (2000).

Scholarship on the origins of the Cold War is extensive and includes Akira Iriye, *The Cold War in Asia: A Historical Introduction* (1974); Bruce Kuniholm, *The Origins of the Cold War in the Middle East* (1980); Madelaine Kalb, *The Congo Cables: The Cold War in Africa—From Eisenhower to Kennedy* (1982); and Michael J. Hogan, *A Cross of Iron: Harry S Truman and the Origins of the National Security State* (1998). For a recent reconsideration of earlier historical viewpoints see Melvyn P. Leffler and David S. Painter, eds., *Origins of the Cold War: An International History* (1994).

Good general histories of the Cold War include Martin Walker, *The Cold War: A History* (1993), and Walter Lafeber, *America, Russia, and the Cold War, 1945–1992* (1993). The latter emphasizes how the Cold War eroded American democratic values. For a look at the Cold War from the Soviet perspective see William Taubman, *Stalin's America Policy* (1981); for the American perspective see John Lewis Gaddis, *Strategies of Containment: A Critical Appraisal of Postwar American National Security Policy* (1982). The Cuban missile crisis is well covered in Graham Allison, *Essence of Decision: Explaining the Cuban Missile Crisis* (1971), and Michael Beschloss, *The Crisis Years: Kennedy and Khrushchev, 1960–1963* (1991). Also see Aleksandr Fursenko and Timothy Naftali, *"One Hell of a Gamble": Khrushchev, Castro, and Kennedy, 1958–1964: The Secret History of the Cuban Missile Crisis* (1997); and the more recent John L. Gaddis, *We Now Know: Rethinking Cold War History* (1997); Mark Mazower, *Dark Continent* (1999); and William Hitchcock,

The Struggle for Europe: The Turbulent History of a Divided Continent 1945–2002 (2003).

The nuclear arms race and the associated Soviet–U.S. competition in space are well covered by McGeorge Bundy, *Danger and Survival: Choices About the Bomb in the First Fifty Years* (1988), and Walter MacDougall, *The Heavens and the Earth: A Political History of the Space Age* (1985). Among the many novels illustrating the alarming impact of the arms race on the general public are Philip Wylie, *Tomorrow!* (1954), and Nevil Shute, *On the Beach* (1970). At a technical and philosophical level, Herman Kahn's *On Thermonuclear War* (1961) had a similar effect.

The end of the European empires is broadly treated by D. K. Fieldhouse, *The Colonial Empires* (1982); a broad view is provided by D. A. Low, *The Egalitarian Moment: Asia and Africa, 1950–1980* (1996); for the British Empire in particular, Brian Lapping, *End of Empire* (1985). For a critical view of American policies toward the decolonized world see Gabriel Kolko, *Confronting the Third World: United States Foreign Policy, 1945–1980* (1988).

For books on some of the specific episodes of decolonization treated in this chapter see, on Algeria, Alistaire Horne, *A Savage War of Peace: Algeria, 1954–1962* (1987); on Africa, H. S. Wilson, *African Decolonization* (1994); and Frederick Cooper, *Decolonization and African Society: The Labor Question in French and British Africa* (1996); on Cuba, Hugh Thomas, *Cuba: The Pursuit of Freedom* (1971); on the Suez crisis of 1956, Keith Kyle, *Suez 1956* (1991); on Britain's role in the Middle East over the period

of the birth of Israel, William Roger Louis, *The British Empire in the Middle East, 1945–1951* (1984); on Vietnam, George Herring, *America's Longest War: The United States and Vietnam, 1950–1975* (1986), and Stanley Karnow, *Vietnam: A History* (1991); and on Latin America, Thomas E. Skidmore and Peter H. Smith, *Modern Latin America*, 5th ed. (2001).

The special cases of Japan and China in this period are covered by Takafusa Nakamura, *A History of Showa Japan, 1926–1989* (1998); John Dower, *Embracing Defeat: Japan in the Wake of World War II* (1999); Marius B. Jansen, *Japan and China: From War to Peace, 1894–1972* (1975); and Maurice Meisner, *Mao's China and After: A History of the People's Republic* (1986). On the consequences of the Great Leap Forward see Jasper Becker, *Hungry Ghosts* (1998); and on the Cultural Revolution see Lynn T. White, *Policies of Chaos: The Organizational Causes of Violence in China's Cultural Revolution* (1989). John Merrill, *Korea: The Peninsular Origins of the War* (1989), presents the Korean War as a civil and revolutionary conflict as well as an episode of the Cold War. Among the hundreds of books on the Arab-Israeli conflict, Charles D. Smith, *Palestine and the Arab-Israel Conflict* (1992), and Trevor N. Dupuy, *Elusive Victory: The Arab-Israeli Wars, 1947–1974* (1978), stand out.

■ Notes

1. From Mark Mazower, *Dark Continent: Europe's Twentieth Century* (New York: Alfred A. Knopf, 1999), 271.

Document-Based Question
Identity and Independence in the Cold War Era

Using the following documents, analyze the experiences that shaped the identity of newly independent nations in Africa and Asia during the Cold War.

DOCUMENT 1
Map 31.1 Cold War Confrontation (p. 827)

DOCUMENT 2
The Vietnamese People at War (photo, p. 828)

DOCUMENT 3
Map 31.2 Decolonization, 1947–1990 (p. 831)

DOCUMENT 4
African Leaders Meet for Conference (photo, p. 833)

DOCUMENT 5
Quote from Malagasy politician Philibert Tsirinana (p. 834)

DOCUMENT 6
Race and the Struggle for Justice in South Africa (Diversity and Dominance, pp. 836–837)

DOCUMENT 7
Bandung Conference, 1955 (photo, p. 840)

In Document 6, how do Steve Biko and Desmond Tutu express different views of South African identity? What additional types of documents would help you understand the experiences that shaped the identity of newly independent nations in Africa and Asia during the Cold War?

Crisis, Realignment, and the Dawn of the Post–Cold War World, 1975–1991

32

Dry Docks Owned by Korea's Hyundai Corporation   Korea's rapid industrialization symbolizes Pacific Rim economic growth.

On Thursday, July 22, 1993, police officers in Rio de Janeiro's banking district attempted to arrest a young boy caught sniffing glue. In the resulting scuffle, one police officer was injured by stones thrown by homeless children who lived in nearby streets and parks. Late the following night, hooded vigilantes in two cars fired hundreds of shots at a group of these children who were sleeping on the steps of a church, killing five of them at the church and two more in a park. The murderers were later identified as off-duty police officers.

At the time more than 350,000 abandoned children lived in Rio's streets and parks, begging, selling drugs, stealing, and engaging in prostitution to survive. In 1993 alone death squads and drug dealers killed more than 400 of them. Few people sympathized with the victims. One person living near the scene of the July shootings said, "Those street kids are bandits, and bandits have to die. They are a rotten branch that has to be pruned."

At the end of the twentieth century the brutality of those children's lives were common in the developing world, where rapid population growth was outstripping economic resources.[1] Problems of violence, poverty, and social breakdown could be found in most developing nations.

In wealthy industrialized nations as well, politicians and social reformers worried about the effects of unemployment, family breakdown, substance abuse, and homelessness. As had been true during the Industrial Revolution in the eighteenth century (see Chapter 22), dramatic economic growth, increased global economic integration, and rapid technological progress in the post–World War II period coincided with growing social dislocation and inequality. Among the most important events of the period were the emergence of new industrial powers in Asia and the precipitous demise of the Soviet Union and its socialist allies.

World population growth and large-scale migrations also created new challenges. Population grew most rapidly in the world's poorest nations, worsening social and economic problems and undermining fragile political institutions. In the industrialized nations the arrival of large numbers of culturally and linguistically distinct immigrants fueled economic growth but also gave rise to anti-immigrant political movements and, in some cases, violent ethnic conflict.

As you read this chapter, ask yourself the following questions:

- How did the Cold War affect politics in Latin America and the Middle East in the 1970s and 1980s?

- What forces led to the collapse of the Soviet Union?

- Why did the gap between rich and poor nations increase in this period?

- What is the relationship between the rate of population growth and the wealth of nations?

- How did technological change affect the global environment in the recent past?

POSTCOLONIAL CRISES AND ASIAN ECONOMIC EXPANSION, 1975–1991

Between 1975 and 1991 wars and revolutions provoked by a potent mix of ideology, nationalism, ethnic hatred, and religious fervor spread death and destruction through many of the world's least-developed regions. These conflicts often had ties to earlier colonialism and foreign intervention, but the character and objectives of each conflict reflected specific historical experiences. Throughout these decades of conflict the two superpowers sought to avoid direct military confrontation while working to gain strategic advantages. The United States and the Soviet Union each supplied arms and financial assistance to nations or insurgent forces hostile to its superpower rival. Once they became linked to the geopolitical rivalry of the superpowers, conflicts provoked by local and regional causes tended to become more deadly and long-lasting. Conflicts in which the rival super powers financed and armed competing factions or parties were called **proxy wars.**

In Latin America the rivalry of the superpowers helped transform conflicts over political rights, social justice, and economic policies into a violent cycle of revolution, military dictatorship, and foreign meddling. In

C H R O N O L O G Y

	The Americas	Middle East	Asia	Eastern Europe
1970	**1964** Military takeover in Brazil **1970** Salvador Allende elected president of Chile **1973** Allende overthrown **1976** Military takeover in Argentina **1979** Sandinistas overthrow Anastasio Somoza in Nicaragua		**1975** Vietnam war ends **1978** China opens its economy	**1978** USSR sends troops to Afghanistan
1980	**1983–1990** Democracy returns in Argentina, Brazil, and Chile	**1979** Islamic Revolution overthrows shah of Iran **1980–1988** Iran-Iraq War	**1986** Average Japanese income overtakes income in United States	**1985** Mikhail Gorbachev becomes Soviet head of state
1990	**1989** United States invades Panama **1990** Sandinistas defeated in elections in Nicaragua	**1989** USSR withdraws from Afghanistan **1990** Iraq invades Kuwait **1991** Persian Gulf War	**1989** Tiananmen Square confrontation **1990s** Japanese recession	**1989** Berlin Wall falls **1989–1991** End of communism in eastern Europe **1990** Reunification of Germany

Iran and Afghanistan resentment against foreign intrusion and a growing religious hostility to modernization led to revolutionary transformations. Here again superpower ambitions and regional political instability helped provoke war and economic decline. These experiences were not universal. During this period some Asian nations experienced rapid transformation. Japan became one of the world's leading industrial powers, while a small number of other Asian economies quickly entered the ranks of industrial and commercial powers.

The collapse of the Soviet system in eastern Europe at the end of the 1980s ended the Cold War and undermined socialist economies elsewhere. As developing and former socialist nations opened their markets to foreign investment and competition, economic transformation was often accompanied by wrenching social change. The world's growing economic interconnectedness coincided with increased inequality. By the early 1990s it was clear that the world's wealthiest industrial nations were reaping most of the benefits of economic integration.

This period also witnessed a great increase in world population and international immigration. Population growth and increased levels of industrialization had a dramatic impact on the global environment. Every continent felt the destructive effects of forest depletion, soil erosion, and pollution. Wealthy nations with slow population growth found it easier to respond to these environmental challenges than did poor nations experiencing rapid population growth.

Revolutions, Repression, and Democratic Reform in Latin America

In the 1970s Latin America entered a dark era of political violence. As revolutionary movements challenged the established order in many nations, democratic governments were overturned by the military. A region of weak democracy in 1960 became a region of military dictatorships fifteen years later. The new authoritarian leaders had little patience with civil liberties and human rights.

The confrontation between Fidel Castro and the government of the United States that had led to the Bay of Pigs invasion and the missile crisis (see Chapter 31) helped propel the region toward crisis. The fact that the Cuban communist government survived efforts by the United States to overthrow it energized the revolutionary left throughout Latin America. Fearful that revolution would spread across Latin America and determined to defeat communism at all costs, the United States increased support for its political and military allies in Latin America. Many of the military leaders who would come to power in this period were trained by the United States.

Brazil was the first nation to experience the full effects of the conservative reaction to the Cuban Revolution. Claiming that Brazil's civilian political leaders could not protect the nation from communist subversion, the army overthrew the democratically elected government of President João Goulart° in 1964. The military suspended the constitution, outlawed all existing political parties, and exiled former presidents and opposition leaders. Death squads—illegal paramilitary organizations sanctioned by the government—detained, tortured, and executed thousands of citizens. The dictatorship also undertook an ambitious economic program that promoted industrialization through import substitution, using tax and tariff policies to compel foreign-owned companies to increase investment in manufacturing.

This combination of dictatorship, violent repression, and government promotion of industrialization came to be called the "Brazilian Solution" in Latin America. Elements of this "solution" were imposed across much of the region in the 1970s and early 1980s, beginning in Chile. In 1970 Chile's new president, **Salvador Allende°,** undertook an ambitious program of socialist reforms to redistribute wealth from the elite and middle classes to the poor. He also nationalized most of Chile's heavy industry and mines, including the American-owned copper companies that dominated the Chilean economy. From the beginning of Allende's presidency the administration of President Richard Nixon (served 1969–1973) worked to organize opposition to Allende's reforms and to overturn his election. Afflicted by inflation, mass consumer protests, and declining foreign trade, Allende was overthrown in 1973 by a military uprising led by General Augusto Pinochet° and supported by the United States. President Allende and thousands of Chileans died in the uprising, and thousands more were illegally seized, tortured, and imprisoned without trial. Once in power Pinochet rolled back Allende's social reforms, dramatically reduced state participation in the economy, and encouraged foreign investment.

In 1976 Argentina followed Brazil and Chile into dictatorship. Isabel Martínez de Perón° became president

after the death of her husband Juan Perón in 1974 (see Chapter 30). Argentina was wracked by high inflation, terrorism, and labor protests. Impatient with the policies of the president, the military seized power and suspended the constitution. During the next seven years the military fought what it called the **Dirty War** against terrorism. More than nine thousand Argentines lost their lives, and thousands of others endured arrest, torture, and the loss of property.

Despite reverses in Brazil, Chile, and Argentina, however, revolutionary movements persisted elsewhere. The high-water mark of the revolutionary movement came in 1979 in Nicaragua with the overthrow of the corrupt dictatorship of Anastasio Somoza. The broad alliance of revolutionaries and reformers that took power called themselves **Sandinistas°.** They took their name from Augusto César Sandino, who had led Nicaraguan opposition to U.S. military intervention between 1927 and 1932. The Sandinistas received significant political and financial support from Cuba and, once in power, sought to imitate the command economies of Cuba and the Soviet Union, nationalizing properties owned by members of the Nicaraguan elite and U.S. citizens.

During his four-year term U.S. president Jimmy Carter (served 1977–1980) championed human rights in the hemisphere and stopped the flow of U.S. arms to regimes with the worst records. Carter sought to placate Latin American resentment for past U.S. interventions by agreeing to the reestablishment of Panamanian sovereignty in the Canal Zone at the end of 1999. He also tried and failed to find common ground with the Sandinistas. In 1981 Ronald Reagan became president and abandoned this policy of conciliation.

Reagan was committed to reversing the results of the Nicaraguan Revolution and defeating a revolutionary movement in neighboring El Salvador. His options, however, were limited by the U.S. Congress, which feared that Central America might become another Vietnam. Congress resisted using U.S. combat forces in Nicaragua and El Salvador and put strict limits on military aid. The Reagan administration sought to roll back the Nicaraguan Revolution by the use of punitive economic measures and by the recruitment and arming of anti-Sandinista Nicaraguans. Called Contras (counterrevolutionaries), this military force was financed by both legal and illegal funds provided by the Reagan administration.

The Contras were unable to defeat the Sandinistas, but they did gain a bloody stalemate by the end of the 1980s. Confident that they were supported by the majority of Nicaraguans and assured that the U.S. Congress

---

João Goulart (juwow go-LARHT)
Salvador Allende (sal-vah-DOR ah-YEHN-day)   **Augusto Pinochet** (ah-GOOS-toh pin-oh-CHET)   **Isabel Martínez de Perón** (EES-ah-bell mar-TEEN-ehz deh pair-OWN)

Sandinistas (sahn-din-EES-tahs)

The Nicaraguan Revolution Overturns Somoza A revolutionary coalition that included Marxists drove the dictator Anastasio Somoza from power in 1979. The Somoza family had ruled Nicaragua since the 1930s and maintained a close relationship with the United States. (Susan Meiselas/ Magnum Photos, Inc.)

was close to cutting off aid to the Contras, the Sandinistas called for free elections in 1990. But they had miscalculated politically. Exhausted by more than a decade of violence, a majority of Nicaraguan voters rejected the Sandinistas and elected a middle-of-the-road coalition led by Violeta Chamorro°.

The revolutionaries of El Salvador hoped to imitate the initial success of the Sandinistas of Nicaragua. Taking their name from a martyred leftist leader of the 1930s, the FMLN (Farabundo Martí° National Liberation Front) organized an effective guerrilla force. The United States responded by providing hundreds of millions of dollars in military assistance annually and by training units of the El Salvadoran army. These investments in military equipment and training failed to curb the Salvadoran military's human rights abuses.

The assassination of Archbishop Oscar Romero and other members of the Catholic clergy by death squads tied to the Salvadoran government as well as the murder of thousands of noncombatants by military units made it difficult for the Reagan administration to sustain its policy of military aid. Knowledge of human rights abuses led the U.S. Congress to place strict limits on the number of U.S. military advisers that could be sent to El Salvador and to try to force political reforms. External events fi-

Violeta Chamorro (vee-oh-LET-ah cha-MOR-roe)   Farabundo Martí (fah-rah-BOON-doh mar-TEE)

nally brought peace to El Salvador. With the electoral defeat of the Sandinistas in Nicaragua and the collapse of the Soviet Union (see below), popular support for the rebels' vision of a socialist El Salvador waned, and the FMLN rebels negotiated an end to the war, transforming themselves into a civilian political party.

The military dictatorships established in Brazil, Chile, and Argentina all came to an end between 1983 and 1990. In each case reports of kidnappings, tortures, and corruption by military governments undermined public support. In Argentina the military junta's foolish decision in 1982 to seize the Falkland Islands—the Argentines called them the "Malvinas"—from Great Britain ended in an embarrassing military defeat and precipitated the return to civilian rule. The Argentine junta had helped President Reagan support the Contras in Nicaragua and believed he would keep Britain's Prime Minister Margaret Thatcher from taking military action. Instead the United States supported the British. With the surrender of the Argentine garrison in the Falklands, military rule in Argentina itself collapsed.

In Chile and Brazil the military dictatorships ended without the drama of foreign war. Despite significant economic growth under Pinochet, Chileans resented the violence and corruption of the military. In 1988 Pinochet called a plebiscite to extend his authority, but the majority vote went against him. A year later Chile elected its first civilian president in eighteen years. Brazil's military initiated a gradual transition to civilian rule in 1985 and four years later had its first popular presidential election. By 1991 nearly 95 percent of Latin America's population lived under civilian rule.

By the end of the 1980s oil-importing and oil-exporting nations in Latin America were in economic trouble. Brazil and other oil importers had borrowed heavily to cover budget deficits caused by high oil prices engineered by OPEC. Oil exporters such as Mexico and Venezuela at first enjoyed a windfall as prices rose. Expecting prices to remain high, they borrowed to increase production and develop refining capacity. When oil prices fell in the 1980s, they were hard-pressed to repay debts. In 1982 Mexico was forced to declare that it could not make debt payments, triggering a world financial crisis. By 1988 Latin American nations owed more than $400 billion to external lenders, and Brazil alone owed $113 billion. Debt remained an impediment to economic development in Latin America into the 1990s.

In 1991 Latin America was more dominated by the United States than it had been in 1975. On a number of occasions in the 1980s the United States used military force to achieve its objectives. In 1983, for example, President Reagan authorized a military invasion of the tiny Caribbean nation of Grenada, using the need to protect a small number of American students from the actions of a pro-Cuban government as justification. Six years later President George H. W. Bush sent a large military force into Panama to overthrow and arrest dictator General Manuel Noriega°, who was associated with both drug smuggling and attacks on U.S. military personnel. These actions were powerful reminders to Latin Americans of prior foreign intervention and occupation (see Chapter 23).

With socialism discredited by the collapse of the Soviet bloc, most Latin American nations introduced economic reforms advocated by the United States that reduced the economic role of the state. Called neoliberalism in Latin America and other developing regions, these free-market policies reduced protections afforded local industries, government social welfare policies, and public-sector employment. Governments sold public-sector industries, like national airlines, manufacturing facilities, and public utilities, to foreign corporations. Popular support has been eroded by a succession of shocks since 1994, and new political movements are demanding an active role for government in the economy (see Diversity and Dominance: The Struggle for Women's Rights in an Era of Global Political and Economic Change).

Manuel Noriega (MAN-wel no-ree-EGG-ah)

Islamic Revolutions in Iran and Afghanistan

Although the Arab-Israel conflict and the oil crisis (see Chapter 31) concerned both superpowers, the prospect of direct military involvement remained remote. When unexpected crises developed in Iran and Afghanistan, however, significant strategic issues came to the foreground. Both countries adjoined Soviet territory, making Soviet military intervention more likely. Exercising post–Vietnam War caution, the United States reacted with restraint. The Soviet Union chose a bolder and ultimately disastrous course.

Muhammad Reza Pahlavi° succeeded his father as shah of Iran in 1941. In 1953 covert intervention by the U.S. Central Intelligence Agency (CIA) helped the shah retain his throne in the face of a movement to overturn royal power. Even when he finally nationalized the foreign-owned oil industry, the shah continued to enjoy special American support. As oil revenues increased following the price increases of the 1970s, the United States encouraged the shah to spend his nation's growing wealth on equipping the Iranian army with advanced American weaponry.

Resentment in Iran against the Pahlavi family's autocracy dated from the 1925 seizure of power by the shah's father. The shah's dependence on the United States stimulated further opposition. By the 1970s popular resentment against the ballooning wealth of the elite families that supported the shah and the brutality, inefficiency, malfeasance, and corruption of his government led to mass opposition.

Ayatollah Ruhollah Khomeini°, a Shi'ite° philosopher-cleric who had spent most of his eighty-plus years in religious and academic pursuits, became the voice and symbolic leader of the opposition. Massive street demonstrations and crippling strikes forced the shah to flee Iran and ended the monarchy in 1979. In the Islamic Republic of Iran, which replaced the monarchy, Ayatollah Khomeini was supreme arbiter of disputes and guarantor of religious legitimacy. He oversaw a parliamentary regime based on European models, but he imposed religious control of legislation and public behavior. Elections were held, but the electoral process was not open to all: monarchists, communists, and other groups opposed to the Islamic Republic were barred from running for office. Shi'ite clerics with little training for government service held many of the high-

Reza Pahlavi (REH-zah PAH-lah-vee)   **Ayatollah Ruhollah Khomeini** (A-yat-ol-LAH ROOH-ol-LAH ko-MAY-nee)   **Shi'ite** (SHE-ite)

Muslim Women Mourning the Death of Ayatollah Khomeini in 1989   An Islamic revolution overthrew the shah of Iran in 1979. Ayatollah Khomeini sought to lead Iran away from the influences of Western culture and challenged the power of the United States in the Persian Gulf.   (Alexandra Avakian/Woodfin Camp & Associates)

est posts, and stringent measures were taken to combat Western styles and culture. Universities were temporarily closed, and their faculties were purged of secularists and monarchists. Women were compelled to wear modest Islamic garments outside the house, and semi-official vigilante committees policed public morals and cast a pall over entertainment and social life.

The United States under President Carter had criticized the shah's repressive regime, but the overthrow of a long-standing ally and the creation of the Islamic Republic were blows to American prestige. The new Iranian regime was religiously doctrinaire. It also was anti-Israeli and anti-American. Khomeini saw the United States as a "Great Satan" opposed to Islam, and he helped foster Islamic revolutionary movements elsewhere, which

threatened the interests of both the United States and Israel. In November 1979 Iranian radicals seized the U.S. embassy in Tehran and held fifty-two diplomats hostage for 444 days. Americans felt humiliated by their inability to do anything, particularly after the failure of a military rescue attempt.

In the fall of 1980, shortly after negotiations for the release of the hostages began, **Saddam Husain°**, the ruler of neighboring Iraq, invaded Iran to topple the Islamic Republic. His own dictatorial rule rested on a secular, Arab-nationalist philosophy and long-standing friendship with the Soviet Union, which had provided him with advanced weaponry. He feared that the fervor of Iran's revolutionary Shi'ite leaders would infect his own country's Shi'ite majority and threaten his power. The war pitted American weapons in the hands of the Iranians against Soviet weapons in the hands of the Iraqis, but the superpowers avoided overt involvement during eight years of bloodshed. Covertly, however, the United States sent arms via Israel to Iran, hoping to gain the release of other American hostages held by radical Islamic groups in Lebanon and to help finance the Contra war against the Sandinista government of Nicaragua. When this deal came to light in 1986, the resulting political scandal intensified American hostility to Iran. Openly tilting toward Iraq, President Reagan sent the United States Navy to the Persian Gulf, ostensibly to protect nonbelligerent shipping. The move helped force Iran to accept a cease-fire in 1988.

While the United States experienced anguish and frustration in Iran, the Soviet Union found itself facing even more serious problems in neighboring Afghanistan. Since World War II the Soviet Union had stayed out of shooting wars by using proxies to challenge the United States. But in 1979 the Soviet Union sent its army to Afghanistan to bolster communist rule against a hodgepodge of local, religiously inspired guerrilla bands that had taken control of much of the countryside.

With the United States, Saudi Arabia, and Pakistan paying, equipping, and training the Afghan rebels, the Soviet Union found itself in an unwinnable war like the one the United States had stumbled into in Vietnam. Unable to justify the continuing drain on manpower, morale, and economic resources, and facing widespread domestic discontent over the war, Soviet leaders finally withdrew their troops in 1989. The Afghan communists held on for another three years. But once rebel groups took control of the entire country, they began to fight among themselves over who should rule.

Saddam Husain (sah-DAHM who-SANE)

우세인 은신쳐 방

파운드폭탄 4발 투하··· 두 아들과 함께 사망 가

─심진지 구축··· 이틀째 시가戰

령이 대중 앞에 나타나거나 애국심   라크 전후 대책
을 고취하는 노래만을 내보내던 방   의에서는 전후
송마저 중단됐다.   영국 주도로

DIVERSITY AND DOMINANCE

THE STRUGGLE FOR WOMEN'S RIGHTS IN AN ERA OF GLOBAL POLITICAL AND ECONOMIC CHANGE

*The struggle for women's rights is one of the most important social movements of the twentieth century. Although fundamental similarities in objectives can be identified across cultural and political boundaries, women in less-developed nations are forced to recognize that their objectives and strategies must take into account international inequalities in power and wealth. In this section Gladys Acosta, a militant Peruvian feminist, discusses the appropriate agenda for this struggle in the era after the fall of the Soviet Union and the rise of **neo-liberalism.***

Neo-liberalism is the term used in Latin America to identify the free-market economic policies advocated by the United States. Among its chief characteristics are an end to the protection of local industries, a reduction in government social welfare policies, a reduction in public-sector employment, a commitment to paying debts to international creditors, and the removal of impediments to foreign investment. Many Latin Americans believe neo-liberalism is a new form of imperialism.

No one can abstain from the debate about the great historical systems of our time. Not even those of us who are trying to change the complex web of human relationships from a feminist perspective. Everywhere people are talking about the end of ideologies. But before we can grasp the significance of current events and their consequences, we need to pinpoint our various doubts and blank spots. Capitalism is the main pivot of our lives because we were born under its influence. It [has] hegemony. . . .

Gender, the main distinction between all people, is ignored in most philosophical, political or economic discussions. The reason for this lies partly in the low level of women's participation, but not entirely, because women are not always aware of the system of submission and repression to which we are subjected against our will. We need to find something which unites women in a gender-specific manner. That doesn't mean sweeping under the carpet all the differences between us, like social position, culture or age. . . .

NEO-LIBERALISM IN ACTION

For those of us who live under the influence of the capitalist system, the situation is different. When I talk of neo-liberalism, I mean austerity measures, foreign debts, and increased liberties for all those who have the power of money at their disposal and the power of repression over those who make demands. We have now reached a new form of capitalist accumulation. The world's economic system is in a state of change and capital has become more concentrated and centralised. I would not go as far as to say countries don't exist anymore but national identities do certainly play a different role now. It is important to understand the dynamics because otherwise historical responsibilities are obscured and we no longer know whom we're fighting against. If we look at the bare face of neo-liberalism from a woman's point of view, we cannot fail to notice its murderous consequences. To create a more humane society we must continue to reject neo-liberalism here and now in the hope of being able to change the dead present into a living future. Under neo-liberalism there is a breathtaking circulation of commodities, but also an exchange of ideas, illusions and dreams. At the moment we're experiencing capitalism's greatest ideological offensive. It's all business: everything is bought and sold and everything has its price.

THE CONSEQUENCES OF NEO-LIBERAL POLITICS

We women play an important role in this ever-more internationalized economy because we represent, as ever, a particularly exploitable workforce. A number of studies have revealed the existence of subcontractor chains who work for transnational companies "informally" and mainly employ women. Basically we are dealing with a kind of integration into the world market which often uses our own homes as its outlet. Obviously, this work is badly paid and completely unprotected and has to be done without any of those social rights which were formerly achieved by trade union struggles. The most important thing for us is to keep hold of just one thread of the enterprise so we can show how the commodities make their way to their final destination. As it advances worldwide, this capitalism also encourages the expansion of certain kinds of tourism. A visible increase in prostitution is part of this, whereby women from poor countries are smuggled into large, internationally-operated rings which exploit them. The reports of Filipina women traded on the West German market send shivers down our spines... What kind of freedom are you talking about there?

HOW THE ADOPTION OF AUSTERITY MEASURES AFFECTS WOMEN'S LIVES

It is obvious that foreign debt is one of the most inhuman forms of exploitation in our countries when one considers the ratio between work necessary for workers' needs and work producing profit for employers. The experts have already explained how the prevailing exchange and investment structures have created international finance systems which keep whole populations in inhuman conditions. Although many people might think it crazy, the development model of the global economy has a marked relation to gender. As long as prices were slapped on some luxury consumer items there weren't any serious problems; but now the snares have been set around basic commodities. Women in every household are suffering every day as a result of impoverished economies and those who are most exposed to the effects of foreign debt are women.

When it comes to shopping, caring for sick children or the impossibility of meeting their schooling costs, the illusion of "leaving poverty behind" evaporates. Yet the problem is not only of an economic nature because under such circumstances the constant tension leads to grave, often lasting exhaustion. The psychosocial damage is alarming. The situation is ready to explode, so to speak. . . . The adoption of austerity measures means a curtailment of the state's commitment to social services with a direct effect on women. Daily life becomes hell for them. The lack of even minimal state welfare presents women (and obviously children too) with crushing working days. There is a constant expenditure of human energy without any hope of rest! No relaxation, no breaks. . . . And if we consider what happens within the family, we notice that women keep the smallest portion of the meagre family income. They give everything to their children or those adults who bring home a pay packet. As a result malnutrition among women is increasing at an alarming rate and their frequent pregnancies represent a superhuman physical achievement.

Women's valiant achievements in defending life and survival are not acknowledged by society. The efforts of women's organisations, whether it be communal kitchens, the glass-of-milk committees [milk distribution among the poor] or health services don't get the appropriate social esteem. The social value of women cannot be calculated. Perhaps in years to come the fate of millions of women who sacrifice everything to support the children and youth of Peru and other countries in Latin America will be acknowledged. We should not ignore the fact that violence of every form...goes hand-in-hand with the difficult situation I have described.[1] It's nothing new for women because the open wounds of sexual violence, abuse at home and the contempt of this *machista* culture, have always featured in our lives and our mothers' lives. The challenge is to prevent these from also affecting our future generations.

AND THE FUTURE?

The neo-liberal offensive is international and demands international opposition strategies combined with political proposals by new social forces which address women's problems. We want to change estimations of our worth and achieve society's acknowledgement of what has been belittled until now as "women's affairs." Such important decisions as the right to the termination of unwanted pregnancies can no longer be ignored on the political stage. We want our place in the political decision-making process; we want to have a say in all problems which concern the Peruvian people and the whole world. We want to be informed so as not to be deceived by those who are used to practising politics for a flock of sheep. This road will be difficult but at least we shall regain the strengths of socialism and create social alternatives which are aimed at changing the destructive technological order as well as eliminating the international division of labour and the sexual hierarchy inherent within it. In so doing we shall try to create democratic structures which include the people in the decision-making process. The barriers thrown up by formal representative structures must be overcome urgently. A new democracy should be founded as the basic prerequisite for the society of the future.

QUESTIONS FOR ANALYSIS

1. What is neo-liberalism?
2. According to Acosta, how does global economic integration fostered by neo-liberalism affect the lives of women as workers?
3. Acosta claims that indebtedness to foreign lenders leads to austerity measures. How does this impact families in poor countries?
4. What does Acosta advocate?

---

[1] In the last report of the Comisaria de mujeres in Lima (the only one in the country at present) 4,800 rapes were filed for 1990, of which 4,200 went to trial. The police commissioner, in reading the document, personally acknowledged the alarming social problem which is posed by the violence of men who are connected to their victims in some way and. which, indeed, persists throughout all levels of society.

Source: Gaby Küppers, ed., *Compañeras. Voices from the Latin American Women's Movement* (London: Latin American Bureau, 1994), 167–172.

Asian Transformation

Japan has few mineral resources and is dependent on oil imports, but the Japanese economy weathered the oil price shocks of the 1970s better than did the economies of Europe and the United States. In fact, Japan experienced a faster rate of economic growth in the 1970s and 1980s than did any other major developed economy, growing at about 10 percent a year. Average income also increased rapidly, overtaking that of the United States in 1986 and surpassing it in the 1990s.

There are some major differences between the Japanese and U.S. industrial models. During the American occupation, Japanese industrial conglomerates known as *zaibatsu* (see Chapter 28) were broken up. Although ownership of major industries became less concentrated as a result, new industrial alliances appeared. There are now six major **keiretsu°** each of which include a major bank and firms in industry, commerce, and construction tied together in an interlocking ownership structure. There are also minor keiretsu dominated by a major corporation, like Toyota, and including its major suppliers. These combinations of companies have close relationships with government. Government assistance in the form of tariffs and import regulations inhibiting foreign competition was crucial in the early stages of development of Japan's automobile and semiconductor industries, among others.

Through the 1970s and 1980s Japanese success at exporting manufactured goods produced huge trade surpluses with other nations, prompting the United States and the European Community to engage in tough negotiations to try to force open the Japanese market. These efforts had only limited success. In 1990 Japan's trade surplus with the rest of the world was double its size in 1985. Many experts assumed that Japan's competitive advantages would propel it past the United States as the world's preeminent industrial economy. But problems appeared at the end of the 1980s and have proved difficult to solve. Japanese housing and stock markets had become highly overvalued, in part because the large trade imbalances increased the monetary supply. Also, the close relationship of government, banks, and industries had led to speculation and corruption that undermined the nation's confidence. As the crisis deepened, the close relationships between industrial enterprises, government, and banks that had helped propel the postwar expansion proved to be a liability. These close ties propped up inefficient companies and made it next to impossible to write off a mountain of nonperforming loans.

The Japanese model of close cooperation between government and industry was imitated by a small number of Asian states in the 1970s. The most important was South Korea, which had a number of assets that helped promote economic development. The combination of inexpensive labor, strong technical education, and substantial domestic capital reserves allowed South Korea to overcome the devastation of the Korean War in little more than a decade. Despite large defense expenditures, South Korea developed heavy industries such as steel and shipbuilding as well as consumer industries such as automobiles and consumer electronics. Japanese investment and technology transfers accelerated this process. Led by four giant corporations, which accounted for nearly half of South Korea's gross domestic product (GDP) and produced a broad mix of goods, the Korean economy began to match Japanese economic growth rates by the 1980s. Hyundai, one of the four giant corporations, manufactured products ranging from supertankers and cars to electronics and housing.

Taiwan, Hong Kong, and Singapore also developed modern industrial and commercial economies. As a result of their rapid economic growth, these three nations and South Korea were often referred to as the **Asian Tigers.** Taiwan suffered a number of political reverses, including the loss of its United Nations seat to the People's Republic of China in 1971 and the withdrawal of diplomatic recognition by the United States. Nevertheless, it achieved remarkable economic progress. In contrast with South Korea, smaller, more specialized companies led development in Taiwan. Also, Taiwan was able to gain a foothold in the economy of the People's Republic of China while maintaining its traditional markets in the United States and South Asia. Between 1955 and 1990 Taiwan's per capita GDP increased from 10 percent of U.S. levels to 50 percent.

Hong Kong and Singapore—both small societies with extremely limited resources—also enjoyed rapid economic development. Singapore's initial economic takeoff was based on its busy port and on banking and commercial services. As capital accumulated in these profitable sectors, this society of around 3 million people diversified by building textile and electronics industries. Singapore's rate of growth in GDP was double that of Japan from 1970 to 1980. Hong Kong's economic prosperity was also tied to its port and to the development of banking and commercial services, which were increasingly involved with China's growing economy. Hong Kong developed a highly competitive industrial sector

---

keiretsu (kay-REHT-soo)

dominated by textile and consumer electronics production. Worried about Hong Kong's reintegration into the People's Republic of China in 1997, local capitalists moved significant amounts of capital to the United States, Canada, and elsewhere, slowing economic growth in Hong Kong.

These **newly industrialized economies (NIEs)** shared many characteristics that helped explain their rapid industrialization. All had disciplined and hardworking labor forces, and all invested heavily in education. For example, as early as 1980 Korea had as many engineering graduates as Germany, Britain, and Sweden combined. All had high rates of personal saving that allowed them to generously fund investment in new technology. In 1987 the saving rates in Taiwan and South Korea were three times higher than in the United States. All emphasized outward-looking export strategies. And, like Japan, these dynamic Pacific Rim economies benefited from government sponsorship and protection. They were also beneficiaries of the extraordinary expansion in world trade and international communication that permitted technology to be disseminated more rapidly than at any time in the past. As a result, newly industrializing nations began with current technologies.

China Rejoins the World Economy

In China after Mao Zedong's death in 1976 the communist leadership introduced comprehensive economic reforms that relaxed state control of the economy, allowing more initiative and permitting individuals to accumulate wealth. Beginning in 1978 the Communist Party in Sichuan province freed more than six thousand firms to compete for business outside the state planning process. The results were remarkable. Under China's leader **Deng Xiaoping°** these reforms were expanded across the nation. China also began to permit foreign investment for the first time since the communists came to power in 1949. Between 1978 and the end of the 1990s foreign investors committed more than $180 billion to the Chinese economy, and McDonald's, Coca-Cola, Airbus, and other foreign companies began doing business there. But more than 100 million workers were still employed in state-owned enterprises, and most foreign-owned companies were segregated in special economic zones. The result was a dual industrial sector—one modern, efficient, and connected to international markets, the other dominated by government and directed by political decisions.

When Mao came to power in 1949, the meaning of the Chinese Revolution was made clear in the countryside, where collective ownership and organization were imposed. Deng Xiaoping did not privatize land, but he did permit the contracting of land to individuals and families, who were free to consume or sell whatever they produced. By 1984, 93 percent of China's agricultural land was in effect in private hands and producing for the market, tripling agricultural output.

Perhaps the best measure of the success of Deng's reforms is that between 1980 and 1993 China's per capita output more than doubled, averaging more than 8 percent growth per year, in comparison with the world average of slightly more than 1 percent and Japan's average of 3.3 percent. This growth was overwhelmingly the result of exports to the developed nations of the West, especially to the United States. Nevertheless, per capita measures of wealth indicated that China remained a poor nation. In the early 1990s China's per capita GDP was roughly the same as Mexico's, about $3,600 per year. By comparison, Taiwan had a per capita GDP of $14,700. What is clear is that economic reforms combined with massive investments and technology transfers from the United States and Japan to propel China into the twenty-first century as one of the world's major industrial powers.

Much of China's command economy remained in place, and the leadership of the Chinese Communist Party resisted serious political reform. Deng Xiaoping's strategy of balancing change and continuity, however, helped China avoid some of the social costs and political consequences experienced by Russia and other European socialist countries that abruptly embraced capitalism and democracy. As Chinese officials put it, China was "changing a big earthquake into a thousand tremors." The nation's leadership faced a major challenge in 1989. Responding to inflation and to worldwide mass movements in favor of democracy, Chinese students and intellectuals, many of whom had studied outside China, led a series of protests demanding more democracy and an end to inflation and corruption. This movement culminated in **Tiananmen° Square,** in the heart of Beijing. Hundreds of thousands of protesters gathered and refused to leave. After weeks of standoff, tanks pushed into the square, killing hundreds, perhaps thousands. Many more protestors were arrested. Although the Communist Party survived this challenge, it was not clear whether rapid economic growth, increasing inequality, high levels of unemployment, and

Deng Xiaoping (dung shee-yao-ping)

Tiananmen (tee-yehn-ahn-men)

massive migration from the countryside to the cities would ultimately trigger a political transformation.

The End of the Bipolar World, 1989–1991

After the end of World War II competition between the United States and the Soviet Union and their respective allies created a bipolar world. Every conflict, no matter how local its origins, had the potential of engaging the attention of one or both of the superpowers. The Korean War, decolonization in Africa, the Vietnam War, the Cuban Revolution, hostilities between Israel and its neighbors, and numerous other events increased tension between the superpowers, each armed with nuclear weapons. Given this succession of provocations, budgets within both blocs were dominated by defense expenditures, and political culture everywhere was dominated by arguments over the relative merits of the two competing economic and political systems.

Few in 1980 predicted the startling collapse of the Soviet Union and the socialist nations of the Warsaw Pact. Western observers tended to see communist nations as both more uniform in character and more subservient to the Soviet Union than was true. Long before the 1980s deep divisions had appeared among communist states. Yugoslavia broke with the Soviet Union in the 1940s; China actually fought a brief border war with the Soviet Union in the 1960s; and the government of newly unified communist Vietnam invaded communist Cambodia in the 1970s. But in general, the once-independent nations and ethnic groups that had been brought within the Soviet Union seemed securely transformed by the experiences and institutions of communism. By 1990, however, nationalism was resurgent, and communism was nearly finished (see the discussion of the Balkans in Chapter 33).

Crisis in the Soviet Union

Under U.S. President Ronald Reagan and the Soviet Union's General Secretary Leonid Brezhnev°, the rhetoric of the Cold War remained intense. Massive new U.S. investments in armaments, including a space-based missile

protection system that never became operational, placed heavy burdens on the Soviet economy, which was unable to absorb the cost of developing similar weapons. Soviet economic problems were systemic; shortages of food, consumer goods, and housing were an ongoing part of Soviet life. Obsolete industrial plants and centralized planning that stifled initiative and responsiveness to market demand led to a declining standard of living relative to the West. Government bureaucrats and Communist Party favorites received special privileges, including permission to shop in stores that stocked Western goods, but the average citizen faced long lines and waiting lists for goods. Soviet citizens contrasted their lot with the free and prosperous life of the West depicted in the increasingly accessible Western media. The arbitrariness of the bureaucracy, the cynical manipulation of information, and deprivations created a generalized crisis in morale.

Despite the unpopularity of the war in Afghanistan and growing discontent, Brezhnev refused to modify his rigid and unsuccessful policies. But he was unable to contain an underground current of protest. In a series of powerful books, the writer Alexander Solzhenitzyn° castigated the Soviet system and particularly the Stalinist prison camps. He won a Nobel Prize in literature but was charged with treason and expelled from the country in 1974. Self-published underground writings (*samizdat°*) by critics of the regime circulated widely despite government efforts to suppress them. The physicist Andrei Sakharov and his wife Yelena Bonner protested the nuclear arms race and human rights violations and were condemned to banishment within the country. Some Jewish dissidents spoke out against anti-Semitism, and many more left for Israel and the United States.

By the time **Mikhail Gorbachev°** took up the reins of the Soviet government in 1985, weariness with war in Afghanistan, economic decay, and vocal protest had reached critical levels. Casting aside Brezhnev's hard line, Gorbachev authorized major reforms in an attempt to stave off total collapse. His policy of political openness (*glasnost*) permitted criticism of the government and the Communist Party. His policy of **perestroika°** ("restructuring") was an attempt to address long-suppressed economic problems by moving away from central state planning and toward a more open economic system. In 1989 he ended the war in Afghanistan, which had cost many lives and much money.

Solzhenitzen (sol-zhuh-NEET-sin)
samizdat (sah-meez-DAHT)   Gorbachev (GORE-beh-CHOF)
perestroika (per-ih-STROY-kuh)

Leonid Brezhnev (leh-oh-NEED BREZ-nef)

The Collapse of the Socialist Bloc

Events in eastern Europe were important in forcing change on the Soviet Union. In 1980 protests by Polish shipyard workers in the city of Gdansk led to the formation of **Solidarity,** a labor union that soon enrolled 9 million members. The Roman Catholic Church in Poland, strengthened by the elevation of a Pole, Karol Wojtyla°, to the papacy as John Paul II in 1978, gave strong moral support to the protest movement.

The Polish government imposed martial law in 1981 in response to the growing power of Solidarity and its allies, giving the army effective political control. Seeing Solidarity under tight controls and many of its leaders in prison, the Soviet Union decided not to intervene. But Solidarity remained a potent force with a strong institutional structure and nationally recognized leaders. As Gorbachev loosened political controls in the Soviet Union after 1985, communist leaders elsewhere lost confidence in Soviet resolve, and critics and reformers in Poland and throughout eastern Europe were emboldened (see Map 32.1).

Beleaguered Warsaw Pact governments vacillated between relaxation of control and suppression of dissent. Just as the Catholic clergy in Poland had supported Solidarity, Protestant and Orthodox religious leaders aided the rise of opposition groups elsewhere. This combination of nationalism and religion provided a powerful base for opponents of the communist regimes. Threatened by these forces, communist governments sought to quiet opposition by seeking solutions to their severe economic problems. They turned to the West for trade and financial assistance. They also opened their nations to travelers, ideas, styles, and money from Western countries, all of which accelerated the demand for change.

By the end of 1989 communist governments across eastern Europe had fallen. The dismantling of the Berlin Wall, the symbol of a divided Europe and the bipolar world, vividly represented this transformation. Communist leaders in Poland, Hungary, Czechoslovakia, and Bulgaria decided that change was inevitable and initiated political reforms. In Romania the dictator Nicolae Ceausescu° refused to surrender power, thus provoking a rebellion that ended with his arrest and execution. The comprehensiveness of these changes became clear in 1990, when Solidarity leader Lech Walesa° was elected

---

Karol Wojtyla (KAH-rol voy-TIL-ah) **Nicolae Ceausescu** (neh-koh-LIE chow-SHES-koo) **Lech Walesa** (leck wah-LESS-ah)
Vaclav Havel (vah-SLAV hah-VEL)

The Fall of the Berlin Wall The Berlin Wall was the most important symbol of the Cold War. Constructed to keep residents of East Germany from fleeing to the West and defended by armed guards and barbed wire, for many in the West it was the public face of communism. As the Soviet system fell apart, the residents of East and West Berlin broke down sections of the wall. Here young people straddle the wall, signaling the end of an era. (Bossu Regis/Corbis Sygma)

president of Poland and dissident playwright Vaclav Havel° was elected president of Czechoslovakia.

Following the fall of the Berlin Wall, a tidal wave of patriotic enthusiasm swept aside the once-formidable communist government of East Germany. In the chaotic months that followed, East Germans crossed to West Germany in large numbers, and government services in the eastern sector nearly disappeared. Some Europeans recalled German militarism earlier in the century and worried about reunification. But there was little concrete opposition, and in 1990 Germany was reunified. Numerous problems followed reunification, including high levels of unemployment and budget deficits, but nearly fifty years of confrontation and tension across the heart of Europe seemed to end overnight.

Soviet leaders looked on with dismay at the collapse of communism in the Warsaw Pact countries. They knew

Map 32.1   The End of Soviet Domination in Eastern Europe   The creation of new countries out of Yugoslavia and Czechoslovakia and the reunification of Germany marked the most complicated changes of national borders since World War I. The Czech Republic and Slovakia separated peacefully, but Slovenia, Croatia, Macedonia, and Bosnia and Herzegovina achieved independence only after bitter fighting.

that similarly powerful nationalist sentiments existed within the Soviet Union as well. The year 1990 brought declarations of independence by Lithuania, Estonia, and Latvia, three small states on the Baltic Sea that the Soviet Union had annexed in 1939. Violent ethnic strife soon erupted in the Caucasus region. Gorbachev tried to accommodate the rising pressures for change, but the tide was running too fast.

The end of the Soviet Union came suddenly in 1991 (see Map 32.2). After communist hardliners botched a poorly conceived coup against Gorbachev, disgust with communism boiled over. Boris Yeltsin, the president of the Russian Republic and longtime member of the Communist Party, led popular resistance to the coup in Moscow and emerged as the most powerful leader in the country. Russia, the largest republic in the Soviet Union,

was effectively taking the place of the disintegrating USSR. With the central government scarcely functioning, nationalism, long repressed by Soviet authorities, reappeared throughout the Soviet Union. In September 1991 the Congress of People's Deputies—the central legislature of the USSR, long subservient to the Communist Party—voted to dissolve the union. In December a loose successor organization with little central control, the Commonwealth of Independent States (CIS), was created. The same month Mikhail Gorbachev resigned.

The ethnic and religious passions that fueled the breakup of the Soviet Union soon challenged the survival of Yugoslavia and Czechoslovakia. The dismemberment of Yugoslavia began with declarations of independence in Slovenia and Croatia in 1991. Two years later Czechoslovakia peacefully divided into the Czech

Map 32.2   The End of the Soviet Union   When Communist hardliners failed to overthrow Gorbachev in 1991, popular anticommunist sentiment swept the Soviet Union. Following Boris Yeltsin's lead in Russia, the republics that constituted the Soviet Union declared their independence.

Republic and Slovakia. East Germany was reunited with West Germany with little violence, but destructive ethnic and religious conflict characterized the transitional period in Armenia, Georgia, and Chechnya as well as the breakup of Yugoslavia (see Chapter 33).

The Persian Gulf War, 1990–1991

The first significant conflict to occur after the breakup of the Soviet Union and the end of the Cold War was the Persian Gulf War. The immediate causes were local and bilateral. Iraq's ruler, Saddam Husain, had borrowed a great deal of money from neighboring Kuwait and sought unsuccessfully to get Kuwait's royal family to reduce the size of this debt. He was also eager to gain control of Kuwait's oil fields. Husain believed that the smaller and militarily weaker nation could be quickly defeated, and he suspected, as a result of a conversation with an American

diplomat, that the United States would not react. The invasion came in August 1990.

The United States convinced the government of Saudi Arabia that it was a possible target of Iraq's aggression. Saudi Arabia, an important regional ally of the United States and a major oil producer, was the key to any military action by the United States. The United States and its allies concentrated an imposing military force of 500,000 in the region. With his intention to use force endorsed by the United Nations and with many Islamic nations supporting military action, President George H. W. Bush ordered an attack in early 1991. Iraq proved incapable of countering the sophisticated weaponry of the coalition. The missiles and bombs of the United States destroyed not only military targets but also "relegated [Iraq] to a pre-industrial age," the United Nations reported after the war. Although Iraq's military defeat was comprehensive, Husain remained in power, and the country was not occupied. In fact Husain crushed an uprising in the months following this defeat. The United States and its key allies then imposed "no-fly" zones that denied Iraq's military aircraft access to the northern and southern regions of the country. As a result, military tensions and periodic armed confrontations continued.

In the United States the results were interpreted to mean that the U.S. military defeat in the Vietnam War could be forgotten and that U.S. military capability was unrivaled. Unable to deter military action by the U.S.-led coalition or to meaningfully influence the diplomacy that surrounded the war, Russia had been of little use to its former ally Iraq, and its impotence was clear.

THE CHALLENGE OF POPULATION GROWTH

For most of human history population growth was viewed as beneficial, and human beings were seen as a source of wealth. Since the late eighteenth century, however, population increases have been viewed with increasing alarm. At first it was feared that food supplies could not keep up with population growth. Then social critics expressed concern that growing population would lead to class and ethnic struggle as numbers overwhelmed resources. By the second half of the twentieth century population growth was increasingly seen as a threat to the environment. Are urban sprawl, pollution, and soil erosion inevitable results of population growth? The questions and debates continue today, but clearly population is both a cause and a result of increased global interdependency.

Demographic Transition

The population of Europe almost doubled between 1850 and 1914, putting enormous pressure on rural land and urban housing and overwhelming fragile public institutions that provided some crisis assistance (see Chapter 26). This dramatic growth forced a large wave of immigration across the Atlantic, helping to develop North and South America and invigorating the Atlantic economy (see Chapter 23). Population growth also contributed to Europe's Industrial Revolution by lowering labor costs and increasing consumer demand.

Educated Europeans of the nineteenth century were ambivalent about the rapid increase in human population. Some saw it as a blessing that would promote economic well-being. Others warned that the seemingly relentless increase would bring disaster. The best-known pessimist was the English cleric **Thomas Malthus,** who in 1798 argued convincingly that unchecked population growth would outstrip food production. When Malthus looked at Europe's future, he used a prejudiced image of China to terrify his European readers. A visitor to China, he claimed, "will not be surprised that mothers destroy or expose many of their children; that parents sell their daughters for a trifle; . . . and that there should be such a number of robbers. The surprise is that nothing still more dreadful should happen."[2]

The generation that came of age in the years immediately following World War II inherited a world in which the views of Malthus were casually dismissed. Industrial and agricultural productivity had multiplied supplies of food and other necessities. Cultural changes associated with expanded female employment, older age at marriage, and more effective family planning had combined to slow the rate of population increase. And by the late 1960s Europe and other industrial societies had made what was called the **demographic transition** to lower fertility rates (average number of births per woman) and reduced mortality. The number of births in the developed nations was just adequate for the maintenance of current population levels. Thus many experts argued that the population growth then occurring in developing nations was a short-term phenomenon that would be ended by the combination of economic and social changes that had altered European patterns.

By the late 1970s, however, the demographic transition had not occurred in the Third World, and the issue of population growth had become politicized. The leaders of some developing nations actively promoted large families, arguing that larger populations would increase national power. These arguments remained a persistent part of the debate between developed and developing nations. Industrialized, mostly white, nations raised concerns about rapid population growth in Asia, Africa, and Latin America. Populist political leaders in those regions asked whether these concerns were not fundamentally racist.

The question exposed the influence of racism in the population debate and temporarily disarmed Western advocates of birth control. However, once the economic shocks of the 1970s and 1980s revealed the vulnerability of developing economies, governments in the developing world jettisoned policies that promoted population growth. Mexico is a good example. In the 1970s the government had encouraged high fertility, and population growth rose to 3 percent per year. By the 1980s Mexico rejected these policies and promoted birth control, with the result that annual population growth fell to 2.3 percent.

Chinese Family–Planning Campaign   Hoping to slow population growth, the Chinese government has sought to limit parents to a single child. Billboards and other forms of mass advertising have been an essential part of the campaign to gain compliance with national family-planning directives.   (Picard/Sipa Press)

World population exploded in the twentieth century (see Table 32.1). Although there are indications that rates of growth are currently slowing, world population still increases by a number equal to the total population of the United States every three years. If fertility rates across the globe remain unchanged, world population will reach 256 billion in 2150, twenty-eight times the 2050 projection found in Table 32.1.

This is not likely. Fertility is already declining in some developing areas. Mortality rates have also increased in some areas as immigration, commercial expansion, and improved transportation facilitate the transmission of disease. The rapid spread of HIV/AIDS is an example of this phenomenon. Less-developed regions with poorly funded public health institutions and with few resources to invest in prevention and treatment experience the highest rates of infection and the greatest mortality. In Russia, for example, new HIV infections rose from under five thousand in 1997 to over ninety thousand in 2001. AIDS has spread at a similar pace in China. But the disease has developed most quickly and with the most devastating results in Africa, the home of 28 million of the world's 40 million infected people.

Unlike population growth in the eighteenth and nineteenth centuries, when much of the increase occurred in the wealthiest nations, population growth at the end of the twentieth century was overwhelmingly in the poorest nations. Although fertility rates dropped in most developing nations, they remained much higher than rates in the industrialized nations. At the same time, improvements in hygiene and medical treatment caused mortality rates to fall, despite recent catastrophies, such as HIV/AIDS. The result has been rapid population growth.

The Industrialized Nations

In the developed industrial nations of western Europe and in Japan at the beginning of the twenty-first century, fertility levels are so low that population will fall unless immigration increases. Japanese women have an average of 1.39 children; in Italy the number is 1.2. Although Sweden tries to promote fertility with cash payments, tax incentives, and job leaves to families with children, the average number of births per

Table 32.1   Population for World and Major Areas, 1750–2050

Population Size (Millions)

Major Area	1750	1800	1850	1900	1950	1995	(estimated) 2050
World	791	978	1,262	1,650	2,521	5,666	8,909
Africa	106	107	111	133	221	697	1,766
Asia	502	635	809	947	1,402	3,437	5,268
Europe	163	203	276	408	547	728	628
Latin America and the Caribbean	16	24	38	74	167	480	809
North America	2	7	26	82	172	297	392
Oceania	2	2	2	6	13	28	46

Percentage Distribution

Major Area	1750	1800	1850	1900	1950	1995	(estimated) 2050
World	100	100	100	100	100	100	100
Africa	13.4	10.9	8.8	8.1	8.8	12	19.8
Asia	63.5	64.9	64.1	57.4	55.6	61	59.1
Europe	20.6	20.8	21.9	24.7	21.7	13	7.0
Latin America and the Caribbean	2.0	2.5	3.0	4.5	6.6	8	9.1
North America	0.3	0.7	2.1	5.0	6.8	5	4.4
Oceania	0.3	0.2	0.2	0.4	0.5	1	0.5

Source: J. D. Durand, "Historical Estimates of World Population: An Evaluation" (Philadelphia: University of Pennsylvania, Population Studies Center, 1974, mimeographed); United Nations, *The Determinants and Consequences of Population Trends*, vol. 1 (New York: United Nations, 1973); United Nations, *World Population Prospects as Assessed in 1963* (New York: United Nations, 1966); United Nations, *World Population Prospects: The 1998 Revision* (New York: United Nations, forthcoming); United Nations Population Division, Department of Economic and Social Affairs, http://www.popin.org/pop1998/4.htm.

woman has fallen to 1.4 in recent years. The low fertility found in mature industrial nations is tied to higher levels of female education and employment, the material values of consumer culture, and access to contraception and abortion. Educated women now defer marriage and child rearing until they are established in careers. An Italian woman in Bologna, the city with the lowest fertility in the world, put it this way: "I'm an only child and if I could, I'd have more than one child. But most couples I know wait until their 30's to have children. People want to have their own life, they want to have a successful career. When you see life in these terms, children are an impediment."[3]

In industrialized nations life expectancy has improved as fertility has declined. The combination of abundant food, improved hygiene, and more effective medicines and medical care has lengthened human lives. In 2000 about 20 percent of the population in the more-developed nations was sixty-five or over. By 2050 this proportion should rise to one-third. Italy soon will have more than twenty adults fifty years old or over for each five-year-old child. Because of higher fertility and greater levels of immigration, the United States is mov-

ing in this direction more slowly than western Europe; by 2050 the median age in Europe will be fifty-two, while it will be thirty-five in the United States.

The combination of falling fertility and rising life expectancy in the industrialized nations presents a challenge very different from the one foreseen by Malthus. These nations generally offer a broad array of social services, including retirement income, medical services, and housing supplements for the elderly. As the number of retirees increases relative to the number of people who are employed, the costs of these services may become unsustainable. Economists track this problem using the PSR (potential support ratio). This is the ratio of persons fifteen to sixty-four years old (likely workers) to persons sixty-five or older (likely retirees). Between 1950 and 2000 the world's PSR fell from twelve to nine. By 2050 it will fall to four. Clearly, nations with the oldest populations, especially Japan and the nations of western Europe, will have to reexamine programs that encourage early retirement as the ratio of workers to retirees drops.

In Russia and other former socialist nations, current birthrates are now actually lower than death rates—

levels inadequate to sustain the current population size. Birthrates were already low before the collapse of the socialist system and have contracted further with recent economic problems. Since 1975 fertility rates have fallen between 20 and 40 percent across the former Soviet bloc. By the early 1980s abortions were as common as births in much of eastern Europe.

Life expectancy has also fallen. Life expectancy for Russian men is now only fifty-seven years, down almost ten years since 1980. In the Czech Republic, Hungary, and Poland, life expectancy is improving in response to improved economic conditions, but most of the rest of eastern Europe has experienced the Russian pattern of declining life expectancy. High unemployment, low incomes, food shortages, and the dismantling of the social welfare system of the communist era have all contributed to this decline.

The Developing Nations

Even if the industrialized nations decided to promote an increase in family size in the twenty-first century, they would continue to fall behind the developing nations as a percentage of world population. At current rates 95 percent of all future population growth will be in developing nations (see Map 32.3 and Table 32.1). A comparison between Europe and Africa illustrates these changes. In 1950 Europe had twice the population of Africa. By 1985 Africa's population had drawn even with Europe's. According to projections, Africa's population will be three times larger than Europe's by 2025. Given the performance of African economies, future generations of Africans will likely experience increased famine, epidemics, and social breakdown.

As the 1990s ended other developing regions had rapid population growth as well. While all developing nations had an average birthrate of 33.6 per thousand inhabitants, Muslim countries had a rate of 42.1. This rate is more than 300 percent higher than the 13.1 births per thousand in the developed nations of the West. The populations of Latin America and Asia were also expanding dramatically, but at rates slower than sub-Saharan Africa and the Muslim nations. Latin America's population increased from 165 million in 1950 to 405 million in 1985 and is projected to reach 778 million in 2025, despite declining birthrates.

In Asia, the populations of India and China continued to grow despite government efforts to reduce family size. Today these two nations account for roughly one-third of the world's population. In China efforts to enforce a limit of one child per family led to large-scale female infanticide as rural families sought to produce male heirs. India's policies of forced sterilization created widespread outrage and led to the electoral defeat of the ruling Congress Party. Yet both countries achieved some successes. Between 1960 and 1982 India's birthrate fell from 48 to 34 per thousand, while China's rate declined even more sharply—from 39 to 19 per thousand. Still, by 2025 both China, which today has 1.13 billion people, and India, with 853 million, will each reach 1.5 billion.

It is unclear whether the nations of Asia, Africa, and Latin America will undergo the lowered fertility and mortality rates experienced in the West during the Industrial Revolution. Yet real progress has occurred, and fertility rates have fallen where women have had access to education and employment outside the home.

Old and Young Populations

Population pyramids generated by demographers clearly illustrate the profound transformation in human reproductive patterns and life expectancy in the years since World War II. Figure 32.1 shows the 2001 age distributions in Pakistan, South Korea, and Sweden—nations at three different stages of economic development. Sweden is a mature industrial nation. South Korea is rapidly industrializing and has surpassed many European nations in both industrial output and per capita wealth. Pakistan is a poor, traditional Muslim nation with rudimentary industrialization, low educational levels, and little effective family planning.

In 2001 nearly 50 percent of Pakistan's population was under age sixteen. The resulting pressures on the economy have been extraordinary. Every year approximately 150,000 men reach age sixty-five—and another 1.2 million turn sixteen. Pakistan, therefore, has to create more than a million new jobs a year or face steadily growing unemployment and steadily declining wages. Sweden confronts a different problem. Sweden's aging population, growing demand for social welfare benefits, and declining labor pool means that its industries may become less competitive and living standards may decline. In South Korea, a decline in fertility dramatically altered the ratio of children to adults, creating an age distribution similar to that of western Europe earlier in the twentieth century. South Korea does not face Pakistan's impossible task of creating new jobs or Sweden's growing demands for welfare benefits for the aged.

The demographic challenges faced by Sweden and other developed nations are less daunting than those confronting the developing nations. Poor nations must overcome shortages of investment capital, poor transportation and communication networks, and low educational levels while they struggle to create jobs. Wealthy,

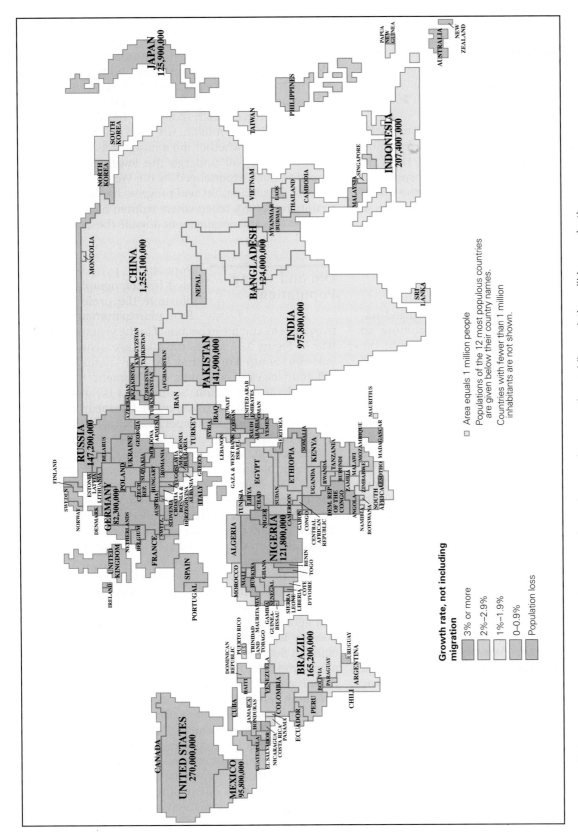

Map 32.3 World Population Growth At current rates of growth, every three years the world's population will increase by the equivalent of a nation the size of the United States. Most of this population increase will be in some of the world's poorest nations. By 2050, for example, Pakistan, a nation of only 40 million in 1950, will surpass the United States and become the country with the world's third largest population. *Source:* National Geographic Maps 1998/10 Map Supplement Population Growth. Used by permission of National Geographic Society.

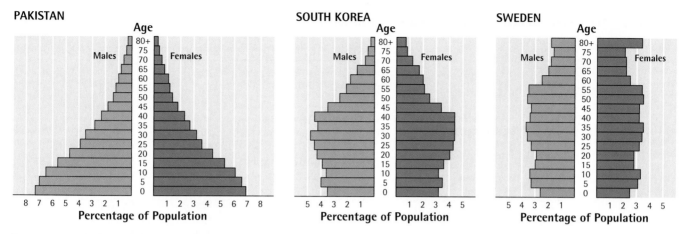

PAKISTAN

SOUTH KOREA

SWEDEN

Figure 32.1 Age Structure Comparison: Islamic Nation (Pakistan), Non-Islamic Developing Nation (South Korea), and Developed Nation (Sweden), 2001 *Source:* U.S. Bureau of the Census, *International Database*, 2001.

well-educated, and politically stable nations can invest in robots and other new technologies to reduce labor needs and increase industrial and agricultural efficiency as their populations age.

The demographic problem and potential technological adjustments are most clearly visible in Japan. Japan has the oldest population in the world, with a current median age of forty-one. Large numbers of young immigrants from poorer nations are entering the work forces of Canada, Germany, the United States, and most other industrialized nations, slowing the aging of these populations. Japan has resisted immigration, instead investing heavily in technological solutions to the problems created by its aging labor force. As of 1994 Japan had 75 percent of the world's industrial robots. Although Japanese industries are able to produce more goods with fewer workers, Japan will still face long-term increases in social welfare payments.

UNEQUAL DEVELOPMENT AND THE MOVEMENT OF PEOPLES

Two characteristics of the postwar world should now be clear. First, despite decades of experimentation with state-directed economic development, most nations that were poor in 1960 were as poor or poorer in 2003. The only exceptions were a few rapidly developing Asian industrial nations and an equally small number of oil-exporting nations. Second, world population increased to startlingly high levels, and most of the increase was in the poorest nations.

The combination of intractable poverty and growing population generated a surge in international immigration. Few issues stirred more controversy. Even moderate voices sometimes framed the discussion of immigration as a competition among peoples. One commentator analyzed the situation this way: "As the better-off families of the northern hemisphere individually decide that having only one or at the most two children is sufficient, they may not recognize that they are in a small way vacating future space (that is, jobs, parts of inner cities, shares of population, shares of market preferences) to faster-growing ethnic groups both inside and outside their boundaries. But that, in fact, is what they are doing."[4]

Large numbers of legal and illegal immigrants from poor nations with growing populations are entering the developed industrial nations, with the exception of Japan. Large-scale migrations within developing countries are a related phenomenon. The movement of impoverished rural residents to the cities of Asia, Africa, and Latin America (see Map 32.3 and Table 32.2) has increased steadily since the 1970s. This internal migration often serves as the first step toward migration abroad.

The Problem of Growing Inequality

Since 1945 global economic productivity has expanded more rapidly than at any other time in the past. Faster, cheaper communications and transportation have combined with improvements in industrial and agricultural technologies to create material abundance that would have amazed those who experienced the first Industrial Revolution (see Chapter 22). Despite this remarkable economic expansion and

Table 32.2 The World's Largest Metropolitan Areas (Population of 10 Million or More)

City	1950	City	1975	City	2000	City	2015
1 New York	12.3	1 Tokyo	19.8	1 Tokyo	26.4	1 Tokyo	26.4
		2 New York	15.9	2 Mexico City	18.1	2 Bombay	26.1
		3 Shanghai	11.4	3 Bombay	18.1	3 Lagos	23.2
		4 Mexico City	11.2	4 Sao Paulo	17.8	4 Dhaka	21.1
		5 Sao Paulo	10.0	5 New York	16.6	5 Sao Paulo	20.4
				6 Lagos	13.4	6 Karachi	19.2
				7 Los Angeles	13.1	7 Mexico City	19.2
				8 Calcutta	12.9	8 New York	17.4
				9 Shanghai	12.9	9 Jakarta	17.3
				10 Buenos Aires	12.6	10 Calcutta	17.3
				11 Dhaka	12.3	11 Delhi	16.8
				12 Karachi	11.8	12 Metro Manila	14.8
				13 Delhi	11.7	13 Shanghai	14.6
				14 Jakarta	11.0	14 Los Angeles	14.1
				15 Osaka	11.0	15 Buenos Aires	14.1
				16 Metro Manila	10.9	16 Cairo	13.8
				17 Beijing	10.8	17 Istanbul	12.5
				18 Rio de Janeiro	10.6	18 Beijing	12.3
				19 Cairo	10.6	19 Rio de Janeiro	11.9
						20 Osaka	11.0
						21 Tianjin	10.7
						22 Hyderabad	10.5
						23 Bangkok	10.1

Source: International Migration Report 2002, United Nations, Department of Economic and Social Affairs, Population Division, "World Urbanization Prospects: The 1999 Revision," p. 6. Reprinted by permission of United States Publications.

growing market integration, the majority of the world's population remains in poverty. The industrialized nations of the Northern Hemisphere now enjoy a larger share of the world's wealth than they did a century ago. The United States, Japan, and the nations of the European Union alone accounted for a startling 74 percent of the world's economy in 1998. The thousands of homeless street children who live among the gleaming glass and steel towers of Rio's banking district, on the other hand, can be seen as a metaphor for the social consequences of postwar economic development.

The gap between rich and poor nations has grown much wider since 1945. But among both groups dramatic changes have resulted from changes in competitiveness, technology transfers, and market conditions. In 2001 Luxemburg and Switzerland had the highest per capita GNI (gross national income)—$39,840 and $35,630, respectively; the U.S. figure was $34,280; and Greece, the poorest nation in the European Union, had a per capita GNI of $11,430. The nations of the former Soviet Union and eastern Europe have per capita GNIs

lower than some developing nations in the Third World. Russia's per capita GNI was $1,750 in 2001, less than Mexico's $5,530, Brazil's $3,070, and South Africa's 2,820, but higher than Bolivia's $950 and the Philippines' $1,030. Among other developing economies, Algeria and Thailand had per capita GNIs of $1,650 and $1,940 respectively. Nigeria, India, and China had GNIs below $1,000. One billion of the world's people, approximately 20 percent, lived on less than $500 a year in 2001. This poverty was concentrated in Africa, Latin America, and Asia.

Wealth inequality within nations also grew. Regions tied to new technologies that provided competitive advantages became wealthier, while other regions lost ground. In the United States, for example, the South and Southwest grew richer in the last three decades relative to the older industrial regions of the Midwest. Regional inequalities also appeared in developing nations. Generally, capital cities such Buenos Aires, Argentina, and Lagos, Nigeria, attracted large numbers of migrants from rural areas because they offered more opportunities,

Garbage Dump in Manila, Philippines   Garbage pickers are a common feature of Third World urban development. Thousands of poor families in nearly every Third World city sort and sell bottles, aluminum cans, plastic, and newspapers to provide household income.   (Geoff Tompkinson/Aspect Picture Library Ltd.)

even if those opportunities could not compare to the ones available in developed nations.

Even in the industrialized world, people were divided into haves and have-nots. The tax reform program put in place during the presidency of Ronald Reagan (served 1981–1989) led to greater wealth inequality in the United States. This trend continued to the present, driven by the stock market boom of the 1990s and another round of tax reforms under President George W. Bush (elected 2001). Wealth inequality is now as great as on the eve of the 1929 stock market crash. Although this trend slowed in the 1990s, the households that make up the wealthiest 5 percent of American society are now relatively richer than at any time in the past. Scholars estimate that the wealthiest 1 percent of households in the United States control more than 30 percent of the nation's total wealth, while the poorest households have average incomes of under $5,000. Even in Europe, where tax and inheritance laws redistributed wealth, unemployment, homelessness, and substandard housing have become increasingly common.

Internal Migration: The Growth of Cities

In developing nations migration from rural areas to urban centers increased threefold between 1925 and 1950, and the pace accelerated after that (see Table 32.2). Shantytowns around major cities in developing nations are commonly seen as signs of social breakdown and economic failure. Nevertheless, city life was generally better than life in the countryside. A World Bank study estimated that three out of four migrants to cities made economic gains. Residents of cities in sub-Saharan Africa, for example, were six times more likely than rural residents to have safe water. An unskilled migrant from the depressed northeast of Brazil could triple his or her income by moving to Rio de Janeiro.

However, as the scale of rural-to-urban migration grew, these benefits proved more elusive. In many West African cities, basic services were crumbling under the pressure of rapid population growth. In 1990 in Mexico City, one of the world's largest cities, more than thirty thousand people lived in garbage dumps, where they scavenged for food and clothing. Worsening conditions and the threat of crime and political instability led many governments to try to slow migration to cities and, in some cases, to return people to the countryside. Indonesia, for example, has relocated more than a half-million urban residents since 1969. Despite some successes with slowing the rate of internal migration, nearly every poor nation still faces the challenge of rapidly growing cities.

Global Migration

Each year hundreds of thousands of men and women leave the developing world to emigrate to industrialized nations. After 1960 this movement increased in scale, and ethnic and racial tensions in the host nations worsened. Political refugees and immigrants faced murderous violence in Germany; growing anti-immigrant sentiment led to a new right-wing political movement in France; and an expanded border patrol attempted to more effectively seal the U.S. border with Mexico. By the 1990s levels of immigration posed daunting social and cultural challenges for both host nations and immigrants.

Immigrants from the developing nations brought host nations many of the same benefits that the great migration of Europeans to the Americas provided a century earlier (see Chapter 23). Many European nations actively promoted guest worker programs and other inducements to immigration in the 1960s, when an expanding European economy first confronted labor shortages. However, attitudes toward immigrants changed as the size of the immigrant population grew and as European economies slowed in the 1980s. Facing higher levels of unemployment, native-born workers saw immigrants as competitors willing to work for lower wages and less likely to support labor unions. However, because cultural and ethnic characteristics have traditionally formed the basis of national identity in many European countries (see Chapter 26), worsening relations between immigrants and the native-born may have been inevitable. Put simply, many Germans are unable to think of the German-born son or daughter of Turkish immigrants as a German.

Because immigrants are generally young adults and commonly retain positive attitudes toward early marriage and large families dominant in their native cultures, immigrants in Europe and the United States have tended to have higher fertility rates than do host populations. In Germany in 1975, for example, immigrants made up only 7 percent of the population but accounted for nearly 15 percent of all births. Although immigrant fertility rates decline with prolonged residence in industrialized societies, the family size of second-generation immigrants is still larger than that of the host population. Therefore, even without additional immigration, immigrant groups grow faster than longer-established populations. The fertility of the Hispanic population in the United States, for example, is lower than the rates in Mexico and other Latin American nations. Nevertheless, Hispanic groups will contribute well over 20 percent of all population growth in the United States during the next twenty-five years.

As the Muslim population in Europe and the Asian and Latin American populations in the United States expand in the twenty-first century, cultural conflicts will test definitions of citizenship and nationality. The United States will have some advantages in meeting these challenges because of long experience with immigration and relatively open access to citizenship. Yet in the 1990s the United States was moving slowly in the direction of restricting immigration and defending a culturally conservative definition of nationality.

TECHNOLOGICAL AND ENVIRONMENTAL CHANGE

Technological innovation powered the economic expansion that began after World War II. New technologies increased productivity and disseminated human creativity. They also altered the way people lived, worked, and played. Because most of the economic benefits were concentrated in the advanced industrialized nations, technology increased the power of those nations relative to the developing world. Even within developed nations, postwar technological innovations did not benefit all classes, industries, and regions equally. There were losers as well as winners.

Population growth and increased levels of migration and urbanization led to the global expansion of agricultural and industrial production. This multiplication of farms and factories intensified environmental threats. At the end of the twentieth century loss of rain forest, soil erosion, global warming, air and water pollution, and extinction of species threatened the quality of life and the survival of human societies. Here again, differences between nations were apparent. Environmental protection, like the acquisition of new technology, had progressed most in societies with the greatest economic resources.

New Technologies and the World Economy

Nuclear energy, jet engines, radar, and tape recording were among the many World War II developments that later had an impact on consumers' lives. When applied to industry, new technology increased productivity, reduced labor requirements, and improved the flow of information that made markets more efficient. Pent-up demand for consumer goods also spurred new research and the development of new technologies. As the Western economies recovered from the war and incomes rose, consumers wanted new products that reduced their workloads or provided entertainment. The consumer electronics industry rapidly developed new products, changes that can be summarized by the music industry's movement from vinyl records to 8-tracks, tapes, CDs, and MP3 technologies.

Improvements in existing technologies accounted for much of the developed world's productivity increases during the 1950s and 1960s. Larger and faster trucks, trains, and airplanes cut transportation costs. Both capitalist and socialist governments built highway systems, improved railroad tracks, and constructed airports. Governments also bore much of the cost of developing and constructing nuclear power plants.

No technology had greater significance than the computer. The first computers were expensive, large, and slow. Only large corporations, governments, and universities could afford them. But by the mid-1980s desktop computers had replaced typewriters in most of the developed world's offices, and the technology continued to advance. Each new generation of computers was smaller, faster, and more powerful than the one before (see Environment and Technology: The Personal Computer).

Computers also altered manufacturing. Small dedicated computers were used to control and monitor machinery in most industries. In the developed world companies forced by competition to improve efficiency and product quality brought robots into factories. Europe quickly followed Japan's lead in robotics, especially in automobile production and mining. The United States introduced robots more slowly because it enjoyed lower labor costs, but has now fully embraced this technology.

The transnational corporation became the primary agent of these technological changes. Since the eighteenth century powerful commercial companies have conducted business across national borders. By the twentieth century the growing economic power of corporations in industrialized nations allowed them to invest directly in the mines, plantations, and public utilities of less-developed regions. In the post–World War II years many of these companies became truly transnational, having multinational ownership and management. International trade agreements and open markets furthered the process. Ford Motor Company not only produced and sold cars internationally, but its shareholders, workers, and managers also came from numerous nations. Symbolic of these changes, the Japanese automaker Honda manufactured cars in Ohio and imported them into Japan, while Germany's Volkswagen made cars in Mexico for sale in the United States.

As transnational manufacturers, agricultural conglomerates, and financial giants became wealthier and more powerful, they increasingly escaped the controls imposed by national governments. If labor costs were too high in Japan, antipollution measures too intrusive in the United States, or taxes too high in Great Britain, transnational companies relocated—or threatened to do so. In 1945, for example, the U.S. textile industry was located in low-wage southern states, dominating the American market and exporting to the world. As wages in the South rose and global competition increased, producers began relocating plants to Puerto Rico in the 1980s, to Mexico after NAFTA went into effect in 1994 (see Chapter 33), and now to China. The relatively low Mexican wages that attracted investments in the early 1990s now appear high in comparison with China's wages. As industries moved around, searching for profits, the governments in the developing world were often hard-pressed to control their actions. As a result, the worst abuses of labor and of the environment usually occurred in poor nations.

Conserving and Sharing Resources

In the 1960s environmental activists and political leaders began warning about the devastating environmental consequences of population growth, industrialization, and the expansion of agriculture onto marginal lands. Assaults on rain forests and redwoods, the disappearance of species, and the poisoning of streams and rivers raised public consciousness. Environmental damage occurred both in the advanced industrial economies and in the poorest of the developing nations. Perhaps the worst environmental record was achieved in the former Soviet Union, where industrial and nuclear wastes were often dumped with little concern for environmental consequences. The accumulated effect of scientific studies and public debate led to national and international efforts to slow, if not undo, damage to the environment.

The Personal Computer

The period since World War II has witnessed wave after wave of technological innovations. Few of them have had a greater impact on the way people work, learn, and live than the personal computer. Until the 1970s most computing was done on large and expensive mainframe computers, and IBM (International Business Machines) dominated the industry. Access to computers was controlled by the government agencies, universities, and large corporations that owned them.

Few anticipated the technological innovations that revolutionized the computer industry in the next two decades. In rapid succession transistors replaced vacuum tubes in mainframes and then silicon chips replaced hard-wired transistors. The race to miniaturize was on. The key development was the microprocessor, a computer processor (in effect the computer's brains) on a silicon chip. Computers became smaller and cheaper as memory chips and microprocessors were made smaller and more powerful. As new companies entered the market, prices fell, and computers became a part of modern consumer culture.

Young physicists, engineers, and mathematicians working for small companies in Massachusetts and California were responsible for nearly all the most important innovations that led to desktops, then laptops, and more recently a variety of hand-held computers. Among the most important of these innovators were Steven Jobs and Stephen G. Wozniak. Part of an enterprising group of hobbyists, they joined forces to introduce the first mass-market home computer with color screen, keyboard, and built-in computing language, the Apple II, in 1977. IBM responded to these developments slowly, but in 1981 introduced its own personal computer, the IBM PC. Although IBM did not continue as the industry leader, the PC would begin a slow process of operating system standardization tied to the meteoric growth of Microsoft.

Each new generation of computers has been more powerful, smaller, and less expensive. A modern 1.8 gigahertz Intel Pentium 4 chip is 3,600 times as fast as the first desktop processor just forty years ago. By the mid-1990s desktop and laptop computers had replaced the mainframe for most uses. The Internet was developed to facilitate defense research in the 1960s. The establishment of the World Wide Web as a graphic interface in the 1990s allowed the smaller, faster computers to become research portals that accessed a vast international database of research, opinion, entertainment, and commerce. The computer revolution and the Web have had a revolutionary impact, allowing individuals and groups—without the support of governments, corporations, or other powerful institutions—to collect and disseminate information more freely than any time in the past (see Chapter 33).

From Mainframe to Laptop   During the last forty years the computer revolution has changed the way we work.   (left: Courtesy, IBM Corporation; bottom: Dagmar Fabricius/Liaison/Getty Images)

Loss of Brazilian Rain Forest   The destruction of tropical rain forest in Brazil demonstrates the growing threat to the environment caused by population growth and economic development. In this photograph we see a view of the Carajas iron mine, where heavy machinery has gouged the landscape, stripping away forest cover to facilitate the extraction of the ore.   (Jacques Jangoux/Peter Arnold, Inc.)

The expanding global population required increasing quantities of food, fresh water, housing, energy, and other resources as the twentieth century ended (see Map 32.4). In the developed world industrial activity increased much more rapidly than population grew, and the consumption of energy (coal, electricity, and petroleum) rose proportionally. Indeed, the consumer-driven economic expansion of the post–World War II years became an obstacle to addressing environmental problems. Modern economies depend on the profligate consumption of goods and resources. Stock markets closely follow measures of consumer confidence—the willingness of people to make new purchases. When consumption slows, industrial nations enter a recession. How could the United States, Germany, or Japan change consumption patterns to protect the environment without endangering corporate profits, wages, and employment levels?

Since 1945 population growth has been most dramatic in the developing countries, where environmental pressures have also been extreme. In Brazil, India, and China, for example, the need to expand food production led to rapid deforestation and the extension of farming and grazing onto marginal lands. The results were predictable: erosion and water pollution. Population growth in Indonesia forced the government to permit the cutting of nearly 20 percent of the total forest area. These and many other poor nations also attempted to force industrialization because they believed that providing for their rapidly growing populations depended on the completion of the transition from agriculture to manufacturing. The argument was compelling: Why

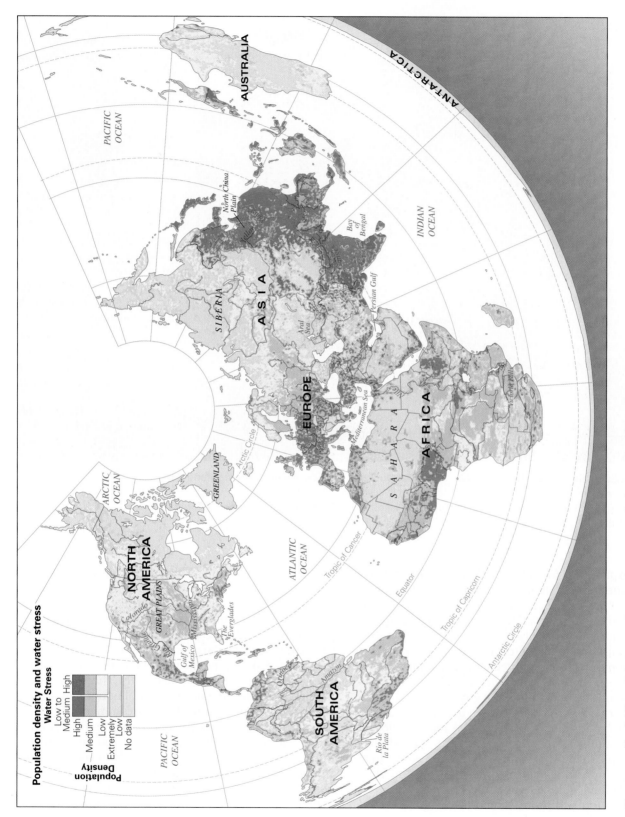

Map 32.4   Fresh Water Resources   This map links population density and the availability of water. Red areas are highly stressed environments where populations use at least 40 percent or more of available water. Less stressed environments are blue. The deeper the shade of red or blue the greater the environmental stress.   *Source: National Geographic, September, 2002. Reprinted by permission of The National Geographic Society.*

should Indians or Brazilians remain poor while Americans, Europeans, and Japanese remained rich?

Responding to Environmental Threats

Despite the gravity of environmental threats, there were many successful efforts to preserve and protect the environment. The Clean Air Act, the Clean Water Act, and the Endangered Species Act were passed in the United States in the 1970s as part of an environmental effort that included the nations of the European Community and Japan. Grassroots political movements and the media encouraged environmental awareness, and most nations in the developed world enforced strict antipollution laws and sponsored massive recycling efforts. Many also encouraged resource conservation by rewarding energy-efficient factories and manufacturers of fuel-efficient cars and by promoting the use of alternative energy sources such as solar and wind power. These efforts were implemented most comprehensively in Europe, where both energy conservation and new technologies like wind turbines were embraced.

Environmental efforts produced significant results. In western Europe and the United States air quality improved dramatically. Smog levels in the United States fell nearly a third from 1970 to 2000, even though the number of automobiles increased more than 80 percent. Emissions of lead and sulfur dioxide were down as well. The Great Lakes, Long Island Sound, and Chesapeake Bay were all much cleaner at the end of the century than they had been in 1970. The rivers of North America and Europe also improved. Still, in the United States more than thirty thousand deaths each year are attributed to exposure to pesticides and other chemicals.

New technologies made much of the improvement possible. Pollution controls on automobiles, planes, and factory smokestacks reduced harmful emissions. Scientists identified the chemicals that threaten the ozone layer, and their use in new appliances and cars began to be phased out.

Clearly, the desire to preserve the natural environment was growing around the world. In the developed nations continued political organization and enhanced awareness of environmental issues seemed likely to lead to step-by-step improvements in environmental policy. In the developing world and most of the former Soviet bloc, however, population pressures and weak governments were major obstacles to effective environmental policies. In China, for example, respiratory disease caused by industrial pollution was the leading cause of death.

Thus it was likely that the industrialized nations would have to fund global improvements, and the cost was likely to be high. Nevertheless, growing evidence of environmental degradation continued to propel reform efforts. The media drew attention to the precipitous shrinkage of Peru's Andean glaciers, which have lost a quarter of their volume in the last three decades; to oil spills, loss of rain forest in Brazil, and deforestation in Indonesia; and to erosion in parts of Africa. A growing, vocal movement pushed reluctant politicians to act.

In Kyoto, Japan, in 1997 representatives from around the world negotiated a far-reaching treaty to reduce greenhouse gases that contribute to global warning. Signed by President Clinton, the treaty was not ratified by the Senate, although it was affirmed by nearly all other industrial nations. Objections in the United States and elsewhere focused on costs. Without broad agreement among the rich nations, the economic and political power necessary for environmental protections on a global scale will be very difficult to institute.

CONCLUSION

The world was profoundly altered between 1975 and 1991. The Cold War dominated international relations to the end of the 1980s. Both the United States and the Soviet Union feared that every conflict and every regime change represented a potential threat to their strategic interests, and every conflict threatened to provoke confrontation between them. As a result, the superpowers were drawn into a succession of civil wars and revolutions. The costs in lives and property were terrible, the gains small. As defense costs escalated, the Soviet system crumbled. By 1991 the Soviet Union and the socialist Warsaw Pact had disappeared, transforming the international stage.

Latin America was pulled into the violence of the late Cold War period and paid a terrible price. The 1970s and 1980s witnessed a frontal assault on democratic institutions, a denial of human rights, and economic decline. This was the period of death squads and Dirty War. With the end of the Cold War, peace returned and democracy began to replace dictatorship.

In the Persian Gulf the end of the Cold War did not lead to peace. Iran and Iraq have experienced deep cycles of political turmoil, war, and foreign threats since the late 1970s.

The world was also altered by economic growth and integration, by population growth and movement, and by technological and environmental change. Led by the postwar recovery of the industrial powers and the remarkable economic expansion of Japan, the Asian Tigers, and more recently China, the world economy grew dramatically. The development and application of new technology contributed significantly to this process. International markets were more open and integrated than at any other time. The new wealth and exciting technologies of the postwar era were not shared equally, however. The capitalist West and a few Pacific Rim nations grew richer and more powerful, while most of the world's nations remained poor.

Population growth in the developing world was one reason for this divided experience. Unable to find adequate employment or, in many cases, bare subsistence, people in developing nations migrated across borders, hoping to improve their lives. These movements often provided valuable labor in the factories and farms of the developed world, but they also provoked cultural, racial, and ethnic tension. Problems of inequality, population growth, and international migration would continue to challenge the global community in the coming decades.

Technology seemed to offer some hope for meeting these challenges. Engineering, financial services, education, and other professions developed an international character, thanks to the communications revolution. Ambitious and talented people in the developing world could now fully participate in global intellectual and economic life. However, most people working in the developing world remained disconnected from this liberating technology by poverty. Technology also bolstered efforts to protect the environment, providing the means to clean auto and factory emissions—even while it helped produce much of the world's pollution. Technology has been intertwined with human culture since the beginning of human history. Our ability to control and direct its use will determine the future.

■ Key Terms

proxy wars
Salvador Allende
Dirty War
Sandinistas
Ayatollah Ruhollah Khomeini
Saddam Husain
neo-liberalism
keiretsu
Asian Tigers
newly industrialized economies (NIEs)
Deng Xiaoping

Tiananmen Square
Mikhail Gorbachev
perestroika
Solidarity
Thomas Malthus
demographic transition

■ Suggested Reading

Among the works devoted to postwar economic performance are W. L. M. Adriaasen and J. G. Waardensburg, eds., *A Dual World Economy: Forty Years of Development Experience* (1989); P. Krugman, *The Age of Diminished Expectations: U.S. Economic Policy in the 1990s* (1990); B. J. McCormick, *The World Economy: Patterns of Growth and Change* (1988); and H. van der Wee, *Prosperity and Upheaval: The World Economy, 1945–1980* (1986).

For Latin America, Thomas E. Skidmore and Peter H. Smith, *Modern Latin America*, 4th ed. (1996), provides an excellent general introduction to the period 1975 to 1991. The literature on the era of repression is large. *Nunca Mas* (1986), the official report of the Argentine government, provides a moving introduction. Also see news stories in 1999 and 2000 about the arrest of Augusto Pinochet in London and the resulting legal proceedings. The movie *Official Story* (available with subtitles or dubbed) offers an effective look at the legacy of the Dirty War in Argentina. For Central America see Walter La Feber, *Inevitable Revolutions: The United States in Central America* (1983).

For the Pacific Rim see Jonathan Spence, *The Search for Modern China* (1990); Edwin O. Reischauer, *The Japanese* (1988); H. Patrick and H. Rosovsky, *Asia's New Giant: How the Japanese Economy Works* (1976); and Staffan B. Linder, *Pacific Century: Economic and Political Consequences of Asian-Pacific Dynamism* (1986).

There are many fine studies of Europe and the Soviet system. See, for example, Richard Sakwa, *The Rise and Fall of the Soviet Union, 1917–1991* (1999). More focused examinations of the Soviet bloc are provided in Gale Stokes, *The Walls Came Tumbling Down: The Collapse of Communism in Eastern Europe* (1993); Barbara Engel and Christine Worobec, eds., *Russia's Women: Accommodation, Resistance, Transformation* (1990); David Remnick, *Lenin's Tomb: The Last Days of the Soviet Empire* (1993); and Charles Maier, *Dissolution: The Crisis of Communism and the End of East Germany* (1997). See also Katherine Verdery, *What Was Socialism, and What Comes Next?* (1996).

The story of the Iranian Revolution and the early days of the Islamic Republic of Iran is told well by Shaul Bakhash, *The Reign of the Ayatollahs: Iran and the Iranian Revolution* (1990). Barnet Rubin, *The Fragmentation of Afghanistan* (1995), provides excellent coverage of the struggle between Soviet forces and the Muslim resistance in that country.

A number of studies examine the special problems faced by women in the postwar period. See, for example, Elisabeth Croll,

Feminism and Socialism in China (1978); J. Ginat, *Women in Muslim Rural Society: Status and Role in Family and Community* (1982); June Hahner, *Women in Latin America* (1976); P. Hudson, *Third World Women Speak Out* (1979); A. de Souza, *Women in Contemporary India and South Asia* (1980); and M. Wolf, *Revolution Postponed: Women in Contemporary China* (1985).

For general discussions of economic, demographic, and environmental problems facing the world see R. N. Gwynne, *New Horizons? Third World Industrialization in an International Framework* (1990); W. Alonso, ed., *Population in an Interacting World* (1987); P. R. Ehrlich and A. E. Ehrlich, *The Population Explosion* (1990); James Fallows, *More Like Us: Making America Great Again* (1989); Paul M. Kennedy, *Preparing for the Twenty-first Century* (1993); W.W. Rostow, *The Great Population Spike and After: Reflections on the 21st Century* (1998); and J. L. Simon, *Population Matters: People, Resources, Environment and Immigration* (1990).

For issues associated with technological and environmental change see M. Feshbach and A. Friendly, *Ecocide in the U.S.S.R.* (1992); John Bellamy Foster, *Economic History of the Environ-ment* (1994); S. Hecht and A. Cockburn, *The Fate of the Forest: Developers, Destroyers, and Defenders of the Amazon* (1989); K. Marton, *Multinationals, Technology, and Industrialization: Implications and Impact in Third World Countries* (1986); S. P. Huntington, *The Third Wave: Demoralization in the Late Twentieth Century* (1993); John R. McNeill, *Something New Under the Sun: An Environmental History of the Twentieth Century World* (2000); and B. L. Turner II et al., eds., *The Earth as Transformed by Human Action: Global and Regional Changes in the Biosphere over the Past 300 Years* (1990).

■ Notes

1. *New York Times,* July 24, 1993, 1.
2. Quoted in Antony Flew, "Introduction," in Thomas Robert Malthus, *An Essay on the Principle of Population and a Summary View of the Principle of Population* (New York: Penguin Books, 1970), 30.
3. "Population Implosion Worries a Graying Europe," *New York Times,* July 10, 1998.
4. Paul Kennedy, *Preparing for the Twenty-first Century* (New York: Random House, 1993), 45.

Document-Based Question
Women's Rights in the Late Twentieth Century

Using the following documents, analyze the political and economic forces that shaped women's rights movements in the late twentieth century.

DOCUMENT 1
The Struggle for Women's Rights in an Era of Global Political and Economic Change (Diversity and Dominance, pp. 854–855)

DOCUMENT 2
Chinese Family Planning Campaign (photo, p. 863)

DOCUMENT 3
Quote from Italian woman (p. 864)

DOCUMENT 4
Figure 32.1 Age Structure Comparison (p. 867)

DOCUMENT 5
Quote on immigration (p. 867)

DOCUMENT 6
Garbage Dump in Manila, Philippines (photo, p. 869)

What passages from Document 1 show that Gladys Acosta is a militant feminist? What additional types of documents would help you understand the political and economic forces that shaped women's rights movements in the late twentieth century?

33

Globalization at the Turn of the Millennium

Lower Manhattan, 11 March 2002 Six months after the terrorist attacks, beams of light commemorated the destroyed twin towers of the World Trade Center and those who perished in them.

The workday began normally at the World Trade Center in lower Manhattan on the morning of September 11, 2001. The 50,000 people who work there were making their way to the two 110-story towers, as were some 140,000 others who visit on a typical day. Suddenly, at 8:46 A.M., an American Airlines Boeing 767 with 92 people on board, traveling at a speed of 470 miles per hour (756 kilometers per hour), crashed into floors 94 to 98 of the north tower, igniting the 10,000 gallons (38,000 liters) of fuel in its tanks. Just before 9:03 A.M. a United Airlines flight with 65 people on board and a similar fuel load hit floors 78 to 84 of the south tower.

As the burning jet fuel engulfed the collision areas, the buildings' surviving occupants struggled through smoke-filled corridors and down dozens of flights of stairs. Many of those trapped above the crash sites used cell phones to say good-bye to loved ones. Rather than endure the flames and fumes, a few jumped to their deaths.

Just before 10 o'clock, temperatures that had risen to 2,300° Fahrenheit (1,260° Celsius) caused the steel girders in the impacted area of the south tower to give way. The collapsing upper floors crushed the floors underneath one by one, engulfing lower Manhattan in a dense cloud of dust. Twenty-eight minutes later the north tower pancaked in a similar manner. Miraculously, most of the buildings' occupants had escaped before the towers collapsed. Besides the people on the planes, nearly 2,600 lost their lives, including some 200 police officers and firefighters helping in the evacuation.

That same morning another American Airlines jet crashed into the Pentagon, killing all 64 people on board and 125 others inside the military complex near Washington, D.C. Passengers on a fourth plane managed to overpower their hijackers, and the plane crashed in rural Pennsylvania, killing all 45 on board.

The four planes had been hijacked by teams of Middle Eastern men who slit the throats of service and flight personnel and seized control. Of the nineteen hijackers, fifteen were from Saudi Arabia. All had links to an extremist Islamic organization, al Qaeda° (the base or foundation), supported by a rich Saudi named Usama bin Laden°, who was incensed with American political, military, and cultural influence in the Middle East. The men were educated and well-traveled, had lived in the United States, and spoke English. Some had trained as pilots so that they could fly the hijacked aircraft.

The hijackers left few records of their personal motives, but the acts spoke for themselves. The Pentagon was the headquarters of the American military, the most technologically sophisticated and powerful fighting force the world had even seen. The fourth plane was probably meant to hit the Capitol or the White House, the legislative and executive centers of the world's only superpower. The Twin Towers may have been targeted because they were the tallest buildings in New York, but they were not just American targets. The World Trade Center housed 430 companies involved in international commerce and finance. Among the dead were people from more than half the countries in the world. New York was the site of the attack, but the World Trade Center was a powerful symbol of the international economy.

The events of September 11 (9/11) can be understood on many levels. The hijackers and their supporters saw themselves as engaged in a holy struggle against economic, political, and military institutions they believed to be evil. They believed so deeply in their mission that they were willing to give their lives for it and to take as many other lives as they could. People directly affected and political leaders around the world tended to describe the attacks as evil acts against innocent victims.

To understand why the nineteen attackers were heroes to some and terrorists to others, one needs to explore the historical context of global changes at the turn of the millennium and the ideological tensions they have generated. While the advancing economic,

---

al Qaeda (ahl KIGH-duh or ahl kuh-EE-duh)   **Usama bin Laden** (oo-SAH-mah bin LAH-din)

political, and cultural integration of the world is welcomed by some, it is hated or feared by others. The unique prominence of the United States in every major aspect of global integration also elicits sharply divergent views.

As you read this chapter, ask yourself the following questions:

- What are the main benefits and dangers of growing political, economic, and cultural integration?

- What roles do religious beliefs and secular ideologies play in the contemporary world?

- How has technology contributed to the process of global interaction?

GLOBAL POLITICAL ECONOMIES

The turn of the millennium saw the intensification of a **globalization** trend that had been building for some time. Growing trade and travel and new technologies were bringing all parts of the world into closer economic, political, and cultural integration and interaction. The collapse of the Soviet Union had completed the dissolution of empires that had been under way throughout the twentieth century. Autonomous national states (numbering about two hundred) became an almost universal norm, and a growing number of them have embraced democratic institutions. The rapid integration of world trade and markets have convinced world leaders of the need to balance national autonomy with international agreements and associations.

The Spread of Democracy

The last decades of the twentieth century saw rapid increases in democratic institutions and personal freedom. In 2003, 140 countries regularly held elections; people in 125 had access to free (or partly free) presses; and most people lived in fully democratic states.[1]

The great appeal of democracy has been that elections are a peaceful way to settle the inevitable differences among a country's social classes, cultural groups, and regions. Although majority votes might swing from one part of the political spectrum to another, democracies tend to encourage political moderation. For example, two of the world's oldest democracies saw two candidates win national elections in the 1990s by moving their political parties closer to the political center (and by exuding great personal charm). In 1992 Bill Clinton was the first Democrat to win the American presidency in twelve years. In 1997 Tony Blair became Great Britain's first Labour Party prime minister in eighteen years.

Very significant democratic gains have been made in the new nations of eastern Europe, where elections have also been more open to electoral mood swings. The Czech Republic, Poland, Romania, Ukraine, and most other formerly communist-ruled states have adopted democratic institutions. Likewise, after a shaky start, political institutions in the Russian Federation have begun to function more smoothly under President Vladimir Putin, elected in 2000.

Latin America has a long history of democracy, but an almost equally long history of authoritarian rule by military and personalist leaders (see Chapter 23). Since 1991, however, democracy has become almost universal in South and Central America. The region has also seen significant shifts in the balance of power within countries. In 2000 Mexican voters elected a reformist president with a centrist agenda, Vincente Fox, ending the half-century rule of the corrupt Institutional Revolutionary Party (PRI). In 2002 leftist Workers' Party candidate Luiz Inácio Lula da Silva° won the presidency of Brazil by appealing to nationalism and popular discontent with the economy. Other populist leaders won elections in Venezuela (1999), Chile (2000), and Argentina (2003).

Democratic governments continued to flourish in Asia. Beginning in 1999 the populous state of Indonesia moved from years of authoritarian and corrupt rule toward much more open political institutions. Since the death of long-time Communist leader Deng Xiaoping in 1997, China, the world's most populous country, has allowed a greater measure of free expression, but democracy is a long way off. India saw a major political shift in 1998 when a Bharatiya Janata Party (BJP) electoral victory ended four decades of Congress Party rule. The BJP success came through blatant appeals to Hindu nationalism, the condoning of violence against India's Muslims, and opposition to the social and economic progress of the Untouchables (those traditionally confined to the dirtiest jobs). The BJP also adopted a belligerent policy against neighboring Pakistan, centering on the two countries' long-standing claims to the state of Kashmir.

In sub-Saharan Africa, democracy has had mixed results. Many elected leaders have used their offices to

Luiz Inácio Lula da Silva (loo-EES ee-NAH-see-oh LOO-lah dah SEAL-vah)

C H R O N O L O G Y		
	Politics	**Economics and Society**
1991	**1992** Yugoslavia disintegrates—Croatia and Slovenia become independent states	**1991** Mercosur free trade association formed
	1992–1995 Bosnia crisis	**1993** Nobel Peace Prize to Nelson Mandela
	1994 Nelson Mandela elected president of South Africa; Tutsi massacred in Rwanda	**1994** North Atlantic Free Trade Agreement adopted
1995	**1995** Nerve gas released in Tokyo subway	**1995** World Trade Organization founded; United Nations women's conference in China
	1997 Hong Kong reunited with China	**1997** Asian financial crisis begins
	1998 Terrorists bomb U.S. embassies in Kenya and Tanzania; India and Pakistan test atomic bombs	
2000	**1999** East Timor secedes from Indonesia (officially independent 2002)	**1999** Nobel Peace Prize to Doctors Without Borders
	2001 Terrorists destroy the World Trade Center and damage the Pentagon on September 11	**2001** Start of global recession
	2002 United Nations weapons inspectors return to Iraq	**2002** Euro the only currency in twelve European countries
	2003 United States and Britain invade and occupy Iraq	

enrich themselves and limit their opponents. Military coups and conflicts over resources such as diamonds have also been distressingly common. Southern Africa, however, has seen democratic progress and a decline in armed conflicts since 1991. A key change came in South Africa in 1994, when long-time political prisoner Nelson Mandela and his African National Congress (ANC) won the first national elections in which the African majority could participate equally. Since then, the lively politics of this ethnically diverse country have been a model of how democracy can resolve conflicts. Also hopeful has been the return to democracy of Nigeria, Africa's most populous state, after decades of military rulers. In 1999, after a succession of military governments, Nigerians elected President Olusegun Obasanjo° (a former coup leader) and a 2003 vote renewed his term, despite serious voting irregularities. In 2002 Kenyans voted out the party that had held power for thirty-nine years.

Democracy is as exceptional in the Middle East as it is in much of Africa. Some once-democratic states such as Algeria have manipulated elections because those in power fear the rising power of Islamic militants. On the other hand, in Turkey, the most democratic Muslim-majority state in the region, a once-strident Islamist

Olusegun Obasanjo (oh-LOO-say-goon oh-bah-SAHN-joh)

party won a parliamentary majority in 2002 by moderating its tone and politics. Women have made gains in recent elections in Morocco, Turkey, and Bahrain. Recent regime changes in Afghanistan and Iraq may mark a move toward more democratic rule in these countries.

As examples later in the chapter will indicate, the growth (or decline) of democracy has only partly been due to internal changes in individual countries. Two international factors have also played important roles: the changed politics of the post–Cold War era and the demands of global economic forces.

Global Politics

Modern nation-states have considerable autonomy under international law. Other nations may intervene in a state's affairs only when seriously threatened or when the state is engaging in extreme human rights abuses. Although necessary to protect smaller, weaker countries from the imperial bullying that was once common, this autonomy greatly complicates international policing and peacekeeping efforts.

After the end of the Cold War, the United Nations struggled to reclaim its roles as defender of human rights and peacekeeper. This was especially noticeable under the leadership of Kofi Annan, who became United

Sectarian Strife in India   Hours after these Hindu youths clambered atop the sixteenth-century Babri Mosque in December 1992 hundreds of angry Hindu nationalists completely demolished the structure. The Hindus claimed the Muslim place of worship in the northern Indian province of Uttar Pradesh had been erected upon the site of a temple commemorating the birthplace of Lord Ram, the incarnation of the Hindu god Vishnu. Thousands died in the riots that followed the razing of the temple. An Indian government archaeological team uncovered the foundation of an earlier temple-like structure.   (Douglas E. Curran/Getty Images)

Nations secretary general in 1997. The members of the United Nations Security Council often had difficulty agreeing on a course of action. Individual countries often acted alone or with their neighbors to resolve conflicts in nearby countries, whether through peaceful negotiation or military intervention. Some interventions restored order and punished wrongdoers, but in other cases people suffered and died by the hundreds of thousands as world leaders hesitated or debated the wisdom and legitimacy of intervening. As the lone superpower, the United States was in a unique position to use its moral leadership, economic power, and military might to defend its national interests and promote the general good. However, interventions also brought charges of American imperialism.

There were some notable peacemaking successes. The United Nations, South Africa, and other countries helped end the long civil war in Mozambique in 1992 and struggled to do the same in Angola, where peace finally returned in 2002. In the 1990s Nigeria, the major military power in West Africa, helped end fighting in Sierra Leone in 1998, and again in 2003 in Liberia, which warlords and embezzlement has made the world's poorest country. The Clinton and George W. Bush administrations had some success in getting aggrieved parties in

Israel, Ireland, and South Asia to negotiate their differences, even though lasting solutions were elusive.

However, in a number of cases the international community had great difficulty in agreeing on when and how to stop civil conflicts and abuses in individual countries. For example, in 1991 the Balkan state of Yugoslavia, which had existed since 1920 and was united by a common language (Serbo-Croatian), dissolved into a morass of separatism and warring ethnic and religious groups. Slovenia and Croatia, the most westerly provinces of Yugoslavia, both heavily Roman Catholic, became independent states in 1992 after brief struggles with federal Yugoslav forces. Reflecting centuries of Muslim, Catholic, and Orthodox competition in the Balkans, the people of the province of Bosnia and Herzegovina were more mixed—40 percent were Muslims, 30 percent Serbian Orthodox, and 18 percent Catholics. The murderous three-sided fighting that broke out with the declaration of Bosnian national independence in 1992 gave rise to **ethnic cleansing,** an effort by one racial, ethnic, or religious group to eliminate the people and culture of a different group. In this case, the Orthodox Serbs attempted to rid the state of Muslims.

At first, no European power acted to stop the growing tragedy in the Balkans. Finally, after much indecision—and extensive television coverage of atrocities and wanton destruction—the United States made a cautious intervention and eventually brokered a tentative settlement in 1995. In 1999 vicious new fighting and ethnic cleansing broke out in the southernmost Yugoslavian province of Kosovo, the ancient homeland of the Serbs, which had become predominantly Muslim and Albanian. When NATO's warnings went unheeded in Kosovo, the United States, with aid from Britain and France, launched an aerial war against Serbia. Suffering few casualties themselves, the NATO allies damaged military and infrastructure targets in Serbia and forced the withdrawal of Serbian forces from Kosovo. A trial of former Serbian president Slobodan Milosevic° at a special tribunal in the Hague on charges of crimes against humanity began in 2002 but was often delayed by his ill health.

Another tragedy unfolded in 1994, when political leaders in the Central African nation of Rwanda incited Hutu people to massacre their Tutsi neighbors. The major powers avoided characterizing the slaughter as genocide because an international agreement mandated intervention to stop genocide. Only after some 750,000 people were dead and millions of refugees had fled into neighboring states did the United States and other powers intervene. Belatedly, the United Nations set up a tribunal to try those responsible for the genocide. In 1998 violence spread from Rwanda to neighboring Congo, where growing opposition and ill-health had forced President Joseph Mobutu from office after over three decades of dictatorial misrule. Various peacemaking attempts failed to restore order. By mid-2003 more than 3 million Congolese had died from disease, malnutrition, and injuries related to the fighting.

Fear that intervention could result in long and costly commitments was one reason the major powers were reluctant to intervene. Nor was it easy to distinguish conflicts that would benefit from forceful intervention from those that might better be resolved by diplomatic pressure. Many conflicts reflected deep-seated differences that were difficult to resolve. Tamil-speaking Hindus in Sri Lanka have waged a merciless guerrilla struggle against the dominant Sinhalese-speaking Buddhists for decades. Militant Hindus and Muslims in South Asia continue a violent struggle over the territories of the state of Kashmir, which was divided between India and Pakistan at their independence in 1947. Sometimes it took decades of international pressure to bring a conflict to an end, as was the case in East Timor (a mostly Catholic former Portuguese colony that

Slobodan Milosevic (SLOH-boh-duhn mee-LOH-seh-vitch)

Indonesia had annexed in 1975), whose people voted to separate from Muslim Indonesia in 1999 and gained full independence in 2002.

Arms Control and Terrorism

In addition to agreements on collective action against genocide and other crimes against humanity (see below), international treaties govern **weapons of mass destruction.** Nuclear, biological, and chemical devices pose especially serious dangers to global security because they can kill large numbers of people quickly.

For a time after international agreements were signed in the 1960s and 1970s (see Chapter 31), considerable progress was made in restricting the testing and spread of nuclear weapons and reducing their numbers. Fear increased when the breakup of the Soviet Union threatened to expand the number of states with nuclear weapons, but in the end only Russia retained nuclear arsenals. Meanwhile, China resumed nuclear weapons tests in 1992.

Anxiety over nuclear proliferation increased in 1998 when India and Pakistan openly tested nuclear bombs and missile delivery systems, acts that raised the stakes in any future conflict between them. Although North Korea was a signatory of the nuclear nonproliferation treaty, it secretly continued nuclear weapons programs and, beginning in 2002, belligerently challenged the rest of the world to try to stop them. Iran and Israel are also believed to have secret nuclear weapons programs. In violation of another agreement, the Bush administration is pushing for new nuclear weapons development in the United States.

Chemical and biological weapons are difficult to detect and can easily be produced in seemingly ordinary chemical and pharmaceutical plants. As part of the settlement of the 1991 Persian Gulf War, United Nations inspectors in Iraq uncovered and destroyed extensive stocks of chemical munitions and plants for producing nerve gas and lethal germs. However, in 1997 the government of Saddam Husain reneged on its agreement to allow United Nations weapons inspectors free access to all sites in Iraq.

What made the proliferation of weapons of mass destruction more worrisome was the fear that such weapons could be used for **terrorism.** Terrorists believe that horrendous acts of violence can provoke harsh reprisals that would win them sympathy or cause the regimes they oppose to lose legitimacy. Terrorism has a long history, but much recent concern focused on the network of terrorist organizations created by **Usama**

The New York Times

"All the News That's Fit to Print"

New England Edition
Boston: Windy, some clearing late. High 37. Mainly clear, brisk. Low 28. Tomorrow, partly sunny and not as cold, much lighter winds. High 42. Weather map appears on Page D12.

VOL. CLIII .... No. 52,698   Copyright © 2003 The New York Times   MONDAY, DECEMBER 15, 2003   ONE DOLLAR

HUSSEIN CAUGHT IN MAKESHIFT HIDE-OUT; BUSH SAYS 'DARK ERA' FOR IRAQIS IS OVER

BETRAYED BY CLAN

Breakthrough Capped a Renewed Effort to Ferret Out Leads

By ERIC SCHMITT

BAGHDAD, Iraq, Dec. 14 — The hunt for Saddam Hussein ended late Saturday with information from a member of his tribal clan.

Seizing Mr. Hussein, a man who one senior general said had 20 to 30 hide-outs and moved as often as every three to four hours, had become a maddening challenge. Eleven previous times in the last several months, a brigade combat team from the Army's Fourth Infantry Division thought it had a bead on Mr. Hussein and began raids to kill or capture him, only to come up empty, sometimes missing its man by only a matter of hours, military officials here said.

But at 8:26 p.m. Saturday, less than 11 hours after receiving the decisive tip, 600 American soldiers and Special Operations forces backed by tanks, artillery and Apache helicopter gunships surrounded two farmhouses, and near one of them found Mr. Hussein hiding alone at the bottom of an eight-foot hole.

He surrendered without a shot.

"He was just caught like a rat," Maj. Gen. Raymond T. Odierno, the commander of the Fourth Infantry Division, told reporters at his headquarters in Tikrit on Sunday. "He could have been hiding in a hundred different places, a thousand different places like this all around Iraq. It just takes finding the right person who will give you a good idea where he might be."

In recent weeks, American officials had started a new effort to draw up a list of people likely to be hiding Mr. Hussein, including bodyguards, former palace functionaries, tribal

Arrest by U.S. Soldiers — President Still Cautious

By SUSAN SACHS

BAGHDAD, Iraq, Dec. 14 — Saddam Hussein, once the all-powerful leader of Iraq, was arrested without a fight on Saturday night by American soldiers who found him crouching in an eight-foot hole at an isolated farm near Tikrit, haggard, dirty and disoriented after eluding capture for nearly nine months.

News of Mr. Hussein's arrest, announced Sunday after being kept secret for 18 hours, electrified Iraq and much of the world, sending joyous Iraqis into the streets with the first real catharsis of liberation since the invasion toppled him in April.

For the Bush administration, which has been struggling to stabilize Iraq, the capture of Mr. Hussein was the most triumphant moment since American forces ousted him.

"In the history of Iraq, a dark and painful era is over," President Bush said in a televised noontime address from Washington. "A hopeful day has arrived. All Iraqis can now come together and reject violence and build a new Iraq." But Mr. Bush was careful to couch his message with caution that Iraq remains violent and dangerous.

American officials said Mr. Hussein was being held in Iraq, but they would not disclose the exact location. They said he had been unresistant in medical tests and other procedures but was not cooperating with interrogators on substantive matters.

American-appointed Iraqi leaders said he would eventually face a war crimes trial, but it was unclear when.

President Bush, in a brief televised speech yesterday. Page A16.

Maj. Gen. Raymond T. Odierno, commander of the Fourth Infantry Division, which captured Mr. Hussein with a force of 600 soldiers, said he was armed with only a pistol and had surrendered without firing a shot. Two AK-47 rifles and $750,000 in American cash were found nearby.

It was an ignominious ending for Mr. Hussein, 66, who survived American attempts to kill him during the invasion and had eluded capture apparently by moving from one dingy hide-out to another.

Whether his arrest will undermine the insurgency against the American-led forces in Iraq is unclear. Hours after his capture but before it was announced publicly, a car bomb killed at least 17 people in a town west of Baghdad. [Page A12.]

Even in hiding, Mr. Hussein had

Continued on Page A12

In the Streets, a Shadow Lifts

By JOHN F. BURNS

Capture of Saddam in Iraq

Acting on a tip from Iraqi sources, American troops captured Saddam Husain in December 2003. The bearded former dictator of Iraq was discovered in a small underground "spider hole" about ten miles southeast of the city of Tikrit. (©New York Times. Reprinted with permission.)

---

bin Laden, a wealthy Saudi. Because his methods were so repugnant, his own family disowned him and Saudi Arabia stripped him of his citizenship, but his anti-American stance and patronage attracted followers throughout the Islamic world. In 1992 bin Laden established himself in Sudan, where he invested in many projects. Suspecting that a pharmaceutical plant near the Sudanese capital Khartoum was being used for making chemical weapons, President Clinton had it destroyed by rockets in 1998, but no evidence of weapons production was found.

After being expelled from Sudan in 1996, bin Laden went to Afghanistan, where he had close ties with the Taliban, a fundamentalist Islamic organization that had taken control of most of that country in 1995. Bin Laden's agents bombed the American embassies in Kenya and Tanzania in 1998 as well as the destroyer USS *Cole,* which was making a port call in Yemen in 2000, before turning to targets in the United States itself. In response to the terrorist attacks of September 2001 and the subsequent panic caused by an unknown terrorist mailing spores of anthrax, a lethal disease, the U.S. government adopted a more aggressive policy against terrorism and weapons of mass destruction. In December 2001, American and other NATO forces joined with Afghan opposition groups to overthrow the Taliban-supported regime in Afghan-

istan, an act that President Bush declared to be the first step in a much larger "war on terrorism."

Such preemptive strikes are clearly speedier than collective action, but the issue of when military intervention is justified became the focus of a huge international debate after President Bush pushed for extension of the war on terrorism against the brutal regime of Saddam Husain in Iraq. Strong opposition to unilateral action came from America's NATO allies France and Germany, as well as from Russia and China. German Chancellor Gerhard Schröder won a close election in September 2002 by campaigning against American imperialism. Faced with this opposition, the Bush administration changed tactics. In November 2002 it persuaded the United Nations Security Council to unanimously pass a resolution ordering the return of United Nations weapons inspectors to Iraq and requiring the Iraqi government to specify what weapons of mass destruction it still possessed. It was a rare moment in which superpower America bowed to the authority of the international body and in which the Security Council acknowledged the need to take firm and forceful action to enforce its resolutions.

When the new United Nations inspectors in Iraq failed to find any evidence of banned weapons, the split widened between those nations wanting to continue inspections and those, led by the United States and Britain, wanting to intervene militarily. Abandoning efforts to gain Security Council authorization, an American-led "coalition of the willing" invaded Iraq in March 2003. On the eve of the invasion, General Brent Scowcroft, a former national security adviser to the elder President George Bush, predicted that the United States would pay a high price for the image of American arrogance and unilateralism that such actions fostered.

By the time the new Persian Gulf war began, the overwhelming international sympathy the United States had received after September 11 had evaporated. Public disapproval ran well over 80 percent in Russia and in NATO allies France, Germany, and Turkey (whose parliament voted not to allow American troops to attack Iraq from Turkish soil). Public opinion in most of the Muslim world was almost unanimously against the intervention. Even in Britain and Poland, which sent troops to Iraq, most people disapproved of the war. Not surprisingly, the war set off large antiwar demonstrations around the world and drew strong criticism from prominent religious leaders.

The war took only six weeks to drive Saddam's regime from power and showcased the technological precision of America's latest bombs and missiles. Iraqi looters did more damage to utility plants, oil well equipment, and government offices than had the bombing. However, the hidden weapons of mass destruction, on whose removal the Bush administration had justified the war, were not found.

In May the Security Council authorized the American and British occupation of Iraq and lifted the sanctions on petroleum exports that had been imposed on the old regime. But American efforts to secure a larger United Nations role in rebuilding Iraq faced resistance from other world powers, who insisted on curbing American control. Meanwhile, sniper attacks and car bombings took a steady toll.

Most Iraqis welcomed the end of Saddam's rule and applauded his capture, but were eager for American occupiers to leave. They criticized the slow pace of restoring electricity and water to the cities and the lack of law and order. They had little faith in the American-nominated Iraqi Governing Council. As in Afghanistan, reestablishing political and civil order in Iraq would be a long and costly process. In September 2003 President Bush announced the price tag for the next year: $87 billion.

The Global Economy

The 1990s opened a new chapter in the history of global capitalism. After the collapse of the long experiment with state-managed socialist economies in eastern Europe and the Soviet Union, free-market capitalism seemed to be the only road to economic growth. Free trade could generate new wealth, but it also brought many problems.

From 1991 to 2000 the world experienced rapid expansion in manufacturing and trade. The burgeoning international trade of the 1990s tied the world more tightly together. Manufactured products were increasingly likely to be the product of materials and labor from many countries. Overall, the already developed economies increased their wealth the most, but the fastest rates of growth were in developing countries and in economies making a transition from communism. Net private capital flows to developing nations rose almost sevenfold between 1990 and 2000. This was not foreign aid. Investors put their funds in countries whose political stability, legal systems, level of education, and labor costs promised the most profitable returns.

The greatest single beneficiary was China. While officially espousing communism, the Chinese government took major steps to open its economy to freer trade and investment. Newly opened markets in eastern Europe and the former Soviet Union also received significant private investment. Stimulated by foreign investment, the Latin American nations of Brazil, Argentina, and Mexico experienced great economic growth. Investors put much less money into the shaky economies and political systems of sub-Saharan Africa, except for countries with significant petroleum resources.

Electronic transfers via the Internet made it possible to invest capital quickly; but when conditions became unfavorable, funds could be withdrawn just as fast. When investors lost faith in Thailand in 1997 and shifted their funds out, the country's currency and stock values plummeted. Political corruption and unrest in Indonesia brought on a similar capital flight the next year, and the widening Asian collapse eventually triggered a serious recession in Japan, business failures in South Korea, and a slowing of economic growth in China.

Government intervention sometimes helped. When Mexico's economy stumbled badly in 1995, U.S. loan guarantees helped it recover rapidly, and by 2001 Mexico had the largest economy in Latin America. However, when Argentina had to abandon its attempt to link its currency to the U.S. dollar in 2001, the value of the Argentine peso plummeted.

Although the largest economies were better able to weather tough times, they were not immune to economic downturns. The extraordinary economic and stock market economic boom of the 1990s cooled in 2000 and plunged deeper into recession in the wake of the September 11 attacks. The rate of growth in world trade fell from 13 percent in 2000 to only 1 percent in 2001.

As Map 33.1 shows, the economic boom of the 1990s

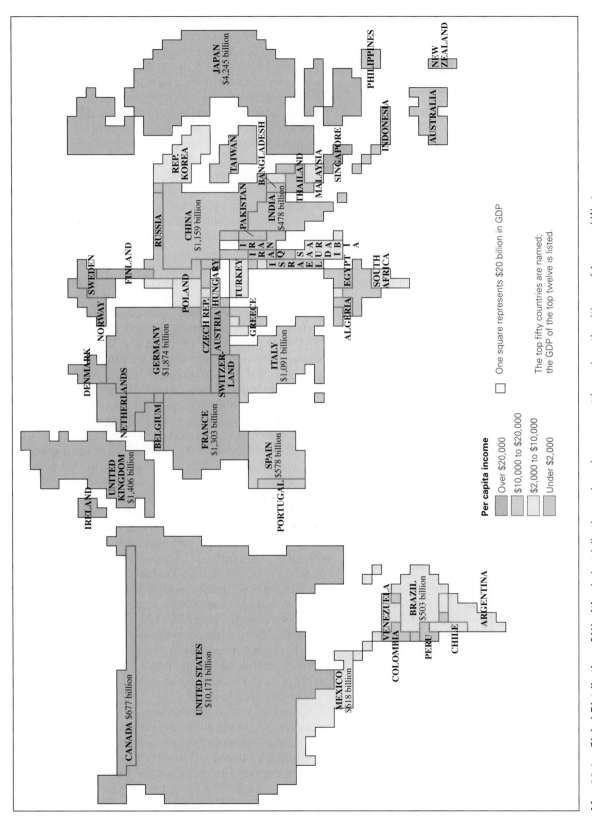

Map 33.1 Global Distribution of Wealth   Industrialization and good government have given the citizens of Japan and Western countries access to tremendous wealth. Elsewhere, warfare and political mismanagement have slowed or reversed economic growth, while high population growth (see Map 32.3) has slowed increases in per capita wealth. In nearly all countries the distribution of wealth among individuals varies tremendously. Wealth is clearly concentrated in some parts of the world, but its geographical distribution is more complex than the often-cited divide between a rich north and a poor south.

did little to change historic disparities in regional economic size and in per capita income in 2002. The gigantic U.S. economy continued to be larger than the economies of the next five countries combined—Japan, Germany, Great Britain, China (including Hong Kong), and France. One person in six lived in a country whose per capita income was over $20,000, while four of every six lived in countries with per capita incomes of under $2,000. Some sixty countries grew poorer in the 1990s, but there were some remarkable overall improvements in the length and quality of life. The average lifespan grew by ten years in three decades. Infant mortality fell by 40 percent and adult illiteracy by 50 percent. However, every day many thousands still died of preventable diseases such as malaria, cholera, and tuberculosis.

Managing the Global Economy

To promote economic growth and reduce their vulnerabilities, many countries joined with their neighbors in free-trade zones and regional trade associations (see Map 33.2). The granddaddy of these is the European Union (EU), most of whose members replaced their coins and bills with a new common currency (the Euro) in 2002. Ten new members from eastern Europe and the Mediterranean were admitted in May 2004. Turkey, Bulgaria, and Romania were hoping to join. Despite the EU's expansion, the North American Free Trade Agreement (NAFTA), which eliminated tariffs among the United States, Canada, and Mexico in 1994, governed the world's largest free-trade zone. A South American free trade zone, Mercosur, created by Argentina, Brazil, Paraguay, and Uruguay in 1991 is the world's third largest trading group. In 2002 Mercosur decided to allow the free movement of people within its area and gave equal employment rights to the citizens of all member states. President Bush promoted a Free Trade Area of the Americas, which would include all the democracies of the Western Hemisphere. Chile was the first to sign on. Other free trade associations operate in West Africa, southern Africa, Southeast Asia, Central America, the Pacific basin, and the Caribbean.

Because of the inequalities and downturns that are intrinsic to capitalism, the global economic bodies that try to manage world trade and finance find it hard to convince poorer nations that they are not only concerned with the welfare of richer countries. In 1995 the world's major trading powers established the **World Trade Organization (WTO)** to replace GATT (see Chapter 31). The WTO encourages reduced trading barriers and enforces international trade agreements. Despite the member-ship of some 150 nations, the WTO has many critics, as became evident in Seattle in 1999, when street demonstrations, partly organized by American labor unions fearful of foreign competition, forced the organization to suspend a meeting. Moreover, the seven richest nations plus Russia form the Group of Eight (G-8), whose annual meetings have an enormous impact on international trade and politics and also attract a variety of protestors.

Countries in economic trouble have little choice but to turn to the international financial agencies for funds to keep things from getting worse. The International Monetary Fund (IMF) and World Bank make their assistance conditional on internal economic reforms that are often politically unpopular, such as terminating government subsidies for basic foodstuffs, cutting social programs, and liberalizing investment. While the bitter pill of economic reform may be good in the long run, it also fuels criticism of the international economic system.

The emphasis on free trade led to changes in the term of government-to-government aid programs. During the Cold War countries had often gained funds for economic development by allying themselves with one of the superpowers. In the decade after the Cold War ended, however, foreign economic aid to poor nations fell by a third. On an African tour in 2000 President Clinton told African countries that the days of large handouts were over and that they would have to rely on their own efforts to expand their economies.

In the face of rising criticism at home and protests at international meetings, world leaders in the 2000s have pledged to increase attention to the problem of economic backwardness, especially in Africa. At a Millennium Summit in September 2000 the states of the United Nations agreed to make sustainable development and the elimination of world poverty their highest priorities. A 2002 United Nations meeting in Monterrey, Mexico, called for special commitments to Africa. Recent G-8 summits endorsed new joint efforts to promote African development. Late in 2002 President Bush proposed a substantial increase in American foreign aid. If funded, his Millennium Challenge Account would increase the amount of nonmilitary foreign aid by 50 percent. First priority would be given to poor countries that cracked down on corruption, promoted civil liberties, increased spending on education and health, and followed free-market economic principles.

Freer trade has also put pressure on developed countries to change domestic aid programs. Though agriculture occupies a small part of the work force in Europe and the United States, agricultural interests are politically powerful. Government subsidies have led to vast overproduction of some products. Some of this surplus

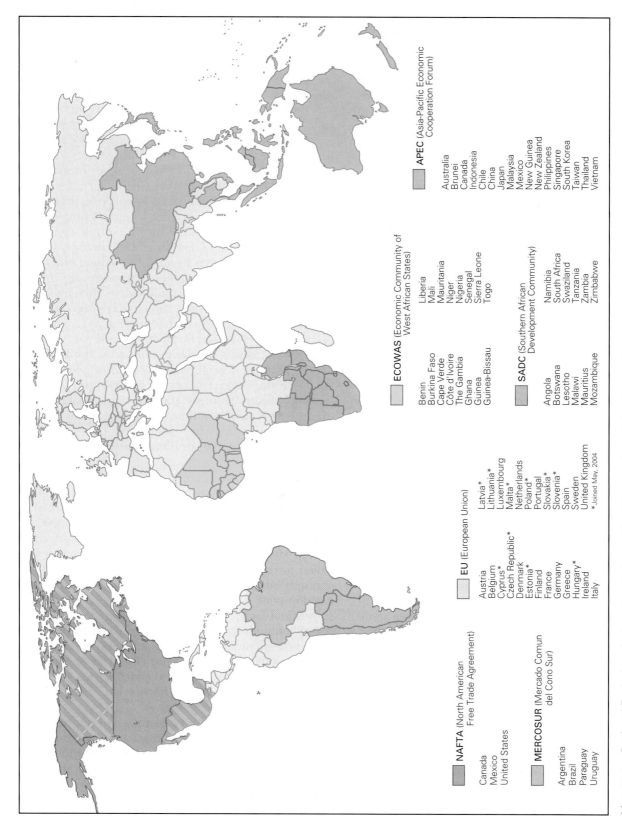

NAFTA (North American
          Free Trade Agreement)

Canada
Mexico
United States

MERCOSUR (Mercado Comun
                del Cono Sur)

Argentina
Brazil
Paraguay
Uruguay

EU (European Union)

Austria   Latvia *
Belgium   Lithuania *
Cyprus *   Luxembourg
Czech Republic *   Malta *
Denmark   Netherlands
Estonia *   Poland *
Finland   Portugal
France   Slovakia *
Germany   Slovenia *
Greece   Spain
Hungary *   Sweden
Ireland   United Kingdom
Italy   * Joined May, 2004

ECOWAS (Economic Community of
            West African States)

Benin   Liberia
Burkina Faso   Mali
Cape Verde   Mauritania
Côte d'Ivoire   Niger
The Gambia   Nigeria
Ghana   Senegal
Guinea   Sierra Leone
Guinea-Bissau   Togo

SADC (Southern African
         Development Community)

Angola   Namibia
Botswana   South Africa
Lesotho   Swaziland
Malawi   Tanzania
Mauritius   Zambia
Mozambique   Zimbabwe

APEC (Asia-Pacific Economic
          Cooperation Forum)

Australia
Brunei
Canada
Indonesia
Chile
China
Japan
Malaysia
Mexico
New Guinea
New Zealand
Philippines
Singapore
South Korea
Taiwan
Thailand
Vietnam

Map 33.2   Regional Trade Associations, 2004   International trade and development are major concerns of governments in developed and developing countries. NAFTA, Mercosur, and the EU are free-trade areas. The other associations promote trade and development.

Cheers for President Clinton in Nigeria In 2000 the first visit to sub-Saharan Africa by a sitting U.S. president brought out large, enthusiastic crowds everywhere, including this one outside the Nigerian capital city Abuja. The enthusiasm for President Clinton reflected his celebrity and his enthusiasm for Africa, but he was unable to promise much in the way of new American aid to this impoverished region. President Bush received a warm welcome when he visited Nigeria in 2003. (Brennan Linsley/AP/Wide World)

food is distributed as famine relief, but critics point out that subsidies to farmers in developed countries actually hurt farmers in poor countries who cannot compete with the artificially low prices that subsidies produce. A WTO meeting collapsed in 2003 when richer countries refused to meet the demands of delegates from poorer states to reduce agricultural subsidies.

TRENDS AND VISIONS

As people around the world faced the opportunities and problems of globalization, they tried to make sense of these changes in terms of their own cultures and beliefs. With 6 billion people, the world is big enough to include a variety of different approaches, from intensely religious or local visions to broad secular views that champion a new universal value system. In some cases, however, conflicting visions fed violence.

A New Age? In 1999 Thomas L. Friedman, a veteran Middle East and international reporter and columnist for the *New York Times*, published a penetrating analysis of the state of the planet. "The world is ten years

old," proclaimed the opening essay of *The Lexus and the Olive Tree*. Friedman argued that the political and economic changes associated with the collapse of the Soviet Empire and the technological advances (computers, satellite and fiber optic communications, and the Internet) that had made possible a huge drop in telecommunications costs had ushered in a new age of political and economic globalization. In his view, global capitalism and American power and values characterized this new era of history, which held the promise (but not the certainty) of increased prosperity, peace, democracy, environmental protection, and human rights.

In Friedman's analysis, the Lexus, a splendidly engineered Japanese luxury car, produced for a global market on a computer-run assembly line of mechanical robots, symbolizes global progress and prosperity, and the international cooperation needed to achieve them. A Middle Eastern symbol, the olive tree, stands for the communal values of family, ethnicity, and religion that give people's lives stability, depth, and meaning.

To Friedman both the Lexus and the olive tree represent important human values, and his book suggests that they are mutually compatible. But his optimism about the new age is guarded. He believes that the benefits of global integration will offset its threats to established order. Still, his years of observation of Middle Eastern conflicts make him wary of the dangers that excessive devotion to parochial ethnic and religious values may pose to global progress. His book is less inclined to criticize the excesses of global capitalism.

The September 11 terrorist attacks that were being planned as Friedman wrote were a clear illustration of the extreme olive-tree mentalities he warned about, as are many other simmering conflicts around the world. The steeper declines in the value of the stock markets generally and especially of telecommunication companies that came in the wake of 9/11 and growing revelations of excessive greed and dishonesty by top executives in key companies shook many people's faith in free-market capitalism. Friedman and others would argue that such events were normal (and self-correcting) aspects of free markets, but they also suggest that the rapid pace of economic growth in the 1990s cannot be counted on. Moreover, the war on terrorism declared by President Bush in the wake of the 9/11 attacks promised to be a long and costly global struggle with an uncertain outcome.

Was Friedman too optimistic in seeing the dawning of an age of great promise? Many who thought so cited *The Clash of Civilizations and the Remaking of the World Order,* in which Harvard political scientist Samuel P. Huntington argues that the end of the Cold War left the world divided into distinct regional civilizations. For Huntington, religious and cultural differences are more likely to shape the future than are globalizing economic, political, and communication forces. It is impossible to predict whether global clashes or global convergence are more likely to dominate the future. Recent trends seem to point in both directions.

Christian Millenarianism

The turn of the millennium was an occasion for some very big parties. It also raised more serious issues. Fearing all sorts of mix-ups, businesses and governments spent vast sums to ensure that computers would recognize dates beginning with 2000. Some religious groups believed that a new era had arrived in which cosmic battles would be waged for the heart and soul of humanity.

Since the calendar now used around the world was devised to count the years since the birth of Jesus Christ, Christians had special reason to celebrate the millennium. The Catholic Church proclaimed the year 2000 a holy year and marked it with all sorts of special celebrations, including a vast gathering at its headquarters in Rome. With some 2 billion adherents, Christianity is the world's largest religious tradition and the most widespread globally (see Map 33.3). Well established in the Americas, Europe, and Africa, Christianity has been spreading rapidly in East Asia; for example, Christians are now more numerous than Buddhists in South Korea. After the fall of the official atheistic communist regime, many Russians returned to the Russian Orthodox Church or joined new evangelical Christian congregations.

As had sometimes happened in the past, some Christians looked for deeper meaning in the calendar change. Many turned to the prophetic account of the end of the world in the final book of the New Testament, the Apocalypse or Book of Revelation. This book foretold that three sets of seven violent struggles would lead to the final triumph of good over evil. With victory achieved, Christ would return to Earth, the good would be taken to Heaven, and the material world would come to an end. Guided by a tradition that held that since God had created the world in six days, the end of the world would come after the passage of six millennia, some Christians held that the year 2000 marked the beginning of the end, and they saw the events around them in terms of these prophecies.

The extent of this Christian **millenarianism** was suggested by the huge sales of the Left Behind series of novels, which described the events foretold in Revelation in vivid present-day settings. By the end of 2001 the ten novels by Tim LaHaye, a Baptist minister, and Jerry B. Jenkins, a syndicated cartoonist, had sold an unprecedented 50 million copies. Whatever the precise strength of Christian millenarianism, its supporters are well organized and skillfully use the Internet and other forms of mass communication to circulate their ideas.

While social scientists are inclined to interpret millenarian and other prophetic beliefs as efforts to find certainty in an uncertain world, believers accept the prophesies in Revelation as the guiding reality of their religious lives. To believers, the proliferation of secular values and permissive attitudes toward moral issues, disturbances in the weather, and the events of 9/11 are all signs of the impending confrontation between good and evil.

Because of their belief that only Christians can be saved, millenarian Christians have stepped up efforts to convert Muslims and Jews. These efforts have caused much resentment in Middle Eastern lands, where some Muslims have assaulted Christian missions. An American missionary in Lebanon was assassinated in 2002 for trying to convert Muslims.

A small part of millenarianism was associated with cult movements that came to violent ends. An armed confrontation with the FBI in Waco, Texas, in 1993 destroyed a small group called the Branch Davidians led by David Koresh. This was followed by ritual murders and collective suicides of members of the Heaven's Gate movement in California in 1997 and of members of the

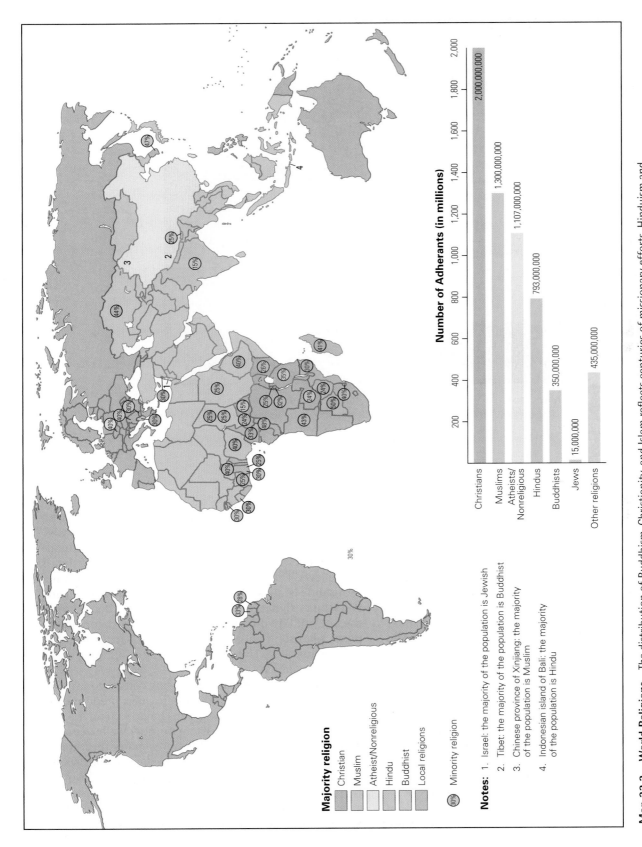

Majority religion

Christian
Muslim
Atheist/Nonreligious
Hindu
Buddhist
Local religions

60% Minority religion

Notes: 1. Israel: the majority of the population is Jewish
2. Tibet: the majority of the population is Buddhist
3. Chinese province of Xinjiang: the majority of the population is Muslim
4. Indonesian island of Bali: the majority of the population is Hindu

Number of Adherants (in millions)

Christians — 2,000,000,000
Muslims — 1,300,000,000
Atheists/Nonreligious — 1,107,000,000
Hindus — 793,000,000
Buddhists — 350,000,000
Jews — 15,000,000
Other religions — 435,000,000

Map 33.3 World Religions The distribution of Buddhism, Christianity, and Islam reflects centuries of missionary efforts. Hinduism and Judaism have expanded primarily through trade and migration. Chinese governments have actively curtailed religious practice. As religion revives as a source of social identity or a rationale for political assertion or mass mobilization, the possibility of religious activism across broad geographic regions becomes greater, as does the likelihood of domestic discord in multireligious states. [Data from *The New York Times 2003 Almanac*, ed. John W. Wright (New York: Penguin Books, 2002), 484–488. Copyright © The New York Times Company, 2002.]

Millennium Celebration in Sydney Australia Uncertainties about what lay ahead for the world in the twenty-first century took a back seat to exuberant festivities as the millennium ended. The sleek modern silhouette of Sydney's opera house and the neon signs of major corporations epitomized the hopes of many. (Sydney Morning Herald/Sipa Press)

Order of the Solar Temple in France and Quebec in 1999. Such movements are easily dismissed as lunatic fringe groups, but they were not alone or uniquely Christian. In 1995 members of Aum Shinrikyo, a Buddhist sect whose founder had predicted that the world would end in 1999, released nerve gas in the Tokyo subway system.

Militant Islam

People in other faiths were also interpreting contemporary events from deeply religious perspectives. In the Jewish calendar a millennial change (the year 6000) will not arrive until 2240 C.E., but many on the religious right in Israel interpret the struggle of modern Israel to survive and prosper in terms of the Biblical accounts of the Israelites' conquests more than four thousand years ago. Some Christian believers have gone to Israel to support Jewish settlers' efforts to reclaim the lands of the ancient Jewish kingdoms. In mid-2003, as President Bush was securing agreement to a new peace plan between Israel and the Palestinian Muslims who have occupied these lands for centuries, a conservative Jewish Israeli cabinet minister insisted that Palestinians must understand that God had given all of these lands to the Jews. The day the new peace plan was signed, ten thousand Israelis demonstrated against recognizing Palestinian rights to any territory that had been part of the ancient kingdom of Israel. Like others before it, the peace plan soon collapsed. For greater security against suicide bombers, Israel began walling off West Bank Palestinian lands.

Muslims have also drawn varying conclusions about the age of globalization. Moderate views predominate, but extreme and intolerant groups have been on the rise. Even though adherents to Islam number well over a billion globally and the numbers are increasing rapidly, many Muslims feel frustrated. The last of the Islamic empires disappeared after the defeat of the Ottoman Empire in the First World War, and three decades of European occupation of former Ottoman lands followed.

Since becoming independent in the 1950s, some Middle Eastern states have earned great wealth from petroleum exports, but per capita income in Muslim-majority countries in 2002 averaged half as much as in the world as a whole. No Muslim state is a major industrial or geopolitical power. The spread of mass media has also fed discontent by making ordinary Muslims more aware of life in the outside world and of the wide gaps in income and privilege within Muslim societies.

This failure of economic, social, and political modernization to advance along the lines envisioned by nationalist leaders of the twentieth century has led many Muslims to seek consolation in their sacred past. For some, it has also encouraged hostility to the seductions of the modern world and a rekindling of the Islamic struggle against non-Muslim infidels. In Indonesia, Nigeria, and other places, Muslim militants have assaulted non-Muslim minorities, often provoking retaliations.

Others have focused their hostility on external enemies. Much resentment centers on Israel, a Jewish state established in a part of the world that had been Muslim for many centuries. Israel's military victories over its Islamic neighbors have been particularly painful, as has been the failure to create the Palestinian state envisaged by the United Nations resolution in 1947. Israel's greater economic prosperity and technological sophistication are also frustrating to its Muslim neighbors.

Because American aid and support have helped Israel acquire the most powerful military force in the Middle East, much Islamic hatred and opposition has been directed against the United States. Many militants also denounce American support for unpopular and undemocratic governments in Muslim-majority countries, especially Saudi Arabia. Although most Muslims admire American technological and cultural achievements, a 2002 poll by the Pew Research Center for the People and the Press found that the majority of Egyptians, Jordanians, and Pakistanis held a "very unfavorable" opinion of the United States. America's extensive aid to Egypt and Pakistan seems to have won it few friends in those countries. The American-led liberation of the Muslim state of Kuwait in the Persian Gulf War of 1990–1991 after a violent takeover by Iraq actually became a rallying issue for many Islamic extremists, in part because of the American use of bases in Saudi Arabia, which they consider sacred territory.

This view of the world order has many roots, but it reflects an ideological vision of Muslims under attack that is widely published in the media in Muslim states and promoted by some Islamic leaders who use religious ideas to justify violent actions. From this perspective the Palestinian suicide bombers in Israel that others call terrorists are martyrs and heroes. Such a vision explains why some Muslims celebrated when the Twin Towers collapsed in New York.

While the actions of militant Muslims are based on their perception of complex realities, it is important to keep in mind that they are also the product of ideologies. A rational explanation of the 9/11 events makes no sense, according to Professor Richard Landes, director of the Center for Millennial Studies, because Usama bin Laden believes he is fighting "in a cosmic battle that pits the warriors for truth against the agents of Satan and evil in this world." Similarly, Bernard Lewis, a respected senior scholar of Islam, argues that for bin Laden "2001 marks the resumption of the war for the religious dominance of the world that began in the seventh century" when Islam was founded.[2] Such beliefs help explain why many Muslims also saw nothing positive in America's overthrow of the oppressive and unpopular Taliban regime in Afghanistan in 2001 and why a high proportion of Muslims regarded the American campaign to oust Saddam Husain from Iraq in 2003 as further American aggression against the Muslim world, rather than as the liberation of Muslims from an oppressive dictator.

Universal Rights and Values

At the same time as these religious visions have gained strength, efforts to promote adherence to universal standards of human rights have also gained wider acceptance. Religious leaders had first voiced the notion that all people are equal, but the modern human rights movement grew out of the secular statements of the French Declaration of the Rights of Man (1789) and the U.S. Constitution (1788) and Bill of Rights (1791). Over the next century, the logic of universal rights moved Westerners to undertake international campaigns to end slave trading and slavery throughout the world and to secure equal legal rights (and eventually voting rights) for women.

International organizations in the twentieth century secured agreement on labor standards, the rules of war, and the rights of refugees. The pinnacle of these efforts was the **Universal Declaration of Human Rights,** passed by the United Nations General Assembly in 1948, which proclaimed itself "a common standard of achievement for all peoples and nations." Its thirty articles condemned slavery, torture, cruel and inhuman punishment, and arbitrary arrest, detention, and exile. The Declaration called for freedom of movement, assembly, and thought. It asserted rights to life, liberty, and security of person; to impartial public trials; and to education, employment, and leisure. The principle of equality was most fully articulated in Article 2:

> Everyone is entitled to all the rights and freedoms set forth in this Declaration, without distinction of any kind, such as race, color, sex, language, religion, or political or other opinion, national or social origin, property, birth or other status.[3]

This passage reflected an international consensus against racism and imperialism and a growing acceptance of the importance of social and economic equality. Most newly independent countries joining the United Nations willingly signed the Declaration because it implicitly condemned European colonial regimes.

The idea of universal human rights has not gone unchallenged. Some have asked whether a set of principles whose origins were so clearly Western could be called universal. Others have been uneasy with the idea of subordinating the traditional values of their culture or religion to a broader philosophical standard. Despite these objections, important gains have been made in implementing these standards.

Besides the official actions of the United Nations and individual states, individual human rights activists, often working through international philanthropic bodies known as **nongovernmental organizations (NGOs),** have been important forces for promoting human rights. Amnesty International, founded in 1961 and numbering a million members in 162 countries by the 1990s, concentrates on gaining the freedom of people who have been tortured or imprisoned without trial and campaigns against summary execution by government death squads or other gross violations of rights. Arguing that no right is more fundamental than the right to life, other NGOs have devoted themselves to famine relief, refugee assistance, and health care around the world. Médecins Sans Frontières (Doctors Without Borders), founded in 1971, was awarded the Nobel Peace Prize for 1999 for the medical assistance it offered in scores of crisis situations.

The rising tendency to see health care as a human right has made a new disease, acquired immune deficiency syndrome (AIDS), the focus of particular attention because its incidence and high mortality rate are closely associated with poverty, and treatments are very expensive. Over 40 million people worldwide are infected with the HIV retrovirus that causes AIDS. Of them, 70 percent live in sub-Saharan Africa (see Figure 33.1). The number of sick and dying is already large enough in some parts of Africa to pose a significant risk to the production of food, the care of the young and elderly, and the staffing of schools. Because sexual promiscuity among young men serving in the armed forces has made them especially likely to be infected, death and incapacitation from AIDS

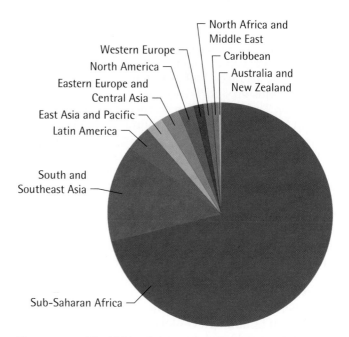

Figure 33.1 World Distribution of HIV/AIDS Cases (2001 estimates) *Source:* United Nations AIDS and World Health Organization, *Report on the Global HIV/AIDS Epidemic* (June 2000).

has significantly imperiled military preparedness in parts of Africa. Great international efforts are being made to provide drugs at a lower cost, so that more Africans can be treated. Because the disease is not contagious except by very intimate contact, education is a more cost-effective way of stemming the spread of AIDS. In Uganda, South Africa, and Ethiopia, for example, education campaigns have reduced the incidence of new HIV infections in targeted groups. An inexpensive drug has also been successful in cutting the transmission of the infection from mother to infant during childbirth.

Other international agreements have made genocide a crime and have promoted environmental protection of the seas, of Antarctica, and of the atmosphere. The United States and a few other nations were greatly concerned that such treaties would unduly limit their sovereignty or threaten their national interests. For this reason the U.S. Congress delayed ratifying the 1949 convention on genocide until 1986. More recently the United States drew widespread international criticism for demanding exemption for Americans from the jurisdiction of the International Criminal Court, created in 2002 to try international criminals, and for withdrawing in 2001 from the 1997 Kyoto Protocol requiring industrial nations to sharply reduce emissions of pollutants that damage the atmosphere (see Environment and Technology: Global Warming). To many nations it seemed as if

Global Warming

Until the 1980s environmental alarms focused mainly on localized episodes of air and water pollution, exposure to toxic substances, waste management, and the disappearance of wilderness. The development of increasingly powerful computers and complex models of ecological interactions in the 1990s, however, made people aware of the global scope of certain environmental problems.

Many scientists and policymakers came to perceive global warming, the slow increase of the temperature of the Earth's lower atmosphere, as an environmental threat requiring preventive action on an international scale. The warming is caused by a layer of atmospheric gases (carbon dioxide, methane, nitrous oxide, and ozone) that allow solar radiation to reach Earth and warm it, but keep infrared energy (heat) from radiating from Earth's surface into space. Called the *greenhouse effect*, this process normally keeps the Earth's temperature at a level suitable for life. However, increases in greenhouse-gas emissions—particularly from the burning of fossil fuels in industry and transportation—have added to this insulating atmospheric layer.

Recent events have confirmed predictions of global temperature increases and melting glaciers and icecaps. Globally, the five warmest years on record were 1995, 1997, 1998, 2001, and 2002. Record heat hit northern Europe in the summer of 2003. Greenland glaciers and Arctic Ocean sea ice melted at record rates during 2002, and a huge section of the Antarctic ice shelf broke up and floated away. Andean glaciers are shrinking so fast they could disappear in a decade, imperiling water supplies for drinking, irrigation, and hydroelectric production. Drought has affected much of the United States in recent years, and in 2002 Australia experienced the "Big Dry," its worst drought in a century.

Despite this evidence, governments of the industrialized countries that produce the most greenhouse gasses have been slow to adopt measures stringent enough to reduce emissions because of the negative effects they believe this could have on their economies. There is also fear that it may be already too late to reverse global warming. The pledges that representatives from 178 countries made at the first Earth Summit in Rio de Janeiro in 1992 to limit their *increase* in greenhouse-gas production have so far been ineffective. Fearing limits on gas emissions could cripple their plans for industrial and economic expansion, many nations hesitated to sign the 1997 Kyoto Protocol, the first international agreement to impose penalties on countries that failed to cut greenhouse-gas emissions. It was a major environmental victory when Japan added its signature in March 2001, but to the consternation of many world leaders President George W. Bush has rejected the agreement. The war on terrorism also appears to have made the environment a lower American priority. Until the destructive effects of global warming, such as the inundation of coastal regions and large cities by rising sea levels, match the destruction of terrorists, the political focus is unlikely to shift.

Flooding in Bangladesh Typhoon-driven floods submerge the low-lying farmlands of Bangladesh with tragic regularity. Any significant rise in the sea level will make parts of the country nearly uninhabitable. (D. Aubert/Sygma)

Americans, with the world's greatest industrial economy, were trying to exempt themselves from standards that they wanted to impose on other nations.

Women's Rights

The women's rights movement, which began on both sides of the North Atlantic in the nineteenth century, became an important human rights issue in the twentieth century. Rights for women became accepted in Western countries and were enshrined in the constitutions of many nations newly freed from colonial rule. . A series of international conferences on the status of women sponsored by the Division for the Advancement of Women of the United Nations have shown the international importance of women's rights at the end of the twentieth century. The first meeting, held in Nairobi, Kenya, in 1985, attracted seventeen thousand women from all over the world. The delegates focused on equal access to education and jobs and on quality-of-life matters such as ending sexual exploitation and gaining control of reproduction. A second conference in Beijing in 1995 also examined a variety of women's issues and perspectives, in some cases to the discomfort of the Chinese government. The Beijing conference recognized the advances that had been made in the status of women and called for efforts to remove remaining obstacles to equality, including those caused by poverty.

Besides highlighting the similarity of the problems women faced around the world, the conferences also revealed great variety in the views and concerns of women. Feminists from the West, who had been accustomed to dictating the agenda and who had pushed for the liberation of women in other parts of the world, sometimes found themselves accused of having narrow concerns and condescending attitudes. Some non-Western women complained about Western feminists' endorsement of sexual liberation and about the deterioration of family life in the West. They found Western feminists' concern with matters such as comfortable clothing misplaced and trivial compared to the issues of poverty and disease.

Other cultures came in for their share of criticism. Western women and many secular leaders in Muslim countries protested Islam's requirement that a woman cover her head and wear loose-fitting garments to conceal the shape of her body, practices enforced by law in countries such as Iran and Saudi Arabia. Nevertheless, many outspoken Muslim women voluntarily donned concealing garments as expressions of personal belief, statements of resistance to secular dictatorship, or defense against coarse male behavior. Much Western criticism focused on the African custom of circumcising girls, a form of genital mutilation that can cause chronic infections or permanently impair sexual enjoyment. While not denying the problems this practice can lead to, many African women saw deteriorating economic conditions, rape, and AIDS as more important issues.

The conferences were more important for the attention they focused on women's issues than for the solutions they generated. The search for a universally accepted women's rights agenda proved elusive because of local concerns and strong disagreement on abortion and other issues. Nevertheless, increases in women's educa-

Beijing Women's Conference in 1995 This gathering of women from every part of the world, under United Nations auspices, illustrated the challenges posed by women's search for equality. The Chinese government, consistent with its policies of suppressing dissent and closely regulating social life, tried to limit press access to the conference. As in many other instances, these efforts to silence or control women's voices on issues like abortion and family planning proved ineffective. (Boulat/Sipa Press)

tion, access to employment, political participation, and control of fertility augured well for the eventual achievement of gender equality.

Such efforts raised the prominence of human rights as a global concern and put pressure on governments to consider human rights when making foreign policy decisions. Skeptics observed, however, that a Western country could successfully prod a non-Western country to improve its human rights performance—for example, by granting women more equal access to education and careers—but that reverse criticism of a Western country often fell on deaf ears—for example, condemnation of the death penalty in the United States. For such critics the human rights movement was not as an effort to make the world more humane but another form of Western cultural imperialism, a club with which to beat former colonial societies into submission. Still, support for universal rights has grown, especially because increasing globalization has made common standards of behavior more important.

GLOBAL CULTURE

Along with the human rights movement, other kinds of cultural globalization were also proceeding rapidly at the turn of the millennium. A global language, a global educational system, and global forms of artistic expression have all come into being. Trade, travel, and migration have made a common culture necessary. Electronic communications that were once confined to members of a jet-setting elite have enabled global cultural influences to move deeper into many societies, and a sort of global popular culture has also emerged. These changes have angered some and delighted others.

The Media and the Message

Although cultural influences from every continent travel around the world, the fact that the most pervasive elements of global culture have their origins in the West raises concerns in many quarters about **cultural imperialism.** Critics complain that entertainment conglomerates are flooding the world's movie theaters and television screens with Western tastes and styles and that manufacturers are flooding world markets with Western goods—both relying on sophisticated advertising techniques that promote consumption and cultural conformity. In this view, global marketing is an especially insidious effort not only to overwhelm the world with a single Western out-

look shaped by capitalist ideology, but also to suppress or devalue traditional cultures and alternative ideologies. As the leader of the capitalist world, the United States is seen as the primary culprit.

But in truth, technology plays a more central role than ideology in spreading Western culture. Even though imperialist forces old and new shape choices, strongly democratic forces are also at work as people around the world make their selections in the cultural marketplace. Thus, a diversity of voices is more characteristic of cultural globalization than the cultural imperialism thesis maintains.

The pace of cultural globalization began to quicken during the economic recovery after World War II. The Hollywood films and American jazz recordings that had become popular in Europe and parts of Asia continued to spread. But the birth of electronic technology opened contacts with large numbers of people who could never have afforded to go to a movie or buy a record.

The first step was the development of cheap transistor radios that could run for months on a couple of small batteries. Perfected by American scientists at Bell Telephone Laboratories in 1948, solid-state electronic transistors replaced power-hungry and less reliable electron tubes in radios and a wide array of other devices. Just as tube radios had spread in Europe and America in the decades before the war, small portable transistor radios, most made in Japan and elsewhere in Asia, spread rapidly in parts of the world where homes lacked electricity.

Because the transistor radios sold in Asia and Africa were designed to receive shortwave broadcasts, they brought people in remote villages the news, views, and music that American, European, Soviet, and Chinese transmitters beamed to the world. For the first time in history, the whole world could learn of major political and cultural events simultaneously. Although such broadcasts came in local and regional languages, many were in English. Electronic audiotape and CD players added to the diversity of music available to individuals everywhere.

Television, made possible by the invention of an electron scanning gun in 1928, became widely available to consumers in Western countries in the 1950s. In poorer parts of the world TVs were not common until the 1980s and 1990s, after mass production and cheap transistors made sets more affordable and reliable. Outside the United States, television broadcasting was usually a government monopoly at first, following the pattern of telegraph and postal service and radio broadcasting. Governments expected news reports and other programming to disseminate a unified national viewpoint.

Government monopolies eroded as the high cost of television production opened up global markets for re-broadcasts of American soap operas, adventure series, and situation comedies. By the 1990s a global network of satellites brought privately owned television broadcasting to even remote areas of the world, and the VCR (videocassette recorder) brought an even greater variety of programs to people everywhere. British programs found a secondary market in the United States, Canada, Australia, and other countries. As a result of wider circulation of programming, people often became familiar with different dialects of English and other languages. People in Portugal, for example, who in the 1960s had found it difficult to understand Brazilian Portuguese, have become avid fans of Brazilian soap operas. Immigrants from Albania and North Africa often arrive in Italy with a command of Italian learned from Italian stations whose signals they could pick up at home.

Further internationalization of culture resulted from satellite transmission of TV signals. Specializing in rock music videos aimed at a youth audience, MTV (Music Television) became an international enterprise offering special editions in different parts of the world. Music videos shown in Uzbekistan°, for example, often featured Russian bands, and Chinese groups appeared in MTV programs shown in Singapore. CNN (Cable News Network) expanded its international market after becoming the most-viewed and informative news source during the 1991 Persian Gulf War, when it broadcast live from Baghdad. Despite CNN's fundamentally American view of the news, its round-the-clock coverage and global resources began to supplant other commercial and government news programming as the best source of information about rapidly developing events. By the new millennium global satellite networks (Fox, Sky) assembled by Rupert Murdock and new regional networks competed for viewers.

The Internet, a linkage of academic, government, and business computer networks developed in the 1960s, became a major cultural phenomenon. Personal computers proliferated in the 1980s, and with the establishment of the easy-to-use graphic interface of the World Wide Web in 1994, the number of Internet users skyrocketed. Myriad new companies formed to exploit "e-commerce," the commercial dimension of the Internet. In the new century many college students spent less time studying conventional books and scholarly resources than they spent exploring the Web for information and entertainment.

Uzbekistan (ooz-BEK-ih-STAN)

As had happened so often throughout history, technological developments had unanticipated consequences. Although the new telecommunications and entertainment technologies derived disproportionately from American invention, industry, and cultural creativity, Japan and other East Asian nations came to dominate the manufacture and refinement of computer devices. In the 1990s Japan introduced digital television broadcasting at about the time that disks containing digitized movies and computer programs with movie-like action became increasingly available. In the early 2000s digital cameras, DVD players, and new generations of cell phones became popular, providing opportunities for companies in a variety of developing countries to capture a corner of the market. In contrast to these rapid changes in technology, Western, especially American, cultural domination of the content of the Web has changed more slowly, but people around the world can adapt the medium to their own purposes.

The Spread of Pop Culture

New technologies changed perceptions of culture as well as its distribution around the world and among different social classes. For most of history, popular culture was folk culture, highly localized ways of dress, food, music, and expression. Only the educated and urban few had access to the riches of a broader "great tradition," such as Confucianism in East Asia or Western culture in Europe and the Americas. The schools of modern nation-states promoted national values and beliefs, and tastes in painting, literature, and art. Governments also promoted a common language or dialect and frequently suppressed local traditions and languages. In a more democratic way, the transistor helped break down barriers and create a global popular culture that transcended regional great traditions and national cultures.

Initially, the content of global **pop culture** was heavily American. Singer Michael Jackson was almost as well known to the youth of Dar-es-Salaam (Tanzania) and Bangkok (Thailand) as to American fans. Basketball star Michael Jordan became a worldwide celebrity, heavily promoted by Nike, McDonald's, and television. American television programs such as Wheel of Fortune and Friends acquired immense followings and inspired local imitations. In the late twentieth century American movies, which had long had great popular appeal, substantially increased their share of world markets. In the 1990s the vast majority of the most popular films in Europe were American made. Many Europeans complained loudly about this American cultural imperialism—and then bought tickets to see the latest Hollywood spectacular.

As with music and fast food, companies spent heavily to promote profitable overseas markets, but the United States did not have a lock on global pop culture. Latin American soap operas, *telenovelas*, have a vast following in the Americas, eastern Europe, and elsewhere. Bombay, India, long the largest producer of films in the world, is now making more films for an international audience, rather than just for the home market. Bruce Lee popularized kung fu (Chinese martial arts) movies. A sophisticated kung fu film, *Crouching Tiger, Hidden Dragon* by Hong Kong-born director Ang Lee, was very popular in the United States and won four Academy Awards for 2000, including one for the best foreign-language film.

In the post–World War II decades American, European, and Japanese companies sought international markets for their products. In the 1970s and 1980s American brand names like Levi's, Coca-Cola, Marlboro, Gillette, McDonald's, and Kentucky Fried Chicken were global phenomena. But in time Asian names—Hitachi, Sony, Sanyo, and Mitsubishi— were blazoned in neon and on giant video screens on the sides of skyscrapers, along with European brands such as Nestlé, Mercedes, Pirelli, and Benetton. The location of manufacturing plants overseas and the acquisition of corporate operations by foreign buyers rendered such global firms as transnational as the products they sell.

The content of international pop culture does not have to remain any more monolithic than the typical McDonald's lunch, which consists of a meat patty named for a German city, potatoes prepared in a French manner, and a soft drink named after the South American coca leaves and West African kola that were its original ingredients. Popular music also became increasingly international. Latin American styles extended their appeal beyond the Americas. The hybrid rhythms known as Afropop spread around Africa and found fans in Europe and the Americas.

Emerging Global Culture

While the globalization of popular culture has been criticized, cultural links across national and ethnic boundaries at a more elite level have generated little controversy. The end of the Cold War reopened intellectual and cultural

Japanese Adult Male Comic Book   After World War II comic magazines emerged as a major form of publication and a distinctive product of culture in Japan. Different series are directed to different age and gender groups. Issued weekly and running to some three hundred pages in black and white, the most popular magazines sell as many copies as do major newsmagazines in the United States.   (Private Collection)

contacts between former adversaries, making possible such things as Russian-American collaboration on space missions and extensive business contacts among former rivals. The English language, modern science, and higher education became the key elements of this **global culture.**

The emergence of English as the first global language depended on developments that had been building for centuries. The British Empire introduced the language to far-flung colonies. When the last parts of the empire gained independence after World War II, most former colonies chose to continue using English as an official language because it provided national unity and a link to the outside world that the dozens or hundreds of local languages could not. After independence, representatives of former British colonies formed the Commonwealth on the basis of their shared language and commercial ties. Newly independent countries that made a local language official for nationalist reasons often found the decision counterproductive. Indian nationalists had pushed for Hindi to be India's official language, but they found that students taught in Hindi were unable to compete internationally because of poor knowledge of English. Sri Lanka, which had made Sinhala its official language in 1956, reversed itself after local reporters revealed in 1989 that prominent officials were sending their children to English-medium private schools.

The use of English as a second language was greatly stimulated by the importance of the United States in postwar world affairs. Individuals recognized the importance of mastering English for successful business, diplomatic, and military careers. After the collapse of Soviet domination, students in eastern Europe flocked to study English instead of Russian. Ninety percent of students in Cambodia (a former French colony) choose to study English, even though a Canadian agency offers a sizable cash bonus if they will study French. In the 1990s China made the study of English as a second language nearly universal from junior high school onwards, but also forced an English-medium school in Hong Kong to teach most subjects in Chinese.

English has become the language of choice for most international academic conferences, business meetings, and diplomatic gatherings. International organizations that provide equal status to many languages, such as the United Nations and the European Union, tend to conduct all informal committee meetings in English. English has even replaced Latin as the working language for international consultations in the Catholic Church. In cities throughout the world, signs and notices are now posted in the local language and English.

The utility of English as a global language is also evident in the emergence of an international literature in English (see Diversity and Dominance: World Literature in English). The trend has been evident for decades in former British colonies in Africa, where most writers use English to reach both a national audience and an international one. Wole Soyinka, the first sub-Saharan African to win the Nobel Prize in literature for 1986, wrote in English, the national language of Nigeria,

V. S. Naipaul Receives the 2001 Nobel Prize for Literature Of Indian descent and Trinidadian birth, Naipaul wrote critically of life in the West Indies, Africa, and the Islamic world. His selection for the world's most prestigious literary prize was a tribute to his talents and diligence and also highlighted the increasing globalization of writing in English. (Jonas Ekstromer/Pool/AP Wide)

rather than his native Yoruba. When Arundhati Roy won the prestigious Booker Prize in 1997 for *The God of Small Things,* a novel set in her native state of Kerala in southwest India, she was part of an English-language literary tradition that has been growing in India for a century. V. S. Naipaul of Trinidad, winner of the Nobel Prize in literature for 2001, is a good example of the way global migration has fostered the use of English. Naipaul's ancestors had emigrated from India in the nineteenth century.

World literature remains highly diverse in form and language, but science and technology have become standardized components of global culture. Though imperialism helped spread the Western disciplines of biology, chemistry, and physics around the world, their popularity continued to expand even after imperial systems ended because they worked so much better than other approaches to the natural world. Their truth was universal even if plants and animals continue to be classified in Latin and the less common elements are called by names originally derived from Latin and Greek. Global manufacturing could not function without a common system of applied science. Because of their scientific basis Western medicine and drugs are increasingly accepted as the best treatments, even though many cultures also use traditional remedies.

The third pillar of global elite culture is the university. The structure and curricula of modern universities are nearly indistinguishable around the world, permitting students today to cross national boundaries as freely as students in the medieval Latin West or the Muslim world. Instruction in the pure sciences varies little from place to place, and standardization is nearly as common in social science and applied sciences such as engineering and medicine. There may be more diversity in the humanities, but professors and students around the world pay attention to the latest literary theories and topics of historical interest.

While university subjects are taught in many languages, instruction in English is spreading rapidly. Because discoveries are often first published in English, advanced students in science, business, and international relations need to know that language to keep up with the latest developments. The global mobility of professors and students also promotes classroom instruction in the most global language. Many courses in the Netherlands and in Scandinavian countries have long been offered in English, and elsewhere in Europe offering more courses in English was the obvious way to facilitate the EU's efforts to encourage students to study outside their countries of origin. When South Africa ended the apartheid educational systems that had required people to study in their own languages, most students chose to study in English.

Because global elite culture is so deeply rooted in years of training, complex institutions, and practical utility, it is less subject to fads and commercial promotion than is global pop culture. Because such elite culture is confined to a distinct minority in most places, it poses little threat to national and folk cultures and, therefore, is much less controversial.

Enduring Cultural Diversity

Although protestors regularly denounce the "Americanization" of the world, a closer look suggests that cultural globalization is more complex and multifaceted. Just as English has largely spread as a second language, so global culture is primarily a second culture that dominates some contexts but does not displace other traditions. From this perspective, American music, fast food, and fashions are more likely to add to a society's options than to displace local culture. In any event, the amount of global change largely rests with the world's 6 billion people.

Japan first demonstrated that a country with a non-Western culture could perform at a high industrial level. Individuality was less valued in Japan than the ability of each person to fit into a group, whether as an employee, a member of an athletic team, or a student in a class. Moreover, the Japanese considered it unmannerly to directly contradict, correct, or refuse the request of another person. From a Western point of view, these Japanese customs seemed to discourage individual initiative and personality development and to preserve traditional hierarchies. Japanese women, for example, even though they often worked outside the home, responded only slowly to the American and European feminist advocacy of equality in economic and social relations. However, the Japanese approach to social relations was well suited to an industrial economy. The efficiency, pride in workmanship, and group solidarity of Japanese workers, supported by closely coordinated government and corporate policies, played a major role in transforming Japan from a defeated nation with a demolished industrial base in 1945 to an economic power by the 1980s.

Japan's success in the modern industrial world called into question the older assumption that successful industrialization required the adoption of Western culture. As awareness of the economic impact of Japanese culture and society began to spread, it became apparent that Taiwan and South Korea, along with Singapore and Hong Kong (a British colony before being reunited with China in 1997), were developing dynamic industrial economies of their own. Other countries seem likely to follow this model.

This does not mean that the world's culture diversity is secure. Every decade a number of languages cease to be spoken, usually as the result of the spread of national languages. Many religious practices are also disappearing in the face of the successful expansion of Islam, Christianity, and other religions, although secular values also play a role. Televised national ceremonies

DIVERSITY AND DOMINANCE

WORLD LITERATURE IN ENGLISH

The linguistic diversity of the world is part of its richness, but it is also an impediment to global communication. In this essay novelist and Indian diplomat Shashi Tharoor explains why he chooses to write in English. His decision to use English is not unusual among writers in India and many other lands where English is not the first language. Mr. Tharoor has worked for the United Nations since 1978. In 2002 he became Under-Secretary-General for Communications and Public Information.

For the record, the national languages of India are Hindi (spoken by 30 percent of the population) and English, which dominates communication among India's elite. Fourteen other languages are official at the provincial level, with English having official status in the provinces of East Bengal, Kerala, and Orissa.

As an Indian writer living in New York, I find myself constantly asked a question with which my American confreres never have to contend: "But whom do you write for?"

In my case, the question is complicated by both geography and language. I live in the United States (because of my work at the United Nations) and I write about India; and I do so in English, a language mastered, if the last census is to be believed, by only 2 percent of the Indian population. There is an unspoken accusation implicit in the question: Am I not guilty of the terrible sin of inauthenticity, of writing about my country for foreigners? . . .

This is ironic, because few developments in world literature have been more remarkable than the emergence, over the last two decades, of a new generation of Indian writers in English.

Beginning with Salman Rushdie's *Midnight's Children* in 1981, they have expanded the boundaries of their craft and their nation's literary heritage, enriching English with the rhythms of ancient legends and the larger-then-life complexities of another civilization, while reinventing India in the confident cadences of English prose. Of the unintended consequences of empire, it is hard to imagine one of greater value to both colonizers and colonized.

The new Indian writers dip into a deep well off memory and experience far removed from those of their fellow novelists in the English language. But whereas Americans or Englishmen or Australians have also set their fictions in distant lands Indians write of India without exoticism, their insights undimmed by the dislocations of foreignness. And they do so in an English they have both learned and lived, an English of freshness and vigor, a language that is as natural to them as their quarrels at the school playground or the surreptitious notes they slipped each other in their classrooms.

Yet Indian critics still suggest that there is something artificial and un-Indian about an Indian writing in English. One critic disparagingly declared that the acid test ought to be, "Could this have been written only by an Indian?" I have never been much of a literary theoretician—I always felt that for a writer to study literature at university would be like learning about girls at medical school—but for most, though not all, of my own writing, I would answer that my works could not only have been written only by an Indian, but only by an Indian *in English*.

I write for anyone who will read me, but first of all for Indians like myself, Indians who have grown up speaking, writing, playing, wooing and quarreling in English, all over India. (No writer really chooses a language: the circumstances of his upbringing ensure that the language chooses him.)

Members of this class have entered the groves of academe and condemned themselves in terms of bitter self-reproach: one Indian scholar, Harish Trivedi, has asserted (in English) that Indian writers in that language are "cut off from the experiential mainstream and from that common cultural matrix . . . shared with writers of all other Indian languages." Dr. Trivedi metaphorically cites the fictional English-medium school in an R. K. Narayan story where the students must first rub off the sandalwood-paste caste marks from their foreheads before they enter its portals: "For this golden gate is only for the déraciné to pass through, for those who have erased their antecedents." [R. K. Narayan (1906–2001) pioneered writing in English in Madras in the 1930s, publishing three dozen novels and many short stories and essays.]

It's an evocative image, even though I thought the secular Indian state was supposed to encourage the erasure of casteism from the classroom. But the more important point is that writers like myself do share a "common cultural matrix," albeit one devoid of helpfully identifying caste marks.

It is one that consists of an urban upbringing and a pan-national outlook on the Indian reality. I do not think this is any less authentically "Indian" than the worldviews of writers in other Indian languages. Why should the rural peasant or the small-town schoolteacher with his sandalwood-smeared forehead be considered more quintessentially Indian than the punning collegian or the Bombay socialite, who are as much a part of the Indian reality?

India is a vast and complex country; in Whitman's phrase, it contains multitudes. I write of an India of multiple truths and multiple realities, an India that is greater than the sum of its parts. English expresses that diversity better than any Indian language precisely because it is not "rooted" in any one region of my vast country. At the same time, as an Indian, I remain conscious of, and connected to, my pre-urban and non-Anglophone antecedents: my novels reflect an intellectual heritage that embraces the ancient epic the Mahabharata, the Kerala folk dance called the ottamthullal (of which my father was a gifted practitioner) and the Hindi B-movies of Bollywood [the large movie-making industry of Bombay], as well as Shakespeare, Wodehouse and the Beatles.

As a first-generation urbanite myself, I keep returning to the Kerala villages of my parents, in my life as in my writing. Yet I have grown up in Bombay, Calicutta and Delhi, Indian cities a thousand miles apart from one another; the mother of my children is half-Kashmiri, half-Bengali; and my own mother now lives in the southern town of Coimbatore. This may be a wider cultural matrix than the good Dr. Trivedi imagined, but it draws from a rather broad range of Indian experience. And English is the language that brings those various threads of my India together, the language in which my wife could speak to her mother-in-law, the language that enables a Calcuttan to function in Coimbatore, the language that serves to express the complexity of that polyphonous Indian experience better than any other language I know.

As a novelist, I believe in distracting in order to instruct—my novels are, to some degree, didactic works masquerading as entertainments. Like Molière I believe that you have to entertain in order to edify. But the entertainment, and the edification, might strike different readers differently.

My first novel, *The Great Indian Novel*, as a satirical reinvention of the Mahabharata inevitably touches Indians in a way that most foreigners will not fully appreciate. But my publishers in the West enjoyed its stories and the risks it took with narrative form. My second, *Show Business*, did extremely well with American reviewers and readers, who enjoyed the way I tried to portray the lives and stories of Bollywood as a metaphor for Indian society. With *India: From Midnight to the Millennium*, an attempt to look back at the last 50 years of India's history; I found an additional audience of Indian-Americans seeking to rediscover their roots; their interest has helped the American edition outsell the Indian one.

In my new novel, *Riot*, for the first time I have major non-Indian characters, Americans as it happens, and that is bound to influence the way the book is perceived in the United States, and in India. Inevitably the English fundamentally affects the content of each book, but it does not determine the audience of the writer; as long as translations exist, language is a vehicle, not a destination.

Of course, there is no shame in acknowledging that English is the legacy of the colonial connection, but one no less useful and valid than the railway, the telegraphs or the law courts that were also left behind by the British. Historically, English helped us to find our Indian voice: that great Indian nationalist Jawaharlal Nehru wrote *The Discovery of India* in English. But the eclipse of that dreadful phrase "the Indo-Anglian novel" has occurred precisely because Indian writers have evolved well beyond the British connection to their native land.

The days when Indians wrote novels in English either to flatter or rail against their colonial masters are well behind us. Now we have Indians in India writing as naturally about themselves in English as Australians or South Africans do, and their tribe has been supplemented by India's rich diaspora in the United States, which has already produced a distinctive crop of impressive novelists, with Pulitzer Prizes and National Book Awards to their names.

Their addresses don't matter because writers really live inside their heads and on the page, and geography is merely a circumstance. They write secure of themselves in heritage of diversity, and they write free of the anxiety of audience, for theirs are narratives that appeal as easily to Americans as to Indians—and indeed to readers irrespective of ethnicity.

Surely that's the whole point about literature—that for a body of fiction to constitute a literature it must rise above its origins, its setting, even its language, to render accessible to a reader anywhere some insight into the human condition. Read my books and those of other Indian writers not because we're Indian, not necessarily because you are interested in India; but because they are worth reading in and of themselves. And dear reader, whoever you are, if you pick up one of my books, ask not for whom I write: I write for you.

QUESTIONS FOR ANALYSIS

1. What does Shashi Tharoor mean when he states that his novels could only have been written in English?

2. What is the relationship between national literature and global literature?

3. What does the author mean when he says that for writers "geography is merely a circumstance"?

Source: Shashi Tharoor, "A Bedeviling Question in the Cadence of English," *New York Times,* July 30, 2001. Copyright © 2001 by The New York Times Co. Reprinted by permission.

or performances for tourists may prevent folk customs and costumes from dying out, but they also tend to standardize rituals that once had many local variations. While it was possible to recognize the nationality of people from their clothing and grooming a century ago, today most urban men dress the same the world over, although women's clothing shows much greater variety. As much as one may regret the disappearance or commercialization of some folkways, most anthropologists would agree that change is characteristic of all healthy cultures. What doesn't change risks extinction.

CONCLUSION

Have we entered a golden age, or is the world descending into a fiery abyss? The future is unknowable, but the study of history suggests that neither extreme is likely. Golden ages and dark ages are rare, and our understanding of our own time is easily swayed by hopes, fears, and other emotions. If the exuberant optimism of the 1990s now seems excessive, the pessimism of the early 2000s may in time seem equally far off the mark.

What is undeniable is that the turn of the millennium has been a time of important global changes. The Iron Curtain that had divided Europe since the end of the Second World War fell, taking with it the tensions and risks of the Cold War. The great Soviet Empire broke up, while dozens of countries joined new economic coalitions. The bastions of communism embraced capitalism with varying degrees of enthusiasm. As trading barriers tumbled, world trade surged, creating new wealth and new inequalities in its distribution.

Aided by new electronic marvels, individuals communicated around the planet and interacted across cultural barriers in ways never before imagined. News of disasters and human rights violations brought more rapid responses than ever before. Culturally, the English language, higher education, and science formed a viable global culture for the elite.

History teaches that change is always uneven. The rate of change in global telecommunications and international economic institutions was notably faster than in international political institutions. The nation-state remained supreme. The structure of the United Nations was little different than at its founding six decades earlier. States resisted limits on their autonomy, and the more powerful ones took unilateral actions, whether supported or opposed by international public opinion. Never before had one state, the United States, stood so far above the rest.

Rather than giving ground to globalization, many older ideas and values continued to be strong. The less powerful adapted slowly, dug in their heals to resist change, or raised voices and fists against it. Protests forced new attention on global poverty, disease, exploitation, and environmental damage that globalization caused or failed to relieve. Adjustments were made, but on the whole change on these fronts also came slowly.

In many places religious fundamentalism, ethnic nationalism, and social conservatism seemed to reach new levels of intensity. In some quarters globalization fomented and fostered violent responses and provoked a new war on terrorism led by the United States. The resulting clashes raised concerns and inspired apocalyptic visions. Adjusting to the new age of globalization would be neither quick nor easy.

■ Key Terms

globalization
ethnic cleansing
weapons of mass destruction
terrorism
Usama bin Laden
World Trade Organization (WTO)
millenarianism
Universal Declaration of Human Rights
nongovernmental organizations (NGOs)
cultural imperialism
pop culture
global culture

■ Suggested Reading

Among those attempting to describe the world at the turn of the millennium are Benjamin R. Barber, *Jihad vs. McWorld: How Globalism and Tribalism Are Reshaping the World* (1995); Thomas L. Friedman, *The Lexus and the Olive Tree* (1999); Samuel P. Huntington, *The Clash of Civilizations and the Remaking of the World Order* (1996); and Paul Kennedy, *Preparing for the Twenty-First Century* (1993).

Recent studies of American military policies and the widening split with Europe include Dana Priest, *The Mission: Waging War and Keeping Peace with America's Military* (2003); Robert Kaplan, *Of Paradise and Power: America and Europe in the New World Order* (2002); Charles A. Kulpchan, *The End of the American Era: U.S. Foreign Policy and the Geopolitics of the Twenty-First Century* (2002); and Joseph S. Nye, Jr., *The Paradox of American Power: Why the World's Only Superpower Can't Go It Alone* (2002).

Mike Moore, a former director-general of the WTO, provides an insider's view of the global economy in *A World Without Walls: Freedom, Development, Free Trade and Global Governance*

(2003). Amy Chua, *World on Fire: How Exporting Free Market Democracy Breeds Ethnic Hatred and Global Instability* (2003), offers a quite different perspective.

Gilles Kepel, *The Revenge of God: The Resurgence of Islam, Christianity and Judaism in the Modern World* (1994), Philip Jenkins, *The Next Christendom: The Coming of Global Christianity* (2002), and Bernard Lewis, *What Went Wrong? The Clash Between Islam and Modernity in the Middle East* (2003), deal with recent religious-political movements. Eugen Weber, *Apocalypses: Prophesies, Cults, and Millennial Beliefs Through the Ages* (1999), provides a deeper historical perspective. The Bosnian crisis is well covered in Susan L. Woodward, *Balkan Tragedy: Chaos and Dissolution After the Cold War* (1995). Other world crises involving international intervention are treated in William J. Durch, ed., *UN Peacekeeping, American Policy, and the Uncivil Wars of the 1990s* (1996). Terrorism is well covered by Bruce Hoffman, *Inside Terrorism* (1998).

Standard reviews of human rights include Thomas Buergenthal, et al., *International Human Rights in a Nutshell,* 3d ed. (2002); Carol Devine and Carol Rae Hansen, *Human Rights: The Essential Reference* (1999); and Jack Donnelly, *International Human Rights,* 2d ed. (1998). Ronald Inglehart and Pippa Norris, *Rising Tide: Gender Equality and Cultural Change Around the World* (2003), surveys the condition of women.

The interrelationships between high culture and popular culture during the twentieth century are treated from different perspectives in Arjun Appadurai, *Modernity at Large: Cultural Dimensions of Globalization* (1996); Peter L. Berger and Samuel Huntington, eds., *Many Globalizations: Cultural Diversity in the Contemporary World* (2002); Tyler Cowen, *Creative Destruction: How Globalization Is Changing the World's Cultures* (2002); and Diana Crane, Nobuko Kawashima, and Kenichi Kawasaka,

eds., *Global Culture: Media Arts, Policy* (2002). Two very readable books by James B. Twitchell detail the rise of popular culture in the United States and present various reactions to this phenomenon: *Carnival Culture: The Trashing of Taste in America* (1992) and *Adcult USA: The Triumph of Advertising in American Culture* (1996). Walter LaFeber, *Michael Jordan and the New Global Capitalism* (1999), explores the relationship between a sports star and global marketing.

Some personal accounts of cultural change are Philippe Wamba, *Kinship: A Family's Journey in Africa and America* (1999); William Dalrymple, *The Age of Kali: Indian Travels and Encounters* (1998); V. S. Naipaul, *Beyond Belief: Islamic Excursions Among the Converted Peoples* (1997); Fergal Keane, *A Season of Blood: A Rwandan Journey* (1995); Nelson Mandela, *Long Walk to Freedom* (1994); and Mark Mathabane, *African Women: Three Generations* (1994).

On global English see David Crystal, *English as a Global Language* (1997); Alistaire Pennycock, *The Cultural Politics of English as an International Language* (1994); and Robert Phillipson, *Linguistic Imperialism* (1992).

■ Notes

1. "Liberty's Great Advance," *The Economist,* June 28–July 4, 2003, pp. 5-6.
2. Richard Landes, "Apocalyptic Islam and bin Laden," available at http://www.mille.org; and Bernard Lewis, "The Revolt of Islam: When Did the Conflict with the West Begin?" *The New Yorker,* November 11, 2001.
3. "Universal Declaration of Human Rights," in *Twenty-five Human Rights Documents* (New York: Center for the Study of Human Rights, Columbia University, 1994), 6.

Document-Based Question
Global Integration

Using the following documents, analyze the factors fostering and hindering the political, economic, and cultural integration of the global community.

DOCUMENT 1
Map 33.1 Global Distribution of Wealth (p. 886)

DOCUMENT 2
Map 33.2 Regional Trade Associations, 2004 (p. 888)

DOCUMENT 3
Map 33.3 World Religions (p. 891)

DOCUMENT 4
Excerpt from the Universal Declaration of Human Rights (p. 894)

DOCUMENT 5
Beijing Women's Conference in 1995 (photo, p. 896)

DOCUMENT 6
World Literature in English (Diversity and Dominance, pp. 902–903)

How does Shashi Tharoor's argument in Document 6 reflect divergent views of the global community? What additional types of documents would help you analyze the factors fostering and hindering the political, economic, and cultural integration of the global community?

Glossary

Abbasid Caliphate Descendants of the Prophet Muhammad's uncle, al-Abbas, the Abbasids overthrew the **Umayyad Caliphate** and ruled an Islamic empire from their capital in Baghdad (founded 762) from 750 to 1258. (*p. 203*)

abolitionists Men and women who agitated for a complete end to slavery. Abolitionist pressure ended the British transatlantic slave trade in 1808 and slavery in British colonies in 1834. In the United States the activities of abolitionists were one factor leading to the Civil War (1861–1865). (*p. 610*)

acculturation The adoption of the language, customs, values, and behaviors of host nations by immigrants. (*p. 614*)

Acheh Sultanate Muslim kingdom in northern Sumatra. Main center of Islamic expansion in Southeast Asia in the early seventeenth century, it declined after the Dutch seized **Malacca** from Portugal in 1641. (*p. 504*)

Aden Port city in the modern south Arabian country of Yemen. It has been a major trading center in the Indian Ocean since ancient times. (*p. 342*)

African National Congress An organization dedicated to obtaining equal voting and civil rights for black inhabitants of South Africa. Founded in 1912 as the South African Native National Congress, it changed its name in 1923. Though it was banned and its leaders were jailed for many years, it eventually helped bring majority rule to South Africa. (*p. 799*)

Afrikaners South Africans descended from Dutch and French settlers of the seventeenth century. Their Great Trek founded new settler colonies in the nineteenth century. Though a minority among South Africans, they held political power after 1910, imposing a system of racial segregation called apartheid after 1949. (*p. 717*)

Agricultural Revolution(s) (ancient) The change from food gathering to food production that occurred between ca. 8000 and 2000 B.C.E. Also known as the Neolithic Revolution. (*pp. 8, 570*)

agricultural revolution (eighteenth century) The transformation of farming that resulted in the eighteenth century from the spread of new crops, improvements in cultivation techniques and livestock breeding, and the consolidation of small holdings into large farms from which tenants and sharecroppers were forcibly expelled. (*p. 570*)

Aguinaldo, Emilio (1869–1964) Leader of the Filipino independence movement against Spain (1895–1898). He proclaimed the independence of the Philippines in 1899, but his movement was crushed and he was captured by the United States Army in 1901. (*p. 725*)

Akbar I (1542–1605) Most illustrious sultan of the Mughal Empire in India (r. 1556–1605). He expanded the empire and pursued a policy of conciliation with Hindus. (*p. 500*)

Akhenaten Egyptian pharaoh (r. 1353–1335 B.C.E.). He built a new capital at Amarna, fostered a new style of naturalistic art, and created a religious revolution by imposing worship of the sun-disk. The Amarna letters, largely from his reign, preserve official correspondence with subjects and neighbors. (*p. 64*)

Alexander (356–323 B.C.E.) King of Macedonia in northern Greece. Between 334 and 323 B.C.E. he conquered the Persian Empire, reached the Indus Valley, founded many Greek-style cities, and spread Greek culture across the Middle East. Later known as Alexander the Great. (*p. 116*)

Alexandria City on the Mediterranean coast of Egypt founded by Alexander. It became the capital of the Hellenistic kingdom of the **Ptolemies.** It contained the famous Library and the Museum—a center for leading scientific and literary figures. Its merchants engaged in trade with areas bordering the Mediterranean and the Indian Ocean. (*p. 117*)

Allende, Salvador (1908–1973) Socialist politician elected president of Chile in 1970 and overthrown by the military in 1973. He died during the military attack. (*p. 850*)

All-India Muslim League Political organization founded in India in 1906 to defend the interests of India's Muslim minority. Led by Muhammad Ali Jinnah, it attempted to negotiate with the **Indian National Congress.** In 1940, the League began demanding a separate state for Muslims, to be called Pakistan. (See also **Jinnah, Muhammad Ali.**) (*p. 803*)

amulet Small charm meant to protect the bearer from evil. Found frequently in archaeological excavations in Mesopotamia and Egypt, amulets reflect the religious practices of the common people. (*p. 19*)

Amur River This river valley was a contested frontier between northern China and eastern Russia until the settlement arranged in Treaty of Nerchinsk (1689). (*p. 522*)

anarchists Revolutionaries who wanted to abolish all private property and governments, usually by violence, and replace them with free associations of groups. (*p. 691*)

Anasazi Important culture of what is now the Southwest United States (1000–1300 C.E.). Centered on Chaco Canyon in New Mexico and Mesa Verde in Colorado, the Anasazi culture built multistory residences and worshiped in subterranean buildings called kivas. (*p. 278*)

aqueduct A conduit, either elevated or underground, using gravity to carry water from a source to a location—usually a city—that needed it. The Romans built many aqueducts in a period of substantial urbanization. (*p. 135*)

Arawak Amerindian peoples who inhabited the Greater Antilles of the Caribbean at the time of Columbus. (*p. 381*)

Arkwright, Richard (1732–1792) English inventor and entrepreneur who became the wealthiest and most successful textile manufacturer of the early **Industrial Revolution.** He invented the water frame, a machine that, with minimal human supervision, could spin many strong cotton threads at once. (*p. 575*)

Armenia   One of the earliest Christian kingdoms, situated in eastern Anatolia and the western Caucasus and occupied by speakers of the Armenian language. (*p. 190*)

Asante   African kingdom on the **Gold Coast** that expanded rapidly after 1680. Asante participated in the Atlantic economy, trading gold, slaves, and ivory. It resisted British imperial ambitions for a quarter century before being absorbed into Britain's Gold Coast colony in 1902. (*p. 718*)

Ashikaga Shogunate (1336–1573)   The second of Japan's military governments headed by a shogun (a military ruler). Sometimes called the Muromachi Shogunate. (*p. 320*)

Ashoka   Third ruler of the **Mauryan Empire** in India (r. 270–232 B.C.E.). He converted to Buddhism and broadcast his precepts on inscribed stones and pillars, the earliest surviving Indian writing. (*p. 161*)

Asian Tigers   Collective name for South Korea, Taiwan, Hong Kong, and Singapore—nations that became economic powers in the 1970s and 1980s. (*p. 856*)

Atahualpa (1502?–1533)   Last ruling Inca emperor of Peru. He was executed by the Spanish. (*p. 398*)

Atlantic Circuit   The network of trade routes connecting Europe, Africa, and the Americas that underlay the Atlantic system. (*p. 469*)

Atlantic system   The network of trading links after 1500 that moved goods, wealth, people, and cultures around the Atlantic Ocean basin. (*p. 458*)

Augustus (63 B.C.E.–14 C.E.)   Honorific name of Octavian, founder of the **Roman Principate,** the military dictatorship that replaced the failing rule of the **Roman Senate.** After defeating all rivals, between 31 B.C.E. and 14 C.E. he laid the groundwork for several centuries of stability and prosperity in the Roman Empire. (*p. 132*)

Auschwitz   Nazi extermination camp in Poland, the largest center of mass murder during the **Holocaust.** Close to a million Jews, Gypsies, Communists, and others were killed there. (*p. 788*)

ayllu   Andean lineage group or kin-based community. (*p. 282*)

Aztecs   Also known as Mexica, the Aztecs created a powerful empire in central Mexico (1325–1521 C.E.). They forced defeated peoples to provide goods and labor as a tax. (*p. 275*)

Babylon   The largest and most important city in Mesopotamia. It achieved particular eminence as the capital of the Amorite king **Hammurabi** in the eighteenth century B.C.E. and the Neo-Babylonian king Nebuchadnezzar in the sixth century B.C.E. (*p. 14*)

balance of power   The policy in international relations by which, beginning in the eighteenth century, the major European states acted together to prevent any one of them from becoming too powerful. (*p. 424*)

Balfour Declaration   Statement issued by Britain's Foreign Secretary Arthur Balfour in 1917 favoring the establishment of a Jewish national homeland in Palestine. (*p. 744*)

Bannermen   Hereditary military servants of the **Qing Empire,** in large part descendants of peoples of various origins who had fought for the founders of the empire. (*p. 668*)

Bantu   Collective name of a large group of sub-Saharan African languages and of the peoples speaking these languages. (*p. 188*)

Batavia   Fort established ca. 1619 as headquarters of Dutch East India Company operations in Indonesia; today the city of Jakarta. (*p. 507*)

Battle of Midway   U.S. naval victory over the Japanese fleet in June 1942, in which the Japanese lost four of their best aircraft carriers. It marked a turning point in World War II. (*p. 782*)

Battle of Omdurman   British victory over the Mahdi in the Sudan in 1898. General Kitchener led a mixed force of British and Egyptian troops armed with rapid-firing rifles and machine guns. (*p. 712*)

Beijing   China's northern capital, first used as an imperial capital in 906 and now the capital of the People's Republic of China. (*p. 310*)

Bengal   Region of northeastern India. It was the first part of India to be conquered by the British in the eighteenth century and remained the political and economic center of British India throughout the nineteenth century. The 1905 split of the province into predominantly Hindu West Bengal and predominantly Muslim East Bengal (now Bangladesh) sparked anti-British riots. (*p. 802*)

Berlin Conference (1884–1885)   Conference that German chancellor Otto von Bismarck called to set rules for the partition of Africa. It led to the creation of the Congo Free State under King **Leopold II** of Belgium. (See also **Bismarck, Otto von.**) (*p. 716*)

Bhagavad-Gita   The most important work of Indian sacred literature, a dialogue between the great warrior Arjuna and the god Krishna on duty and the fate of the spirit. (*p. 162*)

bin Laden, Usama   Saudi-born Muslim extremist who funded the al Qaeda organization that was responsible for several terrorist attacks, including those on the World Trade Center and the Pentagon in 2001. (*p. 883*)

Bismarck, Otto von (1815–1898)   Chancellor (prime minister) of Prussia from 1862 until 1871, when he became chancellor of Germany. A conservative nationalist, he led Prussia to victory against Austria (1866) and France (1870) and was responsible for the creation of the German Empire in 1871. (*p. 695*)

Black Death   An outbreak of **bubonic plague** that spread across Asia, North Africa, and Europe in the mid-fourteenth century, carrying off vast numbers of persons. (*p. 353*)

Bolívar, Simón (1783–1830)   The most important military leader in the struggle for independence in South America. Born in Venezuela, he led military forces there and in Colombia, Ecuador, Peru, and Bolivia. (*p. 594*)

Bolsheviks   Radical Marxist political party founded by Vladimir Lenin in 1903. Under Lenin's leadership, the Bolsheviks seized power in November 1917 during the Russian Revolution. (See also **Lenin, Vladimir.**) (*p. 744*)

Bonaparte, Napoleon.   See **Napoleon I.**

Bornu   A powerful West African kingdom at the southern edge of the Sahara in the Central Sudan, which was important in trans-Saharan trade and in the spread of Islam. Also known as Kanem-Bornu, it endured from the ninth century to the end of the nineteenth. (*p. 480*)

bourgeoisie   In early modern Europe, the class of well-off town dwellers whose wealth came from manufacturing, finance, commerce, and allied professions.   (*p. 413*)

Brant, Joseph (1742–1807)   Mohawk leader who supported the British during the American Revolution.   (*p. 549*)

Brazza, Savorgnan de (1852–1905) Franco-Italian explorer sent by the French government to claim part of equatorial Africa for France. Founded Brazzaville, capital of the French Congo, in 1880.   (*p. 714*)

British raj   The rule over much of South Asia between 1765 and 1947 by the East India Company and then by a British government.   (*p. 634*)

bubonic plague   A bacterial disease of fleas that can be transmitted by flea bites to rodents and humans; humans in late stages of the illness can spread the bacteria by coughing. Because of its very high mortality rate and the difficulty of preventing its spread, major outbreaks have created crises in many parts of the world. (See also **Black Death.**) (*pp. 250, 302*)

Buddha (563–483 B.C.E.)   An Indian prince named Siddhartha Gautama, who renounced his wealth and social position. After becoming "enlightened" (the meaning of *Buddha*) he enunciated the principles of Buddhism. This doctrine evolved and spread throughout India and to Southeast, East, and Central Asia. (See also **Mahayana Buddhism, Theravada Buddhism.**)   (*p. 156*)

business cycles   Recurrent swings from economic hard times to recovery and growth, then back to hard times and a repetition of the sequence.   (*p. 586*)

Byzantine Empire   Historians' name for the eastern portion of the Roman Empire from the fourth century onward, taken from "Byzantion," an early name for Constantinople, the Byzantine capital city. The empire fell to the Ottomans in 1453. (See also **Ottoman Empire.**)   (*p. 138, 219*)

caliphate   Office established in succession to the Prophet Muhammad, to rule the Islamic empire; also the name of that empire. (See also **Abbasid Caliphate; Sokoto Caliphate; Umayyad Caliphate.**)   (*p. 201*)

capitalism   The economic system of large financial institutions—banks, stock exchanges, investment companies—that first developed in early modern Europe. *Commercial capitalism,* the trading system of the early modern economy, is often distinguished from *industrial capitalism,* the system based on machine production.   (*p. 468*)

caravel   A small, highly maneuverable three-masted ship used by the Portuguese and Spanish in the exploration of the Atlantic.   (*p. 384*)

Cárdenas, Lázaro (1895–1970)   President of Mexico (1934–1940). He brought major changes to Mexican life by distributing millions of acres of land to the peasants, bringing representatives of workers and farmers into the inner circles of politics, and nationalizing the oil industry.   (*p. 809*)

Carthage   City located in present-day Tunisia, founded by **Phoenicians** ca. 800 B.C.E. It became a major commercial center and naval power in the western Mediterranean until defeated by Rome in the third century B.C.E.   (*p. 81*)

Caste War   A rebellion of the Maya people against the government of Mexico in 1847. It nearly returned the Yucatán to Maya rule. Some Maya rebels retreated to unoccupied territories where they held out until 1901.   (*p. 609*)

Catholic Reformation   Religious reform movement within the Latin Christian Church, begun in response to the **Protestant Reformation.** It clarified Catholic theology and reformed clerical training and discipline.   (*p. 409*)

Champa rice   Quick-maturing rice that can allow two harvests in one growing season. Originally introduced into Champa from India, it was later sent to China as a tribute gift by the Champa state. (See also **tributary system.**)   (*p. 264*)

Chang'an   City in the Wei Valley in eastern China. It became the capital of the Qin and early Han Empires. Its main features were imitated in the cities and towns that sprang up throughout the Han Empire.   (*p. 143*)

Charlemagne (742–814)   King of the Franks (r. 768–814); emperor (r. 800–814). Through a series of military conquests he established the Carolingian Empire, which encompassed all of Gaul and parts of Germany and Italy. Though illiterate himself, he sponsored a brief intellectual revival.   (*p. 219*)

chartered companies   Groups of private investors who paid an annual fee to France and England in exchange for a monopoly over trade to the West Indies colonies.   (*p. 460*)

Chavín   The first major urban civilization in South America (900–250 B.C.E.). Its capital, Chavín de Huántar, was located high in the Andes Mountains of Peru. Chavín became politically and economically dominant in a densely populated region that included two distinct ecological zones, the Peruvian coastal plain and the Andean foothills.   (*p. 54*)

Chiang Kai-shek (1886–1975) Chinese military and political leader. Succeeded Sun Yat-sen as head of the **Guomindang** in 1923; headed the Chinese government from 1928 to 1948; fought against the Chinese Communists and Japanese invaders. After 1949 he headed the Chinese Nationalist government in Taiwan.   (*pp. 752, 776*)

chiefdom   Form of political organization with rule by a hereditary leader who held power over a collection of villages and towns. Less powerful than kingdoms and empires, chiefdoms were based on gift giving and commercial links.   (*p. 280*)

chinampas   Raised fields constructed along lake shores in Mesoamerica to increase agricultural yields.   (*p. 270*)

city-state   A small independent state consisting of an urban center and the surrounding agricultural territory. A characteristic political form in early Mesopotamia, Archaic and Classical Greece, Phoenicia, and early Italy. (See also **polis.**)   (*p. 16*)

civilization   An ambiguous term often used to denote more complex societies but sometimes used by anthropologists to describe any group of people sharing a set of cultural traits.   (*p. 5*)

Cixi, Empress Dowager (1835–1908)   Empress of China and mother of Emperor Guangxi. She put her son under house arrest, supported antiforeign movements, and resisted reforms of the Chinese government and armed forces.   (*p. 701*)

clipper ship   Large, fast, streamlined sailing vessel, often American built, of the mid-to-late nineteenth century rigged with vast canvas sails hung from tall masts.   (*p. 644*)

Cold War (1945–1991)   The ideological struggle between communism (Soviet Union) and capitalism (United States) for world influence. The Soviet Union and the United States came to the brink of actual war during the **Cuban missile crisis** but never attacked one another. The Cold War came to an end when the Soviet Union dissolved in 1991. (See also **North Atlantic Treaty Organization; Warsaw Pact.**)   (*p. 821*)

colonialism   Policy by which a nation administers a foreign territory and develops its resources for the benefit of the colonial power.   (*p. 713*)

Columbian Exchange   The exchange of plants, animals, diseases, and technologies between the Americas and the rest of the world following Columbus's voyages.   (*p. 431*)

Columbus, Christopher (1451–1506)   Genoese mariner who in the service of Spain led expeditions across the Atlantic, reestablishing contact between the peoples of the Americas and the Old World and opening the way to Spanish conquest and colonization.   (*p. 388*)

Confederation of 1867   Negotiated union of the formerly separate colonial governments of Ontario, Quebec, New Brunswick, and Nova Scotia. This new Dominion of Canada with a central government in Ottawa is seen as the beginning of the Canadian nation.   (*p. 599*)

Confucius   Western name for the Chinese philosopher Kongzi (551–479 B.C.E.). His doctrine of duty and public service had a great influence on subsequent Chinese thought and served as a code of conduct for government officials.   (*p. 45*)

Congress of Vienna (1814–1815)   Meeting of representatives of European monarchs called to reestablish the old order after the defeat of **Napoleon I.**   (*p. 563*)

conquistadors   Early-sixteenth-century Spanish adventurers who conquered Mexico, Central America, and Peru. (See **Cortés, Hernán; Pizarro, Francisco.**)   (*p.394*)

Constantine (285–337 C.E.)   Roman emperor (r. 312–337). After reuniting the Roman Empire, he moved the capital to Constantinople and made Christianity a favored religion.   (*p. 138*)

Constitutional Convention   Meeting in 1787 of the elected representatives of the thirteen original states to write the Constitution of the United States.   (*p. 551*)

contract of indenture   A voluntary agreement binding a person to work for a specified period of years in return for free passage to an overseas destination. Before 1800 most **indentured servants** were Europeans; after 1800 most indentured laborers were Asians.   (*p. 647*)

Cortés, Hernán (1485–1547)   Spanish explorer and conquistador who led the conquest of Aztec Mexico in 1519–1521 for Spain.   (*p. 394*)

Cossacks   Peoples of the Russian Empire who lived outside the farming villages, often as herders, mercenaries, or outlaws. Cossacks led the conquest of Siberia in the sixteenth and seventeenth centuries.   (*p. 529*)

Council of the Indies   The institution responsible for supervising Spain's colonies in the Americas from 1524 to the early eighteenth century, when it lost all but judicial responsibilities.   (*p. 434*)

***coureurs des bois* (runners of the woods)**   French fur traders, many of mixed Amerindian heritage, who lived among and often married with Amerindian peoples of North America.   (*p. 450*)

creoles   In colonial Spanish America, term used to describe someone of European descent born in the New World. Elsewhere in the Americas, the term is used to describe all non-native peoples.   (*p. 440*)

Crimean War (1853–1856)   Conflict between the Russian and Ottoman Empires fought primarily in the Crimean Peninsula. To prevent Russian expansion, Britain and France sent troops to support the Ottomans.   (*p. 660*)

Crusades (1096–1291)   Armed pilgrimages to the Holy Land by Christians determined to recover Jerusalem from Muslim rule. The Crusades brought an end to western Europe's centuries of intellectual and cultural isolation.   (*p. 237*)

Crystal Palace   Building erected in Hyde Park, London, for the Great Exhibition of 1851. Made of iron and glass, like a gigantic greenhouse, it was a symbol of the industrial age.   (*p. 578*)

Cuban missile crisis (1962)   Brink-of-war confrontation between the United States and the Soviet Union over the latter's placement of nuclear-armed missiles in Cuba.   (*p. 829*)

cultural imperialism   Domination of one culture over another by a deliberate policy or by economic or technological superiority.   (*p. 897*)

Cultural Revolution (China) (1966–1969)   Campaign in China ordered by **Mao Zedong** to purge the Communist Party of his opponents and instill revolutionary values in the younger generation.   (*p. 841*)

culture   Socially transmitted patterns of action and expression. *Material culture* refers to physical objects, such as dwellings, clothing, tools, and crafts. Culture also includes arts, beliefs, knowledge, and technology.   (*p. 6*)

cuneiform   A system of writing in which wedge-shaped symbols represented words or syllables. It originated in Mesopotamia and was used initially for Sumerian and Akkadian but later was adapted to represent other languages of western Asia. Because so many symbols had to be learned, literacy was confined to a relatively small group of administrators and **scribes.**   (*p. 22*)

Cyrus (600–530 B.C.E.)   Founder of the Achaemenid Persian Empire. Between 550 and 530 B.C.E. he conquered Media, Lydia, and Babylon. Revered in the traditions of both Iran and the subject peoples, he employed Persians and Medes in his administration and respected the institutions and beliefs of subject peoples.   (*p. 96*)

czar   See **tsar.**

daimyo   Literally, great name(s). Japanese warlords and great landowners, whose armed **samurai** gave them control of the Japanese islands from the eighth to the later nineteenth century. Under the **Tokugawa Shogunate** they were subordinated to the imperial government.   (*p. 511*)

Daoism   Chinese school of thought, originating in the Warring States Period with Laozi (604–531 B.C.E.). Daoism offered an alternative to the Confucian emphasis on hierarchy and duty. Daoists believe that the world is always changing and is devoid of absolute morality or meaning. They accept the world as they find it, avoid futile struggles, and deviate as little as possible from the *Dao,* or "path" of nature. (See also **Confucius.**) (*p. 45*)

Darius I (ca. 558–486 B.C.E.) Third ruler of the Persian Empire (r. 521–486 B.C.E.). He crushed the widespread initial resistance to his rule and gave all major government posts to Persians rather than to Medes. He established a system of provinces and tribute, began construction of Persepolis, and expanded Persian control in the east (Pakistan) and west (northern Greece). (*p. 96*)

Decembrist revolt Abortive attempt by army officers to take control of the Russian government upon the death of Tsar Alexander I in 1825. (*p. 666*)

Declaration of the Rights of Man (1789) Statement of fundamental political rights adopted by the French **National Assembly** at the beginning of the French Revolution. (*p. 555*)

deforestation The removal of trees faster than forests can replace themselves. (*p. 416*)

Delhi Sultanate (1206–1526) Centralized Indian empire of varying extent, created by Muslim invaders. (*p. 328*)

democracy A system of government in which all "citizens" (however defined) have equal political and legal rights, privileges, and protections, as in the Greek city-state of Athens in the fifth and fourth centuries B.C.E. (*p. 107*)

demographic transition A change in the rates of population growth. Before the transition, both birthrates and death rates are high, resulting in a slowly growing population; then the death rate drops but the birthrate remains high, causing a population explosion; finally the birthrate drops and the population growth slows down. This transition took place in Europe in the late nineteenth and early twentieth centuries, in North America and East Asia in the mid-twentieth, and, most recently, in Latin America and South Asia. (*p. 862*)

Deng Xiaoping (1904–1997) Communist Party leader who forced Chinese economic reforms after the death of **Mao Zedong.** (*p. 857*)

development In the nineteenth and twentieth centuries, the economic process that led to industrialization, urbanization, the rise of a large and prosperous middle class, and heavy investment in education. (*p. 616*)

devshirme "Selection" in Turkish. The system by which boys from Christian communities were taken by the Ottoman state to serve as **Janissaries.** (*p. 489*)

dhow Ship of small to moderate size used in the western Indian Ocean, traditionally with a triangular sail and a sewn timber hull. (*p. 338*)

Diagne, Blaise (1872–1934) Senegalese political leader. He was the first African elected to the French National Assembly. During World War I, in exchange for promises to give French citizenship to Senegalese, he helped recruit Africans to serve in the French army. After the war, he led a movement to abolish forced labor in Africa. (*p. 799*)

Dias, Bartolomeu (1450?–1500) Portuguese explorer who in 1488 led the first expedition to sail around the southern tip of Africa from the Atlantic and sight the Indian Ocean. (*p. 386*)

Diaspora A Greek word meaning "dispersal," used to describe the communities of a given ethnic group living outside their homeland. Jews, for example, spread from Israel to western Asia and Mediterranean lands in antiquity and today can be found throughout the world. (*p. 80*)

Dirty War War waged by the Argentine military (1976–1982) against leftist groups. Characterized by the use of illegal imprisonment, torture, and executions by the military. (*p. 850*)

divination Techniques for ascertaining the future or the will of the gods by interpreting natural phenomena such as, in early China, the cracks on oracle bones or, in ancient Greece, the flight of birds through sectors of the sky. (*p. 41*)

division of labor A manufacturing technique that breaks down a craft into many simple and repetitive tasks that can be performed by unskilled workers. Pioneered in the pottery works of Josiah Wedgwood and in other eighteenth-century factories, it greatly increased the productivity of labor and lowered the cost of manufactured goods. (See also **Wedgwood, Josiah.**) (*p. 574*)

driver A privileged male slave whose job was to ensure that a slave gang did its work on a plantation. (*p. 464*)

durbar An elaborate display of political power and wealth in British India in the nineteenth century, ostensibly in imitation of the pageantry of the **Mughal Empire.** (*p. 636*)

Dutch West India Company (1621–1794) Trading company chartered by the Dutch government to conduct its merchants' trade in the Americas and Africa. (*p. 460*)

Edison, Thomas (1847–1931) American inventor best known for inventing the electric light bulb, acoustic recording on wax cylinders, and motion pictures. (*p. 684*)

Einstein, Albert (1879–1955) German physicist who developed the theory of relativity, which states that time, space, and mass are relative to each other and not fixed. (*p. 760*)

El Alamein Town in Egypt, site of the victory by Britain's Field Marshal Bernard Montgomery over German forces led by General Erwin Rommel (the "Desert Fox") in 1942–1943. (*p. 782*)

electricity A form of energy used in telegraphy from the 1840s on and for lighting, industrial motors, and railroads beginning in the 1880s. (*p. 684*)

electric telegraph A device for rapid, long-distance transmission of information over an electric wire. It was introduced in England and North America in the 1830s and 1840s and replaced telegraph systems that utilized visual signals such as semaphores. (See also **submarine telegraph cables.**) (*p. 580*)

encomienda A grant of authority over a population of Amerindians in the Spanish colonies. It provided the grant holder with a supply of cheap labor and periodic payments of goods by the Amerindians. It obliged the grant holder to Christianize the Amerindians. (*p. 439*)

English Civil War (1642-1649) A conflict over royal versus. Parliamentary rights, caused by King Charles I's arrest of his parliamentary critics and ending with his execution. Its outcome checked the growth of royal absolutism and, with the Glorious Revolution of 1688 and the English Bill of Rights of 1689, ensured that England would be a constitutional monarchy. (*p. 422*)

Enlightenment A philosophical movement in eighteenth-century Europe that fostered the belief that one could reform society by discovering rational laws that governed social behavior and were just as scientific as the laws of physics.   (*pp. 412, 542*)

equites   In ancient Italy, prosperous landowners second in wealth and status to the senatorial aristocracy. The Roman emperors allied with this group to counterbalance the influence of the old aristocracy and used the *equites* to staff the imperial civil service.   (*p. 132*)

Estates General   France's traditional national assembly with representatives of the three estates, or classes, in French society: the clergy, nobility, and commoners. The calling of the Estates General in 1789 led to the French Revolution.   (*p. 553*)

Ethiopia   East African highland nation lying east of the Nile River. (See also **Menelik II; Selassie, Haile.**)   (*p. 190*)

ethnic cleansing   Effort to eradicate a people and its culture by means of mass killing and the destruction of historical buildings and cultural materials. Ethnic cleansing was used by both sides in the conflicts that accompanied the disintegration of Yugoslavia in the 1990s.   (*p. 882*)

European Community (EC)   An organization promoting economic unity in Europe formed in 1967 by consolidation of earlier, more limited, agreements. Replaced by the European Union (EU) in 1993.   (*p. 825*)

extraterritoriality   The right of foreign residents in a country to live under the laws of their native country and disregard the laws of the host country. In the nineteenth and early twentieth centuries, European and American nationals living in certain areas of Chinese and Ottoman cities were granted this right.   (*p. 661*)

Faisal I (1885–1933)   Arab prince, leader of the Arab Revolt in World War I. The British made him king of Iraq in 1921, and he reigned under British protection until 1933.   (*p.744*)

Fascist Party   Italian political party created by Benito Mussolini during World War I. It emphasized aggressive nationalism and was Mussolini's instrument for the creation of a dictatorship in Italy from 1922 to 1943. (See also **Mussolini, Benito.**)   (*p. 774*)

fief   In medieval Europe, land granted in return for a sworn oath to provide specified military service.   (*p. 225*)

First Temple   A monumental sanctuary built in Jerusalem by King Solomon in the tenth century B.C.E. to be the religious center for the Israelite god Yahweh. The Temple priesthood conducted sacrifices, received a tithe or percentage of agricultural revenues, and became economically and politically powerful. The First Temple was destroyed by the Babylonians in 587 B.C.E., rebuilt on a modest scale in the late sixth century B.C.E., and replaced by King Herod's Second Temple in the late first century B.C.E. (destroyed by the Romans in 70 C.E.)   (*p. 76*)

Five-Year Plans   Plans that Joseph Stalin introduced to industrialize the Soviet Union rapidly, beginning in 1928. They set goals for the output of steel, electricity, machinery, and most other products and were enforced by the police powers of the state. They succeeded in making the Soviet Union a major industrial power before World War II. (See also **Stalin, Joseph.**)   (*p. 767*)

foragers   People who support themselves by hunting wild animals and gathering wild edible plants and insects.   (*p. 6*)

Franklin, Benjamin (1706–1790)   American intellectual, inventor, and politician He helped negotiate French support for the American Revolution.   (*p. 545*)

free-trade imperialism   Economic dominance of a weaker country by a more powerful one, while maintaining the legal independence of the weaker state. In the late nineteenth century, free-trade imperialism characterized the relations between the Latin American republics, on the one hand, and Great Britain and the United States, on the other.   (*p. 727*)

Fujiwara   Aristocratic family that dominated the Japanese imperial court between the ninth and twelfth centuries.   (*p. 263*)

Funan   An early complex society in Southeast Asia between the first and sixth centuries C.E. It was centered in the rich rice-growing region of southern Vietnam, and it controlled the passage of trade across the Malaysian isthmus.   (*p. 169*)

Gama, Vasco da (1460?–1524)   Portuguese explorer. In 1497–1498 he led the first naval expedition from Europe to sail to India, opening an important commercial sea route.   (*p. 386*)

Gandhi, Mohandas K. (Mahatma) (1869–1948)   Leader of the Indian independence movement and advocate of nonviolent resistance. After being educated as a lawyer in England, he returned to India and became leader of the **Indian National Congress** in 1920. He appealed to the poor, led nonviolent demonstrations against British colonial rule, and was jailed many times. Soon after independence he was assassinated for attempting to stop Hindu-Muslim rioting.   (*p. 803*)

Garibaldi, Giuseppe (1807–1882)   Italian nationalist and revolutionary who conquered Sicily and Naples and added them to a unified Italy in 1860.   (*p. 694*)

Genghis Khan (ca. 1167–1227)   The title of Temüjin when he ruled the Mongols (1206–1227). It means the "oceanic" or "universal" leader. Genghis Khan was the founder of the Mongol Empire.   (*p. 295*)

gens de couleur   Free men and women of color in Haiti. They sought greater political rights and later supported the Haitian Revolution. (See also **L'Ouverture, François Dominique Toussaint.**)   (*p. 561*)

gentry   In China, the class of prosperous families, next in wealth below the rural aristocrats, from which the emperors drew their administrative personnel. Respected for their education and expertise, these officials became a privileged group and made the government more efficient and responsive than in the past. The term *gentry* also denotes the class of landholding families in England below the aristocracy.   (*pp. 144, 415, 459*)

Ghana   First known kingdom in sub-Saharan West Africa between the sixth and thirteenth centuries C.E. Also the modern West African country once known as the Gold Coast.   (*p. 206*)

global culture   Cultural practices and institutions that have been adopted internationally, whether elite (the English language, modern science, and higher education) or popular (music, television, the Internet, food, and fashion).   (*p. 899*)

globalization   The economic, political, and cultural integration and interaction of all parts of the world brought about by increasing trade, travel, and technology.   (*p. 880*)

Gold Coast (Africa)   Region of the Atlantic coast of West Africa occupied by modern Ghana; named for its gold exports to Europe from the 1470s onward.   (*p. 386*)

Golden Horde   Mongol khanate founded by Genghis Khan's grandson Batu. It was based in southern Russia and quickly adopted both the Turkic language and Islam. Also known as the Kipchak Horde.   (*p. 303*)

Gorbachev, Mikhail (b. 1931)   Head of the Soviet Union from 1985 to 1991. His liberalization effort improved relations with the West, but he lost power after his reforms led to the collapse of communist governments in eastern Europe.   (*p. 858*)

Gothic cathedrals   Large churches originating in twelfth-century France; built in an architectural style featuring pointed arches, tall vaults and spires, flying buttresses, and large stained-glass windows.   (*p. 362*)

Grand Canal   The 1,100-mile (1,700-kilometer) waterway linking the Yellow and the Yangzi Rivers. It was begun in the **Han** period and completed during the Sui Empire. (*p. 247*)

"great traditions"   Historians' term for a literate, well-institutionalized complex of religious and social beliefs and practices adhered to by diverse societies over a broad geographical area. (See also **"small traditions."**)   (*p. 185*)

Great Western Schism   A division in the Latin (Western) Christian Church between 1378 and 1417, when rival claimants to the papacy existed in Rome and Avignon. (*p. 370*)

Great Zimbabwe   City, now in ruins (in the modern African country of Zimbabwe), whose many stone structures were built between about 1250 and 1450, when it was a trading center and the capital of a large state.   (*p. 341*)

guild   In medieval Europe, an association of men (rarely women), such as merchants, artisans, or professors, who worked in a particular trade and banded together to promote their economic and political interests. Guilds were also important in other societies, such as the Ottoman and Safavid empires.   (*p. 359*)

Gujarat   Region of western India famous for trade and manufacturing; the inhabitants are called Gujarati.   (*p. 337*)

gunpowder   A mixture of saltpeter, sulfur, and charcoal, in various proportions. The formula, brought to China in the 400s or 500s, was first used to make fumigators to keep away insect pests and evil spirits. In later centuries it was used to make explosives and grenades and to propel cannonballs, shot, and bullets.   (*p. 257*)

Guomindang   Nationalist political party founded on democratic principles by **Sun Yat-sen** in 1912. After 1925, the party was headed by **Chiang Kai-shek,** who turned it into an increasingly authoritarian movement.   (*p. 751*)

Gupta Empire (320–550 C.E.)   A powerful Indian state based, like its Mauryan predecessor, on a capital at Pataliputra in the Ganges Valley. It controlled most of the Indian subcontinent through a combination of military force and its prestige as a center of sophisticated culture. (See also **theater-state.**)   (*p. 162*)

Habsburg   A powerful European family that provided many Holy Roman Emperors, founded the Austrian (later Austro-Hungarian) Empire, and ruled sixteenth- and seventeenth-century Spain.   (*p. 418*)

hadith   A tradition relating the words or deeds of the Prophet Muhammad; next to the **Quran,** the most important basis for Islamic law.   (*p. 209*)

Hammurabi   Amorite ruler of **Babylon** (r. 1792–1750 B.C.E.). He conquered many city-states in southern and northern Mesopotamia and is best known for a code of laws, inscribed on a black stone pillar, illustrating the principles to be used in legal cases.   (*p. 17*)

Han   A term used to designate (1) the ethnic Chinese people who originated in the Yellow River Valley and spread throughout regions of China suitable for agriculture and (2) the dynasty of emperors who ruled from 206 B.C.E. to 220 C.E.   (*p. 139*)

Hanseatic League   An economic and defensive alliance of the free towns in northern Germany, founded about 1241 and most powerful in the fourteenth century.   (*p. 356*)

Harappa   Site of one of the great cities of the Indus Valley civilization of the third millennium B.C.E. It was located on the northwest frontier of the zone of cultivation (in modern Pakistan), and may have been a center for the acquisition of raw materials, such as metals and precious stones, from Afghanistan and Iran.   (*p. 30*)

Hatshepsut   Queen of Egypt (r. 1473–1458 B.C.E.). She dispatched a naval expedition down the Red Sea to Punt (possibly northeast Sudan or Eretria), the faraway source of myrrh. There is evidence of opposition to a woman as ruler, and after her death her name and image were frequently defaced.   (*p. 64*)

Hausa   An agricultural and trading people of central Sudan in West Africa. Aside from their brief incorporation into the Songhai Empire, the Hausa city-states remained autonomous until the **Sokoto Caliphate** conquered them in the early nineteenth century.   (*p. 480*)

Hebrew Bible   A collection of sacred books containing diverse materials concerning the origins, experiences, beliefs, and practices of the Israelites. Most of the extant text was compiled by members of the priestly class in the fifth century B.C.E. and reflects the concerns and views of this group.   (*p. 75*)

Hellenistic Age   Historians' term for the era, usually dated 323–30 B.C.E., in which Greek culture spread across western Asia and northeastern Africa after the conquests of **Alexander** the Great. The period ended with the fall of the last major Hellenistic kingdom to Rome, but Greek cultural influence persisted until the spread of Islam in the seventh century C.E.   (*p. 116*)

Helsinki Accords (1975)   Political and human rights agreement signed in Helsinki, Finland, by the Soviet Union and western European countries.   (*p. 830*)

Henry the Navigator (1394–1460)   Portuguese prince who promoted the study of navigation and directed voyages of exploration down the western coast of Africa.   (*p. 383*)

Herodotus (ca. 485–425 B.C.E.)   Heir to the technique of *historia*—"investigation"—developed by Greeks in the late Archaic period. He came from a Greek community in

Anatolia and traveled extensively, collecting information in western Asia and the Mediterranean lands. He traced the antecedents of and chronicled the **Persian Wars** between the Greek city-states and the Persian Empire, thus originating the Western tradition of historical writing.   (*p. 109*)

Herzl, Theodore (1860–1904)   Austrian journalist and founder of the Zionist movement urging the creation of a Jewish national homeland in Palestine.   (*p. 744*)

Hidalgo y Costilla, Miguel (1753–1811)   Mexican priest who led the first stage of the Mexican independence war in 1810. He was captured and executed in 1811.   (*p. 597*)

Hidden Imam   Last in a series of twelve descendants of Muhammad's son-in-law Ali, whom **Shi'ites** consider divinely appointed leaders of the Muslim community. In occlusion since ca. 873, he is expected to return as a messiah at the end of time.   (*p. 497*)

hieroglyphics   A system of writing in which pictorial symbols represented sounds, syllables, or concepts. It was used for official and monumental inscriptions in ancient Egypt. Because of the long period of study required to master this system, literacy in hieroglyphics was confined to a relatively small group of **scribes** and administrators. Cursive symbol-forms were developed for rapid composition on other media, such as **papyrus.**   (*p. 26*)

Hinduism   A general term for a wide variety of beliefs and ritual practices that have developed in the Indian subcontinent since antiquity. Hinduism has roots in ancient Vedic, Buddhist, and south Indian religious concepts and practices. It spread along the trade routes to Southeast Asia. (*p. 157*)

Hiroshima   City in Japan, the first to be destroyed by an atomic bomb, on August 6, 1945. The bombing hastened the end of World War II.   (*p. 784*)

history   The study of past events and changes in the development, transmission, and transformation of cultural practices.   (*p. 6*)

Hitler, Adolf (1889–1945)   Born in Austria, Hitler became a radical German nationalist during World War I. He led the National Socialist German Workers' Party—the **Nazis**—in the 1920s and became dictator of Germany in 1933. He led Europe into World War II.   (*p. 774*)

Hittites   A people from central Anatolia who established an empire in Anatolia and Syria in the Late Bronze Age. With wealth from the trade in metals and military power based on chariot forces, the Hittites vied with New Kingdom Egypt for control of Syria-Palestine before falling to unidentified attackers ca. 1200 B.C.E. (See also **Ramesses II.**)   (*p. 62*)

Holocaust   Nazis' program during World War II to kill people they considered undesirable. Some 6 million Jews perished during the Holocaust, along with millions of Poles, Gypsies, Communists, Socialists, and others.   (*p. 788*)

Holocene   The geological era since the end of the **Great Ice Age** about 11,000 years ago.   (*p. 10*)

Holy Roman Empire   Loose federation of mostly German states and principalities, headed by an emperor elected by the princes. It lasted from 962 to 1806.   (*pp. 229, 418*)

hoplite   A heavily armored Greek infantryman of the Archaic and Classical periods who fought in the close-packed phalanx formation. Hoplite armies—militias composed of middle- and upper-class citizens supplying their own equipment—were for centuries superior to all other military forces.   (*p. 105*)

horse collar   Harnessing method that increased the efficiency of horses by shifting the point of traction from the animal's neck to the shoulders; its adoption favors the spread of horse-drawn plows and vehicles.   (*p. 236*)

House of Burgesses   Elected assembly in colonial Virginia, created in 1618.   (*p. 446*)

humanists (Renaissance)   European scholars, writers, and teachers associated with the study of the humanities (grammar, rhetoric, poetry, history, languages, and moral philosophy), influential in the fifteenth century and later.   (*p. 365*)

Hundred Years War (1337–1453)   Series of campaigns over control of the throne of France, involving English and French royal families and French noble families.   (*p. 371*)

Husain, Saddam (b. 1937)   President of Iraq from 1979 until overthrown by an American-led invasion in 2003. Waged war on Iran from 1980 to 1988. His invasion of Kuwait in 1990 was repulsed in the Persian Gulf War in 1991.   (*p. 853*)

Ibn Battuta (1304–1369)   Moroccan Muslim scholar, the most widely traveled individual of his time. He wrote a detailed account of his visits to Islamic lands from China to Spain and the western Sudan.   (*p. 328*)

Il-khan   A "secondary" or "peripheral" khan based in Persia. The Il-khans' khanate was founded by Hülegü, a grandson of **Genghis Khan,** and was based at Tabriz in modern Azerbaijan. It controlled much of Iran and Iraq.   (*p. 303*)

import-substitution industrialization   An economic system aimed at building a country's industry by restricting foreign trade. It was especially popular in Latin American countries such as Mexico, Argentina, and Brazil in the mid-twentieth century. It proved successful for a time but could not keep up with technological advances in Europe and North America.   (*p. 813*)

Inca   Largest and most powerful Andean empire. Controlled the Pacific coast of South America from Ecuador to Chile from its capital of Cuzco.   (*p. 286*)

indentured servant   A migrant to British colonies in the Americas who paid for passage by agreeing to work for a set term ranging from four to seven years.   (*p. 446*)

Indian Civil Service   The elite professional class of officials who administered the government of British India. Originally composed exclusively of well-educated British men, it gradually added qualified Indians.   (*p. 636*)

Indian National Congress   A movement and political party founded in 1885 to demand greater Indian participation in government. Its membership was middle class, and its demands were modest until World War I. Led after 1920 by Mohandas K. Gandhi, it appealed increasingly to the poor, and it organized mass protests demanding self-government and independence. (See also **Gandhi, Mohandas K.**) (*pp. 641, 802*)

Indian Ocean Maritime System   In premodern times, a network of seaports, trade routes, and maritime culture linking countries on the rim of the Indian Ocean from Africa to Indonesia.   (*p. 178*)

indulgence The forgiveness of the punishment due for past sins, granted by the Catholic Church authorities as a reward for a pious act. Martin Luther's protest against the sale of indulgences is often seen as touching off the **Protestant Reformation.** (*p. 406*)

Industrial Revolution The transformation of the economy, the environment, and living conditions, occurring first in England in the eighteenth century, that resulted from the use of steam engines, the mechanization of manufacturing in factories, and innovations in transportation and communication. (*p. 569*)

investiture controversy Dispute between the popes and the Holy Roman Emperors over who held ultimate authority over bishops in imperial lands. (*p. 229*)

Irigoyen, Hipólito (1850–1933) Argentine politician, president of Argentina from 1916 to 1922 and 1928 to 1930. The first president elected by universal male suffrage, he began his presidency as a reformer, but later became conservative. (*p. 812*)

Iron Age Historians' term for the period during which iron was the primary metal for tools and weapons. The advent of iron technology began at different times in different parts of the world. (*p. 60*)

iron curtain Winston Churchill's term for the Cold War division between the Soviet-dominated East and the U.S.-dominated West. (*p. 821*)

Iroquois Confederacy An alliance of five northeastern Amerindian peoples (six after 1722) that made decisions on military and diplomatic issues through a council of representatives. Allied first with the Dutch and later with the English, the Confederacy dominated the area from western New England to the Great Lakes. (*p. 449*)

Islam Religion expounded by the Prophet Muhammad (570–632 C.E.) on the basis of his reception of divine revelations, which were collected after his death into the **Quran.** In the tradition of Judaism and Christianity, and sharing much of their lore, Islam calls on all people to recognize one creator god—Allah—who rewards or punishes believers after death according to how they led their lives. (See also **hadith.**) (*p. 201*)

Israel In antiquity, the land between the eastern shore of the Mediterranean and the Jordan River, occupied by the Israelites from the early second millennium B.C.E. The modern state of Israel was founded in 1948. (*p. 74*)

Jackson, Andrew (1767–1845) First president of the United States to be born in humble circumstances. He was popular among frontier residents, urban workers, and small farmers. He had a successful political career as judge, general, congressman, senator, and president. After being denied the presidency in 1824 in a controversial election, he won in 1828 and was reelected in 1832. (*p. 603*)

Jacobins Radical republicans during the French Revolution. They were led by Maximilien Robespierre from 1793 to 1794. (See also **Robespierre, Maximilien.**) (*p. 556*)

Janissaries Infantry, originally of slave origin, armed with firearms and constituting the elite of the Ottoman army from the fifteenth century until the corps was abolished in 1826. (See also **devshirme.**) (*pp. 489, 653*)

jati. See *varna.*

Jesus (ca. 5 B.C.E.–34 C.E.) A Jew from Galilee in northern Israel who sought to reform Jewish beliefs and practices. He was executed as a revolutionary by the Romans. Hailed as the Messiah and son of God by his followers, he became the central figure in Christianity, a belief system that developed in the centuries after his death. (*p. 134*)

Jinnah, Muhammad Ali (1876–1948) Indian Muslim politician who founded the state of Pakistan. A lawyer by training, he joined the **All-India Muslim League** in 1913. As leader of the League from the 1920s on, he negotiated with the British and the **Indian National Congress** for Muslim participation in Indian politics. From 1940 on, he led the movement for the independence of India's Muslims in a separate state of Pakistan, founded in 1947. (*p. 806*)

joint-stock company A business, often backed by a government charter, that sold shares to individuals to raise money for its trading enterprises and to spread the risks (and profits) among many investors. (*p. 415*)

Juárez, Benito (1806–1872) President of Mexico (1858–1872). Born in poverty in Mexico, he was educated as a lawyer and rose to become chief justice of the Mexican supreme court and then president. He led Mexico's resistance to a French invasion in 1863 and the installation of Maximilian as emperor. (*p. 606*)

junk A very large flatbottom sailing ship produced in the **Tang, Ming,** and **Song Empires,** specially designed for long-distance commercial travel. (*p. 257*)

Kamakura shogunate The first of Japan's decentralized military governments. (1185–1333). (*p. 263*)

kamikaze The "divine wind," which the Japanese credited with blowing Mongol invaders away from their shores in 1281. (*p. 319*)

Kangxi (1654–1722) Qing emperor (r. 1662–1722). He oversaw the greatest expansion of the **Qing Empire.** (*p. 519*)

karma In Indian tradition, the residue of deeds performed in past and present lives that adheres to a "spirit" and determines what form it will assume in its next life cycle. The doctrines of karma and reincarnation were used by the elite in ancient India to encourage people to accept their social position and do their duty. (*p. 155*)

keiretsu Alliances of corporations and banks that dominate the Japanese economy. (*p. 856*)

khipu System of knotted colored cords used by preliterate Andean peoples to transmit information. (*p. 282*)

Khomeini, Ayatollah Ruhollah (1900?–1989) Shi'ite philosopher and cleric who led the overthrow of the shah of Iran in 1979 and created an Islamic republic. (*p. 852*)

Khubilai Khan (1215–1294) Last of the Mongol Great Khans (r. 1260–1294) and founder of the **Yuan Empire.** (*p. 310*)

Kievan Russia State established at Kiev in Ukraine ca. 879 by Scandinavian adventurers asserting authority over a mostly Slavic farming population. (*p. 219*)

Korean War (1950–1953) Conflict that began with North Korea's invasion of South Korea and came to involve the United Nations (primarily the United States) allying with South Korea and the People's Republic of China allying with North Korea. (*p. 826*)

Koryo   Korean kingdom founded in 918 and destroyed by a Mongol invasion in 1259.   (*p. 261*)

Kush   An Egyptian name for Nubia, the region alongside the Nile River south of Egypt, where an indigenous kingdom with its own distinctive institutions and cultural traditions arose beginning in the early second millennium B.C.E. It was deeply influenced by Egyptian culture and at times under the control of Egypt, which coveted its rich deposits of gold and luxury products from sub-Saharan Africa carried up the Nile corridor.   (*p. 50*)

labor union   An organization of workers in a particular industry or trade, created to defend the interests of members through strikes or negotiations with employers.   (*p. 690*)

laissez faire   The idea that government should refrain from interfering in economic affairs. The classic exposition of laissez-faire principles is Adam Smith's *Wealth of Nations* (1776).   (*p. 587*)

lama   In Tibetan Buddhism, a teacher.   (*p. 310*)

Las Casas, Bartolomé de (1474–1566)   First bishop of Chiapas, in southern Mexico. He devoted most of his life to protecting Amerindian peoples from exploitation. His major achievement was the New Laws of 1542, which limited the ability of Spanish settlers to compel Amerindians to labor for them. (See also **encomienda**.)   (*p. 437*)

Latin West   Historians' name for the territories of Europe that adhered to the Latin rite of Christianity and used the Latin language for intellectual exchange in the period ca. 1000–1500.   (*p. 350*)

League of Nations   International organization founded in 1919 to promote world peace and cooperation but greatly weakened by the refusal of the United States to join. It proved ineffectual in stopping aggression by Italy, Japan, and Germany in the 1930s, and it was superseded by the **United Nations** in 1945.   (*p. 746*)

Legalism   In China, a political philosophy that emphasized the unruliness of human nature and justified state coercion and control. The **Qin** ruling class invoked it to validate the authoritarian nature of their regime and its profligate expenditure of subjects' lives and labor. It was superseded in the **Han** era by a more benevolent Confucian doctrine of governmental moderation.   (*p. 45*)

"legitimate" trade   Exports from Africa in the nineteenth century that did not include the newly outlawed slave trade.   (*p. 631*)

Lenin, Vladimir (1870–1924)   Leader of the Bolshevik (later Communist) Party. He lived in exile in Switzerland until 1917, then returned to Russia to lead the Bolsheviks to victory during the Russian Revolution and the civil war that followed.   (*p. 744*)

Leopold II (1835–1909)   King of Belgium (r. 1865–1909). He was active in encouraging the exploration of Central Africa and became the ruler of the Congo Free State (to 1908).   (*p. 714*)

liberalism   A political ideology that emphasizes the civil rights of citizens, representative government, and the protection of private property. This ideology, derived from the **Enlightenment**, was especially popular among the property-owning middle classes of Europe and North America.   (*p. 694*)

Library of Ashurbanipal   A large collection of writings drawn from the ancient literary, religious, and scientific traditions of Mesopotamia. It was assembled by the sixth century B.C.E. Assyrian ruler Ashurbanipal. The many tablets unearthed by archaeologists constitute one of the most important sources of present-day knowledge of the long literary tradition of Mesopotamia.   (*p. 74*)

Linear B   A set of syllabic symbols, derived from the writing system of **Minoan** Crete, used in the Mycenaean palaces of the Late Bronze Age to write an early form of Greek. It was used primarily for palace records, and the surviving Linear B tablets provide substantial information about the economic organization of Mycenaean society and tantalizing clues about political, social, and religious institutions.   (*p. 69*)

Li Shimin (599–649)   One of the founders of the **Tang Empire** and its second emperor (r. 626–649). He led the expansion of the empire into Central Asia.   (*p. 245*)

Little Ice Age   A century-long period of cool climate that began in the 1590s. Its ill effects on agriculture in northern Europe were notable.   (*p. 416*)

llama   A hoofed animal indigenous to the Andes Mountains in South America. It was the only domesticated beast of burden in the Americas before the arrival of Europeans. It provided meat and wool. The use of llamas to transport goods made possible specialized production and trade among people living in different ecological zones and fostered the integration of these zones by **Chavín** and later Andean states.   (*p. 55*)

loess   A fine, light silt deposited by wind and water. It constitutes the fertile soil of the Yellow River Valley in northern China. Because loess soil is not compacted, it can be worked with a simple digging stick, but it leaves the region vulnerable to devastating earthquakes.   (*p. 38*)

Long March (1934–1935)   The 6,000-mile (9,600-kilometer) flight of Chinese Communists from southeastern to northwestern China. The Communists, led by **Mao Zedong,** were pursued by the Chinese army under orders from **Chiang Kai-shek.** The four thousand survivors of the march formed the nucleus of a revived Communist movement that defeated the **Guomindang** after World War II.   (*p. 777*)

L'Ouverture, François Dominique Toussaint (1743–1803)   Leader of the Haitian Revolution. He freed the slaves and gained effective independence for Haiti despite military interventions by the British and French.   (*p. 561*)

ma'at   Egyptian term for the concept of divinely created and maintained order in the universe. Reflecting the ancient Egyptians' belief in an essentially beneficent world, the divine ruler was the earthly guarantor of this order. (See also **pyramid**.)   (*p. 25*)

Macartney mission (1792–1793)   The unsuccessful attempt by the British Empire to establish diplomatic relations with the **Qing Empire.**   (*p. 524*)

Magellan, Ferdinand (1480?–1521)   Portuguese navigator who led the Spanish expedition of 1519–1522 that was the first to sail around the world.   (*p. 389*)

Mahabharata   A vast epic chronicling the events leading up to a cataclysmic battle between related kinship groups in early India. It includes the Bhagavad-Gita, the most important work of Indian sacred literature.   (*p. 162*)

Mahayana Buddhism "Great Vehicle" branch of Buddhism followed in China, Japan, and Central Asia. The focus is on reverence for **Buddha** and for bodhisattvas, enlightened persons who have postponed nirvana to help others attain enlightenment. (*p. 157*)

Malacca Port city in the modern Southeast Asian country of Malaysia, founded about 1400 as a trading center on the Strait of Malacca. Also spelled Melaka. (*p. 343*)

Malay peoples A designation for peoples originating in south China and Southeast Asia who settled the Malay Peninsula, Indonesia, and the Philippines, then spread eastward across the islands of the Pacific Ocean and west to Madagascar. (*p. 168*)

Mali Empire created by indigenous Muslims in western Sudan of West Africa from the thirteenth to fifteenth century. It was famous for its role in the trans-Saharan gold trade. (See also **Mansa Kankan Musa** and **Timbuktu**.) (*p. 330*)

Malthus, Thomas (1766–1834) Eighteenth-century English intellectual who warned that population growth threatened future generations because, in his view, population growth would always outstrip increases in agricultural production. (*p. 862*)

Mamluks Under the Islamic system of military slavery, Turkic military slaves who formed an important part of the armed forces of the **Abbasid Caliphate** of the ninth and tenth centuries. Mamluks eventually founded their own state, ruling Egypt and Syria (1250–1517). (*p. 205*)

Manchu Federation of Northeast Asian peoples who founded the **Qing Empire**. (*p. 511*)

Mandate of Heaven Chinese religious and political ideology developed by the **Zhou**, according to which it was the prerogative of Heaven, the chief deity, to grant power to the ruler of China and to take away that power if the ruler failed to conduct himself justly and in the best interests of his subjects. (*p. 43*)

mandate system Allocation of former German colonies and Ottoman possessions to the victorious powers after World War I, to be administered under League of Nations supervision. (*p. 43, 752*)

manor In medieval Europe, a large, self-sufficient landholding consisting of the lord's residence (manor house), outbuildings, peasant village, and surrounding land. (*p. 224*)

mansabs In India, grants of land given in return for service by rulers of the **Mughal Empire**. (*p. 501*)

Mansa Kankan Musa Ruler of Mali (r. 1312–1337). His pilgrimage through Egypt to **Mecca** in 1324–1325 established the empire's reputation for wealth in the Mediterranean world. (*p. 330*)

manumission A grant of legal freedom to an individual slave. (*p. 467*)

Mao Zedong (1893–1976) Leader of the Chinese Communist Party (1927–1976). He led the Communists on the **Long March** (1934–1935) and rebuilt the Communist Party and Red Army during the Japanese occupation of China (1937–1945). After World War II, he led the Communists to victory over the **Guomindang**. He ordered the **Cultural Revolution** in 1966. (*p. 776*)

maroon A slave who ran away from his or her master. Often a member of a community of runaway slaves in the West Indies and South America. (*p. 467*)

Marshall Plan U. S. program to support the reconstruction of western Europe after World War II. By 1961 more than $20 billion in economic aid had been dispersed. (*p. 823*)

Marx, Karl (1818–1883) German journalist and philosopher, founder of the Marxist branch of **socialism**. He is known for two books: *The Communist Manifesto* (1848) and *Das Kapital* (Vols. I–III, 1867–1894). (*p. 690*)

mass deportation The forcible removal and relocation of large numbers of people or entire populations. The mass deportations practiced by the Assyrian and Persian Empires were meant as a terrifying warning of the consequences of rebellion. They also brought skilled and unskilled labor to the imperial center. (*p. 72*)

mass production The manufacture of many identical products by the division of labor into many small repetitive tasks. This method was introduced into the manufacture of pottery by Josiah Wedgwood and into the spinning of cotton thread by Richard Arkwright. (See also **Arkwright, Richard; Industrial Revolution; Wedgwood, Josiah**.) (*p. 574*)

Mauryan Empire The first state to unify most of the Indian subcontinent. It was founded by Chandragupta Maurya in 324 B.C.E. and survived until 184 B.C.E. From its capital at Pataliputra in the Ganges Valley it grew wealthy from taxes on agriculture, iron mining, and control of trade routes. (See also **Ashoka**.) (*p. 160*)

Maya Mesoamerican civilization concentrated in Mexico's Yucatán Peninsula and in Guatemala and Honduras but never unified into a single empire. Major contributions were in mathematics, astronomy, and development of the calendar. (*p. 271*)

Mecca City in western Arabia; birthplace of the Prophet **Muhammad,** and ritual center of the Islamic religion. (*p. 198*)

mechanization The application of machinery to manufacturing and other activities. Among the first processes to be mechanized were the spinning of cotton thread and the weaving of cloth in late-eighteenth- and early-nineteenth-century England. (*p. 575*)

medieval Literally "middle age," a term that historians of Europe use for the period ca. 500 to ca. 1500, signifying its intermediate point between Greco-Roman antiquity and the Renaissance. (*p. 219*)

Medina City in western Arabia to which the Prophet Muhammad and his followers emigrated in 622 to escape persecution in Mecca. (*p. 201*)

megaliths Structures and complexes of very large stones constructed for ceremonial and religious purposes in **Neolithic** times. (*p. 12*)

Meiji Restoration The political program that followed the destruction of the **Tokugawa Shogunate** in 1868, in which a collection of young leaders set Japan on the path of centralization, industrialization, and imperialism. (See also **Yamagata Aritomo**.) (*p. 702*)

Memphis The capital of Old Kingdom Egypt, near the head of the Nile Delta. Early rulers were interred in the nearby **pyramids**. (*p. 25*)

Menelik II (1844–1911) Emperor of Ethiopia (r. 1889–1911). He enlarged Ethiopia to its present dimensions and defeated an Italian invasion at Adowa (1896). (*p. 718*)

mercantilism European government policies of the sixteenth, seventeenth, and eighteenth centuries designed to promote overseas trade between a country and its colonies and accumulate precious metals by requiring colonies to trade only with their motherland country. The British system was defined by the Navigation Acts, the French system by laws known as the *Exclusif*. (*p. 468, 587*)

Meroë Capital of a flourishing kingdom in southern Nubia from the fourth century B.C.E. to the fourth century C.E. In this period Nubian culture shows more independence from Egypt and the influence of sub-Saharan Africa. (*p. 50*)

mestizo The term used by Spanish authorities to describe someone of mixed Amerindian and European descent. (*p. 444*)

Middle Passage The part of the **Atlantic Circuit** involving the transportation of enslaved Africans across the Atlantic to the Americas. (*p. 469*)

millenarianism Beliefs, based on prophetic revelations, in apocalyptic global transformations associated with the completion of cycles of a thousand years. (*p. 890*)

Ming Empire (1368–1644) Empire based in China that Zhu Yuanzhang established after the overthrow of the **Yuan Empire.** The Ming emperor **Yongle** sponsored the building of the Forbidden City and the voyages of **Zheng He.** The later years of the Ming saw a slowdown in technological development and economic decline. (*pp. 312, 517*)

Minoan Prosperous civilization on the Aegean island of Crete in the second millennium B.C.E. The Minoans engaged in far-flung commerce around the Mediterranean and exerted powerful cultural influences on the early Greeks. (*p. 66*)

mit'a Andean labor system based on shared obligations to help kinsmen and work on behalf of the ruler and religious organizations. (*p. 282*)

Moche Civilization of north coast of Peru (200–700 C.E.). An important Andean civilization that built extensive irrigation networks as well as impressive urban centers dominated by brick temples. (*p. 283*)

Moctezuma II (1466?–1520) Last Aztec emperor, overthrown by the Spanish conquistador Hernán Cortés. (*p. 394*)

modernization The process of reforming political, military, economic, social, and cultural traditions in imitation of the early success of Western societies, often with regard for accommodating local traditions in non-Western societies. (*p. 628*)

Mohenjo-Daro Largest of the cities of the Indus Valley civilization. It was centrally located in the extensive floodplain of the Indus River in contemporary Pakistan. Little is known about the political institutions of Indus Valley communities, but the large-scale of construction at Mohenjo-Daro, the orderly grid of streets, and the standardization of building materials are evidence of central planning. (*p. 30*)

moksha The Hindu concept of the spirit's "liberation" from the endless cycle of rebirths. There are various avenues—such as physical discipline, meditation, and acts of devotion to the gods—by which the spirit can distance itself from desire for the things of this world and be merged with the divine force that animates the universe. (*p. 156*)

monasticism Living in a religious community apart from secular society and adhering to a rule stipulating chastity, obedience, and poverty. It was a prominent element of medieval Christianity and Buddhism. Monasteries were the primary centers of learning and literacy in medieval Europe. (*p. 230*)

Mongols A people of this name is mentioned as early as the records of the **Tang Empire,** living as nomads in northern Eurasia. After 1206 they established an enormous empire under **Genghis Khan,** linking western and eastern Eurasia. (*p. 295*)

monotheism Belief in the existence of a single divine entity. Some scholars cite the devotion of the Egyptian pharaoh **Akhenaten** to Aten (sun-disk) and his suppression of traditional gods as the earliest instance. The Israelite worship of Yahweh developed into an exclusive belief in one god, and this concept passed into Christianity and Islam. (*p. 80*)

monsoon Seasonal winds in the Indian Ocean caused by the differences in temperature between the rapidly heating and cooling landmasses of Africa and Asia and the slowly changing ocean waters. These strong and predictable winds have long been ridden across the open sea by sailors, and the large amounts of rainfall that they deposit on parts of India, Southeast Asia, and China allow for the cultivation of several crops a year. (*pp. 152, 326*)

Morelos, José María (1765–1814) Mexican priest and former student of Miguel Hidalgo y Costilla, he led the forces fighting for Mexican independence until he was captured and executed in 1814. (See also **Hidalgo y Costilla, Miguel.**) (*p. 598*)

most-favored-nation status A clause in a commercial treaty that awards to any later signatories all the privileges previously granted to the original signatories. (*p. 669*)

movable type Type in which each individual character is cast on a separate piece of metal. It replaced woodblock printing, allowing for the arrangement of individual letters and other characters on a page, rather than requiring the carving of entire pages at a time. It may have been invented in Korea in the thirteenth century. (See also **printing press.**) (*p. 259*)

Mughal Empire Muslim state (1526–1857) exercising dominion over most of India in the sixteenth and seventeenth centuries. (*p. 500*)

Muhammad (570–632 C.E.) Arab prophet; founder of religion of Islam. (*p. 199*)

Muhammad Ali (1769–1849) Leader of Egyptian modernization in the early nineteenth century. He ruled Egypt as an Ottoman governor, but had imperial ambitions. His descendants ruled Egypt until overthrown in 1952. (*p. 628, 652*)

mulatto The term used in Spanish and Portuguese colonies to describe someone of mixed African and European descent. (*p. 445*)

mummy A body preserved by chemical processes or special natural circumstances, often in the belief that the deceased will need it again in the afterlife. In ancient Egypt the bodies of people who could afford mummification underwent a complex process of removing organs, filling body cavities, dehydrating the corpse with natron, and then wrapping the body with linen bandages and enclosing it in a wooden sarcophagus. (*p. 28*)

Muscovy Russian principality that emerged gradually during the era of Mongol domination. The Muscovite dynasty ruled without interruption from 1276 to 1598. (*p. 526*)

Muslim An adherent of the Islamic religion; a person who "submits" (in Arabic, *Islam* means "submission") to the will of God. (*p. 201*)

Mussolini, Benito (1883–1945) Fascist dictator of Italy (1922–1943). He led Italy to conquer Ethiopia (1935), joined Germany in the Axis pact (1936), and allied Italy with Germany in World War II. He was overthrown in 1943 when the Allies invaded Italy. (*p. 774*)

Mycenae Site of a fortified palace complex in southern Greece that controlled a Late Bronze Age kingdom. In Homer's epic poems Mycenae was the base of King Agamemnon, who commanded the Greeks besieging Troy. Contemporary archaeologists call the complex Greek society of the second millennium B.C.E. "Mycenaean." (*p. 67*)

Napoleon I (1769–1832) Overthrew French Directory in 1799 and became emperor of the French in 1804. Failed to defeat Great Britain and abdicated in 1814. Returned to power briefly in 1815 but was defeated and died in exile. (*p. 557*)

Nasir al-Din Tusi (1201–1274) Persian mathematician and cosmologist whose academy near Tabriz provided the model for the movement of the planets that helped to inspire the Copernican model of the solar system. (*p. 305*)

National Assembly French Revolutionary assembly (1789–1791). Called first as the Estates General, the three estates came together and demanded radical change. It passed the **Declaration of the Rights of Man** in 1789. (*p. 554*)

nationalism A political ideology that stresses people's membership in a nation—a community defined by a common culture and history as well as by territory. In the late eighteenth and early nineteenth centuries, nationalism was a force for unity in western Europe. In the late nineteenth century it hastened the disintegration of the Austro-Hungarian and Ottoman Empires. In the twentieth century it provided the ideological foundation for scores of independent countries emerging from **colonialism.** (*p. 691*)

nawab A Muslim prince allied to British India; technically, a semi-autonomous deputy of the Mughal emperor. (*p. 633*)

Nazis German political party joined by Adolf Hitler, emphasizing nationalism, racism, and war. When Hitler became chancellor of Germany in 1933, the Nazis became the only legal party and an instrument of Hitler's absolute rule. The party's formal name was National Socialist German Workers' Party. (See also **Hitler, Adolf.**) (*p. 774*)

Nehru, Jawaharlal (1889–1964) Indian statesman. He succeeded Mohandas K. Gandhi as leader of the **Indian National Congress.** He negotiated the end of British colonial rule in India and became India's first prime minister (1947–1964). (*p. 804*)

Neo-Assyrian Empire An empire extending from western Iran to Syria-Palestine, conquered by the Assyrians of northern Mesopotamia between the tenth and seventh centuries B.C.E. They used force and terror and exploited the wealth and labor of their subjects. They also preserved and continued the cultural and scientific developments of Mesopotamian civilization. (*p. 71*)

Neo-Babylonian kingdom Under the Chaldaeans (nomadic kinship groups that settled in southern Mesopotamia in the early first millennium B.C.E.), **Babylon** again became a major political and cultural center in the seventh and sixth centuries B.C.E. After participating in the destruction of Assyrian power, the monarchs Nabopolassar and Nebuchadnezzar took over the southern portion of the Assyrian domains. By destroying the **First Temple** in Jerusalem and deporting part of the population, they initiated the **Diaspora** of the Jews. (*p. 85*)

neo-Confucianism Term used to describe new approaches to understanding classic Confucian texts that became the basic ruling philosophy of China from the **Song** period to the twentieth century. (*p. 258*)

neo-liberalism The term used in Latin America and other developing regions to describe free-market policies that include reducing tariff protection for local industries; the sale of public-sector industries, like national airlines and public utilities, to private investors or foreign corporations; and the reduction of social welfare policies and public-sector employment. (*p. 854*)

Neolithic The period of the Stone Age associated with the ancient **Agricultural Revolution(s).** It follows the **Paleolithic** period. (*p. 6*)

Nevskii, Alexander (1220–1263) Prince of Novgorod (r. 1236–1263). He submitted to the invading Mongols in 1240 and received recognition as the leader of the Russian princes under the **Golden Horde.** (*p. 307*)

New Economic Policy Policy proclaimed by Vladimir Lenin in 1924 to encourage the revival of the Soviet economy by allowing small private enterprises. Joseph Stalin ended the N.E.P. in 1928 and replaced it with a series of **Five-Year Plans.** (See also **Lenin, Vladimir.**) (*p. 748*)

New France French colony in North America, with a capital in Quebec, founded 1608. New France fell to the British in 1763. (*p. 450*)

New Imperialism Historians' term for the late-nineteenth- and early-twentieth-century wave of conquests by European powers, the United States, and Japan, which were followed by the development and exploitation of the newly conquered territories for the benefit of the colonial powers. (*p. 708*)

newly industrialized economies (NIEs) Rapidly growing, new industrial nations of the late twentieth century, including the **Asian Tigers.** (*p. 857*)

new monarchies Historians' term for the monarchies in France, England, and Spain from 1450 to 1600. The centralization of royal power was increasing within more or less fixed territorial limits. (*p. 371*)

nomadism A way of life, forced by a scarcity of resources, in which groups of people continually migrate to find pastures and water. (*p. 295*)

nonaligned nations Developing countries that announced their neutrality in the **Cold War.** (*p. 839*)

nongovernmental organizations (NGOs) Nonprofit international organizations devoted to investigating human rights abuses and providing humanitarian relief. Two NGOs won the Nobel Peace Prize in the 1990s: International Campaign to Ban Landmines (1997) and Doctors Without Borders (1999). (*p. 894*)

North Atlantic Treaty Organization (NATO) Organization formed in 1949 as a military alliance of western European and North American states against the Soviet Union and its east European allies. (See also **Warsaw Pact.**) *(p. 822)*

Olmec The first Mesoamerican civilization. Between ca. 1200 and 400 B.C.E., the Olmec people of central Mexico created a vibrant civilization that included intensive agriculture, wide-ranging trade, ceremonial centers, and monumental construction. The Olmec had great cultural influence on later Mesoamerican societies, passing on artistic styles, religious imagery, sophisticated astronomical observation for the construction of calendars, and a ritual ball game. *(p. 52)*

Oman Arab state based in Musqat, the main port in the southwest region of the Arabian peninsula. Oman succeeded Portugal as a power in the western Indian Ocean in the eighteenth century. *(p. 406)*

Opium War (1839–1842) War between Britain and the **Qing Empire** that was, in the British view, occasioned by the Qing government's refusal to permit the importation of opium into its territories. The victorious British imposed the one-sided **Treaty of Nanking** on China. *(p. 668)*

Organization of Petroleum Exporting Countries (OPEC) Organization formed in 1960 by oil-producing states to promote their collective interest in generating revenue from oil. *(p. 844)*

Ottoman Empire Islamic state founded by Osman in north-western Anatolia ca. 1300. After the fall of the **Byzantine Empire,** the Ottoman Empire was based at Istanbul (formerly Constantinople) from 1453 to 1922. It encompassed lands in the Middle East, North Africa, the Caucasus, and eastern Europe. *(pp. 309, 485)*

Páez, José Antonio (1790–1873) Venezuelan soldier who led Simón Bolívar's cavalry force. He became a successful general in the war and built a powerful political base. He was unwilling to accept the constitutional authority of Bolívar's government in distant Bogotá and declared Venezuela's independence from Gran Colombia in 1829. *(p. 603)*

Paleolithic The period of the Stone Age associated with the **evolution** of humans. It predates the **Neolithic** period. *(p. 6)*

Pan-Slavism Movement among Russian intellectuals in the second half of the nineteenth century to identify culturally and politically with the Slavic peoples of eastern Europe. *(p. 665)*

Panama Canal Ship canal cut across the isthmus of Panama by United States Army engineers; it opened in 1915. It greatly shortened the sea voyage between the east and west coasts of North America. The United States turned the canal over to Panama on January 1, 2000. *(p. 730)*

papacy The central administration of the Roman Catholic Church, of which the pope is the head. *(pp. 228 406)*

papyrus A reed that grows along the banks of the Nile River in Egypt. From it was produced a coarse, paperlike writing medium used by the Egyptians and many other peoples in the ancient Mediterranean and Middle East. *(p. 26)*

Parthians Iranian ruling dynasty between ca. 250 B.C.E. and 226 C.E. *(p. 175)*

patron/client relationship In ancient Rome, a fundamental social relationship in which the patron—a wealthy and powerful individual—provided legal and economic protection and assistance to clients, men of lesser status and means, and in return the clients supported the political careers and economic interests of their patron. *(p. 128)*

Paul (ca. 5–65 C.E.) A Jew from the Greek city of Tarsus in Anatolia, he initially persecuted the followers of Jesus but, after receiving a revelation on the road to Syrian Damascus, became a Christian. Taking advantage of his Hellenized background and Roman citizenship, he traveled throughout Syria-Palestine, Anatolia, and Greece, preaching the new religion and establishing churches. Finding his greatest success among pagans ("gentiles"), he began the process by which Christianity separated from Judaism. *(p. 134)*

pax romana Literally, "Roman peace," it connoted the stability and prosperity that Roman rule brought to the lands of the Roman Empire in the first two centuries C.E. The movement of people and trade goods along Roman roads and safe seas allowed for the spread of cultural practices, technologies, and religious ideas. *(p. 134)*

Pearl Harbor Naval base in Hawaii attacked by Japanese aircraft on December 7, 1941. The sinking of much of the U.S. Pacific Fleet brought the United States into World War II. *(p. 782)*

Peloponnesian War A protracted (431–404 B.C.E.) and costly conflict between the Athenian and Spartan alliance systems that convulsed most of the Greek world. The war was largely a consequence of Athenian imperialism. Possession of a naval empire allowed Athens to fight a war of attrition. Ultimately, Sparta prevailed because of Athenian errors and Persian financial support. *(p. 115)*

perestroika Policy of "openness" that was the centerpiece of Mikhail Gorbachev's efforts to liberalize communism in the Soviet Union. (See also **Gorbachev, Mikhail.**) *(p. 858)*

Pericles (ca. 495–429 B.C.E.) Aristocratic leader who guided the Athenian state through the transformation to full participatory democracy for all male citizens, supervised construction of the Acropolis, and pursued a policy of imperial expansion that led to the **Peloponnesian War.** He formulated a strategy of attrition but died from the plague early in the war. *(p. 110)*

Perón, Eva Duarte (1919–1952) Wife of **Juan Perón** and champion of the poor in Argentina. She was a gifted speaker and popular political leader who campaigned to improve the life of the urban poor by founding schools and hospitals and providing other social benefits. *(p. 814)*

Perón, Juan (1895–1974) President of Argentina (1946–1955, 1973–1974). As a military officer, he championed the rights of labor. Aided by his wife **Eva Duarte Perón,** he was elected president in 1946. He built up Argentinean industry, became very popular among the urban poor, but harmed the economy. *(p. 814)*

Persepolis A complex of palaces, reception halls, and treasury buildings erected by the Persian kings **Darius I** and Xerxes in the Persian homeland. It is believed that the New Year's festival was celebrated here, as well as the coronations, weddings, and funerals of the Persian kings, who were buried in cliff-tombs nearby. *(p. 98)*

Persian Wars Conflicts between Greek city-states and the

Persian Empire, ranging from the Ionian Revolt (499–494 B.C.E.) through Darius's punitive expedition that failed at Marathon (490 B.C.E.) and the defeat of Xerxes' massive invasion of Greece by the Spartan-led Hellenic League (480–479 B.C.E.). This first major setback for Persian arms launched the Greeks into their period of greatest cultural productivity. **Herodotus** chronicled these events in the first "history" in the Western tradition.   (*p. 111*)

personalist leaders   Political leaders who rely on charisma and their ability to mobilize and direct the masses of citizens outside the authority of constitutions and laws. Nineteenth-century examples include José Antonio Páez of Venezuela and Andrew Jackson of the United States. Twentieth-century examples include Getulio Vargas of Brazil and Juan Perón of Argentina. (See also **Jackson, Andrew; Páez, José Antonio; Perón, Juan; Vargas, Getulio.**)   (*p. 603*)

Peter the Great (1672–1725)   Russian tsar (r. 1689–1725). He enthusiastically introduced Western languages and technologies to the Russian elite, moving the capital from Moscow to the new city of St. Petersburg.   (*p. 529*)

pharaoh   The central figure in the ancient Egyptian state. Believed to be an earthly manifestation of the gods, he used his absolute power to maintain the safety and prosperity of Egypt.   (*p. 25*)

Phoenicians   Semitic-speaking Canaanites living on the coast of modern Lebanon and Syria in the first millennium B.C.E. From major cities such as Tyre and Sidon, Phoenician merchants and sailors explored the Mediterranean, engaged in widespread commerce, and founded **Carthage** and other colonies in the western Mediterranean.   (*p. 80*)

pilgrimage   Journey to a sacred shrine by Christians seeking to show their piety, fulfill vows, or gain absolution for sins. Other religions also have pilgrimage traditions, such as the Muslim pilgrimage to **Mecca** and the pilgrimages made by early Chinese Buddhists to India in search of sacred Buddhist writings.   (*p. 238*)

Pilgrims   Group of English Protestant dissenters who established Plymouth Colony in Massachusetts in 1620 to seek religious freedom after having lived briefly in the Netherlands.   (*p. 447*)

Pizarro, Francisco (1475?–1541)   Spanish explorer who led the conquest of the **Inca** Empire of Peru in 1531–1533.   (*p. 398*)

Planck, Max (1858–1947)   German physicist who developed quantum theory and was awarded the Nobel Prize for physics in 1918.   (*p. 760*)

plantocracy   In the West Indian colonies, the rich men who owned most of the slaves and most of the land, especially in the eighteenth century.   (*p. 463*)

polis   The Greek term for a **city-state,** an urban center and the agricultural territory under its control. It was the characteristic form of political organization in southern and central Greece in the Archaic and Classical periods. Of the hundreds of city-states in the Mediterranean and Black Sea regions settled by Greeks, some were oligarchic, others democratic, depending on the powers delegated to the Council and the Assembly.   (*p. 104*)

pop culture   Entertainment spread by mass communications and enjoying wide appeal.   (*p. 898*)

positivism   A philosophy developed by the French count of Saint-Simon. Positivists believed that social and economic problems could be solved by the application of the scientific method, leading to continuous progress. Their ideas became popular in France and Latin America in the nineteenth century.   (*p. 588*)

Potosí   Located in Bolivia, one of the richest silver mining centers and most populous cities in colonial Spanish America.   (*p. 437*)

printing press   A mechanical device for transferring text or graphics from a woodblock or type to paper using ink. Presses using movable type first appeared in Europe in about 1450. See also **movable type.**   (*p. 367*)

Protestant Reformation   Religious reform movement within the Latin Christian Church beginning in 1519. It resulted in the "protesters" forming several new Christian denominations, including the Lutheran and Reformed Churches and the Church of England.   (*p. 406*)

proxy wars   During the **Cold War,** local or regional wars in which the superpowers armed, trained, and financed the combatants.   (*p. 848*)

Ptolemies   The Macedonian dynasty, descended from one of Alexander the Great's officers, that ruled Egypt for three centuries (323–30 B.C.E.). From their magnificent capital at Alexandria on the Mediterranean coast, the Ptolemies largely took over the system created by Egyptian pharaohs to extract the wealth of the land, rewarding Greeks and Hellenized non-Greeks serving in the military and administration.   (*p. 117*)

Puritans   English Protestant dissenters who believed that God predestined souls to heaven or hell before birth. They founded Massachusetts Bay Colony in 1629.   (*p. 447*)

pyramid   A large, triangular stone monument, used in Egypt and Nubia as a burial place for the king. The largest pyramids, erected during the Old Kingdom near Memphis with stone tools and compulsory labor, reflect the Egyptian belief that the proper and spectacular burial of the divine ruler would guarantee the continued prosperity of the land. (See also **ma'at.**)   (*p. 25*)

Qin   A people and state in the Wei Valley of eastern China that conquered rival states and created the first Chinese empire (221–206 B.C.E.). The Qin ruler, **Shi Huangdi,** standardized many features of Chinese society and ruthlessly marshaled subjects for military and construction projects, engendering hostility that led to the fall of his dynasty shortly after his death. The Qin framework was largely taken over by the succeeding **Han** Empire.   (*p. 139*)

Qing Empire   Empire established in China by Manchus who overthrew the **Ming Empire** in 1644. At various times the Qing also controlled Manchuria, Mongolia, Turkestan, and Tibet. The last Qing emperor was overthrown in 1911.   (*p. 518*)

Quran   Book composed of divine revelations made to the Prophet Muhammad between ca. 610 and his death in 632; the sacred text of the religion of **Islam.**   (*p. 202*)

railroads   Networks of iron (later steel) rails on which steam (later electric or diesel) locomotives pulled long trains at high speeds. The first railroads were built in England in the 1830s. Their success caused a railroad-building boom throughout the world that lasted well into the twentieth century.   *(p. 681)*

Rajputs   Members of a mainly Hindu warrior caste from northwest India. The Mughal emperors drew most of their Hindu officials from this caste, and **Akbar I** married a Rajput princess.   *(p. 501)*

Ramesses II   A long-lived ruler of New Kingdom Egypt (r. 1290–1224 B.C.E.). He reached an accommodation with the **Hittites** of Anatolia after a standoff in battle at Kadesh in Syria. He built on a grand scale throughout Egypt.   *(p. 65)*

Rashid al-Din (d.1318)   Adviser to the **Il-khan** ruler Ghazan, who converted to Islam on Rashid's advice.   *(p. 305)*

recaptives   Africans rescued by Britain's Royal Navy from the illegal slave trade of the nineteenth century and restored to free status.   *(p. 631)*

reconquest (of Iberia)   Beginning in the eleventh century, military campaigns by various Iberian Christian states to recapture territory taken by Muslims. In 1492 the last Muslim ruler was defeated, and Spain and Portugal emerged as united kingdoms.   *(p. 372)*

Renaissance (European)   A period of intense artistic and intellectual activity, said to be a "rebirth" of Greco-Roman culture. Usually divided into an Italian Renaissance, from roughly the mid-fourteenth to mid-fifteenth century, and a Northern (trans-Alpine) Renaissance, from roughly the early fifteenth to early seventeenth century.   *(pp. 364, 405)*

Revolutions of 1848   Democratic and nationalist revolutions that swept across Europe. The monarchy in France was overthrown. In Germany, Austria, Italy, and Hungary the revolutions failed.   *(p. 564)*

Rhodes, Cecil (1853–1902)   British entrepreneur and politician involved in the expansion of the British Empire from South Africa into Central Africa. The colonies of Southern Rhodesia (now Zimbabwe) and Northern Rhodesia (now Zambia) were named after him.   *(p. 717)*

Robespierre, Maximilien (1758–1794)   Young provincial lawyer who led the most radical phases of the French Revolution. His execution ended the Reign of Terror. See **Jacobins.**   *(p. 556)*

Romanization   The process by which the Latin language and Roman culture became dominant in the western provinces of the Roman Empire. The Roman government did not actively seek to Romanize the subject peoples, but indigenous peoples in the provinces often chose to Romanize because of the political and economic advantages that it brought, as well as the allure of Roman success.   *(p. 134)*

Roman Principate   A term used to characterize Roman government in the first three centuries C.E., based on the ambiguous title *princeps* ("first citizen") adopted by Augustus to conceal his military dictatorship.   *(p. 132)*

Roman Republic   The period from 507 to 31 B.C.E., during which Rome was largely governed by the aristocratic **Roman Senate.**   *(p. 127)*

Roman Senate   A council whose members were the heads of wealthy, landowning families. Originally an advisory body to the early kings, in the era of the **Roman Republic** the Senate effectively governed the Roman state and the growing empire. Under Senate leadership, Rome conquered an empire

of unprecedented extent in the lands surrounding the Mediterranean Sea. In the first century B.C.E. quarrels among powerful and ambitious senators and failure to address social and economic problems led to civil wars and the emergence of the rule of the emperors.   *(p. 127)*

Royal African Company   A trading company chartered by the English government in 1672 to conduct its merchants' trade on the Atlantic coast of Africa.   *(p. 458)*

sacrifice   A gift given to a deity, often with the aim of creating a relationship, gaining favor, and obligating the god to provide some benefit to the sacrificer, sometimes in order to sustain the deity and thereby guarantee the continuing vitality of the natural world. The object devoted to the deity could be as simple as a cup of wine poured on the ground, a live animal slain on the altar, or, in the most extreme case, the ritual killing of a human being.   *(p. 108)*

Safavid Empire   Iranian kingdom (1502–1722) established by Ismail Safavi, who declared Iran a Shi'ite state.   *(p. 495)*

Sahel   Belt south of the Sahara; literally "coastland" in Arabic.   *(p. 185)*

samurai   Literally "those who serve," the hereditary military elite of the **Tokugawa Shogunate.**   *(p. 511)*

Sandinistas   Members of a leftist coalition that overthrew the Nicaraguan dictatorship of Anastasia Somoza in 1979 and attempted to install a socialist economy. The United States financed armed opposition by the Contras. The Sandinistas lost national elections in 1990.   *(p. 850)*

Sanger, Margaret (1883–1966)   American nurse and author; pioneer in the movement for family planning; organized conferences and established birth control clinics.   *(p. 759)*

Sasanid Empire   Iranian empire, established ca. 226, with a capital in Ctesiphon, Mesopotamia. The Sasanid emperors established **Zoroastrianism** as the state religion. Islamic Arab armies overthrew the empire ca. 640.   *(p. 176)*

satrap   The governor of a province in the Achaemenid Persian Empire, often a relative of the king. He was responsible for protection of the province and for forwarding tribute to the central administration. Satraps in outlying provinces enjoyed considerable autonomy.   *(p. 97)*

savanna   Tropical or subtropical grassland, either treeless or with occasional clumps of trees. Most extensive in **sub-Saharan Africa** but also present in South America.   *(p. 185)*

schism   A formal split within a religious community. See **Great Western Schism.**   *(p. 221)*

scholasticism   A philosophical and theological system, associated with Thomas Aquinas, devised to reconcile Aristotelian philosophy and Roman Catholic theology in the thirteenth century.   *(p. 365)*

Scientific Revolution   The intellectual movement in Europe, initially associated with planetary motion and other aspects of physics, that by the seventeenth century had laid the groundwork for modern science.   *(p. 410)*

"scramble" for Africa   Sudden wave of conquests in Africa by European powers in the 1880s and 1890s. Britain obtained most of eastern Africa, France most of northwestern Africa. Other countries (Germany, Belgium, Portugal, Italy, and Spain) acquired lesser amounts.   *(p. 714)*

scribe   In the governments of many ancient societies, a professional position reserved for men who had undergone the lengthy training required to be able to read and write using **cuneiforms, hieroglyphics,** or other early, cumbersome writing systems. (*p. 18*)

seasoning An often difficult period of adjustment to new climates, disease environments, and work routines, such as that experienced by slaves newly arrived in the Americas. (*p. 466*)

Selassie, Haile (1892–1975) Emperor of Ethiopia (r. 1930–1974) and symbol of African independence. He fought the Italian invasion of his country in 1935 and regained his throne during World War II, when British forces expelled the Italians. He ruled **Ethiopia** as a traditional autocracy until he was overthrown in 1974. (*p. 800*)

Semitic Family of related languages long spoken across parts of western Asia and northern Africa. In antiquity these languages included Hebrew, Aramaic, and Phoenician. The most widespread modern member of the Semitic family is Arabic. (*p. 15*)

"separate spheres" Nineteenth-century idea in Western societies that men and women, especially of the middle class, should have clearly differentiated roles in society: women as wives, mothers, and homemakers; men as breadwinners and participants in business and politics. (*p. 688*)

sepoy A soldier in South Asia, especially in the service of the British. (*p. 633*)

Sepoy Rebellion The revolt of Indian soldiers in 1857 against certain practices that violated religious customs; also known as the Sepoy Mutiny. (*p. 636*)

Serbia The Ottoman province in the Balkans that rose up against **Janissary** control in the early 1800s. After World War II the central province of Yugoslavia. Serb leaders struggled to maintain dominance as the Yugoslav federation dissolved in the 1990s. (*p. 653*)

serf In medieval Europe, an agricultural laborer legally bound to a lord's property and obligated to perform set services for the lord. In Russia some serfs worked as artisans and in factories; serfdom was not abolished there until 1861. (*pp. 529, 569*)

shaft graves A term used for the burial sites of elite members of Mycenaean Greek society in the mid-second millennium B.C.E. At the bottom of deep shafts lined with stone slabs, the bodies were laid out along with gold and bronze jewelry, implements, weapons, and masks. (*p. 67*)

Shah Abbas I (r. 1587–1629) The fifth and most renowned ruler of the **Safavid** dynasty in Iran. Abbas moved the royal capital to Isfahan in 1598. (*p. 497*)

Shang The dominant people in the earliest Chinese dynasty for which we have written records (ca. 1750–1027 B.C.E.). Ancestor worship, divination by means of oracle bones, and the use of bronze vessels for ritual purposes were major elements of Shang culture. (*p. 41*)

Shi Huangdi Founder of the short-lived **Qin** dynasty and creator of the Chinese Empire (r. 221–210 B.C.E.). He is remembered for his ruthless conquests of rival states, standardization of practices, and forcible organization of labor for military and engineering tasks. His tomb, with its army of life-size terracotta soldiers, has been partially excavated. (*p. 139*)

Shi'ites Muslims belonging to the branch of Islam believing that God vests leadership of the community in a descendant of Muhammad's son-in-law Ali. Shi'ism is the state religion of Iran. (See also **Sunnis.**) (*pp. 197, 496*)

Siberia The extreme northeastern sector of Asia, including the Kamchatka Peninsula and the present Russian coast of the Arctic Ocean, the Bering Strait, and the Sea of Okhotsk. (*p. 527*)

Sikhism Indian religion founded by the guru Nanak (1469–1539) in the Punjab region of northwest India. After the Mughal emperor ordered the beheading of the ninth guru in 1675, Sikh warriors mounted armed resistance to Mughal rule. (*p. 502*)

Silk Road Caravan routes connecting China and the Middle East across Central Asia and Iran. (*p. 175*)

Slavophiles Russian intellectuals in the early nineteenth century who favored resisting western European influences and taking pride in the traditional peasant values and institutions of the Slavic people. (*p. 665*)

"small traditions" Historians' term for a localized, usually nonliterate, set of customs and beliefs adhered to by a single society, often in conjunction with a **"great tradition."** (*p. 185*)

socialism A political ideology that originated in Europe in the 1830s. Socialists advocated government protection of workers from exploitation by property owners and government ownership of industries. This ideology led to the founding of socialist or labor parties throughout Europe in the second half of the nineteenth century. (See also **Marx, Karl.**) (*p. 690*)

Socrates Athenian philosopher (ca. 470–399 B.C.E.) who shifted the emphasis of philosophical investigation from questions of natural science to ethics and human behavior. He attracted young disciples from elite families but made enemies by revealing the ignorance and pretensions of others, culminating in his trial and execution by the Athenian state. (*p. 113*)

Sokoto Caliphate A large Muslim state founded in 1809 in what is now northern Nigeria. (*p. 627*)

Solidarity Polish trade union created in 1980 to protest working conditions and political repression. It began the nationalist opposition to communist rule that led in 1989 to the fall of communism in eastern Europe. (*p. 859*)

Song Empire Empire in central and southern China (960–1126) while the Liao people controlled the north. Empire in southern China (1127–1279; the "Southern Song") while the Jin people controlled the north. Distinguished for its advances in technology, medicine, astronomy, and mathematics. (*p. 254*)

Songhai A people, language, kingdom, and empire in western Sudan in West Africa. At its height in the sixteenth century, the Muslim Songhai Empire stretched from the Atlantic to the land of the **Hausa** and was a major player in the trans-Saharan trade. (*p. 477*)

Stalin, Joseph (1879–1953) Bolshevik revolutionary, head of the Soviet Communist Party after 1924, and dictator of the Soviet Union from 1928 to 1953. He led the Soviet Union with an iron fist, using **Five-Year Plans** to increase industrial production and terror to crush all opposition. (*p. 766*)

Stalingrad City in Russia, site of a Red Army victory over the German army in 1942–1943. The Battle of Stalingrad was the turning point in the war between Germany and the Soviet Union. Today Volgograd.   (*p. 780*)

Stanley, Henry Morton (1841–1904)   British-American explorer of Africa, famous for his expeditions in search of Dr. David Livingstone. Stanley helped King **Leopold II** establish the Congo Free State.   (*p. 714*)

steam engine   A machine that turns the energy released by burning fuel into motion. Thomas Newcomen built the first crude but workable steam engine in 1712. **James Watt** vastly improved his device in the 1760s and 1770s. Steam power was later applied to moving machinery in factories and to powering ships and locomotives.   (*p. 578*)

steel   A form of iron that is both durable and flexible. It was first mass-produced in the 1860s and quickly became the most widely used metal in construction, machinery, and railroad equipment.   (*p. 682*)

steppes   Treeless plains, especially the high, flat expanses of northern Eurasia, which usually have little rain and are covered with coarse grass. They are good lands for nomads and their herds. Living on the steppes promoted the breeding of horses and the development of military skills that were essential to the rise of the Mongol Empire.   (*p. 185*)

stirrup   Device for securing a horseman's feet, enabling him to wield weapons more effectively. First evidence of the use of stirrups was among the Kushan people of northern Afghanistan in approximately the first century C.E.   (*p. 178*)

stock exchange   A place where shares in a company or business enterprise are bought and sold.   (*p. 415*)

Stone Age   The historical period characterized by the production of tools from stone and other nonmetallic substances. It was followed in some places by the Bronze Age and more generally by the Iron Age.   (*p. 6*)

submarine telegraph cables   Insulated copper cables laid along the bottom of a sea or ocean for telegraphic communication. The first short cable was laid across the English Channel in 1851; the first successful transatlantic cable was laid in 1866. (See also **electric telegraph.**)   (*p. 682*)

sub-Saharan Africa   Portion of the African continent lying south of the Sahara.   (*p. 185*)

Suez Canal   Ship canal dug across the isthmus of Suez in Egypt, designed by Ferdinand de Lesseps. It opened to shipping in 1869 and shortened the sea voyage between Europe and Asia. Its strategic importance led to the British conquest of Egypt in 1882.   (*p. 708*)

Suleiman the Magnificent (1494–1566)   The most illustrious sultan of the **Ottoman Empire** (r. 1520–1566); also known as Suleiman Kanuni, "The Lawgiver." He significantly expanded the empire in the Balkans and eastern Mediterranean.   (*p. 486*)

Sumerians   The people who dominated southern Mesopotamia through the end of the third millennium B.C.E. They were responsible for the creation of many fundamental elements of Mesopotamian culture—such as irrigation technology, **cuneiform,** and religious conceptions—taken over by their **Semitic** successors.   (*p. 15*)

Sunnis   Muslims belonging to branch of Islam believing that the community should select its own leadership. The majority religion in most Islamic countries. (See also **Shi'ites.**)   (*p. 197*)

Sun Yat-sen (1867–1925)   Chinese nationalist revolutionary, founder and leader of the **Guomindang** until his death. He attempted to create a liberal democratic political movement in China but was thwarted by military leaders.   (*p. 751*)

Swahili   Bantu language with Arabic loanwords spoken in coastal regions of East Africa.   (*p. 506*)

Swahili Coast   East African shores of the Indian Ocean between the Horn of Africa and the Zambezi River; from the Arabic *sawahil,* meaning "shores."   (*p. 341*)

Taiping Rebellion (1853–1864)   The most destructive civil war before the twentieth century. A Christian-inspired rural rebellion threatened to topple the **Qing Empire.**   (*p. 670*)

Tamil kingdoms   The kingdoms of southern India, inhabited primarily by speakers of Dravidian languages, which developed in partial isolation, and somewhat differently, from the Aryan north. They produced epics, poetry, and performance arts. Elements of Tamil religious beliefs were merged into the Hindu synthesis.   (*p. 162*)

Tang Empire   Empire unifying China and part of Central Asia, founded 618 and ended 907. The Tang emperors presided over a magnificent court at their capital, Chang'an.   (*p. 245*)

Tanzimat   "Restructuring" reforms by the nineteenth-century Ottoman rulers, intended to move civil law away from the control of religious elites and make the military and the bureaucracy more efficient.   (*p. 656*)

Tecumseh (1768–1813)   Shawnee leader who attempted to organize an Amerindian confederacy to prevent the loss of additional territory to American settlers. He became an ally of the British in War of 1812 and died in battle.   (*p. 608*)

Tenochtitlan   Capital of the Aztec Empire, located on an island in Lake Texcoco. Its population was about 150,000 on the eve of Spanish conquest. Mexico City was constructed on its ruins.   (*p. 275*)

Teotihuacan   A powerful **city-state** in central Mexico (100 B.C.E.–750 C.E.). Its population was about 150,000 at its peak in 600.   (*p. 270*)

terrorism   Political belief that extreme and seemingly random violence will destabilize a government and permit the terrorists to gain political advantage. Though an old technique, terrorism gained prominence in the late twentieth century with the growth of worldwide mass media that, through their news coverage, amplified public fears of terrorist acts.   (*p. 883*)

theater-state   Historians' term for a state that acquires prestige and power by developing attractive cultural forms and staging elaborate public ceremonies (as well as redistributing valuable resources) to attract and bind subjects to the center. Examples include the **Gupta Empire** in India and **Srivijaya** in Southeast Asia.   (*p. 163*)

Thebes   Capital city of Egypt and home of the ruling dynasties during the Middle and New Kingdoms. Amon, patron deity of Thebes, became one of the chief gods of Egypt. Monarchs were buried across the river in the Valley of the Kings.   (*p. 25*)

Theravada Buddhism   "Way of the Elders" branch of Buddhism followed in Sri Lanka and much of Southeast Asia. Therevada remains close to the original principles set forth by the **Buddha;** it downplays the importance of gods and emphasizes austerity and the individual's search for enlightenment. (*p. 157*)

third-century crisis Historians' term for the political, military, and economic turmoil that beset the Roman Empire during much of the third century C.E.: frequent changes of ruler, civil wars, barbarian invasions, decline of urban centers, and near-destruction of long-distance commerce and the monetary economy. After 284 C.E. Diocletian restored order by making fundamental changes. (*p. 135*)

Third World Term applied to a group of developing countries who professed nonalignment during the **Cold War.** (*p. 839*)

three-field system A rotational system for agriculture in which one field grows grain, one grows legumes, and one lies fallow. It gradually replaced two-field system in medieval Europe. (*p. 353*)

Tiananmen Square Site in Beijing where Chinese students and workers gathered to demand greater political openness in 1989. The demonstration was crushed by Chinese military with great loss of life. (*p. 857*)

Tibet Country centered on the high, mountain-bounded plateau north of India. Tibetan political power occasionally extended farther to the north and west between the seventh and thirteen centuries. (*p. 252*)

Timbuktu City on the Niger River in the modern country of Mali. It was founded by the Tuareg as a seasonal camp sometime after 1000. As part of the **Mali** empire, Timbuktu became a major terminus of the trans-Saharan trade and a center of Islamic learning. (*p. 344*)

Timur (1336–1405) Member of a prominent family of the Mongols' Jagadai Khanate, Timur through conquest gained control over much of Central Asia and Iran. He consolidated the status of Sunni Islam as orthodox, and his descendants, the Timurids, maintained his empire for nearly a century and founded the **Mughal Empire** in India. (*p. 304*)

Tiwanaku Name of capital city and empire centered on the region near Lake Titicaca in modern Bolivia (375–1000 C.E.). (*p. 284*)

Tokugawa Shogunate (1600–1868) The last of the three shogunates of Japan. (*p. 512*)

Toltecs Powerful postclassic empire in central Mexico (900–1168 C.E.). It influenced much of Mesoamerica. Aztecs claimed ties to this earlier civilization. (*p. 274*)

trans-Saharan caravan routes Trading network linking North Africa with **sub-Saharan Africa** across the Sahara. (*p. 182*)

Treaty of Nanking (1842) The treaty that concluded the **Opium War.** It awarded Britain a large indemnity from the **Qing Empire,** denied the Qing government tariff control over some of its own borders, opened additional ports of residence to Britons, and ceded the island of Hong Kong to Britain. (*p. 668*)

Treaty of Versailles (1919) The treaty imposed on Germany by France, Great Britain, the United States, and other Allied Powers after World War I. It demanded that Germany dismantle its military and give up some lands to Poland. It was resented by many Germans. (*p. 747*)

treaty ports Cities opened to foreign residents as a result of the forced treaties between the **Qing Empire** and foreign signatories. In the treaty ports, foreigners enjoyed **extraterritoriality.** (*p. 668*)

tributary system A system in which, from the time of the **Han** Empire, countries in East and Southeast Asia not under the direct control of empires based in China nevertheless enrolled as tributary states, acknowledging the superiority of the emperors in China in exchange for trading rights or strategic alliances. (*p. 247*)

tribute system A system in which defeated peoples were forced to pay a tax in the form of goods and labor. This forced transfer of food, cloth, and other goods subsidized the development of large cities. An important component of the Aztec and Inca economies. (*p. 276*)

trireme Greek and Phoenician warship of the fifth and fourth centuries B.C.E. It was sleek and light, powered by 170 oars arranged in three vertical tiers. Manned by skilled sailors, it was capable of short bursts of speed and complex maneuvers. (*p. 112*)

tropical rain forest High-precipitation forest zones of the Americas, Africa, and Asia lying between the Tropic of Cancer and the Tropic of Capricorn. (*p. 185*)

tropics Equatorial region between the Tropic of Cancer and the Tropic of Capricorn. It is characterized by generally warm or hot temperatures year-round, though much variation exists due to altitude and other factors. Temperate zones north and south of the tropics generally have a winter season. (*p. 325*)

Truman Doctrine Foreign policy initiated by U.S. president Harry Truman in 1947. It offered military aid to help Turkey and Greece resist Soviet military pressure and subversion. (*p. 826*)

tsar (czar) From Latin *caesar*, this Russian title for a monarch was first used in reference to a Russian ruler by Ivan III (r. 1462–1505). (*pp. 308, 527*)

Tulip Period (1718–1730) Last years of the reign of Ottoman sultan Ahmed III, during which European styles and attitudes became briefly popular in Istanbul. (*p. 495*)

Tupac Amaru II Member of Inca aristocracy who led a rebellion against Spanish authorities in Peru in 1780–1781. He was captured and executed with his wife and other members of his family. (*p. 453*)

tyrant The term the Greeks used to describe someone who seized and held power in violation of the normal procedures and traditions of the community. Tyrants appeared in many Greek **city-states** in the seventh and sixth centuries B.C.E., often taking advantage of the disaffection of the emerging middle class and, by weakening the old elite, unwittingly contributing to the evolution of **democracy.** (*p. 107*)

Uighurs A group of Turkic-speakers who controlled their own centralized empire from 744 to 840 in Mongolia and Central Asia. (*p. 251*)

ulama Muslim religious scholars. From the ninth century onward, the primary interpreters of Islamic law and the social core of Muslim urban societies. (*p. 207*)

Umayyad Caliphate First hereditary dynasty of Muslim caliphs (661 to 750). From their capital at Damascus, the Umayyads ruled an empire that extended from Spain to India. Overthrown by the **Abbasid Caliphate.** (*p. 202*)

umma The community of all Muslims. A major innovation against the background of seventh-century Arabia, where traditionally kinship rather than faith had determined membership in a community.   (*p. 201*)

underdevelopment   The condition experienced by economies that depend on colonial forms of production such as the export of raw materials and plantation crops with low wages and low investment in education.   (*p. 616*)

United Nations   International organization founded in 1945 to promote world peace and cooperation. It replaced the **League of Nations.**   (*p. 822*)

Universal Declaration of Human Rights   A 1946 United Nations covenant binding signatory nations to the observance of specified rights.   (*p. 893*)

universities   Degree-granting institutions of higher learning. Those that appeared in Latin West from about 1200 onward became the model of all modern universities.   (*p. 364*)

Ural Mountains   This north-south range separates Siberia from the rest of Russia. It is commonly considered the boundary between the continents of Europe and Asia.   (*p. 527*)

Urdu   A Persian-influenced literary form of Hindi written in Arabic characters and used as a literary language since the 1300s.   (*p. 344*)

utopian socialism   A philosophy introduced by the Frenchman Charles Fourier in the early nineteenth century. Utopian socialists hoped to create humane alternatives to industrial capitalism by building self-sustaining communities whose inhabitants would work cooperatively. (See also **socialism.**)   (*p. 588*)

Vargas, Getulio (1883–1954)   Dictator of Brazil from 1930 to 1945 and from 1951 to 1954. Defeated in the presidential election of 1930, he overthrew the government and created Estado Novo ("New State"), a dictatorship that emphasized industrialization and helped the urban poor but did little to alleviate the problems of the peasants.   (*p. 813*)

varna/jati   Two categories of social identity of great importance in Indian history. *Varna* are the four major social divisions: the *Brahmin* priest class, the *Kshatriya* warrior/administrator class, the *Vaishya* merchant/farmer class, and the *Shudra* laborer class. Within the system of *varna* are many *jati*, regional groups of people who have a common occupational sphere, and who marry, eat, and generally interact with other members of their group.   (*pp. 154, 155*)

vassal   In medieval Europe, a sworn supporter of a king or lord committed to rendering specified military service to that king or lord.   (*p. 225*)

Vedas   Early Indian sacred "knowledge"—the literal meaning of the term—long preserved and communicated orally by Brahmin priests and eventually written down. These religious texts, including the thousand poetic hymns to various deities contained in the Rig Veda, are our main source of information about the Vedic period (ca. 1500–500 B.C.E.).   (*p. 152*)

Versailles   The huge palace built for French King Louis XIV south of Paris in the town of the same name. The palace symbolized the preeminence of French power and architecture in Europe and the triumph of royal authority over the French nobility.   (*p. 422*)

Victorian Age   The reign of Queen Victoria of Great Britain (r. 1837–1901). The term is also used to describe late-nineteenth-century society, with its rigid moral standards and sharply differentiated roles for men and women and for middle-class and working-class people. (See also **"separate spheres."**)   (*p. 688*)

Vietnam War   (1954–1975) Conflict pitting North Vietnam and South Vietnamese communist guerrillas against the South Vietnamese government, aided after 1961 by the United States.   (*p. 829*)

Villa, Francisco "Pancho" (1878–1923)   A popular leader during the Mexican Revolution. An outlaw in his youth, when the revolution started, he formed a cavalry army in the north of Mexico and fought for the rights of the landless in collaboration with **Emiliano Zapata.** He was assassinated in 1923.   (*p. 808*)

Wari   Andean civilization culturally linked to **Tiwanaku,** perhaps beginning as a colony of Tiwanaku.   (*p. 285*)

Warsaw Pact   The 1955 treaty binding the Soviet Union and countries of eastern Europe in an alliance against the **North Atlantic Treaty Organization.**   (*p. 826*)

Washington, George (1732–1799)   Military commander of the American Revolution. He was the first elected president of the United States (1789–1799).   (*p. 549*)

water wheel   A mechanism that harnesses the energy in flowing water to grind grain or to power machinery. It was used in many parts of the world but was especially common in Europe from 1200 to 1900.   (*p. 355*)

Watt, James (1736–1819)   Scot who invented the condenser and other improvements that made the **steam engine** a practical source of power for industry and transportation. The watt, an electrical measurement, is named after him.   (*p. 579*)

weapons of mass destruction   Nuclear, chemical, and biological devices that are capable of injuring and killing large numbers of people.   (*p. 883*)

Wedgwood, Josiah (1730–1795)   English industrialist whose pottery works were the first to produce fine-quality pottery by industrial methods.   (*p. 574*)

Western Front   A line of trenches and fortifications in World War I that stretched without a break from Switzerland to the North Sea. Scene of most of the fighting between Germany, on the one hand, and France and Britain, on the other.   (*p. 740*)

Wilson, Woodrow (1856–1924)   President of the United States (1913–1921) and the leading figure at the Paris Peace Conference of 1919. He was unable to persuade the U.S. Congress to ratify the **Treaty of Versailles** or join the **League of Nations.**   (*p. 745*)

witch-hunt   The pursuit of people suspected of witchcraft, especially in northern Europe in the late sixteenth and seventeenth centuries.   (*p. 409*)

Women's Rights Convention   An 1848 gathering of women angered by their exclusion from an international antislavery meeting. They met at Seneca Falls, New York to discuss women's rights.   (*p. 615*)

World Bank   A specialized agency of the United Nations that makes loans to countries for economic development, trade promotion, and debt consolidation. Its formal name is the

International Bank for Reconstruction and Development. (*p. 822*)

World Trade Organization (WTO)   An international body established in 1995 to foster and bring order to international trade.   (*p. 887*)

Wright, Wilbur (1867-1912), and Orville (1871-1948)   American bicycle mechanics; the first to build and fly an airplane, at Kitty Hawk, North Carolina, December 7, 1903.   (*p. 760*)

Yamagata Aritomo (1838–1922)   One of the leaders of the **Meiji Restoration.**   (*p. 704*)

Yi (1392–1910)   The Yi dynasty ruled Korea from the fall of the **Koryo** kingdom to the colonization of Korea by Japan.   (*p. 317*)

yin/yang   In Chinese belief, complementary factors that help to maintain the equilibrium of the world. Yin is associated with feminine, dark, and passive qualities; yang with masculine, light, and active qualities.   (*p. 48*)

Yongle   Reign period of Zhu Di (1360–1424), the third emperor of the **Ming Empire** (r. 1403–1424). He sponsored the building of the **Forbidden City,** a huge encyclopedia project, the expeditions of **Zheng He,** and the reopening of China's borders to trade and travel.   (*p. 313*)

Young Ottomans   Movement of young intellectuals to institute liberal reforms and build a feeling of national identity in the Ottoman Empire in the second half of the nineteenth century.   (*p. 663*)

Yuan Empire (1271–1368)   Empire created in China and Siberia by **Khubilai Khan.**   (*p. 300*)

Yuan Shikai (1859–1916)   Chinese general and first president of the Chinese Republic (1912–1916). He stood in the way of the democratic movement led by **Sun Yat-sen.**   (*p. 751*)

Zapata, Emiliano (1879–1919)   Revolutionary and leader of peasants in the Mexican Revolution. He mobilized landless peasants in south-central Mexico in an attempt to seize and divide the lands of the wealthy landowners. Though successful for a time, he was ultimately defeated and assassinated.   (*p. 808*)

Zen   The Japanese word for a branch of **Mahayana Buddhism** based on highly disciplined meditation. It is known in Sanskrit as *dhyana*, in Chinese as *chan*, and in Korean as *son*.   (*p. 258*)

Zheng He (1371–1433)   An imperial eunuch and Muslim, entrusted by the Ming emperor **Yongle** with a series of state voyages that took his gigantic ships through the Indian Ocean, from Southeast Asia to Africa.   (*pp. 314, 380*)

Zhou   The people and dynasty that took over the dominant position in north China from the **Shang** and created the concept of the **Mandate of Heaven** to justify their rule. The Zhou era, particularly the vigorous early period (1027–771 B.C.E.), was remembered in Chinese tradition as a time of prosperity and benevolent rule. In the later Zhou period (771–221 B.C.E.), centralized control broke down, and warfare among many small states became frequent.   (*p. 43*)

ziggurat   A massive pyramidal stepped tower made of mudbricks. It is associated with religious complexes in ancient Mesopotamian cities, but its function is unknown.   (*p. 19*)

Zoroastrianism   A religion originating in ancient Iran with the prophet Zoroaster. It centered on a single benevolent deity—Ahuramazda—who engaged in a twelve-thousand-year struggle with demonic forces before prevailing and restoring a pristine world. Emphasizing truth-telling, purity, and reverence for nature, the religion demanded that humans choose sides in the struggle between good and evil. Those whose good conduct indicated their support for Ahuramazda would be rewarded in the afterlife. Others would be punished. The religion of the Achaemenid and Sasanid Persians, Zoroastrianism may have spread within their realms and influenced Judaism, Christianity, and other faiths.   (*p. 99*)

Zulu   A people of modern South Africa whom King Shaka united in 1818.   (*p. 625*)

Index